The Ministry of Mĕssiah Yĕshua

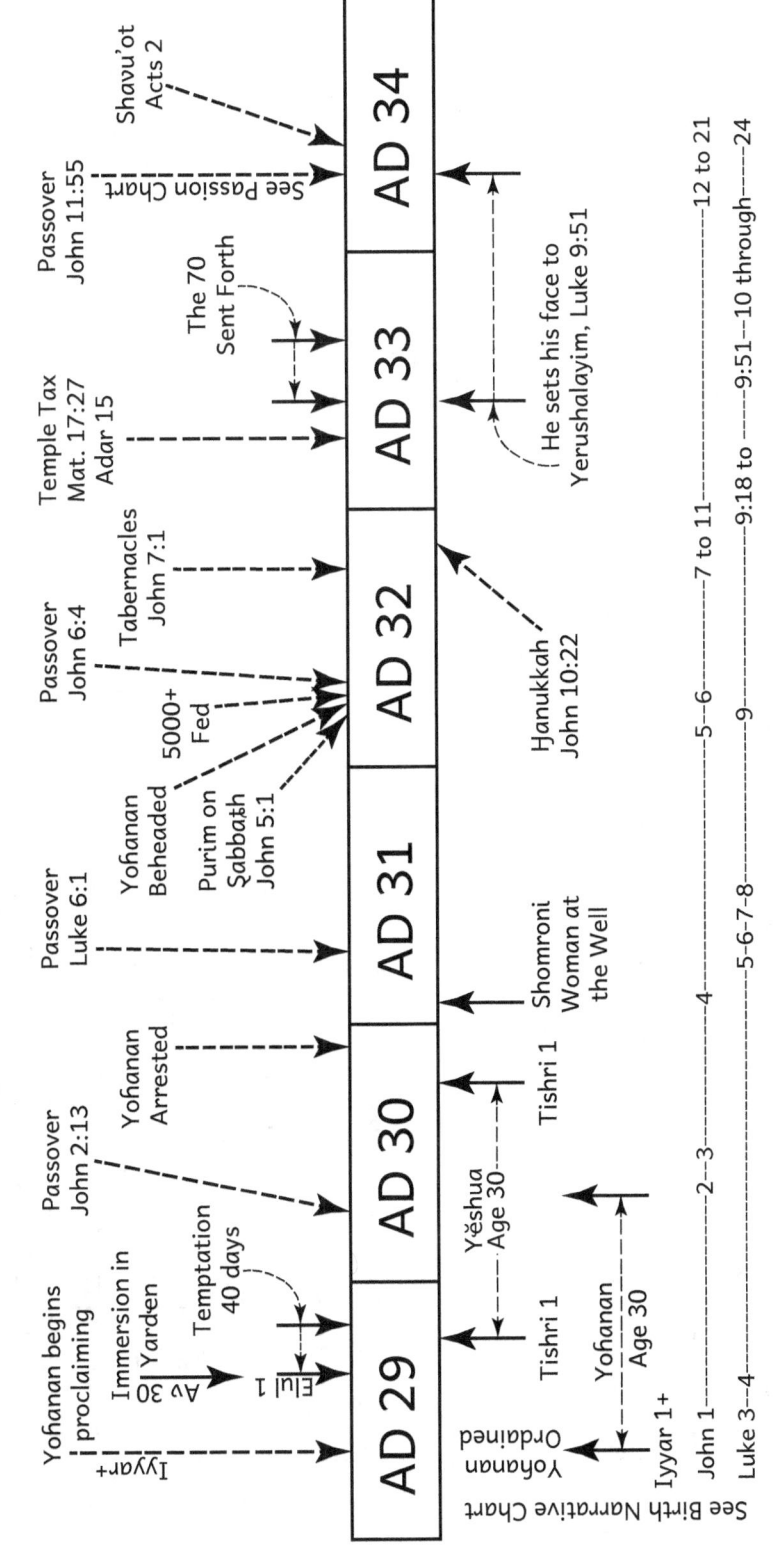

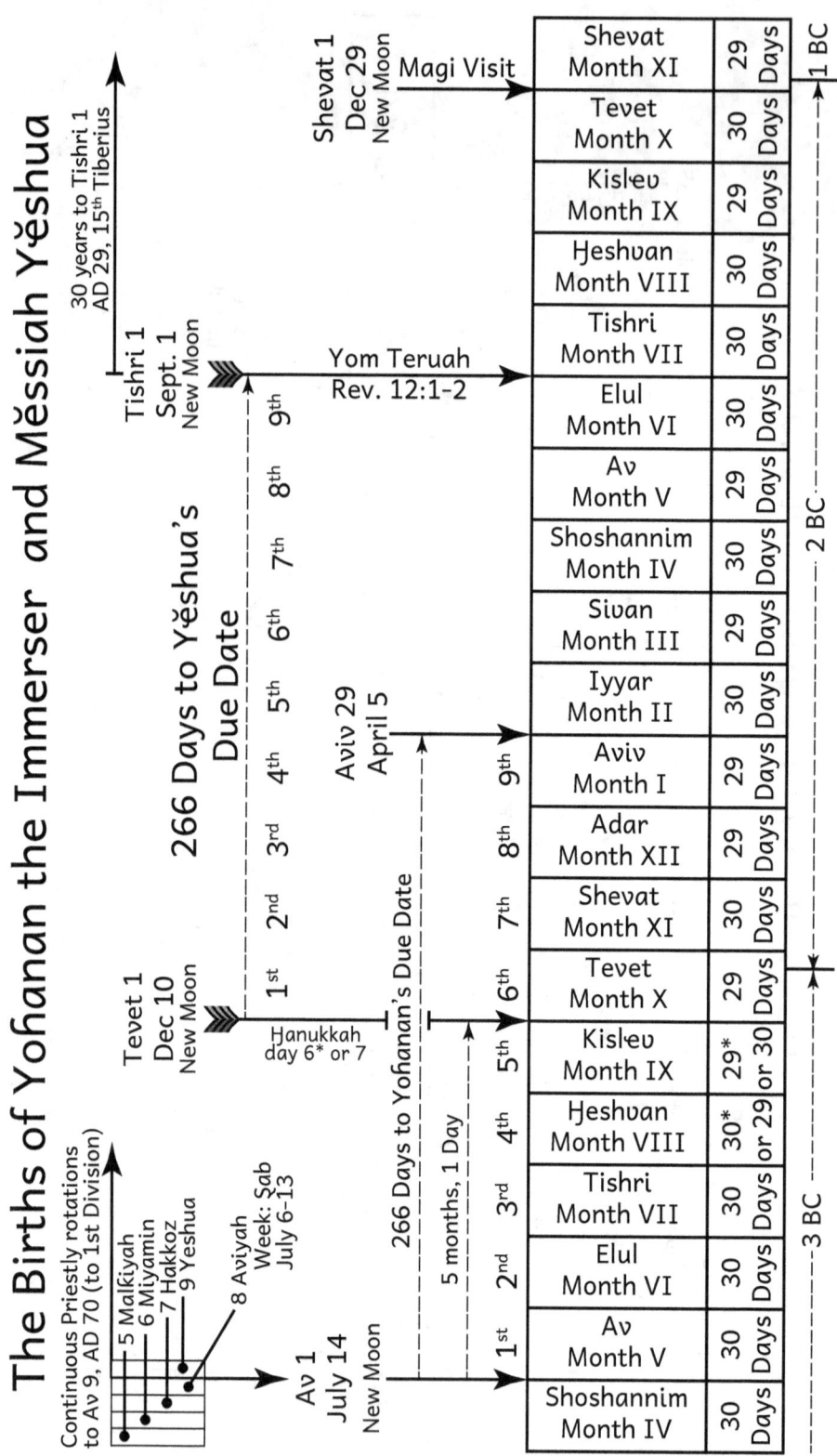

בְּשׂוֹרַת הַמָּשִׁיחַ

בשורת הברית החדשה של משיח
כאמונת המשיח לחדש
את ברית עולם

The Good News

of the New-Made Covenant

of Messiah

According to the Faithfulness of Messiah to Make New the Covenant of Old

Hardcover Edition

The Good News of Mĕssiah
Copyright 2022
Hardcover Edition 0.5.2.5

Published by Daniel Gregg
All Rights Reserved

Translated by Daniel Gregg
For ordering, see:
www.torahtimes.org

Previous page: The social circle of the gnostic heretic Marcion first associated the title 'New Testament' with this book. That he was later judged a heretic should call us to question the legitimacy of that innovation. Also, Marcion's 'canon' was an edited version of Luke-Acts and Paul's letters, omitting the Torah and Prophets, Matthew and the writings of Yoḥanan, because his goal was to remove all influence of what he called the "Old Testament" from what he called the "New Testament." So what is called Christianity owes its basic premise in rejecting the Torah to a man considered a heretic by both Eastern and Western Christianity. Gnostics went too far, however, and also denied the divinity of the Son, and were too radical either in licentiousness or asceticism. Yet they were the majority of Christendom at the time.

A 'testament' (also 'will') was an inheritance document in normal Koine Greek, and this was mistakenly taken for granted by the author of the Alexandrian Letter (see TOC) with prejudice. But among the Greek Jews, the word meant "covenant," a compact with mutal obligations, duties and promises. ▷ In Hebrew and Greek the term 'new' meant something 'made new,' either as to renew or make brand new, or any combination between the two. To make the covenant new means to restore it and update it to new circumstances. Far from being wiped out and replaced, the Torah remains at the center of the new made covenant. And therefore what we call the Evangelists writings should reflect this.

This book therefore is not the "New Testament," nor is this book "The New-Made Covenant." Rather, it is "The Good News of the New-Made Covenant." That is, it is the good news *about* the new-made covenant, the covenant of old made new.

In Hebrew translation this book is the *Besoraṭh Ha-Brit Ha-Ḥadashah*.

The expanded title on the title page is also explained by the notes on 1 Cor. 11:25; Mark 14:24 (cf. Mat. 26:28); Luke 22:19; 2 Cor. 3:6, 14. See also 2 Tim. 3:14-15 notes (cf. Alex. Letter 8:6 on page **558** and 8:7-13; 9:1, 15 notes). On THE FAITHFULNESS OF MESSIAH see the Preface and Rom. 3:22, 26; Gal. 2:16, 20; 3:22, 26; Phil. 3:9.

Edition Info: The major update that occassioned this edition is the full expansion of the ransom truth of Mĕssiah Yĕshua's death and resurrection. Many new notes were added, and portions of existing notes were corrected, mostly where language or wording might appear to accomodate the wrath satisfaction or commercial atonement heresy. Also, the opportunity was taken to add, correct, and clarify many other things.

Table of Contents†

PREFACES
- The Terms of the New-Made Covenant — 9
- Further In-Edition 0.5.2.3 Preface — 11
- Come Let Us Reason Together — 14
- Some Things Hard to Understand — 325

CHARTS
- Notes on the Chronological Charts — 12
- AD 29 to AD 34 Ministry Chart — iii
- The Births of Yoḥanan the Immerser and Mĕssiah Yĕshua — iv
- Daniel 9:24-27 Chart — 619
- Three Days and Three Nights and Resurrection Sabbath — 620
- Restoration of Kingdom Chart — 532
- General End Times Chart — 533
- Ya'aqov's Trouble Chart — 534

WHY DID MESSIAH DIE?
- Forgiveness — 583
- The Relation of Colossians 2:14 to Ephesians 2:15 — 413
- Isaiah 53: The Divine Ransom — 421
- Faithfulness, Forgiveness, and Ransom — 11
- Justify in Koine Greek — 420
- Justify in Biblical Hebrew — 421
- The Meaning of Justify — 588
- The Mystery of Lawlessness — 433
- Works of the Law — 579
- The Rabbis on Merit — 434
- What is Atonement? — 584
- Rabbinic Authority — 74
- Do We Need Tradition? — 603
- Genesis 15:6 and Psalm 106:31 — 384
- Deuteronomy 27:26 — 383

COSMOLOGY
- Genesis 1:1 Corrected — 444
- Cosmological Remarks — 472
- The Ruin Reconstruction Theory Refuted — 323

WRITINGS FALSELY ADDED TO SCRIPTURE
- The Alexandrian Letter Introduction — 539
- The Forged Alexandrian Letter — 547
- The Spurious Ending of Mark — 571
- The Misplaced Adultery Story — 537

---

†The customary books of the Good News are not listed here. The reader should know or memorize their order. This contents is a topically arranged index of supporting materials.

The Spurious Verses Added to Luke	577

THE APPOINTED TIMES OF THE MOST HIGH

Appointed Times Until The Year of Jubilee	593
The New Moon	599
Names of Moons	535
Priestly Rotations	601
Appointed Times vs. Church Counterfeit Holidays	592
The Rabbinic Calendar	536
Pseudo-Enoch Solar Calendar Heresy	601
Lunar Sabbath Heresy	602

WHEN DID MESSIAH DIE AND RISE FROM THE DEAD?

When Did Yĕshua Rise?	436
Resurrection Account Harmony	575
The Year Determined	173
Passion Year Guesses	227
Counting Sabbaths: Leviticus 23:15-16 Explained	173
After Three Days	114
First Day of the Week?	226
The Late One	73
Conting to the Sabbath	451
The Timing of Sabbaths Explained	75

ODDS AND ENDS

Special Letters	536
Nicene Idolatry	489
Which Texts Does the Most High Defend?	386
Quotations	591
Translation Concordance	604
Nomos with and without the article	582
Glossary of Significant Terms	175
Indefinite Future Perfect	597
Grammatical Codes	444
Grammar Points	400
On Circumcision	400
The Rhetorical Negative	228
Faith Designations	382
Execution Timber	73
The use of *one* with Almighty	474
Almighty Son vs. Son of God	174
End Notes	607
Witness To The Truth (Personal Testimony)	425
The Abstract Use of ב and ל	580
Yăhweʜ Appearing to Avraham	445
Apparatus Notes	581
Terminal Corruption	322
The Imperative to hear Mĕssiah's Word	284

9 The Terms of the New-Made Covenant

The Scripture does a great job of explaining everything, so that I don't have to. That is, except when men mistranslate it to make it say something that the Most High did not intend, and then write theology books based on their mistranslations and their heretical interpretations. Indeed, men of religion are in the business of destroying the Word of the Almighty, and in fact, I would have to say that most religion which claims to follow the light represents a greater threat than the threat of evil that so clearly and outwardly appears to be evil. Most of the Christian west, and Christianity itself is on the darkside. They just don't know it. And if you think that what goes by the Messianic Faith or Messianic Judaism isn't also enslaved by the dark side, or in fact in some cases actually helping it out, then I pray that you be given eyes to see clearly dear reader if you do not have them yet. And if you truly follow the true light, which is Mĕssiah Yĕshua, then what you need is a clearer knowledge of the truth, since the willingness to follow the truth is already in you.

Wherever the true light has shone, it has shone for a faithful remnant against the backdrop of a war against the truth by a majority that claims the authority of the light and the mantle of the light, but which in fact is serving the dark side or deeply enslaved by the darkside to false doctrines masquerading as the light. The object here is not to enter into polemic with the false light or its leadership, though I might reason with them a bit as a test to see whether they are enslaved by ignorance or are the spawn of Satan promoting the deception. Those enslaved in ignorance can be rescued. But their masters cannot. At the end of the age, Mĕssiah is going to come and destroy them.

The willingness to do right and follow the truth is with all the faithful, but the faithful have been unwise in accepting things which the false light side presents as light and truth. The false light has in fact exploited the willingness of the faithful to follow the true light by shrouding its evil doctrines in a robe of righteousness.

Now the purpose of explaining the truth clearly and accurately is to break the chains forged by the false light, and to free the faithful it has taken captive. This is about bringing the facts to light, and then not. It is not, because it is really about the power of the Most High through his Spĭrit to rescue the faithful. All facts will be disputed, but the might of the Spĭrit will show who is right in the end. But the Spĭrit requires me to state the facts before he will bear witness to them.

The first term is that which we call "repentance," which has been rendered herein as "being sorry and turning one's heart *from sin.*" The occurrences of this concept are found in the concordance starting on page **604**. The word repentance is not really a mistranslation, but it is regularly misinterpreted. According to its etymology in English, "repentance" originates in a Latin word meaning "to regret" (*penitire*) or "to make sorry" (*poenitire*). The Greek term is μετανοέω, which means *to have a change of heart.* But in the LXX it regularly translates the Hebrew verb נָחַם, which means "to be sorry" or "to regret." Another Hebrew term used to translate this term is לִתְשׁוּבָה, which means 'to turn around.' In as much as this begins in the heart with regretting one's past behavior and seeking to change it, it is correct. So then now the reader can see how I arrived at "being sorry and turning one's heart *from sin.*"

In respect to the terms of everlasting life, if the reader will look the occurrences up, he will see that being sorry and turning one's heart always has to do with regretting one's own evil works and turning his heart away from them. And the inevitable result of this is that he or she will stop practicing the evil they are sorry for. This of course requires the knowledge and conviction in the heart that what one had been doing was wrong and evil. So this is the first term or condition of seeking everlasting life with a view to being released from sin. A release is a dual concept. It means to gain forgiveness, and also to gain freedom from the sin that formerly enslaved us. And it is the Most High that sees the heart and who forgives, and it is the Almĭghty Sŏn who suffered to ransom us from all evil.

The second term is that which we call "faithfulness," which occurs herein translated "faithful," (πιστὸς) "faithfulness," (πίστις) or "to hold faithful" (πιστεύειν) according to whether the Greek is an adjective, noun, or verb. Forms of this word occur more than 500 times. The verb πιστεύειν which I render herein "to hold faithful" is mistranslated in almost all other versions as "to believe." But it is impossible that this word should mean just this and nothing else, because the good news is constantly communicated with this term. If the term meant "to believe" only then it would stand in contradiction to the imperative to be sorry for one's sins and to turn one's heart from sin.

No one is truly saved who thinks their only obligation to Gŏd is to believe that Mĕssiah is his Saviour or that Gŏd forgives his sin, and then who practices no loyalty to him. Though there are many who believe this doctrine and yet hold faithful anyway (because the Spĭrit of Mĕssiah bears witness in them that if they become disloyal they will become enslaved to sin again) this doctrine does contradict what the Scripture teaches. Because when he was asked what was necessary for everlasting life, Mĕssiah's answer was to obey the commandments (Mat. 19:16; Mark 10:17). Paul did not give a different answer, but states in Rom. 2:7 that everlasting life must be sought by doing good. The same was taught in the beginning.

Without a doubt there are many texts one could quote or interpret some other way as to say that holding faithful to Mĕssiah is not necessary for everlasting life. But anyone who ever did trust on this doctrine and continued in sin is not saved. And since it is the case that those who are disloyal cannot be saved, then the most important imperative anyone who claims to follow Mĕssiah can hear is that it is necessary to pledge faithfulness to Him, and to be holding faithful to him.

One can seek assurance of salvation in the doctrines of men, or one can listen to the words of Mĕssiah's emissary, "And by this we are knowing that

we have been knowing him, if we may be keeping his commandments. The one who says, "I have been knowing him," and does not keep his commandments, is a liar, and the truth is not in him; but whoever may be keeping his word, truly in him the love of the Almĭghty has been getting accomplished. By this we know that we are in him: the one who is claiming he remains in him ought himself to be walking in the same way he walked" (1 Yoḣ. 2:3-6). And "If anyone may not be remaining in me, he is going to be thrown out like the branch, and will have been dried up. Then they are gathering them, and casting them into the fire, and it is burning them." (Yoḣ. 15:6).

So it is only consistent with the truth to translate the verb πιστεύειν in agreement with the adjective πιστός from which it is derived. And in fact, upon investigation, I find no evidence that it is derived from the verb πείθω, which means "to persuade," but as with many words the verb is derived from the adjective. And so also in this case the verb for "faithful" is "to be faithful," or to "hold faithful." Certainly in the case of the Hebrew, the noun, the adjective, and the verb are all derived from the same root אָמַן, and here too many tell us the verb means "believe," including Israeli's and Jews who do not know Biblical Hebrew, but who only know late Hebrew which has been corrupted just like Greek.

But a survey of the usage of אָמַן in BH will show that its fundamental meaning is "to support" something or someone. It is used for a mother supporting a child, foster parents supporting a child, physical temple supports. And when it is supporting a person, then it stands for loyalty to that person. Thus, if it is to hold something faithful, then it is to believe the something is valid, but if it is to hold faithful to someone than it stands for loyalty. And in a number of cases of Messiah's words, it appears that both believing something is true or possible and being loyal to him are meant at the same time.

The case of Isaiah 7:9 can instruct us, viz. "אִם לֹא תַאֲמִינוּ כִּי לֹא תֵאָמֵנוּ," "If you will not give support, surely you will not be supported!" If they will not give their support to the Most High, then he will not support them! But if we examine the common translations, none of them can render it consistently.

Finally, if the reader will care to examine Romans 10:8-10, it says there, "But what is it saying? "The Word is near you, in your mouth and in your heart." This is the word of the faithfulness which we are proclaiming, because if you may have confessed with your mouth, Adŏnai Yĕshua, and may have pledged faithfulness in your heart, because the Almĭghty raised him from the dead, you will be rescued. Because by the heart one is confirmed faithful to righteousness, and by the mouth one confesses oneself unto deliverance." The word here that Paul speaks about is the quotation he has given from Deuteronomy 30:14, and this word is the commandments which are written on the heart. So we can see that Paul teaches holding faithful to the Word.

Paul seems to speak against works of the law in several places. It would seem then that he is against being sorry and turning one's heart from sin, since the law identifies what sin is, but the word νόμος has a more common meaning in Greek, and that is *custom*. Anyone with a decent Greek dictionary can look it up. And a little knowledge of Judaism is also necessary to understand what Paul was talking about. You see the Rabbis of the day had this idea that if one did certain good deeds beyond the call of duty, that is beyond what was required, then Gŏd would be persuaded to forgive sins by the extra credit earned by the good deed. And if one lacked these customary deeds, then just by being properly Jewish one could inherit the needed extra credit from Abraham. The customary deeds would always appear to be fulfilling commandments beyond the call of duty, such as extra charity, or extra prayers, or whatever the Rabbis might regard as a penance.

So these works became a system by which Gŏd could be propitiated. This is what Paul was against, because it negated the need for two things. Firstly, it negated in some degree the need to be sorry for and turn the heart from sin. Because if Gŏd could be propitiated by the works, then the demerit could be compensated for, such that Gŏd did not have a loss for the person in the heavenly accounting. Secondly, it negated Gŏd's forgiveness because now the demerit was paid for instead of being forgiven.

But the Scripture prescribes being sorry for and turning the heart from sin to receive forgiveness of sins, and not paying for sin out of extra credit or the treasury of Abraham. The Rabbis' system resulted in a half hearted perfunctory faithfulness, because the unfaithful part could be traded out with the extra credits.

It was only this rabbinic system of merit that Paul was against, and not against being faithful and keeping the commandments. But when some of Paul's converts did not understand the concepts he was against, they were led astray by teachers taking exception to the Sabbath, circumcision, and food laws, and they thought that he was talking about these laws. Eventually they called this "the ceremonial law," and concluded that the ceremonial law was abolished and the moral law remained. The instances of so called ceremonial law nullification are discussed in detail in the notes upon the passages where these questions arise, which the reader can see.

It suffices to point out that νόμος also stands for a "legal norm" as opposed to a legal exception. So when Paul says one is not under the legal norm, he means divine judgment for violating any part of the Torah. We are instead under forgiveness, which is the legal exception. Now if "not under law" should refer only to the ceremonial law, then this leaves us under the moral law. So now lets see how this reads, "you are not under the ceremonial law (but still under the moral law), but under grace." So then is grace given in place of the ceremonial law, but not in place of the moral law? You see than the contradiction? By saying it means the ceremonial law it follows that grace is only given for violating the ceremonial law, because Paul has said nothing about the moral law.

Truly Paul's words concerning the law were spoken about all of it, and not just some little part that Christians desired to have nullified.

Further In-Edition 0.5.2.3 Preface

The greatest knowledge problem to face the faithful in Mĕssiah Yĕshua is the use of corrupt Scripture translations (Jer. 8:8; Hos. 4:6). If one reads the common translations in almost any language, and listens to even a few Christian sermons, the understanding gained from the text is a message of lawlessness (Mat. 7:23). This problem climaxes in Paul's letter to the Romans and Galatians, but it occurs in many other places as well (2 Pet. 3:16). Enough of the translation printed on the page is corrupted to ensure a lawless interpretation in the hands of the lawless, and to confuse the faithful who see the larger context and the contradictions. Knowing Greek is not an assured deliverance. Even if one is educated in Koine Greek, but he uses the church approved definitions of the Greek words, then the message is already corrupted. Both the translations and the dictionaries used to support them were heavily impacted by a tradition of lawlessness resulting in lawless interpretations.

Even the lawful among the lawless have been rendered weak and powerless by this prison of circular reasoning. False tradition supports false definitions in the most used dictionaries, and false dictionaries support false translations, which support false tradition. Where does the loop end? It does not end until the confused admit that they have not seen a viable solution put onto the table of debate, and then are willing to seek an answer through prayer.

But all is not to be lost. For the faithful, for a remnant still able to listen, the hour of redemption from enslavement and persecution through these false teachings has been coming nearer. Top scholars have now unpacked the sense of a key Pauline phrase, "the faithfulness of Mĕssiah" (N.T. Wright, Richard Hays, Daniel Wallace; Rom. 3:26; Gal. 2:16, 20; 3:22, 26; Phil. 3:9.) vs. "faith in Christ" or "the faith of Christ." They have blown a hole in the prison wall. They have ignited a theological war with the prison guards who cling to the corrupted sense of pístis, 'faith,' or even 'belief.' What the lawless are faced with now, if they are paying attention, is the exposure of faulty grammar and lexical sense in some of their key mistranslations at the highest levels of academic competence. The dam really begins to break when we realize that the pístis word group plainly means, "faithful," "faithfulness" and "to hold faithful," in three parts of speech and not "believing," "belief" and "to believe," adjective, noun, and verb.

New Perspective scholars are still trying to come to grips with the meaning of 'justify' (See Appendix XI, and page 588) and 'the customary works' (See Appendix VIII, and 579). The latter is explained to mean Jewish identity markers as the people of Gŏd: Ṣabbaṯh, circumcision, festivals, new moons, clean and unclean, and the Temple and Levitical offerings. You can see it in their raging debate with the classical Reformed party, which wishes to include all moral law in some sense under "works of the law" (page 433). But none of them have a clear solution, because they are committed to a rejection of a good deal of the Law fueled by anti-Jewish prejudices, as well as Christian versions of the same doctrines of appeasement used by Judaism. So, the New Perspective scholars have still not figured out what Paul meant by "customary works," or by the word "justify" and its various forms. Their opponents do not know what it means either.

This translation presents a clear solution. The "customary works," (See Appendix VIII and page 433) refers to the traditional Jewish doctrine of merits, wherein the means of forgiveness is that a merit cancels out a demerit. Even while the Temple stood, this unbiblical understanding was replacing the real meaning of forgiveness. So Paul is only objecting to the unscriptural concept of doing good deeds in order to pay off the bad deeds. Any deed may be done for that goal where a person does not understand real forgiveness. So Paul does not mean legitimate obedience which is motivated by love. He means deeds of merit motivated to earn forgiveness.

On the one hand, obeying the commandments merits eternal life (cf. Rom. 2:7; Exo. 20:6; Lev. 18:5; Mat. 20:16), but on the other the merit of obedience does not atone for sin, or pay for it, or compensate for it. Sin has to be forgiven, and not compensated for by positive deeds or propitiatory sacrifice.

I now come to the word "justify." It is exactly because the translators are still understanding this word to mean acquit, declare righteous, or make righteous that we have a problem. According to Scripture the guilty cannot be acquitted (Exodus 23:7). The guilty may be condemned or forgiven. But the guilty cannot be justified. To acquit the guilty is to declare that they did no wrong. It would mean a false justice. It would be a judicial lie, a mistake. It is the lawless who want to be acquitted, because they do not want to confess their lawlessness.

The clear solution is integrated into this translation. In the first century Koine Greek, as may be demonstrated from usage in Josephus and Cassius Dio the word "justify" meant "to administer justice" to someone, usually in some punitive sense (See page 420). "To justify the guilty" then meant to do justice to them, to punish them. Also in Hebrew, the equivalent verb meant "to get justice" for someone usually with the connotation of a favorable outcome (See page 421). So if your advocate can get justice for you, it may be either an acquittal or a pardon. Clearly if one is **guilty**, the advocate can only get justice via a pardon in the favorable sense. A pardon is forgiveness.

The reason that we have the lawless translation, "justified by faith" (Rom. 5:1, KJV) is that the guilty like hearing that they have been acquitted on the condition of their believing only or trusting the alleged fact of acquittal (2 Tim. 4:3). For this reason the lawless party teaches that no repentance is required for salvation. On the contrary, Paul meant we are "administered justice by Messiah's faithfulness" (Rom. 5:1). His forgiving-justice, if we confess our sins, and turn from them pledging faithfulness to him, is to cancel the penalties against us, to forgive us. Then he ransoms us from the powers of lawlessness, canceling their claim of ownership over us, and cleanses us from sin. See Mat. 20:28, Mark 10:45; Rev. 5:9, Appendix X, page 584, and related passages.

By this fundamental test we can prove that all the "justified by faith" versions are corrupt, and were

translated by men who did not understand the key meaning of "justify" in Koine Greek. The very idea of justifying the guilty before God's court is an abomination to him (Prov. 17:15). It is totally opposed to forgiveness.

The first century Rabbis also evolved a doctrine of acquitting the guilty. They posed the question, "Why was Israel delivered from the armies of Pharaoh at the sea?" The larger party claimed that it was because of the merit of Abraham that they were saved from destruction. This was the house of Shemaiah. The smaller party claimed that it was because of their own merits. This was the doctrine of Abtalyon. And their disciple Hillel taught it both ways. They were teaching that for whatever reason that the Almĭghty would consider not delivering them there that it was because of the merit of Abraham. The merit of Abraham was considered to atone for any deficiency of merit they had. And the proof text was Gen. 15:6 (see page 384).

Going through the sea in Jewish soteriology is the symbol of salvation, to be immersed into the sea, which we understand, to bury the old man with Mĕssiah, and to rise renewed with Mĕssiah. For this reason the doctrine of compensation by merit must be rejected. The Făther forgives, and Mĕssiah died as a ransom to rescue us from the power of sin. By no means is sin compensated for by merit. Only the lawless believe that, like king Saul who believed he could atone for taking spoil by sacrificing the spoil.

At the first, the Roman Church adopted the doctrine of Hillel. It was both ways. But instead of imputing Abraham's faithfulness to the offspring as merits, the Church modified the doctrine to impute Christ's righteousness to his followers in both fact and in law. This doctrine teaches that the infused righteousness of Christ is what acquits one of sin. Later Luther came along and rejected the idea of personal righteousness choosing to believe instead that the Almĭghty is compensated for sin by Christ's righteousness only. This too is nothing but an acquittal based on legal fiction. It is just legalism.

The true good news answers the question, "What must I do to inherit eternal life?" (Mat. 19:16). There is no one commandment that is best, because forgiveness is not by personal compensation (vs. 17). There is no make up deed as Abtalyon taught. And there is no perfection, because all have sinned. Only Gŏd is good (Mark 10:18). Therefore, there is no legal perfection as Shemiah taught. Yet we must hold faithful to Mĕssiah by keeping his commandments, even though we still stumble in ignorance. And those who do so are also given the unmerited loving-kindness of forgiveness of sins through the covenant faithfulness of Mĕssiah (Exo. 20:6). By Mĕssiah's faithfulness the Făther thought it just to forgive, and to ransom us from the Powers into whose hands he had sold us. This is what the true good news is.

For the forgiving justice of the Almĭghty is revealed in the good news from his faithfulness unto our faithfulness, as it has been getting written, the righteous shall live by his faithfulness.

The Good News of Messiah is hereby commended to all the faithful in Mĕssiah. It's publication would need no justification other than the reasons mentioned in this preface.

Notes on the Chronological Charts

The aim here is to relate the seven charts without getting lost in the details, and to give information not presented in the charts. The charts are near the ends of the book, which I will call, *Ministry* (page iii), *Birth* (page iv), *Sabbath Years* (page 619), *Resurrection* (page 620), *Jacob's Trouble* (page 534), *General End Times* (page 533), and the *Restoration* chart (page 532).

❶ The *Sabbath Years* chart is a detail of Daniel 9:24-27 (page 619). This chart lays out the prediction in the book of Daniel that Messiah would come after a specified number of Sabbath years had passed to ransom Yisra'el. The details are explained in my book titled *The Resurrection Day of Messiah Yĕshua*.

The prophecy lays out 70 Sabbath years in relation to the first and second comings of Messiah. Firstly, the prophecy says we are to count the sabbatical years starting with a commandment or decree to rebuild the city of Jerusalem. This happened under Neḥemyah in 445 BC. Then seven Sabbath years pass by until the anointed priest Ezra comes to restore the Sanctuary service. Then sixty-two Sabbath more years pass until the Anointed One, Yeshua, who was cut off in AD 34.

These Sabbath years are called 'sevens' in the prophecy, sometimes mistakenly translated 'weeks,' but in fact Deut. 16:9 says, "the year of the seven *is* the year of the release," (שְׁנַת־הַשֶּׁבַע שְׁנַת הַשְּׁמִטָּה), which is to say the Sabbatical year is called a "seven," so that "sevens" pertains to multiple Sabbath years.

After the Messiah was killed and rose from the dead, the clock counting the Sabbatical years was stopped, and will remain so until the end Messiah is ready to visibly return to receive his kingdom. But this is not unusual in the calculation of the era's of Scripture. The summation of 390 years of sin for Yisra'el and 40 years of Yehudah was the result of starting and stopping the clock multiple times according to when they were sinning and when they were not. And just the same, the clock measuring the Babylonian Dominion for 70 years stopped at 66 ½ years, leaving 42 months for the Babylonian Dominion to be completed. When the final Babylonian Dominion is completed, and the last of the 70 Sabbatical years is counted, then the prophecy promises that iniquity will be declared to be cleansed, and everlasting righteousness will rest upon all Yisra'el. So we still have to wait for it.

The seven sevens mentioned in the prophecy

has this explanation. After seven sevens the anointed priest Ezra comes. After the sixty-two the expected seed of the woman, the Anointed One.

Ezra is the first anointed. Mĕssiah is the second. Neḥemyah governed first, and Ezra second. The gap between the 69th Şabbath year and the 70th should not be unexpected. Yisra'el failed to keep 70 Şabbath years in batches with gaps between them. Neither the 390 or 40 years are thus continuous stretches, but they are the sum of the episodes during which Yisra'el served idols.

They came into the land in 1592 BC. They first observed the seventh year Şabbath after six years of planting and harvest, and the Jubilee Şabbath after 49 years. The Şabbath year clock is set synchronously with creation at 4139 BC. I have published several editions of this chronology before. The new edition is now available (*The Scroll of Biblical Chronology and Ancient Near Eastern History*, Volumes I and II). The Chronology is the spearhead that will break the rationality of all opposition. I may not in the end wield the spear. The Chronology stands independent of this author on the Truth and Word of the Almĭghty. It points to the Truth and the Word, and His Good News. What you see here is only the point of the spear. The majority will rebel because they believe in a false gospel of acquittal and appeasement. The remnant of grain left in that weed patch will be shown the way out of their ignorance. But the day of Yăhweh will test the Assembly. See Rev. 12:14 footnote.

❷ The *Resurrection* chart is a detail of Mĕssiah's suffering in AD 34, at the end of the 62 sevens (page 620). The year AD 34 has a high profile in Church traditions, as also the March 25th date for the first day of unleavened bread that year. This simply confirms what may be calculated. I am persuaded that the emissaries did not write so that the lawless translators and teachers of the last two millennia would corrupt their writings but so that all will be revealed to the house of Yisra'el in the last days, so that they will come trembling out of their exile in the nations to their own land. This will have a cost. The nations will be hardened into implacable rebellion by the fallen Powers and their own arrogance. Whoever professes faith in Mĕssiah will have to decide whether to go with them or to claim their inheritance in Yisra'el, and to do the commandments of Mĕssiah. The peoples will fall into a new dark age, but the kingdom will be glorious. Do not worry about the conversion of the nations. The example of Yisra'el will be the best way to tell them. But if anyone asks, then give them the reason we have hope: Mĕssiah, the Almĭghty Sŏn.

All things worth knowing may be proved, tested, and confirmed. I am no authority except to the one who realizes he can learn something from me until he himself grows up. For a season you may volunteer to regard me as an authority. But I claim no authority over anyone except that given me over my own house. Mĕssiah is your authority.

❸ Now to the *Birth* chart (page iv). The reader will want to consult Luke 1-3 and the notes there under in conjunction with this chart. It took me longer to figure this out than any other part of the chronology, with a wrong turn to 3 BC, and a wrong turn on priestly divisions, because we have inherited lies from our fathers. Mĕssiah was exactly 'almost 30' in AD 29. Luke was not guessing, but stating more exactly. This puts the birth year in 2 BC. Rev. 12:1-2 gives us the exact date: Yom Teruah. The seventh month began Sept. 1 that year (see Appendix I for the calendar rules).

The timing for the birth of Yoḥanan is independently figured in the same year using priestly rotations, which were continuous, with no annual reset. All priests were to eat equally from the altar, and not some more than others. Therefore, we figure from a known date and known priestly division whose service was Av 9, AD 70 back to the division of Aviyah. For the priests well remembered which division served at the fall of the Temple. This leads to Av 1, July 14, a new moon, for the conception of Yoḥanan, and leads to an amazing synchronization of the two births with the remaining facts. The data and the astronomy fit only one way between the constraining dates on both ends (except for two months with no net change effected). I am no prophet, except one who explains what is already written, and no seer, except one who sees what has been seen.

❹ The *Ministry*: see Luke 13:6-9 and the footnote on that text (page iii). Notice all those appointed times in the chart? The Scripture knows nothing of the times invented by the Church, but only those appointed feasts in Scripture, and those coming out of the Jewish tradition: Ḥanukkah and Purim.

❺ Finally, I come to the latest set of charts I have added. First, *Jacob's Trouble* (page 534). This chart should not be considered a divine prediction, but only a human one based on divine predictions given to us in prophecy. Even if some things prove incorrect, I have included the charts because I am certain that a good deal of prophecy is going to come to pass in accord with the principles included in these charts.

I will include here some mention of the fundamental basis for this chart. The first thing I should mention is that it is just over 100 years in the future, because a space in time must be made for the restoration of all Yisra'el to the land. Also, the timing is based on the Jubilee cycle, the third Jubilee from now will be in AD 2133. The "time, times, and half a time" are split into two halves of the final seven years leading up to the Jubilee year. I have determined that "a time" in Old Imperial Aramaic has the same meaning as the Hebrew word "days," in phrases such as "from days to days." "Days" is the Hebrew idiom for exactly one solar year, from spring equinox to spring equinox.

The chart is also designed so that the two witnesses will be able to repeat the sign of Jonah, which will look like the *Resurrection* chart (page 620) in terms of weekdays, but it will be a month before Passover in AD 2130.

❻ Second *General End Times* (page 533). I should note several impressions of this chart I have. I believe that events have been crammed into about as small a time span as they can go.

❼ Third, the *Restoration* chart (page 532).

Come and Reason Together

What is necessary for Salvation? Měssiah gives a direct answer to the Rich Young Ruler in Matthew 19, Mark 10, and Luke 18. What is your answer? Měssiah began with the easiest of the commandments and progressed until he reached those among the hardest: YOU SHALL LOVE YOUR NEIGHBOR AS YOURSELF. Though not quoted in all accounts, it is implicit in Měssiah's command for the young man. This was the commandment he was not keeping to Měssiah's satisfaction. His wealth was not at the disposal of the kingdom of Gŏd. No doubt the young man was already giving the "required" charity and alms as the religious leaders taught. The problem with this is that the leaders had relaxed the Torah and made it easy with a check list of do's. As a result they were putting the Most High at a distance and treating him like a creditor who just needed to be paid his dues by sufficient performance.

But the Almĭghty Sŏn desires our complete pledge of faithfulness, so that we hold faithful to Him in everything he says. Because he loves those who keep his commandments, and he shows mercy and loving kindness to those obeying him, as it is written in the Ten Commandments. See Exodus 20:6. Therefore, forgiveness of sins comes upon being sorry for one's sins and turning one's heart from sin. The young man's sin was giving only the little charity the religious leaders required rather than placing all of it at the disposal of Gŏd's kingdom. His faithfulness was far less than it could have been due to false teaching combined with the desire of his flesh to keep for himself what Gŏd desired to be put to just use. A person in doubt of their forgiveness and their inheritance in the life to come should ponder whether they have complete faithfulness or not.

This is not just about money, which most of us do not have a lot of. It is about our time and our gifts also. Have we submitted all to Him? The religious authorities cannot answer this question for you. Their answer is spiritual abuse for their benefit. Only you can. Because it is the Holy Spĭrit that writes the Torah on the heart. If you want his assurance then listen to Him! And if you listen then you belong to Měssiah, and His Spĭrit will give you the necessary peace and assurance that you remain in his forgiveness, because most of us are less than perfect.

But those who are less than faithful to Měssiah have sought another way to address their sin problem, another way to please Gŏd, and another way to gain assurance. And this is the idea that sufficient charity will atone for one's sins. Judaism calls it zechut. This is what religious leaders teach. They teach your merits or inherited merits from Abraham should be sufficient to cover your demerits. Since this system covers demerit by payment, it requires less than complete faithfulness to Gŏd, and it does not address demerits with repentance and forgiveness. Forgiveness is not debt repayment!

Most of the rest of the world repeats this Jewish error in other ways, and I will focus on the error of Gnostic Christianity, which has repeated this error in its theological philosophy. This error is being counted righteous by the merit of Christ. This is really the same thing as the doctrine of zechut in Judaism. The merit of another is counted to one's account so that the Most High does not view one's sin. As a result, Gnostics teach less than being wholeheartedly faithful to Měssiah is necessary for salvation. In fact they teach that no faithfulness at all is necessary in their most radical sectors.

Therefore, the Gnostics have reinterpreted the Torah and more so the writings of Paul to suit their no-faithfulness salvation. But Gnostics have also reinterpreted the Torah and the Evangelists to conform to their image of Yĕshua[h] (salvation). The Gnostics have corrupted the meanings of all the basic vocabulary, putting faith for faithfulness, believe for holding faithful, justification for the administration of justice, and more, and they have corrupted all their translations to support their doctrines. Even Jewish translations are infected with their disease, which after almost 2000 years has terminally corrupted them, more corrupt than deep state totalitarianism. Gnostic Christianity is more corrupt than communism, and less able to be spiritually rescued.

I counsel them to reconsider what Měssiah said to the young man and not to reinterpret it, because your salvation does depend on understanding him plainly. So for the Christian coming with gnostic arguments and reinterpretations and excuses as to why he or she does not have to obey the Almĭghty, I have only one question. What is necessary for everlasting life? And if the answer isn't to keep the commandments with complete faithfulness to Měssiah, then we are done. I say to them in that case, they need to cut off their book of Hebrews, their Paul, their false chronology of Měssiah's death and resurrection, their false Marcionite redefinition called the New Testament, and their false translations and interpretations of key passages in the Torah and Prophets.

This volume rescues the real Paul and the real canon of Scripture from the Gnostic Beast, but this rescue isn't for the unfaithful. It is for the faithful and the little faithfuls that need to be rescued from the mouth of this roaring beast, and want to be rescued, who live in the wilderness of the nations surrounded by gnostic wolves. Because Gnostic Christianity was never of the truth, and never followed Měssiah. They always practiced lawlessness. They try to propitiate the wrath of Gŏd with payment.

They are the many who claim to believe in Měssiah, but who have instead invented their New Testament, honor the 'Church fathers,' and follow the corrupt theology of Augustine, Anselm, Luther, Calvin, and Lewis Sperry Chafer. In the last day, Měssiah will say to the many. I never knew you.

Mattatyahu

1 ¹The scroll of the begettings of ᵍYĕshuą the Anŏinted, son of David, son of Avraham. ²Avraham₁ fathered Yitsḥaq, and Yitsḥaq fathered Ya'aqov, and Ya'aqov fathered Yehudah and his brothers. ³And Yehudah fathered Perez and Zeraḥ from Tamar. And Perez fathered Ḥezron, and Ḥezron fathered Ram. ⁴And Ram fathered Amminadav, and Amminadav fathered Naḥshon, and Naḥshon fathered Salmon. ⁵And Salmon ᵝfathered Bo̊az from Raḥav, and Bo̊az fathered Ǫved from Ruṭh, and Ǫved fathered Yishai. ⁶And Yishai fathered David₁₄ the king.

⁶ᵇAnd David₁ fathered Ṣolomoṇ from the wife of Uriyah. ⁷And Ṣolomoṇ fathered Reḥavam, and Reḥavam fathered Aviyah, and Aviyah fathered Aṣå. ⁸And Aṣå fathered Yehoshaphaṭ, and Yehoshaphaṭ fathered Yoram, and Yoram fathered Uzziyahu. ⁹And Uzziyahu fathered Yoṭham, and Yoṭham fathered Aḥaz, and Aḥaz fathered Yeḥizqiyahu. ¹⁰And Yeḥizqiyahu fathered Menaṣṣeн, and Menaṣṣeн fathered Amon, and Amon fathered ₁₄Yo'shiyahu. ¹¹And Yo'shiyahu fathered Yekǫnyahu and his brothers, before the time of the deportation to Baḇel.

¹²And after the deportation to Baḇel, Yekǫnyahu₁ fathered She'alti̊'l, and ⁷She'alti̊'l fathered Zerubbavel. ¹³And Zerubbavel fathered Avihud, and Avihud fathered Elyaqim, and Elyaqim fathered Azzur. ¹⁴And Azzur fathered Ẓadoq, and Ẓadoq fathered Yakin, and Yakin fathered Elihud. ¹⁵And Elihud fathered Elazar, and Elazar fathered Mattan, and Mattan fathered Ya'aqov. ¹⁶And Ya'aqov fathered Yoṣeph the husband of Miryam from whom has been born ₁₄Yĕshuą, who is called *the* Anŏinted One. ¹⁷So all the generations from Avraham through David are fourteen generations and from David up to the Baḇeli deportation are fourteen generations. And from the Baḇeli deportation through the Anŏinted are fourteen generations.ˣ

¹⁸And the birth of Yĕshuą the Anŏinted One was *happening* like this: his mother Miryam, having been betrothed to Yoṣeph, before either *of* them came together, was found pregnant from the Holy Spĭrit. ¹⁹And, Yoṣeph her husband, being righteous, and not willing to make her an example, had been decided to dismiss her secretly. ²⁰And, when he considered these things, behold, the Messenger *of* Yăhweн*ᵖ* was seen by him in a dream, saying, "Yoṣeph, son of David,

---

1:1 θ Yĕshuą, Anŏinted, Făther, Sŏn, Spĭrit, Almĭghty, Yăhweн, Aďŏnai, Măster, Aďŏn, Aďŏni, Lŏrd, Sĭr. The breve /˘/ indicates where the texts marked a *nomina sacra*, indicating the divinity of the person titled or named, and additionally that Hebrew may be substituted, viz. Yehŏshuą or Yĕshuą, Măshiaḥ, Aḇḇă, Bĕn or Bĕn, Rŭaḥ, Elŏhim or Ĕl, Aďŏnai, Aďŏn, Aďŏni. It is not known how many nomina sacra there were originally. **1:5** β Ten or more unrecorded generations were skipped at β and also in earlier lists, covering about 300 years. See Deut. 23:3. Between Yoram and Uzziyahu three kings that committed iniquity are skipped: A'ḥaziah, Yoa'sh, A'maziah, and after Yo'shiyahu Yehoyaqim is skipped. David is honored to be counted twice. Yekǫnyah is cut off from the count in vs. 11 (Jer. 22:24; Hag. 2:23) but counted in vs. 12. The 14-14-14 structure was useful as a check sum. **1:12** γ She'alti̊'l was born of kinsman marriage. The ransom father was Neri (Luke 3:27) and mother Yekǫnyahu's widow, because Yekǫnyahu was childless at his death (Jer. 22:30). Zerubbavel also had two fathers. The ransom father was Peḍayah (1 Chron. 3:19) because She'alti̊'l must have been childless at death, and his widow became the wife of Peḍayah. **1:17** χ Notice in vs. 2 & 6, 6b & 10, and 12 & 16, the subscripts 1 & 14. **1:20** ρ cf. 1:1θ. Compare Syriac Marayya: מָרְיָא = ܡܳܪܝܳܐ = ha-Aďŏnai. See Dani̊'l 4:1 for paradigmn: עַמְמַיָּא אֻמַּיָּא וְלִשָּׁנַיָּא. The יָא ending = plural emphatic. The emphatic ending makes

Mattatyahu 2

you should not fear to take Miryam your wife, because he which has been conceived in her is from the Holy Spirit. ²¹And she will bear a Sŏn. And you will call his name Yĕshuą͑, because he will rescue his people from their sins. ²²And all this had been happening so that the thing uttered through the prophet will have been fulfilled, by the mouth of Yăhwęҥ, saying, ²³ 'BEHOLD, THE VIRGIN WILL BE WITH CHILD, AND WILL BEAR A SŎN. AND °THEY WILL CALL HIS NAME ỊMMANU‑ęʹLᵅ,'" (which being translated means, "GŎD IS WITH USᵝ.") ²⁴And when Yoşeph was risen from his sleep, he did as the Messenger of Yăhwęҥ commanded him. And he received his wife, ²⁵and he was not knowing her until from it she gave birth to ᵋthe firstborn Sŏn, and called his name Yĕshuą͑.

2 ¹And, when Yĕshuą͑ was born in Bęṭh‑leħem of Yehuḓah in the days of Herod the king, behold, Magi from the east came alongside ṭo Yerushalayim, saying, ²"Where is he who has been born King of the Yehuḓîm? Because we have seen his star ᵚin the rising, and we have come to worship him." ³And, when Herod the king heard this, he was shaken up, and all Yerushalayim with him. ⁴And having gathered together all the chief priests and scribes of the people, he was inquiring before them where the Anŏinted One is born. ⁵And, they said to him, "In Bęṭh‑leħem of Yehuḓah, because thus it has been getting written through the prophet. ⁶ 'AND YOU BęṬH‑LEḦEM, IN THE LAND OF YEHUḎAH, ARE BY NO MEANS LEAST AMONG THE LEADERS OF YEHUḎAH, because OUT OF YOU WILL GO FORTH A RULERᵅ, WHO WILL SHEPHERD MY PEOPLE YISRA'ęLᵝ.'"

---

the word definite, i.e. *The* lord, and the plural makes it magestic: 'The Lǒrd.' See 1 Cor. 16:22. The poor similarity of *yaʹ* in Marayyaʹ to Yăh is transmutted by false teachers to 'Mar‑Yah.' **1:21** γ יֵשׁוּעַ *Yĕshuą͑*. Yăhwęҥ *is* salvation. **1:23** α Is 7.14 **1:23** β Is 8:8, 10 **1:23** φ "THEY WILL CALL" is correct. Isa. 7:14 does not say "She *will* have called" but "YOU WILL HAVE CALLED," using a different vowel pointing: קָרָאתָ. "YOU" (singular collective) refers to the house of David, which Matthew correctly interprets in the third person plural "they." Singular pronouns are often used in Hebrew to refer to plural entities. Also note that the future perfect in Isaiah is rendered in the simple future by Matthew showing the meaning is future. ▷ 'You' will have called refers to the house of David (Isa. 7:13), and thus transcends the time of Aħaz. Upon the king's refusal to ask for a sign, a sign is predicted anyway, but it is not given to the king. It is given to the house of David, and so did not have to be immediately fulfilled. 'Curd and honey he will eat, because he knows refusing of the bad, and choosing of the good,' because he will be the Almighty Son. Then the son that Yəshaʻyahu brought with him to the meeting with Aħaz is the subject of the prophecy in vs.

7:16-25, and not the future virgin's Son. Immanu'el is addressed in 8:8, 10, but not as the prophesied child of the virgin. He was there to witness the invasion, because he was there before he was born of the Virgin. Then vs. 17 says, "I will have awaited Yăhwęҥ, who is hiding his face from the house of Ya'aqov." This means they will not find him if they keep believing lies. **1:24** ξ See Luke 2:7; Psa. 89:27; Col. 1:15. **1:25** *from it* {le MT—aDLNT} **2:2** ω *also: in the branch.* The Magim meant a helical rising of Jupiter. They observed this twice. The second time was September 1, 2 BC in Virgo, and this was the date of Mĕşşiah's birth. The word used here is ἀνατολή which is used by Zechariah in the LXX to mean the Branch. The word means a "riser" and "rising." A Branch, shoot, or twig is a riser from the earth. See 2:9. **2:6** α Miçah 5:2 וְאַתָּה בֵּית־לֶחֶם אֶפְרָתָה צָעִיר לֹא הֱיוֹת בְּאַלְפֵי יְהוּדָה מִמְּךָ לִי יֵצֵא לִהְיוֹת מוֹשֵׁל בְּיִשְׂרָאֵל וּמוֹצָאֹתָיו מִקֶּדֶם מִימֵי עוֹלָם: β Miçah 5:4: וְעָמַד וְרָעָה בְּעֹז יְהוָה cf. 1 Chron 11:2, 2 Sam 5:2.

⁷Then Herod, as he secretly called the magi, ascertained before them ᵋthe time the star manifested itself. ⁸And as he sent them to Beṭh-leḥem, he said, "Having gone yourselves, search carefully for the child. And when you may find him, report back to me, so that even I, having come, may worship him." ⁹And having heard the king, they went themselves. And behold, the star, which they did see in the Branch, was going before them till, having arrived, it was ᶲstationed up above where the child was. ¹⁰And when they saw the star, they themselves rejoiced exceedingly *with* great joy. ¹¹And as they came into the house, they saw the ᵖchild with Miryam his mother. And when they fell down, they worshiped him. And as they opened their treasures, they carried to him gifts: gold and frankincense and myrrh. ¹²And when they were divinely instructed in a dream not to return to Herod, they departed to their own country through another way. ¹³Yet also, as they departed, behold, the Messenger *of* Yăhwєн is showing himself to Yoṣeph in a dream, saying, "Having risen up, take the child and his mother, and be fleeing to Mitsrayim, and be remaining there until I shall have told you, because Herod is going to seek the child so that he may destroy him."
¹⁴And having raised himself up, he took the child and his mother by night and departed for Mitsrayim, ¹⁵and he was remaining there past the death of Herod, so that what was spoken by Yăhwєн through the prophet would be fulfilled, saying, "OUT OF MITSRAYIM I CALLED MY SONᵛ."
¹⁶Then when Herod saw that he was outwitted by the Magi, he was intensely enraged, and having sent *his men*, he killed all the boys who were in Beṭhleḥem

---

2:7 ξ The first time the star appeared was August 1, 3 B.C. in Leo. It had been a year and five months from that time to the time of Herod's inquiry. **2:9** φ The star, which was Jupiter, stopped. It reached a relative stationary point among the stars. It stood over Beṭh-leḥem from the vantage point of Yerushalayim. The date this happened was Dec. 27-28, 2 B.C. The Magim searched for the child on the 28th. They presented their gifts on XI.1 (Dec. 29), which was the new moon day for Shevaṭ. **2:11** π παιδίον. On page 67 of his book, *The Star that Astonished the World* (1998), Ernest Martin adapts Adam Rutherford's argument from page 433 of *Bible Chronology* (1957), to claim that παιδίον means a 'toddler' vs. βρέφος which means 'infant.' He does this to put Messiah's birth back earlier from the December 2 BC date of the Magim's visit by more than a year, to September 11, 3 BC, since Messiah is called παιδίον in this passage. But the claim that παιδίον means 'toddler' and not just 'child' is proved false when the very same word is used to describe Yoḥanan the Immerser when he was circumcised, only eight days old in Luke 1:59, 66, and 76. Even more astonishing is the occurrence in Luke 2:17 and 2:27 in reference to Messiah himself right after Miryam's days of purification from childbirth. The word παιδίον plainly means 'child' in all these cases, and most certainly not 'toddler.' The very simplest word study and checking of its other uses is sufficient to expose this error. Unlike Martin, this present author spends a lot of time and research examining the arguments he comes up with to see if there are any easy to check facts which would require an assumption to be discarded. ▷ When the Magim visited, Messiah was probably exactly four months and one day old, and certainly not more than four days more or less, because it is how long it took Tzedeq to rise as the bright dawn star on the day of Messiah's birth (Sept. 1, 2 BC) and stop at its first station. Martin is overlooking the obvious birth star of Messiah for a date that had no helical rising (cf. Rev. 22:16). ▷ See also notes on Luke 1:5, 24, 36, and 2:6 where it is explained that Martin's theory contradicts the rotations of the priestly divisions. **2:15** ν Hoş 11:1 וּמִמִּצְרַיִם קָרָאתִי לִבְנִי The source of this prophecy is Num. 24:8: "GŎD BRINGS HIM OUT FROM MITSRAYIM." But the wording is from Hoş. 11:1 because it alludes to Num. 24:8. See also Num. 23:22 אֵל מוֹצִיאָם מִמִּצְרָיִם , 24:8: אֵל מוֹצִיאוֹ מִמִּצְרָיִם. **2:16** φ→in = *from;* ω διετοῦς. The second year of life is the 13ᵗʰ to end of the 24ᵗʰ month. Herod would not have had to kill any boys over 24 months according to the Magim's timetable for the appearances of the star. The word used here is διετοῦς, which does not obviously mean two years old. Rather it means twice-year or double-year. Two years old would be between the start of month 25 and the end of month 36, because age is only counted upon the completion of years.

Mattatyahu 3

and in all its surroundings, ᵠwho where in ᵚthe second year and under, according to the time which he ascertained before the Magi. ¹⁷Then was ᵝfilled up what was spoken through Yirmeyahu the prophet, saying, ¹⁸"A VOICE WAS LISTENED TO IN RAMAH, WEEPING AND GREAT MOURNING, RACH̱EL WEEPING OVER HER CHILDREN. AND SHE WAS DESIRING NOT TO BE COMFORTED, BECAUSE THEY ARE NOT.ᵅ"

¹⁹Yet also, Herod ᵟhaving died, behold, the Messenger *of* Yăhwєh shows himself in a dream to Yos̩eph in Mitsrayim, saying, ²⁰"Having risen up, take the child and his mother, and be going into the land of Yisra'el, because those seeking the child's soul have been dying." ²¹And having arisen, he took the child and his mother, and came into the land of Yisra'el. ²²Yet when he heard that 'Archelaus reigns over Yehud̩ah in place of his father Herod,ᶿ he was afraid to go there. Yet also, having been divinely instructed in a dream, he departed for the regions of Galil, ²³and having come, he dwelled in a city being called Nєtsereth̩, so that it should be fulfilled, what was spoken through the prophets, "HE WILL BE CALLED A NєTSЄRiᵠ."

3 ¹And ᵠin those days comes Yoh̩anan the Immerser, proclaiming in the wilderness of Yehud̩ah, also saying, ²"Be sorry and turn your heart, because the kingdom of the heavens has been coming near." ³Yea, this is he who was spoken about through Yeshayahu the prophet, saying, "THE VOICE OF ONE CRYING IN THE WILDERNESS, MAKE READY THE WAY OF YĂHWЄH, BE MAKING STRAIGHT HIS PATHS.ᵞ" ⁴And, Yoh̩anan himself was wearing a garment of camel's hair, and a leather belt around his waist, and his food was constantly locusts and wild honey.

⁵At that time Yerushalayim was going out to him, and all Yehud̩ah, and all the region around the Yard̩en. ⁶And they were being immersed by him in the river Yard̩en, confessing their sins. ⁷But when he saw many of the Perushim and Tsadduqim coming for immersion, he said to them, "You spawn of vipers, who warned you to flee from the coming wrath? ⁸Therefore you should produce the worthy fruit of being sorry and turning the heart *from sin*. ⁹And you should not think to say to yourselves, 'We have Ȧvraham as our father,' because I say to

---

2:17 β When a non-prediction is said to be filled up it means the theme is added to by another episode that fits the theme. Love fills up the Law, but it must be renewed every day. The 'voice' (vs. 18) is that haunting voice of suffering that weighs down on Yisra'el's heart through the ages. **2:18 α** Jer 31:15. The date for this is probably December 30ᵗʰ, though it could have been late on the 29ᵗʰ. A feast is celebrated by the Church on these days called the *Feast of the Holy Innocents;* Jer. 31:15 sums up all the suffering of Yisra'el. The passage is not a prediction, but it is an historical reference to Yisra'el's suffering, which needs consolation. The consolation is Mєs̩s̩iah̩, because he is hope for the future (cf. Jer. 15:16f). **2:19 δ** Herod died after a lunar eclipse in early 1 BC about a month after killing the children, but afterward was a major war in Yehud̩ah that was not ended until the fall feasts of 1 BC. **2:22 θ** Archelaus reigned 7 years and was deposed in AD 6. **2:23 φ** Zech. 6:12; see also Isa. 11:1; "A NєTSЄR (branch, shoot) FROM HIS ROOTS WILL BEAR FRUIT." Zech. 6:12, "BEHOLD A MAN. A TSEMAH̩ (BRANCH, SHOOT, RISER) *WILL BE* HIS NAME, AND FROM UNDER HIMSELF HE WILL BRANCH OUT. AND HE WILL HAVE BUILT THE TEMPLE OF YĂHWЄH." Also Jer. 23:5; 33:15; Zech. 3:8. "HE WILL BE CALLED A NєTSЄRi" is a fair interpretation of "TSEMAH̩ *WILL BE* HIS NAME" (צֶמַח שְׁמוֹ) Zech. 6:12]]Also καλέω (called) is used as a synonym for what someone is named. **3:1 φ** Starting after the spring equinox in AD 29. **3:3 λ** Isa 40:3]] קוֹל קוֹרֵא בַּמִּדְבָּר פַּנּוּ דֶּרֶךְ יְהוָה יַשְּׁרוּ בָּעֲרָבָה מְסִלָּה לֵאלֹהֵינוּ.

you, that the Almĭghty is able from these stones to raise up children to Ȧvraham. ¹⁰And, now the ax is laid at the root of the trees. Therefore every tree that does not produce good fruit is cut down and is thrown into the fire. ¹¹Truly, I immerse you in water toward being sorry and turning the heart *from sin*, but he who is coming after me is mightier than I, and I am not worthy to carry his sandals. He will immerse you with the Holy Spĭrit and with fire. ¹²His winnowing fork is in his hand, and he will thoroughly cleanse his threshing floor. And he will gather his wheat into the barn, yet the chaff he will burn with unquenchable fire."

¹³Then comes Yĕshuą̊ from Galil upon the Yarden to Yoḣanan, to be immersed by him. ¹⁴And Yoḣanan was preventing him, saying, "I have need to be immersed by you, and you are coming to me?" ¹⁵And when he answered, Yĕshuą̊ said to him, "Allow it now, because in this manner it is fitting for us ᵠto fulfill all righteousness." Then he allows him. ¹⁶And having been immersed, Yĕshuą̊ went up immediately from the water, and behold, the heavens were opened, and he saw the Spĭrit of the Almĭghty descending like a dove coming upon him, ¹⁷and behold, a voice out of the heavens, saying, "This is my beloved Sŏn with whom I am well-pleased."

4

¹Then Yĕshuą̊ was led up into the wilderness by the Spĭrit to be tempted by the Slanderer. ²And having fasted ⌖forty days and forty nights, afterward he was hungry. ³And having come, the tempter said to him, "If you are the Almĭghty

---

3:13 τ Near the last day of A'v. **3:15** ψ *To fulfill all righteousness* (in the infinitive form) means here to show the intent to fulfill all righteousness. See Deut. 6:25. An immersion *into* repentance (vs. 11) *also* makes a positive public proclamation that the one being immersed intends to obey the commandments. Therefore, he says *us* because this purpose is common to all who make this declaration by immersion. Stated positively thus rather than negatively as a need to repent, Yoḣanan permitted the Mĕṣṣiaḣ to be immersed who needed no repentance. See Psa. 40:8 לַעֲשׂוֹת־רְצוֹנְךָ אֱלֹהַי חָפָצְתִּי וְתוֹרָתְךָ בְּתוֹךְ מֵעָי׃

4:2 ⌖ Elul 1 to Tishri 11, AD 29 = dawn August 30 to dawn October 9, AD 29. These dates are the dates of the traditional Jewish fasting period. The historical background of this fast is based on Mosheн fasting for forty days and forty nights, when he ate no bread and drank no water. Mosheн fasted this long three times in a row. The first occasion was after Shavu'ot, when the covenant had been new made on Sabbath, and commenced on Sunday, Sivan 7, lasting until dawn on the 17th day of month IV (dawn June 1, 1632 BC to dawn July 11, 1632 BC). See Deut. 9:9. He came down on the 17th day, and saw their sin. He then fasted concerning their sin another forty days and forty nights (Deut. 9:18). He did not eat or drink. During this time he was in the camp. Since this was an immediate reaction, he must have fasted from the 17th of that month until dawn on the 27th day of Av, which turns out to be the fourth day of the week (Wed, Aug. 20, 1632 BC). Up to this time he did not get a break from fasting. On the following Sabbath, the first day of Elul, he went up the mountain again, and began another forty day and forty night fast! See Deut. 10:1, 10. And this fast lasted until the day after YOM KIPPURIM (till dawn on October 2, 1632 BC). ▷ Now why the break in fasts from dawn on Wednesday to dawn on the Sabbath? Because on the 4th day he was as good as dead in asking for forgiveness for the people, and he had to eat the manna, the bread of life, and then the following Sabbath he ascended the mountain, because he had been heard, and was raised up again. Likewise Messiah died on the fourth day to declare the wiping of our sins, and he rose at dawn on the Sabbath to renew his covenant. The third time on the mountain were written the commandments of the new made tablets. And Mosheн was able to deliver them whole on the day after YOM KIPPURIM. ▷ It is this third round of fasting that Jewish tradition memorializes in the 40 days of repentance, because the result was positive whereas the former two were negative, and on the mount the Most High revealed his name. ▷ Now in AD 29, the month of Elul was 29 days. So how did Yeshua fast for 40? Well it just so happens that YOM KIPPURIM fell that year on a Friday, and he was compelled to fast on Sabbath also. It was then Sunday morning October 9 (Tishri 12) that the Accuser assaulted him in AD 29. ▷ The linking of the fasts has a redemptive purpose, and profound consequences for biblical chronology, because this was not during Lent. It does once again prove that Messiah was born in the fall season.

Mattatyahu 4

Sŏn, command *it* so that these stones will have become bread." ⁴And when he answered, he said, "It has been getting written, 'MAN WILL NOT LIVE ON BREAD ALONE, BUT UPON EVERY WORD THAT PROCEEDS OUT OF THE MOUTH OF YĂHWᵉH.'ᵝ"

⁵Then the Slanderer takes him into the holy city, and he made him stand on the pinnacle of the temple, ⁶and says to him, "If you are the Almĭghty Sŏn, throw yourself down, because it has been getting written, 'HIS MESSENGERS HE WILL COMMAND CONCERNING YOUᶿ' and 'ON THEIR HANDS THEY WILL BEAR YOU UP, LEST YOU MAY STRIKE YOUR FOOT AGAINST A STONE.ᵟ'" ⁷Yĕshuą was saying to him, "Again, it has been getting written, 'YOU SHALL NOT PUT YĂHWᵉH YOUR ALMĬGHTY TO THE TEST.ᵞ'"

⁸Again, the Slanderer takes him to a very high mountain, and shows him all the kingdoms of the world, and their glory. ⁹And he said to him, "All these things will I give you, if having fallen down, you will have worshiped me." ¹⁰Then Yĕshuą says to him, "Be departing, Sąṭan! Because it has been getting written, 'YOU WILL WORSHIP YĂHWᵉH YOUR ALMĬGHTY, AND YOU WILL SERVE HIM ALONE.ᵘ'" ¹¹Then the Slanderer leaves him, and behold, messengers came and were ministering to him.

¹²And ᶠwhen he heard that Yoḥanan was arrested, he withdrew into Galil. ¹³And having left Netsereṯh, having come, he stayed in Kefar-Naḥum, which is by the sea, in the region of Zevulun and Naphtali, ¹⁴so that it may be fulfilled that which was spoken through Yeshayahu the prophet, saying, ¹⁵"THE LAND OF ZEVULUN AND THE LAND OF NAPHTALI BY WAY OF THE SEA, BEYOND THE YARDᵉN, GALIL OF THE NATIONS—¹⁶THE PEOPLE WHO ARE DWELLING IN DARKNESS WILL HAVE SEEN A GREAT LIGHT, AND ON THOSE WHO ARE DWELLING IN A COUNTRY, EVEN IN THE SHADOW OF DEATH, A LIGHT WILL HAVE RISEN *ON THEM*.ᵖ"

¹⁷From that ᶲtime Yĕshuą began to be proclaiming and to be saying, "Be sorry and be turning your heart, because the kingdom of the heavens has been coming near." ¹⁸And walking beside the Sea of Galil, he saw two brothers, Şim'on being called Peter, and Andrew his brother casting a net into the sea, because they were fishermen. ¹⁹And he says to them, "Follow after me, and I will make you fishers of men." ²⁰And immediately, having left the nets, they followed him. ²¹And when he went forward from there he saw two other brothers, Ya'aqov the son of Zavdai, and Yoḥanan his brother in the boat with Zavdai their father, mending their nets. And he called them. ²²And immediately having left the boat and their father, they followed him.

²³And he was going around in all Galil, teaching in their congregations and proclaiming the good news of the kingdom, and healing every disease and every sickness among the people. ²⁴And the report about him went out into all Şyria. And they brought to him all who were sick, having various diseases and suffering pains, and ones being controlled by demons, and ones being epileptics, and paralytics. And he healed them. ²⁵And large crowds followed him from Galil and Decapolis and Yerushalayim and Yehudah and from beyond the Yardᵉn.

4:4 β Deut 8:3. **4:6** θ Psa 91:11; δ Psa 91:12. | **4:14-16** π Isa 9:1-2. **4:17** φ Ṭevet AD 31: 4:17-22.
4:7 λ Deu 6:16. **4:10** μ Deu 6:4, 13; 10:20; 32:43 ⓢ. | **4:23** Shevaṭ AD 31.
4:12 ξ Yoḥanan was arrested in the late fall of AD 30.

Mattatyahu 5

5 ¹And when⁷ he saw the crowds, he went up to the mountain. Even as he sat down, his disciples came to him. ²And when he opened his mouth, he was teaching them, saying:

³"Blessed are the poor in spirit, because theirs is the kingdom of the heavens. ⁴Blessed are those who are mourning, because they will be comforted. ⁵Blessed are the humble, because they will inherit the earth. ⁶Blessed are those hungering and thirsting for righteousness, because they will be satisfied. ⁷Blessed are the merciful, because they will receive mercy. ⁸Blessed are the pure in heart, because they will see the Almĭghty. ⁹Blessed are the peacemakers, because THEY WILL BE CALLED SONS OF THE ALMĬGHTY.ᵠ ¹⁰Blessed are those who have been getting persecuted for righteousness' sake, because theirs is the kingdom of the heavens. ¹¹Blessed are you when they may have insulted you, and may have persecuted you, and may have spoken every evil against you falsely, because of me. ¹²Be rejoicing and be exulting, because your reward is great in the heavens, because likewise they have persecuted the prophets who were before you."

¹³"You are the salt of the earth, but if the salt may have become foolish, with what will it be salted? It is no longer effective for anything, except having been thrown out, to be trampled under *foot* by men. ¹⁴You are the light of the world. A city lying on a hill is not able to be hidden. ¹⁵Neither do they light a lamp, and put it under the peck-container, but on the lampstand, and it gives light to all in the house. ¹⁶Likewise, let your light shine before men, so that they will have seen your good deeds, and will have glorified your Făther who is in the heavens."

¹⁷"You should not suppose˟ that I came to abolish the Law or the Prophets. I came not to abolish, but to fulfill.ᵏ ¹⁸So *a*m*e*n I say to you, ᵋbefore the point that heaven and earth will have passed away, one yod or one serif, no, not by any chance will have passed away from the Law. ¹⁹ᵖ Up to the point that all things will have happened, whoever then will have loosened one of the least of

---

5:1 τ Summer AD 31. **5:9** ψ Hoŝ. 1:10]] יֹאמַר לָהֶם בְּנֵי אֵל־חָי cf. Rom. 9:26. **5:17** χ There are several ways that lawless teachers twist Mat. 5:17-20 to fit their preconceived theology, but all of them have to *think* that the Law was abolished to even begin their re-explanation of the text. **5:17** μ *Fulfill* means to do the Law (cf. Mat. 3:15; 5:19-20; Rom. 8:4; 13:8; 2 Cor. 10:6; Gal. 5:14). It also means *to fulfill* prophecy, which for the Měssiah meant then and into the far future. With respect to the doing, the Torah always remains to be fulfilled again the next time a command should be kept. But also *fulfill* means to finish with respect to teaching. When the Law is fully written on the heart, then teaching is finished. See Jer. 31:33-34. But doing with love remains. Permit no one to redefine this. **5:18** ξ→that = ἕως; the word ἕως has the force of "up to the point that," or "before the point that." The English word "until" has been avoided because it too strongly implies termination when the point is reached. The Greek and Hebrew terms require no termination but simply assert a duration at least till the point mentioned leaving continuation beyond the point open ended. See Gen. 8:5; 26:13; 27:44; 28:15; 39:16; 41:49, "THEN YOSƐF GATHERED GRAIN AS THE SAND OF THE SEA, VERY MUCH, UP TO THE POINT THAT (ἕως) HE CEASED TO NUMBER, BECAUSE IT WAS BEYOND NUMBERING." Clearly, they did not stop gathering after the numbering ceased since it would have been counted if they stopped gathering when they stopped numbering. Sometimes the word has the sense of "past the point that" without saying how far past. See עַד Gesenius. לְעוֹלָם וָעֶד *to the age and past it*. "But, on the other hand, it is not less certain that the sacred writers have not stated the extreme limit in places of this kind, but have mentioned a nearer limit without excluding the time beyond." **5:19** π→happen = ἕως ἂν πάντα γένηται; Or "Up to the point that ever all things will have happened," but the translation is put more idiomatically in English. The clause may end the previous verse or begin the next, and more likely begins the next as it is redundant at the end of the last verse, and only had been placed there by translators seeking to create a lever for interpreters to escape the plain meaning of the text, i.e. "till all be fulfilled."

Mattatyahu 5

these commandments, and likewise may have taught others, will be called least in the kingdom of the heavens, but whoever will have kept and will have taught them, this one will be called great in the kingdom of the heavens. ²⁰Because I say to you, that except your righteousness will have abounded above that of the scribes and Perushim, no, not by any possibility will you have entered the kingdom of the heavens."

²¹"You have heard that it was said to the first ones, 'YOU SHALL NOT COMMIT MURDER,ᵝ' yet also, whoever will have murdered will be held guilty in the judgment. ²²Yet also, I say to you that anyone being angry with his brother will be held guilty in the judgment. Yet also, whoever will have said to his brother, 'Retard,'ᵠ will be held guilty in the Council. And, whoever will have said, 'You ᵠfool,' will be held guilty into the fiery ᵞGeihinnom. ²³If therefore you may be presenting your gift upon the altar, and there you will have been reminded that your brother holds something against you, ²⁴leave there your gift before the altar, and be going your way. First be reconciled to your brother, and then having come, be offering your gift."

²⁵"Be being well disposed toward your adversary at law quickly while you are with him on the way, lest your opponent will have delivered you to the judge, and the judge to the officer, and into prison you are thrown. ²⁶Amen! I say to you: no, not by any possibility will you have come out of there, until you will have paid the last quadrans." ²⁷"You have heard that it was said, 'YOU SHALL NOT COMMIT ADULTERY,ᵝ' ²⁸yet also I say to you, that everyone looking on a woman to lust for her has committed adultery with her already in his heart."

²⁹"And if your right eye makes you stumble, tear it out, and throw it from you, because it is better for you that one of your members will have perished, and your whole body shall not have been thrown into Geihinnom. ³⁰And if your right hand makes you stumble, cut it off and throw it from you, because it is better for you that one of your members will have perished, and your whole body shall not have gone into Geihinnom."

³¹"And, it was said, 'Whoever may have dismissed his woman, HE WILL HAVE GIVEN HER A CERTIFICATE OF DIVORCE.' ³²Yet also, I say to you that everyone who is dismissing his wife, except in the case of the relationship being unlawful, is inducing her to commit adultery. And whoever will have married she who has been getting dismissed is committing adultery."

5:21 β Exo 20:13: לֹא תִּרְצָח, Deu 5:17; **5:22** ψ,ϕ These terms imply moral degeneracy, i.e. godless fool, libtard, demon. **5:22** γ *Geihinnom,* גֵּיא בֶן־הִנֹּם, valley of the son of Hinnom, Josh. 15:8. This was the garbage dump outside Yershalayim where all manner of refuse was tossed including dead bodies of animals and criminals. An eternal fire was kept burning to keep the air from being tainted. See Thayer.

5:27 β Exo 20:14, Deu 5:18: לֹא תִּנְאָף.
5:31 Deu 24:1: וְכָתַב לָהּ סֵפֶר כְּרִיתֻת וְנָתַן

בְּיָדָהּ וְשִׁלְּחָהּ מִבֵּיתוֹ, See Mat 19:3-9 & notes, Luke 16:18 & notes; Mark 10:11-12 & notes; Mal. 2:14-16; ▷ In Judaism it is possible to send a wife away without divorcing her. This is called dismissal. If remarriage occurs then it is technical adultery without the official divorce. Those who dismiss without divorce make their wives commit adultery if they marry another. Dismissal (without divorce) is only allowed if the relationship is unlawful in the first place. Otherwise, the dismisser induces his wife to commit adultery if she has another, or himself if he takes another.

³³"Again, you have heard that it was said to those of old, 'YOU SHALL NOT GIVE A FALSE VOW.μ' And, you shall pay back your vows to Yăhweh. ³⁴Yet also I say to you, not to make oaths in general; as well, not by heaven, because it is the throne of the Almĭghty, ³⁵nor, as well, by the earth, because it is the footstool of his feet, nor, as well, by Yerushalayim, because it is THE CITY OF THE GREAT KING.β ³⁶Nor, as well, by your head should you have taken an oath, because you cannot make one hair white or black. ³⁷And be making your word, 'Yes, yes;' 'No, no', and what exceeds these is from the evil one." ³⁸"You have heard that it was said, 'EYE FOR EYE, AND TOOTH FOR TOOTH.η' ³⁹Yet also I say to you, not to resist the evil one—but whoever strikes you on your right cheek, turn to him the other also." ⁴⁰"And when anyone wants to sue you, and to take your under shirt, leave for him your outer garment also." ⁴¹"And whoever will compel you to go one mile, be going with him two." ⁴²"To him asking of you, give, and do not turn away from him wanting to borrow from you."

⁴³"You have heard that it was said, 'YOU SHALL LOVE YOUR NEIGHBOR,α' and 'SHALL HATE YOUR ENEMY.β' ⁴⁴ᴪYet also I say to you, be loving your enemies, and be praying for those persecuting you,τ ⁴⁵so that you will have been sons of your Făther who is in the heavens, because he makes his sun rise on the evil and the good, and he sends rain on the righteous and the unrighteous. ⁴⁶Because when you may have loved those loving you, what reward have you? Do not even the tax collectors do the same? ⁴⁷And when you may have greeted your brothers only, what do you do more than others? Do not even the nations do the same? ⁴⁸Therefore you shall be blameless, as your heavenly Făther is blameless."

5:33 μ Lev 19:12 **5:35** β Psa 48:2 **5:38** η Exo 21:24f, Lev 24:20, Deu 19:21 עַיִן תַּחַת עַיִן שֵׁן תַּחַת שֵׁן, יָד תַּחַת יָד רֶגֶל תַּחַת רֶגֶל, ὀφθαλμὸν ἀντὶ ὀφθαλμοῦ ὀδόντα ἀντὶ ὀδόντος χεῖρα ἀντὶ χειρός πόδα ἀντὶ ποδός. ▷ The law does not express here a rule of compensatory justice, but a measure of retribution meant to deter further assault. The rule of deterrence was limited to the damage caused, and was so stated in Torah because the contemporary Amorite culture dispensed punitive justice measured by one's class or rank. The Most High does not favor nobility, which is why the Law is so stated. But thus exacting the punitive measure does nothing to restore the unjustly injured party to wholeness again. The loss of the injured party is not restored. But the one who caused the loss is punished. It is therefore complete folly to suppose that retributive justice can somehow compensate the victim of sin, or the Most High, from the loss caused by sin. There is no satisfaction to the injured party that everything has been justly paid for and squared up. For this reason, Messiah tells us not to seek any personal vengeance. It will not even things up or restore harmony. There is, in fact, more restorative power in forgiveness than retribution. Consider Inigo Montoya's famous line in the Princess Bride after the villain offers everything he can give by way of compensation to save his life. It is this, "I want my father back you SOB." The penal substitution theory would have us translate this text as "an eye in the place of an eye" and have us consider justice satisfied by the substitution. That's two blind eyes. But it was a whole eye that was taken, and it is not a whole eye that is replaced, to say nothing of undoing the pain involved in the loss of an eye. A lot more can be said for the merciful justice that Messiah taught (which is according to Torah). He is a ransom in return for many. When we repented, he forgave us, and then when death demanded to kill us, paid the cost exacted by death (the ransom) and then he defeated death by his resurrection. Now he can justly demand that death release us. Thereby Messiah has many whole persons forgiven, purchased from lawlessness, and healed, and not two dead eyes. **5:43** α Lev 19:18 **5:43** β Psa 139:21-22; cf. Deu 29:17-22 **5:44** ᴪ δὲ "A marker with an additive relation, with possible suggestion of contrast: *at the same time* (BDAG δὲ def. no. 3).

Mattatyahu 6

6 ¹Be taking care not to perform your ˣrighteousness before men to be seen by them. Otherwise you have no reward at the side of your Făther who is in the heavens. ²ᵃWhenever, therefore, you may be giving alms, do not sound a trumpet before you, as the hypocrites do in the congregations and in the streets, so that they will have been glorified by men."

²ᵇ"Ămen, I say to you, they have their reward in full. ³But when you give charity, do not let your left hand know what your right hand is doing, ⁴that your charity may be in secret. And your Făther who sees in secret will repay you."

⁵ᵃ"And whenever you may be praying, you will not be as the hypocrites, because they love in the congregations and on the corners of the streets (those who have been taking a stand), to be praying so that they will have been seen by men."

⁵ᵇ"Ămen, I say to you, they have received their reward. ⁶But you, when you may be praying, go into your inner room, and when you have shut your door, pray to your Făther who is hidden, and your Făther who sees what is hidden will repay you."

⁷"And when you are praying, you shall not have used meaningless repetition, as the nations do, because they think that they will be heard because of their many words. ⁸Therefore you will not have been like them, because your Făther has been knowing what you need before you ask him. ⁹Be praying, then, in this way: 'Our Făther who art in heaven, hallowed be your name. ¹⁰Thy kingdom come. Thy will be done, on earth as it is in heaven. ¹¹Give us bread for tomorrow each day. ¹²And forgive us our debts, as we also have forgiven our debtors. ¹³And may you not lead us into testing, but deliver us from evil. [For Thine is the kingdom, and the power, and the glory, forever. Ămen.]'"

¹⁴"Because if you will have forgiven men for their trespasses, your heavenly Făther will also forgive you. ¹⁵But if you will not have forgiven men, then your Făther will not forgive your trespasses."

¹⁶"And whenever you may be fasting, do not be putting on gloomy faces like the hypocrites, because they neglect their appearance in order that they will have been seen fasting by men. Ămen, I say to you, they have their reward in full. ¹⁷But you, when you fast, anoint your head, and wash your face, ¹⁸so that you will not have been seen fasting by men, but by your Făther who is in secret. And your Făther who sees in secret will repay you."

¹⁹"Do not be storing up for yourselves treasures on earth, where moth and rust destroy, and where thieves break in and steal. ²⁰But be storing up for yourselves treasures in heaven, where neither moth nor rust destroys, and where thieves do not break in or steal, ²¹because where your treasure is, there will your heart be also. ²²The lamp of the body is the eye. If therefore your eye may

---

6:1 χ = δικαιοσύνην = צְדָקָה = *charity, alms, good deeds, mercy* BDAG 3b. Charity was one of those works reckoned for righteousness according to Judaism, as a merit for a demerit. This more or less explains why the word righteousness came to be used for alms. Charity, like Papal indulgences was regarded as a compensatory merit. Charity only has its own reward, and none compensating for a lack of loyalty to Mĕşşiaȟ.

be good⁽ᵘ⁾, your whole body will be illuminated. ²³But if your eye may be bad, your whole body will be darkened. If therefore the light that is in you is darkness, how great is the darkness!"

²⁴"No one can serve two masters, because either he will hate the one and love the other, or he will hold to one and despise the other. You cannot serve the Almĭghty and money. ²⁵For this reason I say to you, do not be being anxious for your soul, as to what you will have eaten, or what you will have drunk, nor for your body, as to what you will have put on. Is not life more than food, and the body more than clothing? ²⁶Look at the birds of the air, because they do not sow, neither do they reap, nor gather into barns, and yet your heavenly Făther feeds them. Are you not worth much more than they? ²⁷And which of you by being anxious can add a single cubit to his stature? ²⁸And why are you anxious about clothing? Observe how the lilies of the field grow. They do not toil nor do they spin, ²⁹yet I say to you that not even Şolomon̦ in all his glory got dressed like one of these. ³⁰But if the Almĭghty so arrays the grass of the field, which is alive today and tomorrow is thrown into the furnace, will he not much more do so for you little ᵋfaithful ones?"

³¹"You will not have been anxious then, saying, 'What will we have eaten?' or 'What will we have drunk?' or 'With what will we have gotten dressed?' ³²Because all these things the nations eagerly seek, and because your heavenly Făther has been knowing that you need all these things. ³³But be seeking first the kingdom and his righteousness, and all these things will be added to you. ³⁴Therefore you will not have been anxious for tomorrow, because tomorrow will care for itself. Each day has enough trouble of its own."

7 ¹Do not be judging, so that you will not have been judged, ²because with the judgment you are judging, you will be judged, and with the measure you are measuring, it will be measured to you. ³And, why are you looking at the speck that is in your brother's eye, and are not noticing the log that is in your own eye? ⁴Or how will you say to your brother, 'Allow *me, so that* I will have taken the speck out of your eye,' and behold the log *is* in your own eye? ⁵You hypocrite, first take the log out of your own eye, and then you will see clearly to take the speck out of your brother's eye."

⁶"You shall not have given what is holy to dogs, and you shall not have thrown your pearls before pigs, lest they trample them under their feet, and turn and will have torn you to pieces."

⁷"Be asking, and it will be given to you. Be seeking, and you will find. Be knocking, and it will be opened to you. ⁸For everyone who asks receives, and he who seeks finds, and to him who knocks it will be opened. ⁹Or what man is there

---

6:22 μ A *good eye* is a Hebrew idiom for being generous, a bad for stinginess. See Prov. 22:9. But Yeshua appears to be going beyond outward charity here to the heart of the matter. **6:30** ξ√ ὀλίγος + πιστοί.

Mattatyahu 7

among you, when his son will ask him for a loaf, will give him a stone? ¹⁰Or if he will ask for a fish, he will not give him a snake, will he? ¹¹If you then, being bad, have been knowing how to be giving good gifts to your children, how much more will your Făther, who is in the heavens, give what is good to those asking him!"

¹²"Therefore, however you may be wishing that men may be treating you, so also you be treating them, because this is the law, and *what* the prophets *teach*."

¹³"Enter by the narrow gate, because the gate is wide, and the way is broad that leads to destruction, and many are those who enter by it. ¹⁴Because the gate is small, and the way has been getting troubled that is leading to life, and few are those finding it."

¹⁵"Be guarding against the false prophets, who come to you in sheep's clothing, but inwardly are ravenous wolves. ¹⁶You will know them by their fruits. Grapes are not gathered from thorns, or figs from thistles, are they? ¹⁷Even so, every good tree bears good fruit, but the bad tree bears bad fruit. ¹⁸A good tree cannot produce bad fruit, nor can a bad tree produce good fruit. ¹⁹Every tree that does not bear good fruit is cut down and thrown into the fire. ²⁰So then, you will know them by their fruits.

²¹"Not everyone who says to me, 'Ădŏnai', Ădŏnai,' will enter the kingdom of heaven, but he who does the will of my Făther who is in heaven. ²²Many will say to me on that day, 'Ădŏnai, Ădŏnai, did we not prophesy in your name, and in your name cast out demons, and in your name perform many miracles?' ²³And then I will confess to them, 'I never acknowledged you! BE DEPARTING FROM ME, YOU WHO PRACTICE LAWLESSNESS!ψ'"

²⁴"Therefore everyone who hears these words of mine, and acts upon them, may be compared to a wise man, who built his house on bedrock. ²⁵And the rain descended, and the floods came, and the winds blew, and burst against that house, and it did not fall, because it had been getting founded upon the bedrock. ²⁶And everyone who hears these words of mine, and does not act upon them, will be like a foolish man, who built his house upon the sand. ²⁷And the rain descended, and the floods came, and the winds blew, and burst against that house, and it fell, and great was its fall."

²⁸The result was that when Yĕshuą finished these words, the crowds were amazed at his teaching, ²⁹because he was teaching them as one having authority, and not as their scribes. ⁸·¹And when he came down from the mountain, large crowds followed him.

7:21 η ĂDŎNAI: The combining breve stands for the *nomina sacra* marks in the original texts. The reader may substitute Yăhweн, Măster, Ădŏn, Ădŏni (*my* Ădŏn), Lŏrd (equiv. to L-rd) or even Sĭr, as he or she sees fit or context requires. The use of this word in the translation does not for certain represent how a person quoted would have spoken, but the *nomina sacra* serve several functions: 1. A mark of divinity, 2. To indicate that the proper name is Hebrew, 3. To indicate to the reader who a person is, though the speaker in a text may not fully know. אֲדֹנָי Ădŏnai (intensive plural), i.e. '(my) great Lord' vs. simply ădŏni '(my) lord.' Ădŏnai vs. Ădŏnai. The Masoretes lengthened נִי to נָי as a mark of divinity, which I have retained. **7:23** ψ Psa 6:8] סוּרוּ מִמֶּנִּי כָּל־פֹּעֲלֵי אָוֶן.

8 And behold,ᵗ a leper came to him and bowed down to him, saying, "Ădŏnai, if you may be willing, you are able to make me clean." ³And he stretched out his hand and touched him, saying, "I am willing. Be cleansed." And immediately his leprosy was cleansed. ⁴And Yĕshuą says to him, "Be seeing that you will have told no one, but be going; show *yourself* to the priest, and offer the gift that Moshęh has commanded, for a testimony to them."

⁵And when he entered Kefar-Nahum,ᵛ a centurion came to him, entreating him, ⁶and saying, "Ădŏnai, my servant has been lying paralyzed at home, suffering great pain." ⁷And he said to him, "I will come and heal him." ⁸But the centurion answered and said, "Ădŏnai, I am not worthy that you may come under my roof, but speak the word, and my servant will be healed. ⁹And because I am a man being appointed under authority, having soldiers under myself, and I say to this one, 'Go!' and he goes, and to another, 'Be coming!' and he is coming, and to my servant, 'Do this!' and he is doing it."

¹⁰Now when Yĕshuą heard it, he expressed amazement, and said to those who were following, "Ămen I say to you, I have not found such great affirmation of support with anyone in Yisra'el. ¹¹And I say to you, that many will come from the east and the west, and will recline to eat with Ăvraham, and Yitshąq, and Ya'aqov in the kingdom of the heavens, ¹²but the sons of the kingdom will be cast out into the ᵟuttermost darkness. ᵖUnto that place there will be weeping and gnashing of teeth." ¹³And Yĕshuą said to the centurion, "Be going your way. As you have held *it* faithful, let it have been done for you." And the servant was healed in that hour.

¹⁴And when Yĕshuą came to Peter's home, he saw his mother-in-law, who had been lying and burning with fever. ¹⁵And he touched her hand, and the fever left her, and she arose, and was waiting on him.

¹⁶And when it became late, they brought to him many who were demon-possessed. And he cast out the spirits with a word, and healed all who were ill ¹⁷in order that what was spoken through Yeshąyahu the prophet will have been fulfilled, saying, "HE TOOK OUR INFIRMITIES AND CARRIED AWAY THE DISEASES.ᵝ" ¹⁸Now when Yĕshuą saw large crowds around him, he gave orders to depart to the other side.

¹⁹And a ᵞcertain scribe came and said to him, "Teacher, I will follow you wherever you may be going." ²⁰And Yĕshuą said to him, "The foxes have holes, and the birds of the air have nests, but the Sŏn of Man has nowhere he may be laying his head." ²¹And another of the disciples said to him, "Adŏn, permit me first to go and bury my father." ²²But Yĕshuą says to him, "Be following me, and

---

8:2 τ Winter, AD 31. **8:5** ν Summer AD 31. **8:12** δ or: oblivion **8:12** π Or "Thither." "To that place" instead of "in that place." "In that place," would appear to be influenced by the false doctrine of eternal torment. **8:14-15** Winter AD 31. **8:17** β Isa 53:4 **8:19** λ See Luke 9:57-62. Spring AD 33. At certain points the Evangelists put down episodes as they remembered them without respect to their chronology. Something or other triggered their memory, either theme or subject, and they organized minor episodes on that principle. The time line is sorted according to Luke who was more strict to chronological order. Possibly in this case Matattyahu was thinking of all the prospective disciples Yĕshuą had to deal with in the crowds with which he closed out the last scene.

Mattatyahu 8

leave the dead to bury their own dead." ²³And ⱽwhen he got into the boat, his disciples followed him. ²⁴And behold, there arose a great storm in the sea, so that the boat was covered with the waves, but he himself was asleep. ²⁵And they came and awoke him, saying, "Rescue us, Ădŏnai! We are perishing!" ²⁶And he said to them, "Why are you afraid little faithful ones?" Then he arose and rebuked the winds and the sea, and it became perfectly calm. ²⁷And the men expressed amazement, saying, "What kind of a man is this, that even the winds and the sea obey him?"

²⁸And when he came to the other side into the country of the Gadriyim, two men who were demon-possessed met him as they were coming out of the tombs, who were so very violent that no one could pass by that way. ²⁹And behold, they cried out, saying, "What do we have to do with you, Sŏn of the Almĭghty? Have you come here to torment us before the time?"

³⁰Now there was at a distance from them a herd of many pigs feeding. ³¹And the demons were begging him, saying, "If you cast us out, send us into the herd of pigs." ³²And he said to them, "Be going!" And when they went out, they went away into the pigs. And behold, the whole herd rushed down the steep bank into the sea and perished in the waters. ³³And the herders fled, and having gone into the town, they reported everything, also the *news* of those getting themselves demonized. ³⁴And behold, the whole town went out for a meeting with Yĕshua̧, and when they saw him, they begged him in order that he may depart from their boundaries. ⁹·¹ᵃAnd stepping into a boat, he crossed over and came into his own town.

9 ¹ᵇAnd behold, they were ²bringing to him a paralyzed man, who had been himself lying upon a bed, and Yĕshua̧, seeing their ᵟfaithfulness, said to the paralyzed man, "Be taking courage child. Your sins are getting forgiven." ³And behold, some of the scribes said within themselves, "This man is blaspheming." ⁴And Yĕshua̧, who had been knowing their thoughts said therefore, "Why are you thinking evil in your hearts? ⁵Because which is easier work, to have said, 'Your sins are getting forgiven,' or to have said, 'Be rising, and be walking'? ⁶But so that you will have been knowing that the Sŏn of Man has authority on the earth to be forgiving sins," then he says to the paralytic, "Having risen, take your bed, and be going to your home." ⁷And having risen, he went away to his home. ⁸But when the crowds had seen *it*, they had been awestruck, and had glorified the Almĭghty, who had given such authority to men.

⁹And Yĕshua̧ passing along from there, saw a man, sitting over the tax office called Mattatyahu, and he says to him, "Be following me!" And having risen up, he followed him. ¹⁰And it happened as he was reclining in the house to eat, that

---

8:23 ᵛ Fall, AD 31. Having to cross the lake (8:18) suggested putting this story here to Mattatyahu. **9:2** ᵟ *courage, determination.* **9:2** τ Around Ădar, AD 31. Luke sorts the story into order. Matattyah included it here because Yĕshua̧ going to his own city reminded him of it. **9:9** τ Ădar, AD 31.

behold, many tax-collectors and sinners who came, were reclining together with Yĕshuą and his disciples. ¹¹And the Perushim seeing it, said to his disciples, "Why is your teacher eating with the tax-collectors and sinners?" ¹²But when he heard this, he said, "It is not those who are healthy who need a doctor, but those who are sick. ¹³But go and learn what this means, 'I DESIRE COMPASSION, AND NOT SACRIFICE,ᵠ' because I did not come to call the righteous, but sinners."

¹⁴Then the disciples of Yoḣanan came to him, saying, "Why do we and the Perushim fast, but your disciples do not fast?" ¹⁵And Yĕshuą said to them, "The ᵞsons of the bridal suite cannot mourn as long as the bridegroom is with them, can they? But the days will come when the bridegroom will have been taken away from them, and then they will fast." ¹⁶"And no one puts a patch of unshrunk cloth on an old garment, because the patch pulls away from the garment, and a worse tear is made. ¹⁷Nor do they put young wine into old wineskins. Otherwise the wineskins are bursting, and the wine is poured out, and the wineskins are ruined, but they put young wine into new-made wineskins, and both are preserved."

¹⁸While⁰ he is saying such things to them, behold, there came an official, and bowed down to him, saying, "My daughter just died, but come and lay your hand on her, and she will live." ¹⁹And rising Yĕshuą followed him, and his disciples. ²⁰And behold, there was a woman who was suffering from a blood flow for twelve years, who coming up behind him touched the tassel of his clothing, ²¹because she was saying within herself, "If only I will have touched his garment, I will be delivered." ²²But Yĕshuą, who turned and saw her, said, "Daughter, be taking courage, your faithfulness has been delivering you." And from that hour the woman was delivered. ²³And as Yĕshuą came into the official's house, and saw the flute-players, and the crowd getting themselves into a noisy disorder, ²⁴he was saying, "Be clearing out, because the girl has not died, but she sleeps.ᵖ" And they were ridiculing him. ²⁵But when the crowd was ushered out, when he entered, he took hold of her hand, and the girl was raised. ²⁶And this news went out into all that land.

²⁷And as Yĕshuą passed on from there, two blind men followed him, crying out, and saying, "Have mercy on us, Sŏn of Dauid!" ²⁸And when he was coming into the house, the blind men came up to him, and Yĕshuą said to them, "Do you hold faithful, because I am able to do this?" They said to him, "Yes, Ádŏnai." ²⁹Then he touched their eyes, saying, "Be it done to you according to your support." ³⁰And their eyes were opened. And Yĕshuą sternly warned them, saying, "Be seeing that no one is knowing!" ³¹But they went out, and broadcast about him in all that land. ³²And as they were going out, behold, a mute man, demon-possessed, was brought to him. ³³And after the demon was cast out,

---

9:13 ψ Hoş 6:6: כִּי חֶסֶד חָפַצְתִּי וְלֹא־זָבַח, 1 Şam 15:22: הִנֵּה שְׁמֹעַ מִזֶּבַח טוֹב לְהַקְשִׁיב מֵחֵלֶב אֵילִים;
9:15 γ These were nuptial witnesses, attendants, and friends. **9:18** θ Matattyah leaps over a considerable number of events here, so it is likely that Yĕshuą was repeating the wineskin parable on a later occasion when the official came. Around Kislev AD 31. **9:24** ρ See Luke 8:52.

Mattatyahu 10

the mute man spoke, and the crowds were amazed, saying, "Nothing like this was ever seen in Yisra'el." ³⁴But the Perushim were saying, "He casts out the demons by the ruler of the demons."

³⁵And Yĕshua was going around to all the towns and the villages, teaching in their congregations, and proclaiming the good news of the kingdom, and healing every disease and every sickness. ³⁶And when he saw the crowds, he felt compassion for them, because they had been losing their hides, and had been getting cast off, as sheep having no shepherd. ³⁷Then he says to his disciples, "The harvest is abundant, yet the workers are few. ³⁸Therefore urgently ask the Măster of the harvest, so that he will have sent out workers into his harvest."

10 ¹And calling unto his twelve disciples, he gave them authority over unclean spirits, to cast them out and to heal every disease and every sickness. ²Now the names of the twelve emissaries are these: the first, Şim'on, who is called Peter, and Andrew his brother, and Ya'aqov the one from Zavdai, and Yohanan his brother, ³Philip and Bar-Talmai, Toma and Mattatyahu the tax-gatherer, Ya'aqov the one from Ḥalphai, and Taddai, ⁴Şim'on the Zealot, and Yehudah Ish-Qeriyot, the one who betrayed him.

⁵These twelve Yĕshua sent out instructing them, saying, "You should not go off into the way of the nations, and you should not enter into a town of the Shomronim, ⁶but more⁼ be going to the sheep, who have been getting lost, of the house of Yisra'el. ⁷And going, be proclaiming, saying, 'The kingdom of the heavens has been coming near.' ⁸Be healing the ailing, be raising the dead, be cleansing the lepers, be casting out demons. Freely you have received. Freely give. ⁹You shall not have acquired *additional* gold, or silver, or copper for your belts, ¹⁰or a bag for the journey, or even two tunics, or sandals, or a staff, because the worker is worthy of his food."

¹¹"And into whatever city or village you may have entered, ask who is worthy in it, and remain there until you may have gone away. ¹²And as you enter the house, give it your greeting. ¹³And if the house may be worthy, let your peace come upon it, but if it may not be worthy, let your peace return to you. ¹⁴And whoever may not have received you, or may not have listened to your words, as you go out of that house or that city, shake off the dust from your feet. ¹⁵Amen, I say to you, it will be more bearable for the land of Sedom and Amorah in the day of judgment, than for that town."

¹⁶"Behold, I am sending you off as sheep in the midst of wolves. Therefore be

---

9:35 τ Ţevet (winter), early AD 32.

10:6 π The foregoing negatives are not imperative prohibitions but rather instruct them to place their priority on the house Yisra'el. The house of Yisra'el (בֵּית־יִשְׂרָאֵל) referred to the whole united nation before the divided kingdom (cf. Exo. 16:31), but afterward came to be used distinctively of the northern kingdom. Only in an ideal sense is it used again when sometimes speaking to the house of Yehudah when the speaker wants to include the lost tribes in the scope of his address, even if they are not present (or very few in number), so as to look forward to a reunification of the tribes (cf. Ezek. 37). Though on the present mission the disciples will go to Jews only, Messiah's intention was ultimately to reach all the tribes, which were in fact the non Jewish nations (cf. Gen. 48:19).

getting wise as serpents, and innocent as doves. ¹⁷But be guarding against men, because they will deliver you up to the councils, and whip you in their congregations, ¹⁸and you will even be brought before governors and kings for my sake, as a testimony to them and to the nations. ¹⁹But when they may have delivered you up, you shall not become anxious about how or what you will have spoken, because it will be given to you in that hour, what you shall have spoken. ²⁰Because it is not you who speak, but the Spirit of your Father who speaks in you."

²¹"And brother will deliver up brother to death, and a father a child, and children will rise up against parents, and have them to be put to death. ²²And you will be hated by all on account of my name, but it is the one who endures to the end who will be rescued. ²³But whenever they may be persecuting you in this city, be fleeing to the next, because amen, I say to you: You may not have finished with the cities of Yisra'el, even till when the Son of Man may have come."

²⁴"A disciple is not above his teacher, nor a slave above his master. ²⁵It is enough for the disciple that he will have become like his teacher, and the slave like his master. If they call the head of the house Ba'al-zevul, how much more the members of his household! ²⁶Therefore you shall not have feared them, because nothing has been getting veiled that will not be revealed, and hidden that will not be made known. ²⁷What I tell you in the darkness, declare in the light. And what you hear in the ear, proclaim over the housetops."

²⁸"And do not be getting afraid of those killing the body, but are being unable to kill the soul, but rather be yourselves fearing him who is being able to destroy both soul and body in Geihinnom. ²⁹Are not two sparrows sold for an ⁰assarion? And not one of them will fall to the ground without your Father noticing. ³⁰But even the hairs of your head all have been getting numbered. ³¹Therefore do not be getting afraid. You are of more value than many sparrows."

³²"Everyone therefore who will confess me before men, I will also confess him before my Father who is in the heavens. ³³But whoever will have denied me before men, I will also deny him before my Father who is in the heavens."

³⁴"You shall not have supposed that I came to bring peace on the earth. I did not come to bring peace, so much as a sword, ³⁵because I came to 'SET A MAN AGAINST HIS FATHER, AND A DAUGHTER AGAINST HER MOTHER, AND A DAUGHTER-IN-LAW AGAINST HER MOTHER-IN-LAW. ³⁶And A MAN'S ENEMIES WILL BE THE MEMBERS OF HIS HOUSEHOLD'. ³⁷He who loves father or mother more than

---

10:22 ζ See Eph. 2:5-9. **10:29** ω An assarion is a copper coin equal to 1/16 denarius. A denarius, generally considered a good days wages for a day laborer, has 3.25 grams silver. So 1 assarion = 6.25% days wages. But if one wanted to buy a denarius, it might cost 18 assarion instead of the valuation rate of 16. **10:35-36** μ Micah 7:6 כִּי־בֵן מְנַבֵּל אָב בַּת קָמָה בְאִמָּהּ כַּלָּה בַּחֲמֹתָהּ אֹיְבֵי אִישׁ אַנְשֵׁי בֵיתוֹ.

10:41 π See Rom. 12:6. **11:1** τ Tevet to II Adar, AD 32. During this time Yeshua attended Purim while his disciples were out on the mission he had sent them to do; John 5:1-15.

10:23 ψ Cf. 10:6 π. The "cities of Yisra'el" refers to any cities with populations of the "house of Yisra'el" in them. The mystery of the kingdom is that the scattered seed of Yisra'el was sowed in exile among the nations so that the nations over time became descended from Yisra'el (Gen. 48:19; Rom. 11:25)! So all the cities of the earth are in the cities of Yisra'el. Messiah did not want his emissaries wasting time being persecuted in one city when there were many more to get to, and the subjunctive expresses a doubt that they will reach all of them before he returns to gather Yisra'el back to the land, because whosoever is not returned to the bond of the covenant is bound to remain in the wilderness of the nations when he

Mattatyahu 11

me is not worthy of me. And he who loves son or daughter more than me is not worthy of me. ³⁸And he who does not take his execution timber and follow after me is not worthy of me. ³⁹He who finds his life will lose it, and he who loses his life for my sake will find it."

⁴⁰"He who receives you, receives me, and he who is receiving me, receives the one having sent me. ⁴¹He who receives a ᵗprophet in the name of a prophet will receive a prophet's reward, and he who receives a just man in the name of a just man will receive a just man's reward. ⁴²And whoever in the name of a disciple may have given to one of these little ones only a cup of cold water to drink, amen, I say to you he shall not have lost his reward."

¹¹·¹And it happened when Yĕshua finished giving instructions to his twelve disciples, that he departed from there to teach and proclaim in their cities.

11 ¹ᵇWhen Yohanan in ²prison heard of the deeds of the Anŏinted, he sent a message by his disciples, ³and said to him, "Are you THE COMING ONE, or should we be looking for someone else?" ⁴And Yĕshua answered and said to them, "Go and report to Yohanan what you hear and see! ⁵THE BLIND RECEIVE SIGHT AND THE LAME WALK^φ, the lepers are cleansed and THE DEAF HEAR, and the dead are raised up, and the POOR HAVE THE GOOD NEWS PROCLAIMED TO THEM^β. ⁶And blessed is he who may not have stumbled because of me."

⁷And as these were going away, Yĕshua began to speak to the crowds about Yohanan, "What did you go out into the wilderness to look at? A reed shaken by the wind? ⁸But what did you go out to see? A man who had been getting dressed in luxurious clothes? Behold, those who wear luxurious clothes are in kings' palaces. ⁹But why did you go out? To see a prophet? Yes, I say to you, and one who is more than a prophet!"

¹⁰"This is the one about whom it has been getting written, 'BEHOLD, I SEND MY MESSENGER BEFORE YOUR FACE, WHO WILL PREPARE YOUR WAY BEFORE YOU^β.' ¹¹Amen, I say to you, among those born of women there has not been getting raised up one ᵗmore popular than Yohanan the Immerser, but he who is less popular in the kingdom of the heavens is greater than he."

¹²And from the days of Yohanan the Immerser until now the kingdom of

---

restores Yisra'el. See Yoḥ. 11:52. ▷ Many wish to reinterpret "when the Son of man may have come" to refer to a proposed coming of the Son in spirit to judge the house of Yehudah in AD 70 because they want the dispensation of the 'old covenant' as they put it to end, but this is conjecture on the one point and heresy on the other, since the covenant is the covenant of old new made. So the present interpretation is the spirit of prophecy and much preferable to one which rejects the Messianic intent for re-uniting Yisra'el. See Eph. 3:4 ξ; Jer. 33:14; Mat. 21:43.

11:1b τ Yohanan sent this message in the late spring of AD 31. **11:5** φ Isa 35:5-6 **11:5** β Isa 61:1: לְבַשֵּׂר עֲנָוִים. **11:10** β Mal 4:5 **11:11** τ→popular: Greater and least are used in the sense of popular and less popular. Yohanan was not the greatest of the prophets. Eliyahu was. But Eliyahu was less popular. Měssiah was less popular than Yohanan. Yohanan was so popular because he said the Měssiah was coming after him, and this is what the people wanted to hear. But when Yĕshua came many did not want to hear what he said.

11:12 θ The multitudes were zealously seeking the kingdom. They were coming about the disciples like a siege force. ▷ But Yohanan announced the Měssiah had come. See John 1:29-34.

the heavens is getting ᶿassaulted, and assaulters are plundering it. ¹³Certainly, all the prophets and the Law until Yoḥanan ˣprophesied *such*. ¹⁴And if you care to accept it, he is *an* ᵉEliyahu, (who is about to be coming). ¹⁵He who is having ears, let him be hearing.

¹⁶"But to what will I compare this kindred? It is like children sitting in the market places, who call out to the other children, ¹⁷and say, 'We played the flute for you, and you did not dance. We sang a lament, and you did not mourn.' ¹⁸Because Yoḥanan came neither eating nor drinking, and they say, 'He has a demon!' ¹⁹The Sŏn of Man came eating and drinking, and they say, 'Behold, a gluttonous man and a drunkard, a friend of tax-collectors and sinners!' Yet wisdom is judged rightly by her deeds."

²⁰ᵀThen he began to reproach the cities in which most of his miracles were done, because they did not become sorry to turn their heart *from sin*. ²¹Woe to you, Korazin! Woe to you, Beṯh-Tsaidah! For if the miracles had occurred in Tsor and Tsidon which have occurred in you, they would have become sorry to turn their heart *from sin* long ago in sackcloth and ashes. ²²Nevertheless I say to you, it will be more tolerable for Tsor and Tsidon in the day of judgment than for you. ²³And you, Kefar-Naḥum, will not be exalted to heaven, will you? You will descend to the grave, because if the miracles had occurred in Sedom which have occurred in you, it would have remained to this day. ²⁴Nevertheless I say to you that it will be more tolerable for the land of Sedom in the day of judgment than for you.

²⁵At that time Yĕshua continuing said, "I praise you, Făther, Adŏnai of the heavens and the earth, that you did hide these things from the wise and intelligent and did reveal them to babes. ²⁶Yes, Făther, for thus it was well-pleasing

---

11:13 χ→such: The verb demands us to supply what was being prophesied after *prophesied*, and this is obtained from the preceding verse. ▷ Starting in Gen. 3:15 it was predicted that the serpent would hate the seed of the woman. The law and prophets repeat this prediction many times and ways, and show in the history of Israel the many assaults on the kingdom. See Luke 16:16. **11:14** ε The cloak of Eliyahu fell to Elisha his successor, and then to Yoḥanan (cf. Luke 1:17). But Eliyahu will still come. See Mat. 17:11 and Mark 9:12. Yoḥanan denied he was Eliyahu in person (see John 1:21; cf. Mal. 4:5-6). Eliyahu appears later on the Mount of Transfiguration (see Mat. 17:11-12), and is one of the two witnesses of Mĕssiah's death and resurrection who stand before the Adŏnai of all the earth. He still comes. See Rev. 11:3-13; Zech. 4:14. ▷ John Gill says, "And, as it was usual with the Jews (f), to call Phinehas by the name of Elias, and Elias Phinehas, because of his zeal for the Lord of hosts; for the same reason may John be called by the same name, there being a great resemblance between Elias and him; in their temper and disposition; in their manner of clothing, and austere way of living; in their very great piety and holiness; in their courage and integrity, in reproving vice; and in their zeal and usefulness in the cause of Gŏd, and true religion:" To understand the use of a famous character namesake we only have to consider usages like "modern day Joshua," or "modern day Caleb." Men are so referred to metaphorically in the namesake of their predecessor when they evidence the same characteristics. Mĕssiah assures us that Eliyahu will still come. See Mat. 17:11 and Mark 9:12. Because Mĕssiah comes twice, once to die and rise, and once to set up the kingdom. Yoḥanan was sent first in the spirit and power of Eliyahu. See Luke 1:17. Yoḥanan was only a type of Eliyahu. "Eliyahu the prophet" (cf. Mal. 4:5) still comes. ▷ Many of the commentators try to explain that Mal. 4:5 only meant Yoḥanan and that there will be no future "Eliyahu the prophet" to fulfill the prophecy. This opinion is founded on no other prejudice than a rejection of the literal fulfillment of the promises for the restoration of Yisra'el. **11:20** τ Late Spring AD 31.

Mattatyahu 12

in your sight."

²⁷"All things are handed over to me by my Făther, and no one is knowing the Sŏn, except the Făther, nor is anyone knowing the Făther, except the Sŏn, and whomever the Sŏn may be intending to reveal him."

²⁸"Come to me, all you who are wearying and who have been getting loaded down, and I will give you rest. ²⁹Take my yoke upon you, and learn from me, because I am gentle and humble in heart, and 'YOU WILL FIND REST FOR YOUR SOULS,ᵖ' ³⁰because my yoke is easy, and my load is light."

12

¹In that ᵃseason Yĕshua went on the Şabbaths through the grain fields, and his disciples became hungry and began to pick the grain ears and eat them. ²But when the Perushim saw it, they said to him, "Behold, your disciples do what is not lawful to do on Şabbath." ³But he said to them, "Have you not ᵖread what David did, when he became hungry, he and his companions, ⁴how he entered the house of the Almĭghty, and they ate the consecrated bread, which was not lawful for him to eat, nor for those with him, but for the priests alone?"

⁵"Or have you not read in the Law, that on the Şabbaths the priests in the temple break the Şabbath, and are innocent? ⁶But I say to you, that something greater than the temple is here. ⁷But if you had been knowing what means, "I AM DESIRING COMPASSION, AND NOT A SACRIFICE,ᵋ" you would not have condemned the innocent." ⁸"For the Sŏn of Man is Măster of the Şabbath."

⁹And departing from there, he went into their congregation. ¹⁰And behold, there was a man with a withered hand. And they questioned him, saying, "Is it lawful to heal on the Şabbaths?" in order that they might accuse him. ¹¹And he said to them, "What man will there be among you, who will have one sheep, and if it may have fallen into a pit on the Şabbath, will he not take hold of it, and lift it out?"

¹²"Of how much more value then is a man than a sheep! So then, it is lawful to do good on the Şabbaths." ¹³Then he said to the man, "Stretch out your hand!" And he stretched it out, and it was restored to normal, like the other. ¹⁴But the Perushim went out, and counseled together against him, as to how they might

---

11:28-30 π Jer 6:16, כֹּה אָמַר יְהוָה עִמְדוּ עַל־
דְּרָכִים וּרְאוּ וְשַׁאֲלוּ לִנְתִבוֹת עוֹלָם אֵי־זֶה דֶרֶךְ הַטּוֹב
= וּלְכוּ־בָהּ וּמִצְאוּ מַרְגּוֹעַ לְנַפְשְׁכֶם וַיֹּאמְרוּ לֹא נֵלֵךְ׃

Thus has said Yăhweh, stand at the cross roads, and look! And ask for the paths of old, where is the way of good, and walk on it, and find rest for your souls. Then they said, we will not go.

12:1 α The same season as the embassy from Yohanan, but earlier in the spring. See Luke 6:1. During Passover AD 31. Although it may be presumed that Luke's account describes the scene that set off the arguments of the Perushim, we may infer that the disciples kept up this Şabbath habit during the whole grain harvest season, and therefore Matthew

and Mark say Şabbaths whereas Luke refers to the first incident as on the second first Şabbath. **12:3** ρ 1 Sam. 21:1-6. "THEN THE PRIEST GAVE TO HIM THE HOLY THING, BECAUSE THERE HAD NOT BEEN THERE ANY BREAD EXCEPT THE BREAD OF THE FACES BEING MADE TO TURN ASIDE FROM THE FACE OF YĂHWEH TO SET HOT BREAD ON THE DAY OF ITS BEING TAKEN AWAY" (וַיִּתֶּן־לוֹ
הַכֹּהֵן קֹדֶשׁ כִּי לֹא־הָיָה שָׁם לֶחֶם כִּי־אִם־לֶחֶם הַפָּנִים
הַמּוּסָרִים מִלִּפְנֵי יְהוָה לָשׂוּם לֶחֶם חֹם בְּיוֹם הִלָּקְחוֹ׃). The exchange of the old bread for the hot bread was always done on the Şabbath. This happened on the 4th day of the month of Aviv in the year 1069 BC. **12:7** ξ Hos 6:6 כִּי חֶסֶד חָפַצְתִּי וְלֹא־זָבַח.

destroy him. ¹⁵But Yĕshua, aware of this, withdrew from there.

¹⁵ᵇAnd large crowds followed him, and he healed them all, ¹⁶and warned them, that they should not make him public, ¹⁷in order that what was spoken through Yeshayahu the prophet, might be fulfilled, saying, ¹⁸ˣBEHOLD, MY SERVANT WHOM I HAVE CHOSEN, MY BELOVED IN WHOM MY SOUL IS WELL-PLEASED. I WILL PUT MY SPĬRIT UPON HIM, AND HE WILL ANNOUNCE JUSTICE TO THE NATIONS. ¹⁹HE WILL NOT QUARREL, NOR RAISE AN OUTCRY; NOR WILL ANYONE HEAR HIS VOICE IN THE STREETS. ²⁰A ᵠREED THAT HAS BEEN GETTING BRUISED HE WILL NOT SHATTER, AND A ᵞSMOLDERING WICK HE WILL NOT PUT OUT, TIL WHEN HE MAY HAVE DRIVEN JUSTICE TO VICTORY. ²¹AND ᵋFOR HIS NAME THE ᵡNATIONS WILL WAIT."

²²Then there was brought to him a demon-possessed man who was blind and dumb, and he healed him, so that the dumb man spoke and saw. ²³And all the crowds were amazed, and were saying, "This man cannot be the Sŏn of David, can he?" ²⁴But when the Perushim heard it, they said, "This man casts out demons only by Ba'al-zevul the ruler of the demons."

²⁵And having been knowing their thoughts, he said to them, "Every kingdom divided against itself is being laid waste. And every city or house divided against itself will not stand. ²⁶And if Satan casts out Satan, he is divided against himself. How then will his kingdom stand? ²⁷And if I by Ba'al-zevul cast out demons, by whom do your sons cast them out? Consequently they will be your judges. ²⁸But if I cast out demons by the Spĭrit of the Almĭghty, then the kingdom of the Almĭghty has come upon you."

²⁹"Or how can anyone enter the strong man's house and carry off his property, unless he first may have bound the strong man? And then he will plunder his house."

³⁰"He who is not with me is against me, and he who does not gather with me scatters. ³¹Therefore I say to you, any sin and blasphemy may be forgiven men, but blasphemy against the Spĭrit will not be forgiven. ³²And whoever may have spoken a word against the Sŏn of Man, it will be forgiven him, but whoever may have spoken against the Holy Spĭrit, IT WILL NOT BE FORGIVEN HIM,ᵟ neither in this age, nor as well in the one coming."

³³"Either make the tree good, and its fruit good, or make the tree bad,

---

12:18 χ Isa 42:1-4; Isa. 60:9 **12:20** ψ→bruised: fig. of weak beaten up person **12:20** γ→wick: fig. of person barely hanging onto life. **12:21** ξ In Isa. 42:4, ξ→NAME = *for his law*; τῷ νόμῳ = וּלְתוֹרָתוֹ. But see Isa. 60:9, 'Surely for Me the coastlands will wait (כִּי־לִי אִיִּים יְקַוּוּ) ... and the ships of Tarshish in the lead, to bring your sons from afar, their silver and their gold with them, to the name of Yahweh our Almĭghty, even to the Holy One of Yisrael. Surely He will have beautified You. ▷ The 'name' is the personified embodiment of Mĕssiah, represented by each of the underlined phrases. Isa. 42:4 suggests a connection to Isa. 60:9, and so the quote is finished with a summary of Isa. 60:9, by putting 'his name' for 'Me' (לִי). The mistake belongs to the LXX translators who supposed that Mat. 12:21 was taken from Isa. 42:4, and so they redacted the LXX in Isa. 42:4 to conform to Mat. 12:21. The parallel interpretation suggests that waiting for his name means seeking his Law. See also Rom. 15:12; Isa. 11:10. **12:21** λ Hebrew: coastlands, אִיִּים.

12:32 δ Deu 29:20: לֹא־יֹאבֶה יְהוָה סְלֹחַ לוֹ; cf. Mark 3:29. He speaks of the willful sin against knowledge in the heart which the Spirit bears witness to.

Mattatyahu 12

and its fruit bad, because the tree is known by its fruit. ³⁴You, who are born of snakes, how can you, being evil, speak what is good? Because the mouth speaks out of that which fills the heart. ³⁵The good man out of his good treasure brings forth what is good. And the evil man out of his evil treasure brings forth what is evil. ³⁶And I say to you, that every careless word that men will speak, they will render account for it in the day of judgment. ³⁷Because by your words you will be declared right, and by your words you will be found guilty."

³⁸Then some of the scribes and Perushim answered him, saying, "Teacher, we want to see a sign from you." ³⁹But he answered and said to them, "An evil and adulterous kindred demands a sign, and no sign will be given to it except the sign of Yonah the prophet, ⁴⁰because just as 'YONAH WAS IN THE BELLY OF THE GREAT FISH THREE DAYS AND THREE NIGHTS,ᵅ' so will the Sŏn of Man be THREE DAYS AND THREE NIGHTS^β IN THE HEART OF THE^ρ EARTH.^γ

⁴¹The men of Ninveh will rise up against^θ this kindred during the judgment, and will condemn it because they became sorry and turned their heart at the proclaiming of Yonah, and behold, something greater than Yonah is here. ⁴²The Queen of the South will rise up against this kindred at the judgment and will condemn it, because she came from the ends of the earth to hear the wisdom of Shelomoh, and behold, something greater than Shelomoh is here."

⁴³"Now whenever the unclean spirit may have gone out of a man, it passes through waterless places, seeking rest, and does not find it. ⁴⁴Then it says, 'I will return to my house from which I came', and when it comes, it finds it being unoccupied, having been getting swept, and which has been getting put in order. ⁴⁵Then it goes, and takes along with it seven other spirits more wicked than itself, and they go in and live there. And the last state of that man becomes worse than the first. That is the way it will also be with this evil kindred."

⁴⁶When he *was* ᵋspeaking to the crowds, behold, his mother and brothers had been standing outside, seeking to speak to him. ⁴⁷And someone said to him,

---

12:40 α-β Yonah 1:17; cf. 1 Sam. 30:12. **12:40** ρ Yonah 2:3: בְּלְבַב יַמִּים. **12:40** γ Yonah 2:6: הָאָרֶץ בְּרִחֶיהָ בַעֲדִי לְעוֹלָם. *Heart of the Earth:* recombined Hebrew = suffering + entombment. These two prophetic texts (Yonah 1:17; cf. 1 Sam. 30:12) witness that three nights are required. On the third day texts see Luke 24:46. The third day theme is everywhere in the Torah and Prophets under many guises and in many stories. ▷ It is very important to stress that Mat. 12:40 is on the basis of putting the day before the night, i.e. each calendar day begins at dawn and ends at the next. The day from the beginning was reckoned this way. Each day of creation ends with the night refrain: "THEN THERE IS SETTING. THEN THERE IS DAYBREAK." At daybreak, the number of complete days is counted. The reason there is so much confusion is the popular KJV translation predicated the whole day with the evening and the morning: "And the evening and the morning *were* the first day." It is not a valid translation of the Hebrew. The KJV deleted the verb twice and then added it back in where it does not occur in the text in Gen. 1:5, 8, 13, 19, 23, 31. ▷ The day for every burnt offering is likewise reckoned to dawn: See Lev. 6:9-10; Num. 28:1-4; so also the day of a peace offering, Lev. 7:15. All the places where it is commanded to leave no offering until morning are reckoning the day for the offering from dawn to dawn. The resurrection chart explains how it all fits together. ▷ So Mat. 12:40 is reckoned, day and night, day and night, day and night, 1d, 1n, 2d, 2n, 3d, 3n. The third calendar day is the 3d + 3n, dawn on Friday to dawn on the Şabbath (See Genesis Note on page 444). **12:41** θ Literally, "with." Picture the witnesses and the defendants rising together from seats at the start of a trial. Functional translation. **12:46** ξ Other MSS add "still", but I think not. The narrative follows after an interval in the early summer of AD 31.

"Behold, your mother and your brothers have been standing outside seeking to speak to you." ⁴⁸But he answered the one who was telling him and said, "Who is my mother and who are my brothers?" ⁴⁹And stretching out his hand toward his disciples, he said, "Behold, my mother and my brothers! ⁵⁰Because whoever may have done the will of my Father, who is in the heavens, he is my brother and sister and mother."

13

¹In that day Yĕshua went out of the house, and was sitting beside the sea. ²And large crowds gathered to him, so that he got into a boat and sat down, and the whole crowd had been standing on the beach. ³And he spoke many things to them in parables, saying:

³ᵇ"Behold, the sower went out to sow, ⁴and as he sowed, some seeds fell beside the road, and the birds came and ate them up. ⁵And others fell upon the rocky places, where they did not have much soil, and immediately they sprang up, because they had no depth of soil. ⁶But when the sun rose, they were scorched. And because they had no root, they withered away. ⁷And others fell among the thorns, and the thorns came up and choked them out. ⁸And others fell on the good soil, and yielded a crop, some a hundredfold, some sixty, and some thirty. ⁹He who is having ears, let him be hearing."

¹⁰And the disciples came and said to him, "Why do you speak to them in parables?" ¹¹And when he answered, he said to them, "Because, to you it has been ᵘgetting offered to know the secrets of the kingdom of the heavens, but to ᶿthose it has not been ᵘgetting offered. ¹²Because whoever holds fast, to him will more be given, and he will have an abundance, but whoever does not hold fast, even what he has will be taken away from him. ¹³Therefore I speak to them in parables, because while seeing they do not perceive, and while hearing they do not listen, nor do they understand. ¹⁴And in their case the prophecy of Yeshayahu is fulfilled, which says, ᵞHEARING YOU WILL HEAR, AND NO, YOU SHALL NOT HAVE UNDERSTOOD. AND SEEING YOU WILL SEE, BUT NO, YOU SHALL NOT HAVE PERCEIVED. ¹⁵BECAUSE THE HEART OF THIS PEOPLE ᵠIS DULLED AND THEIR EARS ᵠHARDLY HAVE HEARD, AND THEIR EYES THEY ᵖHAVE CLOSED, LEST THEY MAY HAVE SEEN WITH THEIR EYES, AND MAY HAVE HEARD WITH THEIR EARS, AND THEIR HEART MAY HAVE UNDERSTOOD AND THEY MAY HAVE RETURNED, AND I WILL HEAL THEM.' ¹⁶But blessed are your eyes, because they see, and your ears, because they hear. ¹⁷Amen indeed! I say to you, that many prophets and just men desired to see what you see, and did not see it, and to hear what you hear, and did not hear it."

¹⁸"Hear then the parable of the sower. ¹⁹For everyone hearing the word of

---

13:11 μ or: *will have been getting offered,* gnomic/distributive perfect. See vs. 12, where it is clear that revelation of the secrets is progressively unfolded. **13:11** θ *those ones,* i.e the unproductive soils; see Mark 4:11 += *those outside* τοῖς ἔξω, i.e. whoever is not listening and holding faithful. **13:14-15** λ Isa 6:9f **13:15** φ→dulled = הַשְׁמֵן = *has been made fat;* **13:15** ψ→heard = הַכְבֵּד = *have been made heavy.* or more likely: הַכְבֵּד = *it (the people) has made heavy;* **13:15** ρ→closed = הָשַׁע = *it has made closed.* I very much doubt that the traditional imperative vowel pointing of Isa. 6:10 in the MT is meant to be the only way of reading the text. The hardheartedness is just as much self inflicted.

the kingdom, and who is not putting it together, the evil one is coming and he is snatching away what has been getting sown in his heart. This is the one on whom seed was sown beside the road. ²⁰And the one on whom seed was sown on the rocky places, this is the man who hears the word, and immediately receives it with joy. ²¹Yet he has no firm root in himself, but is only temporary, and when affliction or persecution arises because of the word, immediately he falls away. ²²And the one on whom seed was sown among the thorns, this is the man who hears the word, but the worry of the age, and the deceitfulness of riches choke the word, and it becomes unfruitful. ²³And the one on whom seed was sown on the good soil, this is the man who is listening to the word and putting it together, who indeed bears fruit, and brings forth, some a hundredfold, some sixty, and some thirty."

²⁴He put forward another parable to them, saying, "The kingdom of the heavens may be compared to a man who sowed good seed in his field. ²⁵But while men were sleeping, his enemy came and sowed ᵘdarnel also among the wheat, and went away. ²⁶But when the wheat sprang up and bore grain, then the darnel became evident also. ²⁷And the servants of the landowner came and said to him, 'Sir, did you not sow good seed in your field? How then does it have darnel?' ²⁸And he said to them, 'An enemy did this!' And the servants say to him, 'Do you want us, then, having gone *that* we will have gathered them up?' ²⁹But he said, 'No, lest while you are gathering up the darnel, you may have uprooted the wheat with them. ³⁰Allow both to grow together until the harvest, and in the time of the harvest I will say to the reapers, "First gather up the darnel and bind them in bundles to burn them up, but gather the wheat into my barn."'"

³¹He presented another parable to them, saying, "The kingdom of the heavens is like a mustard seed, which a man took and sowed in his field. ³²And this is littler among all seeds, but when it may have grown, it is larger among the garden plants, and becomes a tree, so that THE BIRDS OF THE AIR come and NEST IN ITS BRANCHES^ϕ." ³³He spoke another parable to them, "The kingdom of the heavens is like leavening, which a woman took, and hid in three pecks of meal, until it was all leavened." ³⁴All these things Yĕshua spoke to the crowds in parables, and he was not speaking to them without a parable, ³⁵so that what was spoken through the prophet might be fulfilled, saying, "I WILL OPEN MY MOUTH IN PARABLES. I WILL POUR OUT WHAT HAS BEEN GETTING HIDDEN FROM THE FOUNDING OF THE WORLD^γ."

³⁶Then he left the crowds, and went into the house. And his disciples came to him, saying, "Explain to us the parable of the darnel in the field." ³⁷And he answered and said, "The one who sows the good seed is the Sŏn of Man, ³⁸and the field is the world, and as for the good seed, these are the sons of the king-

---

13:25 μ At first the darnel looks like the wheat, but when it matures it is revealed. **13:32** ϕ Eze 17:23; 31:6; Dan 4:12, 21. **13:35** γ Psa 78:2.

dom. And the darnel are the sons of the evil one, ³⁹and the enemy who sowed them is the Slanderer, and the harvest is the end of the age, and the reapers are messengers."

⁴⁰"Therefore just as the darnel are gathered up and burned with fire, so will it be at the end of the age. ⁴¹The Sŏn of Man will send forth his messengers, and they will gather out of his kingdom all stumbling blocks, and those practicing lawlessness, ⁴²and THEY WILL CAST THEM INTO THE FURNACE OF FIRE⸱ On the way to that place there will be weeping and gnashing of teeth. ⁴³THEN THE RIGHTEOUS WILL SHINE FORTH AS THE SUN^β in the kingdom of their Făther. He who is having ears, let him be hearing."

⁴⁴"The kingdom of the heavens is like a treasure which had been getting hidden in a field, which when a man had found it, he had hid. And from joy over it he is going and selling all that he has, and buys that field." ⁴⁵"Again, the kingdom of the heavens is like a merchant seeking fine pearls. ⁴⁶And when he had found one pearl of great value, *he had* gone away, *and* he had been selling all that he had been owning, and he had bought it." ⁴⁷"Again, the kingdom of the heavens is like a dragnet cast into the sea, and gathering fish of every kind. ⁴⁸And when it was filled, they drew it up on the shore, and they sat down, and gathered the good fish into containers, but the bad they threw away⸱ ⁴⁹So it will be at the end of the age. The messengers will come forth, and will separate out the wicked from among the righteous, ⁵⁰and will cast them into the furnace of fire. On the way to that place will be weeping and gnashing of teeth. ⁵¹Have you understood all these things?" They said to him, "Yes." ⁵²And he said to them, "Therefore every scribe who has become a disciple of the kingdom of the heavens is like a head of a household, who brings forth out of his treasure things new-made and old." ⁵³And it came about that when Yĕshua finished these parables, he departed from there.

⁵⁴ᵀAnd coming to his home town, he was teaching them in their congregation, so that they became astonished, and said, "Where did this man get this wisdom, and these miraculous powers? ⁵⁵Is not this the carpenter's son? Is not his mother called Miryam, and his brothers, Ya'aqov and Yosef and Şim'on and Yehudah? ⁵⁶And his sisters, are they not all with us? Where then did this man get all these things?" ⁵⁷And they took offense at him. But Yĕshua said to them, "A prophet is not without honor except in his home town, and in his own household." ⁵⁸And he did not do many miracles there because of their faithlessness.

14

¹In that ᵀseason Herod the Tetrarch heard the news about Yĕshua, ²and said to his servants, "This is Yoḥanan the Immerser. He has risen from the dead, and that is why miraculous powers are at work in him."

13:42 ζ Dan. 3:6⟧ יִתְרְמֵא לְגוֹא־אַתּוּן נוּרָא | are the unclean without fins and scales. **13:54-58** τ Winter, AD 31/32. **14:1** τ Late winter, AD 32 in Adar II.
יָקְדְתָּא. **13:43** β Dan 12:3⟧ וְהַמַּשְׂכִּלִים יַזְהִרוּ כְּזֹהַר
הָרָקִיעַ. **13:48** η The bad sea creatures thrown away

Mattatyahu 14

³Because when Herod had Yoḥanan arrested, he bound him, and put him in prison on account of Herodias, the wife of his brother Philip, ⁴because Yoḥanan was saying to him, "It is not lawful for you to have her." ⁵And although he wanted to put him to death, he feared the crowd, because they regarded him as a prophet. ⁶But when Herod's birthday came, the daughter of Herodias danced before them and pleased Herod. ⁷Thereupon he promised with an oath to give her whatever she will have asked. ⁸And having been prompted by her mother, she said, "Give me here on a platter the head of Yoḥanan the Immerser." ⁹And although he was grieved, the king commanded it to be given because of his oaths, and because of his dinner guests. ¹⁰And he sent and had Yoḥanan beheaded in the prison. ¹¹And his head was brought on a platter and given to the girl. And she brought it to her mother. ¹²And his disciples came and took away the body and buried it, and they went and reported to Yĕshua.

¹³Now ᵗwhen Yĕshua heard it, he withdrew from there in a boat, to a lonely place by himself. And when the crowds heard of this, they followed him on foot from the cities. ¹⁴And when he went ashore, he saw a large crowd, and felt compassion for them, and healed their sick.

¹⁵And when it was late, the disciples came to him, saying, "The place is desolate, and the hour is already past, so send the crowds away, that they may go into the villages and may buy food for themselves." ¹⁶But Yĕshua said to them, "They do not need to go away. You give them something to eat!" ¹⁷And they said to him, "We have here only five loaves and two fish." ¹⁸And he said, "Be bringing them here to me." ¹⁹And ordering the crowds to recline on the grass, he took the five loaves and the two fish, and looking up toward heaven, he blessed Yăhweh, and breaking the loaves he gave them to the disciples, and the disciples gave to the crowds, ²⁰and they all ate, and were satisfied. And they picked up what was left over of the broken pieces, twelve full baskets. ²¹And there were about five thousand men who ate, aside from women and children.ᵟ

²²And immediately he made the disciples get into the boat, and go ahead of him to the other side, until he could send the crowds away. ²³And after he sent the crowds away, he went up to the mountain by himself to pray. And when it was late, he was there alone. ²⁴But the boat was already many stadia away from the land, battered by the waves, because the wind was contrary. ²⁵And in the fourth watch of the night he came to them, walking on the sea. ²⁶And when the disciples saw him walking on the sea, they were frightened, saying, "It is a ghost!" And they cried out for fear. ²⁷But immediately Yĕshua spoke to them, saying, "Be taking courage, ˣI AM! Do not be getting afraid." ²⁸And Peter when he answered him, said, "Adŏnai, if it is you, command me to come to you on the water." ²⁹And he said, "Come!" And having stepped down from the boat, Peter walked on the water and came toward Yĕshua.

14:13 τ Toward the end of II Adar, AD 32. **14:19-21** δ AD 32 near the Passover of John 6:4. **14:27** χ = אֲנִי הוּא.

³⁰But seeing the strong wind, he became afraid, and began to be sinking, he cried out, saying, "Yăhwe︭ͪ, rescue me!" ³¹And immediately Yĕshua, having stretched out his hand, took hold of him, and says to him, "Little faithful one, why did you doubt?" ³²And when they got into the boat, the wind stopped. ³³And those who were in the boat worshiped him, saying, "You are truly the Almĭghty Sŏn!" ³⁴And when they crossed over, they came upon the land at Genneisaret. ³⁵And when the men of that place recognized him, they sent into all that surrounding district and brought to him all who were sick. ³⁶And they were begging him that they might just touch the tassel of his cloak, and as many as touched it were cured.

15

¹Thenᵀ some Perushim and scribes are coming to Yĕshua from Yerushalayim, saying,²"For what *reason* are your disciples transgressing the tradition of the elders? Because they do not wash their hands when they may be eating bread." ³And having answered, he said to them, "For what *reason* are you also transgressing the commandment of the Almĭghty by your tradition? ⁴Because the Almĭghty said, 'BE HONORING YOUR FATHER AND YOUR MOTHER,ᶿ' and, 'HE WHO SPEAKS EVIL OF FATHER OR MOTHER, BY DEATH MUST BE ENDING.ᵝ' ⁵But you say, 'Whoever may have said to father or mother, "Anything of mine you might be helped by *is a gift to the Almĭghty*." ⁶No, he will not honor his father ⸀or his mother⸀.' Then you have invalidated the word of the Almĭghty by your tradition." ⁷"You hypocrites, rightly did Yeshayahu prophesy about you, saying, ⁸'THIS PEOPLE DRAWS NEAR TO ME WITH THEIR MOUTH AND WITH THE LIPS THEY HONOR ME, BUT THEIR HEART IS FAR FROM ME. ⁹BUT VAINLY THEY REVERENCE ME, TEACHING AS TEACHINGS THE COMMANDMENTS OF MEN.ᵟ'"

¹⁰And when he called the crowd, he said to them, "Be hearing and be understanding. ¹¹What enters by itself into the mouth is not sharing defilement with the man, but what is going out of the mouth—this is sharing defilement with the man.ᵡ" ¹²Then when they came near, the disciples say to him, "You have been knowing that the Perushim who heard that saying were offended?" ¹³And, when he answered, he said, "Every plant which my heavenly Făther has not planted will be rooted up. ¹⁴Leave them! They are blind guides of the blind. And if a blind man may be guiding a blind man, both will fall into a pit." ¹⁵And when Peter answered, he said to him, "Explain this parable to us." ¹⁶And, he

---

14:30 μ or Adonai. אֲדֹנָי. **15:1** τ Late spring AD 32. **15:4** θ Exo 20:12, Deu 5:16; **15:4** β Exo 21:17 τελευτήσει θανάτῳ (will be ending by death), Lev 20:9: מוֹת יוּמָת = θανάτῳ θανατούσθω, LXX. **15:6** ʹ omit: א D B pc a e syᶜ sa. **15:8** δ Isa 29:13, Col 2:22, Tit 1:14. **15:10-11** χ See extended remarks on Mark 7:2, 15, 19. The key here is that Yĕshua is speaking of defilement of the heart. There are two types of impurity, that which involves intentionality and breaking a command (Type I) and that which involves natural human uncleannesses or cannot involve intentionality (Type II) which includes unwashed hands, and second degree Type I contamination. Only intentional first degree contamination defiles the heart. Nothing entering accidentally or undetectably can contaminate the heart, because the body was designed to eliminate such trivial contaminations. This is just a reminder summary. See notes on Mark for full explanation, and remarks on Acts 10 and remarks on Romans 14.

Mattatyahu 15

said, "So now, are you also without understanding? ¹⁷Are you not understanding that everything that goes by itself[ξ] into the mouth passes into the stomach, and is eliminated? ¹⁸But the things that are going out of the mouth are coming forth from the heart, and these are sharing defilement with a man, ¹⁹because out of the heart come evil thoughts, *for* murders, adulteries, fornications, thefts, false witness, slanders. ²⁰These are the things which are sharing defilement with the man, but to eat with unwashed hands is not sharing defilement with the man."

²¹And Yĕshua went away from there, and withdrew into the district of Tsor and Tsidon. ²²And behold, a Kena'anit woman came out from that region, and was crying out, saying, "Have mercy on me, Adŏnai, Sŏn of David. My daughter is cruelly demon-possessed." ²³But he did not answer her a word. And his disciples came to him and kept asking him, saying, "Send her away, because she is shouting out after us." ²⁴And when he replied, he said, "I was not sent, except to the sheep that have been straying, of the house of Yisra'el." ²⁵But when she came, she was bowing down to him, saying, "Adŏnai, be helping me!" ²⁶And when he answered, he said, "It is not good to take the children's bread and throw it to the dogs." ²⁷But she said, "Yes, Adŏnai, and surely the dogs are eating from the crumbs which are falling from their masters' tables." ²⁸Then Yĕshua answered and said to her, "Woman, your courageous faithfulness is great. Be it done for you as you wish." And her daughter was healed at once.

²⁹And [τ]departing from there, Yĕshua went along beside the Sea of Galil, and having gone up to the mountain, he was sitting there. ³⁰And large crowds came to him, bringing with them those who were lame, crippled, blind, dumb, and many others, and they laid them down beside his feet. And he healed them, ³¹so that the crowd marveled as they saw the dumb speaking, the crippled restored, and the lame walking, and the blind seeing. And they glorified the Almĭghty of Yisra'el.

³²And Yĕshua called his disciples to him, and said, "I feel compassion for the crowd, because they have remained with me now three days and have nothing which they might eat. And I do not wish to send them away hungry, lest they may faint on the way." ³³And the disciples said to him, "Where would we get so many loaves in a desolate place to satisfy such a great crowd?" ³⁴And Yĕshua said to them, "How many loaves do you have?" And they said, "Seven, and a few small fish." ³⁵And he directed the crowd to sit down on the ground. ³⁶And he took the seven loaves and the fish, and giving thanks, he broke them and started giving them to the disciples, and the disciples in turn, to the crowds. ³⁷And they

---

15:17 ξ εἰσπορευόμενον (V-PPM/P-NNS). The middle voice verb translates "goes by itself." This is critically important because the food is not entering the mouth "by itself," but is actively being put there by the person eating. What goes of itself is any undetected contaminations. It is further noted that not everything is eliminated. The contaminations and what the body cannot use are eliminated. So only by translating "by itself," and referring it to the (possible) contaminations on the food can the statement be made true. For the person intends to eat the food and not the unseen contamination. **15:29** τ Early summer AD 32. **15:32-39** μ Here is an illustration. Mĕssiah was in the grave for three days. The seven loaves are for the resurrection day on the Şabbath, and the 4000 are for the 4th day of the week upon which he died. See also Num. 19:12-19; 31:19.

all ate and were satisfied, and they picked up what was left over of the broken pieces, seven large baskets full. ³⁸And those who ate were four thousand men, without women and children. ³⁹And sending away the crowds, he got into the boat, and came to the region of Magdan⁴⁴.

16 ¹And the Perushim and Tsadduqim came up, and testing him asked him to show them a sign from heaven. ²But he answered and said to them, "When it is late, you say, 'It will be fair weather, because the sky is red.' ³And when early, 'There will be a storm today, because the sky is red and threatening.' Do you know how to discern the face of the sky, but cannot discern the signs of the times? ⁴An evil and adulterous kindred seeks after a sign. And a sign will not be given it, except the sign of Yonah^χ." And he left them, and went away.

⁵And the disciples came to the other side and forgot to take bread. ⁶And Yĕshua said to them, "Be looking out and be guarding against the leaven of the Perushim and Tsadduqim." ⁷And they began to discuss among themselves, saying, "It is because we took no bread." ⁸But Yĕshua, aware of this, said, "Little faithful ones, why do you discuss among yourselves that you have no bread? ⁹Do you not yet understand or remember the five loaves of the five thousand, and how many baskets you took up? ¹⁰Or the seven loaves of the four thousand, and how many large baskets you took up? ¹¹How is it that you do not understand that I did not speak to you concerning bread? But be guarding against the leaven of the Perushim and Tsadduqim." ¹²Then they understood that he did not say to beware of the leaven of bread, but of the teaching of the Perushim and Tsadduqim.

¹³Now when^τ Yĕshua came into the district of Caesarea Philippi, he was asking his disciples, saying, "Who do people say that the Sŏn of Man is?" ¹⁴And they said, "Some say Yohanan the Immerser, and others, Ĕliyahu, but still others, Yirmeyahu, or one of the prophets." ¹⁵He said to them, "But who do you say that I am?" ¹⁶And Şim'on Peter answered and said, "You are the Anŏinted, the Sŏn of the Living Almĭghty." ¹⁷And, when Yĕshua answered, he said to him, "Blessed are you, Şim'on son of Yonah, because flesh and blood did not make this revelation to you, but my Făther who is in the heavens. ¹⁸And, I also say to you that you are Peter, and upon this bedrock^ξ I will build my Assembly. And the gates of the grave will not overpower it. ¹⁹I will give you the keys^θ of the kingdom of the heavens, and whatever you may have bound on earth ^π will have been getting bound by heaven, and whatever you may have loosed on earth will

---

16:4 χ This is the greatest sign of all, because the third day theme runs deep in the depths of Scripture. The subjective parts make an objective whole. It can only have been divinely intertwined with Scripture, and the Sŏn exactly fulfills it. He is not denying them a sign, but he is pointing them to the sign that really matters. See Luke 24:46. **16:13** τ About Tevet (Jan), AD 33. **16:18** ξ The revelation of Mĕssiah is the bedrock of the faith. See vs. 16. Peter means a *stone, pebble*. **16:19** π→getting: this simplifies to 'will be bound;' heaven binds in response to the binding on earth. See App. XV. ▷ A key unlocks something. The Revelation of Mĕssiah unlocks the secrets of the kingdom of heaven. There is contingency to whatever should be bound (enforced) or loosed (allowed), but the keys would tell Peter what to bind and loose. The assurance is that he would have the backing of heaven for this.

have been getting loosed by heaven." ²⁰Then he warned the disciples that they should tell no one that he was the Anŏinted One.

²¹From that time Yĕshua the Anŏinted began to show his disciples that it is necessary for him to go to Yerushalayim, and to suffer many things from the elders and the chief priests and the scribes, and to be killed, and ᵞafter three days to rise. ²²And Peter took him aside and began to rebuke him, saying, "Forbid it, Adŏnai! This will never happen to you." ²³But having turned, he said to Peter, "Be going behind me, Satan! You are a stumbling block to me, because you are not setting your mind on the matters of the Almĭghty, but the matters of men." ²⁴Then Yĕshua said to his disciples, "If anyone wishes to have come after me, let him deny himself, and take up his ᶲexecution timber, and be following me, ²⁵because whoever may be wishing to preserve his soul will lose it. But whoever will have lost his soul for my sake will find it. ²⁶Because what will a man be profited, if he may have gained the whole world, yet will have forfeited his soul? Or what will a man give in exchange for his soul? ²⁷Because the Sŏn of Man is going to come in the glory of his Făther with his messengers, and WILL THEN REPAY EVERY MAN ACCORDING TO HIS DEEDS.ᵘ ²⁸Amen, I say to you, there are some of those who have been standing here who no, they will not have tasted death until they have seenᶲ to the Sŏn of Man coming in his kingdom."

17

¹And ᵗafter six days Yĕshua took with him Peter and Ya'aqov and Yohanan his brother, and brought them up to a high mountain by themselves. ²And he was transfigured before them. And his face shone like the sun, and his garments became as white as light. ³And behold, Mosheh and Ĕliyahu appeared to them, talking with him.

⁴And Peter replied and said to Yĕshua, "Adŏnai, it is good for us to be here. If you wish, I will make three shelters here, one for you, and one for Mosheh, and one for Ĕliyahu." ⁵While he *was* still speaking, behold, a bright cloud overshadowed them. And behold, a voice out of the cloud, *was* saying, "This is my beloved Sŏn, with whom I am well-pleased. Be listening to him!" ⁶And when the

---

16:21 γ→days: This text is parallel to Mark 8:31, which says "after three days" in all ancient texts. Codex Bezae (D) and more than a few old Latin texts read "after three days" here. See also Luke 9:22. Clearly the text was changed to read 'the third day' by an ignorant scribe who did not understand how the chronology worked, but Mark 8:31 and a few ancient texts remain to expose the change. **16:24** ξ→timber: A wooden timber used for displaying an execution, but not so large that a strong man could not carry it. See Yoh. 19:31. **16:27** μ Psa 62:12; Prov 24:12; Rom 2:6 **16:28** ξ See *Mark* 9:1; *Luke* 9:27. On idiom cf. Gen. 22:8, 14; 39:23; 41:33; Deu. 33:21; 1 Sam. 16:1, 17; 2 Ki 10:3; Mat. 27:4, 24; Luke 12:15; Acts 18:15. It cannot be the transfiguration, because the promise not to taste death first would be untimely. But it must be seeing to the Son coming in his glory (cf. vs. 27). Yet Seeing cannot be anything that everyone could just passively observe when it happened, because the promise was aimed at some, and also everyone died. It should include the scope of vs. 24, and Messiah left an example (cf. Mat. 26:64; Mark 14:62) by seeing to his kingdom with his own personal sacrifice. In fact, those who killed him saw to it. And these disciples will also see to the kingdom by making personal sacrifice for it, not necessarily martyrdom, but giving all their life, time, and treasure. More than the three were in Yĕshua's audience that day. Seeing is not everything that meets the eye, and in some of the usages above there is no 'to' in the example texts to indicate this. But logical deduction from the context requires us to supply it in English. See Yoh. 11:52; Mat. 21:43. **17:1** τ→days: After the six working days. They went up the mountain on the Şabbath. See Luke 9:28.

disciples heard this, they fell on their faces and were much afraid. ⁷And when Yĕshua came to them, and having touched them, he said, "Arise, and do not be getting afraid." ⁸And lifting up their eyes, they saw no one, except Yĕshua himself, alone.

⁹And as they were coming down from the mountain, Yĕshua commanded them, saying, "You shall have told the vision to no one until the Sŏn of Man may be risen from the dead." ¹⁰And his disciples asked him, saying, "Why then are the scribes saying that Ĕliyahu is needing to have come first?" ¹¹And when he answered, he said, "Ĕliyahu surely is coming himself and will re-establish all things! ¹²But I am saying to you, that 'Ĕliyahu' already came, and they did not acknowledge him, but they did with him as much as they wished. Likewise also, the Sŏn of Man is about to be suffering by them." ¹³Then the disciples put it together that he had spoken to them about Yoḥanan the Immerser.

¹⁴And when they came to the crowd, a man came up to him, falling on his knees before him, and saying, ¹⁵"Adŏnai, have mercy on my son, because he is a lunatic, and is very ill, because he often falls into the fire, and often into the water. ¹⁶And I brought him to your disciples, and they could not cure him." ¹⁷And as he answered, Yĕshua said, "O kindred, unfaithful and having been getting perverted, how long will I be with you? How long will I put up with you? Be bringing him to me as such here." ¹⁸And Yĕshua rebuked him, and the demon came out of him, and the boy was cured at once. ¹⁹Then the disciples came to Yĕshua privately and said, "Why could we not cast it out?" ²⁰And he said to them, "because of the littleness of your faithfulness, because amen, I say to you, if you may be having faithfulness$^\psi$ like a mustard seed, you can say to this mountain, 'Move from here to there,' and it will move, and nothing will be impossible to you. ²¹But this kind does not go out except by prayer and fasting."

²²And while they were gathering together in Galil, Yĕshua said to them, "The Sŏn of Man is about to be delivered into the hands of men, ²³and they will kill him, and after three days he will be raised." And they were deeply grieved.

²⁴And when they came to Kefar-Naḥum, those who collected the two-drachma tax came to Peter, and said, "Does your teacher not pay the two-drachma tax?" ²⁵He said, "Yes." And when he came into the house, Yĕshua spoke to him first, saying, "What do you think, Şim'on? From whom do the kings of the earth collect duties or census head-tax, from their sons or from strangers?" ²⁶And upon his saying, "From strangers," Yĕshua said to him, "Consequently the sons

---

17:9-13 Yoḥanan represented Ĕliyahu because he inherited his mantle. Whatever they did to Yoḥanan is what they would have done to Ĕliyahu if he had actually come then. ▷ We have this manner of speaking in modern times. Sometimes a famous person is referred to by a more well known namesake as a metaphor to describe what they are like. See Mark 9:11f. **17:20** ψ This is a two sided concept, and because divine faithfulness is always assumed and human faithfulness is what is contingent, people almost always think of human faithfulness to the Most High first. Here we must think of divine faithfulness as his support, pledge, or confirmation that something should happen or be done. That is the endeavor has to be supported by divine faithfulness to the goal. But it also takes faithfulness to the Most High to know his mind and to hear the Spirit. See Mark 11:22-24.

17:24-27 The tax was collected in Adar. This was in AD 33.

Mattatyahu 18

are exempt. ²⁷But, lest we may give them offense, go to the sea, and throw in a hook, and take the first fish that comes up. And when you open its mouth, you will find a stater. Take that and give it to them for you and me."

18 ¹At that timeᵀ the disciples came to Yĕshua, saying, "Who then is greatest in the kingdom of the heavens?" ²And he called a child to himself and set him before them, ³and he said, "Amen, I say to you, unless you may have turned and may have become like children, no, you will not have entered the kingdom of the heavens. ⁴Whoever then humbles himself as this child, he is the greatest in the kingdom of the heavens. ⁵And whoever will have received one such child in my name receives me. ⁶But whoever will have caused one of these little ones holding faithful to me to stumble, it is better for him that a heavy millstone may have been hung around his neck, and that he shall have been drowned in the depth of the sea."

⁷"Woe to the world because of its stumbling blocks! Because it is inevitable that stumbling blocks come, but woe to that man through whom the stumbling block comes!" ⁸"And if your hand or your foot causes you to stumble, cut it off and throw it from you. It is better for you to enter life crippled or lame, than having two hands or two feet, to be cast into the enduring fire. ⁹And if your eye causes you to stumble, pluck it out, and throw it from you. It is better for you to enter life with one eye, than having two eyes, to be cast into the fiery Geihinnom. ¹⁰Be seeing that you may not despise one of these little ones ⸀of those holding faithful to me⸁, because I say to you, that their messengers in the heavens continually do behold the face of my Făther who is in the heavens." ¹¹For the Sŏn of man came to rescue that which has been perishing.

¹²"What do you think?ᵀ If any man may have acquired a hundred sheep, and one of them may have gone astray, does he not leave the ninety-nine on the mountains and go and search for the one that is straying? ¹³And if he may have happened to have found it, amen, I am saying to you, he is rejoicing over it more than over the ninety-nine which had not been getting led astray. ¹⁴Likewise it is not the will of your Făther who is in the heavens that one of these little ones will have perished."

¹⁵"And, if ever your brother may have sinned against you, be going and reprove him, between you and him alone. If he may have listened to you, you will have won your brother. ¹⁶And, if ever he may not have listened to you, take one or two more with you, so that BY THE MOUTH OF TWO OR THREE WITNESSES EVERY MATTER MIGHT BE CONFIRMED.ᵝ ¹⁷And, if ever he may have refused to listen to them, tell it to the assembly, and if ever he may have refused to listen even to the assembly, let him be being to you as a pagan and a tax-gatherer. ¹⁸Amen I am saying to you all, as much as ever ye may have bound on earth—it will have been

---

18:1 τ Adar, AD 33. **18:10** ⸀D it; vs. 11: D. **18:12** τ Probably the rest of the chapter belongs to Adar of AD 33. There is a year between 18:1 and 19:1 covered mostly by Luke. **18:16** β Deu 19:15

getting bound in heaven, and as much as ever ye may have loosed on earth—it will have been getting loosed in heaven. ¹⁹Again, truly I am saying to you, that if ever two from you may have agreed on earth about any matter, which if ever they may have asked, it will be done for them from the hand of my Făther who is in the heavens. ²⁰For where two or three have been gathering together into[y] my name, there I am in their midst."

²¹Then Peter came and said to him, "Adŏnai, how often will my brother sin against me and I forgive him? Up to seven times?" ²²Yĕshua said to him, "I do not say to you, up to seven times, but up to seventy times seven. ²³For this reason the kingdom of the heavens may be compared to a certain king who wished to settle accounts with his slaves. ²⁴And when he began to settle them, there was brought to him one who owed him ten thousand talents. ²⁵But since he did not have the means to repay, his lord commanded him to be sold, along with his wife and children and all that he had, and repayment to be made. ²⁶The slave therefore falling down, prostrated himself before him, saying, 'Have patience with me, and I will repay you everything.' ²⁷And the lord of that slave felt compassion and released him and forgave him the debt." ²⁸"But that slave went out and found one of his fellow slaves who owed him a hundred denari, and he seized him and was choking him, saying, 'Pay back what you owe.' ²⁹So his fellow slave fell down and was entreating him, saying, 'Have patience with me and I will repay you.' ³⁰He was unwilling however, but went and threw him in prison until he may have paid back what was owed. ³¹So when his fellow slaves saw what happened, they were deeply grieved and came and reported to their lord all that happened. ³²Then summoning him, his lord said to him, 'You wicked slave, I forgave you all that debt because you begged me. ³³Should you not also have had mercy on your fellow slave, even as I had mercy on you?' ³⁴And his lord, moved with anger, handed him over to the torturers until he may have repaid all that was owed him. ³⁵So will my heavenly Făther also do to you, if each of you will not have forgiven his brother from your heart."

19

¹And it came about that when Yĕshua finished these words, he departed from Galil, and came into the region of Yehudah beyond the Yarden, ²and large crowds followed him, and he healed them there.[τ] ³And some Perushim came to him, testing him, and saying, "Is it lawful for a man to send his wife away for any cause at all?" ⁴And he answered and said, "Have you not read, that he who created them from the beginning MADE THEM MALE AND FEMALE,[α] ⁵and said, 'THEREFORE, A MAN WILL LEAVE FATHER AND MOTHER AND WILL CLEAVE TO HIS WIFE, AND THE TWO WILL BE AS ONE FLESH.'[β] ⁶Consequently they are no longer two, but one flesh. What therefore the Almĭghty has joined together, let

---

18:20 γ 'Into my name' is equivalent to into the divine presence. Scripture says in the place that the Almĭghty chooses, he will cause his name to dwell there, and where the place of his name is, is where the answers to difficult legal cases were to be sought. Binding and loosing refers to legal decisions regarding the matters in Deut. 17:8, either capital cases, personal injury cases, or property disputes. **19:2** τ Late winter in early AD 34. **19:4** α Gen 1:27, 5:2 **19:5** β Gen. 2:24.

Mattatyahu 19

no man be separating." ⁷They say to him, "Why then did Mosheh command to GIVE HER A CERTIFICATE OF DIVORCE AND SEND HER AWAY?ψ ⁸He said to them, "Because of your ˣhardness of heart, Mosheh permitted you to send your wives away, but at the beginning it had not been happening this way. ⁹And I say to you, whoever may have sent his wife away, except for sexual immorality, ʸso that he may marry another woman, is committing adultery." ¹⁰The disciples said to him, "If the relationship of the man with his wife is like this, it is better not to marry." ¹¹But he said to them, "Not all men make room for this statement, but only those to whom it has been getting given. ¹²Because there are eunuchs who were born that way from their mother's womb, and there are eunuchs who were made eunuchs by men, and there are also celibate persons who made themselves celibate for the sake of the kingdom of the heavens. He who is being able to be making a space for it, let him be making a space."

¹³Then some children were brought to him so that he might lay his hands on them and will have prayed, and the disciples rebuked them. ¹⁴But Yĕshua said, "Allow the children, and be not hindering them to come to me, because of such as these is the kingdom of the heavens." ¹⁵And after laying his hands on them, he departed from there.

¹⁶And behold, when one approached him, he said, "Teacher, what good deed shall I have done so that I will have inherited life everlasting?δ ¹⁷And he said to him, "Why are you asking me about the best one? One thing is the best: If you are desiring to enter into life, you must keep the commandments." ¹⁸He says to him, "Which ones?" And Yĕshua said, "YOU SHALL NOT MURDER. YOU SHALL NOT COMMIT ADULTERY. YOU SHALL NOT STEAL. YOU SHALL NOT BEAR FALSE

19:7 ψ Deu 24:1, 3. See also Mat. 5:32. **19:8** χ→heart. This is the case of Deut. 24:3: וּשְׂנֵאָהּ = *and he has hated her*. This would be for any reason at all, but the Law does not approve of it, and condemns it (cf. Mal. 2:14-16 כִּי־שָׂנֵא שַׁלַּח), it only notes it to prohibit a twice divorced woman from returning to the first husband. The valid reasons for seeking a divorce, are **(1)** marital infidelity by either spouse (Mat. 5:32), **(2)** premarital infidelity is discovered when a virgin was expected (Deut. 24:1; cf. Deut. 22:13-21, *a fortiori*), **(3)** refusal to grant marital relations when possible by either spouse (cf. Exodus 21:10; 1 Cor. 7:3-7), **(4)** refusal of the husband to provide food, shelter, and clothing when he is able (cf. Exodus 21:10 *a fortiori*). **(5)** Refusal to repent of any habit that destroys the family: physical abuse, child abuse, or other violence. **(6)** The other spouse is a pagan and wants to leave (1 Cor. 7:15) **(7)** The other spouse is a pagan and refuses to keep the home free of idolatry, or refuses to allow the faithful spouse to obey the commandments of Gŏd. (Deut. 29:18-21, *a fortiori*). **(8)** The community of the faithful is put at risk by the faithful (who should know better) entering into marriages with pagans (cf. Ezra 9-10). ▷ It is not allowed to send a spouse away (called a separation) for any other reason (1 Cor. 7:10-11), but if it happens they may not marry another without the legal divorce, and should see reconciliation if the offenses are not too great or can be forgiven (cf. 1 Cor. 7:11). ▷ There is no law prohibiting a woman writing a bill of divorcement. As far as Scripture is concerned, it would end the moral obligations of marriage just the same as a man who wrote one. But all parties who are Scripturally justified in doing such must realize that civil and religious authorities exert their powers to allow divorce when it shouldn't be and to prohibit it when it is necessary, and carry considerable power to make sure it is done only their way. All their remedies should be exhausted before asserting a truth that they do not acknowledge. Carefully read Mal. 2:14-16. Anyone who is faithless against their spouse commits a grave sin. **19:9** γ→that: καί; *so that*. BDB: 'With a voluntative (cohort. or juss.) וְ expresses an intention, *that* or *so that* (an elegancy by which the too frequent use of לְמַעַן or בַּעֲבוּר is avoided)." וַיִּקַּח a= *that he may take (another)*.
19:16 δ See Mark 10:17-30.

WITNESS. ¹⁹BE HONORING YOUR FATHER AND MOTHER,^θ and YOU SHALL LOVE YOUR NEIGHBOR AS YOURSELF.^λ" ²⁰The young man says to him, "All these things I have kept. What am I still lacking?" ²¹Yĕshua was saying to him, "If you desire to be blameless, be going and sell your possessions and give to the poor, and you will have treasure in the heavens. Then come hither. Be following me." ²²But when the young man heard this statement, he went away grieved, because he was one who owned much property. ²³And Yĕshua said to his disciples, "Amen, I say to you, it is hard for a rich man to enter the kingdom of the heavens. ²⁴And again I say to you, it is easier work for a camel to go through the eye of a needle, than for a rich man to enter the kingdom of the Almĭghty." ²⁵And when the disciples heard this, they were very astonished and said, "Then who can be rescued?" ²⁶And looking upon them Yĕshua said to them, "Beside men this is impossible, but beside the Almĭghty all things are possible."

²⁷Then Peter replied and said to him, "Behold, we have left everything and followed you. What then will there be for us?" ²⁸And Yĕshua said to them, "Amen I say to you, that you who have followed me, in the restoration when the Sŏn of Man will have sat on his glorious throne, you also will sit upon twelve thrones, judging the twelve tribes of Yisra'el. ²⁹And everyone who has left houses or brothers or sisters or father or mother or children or farms for my name's sake, will receive many times as much, and will inherit everlasting life. ³⁰But many who are first will be last, and the last, first.

20

¹For the kingdom of the heavens is like a landowner who went out early in the morning to hire laborers for his vineyard. ²And when he agreed with the laborers a day's wages for the day, he sent them into his vineyard. ³And when he went out about the third hour, he saw others, who had been standing idle in the market place, ⁴and to those he said, 'You also be going into the vineyard, and whatever may be right I will give you.' And so they went. ⁵Again when he went out about the sixth and the ninth hour, he did the same thing. ⁶And about the eleventh hour, when he went out, he found others who had been standing, and he says to them, 'Why have you been standing here idle all day long?' ⁷They said to him, 'Because no one hired us.' He said to them, 'You also be going into the vineyard.'"

⁸"And when it became late, the owner of the vineyard said to his foreman, 'Call the laborers and pay them their wages, beginning with the last group to the first.' ⁹And when those hired about the eleventh hour came, each one received a day's wages. ¹⁰And when those hired first came, they thought that they would receive more, and they also received each one a day's wages. ¹¹And when they received it, they grumbled at the landowner, ¹²saying, 'These last men worked only one hour, and you made them equal to us who have borne the burden and

---

19:19 θ Exo 20:12-16, Deu 5:16-20 **19:19** λ Lev 19:18. The easiest to keep is put first, and then progressively harder until he stops at the most relevant one to the man's condition in terms of the relation of his wealth to his poor neighbors.

the scorching heat of the day.'"

¹³"But he answered and said to one of them, 'Friend, I am doing you no wrong. Did you not agree with me for a day's wages? ¹⁴Take what is yours and be going your way, but I wish to give to this last man the same as to you. ¹⁵Or is it not lawful for me to do what I wish with what is my own? Or is your eye envious because I am generous?' ¹⁶Thus the last will be first, and the first last."

¹⁷And as Yĕshua was about to go up to Yerushalayim, he took the twelve disciples aside by themselves, and on the way he said to them, ¹⁸"Behold, we are going up to Yerushalayim, and the Sŏn of Man will be delivered to the chief priests and scribes, and they will condemn him to death, ¹⁹and they will deliver him to the nations to mock and scourge and fasten him up on an execution timber, and the third day he will rise."

²⁰Then the mother of the sons of Zavdai came to him with her sons, bowing down, and making a request of him. ²¹And he said to her, "What do you wish?" She said to him, "Command that in your kingdom these two sons of mine will have sat, one on your right and one on your left." ²²But as he answered, Yĕshua said, "You have not been knowing what you are asking for. Are you able to drink the cup that I am about to drink?" They said to him, "We are able." ²³He said to them, "My cup you will drink, but to sit on my right and on my left, this is not mine to give, but it is for those for whom it has been getting prepared by my Făther."

²⁴And hearing this, the ten became indignant with the two brothers. ²⁵But Yĕshua called them to himself, and said, "You have been knowing that the rulers of the nations lord it over them, and their great men exercise authority over them. ²⁶It is not so among you, but whoever may be wishing to become great among you will be your servant, ²⁷and whoever may be wishing to be first among you will be your slave, ²⁸just as the Sŏn of Man did not come to be served, but to serve, and to give his life a ˣransom in return for⁺ many."

20:28 χ λύτρον = ransom. The price for gaining the freedom or release of a slave. The cup that Messiah drank is not the cup of divine wrath, but the cup of suffering and death dealt to him by sinful man and the powers of evil in their mission to suppress the revelation of the truth in Messiah. The two sons drank the same cup of suffering as Messiah when they proclaimed the truth concerning the Almighty Son (vs. 22-23). So the cup is not divine wrath against sin. Rather the cup is sin and evil's wrath against the truth. The ransom is the cost exacted by sin and evil even unto death. In order to overcome obstacles put up by sin, sacrifice is necessary, the enduring of insult and ridicule for the sake of the truth, the enduring of every sort of mistreatment without exacting vengeance patiently hoping that some will open their eyes. This is the service that Messiah speaks about. Also included is enduring every sort of privation and emotional grief, and the taking on of risks for the sake of others. All this self sacrifice for the sake of many is the ransoming cost. By also allowing evil to kill Messiah, the Most High was able to even more successfully proclaim the resurrection of the dead and everlasting life unto all who would pledge faithfulness to Him. Messiah makes not only the point that he is the ransom for many through his service, but he also teaches that his followers enter his service with the same expectation, that their sufferings for the truth will benefit the many, just as Paul said to fill up what lacks in the sufferings of Messiah. To this we may also correlate the death and resurrection of the two witnesses in Revelation 11. By the suffering and sacrifice of one, many are benefited by having their eyes opened to the love and long-suffering of the Most High, who is willing to suffer the ravages of sin, even on his own Son (with his consent), in order to draw unrepentant men into repentance when they see the true character of the Almighty, and to put before them the truth of resurrection and everlasting life. ▷ Messiah made his life a ransom "for many," that is he paid the cost for the deliverance of many by his life, his sufferings, and his death. This work cost him suffering and temporary death. He was rewarded with the deliverance of many. Once again, the cost is not exacted by divine wrath (cf. *Mark* 10:45). The ransom is not paying the cost of a penalty of sin. The

²⁹And as they were going out from Yeriḥo, a great crowd followed him. ³⁰And behold, two blind men sitting beside the road, hearing that Yĕshua was passing by, cried out, saying, "Adŏnai, have mercy on us, Sŏn of David!" ³¹And the crowd sternly warned them, so that they will have been silent, but they cried out all the more, saying, "Adŏnai, have mercy on us, Sŏn of David!"

³²And Yĕshua stopped and called them, and said, "What do you want *that* I will have done for you?" ³³They said to him, "Adŏnai, we want for our eyes to be opened." ³⁴And moved with compassion, Yĕshua touched their eyes, and immediately they regained their sight and followed him.

21

¹And when^τ they were approaching Yerushalayim and came to Bethphage, to the Mount of Olives, then Yĕshua sent two disciples, ²saying to them, "Be going into the village opposite you, and immediately you will find a donkey, which has been getting held bound, and a colt with her. Having untied *them*, lead *them* to me. ³And if anyone may have said something to you, you will say that, 'Their Mäster has need of them,' and immediately he will send them." ⁴Now this had been happening so that what was spoken through the prophet

---

ransom is paying the cost to get the message across that the Most High forgives sin without payment. The ransom is a divine cost, and not a divine income to satisfy retribution. Retribution is forgiven. The Son is not paying off a demand to satisfy retributive justice. But his sacrifice is an indication of the cost of turning us back to him. It is the cost as one soldier sacrifices himself for the sake of many in a war, and it is the enemy that demands the sacrifice, and exacts the ransom cost. ▷ Messiah is not ransoming us from the Father's justice. He is ransoming from sin and death after we have repented and are forgiven by the Father. Penal justice is forgiven. Penal justice, such as in the death penalty, was never about undoing the damages. It was about deterring further damages. The wrath of the Almighty upon the wicked does not restore the losses caused by wickedness. Much less, then, does the heretical concept of penal substitution restore divine loss or honor. Yet false teachers seek to restore divine loss by transferring the righteousness of Messiah to the sinner by judicial fiat, so that then, the Most High sees no loss at all. But this is a diabolical lie. Divine loss cannot be erased by legal philosophy. It is real and everlasting. Messiah teaches he is the ransom. This points out the divine loss, but Satan promotes the notion that God's legal wrath is not canceled without payment, and that substitutionary righteousness results in legal acquittal. This again smothers the divine loss and pretends that there is none. It also destroys forgiveness and the unity of the Almighty when taken to logical conclusion. Therefore, flee from those doctrines. **20:28 ϕ** The word 'in return for' ἀντί is corresponding to תַּחַת in Hebrew (cf. Isa. 43:3-4, נָתַתִּי כָפְרְךָ מִצְרַיִם כּוּשׁ וּסְבָא תַּחְתֶּיךָ, I WILL HAVE GIVEN AS YOUR RANSOM EGYPT, AND CUSH, AND SEVA, **IN RETURN FOR** YOU.) See Thayer, "2. indicating exchange." See BDB Lexicon, "*in exchange* or *return for*" (pg. 1065). Also note that the word 'ransom' is explained by a derivative of the verb KaPHaR. We may view the blood of the ransom as the cost of cleansing. The word ἀντί means 'over against' but comes to have the sense of 'in behalf of' (cf. BAG, 1957, BDAG 2000), and 'in return for' (cf. LSJ, Harper: Analytical Greek Lexicon), and 'in exchange for' (e.g. Heb. 12:16; BAG 1957 to BDAG 2000). There was once a war when the commanders called out one out of every two young men to go to war with them. When a certain weakly young man was drafted, his best friend, who wasn't drafted, offered to go in return for his friend. Thus he became the ransom for that man, saving him from death by his self sacrifice to endure the sufferings and risks of war. So also the only kindred Son volunteered to meet up with our transgressions, to war against sin and death, and bear its suffering, in return for, and in behalf of gaining our release from sin's attack to cleanse us through confession and repentance from all sin (See 1 Peter 2:24 notes). So also Messiah sacrifices himself to cleanse his people from all evil. ▷ The ransom cost is exacted by sin and death (cf. Hos. 13:14; Isa. 43:3-4) and the false gods that have seized control of Creation. The ransom cost is the cup of suffering Messiah spoke about, undertaken in the service of fighting for Yisra'el. It is the price that Messiah and the emissaries paid in terms of suffering for the deliverance of the people. **21:1 τ** Şabbaṯh, Aviv 10, AD 34. March 20.

Mattatyahu 21

might be fulfilled, saying, ⁵'SAY^μ TO THE DAUGHTER^ρ OF TSIYON, BEHOLD, YOUR KING IS COMING TO YOU HUMBLE, HAVING BEEN MOUNTED ON A DONKEY, EVEN ON A COLT, SON OF A BEAST OF BURDEN.'

⁶And the disciples went and did just as Yĕshua directed them, ⁷and brought the donkey and the colt, and laid on them their garments, on which he sat. ⁸And most of the crowd spread their garments in the road, and others were cutting branches from the trees, and spreading them in the road. ⁹And the crowds going before him, and those following *after* were crying out, saying, "HOSHA'NA^ψ to the Sŏn of David. HAS BEEN GETTING BLESSED^λ THE COMING ONE IN THE NAME OF YĂHWEĦ. HOSHA'NA^ψ IN^δ THE HEIGHTS!" ¹⁰And when he entered Yerushalayim, all the city was stirred, saying, "Who is this?" ¹¹And the crowds were saying, "This is ^πTHE PROPHET, Yĕshua, from Netsereth in Galil." ¹²And Yĕshua ^γentered the temple and cast out all those who were buying and selling in the temple, and overturned the tables of the moneychangers and the seats of those who were selling doves. ¹³And he said to them, "It has been getting written, 'MY HOUSE SHALL BE CALLED A HOUSE OF PRAYER^α, but you are making it a DEN OF ROBBERS^θ.'"

¹⁴And the blind and the lame came to him in the temple, and he healed them. ¹⁵But when the chief priests and the scribes saw the wonderful things that he did, and the children who were crying out in the temple and saying, "Hosha'na to the Sŏn of David," they became indignant, ¹⁶and said to him, "Are you hearing what these are saying?" And Yĕshua says to them, "Yes. Have you never read, 'OUT OF THE MOUTH OF CHILDREN AND NURSING INFANTS YOU PREPARE PRAISE?'^β ¹⁷And he left them and went out of the city to Beth-Hini, and lodged there.

¹⁸Now in the ^τmorning, when he returned to the city, he became hungry. ¹⁹And seeing a lone fig tree by the road, he came to it, and found nothing on it except leaves only, and he said to it, "No longer will there have come fruit from you into the age." And at once the fig tree withered.

²⁰And ^xseeing this, the disciples were amazed, saying, "How did the fig tree wither at once?" ²¹And Yĕshua answered and said to them, "Amen I say to you, if you may be having faithfulness^φ, and will not have doubted, you will not only do what was done to the fig tree, but even if you may have said to this mountain, 'Be taken up and be cast into the sea,' it will happen. ²²And all, as much ever you will have asked in prayer, holding faithful, you will receive."

²³And when he came into the temple, the chief priests and the elders of the people came to him as he was teaching, and said, "By what authority are you doing

---

21:5 μ Isa 62:11; ρ Zech 9:9. **21:9** ψ Psa 118:25 λ Psa 118:26 δ Psa 148:1 **21:11** π Deut. 18:18; Dan. 9:24: ולחתם חזון ונביא; Yoħ. 3:33. **21:12** γ He entered the Temple on Şabbath and then retired to Beth-Anyah. The next day he entered the Temple again and cast out the merchants. Sunday, Aviv 11, March 21, AD 34. **21:13** α Isa 56:7; θ Jer 7:11. **21:16** β Psa 8:2 **21:18-19** τ The narrative backtracks to Sunday morning. **21:20** x The disciples did not notice Sunday morning when he cursed the fig tree. Nor did they notice on their return to Beth-Anyah in the dark Sunday evening. But they did notice on Monday morning. Monday, Aviv 12. March 22. **21:21** φ Mark 11:22 explains this as 'having the faithfulness of the Almighty,' (q.v.). One has to have both a divine commitment, pledge, or support (πίστιν) to the goal, and be holding faithful (πιστευοντες), vs. 22.

these things, and who gave you this authority?" ²⁴And Yĕshua answered and said to them, "I will ask you one thing too, which if you may have told me, I will also tell you by what authority I do these things. ²⁵The immersion of Yoḣanan was from what source, from heaven or from men?" And they were reasoning among themselves, saying, "If we may have said, 'from heaven,' he will say to us, 'Then why didn't you hold him faithful?' ²⁶But if we may have said, 'From men,' we fear the crowd, because they all hold that Yoḣanan was a prophet." ²⁷And as they answered Yĕshua, they said, "We have not been knowing." He also was saying to them, "Neither am I telling you by what authority I am doing these things."

²⁸"But what do you think? A man was having two children, and having come to the first, he said, 'Child, be going today. Be working in the vineyard.' ²⁹And when he answered, he said, 'I don't want to.' And later, having repented, he went off. ³⁰And when he came to the second, he said the same thing. And when he answered, he said, 'Aye Sir', and he did not go. ³¹Which of the two did the will of his father?" They say, "The first." Yĕshua says to them, "Amen, I say to you that the tax-collectors and harlots are going before you into the kingdom of the Almĭghty. ³²For Yoḣanan came to you in the way of justice^δ and you did not hold him faithful, but the tax-collectors and harlots held him faithful, and you, having seen *this*, did not even repent later to hold him faithful."

³³"Listen to another parable. There was a landowner who PLANTED A VINEYARD AND PUT A WALL AROUND IT AND DUG A WINE PRESS IN IT, AND BUILT A TOWER,^{φ} and rented it out to vine-growers, and went on a journey. ³⁴And when the harvest time approached, he sent his slaves to the vine-growers to receive his produce. ³⁵And the vine-growers took his slaves and beat one, and killed another, and stoned a third. ³⁶Again he sent another group of slaves larger than the first, and they did the same thing to them. ³⁷But afterward he sent his son to them, saying, 'They will respect my son.' ³⁸But when the vine-growers saw the son, they said among themselves, 'This is the heir! Come, we will have killed him, and we shall have seized his inheritance.' ³⁹And they took him, and threw him out of the vineyard, and killed him. ⁴⁰Therefore when the owner of the vineyard will have come, what will he do to those vine-growers?" ⁴¹They said to him, "He will bring those wretches to a wretched end, and will rent out the vineyard to other vine-growers, who will pay him the proceeds at the proper seasons."

⁴²Yĕshua said to them, "Did you never read in the writings, 'THE STONE WHICH THE BUILDERS REJECT, THIS HAS BECOME THE CHIEF CORNER STONE. THIS CAME ABOUT FROM BESIDE YĂHWEḤ, AND IT IS WONDERFUL IN OUR EYES^β.' ⁴³Therefore I say to you, the kingdom of the Almĭghty will be taken away from you, and be given to a nation producing the fruit of it^ω. ⁴⁴And he who falls on this stone will be broken to pieces, but on whomever it may have fallen, it will grind him to dust."

21:32 δ or *righteousness* **21:33** φ Isa 5:1-2. **21:42** β Psa 118:22-23 **21:43** ω This refers to the exiled house of Yisra'el. See Jer. 33:24; Ezek. 37; Eph. 3:4 ξ; Gen. 48:19; Rom. 11:25; 9:22-26; Rev. 7. See Hos. 1:10; 2:23.

Mattatyahu 22

⁴⁵And when the chief priests and the Perushim heard his parables, they understood that he was speaking about them. ⁴⁶And they were seeking to seize him, but they feared the crowds, because they held him to be a prophet.

22 ¹And Yĕshua answered and spoke to them again in parables, saying, ²"The kingdom of the heavens may be compared to a king who gave a wedding feast for his son. ³And he sent out his slaves to call those who had been getting invited to the wedding feast, and they were not willing to come. ⁴Again he sent out other slaves saying, 'Tell those who have been getting invited, "Behold, I have been preparing my dinner. My oxen and my fattened livestock have been getting butchered and everything is ready. Come to the wedding feast."' ⁵But as they paid no attention, they went away, one to his own farm, another to his business, ⁶and the rest, who seized his slaves, mistreated and killed *them*. ⁷But the king was enraged, and when he sent his armies, he destroyed those murderers, and burned their city."

⁸"Then he says to his servants, 'Surely, the wedding *feast* is ready, yet those who had been getting invited were not being worthy. ⁹Be going therefore on the throughways to the byways, and as many as you may ever have found, call to the wedding feast.' ¹⁰And those slaves, having gone out to the byways, gathered together all they found, the evil besides also the good. And the wedding *feast* was filled up with reclining dinner guests."

¹¹"But when the king came in to look over the reclining *guests*, he saw there a man, who had not been getting dressed in wedding clothes, ¹²and he says to him, "Friend,'ᵋ how did you come in here without wedding clothes?' And he was speechless. ¹³Then the king said to the servants, 'Having bound his feet and hands, cast him out into the ᵟuttermost darkness. ᶿTo that place there will be weeping and gnashing of teeth.' ¹⁴For many are called, but few are chosen."

¹⁵Then the Perushim went and counseled together how they might trap him in what he said. ¹⁶And they sent their disciples to him, along with the Herodians, saying, "Teacher, we surely have been knowing that you are true and are teaching the way of the Almĭghty in truth, and are deferring to no one, because you are not being partial to any. ¹⁷Tell us therefore, what are you thinking? Is it lawful to give a census head-tax to Caesar, or not?"

¹⁸But Yĕshua perceived their malice, and said, "Why are you testing me, you hypocrites? ¹⁹Show me the coin used for the census head-tax." And they brought him a dinar. ²⁰And he said to them, "Whose likeness and inscription is this?" ²¹They said to him, "Caesar's." Then he said to them, "Then render to Caesar the things that are Caesar's, and to the Almĭghty the things that are the Almĭghty's." ²²And hearing this, they were amazed, and leaving him, they went away.

22:12 ξ = ἑταῖρε *mate, buddy, chum, pal*. A term used for an unwanted intruder that also means 'friend' in other contexts. **22:13** δ→darkness = oblivion **22:13** θ→place: ἐκεῖ = *thither*.

²³On that ᵗday some Tsadduqim (who say there is no resurrection) came to him and questioned him, ²⁴saying, "Teacher, Mosheh said, 'IF A MAN MAY HAVE DIED, HAVING NO CHILDREN, HIS BROTHER AS NEXT OF KIN WILL MARRY HIS WIFE, AND RAISE UP AN OFFSPRING FOR HIS BROTHER.'ᵝ ²⁵Now there were seven brothers before us. And the first married and died, and having no offspring left his wife to his brother. ²⁶So also the second, and the third, down to the seventh. ²⁷And last of all, the woman died. ²⁸In the resurrection therefore whose wife of the seven will she be? Because they all had her."

²⁹But Yĕshua answered and said to them, "You are erring, who have not been knowing the writings, neither the power of the Almĭghty, ³⁰because in the resurrection they neither marry, nor are given in marriage, but are like messengers in heaven." ³¹"But regarding the resurrection of the dead, have you not read that which was spoken to you by the Almĭghty, saying, ³² 'I AM THE ALMĬGHTY OF AVRAHAM, AND THE ALMĬGHTY OF YITS'HAQ, AND THE ALMĬGHTY OF YA'AQOV?'ᵝ He is not the Almĭghty of the dead, but of the living." ³³And when the crowds heard this, they were astonished at his teaching. ³⁴But when the Perushim heard that he had put the Tsadduqim to silence, they gathered themselves together. ³⁵And one of them, a lawyer, asked him, testing him, ³⁶"Teacher, which is the greatest commandment in the Law?" ³⁷And he said to him, "'YOU SHALL LOVE YĀHWEH YOUR ALMĬGHTY WITH ALL YOUR HEART, AND WITH ALL YOUR SOUL, AND WITH ALL YOUR MIND.'ᵝ ³⁸This is the greatest and foremost commandment. ³⁹The second is like it, 'YOU SHALL LOVE YOUR NEIGHBOR AS YOURSELF.'ᵝ ⁴⁰On these two commandments hang the whole law and the prophets."

⁴¹And while the Perushim had been gathering together, Yĕshua asked them a question, ⁴²saying, "What do you think about the Anŏinted, whose son is he?" They said to him, "The son of David." ⁴³He said to them, "Then how does David in the Spĭrit call him 'Adŏnai,' saying, ⁴⁴ 'SAYS YĀHWEH TO MY ADŎNAI, "BE SITTINGˣ AT MY RIGHTᵘ HAND UNTIL I SHALL HAVE MADE YOUR ENEMIES A FOOTSTOOL FOR YOUR FEET,"ᵥ'? ⁴⁵If David then calls him 'Adŏnai,' how is he his Sŏn?" ⁴⁶And no one was able to answer him a word, nor did anyone dare from that day on to ask him another question.

23

¹Then Yĕshua spoke to the crowds and to his disciples, ²saying, "The scribes and the Perushim have sat down upon the seat of Mosheh. ³All accordingly, whatsoever they should have said to you, do and be observing, but do not be doing according to their deeds, because they *only say so*, and they

---

22:23 τ Aviv 12, Monday, March 22. **22:24** β Deu 25:5; cf. Gen 38:8 **22:32** β Exo 3:6. **22:37** ρ Deu 6:5 **22:39** β Lev 19:18 **22:44** ψ Psa 110:1 **22:44** χ Idiom: seat of power, authority **22:44** μ Idiom: right hand man, helper **23:1-3** But if they speak contrary to Mosheh, then they are not sitting in his seat, but only '*they say*' they sit in his seat, and do not do so. See vs. 3. This is their greatest hypocrisy. We are not commanded to obey those who make a false claim to sit in Mosheh's seat. But we are only commanded to obey them according to when they do really sit in his seat, ruling what he ruled, and saying what he wrote. We may easily prove that no absolute authority was given to them, but only authority contingent upon agreement with scripture: the Perushim commanded that if anyone should confess Yĕshua to be the Mĕssiah, then he was to be put out of the synagogue (cf. Yoḥ. 9:22, 12:42). This then proves that their legitimate authority was limited to teaching what the Scripture actually says. See also Mark 7:5-7; Mat. 15:2; Acts 4:19-20; Titus 1:14; Isa. 29:13-14; Jer. 8:8. The same may be

Mattatyahu 23

do not do so.

⁴ "And they tie up heavy loads, and lay them on men's shoulders, but they themselves are unwilling to move them with so much as a finger. ⁵But they do all their deeds to be noticed by men, because they make wide their ᶲguardians, and make long the tassels of their garments. ⁶And they love the place of honor at banquets, and the chief seats in the congregations, ⁷and respectful greetings in the market places, and being called by men, Rabbi.

⁸"And you should not be called ᵘRabbi, because One is your Teacher, and you are all brothers. ⁹And 'Fatherᵞ you should not call anyone from among yourselves upon the earth, because One is your heavenly Father. ¹⁰And you shall not

---

said for their Rabbinic successors. ▷ In more modern terms, we may observe that many teach *Scripture Only* or many teach the *Bible only*; all accordingly they should have said, do and be observing. Again their authority is limited to when they are actually teaching what Scripture says. They say they teach *Scripture Only*, but do not do so. This is the greatest hypocrisy. ▷ The Rabbis base their claim to absolute authority on Deu. 17:8-13. Rabbinic Judaism claims to be the absolute interpreter of Scripture. They also claim that the unity of the faithful obligates all dissenters to line up with their doctrines. See End Note no. 3: Rabbinical Authority. **23:3** ω *Accordingly:* The logical conjunction makes the command contingent on their abiding in the authority of Mosheh, as well the subjunctive, *should have said.* **23:3** φ *Observing:* It is impossible here to get around the fact that Yeshua is upholding the authority of the Law for observance. It is equally impossible to get around the fact that this instruction was to his disciples and also the fact that they reiterated the validity of all his instructions after his resurrection. **23:3** δ "Deeds" means their traditions, the evil they do, and their teaching, as is plain from his description of their deeds, which are no where commanded in Scripture. **23:3** π→so: (λέγουσιν) is equivalent to 'they claim it.' See λέγω BDAG 2e, and Thayer "2. a. *asseverate, affirm, aver, maintain.*" They claim to sit on the seat of Mosheh. Their hypocrisy is that they say they sit in the seat of Mosheh, but they do not do so: "because they say [they sit in his seat], and do not do [so in fact sit in his seat.] Protestants teach *Scripture Only*, so do all that they should have said accordingly, but not do their teachings, because they only say *it*, but do not practice *Scripture Only!* A Church teaches *Bible only*, but do not do its works, because they only say *bible only*, and do not do *bible only.* ▷ The commentaries say, and the usual translations try to imply, that *they say* mainly means they only say the right things but do not do them. There are several fatal objections to this interpretation, **1.** If they only said to do what the law commanded but did not do them, then no one would listen to them, **2.** They actually said the wrong things: Mat. 23:16, 18. (cf. Mat. 15:2-9, 16:12; Mar. 7:1-13), and **3.** Their chief hypocrisy was in claiming to speak according to Moses, but in fact not doing it. This is the same as the chief hypocrisy of the Church, claiming to be biblical, but in fact not being biblical. But because the Church and Rabbis want to arrogate the authority to determine the interpretation of Scripture, rather than to acknowledge their authority is limited to what Scripture says, they pervert this text and also Deut. 17:8f. **23:5** φ φυλακτήρια = guardians. The choice of word implies that the phylacteries have a superstition attached to them that goes beyond the biblical commandment. See Rashbam on Exo. 13:9: וְהָיָה לְךָ לְאוֹת עַל־יָדֶךָ; cf. Song of Songs 8.6: שִׂימֵנִי כַחוֹתָם עַל־לִבֶּךָ כַּחוֹתָם עַל־זְרוֹעֶךָ. **23:8-12** μ The taking of titles is because men like to equivocate them with actual authority. Titles are a means of falsely laying claim to authority and getting the respect of being an authority by being labeled as such even when the claim is false. Even authorities who have studied to become an authority in a subject abuse their position. An academic title therefore is no more than an advertisement that the one bearing it should know their subject. But it gives no assurance they will not prostitute their learning to the promotion of error. True authority is not a claim or an academic title but the explanation and demonstration of truth by facts which the audience is able to confirm. Academic titles are all too often granted by the erring cabal in power who grant them only after the proselyte submits to their doctrine. Academic titles granted in one place for one reason are often taken to another place by the person bearing them and used to promote all kinds of speculation. **23:9** λ This is not talking about biological fathers. It is talking about elevating a man over a community or school of disciples and calling him father. Such is the title *Abbot* < אָבוֹת.

be called leaders, because One is your Leader, that is, the Anŏinted. ¹¹But the greatest among you will be your servant. ¹²And whoever exalts himself will be humbled. And whoever humbles himself will be exalted.

¹³"But woe to you, scribes and Perushim, hypocrites, because you shut off the kingdom of the heavens from men, because you do not enter in yourselves, nor do you allow those who are entering to go in.

¹⁵"Woe to you, scribes and Perushim, hypocrites, because you travel about on sea and land to make one proselyte. And when he may have become one, you make him twice as much a son of Geihinnom as yourselves.

¹⁶"Woe to you, blind guides, who say, 'Whoever may have sworn by the Temple, that is nothing, yet whoever shall have sworn by the gold of the Temple, he is obligated.' ¹⁷You fools and blind men! Which is more important, the gold, or the Temple that sanctified the gold? ¹⁸And, 'Whoever may have sworn by the altar, that is nothing, yet whoever shall have sworn by the offering upon it, he is obligated.' ¹⁹You blind men, which is more important, the offering or the altar that sanctifies the offering? ²⁰Therefore he who swears by the altar, swears both by the altar and by everything on it. ²¹And he who swears by the Temple, swears both by the Temple and by Him who dwells within it. ²²And he who swears by heaven, swears both by the throne of the Almĭghty and by Him who sits upon it.

²³"Woe to you, scribes and Perushim, hypocrites! Because you tithe mint and dill and cumin, and have neglected the weightier provisions of the Law, justice and mercy and faithfulness. But these are the things you should have done without neglecting the others. ²⁴You blind guides, who strain out a gnat and swallow a camel!

²⁵"Woe to you, scribes and Perushim, hypocrites! Because you clean the outside of the cup and the dish, but inside they are full of robbery and self-indulgence. ²⁶You blind Pharisee! First clean the inside of the cup and the dish, so that the outside of it will have become clean also.

²⁷"Woe to you, scribes and Perushim, hypocrites! Because you are like tombs which have been getting whitewashed, which on the outside appear beautiful, but inside they are full of dead men's bones and all uncleanness. ²⁸Even so you too outwardly appear righteous to men, but inwardly you are full of hypocrisy and lawlessness.

²⁹"Woe to you, scribes and Perushim, hypocrites! Because you build the tombs of the prophets and adorn the monuments of the just, ³⁰and say, 'If we were living in the days of our fathers, we would not have been partners with them in shedding the blood of the prophets.' ³¹Consequently you bear witness against yourselves, that you are sons of those who murdered the prophets. ³²Fill up then the measure of your fathers.

³³"You serpents, you who are born of snakes, how will you have escaped the judgment of Geihinnom? ³⁴Therefore, behold, I am sending you prophets and wise men and scribes. Some of them you will kill and fasten up on an execution

timber, and some of them you will scourge in your congregations, and persecute from city to city, ³⁵so that upon you will have come the guilt of all the righteous blood shed on earth, from the blood of righteous Hevel to the blood of Zeḳaryahu, whom you murdered between the temple and the altar. ³⁶Amen I say to you, all these things will come upon this kindred.

³⁷"Yerushalayim, Yerushalayim, who is killing the prophets and stoning those who have been getting sent to her! How often I wanted to gather your children together, the way a hen gathers her chicks under her wings, and you were unwilling. ³⁸Behold, your house is being left to you desolate! ³⁹Because I say to you, from now on, no, you will not have seen me until you may have said, 'HAS BEEN GETTING BLESSED **THE COMING ONE** IN THE NAME OF YĂHWEH!'"

24

¹And Yĕshua came out from the temple and was going away when his disciples came up to point out the Temple buildings to him. ²And he answered and said to them, "Do you not see all these things? Amen, I say to you, no, not one stone here will have been left upon another, which will not be dislodged^ψ."

³And as he was sitting on the Mount of Olives, the disciples came to him privately, saying, "Tell us, when will these things be, and what will be the sign of your coming presence, and of the end of the age?"

⁴And when he answered, Yĕshua said to them, "Be watching *that* no one may have misled you. ⁵Because many will come in my name, saying, 'I am the Anŏinted,' and will mislead many. ⁶And you will be hearing of wars and rumors of wars. Be discerning, not getting yourselves alarmed, because such is necessary to happen, but not yet is the end. ⁷Because nation will be raised up against nation, and kingdom against kingdom, and down through *various* places there

---

23:39 ψ Psa 118:26. **24:2** ψ This remark pertains exclusively to AD 70, but the answer was given in the usual frame of prophecy where the foothills of a mountain range in the distance are not clearly perceived as distinct nor the long valleys between the foothills and the tall mountains, e.g. the destruction of Babylon (cf. Hos. 6:1-3). In objective terms the disciples have really asked a question with two answers, but the answers are not given separately from the final end, and so also the account in Mark 13 is framed. But Luke was writing with the knowledge of AD 70 in mind, and so is able to sort a near fulfillment of the prophecy out from the far (Luke 21:5-24, q.v.) before returning to the far (Luke 21:25-36). ▷ Every stone of the second Temple was torn down, leaving only its foundation, but it may be perceived in Daniel 9:26 and 27 a destruction followed by a defilement, which would imply a necessary rebuilding before the defilement can take place. And it is clear from Dan. 8:14 that at the end of 2300 daily offerings (or 1150 days) the Holy Place will be restored and righted, so the future structure will not be razed. The Third Temple is still to be rebuilt in a valley not mentioned in this prophecy, and this valley will see the spiritual and physical prosperity of Israel restored before the time of final testing. **24:3** τ Monday afternoon, Aviv 12, March 22. **24:3** μ This question was motivated by Messiah's declaration in vs. 2, and the next two questions by previous teaching they had heard. **24:3** π παρουσίας = advent; As lightning (vs. 27), as flood (vs. 37, 39); of resurrection (1 Cor. 15:23; 1 Thes. 2:19); with holy ones (1 Thes. 3:13); of those still living at far Shofar (1 Thes. 4:15-16; cf. 1 Cor. 15:52); of complete holiness (1 Thes. 5:23; cf. Lev. 16:30); of man of lawlessness' destruction (2 Thes. 2:1; cf. Dan. 9:27). See also James 5:7; 2 Pet. 1:16; 2 Pet. 3:4, 12; 1 Yoḥ. 2:28. Cf. Yoḥ. 6:39, 44, etc. **24:3** η συντελείας τοῦ αἰῶνος = 'completion of the age'; cf. Mat. 13:39-40, 49; 28:20. The disciples had heard these words used before in the explanation of the parable of the sower (q.v.). In that place, these words are only used concerning Messiah's Advent when he sends his angels to gather the wicked to be burned and the righteous into the kingdom. Also, in the LXX 'consummation' (συντελείας) is used in Dan. 9:27, 12:4, 4, 7, 13 (συντέλειαν ἡμερῶν).

will be famines and earthquakes. ⁸But all these things are the beginning of birth pangs. ⁹Then they will deliver you to tribulation, and will kill you, and you will be hated by all nations on account of my name."

¹⁰"And at that time ⁿmany will fall away, and will betray one another and hate one another. ¹¹And many false prophets will arise, and will mislead many. ¹²And because lawlessness is increased, most people's love will grow cold. ¹³But the one who endures to the end, he will be rescued. ¹⁴And this good news of the kingdom will be proclaimed in the whole world for a witness to all the nations, and then the end will comeˣ."

¹⁵Therefore when you may have seen the ABOMINATION OF DESOLATION˞ which was spoken of through Daniel the prophet, having been standing in the holy place (let the reader be understanding), ¹⁶then let those who are in Yehudah be fleeing to the mountains. ¹⁷Let him who is on the housetop not go down to get the things out that are in his house, ¹⁸and let him who is in the field not turn back to get his cloak. ¹⁹But woe to those who are with child and to those who nurse babes in those days!"

²⁰"But be praying that your flight will not have been in the winter, or on a Şabbaṭh, ²¹because then there will be a great tribulation, such as has not been occurring since the beginning of the world until now, nor ever, no, not shall have happened. ²²And unless those days are cut short, no life would be rescued, but for the sake of the chosen those days will be cut short."

²³"Then if anyone may have said to you, 'Behold, here is the Anŏinted,' or 'There,' you shall not have ˣheld *it* faithful. ²⁴Because false Mĕssiahs and false prophets will arise and will show great signs and wonders, so as to mislead, if˞ possible, even the chosen. ²⁵Behold, I have been telling you beforehand. ²⁶If therefore they may have said to you, 'Behold, he is in the wilderness,' you will not have gone forth, or 'Behold, he is in the inner rooms,' you will not have ˣheld *it* faithful. ²⁷Because just as the lightning comes from the east, and flashes even to the west, so will the coming presence of the Sŏn of Man be. ²⁸Wherever the corpse may be, there the vultures will gather."

²⁹"But immediately after the tribulation of those days THE SUN WILL BE DARKENED, AND THE MOON WILL NOT GIVE ITS LIGHT, AND THE STARS WILL FALL

24:10 η The sense is that it will become obvious by some external force or test that they have betrayed the faith. Generally people depart from the love of the truth and accept false doctrines well before it becomes obvious that they have done so. The external force is a test that will force them to choose sides and they will choose evil, hating the righteous and supporting the evil. **24:14** χ This indicates a long delay. See Hos. 6:1-3. **24:15** ξ Dan 9:27: וְהִגְבִּיר בְּרִית לָרַבִּים שָׁבוּעַ אֶחָד וַחֲצִי הַשָּׁבוּעַ יַשְׁבִּית זֶבַח וּמִנְחָה וְעַל כְּנַף שִׁקּוּצִים מְשֹׁמֵם וְעַד־כָּלָה וְנֶחֱרָצָה תִּתַּךְ עַל־שֹׁמֵם. 11:31: וְנָתְנוּ הַשִּׁקּוּץ מְשׁוֹמֵם; 12:11: וּמֵעֵת הוּסַר הַתָּמִיד וְלָתֵת שִׁקּוּץ שֹׁמֵם יָמִים אֶלֶף מָאתַיִם וְתִשְׁעִים. **24:23** χ→faithful = *consider it trustworthy*; **24:24** ξ The NIV adds "that were" so it would read "if that were possible," and by so doing suggests only a theoretical possibility. This is no doubt due to the false doctrine of "once saved always saved." The faithful stand through their faithfulness to Mĕssiah. If they decide to be disloyal then they fall. **24:29** μ Isa 13:10.

Mattatyahu 24

FROM THE HEAVEN", and the powers of the heavens will be shaken, ³⁰and then the sign of the Sŏn of Man will appear in the heaven, and then all the tribes of the earth will mourn, and they will see THE SŎN OF MAN COMING ON THE CLOUDS OF HEAVEN⁹ with power and great glory. ³¹And he will send forth his messengers with A TRUMPET⁸ of great sound and THEY WILL GATHER TOGETHER⁵ his chosen from the four winds, from one boundary of the heavens to the other boundary."

³²"Now learn the parable from the fig tree. When its branch may already have become tender, and it may be putting forth its leaves, you are knowing that summer is near. ³³Even so you too, when you may have seen all these things, be recognizing that he is near, right at the door. ³⁴Amen, I say to you, this ᵘkindred by no means will have passed away, before the point when all these things may have happened. ³⁵The heavens and the earth will pass away, yet my words, no, they will not have passed away."

³⁶"But concerning that day or time no one has been knowing, not even the messengers of the heavens, nor the Sŏn, but the Făther alone. ³⁷Because the coming presence of the Sŏn of Man will be just like the days of Noah. ³⁸Because, as in those days, which were before the flood, they were eating and drinking, they were marrying and giving in marriage, until the day that Noah entered the ark, ³⁹and they did not understand until the flood came and took them all away. So will the coming presence of the Sŏn of Man be. ⁴⁰Then there will be two men in the field. One will be taken, and one will be left. ⁴¹Two women will be grinding at the mill. One is taken, and one is left."

⁴²"Therefore be observing—because you have not been knowing in which day your Adŏnai is coming. ⁴³But be sure of this, that if the head of the house had been knowing at what time of the night the thief was coming, he would have been on the alert and would not have allowed his house to be broken into. ⁴⁴For this reason you be getting yourselves prepared also, because it ᶠmay be in an hour you are not supposing *when* the Sŏn of Man is coming."

⁴⁵"Who then is the faithful and sensible slave whom his master put in charge of his household to give them their food at the proper time? ⁴⁶Blessed is that slave whom his master finds so doing when he comes. ⁴⁷Amen, I say to you, that he will put him in charge of all his possessions. ⁴⁸But if an evil slave may have said in his heart, 'My master is not coming for a long time,' ⁴⁹and will have begun to beat his fellow slaves and may be eating and drinking with drunkards, ⁵⁰then the master of that slave will come on a day when he does not expect and

---

24:30 θ Dan 7:13: חָזֵה הֲוֵית בְּחֶזְוֵי לֵילְיָא וַאֲרוּ עִם־עֲנָנֵי שְׁמַיָּא כְּבַר אֱנָשׁ אָתֵה הֲוָה וְעַד־עַתִּיק יוֹמַיָּא מְטָה וּקְדָמוֹהִי הַקְרְבוּהִי. Seeing vision I had been in visions of the night, and behold with the clouds of the heavens, as a Son of man, coming, he had come, and unto the Ancient of the days he had reached, and before Him, they were made to come near Him. **24:31** δ σάλπιγγος φωνῆς μεγάλης Lev. 25:9 = σάλπιγγος φωνῇ = שׁוֹפָר תְּרוּעָה (cf. Lev. 16:30); 1 Cor. 15:52; 1 Thess. 4:16. **24:31** ζ Dan 12:1-2, 10. **24:34** μ The text points us to Jer. 33:23-26. See also Mark 13:30 and Luke 21:32. See Mat. 5:17-18 on "before the point." הַמִּשְׁפָּחוֹת < γενεά. The LXX omits this text because THE MANY who corrupted the Scripture rejected the promises to Israel and Judah. **24:44** ζ Byz ἤ (V-PSA-3S) = may be; ὅτι ᾗ ὥρα οὐ δοκεῖτε = *beause it-may-be in-hour not you-suppose.*

at a time which he does not recognize, ⁵¹and will cut him in pieces and assign him a place with the hypocrites. On the way to that place there will be weeping and gnashing of teeth."

25

¹At that time, the kingdom of the heavens will be comparable to ten virgins, who took their lamps, and went out to meet the bridegroom. ²And five of them were foolish, and five were prudent. ³Because when the foolish took their lamps, they took no oil with them, ⁴but the prudent took oil in flasks along with their lamps."

⁵"Now while the bridegroom was delaying, they all got drowsy and were sleeping. ⁶But in the middle of the night there had been a cry happening, 'Behold, the bridegroom! Be going out to meet him.' ⁷Then all those virgins rose, and trimmed their lamps. ⁸And the foolish said to the prudent, 'Give us some of your oil, because our lamps are going out.' ⁹But the prudent answered, saying, 'No, there will not have been enough for us and you too. Be getting yourselves gone instead to the dealers and buy some for yourselves.' ¹⁰And while they were going away to make the purchase, the bridegroom came, and those who were ready went in with him to the wedding feast, and the door was shut. ¹¹And later the other virgins also came, saying, 'Adŏnai, Adŏnai, open up for us.' ¹²But he answered and said, 'Amen I say to you, I have not been knowing you.' ¹³Be watching then, because you have not been knowing the day nor the hour."

¹⁴"Because it is just like a man about to go on a journey, who called his own slaves, and entrusted his possessions to them. ¹⁵And to one he gave five ʸtalents, to another, two, and to another, one, each according to his own ability. And he went on his journey. ¹⁶Immediately the one who received the five talents went and traded with them, and gained five more talents. ¹⁷In the same manner the one who received the two talents gained two more. ¹⁸But he who received the one talent went away and dug in the ground, and hid his master's silver."

¹⁹"Now after a long time the master of those slaves came and settled accounts with them. ²⁰And the one who received the five talents came up and brought five more talents, saying, 'Master, you entrusted five talents to me. See, I have gained five more talents.' ²¹His master said to him, 'Well done, good and faithful servant. You were faithful with a few things, I will put you in charge of many things. Enter into the joy of your master.' ²²The one also who received the two talents came up and said, 'Master, you entrusted to me two talents. See, I have gained two more talents.' ²³His master said to him, 'Well done, good and faithful servant. You were faithful with a few things, I will put you in charge of many things. Enter into the joy of your master.'"

²⁴"And the one also who had been taking the one talent came up and said, 'Master, I knew you to be a hard man, reaping where you did not sow, and

---

25:15 γ τάλαντον. One talent is an enormous sum of silver (cf. vs. 18), worth 6,000 denari, about 20 years of a working man's wages. The 5 talents was worth around 100 years of a working man's wages, and the faithful servant returned 200 years of value to his master.

Mattatyahu 25

gathering where you scattered no seed. ²⁵And I was afraid, and went away and hid your talent in the ground. See, you have what is yours.' ²⁶But his master answered and said to him, 'You wicked, lazy servant, you had been knowing that I reap where I did not sow, and gather where I scattered no seed. ²⁷Then you ought to have placed my silver with the money lenders, and on my arrival I would have received what is mine back with interest. ²⁸Therefore take away the talent from him, and give it to the one who has the ten talents.' ²⁹Because unto everyone holding fast more will be given, and he will hold an abundance, but from the one who does not hold fast, even what he does hold will be taken away. ³⁰And cast out the worthless servant into the ᵟuttermost darkness. Thither there will be weeping and gnashing of teeth."

³¹"But when the Sŏn of Man may have come in his glory, and all the messengers with him, then he will sit on his glorious throne. ³²And all the nations will be gathered before him, and he will separate them from one another, as the shepherd separates the sheep from the goats, ³³and he will put the sheep on his right, and the goats on the left."

³⁴"Then the King will say to those on his right, 'Come, you who have been getting blessed of my Făther, inherit the kingdom, which has been getting prepared for you since the founding of the world. ³⁵Because I was hungry, and you gave me something to eat. I was thirsty, and you gave me drink. I was a sojourner, and you invited me in, ³⁶naked, and you dressed me. I was sick, and you visited me. I was in prison, and you came to me.'"

³⁷"Then the righteous will answer him, saying, 'Adŏnai, when did we see you hungry, and feed you, or thirsty, and give you drink? ³⁸And when have we seen you a sojourner, and gathered *you* in, or naked, and dressed you? ³⁹And when did we see you sick, or in prison, and come to you?' ⁴⁰And the King will answer and say to them, 'Amen I say to you, to the extent that you did it to one of these brothers of Mine, even the least of them, you did it to me.'"

⁴¹"Then he will also say to those on his left, 'Be departing from me, *you* who have been getting accursed, into the enduring fire which ˣhas been getting prepared for the Slanderer and his messengers, ⁴²because I was hungry, and you gave me nothing to eat. I was thirsty, and you gave me nothing to drink. ⁴³I was a sojourner, and you did not gather *me* in, naked, and you did not dress me, sick, and in prison, and you did not look in on me.' ⁴⁴Then they themselves also will answer, saying, 'Adŏnai, when did we see you hungering, or thirsting, or a sojourner, or naked, or sick, or in prison, and we did not minister to you?' ⁴⁵Then he will answer them, saying, 'Amen I say to you, to the extent that you did not do it to one of the least of these, you did not do it to me.'" ⁴⁶"Then these will depart for eternal ᵋexcision, and the righteous for eternal life."

25:30 δ→darkness = oblivion
25:41 χ→prepared: personification; cf. Isa. 14:9.
25:46 ε 'Excision' means a cutting off. It derives from the verb κολάζω "Properly, to *curtail, dock, prune*" (LSJ). κόλασις from κολάζω. Friberg: "κολάζω; strictly cut off, lop, trim; hence prune, trim;" Autenrieth, "cut short." ▷ As a noun "excision." Equiv. to the Hebrew verb לִכְרֹת *likrōt* (infinitive form) means "to cut off." See Gen. 17:14; Exodus 12:15, 30:33, 38; 31:14; Lev. 7:20; Deut. 19:1; Exodus 31:14; Lev. 20:3, 5, 6. The

26 ¹And it came about that when Yĕshua finished all these words, he said to his disciples, ²"You have been knowing that ⁵AFTER TWO DAYS the Passover is coming, and the Sŏn of Man is to be delivered up for fastening up on an execution timber."

³Then the chief priests and the elders of the people were gathered together in the court of the high priest, named Qaiyapha. ⁴And they plotted together, so that they might seize Yĕshua by stealth, and might kill him. ⁵But they were saying, "Not during the festival, so that a riot will not have occured among the people."

⁶Now ⁻when Yĕshua was in Beth-Hini, at the home of Şim'on the leper, ⁷a woman came to him with an alabaster vial of very costly perfume, and she poured it on his head as he reclined at the table. ⁸But the disciples were indignant when they saw this, and said, "Why this waste? ⁹Because this perfume could have been sold for a high price and given to the poor."

¹⁰But Yĕshua, aware of this, said to them, "Why do you bother the woman? Because she has done a good deed to me. ¹¹For the poor you have with you always, but you do not always have me, ¹²because when she poured this perfume upon my body, she did it to prepare me for burial. ¹³Amen, I say to you, wherever this good news will have been proclaimed in the whole world, what this woman has done will also be spoken of, in memory of her."

¹⁴Then^μ one of the twelve, named Yehudah Ish-Qeriyot, went to the chief priests, ¹⁵and said, "What are you willing to give me to deliver him up to you?" And they weighed out to him thirty pieces of silver. ¹⁶And from then on he was looking for a good opportunity so that he might betray him.

¹⁷Now on the ⁵headmost *day* ᶿfor the unleavened ones the disciples came to Yĕshua, saying, "Where do you desire *that* we will ᵘhave readied for you to eat the Passover?" ¹⁸And he said, "Be going into the city to a certain man, and say

---

noun of that is verb: בְּרִיתָה keriṭah (Reuben Alcalay). Construct: בְּרִיתַת keriṭat, "cutting off of, excision of."
▷ The old argument of limiting the meaning of eternal here to an age should not be used as it is parallel to everlasting life. Rather the term *kolasis* specifies an excision. Branches are cut off from the life of a tree. They wither and die and then are burned. The excision of the branches is permanent. Nor should the word punishment be conceded in an active sense as it still implies a continuing infliction of pain and suffering. **26:2** ζ→days; Hos 6:2; After two days is the third day. The phrase is intentional to remind us of Genesis 22 and other third day passages. The words were spoken on Monday afternoon (Aviv 12), and so after one day is Tuesday (Aviv 13), and after two days is Wednesday (Aviv 14), when the Passover was sacrificed. This is the third day counting inclusively from Monday. There are several other ways the third day is counted in Scripture. Counting backwards from the resurrection as today, yesterday, the third day makes the crucifixion day the third day. The day of the crucifixion is the third day and so also the day of the resurrection. See Hos. 6:1-3, where "AFTER TWO DAYS" is computed by a calendar day from dawn to dawn. See chart. **26:6** τ Monday evening at supper. **26:14** μ Sometime on Aviv 13, perhaps in the night of March 22-23 or early in the morning, Tuesday, March 23. **26:17** ξ Hebrew: headmost day of, firstmost day of. The Greek is also amenable to this. See Mark 14:12 note. See Exodus 12:15 where the 14th day of the month is so called in the first occurrence of this riddle. The day heading up the feast of unleavened bread, upon which the leaven is removed, is not the first day of the feast, but the day before it. The question was asked just after sunset going into Nisan 14. It was Tuesday, March 23, AD 34. **26:17** θ genitive case, 'of' or 'for.' **26:17** μ I have put a more literal rendition of the aorist subjunctive here.

26:18 γ→doing: The verb ποιῶ is either VSPA (*Let me do, may I do,* or *I may do*) or VIPA (*I am going to do*). VSPA (S=subjunctive) is correct since Yĕshua is expressing a wish and not making a demand or declaring a certainty. It is called the volitive subjunctive, viz. "Let me do the Passover with you with my disciples." The word "wish" expresses the subjunctive, that is, an optative subjunctive, expressing only a hypothetical

Mattatyahu 26

to him: the teacher says, my time is at hand. With you ʸI wish to be doing the Passover with my disciples." ¹⁹And the disciples did as Yĕshua directed them, and readied the Passover.

²⁰Now as it was ᵃbecoming later, he was reclining with the twelve disciples. ²¹And as they were eating, he said, "Amen, I say to you that one of you will betray me." ²²And being deeply grieved, they each one began to say to him, "Surely not I, Adŏnai?" ²³And he answered and said, "He who dipped his hand with me in the bowl is the one who will betray me. ²⁴Surely, the Sŏn of Man goes, just as it has been getting written about him, but woe to that man by whom the Sŏn of Man is betrayed! It would have been good for that man if he had not been born." ²⁵And Yehudah, who was betraying him, replied and said, "Surely it is not I, Rabbi?" He said to him, "You have said it yourself."

²⁶And while they were eating, Yĕshua took bread, and after blessing, he broke it and gave it to the disciples, and said, "Take, eat. This represents my body." ²⁷And when he took a cup and gave thanks, he gave it to them, saying, "Drink from it, all of you, ²⁸because this represents my blood of the covenant, which is poured out for many toward a release from sins. ²⁹But I say to you, no, I will not have drunk from now, from this *cup*, of the fruit of the vine until

---

possibility (cf. Wallace, Syntax, pg. 462). The aspect is durative, so the progressive is translated "be doing." The chronology is secured by more specific statements. These statements may be regarded as chronological parables where one thing is supposed by simple readers, but another thing is the case when everything is read and considered. The meal was a Seder, but it was not at the official time because Mĕssiah was the Passover that year and would not be available to eat it. See Luke 22:16. **26:19** χ The commandment to take a lamb, called the Passŏver, on the 10th day was regarded as being specific to the year of the Exodus like the command to put blood on the door posts. So they got ready at dusk on the 14th by acquiring a Passover suitable for sacrifice the next day and by making or acquiring unleavened bread and the necessary herbs. The dealers in all items for Passover would have been open late this night serving pilgrims to the holy city, and also open early the next day until noon when businesses would close. The lamb would be washed, groomed and fed by the disciples. ▷ The Passover would then be kept ready until they took it up to the Temple to be slaughtered. No doubt it remained tethered just outside the καταλυμά when they went out at midnight. **26:20** α When full dark arrived. Tuesday night. **26:28** φ Cf. Mark 14:24. Notice that the texts omit the word 'new' here, which in any case I would translate 'new made covenant' if it were in the text. This statement represents a covenant renewal, but not just renewal. It is also renewal with modification. This calls us back to Exodus 24:8, "BEHOLD, THE BLOOD OF THE COVENANT WHICH YĀHWEH HAS COVENANTED WITH YOU CONCERNING ALL THESE WORDS." It also recalls Deut. 29:1, "THESE ARE THE WORDS OF THE COVENANT WHICH YĀHWEH HAD COMMANDED MOSHEH TO COVENANT WITH THE SONS OF YISRA'EL IN THE LAND OF MO'AV APART FROM THE COVENANT THAT HE HAD COVENANTED WITH THEM IN HOREV." This text reveals that the covenant is newly made with the people then (cf. Deut. 29:12-15). There are new laws added, laws clarified, and laws repeated in the new making of the covenant. Man was not allowed to add to the covenant, but the Most High was allowed to add to it, modify it, or subtract from it (Deut. 12:32). It is a suzerainty covenant. The lord is in charge of the terms, and the lord only. He was also in charge of when and how the covenant could be reinstated should it ever be broken, and the terms thereof. ▷ When the covenant terms were broken by Yisra'el, the Almighty sold them to their enemies. But Yisra'el repented and he forgave them under the condition that the covenant be new made, and the blood used to restore us so that we can enter the new making is Messiah's. **26:28** ψ εἰς "❶ extension involving a goal, *into, in, toward, to*" (BDAG). For 'sins' we can put 'lawlessness,' personify it, and say the goal is to gain our freedom by paying the ransom cost. See Acts 2:38 ψ.

26:28 χ The new making is effected by the forgiveness of sins, allowing the confessor to enter into the covenant again (Deut. 29:12). The blood of Messiah represents his divine life, because he is Everlasting Life (1 Yoh. 1:2, 5:20). The Life cleanses the record of the judgment against our sins. It blots it out (cf. Col. 1:14). KIPPURIM means *a declaring to be wiped out*. The blood also cleanses us from all unrighteousness (cf. 1 Yoh. 1:9). The physical elements are symbolic of spiritual realities (cf. Yoh. 6:63). The death of Messiah also ransoms us from Lawlessness, from the powers we were sold under because of our

that day when I may be drinking it new-made with you in my Fäther's kingdom."

³⁰And after singing a Psalm, they went out to the Mount of Olives. ³¹Then Yĕshua said to them, "You will all fall away because of me this night, because it has been getting written, 'I WILL STRIKE THE SHEPHERD, AND THE SHEEP OF THE FLOCK WILL BE SCATTERED.' ³²But after I have been raised, I will go before you to Galil.⁰"

³³But Peter answered and said to him, "Even though all may fall away because of you, I will never fall away." ³⁴Yĕshua said to him, "Amen, I say to you that this very night, before the rooster sounds, you will deny me three times." ³⁵Peter says to him, "Even if I may need to die with you, I will not deny you." All the disciples said the same thing too.

³⁶Then Yĕshua came with them to a place called Gaṭh-Ṣemanei, and said to his disciples, "Sit here, while having gone there, I may pray." ³⁷And he took with him Peter and the two sons of Zavdai, and began to be grieved and distressed. ³⁸Then he said to them, "My soul is deeply grieved, to the point of death. Remain here and be keeping watch with me." ³⁹And he went a little beyond them, and fell on his face and prayed, saying, "My Fäther, if it is possible, let this cup pass from me, yet not as I will, but as you will." ⁴⁰And he came to the disciples and found them sleeping, and said to Peter, "So, you could not keep watch with me for one hour? ⁴¹Be keeping watch and be praying, that you will not have entered into testing. The spirit is willing, but the flesh is weak."

⁴²When he went away again a second time, he prayed, saying, "My Fäther, if this cannot pass away unless I may drink it, your will be done." ⁴³And when again he came, he found them sleeping, because their eyes had been getting heavy.

⁴⁴And he left them again, and went away and prayed a third time, saying the same thing once more. ⁴⁵Then he comes to the disciples, and is saying to them, "Are you left sleeping and taking your rest? Behold, the hour has been drawing near, and the Sŏn of Man is being betrayed into the hands of sinners. ⁴⁶Be arising, we should be going. Behold, the one who betrays me has been drawing near."

⁴⁷And while he was still speaking, behold, Yehudah, one of the twelve, came up, accompanied by a great crowd with swords and clubs, from the chief priests and elders of the people. ⁴⁸Now he who was betraying him gave them a sign,

---

sins. Lawlessness took the ransom by taking innocent blood. So the Most High compels them to free us. ▷ The symbolic sacrifice represents divine cost, which became real cost in the circumstances of Messiah's death. At no point should the death of the sacrifice be represented as a payment or appeasement of divine wrath. But the death symbolizes the ransom cost exacted by Lawlessness and death to return the confessor to the Covenant. ▷ In respect to sacrificial symbolism, Messiah's death has the same meaning as the sin and guilt offerings, except that the later were limited to sins of ignorance, and except that it was always divine life that was effecting the cleansing of the human spirit under the figure of the blood. ▷ The other difference is that in the slaying of the Levitical offerings, the action of lawlessness is only symbolized in taking the life of a symbolic ransom. It was a role play to symbolize what happened in reality. Lawlessness exacts the costs of sin. Obviously this point cannot be illustrated by being lawless. However, in Messiah's case, the Most High arranged their propensity to harm him to manifest in Lawlessness acting directly upon Messiah. Therefore, Messiah is the ontological ransom. **26:31** ρ Zech 13:7: הַךְ אֶת־הָרֹעֶה וּתְפוּצֶיןָ. **26:32** θ cf. Mt. 28:7. הֵצֵאן

saying, "Whomever I will have kissed, he is the one. Seize him!" ⁴⁹And immediately he went to Yĕshua and said, "Be rejoicing, Rabbi!" Then he kissed him. ⁵⁰And Yĕshua said to him, "Friend, for what do you come by?" Then they came and laid hands on Yĕshua and seized him.

⁵¹And behold, one of those who were with Yĕshua reached and drew out his sword, and struck the slave of the high priest, and cut off his ear. ⁵²Then Yĕshua says to him, "Put your sword back into its place, because all those having taken up the sword will perish by the sword. ⁵³Or do you think that I cannot appeal to my Făther, and he will at once put at my disposal more than twelve legions of messengers? ⁵⁴How then may the writings be fulfilled, that it is necessary to happen this way?"

⁵⁵At that time Yĕshua said to the crowds, "Have you come out with swords and clubs to arrest me as against a robber? Throughout the day I was sitting in the temple teaching and you did not seize me. ⁵⁶But all this had been happening that the writings of the prophets might be fulfilled." Then all the disciples, having left him, fled.

⁵⁷And those who seized Yĕshua led him away to Qaiyapha, the high priest, where the scribes and the elders were gathered together. ⁵⁸But Peter also was following him at a distance as far as the courtyard of the high priest, and entered in, and sat down with the officers to see the outcome.

⁵⁹Now the chief priests and the whole Sanhedrin kept trying to obtain false testimony against Yĕshua, in order that they might put him to death. ⁶⁰And they did not find any, even though many false witnesses came forward. But later on two came forward, ⁶¹and said, "This man stated, 'I am able to destroy the temple of the Almĭghty and to rebuild it in three days.'" ⁶²And the high priest stood up and said to him, "Do you make no answer? What is it that these men are testifying against you?" ⁶³But Yĕshua kept silent. And the high priest said to him, "I am putting you under oath, down from the living Almĭghty, that you shall tell us whether you are the Anŏinted One, the Almĭghty Sŏn."

⁶⁴Yĕshua said to him, "You have said it yourself. Nevertheless I tell you, because of[α] now you-all will see[β] to THE SŎN OF MAN SITTING AT THE RIGHT HAND OF POWER, AND COMING ON THE CLOUDS OF HEAVEN[δ]."

⁶⁵Then the high priest tore his robes, saying, "He blasphemed! What further need do we have of witnesses? Behold, you have now heard the blasphemy. ⁶⁶What do you think?" They answered and said, "He is deserving of death!" ⁶⁷Then they spat in his face and beat him with their fists, and others slapped him, ⁶⁸and said, "Prophesy to us, Mĕssiah. Who is the one who hit you?"

⁶⁹Now Peter was sitting outside in the courtyard, and a certain servant-girl came to him and said, "You too were with Yĕshua the Galili." ⁷⁰But he denied it before them all, saying, "I have not been knowing what you are talking about."

26:64 δ Dan 7:13; Psalm 110:1. **26:64** α 'from now,' 'based upon now' **26:64** β or 'provide for,' e.g. 'they would see him made king'; cf. Gen. 22:14.

⁷¹And when he went out to the gateway, another servant-girl saw him and said to those who were there, "This man was with Yĕshua of Netsereth." ⁷²And again he denied it with an oath *saying* that, "I have not been knowing the man." ⁷³And a little later those who had been standing by approached. They said to Peter, "Truly, you also are from them, because even the way you talk gives you away." ⁷⁴Then he began to be cursing and swearing, "I have not been knowing the man!" And immediately a rooster sounded. ⁷⁵And Peter remembered the word which Yĕshua had been saying, "Before the rooster sounds, you will deny me three times." And he went out and wept bitterly.

27

¹Now when morning^τ came, all the chief priests and the elders of the people took counsel against Yĕshua to put him to death. ²And they bound him, and led him away, and delivered him up to Pilate the governor.

³Then when Yehudah, who betrayed him, saw that he was condemned, he felt remorse and returned the thirty pieces of silver to the chief priests and elders, ⁴saying, "I have sinned by betraying innocent blood." But they said, "What is that to us? See to that yourself!" ⁵And he threw the pieces of silver into the sanctuary and departed. And he went away and hanged himself.

⁶And the chief priests took the pieces of silver and said, "It is not lawful to put them into the temple treasury, since it is the price of blood." ⁷And they counseled together and with the silver bought the Potter's Field as a burial place for strangers. ⁸For this reason that field has been called the Field of Blood to this day. ⁹Then that which was spoken through the prophet was fulfilled, saying, "AND THEY TOOK THE THIRTY PIECES OF SILVER, THE SPLENDID *amount* WHICH the sons of Yisra'el HAD BEEN VALUING *me* ¹⁰AND THEY GAVE THEM TO THE FIELD OF THE POTTER, AS YĂHWEH DIRECTED ME^ψ." ¹¹Now Yĕshua stood before the governor, and the governor questioned him, saying, "Are you the King of the Yehudim?" And Yĕshua said to him, "It is as you say." ¹²And while he was being accused by the chief priests and elders, he made no answer. ¹³Then Pilate said to him, "Do you not hear how many things they testify against you?" ¹⁴And he did not answer him with regard to even a single charge, so that the governor was quite amazed.

¹⁵Now ^μduring a feast the governor had been getting accustomed to release for the crowd any one prisoner whom they wanted. ¹⁶And they were holding at that time a notorious prisoner, called *Yeshua*^χ Bar-Abba. ¹⁷While therefore they have been gathering together, Pilate said to them, "Whom do you want *that* I will have released for you? *Yeshua*^χ Bar-Abba, or Yĕshua who is called the Anointed One?" ¹⁸For he had been knowing that because of envy they delivered him up. ¹⁹And while he was sitting on the judgment seat, his wife sent to him, say-

---

27:1 τ Wednesday morning, March 24, Aviv 14, AD 34. **27:9-10** ψ Zech 11:12-13: וָאֹמַר אֲלֵיהֶם אִם־טוֹב בְּעֵינֵיכֶם הָבוּ שְׂכָרִי וְאִם־לֹא חֲדָלוּ וַיִּשְׁקְלוּ 13:אֶת־שְׂכָרִי שְׁלֹשִׁים כָּסֶף וַיֹּאמֶר יְהוָה אֵלַי הַשְׁלִיכֵהוּ אֶל־הַיּוֹצֵר אֶדֶר הַיְקָר אֲשֶׁר יָקַרְתִּי מֵעֲלֵיהֶם וָאֶקְחָה שְׁלֹשִׁים הַכֶּסֶף וָאַשְׁלִיךְ אֹתוֹ בֵּית יְהוָה אֶל־הַיּוֹצֵר.
27:15 μ = down through **27:16** λ a few texts. **27:17** χ Vaticanus, and a few other texts.

Mattatyahu 27

ing, "Have nothing to do with that righteous Man, because last night I suffered greatly in a dream because of him." ²⁰But the chief priests and the elders persuaded the crowds that they should ask for Bar-Abba, and Yĕshua they should destroy. ²¹Yet when the governor answered, he said to them, "Which of the two do you want *that* I may release for you?" And they said, "Bar-Abba." ²²Pilate says to them, "Then what will I have done with Yĕshua who is being called the Anŏinted One?" They all said, "Let him be fastened up on an execution timber!" ²³And he said, "Why, what evil has he done?" But they kept shouting all the more, saying, "Let him be fixed up on an execution timber!" ²⁴And when Pilate saw that he was accomplishing nothing, but rather that a riot was starting, he took water and washed his hands in front of the crowd, saying, "I am innocent of this Man's blood. See *to that* yourselves."

²⁵And all the people answered and said, "His blood be on us and on our children!" ²⁶Then he released Bar-Abba for them, but after having Yĕshua scourged, he delivered him so that he could be fastened up on an execution timber.

²⁷Then the soldiers of the governor took Yĕshua into the Praetorium and gathered the whole Roman cohort around him. ²⁸And they stripped him, and put a scarlet robe on him. ²⁹And after weaving a crown of thorns, they put it on his head, and a reed in his right hand, and they kneeled down before him and mocked him, saying, "Be rejoicing, King of the Yehudim!" ³⁰And they spat on him, and took the reed and were beating him on the head. ³¹And after they mocked him, they took his robe off and put his garments on him, and led him away to fasten him up on an execution timber.

³²And as they were coming out, they found a man of Cyrene named Şimʿon, whom they pressed into service so that he might carry his execution-timber.

³³And when they came to a place called Golgoltha, which means place of a poll, ³⁴they gave him wine to drink, which had been getting mixed with GALL, and after tasting it, he was unwilling to drink. ³⁵And when they fastened him up on an execution timber, they divided up his garments among themselves, casting lots. ³⁶And sitting down, they were keeping watch over him there. ³⁷And they put up above his head the charge against him which had been getting written, "THIS IS YĔSHUA THE KING OF THE YEHUDIM."

³⁸At that time two bandits were fastened up on the execution timber with him, one on the ᵃright *hand* and one on the ᵝleft *hand*. ³⁹And those passing by were hurling abuse at him, wagging their heads, ⁴⁰and saying, "You who were going to destroy the temple and rebuild it in three days, rescue yourself! If you are the Almĭghty Sŏn, come down from the execution timber."

⁴¹In the same way the chief priests also, along with the scribes and elders, were mocking him, and saying, ⁴²"He rescued others? He cannot rescue himself. King of Yisraʾel is he? Let him now come down from the execution timber, and we will pledge faithfulness on him. ⁴³HE HAS BEEN TRUSTING ON THE ALMĬGHTY?

27:38 α→right *hand*; β→left *hand*. See Yoh. 19:18, 31-33. **27:43** ψ Psa. 22:8: גֹּל אֶל־יְהֹוָה יְפַלְּטֵהוּ יַצִּילֵהוּ כִּי חָפֵץ בּוֹ.

LET HIM DELIVER now IF HE TAKES PLEASURE IN HIM,^ψ because he said, 'I am the Sŏn of the Almĭghty.'" ⁴⁴And the bandits also, who were fastened up on the execution timber with him, were casting the same insult at him.

⁴⁵Now from the sixth hour darkness fell upon all the land until the ninth hour. ⁴⁶And about the ninth hour Yĕshua cried out with a loud voice, saying, ⸢"ELi, ELi, LAMAH ṢEVAQTANi?" that is, "MY GŎD, MY GŎD, WHY HAVE YOU FORSAKEN ME?⸣" ⁴⁷And some of those who had been standing there, when they heard it, were saying, "This man is calling for Eliyahu." ⁴⁸And straightaway, one of them ran, and took a sponge, filled it as well with vinegar, and affixed it to a reed, giving him a ⸢drink. ⁴⁹Yet the rest of them were saying, "Leave *him* be, *so that* we may see if Eliyahu is going to come rescuing him." ⁵⁰And Yĕshua cried out again with a loud voice, and yielded up his spirit.

⁵¹And behold, the ᵖveil of the temple was torn in two from top to bottom, and the earth shook, and the rocks were split, ⁵²and the tombs were opened, and many bodies of the holy ones who had been sleeping were raised, ⁵³and coming out of the tombs after his resurrection they entered the holy city and appeared to many. ⁵⁴Now the centurion, and those who were with him keeping guard over Yĕshua, when they saw the earthquake and the things that were happening, became very frightened and said, "Truly this was the Almĭghty Sŏn!"

⁵⁵And many women were there looking on from a distance, who had followed Yĕshua from Galil, ministering to him, ⁵⁶among whom was Miryam Ha-Magdalit,

---

27:46 ⸣ Psa 22:1; The Psalm ends with "Because he has not despised, and he has not made to be abhorrent the affliction of the afflicted one, and he has not hidden his face from him, and when he is crying out unto him, he has heard" (vs 24), thus the first line expresses how Messiah felt, but the Most High was not abandoning him. He was working things to raise him from the dead. Messiah was not made sin to suffer judicial wrath, because then he would be justly despised. But the text makes clear the Most High did not regard him as abhorrent. The Father does not turn his back to the Son, but he permits the evil to happen with the aim to make its defeat all the greater by raising him from the dead, and thus by his death will be ransom from deception and evil for whomever will see Messiah's death in the true light. Many more will be drawn to him through the sacrifice and get cleansing from their sin by the life of Messiah.

27:48 ⸣ Two drinks were offered to Mĕssiah during his suffering, (1) Wine and (2) Vinegar. He refused to drink the wine (Mat. 27:34; Mark 15:23) on the basis of Mat. 26:29, Mark 14:25, and Luke 22:18. But the vinegar he did drink (Mat. 27:48; Mark 15:36; Luke 23:36; John 19:29, 30). The prophecy in Psalm 69:21 was fulfilled, "THEN THEY PUT GALL IN MY FOOD. AND FOR MY THIRST THEY MADE ME DRINK VINEGAR." The word for vinegar here is *homets* חֹמֶץ, which in the Septuagint Greek is ὄξος, and is the same word used in all the vinegar texts. Delitzsch correctly puts חֹמֶץ in John 19:29. Vinegar can be made from apples, palms, figs, fermented grain extract. So it was not the fruit of the vine that he drank. Some Vinegar is *hamets* (like malt vinegar, because it is a grain based fermentation), and other vinegar is not (such as apple cider vinegar or wine vinegar), but if you are not sure, then do not use vinegar at Passover. The vinegar used here, on the basis of the prophecy in Psa. 69:21 was *hamets* חָמֵץ. This can be seen in the very root word used: חָמֵץ. ▷ Therefore, Yĕshua consumed a fermented product on the eve of Passover. This shows that the day was the preparation day for Passover, and the feast of unleavened bread had not yet begun. He also actually did refuse wine when it was offered (cf. Mark 15:23, οἴνου). The Hebrew word for grain based leavening agent (yeast) is: שְׂאֹר *se'or*. חָמֵץ *hamets* is a leavened product, such as bread, wine, or beer, made with שְׂאֹר. And חָמֵץ is a vinegar product made from שְׂאֹר. ▷ Both the leavened product, *hamets* and the grain based leavening agent, *se'or*, are forbidden during the seven days of unleavened bread. See Exodus 12:15, "ON THE HEADMOST DAY YOU SHALL MAKE CEASE LEAVENING (*se'or*) FROM YOUR HOUSES, BECAUSE ANYONE EATING LEAVENED PRODUCTS (*hamets*) ALSO WILL HAVE BEEN CUT OFF THAT SOUL FROM YISRA'EL, FROM THE FIRST DAY UNTIL THE END OF THE SEVENTH."

27:51 π→temple: This was the outer veil covering the doors to the holy place showing a panorama of heaven. The outer veil was visible from the crucifixion site (cf. Mark 15:39; Luke 23:45-48; Mat. 27:54), whereas the inner veil was not. Jerome cites the *Epistle of the Nazarenes*, "We read not that the [inner] veil of the

along with Miryam the mother of Ya'aqov and Yosef, and the mother of the sons of Zavdai.

⁵⁷And when it was late, there came a rich man from Ha-Ramatayim, named Yosef, who himself also was a disciple of Yĕshua. ⁵⁸This man went to Pilate and asked for the body of Yĕshua. Then Pilate ordered it to be given over to him. ⁵⁹And Yosef took the body and wrapped it in a clean linen cloth, ⁶⁰and laid it in his own new-made tomb, which he had hewn out in the rock, and he rolled a large stone against the entrance of the tomb and went away. ⁶¹And Miryam Ha-Magdalit was there, and the other Miryam, sitting opposite the grave.

⁶²Now on the ᶿmorrow which is next to the preparation, the chief priests and the Perushim gathered together with Pilate, ⁶³and said, "Sir, we remember that when he was still alive that deceiver said, 'After three days I rise again*.' ⁶⁴Therefore, give orders for the grave to be made secure ^past the third day, lest his disciples, having come, will have stolen him away and will have said to the people, 'He has risen from the dead,' and the last deception will be worse than the first." ⁶⁵Pilate was saying to them, "You have a guard; be going, make it as secure as you have been knowing." ⁶⁶And they went and made the grave secure, by sealing the stone with the guard.

28

¹But *the* ᵋlater of *the* Şabbaŧhs, at the dawning for *the* ᶿFIRST ᵋOF THE ŞABBAŧHS, Miryam Ha-Magdalit and the other Miryam came to look at the grave. ²And behold, a severe earthquake occurred, ᵅbecause the Messenger of Yăhweн descended from heaven and came, rolled away the stone and was sitting up ᵋabove it. ³And his appearance was being like ᵝlightning, and his garment as ^white as snow. ⁴And those guarding shook because of fear of him,

---

temple was rent but that the lintel of the temple of wondrous size collapsed" (Jerome, *Epist. to Hedibia* 120 and *Comm. on Matt.* re 27.51; cf. *Historia Passionis Domini;*). Therefore, the outer veil had to have been ripped in two by its lintel stone when it cracked in two and fell. The outer veil was in front of the doors of the temple to conceal it. It was not a part of the original Tabernacle design or Shelomoh's Temple, but it was added when they built the second temple without any especial commandment. In ancient times, the people were allowed to look through the open doors. According to a rabbinic tradition the temple doors had to be open for a peace offering to be valid: "If a peace-offering is slaughtered before the doors of the temple are opened, it is invalid" (b. Zevachim 55b; y. Shekalim v, 48d; m. Tamid 1-3; m. Yoma 2.). ▷ There are those that regard the tearing of the veil as divine disapproval of the Temple service. They often imagine that the inner veil between the holy place and the most holy place was torn. But the tearing of the outer veil by the lintel coming down would imply that one could see through the open doors. Thus the Temple was revealed to show approval of Mĕssiah's sacrifice. The door was not open enough for the Almȋghty, so he removed the veil to show acceptance of the offering of his Sŏn. Seen this way, there is no disapproval of the Temple. ▷ According to Josephus the veil was embroidered with a panorama of heaven (*War* 5.5.4 §§212-214). When Mark says the veil was "torn asunder" we are supposed to picture "the heavens being torn asunder" (Mark 1:10) and the Fäther saying, "You are my beloved Sŏn, in you I am well-pleased." See Mark 15:38. **27:62** θ Which was the annual Şabbaŧh between Wednesday sunset and Thursday sunset that year. *On the morrow* means in the morning of this Şabbaŧh which was March 25th, Aviv 15. **27:63** x→days: The day is typically regarded as ending at sunset when using this idiom. When the sun set on Wednesday, it was counted to be after one day. When it set on Thursday, after two days, and when it set on Friday, after three days. From the perspective of a calendar day from one dawn to the next dawn, though, Friday night is still in the third calendar day. See Mark 8:31.

27:64 ^ Generally the English word 'until' does not include the endpoint whereas the Hebrew and Greek may. The sense is something like "till past the third day." The guarding was to include the third day and not just be up to it. See Mat. 5:18. See Gesenius and TWOT, "עַד m. (from the root עָדָה to pass over, to go on,...(b) of time. עַד הַיּוֹם הַזֶּה even unto this day, i.e. (the limit being included...)." **28:1** θ cf. Lev 23:15b; ξ→Şabbaŧhs: See also Mark 16:1-2. The seven days of unleavened bread began that year with the annual

and became like dead men. ⁵And when the Messenger began to speak, he said to the women, "Do not be getting yourselves afraid,ᵟ because I have been knowing that you are looking for Yĕshua who had been getting fastened up on an execution timber. ⁶He is not ᵋso here, because he has risen, just as he said. Come, see the place where he was lying. ⁷And having gone quickly, tell his disciples that he has risen from the dead. And behold, he is going before you into Galil, there you will see him. Behold, ᵠI have told you."

⁸And they departed quickly from the tomb with fear and great joy and ran to report it to his disciples. ⁹And behold, Yĕshua met them, saying "Be Rejoicing!" And they came up and took hold of his feet and worshiped him. ¹⁰Then Yĕshua says to them, "Do not be getting yourself afraid. Be going and take word to my brothers so that they will have left for Galil, and there they will see me."

¹¹Now while they were on their way, behold, some of the guard came into the city and reported to the chief priests all that happened. ¹²And when they were gathered together with the elders, ᵋbesides having taken counsel, they gave considerable silver pieces to the soldiers, ¹³and said, "You are to say, 'His disciples came by night and stole him away while we were asleep.' ¹⁴And if this may have been heard by the governor, we will persuade him and keep you out of trouble."

¹⁵And they took the silver and did as they were instructed. And this story was widely spread among the Yehudim, and is to this day.

¹⁶But the eleven disciples proceeded to Galil, to the mountain which Yĕshua designated. ¹⁷And when they saw him, they worshiped, but some have doubted.ᵖ ¹⁸And Yĕshua came up and spoke to them, saying, "All authority has been given to me in heaven and on earth."

Şabbath, starting on Wednesday evening. But the regular Şabbath fell on the third day of the feast. Mattatyahu calls this weekly Şabbath following three days after Mĕssiah's death, "...the late one of the Şabbaths." **28:1** ξ The adjective late ('Οψὲ) is used substantively, which means it is used as a noun. For example, "The late of the men" means the same as "The late one of the men." **28:1** θ = *first day*, or *one day* **28:1** θ = *one* = literally: 'one *day* of the Şabbaths;' *one* (μια) is used by way of Hebraism for '*first*' (cf. Gen. 1:5), and does not on that account mean '<u>a</u> day of the Şabbaths,' but the *number* one in a counting. The gender of μια implies the word *day* to follow.

28:1 θ→ŞABBATHS: The first of the seven Şabbaths in Lev. 23:15. That passage employs a riddle using the word tomorrow. The sheaf is waved in the tomorrow of the annual Şabbath. Then seven Şabbaths are counted in the tomorrow of the annual Şabbath. Then a fiftieth day is counted in the tomorrow of the seventh Şabbath. The resurrection was on the first weekly Şabbath after Passover before dawn, i.e. before the third night ended. See chart **28:1** ζ genitive case, 'of' or 'for' **28:2** α→YahweH: כִּי מַלְאַךְ יְהוָה. The Mĕssenger, some time after the resurrection, timed the rolling away of his stone just so it would happen just when the women arrived, so as to see it finishing up its removal. The stone, of course, was no obstacle to Mĕssiah's getting out of the grave earlier.

28:2 ζ→it: ἐπάνω αὐτοῦ; cf. Dan. 12:6 לְאִישׁ **28:3** β→light- לְבוּשׁ הַבַּדִּים אֲשֶׁר מִמַּעַל לְמֵימֵי הַיְאֹר ning: cf. Dan. 10:6. **28:3** λ→white: Mat. 17:2; cf. Dan. 7:9; Rev. 1:14. **28:5** φ→fear: Luke 1:13; Rev. 1:17. **28:6** ξ→here: οὐκ ἔστιν ὧδε = *such is not the case here*. The remark is calculated to allow for the possibility that Yĕshua was there in a different condition than that just mentioned; cf. Luke 24:6. **28:7** ψ 'I told you': cf. Mat. 26:32, 28:10. **28:12** ξ→counsel: συμβούλιόν τε λαβόντες. Or 'besides deliberating' among themselves. The τε clause refers to what is expected to take place as a matter of course in contrast to the unexpected: they bribed the witnesses to keep silent. See also Mat. 22:10; 27:48. Acts 15:3. **28:17** π Or *some doubt*. Gnomic aorist Matthew is acknowledging that there are some who dispute, whoever they may be. His note serves to reinforce the fact that they really worshiped. The directive to see him in Galil was to all his followers, being above 500. Any doubts of the 12 were resolved prior to this text. See 1 Cor. 15:5.

Mattatyahu 28

¹⁹"Go therefore and make disciples of all the nations, immersing them into the ᵝName of the Fӓther, and of the Sŏn, and of the Holy Spĭrit, ²⁰teaching them to observe all that I myself commanded you, and lo, I am with you all the days until the end of the age.ᶿ"

28:19 β The name of the Almĭghty is what he is known for, and what he is reputed for. See Exodus 33:19; 34:6-7. "YӒHWEH, AN EL COMPASSIONATE, AND GRACIOUS, SLOW TO ANGER, AND GREAT OF MERCY AND FAITHFULNESS, HE WHO WATCHES OVER LOVING-KINDNESS TO THE THOUSANDTH GENERATION, FORGIVING INIQUITY AND TRANSGRESSION, AND SIN, BUT HE WILL SURELY NOT ACQUIT, ATTENDING THE INIQUITY OF THE FATHERS UPON THE SONS, AND UPON THE SONS OF THE SONS, UPON THE THIRD GENERATION AND UPON THE FOURTH," but "DOING LOVING-KINDNESS TO THE THOUSANDTH GENERATION FOR THOSE LOVING ME AND FOR THE ONES KEEPING GUARD OVER MY COMMANDMENTS" (Exodus 20:6). Immersion into this truth is essential to proper immersion. **28:19 δ** The truth to be immersed into, is that Fӓther, Sŏn, and Spĭrit share the same attributes of the Almĭghty's name proclaimed to Mosheh. The words are not a baptismal formula to be recited, but an understanding of who the One Almĭghty is, and who is to be worshiped. For it says, "THEN MOSHEH MADE HASTE. THEN HE BOWED DOWN EARTHWARD. THEN HE MADE HIMSELF WORSHIP" (Exodus 34:8). The baptismal words spoken are an understanding to be immersed into. Commonly immersions were into the Name of Mĕssiah only, which is the same thing. **28:20 θ** Teaching the commandments is essential to immersion in the Name, as is understanding that sin is not absolved or acquitted, but is pardoned for all who continue to confirm their faithfulness to Mĕssiah, "FOR THOSE LOVING ME AND FOR THE ONES KEEPING GUARD OVER MY COMMANDMENTS" (Exodus 20:6). See Acts 2:38. ▷ The doctrine of the "Trinity" should not be called a false doctrine, but a flawed doctrine. Most of those who go this far do so because they have been taught false doctrine: either denying the Deity of Mĕssiah (some secretly so), saying the Spĭrit is not a separate *entity (person), and only Gŏd's power, or saying that man somehow will join the Almĭghty in a "family" only presently consisting of two, or saying that the Almĭghty is a single person, a single entity (modalism). But we fully maintain the deity of the Sŏn and the personality of the Spĭrit, and the exclusiveness of these entities who are One Almĭghty: Fӓther, Sŏn, Holy Spĭrit. There is no Almĭghty before Him, and there shall be none after Him. See 2 Pet. 1:4 for our now and future partaking of the divine nature, and Yoh. 1:1; 16:13; Rev. 5:6. ▷ With the forgoing context stated, I would urge that anyone who quotes the following criticisms include the above paragraph as the preface lest only the critique be understood and not what we actually hold to. The formulation of the Trinity is supposed to be a creedal expression (or summary) of Scriptural truths. However, it is badly worded and badly explained, and this is because most have rejected the Law and Prophets which provide the explanations! It is not *exactly* true. Firstly the title of the doctrine itself is problematic, "Trinity," which means three in a unity. Secondly is the description of the persons of the Fӓther, and the Spĭrit, using the term "person," and "three persons" which only has relevance to human beings. To be sure, the Almĭghty has personal traits. But the unitary human idea of a person can only be applied to the Sŏn, because the Almĭghty Sŏn became and took the form of a man. For this reason it would be technically correct to say the Fӓther and Spĭrit are spiritual *entities. It would be incorrect to be dogmatic about the divisibility, or multiplicity of the entities that make up the deity. What we know of the Almĭghty is only revealed through the Sŏn. If you know the Sŏn then you will know the Fӓther and the mind of the Spĭrit. ▷ The other confusing thing is the truth that there is One Almĭghty. This is only confusing if one first presumes that the Almĭghty is a singular person or if one stumbles on the mistranslation, *'The Almĭghty is One.' For it is quite clear that plural entities may be described as One, viz: "There is one people," and the "people are one." In Hebrew "people" is a singular noun and the verbs singular with it. In Hebrew also, singular pronouns: I, my, you, your, he, his, him may all be used to refer to plural entities, and be used by plural entities. ▷ Therefore, brothers and sisters, beware of anyone who dogmatically says they reject the Trinity. While we ourselves do not subscribe to the creedal language used, the reason they oppose it is not the few minor criticisms of terminology I have pointed out here, but they are opposing it because they believe in the serious heresies I listed above. ▷ We really do not know if Fӓther, Sŏn, and Spĭrit are "three persons," in the human sense of the term person, but only one person of the Sŏn, and a spiritual entity of the Fӓther, and the spiritual entity of the Spĭrit. Insight on this is in Rev. 5:6. See also Isa. 11:2. We really do not need to repeat the creedal phrases, which are inaccurate, but the confessions found in Scripture are sufficient if we understand them, and wherever confessions go beyond what is written in public recital, I advise not repeating those parts.

End Note No. 1: Late

In translating Mat. 28:1 all the rules of grammar and all the norms of lexical meaning have been followed. The first clause in Greek has just three words, "Ὀψὲ δὲ σαββάτων." The first rule followed by all translators is to mentally transpose the second word to the first place in preparation for English translation: δὲ Ὀψὲ σαββάτων. Greek differs from English in placing the conjunction δὲ as the second word of the sentence. However it is translated, this is always done by the translator. Second, I pick definition 4 from BDAG, 3rd edition for this word, "marker of contrast, *but, on the other hand*" (pg. 213). There can be no greater contrast between the narrative ending with the sealing of the tomb and finality of death and the resurrection to follow.

Third, in the same lexicon, BDAG, 3rd edition, the first definition of Ὀψὲ is given as "late." Slater, "1. *late*." Autenrieth, "*late*." Thayer, "*late*." ANLEX, "*late*." Sunday apologists will say "But in context it means end or evening or after." Appealing to context is the Protestant version of the Catholic Magisterium, because they claim to be the context authorities. But truly in the context the normal meaning "late" makes perfect sense.

The next word is σαββάτων. The ending ων is plural. The normal sense of the word is *Şabbaths*. The ending is also in the Greek grammatical inflexion called genitive, usually transposed to the front of a word in English and translated "of." By these normal applications of the rules and normal meanings, we arrive at "But late of Şabbaths." All English translators supply the word "the" as required by English rules: "But the late of the Şabbaths."

Observe that the word late may function as an adverb, "He came late," or an adjective "The late man," or as a noun "The late of the men." The noun-like usage of an adjective or adverb in Greek is called a substantive, because it is not just describing something. It is functioning as a substance: person, place, or thing. In English we append the word "one" to the descriptive word. "But the late one of the Şabbaths." This also is according to the normal rules. The word late is not an adverb in this context because it is not against a verb nor a simple adjective. According to the normal rules, it is a substantive, "the late one." The final translation, "But the later of the Şabbaths" is simply a smoother flowing English equivalent to the literal sense, "But the late one of the Şabbaths."

End Note No. 2: Execution Timber

The word traditionally *cross* is translated *execution timber*, and crucify as *to fasten to an execution timber*. The word timber was chosen in order to broaden the sense as much as possible, i.e. allow the reader to visualize all the ways execution could be by suspending. It was certain that condemned men did not carry T or + or x shaped crosses when they were to be executed. The word σταυρός only means a pale, pole, beam, stave, stake, timber. More generally: a length of wood suitable for execution by suspending the victim from it. No one English word is wholly adequate because English is almost always too specific to a particular method, viz. a stake is sharpened, a beam is only laid horizontal. A pole is vertical. A rod is too thin. A pale implies impalement with a point. Even the word timber has faults. A timber might imply a largeness or length greater than actually used. It should be noted that neither the Latin *crux* or Greek σταυρός implied a crosswise shape. These senses were acquired later to Latin by the constant traditional images.

It is the author's considered opinion that a live tree was used to support the execution timber (cf. Luke 23:31; Gal. 3:13; Acts 5:30; 10:39; 13:29; 1 Pet. 2:24) in a horizontal orientation. Perhaps a notch between branches was used and another major limb lopped off to provide a solid support base for the execution timber. The victims would be nailed to it, and then it would be raised and dropped into the prepared place on the supporting tree. There were three victims on one execution timber (cf. Yoh. 19:31) so that one could walk around the tree and come to the two bandits first yet the Anŏinted be in the middle (cf. Yoh. 19:18, 32-33). However one wishes to think of the event, the traditional three crosses on a hill is as fictional as the typical children's storybook model of Noah's ark. If the reader wishes they may substitute the words cross/crucifixion. Those words connote more succinctly the awfulness of the execution even if the image of how it was done is not so accurate.

End Note No. 3: Rabbinic Authority

See Mat. 23:1-3. The Rabbis have claimed for themselves an extraordinary authority over Yisra'el based on Deut. 17:8-13:

17 ⁸When a matter for judgment is too hard for ᵘ*you* concerning bloodshed, concerning *property* lawsuits, and concerning ᵛinjury cases, matters of divided legal opinion in your ᵞ*gates*, then you ᵗ*will* have risen up, and you *will* have gone to the place which Yăhweн your Almĭghty will choose, ⁹and you *will* have come to the Levitical Priests, and to the judge which will be in those days, and you *will* have inquired, and they *will* have made plain to you the word of the judgment. ¹⁰And you *will* have done according to the mouth of the word which they will make plain to you, from that place which Yăhweн chooses. And you *will* have kept watch to do according to all which they direct you, ¹¹according to the mouth of the Torah which they will direct you, and according to the judgment which they will say to you, you shall do. You shall not turn from the word which they will make plain to you, right or left. ¹²And the ᶿman which will do with presumption to not listen to the priest, the one standing to minister there for Yăhweн your Almĭghty, or the judge, also he *will* have been put to death, and you *will* have purged the evil from Yisra'el. ¹³And all the people will hear. Then they will fear and not act insolently again.

Appeal is made to this text to compel the faithful to follow the Rabbinic calendar using this text as a

---

17:8 μ 'You' here means magistrates or judges appointed in the civil government. **17:8** λ Only certain issues regarding bloodshed (a crime involving the death penalty), civil property dispute (theft or property damage), or personal injuries could be appealed since a miscarriage of justice would have the profoundest consequences for Yisra'el. If judges could not agree on other matters, not involving a capital crime, property dispute or personal injuries, then factions were permitted. The Federal power of Yisra'el's central government was limited to these cases. **17:8** γ The gates of a city were equivalent to the city courts, because this is where the elders sat. The wall of a city was thickest at the gate and as you go through the gate, seating places were built into the passage way. Anyone having a case would bring it there. **17:8** π See App. XV. 'You will have risen up [when the case occurs].'' This English usage is called the 'Indefinite Future Perfect.' It is indefinite because the temporal phrase 'when the case occurs' is omitted. A reader not used to a temporal modifier being omitted after a future perfect may suppose that 'will have' refers to a past event. It does not. Rather the point of view is projected into the future by the 'will' and then the 'have' looks backward in time to an event that is regarded as completed. The point in time looked back to is still in the future of the current present. In Hebrew legal texts the perfect tense is used to refer to the future quite extensively this way, because the legislation is emphatic. You will have done something is more forceful and emphatic than 'you will do such and such.' In ancient Hebrew indefinite future perfect usage did not include a separate word for 'will,' but the speakers of Hebrew were familiar with the perfect being used for the future. This feature of Hebrew is present to a lesser extent in the Greek aorist and Greek perfect, mainly being imposed on Greek through the Hebrew background of the Apostolic Writers. It is the purpose of this translation to introduce a literary <u>change</u> in the development of English to better accommodate the Hebrew idiom, and the Greek influenced by it. I have judged that this is not a bridge too far for English speakers, and indeed, other historical translations have introduced oddities in the past that have merged into English usage. I do not take this step lightly, but because the indefinite future perfect has an enormous apologetical value in the temporal relationships in Scripture. It is a direct consequence of my chronological work.

17:12 θ The man here is the judge (or other persons responsible) that refuse to implement the ruling of the High Court which is according to Torah. **χ** "Resh Lakish also said: A heathen who keeps a day of rest, deserves death, for it is written (Gen. VIII, 22), And a day and a night they shall not rest,

threat. But reading the text, we see that the Rabbis simply do not have jurisdiction, nor is the calendar in the list of cases over which a dispute might arise that justice required appealing to a higher court. The only calendar issue that falls in the jurisdiction of the cases is the seventh day (because breaking it is a capital offense), but the Rabbis say if a non-Jew keeps the Şabbaṭh, then he is worthy of death (Sanhedrin 58B). Even if the high priest in a new Temple declared this, it would not be valid, because it is not according to Scripture. If the high priest speaks not according to the mouth of Torah, then his rulings have no validity or moral force (cf. Acts 4:18-20; 5:27-29; 22:5). So we see that even if the Rabbis had jurisdiction, which they do not, their pronouncements only have authority when they are according to Scripture.

The Rabbis' appeal to *unity* on the basis of arrogated authority is not the same as true unity based on what Scripture says. The Soviet Empire had that kind of unity. When Scripture does not command a thing, then appeal to unity to conform in the thing breaks the command to not go along with a majority in doing evil (cf. Exo. 23:2). Those unifying with a majority on a point will create a humanistic unity, but when it is not based on Scripture, then unity is merely a fleshly goal to avoid persecution. It is not founded on truth.

True unity is based on mutual love and faithfulness between the faithful and a knowledge of the truth in the faithful, the same unity by which the Father, the Son, and the Spirit are one.

---

and a master has said: Their prohibition is their death sentence. Rabina said: Even if he rested on a Monday" (Soncino Translation).

The Timing of Sabbaths Explained

The reader should read the Genesis Note on page 444 first, and then come back to this essay. There it is established that the literal definition of 'day' is dawn to dusk, and that the normal time cycle or calendar day is from dawn to dawn, a day and a night. The Sabbath is implict there as being the night of the sixth calendar day and the daytime of the seventh day. It should be noted that the Hebrew term day is defined in several senses, (1) literally dawn to dusk, the light: Gen. 1:5. (2) A time cycle from dawn to dawn: Gen. 1:5. (3) A time period almost a week: Gen. 2:4. (4) A time period of 1000 years: Gen. 2:17; Hos 6:1-2. (5) An indefinite time called "the day of Yăhweh," (6) The indefinite future in prophecy, "in that day," and (7) a time cycle from evening to evening: Lev. 23:32:

But, on the tenth _day_ after this seventh new moon the _day_ of KIPPURIM it is. A holy convocation it will be for ye. And ye will have afflicted your souls. And ye will have brought near an offering by fire to Yăhweh. And any work you shall not do <u>in the bone of this day</u>, because a _day_ of KIPPURIM it is, to KAPPEYR for ye at the face of Yăhweh your Almĭghty, because any soul who will not afflict itself <u>in the bone of this day</u>, then it shall have been cut off from its people. And any soul which will do any work <u>in the bone of this day</u>, then I will have destroyed that soul from from the midst of its people. Any work ye shall not do, [it is] a statue forever for your generatons in all your dwellings. A sabbath of great sabbathing it is for ye. 32bAnd ye will have afflicted your souls in the ninth _day_ after the new moon in the setting. From setting until setting you shall sabbath your sabbath.

We can read through the whole text using the dawn to dusk definition of day every time the word day is mentioned or implied, but when we come to vs. 32b both the precepts for afflicting the soul and for doing no work get extended backward to the evening of the ninth day. Let us turn to Passover:

⁶And on the fifteenth day after this new moon is the feast of unleavened bread to Yăhweh. Seven days unleavened bread you shall eat. On the first day a holy convocation shall be for ye. Any work of service you shall not do. And ye will have brought near a fire offering to Yăhweh seven days. On the seventh day is a holy convocation. Any work of service you shall not do.

Likewise here we may simply treat each day individually as dawn to dusk. But we read over in Exodus 12:

¹⁵Seven days unleavened bread ye shall eat. On the headmost day you shall make sabbath leaven from your houses, because anyone eating leavened bread also will have been cut off that soul from Yisra'el, from the first day through the seventh day.... ¹⁸In the first _moon_ on the fourteenth day after the new moon, in the setting you shall eat unleavened bread through the day twenty first after the new moon in the setting.

And so the precept to sabbath from unleavened bread is extended backwards to the previous day at sunset and terminated on the last day after sunset.

The nights are clearly included in the statement, *from the first day through the seventh*, but in light of Exodus 12:18, the first night must be the one before the 15th day.

And it can hardly be the case that the night in which the Passover lamb is eaten and in which leaven is forbidden that labor is permitted. So we have to comprehend the annual Sabbaths on the first and seventh days as including the nights before each.

Can you see the pattern? Yăhwen was done with all of his work at evening on the sixth day. He ordered that we afflict our souls on the evening before the day of KIPPURIM. He also commanded that that Sabbath should begin in the evening. He also commanded we cease from leaven on the evening before the 15th day of the first month.

We find the same pattern in the Sabbatical years, which begin with the first day of the seventh month. Fall is analogous to the evening of the year, and spring and summer to the day part of the Sabbath. The spring equinox begins the solar year as the dawn begins the day, so there are two ways of counting a year besides two ways of counting a day.

Nehemiah commanded that the gates be shut to Jerusalem on the evening before the Sabbath, while the shadows were growing long before sunset (Neh. 13:19-20).

Josephus, as translated by William Whiston states:

> And the last [tower] was erected above the top of the Pastophoria, where one of the priests stood of course, and gave a signal beforehand, with a trumpet, *at the beginning of every seventh day*, in the evening twilight, as also at the evening when the day was finished, as giving notice to the people when they were to leave off work, and when they were to go to work again. (War 4.582).[χ]

According to Mark, the Sabbath clearly ends after the sunset.

But in Mark 14:12 it says:

> Now the headmost day for the unleavened ones, (when they would be sacrificing the Passover), his disciples said to him, "Where do you desire going we should ready, so that you may eat the Passover?"

Ordinarily, the head day of Passover is the 14th., which at least includes dawn to dusk. But which night does Mark include in the day? He includes the night before, so that the night and the day he calls the headmost day. If we say the words were uttered on the 14th day in the daylight, then it becomes inexplicable how the next day can be called the preparation day for the Sabbath since the 14th day that year landed on a Wednesday.

So it must be quite clear that that Mark has referred to it being on a day when it was dark, and that the day referred to is a night and a day. Luke also refers to the "day of unleavens" meaning the headmost day when they removed the leaven. And this must be reckoned from evening to evening. So we have two uses of the word 'day' pertaining to this time cycle, from evening to evening.

Luke 24:21 records:

> And we were hoping that it was he who was about to ransom Yisra'el. But indeed, even with all this, the third day, this day passes by, from when these things happened.

More literally, "the third day, this day is passing by." But according to Luke 24:1, "this day" was the Sabbath. And the third day was counted from dawn on Friday to dawn on the Sabbath, according to the day for the ascending offering with the firstfruits on Nisan 16. If the Sabbath were to be counted from dawn, then it is more likely that they would have said, "the third day passed yesterday," or "the third day, this day has been passed." So they were referring to a day that was passing, present tense, at dawn on a day which began in the evening and was still current.

But traditionalists regard it as still the third day when they are speaking which makes no sense since only the end of the third day should have been cause for giving up hope, which means it was passing that day they were speaking at some point on that day before they were speaking.

It is possible that 'day' in 'day of the Sabbaths' refers to the day part belonging to a longer period called the Sabbaths, which are a night and a day. In this respect Matthew 28:1 refers to the Sabbath and then to the day of the Sabbaths (q.v.), which is the seventh day.

χ For the italic words Josephus wrote in Greek, ἑκάστην ἑβδομάδα, 'each week,' and not 'at the beginning of every seventh day.' Whiston was not a very good translator here.

Mark

1 ¹The beginning of the good news of Yĕshua the Anŏinted, the Almĭghty Sŏn, ²even as it has been getting written in the prophets, "BEHOLD, I SEND MY MESSENGER BEFORE YOUR FACE, WHO WILL PREPARE THE WAY OF YOU BEFORE YOU.ᵟ ³THE VOICE OF ONE CRYING IN THE WILDERNESS, MAKE READY THE WAY OF YĂHWEH, BE MAKING STRAIGHT THE PATHS FOR HIM!ᵞ"

⁴Yoḣanan the Immerser ͨappeared in the wilderness announcing an immersion of being sorry and turning the heart toward the release from sins.ᵅ ⁵And all the country of Yehudah was going out to him, and all the people of Yerushalayim, and they were being immersed by him in the Yardᵉn River, confessing their sins. ⁶And Yoḣanan had been getting dressed with camel's hair and a leather belt around his waist, and eating locusts and wild honey. ⁷And he was proclaiming, and saying, "After me One is coming who is mightier than I, and I am not fit to stoop down and untie the strap of his sandals. ⁸I immersed you with water, but he will immerse you with the Holy Spĭrit."

⁹And it came about in those daysᵅ that Yĕshua came from Netseret̩h in Galil, and was immersed by Yoḣanan in the Yardᵉn. ¹⁰And immediately coming up out of the water, he saw the heavens being ᵝtorn asunder, and the Spĭrit like a dove descending upon him, ¹¹and a voice came out of the heavens: "You are my beloved Sŏn; with you I have been well-pleased."

¹²And immediately the Spĭrit drove him out into the wilderness. ¹³And he was in the wilderness ᶓforty days being tempted by Satan, and he was with the wild beasts, and the messengers were ministering to him.

¹⁴And after Yoḣanan was imprisoned,ᶲ Yĕshua came into Galil,ᵚ announcing the good news of the Almĭghty, ¹⁵and saying, "The season has been getting filled up, and the kingdom of the Almĭghty has been nearing. Be sorry, turning your heart and be holding faithful in the good news!"

¹⁶And as he was ᵠgoing along beside the Sea of Galil, he saw Şim'on and Andrew, the brother of Şim'on, casting a net in the sea, because they were fishermen. ¹⁷And Yĕshua said to them, "Follow me, and I will make you fishers of men." ¹⁸And they immediately left the nets and followed him. ¹⁹And going on a little farther, he saw Ya'aqov the son of Zavdai, and Yoḣanan his brother, who were also in the boat mending the nets. ²⁰And immediately he called them, and they left their father Zavdai in the boat with the hired servants, and went away to follow him.

²¹And they went into Kefar-Naḣum, and straightaway on the Şabbat̩hs he entered the congregation and was teaching. ²²And they were amazed at his

---

1:2 δ Mal 3:1; **1:3** γ Isa 40:3. **1:4** τ Mid spring, AD 29. **1:4** α An immersion of being sorry and turning the heart [from sin] teaches under the symbolism of water cleansing the releasing of sins to gain the release from sin called forgiveness. See Mat. 26:28 ψ; Acts 2:38 ψ. Dipping in the cleansing water signifies the need to turn away from the filth of sin. **1:9** α Near the last day of Av, AD 29; **1:10** β→asunder: See Mark 15:38. **1:13** ξ→days: Elul 1 to Tishri 11. See Matthew 4:2 notes. **1:14** φ Late fall, AD 30. **1:14** ω Tevet, AD 31. **1:16** ψ→along: Shevat, AD 31.

teaching, because he was teaching them as one having authority, and not as the scribes. ²³And⁽ᵖ⁾ there had been in their congregation a man with an unclean spirit, and he cried out, ²⁴saying, "What's our business and yours, Yĕshua Ha-Netseri? Have you come to destroy us? I have been knowing who you are—the Holy One of the Almĭghty!" ²⁵And Yĕshua rebuked him, saying, "Be quiet, and come out of him!" ²⁶And throwing him into convulsions, the unclean spirit cried out with a loud voice, and came out of him. ²⁷And they were all amazed, so that they debated among themselves, saying, "What is this? A new-made teaching with authority! He commands even the unclean spirits, and they obey him." ²⁸And straightaway the news about him went out everywhere into all the surrounding district of Galil.

²⁹And straightaway after they came out of the congregation, they came into the house of Şim'on and Andrew, with Ya'aqov and Yoḣanan. ³⁰Now Şim'on's mother-in-law was lying sick with a fever, and straightaway they spoke to him about her. ³¹And he came to her and raised her up, taking her by the hand, and the fever left her, and she waited on them.

³²And when it was later, after the sun set⁽φ⁾, they were bringing to him all who were ill and those who were demon-possessed. ³³And the whole town had been gathering itself at the door. ³⁴And he healed many who were ill with various diseases, and cast out many demons, and he was not permitting the demons to speak, because they had been recognizing him.

³⁵And in the early morning, while it was still dark, he arose and went out and departed to a lonely place, and was praying there. ³⁶And Şim'on and his companions hunted for him, ³⁷and they found him, and said to him, "Everyone is looking for you." ³⁸And he says to them, "Let us be going somewhere else, to the towns nearby, in order that I mighṭ proclaim there also, because that is what I came out for." ³⁹And he went into their congregations throughout all Galil, proclaiming and casting out the demons.

⁴⁰And a leper came to him, imploring him and falling on his knees before him, and saying to him, "If you may be willing, you are able to make me clean." ⁴¹And moved with compassion, he stretched out his hand, and touched him, and said to him, "I am willing. Be cleansed." ⁴²And straightaway the leprosy left him and he was cleansed. ⁴³And he sternly warned him and straightaway sent him away, ⁴⁴and he says to him, "Be seeing that you will have said nothing to anyone, but be going, show yourself to the priest and offer for your cleansing what Mosḣeh commanded, for a testimony to them." ⁴⁵But he went out and began to proclaim it freely and to spread the news about, to such an extent that Yĕshua could no longer publicly enter a city, but he stayed out in unpopulated areas, and they were coming to him from everywhere.

1:23 ψ Omit εὐθεὼς *straightaway*. He had been teaching on several Sabbaths. **1:32** φ This is proof positive that the Sabbath was ended after the sunet had set.

2 ¹And when he came back to Kefar-Naḥum several days afterward, it was heard that he was at home. ²And many were gathered together, so that there was no longer room, even near the door, and he was speaking the word to them. ³And they came, bringing to him a paralytic, carried by four men. ⁴And being unable to get to him because of the crowd, they removed the roof above him, and when they dug an opening, they let down the pallet on which the paralytic was lying. ⁵And Yĕshua seeing their steadfastness said to the paralytic, "My son, your sins are getting forgiven." ⁶But there were some of the scribes sitting there and reasoning in their hearts, ⁷"Why does this man speak that way? He is blaspheming. Who can forgive sins except one, the Almĭghty?"

⁸And immediately Yĕshua, aware in his spirit that they were reasoning that way within themselves, said to them, "Why are you reasoning about these things in your hearts? ⁹Which is easier work, to say to the paralytic, 'Your sins are getting forgiven', or to have said, 'Be rising, and take up your bed and be walking'? ¹⁰But in order that you will have been knowing that the Sŏn of Man has authority on earth to be forgiving sins on the earth," he says to the paralytic, ¹¹"I say to you, be rising, take up your pallet and be going to your home." ¹²And he rose and straightaway took up the pallet and went out in the sight of all, so that they were all amazed and were glorifying the Almĭghty, saying, "We have never seen anything like this."

¹³And he went out again beside the seashore, and all the crowd was coming to him, and he was teaching them.

¹⁴And passing by, he saw Levi the son of Ḥalfai sitting in the tax office, and he says to him, "Be following me!" And he rose and followed him.

¹⁵And it came about that he was reclining in his house, and many tax-collectors and sinners were dining with Yĕshua and his disciples, because there were many of them, and they were following him. ¹⁶And when the Perushi scribes saw that he was eating with the sinners and tax-collectors, they were saying to his disciples, "Why is he eating and drinking with tax-collectors and sinners?" ¹⁷And hearing this, Yĕshua said to them, "It is not those who are healthy who need a doctor, but those who are sick. I did not come to call the righteous, but sinners."

¹⁸And^τ Yoḥanan's disciples and the Perushim were fasting, and they came and said to him, "Why do Yoḥanan's disciples and the disciples of the Perushim fast, but your disciples do not fast?" ¹⁹And Yĕshua said to them, "While the bridegroom is with them, the attendants of the bridegroom do not fast, do they? So long as they have the bridegroom with them, they cannot fast. ²⁰But the days will come when the bridegroom will have been taken away from them, and then they will fast in that day. ²¹No one sews a patch of unshrunk cloth on an old garment. Otherwise the patch pulls away from it, the new-made from the old, and a worse tear results. ²²And no one puts young wine into old wineskins (otherwise the wine will burst the skins, and the wine is lost, and the skins) but

---

2:18 τ Adar, AD 31.

young wine into new-made wineskins."

²³And it came aboutᵀ that he was passing through the grain fields on the Şabbaṭhs, and his disciples began to make their way along while picking the heads. ²⁴And the Perushim were saying to him, "See here, why are they doing what is not lawful on the Şabbaṭhs?" ²⁵And he was saying to them, "Have you never read what David did when he was in need and became hungry, he and his companions, ²⁶how he entered the house of the Almĭghty in the time of Evyatar the high priest, and ate the consecrated bread, which is not lawful to eat except the priests, and he gave also to those who were with him?" ²⁷And he was saying to them, "The Şabbaṭh was made for man, and not man for the Şabbaṭh. ²⁸Consequently, the Sŏn of Man is Măster even of the Şabbaṭh."

3 ¹And he entered again into a congregation, and a man was there with a hand, which had been wasting away. ²And they were watching him, if on the Şabbaṭhs he would healᶿ in order that they might accuse him. ³And he says to the man with the withered hand, "Be rising up in the center!" ⁴And he says to them, "Is it lawful on the Şabbaṭhs to do good or to do harm, to rescue a life or to kill?" But they kept silent. ⁵And after looking around at them with anger, grieved at their hardness of heart, he says to the man, "Stretch out your hand." And he stretched it out, and his hand was restored. ⁶And the Perushim went out and straightaway were taking counsel with the Herodians against him, as to how they could destroy him.

⁷And Yĕshua withdrew to the sea with his disciples, and a great multitude from Galil followed, and also from Yehudah, ⁸and from Yerushalayim, and from Edom, and beyond the Yarden, and the vicinity of Tsor and Tsidon, a great crowd heard of all that he was doing and came to him. ⁹And he told his disciples that a boat should be standing ready for him because of the crowd, in order that they may not be crowding him, ¹⁰because he had healed many, with the result that all those who had afflictions pressed about him so that they might touch him. ¹¹And whenever the unclean spirits beheld him, they would fall down before him and cry out, saying, "You are the Almĭghty Sŏn!" ¹²And he was sternly rebuking them so that they may not make him known.

2:23 τ Passover week, AD 31. See Luke 6:1 where this began, but the disciples made it a habit.
2:24 The basic charge was made on more than one occasion, as the disciples were in the habit of doing this. However, Yĕshua's answer probably was given on just one occasion, and most definitely it was the second first Şabbaṭh (see Luke 6:1), which is the first Şabbaṭh after Passover.
3:2 φ All the Greek texts (except Codex Bezae) add the word αὐτόν, him, after heal. They also all read "Şabbaṭhs" (plural) in the Greek: σάββασιν. The text makes no sense that way. The English translations neglect the plural in Mark 1:21; Mark 2:23, 24; 3:2, 4; Mat. 12:1, 5, 10, 11, 12; 28:1 2x; Luke 4:31; 6:2; 13:10; 24:1; John 20:1, 19. Where we expect a singular, one occurs, such as in the 2nd use of Mat. 12:5; Mat. 12:8; Mat. 24:20; Mark 2:27; Mark 2:28; Mark 16:1; Luke 6:1; Luke 6:5; Luke 6:6; Luke 13:14; Luke 13:16; Luke 14:1; Luke 23:54; 23:56; John 5:9, 10. There is only one extant text I am aware of that appears to use a plural where a singular is expected, i.e. Mat. 12:11. But the oldest mss evidence for this plural is codex Sinaiticus, AD 325-360, which is 275-310 years after Matthew.

¹³And he went up to the mountain and summoned those whom he himself wanted, and they came to him. ¹⁴And he appointed twelve, that they may be with him, and that he may be sending them out to proclaim, ¹⁵and to have authority to cast out the demons.

¹⁶And he appointed the twelve: Şim'on (to whom he gave the name Peter), ¹⁷and Ya'aqov, the son of Zavdai, and Yohanan the brother of Ya'aqov. To them he gave the name Ben-ei-Regesh, which means, "Sons of Thunder", ¹⁸and Andrew, and Philip, and Bar-Talmai, and Mattatyahu, and Toma, and Ya'aqov the son of Halphai, and Taddai, and Şim'on the Zealot, ¹⁹and Yehudah Ish-Qeriyot, who also betrayed him. ²⁰And he came home, and the crowd gathered again, to such an extent that they could not even eat a meal. ²¹And when those close to him heard, they went out to sieze him, because they were saying, "He is beside himself."

²²And the scribes who came down from Yerushalayim were saying, "He is possessed by Ba'al-zevul," and "He casts out the demons by the ruler of the demons." ²³And he called them to himself and began speaking to them in parables, "How can Satan cast out Satan? ²⁴And if a kingdom may have been divided against itself, that kingdom cannot stand. ²⁵And if a house may have been divided against itself, that house will not be able to stand. ²⁶And if Satan has risen up against himself and is divided, he cannot stand, but he is finished! ²⁷But no one can enter the strong man's house and plunder his property unless he first may have bound the strong man, and then he will plunder his house. ²⁸Amen, I say to you, all sins will be forgiven the sons of men, and whatever evil words they may have evilly spoken, ²⁹but whoever may have spoken evilly against the Holy Spirit has no forgiveness ᵖinto the ageᵖ, but is held bound by an enduring sinˣ." ³⁰For they were saying, "He has an unclean spirit."

³¹Andᵗ his mother and his brothers arrived, and standing outside they sent to him, and called him. ³²And a crowd was sitting around him, and they said to him, "Behold, your mother and your brothers are outside looking for you." ³³And answering them, he said, "Who are my mother and my brothers?" ³⁴And looking about on those who were sitting around him, he said, "Behold, my mother and my brothers! ³⁵For whoever may have done the will of the Almĭghty, he is my brother and sister and mother."

4 ¹And he began to teach again beside the sea. And such a very great crowd gathered to him that he got into a boat on the sea and sat down, and the whole crowd was by the sea on the land. ²And he was teaching them many things in parables, and was saying to them in his teaching, ³"Be listening! Behold, the sower went out to sow, ⁴and it came about that as he was sowing, some fell beside the road, and the birds came and ate it up. ⁵And some fell on the rocky ground where it did not have much soil, and straightaway it sprang up because

---

3:29 See Mat. 12:32; Luke 12:10. p-p. Some omit. x. Some read χρισεως = judgment. **3:31** τ See Matthew 12:46-50. Early summer, AD 31.

it had no depth of soil. ⁶And after the sun rose, it was scorched, and because it had no root, it withered away. ⁷And others fell among the thorns, and the thorns came up and choked it, and it yielded no crop. ⁸And others fell into the good soil, and as they grew up and increased, they yielded a crop and produced thirty, sixty, and a hundredfold." ⁹And he was saying, "He who is having ears to be hearing, let him be hearing."

¹⁰And when he was down alone, those around him, *along* with the twelve, were asking him about the parables. ¹¹And he was saying to them, "To you has been getting given the mystery of the kingdom of the Almĭghty, but those who are outside get everything in parables, ¹²IN ORDER THAT SEEING, THEY MAY BE SEEING AND WILL NOT HAVE PERCEIVED, AND HEARING, THEY MAY BE HEARING AND MAY NOT BE UNDERSTANDING, LEST AT SOME TIME THEY MAY HAVE RETURNED AND THEY WILL HAVE BEEN FORGIVEN⁺."

¹³And he said to them, "Have you not been understanding this parable? Then how will you understand any of the parables? ¹⁴The sower sows the word. ¹⁵And these are the ones who are beside the road where the word is being sown, and when they may have heard, immediately Satan comes and takes away the word which has been getting sown in them. ¹⁶And in a similar way these are the ones on whom seed was sown on the rocky places, who, when they may have heard the word, immediately receive it with joy, ¹⁷and they have no firm root in themselves, but they are only temporary, then, when affliction or persecution arises because of the word, immediately they fall away. ¹⁸And others are the ones on whom seed was sown among the thorns. These are the ones who have heard the word, ¹⁹and the worries of the age, and the deceitfulness of riches, and the desires for other things enter in and choke the word, and it becomes unfruitful. ²⁰And those, which are the ones on whom seed was sown on the good soil, are whomever is hearing the word and accepting it, and bearing fruit, thirty, sixty, and a hundredfold."

²¹And he was saying to them, "A lamp is not brought so that it might be put under a peck-measure, is it, or under a bed? Is it not brought so that it may be placed on the lampstand? ²²For nothing is hidden, except so that it will have been revealed, nor has anything been secret, unless also that it shall have come to light. ²³If any one is having ears to be hearing, let him be hearing."

²⁴And he was saying to them, "Be watching out what you are listening to. By your standard of measure it will be measured to you, and more will be given you. ²⁵For whoever holds fast, to him will more be given, and whoever does not hold fast, even what he has will be taken away from him."

²⁶And he was saying, "The kingdom of the Almĭghty is like a man who will

---

4:12 ⳁ Isa 6:9-10. **4:25** This was one of Yĕshua's frequent sayings. The verb ἔχω does not just mean to have something in a passive sense. It also includes the idea of holding onto something. Delitzsch completely missed the point with שֶׁיֶּשׁ־לוֹ and שֶׁאֵין־לוֹ. A proper Hebrew verb to express the right idea is אָחַז. Whoever is intellectually honest with the truth, to him more will be given, and whoever does not hold to it, because he is dishonest with himself and what he already knows, even what truth he has, he will be deprived of.

have scattered seed upon the earth, ²⁷and will be sleeping and will be rising, night and day, and the seed will be sprouting up and will be growing—how, he himself has not been knowing. ²⁸The soil is producing crops by itself, first the blade, then the head, then the full grain in the head. ²⁹But when the crop may have permitted, he immediately is putting in the sickle, because the harvest has been standing by."

³⁰And he was saying, "How shall we have pictured the kingdom of the Almĭghty, or by what parable shall we have presented it? ³¹It is like a mustard seed, which, when it may have been sown upon the soil, though it is smaller than all the seeds that are upon the soil, ³²yet when it may have been sown, grows up and becomes larger than all the garden plants and forms large branches, so that the birds of heaven can nest under its shade."

³³And with many such parables he was speaking the word to them as they were able to hear it, ³⁴and he did not speak to them without a parable, but he was explaining everything privately to his own disciples.

³⁵And on that day,* when it had become later, he says to them, "We should go over to the other side." ³⁶And leaving the crowd, they took him along with them, just as he was, in the boat, and other boats were with him. ³⁷And there arose a fierce gale of wind, and the waves were breaking over the boat so much that the boat was already filling up. ³⁸And he himself was in the stern, asleep on the cushion, and they awoke him and said to him, "Teacher, do you not care that we are perishing?" ³⁹And when he awoke, he rebuked the wind and said to the sea, "Be quieting; you will have been calming yourself down." And the wind died down and it became a great calm. ⁴⁰And he said to them, "Why are you so timid? How is it that you have no firmness?" ⁴¹And they became very much afraid and said to one another, "Who then is this, that even the wind and the sea obey him?"

5

¹And they came to the other side of the sea, into the country of the Gadriyim. ²And when he came out of the boat, immediately a man from the tombs with an unclean spirit met him, ³and he had his dwelling among the tombs. And no one was able to bind him anymore, even with a chain, ⁴because he had often been getting restrained with shackles and chains—the chains having been getting torn asunder by him, and the shackles having been getting shattered, and none had been strong enough to subdue him. ⁵And constantly night and day, among the tombs and in the mountains, he was crying out and gashing himself with stones.

⁶And when he saw Yĕshua from a distance, he ran up and bowed down before him, ⁷and crying out with a loud voice, he said, "What do I have to do with you, Yĕshua, O Sŏn who is the Almĭghty, the Most High? I implore you by the Almĭghty, *that* you will not have tormented me!" ⁸For he was saying to him, "Come out

---

4:35 τ Fall, AD 31. **5:7** Or, "Sŏn, the Almĭghty One, the Most High One;" (υἱὲ τοῦ θΥ τοῦ ὑψίστου). The genitive can be regarded as a genitive of apposition, i.e. "a son [who is] the Almĭghty, [who is] the Most High" (See Wallace, pg. 95). Also Wallace's example, | "εἰς τὰ κατώτερα μέρη τῆς γῆς" (Eph. 4:9), "into the lower parts, [which is] the earth." Also, "in Matt 2:22 we read ἀνεχώρησεν εἰς τὰ μέρη τῆς Γαλιλαίας. The translation might either be "he departed for the regions [of Israel], namely, Galilee" or, "he departed

of the man, you unclean spirit!" ⁹And he was asking him, "What is your name?" And he said to him, "My name is Legion, because we are many." ¹⁰And he was entreating him earnestly so that he will not have sent them out of the country. ¹¹Now there was a big herd of pigs feeding there on the mountain. ¹²And the demons entreated him, saying, "Send us into the pigs so that we might enter them." ¹³And he gave them permission. And coming out, the unclean spirits entered the pigs, and the herd rushed down the steep bank into the sea, about two thousand of them, and they were drowned in the sea. ¹⁴And those pasturing them ran away and reported it in the city and out in the country. And they came to see what it is that had been happening. ¹⁵And coming to Yĕshua, also they do see the demonized man sitting, who had been getting dressed, and showing mental stability, the very one who had been having the legion, and they were afraid. ¹⁶And those who had seen it described to them how it had happened to the demon-possessed man, and all about the pigs. ¹⁷And they began to beg him to depart from their region.

¹⁸And as he was getting into the boat, the man who was demon-possessed was entreating him that he may be with him. ¹⁹And he did not let him, but he says to him, "Be going home to yours and report to them what great things Yăhweh has been doing for you, and how he had mercy on you." ²⁰And he went away and began to proclaim in Decapolis what great things Yĕshua had done for him, and everyone was amazed.

²¹And when Yĕshua crossed over again in the boat to the other side, a great crowd gathered about him, and he stayed beside the seashore. ²²And one of the congregation officials named Ya'ir came up, and upon seeing him, fell at his feet, ²³and implored him earnestly, saying, "My little daughter is at the point of death, wherein having come, you may lay hands on her, so that she will have been delivered, and will have lived."

²⁴And he went off with him, and a great crowd was following him and pressing in on him. ²⁵And a woman who had a hemorrhage for twelve years, ²⁶and had endured much at the hands of many doctors, and had spent all that she had and was not helped at all, but rather had grown worse, ²⁷after hearing about Yĕshua, came up in the crowd behind him, and touched his cloak. ²⁸For she was saying, "If I just will have touched his garments, I will be delivered." ²⁹And immediately the flow of her blood was dried up, and she knew in her body that she had been getting healed of her affliction. ³⁰And immediately Yĕshua, perceiving in himself that the power from him had gone forth, turned around in the crowd and was saying, "Who touched my garments?" ³¹And his disciples were saying to him, "You see the crowd pressing in on you, and you say, 'Who touched me?'" ³²And

---

for the regions that constitute Galilee." (pg. 99-100). Also the phrase "εἰς δόξαν θεοῦ πατρός" (Phil. 2:11) is "to the glory of Gŏd, [who is] Father," or "Gŏd the Father," and not *"Gŏd of the father." It may be stated that υἱὲ τοῦ θΥ is ambiguous, "Son of the Almĭghty," or "Son [who is] the Almĭghty," and I would say the first idea is already implied in the second case, but that the first case in English does not make the point that would be evident in Greek or Hebrew. Therefore, it is better to translate according to the latter case. There is no case in Scripture of the phrase 'Sŏn of Gŏd' being applied to a mere man. It always means or connotes, 'Divine Son.'

he looked around to see the woman who had done this. ³³But the woman, fearing and trembling, who had been knowing what had been happening to her, came and fell down before him, and told him the whole truth. ³⁴And he said to her, "Daughter, your ᶿfaithfulness has been making you well. Be going ᵠinto peace, and be being well of your affliction."

³⁵While he was still speaking, they came from the house of the congregation official, saying, "Your daughter has died. Why trouble the Teacher anymore?" ³⁶But Yĕshua, having heard the word being spoken, says to the congregation ruler, "Do not be getting afraid, only be holding faithful." ³⁷And he allowed no one to follow with him, except Peter and Ya'aqov and Yoḥanan the brother of Ya'aqov.

³⁸And they came to the house of the congregation official, and he beheld a commotion, and people loudly weeping and wailing. ³⁹And entering in, he said to them, "Why make a commotion and weep? The child has not died, but is asleep." ⁴⁰And they were laughing at him. But putting them all out, he took along the child's father and mother and his own companions, and entered the room where the child was.

⁴¹And taking the child by the hand, he said to her, "Talyeta Qumi;" which translated means, "Little girl, I say to you, be rising!" ⁴²And immediately the girl rose and was walking, because she was twelve years old. And immediately they were completely astounded. ⁴³And he gave them strict orders that no one should know about this, and he said *something should* be given her to eat.

6

¹And⁺ he went out from there, and he came into his home town, and his disciples followed him. ²And when the Şabbaṯh came, he began to teach in the congregation, and the many listeners were astonished, saying, "Where did this man get these things, and what is this wisdom given to him, and such miracles as these performed by his hands? ³Is not this the carpenter, the son of Miryam, and brother of Ya'aqov, and Yosei, and Yehudah, and Şim'on? Are not his sisters here with us?" And they took offense at him. ⁴And Yĕshua said to them, "A prophet is not without honor except in his home town and among his own relatives and in his own household." ⁵And he could do no miracle there except that he laid his hands upon a few sick people and healed them. ⁶And he wondered at their unfaithfulness.

⁶ᵇAnd he was going around the villages teaching;ᶝ

⁷Then he calls near the twelve and began to be sending them out two by two,

---

5:34 θ and *faithfulness, steadfastness, holding faithful*. **5:34** ψ εἰς. Physical healing is not just in view here, but the text points strongly in the direction of future spiritual wellness. **5:39** This may sound like deception to some, but it is a parable from Mĕssiah's point of view! He meant that her soul had not died. It was only asleep from his point of view, though her body was dead. It is the second death that destroys both the body and the soul. See Matthew 10:28 and 9:24. Some suppose that sleep refers to her body and that her soul was conscious after death, but the parallelism would require us to apply the denial that she had died to the body also. In that case it would be deception. We must reject the Catholic doctrine of consciousness awakened after death.

6:1 τ Sometime around Kislev, AD 31. See Matthew 13:54-58. **6:6b** ξ Winter, AD 32.

Mark 6

and he was giving them authority over the unclean spirits, ⁸and he instructed them that they may be taking nothing for the road, except only a staff; no bread, no bag, no copper coinage in the*ir* belt, ⁹but having been putting on sandals, and *he added,* "You will not have put on two tunics." ¹⁰And he was saying to them, "Wherever you may have entered into a house, be staying there until you may have left there. ¹¹And whichever place *that* may not have received you, *or even* may not have listened to you, as you are going out from there, shake off the dust under your feet *as a testimony* to them."

¹²And they went out and announced that men should be sorry, turning their heart *from sin.* ¹³And they were casting out many demons and were anointing with oil many sick people and healing them.

¹⁴And king Herod ᵗheard of it, because his name had become well known, and they were saying that, "Yoḥanan the Immerser ᶴhad been getting raised from the dead, and that is why these miraculous powers are at work in him." ¹⁵And others were saying, "He is Ẹliyahu." And others were saying, "He is a prophet, like one of the prophets of old." ¹⁶And, when Herod heard of it, he was saying, "Yoḥanan, whom I beheaded, is risen!"

¹⁷For Herod himself had sent and had Yoḥanan arrested and bound in prison on account of Herodias, the wife of his brother Philip, because he had married her. ¹⁸For Yoḥanan was saying to Herod, "It is not lawful for you to have your brother's wife." ¹⁹And Herodias had been holding a grudge against him and wanted to put him to death and could not do so, ²⁰because Herod was fearing Yoḥanan, having been knowing that he was a righteous and holy man, and so he was keeping him safe. And when he had heard him, he became greatly perplexed, and yet gladly he was hearing him.

²¹And a strategic day came when Herod on his birthday gave a banquet for his lords and military commanders and the leading men of Galil. ²²And when the daughter of Herodias herself came in and danced, she pleased Herod and his dinner guests, and the king said to the girl, "Ask me for whatever you may be wanting and I will give it to you." ²³And he swore to her, "However much, whatever you will have asked me, I will give it to you, up to half of my kingdom." ²⁴And when she went out, she said to her mother, "What will I have asked for?" And, she said, "The head of Yoḥanan the Immerser." ²⁵And immediately, having gone with haste to the king, she asked, saying, "I am wanting that at once, you will have given to me the head of Yoḥanan the Immerser on a plate." ²⁶And although the king was very sorry, yet because of his oaths and because of his dinner guests, he was unwilling to refuse her. ²⁷And immediately the king sent an executioner and commanded him to bring back his head. And he went and

---

6:14 τ Late Adar II, AD 32. **6:14** ζ →raised. A perfect that makes no sense in the present perfect becomes a pluperfect. The actual Greek pluperfect is a secondary tense, which only makes grammatically explicit that which is ambiguous with the Greek perfect, which is by default present perfect progressive, but the present perfect may become past perfect if the context cancels out any notion of the action presently happening. Such is the case here. Yoḥanan was not presently assumed to be rising from the dead, so the action is in the past of the context.

had him beheaded in the prison, ²⁸and brought his head on a platter, and gave it to the girl, and the girl gave it to her mother. ²⁹And when his disciples heard about this, they came and took away his body and laid it in a tomb.

³⁰And the emissaries gathered together with Yĕshua, and they reported to him all that they had done and taught. ³¹And he said to them, "Come away by yourselves to a lonely place and rest a while." (For there were many people coming and going, and they did not even have time to eat.) ³²And they went away in the boat to a lonely place by themselves.

³³And the people saw them going, and many recognized them, and they ran there together on foot from all the cities, and got there ahead of them. ³⁴And when he went ashore, he saw a great crowd, and he felt compassion for them because they were like sheep without a shepherd, and he began to teach them many things.

³⁵And already, having become a late hour,⁺ his disciples, having approached him, were saying that, "The place is desolate, and already it is a late hour. ³⁶Dismiss them, so that having gone into the surrounding countryside and villages, they may buy themselves something they may eat." ³⁷Yet answering, he said to them, "You give them *something* yourselves to eat!" Then they are saying to him, "Having gone, shall we have bought bread with two hundred denari? Then we will give them something to eat!" ³⁸Then he says to them, "How many loaves do you have? Be going; look!" And when they knew, they are saying, "Five, and two fish." ³⁹And he commanded them all to recline party by party on the green grass. ⁴⁰And they laid back plot *by* plot, by hundreds and by fifties. ⁴¹And taking the five loaves and the two fish, looking up to heaven, he blessed *the Almĭghty*, and broke the loaves, and was giving *them* to the disciples, that they may be setting *them* before them, and he divided up the two fish for all. ⁴²And they all ate and were satisfied. ⁴³And they picked up twelve full baskets of the broken pieces, and also of the fish. ⁴⁴And there were five thousand men who ate the loaves.

⁴⁵And immediately he compelled his disciples to step into the boat and to be going before *him* to the other side toward Beṯh-Tsaidah, while he is sending the crowd away. ⁴⁶And having taken leave from them, he departed to the mountain to pray. ⁴⁷And when it had become later, the boat was in the midst of the sea, and he *was* alone on the land. ⁴⁸And when he saw them straining at the rowing, because the wind was against them, at about the fourth watch of the night, he is coming toward them, walking on the sea, and he was intending to pass by them. ⁴⁹But when they saw him walking on the sea, they supposed that it was a ghost, and cried out, ⁵⁰because they all saw him and were frightened. But immediately he spoke with them and says to them, "Be taking courage! I AM!ᵝ Do not be getting frightened!" ⁵¹And he got into the boat with them, and the wind stopped,

---

6:35 τ Near Passover AD 32. **6:50** β I AM (ἐγώ εἰμι) only occurs in absolute usage in Greek when used of or by Yăhweh. See below. Furthermore, the absolute, I AM only translates passages in the LXX where Yăhweh is represented as speaking. ▷ See John 13:19. It is not completely clear if he said אֶהְיֶה *'Ehyeh* or אֲנִי־הוּא *'Ani hu*. Readers of I AM in English or Greek, Ἐγώ εἰμι, at first sight think it refers to I AM in Exodus 3:14 (אהיה). But this is incorrect as I AM is a mistranslation there of the Hiphil אַהְיֶה,

and they were greatly astonished, ⁵²because they had not gained any insight from the incident of the loaves, but their heart had been getting ᶲhardened.

⁵³And when they crossed over they came to land at Ginneisar, and moored to the shore. ⁵⁴And when they came out of the boat, immediately the people

---

which means "I MAKE BECOME," or "I CREATE." See Exodus 3:14 remarks. And it also occurs with a predicate there: "I MAKE BECOME WHAT I MAKE BECOME." The absolute use of Ἐγώ εἰμι occurs in a number of other passages referring only to the Almighty. See below. The Hebrew behind this is אֲנִי־הוּא *Ani hu*, "I AM HE," which only means "I AM HE (Yăhweh)." But the Greek has explained it with Ἐγώ εἰμι, which is an absolute use, "I AM" without a predicate. ▷ The Greek phrase is unique to divine usage, and was chosen to point to the absolute sense of the words, which is apparent in the Hebrew usages of *Ani hu*. If the translation were put, "I am he," then the sense would be lost on most English readers, or if put ἐγώ εἰμι αὐτός lost on Greek speakers. The reference is to Yăhweh. The translation, "I am he" is too likely to be misinterpreted "I am the Měssiah," and the translation "I am He," depends on a written text, and the reader might dismiss the capital He as an opinion. I AM makes the point in English best, but in Hebrew it is more likely that he said אֲנִי־הוּא, which may be translated, "I AM" since the pronoun is sometimes used for the verb "to be." See Deut. 32:39, "I, I AM HE, AND THERE IS NO ALMIGHTY WITH ME" (אֲנִי אָנִי הוּא וְאֵין אֱלֹהִים עִמָּדִי). Also Isa. 43:25, "I, I AM HE WIPING OUT YOUR TRANSGRESSIONS FOR MY SAKE, AND YOUR SINS I WILL NOT REMEMBER" (אָנֹכִי אָנֹכִי הוּא מֹחֶה פְשָׁעֶיךָ לְמַעֲנִי וְחַטֹּאתֶיךָ לֹא אֶזְכֹּר). See other references under Yoh. 13:19. Isa. 52:6, "THEREFORE, MY PEOPLE WILL KNOW MY NAME IN THAT DAY, THAT I AM HE, THE ONE SPEAKING. BEHOLD, IT IS ME" (אֲנִי הוּא, LXX: ἐγώ εἰμι αὐτός). Isa. 43:13, "I AM HE, AND NONE FROM MY HAND IS DELIVERING!" (אֲנִי הוּא וְאֵין מִיָּדִי מַצִּיל). ▷ In Isa 48:12, "ἐγώ εἰμι" stands for "אֲנִי יְהוָה," I am Yăhweh. And a very important point is made about "ἐγώ εἰμι" by scholars, and this is that this absolute use of "I AM" appears nowhere in Greek outside the LXX and NT. In fact, "I AM" is considered meaningless without a predicate. See *I Am He: The Interpretation of Anî Hû in Jewish and Early Christian Literature*, Catrin H. Williams, page 11: "The absolute use of ἐγώ εἰμι is not attested in non-Jewish Greek texts,⁵⁰ and it is also absent from the writings of Josephus and Philo.⁵¹" Catrin Williams also states, "In the Hebrew Scriptures the expression אֲנִי הוּא is primarily encountered in statements pronounced by Yahweh. Indeed, all examples of אֲנִי הוּא in its bipartite form are found in divine declarations" (pg. 15). ▷ It should be noted again that the translators did not choose ἐγώ εἰμι in Greek as an exact translation of *Ani hu*, but to in fact point us to the absolute meaning of the phrase in Hebrew, and the context in which it is used, which are exclusively divine. And again, it has to be emphasized that ἐγώ εἰμι does not occur in ordinary Greek in this absolute sense. ▷ All these "I AM" passages are correctly reproduced "I AM" in English, but we should not regard them as standing for the exact Hebrew in Exodus 3:14. The words are a terse explanation of what must be more carefully understood in the contexts of the passages. In other words, to translate literally in these cases is to convey an incorrect sense. The incorrect sense is, "I he," or "I am he," which would imply that the usage in the original text was ordinary. It is anything but ordinary, and therefore, we have to stick with "I AM" which is literal to the Greek, but not to the underlying Hebrew, except in its exclusive reference to Yăhweh. **6:51** ᶲ The miracle of the loaves was an act of creation by the one who is *A'nî Hū'*, i.e. Yăhweh. See Exodus 3:14. So also the power over the sea showed he was the Creator. Yeshua, in his appearances as the Malakh YHWH concealed his real identity at times. It was also necessary to keep himself mostly concealed after his being begotten as a human until his return to glory because disclosure would jeopardize his mission. This is why the vision in Matthew 17 was to be kept secret, and why the (collective) heart of the disciples (in general) were getting hardened. It was not a sinful hardening, but rather spiritual concealment by the Holy Spirit. Nevertheless, some of the disciples realized the truth, but did not publicize it, or were told not to do so. ▷ Exo. 3:14-15: אֶהְיֶה אֲשֶׁר אֶהְיֶה...כֹּה תֹאמַר לִבְנֵי יִשְׂרָאֵל אֶהְיֶה שְׁלָחַנִי אֲלֵיכֶם...כֹּה־תֹאמַר אֶל־בְּנֵי יִשְׂרָאֵל יְהוָה אֱלֹהֵי אֲבֹתֵיכֶם אֱלֹהֵי אַבְרָהָם אֱלֹהֵי יִצְחָק וֵאלֹהֵי יַעֲקֹב שְׁלָחַנִי אֲלֵיכֶם זֶה־שְּׁמִי לְעֹלָם וְזֶה זִכְרִי לְדֹר דֹּר I = (אֶהְיֶה) I MAKE BE (אֲשֶׁר) WHAT (אֶהְיֶה) MAKE BE... SO YOU WILL SAY TO THE SONS OF YISRAEL I MAKE BE (אֶהְיֶה) HAS SENT ME TO YOU..., SO YOU WILL SAY TO THE SONS OF YISRAEL HE MAKES BE (יְהוָה, YAHWEH), ALMĪGHTY OF YOUR FATHERS, ALMĪGHTY OF AVRAHAM, ALMĪGHTY OF YITSḤAQ, AND ALMĪGHTY OF YA'AQOV, HAS SENT ME TO YOU, AND THIS IS MY NAME FOREVER, AND THIS IS MY MEMORIAL FROM GENERATION TO GENERATION. Exo. 3:15. ▷ Exo. 15:3; Amos 5:8, 9:6: יְהוָה שְׁמוֹ = YAHWEH IS HIS NAME. ▷ Isa. 48:2, 51:15, 54:5; Jer. 10:16; Jer. 31:35, 32:18, 33:2, 46:18, 48:15, 50:34, 51:19; 51:57: יְהוָה צְבָאוֹת שְׁמוֹ. Jer. 23:6: וְזֶה־

recognized him, ⁵⁵and ran about that whole country and began to carry round on their pallets those who were sick, to the place they heard he was. ⁵⁶And wherever he entered villages, or cities, or countryside, they were laying the sick in the market places, and entreating him that they might just touch the tassel of his cloak, and as many as may have touched it were being cured.

7 And˒ the Perushim and some of the scribes gathered together around him when they came from Yerushalayim, ²and they saw that some of his disciples were eating their bread with ˣcommunicable hands, that is, unwashed. ³(For the Perushim and all the ˢYehudim do not eat unless they with fistfuls may have washed their hands, thus observing the traditions of the elders, ⁴and when they come from the market place, they do not eat unless they may have washed *them*, and there are many other things which they have received in order to observe, such as the washing of cups and pitchers and copper pots.)

⁵And the Perushim and the scribes asked him, "Why do your disciples not walk according to the tradition of the elders, but eat their bread with ᵝcommunicable hands?" ⁶And he said to them, "Rightly did Yeshayahu prophesy of you hypocrites, as it has been getting written, "THIS PEOPLE HONORS ME WITH THEIR LIPS, BUT THEIR HEART IS FAR AWAY FROM ME. ⁷But in vain do THEY REVERENCE ME, TEACHING AS DOCTRINES THE PRECEPTS OF MEN.ᵋ"

⁸"Neglecting the commandment of the Almĭghty, you hold to the tradition of men." ⁹He was also saying to them, "You nicely set aside the commandment of the Almĭghty so that you will have preserved your tradition. ¹⁰For Mosheh said, 'BE HONORING YOUR FATHER AND YOUR MOTHER,ᵅ' and, 'HE WHO SPEAKS EVIL OF FATHER OR MOTHER, BY DEATH HE MUST BE ENDING,ᵝ' ¹¹but you say, 'If a man may have said to his father or his mother, anything of mine you might be helped by is Qorban (that is to say, given to the Almĭghty),' ¹²you no longer permit him to do anything for his father or mother, ¹³thus invalidating the word

---

שְׁמוֹ אֲשֶׁר־יִקְרָאוֹ יְהֹוָה צִדְקֵנוּ. See Amos 4:13, 5:27; Zech. 14:9 **7:1** τ Mid spring, AD 32. **7:2** χ→hands: The text says κοιναῖς χερσίν, "common hands." The word κοιναῖς is not used in the LXX (Septuagint) regarding any commandment having to do with unclean things or things regarded as unclean to eat. The word means "shared," or having something "in common." Common hands were <u>defilement sharing</u> hands. They could share uncleanness if they had it. So the more precise meaning in this context is communicable, 'able to communicate.' ▷ If hands became unclean by contact with an unclean substance of any sort, then they were able to communicate the contamination to anything else they touched. But if the hands were immediately washed, then they were not able to communicate the defilement any further, and though unclean till evening, they were not communicable. See Lev. 15:11 where if the hands are not washed, then the person who touched uncleanness of another person has to not only wash his hands, but bathe himself and wash his clothes also. This is because when the hand washing is neglected, the contamination is regarded to have spread to the body and clothes generally or anything else touched. The **unwashed** hands may be <u>sharing defilement</u> (communicable). Lev. 15:11, "AND ANYONE WHO TOUCHES ON HIM, WHO IS DISCHARGING, AND <u>DID NOT RINSE HIS HANDS IN WATER</u>, THEN HE <u>SHALL WASH</u> HIS CLOTHES. ALSO HE <u>SHALL BATHE</u> IN WATER. AND AFTERWARD HE WILL HAVE BEEN UNCLEAN UNTIL THE SETTING." Therefore, the unwashed hands could communicate uncleanness if they had been contaminated. The washing prevented any further sharing of contagion. In the case of eating with unwashed hands, it was only <u>perhaps</u> they were unclean. The washing ended the communicability of possible uncleanness. See Mat. 15; Acts 10; Rom. 14:14, 20. Titus 1:15. **7:3** ζ Used in a geographic sense, of the province of Judea. Judeans. The Galileans ignored these southern rules when it suited them, living as they were at a greater distance from the holy place. **7:5** β cf. 7:2 χ. **7:6-7** ξ Isa 29:13 𝔊 M: מִצְוַת אֲנָשִׁים מְלֻמָּדָה. **7:10** α Exo 20:12, Deu 5:16; **7:10** β Exo 21:17; Lev 20:9.

of the Almĭghty by your tradition, which you have handed down, and you do many things such as that."

¹⁴And after he called the multitude to him again, he was saying to them, "Listen to me, all of you, and understand: ¹⁵there is nothing outside the man which ᵘby itself going into him is able to share defilement with him, but the things proceeding out of a man are the things sharing defilement with the man. ¹⁶If anyone is having ears to be hearing, let him be hearing.ⁿ

¹⁷And when he entered into the house (away from the crowd), his disciples were asking him about the parable. ¹⁸And he says to them, "Likewise are you also without understanding? Do you not understand that anything which ᶲby itself is entering into the man from outside is not able to share defilement with him, ¹⁹ᵃbecause it does not go into his heart, ¹⁹ᵇbut into his stomach, and is eliminated, cleansing all foodsᵠ." ²⁰And he was saying, "That which proceeds out of the man, that is what is sharing defilement with the man. ²¹Because from within, out of the heart of men, evil thoughts are going out: for ʳunlawful sex, theft, adultery, murder, ²²coveting, deceit, wickednessˢ, sensuality, envy, slander, pride *and* foolishness. ²³All these evil things are going out from within. And *any one of them* is sharing defilement with the man.ᵟ"

²⁴And from there he arose and went away to the region of Tsor. And when he entered a house, he wanted no one to know of it, but he could not escape notice. ²⁵But after hearing of him, a woman whose little daughter had an unclean

---

7:15 μ middle voice **7:16** η Some manuscripts omit vs. 16. **7:18** ɸ→itself; here and in 7:15μ, "by itself" (=δι' ἑαυτοῦ, Rom. 14:14) is the reflexive rendition of the middle voice verb. This would correspond to a Niphal stem in Hebrew, meaning "by itself." It does not defile the heart because no intentionality is involved in the intake, and the body has a system for cleansing microscopic impurity.

7:19 ψ The undetected contamination is eliminated by the body's system just as hand washing eliminates outer contamination. The Greek runs thus, "καθαρίζων πάντα τὰ βρώματα", and means "cleansing all the foods." Modern versions extract the words into an editorial remark adding their own words, "*Thus he declared* all foods clean" (ESV). The verb καθαρίζων (cleansing) is illegitimately turned into an adjective. Corrupt versions: ASV, AMP, CEB, CEV, CJB, DLNT, ERV, ESV, ESVUK, EXB, GW, GNT, HCSB, ICB, LEB, TLB, MSG, MOUNCE, NOG, NABRE, NASB, NCV, NET, NIRV, NIV, NIVUK, NLV, NLT, NRSV, NRSVA, NRSVACE, NRSVCE, RSV, RSVCE, VOICE, WEB, GWN, NAB, NJB. **7:21/22** ʳ **D. 7:23** δ The scripture distinguishes between two types of defilement. The first kind (type I) is defilement of the soul, "YOU SHALL NOT MAKE YOUR SOULS ABOMINABLE" (Lev. 11:43-44), which is by eating abominable things (or unnecessary touching of dead bodies), Literally, "NOT YOU SHALL MAKE TO BE THE SOULS OF YOU-ALL ABOMINABLE..." (Lev. 11:43), and "AND NOT YOU SHALL MAKE TO BE UNCLEAN THE SOULS OF YOU ALL" (Lev. 11:44). Since there is a command not to eat those things, it is a sin to defile oneself by them. It defiles the soul. Lev. 11:8, "AND ON THEIR DEAD BODIES YOU SHALL NOT TOUCH." Except by accident, doing this defiles the soul. This type is a sin. ▷ The other type of uncleanness is that which is **natural** to man, caused by monthly cycles, emissions, abnormal discharges, child birth, and diseases. This type II is not a sin to have, but such uncleanness is a sin **only** if transported into the sanctuary (cf. Lev. 15:31). Intercourse renders man and woman ritually unclean. It does not make the soul abominable (polluted, defiled, unclean). It is *only* a sin if transported into the holy places. ▷ Every uncleanness of this second type does not defile the soul itself. Every uncleanness contracted by *second degree* communication of uncleanness is also of this second type, i.e. someone touches a chair that a woman on her cycle sat in. He is unclean. His soul is not defiled. It is only **outward** ritual impurity. It follows further that any sort of *second degree* undetected type I uncleanness does not make the soul impure except when a person recognizes that he broke the commandment and becomes guilty. *Second degree* contamination is that which is transferred from the source by a second object, in this case unclean source to hands, and hands to elsewhere. ▷ Therefore, unwashed hands may only communicate type II uncleanness, which is ritual impurity, but they do not defile food eaten with them so as to render the soul impure. This is because anything forbidden is undetected, and enters only of itself. See Rom 14:14.

spirit, immediately came and fell at his feet. ²⁶Now the woman was a Greek, the Syria-Phoenician kind. And she was asking him, so that he will have cast the demon out of her daughter. ²⁷And he was saying to her, "Let the children be satisfied first, because it is not good to take the children's bread and throw it to the dogs."

²⁸But she answered and says to him, "Yes, Adŏni, but even the dogs under the table feed on the children's crumbs." ²⁹And he said to her, "Because of this answer be going your way. The demon has been ⁿgoing away from your daughter." ³⁰And when she went away to the house,ᵀ she found ʹthe demon having been ⁿgoing away and the daughter, having herself been lying on the bed.ʹ

³¹And again he went out from the region of Tsor, and came through Tsidon to the Sea of Galil, within the region of ᵟTen-Cities. ³²And they brought to him one who was deaf and spoke with difficulty, and they begged him, that he may lay his hand upon him. ³³And he took him aside from the crowd by himself, and put his fingers into his ears, and after spitting, he touched his tongue with the saliva. ³⁴And looking up to heaven with a deep sigh, he said to him, "Ȩṯhpattaḥ!"—That is, "Be opened!" ³⁵And his ears were opened, and the impediment of his tongue was removed, and he was speaking plainly. ³⁶And he ordered them that they may not be telling anyone, but the more he ordered them, the more widely they continued to proclaim it. ³⁷And they were utterly astonished, saying, "He has been doing all things well. He is making even the deaf to be hearing, and the dumb to be speaking."

8 ¹In those days,ᵀ there being again a great crowd, and not having anything they might eat, calling the disciples, he was saying to them, ²"I feel compassion for the crowd because they are sticking with me now three days, and they do not have anything they *possibly* will have eaten. ³And if I may have sent them away hungry to their home, they will faint on the way, and some of them have been ʸcoming from afar."

⁴And his disciples answered him, "Where will anyone be able to find enough to satisfy these men with bread here in a desolate place?" ⁵And he was asking them, "How many loaves do you have?" And they said, "Seven." ⁶And he ordered the crowd to recline on the earth. And taking the seven loaves, giving thanks, he broke them, and was giving them to his disciples so they may be serving, and they served them to the multitude. ⁷They also had a few small fish, and saying a blessing, he ordered these to be served as well. ⁸And they ate and were satisfied,

---

7:29 η see: 7:30 η. **7:30** ᵀ txt 𝔓⁴⁵ D W *f* ¹ 28 it bo^ms vs. ℵ B L Δ *αὐτῆς of her.* **7:30** ʳ txt 𝔓⁴⁵ A W *f* ¹³ 𝔐 sy^h. **7:30** see Mat. 15:22f. **7:30** η the perfect is an unusual case, showing the reluctance of the evil spirit to leave. It was not trespassing on kingdom territory in the first place. It is as if the demon left the daughter when Mĕssiah said so, but tarried at the threshold of the house until it saw the woman returning, and then seeing her renewed spirit and courage, it went out the front door just as the woman was going in, and the woman knew it, or saw it leaving. The recording of these facts indicate that the woman did continue to hold faithful to Mĕssiah. **7:31** δ Δεκαπόλεως = *Decapolis.*

8:1 τ Late spring or early summer, AD 32. **8:3** γ ἥκω or *be present, 'presenting.'*

and they picked up seven large baskets full of what was left over of the broken pieces. ⁹And about four thousand were there, and he sent them away. ¹⁰And immediately he entered the boat with his disciples, and came to the district of Dalmanuta.

¹¹And the Perushim came out and began to argue with him, seeking at his side a sign from heaven, to test him. ¹²And sighing deeply in his spirit, he said, "Why does this kindred seek for a sign? Amen, I am saying to you ᵝtruly a sign will be given to this kindred." ¹³And leaving them, he again embarked and went away to the other side.

¹⁴And they had forgotten to take bread, and did not have more than one loaf in the boat with them. ¹⁵And he was giving orders to them, saying, "Be looking out! Be watching against the leaven of the Perushim and the leaven of Herod." ¹⁶And they were discussing with one another the fact that they had no bread. ¹⁷And Yeshua, when he knew, says to them, "Why are you rationalizing because you are having no bread? Are you not yet realizing or putting it together? Has your heart been getting hardened?ᵋ ¹⁸HAVING EYES, DO YOU NOT SEE? AND HAVING EARS, DO YOU NOT HEAR?ᶿ And do you not remember, ¹⁹when I broke the five loaves for the five thousand, how many baskets full of broken pieces you picked up?" They said to him, "Twelve." ²⁰"And when I broke the seven for the four thousand, how many large baskets full of broken pieces did you pick up?" And they said to him, "Seven." ²¹And he was saying to them, "Do you not yet understand?"

²²And they came to Beth-Tsaidah. And they brought a blind man to him, and

---

8:12 β εἰ = אִם. See Gesenius: "Its primary power I regard as demonstrative, (*Lo! Behold!*) kindred to הֵן (ἤν *en* [contr. fr. εἰ ἄν and ἐάν; also *see there!* cf. LSJ. **VI.**]), Arab. *truly, certainly* ...(The Hebrew interpreters, explain this אִם which they rightly notice to be affirmative, by אָמְנָה, and they consider it shortened from אָמֵן; I should prefer from אָמַר." See BDAG 3rd, 'NColeman, JTS 28, 1927, 159-67 interprets this as strongly positive.' Also it could be 'when,' the 'if' expressing only uncertainty as to timing, Gesenius No. 4: 'a particle of time, *when* (compare the Germ. **wenn** and **wann**, and Engl. *when*). The negative usage was not current in Koine Greek, except in quotations of archaic material. See on Acts 26:23; Gal. 5:11; Ep. Alex 7:15. Coleman's trans. is, 'I tell you truly, there shall indeed be given to this generation a sign!" This trans. makes a lot of sense, especially if the answer was solicited more than once. For they already had heard the full answer: the sign of Yonah. The timing condition was when they would 'get' the sign for themselves.

8:17 ξ Yeshua's identity was being generally (by the Spirit) protected from discovery until the proper time. Most of the disciples were not getting it for this reason, though some did. The concealment was collective. The Messenger of Yahweh previously concealed his identity for strategic reasons. So also the Holy Spirit does now conceal what he does not want yet discovered, and though some with eyes open and listening hard will find it, it will be kept from general view until a time of his own choosing. Mark's theme about their 'getting hardened' is thematic, and a parable in itself. The disciples were not sinners that had no ears to hear like the poor soils in the parable of the sower. And this has to be taken into account, as well as the reason they 'had been getting hardened.' Yeshua knows the reason on the one hand, but on the other he is hoping that some will get it. ▷ Firstly, they picked up 12 smaller baskets (κοφίνους) with an initial cost of 5 loaves. The leftovers exceed the input by sevenfold (12-5 = 7). In the second case they began with 7 and ended with 7 'large baskets' (σπυρίδων). Again the leftovers exceeded, this time in size, but their number was 7, whereas it might have been a different number if the smaller baskets were used. Both miracles were miracles of creation. And after creation was finished, the Almighty declared his creation to be completed on the seventh day. Why were they amazed at the miracle of the sea? It was because they were not understanding who he was. The leftovers are the Creator's signature on his creation, the sign that they were seeking (cf. 11-13). **8:18** θ Jer 5:21.

begged him, so that he may touch him. ²³And taking the blind man by the hand, he brought him out of the village, and after spitting on his eyes, and laying his hands upon him, he asked him, "Do you see anything?" ²⁴And he looked up and said, "I see men, because I am seeing them like trees, walking about." ²⁵Then again he laid his hands upon his eyes, and he looked intently and was restored, and was seeing everything clearly. ²⁶And he sent him to his home, saying, "You will not have even entered the village."

²⁷And᛭ Yĕshua went out, along with his disciples, to the villages of Caesarea Philippi, and on the way he questioned his disciples, saying to them, "Who do people say that I am?" ²⁸And they told him, saying, "Yohanan the Immerser, and others say Ĕliyahu, but others, one of the prophets." ²⁹And he continued by questioning them, "But who do you say that I am?" Peter answered and said to him, "You are the Anŏinted." ³⁰And he warned them that they should be telling no one about him. ³¹And he began to teach them that the Sŏn of Man must suffer many things and be rejected by the elders and the chief priests and the scribes, and be killed, and after three days rise again.ᵠ ³²And he was stating the matter plainly. And Peter took him aside and began to rebuke him. ³³But turning around and seeing his disciples, he rebuked Peter, and said, "Be getting behind me, Satan, because you are not setting your mind on the Almĭghty's interests, but man's."

³⁴And he summoned the multitude with his disciples, and said to them, "If anyone wishes to come after me, let him deny himself, and take up his execution timber, and be following me. ³⁵For whoever may be wishing to rescue his soul will lose it, but whoever will lose his soul for my sake and the good news will rescue it. ³⁶For what does it profit a man to gain the whole world, and forfeit his soul? ³⁷For what will a man have given in exchange for his soul? ³⁸For whoever may have been ashamed of me and my words among this adulterous and sinful kindred, the Sŏn of Man will also be ashamed of him when he may have come in the glory of his Făther with the holy messengers."

9

¹And he was saying to them᛭, "Amen I say to you, there are some of those who have been standing here who, no, they will not have tasted death until they will have seen *to* the kingdom of the Almĭghty, ᶿhaving been coming with power."

²And after six days, Yĕshua took with him Peter and Ya'aqov and Yohanan, and brought them up to a high mountain by themselves. And he was transfigured before them, ³and his garments became radiant and exceedingly white, as no

---

8:27 τ Winter, early AD 33. **8:31** ψ From Messiah's point of view (on the occasion of this utterance), this means after the third literal day, a day being defined as *dawn* to *dusk*, which then is the night after the third day. But this is still in the third *calendar day*, since a calendar day is *dawn* to *dawn*. So to state "*on* the third day" is the same time as *after* three days, keeping the right definition of day in mind for each saying. See parallel passages in Matthew 16:21 and Luke 9:22. Mark also says "after three days" in 9:31. ▷ In Greek and Latin "after three days" means the same as "the third day after," which if counting by hours is between 48 and 72 hours later than when he is killed. The Hebrew idiom only counts *after a day* when a day ends. So count the third day as between 48 and 72 hours after the sun went down on the day he was killed. But Friday to Sunday morning is not more than 42 hours and does not fit either definition.

9:1 τ About Adar, AD 33. **9:1** θ→coming: ἐληλυθυῖαν; the present participle is used in Mat. 16:28 (ἐρχόμενον). See *Luke 9:27* also.

launderer on earth can whiten them. ⁴And Ĕliyahu appeared to them along with Moshˑeh, and they were talking with Yĕshua. ⁵And Peter answered and says to Yĕshua, "Rabbi, it is good for us to be here, and let us have made three shelters, one for you, and one for Moshˑeh, and one for Ĕliyahu," ⁶because he had not been knowing what he should answer, because they had become terrified.

⁷Then a cloud formed, overshadowing them, and a voice came out of the cloud, "This is my beloved Sŏn, be listening to him!" ⁸And all at once they looked around and saw no one with them anymore, but Yĕshua alone.

⁹And as they were coming down from the mountain, he gave them orders that they should not narrate even to one person what they saw, until the Sŏn of Man may have risen from the dead. ¹⁰And they kept the matter to themselves, discussing with one another what 'risen from the dead' could mean.

¹¹And they were asking him, saying that the scribes say that "Ĕliyahu is needing to have come first?" ¹²And he was saying to them, "Ĕliyahu surely, when he will have ᵠfirst come, is re-establishing all things, even re-establishing ^λ how it had been getting written about the Sŏn of Man, that he will have suffered many things, and will have been despised." ¹³But I am saying to you, that also ᵝ'Ĕliyahu' ᵞhas been coming, and they ᵁwill have done to him whatever they were wishing, even as it ᵋhas been getting written against him."

¹⁴And when they came back to the disciples, they saw a large crowd around them, and some scribes arguing with them. ¹⁵And immediately, when the entire crowd saw him, they were amazed, and were running up to greet him. ¹⁶And he asked them, "What are you discussing with them?"

¹⁷And one of the crowd answered him, "Teacher, I brought you my son, possessed with a spirit which makes him mute, ¹⁸and whenever it may have seized him, it dashes him to the ground and he foams at the mouth, and grinds his teeth, and stiffens out. And I spoke to your disciples that they might cast it out, and they have not been able." ¹⁹And he answered them and said, "Unfaithful kindred, how long will I be with you? How long will I put up with you? Be bringing him to me!" ²⁰And they brought the boy to him. And when he saw him, immediately the spirit threw him into a convulsion, and falling to the ground, he was rolling

---

9:12 λ-ρ Unique to Mark. The Baptist did briefly and cryptically mention the suffering of Mĕssiah. See Yoh. 1:29, 36. But here the text refers to Mal. 4:5-6, and thus to the Ĕliyahu of Mat. 17:2; Mark 9:4; Luke 9:30. *First come* (ψ) means first before Mĕssiah's second coming. Ĕliyahu, having come, will re-establish what is written concerning Mĕssiah, as he is eye witness to the death and resurrection of Mĕssiah (along with Moshˑeh). **9:13** β Yeshua spoke prophetically about Ĕliyahu and historically about his namesake the Baptist in the same words, but Matthew and Mark have split up the sense to present one way each to the reader. Matthew sticks with the Baptist. Mark interprets according to Ĕliyahu in the future. Yeshua spoke with a simple perfect in Hebrew בָּא. Matthew took this as past perfect, 'already came' (ἤδη ἦλθεν)

and Mark took this as a present progressive perfect (ἐλήλυθεν) (γ→coming), understood iteratively, because he wishes us to understand the Ĕliyahu that appears multiple times, in the time of Ahav, and again on the mountain with Moshˑeh, at Mĕssiah's resurrection later as one of 'two men,' and before the second advent. The following aorist (ἐποίησαν) (μ→done) is future perfect, cf. וְעָשׂוּ = καὶ ἐποίησαν (cf. Ezek. 25:14). It refers to Rev. 11:7-8. The following imperfect *(they were wishing)* refers to Izavel's intention sworn in the name of the gods (cf. 1 Kings 19:2), and the final perfect (ξ→written) is completely gnomic summing up everything that was and will be written about Ĕliyahu, including Rev. 11:7-8, *has been* (1 Kings 19:2, 10) or *will have been* (Rev. 11).

about and foaming at the mouth. ²¹And he asked his father, "How long a time is it—while this has been happening to him?" And he said, "From childhood. ²²And it has often thrown him both into the fire and into the water so that it may destroy him. But if you can do anything, take pity on us and help us!"

²³And Yĕshua said to him, "'If you are able 'to hold faithful', all things are possible for the one ᵃholding faithful.'" ²⁴Immediately the boy's father cried out and was saying, "I am ᵝholding faithful. Be helping me in my not ᵞholding faithful!"

²⁵And when Yĕshua saw that a crowd was running up *around them*, he rebuked the unclean spirit, saying to it, "You deaf and dumb spirit, I command you, come out of him and you may no longer enter into him." ²⁶And after crying out and throwing him into terrible convulsions, it came out, and the boy became so much like a corpse that most of them said, "He is dead!" ²⁷But Yĕshua took him by the hand and raised him, and he got up.

²⁸And when he came into the house, his disciples were questioning him privately, "Why could we not cast it out?" ²⁹And he said to them, "This kind cannot come out by anything but prayer."

³⁰Andᵗ from there they went out and were going through Galil, and he was not wanting that some shouldˊ come to know *it*. ³¹For he was teaching his disciples and telling them, "The Sŏn of Man is to be delivered into the hands of men, and they will kill him, and when he has been killed, he will rise after three days." ³²But they did not understand this statement, and they were afraid to ask him.

³³And they came to Kefar-Naḥum, and when he was in the house, he was questioning them, "What were you discussing on the way?" ³⁴But they kept silent, because on the way they had discussed with one another which of them was the greatest. ³⁵And sitting down, he called the twelve and said to them, "If anyone wants to be first, he will be last of all, and servant of all." ³⁶And taking a child, he set him before them, and taking him in his arms, he said to them, ³⁷"Whoever may have received one child like this in my name is receiving me, and whoever

---

9:23 ⌜D A 𝔐 πιστεῦσαι. Even though Yeshua has ordered his immediate disciples not to disclose his identity (cf. Mat. 16:20), he expected people to figure it out and pledge loyalty (α) to him from their hearts, because he was the Almĭghty Sŏn (the Mĕssenger of the Covenant). While many coming for healing or exorcism may have had inward doubts, they did not publically display their doubts, but this man did. The man is desperate and his reply is he will hold faithful (have courage β) for the exorcism, and that he wants the help even though he cannot pledge loyalty (γ). By all rights he should be turned away, but a crowd was gathering.

9:30 τ Around Adar 15, AD 33. **9:31** See 8:31. This text is a model case where the scribes changed "after three days" to "on the third day." The texts agreeing with after three days are: ℵ B C* D L Δ Ψ 529. 892. 2427. pc it sy^hmg co. The old Latin Itala breaks this down as: a k q: *post tertium diem*; b c i: *post tres dies*; d-latin (amazingly disagrees): *in tres dies*; Now for the change to τη τρίτη ημερα we see A C³ N X Γ Π f g¹· g²·ᵛˡᵈ l vg go syrˢᶜʰ etᵖ·ᵗˣᵗ arm aeth (Tischendorf); W θ f¹·¹³ Majority aut f l vg sy (Aland-27). The parallel passage is Matthew 17:23. Also Luke has a parallel passage in 9:44, but Luke did not mention the three days. Catching the scribes in the act on this passage and Mark 10:34 gives us a lot more confidence in some of the cases where D and the Itala alone preserve the reading "after three days." See Mark 8:31; 10:34. ▷ Phillip Comfort notes: "The WH NU reading [after three days] has the best documentary support and is the more difficult reading—especially since it says that Jesus would rise from the dead after three days when Jesus' actual entombment lasted only from Friday evening to Sunday morning. Thus, it is easier to say that he arose 'on the third day.' This was likely the motivation behind the variant [the third day], unless it was a harmonization to Matt 17:23, a parallel passage." See Mark 9:31, *New Testament Text And Translation Commentary*, Comfort.

may be receiving me does not receive me, but *also* him who sent me."

³⁸Yoḥanan said to him, "Teacher, we saw someone casting out demons in your name, and we tried to hinder him because he was not following us." ³⁹But Yĕshua said, "Do not be hindering him, because there is no one who will perform a miracle in my name, and be able soon afterward to speak evil of me. ⁴⁰For he who is not against us is for us. ⁴¹For whoever may have given you a cup of water to drink because you are in the name of the Anŏinted One, amen I say to you, no, he shall not have lost his reward."

⁴²"And whoever may have caused one of these little ones holding faithful to me, to stumble, it would be better for him rather if an ᵛass millstone ᶜwere getting hung around his neck, and he ᶿhad been getting cast into the sea. ⁴³And if your hand may be causing you to stumble, cut it off. It is better for you to have entered life crippled, than having your two hands, to have gone into Geihinnom, into the unquenchable fire, ⁴⁴WHERE THEIR WORM DOES NOT DIE, AND THE FIRE IS NOT QUENCHED.ᶲ

⁴⁵"And if your foot may be causing you to stumble, cut it off. It is better for you to have entered life lame, than having your two feet, to be cast into Geihinnom, ⁴⁶WHERE THEIR WORM DOES NOT DIE, AND THE FIRE IS NOT QUENCHED.ᵞ ⁴⁷And if your eye may be causing you to stumble, cast it out. It is better for you to have entered the kingdom of the Almĭghty with one eye, than having two eyes, to be cast into Geihinnom, ⁴⁸WHERE THEIR WORM DOES NOT DIE, AND THE FIRE IS NOT QUENCHED,ᵠ ⁴⁹because all will be 'salted' with fire. Then every sacrifice will be 'salted' with salt. ⁵⁰Salt is good, but if the salt may have become unsalty, with what will you season it? Be having salt in yourselves, and be being at peace with one another."

10

¹And rising up,ᵗ he went from there to the region of Yehudah, and beyond the Yarden, and crowds gathered around him again, and as he had been getting accustomed, he once more was teaching them. ²And some Perushim came up to him, testing him, and were questioning him whether it was lawful for a man to send away a wife. ³And he answered and said to them, "What did Mosheh command you?" ⁴And they said, "Mosheh permitted a man to WRITE A CERTIFICATE OF DIVORCE AND SEND HER AWAY."

⁵But Yĕshua said to them, "Because of your hardness of heart he wrote you this commandment. ⁶But from the beginning of creation, THE ALMĬGHTY MADE THEM MALE AND FEMALE.ᵅ ⁷FOR THIS CAUSE A MAN WILL LEAVE HIS FATHER AND

9:42 ν *donkey.* **9:42** ς *is.* **9:42** θ→been: or were. **9:44** φ Isa 66:24. But this is missing in many texts. **9:46** γ Isa 66:24. But this is missing in many texts. **9:48** ψ Isa 66:24. The passage does not teach eternal conscious torment. The worm eats the dead bodies, so the worm has 'worm consciousness.' But the dead are dead. The fire is not quenched, but it can go out on its own when the fuel has run out. **9:50** The wickedness in the world will be purified by a destruction of fire, but the righteous will be purified by the salt of faithfulness to Yăhweh's commandments, and by the salt of the sanctifying power of the Ruăḥ. Salt purifies, and so his commandments sanctify. The righteous are living sacrifices to the Almĭghty, and they are salted, crucifying the flesh, and living for Yĕshua and his kingdom. See Romans. 12:1-2.

10:1 τ Winter, AD 34. **10:4** Deu 24:1. **10:6** α Gen 1:27

MOTHER, ⁸AND THE TWO WILL BECOME ONE FLESH,ᵝ consequently they are no longer two, but one flesh. ⁹What therefore the Almĭghty has joined together, let no man be separating."

¹⁰And in the house the disciples were questioning him about this again. ¹¹And he said to them, "Whoever may have sent away his wife, ᵞso that he may marry another, is committing adultery against her, ¹²and if *a* ʳwife, ʿmay go out from the husband, ᵞso that another she may marryʾ *then she* is committing adultery⸸."

¹³And they were bringing children to him so that he might touch them, and the disciples rebuked them. ¹⁴But when Yĕshua saw this, he was indignant and said to them, "Allow the children to come to me. Do not be hindering them, because the kingdom of the Almĭghty belongs to such as these. ¹⁵Amen I say to you, whoever may not have received the kingdom of the Almĭghty like a child, no, he will not have entered into it." ¹⁶And he took them in his arms and was blessing them, laying his hands upon them.

¹⁷And when *he was* going forth himself for a journey, one ran up and knelt down *before* him. He was asking, "Good teacher, what may I do so that I will have inherited everlasting life?"ᶳ ¹⁸And Yĕshua said to him, "Why are you calling me good? No one is *perfectly* good except one, the Almĭghty. ¹⁹ "You have been knowing the commandments, 'YOU SHALL NOT MURDER,ᵝ' 'YOU SHALL NOT COMMIT ADULTERY,ᵖ' 'YOU SHALL NOT STEAL,ᵞ' 'YOU SHALL NOT BEAR FALSE WITNESS,ᵡ' 'YOU SHALL NOT DEFRAUD ANYONE.ᵟ' 'BE HONORING YOUR FATHER AND MOTHER.ᶎ' ²⁰And he was saying to him, "Teacher, I have kept all these things from my youth up."

²¹And when he looked into him, Yĕshua loved him, and said to him, "One thing you are lacking. Be going! As much as you possess, sell, and give to the poor, and you will have treasure in heaven, and come hither, be following me."

10:7 β Gen. 2:24. **10:11/12** γ→that: cf. Mat. 19:9 **10:12** ʳshe, αὐτὴ, txt: A D (ˢ θ) f ¹³ 𝔐 latt sy ᵖ·ʰ. **10:12** ʿαπολυση τον ανδρα αυτης και γαμηθη αλλω: A 𝔐 f l vg syᵖ·ʰ = *(and if a wife)* may send away her husband so that she may be married to another *(then she is comitting adultery.)* | txt εξελθη απο του ανδρος και αλλον γαμηση D (θ) f¹³ (28). 565. (700) it. | vs. NA-27: ℵ B (C) L (Δ,Ψ) 892. 2427 pc co. 𝔐 supplied ἀπολύω assuming it meant a legal divorce, but the original is clearly εξερχομαι with D. It is immaterial whether a legal divorce occurs because even with the legal divorce, divorce in order to remarry is adultery. ℵ B C, etc. delete καὶ ahead of γαμήσῃ in order to eliminate the motivation for the divorce and make remarriage for any reason other than immorality illegal. This is clearly a fourth century innovation not present in the earlier texts.

10:17 ξ See Mat. 19:16f; Luke 18:18f; cf. Luke 10:25-28. The conversation was longer than reported by any one Evangelist, and Matthew reports a different side of it than Mark and Luke. ▷ Yĕshua first points out that no one is perfect except the Almĭghty. There is no reason to suppose that the young man did not concede this point. ▷ The conversation then turns to what is the best commandment (cf. Matthew's account), and the answer to this is that there is no best commandment, i.e. there is none which will confer enough merit to cover the demerit of any failing. Judaism at the time concerned itself with extra special deeds for merits that could cancel out demerits. See Appendix VIII. ▷ Yĕshua answers to keep the commandments. Clearly the young man wants to improve his situation, so Yĕshua tells him how, after seeing that he is sincere in heart. He should sell all and follow Yĕshua, thus demonstrating the utmost loyalty to the Almĭghty. Then he will be wholehearted. ▷ And when the young man follows Yĕshua he would learn that the Almĭghty will have forgiven the sins of those loyal to him even though they are not perfect, and even though there is no commandment to make up for sin. **10:19** β Exo. 20:13, Deut. 5:17; ρ Exo. 20:14, Deut. 5:18; γ Exo. 20:15, Deut. 5:19; χ Exo. 20:16, Deut. 5:20; ζ Exo. 20:12, Deu 5:16; δ Lev. 19:13; Deu. 24:14-15. He cites them progressively from the easiest to keep to the harder. Mark includes Mĕssiah saying "defraud not" as a more specific instance of loving his neighbor, and this is to be connected to the directive to dispose his wealth to the poor.

²²And when he became sad upon this word, he went away grieving, because he was one who owned much property.

²³And Yĕshua, looking around, said to his disciples, "How hard it is for those who have been trusting in riches to enter the kingdom of the Almĭghty!" ²⁴And the disciples were amazed at his words. But Yĕshua answered again and said to them, "Children, how hard it is to enter the kingdom of the Almĭghty! ²⁵It is easier work for a camel to go through the eye of a needle than for a rich man to enter the kingdom of the Almĭghty." ²⁶And they were even more astonished and said to him, "Then who can be rescued?" ²⁷Looking upon them, Yĕshua said, "At the side of men it is impossible, but not at the side of the Almĭghty, because all things are possible at the side of the Almĭghty." ²⁸Peter began to be saying to him, "Behold, we have left everything and have been following you." ²⁹Yĕshua said, "Amen I say to you, there is no one who has left house or brothers or sisters or mother or father or children or farms, for my sake and for the good news' sake, ³⁰except that he shall have received a hundred times as much now in the present season, houses and brothers and sisters and mothers and children and farms, along with persecutions, and in the age to come, everlasting life. ³¹But many who are first, will be last, and the last, first."

³²And they were on the road, going up to Yerushalayim, and Yĕshua was walking on ahead of them, and they were amazed, and those who followed were fearful. And again he took the twelve aside and began to tell them what was going to befall him, ³³saying, "Behold, we are going up to Yerushalayim, and the Sŏn of Man will be delivered to the chief priests and the scribes, and they will condemn him to death, and will deliver him to the nations. ³⁴And they will mock him and spit upon him, and scourge him, and kill him, and after three days he will rise again."

³⁵And Ya'aqov and Yohanan, the two sons of Zavdai, came up to him, saying to him, "Teacher, we want that whatever we may ask you, *that* you will have done *it* for us." ³⁶And he said to them, "What do you want, *that* I may do for you?" ³⁷And they said to him, "Grant us that we may sit in your glory, one on your right, and one on your left." ³⁸But Yĕshua said to them, "You have not been realizing what you are asking for. Are you able to drink the cup that I am drinking, or to be immersed with the immersion with which I am getting immersed?" ³⁹And they said to him, "We are able." And Yĕshua said to them, "The cup that I drink you will drink, and you will be immersed with the immersion with which I am immersed. ⁴⁰Yet to sit on my right or on my left, this is not Mine to give,

---

10:34 See 8:31 and 9:31. This text is also a case of scribes being caught in the act of changing *after three days* to *on the third day*. Aland-27 concurs with after: א B C D L Δ Ψ 579. 892. 2427. pc it sy^hmg co. The altered texts to τη τριτη ημερα are in Aland-27: A(*) W θ f^1.13 Majority aur f l vg sy; Or. The parallel passages are Mat. 20:19 and Luke 18:33. It would appear that both Matthew and Luke have finished their accounts with a statement "on the third day" from another place. Genuine "on the third day" or "in three days" passages are also: Luke 24:7, 24:46; Acts 10:40; 1Cor. 15:4. John 2:19 (cf. Mark 14:58; 15:29; Mat. 26:61; Mat. 27:40; John 2:20). See also Luke 13:32; 24:21. "On the third day" or "in three days" statements pertain to the third calendar day (using a dawn to dawn epoch). See Mat. 12:40. "After three days" statements pertain to the night after the third literal day (dawn to dusk) but still in the third calendar day.

but it is for those for whom it has been getting prepared."

⁴¹And hearing this, the ten began to feel indignant with Ya'aqov and Yoḥanan. ⁴²And when he called them to himself, Yĕshua is saying to them, "You have been knowing that those appearing to be ruling the nations are lording over them, and their great men are taking authority over them. ⁴³But it is not likewise among you, but whoever may be wishing to become great among you will be your servant, ⁴⁴and whoever may be wishing to be first among you will be slave of all. ⁴⁵For even the Sŏn of Man did not come to be served, but to serve, and to give his life a ransom in return for many^λ."

⁴⁶And they came to Yeriḥo. And as he was going out from Yeriḥo with his

---

10:45 λ See *Mat.* 20:28; See notes on Rev. 20:10-15. The penalty for sin is death because sin causes death. The penalty is a judicial intervention to prevent sinners from continuing to cause more death. The Most High intervened to prevent man from eating of the tree of life, because it would allow man to become eternally corrupt and eternally dealing death. At first the Most High did not pre scribe death for the murderer, but he banished him. Then murders multiplied and after the deluge he made a law that the murderer should be put to death. Clearly, this judicial intervention was done with the desire to limit the propensity of man to murder. Since punitive justice is exacted in a desire to limit sin's destruction, it should be clear that punitive justice does not satisfy the debt of justice. It is only what can be done to keep the debt from growing greater. The modern notion that one who served his sentence has paid his debt to society is a delusion. Full justice would require the sinner to repair and restore all the damage he did, and make all the suffering he caused disappear. This of course isn't possible because the past and its effects on the present cannot be erased. For this reason the debt cannot be paid. It is logically impossible. The debt can only be forgiven to the repentant. The norm of justice cannot restore life. Please see Gal. 3:21. Zechut or deeds of merit cannot pay the debt either. For this reason the theory of penal substition can never satisfy the demand of full justice where compensatory justice is demanded. ▷ This is why Messiah's death is a ransom and not a payment of judicial penalty. The ransom is the suffering and death visitied upon the Most High. It is the cost he incurrs to save men. The ransom is the cost to gain deliverance for souls. Sin and death exact the cost. Nations, peoples, and men are the the ransom cost. The suffering of the ransomed fills up what is lacking in the sufferings of Messiah. And Messiah was the divine servant, the one who ransoms his people by his blood, his life, his loss, one on the behalf of many. ▷ Messiah suffered FROM our iniquities and not FOR them (which they claim is a legal transfer of sin's judgment to Christ). "And we will have thought him being struck, being made smitten of the Almighty, and being made to be afflicted" (Isa. 53:4b). In other words, this thought is a mistake, because Yĕsha'yahu immediately states the cause of the affliction, "But he is being made to be wounded FROM our transgressions, is being made to be crushed FROM our iniquities, an instruction of our wellness is upon him, and through his stripes will have been healing for us" (Isa. 53:5). "And Yăhweɥ will have caused to meet up with him the iniquity of us all" (Isa. 53:6). "He will have been cut off from the land of the living. FROM the transgressions of my people is a plague to him" (Isa. 53:8). He was innocent, so "Yahweɥ will have been pleased to declare his crushing to be the malady if his soul will make *itself* an offense offering" (Isa. 53:10). Or "make his crushing the malady" (הֶחֱלִי). The malady, disease, illness, here is our sin, which Messiah is carrying. The offense offering carries the sin away from the repentant sinner where it is purged on the altar by the blood. The offering sums up the ransom cost, demonstrates it, indicates it. The blood symbolizes the purging that comes from divine forgiveness. The offering is the advocate getting forgiving (purging) justice for the penitant man. The offering symbolizes the divine cost in separating the sinner from sin, i.e. the cost to bring the sinner into deliverance and leave the sin behind to be purged. ▷ The offering is performing a divine service in removing sin so it can be purged. Messiah is the ransom for many, bearing the cost, bearing the sin away to the place of divine forgiveness to secure the release of the soul captured by sin, because the Son came to serve, not to be served. The offering symbolizes the actual divine longsuffering with our sin, being divine cost in choosing to forgive. ▷ Messiah's resurrection from the dead shows that he carries our sin away, battles it, defeats it, and purges it (1 Yoḥ. 1:9). By no means is the offense offering suffering a divine penalty, or any divine wrath. Rather the offering is doing the service of indicating the divine ransom cost to separate those seeking deliverance from their sin so that the sin can be purged. ▷ By rising from the dead Messiah shows that he is not suffering the penalty of wrath, because this would leave him in the grave. Anselm and others might say that the value of the Son's death is infinite in a finite space of time so that it can pay the unremitted penalty of all sin. But this is heresy on five points, (1) It lays a judicial penalty (wrath) on the innocent to free the guilty contradicting Exodus 23:7, and (2) The wrath of the Father remains unforgiven since it is exacted in payment, (3) a limit on divine cost is set by the resurrection of Messiah, and thus to speak of an infinite outlay of penalty paying is philosophic

disciples and a great crowd, a blind beggar named Bar-Timai, the son of Timai, was sitting beside the road. ⁴⁷And when he heard that it was Yĕshua Ha-Netseri, he began to cry out and say, "Yĕshua, Sŏn of David, have mercy on me!" ⁴⁸And many were sternly rebuking him, so that he would be quiet, but he kept crying out all the more, "Sŏn of David, have mercy on me!"

⁴⁹And Yĕshua stopped and said, "Call him here." And they called the blind man, saying to him, "Be having courage, be rising! He is calling for you." ⁵⁰And casting aside his cloak, he jumped up, and came to Yĕshua. ⁵¹And answering him, Yĕshua said, "What do you want, *that* I may do for you?" And the blind man said to him, "Rabboni, that I will have seen again!" ⁵²And Yĕshua said to him, "Be going. Your ᵋfaithfulness has been making you well." And immediately he regained his sight and was following him on the road.

11

¹And when they are ᵀapproaching Yerushalayim, at Beth-Paggei and Beth-Hini, toward the Mount of Olives, he is sending two of his disciples, ²and says to them, "Be going into the village opposite you, and immediately entering into it, you will find a colt, which ᵑhas been getting held bound there, on which no one yet has ever sat. Untie it and be bringing it here. ³And if anyone may have said to you, 'Why are you doing this?' Say, 'Adŏnai has need of it', and immediately he will send it back here."

⁴And they went away and found a colt, which had been getting held bound, at the door outside in the street. Then they are untying it. ⁵And some of those, who had been standing there, were saying to them, "What are you doing, untying the colt?" ⁶And they spoke to them just as Yĕshua had told them. Then they permitted them. ⁷And they bring the colt to Yĕshua and throw their garments upon it. Then he sat upon it.

⁸And many spread their garments in the road, and others spread leafy branches which they had cut from the fields. ⁹And those going before, and those fol-

---

sophistry of the same sort claiming that divine justice requires the penalty of sin to be suffered eternally, and (4) these views blaspheme the compassion and mercy of the Most High, and profane his name, and as such are rightfully attributed to Satanic deception and counter narrative concerning Messiah's death. (5) Finally, if divine wrath can be suffered by a substitute, then this must include wrath against unrepentance, and therefore the need to repent would be erased. So the logical end is lawlessness, and indeed some who assume this to be so, correctly calculate from the false assumption to acquit the guilty.

10:52 ξ *holding faithful, faithfulness, courage, steadfastness.* The word πιστις covers a range of meaning that cannot be captured by one English word. Here both courage and faithfulness are meant. The present perfect continuous tense strongly hints that his initial courage is not the end of getting well.

11:1 τ Şabbath Aviv 10, March 20, AD 34.

11:2 η→tied. Greek leaves it unclear whether it is one instance of the action or many, as in 'he has been getting sick today' vs. 'has been getting sick from his youth.' The context may resolve it or not. It could mean the colt was just finished getting tied, or that the colt was repeatedly getting tied there all the time. We see that the progressive translation allows for both interpretations. But trying to reduce 'tied' to a resultant continuous state: 'has been tied' prevents either the actual tying action from being viewed as a progressive, or as repeated over time. Modern Koine Greek theory taught in the theological schools is constantly having to decide between the English present tense and the English non-progressive perfect, i.e. 'is standing' vs. 'has stood.' The former betrays the perfect, and the latter the internal aspect of the Greek perfect! The reason for this contradiction is theology. The many want to put the present perfect progressive out of sight because to allow it utterly destroys their lawless theories of salvation. Yes, indeed an entire Greek tense has been corrupted for the sake of false doctrine!

lowing after, were crying out, "HOSHAʻNAʼ!ᵃ HAVING BEEN GETTING BLESSED IS THE COMING ONE IN THE NAME OF YĂHWEH!ᵝ ¹⁰Having been getting blessed is the coming kingdom, the one of our father, David! HOSHAʻNAʼᵅ INᶿ THE HEIGHTS!"

¹¹And he entered Yerushalayim and came into the temple, and after looking all around, he departed for Beṯh-Hini with the twelve, since it was already late.

¹²And on the next day,ᵗ when they had departed from Beṯh-Hini, he became hungry. ¹³And seeing at a distance a fig tree in leaf, he went to see if perhaps he would find anything on it, and when he came to it, he found nothing but leaves, because it was not the season for figs. ¹⁴And he responded and said to it, "May no one eat fruit from you unto time immemorial!" And his disciples were listening.

¹⁵And they came to Yerushalayim. And he entered the temple and began to cast out those who were buying and selling in the temple, and overturned the tables of the moneychangers and the seats of those who were selling doves. ¹⁶And he would not permit that anyone may carry goods through the temple. ¹⁷And he was teaching and he was saying to them, "Has it not been getting written, MY HOUSE SHALL BE CALLED A HOUSE OF PRAYER FOR ALL THE NATIONSᵅ! But you have been making it A ROBBERS' DEN.ᵝ" ¹⁸And the chief priests and the scribes heard this, and were seeking how they might destroy him, because they were afraid of him, because all the crowd was astonished at his teaching. ¹⁹And whenever it became later, they would go out of the city.

²⁰And passing by in the morning,ᵗ they saw the fig tree, which had been getting withered from the roots *up.* ²¹And reminded, Peter says to him, "Rabbi, behold, the fig tree which you cursed has been getting withered." ²²And when Yĕshua answered, he is saying to them, "If you have the faithfulness^π of the Almĭghty, ²³amĕn, I am saying to you, whoever may say to this mountain, 'Be taken up and be cast into the sea,' and will not have doubted in his heart, but may be holding faithful *so*ᵘ that what he says is *going to be* happening, it shall be for him. ²⁴Because of this I say to you, all things, as much as you are praying and asking, be holding faithful *so*ᵘ that you are *going to be* receiving them, and it shall be for you. ²⁵And whenever you may stand praying, be forgiving, if you have anything against anyone, so that your Făther also who is in heaven will have forgiven you your transgressions. ²⁶But if you do not forgive, neither will your Făther who is in heaven forgive your transgressions.^λ

11:9 α Psa 118:25; **11:9** β Psa 118:26, בָּרוּךְ, Qal. Passive. **11:10** α Psa 118:25; **11:10** θ Psa 148:1, בַּמְּרוֹמִים **11:12** τ Sunday, Aviv 11, March 21, AD 34. **11:17** α Isa 56:7; **11:17** β Jer 7:11: הַמְּעָרַת פָּרִצִים הָיָה הַבַּיִת הַזֶּה; **11:20** τ Monday, Aviv 12, March 22, AD 34.
11:22 π. Εἰ ἔχετε πίστιν ΘΥ (Read εἰ with: ℵ D Θ f¹³ 28. 33ᶜ. 565. 700 *pc* it syˢ). See *Mat.* 17:20; *Luke* 17:5-6. *Mat.* 21:22. ▷ If you have the pledge of the Almĭghty. Πίστιν here means the support, promise, faithful pledge or proof that the Most High wants something to be done. But it also includes being faithful to him. See Joshua 10:12-14. Yehoshua was listened to because he knew what the Most High wanted done. In one doubts what he hears from the Spirit, then he will not have the courage to declare it. **11:23, 24** μ. ὅτι. See BDAG ❺ c. This may be read three ways, "hold *it* faithful that" or "holding faithful *so* that," "holding faithful because...." Likewise with vs. 24. All ideas are true. One should hold it faithful that it is allowed to receive what is asked for, and also hold faithful by keeping the commandments, or hold faithful because one knows what should be. See 1 Yoh. 3:22; Yoh. 14:13, 14; 15:16; 16:23, 24, 26. **11:26** λ many texts omit vs. 26.

²⁷And they came again to Yerushalayim. And as he was walking in the temple, the chief priests, and scribes, and elders came to him, ²⁸and were saying to him, "By what authority are you doing these things, or who gave you this authority, that you may be doing these things?" ²⁹And Yĕshua said to them, "I will ask you one question, and you answer me, and then I will tell you by what authority I do these things. ³⁰Was the immersion of Yoḥanan from heaven, or from men? Answer me." ³¹And they were reasoning among themselves, saying, "If we may have said, 'From heaven,' he will say, 'Then why did you not hold him faithful?' ³²But should we have said, 'From men?'" (*then* they were afraid of the multitude, because all were holding that Yoḥanan truly was a prophet.) ³³And answering Yĕshua, they say, "We have not been knowing." And Yĕshua says to them, "Neither do I tell you by what authority I do these things."

12

¹And he began to speak to them in parables: "A man PLANTED A VINEYARD, AND PUT A WALL AROUND IT, AND DUG A VAT UNDER THE WINE PRESS, AND BUILT A TOWER,ᵅ and rented it out to vine-growers and went on a journey. ²And at the harvest time he sent a slave to the vine-growers, in order that he would receive some of the produce of the vineyard from the hand of the vine-growers. ³And they took him, and beat him, and sent him away empty-handed. ⁴And again he sent them another slave, and they wounded him in the head, and treated him shamefully. ⁵And he sent another, and that one they killed, and so with many others, beating some, and killing others. ⁶He had one more to send, a beloved son. He sent him last of all to them, saying, 'They will respect my son.' ⁷But those vine-growers said to one another, 'This is the heir. Come, we will have killed him, and the inheritance will be ours!' ⁸And they took him, and killed him, and threw him out of the vineyard. ⁹What will the owner of the vineyard do? He will come and destroy the vine-growers, and will give the vineyard to others. ¹⁰Have you not even read this text: "THE STONE WHICH THE BUILDERS REJECTED, THIS BECAME THE CHIEF CORNER STONE. ¹¹THIS CAME ABOUT FROM BESIDE YĂHWEH, AND IT IS WONDERFUL IN OUR EYES?"ᵝ ¹²And they were seeking to seize him, and yet they feared the crowd, because they understood that he spoke the parable against them. And so they left him, and went away.

¹³And they sent some of the Perushim and Herodians to him, so that they might trap him in a matter. ¹⁴And when they came, they say to him, "Teacher, we have been knowing that you are true, and there is no deferrence by you for anyone, because you are not looking on the surface of men, but are teaching the way of the Almĭghty *based* upon truth. Is it lawful to pay a census head-tax to Caesar, or not? ¹⁵Shall we have paid *it*, or shall we not have paid *it*?" But he, having been knowing their hypocrisy, said to them, "Why are you testing me? Be bringing me a dinar, so that I might see *it*." ¹⁶And they brought one. And he said to them, "Whose likeness and inscription is this?" And they said to him,

---

12:1 α Isa 5:1-2; **12:10-11** β Psa 118:22-23;

"Caesar's." ¹⁷And Yĕshua said to them, "Render to Caesar the things that are Caesar's, and to the Almĭghty the things that are the Almĭghty's." And they were amazed at him.

¹⁸And some Tsadduqim (who say that there is no resurrection) came to him, and were questioning him, saying, ¹⁹"Teacher, Mosheh wrote for us that if A MAN'S BROTHER HAS DIED, and has left behind a wife, AND HAS NOT LEFT A CHILD, THAT HIS BROTHER SHOULD TAKE THE WIFE, AND SHOULD RAISE UP SEED FOR HIS BROTHER. ²⁰There were seven brothers, and the first took a wife, and dying, left no seed. ²¹And the second one took her, and died, leaving behind no seed, and the third likewise, ²²and so all seven left no seed. Last of all the woman died also. ²³In the resurrection, when they shall have risen again, which one's wife will she be? For all seven had her as wife."

²⁴Yĕshua was saying to them, "Is this not the reason you are being deceived, that you have not been understanding the writings, or even the power of the Almĭghty? ²⁵Because when they will have risen from the dead, they do not as well marry, nor besides are given in marriage, but they are like messengers in heaven. ²⁶But regarding the fact that the dead rise again, have you not read in the scroll of Mosheh, in the passage about the burning bush, how the Almĭghty spoke to him, saying, "I AM THE ALMĬGHTY OF AVRAHAM, AND THE ALMĬGHTY OF YITSHAQ, AND THE ALMĬGHTY OF YA'AQOV?" ²⁷He is not the Almĭghty of the dead so much as for living! You are greatly mistaken."

²⁸And one of the scribes came and heard them arguing, and recognizing that he had answered them well, asked him, "What commandment is the foremost of all?" ²⁹Yĕshua answered, "The foremost is, BE HEARING, YISRA'EL! YĂHWEH IS OUR ALMĬGHTY, YĂHWEH ONLY IS, ³⁰AND YOU SHALL LOVE YĂHWEH YOUR ALMĬGHTY WITH ALL YOUR HEART, AND WITH ALL YOUR SOUL, AND WITH ALL YOUR STRENGTH." ³¹The second is this, "YOU SHALL LOVE YOUR NEIGHBOR AS YOURSELF." There is no other commandment greater than these."

³²And the scribe said to him, "Right, Teacher, you have truly stated that HE ONLY IS, and THERE IS NO OTHER APART FROM HIM, ³³and to LOVE HIM WITH ALL THE HEART AND WITH ALL THE UNDERSTANDING AND WITH ALL THE STRENGTH, and to LOVE ONE'S NEIGHBOR AS HIMSELF, is much more than all burnt offerings and sacrifices."

³⁴And when Yĕshua saw that he had answered intelligently, he said to him, "You are not far from the kingdom of the Almĭghty." And after that, no one would venture to ask him any more questions.

³⁵And Yĕshua answering was saying, as he taught in the temple, "How is

---

12:19 φ Deu 25:5, Gen 38:8. **12:26** η Exo 3:6. **12:27** θ→as: See Thayer, LSJ. The conjunction limits the preceding statement, and does not have to deny it absolutely. *For living* (ζώντων): the participle expresses a purpose. See Wallace pg. 635. "7 Purpose (Telic)...Mat.27:49." The argument Yĕshua makes is that the Almĭghty would not continue saying he was the Almĭghty of the dead unless he planned to raise them back to life. **12:29-30** α Deu 6:4-5; **12:31** δ Lev 19:18. **12:32** θ Deu 6:4 **12:32** ρ Deu 4:35 (אֵין); Isa 45:21 (אֵין זוּלָתִי); **12:33** λ Deu 6:5; Jos 22:5 **12:33** δ Lev 19:18: וְאָהַבְתָּ לְרֵעֲךָ כָּמוֹךָ.

it that the scribes say that the Anŏinted is the son of David? ³⁶David himself said in the Holy Spĭrit, "YĂHWEH SAID TO MY ADŎNAI, 'BE SITTING AT MY RIGHT HAND WHILE I SHALL PUT YOUR ENEMIES BENEATH YOUR FEET.'" ³⁷David himself calls him 'Adŏnai', and so in what sense is he his son?"

³⁷ᵇAnd the great crowd was gladly listening to him. ³⁸And in his teaching he was saying: "Be keeping a look out against the scribes wanting to be walking around in long robes, and *wanting* respectful greetings in the market places, ³⁹and chief seats in the congregations, and the best reclining places at banquets, ⁴⁰who are devouring widows' houses, and for a public show are offering long prayers. These will receive greater condemnation."

⁴¹And he sat down opposite the treasury, and was observing how the crowd was putting copper coinage into the treasury, and many rich people were putting in large sums. ⁴²And a poor widow came and put in two small copper coins, which amount to a quadrans. ⁴³And calling his disciples to him, he said to them, "Amen I say to you, this poor widow put in more than all the contributors to the treasury, ⁴⁴because they all put in out of their surplus, but she, out of her poverty, put in all she owned, all she had to live on."

13

¹And as he was going out of the temple, one of his disciples said to him, "Teacher, behold what wonderful stones and what wonderful buildings!" ²And Yĕshua said to him, "Do you see these great buildings? No, not one stone will have been left upon another which, no, will not have been dislodged."

³And as he was sitting on the Mount of Olives opposite the temple, Peter and Ya'aqov and Yohanan and Andrew were questioning him privately, ⁴"Tell us, when will these things be, and what will be the sign when all these things may be about to be completing?"

⁵And Yĕshua began to say to them, "Be seeing to it that no one will have misled you. ⁶Many will come in my name, saying, 'I AM!' and will mislead many. ⁷And, when you have heard of wars and rumors of wars, do not be getting frightened. Those things must take place, but that is not yet the end. ⁸For nation will arise against nation, and kingdom against kingdom. There will be earthquakes down through *various* places. There will also be famines. These things are merely the beginning of birth pangs.

⁹"But be you guarding yourselves, because they will deliver you to the courts, and you will be flogged in the congregations, and you will stand before governors and kings for my sake, as a testimony to them. ¹⁰And the good news must first be announced to all the nations. ¹¹And when they may be arresting you, delivering you up, do not be getting anxious beforehand *about* what you will

---

12:36 χ Psa 110:1; נְאֻם יְהוָה לַאדֹנִי.

13:1 τ Monday afternoon, Aviv 12, March 22, AD 34. **13:6** γ The better explanation of the difference here with Mat. 24:5 appears to be that Yeshua said, "saying that I am the Anointed One and I AM," (אֲנִי המשיח ואני הוא) and that Mark and Luke chose to report I AM whereas Matthew reported the first claim. Quite a few Messianic claimants have claimed to be I AM, and these were mostly not Jewish, which explains why Luke 21:8 and this pasage report the latter claim, but not Matthew.

have said, but whatever may have been given you in that hour—this be saying, because it is not you who speak, so much as the Holy Spĭrit. ¹²And brother will deliver brother to death, and a father his child, and children will rise up against parents and have them put to death. ¹³And you will be hated by all on account of my name, but the one who endures to the end, he will be rescued.

¹⁴"But whenever you may have seen the abomination of desolation, having been standing where it ought not be (let the reader be understanding), then let those who are in Yehudah be fleeing into the mountains. ¹⁵And let him who is on the housetop not go down, or enter in, to get anything out of his house. ¹⁶And let him who is in the field not turn back to get his cloak. ¹⁷But woe to those who are with child and to those who nurse babes in those days! ¹⁸But be praying that it will not have happened in the winter. ¹⁹For those days will be *a time of* tribulation such as has not been occurring the like since the beginning of the creation which the Almĭghty created, until now, and no, will not have happened. ²⁰And unless Yăhweh will have cut short the ᵋdays, not ever will have been rescued any flesh, but for the sake of the chosen whom he will have chosen, he will have shortened the ᵋdays.

²¹"And then if anyone may have said to you, 'Look, here is the Mĕssiah!' or 'Look, there!' do not be holding *it* faithful, ²²because false Mĕssiahs and false prophets will arise, and will show signs and wonders, in order, if possible, to lead the chosen astray. ²³But be looking. Behold, I have been telling you everything beforehand.

²⁴But in those days, after that tribulation, THE SUN WILL BE DARKENED, AND THE MOON WILL NOT GIVE ITS LIGHT,ᵅ ²⁵AND THE STARS WILL BE FALLINGᵝ from heaven, and the powers that are in the heavens will be shaken. ²⁶And then they will see THE SŎN OF MAN COMING IN CLOUDSᵞ with great power and glory. ²⁷And then he will send forth the messengers, and will gather together his chosen from the four winds, from the farthest end of the earth, to the farthest end of heaven.

²⁸"Now learn the parable from the fig tree. When its branch may already have become tender, and it may be putting forth its leaves, you know that summer is near. ²⁹Even so, you too, when you may have seen these things happening, be recognizing that he is near, right at the door. ³⁰Amᵉn I say to you that no, this kindred shall not have passed away before the point that all these things may have happened.ᶿ ³¹Heaven and earth will pass away, but my words, no, they will not pass away. ³²But concerning that day or time no one has been knowing, not even the messengers in heaven, nor even the Sŏn,ᵟ but the Făther *alone*. ³³Be looking out, be wakeful, because you have not been knowing when the appointed

---

13:20 ξ = *times*. **13:24** α Isa 13:10 **13:24** β Isa 34:4 **13:26** γ Dan 7:13. **13:30** θ See Mat. 24:34 and Luke 21:32. **13:32** δ Then how can the Son be 'all knowing'? Answer: since the Most High does not have to be 'all-knowing,' then neither does the Son. And much is not knowable before being determined. See Deut. 8:1-2; Gen. 6:6; 18:21; 22:12. The Almighty only purposes to keep sufficient knowledge of the present state of all of reality in mind to exercise sufficient control and governance over it. Part of this sufficiency is that the Father could take over this duty so that the Son could become human, keeping the Son's glory in trust for him to take up again later. Likewise, concerning the future, the Almighty does not have an exhaustive determination of which contingency of all contingencies he wishes to take place, but he has a deterministic plan only

time is. ³⁴"It is like a man, away on a journey, who upon leaving his house and putting his slaves in charge, assigning to each one his task, also commanded the doorkeeper, that he may be wakeful. ³⁵Therefore, be keeping wakeful—for you have not been knowing when the master of the house is coming, whether late, or midnight, whether at crowing, or in the morning— ³⁶lest he come suddenly and may have found you asleep. ³⁷And what I say to you I say to all, 'Be keeping wakeful!'"

14

¹And, the Passover and Unleavened Bread was ᵀAFTER TWO DAYS, and the chief priests and the scribes were seeking a way of seizing him by treachery, *so that* they may kill him, ²because they were saying, "Not during the festival, lest there will be a riot of the people."

³And whileᵀ he was in Beṭh-Hini at the home of Şim'on the leper, and reclining, there came a woman with an alabaster vial of very costly perfume of pure spikenard, and she broke the vial and poured it over his head. ⁴But some were being displeased, *muttering* toward themselves, "For why has this waste of the perfume been happening? ⁵For this perfume could have been sold for over three hundred dinars, and *the money* given to the poor." And they were scolding her.

⁶Butᵀ Yĕshua said, "Let her alone. Why do you bother her? She has done a good deed to me. ⁷Because the poor you always have with you, and whenever you may be wishing, you are able to do them good, yet you are not always having me. ⁸She has done what she could. She has anointed my body beforehand for the burial. ⁹And amen, I say to you, wherever the good news will have been announced in the whole world, that also which this woman has done will be spoken of in memory of her."

¹⁰And Yehudah Ish-Qeriyot, who was one of the twelve, went off to the chief priests, so that he may betray him to them. ¹¹And they were glad when they heard this, and promised to give him silver coinage. And he was seeking how he may betray him at an opportune time.

---

for those contingencies necessary to accomplish his spoken prophetic promises and any unspoken promises with himself he has. ▷ Outside of what is needed to govern, the Most High is not subservient to a need to ontologically know all present details, and only in regard to his future promises is a determined contingency tree knowledge accessible. To say otherwise is to make God a slave of his own eternal will, unable to change anything for the better. To say otherwise is to demand we have to accept the present reality as the just will of the Most High, but it clearly is not (cf. Gen. 6:6). ▷ There are those Arminians who insist that the Most High will observe all future outcomes without actually constraining any future moral choice, but we see in Gen. 6:6 that the Most High was grieved by his own decision to make man. The love of the Most High now constrains him to ransom man from death as best may be. Truly, however, the Scripture presents the Most High as able to ignore whatsoever he will in the present, and the future as largely undetermined except in broad outlines, and therefore not a proper reality that is knowable. ▷ Apologists for exhaustive omniscience claim that Messiah had two natures, one divine, and one human, that were united in one person. So they say this statement in Mark 13:32 is only true with respect to his human nature, as if he were operating only in his human nature when he made the statement. But if Messiah be a whole person, what is true of Messiah must also necessarily be true of both his natures, because if not, then someone could argue that the love of Messiah was not one nature or the other. And this of course would destroy the whole purpose of the Almighty becoming man.

14:1 τ Hos 6:2; Gen 22:4; This was spoken on Monday. After one day would be Tuesday. After two would be Wednesday. Wednesday was Aviv 14, the day for sacrificing the Passover. After two days is the third day. The wording reminds us of Genesis 22 and other third day types. See Mat. 26:2. **14:3** τ Monday evening, Aviv 13. **14:6** τ Monday night or early Tuesday, Aviv 13.

¹²Now the ᵉheadmost day for the unleavened ones, (when they would be sacrificing the Passover)ᵡ, his disciples said to him, "Where do you desire going we should ready, so that you ᵖmay eat the Passover?"

¹³Then he sends two of his disciples, and says to them, "Be going into the city, and a man will meet you carrying a pitcher of water. Follow him. ¹⁴And wherever he may have entered, say to the owner of the house, 'The Teacher says, "Where is my guest room where I may eat the Passover with my disciples?"' ¹⁵And he himself will show you a large upper room, having been getting spread ready. And there get ready for us." ¹⁶Then the disciples went out, and came to the city, and found *it* just as he had told them. Then they readied ᵖthe Passover.

¹⁷And when it was laterʸ he came with the twelve. ¹⁸And as they are reclining *at the table* and eating, Yĕshua said, "Am·en I say to you that one of you will betray me—one who is eating with me." ¹⁹They began to be grieved and to say to him one by one, "Surely not I?" ²⁰And he said to them, "It is one of the twelve, one who dips with me in the bowl, ²¹because the Sŏn of Man is going, just as it has been getting written about him, but woe to that man by whom the Sŏn of Man is betrayed! It would have been good for that man if he had not been born."

²²And while they are eating, he took *some* bread, said a blessing, broke *it*, and gave *it* to them, and said, "Take *it*. This ᵉrepresents my body." ²³Then he took a cup, said a prayer of thanksgiving, gave *it* to them, and they all drank from it. ²⁴Then he said to them, "This represents my blood of the ᵀcovenant, which is poured out on behalf ofᶲ many. ²⁵Am·en, I say to you, no, I will not have drunk

---

14:12 ξ→day: Literally, "On the firstest or firstmost day of unleavens" was the 14th of the month. The Greek word πρῶτός was sometimes used comparatively like πρότερος. In Exodus 12:15 the 14th, when they removed the leaven was called the 'headmost' day (and not the first of the seven days). This riddle, like all other riddles is not understood, and so many presume that they asked where to prepare on the 15th day after the time for preparation already passed. The actual time of the supper and arrest was after the end of the 13th day and before dawn on the 14th. The 15th of the month was the *first* day of unleavened bread, but the 14th was the *headmost* day. The same Hebrew root רֹאשׁ means 'head' and with the ending וֹן, it means either headmost (*ro'shon*) or first (*ri'shon*) רִאשׁוֹן depending on the context. The -on ending is an Aramaic intensifier like -im in Hebrew, and so r*'šon came to mean that which immediately precedes as well as the first in a sequence. **14:12** χ They sacrificed the Passover on the 14th day between 1 and 5 pm, so the parallelism clearly shows that the first of the seven days is not meant. Rather the "header day" is meant, the one at the head of the seven days. So it is translated "the day before." In this case the Galileans reckoned the head most day between two sunsets. So the questions were asked shortly after sunset on the 13th day. This reckoning of the head most day is under the influence of the fact that the seven days of unleavened bread are counted from sunset on the 14th to sunset on the 21st. The "day before" unleavened bread is reckoned on the same pattern. Likewise, the first and seventh days of unleavened bread, being Şabbaṯhs, have influenced the understanding of the limits of the headmost day. ρ→eat: The disciples were assuming he would eat the Passover, so this subjunctive is the polite form of "will." They are not framing it as a demand. See Luke 22:16 where Yĕshua says he would not eat it then. The disciples were expressing what they thought would happen. In vs. 14 Yĕshua uses a subjunctive of obligation "should eat," (cf. Wallace, Syntax, pg. 463), and this expresses the idea that they ought to eat it, but he knows he will not be able to eat it.

14:16 π→Passover. This does not say sacrificing the Passover, but means only getting it ready, purchasing, washing, grooming, and feeding. See notes on Matthew 26:17. **14:17** γ As John states, it was the night before the Passover sacrifice. **14:22** ε The text says "is my body," but in Hebrew there is no word for *is*: זֶה הוּא גּוּפִי, *zeh hu' guphi*, and so *is* may not mean *becomes*. But in Greek τοῦτό ἐστιν τὸ σῶμά μου, the word "is" also is used with the sense of "represents." Yĕshua's parables show the same usage: "And the field is the world" (Mat. 13:38) (ὁ δὲ ἀγρός ἐστιν ὁ κόσμος, וְהַשָּׂדֶה הוּא הָעוֹלָם).

14:24 τ Codex Bezae and Aland's 27th omit the word new (καινῆς) on correct scientific principles of textual criticism. However, the sense is not changed, since the covenant Yĕshua speaks of is a renewal of the original covenant with Yisra'el, just as Deuteronomy

from *this cup of* the fruit of the vine until that day when I may be drinking it new-made in the kingdom of the Almĭghty."

²⁶And after singing a hymn, they went out to the Mount of Olives. ²⁷And Yĕshua says to them, "You will all fall away, because it has been written, "I WILL STRIKE THE SHEPHERD, AND THE SHEEP WILL BE SCATTERED.ξ" ²⁸But after I have been raised, I will go before you to Galil."

²⁹But Peter said to him, "Even though all may fall away, yet I will not." ³⁰And Yĕshua said to him, "Amen, I say to you, that you yourself this very night, before the rooster sounds twice, will three times deny me." ³¹But Peter kept saying insistently, "Even if I need to die with you, I will not deny you!" And they all were saying the same thing, too.

³²And they came to a place named Gaṭh-Ṣemanei, and he said to his disciples, "Sit here until I have prayed." ³³And he took with him Peter and Yaʻaqov and Yoḥanan, and began to be very distressed and troubled. ³⁴And he said to them, "My soul is deeply grieved to the point of death. Remain here and be keeping watch." ³⁵And he went a little beyond them, and fell to the ground, and was praying that if it were possible, the hour might pass him by. ³⁶And he was saying, "Abba! Făther! All things are possible for you. Remove this cup from me. Yet not what I will, but what you will."

³⁷And he came and found them sleeping, and said to Peter, "Ṣimʻon, are you asleep? Could you not keep watch for one hour? ³⁸Be keeping watch and be

---

is a renewal and expansion of the Sinai covenant. ▷ See *Mat.* 26:28 note. The Most High's covenant with his people is a suzerainty covenant, which means the lord sets the terms. At any renewal of such a covenant, terms may be expanded, added, updated, or discarded. The people may not modify it. For example, the Tabernacle was replaced by the Temple, and then in Ezekiel 40-48 we see further modifications of the Levitical service. Very little has been discarded. It was the intention at first for the first born sons to be the priests, but circumstances led to the tribe of Levi being chosen for priests. ▷ Not every covenant renewal or re-affirmation need involve a repetition of the covenant sacrifice, which is to say one will suffer the fate of death if the terms are violated. For example the renewal explained by Mosheḥ on the plains of Moʼav did not need new offerings. The covenant sacrifice is a warning. So if we do not crucify the flesh and put the old nature to death, then such a person is cut off from the people. This is what a covenant ratification or renewal sacrifice means. It spells out what will happen if the participants in the covenant do not hold faithful. ▷ Messiah's sacrifice is the same in this respect for the new made covenant of old (בְּרִית עוֹלָם). His blood also signifies a declaration of the wiping out of transgressions and iniquities for the confessor who has strayed from the covenant and wishes to return. This is just as sins of ignorance were symbolically declared to be wiped by the blood of the sin offering, representing divine forgiveness, for those who had not strayed from the covenant. The sin offering and guilt offering were before only generally for declaring cleansing from the burden of sins of ignorance, and not sins that lead to death and excision from the covenant. This does not mean there was no forgiveness before Messiah for serious sins. The YOM KIPPURIM ceremony could only symbolize transgression being removed if there was the reality of forgiveness prior to it. But later it does mean that Messiah's physical blood became symbolic for cleansing relating to such sins committed before his first advent for the confessor, as it is after the first advent. The physical blood is symbolic. The divine life/spirit that the physical blood stands for is the effective one who forgives and cleanses the sin. ▷ Also, Messiah's death is a ransom, because when the covenant was broken, the Most High sold his people into the hands of other nations, whose lords were the fallen spiritutual powers. These powers took the ransom, and so the Most High will demand the ransom release from them. And in general sacrifice concerning sin is an acknowledgement that the sinner's lawlessness has exacted the cost of a ransom for their restoration and release. The slaying of the offering symbolizes the cost charged by the lawlessness. ▷ So once again, the offering is not a satisfaction of divine wrath, but it is an instruction on the ransom cost taken by sin that is borne by the deliverer seeking to heal us (cf. Gen. 3:15). **14:24** φ ὑπὲρ πολλῶν See Mt. 20:28 **14:27** ξ Zech 13:7.

praying, that you may not come into testing. The spirit is willing, but the flesh
is weak."
[39]And again he went away and prayed, saying the same words. [40]And again
when he came, he found them sleeping, because their eyes had been getting
heavy, and they had not been knowing what they should answer him.
[41]And he came the third time, and said to them, "Are you still sleeping and
taking your rest? It is enough! The hour has come. Behold, the Sŏn of Man is
being betrayed into the hands of sinners. [42]Be getting up, we should be going.
Behold, the one betraying me has been drawing near!"
[43]And immediately while he was still speaking, Yehudah, one of the twelve,
came up, accompanied by a crowd with swords and clubs, from before the chief
priests and the scribes and the elders. [44]And, his betrayer had been giving them
a signal, saying, "Whomever I may have kissed, it is he. Seize him, and be leading
him away under guard." [45]And after coming, he immediately went to him, saying,
"Rabbi!" and kissed him. [46]And they laid hands on him, and seized him. [47]But a
certain one of those who had been standing by drew his sword, and struck the
slave of the high priest, and cut off his ear.
[48]And Yĕshua answered and said to them, "Have you come out with swords
and clubs to arrest me, as against a robber? [49]Throughout the day I was with
you in the temple teaching, and you did not seize me." But this has happened
that the writings may be fulfilled. [50]And they all left him and fled. [51]And a certain
young man was following him, who had been clothing himself in nothing but a
linen garment over his naked body, and they seized him. [52]But he left the linen
garment behind, and escaped naked.
[53]And they led Yĕshua away to the high priest, and all the chief priests
and the elders and the scribes gathered together. [54]And Peter followed him at
a distance, right into the courtyard of the high priest, and he was sitting with
the officers, and warming himself at the fire.
[55]Now the chief priests and the whole Council kept trying to obtain testimony against Yĕshua to put him to death, and they were not finding any. [56]For
many were giving false testimony against him, and yet their testimony was not
consistent. [57]And some stood up and were giving false testimony against him,
saying, [58]"We heard him say, 'I will destroy this temple made with hands, and
during three days[μ] I will build another made without hands.'" [59]And not even in
this respect was their testimony consistent.
[60]And the high priest stood up and came forward and questioned Yĕshua, saying, "Do you make no answer? What is it that these men are testifying
against you?" [61]But he kept silent, and made no answer. Again the high priest
was questioning him, and saying to him, "Are you the Anŏinted, the Sŏn, THE
BLESSED ONE?"
[62]And Yĕshua said, "I AM[ρ], and you will see *to* THE SŎN OF MAN SITTING AT

14:58 μ See Yoḥ. 2:19. **14:62** ρ Deu 32:39: אֲנִי אֲנִי הוּא; Isa. 41:4: אֲנִי־הוּא. **14:62** λ Dan 7:13: עִם־עֲנָנֵי שְׁמַיָּא כְּבַר אֱנָשׁ, Psa. 110:1: שֵׁב לִימִינִי.

THE RIGHT HAND OF POWER, and COMING WITH THE CLOUDS OF HEAVEN.ᵔ" ⁶³And tearing his clothes, the high priest said, "What further need do we have of witnesses? ⁶⁴"You have heard the blasphemy. How does it seem to you?" And they all condemned him to be deserving of death.

⁶⁵And some began to spit at him, and to blindfold him, and to beat him with their fists, and to say to him, "Prophesy!" And the officers received him with slaps in the face.

⁶⁶And as Peter was below in the courtyard, one of the servant-girls of the high priest came, ⁶⁷and seeing Peter warming himself, she looked at him, and said, "You, too, were with Yĕshua Ha-Netseri." ⁶⁸But he denied it, saying, "I neither have been knowing nor am I understanding what you are talking about." And he went out onto the porch. And a rooster sounded.

⁶⁹And when the maid saw him, she began once more to be saying to those who had been standing alongside, "This one is from them!" ⁷⁰But again he was denying it. And after a little while, those who had been standing alongside were again saying to Peter, "Surely you are one of them, because you are also Gelili." ⁷¹But he began to be cursing and to be swearing, "I have not been knowing this man you are talking about." ⁷²And immediately, a second time, the rooster sounded. And Peter remembered how Yĕshua had made the remark to him, "Before the rooster sounds twice, you will deny me three times." And he began to weep.

15

¹And immediately, early in the morning,ᵀ when the chief priests held council with the elders and scribes, then the whole Council, having bound Yĕshua, led him away, and delivered him up to Pilate. ²And Pilate questioned him, "You are the King of the Yehudim?" And answering he says to him, "*So you are saying.*" ³And the chief priests were accusing him of many things. ⁴And Pilate was questioning him again, saying, "Do you make no answer? See how many charges they bring against you!" ⁵But Yĕshua made no further answer, so that Pilate was amazed.

⁶Now ᵠduring a feast he used to release for them any one prisoner whom they were asking to excuse. ⁷And, the one being called Bar-Abba had been getting confined with fellow bandits, whoever had been committing murder in the ᶿbandit raid. ⁸And the crowd went up and began asking him to do as he was accustomed to do for them. ⁹And Pilate answered them, saying, "Do you want *that* I shall have released for you the King of the Yehudim?" ¹⁰For he was aware that the chief priests had been delivering him up because of envy. ¹¹Yet the chief priests stirred up the crowd, so that instead he would release Bar-Abba for them. ¹²And answering again, Pilate was saying to them, "Then what will I have done with him whom you call the King of the Yehudim?" ¹³And they shouted back, "Fasten

---

15:1 τ Aviv 14, Wednesday, March 24th, AD 34. **15:6** ψ down through **15:7** θ→raid: Raids by politically motivated bandits or robbers who robbed the despised rich, and robbed, plundered or murdered political enemies. They were Robinhoods who engaged in long term low grade attacks and thievery. According to Luke 23:18-19 the recent raid was in the city.

him up on an execution timber!" ¹⁴But Pilate was saying to them, "Why, what evil has he done?" But they shouted all the more, "Fasten him up on an execution timber!" ¹⁵And wishing to satisfy the crowd, Pilate released Bar-Abba for them. And he handed Yĕshua over, having scourged *him*, so that he could be fastened up on an execution timber.

¹⁶And the soldiers took him away into the palace (that is, the Praetorium). Then they *did* call together the whole cohort. ¹⁷And they *did* array him in purple, and after weaving a crown of thorns, they put it on him. ¹⁸And they began to be saluting him, "Be rejoicing, King of the Yehudim!" ¹⁹And they were beating his head with a reed, and were spitting on him. And bending the knees, they were bowing down to him. ²⁰And when they had mocked him, they took the purple off him, and put his garments on him. Then they *did* lead him out, that they may have fastened him up on an execution timber. ²¹And they *did* press into service a certain one passing by coming from the field, Şim'on of Cyrene (the father of Alexander and Rufus), so that he will have borne his execution timber.

²²Then they *did* bring him to the place Golgoltha, which being translated *is* "Skull Place" ²³And they were offering him wine, which had been getting mixed with myrrh, but he did not take it. ²⁴Then they *did* fasten him up on an execution timber, and *did* divide up his garments, casting lots for them, *to decide* what each may have taken. ²⁵And it was the third hour when they fastened him up on an execution timber. ²⁶And there was the inscription of the charge against him, which had been getting written: "THE KING OF THE YEHUDIM."

²⁷And with him they *did* fasten up on the execution timber two bandits, one off his right *hand* and one off his left *hand*.ᵂ ²⁹And those passing by were hurling abuse at him, wagging their heads, and saying, "Ha! O one destroying the Temple and rebuilding *it* in three days, ³⁰may you have rescued yourself, having descended from the execution timber!" ³¹In the same way the chief priests also, along with the scribes, mocking to others were saying, "Others he rescued. Himself he is not able to rescue. ³²May the Anŏinted, the King of Yisra'el, have descended now from the execution timber, so that we will have seen and we will have pledged faithfulness!" And those who had been getting ᵋfastened on the execution timber with him were insulting him.

³³And when the sixth hour came, darkness came upon the whole land until the ninth hour. ³⁴And at the ninth hour Yĕshua cried out with a loud voice, "ELI, ELI, LAMAH ŞEVAQTANI?"ᵠ which being translated *is*, "MY GŎD, MY GŎD, WHY HAVE YOU FORSAKEN ME?"ᵠ ³⁵And when some of those, who had been standing alongside, heard *it*, they were saying, "Behold, he is calling for Eliyahu." ³⁶And, someone having run, and having filled a sponge with vinegar, having put it on a reed, was giving him a drink, saying, "Ye will have allowed it *that* we may have

---

15:27 ω omit vs. 28 **15:32** ξ→timber: or *crucified.* **15:34** ψ Psa 22:1: אֵלִי אֵלִי לָמָה עֲזַבְתָּנִי, with Mishnaic Hebrew variation, mss D ηλι. See the note on | Matthew 27:46. The Father was not forsaking the Son. There is no heavenly backturning. But the Father looks upon the Son to deliver him through death, because he is the ransom.

Mark 16

seen whether Ĕliyahu comes to take him down."

³⁷And Yĕshua allowed a loud cry, breathed his last. ³⁸And the veil of the temple was torn asunder⁵ into two from top to bottom. ³⁹And when the centurion, who had been standing out in front of him, saw the way he breathed his last, he said, "Truly this man was the Almĭghty Sŏn!"

⁴⁰And there were also some women looking on from a distance, among whom were Miryam Ha-Magdalit, and Miryam the mother of Ya'aqov the younger, and Yosei, and Shelomit, ⁴¹who when he was in Galil, were following him and ministering to him, and there were many other women who came up with him to Yerushalayim.

⁴²And already, it became late, because it was a preparation, that is, before a Ṣabbath,⁰ ⁴³Yosef of Ha-Ramati came, a prominent member of the Council, who himself was waiting for the kingdom of the Almĭghty, and he gathered up courage and went in before Pilate, and asked for the body of Yĕshua. ⁴⁴And Pilate wondered if he already had been dying by this time, and summoning the centurion, he questioned him as to whether he of old had been dying. ⁴⁵And ascertaining this from the centurion, he granted the body to Yosef.

⁴⁶And Yosef, who bought a linen sheet, who took him down, wrapped *him* in the linen cloth, and laid him in a tomb which had been getting hewn out of rock. Then he rolled a stone over the entry of the tomb. ⁴⁷And Miryam Ha-Magdalit and Miryam the mother of Yosei were looking on to see where he had been getting laid.

16

¹And when the ṢABBAṭH⁵ was past⁵, Miryam Ha-Magdalit, and Miryam the mother of Ya'aqov, and Shelomit, ᵂbought spices, that having come, they mighṭ anoint him. ²And very early on the ⁿFIRST OF THE ṢABBAṭHS⁵ they are coming upon the tomb, ʿthe sun still *not* having risenʾ, ³when they were saying to themselves, "Who will roll away the stone for us from the door of the tomb?" ⁴And when they looked up, they are seeing that the stone has been getting rolled away, although it had been extremely large.

15:38 ξ 'Torn asunder': see Mark 1:10 for the key to this text. The veil over the doors leading to the Holy Place was made with a panorama of the heavens. The message in Mark's symbolism is that heaven was opened to accept Mĕssiah's offering. See Mat. 27:51.

15:42 θ There was always a preparation before the annual Passover Ṣabbath. This Ṣabbath was Aviv 15, March 25, AD 34. The text readings vary, 'toward a Sabbath,' 'before a Sabbath,' 'before-Sabbath.'

16:1 ζ Lev 23:11, 15a: מִמָּחֳרַת הַשַּׁבָּת. **16:1** ζ This was the annual Ṣabbath or first day of the feast. See Lev. 23:11. It fell between Wednesday sunset and Thursday sunset in AD 34 on March 25th. ▷ τ They bought the spices between this Ṣabbath and the following weekly Ṣabbath. See Luke 24:1; Mat. 28:1; Yoḥ. 20:1. **16:1** ω The spices were bought between the two Ṣabbaths. They also prepared them then. On the regular Ṣabbath they brought them to the tomb.

See Luke 24:1. Why did they come at the end of the third day just before dawn on Ṣabbath rather than on the same day they prepared the spices? According to Jewish custom a dead person was regarded the same as an sick person and every opportunity to care for the person was taken until it was no longer possible. Others tended to the body on Friday. Since the time they came was the last opportunity, they did not want to miss it, and what was needed was the aromatic spices they prepared. All manner of care for a dead body was permitted on the Ṣabbath according to Jewish traditional law just as if a person had been sick on the Ṣabbath and needed care. **16:2** η = τῆς μιᾶς = the one [day]; lit. 'the one [day] of the Ṣabbaths.' The words τῆς μιᾶς are a Semiticism equiv. to 'the first.' Cf. μιᾶ Gen. 1:5; Mt. 28:1. The gender of μιᾶς necessarily implies the word 'day' like πρώτη; compare Mark 14:12 & Mat. 26:17. **16:2** η→of = *first day of* or *first day for* **16:2** χ See Lev. 23:15b: ...וּסְפַרְתֶּם

⁵And when they entered the tomb, they saw a young man sitting at the right, who had been wearing on himself a white robe, and they were really amazed. ⁶And he says to them, "Do not be getting yourselves awestruck. You are looking for Yĕshua Ha-Natsri, who had been getting fastened up on an execution timber. He has risen. He is not so here. Behold, here is the place where they laid him. ⁷But be going, tell his disciples and Peter, 'He is going before you into Galil. There you will see him, just as he said to you.ᶻ'" ⁸And when they went out, they fled from the tomb, because trembling and amazement had been gripping them, and they said nothing to anyone, because they were being in a state of awe.ᵠ

שֶׁבַע שַׁבָּתוֹת תְּמִימֹת תִּהְיֶינָה. Şabbath, March 27th, 34 AD. The resurrection was early on the Şabbath before the night ended. He returned to life before the the crack of dawn. We may inquire why so stunning a corruption has occurred in those versions which say "first day of the week," when plainly the text says the first day for Sabbaths following Passover that year. We have to realize that the Assemblies soon fell away from the true Good News soon after the passing of the emissaries. Gnostics infiltrated them. The Good News was re-explained to mean acquittal instead of pardon, and absolution instead of forgiveness. See Mat. 28:18-20 notes. **16:2** ᶠTwo solutions regarding the words, "the sun having risen" are presently possible. ▷ The first is to follow the old Latin mss Codex Bobiensis and omit ἀνατείλαντος τοῦ ἡλίου: itᵏ (Codex Bobiensis IV cent < Exemplar 𝔓 II Cent.): *(having risen the sun)*. As is, the phrase is entirely in contradiction to λίαν πρωΐ *(very early)* and ὄρθρου βαθέως *(deep dawn)*; compare Mark 1:35 πρωΐ ἔννυχον λίαν; See *Greek Testament Critical Exegetical Commentary*, Alford Henry, cf. *Cambridge Greek Testament for Schools and Colleges, The Expositor's Greek Testament*. See also Meyer. The Greek word ἐπὶ *(upon)* used with each phrase indicates the arrival time at the tomb, and not departure from their dwellings. To *'come upon'* something does not mean to leave to go to it, but to arrive at it. ▷ The contradiction is acknowledged in the 2nd century exemplar of Codex Bezae, because the editor saw the need to delete λίαν *(very*; also omit: itᵏ) and change the participle to a present participle ἀνατέλλοντος *(rising)*, and besides to change Luke 24:1 to read ηρχοντο επει τὸ μνῆμα *(they were coming to the tomb)* in place of ἦλθον ἐπὶ τὸ μνῆμα *(they came upon the tomb)*, and then to this is added the argument that they left at dawn and arrived at sunrise. Since there is no possible reason why λίαν would be spuriously added since it would only increase the difficulty, it follows that we must question what stands in contradiction to it instead. Codex Bezae's coordinated change at Luke 24:1, viz. επει τὸ μνῆμα *(to the tomb)* is also acknowledgment that ὄρθρου βαθέως *(earliest dawn)* contradicts its defense of ἀνατέλλοντος τοῦ ἡλίου *(is rising the sun)*. It follows then that rather than make edits in three places, only one edit is needed in one place, and that is ἀνατείλαντος τοῦ ἡλίου *(having risen the sun)* may itself be excised. ▷ Codex Bobiensis' interpolation after vs. 2 gives a different apologetic for a third day and night, which clearly derives from a period before the scribes were able to completely collude in their re-explanation of the text. By the fourth century they had settled on the best way to corrupt the text. ▷ The second solution is Beza's conjecture, which appears more probable. Beza observed that Eusebius quoted the text as, "ετι ἀνατείλαντος τοῦ ἡλίου" "still having risen the sun;" As the text makes no sense in this condition, Beza supposed that the word "not" had disappeared from the text. He suggests the original reading was, "ουκετι ἀνατείλαντος τοῦ ἡλίου." **16:7** ζ cf. Mark 14:28; Mat. 28:7.

16:8 φ The book of Mark ends here. The abruptness of his ending meets with his style if we realize that the kind of fear here mentioned is that of awestruck trembling, a catatonic revival of hope. For longer ending and remarks see Appendix II.

End Note: After Three Days

Seven times the Evangelists report that the resurrection would be "after three days" (Mat. 16:21; 17:23; 27:63; Mark 8:31; 9:31; 10:34; Luke 9:22). One time an adversary says it (Mat. 27:63). On three unique occasions, Měssiah says it (1. Mark 8:31; Mat. 16:21; Luke 9:22; 2. Mark 9:31; Mat. 17:23; 3. Mark 10:34. Six times, scribes or translators changed the texts to "in three days." That left only Mark 8:31.

Six times the Evangelists report that the resurrection would be "the third day" (Mat. 20:19; Luke 13:32; Luke 18:33; Luke 24:7; Luke 24:20; Luke 24:46). Almost all of these are in Luke! On three unique occasions, Měssiah said it himself (1. Luke 18:33; Mat. 20:19; 2. Luke 13:32; 3. Luke 24:46). A friendly party says it twice (Luke 24:7; 24:20).

Five times the Evangelists report "in three days" (Yoĥ. 2:19; Mat. 26:61; 27:40; Mark 14:58; 15:29). Only once does Měssiah say it (Yoĥ. 2:19). The other four reports are of the two times adversaries said it.

Three times the sign of Yonah is repeated (Mat. 12:40; 16:4; Luke 11:29). Two are unique.

Four times by Měssiah "after three days" or its equivalent are uniquely stated (Mat: 12:40 (Luke 11:29); Mark 8:31; 9:31; 10:34), or five if we include Mat. 16:4. And but four times "the third day" or its equivalent (Yoĥ. 2:19; Luke 18:33 (Mat. 20:19); Luke 13:32; 24:46.)

The alterations in the "after three days" texts were made by Catholic scribes in the 2nd to 4th centuries. That changes were made is perfect proof that "after three days" does not agree with the Friday-Sunday theory. In Greek and Latin it means "the third day after," i.e. the time after two full days have passed, between 48 and 72 hours. Only one Codex Bezae appears to have escaped all the ravages of the Catholics among Greek texts. Like the lone Torah Scroll found in the Temple, it alone has survived.

The third day texts agree perfectly with the after three day texts. In no case is a third day text parallel with an after three days text. That is, the four occasions Měssiah indicated the third day are separate from the four occasions (or up six) he indicated after three days. When he said the third day, he meant the third calendar day, using a dawn to dawn epoch. When he said after three days, he meant the night in the third calendar day after the third daylight period.

When David returned to Tsiqlag on the third day (1 Sam. 30:1), he and his mighty men found it burned and all they cherished carried away by Amaŀeq (1 Sam. 30:18). The people were ready to stone the Anointed one (1 Sam. 30:6). But the Almĭghty stayed their hand like that of Avraham and said to pursue the enemy. They found the Servant when he had not eaten or drunk water for three days and three nights (1 Sam. 30:12). When they fed him, then his spirit returned to him. Having risen up, the Servant showed them the way to defeat Amaŀeq. "THEN DAVID SMOTE THEM FROM THE DAWN TWILIGHT EVEN UNTIL THE SETTING OF THEIR NEXT DAY" (1 Sam. 30:17). Now it says 'their next day,' because the Servant counts days to dawn, but Amaŀeq did not. Therefore, the Servant of Yăhweĥ was three days and three nights in the grave, and rose near dawn on the Şabbath.

Again, they did not leave Egypt until the break of day (cf. Exodus 12:22; 12:10.). But they went out by night (cf. Deut. 16:1). And the same day is the 15th day of the month (cf. Exodus 13:4; Num. 33:3). So they began to go out at dawn, and arrived at Sukkot in the night following the day, and therefore the day they rested at Sukkot is marked with a special offering, the wave offering, which is the third day from the Passover.

Luke

1 ¹Inasmuch as many have taken in hand to set forth a narrative about the events which have been getting fully borne out among us, ²exactly as they, who from the beginning were eyewitnesses and ministers of the word, have delivered them to us, ³it seemed good to me also, having been carefully following alongside everything from the start successively, to have written for you, most excellent ᶿTheophilus, ⁴so that you may exactly and securely have known concerning the things you were taught.

⁵There was in the days of Herod, king of Yehudah, a certain priest, by name Zekaryahu, from the ᵘdivision of Aviyah, and his wife from the daughters of Aharon, and her name *was* Elisheva. ⁶And they were both righteous before the Almĭghty, walking in all the commandments and ordinances of Yăhweh, blamelessly. ⁷And there was no child for them, because Elisheva was barren, and both had been advancing in their days.

⁸Then it happened in his priestly serving, in the rotation of his division before the Almĭghty, ⁹according to the custom of the priesthood, that his lot fell to burn incense, for which he had to enter into the temple of Yăhweh. ¹⁰And the ᵋwhole

---

1:3 θ *Beloved of the Almĭghty.* See Acts 1:1.

1:5 μ The key to the priestly rotation riddle is given in Deut. 18:8 (חֵלֶק כְּחֵלֶק יֹאכֵלוּ) "*Portion equal to portion they shall eat.*" The rotation was <u>unbroken</u> and <u>continuous</u> to ensure that all 24 divisions served for <u>equal time</u> to eat equally from the offerings, taking one week turns. The rotations did not restart every year in Nisan or Tishri as claimed by many, and the regular rotation was not suspended during feasts, because any such innovation would give the divisions unequal shares from the offerings. All the courses rotated in 24 weeks and restarted in the next 24 weeks with no gaps, no skips, and no annual restarts. Like the seven day week the rotation was perpetual. The correct order of rotations was set forth in *Fasti Sacri*, in 1865 by Thomas Lewin (AD 1805-1877): "The eighth course, which was that of Abijah, would begin on 16th May B.C. 7." (*Fasti*, pg. xxix). ▷ The priestly rotations were founded on the same equality principle as Solomon's rotating twelve month tax system without yearly correction via a 13th month. ▷ How did Lewin compute the division times? The second Temple was destroyed on the first day of the week on the 9th of Av, when the first of the 24 divisions was beginning (cf. Jos. *Ant*; *Seder Olam*). The 9th of Av was Sunday, August 5th, AD 70 by astronomical calculation. Accounting for the rotations backward through time, we arrive here at the service of Aviyah (the 8th division) between noon on Şabbath, July 6, 3 BC and noon on July 13th, which was month IV.23 to IV.30 in 3 BC. Since 1865, Dead Sea Scroll documents have also confirmed the correct Rotation. See Appendix XVII. ▷ The year is nailed down in Luke 3:1 and 23. Since the divisions come up for service twice a year, 24 weeks apart, one of the service weeks in 3 BC must be eliminated to be sure the July 6-13 service is the right one. Now according to the service period to be eliminated from consideration (XI.1-XI.8, Jan 19-26, 3 BC), the five months would be (1) XI.9 to XII.8, (2) XII.9 to I.8, (3) I.9 to II.8, (4) II.9 to III.8), (5) III.9 to IV.8. And the sixth month commences on IV.9. Calculating the term date based on a IV.9 conception date gives us March 14, 2 BC (Nisan 7). This, of course, assumes the five month accounting began as soon as Zekaryahu ended his week of service, and this is proved at 1:25 γ. But March 14, a week before Passover, is still when the latter rains are heavy, and shepherds did not take their flocks to the the fields then. Considering that Bethlehem is at 2543 feet on average, there is still risk even of snow in early March. See 2:8 χ. Nor can the birth be overdue so much as to overcome this obstacle (See 2:6). ▷ As shown by 1:36, however, the new moon day commenced the sixth month of Elisheva, and therefore, we have a final witness that neither she nor Luke started counting five moons in the middle of a month. Luke is counting from a new moon day exactly equivalent to the day that Zekaryahu came off his priestly division. The first service period in 3 BC is eliminated because the day after it is not a new moon day. ▷ Using the sign in Revelation 12:1-2 to work Luke's time line backward from Mĕssiah's birth to Yohanan's conception, we arrive at the same dates for the division of Aviyah. The clues all intersect at the same points. See the *Birth Chart*.

Luke 1

multitude of the people were praying outside at the hour of the incense offering. ¹¹Then the Messenger *of* Yăhweӊ appeared to him, ᶿwho had been standing at the right of the altar of incense. ¹²Then Zeḵaryahu was distressed, having seen, and fear fell upon him.

¹³Then the Messenger said to him, "Be not fearing, Zeḵaryahu, because your request is heard, and your wife Elisheva will bear you a son. Then you will call his name Yoḥanan. ¹⁴Then he will be a joy for you and gladness, and many will rejoice over his birth, ¹⁵because he will be great before Yăhweӊ, and wine or liquor, no, he will not have drunk. And with the Holy Spirit he will be filled while still in his mother's womb. ¹⁶And many of the sons of Yisra'el he will turn back to Yăhweӊ their Almĭghty. ¹⁷And he will go before *him*, at his face, in the spirit and power of Ęliyahu TO RETURN THE HEART OF THE ANCESTORS TO THE CHILDREN,ᶿ and the disobedient to the wisdom of the *ancient* righteous ones, to make ready for Yăhweӊ a people, who have been getting fully outfitted." ¹⁸Then Zeḵaryahu said to the Messenger, "How will I know this? For I am an old man, and my wife has been advancing in her days." ¹⁹Then the Messenger answered and said to him, "I am ˢGavri•el, who has been standing alongside, at the face of the Almĭghty. And I have been sent to speak to you, and to announce this good news to you. ²⁰And behold, you will be keeping silent, even being unable to speak, past which *ever* day these things may have happened, against *the possibility* that you will not have held my words faithful, which will be fulfilled in the time appointed for them."

²¹And the people were awaiting Zeḵaryahu, and were wondering about his delay in the temple. ²²And as he came out, he was unable to speak to them. Then they realized that he had been seeing a vision in the temple, and he was gesturing to them, and he was remaining mute.

1:10 ξ→multitude: The largest crowd. Thus it was Ṣabbath, IV.23 (July 6), about 3 pm. See 1:23. **1:11** θ→incense: Where Yăhweӊ stood when speaking with Mosheh face to face. When speaking as a voice it was from the glory above the ark of the testimony (Exodus 25:22), but when face to face he stood in the Holy Place near the altar of incense. Exodus 30:6, "THEN YOU SHALL REST IT TOWARD THE FACE OF THE CURTAIN (WHICH IS IN FRONT OF THE ARK OF THE TESTIMONY), TOWARD THE FACE OF THE ATONEMENT COVER (WHICH IS UPON THE TESTIMONY), WHERE I MEET WITH YOU." The same place is described three different ways. In 1 Sam. 3:10 Yăhweӊ's Word, taking physical form, "STOOD HIMSELF" in the holy place where he appeared to Samuel. Also it is where Aharon's rod that budded was put (cf. Num. 17:40) and the manna jar (cf. Exo. 16:33-34). **1:11** θ→standing: the pres. perf. continuous put for habitual or customary actions. See Elisabetta Magni, "Intensity, reduplication, and pluractionality in Ancient Greek," *Lexis Journal in English Lexicology*, 10 | 2017.

1:17 φ Mal 4:6 **1:19** ξ Dan. 8:15-16, "AND BEHOLD, ONE WAS STANDING OPPOSITE ME, LIKE THE APPEARANCE OF A STRONG MAN (גֶּבֶר *gaver*). THEN I HEARD THE VOICE OF A MAN (קוֹל־אָדָם *qol-'adam*) IN THE MIDDLE OF THE ULAI. THEN, HE CALLED. THEN GAVRI•EL SAID, 'GIVE UNDERSTANDING TO THIS ONE, OF THE VISION.'" *Gavri•el* (גַּבְרִיאֵל) means "the strong man of Gŏd." "AND THE MAN (וְהָאִישׁ *we-ha-'ish*) GAVRI•EL, WHOM I HAD SEEN IN VISION PREVIOUSLY, HAVING BEEN WEARIED WITH WEARINESS, TOUCHED ME AT THE TIME OF THE AFTERNOON OFFERING" (Dan. 9:21). "AND BEHOLD, ONE MAN DRESSED IN LINEN" (Dan. 10:5). "THEN HE SAID TO THE MAN DRESSED IN LINEN WHO WAS ABOVE THE WATERS OF THE RIVER...." (Dan. 12:7). The reverse title also occurs in Isa. 9:6, 'ĘL GIBBOR' (mighty Gŏd). Here the name means, 'Mighty [one] of Gŏd.' Compare Zech. 1:8-16. Dan. 8:16: 'THE MIGHTY ONE OF GŎD IS THE ONE MAKING UNDERSTOOD THE VISION FOR THIS ONE.' The 'man' speaks of himself indirectly, but is identified by Dan. 7:9-14, and the words in Dan. 8:17-18. See Rev. 1:12-18 and Dan. 10:5-9 and Ezek. 10:2. See Jud. 13:1-2; Gen. 32:24-30.

²³Then it came about, when the days of his priestly service were fulfilled, *that* he went away to his home. ²⁴And after these days Elisheva his wife conceived.ᶻ And she was concealing herself for *the days of* five *new* moons,ᵝ saying that, ²⁵"So thus Yăhweɦ has been doing with me during the days in which he looks upon *me* to take away my disgrace among men,ᵞ."

²⁶And, with the ᵠsixth new moon the Messenger Gavri'el was sent from the Almĭghty into a city of Galil, named Netsereŧh, ²⁷to a virgin, who had been bethrothing herself to a man whose name *was* Yosef, of the house of David. And the virgin's name *was* Miryam. ²⁸And coming in to her, the Messenger said to her, "Be rejoicing, one who has been getting favored! Yăhweɦ is with you." ²⁹But she was quite perplexed at this statement, and kept pondering what kind of greeting this may be.

³⁰Then the Messenger said to her, "Do not be getting afraid, Miryam, because you have found favor at the side of the Almĭghty. ³¹And behold, you will conceive in your womb. Then you will bring forth a son. Then you shall call his name Yĕshua. ³²He will be great, and he will be called the Sŏn of the Most High. Then Yăhweɦ Almĭghty will give him the throne of his father David. ³³Then he will reign over the house of Ya'aqov for *all* the ages. And of his kingdom *there* will be no end."

³⁴And, Miryam said to the Messenger, "How will this be, since I am not knowing a man?" ³⁵And answering, the Messenger said to her, "The Holy Spĭrit will come upon you, and the power of the Most High will overshadow you; for that reason also, the Holy One being begotten will be called the Almĭghty Sŏn. ³⁶And behold, your kinswoman Elisheva, even she has been conceiving a son in her old age. And this new moon, a sixth is, for her being called barren.ᵏ ³⁷Because

---

1:24 ζ His days of service were noon on Ŝabbaŧh, July 6th, 3 BC to noon on Ŝabbaŧh, July 13th, 3 BC. He was returned home on the first day of the 5th month, on July 14th. Yoɦanan was conceived on V.1, the new moon day. First day of the week. **1:24 β** See Appendix XVI. The maximum days of five new moons, since a sixth new moon is at the end (cf. 1:36; Appendix XVI), and women do not count partial months as whole months: 149 days: July 14th-December 9th; Av 1 to Kislev 29 (V.1 to IX.29): Av, Elul, Tishri, Ḥeshvan, Kislev. All in 3 BC. ▷ Also Luke's attention to the detail 'nearly' in 1:56 implies that he means exactly here. **1:25 γ** The reason given here is for her self-concealment. Luke supplies the five new moons from his notation of the time elapsed. We should not think that five new moons is the whole time of concealment, but it is a measure to the first day of the sixth new moon, just as it says, "a son of a year Ŝa'ul is in his reigning, and two years he has reigned over Yisra'el" (1 Sam. 13:1) is not a statement on the whole length of his reign, which was 40 years. Samuel is just bringing the reign up to the 10th day of Tishri that year, which was just the beginning of Ŝa'ul's second year. For without a doubt the her self concealment lasted at least until Miryam reached her sometime after the sixth new moon. ▷ The five new moons are the days that Yăhweɦ is looking on her to remove her shame, and so the key question is, "When did she find out that the Most High was giving attention to her to remove her shame?" The answer is obviously on the day that her husband arrived home after his service. ▷ See 1:36. **1:26 ψ** Tevet 1 (X.1) (December 10th, 3 BC) and the 6th day of Hannukah was the conception date of Mĕssiah. It was the new moon day, and also the third day of the week. ▷ This chronologicum is obviously on the same timeline as the five new moons of concealment, and so according to **1:25 γ** the days are counted from the first day her husband came off his priestly duty.

1:36 μ See 1:26 ψ. The Messenger, who alone knows the conception date, confirms here that she has been with child the whole time starting from the first day her husband came off his duty. ▷ As a second witness to this matter, we should consider that Elisheva had no last menses to base her reckoning on, but only the knowledge from her husband imparted to her on the day she learned he could not speak. It is not the habit of women to use any sort of inclusive counting for moons regarding a pregnancy, but she will chose the

there will not be any utterance impossible, at the side of the Almĭghty." ³⁸Then Miryam said, "Behold, the servant of Yăhweн. Let it be to me according to your utterance." Then the Messenger went away from her.

³⁹And when Miryam rose up in those days, she herself traveled to the hill country with haste, to a town of Yehudah. ⁴⁰Then she entered into the house of Zeḱaryahu. Then she greeted Elisheva. ⁴¹And came about, as Elisheva heard Miryam's greeting, the baby leaped in her womb. Then Elisheva was filled with the Holy Spĭrit. ⁴²And she cried out with a loud voice, and she said, "Thou art she who has been getting blessed among women, and he who has been getting blessed *is* the fruit of your womb! ⁴³And where *is* such *a privilege* for me, that the mother of my Ado̊nai should have come to me? ⁴⁴For behold, as the sound of your greeting came into my ears, the baby leaped in joyfulness in my womb. ⁴⁵And blessed is she who has held faithful, in that there will be a fulfillment of those things which have been getting spoken to her from alongside Yăhweн."

⁴⁶Then Miryam said: "My soul exalts Yăhweн, ⁴⁷and my spirit has rejoiced in the Almĭghty my Rescuer. ⁴⁸Because he has looked upon the humble state of his maidservant, because behold, from this time on all generations will count me blessed. ⁴⁹For the Mighty One has done great things for me, and holy is his name. ⁵⁰AND HIS MERCY IS UPON GENERATION AFTER GENERATION, TOWARD THOSE WHO FEAR HIM.ᵅ ⁵¹He has done mighty deeds with his Arm. He has scattered those who were proud in the thoughts of their heart. ⁵²He has brought down rulers from their thrones, and has exalted those who were humble. ⁵³HE HAS FILLED THE HUNGRY WITH GOOD THINGS,ᵝ and has sent away the rich empty-handed. ⁵⁴He has given help to Yisra'el his servant, in remembrance of his mercy, ⁵⁵as he spoke the promise to our fathers, to Avraham and his offspring for ever." ⁵⁶Then Miryam stayed with her nearly *the days of* three *new* moons, and then returned to her home.

⁵⁷And the time was fulfilled for Elisheva to give birth^λ. Then she brought forth a son. ⁵⁸Then her neighbors and her relatives heard that Yăhweн had displayed his great mercy toward her. Then they were rejoicing with her. ⁵⁹Then it was

---

best date she can to start counting from (which is the one indicated), and add to the moon count on the same date the next month, even if it is not the new moon day. ▷ But "And this new moon, a sixth is to her" (καὶ οὗτος μὴν ἕκτος ἐστὶν αὐτῇ) is peculiarly worded to refer to the new moon day, and all the versions have mistranslated the text to say, "this is the sixth month with her." As worded in Greek, however, the verb "is" does not come in the place supposed. This requires the mention of 'this' μὴν to be something Miryam already knew about, just as the same language is used to Mosheh: "הַחֹדֶשׁ הַזֶּה לָכֶם רֹאשׁ חֳדָשִׁים (Exodus 12:2)" *This new moon is to you first of the new moons*, cf. LXX here. In Hebrew, which must have been used, "This new moon" without an accompanying date, viz.

"the 14th after the new moon" can only mean the new moon day. See Appendix XVI. ▷ The conclusion then is that Elisheva must enjoy a gestation period of five complete months starting with actual new moons leading up the annunciation to Miryam.

1:50 α Psa 103:17: וְחֶסֶד יְהוָה מֵעוֹלָם וְעַד־. **1:53** β Psa. 107:9 עוֹלָם עַל־יְרֵאָיו. **1:57** λ These were 266 days. Month V.1, 3 BC to I.29, 2 BC. The months were 30, 30, 30, 29, 29, 30, 29, 29. The due date for Yoḣanan was Şabbaʈh on the last day of Nisan, April 5, 2 BC. This is exactly 38 weeks after his father came off duty. Elisheva carried Yoḣanan at least 38 weeks. **1:59** ρ According to the due date, 8 days was Şabbaʈh II.7 (April 12, 2 BC).

on the ᶠeighth day they came to circumcise the child, and they were calling his name Zekaryahu, by his father's name. ⁶⁰Then his mother spoke up and said, "No indeed! He will be called Yoḥanan." ⁶¹Then they said to her, "There is no one among your relatives who is called by this name." ⁶²So they were making signs to his father, as to what he wanted him to be called. ⁶³Then he asked for a tablet, and he wrote as follows, "His name is Yoḥanan." Then they were all astonished. ⁶⁴Then at once his mouth was opened and his tongue *loosed*. And he was speaking, blessing the Almĭghty. ⁶⁵Then awe came on all those living around them. And all these matters were being talked about in all the hill country of Yehudah. ⁶⁶Then all who heard *these things* kept *them* in their hearts, saying, "What then will this child turn out to be?" And indeed, the hand of Yăhwe͡h was with him.

⁶⁷And his father, Zekaryahu, was filled with the Holy Spĭrit. Then he prophesied, saying: ⁶⁸"Blessed be Yăhwe͡h, the Almĭghty of Yisra'el, because he will have attended to us and will have accomplished ransom for his people, ⁶⁹and will have raised up a horn of deliverance for us in the house of David his servant—⁷⁰just as he spoke by the mouth of his holy prophets of old—⁷¹DELIVERANCE FROM OUR ENEMIES, AND FROM THE HAND OF ALL WHO HATE US,ᶿ ⁷²to show mercy toward our fathers, and to remember his holy covenant, ⁷³the oath which he swore to Avraham our father, ⁷⁴to grant us that we, being delivered from the hand of our enemies, *may* be serving him without fear, ⁷⁵in holiness and righteousness before him all our days. ⁷⁶And you, child, will be called the prophet of the Most High, because you will go on BEFORE YĂHWE͡H TO PREPARE HIS WAYS,ᵏ ⁷⁷to give to his people the knowledge of deliverance by release from their sins, ⁷⁸because of the compassionate mercy of our Almĭghty, with which he will attend to us: *the* BRANCHᵘ from on high, ⁷⁹TO APPEAR TO THOSE WHO SIT IN DARKNESS AND THE SHADOW OF DEATH,ᵟ to guide our feet into the way of peace." ⁸⁰And the child was growing, and was getting strong in spirit, and he was in the deserts until the day of his ʸpublic installation for Yisra'el.

1:71 θ Psa. 106:10: וְיוֹשִׁיעֵם מִיַּד שׂוֹנֵא. **1:76** λ Mal. 3:1: הִנְנִי שֹׁלֵחַ מַלְאָכִי וַיִּגְאָלֵם מִיַּד אוֹיֵב:; Isa 40:3: קוֹל קוֹרֵא בַּמִּדְבָּר פַּנּוּ דֶּרֶךְ וּפִנָּה־דֶרֶךְ לְפָנַי יְהוָה. **1:78** μ Greek, 'riser.' See Mat. 2:2, 9. Also Zech. 3:8: כִּי־הִנְנִי מֵבִיא אֶת־עַבְדִּי צֶמַח. Zech. 6:12: הִנֵּה־אִישׁ צֶמַח שְׁמוֹ. Ἀνατολή LXX. Jer. 23:5, 33:15. **1:79** δ Isa. 9:1-2. **1:80** γ→installation = ἀναδείξεως.

When they turned 30, sons of priests could be ordained for public service in the holy place (Num. 4:3). The ordination service is described in Exodus 29 and Leviticus 8. The Greek word ἀναδείξεως here corresponds to מִלֻּאִים *being made to be full*, from Lev. 8:33 and Exo. 29:30, and more fully יְמַלֵּא אֶת־יֶדְכֶם *he will make to be your hands full*. The word is translated ordination or consecration, and generally in Greek as installation or inauguration, as in a public office. Without a doubt, therefore, the word refers to Yoḥanan's ordination to become a Cohen. If Yoḥanan was born on his due date in 2 bc (Nisan 29 = April 5), it would be the 15th day of that year. He would then be 30 on Adar 30, (Apr 4) AD 29, which was the 15th day of this year, reckoning years by the sun, and not by the moon. In AD 29, his priestly division was scheduled for I.26 to II.4 (April 30 to May 7). Also, he would have been able to serve as an extra priest at the Passover festival (I.14 to I.21), since all other priests were able to serve alongside the regular divisions when the extra work load of a feast arrived.

Luke 2

2 ¹And it happened in those days that a decree went out from before Caesar Augustus to register all the inhabited earth. ²This first registration happened—of^γ Quirinius' governing Syria. ³And everyone was going to register, each to his own city. ⁴But Yosef also went up from Galil, from the city of Netsereth, into Yehudah, into the town of David, being called Beth-lehem, because of his being of the house and family of David, ⁵in order to register along with Miryam, who had been betrothing herself to him, she being pregnant.

⁶Then it happened that while they were there, ^θ the days were fulfilled for her to give birth. ⁷Then she gave birth to her first-born son.^ξ Then she wrapped him in *linen* strips. ⁷ᵇThen she laid him in a feeding trough, because their space was not *enough* in the accommodation.

⁸And the shepherds were in the same countryside, staying in the field, and keeping the watches^ρ of the night over their flocks.^χ ⁹And the Messenger *of* Yăhweh stood over them, and the glory of Yăhweh shone around them. Then they were greatly frightened. ¹⁰Then the Messenger said to them, "Do not be getting afraid! For behold, I bring you good news of a great joy which will be for all the people. ¹¹For today in the city of David there ^μ will have been born for you a Rescuer, who is the Anŏinted One, Adŏnai. ¹²And this is the sign for you: You will find *the* baby, who will have been getting wrapped in *linen* strips, also lying in a feeding trough."

¹³And suddenly, there was with the Messenger a multitude of the heavenly host praising the Almĭghty, and saying, ¹⁴"Glory to the Almĭghty in the highest, and on earth peace among men of good intention."

¹⁵And it happened as the messengers departed from them into heaven, *that* the shepherds were saying to one another, "We should go straight up to Beth-lehem *right* now, and we will have seen this declaration which has been happening which Yăhweh has made known to us." ¹⁶And they went, having made haste, and disovered besides Miryam and Yosef, even the baby, who was lying in the feeding trough. ¹⁷And having seen *him*, they made *it* known about the declaration which had been told them about this Child. ¹⁸And all those who

---

2:2 γ→ of = (the first) relating to. **2:6** θ→fulfilled: This means 266 days or 38 weeks. From X.1, 3 BC (December 10th) to VII.1, 2 BC is exactly 266 days. The month lengths were 29, 30, 29, 29, 30, 29, 30, 29, 30, and 1 day. In this case the due date and the birth day were exactly the same date. See Revelation 12:1-2. ▷ This piece of data is of immense importance. For it allows us to decisively eliminate Sept. 11, 3 BC as the birth date in conjunction with the priestly rotations. If one counts five whole months, and then 266 days for Miryam's term from when Elisheva's husband came off duty for the previous year, we will find that the birth has to be premature to be on Tishri 1 in 3 BC. And this text contradicts this. ▷ Also this datum does not allow the birth to go over the due date, because it says 'while they were there,' and they were only there to register. **2:6** ξ It was a feast day, Yom Teruah.

2:7b Literally, 'because not was belonging-to-them room in the accommodation.' Therefore, they were compelled to have the birth in the main room of the building where there was also a manger, where animals were sometimes kept when it was cold. They were not denied their needs. It is simply that they had to seek more space when the birth began to happen. See "The Accommodations of Joseph and Mary in Bethlehem: Κατάλυμα in Luke 2.7," STEPHEN C. CARLSON (New Test. Stud. 56, pp. 326-342. © Cambridge University Press, 2010). **2:8** ρ Watches (plural). The implication is that they were just finishing up the final watch and dawn was appearing. **2:8** χ The shepherds took the sheep out just after Passover and brought them into shelter in the month of Ḥeshvan, month VIII, when the rainy season began. **2:11** μ (לְךָ); cf. Isa. 9:6. 'today': Referring to the new moon day after dawn.

heard it wondered about the things which were told by the shepherds to them. ¹⁹But Miryam was preserving all these utterances, pondering them in her heart. ²⁰Then the shepherds returned back, glorifying and praising the Almĭghty for all which they heard and saw, just as it was spoken to them.

²¹And when *the* ᵋeight days were completed for his circumcision, then his name was called Yĕshua, the name he was called by the Messenger before his conception in the womb. ²²And when the days for their ᵞpurification according to the Law of Mosh‑eh were completed, they brought him into Yerushalayim to present him to Yăhweн ²³(even as it has been getting written in the Law of Yăh‑weн, "EVERY FIRST-BORN MALE THAT OPENS THE WOMB SHALL BE CALLED HOLY TO YĂHWEН");ᵅ ²⁴and to offer a sacrifice according to what has been getting spoken in the Law of Yăhweн, "a PAIR OF TURTLEDOVES, OR TWO YOUNG PIGEONS.ᵝ"

²⁵And behold, a man was in Yerushalayim, whose name was Şim'on. And this man was righteous and devout, waiting for the advocate of Yisra'el. And the Holy Spĭrit was being upon him. ²⁶And it was being to him, *as* one who has been getting divinely warned by the Holy Spirit, that he will not have seen death before he will have seen the Anŏinted One of Yăhweн. ²⁷Then he came by the Spĭrit into the temple. And during *the time* when the parents brought in the child Yĕshua, so that they may do according to what had been becoming customary, relating to the Law concerning him, ²⁸evenᵖ he received him into *his* arms. Then he blessed the Almĭghty. Then he said, ²⁹"Now you *may* dismiss your servant, O Adŏnai, according to your declaration, in peace, ³⁰in that my eyes have seen your deliverance, ³¹which you have prepared *to put* before the face of all peoples, ³²A LIGHT OF REVELATION TO THE NATIONS,ᵠ and the glory of your people Yisra'el."

³³And his father and mother were amazed at the things which were being said about him. ³⁴Then Şim'on blessed them. Then he said to Miryam his mother, "Behold, this Child lays himself down for the fall and rise of many in Yisra'el, and for a sign to be spoken against—³⁵and a sword will go through even your own soul—to the end that the deliberations from many hearts may be revealed."

³⁶And there was *there* a prophetess, Hannah the daughter of Penu‑el, from the tribe of Ash‑er, who had been greatly advancing in *her* days, having lived with a husband seven years after her marriage, ³⁷and she *was* a widow eighty-four years. And she was not forsaking the temple, serving night and day with fastings and prayers. ³⁸And at that *very* hour she stood by and was agreeing before the Almĭghty, and was speaking about him to all those who were waiting for the ransom of Yerushalayim. ³⁹ᵃAnd thus they completed everything according to the Law of Yăhweн.

They remarked, that it "has been happening" using the progressive perfect (cf. vs. 15). Mĕssiah was born after dawn. **2:21** ξ Tishri 8, 2 BC (September 8), on the 2nd day of the week. **2:22** γ The days of purification were 7 days and then 33 days for a total of 40 days. See Lev. 12:1-4. These days were Tishri 1 to Ḥeshʋan 10. They were VII.1 to VIII.10. The first day after the days of purification was Şabbath VIII.11 (October 4, 2 BC). **2:23** α Exo 13:2.12.15; **2:24** β Lev 5:11; 12:8. **2:28** ρ the substance of the custom. **2:32** ψ Isa 9:2; 42:6; 49:6, 9; 51:4; 60:1-3; (thematic). **2:39b** μ According to Matthew they

³⁹ᵇThey returned to Galil, to their own city of Netsereth. ⁴⁰And the child was growing and was becoming strong, getting himself filled with wisdom. And the loving-kindness of the Almĭghty was upon him.

⁴¹And his parents were going to Yerushalayim throughout the year. At the Feast of the Passover, ⁴²also when he became twelve, they went up there according to the custom of the Feast. ⁴³And having completed the days, during their returning, the boy Yĕshua stayed behind in Yerushalayim. And his parents did not know, ⁴⁴but having supposed him to be in the caravan, they went a day's journey. And they were seeking for him among their fellow kinsmen and friends. ⁴⁵And when they did not find him, they returned to Yerushalayim, searching for him. ⁴⁶Then it was after three days *that* they found him in the temple, sitting in the midst of the teachers, and listening to them, and asking them questions. ⁴⁷And all hearing him were being amazed at his understanding and his answers. ⁴⁸And when they saw him, they were astonished. Then his mother said to him, "Child, why have you done so to us? Look, your father and I, getting distressed, were searching for you." ⁴⁹Then he said to them, "Why is it that you were searching for me? Had you not been knowing that it is necessary for me to be about matters of my Făther?" ⁵⁰And they did not understood the statement which he spoke to them. ⁵¹Then he went down with them. Then he came to Netsereth. And he was being obedient to them, and his mother was closely guarding all these things in her heart. ⁵²And Yĕshua was advancing in wisdom and stature, and in favor at the side of the Almĭghty and men.

3 ¹And in the fifteenth year of the reign of Tiberius Caesar, when Pontius Pilate was governor of Yehudah, and Herod was Tetrarch of Galil, and his brother Philip was Tetrarch of the region of Ituraea and Trachonitis, and Lysanias was Tetrarch of Abilene, ²in the high priesthood of Ḥanan and Qaiyapha, the word of the Almĭghty came to Yoḥanan, the son of Zekaryahu, in the wilderness.

³Then he came into all the country around the Yarden, proclaiming an immersion of being sorry and turning the heart *from sin*, toward a release from sins, ⁴as it has been getting written in the scroll of the words of Yeshayahu the

---

fled first to Egypt and then returned to their city in Galilee afterward. No Evangelist records every detail. **2:46** ᴜ Yĕshua was 12 in AD 12. They sacrificed the lamb on I.14. (It was on a weekly Şabbath that year). Then I.15 to I.21 was the feast of unleavened bread. The dates were sunset, March 26th, to sunset April 2. On the first day of the week they returned from the feast. Yĕshua was missing. On the second day of the week they retraced their steps to the city. On the third day they located him in the temple. He was lost and found. Yoḥ. 20:26; 2Ki 20:5; 1Sam. 9:20. He died to them. He rose to them. In Greek and Latin "after three days" means the same as "the third day after," which if counting by hours is between 48 and 72 hours after they lost him. **3:1** ʒ The 15th year began in the fall of AD 28 and ended in the fall of AD 29, according to Roman sources. Yĕshua was born on Tishri 1 in the fall of 2 BC. See Rev. 12:1-2. Yoḥanan was conceived 5 months and one day before Yĕshua. See Luke 1:24, 26. The only way to land Yoḥanan's 30th birthday within the limits of Tiberius' 15th year is if Yoḥanan was ordained around I.29 in the spring of AD 29, when his 30th birthday would have to be. Catholic scholars reject the fall birth date for Mĕssiah, not crediting Rev. 12:1-2, and also reject the plain Roman dating of Tiberius' 15th year. They speculate that Luke uses an undocumented coregency. These are the excuses they use to salvage their traditions against the plain sense. ▷ But the coins discovered by archaeologists and collectors, plus the ancient Roman historians, only confirm the standard dates for Tiberius' regnal years. See vs. 23. **3:4-6** θ Isa 40:3-5.

prophet, "THE VOICE OF ONE CRYING IN THE WILDERNESS, 'MAKE READY THE WAY OF YĂHWEH, BE MAKING HIS PATHS STRAIGHT. ⁵EVERY VALLEY WILL BE FILLED, AND EVERY MOUNTAIN AND HILL WILL BE LEVELED OFF. AND THE CROOKED WAY WILL BE STRAIGHTENED, AND THE ROUGH ROADS SMOOTHED. ⁶THEN ALL FLESH WILL SEE THE DELIVERANCE OF THE ALMĬGHTY.ᵟ'"

⁷Therefore, he was saying to the crowds who were going out to be immersed by him, "You brood of vipers, who warned you to flee from the coming wrath? ⁸Therefore bring forth worthy fruits of being sorry and turning the heart *from sin*, and you shall not begin to say to yourselves, 'We have Avraham for our father,' because I say to you that the Almĭghty is able from these stones to raise up children to Avraham. ⁹And also the ax is already laid at the root of the trees. Every tree therefore that does not bear good fruit is cut down and thrown into the fire."

¹⁰And the crowds were questioning him, saying, "Then what shall we have done?" ¹¹And he would answer and say to them, "Let the man who has two tunics share with him who has none. And let him who has food be doing likewise."

¹²And some tax-collectors also came to be immersed, and they said to him, "Teacher, what should we do?" ¹³And he said to them, "Be collecting no more beside that which you have been getting ordered to." ¹⁴And some soldiers were questioning him, saying, "And what about us, what shall we have done?" And he said to them, "You shall not have extorted from even one by force, nor also shall you have accused falsely, and be remaining content with your wages."

¹⁵Now while the people were in a state of expectation and all were wondering in their hearts about Yohanan, as to whether he may be the Anŏinted, ¹⁶Yohanan answered and said to them all, "As for me, I immerse you with water. But One is coming who is mightier than I, and I am not fit to untie the thong of his sandals. He will immerse you with the Holy Spĭrit and fire. ¹⁷And his winnowing fork is in his hand to thoroughly clear his threshing floor, and to gather the wheat into his barn. But he will burn up the chaff with unquenchable fire."

¹⁸So with many other exhortations also he proclaimed the good news to the people.

¹⁹But when Herod the Tetrarch was reproved by him on account of Herodias, his brother's wife, and on account of all the wicked things which Herod had done, ²⁰he added this also to them all, that he locked Yohanan up in prison.

²¹Now it came about when all the people were immersed, that Yĕshua also was immersed, and while he was praying, heaven was opened, ²²and the Holy Spĭrit descended upon him in bodily form like a dove, and a voice came out of heaven, "You are my beloved Sŏn, in you I am well-pleased."

²³And, Yĕshua was ʸnearly thirty years *old when* beginning, as it was getting ʸcustomary to be, the son of Yosef, from Eli, ²⁴from Matthat, from Levi,

---

3:23 Codex Bezae with two corrections from NA-27 (⌐ωσει & ⌐τριάχοντα): ην δε ιης ⌐ωσει ετων ⌐τριάχοντα αρχομενος ως ενομειζετο ειναι | **3:23** γ→thirty: ὡσεὶ Or, *almost* 30. Yĕshua was born on Tishri 1, 2 BC (Sept. 1). See Rev. 12:1-2. His immersion was a month before his 30th birthday, which came

from Malki, from Yannai, from Yosef, ²⁵from Mattatyahu, from Amots, from Nahum, from Hesli, from Naggai, ²⁶from Mahat, from Mattatyahu, from Shim'i, from Yosef, from Yodah, ²⁷from Yohanan, from Reish'a, from Zerubbavel, from ⁿShe'alti'el, from ᵍN'eri, ²⁸from Malki, from Addi, from Qosam, from Elmedan, from Er, ²⁹from Yosei, from Elie'zer, from Yorim, from Mattat, from Levi, ³⁰from Shim'on, from Yehudah, from Yosef, from Yonam, from Elyaqim, ³¹from Mal'ah, from Manna, from Mattatah, from Nathan, from David, ³²from Yishai, from 'Oved, from Bo'az, from Salmon, from Nahshon, ³³from Amminadav, from Ram, from Hetsron, from Perets, from Yehudah, ³⁴from Ya'aqov, from Yitshaq, from Avraham, from Terah, from Nahor, ³⁵from Serug, from Re'u, from Peleg, from Ever, from Shalah, ³⁶fromᵀ Arphakshad, from Shem, from Noah, from Lamek, ³⁷from Methuselah, from Hanok, from Yered, from Mahalal'el, from Qeinan, ³⁸from Enosh, from Seth, from Adam, ᵚfrom the Almighty.

4 ¹And Yeshua, full of the Holy Spirit, returned from the Yarden and was led about by the Spirit in the wilderness ²for forty daysᵀ, being tempted by the Slanderer. And he ate nothing during those days. And when they ended, he became hungry. ³And the Slanderer said to him, "If you are the Almighty Son,

---

on Tishri 1, AD 29. See Luke 4:2. See Luke 3:1. Yohanan was ordained at thirty (Luke 1:80). Four months later Yeshua was almost thirty. Yohanan was born in the spring and Yeshua in the fall. These seasonal facts fit with the 15th year of Tiberius only in the spring to fall of AD 29. This shows that 2 BC was the year of birth for both Yohanan and Yeshua. **3:23** ν < νομίζω. It was customary to become a teacher at age 30. This notice shows that Messiah was almost exactly 30. Luke carefully investigated all his facts, and also because he interviewed Miryam, as is evident from the amount of detail he records, he certainly knew exactly how old Messiah was and his birth date. He does not just say he was 29, but he says "nearly thirty," which is more precise than just saying he was 29. See ὡσεὶ in Friberg (reject D ὡς λ., ANLEX, "nearly." Scholars propose that Luke was indicating a rounded off number because the plainest sense does not agree with the Catholic tradition. This suggests Luke did not know, or did not care, or was concealing the answer. The plain sense is more plausible than such assumptions. **3:23** η-ξ See Mat. 1:12. **3:36** ᵀomit τοῦ Καϊνάν with 𝔓⁷⁵ᵛⁱᵈ (III cent.); D (Codex Bezae, V Cent.). See Steinmann JETS 60/4 (2017): 697-711, "CHALLLENGING THE AUTHENTICITY OF CAINAN, SON OF ARPHACHSHAD." **3:38** ω→Almighty: GNM, CJB, CEV, DARBY, DRA, NTE, TPT, WE, WYC vs. 'son of God' (50 other versions), an almost unforgivable error seeing there is no word for 'son' in the text.ᶜ

3:23 Codex Bezae with two corrections from NA-27 (ᶠὡσεὶ & ᶠτριάκοντα): ην δε ιης ᶠὡσεὶ ετων ᶠτριάκοντα αρχομενος ως ενομειζετο ειναι **3:23** γ→thirty: ὡσεὶ Or, *almost* 30. Yeshua was born on Tishri 1, 2 BC (Sept. 1). See Rev. 12:1-2. His immersion was a month before his 30th birthday, which came on Tishri 1, AD 29. See Luke 4:2. See Luke 3:1. Yohanan was ordained at thirty (Luke 1:80). Four months later Yeshua was almost thirty. Yohanan was born in the spring and Yeshua in the fall. These seasonal facts fit with the 15th year of Tiberius only in the spring to fall of AD 29. This shows that 2 BC was the year of birth for both Yohanan and Yeshua. **3:23** ν < νομίζω. It was customary to become a teacher at age 30. This notice shows that Messiah was almost exactly 30. Luke carefully investigated all his facts, and also because he interviewed Miryam, as is evident from the amount of detail he records, he certainly knew exactly how old Messiah was and his birth date. He does not just say he was 29, but he says "nearly thirty," which is more precise than just saying he was 29. See ὡσεὶ in Friberg (reject D ὡς λ., ANLEX, "nearly." Scholars propose that Luke was indicating a rounded off number because the plainest sense does not agree with the Catholic tradition. This suggests Luke did not know, or did not care, or was concealing the answer. The plain sense is more plausible than such assumptions. **3:23** η-ξ See Mat. 1:12. **3:36** ᵀomit τοῦ Καϊνάν with 𝔓⁷⁵ᵛⁱᵈ (III cent.); D (Codex Bezae, V Cent.). See Steinmann JETS 60/4 (2017): 697-711, "CHALLLENGING THE AUTHENTICITY OF CAINAN, SON OF ARPHACHSHAD." **3:38** ω→Almighty: GNM, CJB, CEV, DARBY, DRA, NTE, TPT, WE, WYC vs. 'son of God' (50 other versions), an almost unforgivable error seeing there is no word for 'son' in the text.ᶜ

4:1 τ From Elul 1 to Tishri 11. The month of Elul that year was 29 days long. The 40th day was on the Sabbath, Tishri 11, just after Yom Kippur. Traditionally, the whole month of Elul and the first ten days of Tishri were set aside for piety relating to repentance culminating on Yom Kippur. It is similar to Lent in the

speak to this stone, so that it will have become bread." ⁴And Yĕshua answered him, "It has been getting written, 'MAN WILL NOT LIVE ON BREAD ALONE.ᵟ'"

⁵And he led him up and showed him all the kingdoms of the world in a moment of time. ⁶And the Slanderer said to him, "I will give you all this authority and its glory, because it had been getting handed over to me, and I am giving it to whomever I may be wishing. ⁷Therefore, if you will have worshiped before me, it will all be yours." ⁸And Yĕshua answered and said to him, "It has been getting written, 'YOU SHALL WORSHIP YĂHWEĤ YOUR ALMĬGHTY AND SERVE HIM ONLY.ᵝ'"

⁹And he led him to Yerushalayim and had him stand on the pinnacle of the temple, and said to him, "If you are the Almĭghty Sŏn, throw yourself down from here, ¹⁰because it has been getting written, 'HE WILL GIVE HIS MESSENGERS CHARGE CONCERNING YOU, TO GUARD YOU,ᵅ' ¹¹and, 'ON THEIR HANDS THEY WILL BEAR YOU UP, LEST YOU MAY STRIKE YOUR FOOT AGAINST A STONE.ᵝ'" ¹²And Yĕshua answered and said to him, "It has been getting said, 'YOU SHALL NOT PUT YĂHWEĤ YOUR ALMĬGHTY TO THE TEST.ᵞ'" ¹³And when the Slanderer finished every temptation, he departed from him until an opportune time.

¹⁴And Yĕshua returned to Galilᵗ in the power of the Spĭrit. And news about him spread through all the surrounding district. ¹⁵And he was teaching in their congregations and was praised by all. ¹⁶And he came to Netsereṯh, where he had been getting brought up. And he went, according to what he had been getting accustomed to, into the congregation, on the day of the Ṣabbaṯhs—that is, he stood up to read. ¹⁷And the scroll of the prophet Yeshayahu was handed to him. And he opened the scroll, and found the place where it had been getting written, ¹⁸"THE SPĬRIT OF YĂHWEĤ IS UPON ME. FOR THIS REASON HE HAS ANOINTED ME, TO PROCLAIM THE GOOD NEWS TO THE POOR. HE HAS BEEN SENDING ME FOR HEALING, FOR THOSE WHO HAVE BEEN GETTING THEIR MINDS SHATTERED, TO PROCLAIM LIBERTY TO THE CAPTIVES, AND RECOVERY OF SIGHT TO THOSE IN A PRISON OF BLINDNESS, (to free those who have been getting broken to pieces, with liberty,) ¹⁹TO PROCLAIM THE YEAR OF YĂHWEĤ'S FAVOR.ᶲ" ²⁰And when he rolled up the scroll, *and* gave it back to the attendant, he sat down. And all the eyes in the congregation were fixing upon him. ²¹And he began to be saying to them, "Today this text has been getting fulfilled in your hearing."

²²And all were speaking well of him, and wondering at the gracious words which were falling from his lips. And they were saying, "Is this not Yosef's son?"

²³And he said to them, "No doubt you will quote this proverb to me, 'Doctor, heal yourself! Whatever we heard was done at Kefar-Naĥum, do here in your home town as well.'" ²⁴And he said, "amen!" I say to you, no prophet is welcome in his home town. ²⁵But I say to you in truth, there were many widows in Yisra'el

---

Church. It appears here that Yĕshua marked the time by fasting. It may be that the final temptation was on the Ṣabbaṯh after Yom Kippur when Yĕshua was at his weakest. Yĕshua was not to use his power of Creation to fulfill his need on that day, but to act as a man must and trust His Fäther. See Mat. 4:2 notes. **4:4** δ Deu 8:3. **4:8** β Deu 6:13, 10:20. **4:10** α Psa 91:11 **4:11** β Psa 91:12 **4:12** γ Deu 6:16. **4:14** τ Tevet, early AD 31. See John 4:35. **4:18-19** ϕ Isa 61:1-2.

Luke 5

in the days of Ěliyahu, when the sky was shut up for three years and *the days of six moons*, when a great famine came over all the land. ²⁶And yet, Ěliyahu was sent to none of them, but only to Tsarphat, in the land of Tsidon, to a woman who was a widow. ²⁷And there were many lepers in Yisra'el in the time of Elisha the prophet. And none of them was cleansed, but only Na'aman the Arammi."

²⁸And all in the congregation were filled with rage as they heard these things. ²⁹And they rose up and cast him out of the city, and led him to the brow of the hill on which their city had been getting built up, in order to throw him down the cliff. ³⁰But passing through their midst, he went his way.

³¹And he came down to Kefar-Naḥum, a city of Galil. And he was teaching them on the Sabbaths. ³²And they were amazed at his teaching, because his message was with authority.

³³And there was a man in the congregation possessed by the spirit of an unclean demon, and he cried out with a loud voice, ³⁴"Ha! What do we have to do with you, Yĕshua of Netsereth? Have you come to destroy us? I have been knowing who you are—the Holy One of the Almĭghty!" ³⁵And Yĕshua rebuked him, saying, "Be quiet and come out of him!" And when the demon threw him down in their midst, he came out of him without doing him any harm. ³⁶And amazement came upon them all, and they were discussing with one another saying, "What is this message? For with authority and power he commands the unclean spirits, and they come out." ³⁷And the report about him was getting out into every locality in the surrounding district.

³⁸And he arose and left the congregation, and entered Şim'on's home. Now Şim'on's mother-in-law was suffering from a high fever. And they made request of him concerning her. ³⁹And standing over her, he rebuked the fever, and it left her. And she immediately arose and waited on them.

⁴⁰And the sun having set, all who had any sick with various diseases brought them to him. And laying his hands on every one of them, he was healing them. ⁴¹And demons also were coming out of many, crying out and saying, "You are the Almĭghty Sŏn!" And rebuking them, he was not allowing them to be speaking, because they had been recognizing him to be the Anŏinted One.

⁴²And when day came, he departed and went to a lonely place. And the crowds were searching for him, and came to him, and tried to keep him from going away from them. ⁴³But he said to them, "I must proclaim the kingdom of the Almĭghty to the other cities also, because I was sent for this purpose." ⁴⁴And he was proclaiming in the congregations of Galil.ᵖ

5 ¹Nowᵀ it came about that while the crowds were pressing around him and listening to the word of the Almĭghty, he had been standing alongside the lake of Genneisaret, ²and he saw two boats, which had been standing beside the lake, and the fishermen who had stepped out of them, were washing their nets.

4:31 τ Winter, AD 31. **4:44** ρ Other MSS read: 'Yehudah': 𝔓⁷⁵. Text based on: A D 𝔐 latt syᵖʰᵐᵍ boᵖᵗ.
5:1 τ Around Adar, AD 31.

³And he got into one of the boats, which was Şim'on's, and asked him to put out a little way from the land. And he sat down and was teaching the crowds from the boat. ⁴And when he ceased speaking, he said to Şim'on, "Put out into the deep water and let down your nets for a catch." ⁵And Şim'on answered and said, "Master, we worked hard all night and caught nothing, but at your bidding I will let down the nets." ⁶And when they did this, they enclosed a great quantity of fish. And their nets were breaking, ⁷and they signaled to their partners in the other boat, for them to come and help them. And they came, and filled both of the boats, so that they began to sink.

⁸But when Şim'on Peter saw that, he fell down at Yĕshua's feet, saying, "Depart from me, because I am a sinful man, Adŏnai!" ⁹For amazement seized him and all his companions because of the catch of fish which they had taken, ¹⁰and so also Ya'aqov and Yoḥanan, sons of Zavdai, who were partners with Şim'on. And Yĕshua said to Şim'on, "Be not fearing, from now on you will be catching men." ¹¹And when they brought their boats to land, they left everything and followed him.

¹²And it came about that while he was in one of the cities, behold, there was a man full of leprosy. And when he saw Yĕshua, he fell on his face and implored him, saying, "Adŏnai, if you may be willing, you are able to make me clean." ¹³And he stretched out his hand, and touched him, saying, "I am willing. Be cleansed." And immediately the leprosy left him. ¹⁴And he ordered him to tell no one, "But go and show yourself to the priest, and make an offering for your cleansing, just as Mosheh commanded, for a testimony to them."

¹⁵But the news about him was spreading even farther, and great crowds were gathering to hear him and to be healed of their sicknesses. ¹⁶But he himself would often slip away to the wilderness and pray. ¹⁷And it came about on one of the days. And he was teaching. And there were sitting Perushim and teachers of the Law, who had been coming from every village of Galil and Yehudah and from Yerushalayim. And the power of Yăhweh was *present* for him to be healing. ¹⁸And behold, *some* men carrying on a bed a man who had been getting paralyzed. And they were trying to bring him in, and to set him down in front of him. ¹⁹And not finding any way they may bring him in because of the crowd, they went up on the roof and let him down through the tiles with his stretcher, right in the center, in front of Yĕshua. ²⁰And when he saw their steadfastness, he said, "Friend, your sins have been getting forgiven you."

²¹And the scribes and the Perushim began to reason, saying, "Who is this man who speaks blasphemies? Who can forgive sins, but the Almĭghty alone?" ²²But Yĕshua, aware of their reasonings, answered and said to them, "Why are you reasoning in your hearts? ²³Which is easier work, to say, 'Your sins have been getting forgiven you,' or to say, 'Be rising and be walking'? ²⁴But in order that you will have been knowing that the Sŏn of Man has authority on earth to be forgiving sins," he said to the one who had been getting paralyzed, "To you, I am saying, be rising, and having taken up your stretcher, be walking yourself to your house." ²⁵And at once, having risen up before them, having taken up

what he was lying on, he went away to his house, glorifying the Almĭghty. ²⁶And they were all seized with astonishment and were glorifying the Almĭghty. And they were filled with awe, saying, "We have seen remarkable things today."

²⁷And after that he went out, and noticed a tax-gatherer named Leui, sitting in the tax office, and he said to him, "Be following me." ²⁸And he left everything behind, and rose and was following him. ²⁹And Leui gave a big reception for him in his house. And there was a great crowd of tax-collectors and other people who were reclining at the table with them.

³⁰And the Perushim and their scribes were grumbling at his disciples, saying, "Why do you eat and drink with the tax-collectors and sinners?" ³¹And Yĕshua answered and said to them, "It is not those who are well who need a doctor but those who are sick. ³²I have not been coming to call the righteous so much as sinners to be sorry and turn their heart *from sin.*"

³³And they said to him, "The disciples of Yoḥanan often fast and offer prayers. The disciples of the Perushim also do the same, but yours eat and drink." ³⁴And Yĕshua said to them, "You cannot make the attendants of the bridegroom fast while the bridegroom is with them, can you? ³⁵Yet, the days will come, even when the bridegroom may have been taken away from them; then they will fast in those days." ³⁶And he was also telling them a parable: No one tears a piece from a new-made garment and puts it on an old garment. Otherwise surely the new-made will tear away, that is, the old will not harmonize. ³⁷And no one puts young wine into old wineskins. Otherwise the young wine will burst the skins, and it will be spilled out, and the skins will be ruined. ³⁸But young wine must be put into new-made wineskins. ³⁹And no one, after drinking old wine wishes for young, because he says, 'The old is good enough.'"

6

¹Now it came about on the ʽsecond firstʼ Şabbaṯhᵀ, he was passing through some grain fields. And his disciples were picking and eating the heads of grain, rubbing them in their hands. ²But some of the Perushim said, "Why do you do what is not lawful on the Şabbaṯhs?"

³And Yĕshua answering them said, "Have you not even read what Dauid did when he was hungry, he and those who were with him, ⁴how he entered the house of the Almĭghty, and took and ate the consecrated bread which is not lawful for any to eat except the priests alone, and gave it to his companions?"

⁵On the same day, seeing one working on the Şabbaṯh day, he said to him, "Man, if you know what you are doing, you are blessed, but if you do not know,

---

6:1 τ The first Şabbaṯh was the first day of unleavened bread (cf. Lev. 23:11, 15; John 19:31) The second first Şabbaṯh was the weekly Şabbaṯh after the first Passover Şabbaṯh. It was also called first because seven Şabbaṯhs were counted after Passover (cf. Lev. 23:15). This year was AD 31. The Passover Şabbaṯh fell on Wednesday that year (sunset March 27th to sunset March 28th). The second first Şabbaṯh was on the weekly Şabbaṯh starting at Friday sundown on March 31st. It was called the ʽsecond firstʼ to clarify which first Şabbaṯh was meant. See Mat. 28:1; Mark 16:2; Luke 18:12; 24:1; Yoḥ. 20:1, 19; Acts 20:7; 1 Cor. 16:2. **6:1** ⌜δευτεροπρωτω A (V) C (V) D (V) Θ Ψ (f13) 𝔐 lat syʰ; Epiph **vs.** 𝔓⁴ (III) ℵ (VI) B (IV) L W, etc. This shows two things (1) the critical text does not always follow textual rules [this is clearly the harder reading], and (2) later texts are correct over earlier texts! The deciding factor was that the critics cannot make sense out of it, therefore they dicarded it. **6:5** η Codex Bezae, vs. 5 to 10b. **6:13** τ Perhaps late Aviv or early Iyyar, AD 31.

you are accursed and a transgressor of the law"."

⁶And it came about on another Şabbath, that he entered the congregation and was teaching. And there was a man there whose right hand was withered. ⁷And the scribes and the Perushim were watching him closely, to see if he healed on the Şabbath, in order that they might find *reason* to accuse him. ⁸And, he had been knowing their rationalizations. And, he said to the man having the withered hand, "Be rising and stand in the middle!" And having arisen, he stood. ⁹And Yĕshua said to them, "I ask you, is it lawful on the Şabbaths to do good, or to do harm, to rescue a life, or to destroy it?" ¹⁰And after looking around at them all, he said to him, "Stretch out your hand!" And he did so. And his hand was restored. ¹⁰ᵇAnd he was saying to them, "The Sŏn of Man is Măster of the Şabbath." ¹¹But they themselves were filled with rage, and discussed together what they wanted done to Yĕshua.

¹²And it was at this time that he went off to the mountain to pray, and he spent the whole night in prayer to the Almĭghty. ¹³And when day came, he called his disciples to him, and chose twelve of them, whom he also named as emissaries: ¹⁴Şim'on, whom he also named Peter, and Andrew his brother, and Ya'aqov and Yohanan, and Philip and Bar-Talmai, ¹⁵and Mattai and Toma, Ya'aqov the son of Halphai, and Şim'on who was called the Zealot, ¹⁶Yehudah the son of Ya'aqov, and Yehudah Ish-Qeriyot, who became a traitor.

¹⁷And he descended with them, and stood on a level place. And there was a great crowd of his disciples, and a great throng of people from all Yehudah and Yerushalayim and the coastal region of Tsor and Tsidon, ¹⁸who had come to hear him, and to be healed of their diseases. And those who were troubled with unclean spirits were being cured. ¹⁹And all the multitude were seeking to touch him, for power was coming from beside him and healing them all.

²⁰And turning his gaze on his disciples, he was saying, "Blessed are you who are poor, for yours is the kingdom of the Almĭghty.

²¹ "Blessed are you who hunger now, for you will be satisfied.

²¹ᵇ "Blessed are you who weep now, for you will laugh.

²² "Blessed are you when men may have hated you, and may have ostracized you, and may have cast insults at you, and may have spurned your name as evil, for the sake of the Sŏn of Man. ²³Be glad in that day, and leap for joy, because behold, your reward is great in heaven, because in the same way their fathers used to treat the prophets.

²⁴ "But woe to you who are rich, because you are receiving your comfort in full.²⁵Woe to you who have been getting well-fed now, for you will be hungry. Woe to you who laugh now, because you will mourn and weep. ²⁶Woe to you when all men may have spoken well of you, because in the same way their fathers used to treat the false prophets.

²⁷ "But I say to you who hear, be loving your enemies, be doing good to those who are hating you, ²⁸be blessing those who are cursing you, be praying for those who are mistreating you. ²⁹Whoever hits you on the cheek, be offering him the other also. And whoever takes away your coat, you shall not have with-

held your shirt from him either. ³⁰Be giving to everyone who is asking of you, and whoever is taking away what is yours, do not be asking it back. ³¹And just as you are wanting that men may be treating you, be treating them in the same way.

³² "And if you love those who love you, what credit is that to you? For even sinners love those who love them. ³³And if you may be doing good to those who are doing good to you, what credit is that to you? For even sinners do the same. ³⁴And if you may have lent to those from whom you expect to receive, what credit is that to you? Even sinners lend to sinners, in order that they will have received back the same amount.

³⁵ "But be loving your enemies, and be doing good, and be lending, expecting nothing in return. And your reward will be great, and you will be sons of the Most High, because he himself is kind to ungrateful and evil men. ³⁶Be becoming merciful, just as your Fǎther is merciful. ³⁷And do not be judging and, no, you shall not be judged. And do not be condemning, and no, you shall not be condemned. Be pardoning, and you will be pardoned.

³⁸ "Be giving, and it will be given to you, good measure, having been getting pressed down, having been getting shaken together, running over, they will pour into your lap. For by your standard of measure it will be measured to you in return."

³⁹And he also spoke a parable to them: "A blind man cannot guide a blind man, can he? Will they not both fall into a pit? ⁴⁰A pupil is not above his teacher, but everyone, after he has been getting fully trained, will be like his teacher. ⁴¹And why do you look at the speck that is in your brother's eye, but do not notice the log that is in your own eye? ⁴²How are you able to say to your brother, 'brother, Allow *that* I may cast out the speck that is in your eye,' when you yourself do not see the log that is in your own eye? You hypocrite, first take the log out of your own eye, and then you will see clearly to take out the speck that is in your brother's eye.

⁴³ "For there is no good tree which produces bad fruit, nor, on the other hand, a bad tree which produces good fruit. ⁴⁴For each tree is known by its own fruit. Because men do not gather figs from thorns, nor do they pick grapes from a briar bush. ⁴⁵The good man out of the good treasure of his heart brings forth what is good. And the evil man out of the evil treasure brings forth what is evil, because his mouth speaks from that which fills his heart.

⁴⁶ "And why do you call me, 'Adǒnai, Adǒnai,' and do not do what I say? ⁴⁷Everyone who comes to me, and hears my words, and acts upon them, I will show you whom he is like: ⁴⁸He is like a man building a house, who dug and excavated and laid a foundation upon the rock. And when a flood rose, the downpour burst against that house and could not shake it, because it had been getting well built. ⁴⁹But the one who has heard, and does not act accordingly, is like a man who built a house upon the ground without any foundation. And the torrent burst against it and immediately it collapsed, and the ruin of that house was great."

7 ¹Then he completed all his discourse in the hearing of the people, he went to Kefar-Naḥum. ²And a certain centurion's slave, who was highly regarded by him, was sick and about to die. ³And, when he heard about Yĕshua, he sent some Yehudi elders asking him, that having come, he may rescue his slave. ⁴And when they came to Yĕshua, they earnestly entreated him, saying that, "He is worthy, *that* you should grant this to him, ⁵because he loves our nation, and he built us our place of congregation."

⁶Now Yĕshua started on his way with them. And when he was already not far from the house, the centurion sent friends, saying to him, "Adŏnai, be not troubling yourself further, because I am not worthy that you may come under my roof. ⁷For this reason I did not even consider myself worthy to come to you, but just say the word, and my servant will be healed. ⁸For I, too, am a man under authority, with soldiers under me. And I say to this one, 'Go!' and he goes, and to another, 'Be coming!' and he is coming, and to my slave, 'Do this!' and he does it."

⁹Now when Yĕshua heard this, he marveled at him, and turned and said to the crowd that was following him, "I say to you, not even in Yisra'el have I found such great trusting loyalty." ¹⁰And when those who were sent returned to the house, they found the slave in good health.

¹¹And it happened on the next *day, that* he went to a town being called Na'in. And his disciples were going along with him, accompanied by a large crowd. ¹²And as he neared the gate of the town—then look, someone was getting carried out, who had been dying, *an* only kindred son of his mother, and she was a widow, and a sizable crowd from the city was with her.

¹³And when Adŏnai saw her, he felt compassion for her, and said to her, "Do not be weeping." ¹⁴And he came up and touched the coffin. And the bearers came to a halt. And he said, "Young man, I say to you, arise!" ¹⁵And the dead man sat up, and began to speak. And Yĕshua gave him back to his mother. ¹⁶And fear gripped them all, and they were glorifying the Almĭghty, saying, "A great prophet has arisen among us!" and, "The Almĭghty has visited his people!" ¹⁷And this report concerning him went out all over Yehudah, and in all the surrounding district.

¹⁸And the disciples of Yoḥanan reported to him about all these things. ¹⁹And summoning two of his disciples, Yoḥanan sent them to Adŏnai, saying, "Are you **THE COMING ONE**, or should we be looking for someone else?" ²⁰And when the men came to him, they said, "Yoḥanan the Immerser has sent us to you, saying, 'Are you **THE COMING ONE**, or should we be looking for someone else?'" ²¹At that very time he cured many people of diseases and afflictions and evil spirits, and he granted sight to many who were blind. ²²And he answered and said to them, "Go and report to Yoḥanan what you have seen and heard. *The* BLIND RECEIVE SIGHT*ᵃ, the* LAME WALK*ᵃ,* the lepers are cleansed, and THE DEAF HEAR*ᵃ;* the dead

---

7:22 *a* Isa 35:5-6: פֶּסַח כָּאַיָּל יְדַלֵּג אָז... תִּפָּתַחְנָה חֵרְשִׁים וְאָזְנֵי עִוְרִים עֵינֵי תִּפָּקַחְנָה אָז.

are raised up, *the* POOR HAVE THE GOOD NEWS PROCLAIMED TO THEM^β. ²³And blessed is whoever *that* may not be offended by me."

²⁴And when the messengers of Yoḥanan left, he began to speak to the crowds about Yoḥanan, "What did you go out into the wilderness to look at? A reed shaken by the wind? ²⁵But what did you go out to see? A man who had been getting dressed in fancy clothing? Behold, those who are splendidly clothed and live in luxury are found in royal palaces. ²⁶But what did you go out to see? A prophet? Yes, I say to you, and one who is more than a prophet. ²⁷This is the one about whom it has been getting written, "BEHOLD, I SEND MY MESSENGER BEFORE YOUR FACE, WHO WILL PREPARE YOUR WAY BEFORE YOU^ψ." ²⁸I say to you, among those born of women, there is no prophet more popular than Yoḥanan, yet he who is less so, in the kingdom of the Almĭghty, is greater than he."

²⁹And when all the people and the tax-collectors heard this, they vindicated the Almĭghty as ones who were immersed with the immersion of Yoḥanan. ³⁰But the Perushim and the lawyers rejected the Almĭghty's counsel for themselves, not having been immersed by Yoḥanan.

³¹"To what then shall I compare the men of this kindred, and what are they like? ³²They are like children who sit in the market place and call to one another, and they say, 'We played the flute for you, and you did not dance. We sang a dirge, and you did not weep.' ³³For Yoḥanan the Immerser had been coming eating no bread nor as well drinking wine, and you are saying, 'He has a demon!' ³⁴The Sŏn of Man has been coming eating and drinking, and you are saying, 'Behold, a gluttonous man, and a drunkard, a friend of tax-collectors and sinners!' ³⁵Yet wisdom is judged rightly by all her children."

³⁶And, one of the Perushim was requesting him, that he may eat with him. And he entered the Perushi's house, and reclined at the table. ³⁷And behold, there was a woman in the city who was a sinner, and when she learned that he was reclining at the table in the Perushi's house, she brought an alabaster vial of perfume, ³⁸and standing behind him beside his feet, weeping, she began to wet his feet with her tears, and kept wiping them with the hair of her head, and kissing his feet, and anointing them with the perfume.

³⁹Now when the Perushi who had invited him saw this, he said to himself, "If this man were a prophet he would know who and what sort of person this woman is who is touching him, that she is a sinner."

⁴⁰And Yĕshua replied and said to him, "Şim'on, I have something to say to you." And he replied, "Say it, Teacher." ⁴¹"A certain moneylender had two debtors, one owed five hundred dinars, and the other fifty. ⁴²When they were unable to repay, he graciously forgave them both. Which of them therefore will love him more?"

⁴³Şim'on answered and said, "I suppose the one whom he forgave more." And he said to him, "You have judged correctly."

⁴⁴And turning toward the woman, he said to Şim'on, "Do you see this woman? I entered your house. You gave me no water for my feet, but she has wet my feet with her tears, and wiped them with her hair. ⁴⁵You gave me no kiss,

but she, since the time I came in, has not ceased to kiss my feet. ⁴⁶You did not anoint my head with oil, but she anointed my feet with perfume, ⁴⁷in favor of which I am saying to you, her many sins have been getting forgiven, because she loved much, but he who is forgiven little loves little." ⁴⁸And he said to her, "Your sins have been getting forgiven." ⁴⁹And those who were reclining at the table with him began to say to themselves, "Who is this man who even is forgiving sins?" ⁵⁰And he said to the woman, "Your faithfulness has been saving you. Be going in peace."

8 ¹And it came about soon afterward, that he was going down through city and village, proclaiming and announcing the good news of the kingdom of the Almĭghty. And the twelve were with him, ²and some women who had been getting healed from evil spirits and sicknesses: Miryam who is being called Ha-Magdalit, from whom seven demons he had been making go out, ³and Yohanah the wife of Kuza, Herod's steward, and Shoshannah, and many others were contributing to their support, out of their private means.

⁴And when a great crowd was coming together, and those from the city were journeying to him, he spoke by way of a parable. ⁵"The sower went out to sow his seed. And as he sowed, some fell beside the road. And it was trampled under foot, and the birds of the air ate it up. ⁶And other seed fell on rocky soil, and as soon as it grew up, it withered away, because it had no moisture. ⁷And other seed fell among the thorns. And the thorns grew up with it, and choked it out. ⁸And other seed fell into the good soil, and grew up, and produced a crop a hundred times as great." Having said these things, he was saying, "He who is having ears to be hearing, let him be hearing."

⁹And his disciples were questioning him as to what this parable may be. ¹⁰And he said, "To you it has been getting offered to know the mysteries of the kingdom of the Almĭghty, but to the rest it is in parables, in order that 'SEEING THEY MAY NOT BE SEEING, AND HEARING THEY MAY NOT BE UNDERSTANDING.'"

¹¹"Now the parable is this. The seed is the word of the Almĭghty. ¹²And those beside the road are those who have heard. Then the Slanderer comes and takes away the word from their heart, lest having held *it* faithful, they may be rescued. ¹³And those on the rocky soil are those who, when they may have heard, receive the word with joy, and these have no firm root. They are holding faithful for a while, and in time of temptation they are getting themselves led away. ¹⁴And the seed which fell among the thorns, these are the ones who have heard, and as they go on their way they are choked with worries and riches and pleasures of this life, and bring no fruit to maturity. ¹⁵And the seed in the good soil, these are the ones who have heard the word in an honest and good heart, and hold it fast, and bear fruit with perseverance."

¹⁶"Now no one after lighting a lamp covers it over with a container, or puts

---

7:22 β Isa. 61:1: לְבַשֵּׂר עֲנָוִים. **7:27** ψ Mal. 3:1 **8:1** τ Early summer, AD 31. **8 10** φ Isa 6:9.

it under a bed, but he puts it on a lampstand, in order that those who come in may be seeing the light. ¹⁷Because nothing is hidden that will not become evident, nor is anything secret that, no, will not have been known and have come to light. ¹⁸Therefore be keeping watch how you listen, because whoever may be holding fast, to him will more be given. And whoever may not be holding fast, even what he thinks himself to be holding, will be taken away from him."

¹⁹And his mother and brothers came to him, and they were unable to get to him because of the crowd. ²⁰And it was reported to him, "Your mother and your brothers have been standing outside, wishing to see you." ²¹But he answered and said to them, "My mother and my brothers are these who hear the word of the Almĭghty and do it."

²²Now it came about on one of those days⸋ that he and his disciples got into a boat, and he said to them, "We should go over to the other side of the lake." And they launched out. ²³But as they were sailing along he fell asleep. And a fierce gale of wind descended upon the lake, and they were being swamped and were being put in danger. ²⁴And they came to him and woke him up, saying, "Măster, Măster, we are perishing!" And having been jolted awake, he rebuked the wind and the surging waves, and they stopped, and it became calm. ²⁵And he said to them, "Where is your courageous faithfulness?" And they were fearful and amazed, saying to one another, "Who then is this, that he commands even the winds and the water, and they obey him?"

²⁶And they sailed to the country of the Gadriyim, which is opposite Galil. ²⁷And when he came out onto the land, he was met by a certain man from the city who was possessed with demons, and who had not put on any clothing for a long time, and was not living in a house, but in the tombs. ²⁸And seeing Yĕshua, he cried out and fell before him, and said in a loud voice, "What do I have to do with you, Yĕshua, Sŏn of the Almĭghty, Most High? I beg you, *that* me you may not torment," ²⁹because he commanded the unclean spirit to come out away from the man, because it had been seizing him many times, and he was bound with chains and shackles and kept under guard, and yet he would burst his fetters and be driven by the demon into the desert.

³⁰And Yĕshua asked him, "What is your name?" And he said, "Legion", because many demons had entered him. ³¹And they were begging him, that he may not command them to depart into the abyss.

³²Now there was a herd of many pigs feeding there on the mountain. And the demons begged him, that he may permit them to enter the pigs. And he gave them permission. ³³And the demons came out from the man and entered the pigs. And the herd rushed down the steep bank into the lake, and were drowned.

³⁴And when the herdsmen saw what had been happening, they ran away and reported it in the city and out in the country. ³⁵And they went out to see what had been happening. And they came to Yĕshua, and found the man from whom

---

8:22 τ Fall, AD 31.

the demons had gone out, sitting down beside the feet of Yĕshua, having been getting dressed, and being in his right mind. And they became frightened. ³⁶And those who had seen it reported to them how the man who was demon-possessed was made well. ³⁷And all the people of the country of the Gadriyim and the surrounding district asked him to depart from them, because they were gripped with great fear. And he got into a boat, and returned.

³⁸But the man from whom the demons had been going out was begging him to be with him, but he sent him away, saying, ³⁹"Be returning to your house and be describing what great things the Almĭghty has done for you." And he went away, proclaiming down through the whole city what great things Yĕshua had done for him.

⁴⁰And as Yĕshua returned, the crowd welcomed him, because they were all waiting for him. ⁴¹And behold, there came a man named Ya'ir, and he was an official of the congregation. And he fell beside Yĕshua's feet, and was entreating him to come to his house, ⁴²because he had *an* only kindred daughter, ʳabout twelve years old, and she ʳwas dying. But as he went, the crowds were pressing against him.

⁴³And a woman living with a flow of blood for twelve years, who ʿno one was able to healʾ, ⁴⁴having approached behind, touched the tassel of his cloak. And immediately her bleeding stopped. ⁴⁵And Yĕshua said, "Who is the one who touched me?" And while they were all denying it, Peter said, "Măster, the crowds are crowding and pressing upon you." ⁴⁶But Yĕshua said, "Someone did touch me, because I knew power had been going out of me." ⁴⁷And when the woman saw that she had not escaped notice, she came trembling and fell down before him, and declared in the presence of all the people the reason why she had touched him, and how she was immediately healed. ⁴⁸And he said to her, "Daughter, your courageous faithfulness has been saving you. Be going in peace."

⁴⁹While he was still speaking, someone close to the congregation official came, saying, "Your daughter ᵡhas been dying! Do not be troubling the teacher anymore." ⁵⁰But when Yĕshua heard this, he answered him, "Do not be getting afraid! Only ᵃhold faithful, and she will be rescued." ⁵¹And when he came to the house, he did not allow anyone to enter with him, except Peter and Yoĥanan and Ya'aqov, and the girl's father and mother. ⁵²Now they were all weeping and lamenting for her, but he said, "Do not be weeping, because she has not died, but she is asleepᵘ." ⁵³And they were laughing at him, having been knowing that she had died. ⁵⁴He, however, took her by the hand and called, saying, "Child, be rising!" ⁵⁵And her spirit returned, and she rose immediately. And he gave orders for something to be given her to eat. ⁵⁶And her parents were amazed, but he instructed them to tell no one what had been happening.

8:42 ʳ D omit ᶠ D *is*. **8:43** ʳ D **8:49** θ→dying. Ambiguous in Greek with no context or no qualifying word like ἤδη. See Mark 15:44; John 19:33. **8:50** α→have courage = *hold*+ *firm, steadfast, faith-ful.* **8:52** μ Yĕshua was seeing the situation in terms of the second death, wherein both body and soul are destroyed. See Mat. 10:28. When Mĕssiah said she had not died, he spoke of her soul, which was only

Luke 9

9 ¹And he called the twelve together, and gave them power and authority over all the demons, and to heal diseases. ²And he sent them out to proclaim the kingdom of the Almĭghty, and to perform healing. ³And he said to them, "Be taking nothing for your journey, neither a staff, nor a bag, nor bread, nor silver, and do not even have two tunics apiece. ⁴And whatever house you may have entered, be remaining there, and be going out from there. ⁵And as many as ever who may not be receiving you, as you are going out from that city, be shaking off the dust from your feet as a testimony against them."

⁶And departing, they were passing down through the villages, proclaiming the good news, and healing everywhere. ⁷Now Herod the Tetrarch heard of all that was happening. And he was greatly perplexed, because it was said by some that Yoḣanan has been raised from the dead, ⁸and by some that Ęliyahu has been manifested, and by others, that one of the prophets of old has risen again. ⁹And Herod said, "I myself had Yoḣanan beheaded, but who is this man about whom I hear such things?" And he was seeking to see him.

¹⁰And when the emissaries returned, they gave an account to him of all that they had done. And taking them with him, he withdrew by himself to a city called Bėṭh-Tsaidah. ¹¹But the crowds were aware of this and followed him. And welcoming them, he was speaking to them about the kingdom of the Almĭghty and curing those who had need of healing.

¹²And, the day began to decline, and, the twelve, having come, said to him, "Send the crowd away, that they, having gone into the surrounding villages and countryside, will have found lodging and will have found provision, because here we are in a desolate place." ¹³Yet, he said to them, "You give them yourselves *something* to eat!" And, they said, "We have no more than five loaves and two fish, unless perhaps, having gone, we will have bought food for all these people." ¹⁴(For there were being about five thousand men.) And, he said to his disciples, "Make them recline to eat in groups of about fifty each." ¹⁵And they did so, and had them all recline. ¹⁶And he took the five loaves and the two fish, and looking up to heaven, he blessed them, and broke them, and kept giving them to the disciples to set before the crowd. ¹⁷And they all ate and were satisfied. And the broken pieces which they had left over were picked up, twelve baskets full.

¹⁸And it came about that while he was praying down alone, the disciples were with him, and he questioned them, saying, "Who do the crowds say that I am?" ¹⁹And they answered and said, "Yoḣanan the Immerser, and others say Ęliyahu, but others, that one of the prophets of old has risen again." ²⁰And he said to them, "But who do you say that I am?" And Peter answered and said, "The Anŏinted, Sŏnᵏ of the Almĭghty." ²¹But he warned them, and instructed them not to tell this to anyone, ²²saying, "It is necessary for the Sŏn of Man to suffer many things, and be rejected by the elders and the chief priests and the scribes, and to be killed, and after three days to rise." ²³And he was saying to

---

'asleep.' Her body had indeed died. **9:20** μ D (892 *pc*) it bo^ms

them all, "If anyone wishes to come after me, let him deny himself, and take up his execution timber daily, and be following me. ²⁴Because whoever may be wishing to have rescued his soul will lose it, but whoever may have lost his soul for my sake, this one will rescue it. ²⁵Because what is a man profited if he gains the whole world, and loses or forfeits himself? ²⁶For whoever may have been ashamed of me and my words, of him will the Sŏn of Man be ashamed when he may have come in his glory, and *the glory* of the Făther and of the holy *angelic* messengers. ²⁷But I say to you truthfully, there are some, who have been standing here who will not have tasted death until they may have seen *to*ᵘ the kingdom of the Almĭghty᾿."

²⁸And almost eight days after these sayings, it came about that he took along Peter and Yoḣanan and Ya'aqov, and went up to the mountain to pray. ²⁹And while he was praying, the appearance of his face became different, and his clothing became white and gleaming. ³⁰And behold, two men were talking with him. And they were Mosheh and E̱liyahu, ³¹who, appearing in glory, were speaking of his departure which he was about to fulfill at Yerushalayim. ³²Now Peter and his companions had been getting heavy with sleep, but when they were fully awake, they saw his glory and the two men, who had been standing with him. ³³And it happened as these were parting from him. Peter said to Yĕshua, "Măster, it is good for us to be here," and "we should make three shelters: one for you, and one for Mosheh, and one for E̱liyahu"—who had not been realizing what he was saying.

³⁴And while he was saying this, a cloud formed and was overshadowing them. And they were afraid as they entered the cloud. ³⁵And a voice came out of the cloud, saying, "This is my Sŏn who has been getting chosen. Be hearing from him!" ³⁶And when the voice had spoken, Yĕshua was found alone. And they kept silent, and reported to no one in those days any of the things which they had been seeing. ³⁷And it came about on the next day, that when they came down from the mountain, a great crowd met him. ³⁸And behold, a man from the crowd shouted out, saying, "Teacher, I beg you to look at my son, for he is my only kindred, ³⁹and behold, a spirit seizes him, and he suddenly screams, and it throws him into a convulsion with foaming at the mouth, and as it mauls him, it scarcely leaves him. ⁴⁰And I begged your disciples, that they may cast it out, and they could not."

⁴¹And Yĕshua answered and said, "O unfaithful kindred, *which* also has been getting perverted, how long will I be with you, and put up with you? Bring your son here." ⁴²And while he was still approaching, the demon dashed him to the ground, and threw him into a convulsion. But Yĕshua rebuked the unclean spirit, and healed the boy, and gave him back to his father. ⁴³And they were all

---

9:27 η See *Mat. 16:28; Mark 9:1;* **9:27** μ Both Mark and Luke omit the words 'the Son of man coming' to make it easier to understand. They would see to the kingdom by taking the good news to the nations, and they will perceive it among them when they pledge faithfulness to Messiah. See Luke 17:21. Both Peter and Yoḣanan ended up doing this.

Luke 9

amazed at the greatness of the Almĭghty.

⁴³ᵇBut while everyone was marveling at all that he was doing, he said to his disciples, ⁴⁴"Let these words sink into your ears, because the Sŏn of Man is going to be delivered into the hands of men." ⁴⁵But they did not understand this statement, and it had been getting veiled from them so that they might not perceive it. And they were afraid to ask him about this statement.

⁴⁶And an argument arose among them as to which of them may be the greatest. ⁴⁷But Yĕshua, who had been knowing what they were thinking in their heart, took a child and stood him by his side, ⁴⁸and said to them, "Whoever may have received such a child in my name receives me. And whoever may have received me receives him who sent me. Because he who is least among you, this is the one who is great."

⁴⁹And Yoḣanan answered and said, "Mǎster, we saw someone casting out demons in your name. And we tried to hinder him because he does not follow along with us." ⁵⁰But Yĕshua said to him, "Do not be hindering him, because he who is not against you is for you."

⁵¹And it was, in the completion the days of his ascending, that he set his face to go to Yerushalayim. ⁵²And he sent messengers before his face. And they went, and they entered a village of the Shomronim, to make arrangements for him. ⁵³And they did not receive him, because he was journeying with his face toward Yerushalayim. ⁵⁴And when his disciples Ya'aqov and Yoḣanan saw *this*, they said, "Adŏnai, do you want us, that we may command fire to come down from heaven and consume them, ʿas also Eliyahu did?'" ⁵⁵But he turned and rebuked them. ʿAnd he said, "You have not been knowing what kind of spirit you are.' ⁵⁶ ʿThe Sŏn of Man did not come to destroy men's lives, but to rescue them."' And they went on to another village.

⁵⁷And as they were going along the road, someone said to him, "I will follow you wherever you may be going." ⁵⁸And Yĕshua said to him, "The foxes have holes, and the birds of the air have nests, but the Sŏn of Man has nowhere he may be laying his head." ⁵⁹And he said to another, "Be following me." But he said, "Permit me first to go and bury my father." ⁶⁰But he said to him, "Allow the dead to bury their own dead, but as for you, having gone, be proclaiming the kingdom of the Almĭghty." ⁶¹And another also said, "I will follow you, Adŏnai, but first permit me to say good-bye to those at home." ⁶²But Yĕshua said to him, "No one, after putting his hand to the plow and looking back, is fit for the kingdom of the Almĭghty^μ."

9:51 τ These began mid spring, AD 33, perhaps in Iyyar. **9:54** ʿ A C D W Θ Ψ f¹.¹³ 33 𝔐 it syᵖ·ʰ boᵖᵗ **9:55** ʿ D it. **9:56** ʿ it. See 2 Kings 1:5-14. The two cases are not the same. They came to arrest Ẹliyahu, and his action was a defensive measure. The Shomronim simply did not want to listen. The disciples were not in danger. **9:59-62** μ What seems cruel or uncaring at first sight is not. Mĕssiah said these things because time was running out, and also because the initial commitment some where making was not the final commitment that would be needed, and if they departed they would never make the total commitment to Mĕssiah. There was no shortage of half-hearted seekers.

10 ¹Now after this the Măster appointed seventy others, and sent them two and two ahead of him to every city and place where he himself was going to come. ²And he was saying to them, "The harvest is plentiful, but the laborers are few. Therefore beg the Măster of the harvest, that he will have sent out laborers into his harvest. ³Be going! Behold, I send you out as lambs in the midst of wolves. ⁴Be carrying no purse, no bag, no shoes, and you will have greeted no one down through the way.

⁵"And whatever house you may have entered, first be saying, 'Peace be to this house.' ⁶And if a son of peace may be there, your peace will rest upon him, but if not, it will return to you. ⁷And be remaining in that house, eating and drinking what is theirs that they give you, because the laborer is worthy of his wages. Do not be moving from house to house."

⁸"And whatever city you may be entering, and they may be receiving you, be eating the things being set before you, ⁹and be healing those in it who are sick, and be saying to them, 'The kingdom of the Almĭghty has been coming near to you.' ¹⁰But whatever city you may have entered and they may not be receiving you, go out into its streets and say, ¹¹'Even the dust of your city which clings to our feet, we wipe off in protest against you. Nevertheless, be knowing this, that the kingdom of the Almĭghty has been coming near.' ¹²I say to you, it will be more tolerable in that day for Sedom, than for that city.

¹³"Woe to you, Korazin! Woe to you, Beth-Tsaidah! For if the miracles were performed in Tsor and Tsidon which occurred in you, they would have been sorry and turned their hearts *from sin* long ago, sitting in sackcloth and ashes. ¹⁴But it will be more tolerable for Tsor and Tsidon in the judgment, than for you.

¹⁵"And you, Kefar-Nahum, will not be exalted to heaven, will you? You will be brought down to the grave! ¹⁶"The one who listens to you listens to me, and the one who rejects you rejects me. And he who rejects me rejects the One who sent me."

¹⁷And the seventy returned with joy,᛫ saying, "Adŏnai, even the demons are subject to us in your name." ¹⁸And he said to them, "I was watching Satan fall from heaven like lightning. ¹⁹Behold, I have been giving you authority to tread upon serpents and scorpions, and over all the power of the enemy, and nothing, no, it will not have injured you. ²⁰Nevertheless, do not be rejoicing in this, that the spirits are subject to you, but be rejoicing that your names have been getting written down in Heaven."

²¹At that very time he rejoiced greatly in the Holy Spĭrit, and said, "I praise you, Făther, Măster of heaven and earth, that you did hide these things from the wise and intelligent and did reveal them to babes. Yes, Făther, for thus it was well-pleasing in your sight. ²²"All things have been handed over to me by my Făther, and no one knows who the Sŏn is except the Făther, and who the Făther is except the Sŏn, and anyone to whom the Sŏn may be willing to reveal him."

10:17 τ Early summer, AD 33. It was a Şabbaṭical year.

²³And turning to the disciples, he said privately, "Blessed are the eyes which see the things you see, ²⁴for I say to you, that many prophets and kings wished to see the things which you see, and did not see them, and to hear the things which you hear, and did not hear them."

²⁵And behold, a certain lawyer stood up and put him to the test, saying, "Teacher, what shall I do to inherit everlasting life?" ²⁶And he said to him, "What has been getting written in the Law? How does it read to you?" ²⁷And he answered and said, "YOU SHALL LOVE YĂHWEH YOUR ALMĬGHTY WITH ALL YOUR HEART, AND WITH ALL YOUR SOUL, AND WITH ALL YOUR STRENGTH, AND WITH ALL YOUR MIND ͣ, and YOUR NEIGHBOR AS YOURSELF ᵝ." ²⁸And he said to him, "You have answered correctly. BE DOING THIS, AND YOU WILL LIVE ᵞ."

²⁹But wishing to justify himself, he said to Yĕshua, "And who is my neighbor?"

³⁰Yĕshua replied and said, "A certain man was going down from Yerushalayim to Yeriho. And he fell among robbers, and they stripped him and beat him, and went off leaving him half dead. ³¹And by chance a certain priest was going down through that road, and when he saw him, he passed by on the other side. ³²And likewise a Levi'i also, when he came down through the place and saw him, passed by on the other side. ³³"But a certain Shomroni, who was on a journey, came upon him. And when he saw him, he felt compassion, ³⁴and came to him, and bandaged up his wounds, pouring oil and wine on them. And he put him on his own beast, and brought him to an inn, and took care of him.

³⁵And on the next day he took out two dinars and gave them to the innkeeper and said, 'Take care of him. And whatever more you may have spent, when I return, I will repay you.' ³⁶Which of these three do you think had been becoming a neighbor of the man who fell into the robbers' hands?" ³⁷And he said, "The one who showed mercy toward him." And Yĕshua said to him, "Be yourself going and be doing the same."

³⁸Now as they were traveling along, he entered a certain village. And a woman named Marta welcomed him into her home. ³⁹And she had a sister called Miryam, who moreover was listening to Adŏnai's word, seated at his feet. ⁴⁰But Marta was distracted with all her preparations. And she came up to him, and said, "Adŏnai, do you not care that my sister has left me to do all the serving alone? Then tell her that she should have helped me!" ⁴¹But Adŏnai answered and said to her, "Marta, Marta, you are worried and bothered about so many things, ⁴²but only a few things are necessary, really only one, for Miryam has chosen the good part, which will not be taken away from her."

11

¹And it happened while he was praying in a certain place ͭ, as he finished, one of his disciples said to him, "Adŏnai, teach us to pray just as Yohanan also taught his disciples." ²And he said to them, "When you may be praying, be saying: 'Our Făther who art in Heaven, hallowed be your name. Your kingdom come. ³Be giving us bread for tomorrow each day. ⁴And forgive

---

10:27 α Deu 6:5; **10:27** β Lev 19:18; **10:28** γ Lev 18:5, Ezek 20:11. **11:1** τ Fall, AD 33.

us our sins, for we ourselves also forgive everyone who is indebted to us. And may you not lead us into testing.'"

⁵And he said to them, "Suppose one of you will have a friend, and will go to him at midnight, and he will have said to him, 'Friend, lend me three loaves, ⁶because a friend of mine has come to me from a journey, and I have nothing to set before him'. ⁷And from inside he will answer, and will have said, 'Do not be making trouble for me! The door has already been getting shut and my children and I are in bed. I cannot get up and give you anything.' ⁸I tell you, even though he will not get up and give him anything because he is his friend, yet because of his persistence he will get up and give him as much as he needs.

⁹"And I say to you, be asking, and it will be given to you. Be seeking, and you will find. Be knocking, and it will be opened to you. ¹⁰Because everyone who asks, receives, and he who seeks, finds. And to him who knocks, it will be opened.

¹¹"Now suppose one of you fathers is asked by his son for a fish. He will not give him a snake instead of a fish, will he? ¹²Or if he is asked for an egg, he will not give him a scorpion, will he? ¹³If you then, being bad, have been knowing how to give good gifts to your children, how much more will your heavenly Făther give the Holy Spĭrit to those who ask him?"

¹⁴And he was casting out a demon, and it was mute. And it happened when the demon went out, the mute man spoke. And the multitudes marveled. ¹⁵But some of them said, "He casts out demons by Baʻal-zevul, the ruler of the demons." ¹⁶And others, to test him, were demanding at his side a sign from heaven.

¹⁷But he had been knowing their thoughts, and said to them, "Any kingdom divided against itself is laid waste. And a house divided against itself falls. ¹⁸And if Satan also is divided against himself, how will his kingdom stand? For you say that I cast out demons by Baʻal-zevul. ¹⁹And if I by Baʻal-zevul cast out demons, by whom do your sons cast them out? Consequently, they will be your judges. ²⁰But if I cast out demons by the finger of the Almĭghty, then the kingdom of the Almĭghty has come upon you.

²¹"When a strong man, who has been fully arming himself, may be guarding his own homestead, his possessions are undisturbed, ²²yet when someone stronger than he, having attacked, may have gotten victory over him, he takes away from him all his armor on which he had been trusting, and distributes his plunder. ²³He who is not with me is against me. And he who does not gather with me, scatters.

²⁴"When the unclean spirit may have gone out of a man, it passes through waterless places seeking rest, and not finding any, it says, 'I will return to my house from which I came.' ²⁵And when it comes, it finds it has been getting swept and has been getting put in order. ²⁶Then it goes and takes along seven other spirits more evil than itself, and they go in and live there. And the last state of that man becomes worse than the first."

²⁷And it came about while he said these things, one of the women in the crowd raised her voice, and said to him, "Blessed is the womb that bore you,

and the breasts at which you nursed." ²⁸But he said, "On the contrary, blessed are those who hear the word of the Almĭghty, and observe it."

²⁹And as the crowds were increasing, he began to say, "This kindred is a wicked kindred. It seeks for a sign, and yet no sign will be given to it but the sign of Yonah. ³⁰For just as Yonah became a sign to the people of Ninveh, so will the Sŏn of Man be to this kindred. ³¹The Queen of the South will rise up against the men of this kindred at the judgment and condemn them, because she came from the ends of the earth to hear the wisdom of Shelomoh. And behold, something greater than Shelomoh is here. ³²The men of Ninveh will stand up against this kindred at the judgment and condemn it, because they became sorry and turned their hearts *from sin* at the proclaiming of Yonah. And behold, something greater than Yonah is here.

³³"No one, after lighting a lamp, puts it away in a cellar, nor under a peck-measure, but on the lampstand, in order that those who enter may be seeing the light. ³⁴The lamp of your body is your eye. When your eye may be clear, your whole body also is full of light, but when it may be bad, your body also is full of darkness. ³⁵Therefore, be looking out that the light in you may not be darkness. ³⁶If therefore your whole body is full of light, with no dark part in it, it will be wholly illumined, as when the lamp may be illumining you with its rays."

³⁷And while he spoke, a Perushi requests him, that he may eat breakfast with him. And he went in, and reclined at the table. ³⁸And when the Perushi saw it, he was surprised that he had not first ceremonially washed before the meal. ³⁹But Adŏnai said to him, "Now you Perushim clean the outside of the cup and of the platter, but inside of you, you are full of robbery and wickedness. ⁴⁰You foolish ones, did not he who made the outside make the inside also? ⁴¹But give that which is within as charity, and then all things are clean for you.

⁴²"But woe to you Perushim! For you pay tithe of mint and rue and every kind of garden herb, and yet disregard justice and the love of the Almĭghty, but these are the things you should have done without neglecting the others.

⁴³"Woe to you Perushim! For you love the front seats in the congregations, and the respectful greetings in the market places. ⁴⁴"Woe to you! For you are like concealed tombs, and the men who are walking over them have not been knowing."

⁴⁵And one of the lawyers said to him in reply, "Teacher, when you say this, you insult us too." ⁴⁶But he said, "Woe to you lawyers as well! For you weigh men down with burdens hard to bear, while you yourselves will not even touch the burdens with one of your fingers. ⁴⁷"Woe to you! For you build the tombs of the prophets, and it was your fathers who killed them. ⁴⁸Consequently, you are witnesses and approve the deeds of your fathers, because it was they who killed them, and you build their tombs. ⁴⁹For this reason also the wisdom of the Almĭghty said, 'I will send to them prophets and emissaries, and some of them they will kill and some they will persecute, ⁵⁰in order that the blood of all the prophets, which have been getting shed since the foundation of the world,

may be charged against this kindred, ⁵¹from the blood of Hevel to the blood of Zekaryahu, who perished between the altar and the house of the Almĭghty. Yes, I tell you, it will be charged against this kindred.'

⁵²"Woe to you lawyers! For you have taken away the key of knowledge. You did not enter in yourselves, and those who were entering in you hindered."

⁵³And when he left there, the scribes and the Perushim began to be very hostile and to question him closely on many subjects, ⁵⁴laying in wait, to catch him *in* something out of his mouth.

12

¹Under these circumstances, after so many thousands of the crowd had gathered together that they were stepping on one another, he began to be saying to his disciples first *of all*, "Be keeping yourselves from the leaven of the Perushim, which is hypocrisy. ²But there is nothing which has been getting covered up that will not be revealed, and hidden that will not be known. ³Accordingly, whatever you have said in the dark will be heard in the light, and what you have whispered in the inner rooms will be proclaimed upon the housetops.

⁴"And I say to you, my friends, you shall not have been afraid of those who kill the body, and after that have no more that they can do. ⁵Yet, I will warn you whom you shall have feared. Fear the One who after he has killed has authority to cast into Geihinnom. Yes, I tell you, fear him! ⁶Are not five sparrows sold for two cents? And yet not one of them is, *or* has been getting forgotten before the Almĭghty. ⁷But the very hairs of your head have all been getting numbered. Do not be fearing. You are of more value than many sparrows."

⁸"And I say to you, everyone who may have confessed me before men, the Sŏn of Man will confess him also before the angelic messengers of the Almĭghty, ⁹but he who denies me before men will be denied before the angelic messengers of the Almĭghty. ¹⁰And everyone who will speak a word against the Sŏn of Man, it will be forgiven him, but he who blasphemes against the Holy Spĭrit, it will not be forgiven him.ᵝ

¹¹"And when they may be bringing you before the congregations and the rulers and the authorities, you should not become anxious about how or what you shall have spoken in your defense, or what you shall have said, ¹²because the Holy Spĭrit will teach you in that very hour what you is necessary to say."

¹³And someone in the crowd said to him, "Teacher, tell my brother to divide the family inheritance with me." ¹⁴But he said to him, "Man, who appointed me a judge or arbiter over you?" ¹⁵And he said to them, "Be looking closely, and be

---

12:10 β See Mark 3:29; Mat. 12:31. The sin committed in the heart against certain knowledge borne witness to by the Spirit of the Most High, and under no coercion has no forgiveness, but is a sin unto death because it was not committed in ignorance. See 1 Yoḣ. 5:16. Such a sin can bind a person into bondage for a very long time from which there is no release/forgiveness. A person who sins in ignorance or by coercion is still under divine loving-kindness if he his faithful. But a person who sins willfully against a Spirit borne witness of knowledge to the truth is under divine wrath. Messiah never said anyone had committed this sin, but he warned against it. If any one thinking they have committed this sin finds confession and repentance, then it may be later judged that they had not committed this sin in the first place. But this is my opinion. It certainly will not be forgiven in any age without repentance.

guarding yourselves against every form of greed, because not even when one has an abundance does his life consist of his possessions."

¹⁶And he told them a parable, saying, "The land of a certain rich man was very productive. ¹⁷And he began reasoning to himself, saying, 'What will I have done, since I have no place to store my crops?' ¹⁸And he said, 'This is what I will do: I will tear down my barns and build larger ones, and there I will store all my grain and my goods. ¹⁹And I will say to my soul, "Soul, you have many goods laid up for many years to come. Be resting, eat, drink and be getting yourself merry."' ²⁰But the Almĭghty said to him, 'You fool! This very night your soul is required of you. And now who will own what you have prepared?' ²¹So is the man who lays up treasure for himself, and is not rich toward the Almĭghty."

²²And he said to his disciples, "For this reason I say to you, do not be getting anxious for the soul, as to what you will have eaten, nor yet for your body, as to what you will have put on. ²³For life is more than food, and the body than clothing. ²⁴Consider the ravens, because they neither sow nor reap. And they have no storeroom nor barn. And yet the Almĭghty feeds them. How much more valuable you are than the birds! ²⁵And which of you by being anxious can add a single cubit to his life's span? ²⁶If then you cannot do even a very little thing, why are you anxious about other matters? ²⁷Consider the lilies, how they grow. They neither toil nor spin, but I tell you, not even Shelomoh in all his glory had gotten dressed like one of these. ²⁸But if the Almĭghty so arrays the grass in the field, which is alive today and tomorrow is thrown into the furnace, how much more will he clothe you, little faithful ones!

²⁹"And do not be seeking what you may eat, and what you may drink, and do not be worrying. ³⁰For all these things the nations of the world eagerly seek, but your Făther has been knowing that you need these things. ³¹However, be seeking his kingdom, and these things will be added to you. ³²Do not be getting yourselves afraid, little flock, for your Făther has been well pleased to give you the kingdom. ³³Sell your possessions and give to charity. Make yourselves purses which do not wear out, an unfailing treasure in heaven, where no thief comes near, nor moth destroys. ³⁴For where your treasure is, there will your heart be also.

³⁵"Be letting your waist be having been getting girded, and your lamps be burning. ³⁶And be like men who are waiting for their master whenever he may have returned from the wedding feasts, such that when he came and knocked, they have immediately opened for him. ³⁷Blessed are those slaves whom the master will find on the alert when he comes. Amen I say to you, that he will gird himself to serve, and have them recline at the table, and will come up and wait on them. ³⁸Whether he may have come in the second watch, or even in the third, and may have found them so, blessed are those slaves.

³⁹"And be knowing this, that if the head of the house had been knowing at what hour the thief was coming, he would not have allowed his house to be broken into. ⁴⁰You too, be getting yourselves ready, because the Sŏn of Man

---

12:40 φ ᾖ (V-PSA-3S): ὅτι ᾖ ὥρᾳ οὐ δοκεῖτε = *because it may be in an hour not you are supposing.* But not ᾗ (RelPro-DFS). Or *Because it may be in an hour you are not expecting. The Son of man is coming!*

⁕may be coming in an hour that you are not expecting."

⁴¹And Peter said, "Adŏnai, are you addressing this parable to us, or to everyone else as well?" ⁴²And the Măster said, "Who then is the faithful and sensible steward, whom his master will put in charge of his servants, to give them their rations at the proper time? ⁴³Blessed is that slave whom his master finds so doing when he comes. ⁴⁴Truly I say to you, that he will put him in charge of all his possessions. ⁴⁵But if that slave may have said in his heart, 'My master delays to be coming,' and he shall have been a boss to beat the menservants and the maidservants, besides eating and drinking, also being drunk, then ⁴⁶the master of that slave will come on a day when he does not expect him, and at an hour he does not know, and will cut him in pieces, and will assign his portion with the unfaithful. ⁴⁷And that slave who knew his master's will and did not get ready or act in accord with his will, will receive many lashes, ⁴⁸but the one who did not know it, and committed deeds worthy of a flogging, will receive but few. And from everyone who has been given much, will much be required, and to whom they entrusted much, from his hand they will ask all the more."

⁴⁹"I have come to cast fire upon the earth. And how I wish it were already kindled! ⁵⁰But I have an immersion to undergo, and how distressed I am until whenever, it may have been accomplished! ⁵¹Do you suppose that I came to grant peace on earth? I tell you, no, not so much as division, ⁵²because from now on they will be five in one house, who have been dividing themselves, three against two, and two against three. ⁵³They will be divided, father against son, and son against father, mother against daughter, and daughter against mother, mother-in-law against daughter-in-law, and daughter-in-law against mother-in-law."

⁵⁴And he was also saying to the crowds, "When you may have seen a cloud rising in the west, immediately you say, 'A shower is coming,' and so it turns out. ⁵⁵And when you see a south wind blowing, you say, 'It will be a hot day,' and it turns out that way. ⁵⁶You hypocrites! You have been knowing how to be analyzing the appearance of the earth and the sky, but why have you not been knowing how to be analyzing this present time?

⁵⁷And why do you not even on your own initiative judge what is right? ⁵⁸For as you are going with your opponent *to appear* before the magistrate, on your way there make an effort to have been getting released from him, in order that he may not be dragging you before the judge, and the judge turn you over to the constable, and the constable throw you into prison. ⁵⁹I say to you, no, you shall not have gotten out of there until you may have paid the very last cent."

13

¹Now on the same occasion there were some coming by who reported to him about the men of Galil, whose blood Pilate had mingled with their sacrifices.ᵀ ²And when he answered, he said to them, "Are you supposing that

---

13:1 τ This happened at Sukkot, AD 33.

Luke 13

these men of Galil became sinners *more so* to the side all men of Galil, because they have been suffering these things? ³I tell you, no, but unless you may be sorry, and be turning your hearts *from sin*, you will all likewise perish."

⁴"Or do you suppose that those eighteen on whom the tower in Şiloam fell and killed them, became debtors *more so* beside all the men who live in Yerushalayim? ⁵I tell you, no, but unless you will have been sorry and have turned your hearts *from sin*, you will all likewise perish."

⁶And he was telling this parable: "A certain man was having a fig tree that had been getting planted in his vineyard. Then he came looking for fruit on it, and did not find *any*. ⁷And he said to the vineyard-keeper, 'behold, for three years I have come looking for fruit on this fig tree without finding any. Cut it down! Why does it even use up the ground?' ⁸And he answered and said to him, 'Let it alone, sir, for this year too, until when I may have dug around it and may have thrown in fertilizer. ⁹And if it may have produced in the year coming, fine, and if not, surely cut it down.'"

¹⁰And he was teaching in one of the congregations on the Şabbaṯhs. ¹¹And behold, there was a woman who for eighteen years had had a sickness caused by a spirit. And she was bent double, and could not straighten up at all. ¹²And when Yĕshua saw her, he called *her* over and said to her, "Woman, you will have been getting freed from your sickness." ¹³And he laid his hands upon her. And immediately she was made erect again, and was glorifying the Almĭghty.

¹⁴And the congregation official, indignant because Yĕshua had healed on the Şabbaṯh, was saying to the multitude in response, "There are six days in which work should be done. Therefore having come during these *days*, be getting healed, and not on the day of the Şabbaṯh." ¹⁵But the Măster answered him and said, "You hypocrites, does not each of you on the Şabbaṯh untie his ox or his donkey from the stall, and lead him away to water him? ¹⁶And this woman, a daughter of Avraham as she is, whom Satan had bound for eighteen long years, should she not have been released from this bond on the day of the Şabbaṯh?" ¹⁷And as he said this, all his opponents were being humiliated. And the entire crowd was rejoicing over all the glorious things being done by him.

¹⁸Therefore he was saying, "What is the kingdom of the Almĭghty like, and to what will I compare it? ¹⁹It is like a mustard seed, which a man took and threw into his own garden. And it grew and became a tree. And THE BIRDS OF THE AIR NESTED IN ITS BRANCHES^ϕ."

²⁰And again he said, "To what shall I compare the kingdom of the Almĭghty? ²¹It is like leaven, which a woman took and hid in three pecks of meal, until it was all leavened."

²²And he was passing down through cities and villages, teaching, and pro-

---

13:6-9 The parable gives us the length of Měssiah's ministry. It is four years. The first three years were between the Passovers, 30-31, 31-32, 32-33. The final year is between the Passover of AD 33 and that of AD 34. It was during this final year that the parable was spoken. Měssiah's most extensive ministry efforts were made in this year. See Luke 9:51.

13:19 ϕ Ezek 17:23.

ceeding on his way to Yerushalayim. ²³And someone said to him, "Adŏnai, are there just a few who are being rescued?" And he said to them, ²⁴"Be yourselves struggling to enter by the narrow door, because many, I tell you, will seek to enter and will not be able. ²⁵Once the head of the house may have risen up and may have shut the door, and you shall have begun to have been standing outside, even to be knocking on the door, saying, 'Adŏnai, Open up to us!' then having answered, he will say to you, 'I have not been knowing where you are from.'

²⁶Then you will begin to say, 'We ate and drank in your presence, and you taught in our streets', ²⁷and he will say, 'I tell you, I have not been knowing where you are from. DEPART FROM ME, ALL YOU WORKERS OF INJUSTICE.'ᵃ ²⁸Unto that place there will be weeping and gnashing of teeth when you see Avraham and Yitsḥaq and Ya'aqov and all the prophets in the kingdom of the Almĭghty, but yourselves being cast out. ²⁹And they will come from east and west, and from north and south, and will recline at the table in the kingdom of the Almĭghty. ³⁰And behold, some are last who will be first and some are first who will be last."

³¹Just at that time some Perushim came up, saying to him, "Be getting yourself away from here, because Herod wants to kill you." ³²And he said to them, "Having gone, tell that fox, 'behold, I cast out demons and perform cures today and tomorrow, and the third day I am getting finished.'ᵖ

³³Nevertheless I must journey on today and tomorrow and the next day, because it cannot be that a prophet should perish outside of Yerushalayim.

³⁴"Yerushalayim, Yerushalayim, the city that kills the prophets and stones those who have been getting sent to her! How often I wanted to gather your children together, just as a hen gathers her brood under her wings, and you would not have it! ³⁵Behold, your house is being abandoned to you. And, I am saying to you, no, you shall not have seen me, until *the time* has come when you shall have said, 'He HAS BEEN GETTING BLESSED, **THE COMING ONE** IN THE NAME OF YĂHWEH!'"ᵠ

14

¹And it came about when he went into the house of one of the leaders of the Perushim on the Ṣabbath to eat bread, that they were watching him closely. ²And there, in front of him was a certain man suffering from dropsy. ³And Yĕshua answered and spoke to the lawyers and Perushim, saying, "Is it lawful to heal on the Ṣabbath, or not?" ⁴But they kept silent. And he took hold of him, and healed him, and sent him away. ⁵And he said to them, "Which one of you, *if* a son or an ox will fall into a well, also will not immediately pull him out on the day of the Ṣabbath?" ⁶And they could make no reply to such things.

⁷And he was speaking a parable to those who had been getting invited, re-

---

13:27 α Psa 6:8-9, Mat 7:23. **13:32** ρ In this riddle, Mĕssiah is telling us about his impending death. The word 'tomorrow' means hereafter. It also shows how three days are counted. They are counted inclusively. Today, tomorrow, the third day. Likewise Scripture counts backwards: today, yesterday, the third day. The three days were Wednesday dawn to Thursday dawn, day 1. Thursday dawn to Friday dawn, day 2. Friday dawn to Ṣabbath dawn, day 3. The resurrection was before dawn on the Ṣabbath. The verb is passive/reflexive, suggesting something will happen to him on the third day. He speaks of both his death and resurrection. See Hos. 6:1-3. **13:35** ψ Psa 118:26: בָּרוּךְ הַבָּא בְּשֵׁם יְהוָה.

marking on how they were picking out firstmost reclining places, saying to them, ⁸"When you may have been invited by someone to wedding feasts, you should not recline in the headmost place, lest someone more distinguished than you may be *or* has been getting invited by him, ⁹and he who invited you both will come and say to you, 'Give place to this man,' and then in disgrace you proceed to occupy the last place. ¹⁰But whenever you may have been invited, *having* gone, recline at the last place, so that when the one who has been inviting you may have come, he will say to you, 'Friend, move up higher', then you will have honor in the sight of all those reclining with you. ¹¹For everyone who exalts himself will be humbled, and he who humbles himself will be exalted." ¹²And, he was also saying to the one who had been inviting him, "When you may be making a dinner or a supper, do not be calling your friends nor even your brothers nor even your relatives nor even rich neighbors, lest ever they also will have invited you in return, and repayment will have come to you. ¹³But whenever you may be making a reception, be inviting the poor, the crippled, the lame, the blind, ¹⁴and you will be blessed, since they do not have the means to repay you, because you will be repaid at the resurrection of the righteous."

¹⁵And when one of those who were reclining at the table with him heard this, he said to him, "Blessed is everyone who will eat bread in the kingdom of the Almĭghty!"

¹⁶But he said to him, "A certain man was giving a big dinner, and he invited many. ¹⁷And at the dinner hour he sent his slave to say to those who had been getting invited, 'Be coming, because it is already ready.' ¹⁸But they all as one began to be excusing themselves. The first said to him, 'I have bought a field and I have the need, *to have* gone out, to see it. I am begging you, be holding that I have been getting excused.' ¹⁹And another said, 'I have bought five yoke of oxen, and I am going to try them *out*. I am begging you, be holding that I have been getting excused.' ²⁰And another said, 'I have married a wife, and for that reason I am not able to come.' ²¹And the slave came back and reported this to his master. "Then the head of the household became angry and said to his slave, 'Go out at once into the streets and lanes of the city and bring in here the poor and crippled and blind and lame.' ²²And the slave said, 'Master, what you commanded has been happening, and still there is room.' ²³And the master said to the slave, 'Go out into the highways and along the hedges, and compel them to come in, that my house may be filled! ²⁴For I tell you, none of those men who had been getting invited will taste of my dinner.'"

²⁵Now great crowds were going along with him. And he turned and said to them, ²⁶"If anyone comes to me, and does not hate his own father and mother and wife and children and brothers and sisters, still *more* as well even his own life, he is not able to be my disciple. ²⁷Whoever does not carry his own execution timber and come after me cannot be my disciple. ²⁸"For which one of you, when he wants to build a tower, does not first sit down and calculate the cost, to see

if he has enough to complete it? ²⁹Otherwise, when he has laid a foundation, and is not able to finish, all who observe will have begun to be ridiculing him, ³⁰saying, 'This man began to be building and was not able to finish.'

³¹"Or what king, when he sets out to meet another king in battle, will not first sit down and take counsel whether he is strong enough with ten thousand men to encounter the one coming against him with twenty thousand? ³²Or else, while the other is still far away, he sends a delegation and asks terms of peace.

³³"So therefore, no one of you can be my disciple who does not give up all his own possessions. ³⁴Therefore, salt is good, yet if ever even the salt may have become a foolishness, with what will it be seasoned? ³⁵It is useless either for the soil or for the manure pile. It is thrown out. He who is having ears to be hearing, let him be hearing."

15 ¹Now all the tax-collectors and the sinners were coming near him to listen to him. ²And besides the Perushim, also the scribes were grumbling, saying that, "This man is welcoming sinners and is eating with them."

³And he told them this parable, saying, ⁴"What man among you, having a hundred sheep and who has lost one of them, does not leave the ninety-nine in the open pasture, and go after the one which has been perishing, until he may have found it? ⁵And when he has found it, he lays it on his shoulders, rejoicing. ⁶And after he has come into the house, he calls together his friends and his neighbors, saying to them, 'Rejoice with me, because I have found my sheep which had been perishing!' ⁷I tell you that in the same way, there will be more joy in heaven over one sinner who is being sorry and turning his heart *from sin*, than over ninety-nine righteous persons who have no need of being sorry and turning their hearts *from sin*.

⁸"Or what woman, if she has ten silver coins and may have lost one coin, does not light a lamp and sweep the house and search carefully until she may have found it? ⁹And when she has found it, she calls together her friends and neighbors, saying, 'Rejoice with me, for I have found the coin which I had lost!' ¹⁰In the same way, I tell you, there is joy in the presence of the messengers of the Almĭghty over one sinner who is being sorry and turning his heart *from sin*."

¹¹And he said, "A certain man had two sons. ¹²And the younger of them said to his father, 'Father, give me the share of the estate that falls to me.' And he divided his wealth between them. ¹³And not many days later, the younger son gathered everything together and went on a journey into a distant country, and there he squandered his estate with loose living.

¹⁴Now when he had spent everything, a severe famine occurred down through that country, and he began to be in need. ¹⁵"And he went and attached himself to one of the citizens of that country, and he sent him into his fields to feed pigs. ¹⁶And he was longing to fill his stomach with the pods that the pigs were eating, and no one was giving anything to him.

¹⁷"But coming to himself, he said, 'How many of my father's hired men have

more than enough bread, but I am dying here with hunger! ¹⁸'I will get up and go to my father, and will say to him, "Father, I have sinned against heaven, and in your sight. ¹⁹I am no longer worthy to be called your son. Make me as one of your hired men."' ²⁰And he got up and came to his father.

²⁰ᵇ"But while he was still a long way off, his father saw him, and felt compassion for him, and ran and embraced him, and kissed him. ²¹And the son said to him, 'Father, I have sinned against heaven and in your sight. I am no longer worthy to be called your son.' ²²But the father said to his slaves, 'Quickly bring out the best robe and put it on him, and put a ring on his hand and sandals on his feet. ²³And be bringing the fattened calf, kill it, and having eaten we shall have been merry, ²⁴because this son of mine was being dead, and has lived again. He was being one who had been perishing, and has been found.' And they began to be merry.

²⁵"Now his older son was in the field, and when he came and approached the house, he heard music and dancing. ²⁶And he summoned one of the servants and was inquiring what these things may be. ²⁷And he said to him, 'Your brother has come, and your father has killed the fattened calf, because he has received him back safe and sound.' ²⁸But he became angry, and was not willing to go in. "And his father came out and was entreating him. ²⁹But he answered and said to his father, 'Look! For so many years I have been serving you, and I have never neglected a command of yours. And yet you have never given me a kid, so that I may have been merry with my friends, ³⁰but when this son of yours came, who has devoured your wealth with harlots, you killed the fattened calf for him.'

³¹And he said to him, 'My child, you have always been with me, and all that is mine is yours. ³²'Yet, to be merry and to be joyful was fitting, in that this brother of yours had been dead and has lived, and had been perishing and was found.'"

16

¹Now he was also saying to the disciples, "There was a ᵋcertain rich man who was having a steward, and this steward was reported to him as squandering his possessions. ²"And he called him and said to him, 'What is this I hear about you? Give an account of your stewardship, for you can no longer be steward.'

³"And the steward said to himself, 'What shall I have done, since my master is taking the stewardship away from me? I am not strong enough to dig. I am ashamed to beg. ⁴I know what I shall have done, so that when I may have been removed from the stewardship, they shall have received me into their homes.'

⁵"And he summoned each one of his master's debtors, and he was saying to

---

16:1 τ Winter, AD 34. **16:1** ξ→rich man: The character is fictional. See Luke 10:30; 12:16; 14:16; 15:11; 16:1; 18:12 19:12; 20:9; this is one of many parables introduced with the words, 'a certain man,' Ἄνθρωπός τις, or similar words to indicate a story is coming. Quite frequently Yĕshua tells the story but never says it is a 'parable.' The stories are often, but not always introduced with the words 'And he was speaking a parable to them...' by the evangelists. In a good number of cases, it is left to the original audience or to the nature of the story itself for hearers to figure out that it is a parable. What we call fiction literature today, or even historical fiction is a version of the same sort of story telling. Other literary

the first, 'How much do you owe my master?' ⁶And he said, 'A hundred measures of oil.' And he said to him, 'Take your letter promising to repay, and sit down quickly and write fifty.' ⁷Then he said to another, 'And how much do you owe?' And he said, 'A hundred measures of wheat.' He said to him, 'Take your letter promising to repay, and write eighty.'

⁸"And his master praised the unrighteous steward because he had acted shrewdly, because the sons of this age are more shrewd *in relation* to their own kindred than the sons of light.

⁹"And I say to you, make friends for yourselves by means of the wealth of unrighteousness, that when it may have failed, *then* they may have received you in the everlasting tents. ¹⁰He who is faithful in a very little thing is faithful also in much. And he who is unrighteous in a very little thing is unrighteous also in much. ¹¹If therefore you have not been faithful ones with unrighteous wealth, who will hold you faithful? ¹²And if you have not been faithful ones in that which is another's, who will give you that which is your own? ¹³No servant can serve two masters, because either he will hate the one, and love the other, or else he will hold to one, and despise the other. You cannot serve the Almĭghty and wealth."

¹⁴And, the Perushim, being lovers of ᵅmoney, were hearing all these things, and they were ridiculing him. ¹⁵And he said to them, "You are those who are justifying yourselves in the sight of men, but the Almĭghty knows your hearts. Because that which is exalted among men is an ᵝabomination in the sight of the Almĭghty. ¹⁶The Law and the prophets until Yoḣanan ᶿhave prophesied *it*. From that time the good news of the kingdom of the Almĭghty is getting proclaimed, and all carry out an ᵞattack against it. ¹⁷It is yet easier work for heaven and earth

---

forms are satire and fables. **16:14** α *silver.* **16:15** β See Ezek. 34:1-31; Deut. 17:1; Deut. 25:13-16; Prov. 11:1, 20; Prov. 16:5; 17:15; Mal. 1:6-14; Jer. 8:8; Cf. Mat. 23; Isa. 29:11-14; Mat. 3:7-10, 23; Luke 3:7-9. **16:16** θ→it: επροφητευσαν Codex D (Θ) pc vg^ms sy^c; cf. Mat. 11:13. Or *have preached about it, have predicted it.* Often in Greek a pronoun telling us the verb refers to what immediately precedes is left off, as also in Mark 14:22 (NKJV, DLNT, NASB) or Mat. 24:23, 26. ▷ The awful behavior of the Perushim was thoroughly warned against and predicted. They were the sheep traders who became shepherds for profit (cf. Isa. 29:11-14; Ezek. 34:1-31; Jer. 8:8; Mal. 1:6-14; Zech. 11:4-17; Mat. 3:7-10, 23; Luke 3:7-9). They opposed Yăhwe̱ḣ's Anointed (Psa. 2:1-12; cf. 2Sam. 19:21). All these prophesies reached a peak of fulfillment as soon as Yoḣanan finished testifying who the Mĕssiah was, as Satan mobilized his assets to opposition. **16:16** γ See vs. 14-15 for the immediate attack. πᾶς εἰς αὐτὴν βιάζεται (V-PIM-3S) = *everyone against it is forcing himself.* Or 'contending himself,' 'arguing himself vehemently' (LSJ). 'Everyone' here means all the enemies of the kingdom in the same class as the Perushim, wherever they may be found, and have an opportunity to attack the kingdom, either from without or within, because wherever the kingdom was announced, though many gladly heard the message, opposition also was stirred up everywhere. For the prediction of this situation see Mic. 7:6 (cf. Mat. 10:35-36). See J.P. Lange. ▷ Yoḣanan was the last of the prophets before Mĕssiah to prophesy against them, which Yeshua pointedly reminds them by including him at the end of his saying, because they rejected Yoḣanan. ▷ The usual supposition holds βιάζεται to mean people seeking the kingdom pressing their way 'into it' en-mass. This interpretation owes its pedigree to the deletion of the word 'prophesied' by anti-Law heretics, and leaves the sense entirely disconnected from the context (so the commentaries admit). **16:17** π He means not that no copy error can be made, but that the whole is legally valid as long as heaven and earth remain. For example Psa. 145:13b is missing from the Hebrew, and missing from most English translations, but only present in the LXX and some English translations like the ESV. The missing acrostic verse for nun נֶאֱמָן, ב, is proof that scribal blunders can happen.

to pass away than for one stroke of a letter of the Law to fail.ᵖ ¹⁸Everyone who is sending his wife away and is marrying another is committing adultery. And he who is marrying she who has been getting sent awayᵀ is committing adultery.ʕ"

¹⁹"Now there was a certain rich man, and he was getting arrayed in purple and fine linen, making himself merry in splendor throughout the day. ²⁰And a certain poor man named Elazar had been getting tossed down at his gate, one who has been getting afflicted with sores, ²¹and longing to be fed with the crumbs which were falling from the rich man's table, but even the dogs were coming and licking his sores. ²²Now it came about that the poor man died and he was carried away by the angelic messengers to Avraham's bosom. And the rich man also died and was buried.

²³"And in the grave he lifted up his eyes, being in torment, and saw Avraham far away, and Elazar in his bosom. ²⁴And when he cried out, he said, 'Father Avraham, have mercy on me, and send Elazar, that he may dip the tip of his finger in water and shall have cooled off my tongue, because I am in agony in this flame.'ᵠ ²⁵But Avraham said, 'Child, remember that during your life you received your good things, and likewise Elazar bad things, but now he is being comforted here, and you are in agony. ²⁶'And besides in all these things, between us and you a great chasm has been getting fixed, in order that those who are wishing to come over from here to you will not be able, and that none may be crossing over from there to us.'

²⁷"And he said, 'Then I beg you, Father, that you will have sent him to my father's house—²⁸because I have five brothers—that he may be warning them, lest they also will have come to this place of torment.' ²⁹But Avraham said, 'They hold to Mosheh and the prophets. They must listen to them.' ³⁰But he said, 'No, Father Avraham, but if someone may have gone to them from the dead, they will be sorry and turn their hearts *from sin*!' ³¹But he said to him, 'If they are not listening to Mosheh and the prophets, neither will they be persuaded if someone may have risen from the dead.'"

16:18 ζ See Mat. 5:32; 19:9; Mark 10:11-12. It was a common practice for a husband to send away a wife without granting a proper 'certificate of divorce,' either to gain a financial advantage, or out of pure spite. Such a man who remarried became 'polygamous.' The religious authorities, because it was advantageous to them, did not class this kind of polygamy as adultery. But Yĕshua clarified that it was adultery. The Law permitted voluntary polygamy to exist (without approving it), but not the sort the Perushim were allowing to justify *de facto* adultery. ▷ Omitting a bill of divorcement was an act of bad faith regarding a former spouse if the husband remarried. That kind of 'polygamy' is really adultery. And if the wife remarried she could be charged with adultery also without the bill. Luke's use of present participles 'sending away...and is marrying' suggests the same thing as Mat. 19:9 and Mark 10:11-12, i.e. that the intent was to send away in order to remarry. Luke's use of the Greek perfect after the present participle, 'he who is marrying she who has been getting sent away' also suggests a precipitous change of partners indicating the reason was to seek another woman all along. So even if a bill of divorcement was written, it is adultery based on the intent.

16:24 ψ See note on 16:1. In this story Yĕshua is taking poetic license to use the more Greek notion of "Hades" in Rabbinical legend rather than the usual biblical sense of "grave" for this word. We are not told how long the torment lasts, but we may suppose that the worst condemned are being marched in a line down a road winding through the fires that singe and burn them on their way to the hottest part of the fires into which the angels cast them to be consumed.

17 ¹And he said to his disciples, "It is inevitable that tripping hazards should come, but woe to him through whom they come! ²It is more profitable for him if a millstone is getting hanged around his neck, and he has been getting thrown into the sea than that he may have tripped one of these little ones.

³Be keeping your guard! If your brother may have sinned, rebuke him. And if he may have become sorry and turned his heart *from sin*, forgive him. ⁴And if he may have sinned against you seven times a day, and may have returned to you seven times, saying, 'I am sorry,' you will forgive him."

⁵And the emissaries said to the Măster, "Increase our ᵖfaithfulness!" ⁶And the Măster said, "If you have faithfulnessᵖ like a mustard seed, you would say to this mulberry tree, 'Be uprooted and be planted in the sea', and it would obey you. ⁷But which of you, having a slave plowing or tending sheep, will say to him when he has come in from the field, 'Come immediately and sit down to eat'? ⁸But will he not say to him, 'Prepare something I may eat, and having put on an apron, be serving me until I may have eaten and may have drunk. And after these things, you will eat and drink'? ⁹He does not thank the slave because he did the things which were commanded, does he? ¹⁰So you too, when you may have done all the things which you have been commanded, be saying, 'We are unworthy slaves. We have been doing only that which we were being obligated to do.'"

¹¹And it came about while he was on the way to Yerushalayim, that he was passing between Shomron and Galil. ¹²And as he entered a certain village, ten leprous men who stood at a distance met him, ¹³and they raised their voices, saying, "Yĕshua, Măster, have mercy on us!" ¹⁴And when he saw them, he said to them, "Go and show yourselves to the priests." And it came about that as they were going, they were cleansed. ¹⁵Now one of them, when he saw that he was healed, turned back, glorifying the Almĭghty with a loud voice, ¹⁶and he fell on his face beside his feet, giving thanks to him. And he was Shomroni. ¹⁷And Yĕshua answered and said, "Were there not ten cleansed? But the nine—where are they? ¹⁸Was no one found who turned back to give glory to the Almĭghty, except this foreigner?" ¹⁹And he said to him, "Having arisen, be going. Your faithfulness has been saving you."

²⁰Now having been questioned by the Perushim as to when the kingdom of the Almĭghty was coming, he answered them and said, "The kingdom of the Almĭghty is not coming with signs to be observed, ²¹nor will they say, 'Look, here it is!' or, 'There it is!' For behold, the kingdom of the Almĭghty is in your midst."

17:5 π = *courage; a holding faithful* (in the face of a challenge): The component being sought after here is "courage," the courage to act on right convictions. A mustard seed is small, but when it grows it steadfastly reaches a very large size. The small one has the courage to do great things. Courage is directed inwardly to summon the chutzpah to banish fear, uncertainty, and doubt coming from the heart, in order to sacrifice oneself for the greater goal. It is certainly an important component of faithfulness. The mind through truth provides the heart the inner support to act with courage and silence fear, knowing that the Almĭghty is backing you up. Courage is the fidelity of the will to banish fears and doubts in the heart keeping one from the righteous goal. The opposite concept is cowardliness. The coward, due to fear, does not summon the inner support to do what is right. **17:5 π** = also, 'a pledge,' or 'commitment' from

²²And he said to the disciples, "The days will come when you will long to see one of the days of the Sŏn of Man, and you will not see it. ²³And they will say to you, 'Look there! Look here!' You shall not have left, and you shall not have pursued them. ²⁴For just as the lightning, when it flashes out of one part of the sky, shines to the other part of the sky, so will the Sŏn of Man be in his day. ²⁵But first he must suffer many things and be rejected by this kindred."

²⁶"And just as it happened in the days of Noah, so it will be also in the days of the Sŏn of Man: ²⁷they were eating, they were drinking, they were marrying, they were being given in marriage, until the day that Noah entered the ark, and the flood came and destroyed them all. ²⁸It was the same as happened in the days of Lot: they were eating, they were drinking, they were buying, they were selling, they were planting, they were building, ²⁹but on the day that Lot went out from Sedom it rained fire and brimstone from heaven and destroyed them all. ³⁰It will be just the same on the day that the Sŏn of Man is revealed. ³¹On that day, let not the one who is on the housetop and whose goods are in the house go down to take them away. And likewise let not the one who is in the field turn back. ³²Be remembering Lot's wife. ³³Whoever may have ᵋsought to keep his life for himself will lose it, and whoever may have ᵂlost his soul will keep it alive. ³⁴I tell you, on that night there will be two men in one bed. One will be taken, and the other will survive. ³⁵There will be two women grinding at the same place. One will be taken, and the other will be left. ³⁶Two men will be in the field. One will be taken and the other will be left." ³⁷And answering they said to him, "Where, Adŏnai?" And he said to them, "Where the body is, there also will the vultures be gathered."

18

¹And, he was telling them a parable to show that at all times they ought to pray and not to lose heart, ²saying, "There was in a certain city a judge who did not fear the Almĭghty, and did not respect man. ³And there was a widow in that city, and she kept coming to him, saying, 'Give me legal protection from my opponent.' ⁴And for a while he was unwilling, but afterward he said to himself, 'Even though I do not fear the Almĭghty nor respect man, ⁵yet because this widow bothers me, I will give her legal protection, lest by continually coming she may be wearing me out.'" ⁶And Adŏnai said, "Hear what the unrighteous judge said. ⁷And, shall the Almĭghty no not have executed justice for his chosen, who are crying to him day and night, or he be delaying *long* over them? ⁸I tell

---

Gŏd, as explained in Mark 11:22. **17:33** ξ or *required, demanded* **17:33** λ or *sacrificed.* See Rom. 12:1.

18:8b λ LSJ ἄρα "1. then, straightaway, at once." The inferential particle stands in the second position in the sentence in Codex Bezae, vz: πλην αρα ο υιος του ανθρωπου ελθων ευρησει πιστιν επι της γης. The reading is omitted from the NA-26, and NA-27 apparatuses. Codex Bezae likewise omits the definite article here before faithfulness. This could also be translated *loyalty, steadfastness, holding faithful.* Be-

cause he does not delay justice too long, his people will remain loyal to him. See Hab. 2:3, "HE WILL NOT BE TOO LATE." He said that the gates of Hell would not prevail over the Assembly (Mat. 16:18), so there is no doubt that faithfulness will be found on the earth, and therefore, Yĕshua would not have doubted it. The point of his remark is that he will not delay justice so long that no faithful will be discovered on the earth. The reading is according to Codex Bezae, and there are several other Latin texts that give similar readings according to Tischendorf's Critical Apparatus.

you that he will execute justice for them speedily. ⁸ᵇMoreover ^λstraightaway, the Sŏn of Man having come, will find faithfulness on earth!"

⁹And he also told this parable concerning certain ones, those who had been trusting upon themselves that they are righteous, and despising others: ¹⁰"Two men went up into the temple to pray, one a Perushi, and the other a tax-gatherer. ¹¹The Perushi stood and was praying thus to himself, 'Almĭghty, I thank you that I am not like other people: swindlers, unjust, adulterers, or even like this tax-gatherer. ¹²'I fast twice ˣmore than the Ṣabbaṭh. I pay tithes of all that I get.'

¹³But the tax-gatherer, who had been standing some distance away, was even unwilling to lift up his eyes to heaven, but was beating his breast, saying, 'Almĭghty, be merciful to me, the sinner!' ¹⁴I am saying to you, went down this one to his house, who had been ᶲcorrectly judging himself, *compared alongside the other, because everyone who exalts himself will be humbled, but he who humbles himself will be exalted.*"

¹⁵And they were bringing even their infants to him so that he may be touching them, yet when the disciples saw it, they were rebuking them. ¹⁶But Yĕshua called for them, saying, "Permit the children to come to me, and do not be hindering them, for the kingdom of the Almĭghty belongs to such as these. ¹⁷Amen I say to you, whoever may not have received the kingdom of the Almĭghty like a child shall not have entered it at all."

¹⁸And a certain ruler questioned him, saying, "Good Teacher, what shall I do that I may inherit everlasting life?" ¹⁹And Yĕshua said to him, "Why do you call

---

18:12 χ lit. 'I fast twice of the Ṣabbaṭh.' This may be a genitive of comparison. He fasts twice more than or longer than the Ṣabbaṭh. The motivation for the saying is the Pharisees who one upped themselves over those who fasted on the Sabbath (as in Essenes) by saying they fasted twice more than they. Δις means 'double' (John Allen Giles, *A Lexicon of the Greek Language: For the Use of Colleges and Schools*). Thus: "I fast double of the Ṣabbaṭh." Or it may be a genitive of association, viz. "I fast twice with/in relation to the Ṣabbaṭh." Some Perushim fasted Monday's and Thursdays, two days before and two days after the Ṣabbaṭh, putting one eating day between the Ṣabbaṭh and the fast day, on each side of the Ṣabbaṭh. Even the classical ablative might be possible here, "I fast twice off of/from the Ṣabbaṭh." The Greek text might represent the Hebrew idiom לַשַּׁבָּת or בשבת, 'unto Ṣabbaṭh,' but this case is not clearly one of counting to the Ṣabbaṭh, so it remains uncertain. See also "Counting to Ṣabbaṭh" on page 451. There is no clear proof here that Ṣabbaṭh means week, as may be seen from those who render, "I fast twice on the Ṣabbaṭh" (cf. Latin Vulgate, Jubilee 2000 Bible), which sense is also possible, skipping two meals, and taking the third just before Ṣabbaṭh. Aside from the seven places that μ. σαββάτων is mistranslated (Mat. 28:1; Mark 16:2; Luke 24:1; John 20:1, 19; Acts 20:7; and 1 Cor. 16:2), proof for the meaning 'week' is confined to late Psalm titles, late versions of the LXX in Lev. 23:15-16 and 25:8. Lev. 25:8 does not support the meaning *week*, but "And you will have counted for yourself seven Ṣabbaṭhs from the years, [and] seven years, seven times. And they will have been for you the days for seven Ṣabbaṭhs from the years, nine and forty years." From: A genitive of source, *taken from*. For: a genitive of measure, *measured by*. (See Denio, F. B. "The Relations Expressed by the Genitive in Hebrew." *Journal of Biblical Literature*, vol. 19, no. 2, 1900, pp. 107-113.)

18:14 ᶲ מְצַטְדֵּק = *administering justice for oneself, getting oneself administered justice*. Compare 2 Sam. 15:4: וְהִצְדַּקְתִּיו = *and I will have been administering justice for him*. Abşalom meant that he would act as their lawyer or advocate and try to get favorable justice for their cases. ᶲ δεδικαιωμένος = שֶׁהָיָה מִצְטַדֵּק = *who has been (correctly, favorably) getting himself justice*. Middle Passive. ▷ To be 'justiced' in Greek usually has a bad sense, 'to punish,' but here we are dealing with the translation of a Hebrew original. So the sense here is favorable or competent advocacy. **18:14** ᶲ→himself: or *getting made righteous*. Or *getting help with justice*. All these senses are correct, and are a unified semantic domain to the original speakers, but in English we have to highlight the sense most agreeable to the context.

Luke 18

me good? No one is *perfectly* good except one, the Almĭghty. ²⁰You have been knowing the commandments, 'YOU S'HALL NOT COMMIT ADULTERY, YOU S'HALL NOT MURDER, YOU S'HALL NOT STEAL, YOU S'HALL NOT BEAR FALSE WITNESS, BE HONORING YOUR FATHER AND MOTHER.ᵟ'" ²¹And he said, "All these things I have kept from my youth." ²²And when Yĕshua heard this, he said to him, "One thing you still lack. Sell all that you possess, and distribute it to the poor, and you will have treasure in the heavens, then come hither. Be following me." ²³But when he had heard these things, he became very sad, because he was extremely rich.

²⁴And Yĕshua looked at him and said, "How hard it is for those who are wealthy to enter the kingdom of the Almĭghty! ²⁵For it is easier work for a camel to go through the eye of a needle, than for a rich man to enter the kingdom of the Almĭghty." ²⁶And they who heard it said, "Then who can be rescued?" ²⁷But he said, "The things impossible at the side of men are possible at the side of the Almĭghty."

²⁸And Peter said, "Behold, we have left our own homes, and followed you." ²⁹And he said to them, "Amen I say to you, there is no one who has left house or wife or brothers or parents or children, for the sake of the kingdom of the Almĭghty, ³⁰who shall not have received back many times as much in this time and in the coming age, everlasting life."

³¹And he took the twelve aside and said to them, "Behold, we are going up to Yerushalayim. And all things which have been getting written by the prophets will be accomplished by the Sŏn of Man. ³²For he will be delivered to the nations, and he will be mocked and he will be spit upon, ³³and scourging, they will kill him. And the third day he will rise." ³⁴And they understood none of these things, and this declaration had been getting hidden from them, and they were not comprehending the things being said.

³⁵And it came about that as he was approaching Yeriho, a certain blind man was sitting beside the road, begging. ³⁶Now hearing a crowd going by, he was inquiring what this may be. ³⁷And they told him that Yĕshua of Netsereṯh was passing by. ³⁸And he called out, saying, "Yĕshua, Sŏn of David, have mercy on me!" ³⁹And those who led the way were rebuking him, so that he will have kept quiet, but he was crying out all the more, "Sŏn of David, have mercy on me!" ⁴⁰And Yĕshua stopped and commanded that he be brought to him. And when he had come near, he questioned him, ⁴¹"What do you want, *that* I will have done for you?" And he said, "Adŏnai, that I will have seen again!" ⁴²And Yĕshua said

---

18:20 ᵟ Exo 20:12-16, Deu 5:16-20. The point was that this rich man, though interested in following Mĕssiah and in being perfect, somehow felt less than perfect, and incomplete. It was pointed out that only Almĭghty is perfect, (naturally excepting the Almĭghty Sŏn and other unfallen beings in heaven who were not men). What the man lacked was ultimate loyalty to the Almĭghty, which with the revelation of the kingdom meant the affirmation of faithfulness to the Sŏn. The problem is that in practice, the man was more loyal to his wealth than to the King whose subject he was, and whom he must use it for. The King in his estimation was just like an official that must be satisfied by keeping the rules and then he can get on with his own life short of total love and loyalty for the King. One cannot be more loyal to something other than Mĕssiah and expect to have assurance of his love at the same time. See Deut. 6:4-5 and 1 John 2:3-4.

to him, "Receive your sight. Your faithfulness has been saving you." ⁴³And immediately he regained his sight, and was following him, glorifying the Almĭghty. And when all the people saw it, they gave praise to the Almĭghty.

19

¹And he entered and was passing through Yeriho․ ²And behold, there was a man called by the name of Zakkai. And he was a chief tax-gatherer, and he was rich. ³And he was trying to see who Yĕshua was, and he was unable because of the crowd, for he was small in stature. ⁴And he ran on ahead and climbed up into a sycamore tree in order that he may see him, for he was about to pass through that way. ⁵And when Yĕshua came to the place, he looked up and said to him, "Zakkai, hurry and come down, because today I must stay at your house."

⁶And he hurried and came down, and received him gladly. ⁷And when they saw it, they all were grumbling, saying, "He has gone to be the guest beside a man who is a sinner." ⁸And Zakkai stopped and said to the Măster, "Behold, Adŏnai, half of my possessions I will give to the poor, and if I have defrauded anyone of anything, I will give back four times as much." ⁹And Yĕshua said to him, "Today deliverance has come to this house, because he, too, is a Sŏn of Avraham. ¹⁰For the Sŏn of Man has come to seek and to rescue that which has been perishing."

¹¹And while they were listening to these things, he went on to tell a parable, because he was near Yerushalayim, and they supposed that the kingdom of the Almĭghty was going to appear immediately. ¹²He said therefore, "A certain nobleman went to a distant country to receive a kingdom for himself, and then return. ¹³And he called ten of his slaves, and gave them ten ᵘminas, and said to them, 'Do business with this until I come back.' ¹⁴But his citizens hated him, and sent a delegation after him, saying, 'We do not want this man to reign over us.'

¹⁵"And it came about that when he returned, after receiving the kingdom, he ordered that these slaves, to whom he had been giving the silver coin, be called to him in order that he might find out what business they had done. ¹⁶And the first appeared, saying, 'Master, your mina has made ten minas more.' ¹⁷And he said to him, 'Well done, good slave, because you have been faithful in a very little thing, be having authority over ten cities.' ¹⁸And the second came, saying, 'Your mina, master, has made five minas.' ¹⁹And he said to him also, 'And you over five cities *will be getting authority*.'

²⁰"And another came, saying, 'Master, behold your mina, which I kept put away in a handkerchief, ²¹because I was afraid of you, because you are an exacting man. You take up what you did not lay down, and reap what you did not sow.' ²²He says to him, 'By your own words I will judge you, you evil slave. You had been knowing that I am a harsh man, taking up what I did not lay down, and reaping what I did not sow?! ²³Then why did you not put the silver coin in

---

19:1 τ Late Adar or the first week of Aviv, AD 34. **19:13** μ 1 μνᾶς = 100 denari, 100 days wages.

the bank, and having come, I would have collected it with interest?' ²⁴And he said to those who had been standing alongside, 'Take the mina away from him, and give it to the one who has the ten minas.' ²⁵And they said to him, 'Master, he has ten minas already.' ²⁶I tell you, that to everyone who holds fast will more be given, but from the one who does not hold fast, even what he does have will be taken away. ²⁷But these enemies of mine, who did not want me to reign over them, bring them here and slay them in my presence."

²⁸And after he said these things, he was going on ahead, ascending to Yerushalayim. ²⁹And it came about that when he approached Beth-Paggei and Beth-Hini, near the mount that is called Olivet, he sent two of the disciples, ³⁰saying, "Be going into the village opposite you, in which entering you will find a colt, which has been getting held bound, on which no one yet has ever sat. Untie it, and bring it here. ³¹And if anyone may be asking you, 'Why are you untying it?' thus shall you speak, that 'Yăhweh has need of it.'" ³²And having departed, those who had been getting sent, found it just as he had told them. ³³And as they were untying the colt, its owners said to them, "Why are you untying the colt?" ³⁴And they said, "Yăhweh has need of it."

³⁵And they brought it to Yĕshua, and they threw their garments on the colt, and put Yĕshua on it. ³⁶And as he was going, they were spreading their garments in the road. ³⁷And as he was now approaching, near the descent of the Mount of Olives, the whole multitude of the disciples began to praise the Almĭghty joyfully with a loud voice for all the miracles which they had seen, ³⁸saying, *it is* "HE WHO HAS BEEN GETTING BLESSED, **THE COMING ONE**, THE KING IN THE NAME OF YĂH-WEH^ψ, Shalom in heaven and glory in the heights!" ³⁹And some of the Perushim in the crowd said to him, "Teacher, rebuke your disciples." ⁴⁰And he answered and said, "I tell you, if these become silent, the stones will have been crying out!" ⁴¹And when he approached, he saw the city and wept over it, ⁴²saying, "If *only* you would have known, even you, in this day, the things which make for peace! But now they have been hidden from your eyes. ⁴³For the days will come upon you when your enemies will throw up a bank before you, and surround you, and hem you in on every side, ⁴⁴and will level you to the ground and your children within you, and they will not leave in you one stone upon another, because you did not recognize the time of your visitation."

⁴⁵And he entered the temple and began to cast out those who were selling,^τ ⁴⁶saying to them, "It has been getting written, 'AND MY HOUSE SHALL BE A HOUSE OF PRAYER,^α' but you have made it a ROBBERS' DEN.^β" ⁴⁷And he was teaching daily in the temple, but the chief priests and the scribes and the leading men among the people were trying to destroy him, ⁴⁸and they could not find anything that they might do, for all the people were hanging upon his words.

19:31 τ Şabbath, Aviv 10, March 20, AD 34. **19:38** ψ Psa 118:26. **19:45** τ Sunday, Aviv 11, March 21, AD 34. He had gone into the temple at the end of Şabbath, but he retired that day. **19:46** α Isa 56:7 **19:46** β Jer 7:11.

20 ¹And it came about on one of the days,ᵗ while he was teaching the people in the temple and proclaiming the good news, that the chief priests and the scribes with the elders confronted him, ²and they spoke, saying to him, "Tell us by what authority you are doing these things, or who is the one who gave you this authority?"

³And he answered and said to them, "I will also ask you a question, and you tell me: ⁴Was the immersion of Yoḥanan from heaven or from men?" ⁵And they reasoned among themselves, saying, "If we may have said, 'from heaven,' he will say, 'Why did you not hold him faithful?' ⁶But if we may have said, 'From men,' all the people will stone us to death, for they have been getting persuaded that Yoḥanan was a prophet." ⁷And they answered themselves not to have been knowing where *it came from.* ⁸And Yĕshua said to them, "Neither will I tell you by what authority I do these things."

⁹And he began to tell the people this parable: "A man planted a vineyard and rented it out to vine-growers, and went on a journey for a long time. ¹⁰And at the harvest time he sent a slave to the vine-growers, in order that they will give him some of the produce of the vineyard, but the vine-growers beat him and sent him away empty-handed. ¹¹And he proceeded to send another slave. And they beat him also and treated him shamefully, and sent him away empty-handed. ¹²And he proceeded to send a third. And this one also they wounded and cast out.

¹³"And the owner of the vineyard said, 'What shall I have done? I will send my beloved son. Perhaps they will respect him.' ¹⁴But when the vine-growers saw him, they reasoned with one another, saying, 'This is the heir! We will have killed him that the inheritance may become ours.' ¹⁵And they threw him out of the vineyard and killed him. What, therefore, will the owner of the vineyard do to them? ¹⁶He will come and destroy these vine-growers and will give the vineyard to others." And when they heard it, they said, "May it never be!" ¹⁷But he looked at them and said, "What then is that which has been getting written: 'THE STONE WHICH THE BUILDERS REJECTED, THIS BECAME THE CHIEF CORNER STONE'ᵖ? ¹⁸Everyone having fallen on that stone will batter himself, but on whomever it may have fallen, it will pulverize him like dust."

¹⁹And the scribes and the chief priests tried to lay hands on him that very hour, and they feared the people, because they understood that he spoke this parable against them.

²⁰And as they watched, they sent spies feigning themselves to be sincere, in order that they might catch him in some matter, so as to deliver him up to the rule and the authority of the governor.

²¹And they questioned him, saying, "Teacher, we have been knowing that you are speaking and teaching straightly, and you are not favoring appearances, but are teaching the way of the Almĭghty in truth. ²²"Is it lawful for us to have

---

20:1 τ On Monday, March 22. Nisan 12. **20:18** ρ Psa 118:22: אֶבֶן מָאֲסוּ הַבּוֹנִים הָיְתָה לְרֹאשׁ פִּנָּה.

paid taxes to Caesar, or not?" ²³Yet, as he discerned their trickery, he said to them, ²⁴"Show me a dinar. Whose likeness and inscription does it have?" And they said, "Caesar's." ²⁵And, he said to them, "Then pay back to Caesar the things that are Caesar's, and to the Almĭghty the things that are the Almĭghty's." ²⁶And they were unable to catch him in a saying in the presence of the people. As they wondered about his answer, they kept silent.

²⁷Now there came to him some of the Tsadduqim (who say that there is no resurrection), ²⁸and they questioned him, saying, "Teacher, Mosheh wrote for us that IF A MAN'S BROTHER MAY HAVE DIED, having a wife, AND HE MAY BE CHILDLESS, HIS BROTHER SHALL HAVE TAKEN THE WIFE AND SHALL HAVE RAISED UP OFFSPRING TO HIS BROTHER.^δ ²⁹Now there were seven brothers. And the first took a wife, and died childless, ³⁰and the second ³¹and the third took her. And in the same way all seven died, leaving no children. ³²Finally the woman died also. ³³In the resurrection therefore, which one's wife will she be? For all seven had her as wife."

³⁴And Yĕshua said to them, "The sons of this age give in marriage and are married, ³⁵but those who are judged worthy to attain to that age and the resurrection from the dead, neither give in marriage, nor are married. ³⁶Yea, neither can they die anymore, for ^γthe same as angelic messengers are—even ^Tsons of Gŏd,^θ being sons of the resurrection.

³⁷"But that the dead are raised, even Mosheh showed, in the passage about the burning bush, where he calls Yăhweh THE ALMĬGHTY OF AVRAHAM, AND THE ALMĬGHTY OF YITSHAQ, AND THE ALMĬGHTY OF YA'AQOV.^θ ³⁸Now he is not the Almĭghty of the dead but of the living, ^ζbecause all live ^ωby Him."

³⁹And some of the scribes answered and said, "Teacher, you have spoken well." ⁴⁰For they did not dare to question him any longer about anything. ⁴¹And he said to them, "How is it that they say the Anŏinted is David's son? ⁴²For David himself says in the scroll of Psalms, "YĂHWEH SAID TO MY ADŎNAI, 'BE SITTING AT MY RIGHT HAND ⁴³WHILE I SHALL HAVE MADE YOUR ENEMIES A FOOTSTOOL FOR YOUR FEET.'" ⁴⁴David therefore calls him 'ADŎNAI,' and how is he his son?"_ψ

⁴⁵And while all the people were listening, he said to the disciples, ⁴⁶"Be on guard against the scribes, who are wanting to be walking around in long robes, and loving respectful greetings in the market places, and the chief seats in the

---

20:28 δ Deu 25:5, Gen 38:8. **20:36** γ→messengers: ἰσάγγελοι ἴσος + ἄγγελος. Isos: Equal, identical, equivalent. **20:36** ᵀomit 'sons' Codex D pc it vg^ms sy^s, but Codex D altered to the dative: τω θεω. See Psa. 82:6: אֲנִי־אָמַרְתִּי אֱלֹהִים אַתֶּם וּבְנֵי עֶלְיוֹן כֻּלְּכֶם (θεοί ἐστε καὶ υἱοί). **20:36** θ sons of 'Gŏd' have divine like powers relative to men, but have not the omnipotence of the Creator. See Isa. 44:6: וּמִבַּלְעָדַי אֵין אֱלֹהִים. The word 'Elohim' may mean 'Almĭghty,' 'almighty' 'very powerful' (cf. Exo. 7:1), but it seems scribes put in vowels to keep אל from being used of anyone other than Gŏd, viz. אֵיל אֵילִים. See Isa. 43:10: לְפָנַי לֹא־נוֹצַר אֵל וְאַחֲרַי לֹא יִהְיֶה.

20:37 θ Exo 3:6. **20:38** ζ→Him. See Luke 8:52; Mat. 10:28; Rev. 2:11, 20:6,14, 21:8. It seems the first death only kills the body, and not the soul of the man. **20:37** ω→Him = αὐτῷ. The meaning of the dative is not clear, 'by Him,' 'in Him,' 'to Him.' But what does seem clear is that the spiritual souls of the physically dead are in some sense alive to Gŏd, even if they sleep in death. **20:43** ψ Psa. 110:1: נְאֻם יְהוָה לַאדֹנִי שֵׁב לִימִינִי עַד־אָשִׁית אֹיְבֶיךָ הֲדֹם לְרַגְלֶיךָ.

congregations, and best reclining places at banquets, ⁴⁷who devour widows' houses, and for a public show are offering long prayers. These will receive greater condemnation."

21

¹And he looked up and saw the rich putting their gifts into the treasury. ²And he saw a certain poor widow putting in two small copper coins. ³And he said, "Truly I say to you, this poor widow put in more than all of them, ⁴because they all out of their surplus put into the offering, but she out of her poverty put in all that she had to live on."

⁵And while some were talking about the temple,ᵀ that it has been getting adorned with beautiful stones and votive gifts, he said, ⁶"As for these things which you are looking at, the days will come in which there will not be left one stone upon another which will not be dislodged." ⁷And they questioned him, saying, "Teacher, when therefore will these things be? And what will be the sign when these things may be about to be happening?"π

⁸And he said, "Be seeing to it that you may not have been misled, because many will come in my name, saying, 'I AM,' and, 'The time has been drawing near'; you shall not have gone after them. ⁹And when you may have heard of wars and disturbances, you shall not be terrified, because these things must take place first, but the end does not follow immediately."

¹⁰Then he continued by saying to them, "Nation will rise against nation, and kingdom against kingdom. ¹¹As well as great earthquakes, also down through *various* places famines and epidemics will occur. Besides terrors, also there will be great signs from heaven. ¹²But before all these things, they will lay their hands on you and will persecute you, delivering you to the congregations and prisons, bringing you before kings and governors for my name's sake.

¹³It will lead to an opportunity for your testimony. ¹⁴So make up your minds not to prepare beforehand to defend yourselves, ¹⁵because I will give you utterance and wisdom which none of your opponents will be able to resist or refute. ¹⁶But you will be delivered up even by parents and brothers and relatives and friends, and they will put some of you to death, ¹⁷and you will be hated by all on account of my name. ¹⁸Yet, no, not a hair of your head shall have perished.

¹⁹By your endurance you will have gained your souls.

²⁰"But when you may have seen Yerushalayim surrounded by armies, then recognize that her desolation has been drawing near." ²¹Then let those who are in Yehudah be fleeing into the mountains, and let those who are in the midst of the city be putting themselves at a distance, and let not those who are in the

---

21:5 τ Monday afternoon, Aviv 12. March 22, AD 34. **21:5** π See Mat. 24:3. Luke is writing not long after the events took place, mainly after political hatreds have subsided. With the knowledge of AD 70 he is able to sort out the foothills applying to AD 70 from the mountains at the end of the age. Therefore he has simplified the question so that it is aimed only at the AD 70 part of the prediction. **21:20** μ Luke leaves out the the ABOMINATION OF DESOLATION because he has only AD 70 in mind here. After the desolation the future Temple is restored (cf. Dan. 9:27; 8:14). But in AD 70 the second Temple was razed.

country be going into the city, ²²because these are days of vengeance, to fulfill all things which have been getting written.

²³Woe to those who are with child and to those who nurse babes in those days, because there will be great distress upon the land, and wrath to this people, ²⁴and they will fall by the edge of the sword, and will be led captive into all the nations. And Yerushalayim will be trampled under foot by the nations until the times of the nations may have been fulfilled.^λ

²⁵"And there will be indications in sun and moon and stars, and upon the earth anguish of nations in dismay, like a roaring of the sea and the surf, ²⁶men fainting from fear and the expectation of the things which are coming upon the world, because the powers of the heavens will be shaken. ²⁷And then they will see THE SŎN OF MAN COMING IN A CLOUD^χ with power and great glory. ²⁸But when these things begin to take place, straighten up and lift up your heads, because your ransom release is drawing near."

²⁹And he told them a parable: "Behold the fig tree and all the trees, ³⁰as soon as they may have put forth leaves, you see it and know for yourselves that summer is now near. ³¹Even so you, too, when you may have seen these things happening, be knowing that the kingdom of the Almĭghty is near. ³²Amen I say to you, this kindred, no, may not have passed away, going past when all things shall have happened.^ξ ³³Heaven and earth will pass away, but my words will not pass away.

³⁴"Be keeping guard, that your hearts may not have been weighted down with dissipation and drunkenness and the worries of life, and that that day may have sprung on you suddenly like a trap, ³⁵because it will come upon all those who dwell on the face of all the earth. ³⁶But be keeping watch in every appointed time, praying, so that you will have been judged worthy to flee all these things that are going to be happening, and to stand before the Sŏn of Man."

³⁷Now during the day he was teaching in the temple,^τ but at evening he would go out and spend the night on the mount that is called Olivet. ³⁸And all the people would get up early in the morning to come to him in the temple to listen to him.

22

¹Now the Feast of Unleavened Bread, which is called the Passover, was approaching. ²And the chief priests and the scribes were seeking how they might put him to death, but they were afraid of the people.

³And Satan entered into Yehudah who was called Ish-Qeriyot, belonging to the number of the twelve. ⁴And he went away and discussed with the chief priests and officers how he might betray him to them.^τ ⁵And they were glad, and agreed to give him silver. ⁶And he consented, and was seeking a good opportunity to

---

21:24 λ Luke is writing with AD 70 in mind, but this could also refer to AD 135 and the final scattering of the tribe of Yehudah. The times of the nations are during the hiatus of Israel and Judah's final exiles. The long valley of Israel's pre-millennial restoration is omitted, and Luke moves immediately onward to the time of the final testing and the second advent.
21:27 χ Dan 7:13. **21:32** ξ See Endnotes, page 607.
21:37 τ Sabbath, Sunday, Monday, and Tuesday.
22:4 τ Monday night, or very early Tuesday.

betray him to them apart from the multitude.

⁷Then came the ᵗheadmost day of the unleavened ones, on which it was necessary to sacrifice the Passover. ⁸And he sent Peter and Yoḥanan, saying, "Having gone, ready for us the Passover, so that we ᵝmay have eaten." ⁹And they said to him, "Where do you desire we will have gotten ready?" ¹⁰And he said to them, "Behold, when you have entered the city, a man will meet you carrying a pitcher of water. Follow him into the house that he enters. ¹¹And you shall say to the owner of the house, 'The Teacher says to you, "Where is the guest room in which I may eat the Passover with my disciples?" ¹²And he will show you a large upper room, which has been getting furnished. Get ready there.'" ¹³And they departed and found everything just as he had been telling them. And they ᵞreadied the Passover.

¹⁴And when the hour came he reclined *at the table*, and the emissaries with him. ¹⁵And he said to them, "Desiring I have desired this: to eat ᵘthe Passover with you before I suffer. ¹⁶However, I say to you, no, I will not have eaten from it^λ until when it will have been ʿeaten new-madeʾ in the kingdom of the Almĭghty." ¹⁷And when he took a cup and gave thanks, he said, "Take this and share it among yourselves. ¹⁸Truly I say to you, that no, I shall not have drunk from now, from *this cup*, of the fruit of the vine until the kingdom of the Almĭghty may have come." ¹⁹And when he took some bread and gave thanks, he broke it, and gave it to them, saying, "This represents my body."ᵀ

²¹"But behold, the hand of the one betraying me is with me on the table. ²²For indeed, the Sŏn of Man according to what has been getting determined is going, but woe to that man by whom he is betrayed!" ²³And they began to discuss among themselves which one of them it may be who was going to do this thing.

²⁴And there arose also a dispute among them as to which one of them was regarded to be greatest. ²⁵And he said to them, "The kings of the nations lord it over them. And those who have authority over them are called 'Benefactors.'

22:7 τ→Bread: Codex Bezae reads "day of the Passover." The date was nevertheless immediately after sunset at the end of the 13th day of the month, which was March 23, AD 34. See Matthew 26:17 and Mark 14:12. The 14th day may be termed unleavened bread because upon it the leaven is removed, but it is not one of the seven days of unleavened bread. It is the firstest day or headmost day of the feast, the day heading up the feast of unleavened bread. Exodus 12:15: בַּיּוֹם הָרִאשׁוֹן תַּשְׁבִּיתוּ שְּׂאֹר מִבָּתֵּיכֶם. **22:8** β Yĕshua was stating the subjunctive here as an obligation, or even an optative, "that we wish to eat," expressing a hypothetical subjunctive (cf. Wallace, Syntax, page 462). The disciples took it as "may eat." See Mark. The subjunctive covers all these ideas, and is therefore ambiguous. The context tells us that he did not eat it. See vs. 16. **22:13** γ→Passover: or "prepared the Passover" in which case this would mean preparing it for sacrifice, feeding, washing, grooming, keeping. **22:15** μ Ἐπιθυμίᾳ ἐπεθύμησα τοῦτο, Or "desired to eat this Passover," in which case he would be noting the lamb being kept ready, or else using the term Passover in a loose and broad sense of the season. The chronology is made plain in John 13:1. **22:16** λ This shows that the last supper was the night before the Passover Seder. He would not be there at the official time. Other manuscripts were changed to read "no longer eat" as if he were already eating it. These scribes did not understand the idiom for the headmost day of the feast originally in Exodus 12:15, and so they mistakenly assumed that the supper was on the first day of unleavened bread. ▷ ʳ D: ΚΑΙΝΟΝ ΒΡѠΘΗ | or *fulfilled*. **22:19** ᵀ The last part of vs. 19 and all of vs. 20 formed no part of the original mss in my judgment. Codex Bezae (D) omits all the way to vs. 21. The phrase "Do this in remembrance of me,"

Luke 22

²⁶But not so with you, but let him who is the greatest among you be becoming as the youngest, and the leader as the servant. ²⁷For who is greater, the one who reclines at the table, or the one who serves? Is it not the one who reclines at the table? But I am among you as the one who serves.

²⁸"And you are those who have been remaining with me in my trials. ²⁹And just as my Fǎther has granted me a kingdom, I grant you ³⁰that you may be eating and drinking at my table in my kingdom, and you will sit on thrones judging the twelve tribes of Yisra'el.

³¹"Şim'on, Şim'on, behold, Satan has demanded permission to sift you like wheat, ³²but I have prayed for you, that your faithfulness will not have failed. And you, when once you have turned again, strengthen your brothers." ³³And he said to him, "Adǒnai, with you I am ready to go both to prison and to death!" ³⁴And he said, "I say to you, Peter, the rooster will not sound today until you shall have denied three times having been knowing me."

³⁵And he said to them, "When I sent you out without purse and bag and sandals, you did not lack anything, did you?" And they said, "No, nothing." ³⁶And he said to them, "But now, let him who has a purse take it along, likewise also a bag, and let him who has no sword sell his robe and buy one. ³⁷For I tell you, that this which has been getting written must be fulfilled in me, 'AND HE WAS CONSIDERED WITH TRANSGRESSORS,ᵟ' because that which refers to me has its fulfillment." ³⁸And they said, "Adǒnai, look, here are two swords." And he said to them, "It is enough."

³⁹And he came out and proceeded as was his custom to the Mount of Olives. And the disciples also followed him. ⁴⁰And when he arrived at the place, he said to them, "Be praying that you may not enter into temptation." ⁴¹And he withdrew from them about a stone's throw, and he knelt down and was praying, ⁴²saying, "Fǎther, if you are willing, remove this cup from me, yet not my will, but let yours be getting done."

⁴³Now a messenger from heaven appeared to him, strengthening him. ⁴⁴And being in agony he was praying very fervently. And his sweat became as drops of blood, falling down upon the ground.ᵘ ⁴⁵And when he rose from prayer, he came to the disciples and found them sleeping from sorrow, ⁴⁶and said to them, "Why are you sleeping? Rise! Be praying that you will not have entered into testing."

⁴⁷While he was still speaking, behold, a crowd came, and the one called Yehudah, one of the twelve, was preceding them. And he approached Yěshua to kiss him. ⁴⁸But Yěshua said to him, "Yehudah, are you betraying the Sǒn of Man with a kiss?" ⁴⁹And when those who were around him saw what was going to happen, they said, "Adǒnai, shall we strike with the sword?" ⁵⁰And a certain one of them struck the slave of the high priest and cut off his right ear. ⁵¹But Yěshua

---

we do not have to doubt was said, but Luke did not record it. Paul records it in 1 Cor. 11:25. ▷ Vs. 18 || to Mark 14:25. Vs. 19 comes prior to vs. 17. See Appendix. **22:37** ᵟ Isa 53:12: וְאֶת־פֹּשְׁעִים נִמְנָה. **22:43-44** μ Hematidrosis: a rare but real condition. It seems vs. 43-44 were deleted in some mss by docetic factions.

answered and said, "Enough of this!" And he touched his ear and healed him.

⁵²And Yĕshua said to the chief priests and officers of the temple and elders who had come against him, "Have you come out with swords and clubs as against a robber? ⁵³While I was with you through the day in the temple, you did not lay hands on me, but this hour and the power of darkness are yours."

⁵⁴And having arrested him, they led him away, and brought him to the house of the high priest, but Peter was following at a distance. ⁵⁵And when they kindled a fire in the middle of the courtyard, and sat down together, Peter was sitting among them. ⁵⁶And a certain servant-girl, seeing him as he sat in the firelight, and looking intently at him, said, "This man was with him too." ⁵⁷But he denied it, saying, "Woman, I have not been knowing him."

⁵⁸And a little later, another saw him and said, "You are one of them too!" But Peter said, "Man, I am not!" ⁵⁹And after about an hour had passed, another man was insisting, saying, "Certainly this man also was with him, for he is a Gelili too." ⁶⁰But Peter said, "Man, I have not been knowing what you are talking about." And immediately, while he was still speaking, the rooster sounded. ⁶¹And Adŏnai turned and looked at Peter. And Peter remembered the word of Adŏnai, how he had told him, "Before the rooster sounds today, you will deny me three times." ⁶²And he went out and wept bitterly.

⁶³And the men who were holding Yĕshua in custody were mocking him, and beating him, ⁶⁴and they blindfolded him and were asking him, saying, "Prophesy, who is the one who hit you?" ⁶⁵And they were saying many other things against him, blaspheming.

⁶⁶And ᵗwhen it became day, the elders-assembly of the people were gathered together, as well as the chief priests and the scribes. And they led him away to their council *chamber*, saying, ⁶⁷"If you are the Anŏinted, tell us." But he said to them, "If I may have told you, no, you shall not have held *it* faithful, ⁶⁸and if I may have asked a question, no, you shall not have answered. ⁶⁹But from now on ᶲTHE SŎN OF MAN ᵖWILL BE SEATED AT THE RIGHT HAND OF THE ᶳPOWER, THE ALMĬGHTY." ⁷⁰And they all said, "Are you the Almĭghty Sŏn, then?" And he was saying to them, "You are saying *it*, because I AM." ⁷¹And they said, "What further need do we have of testimony? For we have heard it ourselves from his own mouth."

23

¹Then the whole body of them arose and brought him before Pilate. ²And they began to accuse him, saying, "We found this man misleading our nation and forbidding to pay taxes to Caesar, and saying that he himself is the Anŏinted, a King."

³And Pilate asked him, saying, "Are you the King of the Yehudim?" And he answered him and said, "It is as you say." ⁴And Pilate said to the chief priests

---

22:66 τ Wednesday, Nisan 14. March 24th, AD 34. **22:69** φ Dan 7:13; **22:69** π Psa 110:1 נְאֻם יְהוָה לַאדֹנִי שֵׁב לִימִינִי; **22:69** ζ 'The Power' is a substitution for the divine name. 'The Almĭghty' is an appositional genitive inserted by Luke to explain that 'the Power' refers to Gŏd, which Mat. 26:64, and Mark 14:62 leave out.

and the crowds, "I find no guilt in this man."

⁵But they kept on insisting, saying, "He stirs up the people, teaching all over Yehudah, starting from Galil, even as far as this place."

⁶But when Pilate heard it, he asked whether the man was a Gelili. ⁷And when he learned that he belonged to Herod's jurisdiction, he sent him to Herod, who himself also was in Yerushalayim at that time.

⁸Now Herod was very glad when he saw Yĕshua, because he was wanting to see him for a long time, because he was hearing about him and was hoping to see some sign performed by him. ⁹And he questioned him at some length, but he answered him nothing. ¹⁰And, the chief priests and the scribes had been standing there, accusing him vehemently. ¹¹And, when he despised him, even Herod (with his soldiers), also having insulted *him*, having dressed *him* in a gorgeous robe, sent him back to Pilate. ¹²As well, Herod and Pilate became friends with one another that very day. For before they were at enmity with each other.

¹³And Pilate summoned the chief priests and the rulers and the people, ¹⁴and said to them, "You brought this man to me as one who incites the people to rebellion, and behold, having examined him before you, I have found no guilt in this man regarding the charges which you make against him. ¹⁵But not even Herod! Because he sent him back to us, and behold, nothing worthy of death is *or* has been getting committed by him. ¹⁶Therefore, when he is disciplined, I will release him."

¹⁷And, an obligation he was having to be releasing to them one prisoner ˣduring a feast. ¹⁸And they cried out all together, saying, "Be taking this man away, and release for us Bar-Abba!" ¹⁹(He was one who was thrown into prison for a certain bandit raid made in the city, and for murder.)

²⁰And Pilate, wanting to release Yĕshua, addressed them again, ²¹but they kept on calling out, saying, "Be fastening him up on an execution timber! Be fastening him up on an execution timber!ᵖ ²²And he said to them the third time, "Why, what evil has this man done? I have found in him no guilt demanding death. I will therefore punish him and release him."

²³But they were insistent, with loud voices asking that he be fastened up on an execution timber. And their voices were prevailing. ²⁴And Pilate pronounced sentence that their demand should be granted. ²⁵And he released the man they were asking for, who had been getting himself cast into prison for a bandit raid and murder, but he delivered Yĕshua to their will.

²⁶And when they led him away, they laid hold of one Şim'on of Cyrene, coming in from the country, and placed on him the execution timber to carry behind Yĕshua. ²⁷And there were following him a great crowd of the people, and of women who were mourning and lamenting him.

²⁸But Yĕshua turning to them said, "Daughters of Yerushalayim, be not weeping for me, but be weeping for yourselves and for your children. ²⁹For behold, the days are coming when they will say, 'Blessed are the barren, and the wombs that never bore, and the breasts that never nursed.' ³⁰Then they will begin TO

23:17 x down through **23:21** p *Be crucifying! Be crucifying him!*

SAY TO THE MOUNTAINS, 'FALL ON US,' AND TO THE HILLS, 'COVER US.'ᶿ ³¹For if they do these things on the ᶥgreen tree, what shall have happened on the dry?"

³²And two others also, who were criminals, were being led away to be put to death with him.

³³And when they came to the place called the skull, there they fastened him up on an execution timber and the criminals, one on the right *hand* and the other on the left *hand*.

³⁴But Yĕshua was saying, "Făther, forgive them, because they have not been knowing what they are doing." And they cast lots, dividing up his garments among themselves. ³⁵And the people had been standing by, looking on. And even the rulers were sneering at him, saying, "He rescued others. Let him rescue himself if this is the Anŏinted of the Almĭghty, his Chosen One."

³⁶And the soldiers also mocked him, coming up to him, offering him vinegar, ³⁷and saying, "If you are the King of the Yehudim, rescue Yourself!"

³⁸Now there was also an inscription above him, "THIS IS THE KING OF THE YEHUDIM." ³⁹And one of the criminals who were fastened up on an execution timber there was hurling abuse at him, saying, "Are you not the Anŏinted? Rescue yourself and us!"

⁴⁰But the other answered, and rebuking him said, "Do you not even fear the Almĭghty, since you are under the same sentence of condemnation? ⁴¹And we indeed justly, because we are receiving what we deserve for our deeds, but this man has done nothing wrong."

⁴²And he was saying, "Yĕshua, remember me when you may have come into your kingdom!" ⁴³And he said to him, "Amen, to you I am saying today, *that* you will be with me in Paradiseᶯ."

⁴⁴And it was now about the sixth hour, and darkness fell over the whole land until the ninth hour, ⁴⁵the sun being obscured. And the veil of the temple was torn in two. ⁴⁶And Yĕshua, crying out with a loud voice, said, "Făther, INTO YOUR HANDS I ENTRUST MY SPIRITᵠ." And having said this, he breathed his last.

23:30 θ Hos 10:8 , Isa 2:19, 20. **23:31** ξ A green tree represents the righteous. A dry tree the wicked. If a righteous man is so treated then what will be done with the wicked. See Ezek. 20:47; 21:3. Mĕssiah is more specific than the idiom requires here. He says "on (in) a green tree." So not only is the figure meant, but also that they were going to suspend him in a green tree.

23:42-43 η Notice that the repentant bandit requests to be remembered when Mĕssiah comes in his kingdom, and not while he is in the grave. Mĕssiah's word confirms this because he uses the word Paradise, a word of Persian origin meaning garden. The grave was no sort of garden. ▷ In Deut. 30:18, he says, "I HAVE MADE DECLARED TO YOU TODAY THAT PERISHING YOU WILL PERISH...." (הִגַּדְתִּי לָכֶם הַיּוֹם כִּי) (אָבֹד תֹּאבֵדוּן) But they did not perish that day. Rather the sense is "I MAKE PLAIN TO YOU RIGHT NOW...." According to the Hebrew idiom, Mĕssiah said, "I say to you RIGHT NOW," because the bandit's newly asserted fidelity to Mĕssiah and regret for his sins had right then altered his destiny from death to life. See 2 Cor. 5:1-8. Phil. 1:23. ▷ Today: all that is necessary in Yĕshua's speech here to place 'today' with the preceding clause is a pause in his speech (See Deut. 30:18; 32:46. Delitzsch translates: כִּי הַיּוֹם but I would translate הַיּוֹם כִּי just to show that Delitzsch biased his translation). In this sense, the utterance becomes an emphatic promise or is given heightened officious importance, "I say (declare) to you this day...." ▷ It may be possible however to view the term 'today' as representing the entire messianic age in the same sense that the term day in "IN THE DAY THAT YOU EAT IT, YOU SHALL SURELY DIE" represents time till the death of Adam. Objectively the robber sleeps in that day until the resurrection. Subjectively, he is raised right after he dies. ▷ If all else fails with someone who is contrary, then point to the general trend in Scripture that the dead sleep until he returns, and make this passage an exception like the case of Mosheh and Eliyahu. **23:46** ψ Psa 31:5: בְּיָדְךָ אַפְקִיד רוּחִי.

⁴⁷Now when the centurion saw what happened, he was praising the Almĭghty, saying, "Certainly this man was innocent." ⁴⁸And all the crowds who came together for this spectacle, when they observed what happened, were returning, beating their breasts. ⁴⁹And all his acquaintances and the women who accompanied him from Galil, had been standing at a distance, seeing these things.

⁵⁰And behold, a man named Yosef, who was a member of the Council, a good and righteous man ⁵¹(this one had not been consenting to their advice and action), a man from Har-Matayim, a city of the Yehudim, who was waiting for the kingdom of the Almĭghty. ⁵²This man went to Pilate and asked for the body of Yĕshua. ⁵³And he took it down and wrapped it in a linen cloth, and laid him in a tomb cut into the rock, where no one was ever getting laid. ⁵⁴ᵃAnd it was the day of preparation. ⁵⁴ᵇʳThen the Ṣabbath ᵠWAS DAWNING.ˀ

24

⁵⁴ᵇAnd, having followed *him*^λ throughout *his ministry*, ⁵⁵the women (who had been been coming with him out of Galil) ᵟsaw the tomb and how his body was laid, ⁵⁶and having returned, they prepared spices and perfumes. ⁵⁶ᵇAnd on the one ṢABBAṭHᵅ they ᵖrested,ᵀ ²⁴·¹but on the ᶿFIRST OF THE ṢABBAṭHSᵝ,

---

23:54b ψ→dawning: See Mat. 28:1; Hos. 6:3: בְּשַׁחַר נָכוֹן מוֹצָאוֹ. ▷ Mark ends suddenly on a note of stunned amazement (16:8). Here also Luke makes an unexpected literary turn. He jumps from the day of preparation all the way to the time just after the resurrection. He has jumped past the annual Sabbath all the way to the Resurrection Sabbath. And so vs. 54a-54b give a concise endpoints for Messiah's death and resurrection. ▷ This type of sudden summary is to quickly give us a sight of the anticipated moment. (This literary device is also seen in Mat. 21:18-20. It seems that no time has passed after the fig tree was cursed. But Mark 11:12-14, 20-21f makes it clear that a whole day passed before Mĕssiah was questioned about the tree. In like manner, Exodus 19 omits to mention three days of travel in the wilderness before they reach Sinai.) ▷ In 54b, Luke backtracks to tell about the women. Then he brings us up to "deep dawn" again. His literary method is similar to shows where a narrator announces an interesting tidbit to come. Then there is a break (for tea or lunch) and then the narrator repeats the story and brings the narrative up to the interesting moment again. **23:54b** ʳCodex Bezae D 05, d, c read, 'And, it had been the day before a Sabbath' (ην δε η ημερα προσαββατου). This is an easy and tempting solution, but the harder reading is ἐπέφωσκεν, and it appears to me that Codex D's reading was first proposed in the II cent., and then thought better later to interpret ἐπέφωσκεν to mean dusk; ἐπέφωσκεν undoubtedly was the original reading, as there is no accounting for it as an error since it presents its own difficulty! ▷ 'Dawning' ἐπέφωσκεν is necessarily assumed to be evening in the corrupted chronology (Friday-Sunday). Nowhere in Greek does the word mean anything less specific than 'dawn,' as it is a compound word, 'up lighting' or 'lighting up.' Translators cover the *faux pas* with words such as 'drew near,' 'beginning,' and the like. ▷ The chapter clearly ends here because we are introduced to the women in the next where the time line reaches backward to their following Yeshua around in his ministry.

The chapter has been begun in 23:54b, now designated 24:54b, etc. **24:54b** λ Κατα-κολουθήσασαι, Κατα = throughout, about, around, after, down through. As in Acts 16:17. Luke does not mean simply following from the cross to the tomb for which the compound word would be needless, as vs. 55 (αἵτινες ἦσαν συνεληλυθυῖαι αὐτῷ ἐκ τῆς Γαλιλαίας) makes clear, but which he does mean in vs. 24:56 by the word 'returned'. The long introduction before the main verb 'saw' (**24:55** δ) is the logical place to begin ch. 24. The traditional location of vs. 1 is actually in the middle of a sentence (⁵⁶ᵇΚαὶ τὸ μὲν...ᵗτῇ δὲ μιᾷ). **24:56b** α Lev 23:11, 15a; **24:56b** ρ Lev 23:7 **24:56b** ᵀD omits κατὰ τὴν ἐντολήν, 'according to the commandment.' Bezae's last scribe believed Friday-Sunday (cf. 23:54b; Mark 16:2). The omitted phrase does no harm to his view, so it is not likely that he deleted it. It is therefore probable that his exemplar (ca. AD 170) lacked it. But omission is less secure because only Bezae lacks it. Should it be original, it would refer to Lev. 23:7. Should it be added, it would be motivated by the Sunday tradition to clarify the Ṣabbath mentioned as the weekly Ṣabbath. **24:1** θ→of = *first day of* or *first day for*. Literally, "the [number] one [day] of the Sabbaths." **24:1** β Lev 23:15b. **24:1** χ Or "at deep dawn." Genitive of time. Wallace pg. 122. See Mark 16:2. **24:1** ψ→dawn: ὄρθρου βαθέως: A phrase meaning the earliest dawn, which should reconnect us with 23:54a. See Meyer. Cf. John 20:1, "while still dark;" Mat. 28:1, "at the dawning;" Mark 16:2, "very early." See Hosea 6:3. **24:1** γ The spices (ἀρώματα) are "any kind of fragrant substance, fragrant spice/

ˣin ᵠdeep dawn, they came upon the tomb, bringing the ʸspices which they had prepared. ²And they found the stone has been rolling away from the tomb, ³and when they entered, they did not find the body of Adŏnai Yĕshua.

⁴And it happened that while they were perplexed about this, behold, ᶻtwo men suddenly stood near them in dazzling apparel, ⁵and as the women were terrified and bowed their faces to the ground, the men said to them, "Why do you seek the living One among the dead? ⁶He is not so here, but he has risen. Remember how he spoke to you while he was still in Galil, ⁷saying that the Sŏn of Man must be delivered into the hands of sinful men, and be fastened up on an execution timber, and the third day rise again."

⁸And they remembered his words, ⁹and returned from the tomb and reported all these things to the eleven and to all the rest. ¹⁰Now they were Miryam Magdalene and Yohanna and Miryam the mother of Ya'aqov. Also the other women with them were telling these things to the emissaries.

¹¹And these words appeared to them as nonsense, and they were holding them to be unfaithful. ¹²But when Peter arose, he ran to the tomb, and when he stooped sideways, he sees the linen wrappings alone. And he went away, wondering to himself what had been happening.

¹³And behold, two of them were going that very day to a village named Emmaus, which was ᵘseven miles from Yerushalayim. ¹⁴And they were conversing with each other about all these things which had been coming together. ¹⁵And it came about that while they were conversing and discussing, Yĕshua himself approached, and was traveling with them. ¹⁶But their eyes were prevented from recognizing him.

¹⁷And he said to them, "What are these words that you are exchanging

---

salve/oil/perfume" (BDAG, 3rd edition). ▷ The Friday-Sunday chronology has the women arriving at less than 40 hours from the moment of death. What is not explained is why they went so early in the morning since < 40 hours is no where near the deadline for a last anointing. What also is not explained is why the women would go out after dark at the end of Şabbaṭh to buy spices (Mark 16:1) or so early in the morning if there was no rush to get to the tomb. Normally, any decay would not prevent a final anointing until after 72 hours. From his death on Wednesday to his resurrection just before dawn on the Şabbaṭh is a period of about 63 hours which is near enough to the ending time for a final anointing. The women chose that time because it was the last time they could discreetly visit the tomb with no one noticing. In the early dawn while it was still dark on the morning of Şabbaṭh very few people would be up and about. Although their anointing work was permitted by Rabbinic rulings, they wanted it quiet and in the cool of the day. ▷ Mishnah Şabbaṭh 23.5, "One may perform all the requirements for a corpse [on Şabbaṭh]: [One may] anoint and wash him, provided one does not move a limb." Obviously this ruling applies to a body already in a tomb and not just not someone who has died on Şabbaṭh and has to be moved to a tomb. It was expected that anointings could be performed on the Şabbaṭh after the main burial or embalming was already done. Respect for and care of the dead was on the same level of duty as care for a sick person who needed tending, because it was assumed that the soul took several days to depart. Some Jewish traditions specify three to seven days. Mishnah Şabbaṭh 151b, "One should not close the eyes of a dead person, nor on a weekday while the soul is departing." For this reason tending the dead was not considered prohibited work. Even though Scripture says Mĕssiah gave up his spirit, customary beliefs assumed it might linger at the body for several days. Even though the belief is subjective and some Jews doubted it, the practice was to error on the side of caution and safety and care for the dead, even to the point that people would assume that neglect of the dead was a spiritual demerit.

24:4 ζ→men: It is my opinion that these men were Mosheh and Eliyahu, who are the two witnesses. **24:13** τ Şabbaṭh afternoon, March 27th, AD 34. **24:13** μ→miles: It takes about 2 hours and 20 minutes to walk this distance at a walking speed of 20 minutes per mile. 4.5 miles per hour is the maximum walking speed without jogging. At this speed the return trip would take 1.5 hours. Jogging is 5.5 miles per hour. Time to return would be 1.27 hours. If therefore, they returned at 4 p.m. or even 4:30 p.m. they would have time to return on the same day.

with one another as you are walking?" And they stood still, looking sad. ¹⁸And one of them, named Cleopas, answered and said to him, "Are you the only one visiting Yerushalayim and unaware of the things which have happened here in these days?" ¹⁹And he said to them, "What things?" And they said to him, "The things about Yĕshua from Netsereth, who was a prophet mighty in deed and word in the sight of the Almĭghty and all the people, ²⁰besides *also* how the chief priests and our rulers delivered him up to the sentence of death, and fastened him to an execution timber.

²¹And we were hoping that it was he who was about to ransom Yisra'el. But indeed, even with all this, the time is passing a third day this day, from when these things happened.

²²But also some women from us amazed us, who happened to arrive at dawn at the tomb, ²³and not having found his body, they came, saying also to have been seeing a vision of messengers, who are saying him to be living. ²⁴And some of those who were with us went to the tomb and found it just exactly as the women also had said, but him they did not see."

²⁵And he said to them, "Foolish men and slow of heart to hold faithful, based upon all that the prophets have spoken! ²⁶Was it not necessary for the Anŏinted to suffer these things and to enter into his glory?"

²⁷And beginning with Mosheh and with all the prophets, he explained to them the things concerning himself in all the writings.

²⁸And they approached the village where they were going, and he acted as though he would go far away.ᵠ ²⁹And they urged him, saying, "Stay with us, for it is getting toward setting, and the day has already been declining." And he

---

24:21 {db le MT–pYLT} KJV: ***Today is the third day*** is an impossible translation since (1) it deletes the verb, and (2) [is] is interpolated between two substantives in the accusative case which is also impossible. Translations immitating this, equally impossible are ASV, AMP, AMPC, BRG, CSB, CJB, DARBY, DLNT, DRA, EHV, ESV, ESVUK, EXB, GNV, GW, GNT, HCSB, ICB, ISV, PHILLIPS, JUB, AKJV, LEB, MSG, MEV, MOUNCE, NOG, NABRE, NASB, NASB1995, NCB, NCV, NET, NIRV, NIV, NIVUK NKJV, NMB, NRSV, NRSVA, NRSVACE, NRSVCE, NTE, OJB, RGT, RSV, RSVCE, TLV, VOICE, WEB, WYC. Translations impossible for other reasons: CEB, CEV, ERV, TLB, NLV, NLT, WE.

Only YLT renders the verb: ***this third day is passing to-day***, but it is impossible since it makes this third day the subject when it is the object in the accusative case. Simply by translating *time is passing today this third day* exposes the tautalogous corruption of making *this* an adjective instead of a substantive. With respect to the Friday-Sunday heresy, every one of these translations is open to the fatal objection as to why the two men would even make an issue of the time since by all these translations the time would not be past.

With respect to a Wednesday to Saturday afternoon duration in the tomb, and the women going to the tomb on Sunday morning, and the remark in vs.

21 being made on Sunday, it fails utterly to agree with any of the above versions. But it also fails to agree with the legitimate translation above. To make it agree would require a past tense, e.g. ***the time has passed a third day this day***, because at no time on Sunday was the third day passing. But it does agree with the Resurrection at dawn on the Sabbath, because then the remark would be made on the Sabbath. Only then is the time passing a third day on that very Sabbath when they made the remark.

The literal sense is: ***third, this day, it is passing***, which expands to: ***[the] third [day], this day [time] is passing***. In more English order: ***it (time) is passing the third day, this day***. See *Expositor's Greek Testament*: "Other suggestions are that χρόνος or ὁ Ἰησοῦς is to be understood." ▷ τρίτην = [the] *third [one]*, which is the third of the three days. As the first object of the verb ἄγει, τρίτην is standing in the accusative case, so the sense is "*it (the time) is passing a third day.*" The subject of the verb ἄγει is *it* (the time allotted, χρόνος) is passing a third day. ▷ ταύτην ἡμέραν = *this day*, which is the Sabbath (cf. 24:1, 23:54b). As the second object of the verb, ταύτην ἡμέραν is standing in the accusative case, and the sense is "*it (the time) is passing this day.*" Thus with combined objects, "It (*the time allotted*) is passing **a third this day**...." ▷ The third day is reckoned as usual a third

went in to stay with them.

³⁰And it happened when he reclined at the table with them, he took the ᵃbread and blessed it, and breaking it, he was giving it to them. ³¹And their eyes were opened and they recognized him. And he vanished from their sight.

³²And they said to one another, "Were not our hearts burning within us while he was speaking to us on the road, while he was explaining the writings to us?" ³³And having risen up that very hour, they returned to Yerushalayim, and found the eleven, having been gathering together, and those who were with them, ³⁴saying that, "Adŏnai has really risen, and has appeared to Şim'on." ³⁵And they were relating their experiences on the road and how he was recognized by them in the breaking of the bread.

³⁶And while they were telling these things, he himself stood in their midst.ᵗ ³⁷But they were startled and frightened and thought that they were seeing a spirit. ³⁸And he said to them, "Why are *and* have you been getting troubled, and why do doubts arise in your hearts? ³⁹SEE my hands and my feet, BECAUSE MYSELF I AM.ᵠ Touch me and see, for a spirit does not have flesh and bones as you see that I have."

⁴⁰And when he said this, he showed them his hands and his feet. ⁴¹And while they still could not give support to it for joy and were wondering, he said to them, "Have you anything here to eat?" ⁴²And they gave him a piece of a broiled fish. ⁴³And he took it and ate it before them.

⁴⁴Now he said to them, "These are my words which I spoke to you while still being with you, that it is necessary to fulfill all things which have been getting written in the Law of Mosheh and in the Prophets and Psalms about me.

⁴⁵Then he opened their minds to be understanding the writings, ⁴⁶and he said to them, "Thus it has been getting written, that the Anŏinted should suffer and

---

calendar day from dawn on Friday to dawn on the Sabbath, counting inclusively from the first calendar day between dawn Wednesday and dawn Thursday. The second day was dawn Thursday to dawn Friday. So the third day expired at dawn on the Sabbath. ▷ When on that Sabbath did the third day expire. If we say at sunset the beginning of the Sabbath, then they would have had to say, "a third one yesterday passes by." If we say at sunset ending the Sabbath, then why are they concerned? Because the time has not yet run out. But if we say at sunrise on the Sabbath, then the best they can do is say what they said. ▷ ἄγει. The translations ignore the verb (q.v. supra). It is present tense and active (V-PIA-3S). In place of the verb, the translators treat the two accusatives as if they are two nominatives to be equated, viz. "a third day is this day," e.g. Yoḥ. 19:31: μεγάλη ἡ ἡμέρα ἐκείνου = great [is] that day. *Vincent's Word Studies* (Vol. I 1886 & 1888) exposes the error in omitting the verb, which I cite, **"To-day is the third day**...cannot be neatly rendered. Literally it is, "He (*Christ*) is passing (ἄγει) this day as the third." But Vincent's attempt is also tautologous. ▷ See Endnote on page 608. **24:28** ψ This was literally true since he was going to return to the Fäther.

24:30 α The bread was unleavened since it was only the third day of the feast of unleavened bread. This confirms that the common Greek word for bread ἄρτον could mean any kind of bread including unleavened. Likewise the Hebrew word לֶחֶם may also mean any kind of bread, including that which is unleavened. Both words are used in the priestly ordination ceremony for unleavened bread independently of the word unleavened. They mention the bread in Luke 24:35 in the presence of the other disciples, who being Jewish, assume that it is unleavened. Since Yĕshua tied the bread at the last supper to his body symbolically, it is all but certain that it was the bread of affliction, and it was indeed customary with many to eat unleavened bread the whole of Nisan 14 as well as the seven days of the feast. **24:36** τ This was still on Şabbath. See John 20:19.

24:39 ψ {le MT—pYLT} ▷ Read here with Majority text: ἴδετε...ὅτι αὐτὸς ἐγώ εἰμι (A W Θ Ψ f¹·¹³ 𝔐 aur). This is as embedded repetition of Deut. 32:39: רְאוּ ... כִּי אֲנִי אֲנִי הוּא. See now because I, I [am] He, and there is no Almighty besides me. In fact

Luke 24

rise again from the dead the ᵉthird day; ⁴⁷and that being sorry and turning the heart *from sin* toward release from sins should be proclaimed in his name to all the nations, beginning from Yerushalayim. ⁴⁸You are witnesses of these things. ⁴⁹And behold, I am sending forth the promise of my Father upon you, but you are to stay in the city until you shall have been clothed with power from on high."

⁵⁰And he led them out as far as Beth-Hini, and he lifted up his hands and blessed them. ⁵¹And it came about that while he was blessing them, he parted from them. ⁵²And they returned to Yerushalayim with great joy, ⁵³and were continually in the temple, praising the Almighty.

Luke's translation is better than the LXX, viz. ἴδετε ἴδετε ὅτι ἐγώ εἰμι, because Luke captures Yĕshua's first אֲנִי from the Hebrew with αὐτός, which is typically translated 'myself,' e.g. NIV Deut. 32:39. The word αὐτός, 'myself' is not an object of the verb. This is plain by the word order because it stands in the nominative case before ἐγώ. Thus αὐτός ἐγώ represents אֲנִי אֲנִי. Some of the texts alter this to ἐγώ αὐτός, "I myself," (D c e vg^cl) but again this merely emphasizes the subject. This is the very first of seven (אֲנִי הוּא) *Ani Hu* passages in Scripture. They are Deut. 32:39; Isa. 41:4; 43:10, 13; 46:4; 48:12; 52:6. The scribes that changed the word order ($\mathfrak{P}^{75}$ א B L) did not understand the reference and thought Luke's text was bad grammar.

24:46 ξ→day: See also 1 Cor. 15:4. *According to the 'Scriptures'* means many texts, not just a few. According to the types Mĕssiah suffered on the 'THIRD DAY' (Gen 22:4; 40:20) and rose on the 'THIRD DAY' (Gen. 22:4; 40:20). The third day is 'AFTER TWO DAYS' (Hos. 6:1-3; Mat. 26:2; Mark 14:1), and "WITHIN THREE DAYS" (Gen 40:13; 19). This means when counting calendar days from the crucifixion that one must count inclusively. The day of the crucifixion counts as day one. (This is only possible with Matthew 12:40 when the calendar day is from daybreak to daybreak, according to the Scriptural day which begins in the morning.) See also Mat. 20:19; Luke 13:32; 18:33; 24:7; Yoh. 2:19. ▷The thematic types call the crucifixion day the 'THIRD DAY,' as the day when grief is realized, and likewise the 'THIRD DAY' when life is spared, indicating resurrection: Gen. 22:4; 40:20; 42:17-18; Exodus 10:22, 23; 19:16-19; Num. 19:12. Joshua 1:11, 3:2; 2:16, 22; 1 Kings 17:1, 18:1; 2 Kings 20:5; 1Sam 30:1, 12; Jonah 1:17, 2:1-2; Hos. 6:1-2; Esther 4:16; 5:1. Luke 2:46; Acts 9:9. Also types involving the third year: 2 Sam. 21:1; 1 Kings 18:1. Involving three months: Gen. 38:24; Exodus 2:2; 2 Sam. 6:11; 1 Chron. 13:14; Amos 4:7. Three years, three months, three days: 2 Sam. 24:13; 1 Chron. 21:12. Thirty: Gen. 41:46; Exodus 21:32; Num. 29:29; Deut. 34:8; Judges 14:11-19; 20:31, 39. More third day passages: Gen. 31:22; 34:25; Three and Seven: Num. 19:12, 19; 31:19. Third generation: Deut. 23:8. And more: Judges 20:30; 2 Sam. 1:2; 1 Kings 3:18; 1 Kings 12:12; 20:5-8; 2 Chron. 10:12. ▷ It would take another whole book and years of reserach to catalogue and come to an end of all the three types about Mĕssiah encoded into Scripture. Matters branch many ways as each passage tells its own death and life or life and death story. Each passage may by analyzed, dissected, and studied looking for the messianic theme. It is not something man could have put there, but the Spirit of the Almĭghty put it there. ▷ 1Samuel 4:7 and 14:21 tells how to count three days backwards, "FOR IT WAS NOT LIKE THIS YESTERDAY OR THREE DAYS AGO": אֶתְמוֹל שִׁלְשֹׁם *ethmol shilshom*. Also Gen 31:2,5: 'AS YESTERDAY, OR THREE DAYS AGO' כִּתְמוֹל שִׁלְשׁוֹם *citmol shilshom*. And Exodus 4:10, 'ALSO YESTERDAY, ALSO ON THE THIRD DAY' גַּם מִתְּמוֹל גַּם מִשִּׁלְשֹׁם *gam mitmol mishishom*. See also Exodus 5:7, 8. Exodus 5:14. 'AS YESTERDAY, THIRD DAY, ALSO YESTERDAY, ALSO TODAY.' Also Ex. 21:29. ▷ If there is any doubt here, the LXX gives the meaning, ὡς ἐχθὲς καὶ τρίτην ἡμέραν (Gen. 31:2, 5); ἐχθὲς καὶ τρίτην ἡμέραν (Exo 5:7), 'AS YESTERDAY AND THE THIRD DAY.' There are some 25 verses with this idiom. The key point is that in Hebrew the 'day before yesterday' is always identified as the 'third day'; the counting is inclusive. 'Today' is the first day, 'yesterday' is the second, and the 'third day' is the third. The same works for counting forward, 'TODAY AND TOMORROW' (Exo 19:10) and 'LET THEM BE READY FOR THE THIRD DAY.' Uriah's death sentence is issued on the third day (cf. 2Sam. 11:12-14). Yĕshua himself speaks this way, 'today and tomorrow, and the third day' (Luke 13:32) σήμερον καὶ αὔριον καὶ τῇ τρίτῃ. ▷ See "Third Day Note Continued" on page 176.

End Note No. 1: The Year Determined

¹Luke supplies us with the facts necessary to determine the year Yoḥanan came preaching and when Yĕshua turned 30. See Luke 3:1, 23. ²The conclusion is Mĕssiah turned 30 in on Tishri 1, AD 29. ³Calculating backward, one finds his birth on Tishri 1, 2 BC.

⁴Examining the ministry chart, note that a baptism date in the summer of AD 29 leads to Passover of AD 30 for the Passover of Yoḥ. 2:13. ⁵Yoḥanan records the remark made in the story of the woman at the well, Yoḥ. 4:35. This shows that a year elapsed to the Passover of Luke 6:1. ⁶In Yoḥ. 5 we have the coincidence of the feast of Purim on the weekly Ṣabbath which is a way point for AD 32. ⁷Another year takes us by the Passover of Yoḥ. 6:4, then Tabernacles in Yoḥ. 7:1, and finally to the Temple tax scene in Mat. 17:27, around Adar 15, just one year after Yoḥ. 5. ⁸Luke's long travel log (starting in 9:51) takes us past Passover AD 33, and finally the time line comes to the final Passover in Yoḥ. 11:55. ⁹The parable in Luke 13:6-9 confirms the total time of the public ministry of Mĕssiah at four years, Passover AD 30 to Passover AD 34.

¹⁰When we come to calculate the month of Adar for AD 34, we find it at 30 days. ¹¹No matter what the weather may have been like the month of Nisan started the next day. There is therefore no reason to doubt that the first day of unleavened bread fell onto March 25th, a Thursday in AD 34.

¹²According to the plain sense, then, Mĕssiah died on the preparation of the Passover, the day before March 25th, AD 34, which was Nisan 14. ¹³The third day types, i.e. today, tomorrow, and the third day he is perfected (Luke 13:32) lead logically to the resurrection on the first of the Ṣabbaths after Passover. ¹⁴All these conclusions figure according to the norms or plain sense of each contributing Scripture.

End Note No. 2: Lev. 23:15 Explained

¹The Resurrection Ṣabbath is literally translated, "The first of the Ṣabbaths" in all four Evangelists. ²The usage is explained by Lev. 23:15-16. Seven Ṣabbaths were counted off starting with the first one after Passover: "AND YE *WILL* HAVE COUNTED FOR YOURSELVES IN THE TOMORROW OF THE ṢABBATH, FROM THE DAY OF YOUR BRINGING THE SHEAF OF THE WAVE OFFERING: SEVEN REGULAR ṢABBATHS SHALL BE UNTIL IN THE TOMORROW OF THE SEVENTH ṢABBATH YOU *WILL* HAVE COUNTED A FIFTIETH DAY." ³ "In the tomorrow" is an idiom for in the time after.

⁴The Ṣabbath after which the seven Ṣabbaths were counted was the first day of unleavened bread, also called the first Ṣabbath of the feast (Lev. 23:11, 15). ⁵Accordingly two days came to be called the first Ṣabbath, the 15th of Nisan and the weekly Ṣabbath after it. ⁶See Luke 6:1 and Mat. 28:1.

⁷Some Jews still count seven Ṣabbaths after Passover, but while interpreting Lev. 23:11 as the weekly Ṣabbath. ⁸The Rabbis, however, interpret it to mean the annual Passover Ṣabbath. ⁹Plainly the Evangelists agreed with the Rabbis in counting after the annual Ṣabbath (cf. Yoḥ. 19:31; Mark 16:1; Luke 24:1; Mat. 28:1). For all the Evangelists call the first day of unleavened bread "the Ṣabbath." ¹⁰Plainly also the Evangelists agree with those Jews who still today actually count the seven Ṣabbaths.

¹¹All the words in their normal senses agree with seven Ṣabbaths being literally counted. ¹²But there are those Sunday apologists who will argue that the literal translation breaks the grammar rules. This is not true. See Acts 20:6-7 notes for refutation of that claim. Sunday apologists also say that, "first *day* of the Ṣabbaths" is a Hebrew idiom for "first of the week," but this is not true either because the Hebrew idiom requires the word Ṣabbath to be literal as well as singular. See Luke 18:12. Also the LXX consistently renders the Hebrew ב or ל with a full preposition, when counting *months to months*, *days to days*, *years to years* (εἰς, ἐξ, ἐν, καθ', ἐκ, or κατ'). One of these prepositions would be expected.

For example, *μιαν εις το σαββατον, *μια εν τω σαββατω, *μιαν κατ' το σαββατον. Without the preposition εν τη μια ημερα των σαββατων is simply specifying a particular *Ṣabbath day* (ημερα των σαββατων). See Acts 20:7; Luke 18:12; and Counting to the Sabbath, page 451.

Everywhere the Church has put up a false translation or interpretation which seems a formidable barrier to any other view, a way of escape has opened up for us. The escape route agrees with the normal sense of words. It obeys the grammar rules. It leads us to observe Gŏd's law and to find his Law hidden in the Evangelists. The way of escape makes sense out of everything chronological in Scripture. The path lies open, dry ground through the sea.

Almighty Son vs. Son of God

The word *son* is used in Hebrew to denote a kinship relationship. In non literal uses the attributes of whatever something is said to be the *son of* are ascribed to whoever the *son* is. That is "son of X" means the qualities of X are being ascribed to whoever is called "the son of X." This can be transformed into "the son, the X one" or "the X son." Before the transformation X is a noun, and afterward it gets used an adjective, thus "a son of wood-working" means "a wood-working son." And "a son of might" (בֶּן־חַיִל) means "a mighty son." Sometimes the same nouns work as both nouns and adjectives. It is simply where you put them in relation to the words they modify.

So far, I have just showed a normal genitive of apposition. But the word "son" is special. It's meaning is generalized to mean *kindred* in an abstract sense. Thus 'a son of might' means 'a kindred of might' the same as "mighty kindred," of the same kind, genus, or type as the mighty. So the Hebrew word *son* uniquely ascribes. It has a grammatical function of its own. For this reason it is also not under the restrictions that govern ordinary Greek appositional usage.

So anytime the adjective use of X makes sense an appositional, or equative meaning, is possible. One can test this with the words *who is*, or *which is*, viz. 'the son [who is] X,' replacing 'of' with *who is* or *which is*, e.g. '*the son [who is] mighty* (בֶּן־חַיִל).

There is one restriction on this, and also one warning. Firstly the warning: the construct or genitive relation may still be another type of genitive, such as origin or produced by. So it is possible for this construction to be ambiguous. In normal construct relations, if the coverted form does not make the same sense as the converted form, then the converted form (equative usage) is not likely. But the use of the word 'son' tosses this rule out the window because it is used in the sense of 'kin,' as if "son of X" meant "kin of X," or "related to being X." This means that the meaning of "son of X" may mean "son [who is] X" even when "son of X" makes another sense. The solution to which it is must then be sought in the larger context.

Secondly the restriction. If son is plural, i.e. sons, then equative apposition is only possible in the sense where X is a plural of number. English will ignore this rule because adjectives do not have to agree in number in English, but Hebrew and Greek require agreement. So the *who is/which is* test is only valid with number agreement. Thus בְּנֵי־חַיִל *sons of might* = sons [who are] mighty (ones). English will be satisfied with "sons [who are] mighty," but X must be understood to agree in number with 'son' or 'sons' in Hebrew. This means that *sons of elohim* בְּנֵי אֱלֹהִים may not be understood as **sons [who are] Almighty*, because the equivalent adjective construction in Greek and Hebrew would require *elohim* to be a plural of number, and thus it could not be intensive, *Almighty*, but it would have to mean *mighty ones*. Thus *sons of elohim* can only be read appositionally as "sons [who are] mighty," i.e. understood *mighty ones*. Construct, or genitive apposition allows the number not to be specified in X, but it should not be understood to mean differently than if a formal adjective noun construction is used.

So if we understand *sons of elohim* as an equative genitive *sons [who are] elohim*, the word *elohim* is forced by this context into a plural of number: *sons [who are] mighty ones*. So *sons of elohim* cannot assume this sense **sons [who are] Almighty* or **almighty sons*. For this reason, it is apologetically wrong to claim that *ben elohim* does not ascribe divinity because *bene elohim* does not.

When *elohim* is a plural of number or the singular *el* is used of beings other than the Most High, the reference is to being(s) with supra human powers infinitely less than ominpotence, but having immortality. All angels, good and bad, fit into this category. They are all created, and those who became evil will be ended with the judgment of death.

The sons of the Almighty are generated or produced by the Almighty, that is created, but the Son Almighty is the kin of the Almighty, and is not generated. For this reason Yohanan uses the term μονογενής *only kindred* Son or Almighty to explain the sense of Ben Elohim. But the Gnostics corrupted the translations to mean only *generated* or only *begotten*, and while scholars are admitting that μονογενής does not mean this, the Church is unwilling to humble itself and admit its error because of its investment into the Nicene Creed and other Gnostic doctrines.

Glossary of Significant Terms
Selected terms in order of frequency grouped by Greek terms

πιστεύειν^v, πίστις^v, πιστός^a, 544x.

TO HOLD FAITHFUL: This verb is the correction to the mistranslation *believe*, mainly used of holding faithful to Mĕssiah Yĕshua, the Almĭghty Sŏn. The proof of true loyalty is by keeping his commandments. Secondarily it is used of holding faithful an assertion or truth claim, e.g. to hold faithful to the prophets means to *believe* them. ❶ *[definition suppressed]* (BDAG). הֶאֱמִין.

FAITHFULNESS: A noun, which is the quality of holding faithful. See *to hold faithful*. Mistranslated *faith* or *belief*. ❶ *faithfulness* (BDAG). אֱמוּנָה.

FAITHFUL: The adjective form of above is sometimes mistranslated *believer*. ❶ *faithful* (BDAG). נֶאֱמָן.

δικαιόω^v, δικαιοσύνη^n, 131x.

¹TO ADMINISTER JUSTICE: This is the correction to the mistranslation *justify*. The verb refers to the action of a judge judging, to make or determine a decision in a given case, whether for guilt or innocence and whether to punish or forgive. The term does not indicate the outcome of the case, and certainly has nothing to do with justifying the sinner, acquitting the sinner, or declaring the sinner innocent. Archaic English verb *to justice*. ❶ *do justice* (BDAG). לְהַצְדִּיק.

¹ADMINISTRATION OF JUSTICE: The noun is used in a specific sense of *justice*. The activity of a judge administering justice. See *to administer justice*. ❷ *quality of juridical correctness* (BDAG). לִצְדָקָה.

JUSTICE: Misunderstood as *justification*, this noun means the same thing as being administered justice. See above. But it also has a broader sense of denoting justice in general. Equivalent to *righteousness*. ❶ *justice* (BDAG). ❸ *righteousness* (BDAG). צֶדֶק, צְדָקָה.

²TO ADMINISTER JUSTICE: Also refers to Mĕssiah's faithfulness jointly working with our faithfulness the inward change necessary to produce righteousness. Thus equivalent to being made holy or being cleansed from unrighteousness.

²ADMINISTRATION OF JUSTICE: See to administer justice no. 2. The activity of Messiah cleansing us from sin, and making us right again in cooperation with our faithfulness.

τετελεσμένος μέλλοντας, 158x.

WILL HAVE: Future perfective and gnomic usages (translated in the English present tense) of the Greek aorist and perfect. 143x.

WOULD HAVE: Future in past. 15x.

νόμος, 68x/196x. ❶ *custom, rule, norm* (BDAG). נִמּוּס.

WHAT IS CUSTOMARY: This noun is the correction to the mistranslation *law*. It refers to two things in Paul's usage, often not distinguished, and sometimes referring to both in a given usage. (1a) Judaism's doctrine of zechut, whereby good deeds that are not strictly required by Torah may be applied to bad deeds, called demerits, to cancel them out, so that Gŏd will not judge the sinner. (1b) Also the doctrine of zechut teaches that Jews may inherit the merits of the fathers, chiefly Abraham, if personal merit is not enough to cancel out the demerits of the individual Jew. (2) It refers to the curses in Deut. 27-28, which became customary over time as Israel fell into greater and greater transgression. The judgment of the unfaithful is what is customary. The helping words [what is] custom[ary] are explained on page 582. 35x.

CUSTOMARY: See *what is customary* definition 1a-1b. Mainly used with the word *works* in the combination *customary works*. Sometimes supplied by the translator to explain works. ❶ *custom* (BDAG). Converted to an adjective by genitive of quality, viz. *works of custom* means *customary works*. 13x.

NORM: Paul uses the term to refer to a social norm or habit outside the sphere of law. Rom. 5:20; 7:21, 23, 25; 8:1; 1 Cor. 15:56. ❶ *norm* (BDAG). 7x.

CUSTOMARY NORM: see what is customary definition 1 & 2. The article places the emphasis, which in English is conveyed by the redundant synonym. ❶ *custom , norm* (BDAG). 9x.

CUSTOM: used by Paul in an indefinite sense twice. Rom. 3:27; Gal. 3:21. ❶ *custom* (BDAG). 3x.

RULE: approaches the sense of principle in Rom. 3:27. ❶ *rule, principle* (BDAG). 1x.

μετανοίας, μετανοέω, 56x.

BEING SORRY AND TURNING THE HEART: an expanded definition of repentence based on the Hebrew and bringing out the meaning of the Greek term in proper context. *Being sorry* means to be sorry for *sin* and *turning the heart* means to turn the heart from *sin*. This definition is counter to the definition which claims these words only mean *a change of mind to believe essential truth*. On the contrary, the word concerns a change of mind about sin and sinning, and not about inteluctual facts. Equal to נָחַם and תְּשׁוּבָה.

καινός, 42x.

NEW MADE: mistranslated *new*. this definition is meant to convey a degree of ambiguity necessary to understand the new made covenant.

YY τοῦ ΘY, 42x.

ALMĪGHTY SŎN: The translation Sŏn of Gŏd does not communicate well in English the proper sense, 'kin of God', which is to say divine Son. בן אלהים.

λογίζομαι, 41x

TAKE INTO ACCOUNT: vs. *impute*. When he administers justice the Most High takes into account the pledge of faithfulness upon genuine repentence, and forgives the sinner. We should have peace through holding faithful. Extra merit (zechut) is not needed in our account to cancel demerit. The Almīghty Sŏn has no need to be paid off by someone's merit in order to forgive, or ancestors or anyone else. His wrath is forgiven, not paid off, because he ransoms, and cleanses, and the final cleansing we wait for by faithfulness. Gal. 5:5. חשב.

λύτρον, λυτρόω, ἀντίλυτρον, ἐξαγοράζω, ἀπολύτρωσις, λύτρωσις, 20x

RANSOM: usually mistranslated by some form of the word *redeem*. Mĕssiah's ransom is the cost in the flesh of a larger cost paid by the Făther, the Sŏn, and the Spĭrit to rescue us from the hand of lawlessness. The cost is exacted by lawlessness while he bears with our sins, forebearing judgment while we damage everything with sin. The Most High could not avoid this cost because his love requires him to allow time for repentance so that he can have mercy. Messiah's death has nothing to do with making a payment to the Făther to satisfy divine wrath. This view was invented by Augustine, Anselm and the Calvinists. גאל and כֹּפֶר and פדה.

γενεά, 29x

KINDRED: mistranslated *generation*. משפחה.

μονογενής, 10x

ONLY KINDRED: mistranslated *only begotten* before 1950 and *only* after 1950. The term describes the Sŏn's divine kinship to the Făther and vice versa. Greek explanation of יחיד and בן אלהים.

Third Day Note Continued

All of the aforementioned passages with the word שִׁלְשׁוֹם *shilshom* are mistranslated in the English versions. The word is a joining of two Hebrew words, *shelosh* and *yom* to form the contraction *shilshom*. It is always placed as the day before yesterday, thus counting backwards inclusively from 'today,' or the day after tomorrow, counting forward inclusively from today. ▷ So if one starts on the day of the resurrection counting back: Friday sunrise to Ṣabbath sunrise is 'today' (using the daybreak day). Thursday sunrise to Friday sunrise is 'yesterday', and Wednesday sunrise to Thursday sunrise is 'the third day.' Or counting forward, the day of the crucifixion (Wed sunrise to Thursday sunrise) is day 1; and Thursday sunrise to Friday sunrise is day 2; and Friday sunrise to Ṣabbath sunrise is day three. ▷ The three days Wed. Daytime, Thur. Daytime, Friday Daytime. The three nights are Wed night, Thur night, Friday night. This satisfies Matthew 12:40, because the scripture also counts days and nights inclusively. One may have part of the first day and part of the last night. Yĕshua counts this as, 'today and tomorrow and the next day...for it cannot be that a prophet should perish outside of Jerusalem' (Luke 13:33). For he says, 'and on the third day I will be finished' (Luke 13:32). And he said, 'it is finished' (John 19:30). So whatever events happen 'today' such as Yĕshua's dying, then the third day is counted inclusively from then. ▷ Yĕshua died on the 4th day of the week. That day must be included in the counting. There are no exceptions in the typology of the third day. None. Thus, for instance, he could not have died on Wednesday and then be raised at any time after dawn on the Ṣabbath. For that would exceed three calendar days (daybreak to daybreak), or any other way one wants to reckon a day. Yĕshua was raised in the night after the third day, which still belongs to the third calendar day. Sometimes Yĕshua would say, 'after three days', but what he meant was the night after the third twelve-hour day (Friday, dawn to dusk), which was Friday night. Next to Salvation itself, this teaching is the most important teaching of the entire scriptures. See 1 Cor. 15:1-4. See Genesis Note on page 444.

Yohanan

1 ¹In the beginning ᵃhad been^ην the Word.^λ And the Word had been^ην next to the Almighty. And Almĭghty^β the Word ^δhas been^ην. ²This one had been^ην in the beginning next to the Almighty. ³All things through^ε him have become, and without^ρ him has become not even one thing, which has been becoming. ⁴In him life has been^ην, and the life has been^ην the light of men, ⁵and the light in the darkness is shining, and the darkness has not ^ωovercome it. ⁶There came a man, who ^εhad been getting sent ^νfrom before the Almighty. His name *was* Yohanan. ⁷This one came as a witness, so that he may bear witness about the light, so that all may hold faithful through him. ⁸That one had not been^ην the light, but *came* so that he may bear witness about the light, ⁹the true light, which is enlightening every man, *that* has been^ην coming into the world. ¹⁰He has been^ην in the world, and the world through him became, but the world did not know him.

¹¹Unto they which belonged to him, he came, and they which belonged to him did not receive him. ¹²But to as many as receive him, he gives to them the ability to become children of the Almighty, to those holding faithful to His Name. ¹³Who not from ^θblood *lines*, and not from the desire of the ^μflesh, and not from

---

1:1 α= ἦν. Or *had been existing, was being*. Also "At the very first...." (בְּרִאשׁוֹנָה הָיָה אֶת הַדָּבָר). Or "In the firstest," "At the firstmost was the Word." Cf. 1:1 δ. Compare Isa. 44:6, "I AM FIRSTMOST AND LASTMOST. AND WITHOUT ME THERE IS NO ALMĬGHTY." Also Isa. 43:10, "AT MY FACE NO GŎD HAS BEEN FORMED, AND AFTER ME NONE WILL BE." See also Rev. 1:8, 17. The Sŏn says in Isa. 48:16, "FROM THE TIME OF ITS BEING, THERE I [HAD BEEN], AND NOW ADŎNAI YĂHWEH HAS SENT ME AND HIS SPIRIT." See 2 Peter 2:4. The person called the Sŏn of the Almighty has always been. See Yoh. 16:13 note. **1:1** λ *Word*. See Rev. 19:13. See 1 Sam. 3:7, 10, 21. The Word appeared. The "Word" (מימרא) was used in the Aramaic Targums as a euphemism for Yăhweh whenever the interpreters felt the descriptions were too anthropomorphistic. Like using Ha-Shem as a way of avoiding saying the divine name, Yohanan points out the truth behind the usage of THE WORD. **1:1** β The word "Almighty" is used as an adjective attributing the characteristics of divinity to the Word but not identifying the Almighty Sŏn as the same person as the Făther. See note on Mat. 28:20. Cf. Mark 15:39; Isa. 53:1. The original word order is: 'And Almĭghty, has been the word,' to emphasize Almĭghty. ▷ The original languages allow both a noun and adjective use of Θεός/אֱלֹהִים. The reason the English translators prefered the English noun God to a word like Almighty which is more accurate to the original text is due to English translators wanting to shore up the one being doctrine in the Nicene Creed. Eng. adj. use is rare, e.g. 'god son,' and not in the correct sense to be used. **1:1** δ = ἦν =*has been* (= הָיָה). Strictly speaking the Greek imperfect is a past continuous. Yoh. 1:1 has little to say about the present state of the 'Word;' but we may be sure that whatever divine attributes of the Word were necessarily minimized in order to take on flesh and the human nature, that the Word is still identified as Almighty. The present Almightiness of the Son is made plain in Yoh. 1:18, q.v., and Yohanan's use of the present tense in vs. 5 and 9. The translation ἦν = *was* in English in equative uses tends to close the door on present continuance of the assertion. Thus it is best rendered 'has been' when we wish to leave open the possibility of the present truth of the assertion. **1:3** ε-ρ All created things, by his consent, had their origin. **1:5** α κατέλαβεν. Or "understood" or "grasped." **1:6** ε ἀπεσταλμένος. The pluperfect is on account of this account being written long after Yohanan was dead. The progressiveness of the verb pertains to the Prophet being constantly dispatched by the Spĭrit to clear the way for Měssiah. **1:6** η παρὰ = *from beside, from alongside,* מלפני. Yohanan was getting told what to say on a regular basis by the Spirit concerning the coming kingdom, as if he were before the throne of Gŏd being constantly dispatched as the advance messenger before the Měssiah himself. This is the force of the perfect participle. **1:9** ην He had come as the Messenger of Yăhweh appearing to many. **1:13** θ i.e. not from, race, nobility, or nationality. **1:13** μ not the begetting of marital relations **1:13** δ not begetting by an adoptive procedure (Barnes). But begetting by the word of the Almĭghty sown into the hearts of men, who if they accept it are getting begotten of the Almighty.

Yoḥanan 1

the desire of ᵒman, but *who* from the Almĭghty arę begotten. ¹⁴And the Word has become flesh. And he has tented in the midst of us. And we saw his glory, the glory like an only kindred^ψ from beside the Fäther, full of loving-kindness and ᵖfaithfulness.

¹⁵And Yoḥanan is testifying about him, and he has been crying out, saying, "This one is^η *he of* whom I spoke: 'the one after me coming, ᵝbefore me has been appearing, because he ᶿhas been^η over me,'" ¹⁶because^τ from his fullness we have all also received loving-kindness, ᵘafter loving-kindness, ¹⁷ᵃbecause^ϛ the Law has been given through Mosħeh. ¹⁷ᵇThe^ι loving-kindness and ᵛthe ᵖfaithfulness ^π revealed therein, always through Yĕshua the Anöinted ^η have been carried out.

1:14 ψ *Only kindred:* See 1 Yoḥ. 4:9 & Yoḥ. 5:44. Modern versions add 'Son' after deleting 'kindred.' **1:14** ρ cf. 1:17b ρ. **1:15** β→appearing: See on 1:30. The translation of ἔμπροσθέν μου γέγονεν, in any terms of rank, e.g. 'is preferred before me' is surely wrong, as the perfect γέγονεν would imply that Mĕssiah had gained rank sometime in the past over Yoḥanan. It cannot be justified, because Mĕssiah hardly had a following at this time. Nor can it be taken that Mĕssiah had rank in absolute terms because the verb γέγονεν requires a change to take place. Imagine if the verb γίνομαι had been used in John 1:1 instead of εἰμί. Arians would be rejoicing. **1:15** θ→me, πρῶτός μου ἦν, with the verb εἰμί in play, it is possible to assign an unchanging status. Over the objection that it is not present tense, the final clause supplies the reason for the past manifestation of Mĕssiah in the many Christophanies in the Law and Prophets, because Mĕssiah took precedence by virtue of his divine nature! His present outranking of Yoḥanan is entirely unnecessary to make the point. The same objection could be lodged against John 1:1c for saying the Son 'was' (past tense) Almĭghty (θεὸς ἦν ὁ λόγος). The sense is valid when the point that he 'is' (present tense) Almĭghty is omitted. So ὅτι πρῶτός μου ἦν is a valid reference to past rank even though it does not cover the present rank. ▷ The real reason this text fell into confusion is the total denial of gnostic Christianity of the manifestation of Mĕssiah in the Law and Prophets, (a matter that was worsened by Augustine who went along with them), who attributed every appearance to mere angels The notion of the Latin perfect was used to destroy the Greek perfect, which is present perfect progressive, unlike the Latin. Therefore, 'before me has been coming' was changed to 'before me has come' and changed from meaning of repeated coming to simple superior rank.

1:16 τ The ὅτι (seeing that) of vs. 16 read by Aland is undoubtedly correct. It has the sense of γὰρ or כִּי, supplying the explanation of "before me" in vs. 15. **1:16** μ *After:* the LXX generally uses ἀντὶ parallel to the Hebrew word תַּחַת *tahat*, meaning *under*, to denote one administration *after* an older one. A king reigns *tahat* king (Gen. 36:33, תַּחְתָּיו). The son of the high priest serves *under* (i.e. *after*) his father (Lev. 16:32). ▷ Yoḥanan has to be deciphered this way, "Because from Mĕssiah's abundance (fullness) we have received his loving-kindness (forgiveness of sin) after his first loving-kindness called the Law, and we received the later loving-kindness because the first-loving kindness was given by Mĕssiah through his servant Mosħeh." The first kindness of Torah is foundational to the second kindness of forgiveness. The first mercy is the basis of, and allows for the second mercy. His forgiveness is loving-kindness built upon his previous restorative action, the Law, which is for life. **1:17a** ϛ The conjunction ὅτι (because) supplies the explanation of 'after loving-kindness.' Vs. 17a explains 'after loving-kindness.' Vs. 17b explains both the former and later loving-kindness were implemented by Yĕshua. **1:17a** ϛ ὅτι = *in that* (more literal). The word means 'because' or 'that.' **1:17b** ι reject δε 𝔓⁶⁶. The conjunction δε was probably added to support opposing vs. 17b to 17a. **1:17b** ν: Literally, "the loving-kindness and the faithfulness…." The definite articles, the and the, indicate the mercy and covenant faithfulness first promised in the Law and Prophets, which are carried out by Mĕssiah. They have always been carried out by Mĕssiah as the Mĕssenger of Yäh-weḥ. His loving-kindness was revealed and promised in the giving of the Law plainly stated in Deut. 30:15-16, Exodus 20:6; 33:19; 34:6-7. And Mĕssiah appeared on Mt. Sinai also and was seen by the elders of Yisra'el. The Mĕssiah is the living personal and original source of the Law. He is the one that brought it to be. See Ex. 24:10-11. See Ex. 23:20: Yisra'el is exhorted to obey the voice of Messiah. **1:17b** ρ In Exodus 34:6 appears: חֶסֶד וֶאֱמֶת *ḥesed ve-emeṯh* = ἡ χάρις καὶ ἡ ἀλήθεια. Truth (*emeṯh*) here is not in an abstract sense, but *reliability, dependability, faithfulness*. The text is focusing on the Almĭghty's covenant faithfulness being carried out by Mĕssiah, which is not just an abstract truth. In Exodus 34:6 the better versions have **faithfulness** translated for ἀλήθεια, אמת: CEB, ESV, ESVUK, EXB, GNT, ICB, LEB, NCV, NET, NIV, NIVUK, NLT, NRSV, RSV. **1:17b** π→therein: All the versions try to oppose vs. 17b to 17a by inserting 'but' between them or by so constructing the passage to imply such, except CEB, DLNT, and GNM out of over 50 versions. The TLB exposes the translators hatred of the Law

¹⁸The Almĭghty ᵝno one has ever been ᵅseeing. The only ᵝkindred ᵖAlmĭghty, ᵠTHE ONE BEING in the embrace of the Făther, that one ᵋreveals him.

¹⁹And this is the witness of Yoḣanan when the Yehudim from Yerushalayim sent unto him priests and Leviyim that they may ask him, "Who are you?" ²⁰Then he confessed, and did not deny. Then he confessed thusly: "I am not the Anŏinted." ²¹Then they asked him, "Who then are you? Are you Ęliyahu?" Then he says, "I am not." "Are you THE PROPHET?" Then he answered, "No." ²²Then they said to him, "Who are you, that we may give the answer to those who sent us. What are you saying about yourself?" ²³(He was saying, "I am 'THE VOICE CALLING IN THE WILDERNESS: CLEAR THE WAY FOR YĂHWEH,'" even as Yeshayahu the prophet said.) ²⁴And those who had been getting sent were from the Perushim. ²⁵Then they asked him. Then they said to him, "ᵝWhy then are you immersing, if you are not the Anŏinted, nor Ęliyahu, nor THE PROPHET?"

²⁶Yoḣanan answered them, saying, "I am immersing in water. In the midst of you, one has been standing, who you have not been recognizing: ²⁷the one coming after me, of whom I am not worthy that I may untie the strap of his sandal. ²⁸These things, in Beṯh Anyah, happened across the Yarden, where Yoḣanan was immersing.

²⁹On the next day, he is seeing Yĕshua coming toward him. Then he says, "Behold, the lamb of the Almĭghty, the one ᵅbearing the sin of the world. ³⁰This

---

most clearly: 'For Moses gave us only the Law with its rigid demands and merciless justice, while Jesus Christ brought us loving forgiveness as well.' Deceivers add many words and rearrange whole sentences to add hate of the Law to their translations while hiding the fact that their hatred is not found in the original text they are supposedly translating. **1:17b** η Lit. *has happened, has become.* It is not uncommon to see a verb in Hebrew or Greek indicating a singular subject when a compound subject is supplied. The verb is gnomic (timeless) in that it refers to every time love and faithfulness have come to pass. Mĕssiah's apperance on Mt. Sinai was his first advent to the assembled nation.

1:18 θ It was the Sŏn who appeared when Yăhweh was seen in the form of a man or the form of an angel. The Făther is hidden and is revealed only by the Sŏn. **1:18** α cf. אֵין רָאֹה רָאָה. Heb. equiv. to Greek perfect. **1:18** β✓ μονογενής. See explanation on 1 Yoḣ. 4:9; **1:18** ξ The aorist ἐξηγήσατο is strictly gnomic (untensed, referring to all times) a function carried out in English by the present tense, hence in strict English, *that one relates, expresses, reveals.* But we may also trans. a future perfective sense under the influence of Hebrew, which expresses untensed universal statements using the perfect for the future: *that one will have related* him. Will transports us to the future of all presents, and have points back to all past time making the statement refer to all time.

1:18 ϕ being: ὤν. The present participle completes the picture of Yoḣ. 1:1. The Sŏn still is Almĭghty. An equally valid translation is: *The only kindred Almĭghty*

who is in the embrace of the Father. **1:18** ρ Θεὸς = ΘC: 𝔓⁶⁶ 𝔓⁷⁵ ℵ* B C* L pc sy^hmg Or^pt Did; D vac. Shortening μονογενής Θεός to 'only Gŏd' denies the Father is Gŏd (e.g. ESV). Translation of γενής (*kindred*) must be included. ▷ See Yoḣ. 5:44. ▷ It may be equally pointed out that 'only kindred' by itself affirms deity, because the kinship is composed of deity. All other kinships are not 'only' kinships. See 1:34.

1:21 ι Dan. 9:24: TO AFFIX SEAL TO THE VISION AND PROPHET (וְלַחְתֹּם חָזוֹן וְנָבִיא); Deut. 18:18.

1:23 α Isa. 40:3 **1:25** β They did not think Yoḣanan had sufficient authority to add the immersion of repentance to the Torah because they did not believe he was a prophet of any sort. See Deut. 12:32. But he was a prophet who received immersion from the Almĭghty. The commandment not to add is addressed to men and not to the Almĭghty himself. The command to immerse came from Him. See vs. 33. The teaching that forgiveness requires repentance was already in the Torah. But immersion was chosen as a new symbol to make the public confession that one was repenting and would receive the teaching of Mĕssiah when he was revealed. Immersion also allows women to confess the faith with an outward sign, whereas circumcision was limited to men. All Israel, being in exile, is figuratively immersed in the Yarden before arriving on the plains of Gilgal.

1:29 α = נָשָׂא, or *carrying away.* 'Bearing' means to suffer the ill effects of sin (cf. Isa. 53: 5). *Carring away* ranges from forgiveness/sanctification to eschatological removal of sin from the world system by

is he about whom I have said, ⟨After⁺ me is coming a man, who ᵝbefore me ᵞhas been appearing, because he has been^ην ᵖtaking precedence ᶿover me.' ³¹And I had not been recognizing him. But so that he may be revealed to Yisra'el, because of this, I came immersing in water.'"

³²Then Yoḥanan testified, saying that, "ᵅI had myself been observing the Spĭrit descending as a dove out of heaven.ᵝ Then it remained upon him. ³³And I had not previously been recognizing him. But the one who sent me to be immersing in water, that one said to me, 'Upon whoever you will have seen the Spĭrit descending and remaining upon him, this one is he who is immersing in the holy Spĭrit.' ³⁴And I ᶲhave been seeing and I ᵞhave been testifying that this is the ᵠAlmĭghty Sŏn."

³⁵Then it was the next day^τ. Again Yoḥanan had been standing, and two of his disciples. ³⁶When he looked at Yĕshua walking about, he says, "Behold, the lamb of the Almĭghty!" ³⁷And his two disciples heard him speaking. Then they followed Yĕshua. ³⁸And when Yĕshua turned, and saw them following him, he says to them, "What are you seeking?" And they said to him, "Rabbi, (which means, being translated, "teacher,") where are you staying?" ³⁹Then he says to them, "Be coming, and you will see!" So they came. Then they saw where he is

---

converting sinners or destroying the wicked. **1:30** ζ Yoḥanan repeats this phrase 2x in whole, and 1x in part fitting 3 contexts (1:15, 27, 30; cf. Mat. 3:11; Mk. 1:7). In the first two scenes Yĕshua is not present. The phrase, therefore, is a well thought out, planned riddle used repeatedly. Ὀπίσω (ϕ) may mean 'behind' in a spatial sense, but such a sense would require Yĕshua to be present in all cases and literally behind Yoḥanan the Immerser. Therefore, it means *after* in respect to time. **1:30** β→me ἔμπροσθέν μου = לְפָנַי = at my face. Clearly used in Isa. 43:10 with respect to time 'before:' לְפָנַי לֹא־נוֹצַר אֵל וְאַחֲרַי לֹא יִהְיֶה = *Before me not has been formed a God, and after me none will be*. The perfect verb γέγονεν makes it difficult to interpret β as denoting rank or precedence, because we would expect the verb ἐστιν for such a sense. Γίνομαι denotes a change of state. It cannot mean Yĕshua had gained more rank than Yoḥanan because Yĕshua was barely calling his first disciples then (cf. Yoḥ. 1:35ff, 2:11; 4:1). It thus denotes 'has been manifested.' **1:30** γ→appearing; or 'has been coming.' This Greek perfect is distributive. See Gen. 16:7; 18:1; 22:11; Jos. 5:13. **1:30** π→precedence = πρῶτός = *first, headmost*. **1:30** θ→me = μου = *of me*. **1:31** ω This was said four days before the wedding in Yoḥ. 2:1. How many days the wedding lasted is not stated. After the wedding, in Yoḥ. 2:12 elapsed 'not many days,' and in 2:13, the Passover 'had been near.' If we allow six days for events in Yoḥ. 1, a week for the wedding, and two weeks for Yoḥ. 2:12, then surely these events happened not more than 30 days before Passover in AD 30. Mĕssiah was immersed on the last day of Av in AD 29, then spending 40 days in the wilderness, so at least six full months passed between his immersion and this appearance when Yoḥanan spoke these words.

1:32 α→observing: הַבֵּט הִבַּטְתִּי Τεθέαμαι intensive perfect. **1:32** β He saw this the last day of Av, AD 29. **1:34** ϕ→seeing: ἑώρακα (V-RIA-1S) present perfect, since the 'seeing' (רָאֹה רָאִיתִי) includes spiritual perception of the Spirit 'remaining upon him.' **1:34** γ→testifying: הָעֵד הַעִדֹתִי. He gives a completed testimony repeatedly. **1:34** ψ✓ ὁ υἱὸς τοῦ ΘΥ = the Son, [of] the Almĭghty one = הַבֵּן הָאֱלֹהִים. The meaning is 'the divine Son,' the same as בֶּן־אֱלֹהִים. These words are not used for mere men. Luke 3:38 is no exception since the word 'son' does not appear in the text. But see Dan. 3:25: לְבַר־אֱלָהִין. In Hebrew בֵּן (son) has the same meaning as the word 'kin,' in non literal usage, e.g. son of might = mighty son = one kin of the mighty, viz. sons of the prophets are prophetic sons or kindred. Any non literal usage, "son of X" ascribes the quality of X to whoever son refers to. In Greek all the usages are genitives of apposition, where one thing is ascribed to the other, but we have to take son in the meaning of the Hebrew to see it. Thus: kin of the Almĭghty = Almĭghty kin = the kin/son [who is] Almĭghty. See Daniel Wallace, pg. 97. ▷ 'Only kindred' explains 'Son of the Almĭghty,' to mean kin of Elohim, or elohim kin. See 1:18; 5:44. **1:35** τ AD 30, three days before the wedding (cf. 2:1).

staying, and beside him they stayed that day. And the hour had been⁽ⁿᵛ⁾ about the tenth. ⁴⁰And Andrew, the brother of Şim'on Peter, was⁽ⁿᵛ⁾ one from the two which had heard beside of Yoḥanan, and who followed him. ⁴¹This one is finding firstly his own brother Şim'on. And he is saying unto him, "We have been discovering the Măshiaḥ!", which is getting translated "Anŏinted." ⁴²He led him to Yĕshua. When Yĕshua looked at him, he said, "You are Şim'on son of Yoḥanan. You will be called Keipha," which is translated Peter.

⁴³And on the next day, he wanted to go out toward Galil. And he finds Philip. And Yĕshua says to him, "Be following after me." ⁴⁴And Philip had been⁽ⁿᵛ⁾ from Beṭh-Tsaidah, the city of Andrew and Peter. ⁴⁵And Philip is finding Neṭhani'el. Then he is saying to him, "Him whom Mosheh wrote *about* in the Law and the Prophets, we have been discovering: Yĕshua son of Yosef from Netsereṭh!" ⁴⁶Then Neṭhani'el said unto him, "Can there be anything good from Netsereṭh?" And Philip says unto him, "Be coming and see!" ⁴⁷He saw Neṭhani'el coming toward him. Then he says about him, "Behold, truly a Yisra'eli in whom there is no ᵋguile." ⁴⁸Then Neṭhani'el says to him, "From where are you knowing me?" Then Yĕshua answered, and he said to him, "Before Philip called you, while you are being under the fig tree, I saw you!ᵘ" ⁴⁹Then Neṭhani'el replied to him, "Rabbi, you are the Almĭghty Sŏn! You are the King of Yisra'el!" ⁵⁰Then Yĕshua replied. And he said to him, "Because I said to you 'I saw you under the fig tree,' you pledge faithfulness? Greater things than these you will see!" ⁵¹Then he is saying to him, "Amen, amen! I am saying to all of you, 'You will see heaven, having been opening, and THE MESSENGERS OF THE ALMĬGHTY ASCENDING AND DESCENDING^β upon the Sŏn of man.'"

2 ¹On the third day,ᵗ there was⁽ⁿᵛ⁾ a wedding in Qanah, which is in Galil. And the mother of Yĕshua was there. ²And also Yĕshua and his disciples were invited to the wedding. ³Then when the wine ran out, the mother of Yĕshua says to him, "They have no wine!" ⁴And Yĕshua says to her, "What *is it* to me and you, woman? My time has not yet come." ⁵Then his mother says to the servants, "Whatever he may be saying to you, do!" ⁶And there were there six stone jars, being laid out according to the cleansing of the Yehudim, each one having a capacity of up to two or three measures.

⁷Then Yĕshua says to them, "Fill the jars with water." Then they filled them up to the topmost. ⁸Then he says to them, "Draw now, and be bringing it to the banquet master." ⁹And when the banquet master tasted the water, which had been becoming wine, and he had not been knowing from where it is, but the servants had been knowing, (the ones who had been drawing the water), then the banquet master calls the bridegroom. ¹⁰Then he is saying to him, "Every man

---

1:47 ξ Neṭhani'el saw no need to conceal his opinion (cf. vs. 46) **1:48** μ A fact which no one but Gŏd and Neṭhani'el could know. Fig trees provided shade, and were customary places for rest, prayer, and meditation, and the study of Scripture, and also are an idiom for one's own home: cf. 1 Ki. 4:25; Zech. 3:10; Mal. 4:4. **1:51** β Gen 28:12

2:1 τ The third day from 1:43, inclusive count.

firstly the good wine is setting out. And when they may have been made to drink fully, the less valuable. You have been keeping the best wine until now!" ¹¹This, the first of the signs, Yĕshua did in Qanah, which is in Galil. Then he revealed his glory. And his disciples confirmed *their* faithfulness to him.

¹²After this, he went down to Kefar-Naḥum, he and his mother, and his brothers, and his disciples. And there they stayed not many days. ¹³And the Passover⸝ of the Yehudim was near.

¹³ᵇThen Yĕshua went up to Yerushalayim. ¹⁴And he found in the Temple, those selling oxen, and sheep, and doves, and the money changers sitting. ¹⁵Then he made a whip from cords. And he drove all of them from the Temple. Besides the sheep and the oxen, also the coinage of the exchangers he poured out, and the tables he overturned. ¹⁶And unto the sellers of the doves, he said, "Carry these away from here! Do not be making my Fӑther's house a house of commerce!" ¹⁷And his disciples remembered, that it has been getting written—*yea* it is: "ZEAL FOR YOUR HOUSE HAS EATEN ME!⸝" ¹⁸Then the Yehudim responded. And they said to him, "What sign are you showing us, since you are doing these things?" ¹⁹Then Yĕshua answered. And he said to them, "Destroy this Temple, and within three days I will raise it." ²⁰And the Yehudim said, "Forty and six years has been built this Temple, and you within three days will raise it?!," ²¹But, he had been speaking about the Temple of his body. ²²So, when he had been risen from the dead, his disciples had been reminded that he was saying this to them. And they have held faithful to the Scripture, and to the word which Yĕshua spoke.

²³And as he was in Yerushalayim during the Passover, during the feast many pledged faithfulness to his name, seeing the signs which he was doing. ²⁴And he, Yĕshua, was not himself pledging faithfulness to them, in his knowing all of them, ²⁵and since he was having no need that anyone should testify about ᵅthe man, because he was knowing what was in ᵝthe man.

3

¹Then there was a man from the Perushim, and ᵝNaqdimon was his name, a ruler of the Yehudim. ²This one had come to him at night. And he said to him, "Rabbi, we have been knowing that from the Almĭghty you have been coming, a teacher, because no one is able to be doing these signs which you are doing, unless the Almĭghty should be with him!"

³Then Yĕshua answered. And he said to him, "Amen, amen, I am saying to you, except one shall have been begotten from above, he is not able to see the Kingdom of the Almĭghty." ⁴Then Naqdimon says to him, "How is a man able to be born in his being old? He is not able to enter into his mother's womb a second time and to be born, is he?"

2:13 ς Passover, AD 30. **2:17** φ Psa 69:9. **2:20** θ Herod was appointed king on September 30th, AD 40. According to Josephus the feast of Tabernacles fell at the completion of the Temple on the same date as Herod's appointment. In 17 B.C. Tishri 15, the first day of Sukkot fell on September 30. Forty-six years count from Tishri 15, 17 B.C. to Tishri 15, AD 30. Between Sukkot AD 29 and Sukkot AD 30 was the 46th year that the Temple had been built. **2:25** α Yoḥannan speaks of the Son of Man. **2:25** β Yoḥannan speaks of Adam. **3:1** β Naqdimon Ben Gurion was responsible for water distribution in Yerushalayim during feasts according to Jewish sources.

⁵And Yĕshua answered, "Amen, amen, I say to you, unless a man may be begotten from water and Spĭrit, he is not able to enter into the kingdom of the Almĭghty! ⁶That which has been getting begotten from the flesh, flesh becomes, and that which has been getting begotten from the Spĭrit, spirit becomes. ⁷You should not have been amazed that I have said to you, 'It is necessary for all of you to be begotten from above!' ⁸The Spĭrit where he wills is blowing, and the sound of it you are hearing, but you have not been knowing from where it is coming, and whither it is going. So is everyone who has been getting begotten from the Spĭrit^μ."

⁹Then Naqdimon answered. And he said unto him, "How are these things able to be?" ¹⁰Then Yĕshua answered. And he said unto him, "Are you the teacher of Yisra'el, and these things you are not knowing? ¹¹Amen, amen, I am saying to you that which we have been knowing, we are speaking, and that which we have been seeing, we are testifying, and our testimony you are not receiving. ¹²If earthly things I have spoken to you, and you are not confirming *your* faithfulness, how will you confirm *your* faithfulness if I may have spoken to you about heavenly things?" ¹³And no one ᶿhas been ascending into heaven, except he which descended from heaven, the Sŏn of man, ᵖTHE ONE BEING in heaven.

¹⁴And as Mosheh had made raised high THE SERPENT IN THE WILDERNESS^α, so it is necessary, to make raised high the Sŏn of man, ¹⁵so that anyone holding faithful in him may be inheriting life everlasting. ¹⁶For the Almĭghty has so *greatly* loved the world, that he gave his ᵝonly kindred Sŏn, so that anyone ᵞconfirming ᵟfaithfulness ᵋto him will not have perished, but may be ᵞinheriting everlasting life.

¹⁷Because, the Almĭghty has not sent his Sŏn into the world so that he may be judging the world, but so that the world may be rescued by him. ¹⁸The one holding faithful to him is not ᵑgetting judged, but the one who is not ᵒnow con-

---

3:5-8 μ See Romans 12:1-2. The Rŭaḥ speaks subjectively into the heart of the faithful, and very often a person does not know if they are recalling something or hearing a thought foreign to himself. That the Spĭrit spoke has to be confirmed by other objective witnesses to the truth of what was said. In rare cases, it may become clear to a person that the Spĭrit is speaking in his mind, but he normally works like the wind. You cannot see him, but can only hear him, and you don't know where something is going until it is objectively verified. The Spĭrit speaks for our benefit to sanctify us and also to us for the benefit of others to sanctify them. Everyone who walks with the Almĭghty, listening to the Spĭrit, therefore, is reborn step by step into the image of Mĕssiah. The leading of the Spĭrit should be obeyed, because He will point out how we should apply the commandments. Whoever responds will be given more. This is what it means to be getting begotten from above. **3:13** θ→ascending: The English progressive perfect may mean that someone started ascending in the past, and is still in the process of ascending. This is not what is meant because the Greek perfect excludes this idea. Rather it may also mean someone has made complete ascension in the past on multiple occasions. And this is what is meant. See Wallace pg. 580. English would customarily use a present tense for this kind of gnomic use, "No one ascends into heaven, except he which descended." Mĕssiah's visitations as מַלְאַךְ יְהוָה (the Mĕssenger of Yăhweh) are meant, or otherwise in the form of a man (cf. Gen. 18:1; 32:24; Jos. 5:13). **3:13** ρ→heaven: omitted by some texts.

3:14 α Num. 21:4-9. But later the serpent was worshiped. See 2 Kings 18:4, where it is called: *nehushtan*. **3:16** β→kindred: See explanation on 1 Yoḥ. 4:9. Also in 3:18. The Sŏn is kin to the Făther, that is he is the only Sŏn having the same Almĭghty nature. This point is important because no one who pledges loyalty to the Sŏn while denying his kinship with the Făther has true fidelity to Gŏd. See Yoḥ. 1:18. **3:16** γ *promising, pledging, affirming;* δ *loyalty; fealty; fidelity;* ε *to, into, for;* **3:16** γ→δ or *holding faithful.* The meaning of πιστεύων εἰς αὐτὸν (pisteuon eis auton) is not simply "who believes in him," by rather who pledges fidelity to him, —affirms loyalty to him, — affirms or confirms faithfulness to him, who is holding

firming his faithfulness has been getting judged, because he has not been holding faithful to the name of the ᵒonly kindred Almĭghty Sŏn. ¹⁹And this is the judgment, because the light has been coming into the world, but men have loved more the darkness than the light, because their deeds have been evil. ²⁰Because every one working injustice is hating the light, and he does not come unto the light, so that his deeds will not have been reproved. ²¹But the one doing the truth, he is coming unto the light, so that his deeds will have been revealed, because according to the Almĭghty they are *and* haveᵖ been getting done.

²²Then it was after these things. Then Yĕshua came, and his disciples, into the land of Yehudah, and there he was sojourning with them, and he was immersing. ²³And also Yohanan was immersing in Aenon near to Şalem, because many waters were there. And they were coming alongside. And they were immersing themselves, ²⁴because Yohanan had not yet been getting thrown into the prison.

²⁵Therefore, there occurred a dispute from the disciples of Yohanan with a Yehudi about purification. ²⁶Then they came unto Yohanan. And they said to him, "Rabbi, he who was with you across the Yarden, for whom you have been testifying, behold this one is immersing, and all are coming unto him!"

²⁷Then he answered. And he said, "A man is not being able to be receiving *anything*, except it may be what has been getting offered to him from heaven." ²⁸You yourselves, to me are testifying that I said, 'I am not the Anŏinted One', but that having been getting sent—I am, before the face of that one. ²⁹He who is having the bride is the bridegroom. And the friend of the bridegroom, who has been standing and listening for him, with joy is rejoicing, because of the voice of the bridegroom. Therefore, this my joy has been getting filled up. ³⁰That one needs to be fruitful, and I to be diminished. ³¹He who is coming from above, above *the face of all* is. He being from the earth, from the earth is, and from the earth is speaking. He which out of heaven is coming, up above *the face of all* is."

³²That which he has been seeing, and heard, this one is testifying, and his testimony none takes away. ³³He who has received his witness has ᵃsealed that the **Almĭghty** is trueᵏ, ³⁴**whom** indeed the Almĭghty has sent. The words of the Almĭghty he speaks, because He gives the Spĭrit without measure *to Him.* ³⁵The

---

faithful to him. The Biblical Hebrew sense is "makes/gives support unto him," from the Hiphil of אָמַן. The words may also mean only to believe a fact or assertion but only when a fact or assertion is the object of the verb, viz. I support what you say vs. I support you, or I give my support to you. The last two uses have a personal object, and mean much more than simple belief or even trust. They mean a pledge of loyalty, fidelity, an affirmation to be faithful to the person, or the confirmation that such faithfulness exists. Yohanan very emphatically uses the word "to" or "into" (εἰς) to specify fidelity to the person of Mĕssiah, i.e. not 'holds [it] faithful that [such and such is true]', but 'holds faithful to' Mĕssiah.

3:16 λ see 1 Yoh. 5:12; cf. Heb. נָחַל.

3:18 η Present tense, but also used futuristically as in 'going to be judged.' **3:18** α πιστεύων ἤδη. Literally, 'confirming faithfulness now;' the adverb modifies πιστεύων and not κέκριται. Having them "already condemned" while they still may turn comes from the Calvinist heresy. **3:18** ο√ μονογενοῦς. See 1 Yoh. 4:9. The translation of τοῦ μονογενοῦς υἱοῦ τοῦ θεοῦ may also be "the only kindred Son, the Almighty One (Simple Apposition). **3:21** ρ expanded periphrasis.

3:33 α See Yoh. 6:14; Dan. 9:24, "TO SEAL (confirm, certify) THE VISION AND THE PROPHET."

3:33 μ ὁ θεὸς ἀληθής ἐστιν, ὃν γὰρ ἀπέστειλεν ὁ θεὸς See Yoh. 1:18; 3:16, 18; 17:3. Isa. 48:16: DRAW NEAR TO ME! LISTEN TO THIS! I HAVE NOT BEEN SPEAKING FROM THE BEGINNING IN SECRET. FROM THE TIME OF ITS BECOMING, THERE I AM. SO

Fäther is loving the Sŏn, and has been putting all things into his hand. ³⁶He who is holding faithful to the Sŏn is ᵞinheriting everlasting life, but he who is disobeying the Sŏn will not see life, but the wrath of the Almĭghty remains over him.

4 ¹Therefore ᵅwhen Yĕshua knew that the Perushim had heard that Yĕshua was making, and immersing, more disciples than Yoḣanan, ²(although Yĕshua himself was not immersing, but his disciples), ³then he left Yehudah. And he departed again into Galil. ⁴And it was necessary for him to pass by way of Shomron. ⁵Then he comes to a city of Shomron, being called Suḱar, near the territory that Ya'aqov gave to his son Yosef. ⁶And Ya'aqov's well was there. Therefore Yĕshua, having been laboring from his journey, was sitting in that condition upon the well. It was about the sixth hour.

⁷Then there comes a woman of Shomron to draw water. And Yĕshua says unto her, "Give me a drink," ⁸because his disciples had earlier been going away into the city that they may buy food. ⁹Then the Shomronit woman says to him, "For what reason, since you are Yehudi, are you asking beside me for a drink, when I am a Shomronit woman?" (Because Yehudim are not having any business with Shomronim.) ¹⁰Yĕshua answered and said to her, "If you had been knowing the gift of the Almĭghty, and who it is who says to you, 'Give me a drink,' you would have asked him, and he would have given you living water."

¹¹She says to him, "Sir, you have nothing to draw with and the well is deep. Where then do you get that living water? ¹²You are not greater than our father Ya'aqov, are you, who gave us the well, and drank of it himself, and his sons, and his cattle?" ¹³Yĕshua answered and said to her, "Everyone who drinks of this water will thirst again, ¹⁴but whoever may have drunk of the water that I will give him will not thirst forever, but the water that I will give him will become in him a well of water springing up to everlasting life."

¹⁵The woman says to him, "Sir, give me this water, so I may not be thirsting, nor may be coming all the way here to be drawing." ¹⁶He says to her, "Be going, call your husband, and come here." ¹⁷The woman answered and said, "I have not a husband." Yĕshua says to her, "You have well said, 'A husband'—'I have not', ¹⁸because you have had five husbands, and the one whom you now are having is not your husband. This you have been speaking truly."

¹⁹The woman says to him, "Sir, I perceive that you are a prophet. ²⁰Our fathers worshiped in this mountain, and you say that in Yerushalayim is the place where men ought to worship." ²¹Yĕshua says to her, "Be holding faithful ᵦto me woman, in that an hour is coming when neither in this mountain, nor in Yerushalayim, will you worship the Fäther. ²²You worship that which you have not been knowing. We worship that which we have been knowing, because de-

---

THEREFORE ADŎNAI YÄHWEḤ HAS BEEN SENDING ME AND HIS SPĬRIT. See 4:34 ψ. **3:36** λ see 1 Yoḣ. 5:12.

4:1 α Tevet, AD 31. **4:21** β Yoḣanan has omitted the clarifying εἰς, so *me* could be a direct object, thus the imperative may be to hold Yeshua faithful in what he is saying. But the statement is ambiguous and also means to hold faithful to him, and in that case the conjunction, ὅτι, *in that,* gives a reason to hold faithful to him. It means both *because* and *that. In that* covers both meanings.

Yohanan 4

liverance is from the Yehudim. ²³But an hour is coming, and now is, when the true worshipers will worship the Făther in spirit and truth, because such people the Făther seeks to be his worshipers. ²⁴The Almĭghty is Spĭrit, and those who worship him must worship in spirit and truth."

²⁵The woman says to him, "I have been knowing that Măshiaḥ is coming (he who is being called the Anŏinted). When that One may have come, he will declare all things to us." ²⁶Yĕshua says to her, ψ"It's me, the one speaking to you."

²⁷And at this point his disciples came, and they were amazed that he was speaking with a woman, yet no one said, "What do you seek?" or, "Why do you speak with her?" ²⁸So the woman left her water pot, and went into the city, and says to the men, ²⁹"Come, see a man who told me all the things that I have done. Could this one be the Anŏinted?" ³⁰They went out of the city, and were coming to him.

³¹Meanwhile, the disciples were requesting him, saying, "Rabbi, eat." ³²But he said to them, "I am having food to eat that you have not been knowing about." ³³The disciples therefore were saying to one another, "No one brought him anything to eat, did he?" ³⁴Yĕshua says to them, "My food is that I may have done the will of him who sent me ψ, and *that* I should have accomplished his work. ³⁵Do you not say, 'There are yet four moons, and then comes the harvest ζ? Look, I say to you, lift up your eyes, and look on the fields, that they are white for harvest. ³⁶Already he who reaps is receiving wages, and is gathering fruit for life everlasting, so that he who sows and he who reaps may be rejoicing together. ³⁷Because in this case the saying is true, 'ONE SOWS, AND ANOTHER REAPS.'γ ³⁸I sent you to be reaping that for which you have not been laboring. Others have been laboring, and you have been entering into their labor."

³⁹And from that city many of the Shomronim confirmed faithfulness to him because of the word of the woman who testified, "He told me all the things that I have done." ⁴⁰So when the Shomronim came to him, they were asking him to stay at their side, and he stayed there two days. ⁴¹And many more confirmed *their* faithfulness because of his word. ⁴²But to the woman, they were saying, "It is no longer because of what you said that we are confirming *our* faithfulness, because we have been hearing for ourselves and having been discerning that this One is truly the Rescuer of the world."

⁴³And after the two days he went forth from there into Galil. ⁴⁴For Yĕshua himself testified that a prophet has no honor in his own country. ⁴⁵So when he came into Galil, the men of Galil received him, having been seeing as much as he had done in Yerushalayim during the feast, because they themselves also went to the feast.

4:26 ψ ἐγώ εἰμι. Possibly another case of I AM (cf. Isa. 52:6: אֲנִי־הוּא הַמְדַבֵּר), but this would not be apparent to the woman, because the suggested predicate is, "the Anŏinted One.' **4:34** ψ *And now Adŏnai Yăhweḥ has been sending me and his Spĭrit.* Isa. 48:16. Waltke-O'Connor 30.1d.1-3. Constative, aka. progressive perfect. See 3:33 μ. **4:35** ζ Therefore it was winter. The first harvest remark is literal. The fields being already white is figurative of the time for a spiritual harvest. **4:37** γ Mic 6:15, Deu 28:39; Jos 24:13, Deu 6:11.

⁴⁶He came therefore again to Qanah of Galil where he had made the water wine.ᵝ And there was a certain royal official, whose son was sick at Kefar-Naḥum. ⁴⁷When he heard that Yĕshua had come out of Yehudah into Galil, he went to him, and was requesting him that he may come down and heal his son, because he was at the point of death. ⁴⁸Yĕshua therefore said to him, "Unless you may have seen signs and wonders, no, you will not have pledged *your* faithfulness." ⁴⁹The royal official says to him, "Sir, come down before my child dies." ⁵⁰Yĕshua says to him, "Be going. Your son lives." The man held faithful the word which Yĕshua spoke to him, and he started off. ⁵¹And as he was now going down, his servants met him, saying that his son was living. ⁵²So he asked alongside them the hour when he began to get better. They said therefore to him, "Yesterday at the seventh hour the fever left him." ⁵³So the father knew that it was at that hour in which Yĕshua said to him, "Your son lives," and he ᵃaffirmed *his* loyalty, and his whole household. ⁵⁴This is again a second sign that Yĕshua performed, when he had come out of Yehudah into Galil.

5

¹After these things there was a feast of the Yehudim, and Yĕshua went up to Yerushalayim.ᵝ ²Now there is in Yerushalayim by the sheep gate a pool, which is called in Hebrew Beṯh-Ḥasda, having five porticoes. ³In these lay a multitude of those who were sick, blind, lame, and withered,ᶿ [awaiting the moving of the water, ⁴because a messengerᶓ at *propitious* times was descending into the pool, and he was stirring up the water. So the one who first entered after the stirring of the water was getting well in whatever disease he was just then getting held by.] ⁵And a certain man was there, who was thirty-eight years in his sickness. ⁶When Yĕshua saw him lying there, and knew that he had already been there a long time, he says to him, "Do you wish to get well?" ⁷The sick man answered him, "Sir, I do not have a man so that, when the water may have been stirred up, he may have cast me into the pool, but into which going myself, another steps down before me."

⁸Yĕshua says to him, "Be arising, take up your pallet, and be walking." ⁹And immediately the man became well, and took up his pallet and was walking. Now it was the Ṣabbaṯh on ᵝthat day. ¹⁰Therefore, the Yehudim were saying to him who had been getting healed, "It is the Ṣabbaṯh, and it is not permissible for you to carry your pallet." ¹¹But he answered them, "He who made me well was the one who said to me, 'Take up your pallet and be walking.'" ¹²They asked him, "Who is the man who said to you, 'Take it up, and be walking'?" ¹³But the one being healed had not been knowing who it is, because Yĕshua had slipped away, there being a crowd in the place.

¹⁴After these events Yĕshua finds him in the temple, and said to him, "Look,

---

4:46 β Winter, AD 31. **4:53** α→loyalty: cf. vs. 50; only this time the support is to Yĕshua as personal loyalty and not just to his word.
5:1 β Purim. AD 32. **5:3** θ The place was a pagan shrine dedicated to the god of healing for Greeks and Romans living in or visiting the city. Mss lack the end of vs. 3 and all of vs. 4; **5:4** ξ a rebel spirit **5:9** β The feast fell on Ṣabbaṯh, March 15th, AD 32. This was II Adar,

you have been getting well. Be not sinning anymore, so that something worse will not have happened to you." ¹⁵The man went away, and told the Yehudim that it was Yěshua who had made him well. ¹⁶And for this reason the Yehudim were persecuting Yěshua, because he was doing these things on the Ṣabbaṭh.

¹⁷But he answered ᵅthem, "My Fǎther is working until now, and I myself am ᵝworking." ¹⁸For this cause therefore the Yehudim were seeking all the more to kill him, because he not only was loosing the Ṣabbaṭh, but also was calling the Almǐghty his own Fǎther, making himself equal with the Almǐghty.

¹⁹Yěshua therefore answered and was saying to them, "Amˑen, amˑen, I am saying to you, ᶠno, the Sǒn is ᵅnot able to be doing ᵝyet ʸone *miracle* of himself, unless *it is* something he may be seeing the Fǎther doing, because whatever that one may be doing, these things the Sǒn also is doing likewise. ²⁰For the Fǎther loves the Sǒn, and shows him all things that he himself is doing, and greater deeds than these will he show him, that you may be wondering."

²¹"Because just like the Fǎther is raising the dead and is giving them life, even so the Sǒn also ʸis offering life to whom he wishes, ²²and because no, the Fǎther is judging none, but he has been yielding all the judgment to the Sǒn, ²³in order that all may be honoring the Sǒn, even as they honor the Fǎther. He who does not honor the Sǒn does not honor the Fǎther who sent him. ²⁴Amˑen, amˑen, I am saying to you that the one who is listening to my word, and who is ᵅholding faithful *to* him who sent me, is ᵞinheriting everlasting life, and goes not to judgment, but ᵝhas been getting removed from the death to life."

Adar Shˑeni. **5:17** α The objections of the Perushim caught up with Yěshua after he returned back to Galil, and that is where he stated his responses. **5:17** β The work he was doing was based on the law in Deut. 22:4 that an animal in a ditch could be rescued. It must be assumed that whatever day it happens does not matter. By reasoning from the lesser to the greater, a son, or a sick or ill person could be rescued on the Ṣabbaṭh also if they could be made well. **5:19** ξ οὐ; the first 'no' denies part of the accusation in vs. 18. The Sǒn is not equal to the Fǎther in regards to ability, because the Sǒn has set to the side his glory and power while upon earth. Yěshua has sidestepped the issue of his identity though, allowing it to be hinted at while giving them an answer by which they will misdirect themselves. He is in fact equal to the Fǎther in who he is, the Almǐghty Sǒn. **5:19** αβγ = οὐδὲν; this word is injudiciously translated 'nothing,' here by most, which it may mean, but more precisely, it means 'not yet one.' It therefore does not mean nothing at all, but refers to the topic of conversation about how he is able to do the wonders the Jews are witnessing. In no *thing*, 'thing' is in fact supplied by the translator, but we may supply whatever the context suggests. The word is put as *none* in the Lexicon, which is a contraction of 'not one.' The Greek is a contraction of 'not yet one.' ▷ It was not necessary for the Sǒn to go out on his own independent of the Fǎther in doing miracles, which he could do, but willed not to, because he would live as a man. Therefore, the Fǎther informed the Sǒn what was needed, and the Sǒn did on the human level whatever was necessary to show a miracle was coming via the Sǒn, and the Fǎther exercised his power to do it on behalf of the Sǒn. **5:21** γ→offering; or a completely futuristic present: *is going to give* or possibly *is giving*, but then it would be '2. Mostly Futuristic' (cf. Wallace, Syntax, pg. 537), the giving has begun with his impartation of the word of life to his disciples. We may likewise take *is going to inherit (have)* in vs. 24 and elsewhere. ▷ The passage is not an OSAS passage because the continuance of Gǒd's distributed acts of removal from death, each in itself viewed as completed, is dependent on "holding faithful;" like Israel during the Judges, each deliverance is complete, but when they stopped being faithful he stopped delivering them. **5:24** α→to: *holding faithful to,* or *holding faithful;* this depends on whether the dative is that of direct object or indirect object. Yoḥanan usually adds εἰς when he means 'holds faithful to.' **5:24** λ see 1 Yoḥ. 5:12. **5:24** β→removed: *Removed* here is parallel to *rescued* in Eph. 2:8. Each instance of 'getting removed' from death is complete, but final removal from death has not yet happened. The gnomic/distributive use of the Greek perfect is congruent to the gnomic use of the Hebrew (future) perfect.

Yoḥanan 5

[25] "Am·en, am·en, I am saying to you, a time ⁿis coming and θnow is, when the dead will hear the voice of the Almĭghty Sŏn, and those who listened will live. [26] For just as the Făther has life within himself, so also to the Sŏn he gives ξ life, to have within himself, [27] and he gives him power to execute judgment, because he is the Sŏn of Man.ᵞ [28] Do not be wondering about this, because a time is coming, in which all who are in the tombs will hear his voice, [29] and will come forth. Those who did the good deeds to a resurrection of life, those who committed the evil deeds to a resurrection of judgment."

[30] "I ᶲdare not do anything on my own authority. As I hear, I judge. And my judgment is just, because I do not seek my own will, but the will of him who sent me." [31] "If I may be testifying ᵅall around, ᵝby myself, my testimony is not ⁿobvious. [32] There is another giving testimony about me, and I have been knowing that the testimony which he is testifying about me is ⁿobvious."

[33] "You have been sending unto Yoḥanan, and he has been testifying to the truth. [34] Yet I am not taking the witness from beside man, unless it be that I say these things that you may be rescued. [35] He has beenᶯᵛ the lamp, the one burning itself, and the one shining and you were willing to rejoice for an hour in his light.ᵗ"

5:25 η→coming: he speaks of the physically dead being raised to life after his resurrection. **5:25** θ→is: Mĕssiah is speaking of those he literally raised, 'now', being while he was still with us. **5:26** ξ ✓ *will have*. The perfective aorist is used gnomically, without respect to time. The English present tense is used to express this. ▷ The Făther gives life to the Sŏn because the Sŏn will loose his life. Giving life means restoring life. The kind of life restored is the Everlasting Life, the same kind of Life in the Făther. As the Everlasting Life, the Sŏn has the power to restore life in himself. As the son of Man, the Sŏn set aside his power of Everlasting Life, so for the Făther to give life to the Sŏn means to reconnect him to it. When the Sŏn prayed before the resurrection of Elazar, the Făther reconnected him (long enough) to his power of Everlasting so that he could raise Elazar. And also at other times he raised the dead. This is different from Eliyahu raising the dead, because in Eliyahu's case the miracle was done for him by the Almĭghty. As son of man, the Sŏn did have many miracles done on his behalf. **5:27** γ→man: *Son* has two senses. That one which was from everlasting, the Almĭghty's Kin (בן אלהים), became flesh in his position as the son at a point in time. This sonship was a newly begotten status or role (Psa. 2:7, הַיּוֹם יְלִדְתִּיךָ), as was the fatherhood of the one he calls Făther. For no one is father until he begets. So father has dual use also. The Most High assumed these positional relationships so that the divine Sŏn could descend from heaven to be the son of Man. ▷ As the divine Sŏn (kin) the Sŏn has no dependency on the Făther (17:3), but is Almĭghty in himself, but having emptied himself of his power, he is dependent for its restoration, remaning Almĭghty as to identity of his self, but not having the power of it except when the Făther restores it. Therefore, the text does not teach the false doctrine of eternal generation.

5:30 ᶲ δύναμαι. Dare not: See LSJ. Also "have no legal right." The Făther has given the judgment of life to the Sŏn, but it is not his own exclusive authority. It is the shared authority of the Almĭghty, and not a separate authority derived only from his human nature. F 4:34 ψ. **5:31** α or *all round;* The word περὶ is taken as an adverb (cf. LSJ E.); the literal sense would be suggested by a pause after the words: μαρτυρῶ περὶ. **5:31** β ἐμαυτοῦ = *of myself, from myself.* One witness may yet be true, therefore the 'if' proposal is to exclude the possibility of another witness, "if I may be witnessing *in every respect,* by myself..." **5:31** η ἀληθής = *unconcealed (transparent, obvious),* but אֱמֶת = *firm, trustworthy, faithful, true.* Clearly a case of dynamic equiv. from Hebrew to Greek, and the English word 'true' is inadequate.

5:33-35 τ Having returned to Galil in late Adar II, AD 32, Yĕshua will learn that Yoḥanan has been murdered as this certainly happened just before the feeding of the 5000 (cf. Luke 9:7 fol.). Our text implies that Yoḥanan is either still alive or if not, then only very recently murdered. The text is almost a eulogy. See 1:1 δ.

Yoḥanan 6

³⁶"Yet the testimony which I have is greater than that of Yoḥanan, because the deeds which the Făther has been giving me, that I may accomplish them, the same work^γ that I am doing—it is testifying about me, that the Făther has been sending me." ³⁷"And the Făther who has sent me, that one has been testifying about me. Besides neither his **voice** at any time have you been listening to, nor as well his **form**^μ have you been perceiving. ³⁸And you do not have his **word** in you remaining, because that which^μ that one has sent—to this one you are not holding faithful."

³⁹"You search the writings, because you think that in them you are inheriting everlasting life, and it is these bearing witness about me, ⁴⁰and you are unwilling to come to me, that you may be inheriting life." ⁴¹"I do not take glory at the side of men, ⁴²but I have surely been knowing you: that you do not have the love of the Almĭghty in yourselves. ⁴³I have been coming in my Făther's name, and you are not receiving me. If another may have come in his own name, you will receive him. ⁴⁴How are you able to hold faithful *while* receiving glory at the side of one another, and you are not seeking the ᵟGlory that is from the side of the only ᵘkindred Almĭghty?" ⁴⁵"Do not be thinking that I will accuse you before the Făther. The one who accuses you is Mosheн, to whom you have been hoping, ⁴⁶because if you were holding faithful *to* Mosheн, you would have been holding faithful *to* me, because that one has written about me. ⁴⁷But if you are not holding faithful ᵅto that one's writings, how will you hold faithful ᵅto my words?"

6 ¹After these things Yĕshua went away to the other side of the Sea of Galil (Tiberias). ²And a great crowd was following him, because they were seeing the signs which he was performing on those who were sick. ³And Yĕshua went up on the mountain, and there he sat with his disciples.

⁴Now the ᶲPassover, the feast of the Yehudim, was near. ⁵Yĕshua therefore lifting up his eyes, and seeing that a great crowd was coming to him, said to

---

5:36 γ intensive plural **5:37** μ or *image*. **5:38** μ The relative pronoun points to the bold words, but its gender is attracted to natural gender. **5:44** δ "Glory" here refers to Mĕssiah. Mĕssiah is the glory of the only Elŏhim. He does not share his Glory with other *elohim*. See Yoḥ. 1:14. **5:44** μ√ μονογενοῦς. Read 'only kindred' with Byzantine MSS *Codex Purpureus Petropolitanus* N 022 (ca. AD 525-575, large letters, text: silver ink, gold ink for nomina sacra) and MSS 1071 (12th century). Clark mentions two Slavonic MSS with the reading also. 𝔓⁶⁶,⁷⁵ B W a b sa ac² pbo bo^pt omit Θεοῦ leaving the text unintelligible: 'beside the only one." The KJV trans. realized the received text denies the Son's divinity, so they mis-translated τοῦ μόνου θεοῦ to say "Gŏd only" followed by other versions including CJB. The Gnostic scribes interpreted μονογενοῦς to mean 'only begotten' which becomes a tautology here if interpreted so. It it inexplicable how a reading that did not make sense to them got added to the text by them. So μονογενοῦς Θεοῦ must be original (by the rule of the harder reading). So first γενοῦς was deleted (failing to fix the problem noted by the KJV), and then Θεοῦ leaving, 'only' or 'only [*Son*]' to be supposed (which also fails to fix the problem since too many MSS still have Θεοῦ). The solution is to restore γενοῦς to the text, 'only <u>kindred</u> Almĭghty,' and this applies to the Father, giving the complement of 1:18. As the Son is the only kindred Almĭghty to the Almĭghty (1:18), so the Almĭghty is the only kindred Almĭghty to the Son (5:44). This text kills the Nicene Creed. **5:47** α It is not easy to decide if the dative is a direct object or indirect object. It seems that Yoḥanan means both. In the end it makes no difference since his words say to do his words.

6:4 ϕ Passover, AD 32. In view of the attempt on his life after healing the invalid, Yĕshua did not publicly attend any feasts until Sukkot in AD 32, though he may have attended secretly if possible.

Philip, "Where will we have bought bread, that these will have eaten?" ⁶And this he was saying to test him, because he himself had been knowing what he was intending to do. ⁷Philip answered him, "Two hundred dinars worth of bread is not sufficient for them, that everyone will have received a little." ⁸One of his disciples, Andrew, Şimʻon Peter's brother, said to him, ⁹"There is a lad here who has five barley loaves and two fish, but what are these for so many people?"

¹⁰Yĕshua said, "Have the people sit down." Now there was much grass in the place. So the men sat down, in number about five thousand. ¹¹Yĕshua therefore took the loaves, and having given thanks, he distributed to those who were seated, and likewise also of the fish as much as they wanted. ¹²And when they were filled, he said to his disciples, "Gather up the leftover fragments, so that nothing will have been lost." ¹³And so they gathered them up, and filled twelve baskets with fragments from the five barley loaves which were left over by those who had been eating. ¹⁴When therefore the people saw the sign which he had performed, they said, "This is of a truth THE PROPHET, **THE COMING ONE** into the world."

¹⁵Yĕshua therefore perceiving that they were intending to come and take him by force, so that they may make him king, withdrew again to the mountain by himself alone. ¹⁶And as it became later, his disciples went down to the sea, ¹⁷and having stepped into a boat, they were going across the sea to Kefar-Naḥum. And ⸤the darkness overtook them⸥, and Yĕshua had notᵀ been coming to them. ¹⁸Besides the sea, by a strong wind blowing, was being stirred up. ¹⁹When therefore they had been rowing about three or four miles, they beheld Yĕshua walking on the sea and drawing near to the boat, and they were frightened. ²⁰But he said to them, "I AMˣ. Do not be getting afraid." ²¹They were willing therefore to receive him into the boat, and immediately the boat was at the land to which they were going.

²²The next day the crowd that had been standing on the other side of the sea saw that there was no other small boat there, except one, and that Yĕshua had not entered with his disciples into the boat, but that his disciples had gone away alone. ²³There came other small boats from Tiberias near to the place where they ate the bread after Adŏnai had given thanks. ²⁴When the crowd therefore saw that Yĕshua was not there, nor his disciples, they themselves got into the small boats, and came to Kefar-Naḥum, seeking Yĕshua.

6:17 ᶠ D א vs: *And it has already been becoming dark* **6:17** ᵀ ουχ vs. ουπω

6:20 χ The first of the seven אֲנִי הוּא *Ani Hu* utterances that Yoḥanan records were spoken by Mĕssiah (❶ 6:20; ❷ 8:24; ❸ 8:28; ❹ 8:58; ❺ 13:19; ❻ 18:5-6; ❼ 18:8). There are exactly seven *Ani Hu* utterances in the Tanakh (❶ Deu. 32:39; ❷ Isa. 41:4; ❸ Isa. 43:10; ❹ Isa. 43:13; ❺ Isa. 46:4; ❻ Isa. 48:12; ❼ Isa. 52:6). "See now I, I AM, and there is no Almĭghty besides me" (Deu. 32:39), "From the beginning I am Yăhweн, the firstmost and the lastmost. I AM." "You are my witnesses, an utterance of Yăhweн and my Servant, whom I have chosen, so that you may know and hold faithful to Me that I AM. At my face has been formed no God, and after me none will be" (Isa. 43:10). "Also, from *the beginning of* time I AM" (Isa. 43:13, cf. ἀπ' ἀρχῆς). "Even until aged I AM, even until greyed I will carry you" (Isa. 46:4). "I AM, I am firstmost, also I am lastmost" (Isa. 48:12). "I AM the one speaking. Behold I" (Isa. 52:6).

Yoḥanan 6

²⁵And when they found him on the other side of the sea, they said to him, "Rabbi, when have you been getting here?" ²⁶Yĕshua answered them and said, "Am·en, am·en, I say to you, you seek me, not because you saw signs, but because you ate of the loaves, and were filled. ²⁷Do not be working for the food which perishes, ᵏbut for the food which endures to everlasting life, which the Sŏn of Man will give to you, because on him the Făther, even the Almĭghty, has set his seal." ²⁸They said therefore to him, "What may we be doing, that we may be working the works of the Almĭghty?" ²⁹Yĕshua answered and said to them, "This is the **work** of the Almĭghty, that you should be holding faithful to **that one which** he has sent."

³⁰They said therefore to him, "What then do you do for a sign, that we shall have seen, and shall have held you faithful? What sign are you working? ³¹Our fathers ate the manna in the wilderness, even as it is what has been getting written, 'HE GAVE THEM BREAD OUT OF HEAVEN TO EAT⁵.'" ³²Yĕshua therefore said to them, "Am·en, am·en, I am saying to you, Mosh·eh has not been giving you the bread out of heaven, but it is my Făther who is giving you the true bread out of heaven. ³³Because the bread of the Almĭghty is that which comes down out of heaven, and gives life to the world."

³⁴They said therefore to him, "Adŏnai evermore give us this bread." ³⁵Yĕshua said to them, "I am the bread of life. He who comes to me, no, he shall not have hungered, and the one ᶿholding faithful to me, no, he will not ever thirst. ³⁶But I said to you, that you have been seeing me, and yet are not ᶿholding faithful. ³⁷Anyone the Făther ᵅis giving to me ᵝwill have come to me, and the one who is coming to me I will certainly not cast out. ³⁸Because I have been coming down from heaven, not that I may be doing my will, but the will of him who sent me. ³⁹And this is the will of him who sent me, that of all that he has been giving me I may lose none, but may raise the same up on the last day. ⁴⁰Because this is the will of my Făther, that everyone beholding the Sŏn and who is holding faithful to him, ᵠshall be inheriting everlasting life. And I myself will raise him up on the last day."

⁴¹The Yehudim therefore were murmuring about him, because he said, "I am the bread that came down out of heaven." ⁴²And they were saying, "Is not this Yĕshua, the son of Yos·ef, whose father and mother we have been knowing? How

---

6:27 λ The conjunction αλλα "but" introduces a limitation or qualification to the denial in the previous phrase, equivalent to the sense of "unless" or "not only...but also," or as Thayer expresses it in a rhetorical fasion, "not so much...as." This text beautifully illustrates this sense because it is undeniable that we must continue to work for our daily food. Similar usages are often wrongly taken by interpreters treating denial statements before this conjunction as absolute denials rather than qualified denials. Liddell and Scott introduce this conjunction with the words, "used adversatively to limit or oppose words, sentences, or clauses." See endnote no. 3. **6:31** ξ Psa 78:24, Exo 16:15. **6:35** θ→faithful: or *confirming faithfulness;* **6:37** α See Rotherham. The present tense should be emphasized here as progressive. **6:37** β ἥξω: See Rotherham. BDAG, 3rd, "since it has the meaning of a perfect, its conjugation sometimes has perfect forms;" "have come;" Consult LSJ: "and fut. ἥξω as fut. pf., I shall have come." **6:40** ψ→inherit: or *may be having* (ἔχῃ V-PSA-3S). The present subjunctive is a future equivalent.

does he now say, 'I have been descending out of heaven'?" ⁴³Yĕshua answered and said to them, "Do not be murmuring among yourselves. ⁴⁴No one can come to me, unless the Făther who sent me ᵠmay have drawn him, and I will raise him up on the last day. ⁴⁵It is what has been getting written in the prophets, 'AND THEY WILL ALL BE TAUGHT OF THE ALMĬGHTYᵖ.' Everyone who has listened and learned at the side of the Făther, comes to me, *and* ⁴⁶not because any one has been seeing the Făther, except THE ONE BEING from the side of the Almĭghty. That one has been seeing the Făther."

⁴⁷"Am·en, am·en, I say to you, he who is ᵝholding faithful ᶿis inheriting everlasting life. ⁴⁸I am the bread of life. ⁴⁹Your fathers ate the manna in the wilderness, and they died. ⁵⁰This one is the bread which comes down out of heaven, so that one may eat of it and shall not have ᵖdied. ⁵¹I am the living bread that came down out of heaven. If anyone will have eaten of this bread, he will live forever, and the bread also which I will give, is my flesh on behalf of the life inᵑ the world."

⁵²The Yehudim therefore were arguing with one another, saying, "How can this man give us his flesh to eat?" ⁵³Yĕshua therefore said to them, "Am·en, am·en, I say to you, unless you may have eaten the flesh of the Sŏn of Man and may have drunk his blood, you have no life in yourselves. ⁵⁴He who eats my flesh and drinks my blood is inheriting everlasting life, and I will raise him up on the last day. ⁵⁵Because my flesh is true food, and my blood is true drink. ⁵⁶He who eats my flesh and drinks my blood abides in me, and I in him. ⁵⁷As the living Făther sent me, and I live because of the Făther, so he who eats me, he also will live because of me. ⁵⁸This is the bread which came down out of heaven, not as the fathers ate, and died. He who eats this bread will live forever."

⁵⁹These things he said in the congregation, as he taught in Kefar-Naḥum. ⁶⁰Many therefore of his disciples, when they heard this said, "This is a difficult statement! Who can listen to it?" ⁶¹And, Yĕshua, having been knowing in himself that his disciples are grumbling about this, said to them, "Is this causing you to stumble? ⁶²What then if you should be beholding the Sŏn of Man ascending where he was before? ⁶³It is the Spĭrit who is giving life! The flesh is profiting nothing. The words that I have been speaking to you are spirit and are life."

⁶⁴But there are some from you who are not holding faithful." Because Yĕshua had been knowing ᵅsince the ᵝbeginning who they were who would never be

---

6:44 ψ→drawn: aorist subjunctive: ἑλκύσῃ or "may draw." The idea of drawing is that of getting a large beast to follow along on a small rope. The beast has to be willing and can easily overpower the rope and yank it out of the hand of the owner if it has a mind to. **6:45** π Isa 54:13; Jer. 31:33-34. **6:47** β→faithful: or 'confirming faithfulness.' **6:47** θ→inheriting. See 1 Yoḥ. 5:12. **6:50** ρ i.e. final death; the second death. **6:51** λ or 'for.' Other versions, "so that the world may have life," which is based on rendering the genitive "for." The common rendering "on behalf of the life of the world," or "for the life of the world" suggests universalism by way of an exchange, and is not at all the same as 1 Yoḥ. 2:2, "concerning the whole world" in regard to purging sin, because the final purging is by fire. Only "for" or "in" is logically possible. The genitive is hard for people to grasp, but in a statement such as "the life of the party" one can understand it to mean the life "in" the party, i.e. the person who is the lead actor. According to Yoḥ. 11:51-52, Messiah's death is on behalf of the many, the house of Yehuḓah and the house of Yisra'el. And this is the life in the world, the dry bones that will be raised up.

6:64 α ἐξ = *since, from.* See LSJ. **6:64** β See

holding faithful, and who it was that would betray him. ⁶⁵And he was saying, "For this reason I have been saying to you, that no one is able to come to me, unless it may be what has been getting offered to him from the Făther."

⁶⁶As a result of this many of his disciples withdrew, and were not walking with him anymore. ⁶⁷Yĕshua said therefore to the twelve, "You do not want to go away also, do you?" ⁶⁸Şim'on Peter answered him, "Adŏnai, to whom will we go? You have words of everlasting life. ⁶⁹And we have been holding faithful, and we have been knowing, that you are the holy one of the Almĭghty." ⁷⁰Yĕshua answered them, "Did I myself not choose you, the twelve? And yet one of you is a devil!" ⁷¹Now he meant Yehudah the son of Şim'on Ish-Qeriyot, because he, one of the twelve, was going to betray him.

7 ¹And after these things Yĕshua was walking in Galil, because he was unwilling to walk in Yehudah, because the Yehudim were seeking to kill him. ²And, the feast of the Yehudim, the Feast of Tabernacles, was near. ³His brothers therefore said to him, "Depart from here, and be going into Yehudah, that your disciples also will behold your deeds which you are doing, ⁴because no one does anything in secret, when he himself seeks to be in public. If you do these things, show yourself to the world," ⁵because not even his brothers were confirming loyalty to him.

⁶Yĕshua therefore says to them, "My time is ᵃnot yet coming by, but your time is always opportune. ⁷The world cannot hate you, but it hates me because I testify about it, that its deeds are evil. ⁸You go up to the feast. I am ᵃnot yet going up to this feast because my time has not been filling up." ⁹And, having said these things to them, he stayed in Galil.

¹⁰And, just as his brothers went up to the feast, then he himself also went up, not publically, but as in disguise. ¹¹The Yehudim therefore were seeking him at the feast, and were saying, "Where is he?" ¹²And there was much murmuring among the multitudes concerning him. Some were saying, "He is good." Others were saying, "No, on the contrary, he deceives the crowd." ¹³However, no one was speaking publically about him for fear of the Yehudim.

¹⁴And now, being the middle of the feast, Yĕshua went up into the temple, and was teaching. ¹⁵The Yehudim therefore were wondering, saying, "How has this man been getting to know letters when he has not been studying?" ¹⁶Yĕshua therefore answered them, and said, "My teaching is not mine *only*, but *also* his who sent me. ¹⁷If any man may be willing to be doing his will, he will know about the teaching, whether it is of the Almĭghty, or *whether* I am speaking from myself. ¹⁸He who speaks from himself seeks his own glory; yet, he who is seeking the glory of the One who sent him, he is a true one, and there is no unrighteousness

---

Yoh. 6:5, 15, 26; he means since the beginning of the feeding of the 5000, and apparently at the same time the betrayer turned away from Messiah in his heart; **6:66-71** τ These things wind up before Shavu'ot.

AD 32. Yĕshua probably skipped this feast due to the threat on his life. **7:2** τ Sukkot, AD 32 in the fall. **7:6 & 8** α→yet = οὔπω. **7:16** ρ See Yoh. 6:27

in him. ¹⁹Mosh‧eh has not been bestowing the Law on you! Indeed, none of you is keeping the Law! Why are you seeking to kill me?"

²⁰The crowd replied, "You have a demon! Who seeks to have you killed?" ²¹Yĕshua answered and said to them, "I did one deed, and you are all wonder struck because of this. ²²Mosh‧eh has been giving you circumcision (not because it is from Mosh‧eh, but from the fathers), and on the Ṣabbaṭh you circumcise a man. ²³If a man receives circumcision on the Ṣabbaṭh, so that the Law of Mosh‧eh will not have been broken, are you angry with me because I made an entire man well on the Ṣabbaṭh? ²⁴Do not be judging according to appearance, but be judging with righteous judgment."

²⁵Therefore some of the people of Yerushalayim were saying, "Is this not the man whom they are seeking to have killed? ²⁶And look, he is speaking publicly, and they are saying nothing to him. Perhaps, the rulers truly have realized that this is the Anŏinted One? ²⁷But, we have been knowing ᵖwhere this man is from. Yet, whenever the Anŏinted One may be coming, no one is going to know ᵖwhere he is from."

²⁸Yĕshua therefore shouted out in the temple, teaching and saying, "But you have been knowing me. And you have been knowing where I am from. And from myself I have not been coming, but he who sent me is faithful, whom you have not been knowing. ²⁹I have been knowing him, because from beside him I am, and he has sent me."

³⁰They were seeking therefore to sieze him. Even so, no man laid his hand on him, because his time had not been coming yet. ³¹Yet also, many from the crowd held faithful to him, and they were saying, "When the Anŏinted may come, he will not perform more signs than what this man has done!"

³²The Perushim heard the multitude muttering these things about him, and the chief priests and the Perushim sent officers that they might seize him. ³³Yĕshua therefore said, "For a little while longer I am with you, then I go to him who sent me. ³⁴You will seek me, and will not find me, and where I am, you are not able to come." ³⁵The Yehudim therefore said to themselves, "Where is he about to go, that we will not find him? He is not about to go to the Dispersion among the Greeks, even to teach the Greeks, is he? ³⁶What is this statement that he said, that 'You will seek me, and will not find °me, and where I am, you are not able to come'?"

³⁷And, on the ᶲlast day, the great day of the feast, Yĕshua had been standing up, and he shouted out, saying, "If any man may be thirsting, let him be coming to me and be drinking. ³⁸He who is confirming faithfulness to me, as the Scripture has said, FROM THE BELLY OF HIM WILL FLOW RIVERS OF LIVING WATER.ᵝ" ³⁹But

---

7:27 π They are expressing the Jewish belief that the origins of the Mĕssiah would be in some way mysterious; they were in a way correct. Yoḥanan has chosen to frame the question as one of place. The mystery is disclosed in the following verses. **7:37** ϕ→day: Tishri 22, the 8th day. Friday, October 17, AD 32. Yallop A-D. *Great day:* Cf. Yoḥ. 19:31. This would be the last day for the traditional water libation. **7:38** β There is no quotation from the Scripture that will follow these exact words, but a combination of Scriptures will teach the meanings of the utterance. The words "from his belly" are the most perplexing of the whole utterance, since they seem to be found nowhere. The reason that the words have remained

Yoḣanan 8   196

this he spoke about the Spĭrit, who those who held faithful to him were going to be receiving. For the Spĭrit had not yet been *poured out*, because Yĕshua was not yet glorified. ⁴⁰Some of the crowd therefore, when they heard these words, were saying, "This truly is THE PROPHET͟." ⁴¹Others were saying, "This is the Anŏinted One." And, others were saying, "Surely the Anŏinted does not come from Galil? ⁴²Has not the writing said that THE ANŎINTED COMES FROM THE OFFSPRING OF DAUID, AND FROM Bҽ̱tH-LE̱'HEM͟, the village where David was?" ⁴³So there arose a division in the crowd because of him. ⁴⁴And some of them were wanting to have him seized, but no one laid hands on him.

⁴⁵The officers therefore came to the chief priests and Perushim, and they said to them, "Why did you not bring him?" ⁴⁶The officers answered, "Never did a man speak the way this man speaks." ⁴⁷The Perushim therefore answered them, "Have even you been getting deceived? ⁴⁸Not one of the rulers or Perushim has confirmed loyalty to him, *has he*? ⁴⁹But this crowd which knows not the Law is accursed." ⁵⁰ But Naqdimon said to them, (he who came to him before, being from them), ⁵¹"Our Law does not judge a man, unless it first may have heard at his side and may have known what he is doing!" ⁵²They answered and said to him, "You are not also from Galil, *are you*? Search, and see that no prophet arises out of Galil͟."

8 ¹²Again therefore Yĕshua spoke to them, saying, "I am the ᵖlight of the world. He who follows me, no, he shall not have walked in the darkness, but he will posses the light of life."

¹³The Perushim therefore said to him, "You are bearing witness of yourself. Your witness is not ᵃreliable." ¹⁴Yĕshua answered and said to them, "Even if I may be bearing witness about myself, my witness is reliable, because I have been knowing where I came from, and where I am going, but you have not been

---

perplexing rests on the fact that the many have rejected the restored Temple of the future. But the interpretation of the passage flows into Temple imagery just as the reverse metaphor: Temple imagery flowed into Mĕssiah. The Temple is a metaphor for the body of Mĕssiah (cf. Yoḣ. 2:19-22). Now the belly of him (τῆς κοιλίας αὐτοῦ) is part of the body. The belly has been used metaphorically before to mean the hollow of the grave. In Yonah 2:2 the belly of the fish becomes the belly of She'ol, where the body of Mĕssiah was for three days and three nights. So here also to decipher the riddle we have to realize that the belly is part of his body-Temple *and* the Temple he will rebuild (cf. Zech. 6:13). Read as follows, "from the Temple of him." Now we have three applications, (1) His belly = part of his Temple to be rebuilt (2) His belly = the inward part of the Temple (Mĕssiah himself,) (3) his belly = the inward part of the Temple of the faithful one (We are his Temple). ▷ First, living water flows from under the threshold of the Temple turning into rivers of water (cf. Ezek. 47:1). The place under the threshold is the hollow or belly of the Temple. This is where the Spĭrit of the Almĭghty came to rest (Ezek. 9:3; 10:4). The water that flows from there joins up with the water from the throne of the Almĭghty (cf. Zech 14:8; 13:1; Ezek. 47:8-12). On its banks grow the trees of life as the trees of life grow on the same river system coming from the throne. The water divinely multiplies *as it flows*. ▷ Second, the water of the Spĭrit flows from Mĕssiah himself. Isa. 44:3 says, "FOR I WILL POUR WATER UPON THE THIRSTY, AND STREAMS UPON THE DRY GROUND. I WILL POUR MY SPĬRIT UPON YOUR SEED AND MY BLESSING UPON YOUR OFFSPRINGS, AND THEY WILL HAVE BRANCHED OUT IN THE MIDST OF GRASS, AS WILLOWS BY STREAMS OF WATER." ▷ Thirdly, the water of the Spĭrit flows from the faithful, Isa. 58:11, "AND YOU WILL HAVE BEEN LIKE A WATERED GARDEN, AND AS AN OUTLET OF WATERS, WHICH WATERS NEVER PROVE FALSE." See Yoḣ. 4:14; Psa. 36:8-9; Prov. 4:23. **7:40** ξ Dan 9:24; Deut. 18 **7:42** φ Mic 5:1-4, Psa 89:3-5, 132:11. **7:52** ᵀ John 7:53-8:11 belongs to the disputed adultery story. See Appendix III for discussion and text.

knowing where I am coming from, or where I am going. ¹⁵You are judging according to the flesh. Not I. I am judging no one. ¹⁶But even if I may be judging, my judgment is true, because I am not alone in it, but I and he who sent me, *the* Fäther. ¹⁷But also in the Law ᵝfor you it has been written, that THE TESTIMONY OF TWO MEN IS RELIABLE.ᵞ" ¹⁸"I am he who bears witness of myself, and the Fäther who sent me bears witness of me." ¹⁹And so they were saying to him, "Where is your Fäther?" Yĕshua answered, "Neither me you have been knowing, nor my Fäther. If you had been knowing me, you would have been knowing my Fäther also." ²⁰These words he spoke in the treasury, as he taught in the temple, and no one seized him, because his time had not been coming yet.

²¹He said therefore again to them, "I go away, and you will seek me, and you will die in your sin. Where I am going, you cannot come." ²²Therefore the Yehudim were saying, "Surely he will not kill himself, will he, since he says, 'Where I am going, you cannot come'?" ²³And he was saying to them, "You are from below. I am from above. You are of this world. I am not of this world. ²⁴Therefore I said to you, that you will die in your sins, because except you may hold faithful, *through* seeing that ⁺I AM, you will die in your sins."

²⁵And so they were saying to him, "Who are you?" Yĕshua said to them, "What have I been saying to you from the beginning? ²⁶I have many things to speak and to judge concerning you, but he who sent me is true, and the things which I heard from him, these I speak to the world." ²⁷They did not realize that he was speaking to them about the Fäther. ²⁸Yĕshua therefore said, "When you shall have lifted up the Sŏn of Man, then you will know that I AM, and I do

---

8:12 ρ Also on the last great day would be the last day for the lighting of the four great lampstands in the court of the women. These lamps were so large that they could be seen all over Yerushalayim. **8:13** α They are not denying that one witness cannot possibly be objectively true. They are making a legal argument. One witness is not regarded as reliable when a legal case is being tried. The word "true" in Hebrew is אֱמֶת *emet*, which is based on the root אָמַן *aman* meaning support or confirm. This is how Yoḣanan is using the word ἀληθής. Something that is not ἀληθής or אֱמֶת is something not "confirmable" or "supportable" in a legal court. What is not ἀληθής is not supportable by other present evidence, but it may nevertheless be true. **8:17** β Yĕshua is technically exempt from necessity of having a second witness (cf. vs. 14) because he is the Sŏn of the Almīghty. Nevertheless, He argues that the Fäther (not being man) is the second witness. The Fäther is greater than mere man, so this second witness meets the requirement of the Torah by the rule of light and heavy. This is why he says "Law for you," because he is exempt from it by his status, just as a farmer is exempt from laws for the priests, or a merchant is exempt from laws for the king. The Almīghty is exempt from laws that apply only to fallible man. See 10:34, 15:25. The words τῷ ὑμετέρῳ are not possessive, and no mss omits them. The grammar solves the problem in this text. It does not mean "your law" here, but "the law for you. **8:17** γ Deu 17:6, 19:15. **8:24** φ See Mark 6:50; Yoḣ. 13:19.

8:28 ψ The Sŏn was as to his identity, Almīghty, but he left all of the glory not compatible with becoming human with his Fäther (cf. Phil. 2:7). He left his infinite power in trust with the Fäther, as well as an infinite degree of his divine knowledge, but the disposition of his love and faithfulness was unaffected by the human limitation, or the corrupt environment he was born into, chiefly through the protection of the Spĭrit from erring in ignorance due to his human position (cf. Rom. 5:14). He would just have to exercise those traits humanly, and prove that as a human it was possible to exercise those traits, because the Most High did create humanity in his image with the design that he should be able to exercise love and faithfulness upon reaching maturity. Therefore, he became dependent on the Fäther for both the power he needed and the knowledge needed to apply it to good effect. ▷ The testing of the Sŏn as a mature human was to give proof to the world that the righteousness of the Most High could operate at the human level, when the human was in communication with the Spĭrit. Obviously the Most

nothing from myself[ψ], but I speak these things as the Făther taught me. ²⁹And he who sent me is with me. He has not left me alone, because I always do the things that are pleasing to him." ³⁰As he spoke these things, many confirmed faithfulness to him. ³¹Therefore Yĕshua was saying to those Yehudim who had been pledging faithfulness to him, "If you will remain in my word, you are truly disciples of mine, ³²and you will know the truth, and the truth will make you free."

³³They answered him, "We are Avraham's offspring, and have never yet been serving as slaves to anyone. How is it that you say, 'You will become free'?" ³⁴Yĕshua answered them, "Amen, amen, I say to you, everyone who commits sin is the slave of sin. ³⁵And the slave does not remain in the house forever. The son does remain forever. ³⁶If therefore the Sŏn shall have made you free, you will be free indeed. ³⁷I have been knowing that you are Avraham's offspring, yet you seek to kill me, because my word has no place in you. ³⁸I am speaking the things which I have been seeing from alongside my Făther. Therefore you also are doing the things which you heard alongside your father."

³⁹They answered and said to him, "Avraham is our father." Yĕshua said to them, "If you are Avraham's children, do the deeds of Avraham. ⁴⁰But now, you are seeking to kill me, a man who has been telling you the truth, which I have heard from alongside the Almĭghty. This Avraham did not do. ⁴¹You are doing the deeds of your father." They said to him, "We have not been getting begotten from fornication. We have one Făther, even the Almĭghty."

⁴²Yĕshua said to them, "If the Almĭghty were your Făther, you would be loving me, because I proceeded forth and have been coming from the Almĭghty, because I have not been coming on my own, but that one sent me. ⁴³Why do you not understand what I am saying? It is because you cannot hear my word." ⁴⁴"You are of your father the Slanderer, and you are wanting to be doing the desires of your father. That one has been a murderer from the beginning, and has not been standing in the truth, because there is no truth in him. Whenever he may be speaking a lie, he is speaking on his own, because he is a liar, and the father of such. ⁴⁵And, because I speak the truth, you are not holding me faithful[π]. ⁴⁶Which one of you convicts me of sin? If I speak truth, why are you not holding me [π]faithful? ⁴⁷THE ONE BEING from the Almĭghty hears the words of the Almĭghty. For this reason you do not hear them, because you are not from the Almĭghty."

⁴⁸The Yehudim answered and said to him, "Do we not say rightly that you are a Shomroni and have a demon?" ⁴⁹Yĕshua answered, "I do not have a demon, but I honor my Făther, and you dishonor me. ⁵⁰But I do not seek my glory. There is one who seeks and judges. ⁵¹Amen, amen, I say to you, if anyone will have kept my word, he shall not have looked upon death forever." ⁵²The Yehudim said to him, "Now we *really* have been knowing that you have a demon. Avraham died, and the prophets also, and you say, 'If anyone will have kept my word,

---

High was confident of this result. ▷ So the next time someone brings up human inability (cf. Rom. 2:7), tell them the Son was able.

8:45, 46 π or 'not holding faithful to me."

he shall not have tasted death forever.' ⁵³Surely you are not greater than our father Avraham, who died? The prophets died too. Whom do you make yourself out to be?"

⁵⁴Yĕshua answered, "If I may have glorified myself, my glory is nothing. It is my Făther who glorifies me, of whom you say, 'He is our Almĭghty', ⁵⁵and you have not been knowing him, but I have been knowing him, and if I would have said that I have not been knowing him, I would be a liar like you, but I have been knowing him, and I am keeping his word. ⁵⁶Your father Avraham rejoiced that he will ⸤have been seeing⸥ my day, and he perceived *it* and was gladdened." ⁵⁷The Yehudim therefore said to him, "You are not yet fifty years old, and you have been seeing Avraham?" ⁵⁸Yĕshua said to them, "Amen, amen, I say to you, before Avraham was born, I AM·ᵡ." ⁵⁹Therefore they picked up stones, that they may throw *them* at him, but Yĕshua hid himself, and went out of the temple.

9

¹And⸋ as he passed by, he saw a man blind from ᶿbirth. ²And his disciples asked him, saying, "Rabbi, who sinned, this man or his parents, that he should have been begotten blind?" ³Yĕshua answered, "It is neither that this man sinned, nor his parents. ⸤But so that the works of the Almĭghty will have been displayed in him, ⁴we need to be working the works of him who sent me, as long as it is day. Night is coming, when no man can be working. ⁵While I may be in the world, I am the light of the world." ⁶When he had said this, he spit on the ground, and made clay of the spit, and applied the clay to his eyes, ⁷and he said to him, "Be going, wash in the pool of ᵠṢiloam," (which is translating: has been getting sent). And so he went away and washed, and came back seeing.

⁸The neighbors therefore, and those who previously saw him as a beggar, were saying, "Is not this the one who used to sit and beg?" ⁹Others were saying, "This is he." And others ⸤were saying "no," but⸥ that, "He is like him." He was saying, "I am·ᵘ." ¹⁰Therefore they were saying to him, "How then were your

---

8:58 χ Or, "I am HE" meaning the Holy One, the Almĭghty One, אֲנִי הוּא. See 13:19. See Mark 6:50 β. Strictly speaking the words are equivalent to אֲנִי הוּא which places the chief emphasis on identification between Mĕssiah and the Almĭghty. In other words, he is the same one as the "HE" who is Yăhweh Almĭghty. ▷ He is the same one as the Mĕssenger of Yăhweh of old, being in identity Gŏd, but in actuality existing as a human. The theology behind this is called KENOSIS, or 'emptying.' From time to time, during his ministry, however, his divine power was displayed, with the guidance of the Făther, to use it periodically, to show who he really was. His divine omnipotence was held in trust by the Făther, so that when it was used, it was jointly done. But when the Son is glorified, his divinity is not dependent on the Făther. ▷ Consider the divine name, Yahwej, (יְהֹוָה) which means "he makes become," and that the Most High does not always have to be creating. In fact, he rested on the seventh day. So likewise the Sŏn, for our sakes, ceased from his glory to reach us on our level. Consider also, that through death, the Făther is able to restore his soul, though truly speaking, it was the first death, and this does not involve destruction of both the body and soul. In fact, there seems to be a hint of divine preservation even in death, because his body did not see decay. ▷ We should also consider that arguments over the deity of Messiah tend to focus on his exercise of exclusivly divine attributes at all times, or possessing them at all times, rather than his identity, that is, who he is. And I think that Satan is much more occupied with getting people to deny who he is rather than just how much divine power he set aside in becoming human. I think who he is is the essential truth.

9:1 ⸋ Fall AD 32, perh. Ḥeshvan. **9:3** ν ἀλλ' ἵνα: join to vs. 4. **9:7** ψ perh. שְׁלוּחִים. Isa. 8:6. מֵי הַשִּׁלֹחַ הַהֹלְכִים = *waters of the one being sent which are flowing*. **9:1** θ lit. *from begetting*. The sense covers conception to birth. **9:9** μ Not an exception to 8:58.

eyes opened?" ¹¹He answered, "The man who is called Yĕshua made clay, and anointed my eyes, and said to me, 'Be going to Şiloam, and wash,' so I went away and washed, and I received sight." ¹²And they said to him, "Where is he?" He said, "I have not been knowing."

¹³They brought him who was formerly blind to the Perushim. ¹⁴Now it was a Şabbath on the day when Yĕshua made the clay, and opened his eyes. ¹⁵Therefore again, the Perushim were asking him also how he received his sight. And he said to them, "He applied clay to my eyes, and I washed, and I see." ¹⁶Therefore some of the Perushim were saying, "This man is not from beside the Almĭghty, because he does not keep the Şabbath." But others were saying, "How can a man who is a sinner perform such signs?" And there was a division among them. ¹⁷They said therefore to the blind man again, "What do you say about him, since he opened your eyes?" And he said, "He is a prophet."

¹⁸The Yehudim therefore did not hold it faithful about him, that he was blind, and had recovered sight, until they called the parents of him who has recovered sight, ¹⁹and questioned them, saying, "Is this your son, who you say was begotten blind? Then how does he now see?" ²⁰His parents answered them and said, "We have been knowing that this is our son, and that he was begotten blind, ²¹but how he is now seeing, we have not been knowing, or who opened his eyes, we have not been knowing. Ask him. He is of age, he will speak about himself." ²²His parents said this because they were afraid of the Yehudim, because the Yehudim had already been agreeing with themselves, that if anyone may have confessed him to be the Anŏinted One, he shall have been put out of the congregation. ²³For this reason his parents said, "He is of age. Ask him."

²⁴So a second time they called the man who was blind, and said to him, "Give glory to the Almĭghty. We have been knowing that this man is a sinner." ²⁵That one therefore answered, "Whether he is a sinner, I have not been knowing. One thing I have been knowing, that being blind, now I am seeing." ²⁶They said therefore to him, "What did he do to you? How did he open your eyes?" ²⁷He answered them, "I told you already, and you did not listen. Why are you wanting to be hearing *it* again? You are not wanting to become his disciples also?"

²⁸And they reviled him, and said, "You are his disciple, but we are disciples of Mosheh. ²⁹We have been knowing that the Almĭghty has been speaking to Mosheh^λ, but as for this man, we have not been knowing where he is from." ³⁰The man answered and said to them, "Surely, in this is an amazing thing, that you have not been knowing where he is from, and yet he opened my eyes. ³¹We have been knowing that THE ALMĬGHTY IS NOT HEARING SINNERS^α, but IF ANYONE

See Mark 6:50 β. When the question is, "Are you the man that was blind?" with answer "I am," then the object of the verb is in the question. **9:29** λ pres. perf. prog. Many Jews according to legend believed Moses was raised from the dead or translated to heaven without dying (cf. Jos. Ant. 4:326); They would in fact be correct to imply that Moses was still on speaking terms with the Almĭghty, as shown by the transfiguration accounts, or assumed by their legend, but his testimony was and will be to look to Mĕssiah. **9:31** α Psa 66:18, Isa 1:15. **9:31** β Psa 145:19, Prov 15.8.29.

MAY BE GŎD FEARING, AND MAY BE DOING HIS WILL, HE IS HEARING THIS ONE.ᵝ ³²From time immemorial it has not been heard that anyone opened the eyes of a person who had been getting begotten blind. ³³If this man were not from beside the Almĭghty, no, he could have been getting empowered to be doing nothing."

³⁴They answered and said to him, "You were begotten entirely in sins, and are you teaching us?" And they put him out. ³⁵Yĕshua heard that they had put him out, and finding him, he said, "Are you pledging faithfulness to the Sŏn of Man?" ³⁶He answered and said, "And who is he, Adŏni, that I may confirm faithfulness to him?" ³⁷Yĕshua said to him, "Yea, you have been seeing him, and the one who is talking with you is that one." ³⁸And he said, "Adŏnai, I confirm *my* loyalty." Then he worshiped him.

³⁹And Yĕshua said, "For judgment I came into this world, that those who are not seeing may be seeing, and so that those who are seeing will have become blind." ⁴⁰Those of the Perushim who were with him heard these things, and said to him, "We are not blind too, are we?" ⁴¹Yĕshua said to them, "If you were blind, you would have been having no sin, but since you say, 'We are seeing,' your sin is remaining."

10

¹Amʻen, amʻen, I am saying to you, he who is not entering by the door into the fold of the sheep, but is climbing up some other way, he is a thief and a robber. ²But he who is entering by the door is *the* shepherd of the sheep. ³To him the doorkeeper is opening, and the sheep are hearing his voice, and he is calling his own sheep by name, and is leading them out. ⁴When he may have put forth all his own, he is going before them, and the sheep are following him because they have been knowing his voice. ⁵And a stranger they simply will not follow, but will flee from him, because they have not been knowing the voice of strangers."

⁶This parable Yĕshua spoke to them, yet they did not know what those things were which he was saying to them. ⁷Yĕshua therefore said to them again, "Amʻen, amʻen, I am saying to you, I am the door of the sheep. ⁸All, as many as that came before me are thieves and robbers, but the sheep did not hear them. ⁹I am the door. If anyone may have entered through me, he will be rescued, and will go in and out, and will find pasture. ¹⁰The thief is not coming, except that he will have stolen, and will have slaughtered, and will have destroyed. I came that they may be having life, and may be having it abundantly."

¹¹"I am the good shepherd. The good shepherd is laying down his life on behalf of the sheep. ¹²He who is a hireling, and not a shepherd, who is not the owner of the sheep, sees the wolf coming, and leaves the sheep, and is fleeing, and the wolf is snatching them, and scattering them. ¹³Surely, he is a hireling, and is not caring about the sheep himself. ¹⁴I am the good shepherd. And I am knowing my own, and my own are knowing me, ¹⁵even as the Făther is knowing me and I am knowing the Făther, and I am laying down my soul on behalf of

Yoḥanan 10

the sheep. ¹⁶And I do have other sheep, which are not of this fold. Also those, I need to gather, and they will hear my voice, and they will become one flock, with one shepherd."

¹⁷"For this reason the Făther is loving me, because I am laying down my soul that I may receive it again. ¹⁸No one is taking it away from me, but I am laying it down on my own *initiative*. I have authority to lay it down, and I have authority to take it up again. This commandment I received from beside my Făther." ¹⁹There arose a division again among the Yehudim because of these words. ²⁰And many from them were saying, "He has a demon and is insane. Why are you listening to him?" ²¹Others were saying, "These are not the sayings of one being demon-possessed. A demon cannot open the eyes of the blind!"

²²At that time the feast of the ᵋḤanukkah took place in Yerushalayim. ²³It was winter, and Yĕshua was walking in the temple in the porch of Shelomoh. ²⁴The Yehudim therefore surrounded him, and were saying to him, "How long are you going to hold our souls in suspense? If you are the Anŏinted, tell us plainly." ²⁵Yĕshua answered them, "I told you, and you are not pledging faithfulness. The deeds that I am doing in my Făther's name, these are bearing witness about me. ²⁶But you are not pledging faithfulness because you are not from my sheep. ²⁷My sheep are hearing my voice, and I am knowing them, and they are following me, ²⁸and I am offering everlasting life to them, and no, they will not have perished forever, and no one will snatch them out of my hand. ²⁹My Făther, who has been giving them to me, is greater than all, and no one is able to be snatching them out of the Făther's hand. ³⁰I and the Făther are the same ᵘ."

10:16 The other sheep are the lost house of Yisraʾel. Gen. 48:19; Isa. 49:6; Eze. 37:19; cf. Zech. 11:14.

10:22 ξ ἐνκαίνια = חֲנֻכָּה = *dedication*, e.g. Neh. 12:27, LXX. December 18-25, AD 32. Kislev 25-Tevet 3; borrowed from Hebrew to Greek to English. Why is it permitted to observe Ḥanukkah, which is a traditional Jewish holiday commemorating a historical event, but it is not permitted to honor Christmas traditions? Deuteronomy 12:29-32 explains that many customs are relics with a past of idolatry and immoral pagan practices. Christianity has often uncritically adopted the pagan customs with a new narrative dedicating the customs to God. But this is exactly what the Torah says *not* to do. It is granted that the new narrative absolves those involved from the former paganism, but it still nevertheless offends the Most High to do this! He wants us to observe holy days that he designed for us with his redemptive narrative. ▷ And with Christmas and Easter it is worse than merely baptizing pagan custom. Baptizing pagan custom is simply an attempt to re-explain it in acceptable terms. But these two Christian traditions do not merely re-explain paganism in the service of God. They are frontal assaults on the appointed times we ARE commanded to observe. Easter Sunday is an attack on the Resurrection Sabbath, the solemnity of firstfruits, and also the Sabbath itself, and indirectly Passover also. And Christmas is an attack on the Feast of Trumpets (aka Rosh Hashanah), when Mĕssiah truly was born, and the entire instruction about this in Matthew and Luke. Christmas and Easter are two holidays commanded and ordered by the Church to *foil* biblical holy days. ▷ And in the end, the Church has not succeeded in baptizing pagan custom into the truth. They have in fact, along with it, changed the theology and meaning of Messiah's death to a pagan interpretation, especially in the Western Church via Augustine, Anselm, and Calvin.

10:30 μ His meaning is *I and the Făther are the same* in this respect, according vs. 28-29, that no one is able to snatch his faithful ones out of his hand, with the obvious implication that the Sŏn has the same power as the Făther to protect his own. ▷ By 'one' he is referring to a commonality of divine nature; cf. Gen. 11:1. The Sŏn is a separate person or existence with the same divine nature as the Făther, and not an emanation or generation of the Făther. The Făther and Sŏn relate to each other on the basis of love and faithfulness, and just as the Most High relates to himself, so also he wishes for us to relate to him. ▷ Later Christianity and Judaism defined the Most High as one indivisible being, but this idea was based on the Greek philosophy of perfection, and is not supported by the Scriptures. See Yoḥ. 17:3.

³¹The Yehudim took up stones again, so that they could stone him. ³²Yĕshua answered them, "I showed you many good deeds from the Făther. For which deed of these are you stoning me?" ³³The Yehudim answered him, "For a good deed we are not stoning you, but for blasphemy, even because you, being a man, are making yourself *to be the* ᶿAlmĭghty." ³⁴Yĕshua answered them, "Is it not what has been getting written in ᵁthe Law, 'I SAID, YOU ARE GODS⸢ᵋ⸣? ³⁵If he called those ones ᶜgods, to whom the **Word** of the Almĭghty had come, (and the Scripture cannot be broken), ³⁶**who** the Făther declared to be holy, and has sent into the world, you are saying, 'You are blaspheming,' because I said, ᴾ'I am the Almĭghty Sŏn'?" ³⁷"If I am not doing the deeds of my Făther, be not holding faithful *to* me, ³⁸yet, I am doing *them*; even if you may not be holding faithful *to* me, *then* be holding faithful the deeds, so that you will have known, and may be holding faithful, because the Făther *is* in me, and I in the Făther."

³⁹Therefore they were seeking again to seize him, and he went out of their hand. ⁴⁰And he went away again beyond the Yarden to the place where Yoḥanan was first immersing, and he stayed there. ⁴¹And many came to him and were saying that, "Surely, Yoḥanan performed not even one sign, yet all things Yoḥanan said about this one have been true." ⁴²And many confirmed faithfulness to him there.

11

¹Now ᵗ a certain man was sick, Elazar of Beṯh-anyah, the village of Miryam and her sister Marta. ²And it was the Miryam who anointed the Măster with ointment, and wiped his feet with her hair, whose brother Elazar was sick. ³The sisters therefore sent to him, saying, "Adŏnai, behold, he whom you love is sick." ⁴Yet, when Yĕshua heard it, he said, "This sickness is not unto death, ˣunless *it is* for the glory of the Almĭghty, so that the Almĭghty Sŏn will have been glorified by it."

⁵Now Yĕshua loved Marta, and her sister, and Elazar. ⁶When therefore he heard that he was sick, he stayed then two days longer in the place in which he was. ⁷Then after this, he is saying to the disciples, "Let us be going into Yehudah again." ⁸The disciples are saying to him, "Rabbi, the Yehudim now have been seeking to stone you, and again you are going there?" ⁹Yĕshua answered, "Are there not twelve hours in the day? If anyone may be walking in the day, he is

---

10:33 θ In the Hebrew discussion, the word would have been *Elohim* in all its usages, but the Greek translation varies between plural and singular to show when 'Almĭghty' vs. 'gods' is meant. **10:34** μ Omit "your" before Law. 𝔓⁴⁵ ℵ* D Θ *pc* it syˢ; Cyp. See 15:25, 8:17. **10:35** ζ These other 'gods' were *elohim*, meaning mighty-ones. They were immortal and had powers far exceeding humans, but they were not omnipotent like the Almĭghty. In the eyes of humans they would be termed *elohim*, technically demi-gods. Mĕssiah is not citing the text as if he were only one of these, and if he were defending himself on that basis. He cites the text only to raise the topic in Psa 82:1. He is the Almĭghty who stands in the council of El, i.e. that special one who is the kindred Sŏn to the Făther, the only kindred Almĭghty. See Yoḥ. 1:18; 3:16. They did not want to discuss it. **10:34** ξ "THE ALMĬGHTY IS STANDING IN THE COUNCIL OF GŎD. IN THE MIDST OF THE GODS HE JUDGES" (Psa. 82:1). Mĕssiah opened the topic with citing Psa 82:6, but the heart of the argument is in Psa. 82:1. But there are many others like it that show two divine persons mentioned in the same text. His opponents did not want to discuss it. See Isa. 48:16; Gen. 19:24; 32:30; 48:16. **10:36** ρ 'בֶן־הָאֱלֹהִים אָנִי.' **11:1** τ Winter, early AD 33.

11:4 χ The conjunction could also be translated, *except, if not,* or *but.* Mĕssiah's denial in the

not stumbling, because he is seeing the light of this world. ¹⁰Yet, if anyone may be walking in the night, he is stumbling, because the light is not in him."

¹¹These things he said, and after that he is saying to them, "Our friend Elazar has been sleeping, but I go, that I may awaken him." ¹²The disciples therefore said to him, "Adŏnai, if he has been sleeping, he will recover." ¹³Yet, Yĕshua had been speaking about his death, but they thought that he was speaking of the resting of sleep.

¹⁴Then Yĕshua therefore said to them plainly, "Elazar is dead, ¹⁵and I am rejoicing for your sakes, so that you will have ᵘconfirmed your faithfulness because I was not there, but let us be going to him." ¹⁶Toma, being called Didumos, said to his fellow disciples, "Let us also be going, so that we will have died with him."

¹⁷So when Yĕshua came, he found that he had already been in the tomb four days. ¹⁸Now Bĕth-anyah was near Yerushalayim, about fifteen stadia off, ¹⁹and many of the Yehudim had been coming to Marta and Miryam, that they may console them concerning their brother. ²⁰Marta therefore, when she heard that Yĕshua was coming, went to meet him, but Miryam still sat in the house.

²¹Marta therefore said to Yĕshua, "Adŏnai, if you were here, my brother would not have died. ²²Even now I have been knowing that whatever you may have asked of the Almĭghty, the Almĭghty will give you." ²³Yĕshua said to her, "Your brother will rise again." ²⁴Marta said to him, "I have been knowing that he will rise again in the resurrection on the last day." ²⁵Yĕshua said to her, "I am the resurrection and the life. He who is holding faithful to me, even if he may have died, will live *again*, ²⁶and everyone living and holding faithful to me, no, ᵝhe shall not have died forever. Do you hold ᵗthis faithful?" ²⁷She said to him, "Yes, Adŏnai. ᵘI have surely been holding faithful, because you are the Anŏinted, the Almĭghty Sŏn, he who comes into the world."

²⁸And when she had said this, she went away, and called Miryam her sister, saying secretly, "The Teacher is coming by, and is calling for you." ²⁹And when she heard it, she arose quickly, and was coming to him. ³⁰Now Yĕshua had not been coming into the village yet, but was still in the place where Marta met him. ³¹Then the Yehudim, who were with her in the house and consoling her, when they saw that Miryam had quickly risen and gone out, did follow her, supposing that she was going to the tomb that she may weep there.

³²Therefore, when Miryam came where Yĕshua was, she saw him, and fell

---

main clause is qualified or limited by the ἀλλ᾽ (, אֶלָּא, אִם־לֹא) clause: he will not die unless Gŏd is glorified by it. **11:15** μ or *proved, provided evidence for*. Josephus and Philo also use the noun form in the sense of *evidence* or *proof*. Heb. וְנָתַן Hiphil: *make, give, or provide support* for someone or something, thus confirm.

11:26 β→forever: μὴ ἀποθάνῃ εἰς τὸν αἰῶνα. Compare Yoh. 8:51-52. Elazar died again after being raised. So also others. The language allows for one who is holding faithful to temporarily die. Only 'to die forever' is being denied. **11:26** τ τοῦτο. He asked about believing an assertion. She answered with a confirmation of her loyalty. This is a case where holding faithful to important facts is equivocated with ultimate loyalty. Being a sensitive person, her answer was framed in terms of ultimate loyalty. **11:27** μ→faithful = הֶאֱמַן הֶאֱמַנְתִּי. Greek: *I have been holding faithful*, with emphasis on the continuing fact of it, thus the progressive perfect tense is used.

at his feet, saying to him, "Adŏnai, if you were here, my brother would not have died." ³³When Yĕshua therefore saw her weeping, and the Yehudim who came with her, also weeping, he was deeply moved in spirit, and was troubled, ³⁴and said, "Where have you been putting him?" They said to him, "Adŏnai, be coming and see." ³⁵Yĕshua wept.

³⁶And so the Yehudim were saying, "Behold how he loved him!" ³⁷Yet, some of them said, "This one was not able, who opened the eyes of the blind, to have made *it* so that this one may not have died!"

³⁸Therefore Yĕshua being deeply moved again within, came to the tomb. Now it was a cave, and a stone was lying against it. ³⁹Yĕshua says, "Remove the stone." Marta, the sister of the one who had been expiring, is saying to him, "Adŏnai, by this time there will be a stench, because it is four days."

⁴⁰Yĕshua says to her, "Did I not say to you, that if you ᶲshall hold faithful, you will see the glory of the Almĭghty?" ⁴¹And so they removed the stone. And Yĕshua raised his eyes upward, and said, "Făther, I am thanking you that you hear me. ⁴²And I had been knowing that you are hearing me always, but because of the multitude, who have been standing around, I have said it, so that they will have ᵚconfirmed *their* loyalty, ᵋthrough seeing that you have sent me."

⁴³And when he had said these things, he cried out with a loud voice, "Elazar, come forth." ⁴⁴He who had been dying came forth, who had been getting bound feet and hands with wrappings, and his face had been getting wrapped around with a cloth. Yĕshua said to them, "Unbind him, and let him go." ⁴⁵Many therefore of the Yehudim, who had come to Miryam and beheld what he had done, confirmed faithfulness to him.

⁴⁶But some of them went away to the Perushim, and told them the things which Yĕshua had done. ⁴⁷Therefore the chief priests and the Perushim convened the Sanhedrin, and were saying, "What are we doing? For this man is performing many signs. ⁴⁸If we let him go on like this, all men will confirm faithfulness to him, and the Romans will come and take away both our place and our nation."

⁴⁹But a certain one of them, Qayafa, being high priest that year, said to them, "You have been knowing nothing at all, ⁵⁰nor are you taking into account that it is expedient for you that one man will have died on behalf ofᵚ the people, and that the whole nation will not have perished." ⁵¹Now this he did not say on

---

11:40 ϕ→faithful: or *may hold firm, may keep steadfast*. He isn't asking her to completely trust it will happen then, but he is asking her to have enough courage to go through with his plan. So she consented to the removal of the stone. **11:42** ω→loyalty: 1. in the sense of 'to provide evidence' or 'proof' for staying loyal, or 2. initial affirming/pledge of faithfulness, or 3. held *it* faithful (i.e. that Yeshua did the miracle). **11:42** ξ ὅτι = בַּאֲשֶׁר = *in that, seeing that, because*. Or ὅτι = *that: held [it] faithful (believed) that you have sent me*. It is certain that original speakers and readers perceived the sense as a totality and not as exclusive choices. Thus all of the above is included in the affirmation.

11:50 ψ ὑπὲρ. Cf. vs. 51. See 18:14. The observation in vs. 48 was quite correct. If Messiah had continued to win disciples without meeting up with the internal transgression and corruption of Yisra'el's leadership, the Romans would come and take away their place and nation due to the mounting internal conflict. Continued in Endnotes, page 609.

his own initiative, but being high priest that year, he prophesied that Yĕshua was going to die on behalf of the nation, ⁵²and not on behalf of the nation only, but that he might also gather together into ˣone the children of the Almĭghty who had been getting scattered abroad. ⁵³So from that day on, they planned together that they may kill him. ⁵⁴Yĕshua therefore no longer continued to walk publicly among the Yehudim, but ʳwent away from there to the country near the wilderness, into a city called Ephrayim and there he stayed with the disciples.

⁵⁵Now the ʳPassover of the Yehudim was at hand, and many went up to Yerushalayim out of the country before the Passover, so that they may purify themselves. ⁵⁶Therefore they were seeking for Yĕshua, and were saying to one another, when they had been standing in the temple, "What do you think, that no, he may not have come to the feast?" ⁵⁷Now the chief priests and the Perushim had been putting out warrants, (that if anyone may have known where he was, he will have reported it) so that they may seize him.

12

¹Then Yĕshua, ᵝsix days before the Passover, came to Beṭh-anyah where Elazar wasᶲ, who Yĕshua had raised from the dead. ²Then they made him a dinner there, and Marta was serving, but Elazar was one of those reclining at the table with him. ³Miryam therefore took a pound of very costly perfume of pure spikenard, and anointed the feet of Yĕshua, and wiped his feet with her hair, and the house was filled with the fragrance of the perfume. ⁴But Yehudah

---

11:52 χ ἕν = יַחַד = Yaḥad. Yoḥanan is alluding to the two sticks prophecy here. See Ezek. 37:22; Deut. 33:5: *And he will be king among the upright ones, at the gathering of the heads of the people as One, the tribes of Yisra'el.* See Gal. 3:28. **11:54** τ At the beginning of AD 33. Then from here he retreated to Caesarea Philippi. **11:55** τ AD 34. Most of the missing year is filled in by Luke. The text raises the question why Yoḥanan thought it was necessary to specify the Passover of the Jews. He does so in 2:13, 6:4, and here in 11:55. The point is made in the first text that Yĕshua went up at this time. Some have charged Yoḥanan with antisemitism, so as to imply he observes a different Passover and so must specify that a Jewish one is meant in his history. But this explanation is idle speculation without regard for the times, and is founded on the assumption that the Messianic Faith rejected the Law. The true explanation is undoubtedly that Yoḥanan wanted to promote the Jewish calculation of Passover over and against a widespread non-Jewish sectarian corruption. ▷ For Yoḥanan wrote his book at a time when the Messianic Faith had begun to diverge into different sects primarily among non-Jews, many misunderstanding the other Evangelists, and observing Passover at the wrong times disregarding the Jewish example. His point is that Yĕshua and his disciples observe Passover with the Jews and further that it is the Judean Passover that was at the correct time vs. other sects, such as the Essene Passover, because at that time the Jews were still observing the months according to the sighting of the new moon, and the year was still set so that the first day of the feast would not occur before the equinox. Some factions of the Messianic Faith had an unhealthy attraction to the book of pseudo-Enoch, the book of Jubilees, and other literature promoting the corrupt Qumran Calendar. ▷ Yoḥanan clearly recognized the problems and set out to correct these sectarian errors on the correct timing of Passover and the fact that the last supper was before the Passover. Yoḥanan also set out to rebuke the anti-law theology of gnostic sects and to return many to a clearer understanding of the Messianic Faith.

12:1 β→Passover: The Passover means the time of the sacrifice, the afternoon of Nisan 14. Counting back six days brings us to Nisan 8. This makes Nisan 13 the day before Passover and Nisan 12 two days before Passover, which agrees with Mark 14:1 and Mat. 26:2. I reckon then that this journey was on Nisan 8, a Thursday. They had a late supper, and the dinner (12:2-11) was served on Friday afternoon, Nisan 9. **12:1** β→days: The six days causes terrible problems for the Friday crucifixion chronology. The scribe of 𝔓⁶⁶ detected this and changed his text to read "five" instead of six. **12:1** ϕ After Elazar was raised, he Miryam and Marta retired to a village somewhere in Galilee of unknown location (Luke 10:38-42). Marta had many worries at the time, and these proved valid. The Pharisees laid a plot on Elazar's life. Yĕshua stopped by on his last journey to Jerusalem in the fall of

Ish-Qeriyot, one of his disciples, who was intending to betray him, said, ⁵"Why was this perfume not sold for three hundred dinars, and given to poor people?" ⁶Now he said this, not because he was concerned about the poor, but because he was a thief, and as he had the money-box, he used to pilfer what was put into it.

⁷Yĕshua therefore said, "Let her alone, in order that she will have kept *the rest of* it for the day of my burial. ⁸For the poor you always have with you, but you do not always have me."

⁹The great crowd therefore of the Yehudim learned that he was there, and they came, not for Yĕshua' sake only, but that they will also have seen Elazar, who he raised from the dead. ¹⁰Yet, the chief priests had held counsel that they should put Elazar to death also, ¹¹because on account of him many of the Yehudim were going away, and were confirming faithfulness to Yĕshua.

¹²On the ᶿnext day the great crowd who had come to the feast, when they heard that Yĕshua was coming to Yerushalayim, ¹³took the branches of the palm trees, and went out to meet him, and were crying out, "HOSHA'NA!ᵅ HAVING BEEN GETTING BLESSED IS **THE COMING ONE** IN THE NAME OF YĂHWEH,ᵝ even THE KING OF YISRA'EL.ᵟ" ¹⁴And Yĕshua, when he found a young donkey, sat on it, even as it is what has been getting written, ¹⁵"BE FEARING NOT, DAUGHTER OF TSIYON. BEHOLD, YOUR KING IS COMING, SEATED ON A DONKEY'S COLT.ᵘ"

¹⁶These things his disciples did not understand at the first, but when Yĕshua was glorified, then they remembered that these things had been getting written about him, and that they did these things to him. ¹⁷Accordingly, the multitude being with him, when he called Elazar out of the tomb, and raised him from the dead, was testifying. ¹⁸Because of this ᶲa multitude ᶓmet up with him, because they heard about ᵝthis, *about* ᵝhim ᵟwho had been doing the sign. ¹⁹The Perushim therefore said to themselves, "You see that no, you are gaining no one. Look, the world has gone after him!"

²⁰Now there were certain Greeks among those who were going up, that they may worship at the feast. ²¹These therefore came to Philip, who was from Beth-tsaidah of Galil, and were asking him, saying, "Sir, we wish to see Yĕshua." ²²Philip came and told Andrew. Andrew and Philip came, and they told Yĕshua. ²³And Yĕshua answered them, saying, "The ˣhour has been coming, wherein the Sŏn of Man may be glorified. ²⁴Amen, amen, I say to you, unless a grain of wheat, having fallen into the earth, may have died, it remains by itself alone, yet if it may have died, it bears much fruit. ²⁵He who loves his life is losing it, and he who hates his life in this age will keep it to life everlasting. ²⁶If anyone may be serving me, let him be following me, and where I am, there will my servant

---

AD 33. Here they laid plans to return to their old house at Bethany for a season just before the Passover of AD 34. Many saw the evidence that Elazar was raised and confirmed their faithfulness to Mĕssiah at that time.

12:12 θ→day: Şabbath, Nisan 10, AD 34. March 20. **12:13** α Psa 118:25. **12:13** β Psa 118:26. **12:13** δ

Zeph 3:15. **12:15** μ Zech 9:9. **12:18** φ txts omit ὁ **12:18** ξ txts omit καί. **12:18** β double accusative. 'this' should not be transposed to 'sign.' It had been a year since the raising of Elazar. **12:18** δ→done = who had been doing. **12:23** χ = *time*. Greek uses the word 'hour' as its general word for 'time,' like Hebrew 'day.'

also be. If anyone may be serving me, the Făther will honor him.

²⁷"Now my soul has been getting troubled, and what shall I have said, 'Făther, rescue me from this hour?' But for this purpose I came to this hour. ²⁸Făther, glorify your name." There came therefore a voice out of heaven: "I have both glorified it, and will glorify it again." ²⁹The crowd, therefore, which had been standing by and heard *it*, were saying, "thunder has been occurring." Others were saying, "A messenger has been speaking to him." ³⁰Yĕshua answered and said, "This voice had not been happening for my sake, but for your sakes. ³¹*As it stands* now, the judgment is upon this world. Now *it is that* the ruler of this world will be cast out. ³²And I, if I shall have been lifted up from the earth, will draw all men to myself." ³³But he was saying this to indicate the kind of death by which he was to die.

³⁴The crowd therefore answered him, "We have heard out of the Law that THE ANŎINTED IS TO REMAIN FOREVER". And how can you say, 'The Sŏn of Man must be lifted up'? ³⁵Yĕshua therefore said to them, "For a little while longer the light is among you. Be walking while you have the light, that darkness will not have overtaken you. And he who is walking in the darkness has not been knowing where he goes. ³⁶While you have the light, be holding faithful to the light, in order that you will have become sons of light." These things Yĕshua spoke, and he departed and hid himself from them.

³⁷Yet, though he had been performing so many signs before them, they were not confirming faithfulness to him, ³⁸so that the word of Yeshayahu the prophet may be fulfilled, which he spoke, "YĂHWEḤ, WHO HOLDS FAITHFUL OUR REPORT? AND TO WHOM HAS THE ARM OF YĂHWEḤ BEEN REVEALED?"_ϕ_ ³⁹For this cause they were not able to pledge faithfulness, because Yeshayahu said again, ⁴⁰"HE ᵝHAS BEEN BLINDING THEIR EYES, AND HE ᵞHAS HARDENED THEIR HEART, SO THAT THEY MAY NOT HAVE SEEN WITH THEIR EYES, THEN THEY SHALL HAVE PERCEIVED WITH THEIR HEART, AND MAY HAVE RETURNED, AND I WILL HEAL THEM^α."

⁴¹These things Yeshayahu said when he saw his glory, and he spoke of him. ⁴²Nevertheless many even of the rulers affirmed faithfulness to him, but because of the Perushim they were not publicly agreeing, lest they will have been put out of the congregation, ⁴³because they loved the approval of men rather than the approval of the Almĭghty.

⁴⁴And Yĕshua cried out and said, "He who confirms faithfulness to me is not confirming faithfulness to me only, but also to him who sent me. ⁴⁵And he who is looking at me is looking at the One who sent me. ⁴⁶I have been coming as light into the world, that everyone who confirms faithfulness to me may not have remained in darkness.

⁴⁷And if anyone may have heard my sayings, and may not have kept them,

---

12:34 η 2 Sam 7:13; Psa 89:30.37; Eze 37:25; Psa 110:4; Isa 9:7. **2:38** ϕ Isa 53:1. **12:40** α Isa 6:9-10. **12:40** β→blinded = הֵשַׁע. **12:38** γ→hardened = will have made fat = הִשְׁמֵן. See Mat. 13:15. There appear to be two basic ways of reading the Isa. text, either of external hardening of the heart or of self induced hardening of the heart. One leads to the other.

I do not judge him, because I did not come that I may judge the world, but that I may rescue the world. ⁴⁸He rejecting me, and receiving not my sayings, has one judging him. The word which I have spoken is what will judge him at the last day. ⁴⁹For I have not spoken by myself, BUT THE FĂTHER HIMSELF WHO SENT ME HAS BEEN GIVING ME COMMANDMENT, WHAT I SHOULD SAY, AND WHAT I SHOULD SPEAK.ᵘ ⁵⁰And I have been knowing that his commandment is everlasting life. Therefore the things I am speaking, I speak just as the Făther has been telling me."

13 ¹Now beforeᵀ the Feast of the Passover, Yĕshua—who had been knowing that his time has come, that he would depart out of this world to the Făther, who loved his own who were in the world, (to the end he loved them), ²and supper happening, the Slanderer already having been putting it into the heart of Yehudah Ish-Qeriyot, *the son* of Şim'on, that he will have betrayed him, ³who had been knowing that the Făther has given all things to him, into *his* hands, and that he had come forth from the Almĭghty, and near to the Almĭghty he is going off, ⁴raises himself from the supper, and lays aside his garments, and having taken a cloth apron, wrapped himself about.

⁵Then he is pouring water into the basin, and began to be washing the disciples' feet, and to be wiping them with the cloth apron which he had been wrapping around himself. ⁶And so he came to Şim'on Peter. He said to him, "Adŏnai, do you wash my feet?" ⁷Yĕshua answered and said to him, "What I do, you have not been understanding now, but you will understand after these things." ⁸Peter said to him, "No, you will not have washed my feet!" Yĕshua answered him, "If I will not have washed you, you have no part with me." ⁹Şim'on Peter said to him, "Adŏnai, not my feet only, but also my hands and my head."

¹⁰Yĕshua is saying to him, "He who has been bathing is not having the need, except to wash the feet, but is completely clean, and you are clean, but not all." ¹¹For he had been knowing the one betraying him. For this reason he said, "You are not all clean."

¹²And so when he had washed their feet, and had taken his garments, and had reclined at the table again, he said to them, "Do you know what I have been doing for you? ¹³You call me Teacher and the Măster, and you are right, because so I am. ¹⁴If I then, the Măster and the Teacher, have washed your feet, you also ought to wash one another's feet, ¹⁵because an example I have given you, that even as I did for you, also you should be doing."

12:49 μ Deu 18:18.
13:1 τ At the end of Aviv 13 after dark. Tuesday night. The statement that it was before the Passover is confirmed in 19:14 where it says it was the preparation for the Passover, and in 18:28 where the Passover had not yet been eaten, and likewise in 19:31 where they were urgent to get Mĕssiah's execution finished before the annual Sabbath. They would never have been so urgent if the execution had been on the first day of unleavened bread. For then the holy day would already be defiled. Finally, the disciples supposing something might be purchased during the last supper (cf. 13:29; Neh. 10:31) along with other facts make it certain that the supper happened before Passover. The attendant mistranslations and misinterpretations of the other Evangelists fairly yield to correction as shown in the relevant passages. ▷ Yoḥ. 13:1-4 is one long sentence, the appositives all being marked by participles, conjunctions, or prepositions (e.g.). Yĕshua's name in vs. 1 is the subject. The sentence completes with the main verb at vs. 4: ἐγείρεται = raises himself

Yoḥanan 13

¹⁶"Amen, amen, I am saying to you, a slave is not greater than his master. Neither is an emissary greater than the one who sent him. ¹⁷If you have been understanding these things, you are blessed if you may be doing them."

¹⁸"I do not speak of all of you. I have been knowing whom I have chosen, but it is that the text may be fulfilled, 'HE WHO EATS MY BREAD HAS LIFTED UP HIS HEEL AGAINST ME.'ᵠ ¹⁹From now on I am telling you before it has happened, so that when it will have happened, you will have held faithful, in that ᵞI AM. ²⁰Amen, amen, I say to you, he who receives whomever I may have sent receives me, and he who receives me receives him who sent me."

²¹When Yĕshua had said this, he became troubled in spirit, and testified, and said, "Amen, amen, I say to you, that one of you will betray me." ²²The disciples were looking at one another, at a loss to know of which one he was speaking. ²³There was reclining on Yĕshua's breast one of his disciples, whom Yĕshua loved. ²⁴Shim'on Peter therefore gestured to him, and said to him, "Tell us who it is of whom he is speaking." ²⁵He, leaning back thus on Yĕshua' breast, said to him, "Adŏnai, who is it?" ²⁶Yĕshua therefore answered, "That is the one for whom I will dip the morsel and give it to him." So when he had dipped the morsel, he took and gave it to Yehudah, the son of Şim'on Ish-Qeriyot.

²⁷And after the morsel, Satan then entered into him. Yĕshua therefore said to him, "What you do, do quickly." ²⁸Now no one of those reclining at the table knew for what purpose he had said this to him. ²⁹For some were supposing, because Yehudah had the money box, that Yĕshua was saying to him, "Buyᶿ the things we have need of for the feast", or else, that he should give something to the poor. ³⁰And so after receiving the morsel he went out immediately, and it was night.

³¹When therefore he had gone out, Yĕshua said, "Now the Sŏn of Man will have been glorified, and the Almĭghty will have been glorified in him. ³²If the Almĭghty will have been glorified in him, the Almĭghty will also glorify him in

---

(middle voice). It is thus perfectly clear that the whole occasion was 'before the Passover.'

13:18 ψ Psa 41:9. **13:19** γ→AM: At first sight, it would seem to most readers that "I AM" is taken from Exodus 3:14, but this not the case (see on Mark 6:50). "THUS YOU SHALL SAY TO THE SONS OF YIS-RA'EL, **I MAKE BE** HAS SENT ME UNTO YOU" (Exodus 3:14b). The Hebrew אֶהְיֶה means "I make be," or "I make happen." What Yĕshua says here is: אֲנִי־הוּא, "I AM," which is equivalent of the literal Greek ἐγώ εἰμι in terms of LXX usage. ▷ I AM and I AM THE ONE WHO MAKES BE," refer to the Almighty, but the former is a function of identity, and the latter of nature. ▷ One might translate, "I am he," but it means, "I am Yăhweḥ," and not simply I am the Mĕssiah. ▷ "I AM" without a separate pronoun "he", which is absent in the Greek, better makes the point that he is saying he is Yăhweḥ. The bridge between ἐγώ εἰμι and the divine name may be connected contextually via "I AM HE" (אֲנִי־הוּא) in the following passages. ▷ See Isa. 41:4 (LXX: ἐγώ εἰμι), "I YĀHWEḤ AM THE FIRSTMOST, AND THE LASTMOST, I AM HE" (אֲנִי־הוּא, ἐγώ εἰμι). Also Isa. 43:10, "I AM HE, AT MY FACE NO GŎD HAS BEEN FORMED, AND AFTER ME NONE WILL BE" (I am He: אֲנִי הוּא, ἐγώ εἰμι). And Isa. 43:13, "EVEN BEFORE DAY EXISTED, I AM HE." Isa. 46:4, "AND ONWARD YOUR OLD AGE, I AM HE." Isa. 48:12, "I AM HE, I AM FIRST, YEA I AM LAST" (אֲנִי הוּא, ἐγώ εἰμι). Isa. 52:6, "I AM HE, THE ONE MAKING BE SPOKEN, LOOK IT'S ME" (אֲנִי הוּא, ἐγώ εἰμι). The connection is also made in the LXX of Isa. 45:18, "ἐγώ εἰμι καὶ οὐκ ἔστιν ἔτι" = "I AM YĀHWEḤ, AND NONE YET" (אֲנִי יְהוָה וְאֵין עוֹד). Also Isa. 51:12, "I, I AM HE…" (אָנֹכִי אָנֹכִי הוּא, ἐγώ εἰμι ἐγώ εἰμι.) See note on Mark 6:50.

13:29 θ This proves without a doubt that it was Nisan 14 on which the last super occurred. For the buying and selling of food was prohibited on Nisan 15. See Nehemiah 10:31.

himself, and will glorify him straightaway. ³³Little children, I am with you a little while longer. You will seek me, and as I said to the Yehudim, I now say to you also, 'Where I am going, you cannot come.'"

³⁴"A new-made commandment I am giving to you, that you shall be loving one another, even as I have loved you, that you also should be loving one another. ³⁵By this all will know that you are my disciples, if you may be having love for one another^φ."

³⁶Şim'on Peter said to him, "Adŏnai, where are you going?" Yĕshua answered, "Where I go, you cannot follow me now, but you will follow later." ³⁷Peter said to him, "Adŏnai, why can I not follow you right now? I will lay down my life on behalf of you." ³⁸Yĕshua answered, "Will you lay down your life on behalf of me? Amen, amen, I say to you, a rooster shall not have sounded, until for it you deny me three times.

14

Let not your heart be getting troubled. Be holding faithful to the Almĭghty and be holding faithful to me. ²In my Făther's house are many dwellings. If it were not so, would I have told you that I go to prepare a place for you? ³And if I shall have gone, and shall have prepared a place for you, I am coming again, and will receive you to myself, so that where I am you may be also. ⁴And where I am going, you have been knowing the way."

⁵Toma says to him, "Adŏnai, we have not been knowing where you are going. How are we able to have been knowing the way?" ⁶Yĕshua said to him, "I am the way, and the truth, and the life. No one comes to the Făther, except through me." ⁷ "If you have been knowing me, even my Făther you will know. From just now you are knowing him, and have been seeing him."

⁸Philip says to him, "Adŏnai, show us the Făther, and it is enough for us." ⁹Yĕshua says to him, "So long a time I am being with you, and you have not been knowing me, Philip? The one who has been seeing me has been seeing the Făther. How are you saying, 'Show us the Făther'? ¹⁰Are you not ^πholding faithful,

---

13:34-35 φ Love your neighbor as yourself is the second greatest commandment, and there are no greater commandments than this one and the commandment to love the Almĭghty. See Mark 12:31. But there is a question, "Who is my neighbor?" See Luke 10:29. So Mĕssiah gives us some guidelines on the meaning of the commandment which has been unjustly limited by human rationalizations and fears. Firstly, he already taught that our neighbor is not just those who love us or who can pay us back or who it is convenient to assist. Even those who hate us and persecute us might be included. Even our enemies can be included. He did not mean all, but the Spĭrit will show us which ones. There is another commandment to flee from persecution. See Mat. 10:23. There is another commandment to shake off the dust from our feet for those who reject the good news. See Luke 9:5. Obviously these people are not going to be so much our neighbors. Obviously helping some people is going to make enemies of others whom we may have to fight. ▷ The new-made commandment is a further refinement of "Who is my neighbor?" It is a guideline for appropriating our love, because the Almĭghty also has to appropriate his love. See Exodus 20:6; John 14:21; 15:10. The answer is that we are to especially love the household of the faith (Gal. 6:10) who are the disciples and followers of Mĕssiah. This then is the fresh and new understanding of the old commandment. These people are especially our neighbors. See 1 John 2:7-11.

14:10 π or *holding [it] trustworthy, considering [it] trustworthy;* **14:10** ω or *because, seeing that.* 'Seeing that' is a translation in between 'that' and 'because.' It is possible that an ὅτι (בְּ) clause supplies reasonable evidence confirming one's faithfulness to Mĕssiah, especially when the evidence is so profound that it motivates loyalty, and such should be the case

ᵃ"seeing that I am in the Făther, and the Făther is in me? The words that I say to you I do not speak on my own, but the Father abiding in me does his deeds."

¹¹"Be holding faithful ᵠto me, through seeing that I am in the Făther, and the Făther is in me. If not, be holding faithful on account of the deeds themselves. ¹²Am̌en, am̌en, I am saying to you, the one holding faithful to me, the deeds which I am doing he will do also. And greater than these he will do, because I go to the Făther."

¹³And whatever you may have asked in my name*ᵘ*, that will I do, so that the Făther may be glorified in the Sŏn. ¹⁴If you will have asked me anything in my name, I will do it— ¹⁵if you may be loving me—keepᵚ my commandments!

¹⁶"And I will ask the Făther, and he will give you another Advocate, that he may be with you forever, ¹⁷who is the Spǐrit of truth, who the world cannot receive, because it does not behold him or know him. You know him because he remains beside you, and will be in you. ¹⁸I will not leave you orphans. I will come to you. ¹⁹In a little while the world will see me no longer, but you will see me. Because I live, you will live also. ²⁰In that day you will know that I am in my Făther, and you in me, and I in you. ²¹He who has my commandments and keeps them, he it is who loves me, and he who loves me will be loved by my Făther, and I will love him, and will disclose myself to him."

²²Yehudah (not Ish-Qeriyot) said to him, "Adŏnai, then what has been happening that you are about to disclose yourself to us, and not to the world?" ²³Yĕshua answered and said to him, "If anyone may be loving me, he will keep my word. And my Făther will love him, and we will come to him, and we will make our dwelling beside him. ²⁴He who is not loving me is not keeping my words, and the word which you are hearing is not mine *only*, ᵃbut it is the Făther's who sent me.

²⁵"These things I have been speaking to you, while dwelling beside you. ²⁶But the Counselor, the Holy Spǐrit, whom the Făther will send in my name—that one will teach you all things, and he will cause you to remember all that I say to you.

---

with the disciples witnessing Mĕssiah, and talking and walking with him for four years. It is therefore not certain that the text means holding the mere fact that the Mĕssiah is in the Făther, and the Făther in Mĕssiah, trustworthy. Rather seeing Mĕssiah results in the knowledge of the Almighty, and this is the instructional pattern by which we hold faithful to Him (cf. Jer. 31:32-34). If we see him as he is, then we will be like him. The question is rhetorical. Of course Philip is holding faithful because he has observed the Son. Also the question in vs. 9 is rhetorical. Philip knew him, and the Făther as a result. He simply did not connect the intellectual dots.

14:11 ψ The lack of the preposition before the dative case makes the use of the verb ambiguous. It could refer to holding Mĕssiah trustworthy, but appears that 'holding faithful to him' is really meant. The interpretation of the conjunction as 'because' is reinforced by the parallel διά at the end of the verse, and the explicit use of the preposition εἰς in the next verse.

14:13 μ or 'according to my name,' or 'in connection to' it. The name of Messiah is not a magic charm at the end of a prayer to make it happen. The pronunciation, form of, or even saying his name is not so important as knowing his name. But knowing his name means to know his character and what he is like. To be in the name of Messiah requires holding faithful to Messiah. To bear his name means to represent him. To know it means to keep his commandments. His name is his reputation. To be in it means to uphold it. See also *Mark* 11:22. **14:15** ω τηρήσατε, 'you must keep' or τηρήσετε 'you will keep,' or τηρήσητε 'you should keep.'

14:24 α The Greek conjunction is not only used to oppose statements, but also to limit a preceding statement with a qualification. Sometimes a negative is used this way in Hebrew as in Exodus 6:3-4, "AND BY MY NAME YĂHWEH I HAD NOT [ONLY] MADE MYSELF KNOWN TO THEM, BUT ALSO I HAD MADE STAND MY COVENANT WITH THEM...."

²⁷"Shalom I leave with you. My peace I give to you. Not as the world gives, do I give to you. Let not your heart be getting troubled, nor let it be fearing. ²⁸You heard that I said to you, 'I go away, and I come to you.' If you were loving me, you would be joyful, because I am going to the Făther. For the Făther is ᶲgreater than me.

²⁹"And now I have been telling you before it happens, that when it may have happened, you will have held faithful. ³⁰I will not speak much longer with you, because the one ruling the world system is coming, and he holds nothing over me, ³¹except that the world will have known that I am loving the Făther, and even as the Făther has commanded me, so I am doing. Be rising, we should be going from here.

15

¹"I am the true vine, and my Făther is the cultivator. ²Every branch in me not bearing fruit, he is taking away. And every one bearing fruit, he is cleaning it off, so that it may be bearing more fruit. ³You are already clean through the word which I have been speaking to you. ⁴Remain in me, and I in you. As the branch is not able to be bearing fruit by itself, unless it may be remaining in the vine, so not even you *can*, unless you may be remaining in me.

⁵"I am the vine; you are the branches. The one remaining in me, and I in him, is bearing much fruit. For apart from me you are able to be doing nothing. ⁶If anyone may not be remaining in me, he is going to be thrown out like the branch, and will have been dried up. Then they are gathering them, and casting them into the fire, and it is burning *them*.

⁷"If you may have remained in me, and my words may have remained in you, whatever you may be desiring, ask, and it will happen for you. ⁸By this my Făther will have been glorified, that you may be bearing much fruit, and will have become my disciples.

⁹"Just as the Făther loves me, so also I love you. Remain in my love. ¹⁰If you may have kept my commandments, you will remain in my love, just as I have been keeping my Făther's commandments, and remain in his love. ¹¹These things I have been speaking to you, so that my joy may be in you, and so that your joy will have been full.

¹²"This is my commandment, that you shall be loving one another, just as I have loved you. ¹³Greater love no one is having than this, that one may lay down his soul on behalf of his friends. ¹⁴You are my friends, if you may be doing what I am commanding you. ¹⁵No longer *will* I keep calling you servants, because the servant has not been knowing what his master is doing, but I will have been calling you friends, because all things that I have heard from beside my Făther I have made known to you. ¹⁶You did not choose me, but I chose you, and ap-

---

14:28 ᶲ Cf. Hos. 5:14-6:3. Greater than me: this means that the Sŏn having assumed a lower position by taking the form of man, and limiting himself thereto, is less exalted than the Făther. But upon returning to the Făther, the Sŏn will take up again the glory and exaltedness which were his from time everlasting. The transformation can be witnessed in Revelation 1:13-18. Therefore, the disciples should have joy for the Sŏn that he will soon take up that which he has put aside to suffer alongside men as a man. And then returning in glory, he will put down all his enemies and settle the faithful into his kingdom.

15:16 δ See 14:13; *Mark* 11:22.

pointed you, that you may be going and bearing fruit, and that your fruit may be remaining, so that whatever you may have asked the Fǎther in my name,⁸ he shall have given to you. ¹⁷These things I am commanding you, that you may be loving one another.

¹⁸"If the world is hating you, you are knowing that it has been hating me before you. ¹⁹If you were of the world, the world would love its own, but because you are not of the world, but I chose you out of the world, therefore the world hates you. ²⁰Be remembering the word that I said to you, 'A slave is not greater than his master.' If they persecuted me, they will also persecute you. If they kept my word, they will keep yours also. ²¹But all these things they will do to you because of my name, in that they have not been knowing the One who sent me.

²²"If I had not come and spoken to them, they would not have been having sin, but now they are having no excuse for their sin. ²³The one who is hating me also is hating my Fǎther. ²⁴If I did not do among them the deeds which no one other did, they would not have been having sin, but now also they have been seeing, and they have been hating me and my Fǎther. ²⁵But *this is* where the word will have been fulfilled that has been getting written in the ʸLaw, 'THEY HATED ME WITHOUT REASON.'ᵝ ²⁶When the Counselor will have come, he whom I will send to you from beside the Fǎther—the Spirit of truth, who from beside the Fǎther is going forth, that one will bear witness about me, ²⁷and you are *about to be* bearing witness also, because you are with me ᶠat the beginning.

16

¹"These things I have been saying to you, so that you will not have stumbled. ²They will make you outcasts from the congregation, but an hour is coming that everyone having killed you shall have thought *himself* to be offering a service to the Almǐghty. ³And these things they will do, because they have not known the Fǎther, or me. ⁴But these things I have been saying to you, that when their hour may have come, you may be remembering that I told you *of them*. And, these things I did not say to you at the beginning, because I was with you.

⁵"But now I am going to him who sent me, and none of you asks me, 'Where are you going?' ⁶But because I have been saying these things to you, sorrow has been filling your heart. ⁷But I tell you the truth, it is to your advantage that I shall have gone away, because if I shall not have gone away, the Counselor will not come to you, yet if I shall have gone, I will send him to you.

⁸"And he, when he comes, will convict the world concerning sin, and justice, and judgment— ⁹concerning sin, because they are not confirming faithfulness to me, ¹⁰and concerning justice, because I go to the Fǎther, and you no longer behold me, ¹¹and concerning judgment, because the ruler of this world will have been getting judged.

15:25 γ Omit "their" before Law: 𝔓⁶⁶. See Al- and. See 10:34 and 8:17. **15:25** β Psa 35:19, 69:4-5, 109:3 **15:27** ξ = *from, ἀπ'*; i.e. from the beginning of the messianic mission of the kingdom of the Almǐghty.

¹²"I have many more things to say to you, but you cannot bear them now. ¹³But when he, the Spirit of truth, will have come, he will guide you into all the truth, because he will not speak on his own initiative, but whatever he hears, he will speak, and he will disclose to you what is to come. ¹⁴He will glorify me, because he will take of mine, and will disclose it to you. ¹⁵All things that the Fäther has are mine. Therefore I said that he takes of mine, and will disclose it to you.

¹⁶"A little while, and you will no longer behold me, and again a little while, and you will see me." ¹⁷Some of his disciples therefore said to one another, "What is this thing he is telling us, 'A little while, and you will not behold me, and again a little while, and you will see me', and, 'because I go to the Fäther'?" ¹⁸So they were saying, "What is this that he is saying, 'A little while'? We have not been knowing what he is talking about."

¹⁹Yĕshua knew that they wished to question him, and he said to them, "Are you deliberating together about this, that I said, 'A little while, and you will not behold me, and again a little while, and you will see me'? ²⁰Amen, amen, I say to you, that you will weep and lament, but the world will rejoice. You will be sorrowful, but your sorrow will be turned to joy. ²¹Whenever a woman may be birthing, she is having pain, because her hour has come, but when she may have given birth to the child, she is remembering the anguish no more, for joy that *a human child* has been born into the world. ²²Therefore you too now have sorrow, but I will see you again, and your heart will rejoice, and no one takes your joy away from you.

²³"And in that day you will ask me no question. Amen, amen, I say to you, if you shall have asked the Fäther for anything in my name^χ, he will give it to you. ²⁴Until now you have asked for nothing in my name^χ. Be asking, and you will receive, that your joy may be that which has been getting filled up.

²⁵"These things I have been saying to you in comparisons. An hour is coming when I will speak no more to you in parables, but will tell you plainly of the Fäther. ²⁶In that day you will ask in my name^χ, and I do not say to you that I will request the Fäther on your behalf. ²⁷For the Fäther himself is loving you, because ᵅyou have been loving me, and *because* ᵝyou have been holding faithful, because I came forth from beside the Fäther.

²⁸"I came forth from beside the Fäther, and have been coming into the world. I am leaving the world again, and going to the Fäther."

²⁹His disciples said, "Lo, now you are speaking plainly, and are not using a figure of speech. ³⁰Now we have been knowing that you have been knowing all *things*, and are having no need that anyone may be questioning you. By this we

---

16:12-15 The Spĭrit is described as hearing, speaking, disclosing. The Spĭrit therefore is not a mere force or power extended by the Fäther, but a conscious being that extends through space. He is Almĭghty like the Fäther and the Sŏn, but not the same *entity. There is one Almĭghty of more than one *entity, but only the *entity who is the Sŏn became exactly one person as we understand the meaning of a person from our own existence. See Rev. 5:6 for more on the Holy Spĭrit. See Rom. 8:26-27; Isa. 48:16.

16:23-26 χ (3x): See *14:13*; Mark 11:22.
16:27 α *ye have surely been loving me* אָהֹב אֲהַבְתֶּם
אֹתִי. **16:27** β *ye have surely been holding faithful*

are holding faithful, because you have come forth from the Almĭghty."

³¹Yĕshua answered them, "Are you now holding faithful? ³²Behold, an hour is coming, and has been coming, wherein you will have been scattered, each to his own, and I alone shall have been forsaken, and yet I am not alone, because the Făther is with me.

³³"These things I have been speaking to you, that in me you may be having peace. In the world you are having tribulation, but be taking courage. I have been getting victory over the world."

17

¹These things Yĕshua spoke. And when he lifted up his eyes to heaven, he said, "Făther, the hour has been coming. Glorify your Sŏn, wherein the Sŏn will have glorified you, ²even as you gave him authority over all flesh, so that to everyone you have and will have been giving him, he will have given to them everlasting life. ³And this is everlasting life, that they may be knowing you, **the one alone**ᵏ **being true Almĭghty** and **who** you have sent, Yĕshua the Anŏinted One.

⁴"I glorified you on the earth, the work having accomplished which you have been giving me that I may do. ⁵And now glorify me, thou Făther, alongside yourself, with the glory which I was having alongside you before the world was^β.

⁶"I manifested your name to the men whom you gave me out of the world. Yours they have been, and to me you gave them, and they have been keeping your word. ⁷Now they have been knowing that everything you have been giving me, from alongside you is, ⁸because the words which you gave me I have been giving to them, and they have received them, and have truly understood that I came forth from alongside you, and they hold faithful, because you did send me.

⁹"I ask concerning them. I do not ask concerning the world, but concerning those whom you have been giving me, because they are yours. ¹⁰And all my things are yours, and your things, mine, and I have and will have been receiv-

---

הָאָמֵן הָאֱמַנְתֶּם. The Greek perfect is for emphatic use in cases like this. Typically Hebrew uses infinitive absolute before the main verb to impart emphasis.

17:3 μ μόνον. Same word meaning **alone** twice used in 16:32, where the term means *isolated*. 'Alone' means 'by himself,' 'isolated,' or on his own power, without dependency. In Greek **'who'** is a relative pronoun (ὅν), and by the normal rule it agrees with **the alone true Almĭghty** in gender and number. Good English is too deficient to reflect the precision of the Greek, so I have bolded the phrases to show the antecedent of **who** where the agreement rule holds This statement makes it clear that the Son is not a dependent emanation or projection of the Father. The words 'the alone true Almĭghty' are equivalent to 'the independently real Almĭghty.' The Son may choose dependence temporarily, but his prayer is that we may be knowing him as being alone true Almĭghty, which will be the case when we see him in his glory.' Yĕshua reveals a multi being unity in vs. 11 and 22. See Col. 1:19, 2:9. ▷ The text can be unpacked into *that they may be knowing you, the alone true Almĭghty, and the alone true Almĭghty you have sent, Yĕshua the*

Anŏinted One. This is because the statement is not about a claim that the Almĭghty is one being, but it is a claim that both Făther and Sŏn are by themselves the separately true Almĭghty. The word 'true' is used here not in the sense of a fact, but in the sense of 'really is.' ▷ Understood this way, this text is a flat out rejection of the 'one essence/substance' doctrine from the council of Nicea. ▷ In normal Greek, the relative pronoun *whom* (ὅν) agrees in gender and number with an antecedent noun phrase or other substantive phrase, but its case is determined by its own clause. The pronoun ὅν connects to τὸν μόνον ἀληθινὸν θεόν: *the alone true Almĭghty* as the only antecedent to plug into the *whom* slot: **and the alone true Almĭghty you have sent, Yĕshua the Anŏinted One** (cf. Wallace, GGBB, pg. 335-336). The translation *only true* denies the divinity of the Son, but adherents to the Nicene Creed cannot accept the real explanation given above, because it asserts Father and Son are similarly divine while not being one being, and this is proven in that Messiah prays that we may be one as the Father and Son are one. **17:5** β = is. See Yŏh. 1:18.

ing glory through them. ¹¹And I am going to be no more in the world, and they themselves are in the world, and I am coming to you. Holy Făther, keep them in your name, ʿwhom you have been giving me, that they may be ᵋone, even as we. ¹²While I was with them, I was keeping them in your name ʿwhom you have been giving me, and I guarded them, and not one of them perished except ᵝTHE SON OF PERDITION, wherein the Scripture will have been fulfilled. ¹³Yet now I am coming to you, and these things I am speaking in the world, that they may be having my joy, which has been getting filled up within them.

¹⁴"I have been giving them your word, and the world has hated them, because they are not of the world, even as I am not of the world. ¹⁵I do not ask that you shall have taken them out of the world, but that you may have kept them from the evil one. ¹⁶They are not of the world, even as I am not of the world. ¹⁷Sanctify them in the truth. Your word is truth. ¹⁸As you did send me into the world, I also have sent them into the world. ¹⁹And on behalf of them I am keeping myself holy, so that they themselves also may be those who have been getting made holy in truth.

²⁰"I do not ask concerning these alone, but concerning those also pledging faithfulness through their word, ²¹that they may all be united, even as you, Făther, are with me, and I with you, that they also may be with us, that the world may be pledging faithfulness, because you have sent me.

²²"And I, the glory, which you have and will have been giving me, I will have been giving to them, that they may be one, ᵋeven as we are one, ²³I with them, and you with me, so that they may be those who have been getting perfected unto unity, that the world may be knowing that you have sent me, and *that* you lǫve them, *who hold faithful to me*, even as you lǫve me.

²⁴"Făther, such that you have and will have been giving me, I am desiring that where I am, these also may be with me, that they may be beholding my glory which you have and will have been giving me, because you loved me before the founding of the world. ²⁵Righteous Făther, although the world does not know you, yet I know you, and these know that you sent me, ²⁶and I make your name known to them. That is, I will make it known, so that the love *with* which you lǫve me may be in them, and I in them."

18

¹When Yĕshua had spoken these words, he went forth with his disciples over the ravine of the Qidron, where there was a garden, into which he himself entered, and his disciples. ²And, Yehudah also, the one betraying him, had been knowing the place, because Yĕshua had often met there with his disciples. ³Yehudah then, having received a company, and officers from the chief priests and the Perushim, came there with lanterns and torches and weapons.

17:11 ξ Mĕssiah is revealing here in what sense he and the Făther are one, so also the faithful may become one. **17:12** ς read οὓς, not ᾧ; see vs. 6; cf. Phil. 2:9. **17:12** β Psa 109:8-17, 41:9.

17:22 ξ→one: The *shema* commands an imperative: "Hear Yisrael Yăhweн [is] our Almighty, Yăhweн alone." The shema did not define Elohim in terms of one being. The "God is one being" theology of late Judasim and 4th century Christianity is contradicted by Mĕssiah who reveals a different sense of unity having nothing to do with one being theology since apparently

⁴Yĕshua therefore, who had been knowing all those things coming upon him, when he went forth, said to them, "Whom do you seek?" ⁵They answered him, "Yĕshua Ha-Natsri." He is saying to them, "I AM." And, Yehudah also, the one betraying him, had been standing with them. ⁶When therefore he said to them, "I AM," they drew back, and fell to the ground.

⁷Again therefore he asked them, "Whom do you seek?" And they said, "Yĕshua Ha-Natsri." ⁸Yĕshua answered, "I told you that 'I AM.' If therefore you seek me, let these go their way," ⁹that the word will have been fulfilled which he spoke, "Of those whom you have been giving me I lost not one."

¹⁰Şimʻon Peter therefore having a sword, drew it, and struck the high priest's slave, and cut off his right ear, and the slave's name was Malkos. ¹¹Yĕshua therefore said to Peter, "Put the sword into the sheath. The cup which the Făther has been giving to me, shall I not have drunk it?"

¹²So the company and the commander, and the officers of the Yehudim, arrested Yĕshua and bound him, ¹³and led him to Ḥanan first, because he was father-in-law of Qaiyapha, who was high priest that year. ¹⁴Now Qaiyapha was the one who had advised the Yehudim that it was expedient for one man to die on behalf of the people. ¹⁵And Şimʻon Peter was following Yĕshua, and so was another disciple. Now that disciple was known to the high priest, and entered with Yĕshua into the court of the high priest, ¹⁶and Peter had been standing at the door outside. So the other disciple, who *was* known to the high priest, went out and spoke to the doorkeeper, and brought in Peter. ¹⁷The slave-girl therefore who kept the door said to Peter, "You are not also one of this man's disciples, are you?" He said, "I am not." ¹⁸And the slaves and the officers had been standing, having been making a fire of hot coals, because it was cold and they were warming themselves, and Peter also was with them, who had been standing and warming himself.

¹⁹The high priest therefore questioned Yĕshua about his disciples, and about his teaching. ²⁰Yĕshua answered him, "I have been speaking openly to the world. I constantly taught in congregations, and in the Temple, where all the Yehudim are coming together, and I spoke nothing in secret. ²¹Why are you questioning me? Question those who have been hearing what I spoke to them. Behold, these have been knowing what I said."

²²And when he had said this, one of the officers, who had been standing by, gave Yĕshua a blow, saying, "Is that the way you are answering the high priest?" ²³Yĕshua answered him, "If I have spoken mistakenly, testify about the mistake, but if correctly, why are you striking me?" ²⁴Ḥanan therefore sent him, who had been getting held bound, to Qaiyapha the high priest.

²⁵And, Şimʻon Peter had been standing and warming himself. They said therefore to him, "You *are* not also one of his disciples, are you?" He denied it, and said, "I am not." ²⁶One of the slaves of the high priest, being a relative of the

---

the faithful can participate in the same unity as the Almĭghty has. **18:19-21** He means he did not tell the world one teaching, and then keep a secret teaching for his disciples, as often cultists will do to lure the unsuspecting into their secret teachings. **18:25-27** The final cock crow. I believe this was a real rooster,

one whose ear Peter cut off, said, "Did I not see you in the garden with him?" ²⁷Peter therefore denied it again. And immediately the rooster sounded.

²⁸They led Yĕshua therefore from Qaiyapha into the Praetorium, and it was early. And they themselves did not enter into the Praetorium in order that they will not have been defiled, but may eat the ᵀPassover. ²⁹Pilate therefore went out to them, and said, "What accusation do you bring against this Man?"

³⁰They answered and said to him, "If this Man were not an evildoer, we would not have delivered him up to you." ³¹Pilate therefore said to them, "Take him yourselves, and judge him according to your Law." The Yehudim said to him, "We are not permitted to put anyone to death," ³²that the word of Yĕshua will have been fulfilled, which he spoke, signifying by what kind of death he was about to die.

³³Pilate therefore entered again into the Praetorium, and summoned Yĕshua, and said to him, "Are you the King of the Yehudim?" ³⁴Yĕshua answered, "Are you saying this on your own initiative, or did others tell you about me?" ³⁵Pilate answered, "I am not a Yehudi, am I? Your own nation and the chief priests delivered you up to me. What have you done?"

³⁶Yĕshua answered, "My kingdom is not of this world. If my kingdom were of this world, then my servants would be fighting, so that I will not have been delivered up to the Yehudim, yet now, my kingdom is not from this place."

³⁷Pilate therefore said to him, "No then? You are a king!" Yĕshua answered, "You are saying that 'a king I am.' For this I have been getting brought forth, and for this I have been coming into the world, so that I will have borne witness to the truth. Everyone being from the truth hears my voice." ³⁸Pilate said to him, "What is truth?"

³⁸ᵇAnd when he had said this, he went out again to the Yehudim, and said to them, "I find no guilt in him. ³⁹But you have a custom, that I shall have released someone for you at the Passover. Do you wish then I shall have released for you the King of the Yehudim?" ⁴⁰Therefore they cried out again, saying, "Not this Man, but Bar-Abba." Now Bar-Abba was a bandit.

19

¹Then Pilate therefore took Yĕshua, and scourged him. ²And when the soldiers wove a crown of thorns, they put it on his head, and they dressed him in a purple robe. ³Then they were coming up to him, and were saying, "Be rejoicing, King of the Yehudim!", and were giving him slaps.

⁴And Pilate came out again, and said to them, "Behold, I am bringing him out to you, that you will have known that I find no guilt in him." ⁵Yĕshua therefore came out, wearing the crown of thorns and the purple robe. And Pilate said to them, "Behold, the Man!"

⁶When therefore the chief priests and the officers saw him, they cried out, saying, "Fasten him to an execution timber! Fasten him to an execution timber!" Pilate said to them, "Take him yourselves, and fasten him to an execution timber,

---

caged somewhere. The first cock crow was the alarm for the changing of the watch at about 3 a.m. This cock crow was just after the crack of dawn.

because I find no guilt in him."

⁷The Yehudim answered him, "We have a Law, and by that Law he ought to die because he made himself out to be the Almĭghty Sŏn." ⁸When Pilate therefore heard this statement, he was the more afraid.

⁹And he entered into the Praetorium again, and said to Yĕshua, "Where are you from?" But Yĕshua gave him no answer. ¹⁰Pilate therefore is saying to him, "You do not speak to me? Have you not been knowing that I have authority to release you, and I have authority to fasten you to an execution timber?"

¹¹Yĕshua answered, "You would be having no authority over me, not even any unless it had been getting given you from above. For this reason someone who is delivering me up to you has the greater sin." ¹²As a result of this Pilate was seeking to release him, but the Yehudim cried out, saying, "If you may have released this man, you are no friend of Caesar! Everyone who makes himself out to be a king opposes Caesar!" ¹³When Pilate therefore heard these words, he brought Yĕshua out, and sat down on the judgment seat at a place called The Pavement, but in Hebrew, Gabbetha.

¹⁴Now it was the ʸpreparation of the Passover. It was about the third hour. And he said to the Yehudim, "Behold, your King!" ¹⁵They therefore cried out, "Away with him, away with him, fasten him to an execution timber!" Pilate said to them, "Shall I have fastened your King to an execution timber?" The chief priests answered, "We have no king but Caesar!"

¹⁶So he then delivered him to them that he would be fastened to an execution timber. ¹⁷They took Yĕshua therefore, and he went out, bearing his own execution timber, to the place called the Place of the ʸPoll, which is called in Hebrew, Golgotha. ¹⁸There they fastened him to an execution timber, and with him two other men, on one hand and on the other hand, and Yĕshua in ᵋbetween. ¹⁹And Pilate wrote an inscription also, and put it on the execution timber. And it had been getting written, "Yĕshua ᶿHa-Natsri, the King of the Yehudim.ⁿ" ²⁰Therefore this inscription many of the Yehudim read, because the place was near the city where Yĕshua was fastened to an execution timber. And it had been getting written in Hebrew, Roman, and in Greek. ²¹And so the chief priests of the Yehudim were saying to Pilate, "Do not be writing, 'The King of the Yehudim,' but that, 'He said, I am King of the Yehudim.'" ²²Pilate answered, "What I have

---

18:28 π The first Passover offering, killed after noon on the 14th day is here meant. See 19:31. **19:14** γ Nisan 14, March 24, AD 34. A Wednesday. The third hour: See Mark 15:25. Read *third* instead of *sixth*: ²א Dˢ L Δ Ψ / 844 pc. Yoḥanan was written well after scribes were familiar with the other three Evangelists. The error is to be explained by them having the sixth hour fixed in their minds from Mat. 27:45, Mark 15:33, or Luke 23:44 when they were lazily copying John. Nor can the sixth hour and Mark's third hour have been so imprecise as to overlap. Yoḥanan's accuracy is better than that (cf. Yoḥ. 1:39; 4:6, 52.). **19:17** γ "Head" cf. 2 Sam 15:32 עַד הָרֹאשׁ, (and 2 Sam 16:1 מֵהָרֹאשׁ). **19:18** ξ See LXX Exodus 17:12: ἐντεῦθεν.

מְזֶה. The following arrangement seems to best explain the facts: One execution timber was used (cf. 19:31) supported horizontally through the tree branches (cf. Luke 23:31; Acts 5:30; 13:29; Gal. 3:13; 1 Pet. 2:24), perhaps cut or lopped at points to make easier the placement of the execution timber. At the center of it was the Anointed facing the temple his feet next to the front of the trunk hands spread and nailed to the timber. On the back side of the timber opposite each hand of his is nailed each robber facing away from the temple, and their feet on the uphill side of the trunk (cf. 19:32-33). **19:19** η Psa. 2:6-7, 12; Isa. 9:6-7. **19:19** θ = the branch: Jer. 23:5-6; Isa. 11:1. **19:24** ψ Psa 22:18.

been writing I have been writing."

²³The soldiers therefore, when they had fastened Yĕshua to an execution timber, took his outer garments and made four parts, a part to every soldier and also the tunic. Now the tunic was seamless, woven in one piece. ²⁴They said therefore to one another, "Let us not have torn it, but we shall have cast lots for it, to decide whose it will be," wherein the writing will have been fulfilled, "THEY DIVIDED MY OUTER GARMENTS AMONG THEM, AND FOR MY CLOTHING THEY CAST LOTS^ψ."

²⁵Therefore the soldiers did these things. And, there had been standing beside the execution timber of Yĕshua, his mother, and his mother's sister, Miryam the wife of Clopas, and Miryam Ha-Magdalit. ²⁶When Yĕshua therefore saw his mother, and the disciple whom he was loving, who had been standing alongside, he is saying to his mother, "Woman, behold, your son!" ²⁷Then he says to the disciple, "Behold, your mother!" And from that hour the disciple took her into his own household.

²⁸After this, Yĕshua, who had been knowing that all events already had been getting finished, so that the Scripture will have been finished, says, "I am thirsty." ²⁹A jar full of vinegar was standing there. So they put a sponge full of the vinegar upon a branch of hyssop, and brought it up to his mouth. ³⁰When Yĕshua therefore had received the ᵝVINEGAR, he said, "It ᶿhas been getting finished!" And he bowed his head, and gave up his spirit.

³¹The Yehudim therefore, because it was the day of preparation, so that the bodies will not have remained on the execution timber^β on the Şabbath (because that ŞABBAŧH^θ was great)^δ, had asked Pilate that their legs may be broken, and that they may be taken away. ³²The soldiers therefore came, and broke the legs of the first man, and of the other man who was fastened up on the execution timber with him,^γ ³³and, when they came upon Yĕshua, when they saw that he had already been dying, they did not break his legs, ³⁴but one of the soldiers

---

19:30 β Psa 69:21. **19:30** θ Τετέλεσται or *will have*. See Wallace pg. 580, Gnomic Perfect. See 2 Tim. 4:7. The word may also mean 'paid,' (cf. BAG, 1957). If so, he means his suffering in the flesh is almost finished. But by no means is it the end of divine suffering in the Spirit (cf. Gen. 6:6-7). It also means the end of the personal price he is paying as part of the ransom given by the Most High. See Isa. 43:3. It is not a price charged by divine judicial wrath. It is the price charged by the destructiveness of sin; cf. Hos. 13:14. It is the price and risk that men face and pay when they go to war to defend their country or rescue their people. They are suffering the cost to ransom what and whom they are defending from death and destruction. This cost is not charged lawfully. It is the cost extorted by lawlessness. But more likely he means another iteration of Scripture is being fulfilled. **19:31** θ Lev 23:11, 15a. **19:31** β The word σταυροῦ here is in the singular, "timber." See vs. 18. Just one execution timber was used. See 19:18, 32-33. **19:31** δ March 25th, AD 34. The annual Şabbath began at sunset on Wednesday March 24th. See Lev. 23:11, 15; Luke 23:56b-24:1 (cf. Mat. 28:1); Mark 16:1 (cf. Mark 16:2). The annual Şabbath is the great Şabbath (cf. Yoh. 7:37). In Jewish and Catholic tradition this has been changed. The Rabbis changed it to the Şabbath before Passover, and the Church to the Şabbath after "Good Friday," where they argue that what makes a Şabbath great is when a feast day falls on it. Similarly they argue that preparation of the Passover means Friday of Passover week. But these interpretations are speculations invented to get themselves out of difficulty with their chronological theories which are founded on lawlessness. **19:32** γ The word συσταυρωθέντος means to affix to an execution timber with someone else. See Rom. 6:6; Gal. 2:19. Mar. 15:32; Mat. 27:44. The facts seem to indicate the soldiers came to the back side of the tree first on the uphill side. Perhaps the senior officers were uphill and the junior officers were down hill tending the crowd. See 19:18.

19:33 λ Yohanan points to the blood and water as evidence of Mĕssiah's death. See 1 Yoh. 5:6. It is a myth that the Jews would not certify someone was dead unless it was for a full three days. This was only in cases where the body was not obviously damaged

pierced his side with a spear, and immediately there came out blood and water.ᴧ ³⁵And he who had been seeing has been testifying, and his testimony is true, and that one has been knowing that he is speaking the truth, so that you also may be pledging faithfulness. ³⁶For these things came to pass, so that the writing will have been fulfilled, "NOT A BONE OF HIM WILL BE BROKEN.ᶠ" ³⁷And again another writing says, "THEY WILL LOOK TO HIM WHOM THEY PIERCED.ᶿ"

³⁸And after these things Yosef of Ha-Ramati, being a disciple of Yĕshua, but who had been concealing himself, for fear of the Yehudim, asked Pilate that he may take away the body of Yĕshua, and Pilate granted permission. He came therefore, and took away his body.

³⁹(And Naqdimon came also, who had first come to him by night, bringing a mixture of myrrh and aloes, about a hundred pounds weight. ⁴⁰And so they took the body of Yĕshua, and bound it in linen wrappings with the spices, as is the burial custom of the Yehudim.)

⁴¹And, there was in the place, where he was fastened to an execution timber, a garden, and in the garden a new-made tomb, in which none had yet been getting put. ⁴²There, because of the preparation of the Yehudim, because the tomb was near, they had put Yĕshua.

20

¹Now on the FIRSTᵘ OF THE ṢABBAṮHSⁿ Miryam Ha-Magdalit, is herself coming early, darkness still being,ᵋ to the tomb, ᵖwhen she sees the stone having been ᵞgetting removed from the tomb. ²And so she is runningᵏ and

---

in a way to produce death.
19:36 ξ Psa 34:20, Num 9;12, Exo 12:46.
19:37 θ Zech 12:10. **19:39-40** At first Yĕshua was buried in a simple linen sheet. After the annual Ṣabbaṯh they went to the grave and did a proper embalming.
20:1 μ = Τῇ δὲ μιᾷ = Lit. "Yet on the [number] one [day]." "On the one" is a Semiticism for "on the first." Cf. Gen. 1:5. The gender of μιᾷ implies the word 'day' (compare πρώτῃ ἡμέρᾳ Mark 14:12 to Mat. 26:17 where ἡμέρᾳ is omitted). This does not mean 'day' should be printed in the text though. It is certain that σαββάτων by further Semiticism decodes to שבתות (cf. Lev. 23:15). The ending -ων is also used on the gen. plural of fem. nouns, so that in these cases σαββάτων may be regarded as the feminine Semiticism of שבתות. Precedent has already been set for such a decoding in the first place because σάββατα is already by Semiticism representing the singular שבתא, 'the Ṣabbaṯh,' and not the plural it appears to be to anyone unacquainted with the Aramaic origin of שבתא, ܫܒܬܐ. Thus it is equally possible that -ων represents the Hebrew -ות. The simplest Hebrew version of this phrase would then be: אַחַת הַשַּׁבָּתוֹת. See Neh. 10:33 where τῶν σαββάτων translates הַשַּׁבָּתוֹת. It is greater step for the -α suffix on σάββατα to represent Aramaic 'the' (א) than for -ων to be taken as fem. plural in these cases rather than the usual neuter. There is no good reason Ṣabbaṯh cannot be additionally declined as a Greek feminine in the case of this semiticism. **20:1** η Lev 23:15b; See App XII. This was the first of seven Ṣabbaṯhs which were counted after Passover. See Leviticus 23:15. See Mat. 28:1; Mark 16:1-2; Luke 24:56b-24:1; John 20:19; Acts 20:6-7; 1 Cor. 16:2; Rev. 1:10. See also Col. 2:16; Gal. 4:10; Romans 14:5-6. **20:1** ε It was still dark when the resurrection occurred, because that night was the third night (cf. Mat. 12:40). The resurrection was before any of them arrived during the dawn darkness, as the messengers informed them that Yĕshua was not there (οὐκ ἔστιν ὧδε cf. Mat. 28:6; Mark 16:6; Luke 24:6). **20:1** ρ וְהִיא רֹאָה. The immediacy of the present tense suggests a waw conjunctive for καὶ βλέπει. Yohanan is not concerned about when she left to go to the tomb, and his καί is not calculated to suggest an interval of time, but rather that she saw the stone moving in the same time-frame set before. He emphasizes when she arrived and the dark conditions then. It was not completely dark though, because the moon was 89% full in the west, light enough to keep from blundering into objects in the early dawn. The tomb was near the crucifixion site with a view of the Temple from the Mt. of Olives, on the west side. They may have seen the morning star rise on their way to the tomb if they came from the east side of the Mt. of Olives, which is

is coming to Şim'on Peter, and to the other disciple whom Yĕshua was loving, and is saying to them, "They have taken away my Adŏnai out of the tomb, and we have not been knowing where they have laid him."

³Peter therefore went forth, and the other disciple, and they were going to the tomb. ⁴And the two were running together, and the other disciple ran ahead faster than Peter, and came to the tomb first, ⁵and stooping and looking in, he saw the linen wrappings lying there, but he did not go in.

⁶Şim'on Peter therefore also came, following him, and entered the tomb, and he beheld the linen wrappings lying there, ⁷and the face-cloth, which was on his head, not lying with the linen wrappings, but which had been getting wrapped up in one place. ⁸So the other disciple who had first come to the tomb entered then also, and he saw and he held *it* faithful. (⁹For they had not yet been understanding the Scripture, that he needs to rise from the dead.)

¹⁰So the disciples went away again to ᵖthem. ¹¹But Miryam had been standing outside the tomb weeping, and so, as she wept, she stooped and looked into the tomb, ¹²and she sees two messengers in white sitting, one at the head, and one at the feet, where the body of Yĕshua had been lying. ¹³And they are saying to her, "Woman, why are you weeping?" She is saying to them, "Because they have taken away my Adŏnai, and I have not been knowing where they have laid him."

¹⁴When she had said this, she turned backwards, and sees Yĕshua, who had been standing there, and had not been knowing that it was Yĕshua. ¹⁵Yĕshua said to her, "Woman, why are you weeping? Whom are you seeking?" Supposing him to be the gardener, she said to him, "Sir, if you have carried him away, tell me where you have laid him, and I will take him away."

¹⁶Yĕshua is saying to her, "Miryam!" When she turned around, that one is saying to him in Hebrew, "Rabboni!" (which means, Teacher). ¹⁷Yĕshua is saying to her, "Don't be clinging to me, because ᵝnot yet, have I been ascending to the Father, but be going to my brothers, and say to them, 'I am ᵞascending *soon* to my Father and your Father, and my Almĭghty and your Almĭghty.'" ¹⁸Miryam

---

likely. **20:1** γ→removed. Very probably they saw the stone just rolling to a stop in the moonlight after the earthquake, which was timed to their arrival to open the tomb and stun the guard. The trans. could also be *having being removed*, but this still suggests the action is still occurring, as the Greek perfect almost always does. **20:2** μ Yoḥanan skips over the Mĕssenger's message outside the tomb, and the two men inside straight on to when Miryam left to report to Peter after noticing the body was gone. **20:10** ρ = ἑαυτοὺς = *themselves*: to where the other disciples were. The trans. 'home' or 'homes' is misleading.

20:17 ρ→me: "The tense is present, and the prohibition is, therefore, not of an individual act, but of a continuance of the act, of the habit, 'Do not continue clinging to Me'" (John Ellicot, 1905). **20:17** β.1→ascending; No doubt he had allowed her to hold him for a sufficiently appropriate space of time, and the meaning here is the same as "Stop clinging to me, I'm not saying goodbye just yet!" But he met them many other times during a space of forty days. **20:17** β.2→ascending: οὔπω γὰρ ἀναβέβηκα = not yet indeed have I been ascending, i.e. he is not in the middle of leaving yet, but he is soon ascending, and he needs the message to go out before he does so that all disciples can come and see him off. **20:17** γ The present tense is used in Greek to indicate the urgency of a future event or its nearness. The adverb 'soon' has been supplied to clarify the idea. Someone says, 'I am going up the road' just before he is going up the road. **20:17** The scene reminds us of Gen. 32:26, "MAKE ME SENT, BECAUSE THE DAWN ASCENDS" (שַׁלְּחֵנִי כִּי עָלָה הַשָּׁחַר). The ascension he is speaking of is to his Father, and not his ascending from the grave, which he exited at the earliest dawn (כְּשַׁחַר נָכוֹן מוֹצָאוֹ).

Ha-Magdalit is coming, announcing to the disciples, "I have been seeing Adŏnai," and that he had said these things to her.

¹⁹Therefore *it* being ᵚlater on that day, ᶘTHE FIRST OF THE ṢABBAṯHS, and when the doors had been ʳkept shut, where the disciples were staying, for fear of the Yehudim, Yĕshua came and stood in their midst, and is saying to them, "Peace be with you." ²⁰And when he had said this, he showed them both his hands and his side. The disciples therefore rejoiced when they saw Adŏnai.

²¹Yĕshua therefore said to them again, "Peace be with you! Even as the Fă-ther has been sending me, I also am sending you." ²²And when he had said this, he breathed on them, and is saying to them, "Receive the Holy Spirit. ²³If you will have tolerated the sins of some, their sins will have been getting tolerated for them. If of some you may be holding, they will have been getting held."

²⁴But Toma, one of the twelve, called Didumos, was not with them when Yĕshua came. ²⁵The other disciples therefore were saying to him, "We have been seeing Adŏnai!" But he said to them, "Unless I may have seen in his hands the imprint of the nails, and may have put my finger into the place of the nails, and may have put my hand into his side, no, I will not have held *it* faithful."

²⁶And after eight days,ᶳ his disciples were keeping inside again, and Toma with them. *Then* Yĕshua comes, the doors having been kept shut. And he stood in their midst, and said, "Peace be with you." ²⁷Then he is saying to Toma, "Be bringing here your finger, and see my hands, and be bringing here your hand, and put it into my side, and be becoming not faithless, but *be* faithful!" ²⁸Toma answered and said to him, "My Adŏnai and my Almĭghty!" ²⁹Yĕshua is saying to him, "Because you have been seeing me, you have been holding faithful. Blessed are those who when they have not seen, also will have ᶲpledged faithfulness."

³⁰Surely many other signs therefore Yĕshua also performed in the presence of the disciples, which are not those which have been getting written in this scroll, ³¹but these have been getting written that you may be holding faithful,

---

The ascension day is in Acts 1:9-11.

20:19 ω = *later*. The concept of "evening" in Hebrew is that of growing dark, or the receding of the light. So time in the afternoon is considered evening as well as twilight between sunset and full dark. Evening shadows grow long, which is to say in the afternoon, and so it was still on that Ṣabbath. See Mat. 28:1; Mark 16:2; Luke 24:1; Acts 20:7. **20:19** ʆ→ṢABBAṯHS: Lev 23:15b; The first Ṣabbaṯh after Passover, March 27th, AD 34. ▷ There was a pious Hebrew idiom for counting days to the Ṣabbaṯh in the DSS, 4Q252: יוֹם רביעי לשבת col. 1, line 11. and also באחד בשבת, col. 1, line 4. But but that idiom is counting days "to Ṣabbaṯh" or "unto Ṣabbaṯh," so Ṣabbaṯh does not mean week. The idiom would be pointless if it did, and there are already Hebrew and Greek words for week. But our Greek passages correspond to, "first of the Ṣabbaṯhs," and not to this Qumranite idiom because the Greek corresponds to a construct: אַחַת הַשַּׁבָּתוֹת, which means *first of the Sabbaths*. **20:19** ʳ *being, get-*

ting. The progressive nature of the perfect underlines the continuous state of the doors being shut, but this state was interrupted whenever anyone had to go in or out, as Peter and Yoḥanan had at dawn. The proper idea is *kept shut* in that the doors were not left open after use. This is the same as the iterative idea of 'getting shut.' 'Keep the door' shut on a cold day is not an order never to go out or in, but an order not to leave the door open when not in use.

20:26 ʆ The next Ṣabbaṯh starting at the same hour. Hebrew and English count days *after* an event by the customary start of a 24 hour calendar day always giving the appearance of exclusive counting. Greek and Latin may count from the *hour* of the event sometimes giving an appearance of inclusive counting. Eight days after the first meeting would commence on the same day of the next week at the same hour. Luke counts eight days from one Ṣabbaṯh to the next the same way. See Luke 9:28. Yoḥanan and Luke were narrating for a Greek audience. **20:29** ɸ→faithful: or *held faithful*. Toma had not held *it* faithful when he saw not.

because Yĕshua is the Anŏinted, the Almĭghty Sŏn, and so that holding faithful, you may be having life in his name.

21

¹After these things Yĕshua manifested himself again to the disciples at the Sea of Tiberias, and he manifested himself in this way. ²There were together Şimʻon Peter, and Toma called Didumos, and Neṯhaniʼel of Qanah in Galil, and the sons of Zavdai, and two others of his disciples.

³Şimʻon Peter said to them, "I am going fishing." They said to him, "We will also come with you." They went out, and got into the boat, and that night they caught nothing. ⁴And, when the morning came, Yĕshua stood on the beach, nevertheless the disciples had not been knowing that it is Yĕshua. ⁵Yĕshua therefore says to them, "Children, you do not have any fish?" They answered him, "No." ⁶And he said to them, "Cast the net to the right-hand side of the boat, and you will find *a catch*." They cast therefore, and *then* they were not being strong enough to haul it in because of the multitude of fish.

⁷That disciple therefore whom Yĕshua loved said to Peter, "It is Adŏnai." And so when Şimʻon Peter heard that it was Adŏnai, he put his outer garment on (because he was stripped for work), and threw himself into the sea. ⁸But the other disciples came in the little boat, for they were not far from the land, but about one hundred yards away, dragging the net full of fish. ⁹And so when they got out upon the land, they saw a charcoal fire already laid, and fish placed on it, and bread. ¹⁰Yĕshua said to them, "Bring some of the fish which you have now caught." ¹¹Şimʻon Peter went up, and drew the net to land, full of large fish, a hundred and fifty-three, and although there were so many, the net was not torn.

¹²Yĕshua is saying to them, "Come and have breakfast." None of the disciples were daring to question him, "Who are you?" having been knowing that it was Adŏnai. ¹³Yĕshua is coming and taking the bread, and is giving *it* to them, and the fish likewise. ¹⁴This was now the third time that Yĕshua was manifested to the disciples, having been raised from the dead.

¹⁵So when they had finished breakfast, Yĕshua says to Şimʻon Peter, "Şimʻon, son of Yohanan, are you loving me more than these?" He says to him, "Yes, Adŏnai, you have been knowing that I am your dear friend." He says to him, "Be pasturing my lambs." ¹⁶He says to him again a second time, "Şimʻon, son of Yohanan, are you loving me?" He says to him, "Yes, Adŏnai, you have been knowing that I am your dear friend." He says to him, "Be shepherding my sheep." ¹⁷He says to him the third time, "Şimʻon, son of Yohanan, are you loving me?" Peter was grieved because he said to him the third time, "Are you loving me?" And he said to him, "Adŏnai, you have been knowing all things. You are knowing that I am your dear friend." Yĕshua says to him, "Be pasturing my sheep.

¹⁸"Amen, amen, I am saying to you, when you were younger, you were dressing yourself, and were walking wherever you were wishing, yet when you may have grown old, you will stretch forth your arms, and someone else will dress you, and will carry you where you are not wishing." ¹⁹Now this he said, signifying by what kind of death he will glorify the Almĭghty. And when he had

spoken this, he is saying to him, "Be following me!"

²⁰Peter, turning around, sees the disciple whom Yĕshua was loving following, the one who also had leaned back on his breast at the supper, and said, "Adŏnai, who is the one who is betraying you?" ²¹Peter therefore, when he saw this one, says to Yĕshua, "Adŏnai, and what about this one?" ²²Yĕshua says to him, "If I may be wanting him to be remaining until I am coming, what is that to you? You be following me!" ²³This word therefore went out among the brothers that that disciple is not going to be dying, yet Yĕshua has not said to him that he is not going to be dying, but only, "If I may be wanting him to be remaining until I am coming, what is that to you?"

²⁴This is the disciple who is testifying about these things, and he who wrote these things. And we have been knowing that his testimony is true. ²⁵Yet there are also many other things which Yĕshua did, which if each one may be being written, I am supposing not even the world itself will have space for the scrolls being written.

End Note No. 1: First Day of Week?

The usage of μιᾷ τῶν σαββάτων for "first day of the week" does exist in Ecclesiastical Greek and similarly *prima sabbatorum* in Ecclesiastical Latin. But such usages were not current in the primitive Faith of the Evangelists or contemporary usage. See Acts 20:6-7 notes; Luke 18:12 notes; See Counting to the Sabbath, page 451. What we can say about the usage of the sense "week" in the Greek Septuagint in Lev. 23, 25 and in Psalm titles is it is of unknown provenance, and that none of these usages have ever been proved to be earlier than the 2nd to 4th centuries AD. Day of the week superscriptions do not show in the Qumran LXX texts, and they do not occur in the Hebrew text. It is likely that an early Catholic familiar with the Jewish Psalm reading schedule redacted the Ecclesiastical Greek phrases into the Psalms. Sometimes a pious Jewish usage found in Seder Olam and at Qumran (4Q252ˣ, 4Q320) is claimed to support the "first day of the week" interpretation. This usage occurs only in Hebrew as אחד בשבת or אחד לשבת. It means "one unto the Şabbaṭh," i.e. "first day to the Şabbaṭh." But this usage does not obviously translate to μιᾷ τῶν σαββάτωνᵠ.

E.A. Sophocles suggested an ablative sense "first day *after* the Şabbaṭh," (i.e. *from* it) which at times was adopted by translators. This runs into the problem that the usual idiom "day of the Şabbaṭhs" is not ablative. A second problem is that the Hebrew idiom counts *to* a coming Şabbaṭh and not *from* a past one. Thus 'one day *from* the Şabbaṭh' would be Friday when referencing a coming Şabbaṭh, and obviously the resurrection wasn't on Friday.

It is quite obvious that Şabbaṭh was not used for 'week' in Hebrew, because there was already a word for week: שָׁבֻעַ. For this word, the Greek ἕβδομα was employed. See Gen. 29:27, 28; Dan. 10:2, "three weeks" (שְׁלֹשָׁה שָׁבֻעִים = τρεῖς ἑβδομάδας). As with the Hebrew the root of the word week is based on seven or seventh: ἑβδόμη.

χ 4Q252: יום רביעי לשבת. ψ Among Greek only experts the tendency was to take the genitive in the classical sense as a partitive, "One day after the Şabbaṭh," but this would require the preposition ἐκ in the Koine or the classical ablative, and runs directly contrary to the idiom found at Qumran. The simple genitive strongly resists importing the idea "to" or "unto" a point in time. This is why translators have solved their problem by changing the lexical meaning of the plural σαββάτων to the singular week, but this solution also contradicts the Qumran usage which was intended to highlight the Şabbaṭh and not to assume a new meaning of the word. See "Counting to Şabbaṭh" on page 451.

End Note No. 2: Passion Date Gueses[x]

Promiment Attempts to Date Christ's Birth and Death (200-1600)

Author	Birth	Passion	Year
Hippolytus	*2 BC*	*25 Mar*	AD 29
De pascha computus	4 BC	9 Apr	AD 28
Victorius of Aquitaine	-	26 Mar	AD 28
Bede the Venerable	1 BC	*25 Mar*	*AD 34*
Claudius of Turn	1 BC	21 Mar	*AD 34*
Abbo of Fleury	21 BC	*25 Mar*	AD 12
Heriger of Lobbes	AD 9	23 Mar	AD 42
Gerland	AD 8	23 Mar	AD 42
Marianus Scottus	22 BC	*25 Mar*	AD 12
Heimo of Bamberg	33 BC	*25 Mar*	AD 01
Reinher of Paderborn	AD 1	26 Mar	*AD 34*
Albert the Great	-	*25 Mar*	*AD 34*
Roger Bacon	AD 1	03 Apr	AD 33
Robert of Leicester	-	23 Mar	AD 42
Jean des Murs	AD 1	03 Apr	AD 33
Alfonso Tostado	1 BC	03 Apr	AD 33
Paul of Middelburg	AD 2	30 Mar	AD 36
Joh. Lucidus Samotheus	1 BC	03 Apr	AD 33
Christian Massaeus	AD 1	*25 Mar*	AD 35
Onofrio Panvinio	1 BC	26 Mar	*AD 34*
Gerhard Mercator	*2 BC*	02 Apr	*AD 34*
Matthaeus Beroaldus	1 BC	03 Apr	AD 33
Paul Crusius	*2 BC*	03 Apr	AD 33
J.J. Scaliger (1583)	*2 BC*	23 Apr	*AD 34*
J.J. Scaliger (1598)	3 BC	03 Apr	AD 33
AD 34 = 7x	25 Mar = 7x	2 BC = 4x	

[x] C. Philipp E. Nothaft, *Dating the Passion*, Brill, 2012, Appendix.

25 March, AD 34 is the correct date for the Annual Šabbaṯẖ (cf. Yoḥ. 19:31), which date stuck in tradition before Yohanan corrected them and said it was on Nisan 14 (March 24, AD 34). The AD 33 dates came late and are a result of the discovery that Nisan 15 could not fall on Friday in AD 34. A case can be made here that 25 Mar, AD 34 is the traditional date due to misreading Mat. 26:17 and Mark 14:12.

End Note No. 3: The Rhetorical Negative

This is continued from the note on Yoḥ. 6:27, which the reader should read first. The rhetorical use of "no/not...but" statements is reinforced by a Jewish tendency toward sarcasm and attention getting shock statements in argumentative discourse. We see this in Mat. 22:32, "He is not *only* the Almĭghty of the dead, but *also* of the living." I have here clarified the sense with 'only' and 'also.' See also Mark 12:27 and Luke 20:38. A similar statement occurs in Exodus 6:3, "And then I appeared to Avraham, to Yitsḥaq, and to Ya'aqov in El Shaddai and my name Yăhweḥ. I had not *just* been known to them, but also I had made stand my covenant with them...." It is a witness to the power of tradition that no translation has this verse correct. It is obvious that the patriarchs knew and used the name, because it occurs in the dialogue of the patriarchs (cf. Gen. 14:22; 27:7; 28:16). Mosḥeh's mother Yoḵeved had the theophoric element at the beginning of her name, but it is acknowledged that the custom of theophoric names developed after the Exodus after Mosḥeh's renaming of Hoshea to Yehoshua.

This shows that in that form it was not a sacrilege to have a theophoric name. The text reads בְּאֵל שַׁדָּי וּשְׁמִי יְהֹוָה, "in El Shaddai and my name Yăhweḥ." The translators construed the word 'and' to mean 'but,' added the word 'by,' and split off the clause onto the next sentence, so to say, "but by my name...." This is not what it says. This mistake is as old as the LXX. The mistake was caused by not recognizing the rhetorical use of לֹא..וְגַם, 'not [only]...but also.' And we see that 'also' was already supplied by the text. The satanic documentary hypothesis seizes this error for its foundation. And it is an assumption too far to suppose that Mosḥeh edited the name into the mouths of the patriarchs besides others.

The rhetorical use of οὐκ ... ἀλλ' also has application in Yoḥ. 7:16, Ga, 1 Cor. 7:19, and Gal. 5:6. We may translate the Greek ἀλλά 'but' as 'except when' or 'unless.' This can be seen in the Aramaic equivalent אֶלָּא, a contraction of אֵן לָא or in Hebrew אִם לֹא. This lends itself to meaning, "if not" or "when not." See Jastrow אֶלָּא.

Acts

1 ¹Certainly ᶿO Theophilos, I composed the first account about all that Yĕshua began to do besides also to teach ²until that day ⸤he was taken up, when he gave orders to the emissaries, whom he had chosen through the Holy Spĭrit, and directed *them* to proclaim the good news.⸥ ³To these he also presented himself alive, after his suffering, by many convincing proofs, appearing to them over a period of ᵣforty days, and speaking of the things concerning the kingdom of the Almĭghty.

⁴And ⸤being corralled with them⸥, he commanded them not to leave Yerushalayim, but to wait for what the Făther had promised, which, he said, "you have heard ⸤²spoken through my mouth⸥, ⁵because Yohanan certainly immersed with water, but you will be immersed with the Holy Spĭrit, ⸤indeed which you are about to be receiving⸥, after not many of these days, ⸤²just as far as the fiftieth⸥." ⁶And so when they had come together, they were asking him, saying, "Adŏnai, are you at this time restoring the kingdom to Yisra'el?" ⁷ʳAnd he said to them, "It is not of you to learn the times or epochs which the Făther has fixed by his own authority, ⁸but you will receive power when the Holy Spĭrit has come upon you. And you will be my witnesses, besides in Yerushalayim and ᵀall Yehudah and Shomron, even to the remotest part of the earth."

⁹And ⸤having said what things he had, a cloud came under him, and he was carried off⸥ out of their sight. ¹⁰And as they were gazing intently into the sky, *as he was* departing, then behold, two men had been standing alongside them, *each* in a white robe, ¹¹who also said, "Men of Galil, why have you been standing looking into heaven? This Yĕshua, who has been taken up from you into heaven, will come in just the same way as you have watched him go.ᵀ"

¹²Then they returned to Yerushalayim from the mount called Olives, which is near Yerushalayim, a Şabbaᵵh day's journey away. ¹³And when they had en-

---

1:1 θ→Theophilos: *O Beloved of the Almĭghty.* Or *Friend of the Almĭghty.* Possibly Isa. 41:8 = אַבְרָהָם אֹהֲבִי; & 2Chron. 20:7 = אַהֲבְךָ לְעוֹלָם; James 2:23: φίλος θεοῦ ἐκλήθη = *beloved of the Almĭghty he was called.* Cf. Dan. 10:11, 19: אִישׁ־חֲמֻדוֹת. φίλος both in pass. sense (*beloved, dear*) and active; cf. BDAG 3rd, LSJ. Cf. Neh. 13:26: וְאָהוּב לֵאלֹהָיו = *and beloved of his Almĭghty.* ▷ Luke-Acts were literary works from the start for the general benefit of the faithful, a fact somewhat disguised by the use of the name 'Theophilos,' which is quite in character with his means of concealing certain truths that have to be deciphered. The missing 'title' should be noted here (cf. Luke 1:3). Theophilos may represent a real patron of Luke's work, but the address applies to all the faithful, and it appears that Luke intended it this way. **1:2** ⸤ και εκελευσε κηρυσσειν το ευαγγελιον D (gig t) sy^hmg (sa mae). **1:3** He first appeared after his resurrection on the Şabbaᵵh, March 27th, AD 34, the 17th of Aviv. Forty days carries us to Wednesday, May 5, AD 34. **1:4** ⸤συναλισκομενος D cf. Micah 2:12-13. **1:4** ⸤² φησιν δια του στοματος D* pc vg^cl. **1:5** ⸤και ο μελλετε λαμβανειν D* it; Aug^pt **1:5** ⸤² εως της πεντηκοστης D* sa mae; Eph Cass Aug^pt **1:9** ⸤D: και ταυτα ειποντος αυτου, νεφελη υπεβαλεν αυτον, και απηρθη απο οφθαλμων αυτων = *and these-things having-said of-him, a-cloud under-laid him, and he was borne off from eyes of-them.* See Psa. 104:3; Deu. 33:26; Dan. 7:11.▷ He rides the clouds.

tered, they went up into the upper room, where they were staying, besides Peter and Yoḥanan and Ya'aqov and Andrew; *also* Philip and Toma; Bar-Talmai and Mattai; Ya'aqov *the son* of Ḥalphai, and Şim'on the Zealot, and Yehudah *the son* of Ya'aqov. ¹⁴These all with the same heart were continually devoting themselves to prayer, along with the women ⸢and children⸣, and Miryam the mother of Yěshua, and with his brothers.

¹⁵And during these days, Peter stood up in the midst of the ⸢disciples (there were besides, in the same place, a ᵛhost of names, being ⸢about one hundred and twenty persons), and said, ¹⁶"Men, brothers, it ⸢is necessary to let the writing be fulfilled: ⸢the matter⸣ which the Holy Spirit spoke *about* beforehand through the mouth of David about Yehudah, the one who became a guide to those who arrested Yěshua, ¹⁷because he had been getting counted among us, and he had received a share of this ministry." ¹⁸(Indeed then, this one acquired a field from ⸢his wage for an unjust deed, and when he fell headlong, he burst open in the middle and all his intestines poured out, ¹⁹⸢which also became known to all those dwelling in Yerushalayim, so besides that field was called in their ᵀdialect ᵞḤeqeldama, that is, *the* Field of Blood.) ²⁰"For it has been getting written in the scroll of Psalms, 'LET HIS HOMESTEAD BE MADE DESOLATE, AND LET NO MAN BE DWELLING IN IT,ᵅ' and, 'HIS OFFICE LET ANOTHER MAN TAKEᵝ.' ²¹Therefore it is necessary, from the men who have accompanied us all the time that Adŏnai Yěshua ⸢the Anointed One⸣ went in and went out among us, ²²who began from the immersion of Yoḥanan until the day that he was taken up from us—to make one of these a witness of his resurrection with us." ²³And they put forward two men, Yosef called Bar-Şabba, (who was also called Eustace), and Mattiyah. ²⁴And they prayed, and said, "You, Yăhweh, who know the hearts of all men, show which one of these two you have chosen ²⁵to occupy this ministry and emissaryship from which Yehudah turned aside to go to his own place." ²⁶And they gave ᵟlots for them, and the ᵟlot fell to Mattiyah, and he was voted with the eleven emissaries.

2 And in the ᵋcompletion of the ⸢days for ᵗShavu'ot, they were all together in the same place. ²And °behold, there suddenly happened from heaven a noise like a violent, rushing wind, and it filled ⸢all the building where they were ⸢seating themselves. ³And there appeared to them tongues as of fire distributing

---

1:14 ⸢D. **1:15** ⸢D 𝔐 it etc. **1:15** ν→names: or *crowd of names*. This turn of expression is derived from a Hebrew idiom for important persons. See Rev. 11:13. These were the persons that helped Měssiah in his ministry. **1:16** ⸢D* lat; Irᵃᵗ. **1:19** ⸢D ℵ* syᵖ **1:19** ᵀ D latt ℵ B* omit ἰδίᾳ. **1:19** γ Ἀκελδαιμάχ = חֲקַל אֲדָם (Aramaic). **1:20** α Psa 69:25. **1:20** β Psa 109:8. **1:21** ⸢D pc sy mae. **1:26** ζ *votes*. **1:26** δ *vote*. **2:1** ⸢τας ημερας = *the days*: latt syᵖ mae. ▷ The entire Latin tradition and the Peshitta agree that the text read 'the days.' Mae = Middle Egyptian. Codex Bezae represents a 2nd cent. radical reading on the way to the 4th cent. reading, it's object being to place Acts 2 before Shavu'ot. The 4th cent. versions make 'completion' refer to the 50th day alone, i.e. the completing the 50th day from the point it started to its end; cf. YLT; DLNT. This allows avoiding the idea of completion referring to counting out seven days seven times. It also allows συμπληροῦσθαι to be reinterpreted the same way many try to reinterpret πληρῶσαι in Mat. 5:17. ▷ The 'days' being completed are those of seven

themselves, and ⌜as well ⌜they seated on each one of them. ⁴And they were all filled with the Holy Spĭrit and began to be speaking with other tongues, even as the Spĭrit was giving them something to be uttering.

⁵⌜In Yerushalayim there were ⁿdwelling Yehudim, devout men⌝, from every nation of those under heaven. ⁶And when this sound occurred, the crowds came together, and were bewildered, because they were hearing each one ⌜speaking in languages⌝. ⁷And they⁀ were amazed and marveled, saying ⌜to one another⌝, "Why, are not all these who are speaking men of Galil? ⁸And how is it that we hear each ⌜our language⌝ to which we were born?

⁹"Parthians and Medes and Elamites, and residents of Mesopotamia *and* Yehudah besides also Cappadocia, Pontus and Asia, ¹⁰Phrygia besides also Pamphylia, Mitsrayim and the districts of Libya down from Cyrene, and visitors from Rome, Yehudim besides also proselytes, ¹¹Cretans and ⌜Arabs! We hear them in our own tongues speaking of the mighty deeds of the Almĭghty." ¹²And they all continued in amazement and great perplexity ⌜about what had been happening⌝, saying to one another, "What does this mean?" ¹³But others were mocking and saying that, "Such as have been getting full of sweet wine, ⌜these are."

¹⁴But ⌜then Peter, taking his stand with the eleven, raised his voice and ⌜said, "Men of Yehudah, and all you who live in Yerushalayim, let this be getting known to you, and give heed to my words, ¹⁵because these men are not drunk, as you suppose, because it is the third hour of the day, ¹⁶but this is what has been getting spoken of through the prophet Yo'el:

¹⁷"And it will be in the latter days, says the Almĭghty, 'THAT I WILL POUR FORTH OF MY SPĬRIT UPON ALL MANKIND. AND YOUR SONS AND YOUR DAUGHTERS WILL PROPHESY, AND YOUR YOUNG MEN WILL SEE VISIONS, AND YOUR OLD MEN WILL DREAM DREAMS. ¹⁸EVEN UPON MY SERVANTS, BOTH MEN AND WOMEN, I WILL IN THOSE DAYS POUR FORTH OF MY SPĬRIT. THEY WILL PROPHESY. ¹⁹AND I WILL PUT WONDERS IN THE HEAVEN ABOVE, AND SIGNS ON THE EARTH BENEATH, BLOOD, AND FIRE, AND VAPOR OF SMOKE. ²⁰THE SUN WILL BE TURNED INTO DARKNESS, AND THE MOON INTO BLOOD, BEFORE THE GREAT AND GLORIOUS DAY OF YĂHWEH

---

weeks, seven sevens of days, which is 49 days. When these days are completed, then the 50th day is the feast of weeks (sevens). The days are dawn to dawn. At dawn at the junction of the 49th and 50th day, the 49 days are complete. The Ṣabbath for it starts with sunset on the 49th day. The 50th day arrives at dawn. ▷ This year it was on Friday, May 14th. Sivan 7. **2:1 ε** = *getting totally filled up;* See Deut. 16:9, 16; Exo. 34:22. Esp. Num. 28:26: ἐν τῷ συμπληροῦσθαι τας ημερας = בְּשָׁבֻעֹתֵיכֶם. It is as if, 'in/with weeks for Shavuot/50th day' had been written = 'with your weeks a holy convocation' (Num. 28:26: בְּשָׁבֻעֹתֵיכֶם מִקְרָא־קֹדֶשׁ). Only weeks are ciphered as 'days.' Cf. Exo. 13:10, so many 'days' for a year, and Shavuot, the 50th day, is celebrated with the weeks getting totally filled up first. **2:1** ⌜D **2:1** π *Shavu'ot = Pentecost, the fiftieth day*. Besides a command to count 50 days, there is a command to count seven weeks, seven days seven times, and also a command to count seven Sabbaths. The very first Shavu'ot is the feast that Yisrael went into the wilderness after the Exodus to celebrate. Events on it are found in Exodus 20-24. In that year, the feast came upon the weekly Sabbath, and it was upon this day that the Law was given to Yisrael. **2:5** η That they were dwelling in the city implies that they had a longer stay than just to keep the feast. After long journeys they would stay as long as they could afford to study and learn. **2:5** ⌜D. **2:17-21** ψ Joel 2:28-32.

Acts 2

WILL COME. ²¹AND IT WILL BE, THAT EVERYONE WHO MAY HAVE CALLED ON THE NAME OF YĂHWEH WILL BE RESCUED^ψ.'

²² "Men! Sons of Yisra'el! Hear these words: Yĕshua Ha-Natsri, *a* man who had been getting proved to you by the Almĭghty with miracles and wonders and signs which the Almĭghty did through him in your midst, just as you yourselves have been knowing— ²³this one—within the ᵝdeliberation, which has been getting ᵟdetermined, and within the ᵖforeknowledge of the Almĭghty, *being* betrayed, through the hands of lawless ones, *who* crucified *him,* you lifted *him* up.

²⁴"And the Almĭghty raised him up again, releasing the labor pains of death, since it was impossible for him to be held in its power. ²⁵Because David says of him, 'I WAS ALWAYS BEHOLDING YĂHWEH NEXT TO ME, BECAUSE HE IS AT MY RIGHT HAND, THAT I S'HALL NOT HAVE BEEN SHAKEN. ²⁶THEREFORE MY HEART WAS GLAD AND MY TONGUE REJOICED. MOREOVER MY FLESH ALSO WILL ABIDE IN HOPE, ²⁷BECAUSE YOU WILL NOT ABANDON MY SOUL TO THE GRAVE, NOR ALLOW YOUR HOLY ONE TO UNDERGO DECAY. ²⁸YOU HAVE MADE KNOWN TO ME THE WAYS OF LIFE. YOU WILL MAKE ME FULL OF GLADNESS WITH YOUR PRESENCE^ψ.'

²⁹"Men! Brothers! *It is now* allowed *for me* to speak plainly to you about the patriarch David, in that although he died and was buried, and his tomb is with us until this day, ³⁰certainly being a prophet, and one who had been knowing that the Almĭghty swore to him with an OATH TO SEAT ONE FROM THE FRUIT OF HIS LOIN UPON HIS THRONE,ᵟ ³¹when he looked ahead, spoke about the resurrection of the Anŏinted One, in that he was neither abandoned to the grave, nor did his flesh decay. ³²This Yĕshua, the Almĭghty raised up again, to which we are all witnesses.

³³"Therefore having been exalted to the right hand of the Almĭghty, besides having taken beside the Fäther the promise of the Holy Spĭrit, he has poured forth this which you both see and hear, ³⁴because it was not David who ascended into heaven, but he himself says, 'YĂHWEH SAID TO MY ADŎNAI, "BE SITTING AT MY RIGHT HAND ³⁵UNTIL I S'HALL HAVE MADE YOUR ENEMIES A FOOTSTOOL FOR YOUR

2:23 β βουλή = *counsel, deliberation.* **2:23** δ ὁρίζω *defined, determined, delineated, demarcated.* See LSJ: to mark off, or lay out a boundary. **2:23** π πρόγνωσις or *predetermination* (BDAG, 3rd, pg. 867). 'Within the deliberation which has been getting determined,' means applying the divine counsel to select among contingencies of what may happen to bring to pass what did happen. ▷ The divine foreknowledge consists of unchangeable decisions, formed out of past deliberations, by Gŏd to cause specific things to happen in the future (but not all things), and whatever may be logically predicted from processes in the present unaffected by the decisions of others. ▷ The pres. perfect progressive 'which has been getting determined' means there is an element of the divine will which already has been determined, and an element which still is being determined. The essential parts of the divine plan are already determined. But the plan is progressively fine tuned after the decisions of other created beings with the power of choice become known. Those trying to make decisions outside of the essential divine will, which is already fixed in foreknowledge, discover that their freedom to choose is blocked. Those making decisions within the essential plan are allowed to do so, and when these decisions are fixed, the predictable results are added to the divine knowledge, and the new contingency trees become the subject of new divine deliberation. ▷ Before time ran out for the betrayer to repent, Gŏd knew he could find another unrepentant person to fulfill his will. After time ran out, the betrayer was under judgment, and should he have tried to change course, he would have found himself in bondage to his earlier intent. Either way, Gŏd knew Mĕssiah would be betrayed.

2:25-28 ψ Psa. 16:8-10; **2:30** δ Jer 33:17-22; **2:34-35** ψ Psa 110:1.

FEET.ᵠ.'" ³⁶Therefore let all the house of Yisra'el be knowing for certain that the Almĭghty designates him both Adŏnai and *the* Anŏinted—this Yĕshua whom you fastened to an execution timber."

³⁷Now when they heard this, they were pierced to the heart, and said besides to Peter, also *to* the rest of the emissaries, "Brothers, what shall we have done?" ³⁸And Peter said to them, "Be sorry, and turn your hearts *from sin*, and let each one from you all be ᵝimmersed in the name of Yĕshua the Anŏinted, toward the releaseᵠ from the sins of you all. And you will receive the gift of the Holy Spĭrit, ³⁹because the promise is for you and your children, and for all who are far off, as many as Yăhwєн our Almĭghty will have called to himself."

⁴⁰Besides with many other words he solemnly testified, also he was exhorting them, saying, "Rescue yourselves from this perverse kindred!"

⁴¹So then, those who had received his word were immersed, and there were added that day about three thousand souls.

⁴²And they were continually devoting themselves to the emissaries' teaching and to fellowship, to the breaking of bread and to prayer. ⁴³And, awe was coming on every soul; as well, many wonders and signs were taking place through the emissaries. ⁴⁴And all those holding faithful were together, and had all things in common. ⁴⁵And they were selling their property and possessions, and were sharing them with all, for anyone having a need. ⁴⁶And day by day continuing with the same heart in the Temple, besides breaking bread from house to house, they were taking their meals together with gladness and sincerity of heart, ⁴⁷praising the Almĭghty, and having favor with all the people. And Yăhwєн was adding to their number day by day those who were being rescued.

2:38 β The 'name' is explained in Exodus 34:6-7, and how to be immersed in it in Exodus 20:6. The faithfulness of the Most High is the cause of forgiveness and cleansing from sin. If we repent and renew our faithfulness, he is faithful and just to forgive and cleanse. ▷ Immersion has a more abstract definition than just water baptism, which is symbolic, which is just a sign to proclaim the spiritual reality (cf. Mat. 3:11; 20:22-23; Luke 12:50). "To be immersed into" anything may mean, fire, the Holy Spĭrit, suffering, a teaching, the teaching about Mĕssiah, and Mĕssiah's commandments. Immersion signifies being dipped into something. Being immersed in the name specifies His teaching in general. Being "immersed into the release from your sins" is more specifically the teaching of the reality of forgiveness and cleansing that occurs upon repentance. ▷ Release does not just mean cancellation of a penalty. It also means taking away sin itself. ▷ See Mat. 28:18-20. **2:38** ψ ἄφεσις "❶ *the act of freeing and liberating from something that confines, release* from captivity (BDAG)." See Mat 26:28 ψ. As such this word does not only refer removal of a penalty, not only to forgiveness or pardon. It refers to removal and cleansing from sin itself. ▷ But the mystery of iniquity teaches Christians that they can neglect their own faithfulness and trust in the symbol itself to give them forgiveness, but without a faithful response, there is no release from sin itself, and the symbol quickly becomes a means of divine appeasement. In as much as Christianity teaches symbol over spiritual reality, it is putting people into intellectual bondage to a system of appeasing the Most High with symbol in place of true repentance. ▷ Particular points of the law are often turning into magical charms, such as just saying the name "correctly," or just "believing only." Even calendars have been used this way. If someone emphasizes something to the exclusion of all else in order to gain acceptance, and then condemns others who don't share that emphasis, then they are not getting immersed into a release from sins, and not only that, but because they have missed the real Spirit, they become vulnerable to the powers and err greatly in understanding the commandments themselves. And for us, the degree of their error in regard to the commandments is a sign for us that they have not understood the good news, and are really engaging in a cycle of appeasement and condemnation.

Acts 3

3 Now Peter and Yoḥanan were going up to the Temple at the ᵘninth hour, the hour of prayer. ²And a certain man who was lame from his mother's womb was being carried along, whom they used to set down every day at the gate of the Temple which is called Beautiful, in order to beg alms along the side of those who were entering the Temple.

³And when he saw Peter and Yoḥanan about to go into the Temple, he was asking to receive alms. ⁴And Peter, along with Yoḥanan, fixed his gaze upon him and said, "Look at us!" ⁵And he was giving them his attention, expecting to receive something from beside them. ⁶But Peter said, "I do not possess silver and gold, but what I do have I give to you: In the name of Yĕshua the Anŏinted Ha-Natsri, be walking!" ⁷And seizing him by the right hand, he raised him up. And immediately his feet and his ankles were strengthened.

⁸And leaping up, he stood and was walking! And he entered into the Temple with them, walking and leaping and praising the Almĭghty. ⁹And all the people saw him walking and praising the Almĭghty, ¹⁰and they were recognizing him, in that this one was the one sitting at the Beautiful Gate of the Temple for alms, and they were filled with wonder and amazement at what had been befalling him.

¹¹And while he was clinging to Peter and Yoḥanan, all the people ran together to them at the place called the portico of Shelomoh, full of amazement.

¹²But when Peter saw this, he replied to the people, "Men, sons of Yisra'el, why are you wondering at this, or why are you gazing at us, as *if* by our own power or piety we have been making him to be walking? ¹³THE ALMĬGHTY OF AVRAHAM, YITSḤAQ, AND YAʻAQOV, THE ALMĬGHTY OF OUR FATHERS,ᵋ has glorified his servant Yĕshua, the one whom you delivered up, and disowned in the presence of Pilate, when he had decided to release him. ¹⁴But you disowned the Holy and Righteous One, and asked for a murderer to be granted to you, ¹⁵but put to death the Prince of life, the one whom the Almĭghty raised from the dead, a fact to which we are witnesses. ¹⁶And by the ᵞfaithfulness of His name, this one whom you are seeing and have been knowing — His name has made him strong, and the ᵞfaithfulness which is through Him, has given him this wholeness before all of you. ¹⁷"And now, brothers, I have been knowing that you acted in ignorance, just as your rulers did also. ¹⁸But the things which the Almĭghty announced beforehand by the mouth of all the prophets, that his Anŏinted should suffer, he has thus fulfilled.

¹⁹"Be sorry and turn your hearts *from sin* therefore. And return, to have your sins wiped away, ²⁰in order that times of refreshing will have come from the presence of Yăhweh, and that he will have sent the one who has been getting appointedᵝ for you: Yĕshua, the Anŏinted, ²¹whom heaven must receive until the time of the restoration of all things, about which the Almĭghty has spoken by the mouth of his holy prophets since time immemorial. ²²Mosheh said, 'YĂHWEH

3:1 μ This was the hour of the incense offering between the settings in the Temple. **3:13** ξ Exo. 3:16. **3:16** γ or *reliability*. Covenant faithfulness. **3:20** β As the parable says, Mĕssiah went away to receive his kingdom from the Father. **3:22-23** δ Deut. 18:15-20

Your Almĭghty will raise up for you a prophet like me from your brothers. To him you will give heed in everything, as much as he may have said to you. ²³And, it will be that any soul, if it may not have heeded that prophet, will be utterly destroyed from among the people.ᵟ' ²⁴And likewise, all the prophets who have spoken, since Shemuʼel and his successors, also announced these days.

²⁵"It is you who are the sons of the prophets, and of the covenant which the Almĭghty made with your fathers, saying to Avraham, 'And in your seed all the families of the earth will be blessed.' ²⁶For you firstly, the Almĭghty raised up his Servant, and sent him, blessing you by turning each one from your wicked ways."

4 ¹And as they were speaking to the people, the priests and the captain of the Temple guard, and the Tsadduqim, came upon them, ²being greatly disturbed because they were teaching the people and proclaiming by Yĕshua the resurrection from the dead. ³And they laid hands on them, and put them in prison until the next day, because it was already evening. ⁴But many of those who had heard the message pledged faithfulness. And the number of the men came to be about five thousand.

⁵And it came about on the next day, that their rulers and elders and scribes were gathered together in Yerushalayim; ⁶and Ḥanan the high priest was there, and Qaiyapha and Yoḥanan and Alexander, and all who were of high-priestly descent. ⁷And when they had placed them in the center, they were inquiring, "By what power, or in what name, have you done this?"

⁸Then Peter, filled with the Holy Spĭrit, said to them, "Rulers and elders of the people, ⁹if we are being examined today for a benefit done to a crippled man, as to how this one has been getting delivered, ¹⁰let it be getting known to all of you, and to all the people of Yisraʼel, that by the name of Yĕshua the Anŏinted Ha-Natsri, whom you fastened to an execution timber, whom the Almĭghty raised from the dead—by this name this man has been standing here before you in good health.

¹¹"He is the stone which was rejected by you, the builders, but which became the very corner stone.ᵅ ¹²And there is deliverance in no one else, because there is no other nameᵝ under heaven that has been getting given to men, by which one needs to be rescued."

¹³Now as they observed the confidence of Peter and Yoḥanan, and understood that they were uneducated and untrained men, they were being amazed. Besides they were recognizing them, because they were with Yĕshua. ¹⁴As well as seeing the man with them, who had been standing *there*, who had been getting healed, they were having nothing to contradict *it* with. ¹⁵But when they

---

3:25 η Gen. 12:3; 22:18; 26:4; 28:14   **4:11** α Psa 118:22, Isa 28:16   **4:12** β Hos 13:4, Exo 34:5-8

had ordered them to go aside out of the Council, they were conferring with one another, ¹⁶saying, "What shall we have done with these men? Because the fact that a known miracle had been happening through them is apparent to all who live in Yerushalayim, and we cannot deny it. ¹⁷But in order that it will not have spread any further among the people, we shall have warned them to speak no more to any man in this name."

¹⁸And when they had summoned them, they commanded them not to speak or teach at all in the name of Yĕshua. ¹⁹But Peter and Yoḥanan answered and said to them, "Whether it is right in the sight of the Almĭghty to give heed to you rather than to the Almĭghty, you be the judge, ²⁰because we cannot stop speaking what we have seen and heard."

²¹And when they had threatened them further, they let them go (finding no basis on which they might punish them) on account of the people, because they were all glorifying the Almĭghty for what had been happening, ²²because the man was more than forty years old on whom this sign of curing had been happening.

²³And when they were released, they went to their own companions, and reported all that the chief priests and the elders had said to them. ²⁴And when they heard this, they lifted their voice near to the Almĭghty with the same heart and said, "Adŏnai, it is YOU WHO DID MAKE THE HEAVEN AND THE EARTH AND THE SEA, AND ALL THAT IS IN THEM,ᵅ ²⁵who by the Holy Spĭrit, through the mouth of our father David your servant, did say, 'WHY DO THE NATIONS RAGE, AND THE MASSES DEVISE FUTILE THINGS?²⁶THE KINGS OF THE EARTH TAKE THEIR STAND, AND THE RULERS WERE GATHERED TOGETHER AGAINST YĂHWEH, AND AGAINST HIS ANŎINTED^β.' ²⁷For truly in this city there were gathered together against your Holy Servant Yĕshua, whom you did anoint, besides Herod and Pontius Pilate, along with the nations, also the people of Yisra'el, ²⁸to do whatever your hand and your purpose marked out beforehand to occur. ²⁹And now, Yăhweh, take note of their threats, and grant that your servants may speak your word with all confidence, ³⁰while you extend your hand to heal, and signs and wonders take place through the name of your Holy ᵛServant Yĕshua."

³¹And when they prayed, the place was shaken, in which they had been gathering together, and they were all filled with the Holy Spĭrit, and were speaking the word of the Almĭghty with boldness.

³²And the congregation of those who had pledged faithfulness were of one heart and soul, and not one of them had claimed anything belonging to him to be his own, but all things were common property to them. ³³And with great power the emissaries were giving witness to the resurrection of Adŏnai Yĕshua, besides also, abundant loving-kindness having been upon them all, ³⁴because there was not a needy person among them, because all who were owners of land or houses would sell them and bring the proceeds of the sales, ³⁵and lay them beside the

---

4:24 α Exo 20:11; **4:25-26** β Psa 2:1-2 **4:30** ν See Isa. 37:35; 44:21; 49:6. Compare LXX with GNT; παῖδά μου = עַבְדִּי.

emissaries' feet. And they would be distributed to each, as any had need. ³⁶And Yosef, a Leviʹi of Cyprian birth, who was also called Bar-Nabba by the emissaries, (which translated means, "son of encouragement"), ³⁷and who owned a tract of land, sold it and brought the money and laid it at the emissaries' feet.

5 But a certain man named Ḥananyah, with his wife Ṣappirah, sold a piece of property, ²and kept back some of the value for himself, (also his wife had been knowing *it*) and bringing a portion of it, he laid it beside the emissaries' feet. ³But Peter said, "Ḥananyah, why has Satan filled your heart to lie to the Holy Spĭrit, and to keep back some of the value of the land? ⁴While it remained unsold, did it not remain your own? And after it was sold, was it not under your control? Why is it that you have conceived this deed in your heart? You have not lied to men, but to the Almĭghty."

⁵And as he heard these words, Ḥananyah fell down and breathed his last, and great fear came upon all who heard of it. ⁶And the young men arose and covered him up, and after carrying him out, they buried him.

⁷Now there elapsed an interval of about three hours, and his wife came in, who had not been knowing what had been happening. ⁸And Peter responded to her, "Tell me whether you sold the land for such and such a value?" And she said, "Yes, that was the value." ⁹Then Peter said to her, "Why is it that you have agreed together to put the Spĭrit of Yăhweн to the test? Behold, the feet of those who have buried your husband are at the door, and they will carry you out as well." ¹⁰And she fell immediately at his feet, and breathed her last. And the young men came in and found her dead, and they carried her out and buried her beside her husband. ¹¹And great fear came upon the whole assembly, and upon all who heard of these things.

¹²And at the hands of the emissaries many signs and wonders were taking place among the people, and they were all with the same heart in Shelomoh's portico. ¹³But none of the rest dared to associate with them. However, the people held them in high esteem. ¹⁴And all the more were being added, holding faithful to Yăhweн. Crowds of men besides also women were constantly added to their number, ¹⁵to such an extent that they even carried the sick out into the streets and laid them on cots and pallets, so that when Peter came by, at least his shadow might fall on any one of them. ¹⁶And also the people from the cities in the vicinity of Yerushalayim were coming together, bringing people who were sick or afflicted with unclean spirits, and they were all being healed.

¹⁷But the high priest rose up, along with all his associates, (that is the sect of the Tsadduqim), and they were filled with jealousy. ¹⁸And they laid hands on the emissaries, and put them in a public prison.

¹⁹But the Messenger of Yăhweн during the night opened the gates of the prison; besides taking them out he said, ²⁰"Be going, and having stood, be speaking to the people in the Temple the whole message of this Life." ²¹And upon hearing this, they entered into the Temple about daybreak and were teaching.

Acts 5

²¹ᵇNow when the high priest and his associates had come, they called the Council together, even all the Senate of the sons of Yisra'el, and sent orders to the prison house for them to be brought. ²²But the officers who came did not find them in the prison. And they returned and reported back, ²³saying, "We found the prison house having been getting locked with all security, and the guards having been standing at the doors, but when we opened up, we found no one inside." ²⁴Now as they heard these words, besides the captain of the Temple guard and the chief priests, they were perplexed concerning them, *and what this may come to.*

²⁵But when someone came by, he announced to them, "Behold, the men whom you put in the prison are in the Temple, having been standing and teaching the people!" ²⁶Then the captain went along with the officers and proceeded to bring them back without violence (because they were afraid of the people, lest they would be stoned). ²⁷And when they had brought them, they stood them before the Council. And the high priest questioned them, ²⁸saying, "We gave you strict orders not to continue teaching in this name, and behold, you have been filling Yerushalayim with your teaching, and intend to bring this man's blood upon us."

²⁹But Peter and the emissaries answered and said, "We must obey the Almĭghty rather than men. ³⁰The Almĭghty of our fathers raised up Yĕshua, whom you had put to death by suspending upon a tree. ³¹He is the one whom the Almĭghty exalted to his right hand as Prince and Rescuer, to ᵋoffer to Yisra'el *the chance for* being sorry and turning the heart, and release from sins. ³²And we are witnesses of these things. And so is the Holy Spĭrit, whom the Almĭghty has given to those who obey him."

³³But when they heard this, ᵅthey were getting enraged and were intending to kill them, ³⁴but having stood up in the Council, a certain Perushi by the name Gamli'el, a teacher of the Law, respected by all the people, ordered to put the men outside for a short time; ³⁵besides⁽ᵝ⁾ *that* he had said to them, "Men of Yisra'el, be taking care what you propose to do with these men, ³⁶because some time ago Theudas rose up, claiming to be somebody, and a group of about four hundred men joined up with him. And he was slain. And all who were trusting him were dispersed and came to nothing. ³⁷After this man, ᵞYehudah of Galil rose up in the days of the census, and drew away some people after him. He too perished, and all those who were trusting him were scattered. ³⁸And so in the present case, I am saying to you, stay away from these men and let them alone, because if this plan or action may be of men, it will be overthrown, ³⁹but if it is of the Almĭghty, you will not be able to overthrow them, or else you may

---

5:31 ε δοῦναι < δίδωμι: LSJ: *offer.* **5:33** α→enraged: *they had been getting sawn through; ...cut through.* **5:35** β The unusual element is that Gamli'el stood up in the first place to make the argument. What was known and assumed was the history he reported. **5:37** γ Rabbi Yehudah's sedition was in 2 BC during the census (cf. Luke 2:1). It turned into active rebellion when his disciples tore down the eagle Herod put over the great gate of the Temple in Jan. 1 BC. Herod executed Yehudah and his fellow scholar Mattatyahu by burning. After Herod's death, the revolt was renewed, and the Romans under Quinctilius Varus put it down.

even have been found fighting against the Almĭghty."

⁴⁰And they were persuaded by him. And after calling the emissaries in, they flogged them and ordered them to speak no more in the name of Yĕshua, and then released them. ⁴¹So they went on their way from the presence of the Council, rejoicing that they were considered worthy to suffer shame over his name, ⁴²besides every day in the Temple, also from house to house, they were not ceasing teaching and proclaiming the Anŏinted Yĕshua.

6 Now at this time while the disciples were increasing, a complaint arose on the part of the Greek speaking Yehudim against the Hebrew speaking Yehudim, because their widows were being overlooked in the daily serving. ²And the twelve summoned the congregation of the disciples and said, "It is not desirable for us to neglect the word of the Almĭghty in order to serve tables. ³But select from among you, brothers, seven men of good reputation, full of the Spĭrit and of wisdom, whom we may put in charge of this task. ⁴But we will devote ourselves to prayer, and to the ministry of the word."

⁵And the statement found approval with the whole congregation. And they chose Stephen, a man full of faithfulness and of the Holy Spĭrit, and Philip, Prochorus, Nicanor, Timon, Parmenas and Nicolas, a proselyte from Antioch. ⁶And these they brought before the emissaries, and after praying, they laid their hands on them.

⁷And the word of the Almĭghty kept on spreading, and the number of the disciples continued to increase greatly in Yerushalayim, besides a great host of the priests having been obedient to the pledge of faithfulness.

⁸And Stephen, full of loving-kindness and power, was performing great wonders and signs among the people. ⁹But some men from what was called the Congregation of the Freedmen, including both Cyrenians and Alexandrians, and some from Cilicia and Asia, rose up and disputed with Stephen. ¹⁰And yet they were unable to cope with the wisdom and the Spĭrit with which he was speaking.

¹¹Then they secretly induced men to be saying, "We have been hearing him speak blasphemous words against Mosh‛eh and the Almĭghty." ¹²Besides *also* they had stirred up the people, the elders and the scribes, and having stood over him, they had dragged him away, and had lead *him* before the Council. ¹³Besides *also* they put forward false witnesses saying, "This man ceaselessly is speaking words against the holy place, and the Law, ¹⁴because we have been hearing him say that this Natsri, Yĕshua, will destroy this place and alter the customs which Mosh‛eh handed down to us."

¹⁵And fixing their gaze on him, all who were sitting in the Council saw his face like the face of a messenger.

Acts 7

7 ¹And the high priest said, "Are these things so?" ²And he said, "Hear me, brothers and fathers! The Almĭghty of glory appeared to our father Avraham when he was in ᵞAram-Naharayim, before⁰ he lived in Ḥaran, ³and said to him, 'Depart from your country and your relatives, and come into the land that I shall have shown you.ᵞ' ⁴Then he departed from the land of the Kasdimˣ, and settled in Ḥaran. And from there, after his father died⁰, the Almĭghty removed him into this country in which you are now living. ⁵And he gave him no inheritance in it, not even a foot of ground. And yet, even when he had no child, he promised that he would give it to him as a possession, and to his seed after him⁰. ⁶But the Almĭghty spoke to this effect, that his seed would be aliens in a foreign land, (and that they would be enslaved and mistreated); four hundred years. ⁷'And whatever nation to which they will be in bondage I myself will judgeᵘ,' said the Almĭghty, 'and after that they will come out and serve me in this placeᵘ.' ⁸And he gave him the covenant of circumcision. And so Avraham became the father of Yitsḥaq, (and circumcised him on the eighth day), and Yitsḥaq of Yaʿaqov, and Yaʿaqov of the twelve patriarchs.

⁹"And the patriarchs became jealous of Yosef and sold him into Mitsrayim. And yet the Almĭghty was with him, ¹⁰and rescued him from all his afflictions, and granted him favor and wisdom in the sight of Pharaoh, king of Mitsrayim. And he made him governor over Mitsrayim and all his household. ¹¹Now a famine came over all Mitsrayim and Kenaʿan, and great affliction, and our fathers could find no food. ¹²But when Yaʿaqov heard that there was grain in Mitsrayim, he sent our fathers there the first time. ¹³And on the second visit Yosef made himself known to his brothers, and Yosef's family was disclosed to Pharaoh. ¹⁴And Yosef sent word and invited Yaʿaqov his father and all his relatives to come to him, seventy-five persons in all. ¹⁵And Yaʿaqov went down to Mitsrayim and there passed away, he and our fathers. ¹⁶And from there they were removed to Shekem, and laid in the tomb which Avraham had purchased for a sum of money at the side of the sons of Ḥamor in Shekem.

¹⁷"But as the time of the promise was approaching, which the Almĭghty had assured to Avraham, the people increased and multiplied in Mitsrayim, ¹⁸until there arose another king over Mitsrayim who had been knowing noth-

---

7:2 γ = *Aram of the two rivers.* **7:2** θ He appeared to him in Ur; cf. Gen. 15:7; Neh. 9:7 **7:2** χ This was 430 years before the Exodus, and five years before he left the town of Ḥaran. In vs. 6, 400 years was from when Yitsḥaq was born to the Exodus. **7:3** λ Gen. 12:1; **7:5** δ Gen. 13:15, 17:8, 48:4.

7:4 φ *After his father died* (μετὰ τὸ ἀποθανεῖν τὸν πατέρα αὐτοῦ). Teraḥ died at age 205, and Avraham was 75 in that year when he departed from Ḥaran. But many chronologies err by 60 years when they assume that Avraham was born when Teraḥ was 70 (cf. Gen 11:26). They were too hasty in judging this case to be unlike that of Shem (Gen. 5:32; Gen. 11:10), and the clue is given in the same chapter at 11:10! What they have overlooked is that the death notice for Teraḥ (Gen. 11:32) is displaced from the customary position established in Genesis 5, where all the death notices are biographical summaries out of chronological order. Since Genesis 11:28-31 comes before vs. 32, it is clear that 11:32 is part of the narrative and must come in chronological order. This is more fully explained in *The Scroll of Biblical Chronology*, Vol. II.

7:6-7 μ Gen 15:13-16 **7:18** ζ Exo 1:8

ING ABOUT Yos‑ef.ʲ ¹⁹It was he who took shrewd advantage of our family clan, and mistreated our fathers so that they would expose their infants and they would not survive.

²⁰"And it was at this time that Mosheh was born, and he was lovely in the sight of the Almĭghty, and he was nurtured *the days of* THREE MOONS in his father's home. ²¹And after he was exposed, Pharaoh's daughter took him away, and nurtured him as her own son. ²²And Mosheh was educated in all the learning of Mitsrayim, and he was a man of power in words and deeds.

²³"But when he fulfilled the age of forty, it entered his mind to visit his brothers, the sons of Yisra'el. ²⁴And when he saw one being treated unjustly, he defended him and took vengeance for the oppressed person by striking down the Mitsri. ²⁵And he supposed that his brothers understood that the Almĭghty was granting them deliverance through him, but they did not understand. ²⁶Besides on the following day, he appeared to those quarreling, and he was exhorting them to *make* peace, having said, 'MEN, YOU ARE BROTHERS, WHY DO YOU INJURE ONE ANOTHER?'η ²⁷But the one who was injuring his neighbor pushed him away, saying, 'WHO MADE YOU A RULER AND JUDGE OVER US? ²⁸YOU DO NOT MEAN TO KILL ME AS YOU KILLED THE MITSRI YESTERDAY, DO YOU?'ϕ ²⁹And at this remark Mosheh fled, and became an alien in the land of Midyan, where he became the father of two sons.

³⁰"And after forty years had passed, the Messenger *of* Yăhweh appeared to him in the wilderness of Mount Sinai, in the flame of a burning thorn bush. ³¹And when Mosheh saw it, he was marveling at the sight, and as he approached to look more closely, there came the voice of Yăhweh, ³²'I AM THE ALMĬGHTY OF YOUR FATHERS, THE ALMĬGHTY OF AVRAHAM AND YITS'HAQ AND YA'AQOV.'ξ And Mosheh shook with fear and would not venture to look. ³³But Yăhweh said to him, 'TAKE OFF THE SANDALS FROM YOUR FEET, BECAUSE THE PLACE ON WHICH YOU HAVE BEEN STANDING IS HOLY GROUND. ³⁴I HAVE CERTAINLY SEEN THE OP-PRESSION OF MY PEOPLE IN MITSRAYIM, AND HAVE HEARD THEIR GROANS, AND I HAVE COME DOWN TO DELIVER THEM. COME NOW, AND I SHALL HAVE SENT YOU TO MITSRAYIM.'

³⁵"This Mosheh whom they rejected, saying, 'WHO MADE YOU A RULER AND A JUDGE?'α is the one whom the Almĭghty had been sending to be both a ruler and a REDEEMER^ψ with the help of the Messenger who appeared to him in the thorn bush. ³⁶This man led them out, performing wonders and signs in the land of Mitsrayim and in the ʸRed Sea and in the wilderness for forty years. ³⁷This is the Mosheh who said to the sons of Yisra'el, 'THE ALMĬGHTY WILL RAISE UP FOR YOU A PROPHET LIKE ME FROM YOUR BROTHERS.'β ³⁸This is the one who was in the congregation in the wilderness together with the Messenger who was speaking to him on Mount Sinai, and who was with our fathers, and he received living

---

7:26 η Exo 2:13 **7:27-28** ϕ Exo 2:14 **7:32** ξ | **7:35** ψ cf. Exo 6:6: וְגָאַלְתִּי. **7:36** γ→Sea: LXX for: Exo 3:16 **7:33-34** ρ Exo 3:5, 7-8, 10 **7:35** α Exo 2:14 | יָם סוּף. End Sea. Gulf of Aqaba. **7:37** β Deu 18:15.

oracles to pass on to you.

³⁹"And our fathers were unwilling to be obedient to him, but pushed him away, and in their hearts turned back to Mitsrayim, ⁴⁰saying to Aharon, 'MAKE FOR US GODS WHO WILL GO BEFORE US, BECAUSE THIS MOSHEH WHO LED US OUT OF THE LAND OF MITSRAYIM—WE HAVE NOT BEEN KNOWING WHAT HAPPENED TO HIM.' ⁴¹And at that time they made a calf and brought a sacrifice to the idol, and were rejoicing in the works of their hands.

⁴²"But the Almighty turned away and delivered them up to serve the host of heaven, as it has been getting written in the scroll of the prophets, 'THE SACRIFICES AND TRIBUTE OFFERING YOU HAD BROUGHT NEAR TO ME IN THE WILDERNESS FORTY YEARS O HOUSE OF YISRA'EL? ⁴³BUT YOU HAVE TAKEN UP ⁺SIKKUΤH YOUR KING, AND KIYWAN YOUR IMAGES, THE STAR OF YOUR GODS, WHICH YOU HAVE MADE FOR YOURSELVES. AND I WILL HAVE EXILED YOU FROM BEYOND DAMASEQ.'

⁴⁴"The tabernacle with the testimony was with our fathers in the wilderness, just as he who spoke to Mosheh directed him to make it according to the pattern which he had been seeing. ⁴⁵And having received it in their turn, our fathers brought it in with Yehoshua when dispossessing the nations whom the Almighty drove out before our fathers, until the time of David.

⁴⁶"And David found favor in the Almighty's sight, and asked to find a dwelling place for the Almighty of Ya'aqov. ⁴⁷But it was Shelomoh who built a house for him. ⁴⁸However, the Most High does not dwell in houses made by human hands, just as the prophet says, ⁴⁹'HEAVEN IS MY THRONE, AND EARTH IS THE FOOTSTOOL OF MY FEET. WHAT KIND OF HOUSE WILL YOU BUILD FOR ME?' SAYS YĂHWEH. 'OR WHAT PLACE IS THERE FOR MY REPOSE? ⁵⁰WAS IT NOT MY HAND WHICH MADE ALL THESE THINGS?'

⁵¹"You stiff-necked men, and uncircumcised in heart and ears! You are always resisting the Holy Spirit. You are doing just as your fathers did. ⁵²Which one of the prophets did your fathers not persecute? And they killed those who had previously announced the coming of the Righteous One, whose betrayers and murderers you have now become, ⁵³you who received the Law attended by ranks of messengers, and yet did not keep it!"

7:40 δ Exo. 31:1. **7:42** μ→away: After relating the episode of the golden calf, Stephen jumps ahead in history straightaway to the exile of the northern kingdom which was carried away in stages by the kings of Assyria. This is related in 2 Kings 17:6-18. **7:42-43** ε Amos 5:25-27. **7:42** ω I have taken the translation here from the Hebrew of Amos 5:25-27 because it seems the Greek in Acts here is corrupt, which appears to be assimilated to the LXX here. The LXX mistakenly took Amos 5:25 as a question demanding a 'no' answer, rather than a statement (μὴ σφάγια καὶ θυσίας, as if: הַזְבָחִים). Reverted to the Hebrew here (הִזְבַחְתֶּם). **7:43** φ The LXX translator thought that Sikkuth was the word Sukkoth, tabernacle. They were probably not aware that it was the name of a Mesopotamian god. Further the words "your king" where turned to Μολοχ which requires a slight error to be imputed to the Hebrew text. Again, I think not. Sikkuth is identified with Ninurta, a high ranking star deity. And Kiywan the Saturn deity, with which the Greek Ραιφαν agrees. The Greek text deviates from Damaseq putting Bavel, and this may not be an error. Stephen may simply be giving a dynamic sense of the text since Bavel is beyond Damaseq. **7:49-50** λ Isa. 66:1-2. **7:53** δ εἰς διαταγὰς ἀγγέλων = *with orders of messengers*. The ordering means "rank" or "arrangement", or "array", and not that they actually "ordered" the commandments. Cf. Dan. 7:10. Yăhweh himself spoke the Law.

⁵⁴Now when they heard this, they were enraged, and they were gnashing their teeth at him. ⁵⁵But being full of the Holy Spĭrit, he gazed intently into heaven and saw the glory of the Almĭghty, and Yĕshua who had been standing at the right hand of the Almĭghty. ⁵⁶And he said, "Behold, I am seeing the heavens, which have been opening up, and the Sŏn of Man, who has been standing at the right hand of the Almĭghty."

⁵⁷But they cried out with a loud voice, and covered their ears, and they rushed upon him with the same passion. ⁵⁸And when they had driven him out of the city, they were stoning him, and the witnesses laid aside their robes beside the feet of a young man named Şa'ul.

⁵⁹And they went on stoning Stephen as he called upon Yăhweн and said, "Adŏnai Yĕshua, receive my spirit!" ⁶⁰And falling on his knees, he cried out with a loud voice, "Yăhweн, may you not have held this sin against them!" And having said this, he fell asleep.

8 ¹And Şa'ul was approving during his execution. And on that ᵗday a great persecution arose against the Assembly in Yerushalayim. And they were all scattered down through the country sides of Yehudah and Shomron, except the emissaries. ²And some devout men buried Stephen, and made a great lamentation over him. ³But Şa'ul was ravaging the Assembly, going down into the houses, and dragging off besides men also women. He was putting them in prison.

⁴Therefore, those who were scattered went about proclaiming the word. ⁵And Philip went down to the city of Shomron and was proclaiming the Anŏinted to them. ⁶And the crowds were with the same heart holding close to what was being said by Phillip, while listening to him and observing the signs which he was doing, ⁷because in the case of many who had unclean spirits, they were coming out of them shouting with a loud voice. And many who had been getting paralyzed and lame were healed. ⁸And there was much rejoicing in that city.

⁹Now there was a certain man named Şim'on, who beforehand was practicing magic in the city, and amazing the Shomroni nation, claiming himself to be someone great. ¹⁰And they all, from smallest to greatest, were giving attention to him, saying, "This man is what is called the Great Power of the Almĭghty." ¹¹And they were giving him attention because for a considerable time *he was known* to have been astounding them with magic arts.

¹²But when they affirmed Philip faithful proclaiming the good news about the kingdom of the Almĭghty and the name of Yĕshua the Anŏinted, they were being immersed, men besides also women. ¹³And even Şim'on himself pledged faithfulness, and after being immersed, he continued on with Philip. Besides observing signs and great miracles taking place, he himself was amazed.

¹⁴Now when the emissaries in Yerushalayim heard that 'Shomron has been receiving the word of the Almĭghty,' they sent them Peter and Yoĥanan, ¹⁵who

---

8:1 τ Late summer or early fall, AD 34. **8:16** ζ = *it*. **8:16** θ The descent of the Holy Spirit in Acts 2

Acts 8

came down and prayed for them, that they might receive the Holy Spirit, ¹⁶because ʲhe had not yet upon any one of them been ᵍfalling. And they who had been getting immersed were only beginning into the name of Adŏnai Yĕshua. ¹⁷Then they were laying their hands on them, and they were receiving the Holy Spirit.

¹⁸Now when Şim'on saw that the Spirit was bestowed through the laying on of the emissaries' hands, he offered them money, ¹⁹saying, "Give this authority to me as well, so that everyone on whom I may have laid my hands may be receiving the Holy Spirit." ²⁰But Peter said to him, "May your silver perish with you, because you thought you could obtain the gift of the Almĭghty with commerce! ²¹You have no part or portion in this matter, because your heart is not right before the Almĭghty. ²²Therefore be sorry and turn your heart from this wickedness of yours, and pray to Yăhwєн that if possible, the intention of your heart may be forgiven you. ²³Because I see that you are in the gall of bitterness and in the bondage of iniquity." ²⁴So Şim'on replied and said, "Plead yourselves on my behalf to Yăhwєн, so that nothing will have come upon me of what you have been speaking."

²⁵And so, when they had thoroughly testified and spoken the word of Yăhwєн, they were returning to Yerushalayim; besides *also* they were proclaiming the good news to many villages of the Shomronim.

²⁶But the Messenger *of* Yăhwєн spoke to Philip saying, "Arise and be going down south on the road that descends from Yerushalayim to Azzah." This is a desert road. ²⁷And he arose and went, and behold, there was an Ethiopian eunuch, a court official of Candace, queen of the Ethiopians, who was in charge of all her treasure. And he had been coming to Yerushalayim to worship. ²⁸Besides *also* he was returning and sitting in his chariot, and was reading the prophet Yeshayahu. ²⁹And the Spirit said to Philip, "Go up and join this chariot." ³⁰And when Philip had run up, he heard him reading Yeshayahu the prophet, and said, "Do you understand what you are reading?" ³¹And he said, "Well, how could I, unless someone guides me?" Besides *also* he invited Philip to come up and sit with him.

³²Now the passage of the text which he was reading was this: "HE WAS LED AS A SHEEP TO SLAUGHTER, AND AS A LAMB BEFORE ITS SHEARER IS SILENT, SO HE IS NOT GOING TO OPEN HIS MOUTH. ³³WITH HUMILIATION A JUST JUDGMENT WAS DENIED HIM. WHO WILL PONDER IT OF HIS KINDRED? FOR HIS LIFE IS REMOVED FROM THE EARTH." ³⁴And the eunuch answered Philip and said, "Please tell me, of whom does the prophet say this? Of himself, or of someone else?" ³⁵And Philip opened his mouth, and beginning from this text he proclaimed Yĕshua to him.

³⁶And as they went down the road they came to some water, and the eunuch

---

on the Jewish faithful set them apart from other Jews who had not received Mĕssiah. See Acts 2:38-39. So also it was considered necessary for those 'far off' (μακρὰν) to show tangible evidence of this promise, so that the faithful would be united into one people, so that the old factions would not divide them. The extraordinary delay in the Spirit here is so that Jewish leadership would be established at the beginning over and against Samaritan claims of priority. **8:32-33** η Isa 53:7-8 **8:37** Accept vs. 37: ᶠE, 36. 323. 453. 945. 1739. 1891. *pc* (it vg^d sy^{h**} mae; Ir Cyp).

said, "Look! Water! What prevents me from being immersed?" ³⁷ ʳAnd, he said to him, "If you are holding faithful from all your heart, it is permitted." And he answered, "I am holding faithful ʳto the Anŏinted One, the Almĭghty Sŏn.ʾ ³⁸And he ordered the chariot to stop, and they both went down into the water, besides Philip also the eunuch, and he immersed him. ³⁹And when they came up out of the water, the Spĭrit of Yăhwej snatched Philip away. And the eunuch saw him no more, but went on his way rejoicing. ⁴⁰But Philip found himself at Ashdod, and as he passed through he was proclaiming the good news to all the cities, until he came to Caesarea.

9

¹Now Şa'ul, still breathing threats and murder against the disciples of Adŏnai, went to the high priest, ²and asked for letters from his hand to the congregations at Dammeseq, so that if he may have found any belonging to the way, men, besides also women, he may bring them, who had been getting held bound, to Yerushalayim.

³And it came aboutᵀ that as he journeyed, he was nearing Dammeseq. Besides suddenly a light from heaven had shone around him, ⁴and *having* fallen upon the ground, *also* he had heard a voice saying to him, "Şa'ul, Şa'ul, why are you persecuting me?" ⁵And he said, "Who are you, Adŏnai?" And he said, "I am Yĕshua whom you are persecuting, ⁶but rise, and enter the city, and it will be told you what you must do."

⁷And, the men traveling with him hadʿ been standing speechless, hearing the voice, but seeing no one. ⁸And Şa'ul got up from the ground, and though his eyes had been getting opened, he could see nothing. And leading him by the hand, they brought him into Dammeseq. ⁹And he was three days without sight, and neither ate nor drank.

¹⁰Now there was a certain disciple at Dammeseq, named Hananyah, and Yăhwej said to him in a vision, "Hananyah!" And he said, "Behold, here am I, Yăhwej." ¹¹And Yăhwej said to him, "Arise and go to the street called Straight, and ask at the house of Yehudah for a man from Tarsus named Şa'ul, because behold, he is praying, ¹²and he has seen in a vision a man named Hananyah come in and lay his hands on him, so that he may regain his sight."

¹³But Hananyah answered, "Yăhwej, I have heard from many about this man, how much harm he did to your holy ones at Yerushalayim, ¹⁴and here he has authority from the chief priests to bind all who call upon your name."

¹⁵But Yăhwej said to him, "Be going, because he is my chosen instrument, to bear my name before the nations, besides also kings, besides the sons of Yisra'el. ¹⁶Indeed, I will show him how much it is necessary for him to suffer

---

8:37 ᵀCⲰⲐⲎⲤⲈⲒ E itᵉ Bedeᵐˢ = VIFA-3S *he will rescue [you]*. Reject. **8:37** ʳⲈⲒⲤ Eᵛⁱᵈ itᵉ Bedeᵐˢ. Accept.

9:3 τ Spring AD 36; 14 years to Acts 15 in AD 49; cf. Gal. 2:1. The 14 years is an extension of the 3 years of Gal. 1:18; Paul went to Damascus in AD 36, was converted (vs. 17-19), went into Arabia (vs. 22a), returned to Damascus, confounded the Jews in AD 38 (vs. 22b), escaped (vs. 25), then visited Peter on his first visit to Jerusalem in AD 39 (vs. 27).

over my name."

¹⁷Then Ḥananyah departed and entered the house, and after laying his hands on him said, "Brother Şa'ul, Adŏnai Yĕshua, who appeared to you on the road by which you were coming, has been sending me so that you will have regained your sight, and will have been filled with the Holy Spĭrit." ¹⁸And immediately there fell from his eyes something like scales. He saw again, besides also *having* risen up, he was immersed, ¹⁹and having taken food and he gained strength.

¹⁹ᵇAnd he appeared *for* some days with the disciples in Dammeseq, ²⁰and straightaway he was proclaiming Yĕshua in the congregations, *saying*, "He is the Almĭghty Sŏn." ²¹And all those hearing him were being amazed, and were saying, "Is this one not he who laid waste in Yerushalayim those calling upon this name? And he had been coming here for this *reason*, so that, having been getting *them* held bound, he may have led them before the chief priests!"

²²ᵃAnd, Şa'ul was getting himself more empowered 'in the word,' ²²ᵇand was confounding the Yehudim dwelling in Dammeseq, *by* proving that this *Yĕshua is the Anŏinted One.* ²³And as sufficient days were getting fulfilled, the Yehudim plotted together to do him in, ²⁴but their plot became known to Şa'ul. And they were also watching the gates day besides also night so that they may kill him, ²⁵but his disciples took him by night through the wall. They let him down, lowering him in a large basket.

²⁶And when he had come to Yerushalayim, he had attempted to join the disciples. And they were all afraid of him, not holding *it* faithful that he was a disciple. ²⁷But Bar-Nabba took hold of him and brought him to the emissaries and described to them how he had seen Yăhweн on the road, and that he had talked to him, and how at Dammeseq he had spoken out boldly in the name of Yĕshua. ²⁸Then he was with them going in, and going out of Yerushalayim, speaking out boldly in the name of Yăhweн. ²⁹He was talking besides also debating with the Greek Yehudim, but they had undertaken to do him in. ³⁰But when the brothers learned of it, they brought him down to Caesarea and sent him away to Tarsus.

³¹So the assembly throughout all Yehudah and Galil and Shomron enjoyed peace, being built up, and going on in the fear of Yăhweн and in the comfort of the Holy Spĭrit, it continued to increase.

³²Then it came about that as Peter was traveling through all those parts, he came down also to the holy ones who lived at Lod. ³³And there he found a certain man named Aeneas, lying on a bed more than eight years, who had been getting paralyzed. ³⁴And Peter said to him, "Aeneas, Yĕshua the Anŏinted heals you. Arise, and make your bed." And immediately he arose.

³⁵Then all who lived at Lod and Sharon saw him, and they turned to Yăhweн. ³⁶Now in Yafo there was a certain disciple named Taviṭha (which translated in Greek is called Dorcas). She was full of good deeds and charity, which she was doing. ³⁷Then it came about at that time that she fell sick and died, and when

---

9:22a 'C E pc h l p (mae).

they had washed her body, they laid it in an upper room. ³⁸And since Lod was near Yafo, the disciples, having heard that Peter was there, sent two men to him, entreating him, "You shall not have delayed to come to us."

³⁹And Peter arose and went with them. And when he had come, they brought him into the upper room. And all the widows stood beside him weeping, and showing all the tunics and garments that Dorcas used to make while she was with them. ⁴⁰But Peter sent them all out and knelt down and prayed, and turning to the body, he said, "Tavita, arise." And she opened her eyes, and when she saw Peter, she sat up. ⁴¹And he gave her his hand and raised her up. And calling the holy ones and widows, he presented her alive. ⁴²And it became known all over Yafo, and many pledged faithfulness upon Yăhweĥ. ⁴³And it came about that he stayed many days in Yafo at the side of a certain tanner, Şim'on.

10

¹And there was a certain man at Caesarea named Cornelius, a centurion of what was called the Italian cohort, ²a devout man, and one who feared the Almĭghty with all his household, and he gave many alms to the people, and prayed to the Almĭghty continually. ³About the ninth hour of the day he clearly saw in a vision the ᵘMessenger, the Almĭghty One, come to him, and say to him, "Cornelius!" ⁴And fixing his gaze upon him and being much alarmed, he said, "What is it, ʸAdŏnai?" And he said to him, "Your prayers and alms have ascended as a memorial before the Almĭghty. ⁵And now dispatch some men to Yafo, and send for a man named Şim'on, who is also called Peter. ⁶He is staying at the side of a certain tanner named Şim'on, whose house is by the sea."

⁷And when the Messenger who was speaking to him had departed, he summoned two of his servants and a devout soldier of those who were in constant attendance upon him, ⁸and after he had explained everything to them, he sent them to Yafo.

⁹And on the next day, as these are making their journey, and approaching the city, Peter went up on the housetop around the sixth hour to pray. ¹⁰And he became hungry and was desiring to eat, but while they *were* making preparations, he fell into a trance. ¹¹And he is beholding heaven, which had been opening itself up, and a certain object like a great sheet coming down, lowered by four corners to the ground, ¹²and there were in it all kinds of four-footed animals and crawling creatures of the earth and birds of the air. ¹³And a voice came to him, "Arise, Peter, kill and eat!" ¹⁴But Peter said, "By no means, Sir, because I

10:3 μ→Almĭghty: messenger of the Almĭghty: מַלְאַךְ הָאֱלֹהִים. Compare Judges 6:20. I believe this was THE Messenger. Luke is very careful in the way he places his clues. **10:4** γ or "Adon" or "Adŏnai." Even if the messenger was the Almĭghty Sŏn it is not clear if Cornelius would have recognized him. The Sŏn did not always mean to disclose himself without being directly asked (cf. Judges 13:18). When he appeared after his resurrection he was not always recognized. See 10:22.

10:12 ζ The sheet contained all kinds, which is to say both clean and unclean animals. We may suppose many unclean animals surrounding a few clean. See Mat. 15, Mark 7, Rom. 14. **10:14** Compare Ezekiel 4:12-15. **10:14** η Codex Bezae (D GA_05): **KOINON H AKAΘAPTON**. This variant (חֹל אוֹ טָמֵא) is unreported in NA-27. See Acts 11:8, "sharing defilement or unclean" (κοινὸν ἢ ἀκάθαρτον). Many translators,

have never eaten anything sharing defilement ⁿor unclean."

¹⁵And again a voice came to him a second time, "What the Almīghty has cleansed, you must not be making share defilement." ¹⁶And this happened three times. And immediately the object was taken up into heaven.

¹⁷And while Peter was being greatly perplexed in himself as to what the vision which he had seen may be, behold, the men who had been getting sent along by Cornelius, having asked directions for Şim'on's house, appeared at the gate. ¹⁸And calling out, they were asking whether Şim'on, who was also called Peter, was staying there. ¹⁹And while Peter was reflecting on the vision, the Spīrit said to him, "Behold, three men are looking for you. ²⁰But having arisen, step down *stairs*, and be traveling with them without doubting, because I have been sending them along."

²¹And Peter went down to the men and said, "Behold, I am the one you are looking for. What is the reason for which you are being by?"

²²And they said, "Cornelius, a centurion, a righteous and the Gŏd-fearing man, besides being well attested by the entire nation of the Yehudim, was divinely instructed by *the* Holy Messenger to send for you to come to his house and hear a message at your side." ²³ᵃAnd so he invited them in and gave them lodging.

²³ᵇAnd on the next day he arose and went away with them, and some of the brothers from Yafo accompanied him.

²⁴And on the following day he entered Caesarea. Now Cornelius was waiting for them, and had called together his relatives and close friends. ²⁵And when it came about that Peter entered, Cornelius met him, and ᵠfell at his feet and honored him. ²⁶But Peter raised him up, saying, "Stand up! I too am just a man."

²⁷And holding conversation with him, he entered, and he is finding many people, who have been coming together. ²⁸Besides *also* he was saying to them, "You yourselves are knowing how ᵟtaboo it is for a man who is a Yehudi to be associating or to be coming near another nation, when the Almīghty has shown

---

not understanding the difference, try to treat the two words as synonyms. Shared defilement occurs when something clean is associated with something regarded as unclean. Clean food served in a non-Jewish house was regarded as **KOINON** (common, חֹל) i.e. having 'shared defilement' and is not the same as things that are **ΑΚΑΘΑΡΤΟΝ** (unclean, טָמֵא): cf. Lev. 10:10; 1Sam. 21:5, 6; Ezek. 22:26; 42:20; 44:23; 48:15.

10:15 Things sharing defilement and unclean are here two categories. The unclean creatures are so by nature. The rest, even if they be clean beasts were supposed to be common, that is unclean by shared association with the unclean. In the Rabbinic view "uncleanness" was communicated by associations far exceeding the Scriptural limits. Peter was not to consider the uncleanness of the unclean beasts to be shared with the clean beasts associated with them. The faithful non-Jew was thus to be considered clean even though he had to dwell in the midst of the unclean. See 11:9. **10:25** ψ→honored: This word is used "of the Oriental fashion of making the salām or prostrating oneself before kings and superiors... to make obeisance" (Liddell). Peter was mildly irked at the custom which Jews did not practice due to its ambiguity with worship.

10:28 δ *Taboo*: ἀθέμιτον; or forbidden, illicit. But it was not unlawful according to the Law. Peter is referring to Jewish tradition **10:28** θ→sharer: κοινὸν = *shared*. מְחַלֵּל; *one who is making to be common*. A carrier of defilement without being the source of it.

10:28 γ *unclean*: that is, he should not assume it, because all non-Jews were unclean in the traditional Jewish definition. Peter now had to assume that a given non-Jew could be clean, and thus he could not call anyone unclean or common in the traditional sense. Peter does not mean that all men are "clean" in the Scriptural sense. They can be unclean in the proper sense of the word. See 1Cor. 7:14; Phil. 3:2; Rev. 21:27, 22:15.

me not to be calling any man ⁹a defilement sharer or ʸunclean. ²⁹Therefore surely without contradiction I came, when I was sent after. So I ask myself for what matter you have sent after me."

³⁰And Cornelius said, "From the fourth day until this hour, I was praying in my house during the ninth hour. And behold, a man stood before me in shining garments, ³¹and he said, 'Cornelius, your prayer has been heard and your alms have been remembered before the Almĭghty. ³²Send therefore to Yafo and invite Şim'on, who is also called Peter, to come to you. He is staying at the house of Şim'on the tanner beside the sea.' ³³And so I sent to you forthwith. Besides you have acted graciously, by having come. Now then, we are all present before the Almĭghty to hear all that you have been getting commanded by Adŏnai."

³⁴And opening his mouth, Peter said: "I most certainly understand now that the Almĭghty is not one to show partiality, ³⁵but in every nation the one fearing him and working righteousness is acceptable to him."

³⁶"The word which he sent to the sons of Yisra'el, proclaiming peace through Yĕshua the Anŏinted (he is Adŏnai of all)—³⁷you yourselves have been knowing, that is what took place throughout all Yehudah, starting from Galil after the immersion which Yoħanan proclaimed. ³⁸You know of Yĕshua of Netsereṯh, how the Almĭghty anointed him with the Holy Spĭrit and with power, and how he went about doing good, and healing all who were oppressed by the Slanderer, because the Almĭghty was with him."

³⁹"And we are witnesses of all the things he did besides in the land of the Yehudim also in Yerushalayim. And they also put him to death by suspending him upon a tree. ⁴⁰The Almĭghty raised him up on the third day, and granted that he should become visible, ⁴¹not to all the people, but to witnesses who had been getting chosen beforehand by the Almĭghty, that is, to us, who ate and drank with him after he arose from the dead."

⁴²"And he ordered us to proclaim to the people, and thoroughly to testify that this is the One who has been getting appointed^β by the Almĭghty as Judge of the living and the dead. ⁴³About this one, all the prophets testify, concerning release from sins, to be received through his name, by everyone holding faithful to him."

⁴⁴While Peter was still speaking these words, the Holy Spĭrit fell upon all those who were listening to the message. ⁴⁵And the faithful ones from the circumcision, as many as who had come with Peter, were amazed, because the gift of the Holy Spĭrit had been getting poured out upon the nations also. ⁴⁶For they were hearing them speaking with languages and exalting the Almĭghty.

⁴⁶ᵇThen Peter responded, ⁴⁷"Surely no one can refuse the water for these to be immersed who have received the Holy Spĭrit just as we did, can he?" ⁴⁸And he ordered them to be immersed in the name of Yĕshua the Anŏinted. Then they asked him to stay on for a few days.

10:42 β As the parable says, Mĕssiah went away to receive his kingdom from the Father. See Luke 19:12, 15.

Acts 11

11 ¹Now the emissaries and the brothers who were down through Yehudah heard that the nations also had received the word of the Almĭghty. ²And when Peter came up to Yerushalayim, those who were circumcised took issue with him, ³saying, "You went to uncircumcised men and ate with them!?"

⁴But Peter began speaking and proceeded to explain to them in orderly sequence, saying, ⁵"I was in the city of Yafo praying. And in a trance I saw a vision, a certain object coming down like a great sheet lowered by four corners from the heaven, and it came right down to me. ⁶And when I had fixed my gaze upon it and was observing it I saw the four-footed animals of the earth and the wild beasts and the crawling creatures and the birds of the air. ⁷And I also heard a voice saying to me, 'Arise, Peter! Kill and eat.' ⁸But I said, 'By no means, Sir, for nothing sharing defilement ᵟor unclean has ever entered my mouth.' ⁹But a voice from heaven answered a second time, 'What the Almĭghty has cleansed, you shall not be making share defilement.' ¹⁰And this happened three times, and everything was drawn back up into heaven."

¹¹"And behold, at that moment three men stood before the house in which we were, who had been getting sent to me from Caesarea. ¹²And the Spĭrit told me to go with them without misgivings. And these six brothers also went with me, and we entered the man's house. ¹³And he reported to us how he had seen the Messenger standing in his house, and saying, 'Send to Yafo, and have Şim'on, who is also called Peter, brought here. ¹⁴And he will speak words to you by which you will be rescued, you and all your household.'"

¹⁵"And as I began to speak, the Holy Spĭrit fell upon them, just as he did upon us at the beginning. ¹⁶And I remembered the word of Adŏnai, how he used to say, 'Yoḥanan immersed with water, but you will be immersed with the Holy Spĭrit.' ¹⁷If the Almĭghty therefore has given to them the same gift as also to us, who have pledged faithfulness upon Adŏnai Yĕshua the Anŏinted, who was I that I could stand in the Almĭghty's way?"

¹⁸And when they heard this, they fell silent, and glorified the Almĭghty, saying, "Well then, the Almĭghty has offered to the nations also *the chance for being sorry and turning of the heart that leads to life*."

¹⁹So then those who were scattered because of the persecution that arose in connection with Stephen made their way to Phoenicia and Cyprus and Antioch, speaking the word to no one except to Yehudim alone. ²⁰But there were some of them, men of Cyprus and Cyrene, who came to Antioch and were speaking to the Greeks also, proclaiming Adŏnai Yĕshua. ²¹And the hand of Yăhweʜ was with them, besides *also* a large number having pledged faithfulness, had turned to Yăhweʜ.

²²And the news about them reached the ears of the assembly at Yerusha-

---

11:8 ᵟ See 10:14, 28. Here Peter used the word "or" which shows that two categories are meant. The unclean was defiled by nature. The common was not defiled by nature, but only by association. Peter was not to consider the faithful non-Jews unclean because of their shared association with unclean Gentiles. See 10:15.

layim, and they sent Bar-Nabba off to Antioch. ²³Then when he had come and witnessed the loving-kindness of the Almĭghty, he rejoiced and was encouraging them all with resolute heart to remain true to Yăhweн, ²⁴because he was a good man, and full of the Holy Spĭrit and of faithfulness. And considerable numbers were brought to Yăhweн.

²⁵And he left for Tarsus to look for Şa'ul, ²⁶and when he found him, he brought *him* to Antioch. And it turned out for them, indeed *for* an entire year, to be gathered with the assembly, and to teach an ample crowd, besides *for* the disciples firstly in Antioch to take the name of ˣMessianics.

²⁷Now at this time some prophets came down from Yerushalayim to Antioch. ²⁸And one of them named Agav stood up and was indicating by the Spĭrit that there would certainly be a great famine all over the inhabited land. And this took place in the reign of Claudius.ᵗ ²⁹And in the proportion that any of the disciples had means, each of them determined to send a contribution for the relief of the brothers living in Yehudah. ³⁰And this they did, sending it in charge of Bar-Nabba and Şa'ul to the elders.

12

¹Now about that time Herod the king laid hands on some from the Assembly, in order to harm them. ²And he had Ya'aqov the brother of Yoнanan put to death with a sword. ³And when he saw that it pleased the Yehudim, he proceeded to arrest Peter also. Now it was the days of Unleavened Bread.ᵗ ⁴And when he had seized him, he put him in prison, delivering him to four squads of soldiers to guard him, intending after the Passover to bring him out before the people. ⁵So Peter was kept in the prison, but prayer for him was getting brought intensely by the Assembly near to the Almĭghty.

⁶And when Herod was about to bring him forth, in that night Peter was sleeping between two soldiers where he had been getting held bound with two chains. Besides guards in front of the door were watching over the prison. ⁷And behold, the Messenger *of* Yăhweн suddenly appeared, and a light shone in the cell, and he struck Peter's side and roused him, saying, "Get up quickly." And his chains fell off his hands. ⁸And the Messenger said to him, "Gird yourself and put on your sandals." And he did so. Then he says to him, "Throw your cloak around you and be following me."

⁹And when he went out, he was following, and he had not been knowing that what was being done by the Messenger was real, but thought he was seeing a

---

11:26 Χ or *Christians:* The word means 'anointedians,' sing. 'anointedian,' (or anointian(s)). The ending 'ians' (-ιανούς, -ιανός, -ιανòν) is gentilic, akin to adding 'ite' (someone of) to Israel to for "Israelite," (someone of Israel) or 'n' to Australia to form Australian. ▷ While the word has sense in Greek, it has none in English left in its Greek form, just as the Hebrewized English of the same term "Messianic" lacks the meaning 'anoint' in English. The term may mean ones of or related to the Anointed One, or ones who are anointed (through the Anointed One), the last sense being more proper but less perceived. See Psa. 105:15 and 1 Yoн. 2:20, 27 (χρῖσμα); the faithful are in fact 'anointed.' ▷ See 1 Peter 4.16; Acts 26:28. Psalm 105:15: מְשִׁיחָי, *Meshikhai* = *MY ANOINTED ONES.* See endnote No. 1 for Galatians. **11:28** ψ The famine was 44-45 AD. **12:3** τ AD 43.

12:23 τ AD 44. **13:1** ρ Greek Νίγερ from Latin

vision. ¹⁰And when they had passed the first and second guard, they came to the iron gate that leads into the city, which opened for them by itself. And they went out and went along one street, and immediately the Messenger departed from him. ¹¹And when Peter came to himself, he said, "Now I have been knowing for sure that Yăhweɧ has sent forth his Messenger and rescued me from the hand of Herod and all the expectation of the people of the Yehudim."

¹²Besides when he realized this, he went to the house of Miryam, the mother of Yoɧanan, who is called Mark, where many had been getting gathered together and *have been* praying among themselves. ¹³And when he knocked at the door of the gate, a servant-girl named Rodi came to answer. ¹⁴And when she recognized Peter's voice, because of her joy she did not open the gate, but when she ran in, she reported Peter to have been standing in front of the gate. ¹⁵And they said to her, "You are out of your mind!" But she kept insisting that it was so. And they kept saying, "It is his messenger." ¹⁶But Peter continued knocking, and when they had opened, they saw him and were amazed. ¹⁷But motioning to them with his hand to be silent, he described to them how Yăhweɧ had led him out of the prison. Besides *also* he said, "Report these things to Ya'aqov and the brothers." And he departed and went to another place.

¹⁸Now when day came, there was no small disturbance among the soldiers as to what could have become of Peter. ¹⁹And when Herod had searched for him and had not found him, he examined the guards and ordered that they be led away to execution. And he went down from Yehudah to Caesarea and was spending time there.

²⁰Now he was very angry with the people of Tsor and Tsidon. And with the same heart they were coming along to him, and having persuaded Blastus the king's chamberlain, they were asking for peace, because their country was fed by the king's country. ²¹And on an appointed day Herod, having put on his royal apparel, took his seat on the platform and was delivering an address to them. ²²And the people kept crying out, "The voice of a Gŏd and not of a man!" ²³And immediately the Messenger *of* Yăhweɧ struck him because he did not give the Almĭghty the glory, and he was eaten by worms and died.

²⁴But the word of Yăhweɧ continued to grow and to be multiplied. ²⁵And Bar-Nabba and Şa'ul returned from Yerushalayim when they had fulfilled their mission, taking along with them Yoɧanan, who was also called Mark.

13 Now there were in Antioch, down from the assembly around there, prophets and teachers besides Bar-Nabba, also Şim'on who was called ᵖBlack, and Lucius of Cyrene, besides Menaɧem*ᵘ* who was brought up with Herod the Tetrarch, and Şa'ul. ²And while they were ministering to Yăhweɧ and fasting, the Holy Spĭrit said, "Set apart for me Bar-Nabba and Şa'ul for the work to which

---

meaning 'black.' **13:1** μ Not the Menaɧem mentioned in Josephus and the Talmud. Cf. Jos. Ant. 15.10.5: 15:373-374 and B.T. Chagigah 16b.10, but possibly a son or grandson of this man was a close friend of Antipas.

I have been getting them called." ³Then, when they had fasted and prayed and laid their hands on them, they sent them away.

⁴So, being sent out by the Holy Spirit, they went down to Seleucia, besides from there, they sailed away to Cyprus. ⁵And when they reached Salamis, they were proclaiming the word of the Almĭghty in the congregations of the Yehudim, and they also had Yoḥanan as their helper. ⁶And when they had gone through the whole island as far as Paphos, they found a certain magician, a Yehudi false prophet whose name was Bar-Yeshua, ⁷who was with the proconsul, Sergius Paulus, a man of intelligence. This man summoned Bar-Nabba and Şa'ul and sought to hear the word of the Almĭghty.

⁸But Alima the magician (for thus his name is translated) was opposing them, seeking to turn the proconsul away from the pledge of faithfulness. ⁹But Şa'ul, who was also known as Paul, filled with the Holy Spirit, fixed his gaze upon him, ¹⁰and said, "You who are full of all deceit and fraud, you son of the Slanderer, you enemy of all justice, will you not cease to make crooked the straight ways of Yăhweh? ¹¹And now, behold, the hand of Yăhweh is upon you, and you will be blind and not see the sun for a time." So immediately a mist and a darkness fell upon him, and he went about seeking those who would lead him by the hand. ¹²When the proconsul saw what had been happening, he pledged faithfulness, being amazed at the teaching of Yăhweh.

¹³Now Paul and his companions put out to sea from Paphos and came to Perga in Pamphylia, and Yoḥanan left them and returned to Yerushalayim. ¹⁴But going on from Perga, they arrived at Pisidian Antioch, and on the day of the Şabbaṭhs they went into the congregation and sat down. ¹⁵And after the reading of the Law and the prophets the congregation officials sent to them, saying, "Brothers, if you have any word of exhortation for the people, be saying it."

¹⁶And Paul stood up, and motioning with his hand, he said, "Men of Yisra'el, and you who fear the Almĭghty, listen! ¹⁷The Almĭghty of this people Yisra'el chose our fathers, and made the people great during their stay in the land of Mitsrayim, and with an uplifted arm he led them out from it. ¹⁸And for a period of about forty years he put up with them in the wilderness. ¹⁹And when he had destroyed seven nations in the land of Kena'an, he caused them to inherit their land. ²⁰And after these things, about four hundred and fifty years, he gave them judges, until Shemu'el the prophet.˙ ²¹And then they asked for a king, and the Almĭghty gave them Şa'ul the son of Qish, a man of the tribe of Binyamin, for forty years.˙ ²²And after he had removed him, he raised up Dauid to be their king, concerning whom he also testified and said, 'I HAVE FOUND DAUID THE SON OF YISHAI, A MAN AFTER MY HEART'ᵠ, who will do all my will.'"

13:20 τ 1566 B.C. to 1117 B.C. The 450 years are the sum of all figures in the book of Judges up to Shemu'el. The text says 'about' because the period of the elders is included in the time span, and this period requires a very complex calculation using Şabbaṭical years to determine that it is 20 years. It is not plainly stated in the text. **13:21** τ1103-1063 B.C. 2 Samuel 2:10, "a son of forty years," i.e. his father's kingdom. **13:22** ψ 1 Sam 13:14, Psa 89:20

²³"From the offspring of this man, according to promise, the Almĭghty has brought to Yisra'el a Rescuer, Yĕshua, ²⁴after Yoḥanan had proclaimed before his coming an immersion of being sorry and turning of heart *from sin* to all the people of Yisra'el. ²⁵And while Yoḥanan was completing his course, he kept saying, 'What do you suppose that I am? I am not he. But behold, one is coming after me the sandals of whose feet I am not worthy to untie.'"

²⁶"Brothers, sons of Avraham's family, and those among you who fear the Almĭghty, to us the word of this deliverance is sent out, ²⁷because those who live in Yerushalayim, and their rulers, recognizing neither him nor the utterances of the prophets, which are being read down through every Ṣabbaṯh, fulfilled these by condemning him. ²⁸And though they found no ground for putting him to death, they asked Pilate that he be executed. ²⁹And when they had finished all such things that had been getting written about him, they took him down from the tree and laid him in a tomb."

³⁰"Yet, the Almĭghty raised him from the dead, ³¹and for many days he appeared to those who came up with him from Galil to Yerushalayim, who are now his witnesses to the people."

³²"And we are proclaiming to you the good news, the promise made to the fathers, ³³that this *promise*, the Almĭghty has been fully fulfilling for their children, even us, *by* having raised up Yĕshua, as also it had been getting written in the second Psalm, 'YOU ARE MY SŎN. TODAY I HAVE BEEN BRINGING YOU FORTH.ᶿ' ³⁴And since he raised him up from the dead, (who is no more going to be returning *to death*, to decay), *now* likewise he has been speaking: {I WILL GIVE ᵝHIM—ᵅTO YE—ᵞA COVENANT OF OLD, THE KINDNESSES RELATING TO DAUID, THE FAITHFUL ONES.' ³⁵Therefore he also says in another Psalm, 'YOU WILL NOT ALLOW YOUR KIND ONE TO UNDERGO DECAY.ᵖ' ³⁶Because David, after he had served the purpose of the Almĭghty in his own generation, fell asleep, and was laid among his fathers, and underwent decay, ³⁷but he whom the Almĭghty raised did not undergo decay."

³⁸"Therefore let it be getting known to you men, brothers, that through this one release from sins is being proclaimed to you, even from all which you are not able by the Law of Mosheh to be administered ˣjustice. ³⁹By this one everyone holding faithful is getting himself administered ᵟjusticeᵘ."

13:33 θ Psa 2:7 **13:34** ξ→give: Isa. 55:4 לְאֻמִּים נְתַתִּיו נָגִיד **13:34** β supply *him*. **13:34** α→ones. Isa 55:3. **13:34** γ→old: בְּרִית עוֹלָם. Isa 55:3, διαθήκην αἰώνιον τὰ ὅσια Δαυὶδ τὰ πιστά; cf. Isa 42:6: וְאֶתֶּנְךָ לִבְרִית עָם לְאוֹר גּוֹיִם. Luke 1:72; Lev. 26:42, 45 **13:35** ρ Psa 16:10.

13:38 ℵ√ The great attack of Satan on forgiveness of sins is to deceive people that a sacrifice is required for forgiveness. But after forgiveness, sacrifice is symbolic of the removal of sin by Gŏd, and the ransom cost exacted by sin in dealing with it. But Gŏd forgives those repenting before the lesson. Sacrifice does not forgive. It only teaches a lesson. But people have been deceived into thinking that their baptism, their circumcision, or some legal procedure effected by ritual or sacrifice is the basis of forgiveness. ▷ The point here then is that the Most High judges when it is just to adminster forgiveness, which he does so in view of repentance. Forgiveness is not administered by the Levitical Law. It is administered by Mĕssiah, because he is the Almĭghty Sŏn. The sacrificial law teaches the lesson, at the end of which is the refrain, "And he has been forgiven," that is to say, the sacrifice is just an assurance or declaration that Gŏd has forgiven. Spiritual cleansing of sin is also administered by Messiah, as well as teaching us in the heart how to

⁴⁰"Be watching therefore, so that what has been getting spoken of in the prophets will not have come upon you, ⁴¹'BEHOLD, YOU SCOFFERS, AND WONDER,

---

be righteous. So the Law does not administer forgiveness. Baptism does not. Circumcision does not. Faith does not. But Messiah administers forgiveness and works the spiritual change through our cooperation. ▷ But what about 'atonement?' they will say: KIPPURIM means "a declaring to be wiped," i.e. it is a sacrificial procedure that formally instructs us of our forgiveness (declares it), illustrates the divine ransom from death, and divine cleansing from sin. The procedure is symbolic of spiritual reality: A person is forgiven when they repent, and the heart jointly cleansed with the Holy Spirit, but this administration of justice is an instructive formality through the sacrifice, declaring the invalidity of death's claim against us, and declaring the heart cleansed. Actual forgiveness almost always happens before the associated ritual declares it, beginning at which point the person admits guilt and changes course. The law provided for sacrificial declarations of wiping of our sin in cases of lesser sins of ignorance. But no such formal administration of justice was prescribed for serious transgressions and iniquities, except prophetically speaking pointing to Messiah. **13:39** δ√ Unlike Greek δικαιόω which usually connotes justice in negative terms, the Hebrew sense (Hiphil of צָדַק) connotes a favorable justice. In English this might be termed "to get justice for someone" (הִצְדִּיק). The relevant sense occurs in 2 Sam. 15:4. HALOT defines the term as: "1. to **obtain rights** [justice] **for**" and cites 2 Sam. 15:4; Isa. 50:8; Psa. 82:3; Dan. 12:3; "2. to **assist someone toward his rights**" and cites Isaiah 53:11! BDB has "1. *do justice*, in administering law." This means that the just one administers favorable justice. In his role as advocate for the guilty, Messiah's death stands for two things, (1) an epitome of actual divine suffering in regard to bearing our sin and cost in cleansing it, and (2) a guilt offering symbolizing the first point in the same way that lesser offerings make the same point. With respect to No. 1, there is a difference. The lesser offerings were not acts of lawlessness, but only a symbolic role play of the effect of lawlessness and the cost to be ransomed from it. We may suppose in the symbolism that the lawlessness is diverted (or transferred) to the offering by laying hands on it. Through death, lawlessness collects the ransom. We must think here of the intrinsic destruction of sin and the offering as a ransom. But In the case of Messiah, we are given a window on actual lawlessness exacting some of the cost caused by sin against his flesh. In the injustice done to Messiah, veil is pulled back so we can see a close up of the already existing divine suffering in the spiritual realm in the physical realm. Having allowed us to see this effect on his human self, the Most High took advantage of the fact that Lawlessness had done to Messiah what lawful sacrifices only showed in symbolism. He designated Messiah a guilt offering, or he regarded it as such. As a guilt offering Messiah's death represents the cost of our sin. His blood represents the cost of our cleansing. It represents a legal declaration of wiping our penalty and the removal of our sin. So Messiah's offering operates the same way as the sin offering and guilt offering, except it is not limited to sins of ignorance. And with the exception made in the first point that Lawlessness is shown to have taken the cost, and not just a symbolism of it with the lesser legal offering. ▷ The normative Greek sense may be generalized to include the favorable justice of pardon, and the KIPPURIM 'officially' declares the penalty wiped by symbolically ransoming us from death. The sacrificial aspect of Messiah's death is indicative of what is really happening in the spiritual realm. See Appendix X. **13:41** η Hab. 1:5.

13:39 μ Formal justicing for sins of disloyalty, among the faithful of old who repent, only came when Messiah died. That is, there was a long gap of time between their forgiveness and the declaration of wiping through Messiah's ransom from death. The second goat signified for the forgiven that iniquity is removed from the sinner and the community. ▷ The Father agreed to forgive our transgressions, and ransom us from the powers keeping us in bondage. He administering his justice this way, forgiving the faithful benevolently (without collecting a payment to himself). ▷ The ransom does not represent a payment required by the Father, but a payment exacted by the Lawlessness keeping us in bondage. ▷ The offering does not 'justify' the sinner, unless we go back to Middle English, to a meaning common with earlier Greek and Latin: to administer justice. Sin is not paid for by the offering, and the justice administered is forgiveness in view of confession and repetance. All pecuniary examples are also incorrect. The ransom is not the satisfaction of a debt like a monetary debt. In such cases the one owed the debt is fully compensated, and has no net loss. ▷ But the Father truly forgives. He bears a permanent loss from our sin and the sins of mankind that cannot be satisfied or repaid by any means. The ransom shows him bearing the cost. So we are truly pardoned. Because the Sŏn made a ransom exacted by Lawlessness, all judgment of Lawlessness will be turned over to the Sŏn. ▷ He does not perfectly keep the law *on our behalf* either, because the Father forgives. The Father does not accept impossible compensation. That is just legalism. Vicarious righteousness (merit) is a legal trick stretching all the way from the false rabbinical doctrine of zeḵuth to the legal righteousness of Luther. It does not reduce the Almĭghty's loss from our sins. But to us he decides for a benevolent justice without works by his covenant faithfulness. He collects no payment. ▷ To us who are pardoned, he wants us to become righteous. Perfection does not come instantly, but it comes at the end,

AND PERISH, BECAUSE I AM ACCOMPLISHING A WORK IN YOUR DAYS, A WORK WHICH, NO, YOU SHALL NOT HAVE HELD FAITHFUL, THOUGH SOMEONE MAY BE DESCRIBING IT TO YOU^η.'"

⁴²And as Paul and Bar-Nabba were going out, the people kept begging that these things *may* be spoken to them the next Ṣabbath. ⁴³Now when the congregation had broken up, many of the Yehudim and of the God-fearing proselytes followed Paul and Bar-Nabba, who, speaking to them, were persuading them to continue in the loving-kindness of the Almĭghty.

⁴⁴And the next Ṣabbath nearly the whole city assembled to hear the word of the Almĭghty. ⁴⁵But when the Yehudim saw the crowds, they were filled with jealousy, and were contradicting the things spoken by Paul, and were blaspheming. ⁴⁶Besides, Paul and Bar-Nabba having spoken out boldly, they *also* said, "It was necessary that the word of the Almĭghty should be spoken to you first. Since you repudiate it, and judge yourselves unworthy of everlasting life, behold, we are turning to the nations. ⁴⁷For thus Yăhwej has been commanding to us, 'I HAVE BEEN SETTING YOU AS A LIGHT FOR THE NATIONS, THAT YOU SHOULD BRING DELIVERANCE TO THE END OF THE EARTH^ψ.'"

⁴⁸And hearing this, the nations were rejoicing and were glorifying the Word of Yăhwej. Then they pledged faithfulness, as many as ^ξhad been disposing themselves to seek everlasting life. ⁴⁹And the word of Yăhwej was being spread through the whole region.

⁵⁰But the Yehudim aroused the devout women of prominence and the leading men of the city, and instigated a persecution against Paul and Bar-Nabba, and drove them out of their district. ⁵¹But they shook off the dust of their feet in protest against them and went to Iconium. ⁵²Besides *also* the disciples were themselves filled with joy and with the Holy Spĭrit.

14

¹And it came about that in Iconium they entered the congregation of the Yehudim together, and spoke in such a manner that a great number pledged faithfulness from among the Yehudim, as well as also of the

---

when he raises the dead and we put on immortality. Do you want to become righteous? Then hold faithful to Mĕssiah from your heart, and do the things that show loyalty to him. **13:47** ψ Isa 49:6.

13:48 ξ→*themselves*. Or *had been determining themselves*. The idea is that they set their own minds to it. The Greek verb is middle or passive. Clearly the middle (reflexive sense: determined *themselves*) is correct. The Almĭghty does not rule the will of man by fate, but he allows freedom, which then he puts to the test. See Deut. 8:1-2; Gen. 6:6; 18:21; 22:12. ▷ The ἦσαν τεταγμένοι is a periphrastic construction, i.e. imperfect + perfect. This has contextual the force of the pluperfect (cf. Wallace, pg. 648). This suggests that they set their dispositions prior to confirming their faithfulness, and prior to hearing Paul's final rejoinder to the Jews about the good news being announced to them first, but which upon their refusal was offered to the nations. Thus, the pluperfect is not prior to their hearing the good news, when they disposed themselves to listen, but it is prior to Paul's more pointed appeal to the nations upon the Jewish refusal. For by the time he made it, the whole city had been listening to him for some while. The point of the pluperfect is simply to emphasize that they had been setting their dispositions already before the final rejoinder. ▷ Moulton's Analytical Lexicon supplies the translation *disposed* instead of "appointed" or "ordained." Timothy Friberg's Analytical Lexicon also supplies, "as many as had become disposed toward eternal life." ▷ The Greek perfect is equivalent to the English perfect progressive, almost exactly so. So they were disposing themselves all along while listening to Paul.

Greeks. ²But the disobedient Yehudim stirred up and poisoned the hearts of the non-Jews against the brothers. ³Therefore they consumed a considerable time there speaking boldly for Yăhweh, who was bearing witness to the word of his loving-kindness, granting that signs and wonders be done by their hands. ⁴But the multitude of the city was divided, and some sided with the Yehudim, and some with the emissaries.

⁵But when a violent rage came over the pagans besides also the Yehudim with their rulers, to mistreat and to stone them, ⁶they became aware of it and fled to the cities of Lycaonia, Lystra and Derbe, and the surrounding region. ⁷And there they continued to proclaim the good news.

⁸And at Lystra there was sitting a certain man, without strength in his feet, lame from his mother's womb, who had never walked. ⁹This man was listening to Paul as he spoke, who, when he had fixed his gaze upon him, and had seen that he had the faithfulness to be made well, ¹⁰said with a loud voice, "Stand upright on your feet." And he leaped up and was walking. ¹¹Besides the crowds having seen what Paul had done, they *also* raised their voice, saying in the Lycaonian language, "The gods have become like men and have come down to us."

¹²Besides they were calling Bar-Nabba, Zeus, but Paul, Hermes, because he was the chief speaker. ¹³Besides the priest of Zeus, whose Temple was just outside the city, having brought oxen and garlands to the gates, wanted to offer sacrifice with the crowds.

¹⁴But when the emissaries, Bar-Nabba and Paul, heard of it, they tore their robes and rushed out into the crowd, crying out ¹⁵and saying, "Men, why are you doing these things? We are also men of the same nature as you, and proclaim the good news to you in order that you should turn from these vain things to a living Almĭghty, WHO MADE THE HEAVEN AND THE EARTH AND THE SEA, AND ALL THAT IS IN THEM,ᵞ ¹⁶who during the generations which have been going by, he suffered all the nations to be going their own ways, ¹⁷and yet he did not leave himself without witness, in that he did good and gave you rains from heaven and fruitful seasons, satisfying your hearts with food and gladness." ¹⁸And even saying these things, they with difficulty restrained the crowds from offering sacrifice to them.

¹⁹But Yehudim came from Antioch and Iconium, and having persuaded the crowds, they stoned Paul and dragged him out of the city, supposing him to have been dying. ²⁰But while the disciples stood around him, he arose and entered the city. And the next day he went away with Bar-Nabba to Derbe.

²¹Besides having proclaimed the good news to that city and having made many disciples, they *also* returned to Lystra and to Iconium and to Antioch, ²²strengthening the souls of the disciples, encouraging them to continue in the pledge of faithfulness, and because, through many tribulations it is necessary for us to enter the kingdom of the Almĭghty. ²³And when they had chosen elders

---

14:15 γ Exo 20:11

for them in every assembly, having prayed with fasting, they committed them to Yăhweн, to whom they had been holding faithful.

²⁴And they passed through Pisidia and came into Pamphylia. ²⁵And when they had spoken the word in Perga, they went down to Attalia, ²⁶and from there they sailed to Antioch, from where they had been getting committed to the loving-kindness of the Almĭghty for the work that they had accomplished.

²⁷And when they had arrived and gathered the assembly together, they were reporting all things that the Almĭghty had done with them and how he had opened the door of ᵖfaithfulness to the nations. ²⁸And they spent a long time with the disciples.

15

¹And some men came down from Yehudah and were teaching the brothers, "If you ˣare not circumcised according to the custom of Mosheh, you ᵑcannot be rescuedˡ." ²And when Paul and Bar-Nabba had great dissension and debate with them, they determined that Paul and Bar-Nabba and certain others of them should go up to Yerushalayim to the emissaries and elders concerning this issue. ³Therefore, being helped forward by the assembly, they were going throughout besides Phoenicia also Shomron, describing in detail the conversion of the nations, and were bringing great joy to all the brothers. ⁴And when they arrived at Yerushalayim, they were received by the assembly and the emissaries and the elders. Besides *also* they reported all that the Almĭghty had done with them.

⁵But stood up some of those from the party of the Perushim, who had been holding faithful, saying that, "It is necessary to be circumcising them, ᵝbesides to be commanding *them* to be keeping the law of Mosheh."

⁶Were ᵗgathered together besides the emissaries also the elders to look into this matter. ⁷And after there was much debate, Peter stood up and said to them, "Brothers, you know that in the early days the Almĭghty made a choice among you, that by my mouth the nations should hear the word of the good news also, to pledge faithfulness. ⁸And the Almĭghty, who knows the heart, has borne witness to them, giving them the Holy Spĭrit, just as he also did to us, ⁹and he has made no distinction between us besides, even for them because of ᵠ the pledge of faithfulness having ᶿpurified their hearts. ¹⁰Now therefore why do you put the Almĭghty to the test by placing upon the neck of the disciples a yoke which neither our fathers nor we have been able to bear? ¹¹But we hold faithful to be rescued through the loving-kindness of Adŏnai Yĕshua, in the same way as they also are."

14:27 π or 'the door of the Faith.' **15:1** χ η and λ. See Endnote 15:1 χ, page 610. **15:5** β τε = *besides, as well as;* See Endnote 15:5 β page 610. **15:9** ψ τῇ πίστει, or "with the pledge of f." See Endnote 15:9 ψ page 611. **15:6** τ AD 49 near Shavu'ot.

15:9 θ→hearts: Pagans are in darkness of uncertainty, fear, doubt, and guilt due to their rebellion and sin. By pledging faithfulness, repenting from sin and getting the forgiveness of sins, their hearts are purified from rebellion and the condemnation it brings. This purification does not mean perfection, but coming

¹²And all the gathering fell silent, and they were listening to Bar-Nabba and Paul as they were relating what signs and wonders the Almĭghty had done through them among the nations.

¹³And after they had stopped speaking, Yaʻaqov answered, saying, "brothers, listen to me. ¹⁴Şimʻon has related how the Almĭghty first concerned himself about taking from among the nations a people for his name. ¹⁵And with this the words of the prophets agree, just as it has been getting written, ¹⁶"AFTER THESE THINGS I WILL RETURN, AND I WILL REBUILD THE TABERNACLE OF DAᴜID WHICH HAS BEEN FALLING, AND THAT WHICH HAS BEEN GETTING UNDERMINED I WILL REBUILD, AND I WILL MAKE IT STRAIGHT AGAIN, ¹⁷IN ORDER THAT THE REMNANT OF MANKIND ᴡILL HAVE SOUGHT YĂHWEḤ, AND ALL THE NATIONS UPON WHOM WILL HAVE BEEN GETTING CALLED MY NAME UPON THEM, ¹⁸SAYS YĂHWEḤ, WHO IS DOING THESE THINGS$^\psi$, things known from time immemorial."

¹⁹Therefore it is my judgment that we do not trouble those who are turning to the Almĭghty from among the nations, ²⁰but that we write to them that they keep themselves from the defilements of idols and from fornication and from what is strangled and from blood. ²¹For Mosheh from ancient generations has those throughout the $^\eta$cities proclaiming him, since he is read in the congregations throughout every Şabbaṭh."

²²Then it seemed good to the emissaries and the elders, with the whole assembly, to choose men from among them to send to Antioch with Paul and Bar-Nabba, Yehudah called Bar-Şabba, and Sila, leading men among the brothers, ²³having written through their hand thus, "The emissaries and the brothers who are elders, to the brothers down through Antioch and Syria and Cilicia who are from the nations, greetings. ²⁴Since we have heard that some of our number have disturbed you with their words, unsettling your souls$^\intercal$, to whom we gave no instruction, ²⁵it seemed good to us, having become of the same heart, to select men to send to you with our beloved Bar-Nabba and Paul, ²⁶men who have been setting aside their souls on behalf of the name of our Adŏnai Yĕshua the Anŏinted. ²⁷Therefore we have been sending Yehudah and Sila, who themselves will also report the same things by word of mouth."

²⁸"Indeed it seemed good to the Holy Spĭrit and to us to lay upon you no more burden except these necessities: ²⁹that you keep yourselves away from idol sacrifices, and blood, and things strangled, and from fornication, from which things keeping yourselves free well you will do. *May ye be those who have been getting strong!*"

³⁰So, when they were sent away, they went down to Antioch, and having

---

from paganism to the basics of faithfulness is a huge life changing experience for converts.

15:18 ψ Amos 9:11-12 𝔊 **15:21** η = city. Generic. **15:24** ⊤late MSS add: *saying to be circumcised and to keep the Law:* C E Ψ (1175) 1739 𝔐 (gig) sy; (Ir^{lat}) vs. txt: 𝔓$^{33.45vid74}$ ℵ A B D 33. 81 629 2344 it^{ar} it^c it^d it^{dem} it^l it^p it^{ph} it^{ro} it^w vg cop^{sa} (cop^{bo}) Origen^{lat} Apostolic Constitutions, Amphilochius, Epiphanius, Vigilius WH NR CEI Riv TILC Nv NM; the evidence against this deliberate addition is overwhelming. **15:28** The list does not include obvious commandments that everyone knew, but only necessary things that the new

gathered the congregation together, they delivered the letter. ³¹And when they had read it, they rejoiced because of its encouragement. ³²Yehudah besides also Sila, also being prophets themselves, encouraged and strengthened the brothers with a lengthy message. ³³And after they had spent time there, they were sent away from the brothers in peace to those who had sent them out. ³⁴But it seemed good to Sila to remain there. ³⁵But Paul and Bar-Nabba stayed in Antioch, teaching and proclaiming, with many others also, the word of Yăhweн.

³⁶And after some days Paul said to Bar-Nabba, "Having returned, surely we shall have visited the brothers throughout every city in which we proclaimed the word of Yăhweн, and see how they are." ³⁷And Bar-Nabba was desirous of taking Yoḥanan, called Mark, along with them also. ³⁸But Paul kept insisting that they should not take him along who had deserted them in Pamphylia and had not gone with them to the work.

³⁹And there arose such a sharp disagreement that they separated from one another. As also Bar-Nabba having taken Mark with him, sailed away to Cyprus, ⁴⁰so Paul having chosen Sila departed, having been committed by the brothers to the loving-kindness of Yăhweн. ⁴¹And he was traveling through Syria and Cilicia, strengthening the assemblies.

16

¹And he came also to Derbe and to Lystra. And behold, a certain disciple was there, named Timothy, the son of a Yehudit woman who was one of the faithful, but his father was a Greek, ²and he was well spoken of by the brothers who were in Lystra and Iconium. ³Paul wanted this one to go with him. Then when he took him, he circumcised him ᵞthrough the Yehudim being in those regions, because they all had been knowing that his father was a Greek.

⁴Now while they were passing through the cities, they were delivering the decrees, which had been getting decided by the emissaries and elders who were in Yerushalayim, for them to be guarding. ⁵So the assemblies were being strengthened in the pledge of faithfulness, and were increasing in number daily.

⁶And they passed through the Phrygian and Galatian region, having been forbidden by the Holy Spirit to speak the word in Asia. ⁷And when they had come down through Mysia, they were trying to go into Bithynia, and the Spirit of Yĕshua did not permit them, ⁸and passing by Mysia, they came down to Troas.

⁹And a vision appeared to Paul in the night. A certain man of Macedonia had been standing and appealing to him, and saying, "Come over to Macedonia and help us." ¹⁰And when he had seen the vision, immediately we sought to go into Macedonia, concluding that the Almĭghty has been getting us called to proclaim

---

faithful would be tempted to neglect that would imperil their salvation.

16:3 ᵞ Διὰ τοὺς Ἰουδαίους has been translated by others "because of the Jews," and then made into an argument that Paul was only appeasing their 'ethnocentric custom.' But διὰ in the accusative may mean all the things it means when used with the genitive (cf. LSJ B. 1. *through, among, by aid of, service*). Paul used their services so that everyone would know that Timothy was circumcised just as they knew he wasn't at first. Possibly this text is a concealment text, because it could be read the way the many do. What is prevented here is the insertion of their interpretation into the text. See Gal. 5:11; Mark 8:12; Acts 26:23;

the good news to them.

¹¹Therefore putting out to sea from Troas, we ran a straight course to Samothrace, and on the day following to Neapolis, ¹²and from there to Philippi, which is a leading city of the district of Macedonia, a Roman colony. And we were in this city, having consumed some days. ¹³Besides^α on the day of the Şabba‡hs, we went outside the gate beside the river, where we were accustomed for prayer to be, and having sat down, *also* we^β were speaking to the women who had assembled.

¹⁴And a certain woman named Lydia, from the city of Thyatira, a seller of purple fabrics, a worshiper of the Almĭghty, was listening, and Yăhweн opened her heart to respond to the things spoken by Paul. ¹⁵And when she and her household were immersed, she urged us, saying, "If you have been judging me being faithful to Yăhweн, having come into my house, be staying." And she prevailed upon us.

¹⁶And it happened that as we were going to the place of prayer, a certain slave-girl having a spirit of divination met us, who was bringing her masters much profit by fortunetelling. ¹⁷Following after Paul and us, she kept crying out, saying, "These men are servants of the Almĭghty, Most High, who are proclaiming to you the way of deliverance." ¹⁸And she continued doing this for many days. But Paul was greatly annoyed, and turned and said to the spirit, "I command you in the name of Yĕshua the Anŏinted to come out of her!" And it came out at that very moment.

¹⁹But when her masters saw that their hope of profit was gone, they seized Paul and Silа and dragged them into the market place before the authorities, ²⁰and when they had brought them to the chief magistrates, they said, "These men are throwing our city into confusion, being Yehudĭm, ²¹and are proclaiming customs which it is not lawful for us to accept or to observe, being Romans."

²²And the crowd rose up together against them, and the chief magistrates tore their robes off them, and proceeded to order them to be beaten with rods. ²³Besides having laid many blows upon them, they threw them into prison, commanding the jailer to guard them securely. ²⁴And he, having received such a command, threw them into the inner prison, and fastened their feet in the stocks.

²⁵But about midnight Paul and Silа were praying and singing hymns of praise to the Almĭghty, and the prisoners were listening to them. ²⁶And suddenly there came a great earthquake, so that the foundations of the prison house were shaken, and immediately all the doors were opened, and everyone's chains were unfastened. ²⁷And when the jailer was roused out of sleep, and when he saw

---

Gal. 2:5. Timothy should have been circumcised on the eighth day, even though his father was exempt.

16:13 α The conjunctive adverb (α τέ = *besides, as, as also*) has here the idea of 'as usual'; where *also* is supplied (β) a comparison with something out of the ordinary is introduced. The missing conjunction before the last clause in Greek makes this clearer in Greek.

The idea is besides the ordinary or expected thing, then this also happened. The indicative tense earlier in vs. 13 makes it difficult for the English reader. If we reduce it to a participle, it is easy to understand, "Besides on the day of the Şabba‡hs, <u>having gone outside the gate beside the river</u>, where we were accustomed to have prayer, and having sat dawn, we were speaking

the prison doors which had been getting opened, *then with* his sword drawn he was getting ready to be killing himself, supposing the prisoners to have been escaping. ²⁸But Paul cried out with a loud voice, saying, "You shall not yet have done yourself any harm, because we are all here!"

²⁹And he called for lights and rushed in and, trembling with fear, he fell down before Paul and Sila, ³⁰and after he brought them out, he said, "Sirs, what is it necessary for me to be doing so that I will have been rescued?"

³¹And they said, "Hold faithful upon Adŏnai Yĕshua, and you will be rescued, you and your household." ³²And they spoke the word of Yăhweh to him together with all who were in his house.

³³And he took them that very hour of the night and washed their wounds, and immediately he was immersed, he and all his household. ³⁴Besides having brought them into his house, he set food before them and rejoiced greatly, having been pledging faithfulness *to* the Almĭghty with his whole household.

³⁵Now when day came, the chief magistrates sent their policemen, saying, "Release those men." ³⁶And the jailer reported these words to Paul, saying, "The chief magistrates have been sending that you should be released. Now therefore, come out and be going in peace." ³⁷But Paul said to them, "They have beaten us in public without trial, men who are Romans, and have thrown us into prison, and now are they sending us away secretly? No indeed! But let them come themselves and bring us out."

³⁸And the policemen reported these words to the chief magistrates. And they were afraid when they heard that they were Romans, ³⁹and they came and appealed to them, and when they had brought them out, they kept begging them to leave the city. ⁴⁰And they went out of the prison and entered the house of Lydia, and when they saw the brothers, they encouraged them and departed.

17

¹Now when they had traveled through Amphipolis and Apollonia, they came to Thessalonica, where there was a congregation of the Yehudim. ²And according to what Paul had been getting accustomed to, he went to them, and for three Şabbaths reasoned with them from the writings, ³explaining and giving evidence that the Anŏinted had to suffer and rise again from the dead, and saying, "This Yĕshua whom I am proclaiming to you is the Anŏinted." ⁴And some of them were persuaded and joined Paul and Sila, besides a great multitude of the Gŏd fearing Greeks, besides a number of the leading women.

⁵But the Yehudim, becoming jealous and taking along some wicked men from the market place, formed a mob and set the city in an uproar, and coming upon the house of Yason, they were seeking to bring them out to the people. ⁶And when they did not find them, they were dragging Yason and some brothers before the city authorities, shouting, "These men who have upset the world are coming by here also. ⁷And Yason has been receiving them under *his* roof, and they all act contrary to the decrees of Caesar, saying that there is another king, Yĕshua." ⁸And they stirred up the crowd and the city authorities who heard these things.

⁹And when they had received a pledge from the hand of Yason and the others, they released them.

¹⁰And the brothers immediately sent besides Paul, also Sila away by night to Berea. And when they arrived, they went into the congregation of the Yehudim. ¹¹Now these were more noble-minded than those in Thessalonica, because they received the word with great eagerness, examining the writings daily, to see whether these things were so. ¹²Many of them therefore pledged faithfulness, also *many* from prominent Greek women, and men, not a few.

¹³Yet as the Yehudim of Thessalonica had come to know that the word of the Almĭghty was proclaimed by Paul in Berea also, they came there likewise, agitating and stirring up the crowds. ¹⁴And then immediately the brothers sent Paul out, to go as far as the sea. Even so, had remained besides Sila, also Timothy. ¹⁵And, those conducting Paul brought him as far as Athens, and having taken a command for Sila and Timothy, that quickly they shall have come to him, they were departing.

¹⁶Now while Paul was waiting for them at Athens, his spirit was being provoked within him as he was beholding the city full of idols. ¹⁷So he was reasoning in the congregation with the Yehudim and the proselytes, and in the market place throughout every day with those who happened to be present.

¹⁸And also some of the Epicurean and Stoic philosophers were conversing with him. And some were saying, "What would this idle babbler wish to say?" Others: "He seems to be a proclaimer of strange deities," because he was proclaiming Yĕshua and the resurrection. ¹⁹Besides they took him and brought him to the Areopagus, saying, "May we know what this new-made teaching is which you are proclaiming? ²⁰Because you are bringing some strange things to our ears. We want to know therefore what these things mean." ²¹(Now all the Athenians and the strangers visiting there used to spend their time in nothing other than telling or hearing something new-made.)

²²So Paul stood in the midst of the Areopagus and said, "Men of Athens, I observe that you are very religious in all respects, ²³because while passing through and examining the objects of your worship, I also found an altar on which had been getting written, 'to an unknown Gŏd.' Whom therefore you are worshipping without knowing, this one I am proclaiming to you."

²⁴"The Almĭghty who made the world and all things in it, since he is Adŏnᴇi of heaven and earth, does not dwell in temples made with hands. ²⁵Neither is he served by human hands, as though he needed anything, since he himself gives to all life and breath and all things."

²⁶"Besides he made from one man every nation of mankind to be dwelling on all the face of the earth, having set opportune times, which have been getting arranged, and the boundaries of their habitation, ²⁷so they would be seeking the Almĭghty, if perhaps they may grope for him and may find him, though he is not far from each one of us, ²⁸because in him we live and move and exist, as even

some of your own poetsᵖ have been saying, 'For we also are his kindred.' ²⁹Being then the kindred of the Almĭghty, we ought not to think that the Divine Nature is like gold or silver or stone, an image formed by the art and thought of man."

³⁰"Therefore having disregarded the times of ignorance, the Almĭghty is now declaring to men, that all everywhere should be sorry and be turning their hearts *from sin,* ³¹because he has fixed *a* day in which he will judge the world in justice through a Man whom he has appointed, having offered a faithful proof to all men by raising him from the dead."

³²Now when they heard about the resurrection of the dead, some were sneering, but others said, "We will hear you again concerning this."

³³So Paul went out of their midst. ³⁴But some men joined him and pledged faithfulness, among whom also were Dionysius the Areopagite and a woman named Damaris and others with them.

18

After these things he left Athens and went to Corinth. ²And he found a certain Yehudi named Aquila, a native of Pontus, having recently been coming from Italy with his wife Priscilla, because Claudius had been ordering all the Yehudim to be distanced from Rome.ᵟ He came to them, ³and because he was of the same trade, he stayed beside them and they were working, because by trade they were tent-makers.

⁴And he was reasoning in the congregation down through every Şabbaţh. And he was persuading besides Yehudim also Greeks. ⁵Now as Sila besides also Timothy came down from Macedonia, Paul was holding strictly to the word, thoroughly testifying to the Yehudim that Yĕshua was the Anŏinted. ⁶And when they resisted and blasphemed, he shook out his garments and said to them, "Your blood be upon your own heads! I am clean. From now on I will go to the nations."

⁷And he departed from there and went to the house of a certain man named Titius Eustace, a worshiper of the Almĭghty, whose house was next to the place of congregation. ⁸And Crispus, the leader of the congregation, confirmed faithfulness to Yăhweĥ with all his household, and many of the Corinthians when they heard were pledging faithfulness and being immersed.

⁹And Yăhweĥ said to Paul in the night by a vision, "Be not fearing, but be speaking and you shall not have kept silent, ¹⁰because I am with you, and no man will attack you in order to harm you, because I have many people in this city." ¹¹And he settled there a year and six moons,ᵗ teaching the word of the Almĭghty among them.

¹²But while Gallio was proconsul of Achaia,ᵟ the Yehudim with the same passion rose up against Paul and brought him before the judgment seat, ¹³saying, "This man persuades men to worship the Almĭghty beside the law." ¹⁴But when Paul was about to open his mouth, Gallio said to the Yehudim, "If it were a matter

---

to the women...." Ordinarily they would go out, sit down, have prayer and not speak to the women.
17:28 ρ See Titus 1:12; Jude 1:14. **18:2** δ The expulsion was in AD 49. Paul met up with them in the fall of AD 50, or very early in AD 51. **18:11** τ From about Jan, AD 51 to June or July AD 52. **18:12** τ AD 51-52.

of wrong or of vicious crime, Yehudim, it would be reasonable for me to put up with you, ¹⁵but if there are questions about words and names and your own Law, look after it yourselves. I am unwilling to be a judge of these matters." ¹⁶And he drove them away from the judgment seat. ¹⁷And they all took hold of Sosthenes, the leader of the congregation, and were beating him in front of the judgment seat. And Gallio was not concerned about any of these things.

¹⁸And Paul, having remained many days longer, took leave of the brothers and put out to sea for Syria, and with him were Priscilla and Aquila. In Cenchrea he had his hair cut, because he was keeping a vow.

¹⁹And they came to Ephesus, and he left them there. Now he himself entered the congregation and reasoned with the Yehudim. ²⁰And when they asked him to stay for a longer time, he did not consent, ²¹but taking leave of them and saying, "I will return to you again if the Almĭghty wills," he set sail from Ephesus.

²²And when he had landed at Caesarea,ᵞ he went up and greeted the assembly, and went down to Antioch.

²³And having spent some time there, he departed and passed successively through the Galatian region and Phrygia, strengthening all the disciples.ᵋ

²⁴Now a certain Yehudi named Apollos, an Alexandrian by birth, an eloquent man, came to Ephesus. And he was mighty in the writings. ²⁵This man had been getting instruction in the way of Yăhwєh, and being fervent in spirit, he was speaking and teaching accurately the things concerning Yĕshua, being acquainted only with the immersion of Yoḣanan. ²⁶Besides he began to speak out boldly in the congregation. But when Priscilla and Aquila heard him, they took him aside and explained to him the way of the Almĭghty precisely.

²⁷Then when he wanted to go across to Achaia, the brothers encouraged him and wrote to the disciples to welcome him. And when he had arrived, he helped greatly those who had been holding faithful through Yăhwєh's loving kindness, ²⁸because he powerfully refuted the Yehudim in public, demonstrating by the writings that Yĕshua was the Anŏinted.

19

¹And it came about that while Apollos was at Corinth, Paul having passed through the upper country came to Ephesus, and found some disciples. ²Besides he said to them, "Did you receive the Holy Spĭrit when you pledged faithfulness?" And they said to him, "No, we have not even heard whether there is a Holy Spĭrit. ³Besides he said, "Into what then were you immersed?" And they said, "Into Yoḣanan's immersion." ⁴And Paul said, "Yoḣanan immersed an immersion of being sorry and turning their hearts *from sin*, for the people, saying they shall have affirmed faithfulness to the one coming after him, that is to Yĕshua.

⁵So having heard, they were immersed into the name of Adŏnai Yĕshua. ⁶And when Paul had laid his hands upon them, the Holy Spĭrit came on them;

18:22 γ Late summer, AD 52. **18:23** ξ Winter, AD 53.

besides they were speaking with languages and prophesying. ⁷And there were in all about twelve men.

⁸And he entered the congregation and continued speaking out boldly for three moons, reasoning and persuading them about the kingdom of the Almĭghty. ⁹But when some were hardening and were disobeying, speaking evil of the Way before the multitude, he withdrew from them and took away the disciples, reasoning daily in the school of Tyrannus. ¹⁰And this took place for two years,ᵟ so that all who lived in Asia heard the word of Yăhwe**H**, Yehudim besides also Greeks.

¹¹Besides the Almĭghty was performing extraordinary miracles by the hands of Paul, ¹²so that handkerchiefs or aprons were even carried from his body to the sick, and the diseases left them besides the evil spirits leaving.

¹³But also some of the Yehudi exorcists, who went from place to place, attempted to name over those who had the evil spirits the name of Adŏnai Yĕshua, saying, "I adjure you by Yĕshua whom Paul proclaims." ¹⁴And seven sons of one Seqᵉvah, a Yehudi high priest, were doing this. ¹⁵And the evil spirit answered and said to them, "I recognize Yĕshua, and I know about Paul, but who are you?" ¹⁶And the man in whom was the evil spirit leaped on them and subdued all of them and overpowered them, so that they fled out of that house naked and having been getting wounded.

¹⁷And this became known to all, Yehudim besides also Greeks, who lived in Ephesus. And fear fell upon them all and the name of Adŏnai Yĕshua was getting magnified. ¹⁸Many, as well of those who had been pledging faithfulness were coming, confessing and disclosing their practices. ¹⁹And, a substantial number those who practiced magic brought their scrolls together and were burning them in the sight of all. And they counted up the price of them and found it fifty thousand pieces of silver. ²⁰So the word of Yăhwe**H** was growing mightily and prevailing.

²¹Now after these things were finished, Paul purposed, by the Spĭrit, to go to Yerushalayim after he had passed through Macedonia and Achaia, saying, "After I have been there, I must also see Rome." ²²And having sent into Macedonia two of those who ministered to him, Timothy and Erastus, he himself stayed in Asia for a while.

²³And about that timeˣ there arose no small disturbance concerning the Way, ²⁴because a certain man named Demetrius, a silversmith, who made silver shrines of Artemis, was bringing no little business to the craftsmen. ²⁵These he gathered together with the workmen of similar trades, and said, "Men, you know that our prosperity depends upon this business. ²⁶And you see and hear that not only in Ephesus, but in almost all of Asia, this Paul has persuaded and turned away a considerable number of people, saying that gods made with hands are no gods at all. ²⁷But not only is there danger that this trade of ours may fall into disrepute, but also that the temple of the great goddess Artemis may

---

19:8 τ Late spring to early summer, AD 53. **19:10** δ Fall, AD 53, to Fall AD 55.
19:23 χ Fall, AD 56. See Acts 20:31.

be considered as nothing, besides also *that* they are tearing down her majesty, whom all of Asia and the world worship."

²⁸And when they heard this and were filled with rage, they were crying out, saying, "Great is Artemis of the Ephesians!" ²⁹And the city was filled with confusion; besides they rushed with the same passion into the theater, dragging along Gaius and Aristarchus, Paul's traveling companions from Macedonia. ³⁰And when Paul wanted to go into the assembly, the disciples would not let him. ³¹And also some of the Asiarchs⁷ who were friends of his sent to him and repeatedly urged him not to venture into the theater.

³²Others, surely then another were shouting something, because the assembly had been getting confused, and the majority had not been knowing for what cause they had been coming together. ³³And some of the crowd concluded it was Alexander, since the Yehudim had put him forward. And having motioned with his hand, Alexander was intending to make a defense to the assembly. ³⁴But when they recognized that he was a Yehudi, a single outcry arose from them all as they shouted for about two hours, "Great is Artemis of the Ephesians!"

³⁵And after quieting the crowd, the town clerk said, "Men of Ephesus, what man is there after all who does not know that the city of the Ephesians is guardian of the temple of the great Artemis, and of the image which fell down from heaven? ³⁶Since then these are undeniable facts, it is being necessary for you, having been keeping calm, to be under control, and to be doing nothing precipitous, ³⁷because you have brought these men here who are neither robbers of temples nor blasphemers of our goddess."

³⁸"So then, if Demetrius and the craftsmen who are with him have a complaint against any man, the courts are in session and proconsuls are available. Let them be bringing charges against one another. ³⁹And if you want anything beyond this, it will be settled in the lawful assembly, ⁴⁰because indeed we are in danger of being accused of a riot in connection with today's affair, since there is no real cause for it. And in this connection we will be unable to account for this disorderly gathering."

⁴¹And after saying this he dismissed the assembly.

20

¹And after the uproar had ceased, Paul sent for the disciples, and when he had exhorted them and taken his leave of them, he departed to go to Macedonia.

²And when he had gone through those districts and had given them much

---

19:31 η "Each of the cities of proconsular Asia, at the autumnal equinox, assembled its most honorable and opulent citizens, in order to select one to preside over the games to be exhibited that year, at his expense, in honor of the gods and the Roman emperor. Thereupon each city reported the name of the person selected to a general assembly held in some leading city, as Ephesus, Smyrna, Sardis. This general council, called το κοινον, selected ten out of the number of candidates, and sent them to the proconsul; and the proconsul, apparently, chose one of these ten to preside over the rest. This explains how it is that in Acts, the passage cited several Asiarchs are spoken of, while Eusebius mentions only one; (perhaps also the title outlasted the service)." Thayer.

20:3 ζ Winter, AD 57. **20:6 λ** The feast was

exhortation, he came to Greece; ³besides having spent three moons; and when a plot was formed against him by the Yehudim, as he was about to set sail for Syria, he himself had a reason to return through Macedonia. ⁴And he was accompanied by Sopater of Berea, the son of Pyrrhus, and by Aristarchus and Secundus of the Thessalonians, and Gaius of Derbe, and Timothy, and Tychicus and Trophimus of Asia.

⁵But these had gone on ahead and were waiting for us at Troas. ⁶And we sailed during the days of Unleavened Bread from Philippi. And we came to them unto Troas, up to five days, where we used up the seven days.^λ

⁷And on the FIRST OF THE ṢABBAᴛHS^ψ, when we ^θhad been getting gathered together to break bread, Paul kept on talking to them, intending to be departing in the morning. And besides he was stretching out the word as far as ^μmidnight. ⁸Yet there were many ^ρlamps in the upper room where we ^θhad been getting gathered together. ⁹And there was a certain young man named Eutychus sitting on the window sill, sinking into a deep sleep. And as Paul kept on talking, he was overcome by sleep and fell down from the third floor, and was picked up dead. ¹⁰But Paul went down and fell upon him and after embracing him, he said, "Do not be getting troubled, because his life is in him." ¹¹And when he went

---

Aviv 15-21, starting on Ṣabbaṯh, April 9 and ending on Friday, April 15. They sailed during the week between the Ṣabbaṯhs, arriving on the 5th day of the feast, Wednesday, April 13th. They used up the remaining of the seven days of the feast in Troas. After the 7th day of the feast came the first Ṣabbaṯh after Passover, the Resurrection Ṣabbaṯh. See also Mat. 28:1; Mark 16:1-2; Luke 24:1; Yoḥ. 20:1, 19; 1 Cor. 16:2; Rev. 1:10. **20:6 λ** The feast was Aviv 15-21, starting on Ṣabbaṯh, April 9 and ending on Friday, April 15. They sailed during the week between the Ṣabbaṯhs, arriving on the 5th day of the feast, Wednesday, April 13th. They used up the remaining of the seven days of the feast in Troas. After the 7th day of the feast came the first Ṣabbaṯh after Passover, the Resurrection Ṣabbaṯh. See also Mat. 28:1; Mark 16:1-2; Luke 24:1; Yoḥ. 20:1, 19; 1 Cor. 16:2; Rev. 1:10. ▷ The supposition that they began the meeting in the daytime is confirmed by the twice repeated perfect participles in vs. 7θ and 8θ. The text presents Paul's talking into the night as an unusual occurrence, also confirming that his message had begun in the daytime. **20:7 ψ** = τῇ μιᾷ τῶν σαββάτων. *On the first day of the Ṣabbaṯhs.* This was the first Ṣabbaṯh day after Passover. ▷ The word 'day' (ἡμέρα) is necessarily included, implied by the feminine gender of μιᾷ. A comparison of Mark 14:12 (πρώτῃ ἡμέρᾳ τῶν ἀζύμων) and Mat. 26:17 (πρώτῃ τῶν ἀζύμων) shows that the word 'first' (πρώτῃ) implies the word day, since ἡμέρα is included by Mark, but omitted at the same place by Matthew. Both texts speak of the same day. Therefore the sometimes italicized inclusion of the word 'day' in the translations is correct. With perfect grammatical symmetry, also μιᾷ τῶν σαββάτων is the same day as μιᾷ ἡμέρᾳ τῶν σαββάτων supplying the optional word 'day' (ἡμέρᾳ). ▷ Also, 'one' (μιᾷ) needs the word 'day' due to its gender not being in agreement with σαββάτων, which rules would require the neuter form of 'one' (ενος or εν) without it instead of μιᾷ. By including the implied noun 'day' after the adjective 'first' a requirement of the adjective 'first' to agree with the noun 'Ṣabbaṯhs' disappears according to the grammar rules. ▷ Also, 'one' (μιᾷ) is a Hebraism for 'first' (πρώτῃ). This is so because the Hebrew word אחת is used both for 'one' and 'first.' So the meaning is the same as if πρώτῃ ἡμέρᾳ τῶν σαββάτων had been written. Now compare this with Acts 13:14 and 16:13 (ἡμέρᾳ τῶν σαββάτων) = "day of the Ṣabbaṯhs" and it will be seen by Luke 22:7 (ἡμέρα τῶν ἀζύμων) that the difference made by 'first' (πρώτῃ, μιᾷ) is to point out a specific 'day of the Ṣabbaṯhs' or 'day of unleavens.' **20:7 μ** Paul's exhortations began on the Ṣabbaṯh, but continued into the night.

20:7 θ The perf. participle implies an iterative habit. **20:8 ρ** Perhaps the fumes contributed to the accident. **20:8 θ** cf. vs. 7. The perfect here is further explained by the holy convocation for the last day of the feast, which was on the day immediately before the first of the Ṣabbaṯhs that year. Perhaps also Paul had held some teaching sessions on days 5 and 6 of the

back up, and broke the bread and ate, *then* as well he talked *a long while* until daybreak. This way he departed. ¹²And they led away the boy alive, and were encouraged^π not a little.

¹³But we, going ahead to the ship, set sail for Assos, intending from there to take Paul on board, because so he had been arranging it. He was intending himself to be going by foot. ¹⁴And when he met us at Assos, we took him on board and came to Mitylene. ¹⁵And sailing from there, we arrived the following day opposite Chios. And the next day we crossed over to Samos. And the day following we came to Miletus, ¹⁶because Paul had been deciding to sail past Ephesus in order that he may not have used up time in Asia, because he was hurrying to be in Yerushalayim, if possible, on the day of the Fiftieth.

¹⁷And from Miletus he sent to Ephesus and called to him the elders of the assembly. ¹⁸And when they had come to him, he said to them, "You yourselves know, from the first day that I set foot in Asia, how I was with you the whole time, ¹⁹serving Yăhweн with all humility and with tears and in trials having befallen me through the plots of the Yehudim, ²⁰how I did not shrink from declaring to you anything that was profitable, and teaching you publicly and from house to house, ²¹thoroughly testifying to Yehudim besides also Greeks of being sorry and turning the heart *from sin*, to the Almĭghty and faithfulness to our Adŏnai Yĕshua the Anŏinted.

²²"And now, behold, having been getting held bound by the Spĭrit, I am on my way to Yerushalayim, not having been knowing what will happen to me there, ²³except that the Holy Spĭrit testifies earnestly to me throughout the cities, saying that bonds and afflictions await me. ²⁴But I do not consider my life of any account as dear to myself, in order that I may finish my course, and the ministry which I received from beside Adŏnai Yĕshua, to testify thoroughly of the good news of the loving-kindness of the Almĭghty.

²⁵"And now, behold, I have been knowing that all of you, among whom I went about proclaiming the kingdom, will see my face no more. ²⁶Therefore I testify to you this day, that I am clear of the blood of all of you, ²⁷because I did not shrink from declaring to you the whole purpose of the Almĭghty.

²⁸"Be guarding yourselves and all the flock, among which the Holy Spĭrit has made you overseers, to shepherd the Assembly of the Almĭghty which he acquired with the blood of his own^ψ. ²⁹I have been knowing that after my departure savage wolves will come in among you, not sparing the flock. ³⁰And from among your own selves men will arise, speaking things that have been getting ^ξtwisted around, to draw away the disciples after them. ³¹Therefore be keeping alert,

---

feast. **20:12** π or 'comforted.' **20:28** ψ The Almĭghty Sŏn is the flesh and blood of the Almĭghty, because the Sŏn is his only kindred. **20:30** ξ→around = διαστρέφω = thoroughly twist; or *misinterpreted, perverted*. Δια = *through, thoroughly* + στρέφω = *turn, twist*. LSJ: *twist about*. This prediction has been fulfilled as translators have sown a multitude of doctrinal stumbling blocks in Scripture which support the heresy of the many (cf. Jer. 8:8). **20:31** τ Fall AD 53 to fall AD 56. **20:32** ψ→sanctified; an equally valid trans: *who have been making themselves holy*.

remembering that night and day for a period of ʈthree years I did not cease to educate each one with tears. ³²"And now I commend you to the Almĭghty and to the word of his loving-kindness, which is able to build you up and to give you the inheritance among all those ᵠwho have been getting made holy.

³³"I have coveted no one's silver or gold or clothes. ³⁴You yourselves know that these hands ministered to my own needs and to the men who were with me. ³⁵In everything I showed you that by working hard in this manner you must help the weak, besides remember the words of Adŏnai Yĕshua, that he himself said, 'It is more blessed to give than to receive.'"

³⁶And when he had said these things, he knelt down and prayed with them all. ³⁷And they were weeping aloud and embraced Paul, and repeatedly kissed him, ³⁸grieving especially over the word which he had been speaking, that they should see his face no more. And they were accompanying him to the ship.

21 And when it came about that we had parted from them and had set sail, we ran a straight course to Cos and the next day to Rhodes and from there to Patara, ²and having found a ship crossing over to Phoenicia, we went aboard and set sail. ³And when we had come in sight of Cyprus, leaving it on the left, we kept sailing to Syria and landed at Tsor, because there the ship was to unload its cargo. ⁴And after looking up the disciples, we stayed there seven days, yet they were telling Paul through the Spĭrit not to set foot in Yerushalayim. ⁵And when it came about that our days there were ended, we departed and started on our journey, while they all, with wives and children, escorted us until we were out of the city. And after kneeling down on the beach and praying, we said farewell to one another. ⁶Then we went on board the ship, and they returned home again.

⁷And when we had finished the voyage from Tsor, we arrived at Ptolemais, and after greeting the brothers, we stayed at their side for a day. ⁸And on the next day we departed and came to Caesarea. Then entering the house of Philip the evangelist, who was one of the seven, we stayed at his side. ⁹And this man had four virgin daughters who were prophetesses.

¹⁰And as we were staying there for many days, a certain prophet named Agav came down from Yehudah. ¹¹And coming to us, he took Paul's belt and bound his own feet and hands, and said, "This is what the Holy Spĭrit says: 'In this way the Yehudim at Yerushalayim will bind the man who owns this belt and deliver him into the hands of the nations.'" ¹²And when we had heard this, we besides also the local residents were begging him not to go up to Yerushalayim. ¹³Then Paul answered, "What are you doing, weeping and breaking my heart? Because I am ready not only to be bound, but even to die at Yerushalayim over the name of Adŏnai Yĕshua." ¹⁴And since he would not be persuaded, we fell silent, remarking, "The will of Yăhweн be getting done!"

¹⁵And after these days we got ready and started on our way up to Yerushalayim. ¹⁶And some of the disciples from Caesarea also came with us, taking us to

Mnason of Cyprus, a disciple of long standing alongside whom we could lodge. ¹⁷And when we had come to Yerushalayim, the brothers received us gladly. ¹⁸And now the following day Paul went in with us to Ya'aqov, besides all the elders had come by. ¹⁹And after he had greeted them, he was relating one by one the things which he had done among the nations through his ministry.

²⁰And when they heard it they were glorifying the Almĭghty; besides, they said to him, "You see, brother, how many thousands there are of the Yehudim of those who have been holding faithful, and they are all zealous for the Law. ²¹And they have been told about you, 'that you are teaching all the Yehudim who are down through the nations to forsake Mosheh, telling them not to circumcise their children nor to walk according to the customs.⁹'

²²"What, then, is to be done? They will certainly hear that you have been coming. ²³Therefore do this that we tell you. We have four men who are under a vow. ²⁴Take them and purify yourself along with them, and pay their expenses in order that they may shave their heads, and all will know that there is nothing to the things which they have been getting told about you, but that you yourself also walk orderly, keeping the Law.

²⁵"But concerning the nations who have been pledging faithfulness, weᵀ ⌜wrote, ⌜having decided that they should be on guard against⌝, besides food sacrificed to idols, also blood, and from what is strangled and from prohibited sexual relations.⁸""

²⁶Then Paul took the men, and the next day, purifying himself along with them, went into the Temple, giving notice of the completion of the days of purification, until the sacrifice would be offered on behalf of each one of them.

²⁷And when the seven days were almost over, the Yehudim from Asia, upon

---

21:21 θ Ya'aqov is here reporting not the opinion of the Yehudim who affirmed faithfulness, but the words of the false witnesses that were trying to influence them. **21:25** ᵀD: οὐδὲν ἔχουσιν λέγειν πρὸς σε· ἡμεῖς γὰρ. **21:25** ⌜ἀπεστείλαμεν D B C*; **21:25** ⌜κρίναντες μηδὲν τοιοῦτον τηρεῖν αὐτοὺς εἰ μὴ φυλάσσεσθαι αὐτοὺς (*having decided they should keep no such thing, save only they should guard themselves [from]*). NA-27/28 omit. The addition of the omitted words was a deliberate attack on the Law by corrupt scribes. **21:25** δ The rumors were charging Paul with rebellion. Because Paul was born Yehudi, he is held to a higher standard than those just introduced to the faith from paganism. We should note however, that Yoḥanan writing to second and third generation faithful many years later also holds them to a higher standard. Paul did not neglect the teaching of Torah. His willingness to agree with Ya'aqov shows that he kept the Ṣabbaṭhs and feast days, and the clean and unclean laws, and further that he supported the Levitical priests and the Temple in Yerushalayim. Paul is not agreeing to the manner in which the false charges were framed, nor is Ya'aqov, but only to disproving the main point, that Paul had forsaken the Law, which in the eyes of the faithful Yehudim was the only material point. ▷ The Council only defined the duties of initial repentance for pagans so that they could be saved. The prohibitions were exactly those sins that Greek and Roman pagans were in the habit of committing. But Greeks and Romans also had a much more extensive cultural moral code that they knew they should follow, and this moral code overlapped large portions of the Law. One cannot lie, cheat, steal, murder, commit adultery, etc and truly affirm faithfulness to Mĕssiah. These things were omitted from the decree because they were understood, and were taken for granted by Greeks and Romans. Yet refraining from them is necessary to faithfulness. The point then is that omission of a commandment from the decree does not imply there is no obligation to the commandment either in respect to salvation or in respect to sanctification after salvation. ▷ False teachers, therefore have interpreted the decree to mean such things as Ṣabbaṭh or circumcision or the laws of clean and unclean, or that ritual purity laws are abolished for the faithful, or for non-Yehudi faithful. But they have not understood that the decree is only a measure of merciful leniency,

seeing him in the Temple, were stirring up all the crowds and laid hands on him, ²⁸crying out, "Men of Yisra'el, be running to our cry! This is the man who proclaims to all men everywhere against our people, and the Law, and this place; furthermore besides, Greeks he has even brought into the Temple and has been defiling this holy place^ψ," ²⁹because they had previously been seeing Trophimus the Ephesian in the city with him, and they supposed that Paul had brought him into the Temple.

³⁰Besides, all the city was stirred up, and the people rushed together, and taking hold of Paul, they dragged him out of the Temple, and immediately the doors were shut. ³¹Besides seeking to kill him, a report came up to the commander of the cohort that all Yerushalayim was in confusion. ³²And at once he took along soldiers and centurions, and ran down to them. And when they saw the commander and the soldiers, they stopped beating Paul.

³³Then the commander came up and took hold of him, and ordered him to be bound with two chains, and he was asking who he may be and what it is he has been doing.^τ ³⁴But among the crowd some were shouting one thing and some another, and when he could not find out the facts on account of the uproar, he ordered him to be brought into the barracks. ³⁵And when he got to the stairs, it befell him to be carried by the soldiers because of the violence of the mob, ³⁶because the multitude of the people kept following behind, crying out, "Be taking him away!"

³⁷Besides being about to be brought into the barracks, Paul was saying to the commander, "May I say something to you?" And he said, "Do you know Greek? ³⁸Then you are not the Egyptian who some time ago stirred up a revolt and led the four thousand men of the Assassins out into the wilderness?" ³⁹But Paul said, "I am a Yehudi of Tarsus in Cilicia, a citizen of no insignificant city, and I beg you, allow me to speak to the people."

⁴⁰And when he had given him permission, Paul, having been standing on the stairs, motioned to the people with his hand, and when there was a great hush, he spoke to them in the Hebrew language, saying:

22

¹"Brothers and fathers, hear now my defense to you." ²And when they heard that he was addressing them in the Hebrew language, they became even more quiet. And he said, ³"I am a Yehudi, having been getting begotten in Tarsus of Cilicia, but having been getting raised in this city, having been getting educated beside the feet of Gamli'el, strictly according to the Law

---

and not a comprehensive definition of obligations. **21:28** ψ All the charges were false. For it should be noted that the Yehudim from Asia were willing to create riots, conspire with pagans, and commit murder in order to stop the good news of Mĕssiah from being announced to Yehudim and non-Yehudim. By their definition, proclaiming Mĕssiah is against Yisra'el, and against the Law, and the Temple. This is what they wanted Yehudim and non-Yehudim to believe about the good news. And even to this day, these charges are what they want people to believe, and they have conspired with lawless teachers who have infiltrated the faith to promote the same myths, even corrupting translations of Scripture, both in the Torah and Prophets, and in the Emissaries' Writings. **21:33** τ Paul's arrest was just after Shavu'ot AD 57.

of our fathers, being zealous for the Almĭghty, just as you all are today, ⁴who this way I persecuted to the death, binding and putting men besides also women into prisons, ⁵as also the high priest and all the council of the elders can testify, from the hand of whom, having received letters to the brothers, to Dammeseq I was journeying to bring also the ones being there, when they had been getting held bound, to Yerushalayim so that they will have been punished.

⁶"And it came about that as I was on my way, approaching Dammeseq about noontime, a very bright light suddenly flashed from heaven all around me; ⁷I fell, besides, to the ground and heard a voice saying to me, 'Şa'ul, Şa'ul, why are you persecuting me?' ⁸And I answered, 'Who are you, Adŏnai?' He said as well to me, 'I am Yĕshua Ha-Natsri, whom you are persecuting.' ⁹But those who were with me beheld the light, to be sure, but did not understand the voice of the one who was speaking to me. ¹⁰And I said, 'What shall I have done, Adŏnai?' And Yăhweн said to me, 'Having arisen, be going on into Dammeseq, and there you will be told of all that has been getting appointed for you to do.' ¹¹But since I could not see because of the brightness of that light, I was led by the hand by those who were with me, and came into Dammeseq.

¹²"And a certain Ḥananyah, a man who was devout according to the Law, and well spoken of by all the Yehudim who lived there, ¹³came to me, and standing near said to me, 'Brother Şa'ul, receive your sight!' And at that very time I looked up at him. ¹⁴And he said, 'The Almĭghty of our fathers has appointed you to know his will, and to see the righteous one, and to hear an utterance from his mouth, ¹⁵because you will be a witness for him to all men of what you have been seeing and have heard. ¹⁶And now why do you delay? Arise, and immerse yourself! You yourself should wash away your sins, as one who has called upon his name.'

¹⁷"And it came about when I returned to Yerushalayim and was praying in the Temple, that I fell into a vision, ¹⁸and I saw him saying to me, 'Make haste, and get out of Yerushalayim quickly, because they will not accept your testimony about me.' ¹⁹And I said, 'Yăhweн, they themselves are understanding that I was imprisoning and beating, down throughout the congregations, those holding faithful upon you. ²⁰And when the blood of your witness Stephen was being shed, I also had been standing by approving, and watching out for the cloaks of those who were slaying him.' ²¹And he said to me, 'Be going! Because I will send you far away to the nations.'"

²²And they listened to him up to this statement, and then they raised their voices and said, "Be taking such a fellow away from the earth, because he should not be allowed to live!" ²³Besides, as they were crying out and throwing off their cloaks and tossing dust into the air, ²⁴the commander ordered him to be brought into the barracks, stating that he should be examined by scourging so that he may know for what cause they were shouting against him that way.

²⁵And when they stretched him out with thongs, Paul said to the centurion who had been standing by, "Is it lawful for you to scourge a man who is a Ro-

Acts 23

man and uncondemned?" ²⁶And when the centurion heard this, he went to the commander and told him, saying, "What are you about to do? For this man is a Roman." ²⁷And the commander came and said to him, "Be telling me, are you a Roman?" And he said, "Yes." ²⁸And the commander answered, "I acquired this citizenship with a large sum of money." And Paul said, "But I actually had been getting begotten *a citizen*." ²⁹Therefore those who were about to be examining him immediately let go of him, and the commander also was afraid when he found out that he was a Roman, and because he had been having him bound.

³⁰But on the next day, wishing to know for certain why he was accused by the Yehudim, he released him and ordered the chief priests and all the Council to assemble, and brought Paul down and set him before them.

23

¹And Paul, looking intently at the Council, said, "Brothers, I have been living as a citizen with a perfectly good conscience before the Almĭghty up to this day." ²And the high priest Ḥananyah commanded those who had been standing beside him to strike him on the mouth. ³Then Paul said to him, "The Almĭghty is going to strike you, O wall which has been getting whitewashed! And do you sit to try me according to the Law, and in violation of the Law order me to be struck?"

⁴But those who had been standing alongside said, "Do you revile the Almĭghty's ᵖʰigh priest?" ⁵Besides Paul was saying, "I had not been knowing, brothers, that he was high priest, because it has been getting written, 'YOU SHALL NOT SPEAK EVIL OF A RULER OF YOUR PEOPLE.ᵟ'"

⁶But perceiving that one part were Tsadduqim and the other Perushim, Paul was crying out in the Council, "Brothers, I am a Perushi, a son of Perushim. For the hope, even of the resurrection of the dead, I am getting judged!" ⁷And as he said this, there arose a dissension between the Perushim and Tsadduqim, and the assembly was divided. ⁸For the Tsadduqim say that there is no resurrection, nor an angelic messenger, nor a spirit, but the Perushim acknowledge them all. ⁹And there arose a great uproar, and some of the scribes of the Perushi party stood up and were arguing heatedly, saying, "We find nothing wrong with this man. Suppose a spirit or an angelic messenger has spoken to him?" ¹⁰And as a great dissension was developing, the commander was afraid Paul would have been torn to pieces by them and ordered the troops to go down and take him away from them by force, besides bringing him into the fortress.

¹¹But on the night following, Yăhweḥ stood at his side and said, "Be having courage, because as you have thoroughly witnessed about me to Yerushalayim, so likewise it is necessary for you to witness to Rome also."

¹²And when it was day, the Yehudim formed a conspiracy and bound them-

---

23:4 π Ḥananyah was an ex-High Priest (AD 46-52). He was not in fact the ruling High Priest at the time. The High Priest was actually a man named Yehonaṯhan, who was murdered in the Temple by *Sicarri* in AD 57. So the office was either vacant at Paul's trial and Ḥananyah was just filling in, or Yehonaṯhan was still alive. **23:5** δ Exo 22:28.

selves under an oath, saying that they would neither eat nor drink until when they may have killed Paul. ¹³And there were more than forty who formed this plot. ¹⁴And they came to the chief priests and the elders, and said, "We have bound ourselves under a solemn oath to taste nothing until we may have killed Paul. ¹⁵Now, therefore, you and the Council notify the commander in order that he will have led him down to you, as though you were going to determine his case by a more thorough investigation, and we for our part are ready to slay him before he comes near the place."

¹⁶But the son of Paul's sister heard of their ambush, and he came and entered the barracks and told Paul. ¹⁷And Paul called one of the centurions to him and said, "Be leading this young man off to the commander, because he has something to report to him." ¹⁸So he took him and led him to the commander and said, "Paul the prisoner called me to him and asked me to lead this young man to you since he has something to tell you." ¹⁹And the commander took him by the hand and stepping aside, was inquiring of him privately, "What is it that you have to report to me?" ²⁰And he said, "The Yehudim have agreed to ask you, so that you will have led Paul down tomorrow to the Council, as though they were going to ask somewhat more thoroughly about him. ²¹Therefore, you shall not have been persuaded by them, because more than forty of them are lying in wait for him, who have bound themselves under a curse not to eat or drink until they slay him, and now they are ready and waiting for the promise from you."

²²Therefore the commander let the young man go, instructing him, "Tell no one that you have notified me of these things."

²³And he called to him two of the centurions, and said, "Get two hundred soldiers ready by the third hour of the night so that they may proceed to Caesarea, with seventy horsemen and two hundred spearmen, ²⁴besides mounts to stand by, so that having mounted Paul they may have safely delivered him to Felix the governor." ²⁵And he wrote a letter having this form:

²⁶"Claudius Lysias, to the most excellent governor Felix, greetings. ²⁷When this man was arrested by the Yehudim and was about to be slain by them, I came upon them with the troops and rescued him, having learned that he was a Roman. ²⁸Besides wanting to ascertain the charge for which they were accusing him, I brought him down to their Council, ²⁹and I found him to be accused over questions about their Law, but under no accusation deserving death or imprisonment. ³⁰And when I was informed that there would be a plot against the man, I sent him to you at once, also instructing his accusers to bring charges against him before you."

³¹So the soldiers, in accordance with what had been getting ordered to them, took Paul and brought him by night to Antipatris. ³²But the next day, leaving the horsemen to go on with him, they returned to the barracks. ³³And when these had come to Caesarea and delivered the letter to the governor, they also presented Paul to him. ³⁴And when he had read it, he asked from what province

he was, and when he learned that he was from Cilicia, ³⁵he said, "I will give you a hearing after your accusers may have arrived also," giving orders for him to be kept in Herod's Praetorium.

24

¹And after five days the high priest Ḥananyah came down with some elders, with a certain attorney named Tertullus, and they brought charges to the governor against Paul. ²And after Paul was summoned, Tertullus began to accuse him, saying to the governor, "Since we have through you attained much peace, and since by your providence reforms are being carried out for this nation, ³we welcome this, in every way, besides also everywhere, most excellent Felix, with all thankfulness. ⁴Yet, that I may not be wearying you any further, I am begging you to have heard us briefly, by your fairness.

⁵"Because we have found this man a real pest and stirring up rebellion among all the Yehudim down throughout the world, besides *being* a ringleader of the sect of the Netsarim. ⁶And he even tried to desecrate the Temple, and then we arrested him. And we wanted to judge him according to our own Law. ⁷But Lysias the commander came along, and with much violence took him out of our hands, ⁸ordering his accusers to come before you. At his side, examining him yourself concerning all these matters, you will be able to ascertain the things of which we accuse him." ⁹And the Yehudim also joined in the attack, asserting that these things were so.

¹⁰And when the governor had nodded for him to speak, Paul, as well, responded: "Knowing that for many years you have been a judge to this nation, I cheerfully make my defense, ¹¹since you can take note of the fact that no more than twelve days ago I went up to Yerushalayim to worship. ¹²And neither in the Temple, nor in the congregations, nor besides down through the city itself did they find me carrying on a discussion with anyone or causing a riot. ¹³Nor can they prove to you the charges of which they now accuse me.

¹⁴"But this I admit to you, that down the way which they call a sect I do serve the Almĭghty of our fathers, holding faithful everything that is in accordance with the Law, and that has been getting written in the prophets, ¹⁵having a hope in the Almĭghty, which these men cherish themselves, that there will certainly be a resurrection of the righteous besides also the wicked. ¹⁶In view of this, I also do my best to maintain always a blameless conscience before the Almĭghty and men.

¹⁷"Now after many years I came to bring alms to my nation and to present offerings, ¹⁸in which they found me occupied in the Temple, having been purifying myself, without any crowd or uproar. But there were certain Yehudim from Asia—¹⁹who ought to be coming by before you, and to be making accusation, if they should be having anything against me. ²⁰Or else let these men themselves tell what misdeed they found when I stood before the Council, ²¹other than for this one statement which I shouted out while having been standing among them, 'For the resurrection of the dead I am on trial before you today.'"

²²But Felix put them off, who had been knowing *more* exactly about the

way, saying, "When Lysias the commander will have come down, I will decide your case," ²³having given orders to the centurion to guard him, besides to have some freedom, and not to prevent any of his friends from ministering to him.

²⁴But some days later, Felix arrived with Drusillah, his wife who was Yehudit, and sent for Paul, and heard him speak about faithfulness to the Anŏinted Yĕshua. ²⁵And as he was discussing justice, self-control and the judgment to come, Felix became frightened and said, "Be going away for the present, and when I find time, I will summon you." ²⁶At the same time too, he was hoping that money would be given him by Paul. Therefore he also sent for him quite often and conversed with him.

²⁷But two years having been completed, Felix had taken a successor, Porcius Festus. Wishing, besides, to grant himself a favor to the Yehudim, Felix had left Paul, who had been getting held bound.

25

¹Festus therefore, having arrived in the province, three days later went up to Yerushalayim from Caesarea. ²Besides, the chief priests and the leading men of the Yehudim having revealed charges to him against Paul, also they were begging him, ³requesting a concession against Paul, that he might send for him, at Yerushalayim (at the same time, setting an ambush to kill him down through the way). ⁴Festus then answered that Paul was being kept in custody at Caesarea and that he himself was about to leave shortly. ⁵"Therefore," he said, "let the influential men among you go there with me, and if there is anything wrong about the man, let them be prosecuting him."

⁶And after he had spent not more than eight or ten days among them, he went down to Caesarea, and on the next day he took his seat on the tribunal and ordered Paul to be brought. ⁷And after he had arrived, the Yehudim who had been coming down from Yerushalayim stood around him, bringing many and serious charges against him which they could not prove, ⁸while Paul said in his own defense, "I have committed no offense either against the Law of the Yehudim or against the Temple or against Caesar."

⁹But Festus, wishing to do the Yehudim a favor, answered Paul and said, "Are you willing to go up to Yerushalayim and stand trial before me on these charges?" ¹⁰But Paul said, "I have been standing before Caesar's tribunal, where I ought to be tried. I have done no wrong to the Yehudim, as you also very well know. ¹¹Surely if then I am doing wrong, and have been practicing anything worthy of death, I am not refusing to die, but if none of those things is true of which these men accuse me, no one can hand me over to them. I appeal to Caesar." ¹²Then when Festus had conferred with his council, he answered, "You have been calling on Caesar, up to Caesar you will go."

¹³Now when several days had elapsed, King Agrippa and Berniqah arrived at Caesarea, and paid their respects to Festus. ¹⁴And while they were spending

---

24:27 Fall AD 57 to fall AD 59.

many days there, Festus laid Paul's case before the king, saying, "There is a certain man who had been getting left a prisoner by Felix, ¹⁵and when I was at Yerushalayim, the chief priests and the elders of the Yehudim brought charges against him, asking for a sentence of condemnation upon him. ¹⁶And I answered them that it is not the custom of the Romans to hand over any man before the accused meets his accusers face to face, besides, has an opportunity to make his defense against the charges. ¹⁷And so after they had come together here, I made no delay, but on the next day took my seat on the tribunal, and ordered the man to be brought.

¹⁸"And when the accusers stood up, they were bringing charges against him not of such crimes as I was expecting, ¹⁹but they were having some controversies with him about their own religion, and about a certain Yĕshua, who had been dying, whom Paul was professing to be alive. ²⁰And being at a loss how to investigate such matters, I asked whether he was willing to go to Yerushalayim and there stand trial on these matters. ²¹But when Paul appealed to be held in custody for the Emperor's decision, I ordered him to be kept in custody until when I will have sent him to Caesar."

²²And Agrippa said to Festus, "I also would like to hear the man myself." "Tomorrow," he said, "you will hear him."

²³And therefore, on the morrow, Agrippa and Berniqah having come with great pomp, and having entered the audience hall, besides with the commanders, and the prominent men of the city, then Festus having ordered, Paul was brought in. ²⁴And Festus said, "King Agrippa, and all you gentlemen here present with us, you behold this man about whom all the people of the Yehudim appealed to me, besides in Yerushalayim also here, loudly declaring that he ought not to live any longer. ²⁵But I have understood him to have been committing nothing worthy of death, and since he himself appealed to the Emperor, I decided to send him. ²⁶Yet I have nothing definite about him to write to my lord. Therefore I have brought him before you all and especially before you, King Agrippa, so that after the investigation has taken place, I shall have had something which I may write. ²⁷For it seems absurd to me in sending a prisoner, not to indicate also the charges against him."

26

¹And Agrippa said to Paul, "You are permitted to speak for yourself." Then Paul stretched out his hand and proceeded to make his defense:

²"In regard to all the things of which I am accused by the Yehudim, I have been considering myself fortunate, King Agrippa, that I am about to make my defense before you today, ³especially because you are an expert in all the customs according to the Yehudim besides also controversies. Therefore I beg you to listen to me patiently.

⁴"Surely then, all Yehudim have been perceiving my manner of life, which *is* since *my* youth, which from the beginning has happened among my own nation, besides in Yerushalayim, ⁵who are knowing me *from* before, from the start, if

they may be willing to be testifying, that I lived *as a* Perushi according to the strictest sect of our worship system. ⁶And now I have been standing getting judged for the hope of the promise made by the Almĭghty to our fathers, ⁷the promise to which our twelve tribes hope to attain, as they earnestly serve the Almĭghty night and day. And for this hope, *O* King, I am being accused by Yehudim. ⁸Why is it getting judged unfaithful at your side if the Almĭghty does raise the dead?

⁹"So then, I thought to myself that I had to do many things hostile to the name of Yĕshua Ha-Natsri, ¹⁰which also I did in Yerushalayim. And many besides of the holy ones, I in prisons had locked up, the authority having received from the hand of chief priests. As well when they were being put to death I cast my vote against them. ¹¹And as I punished them often down throughout all the congregations, I tried to force them to blaspheme. Besides being furiously enraged at them, I was pursuing them even as far as foreign cities.

¹²"While so engaged as I was journeying to Dammeseq with the authority and commission of the chief priests, ¹³at midday, *O* King, I saw down through the road a light from heaven, brighter than the sun, shining all around me and those who were journeying with me. ¹⁴Besides all of us having fallen to the ground, I heard a voice saying to me in the Hebrew language, 'Ṣa'ul, Ṣa'ul, why are you persecuting me? It is hard for you to kick against the goads.' ¹⁵And I said, 'Who are you, Adŏnai?' And Yăhwe**н** said, 'I am Yĕshua whom you are persecuting. ¹⁶But arise, and stand on your feet, because for this purpose I have been seen by you, to appoint you a minister and a witness, besides of that which you have seen me *to be*, as well as of which things I will be seen *to be* by you, ¹⁷delivering you from the people and from the nations, into which I am sending you, ¹⁸to open their eyes for turning *them* from darkness to light, and from the dominion of Satan to the Almĭghty, for their receiving release from sins, and an inheritance among those who have been making themselves holy by faithfulness, which is to Me.'

¹⁹"Consequently, King Agrippa, I did not become disobedient to the heavenly vision, ²⁰but was declaring to those in Dammeseq first, besides also those in Yerushalayim, besides all the region of Yehudah, and to the nations, to be sorry, turning the heart *from sin*, and to turn to the Almĭghty, performing deeds worthy of being sorry and turning the heart *from sin*. ²¹For this reason some Yehudim seized me in the Temple and tried to put me to death. ²²And so, having obtained help from the Almĭghty, until this day I have been standing being witness to small besides also great, saying nothing other, besides what the prophets and Mosheh have said was going to be happening, ²³if whenᵖ the Anŏinted One is suffering—if whenᵉ as the ᵠheadmost *one* from the resurrection of the dead, he is going to preach light, besides to the people *of Yisra'el*, even to the nations."

26:19 ε dissuaded [from] **26:23** ε Paul's second εἰ 'if when' applies only to the question of whether the nations are to be included in the proclamation of Mĕssiah. This was the point that set off the riot in Acts 21:21-23 when Paul was arrested. **26:23** ρ The first εἰ only sets the context leading to the second 'if.' By so constructing his sentence Paul has bypassed the question of the resurrection of Mĕssiah in his trial, and his suffering, and gone straight to the substance of the riot, which was the opinion that Mĕssiah would

²⁴And while Paul was saying this in his defense, Festus said in a loud voice, "Paul, you are out of your mind! Your great learning is driving you mad." ²⁵But Paul said, "I am not out of my mind, most excellent Festus, but I utter words of sober truth, ²⁶because the king knows about these matters, and I speak to him also with confidence, since I am persuaded that none of these things escape his notice, because this has not been getting done in a corner. ²⁷King Agrippa, do you hold the prophets faithful? I have been knowing that you do support *them*." ²⁸And Agrippa replied to Paul, "In *such* a short time will you persuade me to become a ʸMessianic?" ²⁹And Paul said, "I would to the Almĭghty, that whether in a short or long time, not only you, but also all who hear me this day, *may* become such as I am, except for these chains."

³⁰Besides the king arose also the governor; besides Berniqah also those who were sitting with them, ³¹and when they had drawn aside, they were talking to one another, saying, "This man is not doing anything worthy of death or imprisonment." ³²And Agrippa was saying to Festus, "This man was being able to have been getting set free if he had not been calling upon Caesar."

27 ¹And when it was decided that we should sail for Italy, they proceeded to deliver besides Paul also some other prisoners to a centurion of the Augustan cohort named Julius. ²And embarking in an Adramyttian ship, which was about to sail to the regions down the coast of Asia, we put out to sea, accompanied by Aristarchus, a Macedonian of Thessalonica. ³And the next day we put in at Tsidon; besides Julius having treated Paul with consideration, allowed him to go to his friends and receive care. ⁴And from there we put out to sea and sailed under the shelter of Cyprus because the winds were contrary. ⁵Besides the open sea, down by *the coasts of* Cilicia and Pamphylia, having sailed, we came down to Myra of Lycia.

⁶And there the centurion found an Alexandrian ship sailing for Italy, and he put us aboard it. ⁷And when we had sailed slowly for a good many days, and with difficulty had arrived down from Cnidus, since the wind did not permit us to go farther, we sailed under the shelter of Crete, down from Salmone, ⁸besides with difficulty sailing past it we came to a certain place called Fair Havens, near which was the city of Lasea.

---

proclaim himself to the nations. Since the opinion was not punishable in the least, it was a point he could win on, and he did win on it, except he appealed to Caesar.

26:23 θ πρῶτος = first one (adj. substantive), where first is meant in terms of rank or importance, as in 'first fruits,' being the chiefest or best to be offered. Compare 1 Cor. 15:23; cf Psa. 89:27; Col. 1:15, 18. By no means was Mĕssiah the first in order to be raised. For we have Moses mentioned alive before the resurrection of Mĕssiah (Mat. 17:3), and we have a multitude of holy ones raised at the time he died, who did remain in their tombs until he was raised, but nonetheless, they were raised first. See Mat. 27:52; 2 Kings 13:21 where a man thrown into Elisha's grave was raised from the dead. How much more then does Mĕssiah raise the dead even in death by the power of the Spĭrit. ▷ The use of εἰ may be strongly affirmative (cf. LSJ: '**VI.** in citing a fact as a ground of argument or appeal, *as surely as, since.*'). This is according to Hebrew usage (cf. Mark 8:13; Gal. 5:11). **26:28** γ מְשִׁיחִי = Meshikhi = Χριστιανὸν. Mĕssiah with a gentilic ending, like adding /i/ to Yisra'el to form Yisra'eli. Literally the term means 'anointedians.' See Acts 11:26.

⁹And when considerable time had passed and the voyage was now dangerous, since even the ᵘfast already had been passing by, Paul was admonishing them, ¹⁰and said to them, "Men, I perceive that the voyage will certainly be attended with damage and great loss, not only of the cargo and the ship, but also of our lives."

¹¹But the centurion was getting persuaded by the pilot and the captain of the ship, more than by what was being said by Paul. ¹²And because the harbor was not suitable for wintering, the majority reached a decision to put out to sea from there, if somehow they could reach ᵠPhoenix, a harbor of Crete, looking down from the southwest wind and down from the northwest wind, and spend the winter there. ¹³And when a moderate south wind came up, supposing that they had been seizing the initiative, they weighed anchor and were sailing along Crete, close to shore. ¹⁴But before very long there rushed down from the land a violent wind, called the northeaster. ¹⁵And when the ship was caught in it, and could not face the wind, we gave way to it, and let ourselves be driven along.

¹⁶And running under the shelter of a small island called Cauda, we were scarcely able to get the ship's boat under control. ¹⁷And after they had hoisted it up, they used supporting cables in undergirding the ship, besides fearing that they might run aground on the shallows of Syrtis, they let down the sea anchor, and so let themselves be driven along. ¹⁸The next day as we were being violently storm-tossed, they began to jettison the cargo. ¹⁹And on the third day they threw the ship's tackle overboard with their own hands. ²⁰And since neither sun nor stars appeared for many days, besides no small storm was assailing us, from then on all hope of our being rescued was gradually abandoned.

²¹Besides when they had gone a long time without food, then Paul stood up in their midst and said, "Men, you ought to have followed my advice and not to have set sail from Crete, besides to have incurred this damage and loss. ²²And yet now I urge you to be cheerful, because there will be no loss of life among you, but only of the ship, ²³because this very night the Messenger of the Almighty to whom I belong and whom I serve stood before me, ²⁴saying, 'Do not be getting afraid, Paul! You must stand before Caesar, and behold, the Almighty has been favoring for you all those who are sailing with you.' ²⁵Therefore, be cheering up men, because I hold faithful to the Almighty, in that thus it will be exactly as it has been getting told to me. ²⁶But we must run aground on a certain island."

²⁷But when the fourteenth night had come, as we were being driven about in the Adriatic Sea, about midnight the sailors were surmising that they were approaching some land. ²⁸And they took soundings, and found it to be twenty fathoms. And a little farther on they took another sounding and found it to be fifteen fathoms. ²⁹Fearing besides lest we will have run aground somewhere on the rocks, having cast four anchors from the stern, they were praying for day to come.

27:9 μ Yom Kippur, AD 59 was on October 7th. **27:12** ψ Modern Loutro, Crete.

Acts 28

³⁰And as the sailors were trying to escape from the ship, and had let down the ship's boat into the sea, on the pretense of intending to lay out anchors from the bow, ³¹Paul said to the centurion and to the soldiers, "Unless these men will have remained in the ship, you yourselves cannot be rescued." ³²Then the soldiers cut away the ropes of the ship's boat, and let it fall away.

³³And until the day was about to dawn, Paul was encouraging them all to take some food, saying, "Today is the fourteenth day that you have been constantly watching and going without eating, having taken nothing. ³⁴Therefore I encourage you to take some food, because this is for your preservation, because not a hair from the head of any of you will perish."

³⁵And having said this, he took bread and gave thanks to the Almĭghty in the presence of all, and he broke it and began to eat. ³⁶And all of them were encouraged, and they themselves also took food. ³⁷And all of us in the ship were two hundred and seventy-six persons. ³⁸And when they had eaten enough, they were lightening the ship by throwing out the wheat into the sea.

³⁹And when day came, they could not recognize the land, but they did observe a certain bay with a beach, and they resolved to drive the ship onto it if they could. ⁴⁰And casting off the anchors, they left them in the sea while at the same time they were loosening the ropes of the rudders, and hoisting the foresail to the wind, they were heading for the beach. ⁴¹But striking a reef where two seas met, they ran the vessel aground, and the prow stuck fast and remained immovable, but the stern was being broken up by the force of the waves.

⁴²And the soldiers' plan was that they should kill the prisoners, that none of them, having swam away, will have escaped, ⁴³but the centurion, wanting to bring Paul safely through, kept them from their intention; besides, he commanded that those being able to swim should jump overboard first and get to land, ⁴⁴and the rest should follow, some on planks, and others on various things from the ship. And thus it happened that they all were brought safely to land.

28

¹And when they were brought safely through, then we found out that the island was called Malta. ²Besides, the natives afforded us unusual kindness, because they kindled a fire and welcomed us all, because of the rain that had been standing over *us* and because of the cold.

³But when Paul had gathered a bundle of sticks and laid them on the fire, a viper came out because of the heat, and fastened on his hand. ⁴And when the natives saw the creature hanging from his hand, they were saying to one another, "Undoubtedly this man is a murderer, and though he has been rescued from the sea, justice has not allowed him to live." ⁵However he shook the creature off into the fire and suffered no harm.

⁶But they were expecting that he was about to swell up or suddenly fall down dead. But after they had waited a long time and had seen nothing unusual happen to him, they changed their minds and were saying that he was a god.

⁷Now in the neighborhood of that place were lands belonging to the leading

man of the island, named Publius, who welcomed us and entertained us courteously three days. ⁸And it came about that the father of Publius was lying in bed afflicted with recurrent fever and dysentery. And Paul went in to see him, and after he had prayed, he laid his hands on him and healed him. ⁹And after this had happened, the rest of the people on the island who had diseases were coming to him and getting cured. ¹⁰And they also honored us with many marks of respect. And when we were setting sail, they supplied us with all we needed.

¹¹And at the end of three moons^τ we set sail on an Alexandrian ship which had been passing winter at the island, and which had the twin brothers for its figurehead. ¹²And after we put in at Syracuse, we stayed there for three days. ¹³And from there we sailed around and arrived at Rhegium, and a day later a south wind sprang up, and on the second day we came to Puteoli. ¹⁴There we found some brothers, and were invited to stay at their side for seven days, and so we came to Rome. ¹⁵And the brothers, when they heard about us, came from there as far as the Market of Appius and Three Inns to meet us, and when Paul saw them, he thanked the Almĭghty and took heart. ¹⁶And when we entered Rome, Paul was allowed to stay by himself, with the soldier who was guarding him.

¹⁷And it happened that after three days he called together those who were the leading men of the Yehudim, and when they had come together, he was saying to them, "Brothers, though I had done nothing against our people, or the customs of our fathers, yet I was delivered prisoner from Yerushalayim into the hands of the Romans. ¹⁸And when they had examined me, they were willing to release me because there was no ground for putting me to death. ¹⁹But when the Yehudim objected, I was forced to appeal to Caesar, not that I had any accusation against my nation. ²⁰For this reason therefore, I requested to see you and to speak with you, because I am wearing this chain for the sake of the hope of Yisra'el."

²¹And they said to him, "We have neither received letters from Yehudah concerning you, nor have any of the brothers come here and reported or spoken anything bad about you. ²²But we desire to hear at your side what your views are, because concerning this sect, it is known to us that it is spoken against everywhere."

²³And when they had set a day for him, they came to him at his lodging in large numbers. And he was explaining to them by thoroughly testifying about the kingdom of the Almĭghty, besides persuading them concerning Yĕshua, as well as from the Law of Mosheh, and the Prophets, from morning until evening.

²⁴And some were persuaded by the things being spoken, but others were not holding faithful. ²⁵And when they did not agree with one another, they were leaving after Paul had spoken one last word, "The Holy Spĭrit rightly spoke through Yeshayahu the prophet to your fathers, ²⁶saying, 'GO TO THIS PEOPLE AND YOU WILL HAVE SAID, HEARING YOU WILL HEAR, AND NO, YOU SHALL NOT HAVE UN-

---

28:11 τ January or Feb, AD 60.

DERSTOOD, AND SEEING YOU WILL SEE, AND NO, YOU SHALL NOT HAVE PERCEIVED, ²⁷BECAUSE THE HEART OF THIS PEOPLE HAS BECOME DULL, AND WITH THEIR EARS THEY SCARCELY HEAR, AND THEY HAVE CLOSED THEIR EYES, LEST THEY MAY HAVE SEEN WITH THEIR EYES, AND MAY HAVE HEARD WITH THEIR EARS, AND MAY HAVE UNDERSTOOD WITH THEIR HEART AND MAY HAVE RETURNED, AND I WILL HEAL THEM^ψ.' ²⁸Let it be getting known to you therefore, that this deliverance of the Almĭghty has been sent to the nations. They will also listen." ³⁰And he remained there two whole ᵋyears in his own rented place, and was welcoming all that came in to him, ³¹proclaiming the kingdom of the Almĭghty, and teaching the things about Adŏnai Yĕshua *the* Anŏinted with all boldness unhindered.

28:27 ψ Isa 6:9-10 **28:30** ᵋ Spring AD 60 to spring AD 62.

The Imperative to Hear Messiah's Word

²⁰Behold, I am sending My Messenger at your faces to keep watch over you in the way, and to cause you to come into the place which I have established. ²¹Watch yourself before his face, and listen to his voice. Do not create bitterness against him, because he will not endure your transgressions, because My Name is in the midst of him. ²²Because, if listening you will listen to his voice, and you will have done all that I am speaking, then I will have been the enemy of your enemies, and I will have become adversary of your adversaries. ²³Because my Messenger will go at your faces, and he will have caused you to come to the Emori, and the Ḥitti, and the Perizzi, and the Kena'ani, the Ḥivvi and the Yevusi, and I will have cut it off. EXODUS 23:20-23.

Adŏnai Yăhweh has been sending me, and his Spĭrit. ISAIAH 48:16. And no one has been ascending into heaven, except he which descended from heaven, the Sŏn of man, the one being in heaven. YO'HANAN 3:13. See also Exo. 32:34.

¹Behold, I am sending My Messenger, and he will have cleared the way at My face, and suddenly he will come to his Temple, the Adŏn whom you are seeking, even the Messenger of the Covenant, whom you delight in. Behold he is coming Yăhweh of Armies has said. MALACHI 3:1.

Now surely someone will say that Mal. 3:1 refers to Yoḥanan the Immerser, and this is so, but to say so and to overlook the greater reference to Messiah is like looking at the Cyrus passages in Isaiah and saying they do not refer to Messiah. They surely do. The language of Malachi 3:1 is so strikingly similar to that of Exodus 23:20 that it is obvious the subject is the same person. This also requires us to look at Malachi 1:1:

The weight of the Word of Yăhweh to Yisra'el, by the hand of My Messenger. I have loved you all has said Yăhweh.

Do we suppose the prophet speaks only of himself here? This is most unlikely considering the prior use of the term My Messenger. The word refers first and foremost to the Messenger of the Covenant. Indeed, after considering just these two passages, I do believe there are no remaining passages that do not refer to either My Messenger or the Messenger Yăhweh as being a mere angel or human messenger.

The importance of this cannot be understated. The Messenger in the Torah whom we are charged to listen to and obey is none other that the Messenger of Yăhweh, who became the Messiah, Yĕshua.

Formerly, we were told that the go to passage for finding a directive to listen to the Messiah is found in Deut. 18. Listening does not just mean believing in him. It means obeying him, because that is what listening means in Hebrew. He will not tolerate transgressions when he is present. And in fact, he withdrew from Yisra'el because of transgression, because if he had stayed he would have had to destroy the transgressors.

So you see, his absence is a season to repent and be forgiven before he comes. So you see the house of Yehudah has been bitter against the Messenger by rejecting his visitation, beginning at the Temple in the Holy City in AD 30, where he said he would tear down the Temple of his Body and rebuild it in three days.

Yet also the house of Yisra'el has been bitter against Messiah because they have rejected his Torah, his regulations for life that he gave on Mt. Sinai. So then it is imperative to hold faithful to the commandments of the Messenger. Because he is the choice cornerstone that the builders rejected, and whoever holds faithful to Him will not have to hurry away to find a hole in the ground when he comes. For coming he will come, and his judgment is with him, and all who made their covenant with death will be put to shame, and they will be ground to powder under his feet.

Romans

1 ¹Paul, a servant of the Anŏinted Yĕshua, called as an emissary, who has been getting set apart for the good news of the Almĭghty ²which he promised beforehand through his prophets in the holy writings, ³about his Sŏn, who was born from the seed of David according to the flesh, ⁴who has been ᵋmarked *as* the Almĭghty Sŏn with power according to the ˣSpĭrit of holiness, by his resurrection from the dead, Yĕshua the Anŏinted, our Adŏnai, ⁵through whom we have received loving-kindness and ambassadorship,ᵅ to bring about a ᶲfaithful listening among all the nations on behalf of his name, ⁶among whom you also are called by Yĕshua the Anŏinted. ⁷To all those living in Rome, beloved of the Almĭghty, called holy ones. Loving-kindness to you and peace from our Almĭghty Făther, and Adŏnai Yĕshua the Anŏinted.

⁸First indeed, I am giving thanks to my Almĭghty through Yĕshua the Anŏinted for all of you, because your faithfulness is being proclaimed in all the world. ⁹Because the Almĭghty is my witness, whom I am serving in my spirit in connection to the good news of his Sŏn, as to how unceasingly I am making mention of you, ¹⁰always in my prayers asking if somehow now at last I will succeed by the will of the Almĭghty to come to you. ¹¹Because I am longing to see you, so that I will have imparted some spiritual gift to you, that you may be established. ¹²And this is so that we may be encouraged together with you, through each other's faithfulness, yours as well as even mine. ¹³But I am not wanting you to be unaware, brothers, that often I set plans before the present (and I was prevented until now) to come to you, so that I may have some fruit among you also, even as among the rest of the nations.ᵘ

¹⁴To Greeks, besides also to Barbarians, to educated besides also to the unlearned, a debtor I am. ¹⁵So, for my part I am also eager to announce the good news to you who are in Rome.

¹⁶Because I am not ashamed of the good news, since it is the power of the Almĭghty for deliverance to everyone holding faithful,ᵅ besides for the Yehudi firstly, also for the Greek, ¹⁷because the justiceᶿ of the Almĭghty in it is revealed from faithfulnessᵋ to faithfulness,ᶲ even as it has been getting written, "BUT THE RIGHTEOUS ONE BY ᵚFAITHFULNESS WILL LIVE.ᶲ"

1:4 ξ or *pointed out* **1:4** χ Rŭakh HaQodesh **1:5** α or *emissaryship*. Paul includes the other emissaries within his focus to the nations, because their mission also was intended to reach the nations, just not so directly as his. **1:5** φ or *hearing of [Gŏd's] faithfulness*. **1:13** μ See 15:22. **1:16** α Specifically holding faithful means to return to the Almĭghty's Law, his Torah Instruction for life, containing his commandments, because the one who does them will live by them (Lev. 18:5; Rom. 2:7). This is necessary for all who seek everlasting life (Mat. 19:16; Mark 10:17). The divine offer of forgiveness is open to both Jew and non-Jew, both to the house of Yehudah, and the scattered house of Yisra'el, and all the nations, who have mixed with Yisra'el, and even to all who only eat crumbs under the table. There is no limit on who can be ransomed from lawlessness, if only they would seek the Most High and pledge their faithfulness through his ransomer Mĕssiah Yĕshua. **1:17** θ✓ This is not the strict punitive justice of the western Church, because divine righteousness (or justice) includes the divine choice for benevolent justice (Rom 3:24) of mercy and forgiveness when the circumstances call for it. The necessary circumstance is a return to faithfulness in repentance by lost Yisra'el. Everyone holding faithful to Messiah will be getting a ransom release from sin and death. Messiah ransoms us from the hand of lawlessness by his power, even up to and including

Romans 2

¹⁸This is because the fierce anger of the Almĭghty is revealed from heaven upon all the evil and injustice of men, who^μ are holding back the truth by injustice, ¹⁹because that which is known about the Almĭghty is manifested among them, because the Almĭghty makes it manifest to them, ²⁰because the unseen things about him, from the creation of the universe, *even by the things made are being understood, and are perceived*, besides his everlasting power and divinity, so that they should be without excuse.

²¹Because as those that know the Almĭghty, they do not glorify him as Almĭghty or give thanks. But they have become worthless in their reasonings, and their senseless heart has become darkened. ²²Claiming to be wise, they have become foolish, ²³and have exchanged the glory of the incorruptible Almĭghty for an image of corruptible man and birds and four-footed beasts and reptiles.

²⁴Therefore the Almĭghty has given them over to the evil lusts of their hearts, to the uncleanness of dishonoring their bodies with themselves, ²⁵who have changed the truth of the Almĭghty into a lie, and have been worshiping and serving the creature beside the one who has created, who is blessed for all the ages. Am·en.

²⁶Because of this the Almĭghty has given them over to dishonorable passions. For as their females have exchanged the natural function for that which is beside nature, ²⁷likewise besides, also the males, having left the natural function of the female, have burned in their desire toward one another, males with males working for shame. And the reward (which was necessary) of their error, they are receiving back into themselves. ²⁸And even as they have approved not the Almĭghty for holding fast, in true knowledge, the Almĭghty has given them over to a worthless mind for doing those things which are not proper, ²⁹who have been getting themselves filled with all injustice, wickedness, greed, evil, *and who are* full of envy, murder, strife, deceit, malice, *being* gossips, ³⁰slanderers, haters of the Almĭghty, insolent, arrogant, boastful, inventors of evil, disobedient to parents, ³¹without moral sense, traitors, lacking in natural love, *and* unmerciful, ³²who the penalty of the Almĭghty fully know, that those doing such things are worthy of death. And not only are they doing them, but also altogether they are giving a good approval to the ones practicing them.

2 ¹Therefore, you are without excuse, O man, every one judging, because in the thing which you are judging the other, you are condemning yourself, because you are doing the same things. ²And we have been knowing that the judgment

---

the cost of his own blood, which he also expends to cleanse us from all sin. ▷ Justice here is the divine option of favorable justice. It is the justice apart from the norm of strict justice, and apart from the norm of paying a punitive debt, or the heretical norm of compensatory deeds. It is not the justice of appeasement, because the object of Messiah's self sacrifice is to ransom man from sin and to cleanse him from it. The Most High is not being propitiated. KIPPURIM is to rescue man from sin, and not to placate the wrath of God, which is reserved only for the unrepentant, who cannot be separated from their sin in the day of judgment. **1:17** ε *Mĕssiah's faithfulness* **1:17** ρ *our faithfulness;* **1:17** ω Salvation is for anyone pledging loyalty to Mĕssiah. Gŏd's justice in mercy (1:17 θ) is revealed from Mĕssiah's ransoming faithfulness (ε). We respond with our faithfulness (ρ). The Hab. 2:4 quote refers to our and Mĕssiah's faithfulness put together. Our deliverance is acomplished by the synergism (working together) of his faithfulness and our faithfulness. **1:17** φ Hab. 2:4. **1:18** μ Paul is not speaking of the faithful here, and so he qualifies his statement.

of the Almĭghty is according to truth, upon those practicing such things. ³But are you taking into account this, O man, who are judging those practicing such things and doing the same yourself, that you will escape the judgment of the Almĭghty? ⁴Or do you despise the riches of his goodness, and his forbearance and long-suffering, without knowing that the kindness of the Almĭghty is leading you to being sorry and turning your heart *from sin*?

⁵But according to your stubbornness and unrepentant heart you are treasuring wrath for yourself in the day of wrath and revelation of the just judgment of the Almĭghty, ⁶WHO WILL REWARD EVERYONE ACCORDING TO HIS DEEDS.ᵅ ⁷Indeed, to those who by patient endurance in ⁿgood work, are seeking glory and honor and incorruptibleness: ᵞeverlasting life, ⁸but to those acting from selfish ambition and being disobedient to the truth, that is, being obedient to unrighteousness, he will pay back wrath and anger, ⁹tribulation and distress—upon every soul of man who is practicing evil, besides first for the Yehudi, also for the Greek, ¹⁰but glory and honor and peace to everyone that is ᵟworking good, besides first to the Yehudi, also to the Greek.

¹¹Because there is no favoritism alongside the Almĭghty, ¹²because as many as ᵅlawless sin, *as* ᵅlawless also will be destroyed. Also as many as sin ᵞwhile being lawful, through the Law will be judged, ¹³because not the hearers of the Law are righteous before the Almĭghty, but the doers of the Law will be ᵟdeclared righteous. ¹⁴For when nations, who do not have the Law, may be naturally doing the things of the Law, these, not having the Law, to themselves are law, ¹⁵who are indicating the work of the Law written in their hearts;ᵋ their conscience bearing witness and their thoughts accusing, one with another, or also defending them, ¹⁶in connection to the day when the Almĭghty will be judging the secrets of men,

---

2:6 α Psa 62:12 **2:7** η See 1 Tim. 6:12, 19. **2:7** γ Everyone is rewarded according to their works, just not on the principles of zechut, which Paul opposes (and which Paul means when he speaks disparagingly of works), because it attempts to purchase forgiveness with good deeds. But for those loving the Most High and keeping his commandments, He shows loving-kindness and mercy. Please see Exodus 20:6. And to seek eternal life one must be seeking to obey the commandments. ▷ Adversaries of the truth hold this verse to be a hypothetical statement, or more commonly try to sandwich the verse into their context of Calvinistic doctrines, total depravity, predestination and regeneration such that the good works are not a genuine human response, but a gift of a false god who is controlling all the strings of his puppets. Thus they explain this text that it only appears that eternal life is contingient on good works, and that the works are really being done for them. **2:10** δ In quoting Psa. 62:12 (2:6α), Paul teaches that good work is necessary for everlasting life. See Mat. 19:16-17; Mark 10:17 ff; 1 Yoḥ. 2:3-6; Yoḥ. 14:21; 15:1-10; Deut. 8:1-2; 30:11-14. Rom. 10:5-13; Gal. 5:21; Lev. 18:5; Hab. 2:4.

2:12 α 2x Adverb and substantive adjective **2:12** γ ἐν νόμῳ The text says literally, 'in law' which means abiding in law or being instructed in it. The mistranslation 'under law' was deliberately foisted on the text to shift Paul's contrast away from lawless vs. lawful to those not subject to law (without law) vs. those subject to law (under it). This subtle deception is a wedge by which the Church seeks to exempt itself from the Torah. This deception was also put on Romans 3:19 q.v. ▷ For those within the sphere of the Torah, Paul did not use the word "destroyed," but he says judged through Torah, which too many perceive as the same condemnation as destroyed because they are taught the Torah only condemns. It does not. See Exodus 20:6 for direct disproof of this belief. If the Almĭghty finds the faithful guilty of sin, then the operation of the Torah allows him to pardon or forgive the person if they repent, and indeed this will be the case for those held faithful. **2:13** δ Paul distinguishes two classes of people here, the lawless and the lawful. The lawless will be summarily condemned to death. But those who sin, yet having lawful attitudes, will be judged by it whether Jew or non Jew. **2:15** ξ *Written in their hearts* refutes total depravity. The nations here represent man without the truth of the Torah, before they come to know the Most High of Yisra'el (contra Augustine).

according to my good news, through the Anŏinted Yĕshua.

¹⁷But if you are calling yourself Yehudi and are finding rest in the Law and are rejoicing in the Almĭghty, ¹⁸and know his will and are approving things making a difference, being instructed out of the Law, ¹⁹having been trusting yourself besides to be a guide of the blind, a light of those in darkness, ²⁰a corrector of the foolish, a teacher of the immature, having the structural form of knowledge and of the truth in the Law, ²¹who then are teaching another, are you not teaching yourself? You who are proclaiming do not steal, are you stealing? ²²You who are saying do not commit adultery, are you committing adultery? You who are abhorring idols, are you robbing temples? ²³You who are boasting in the Law, through transgression of the Law, are you dishonoring the Almĭghty? ²⁴since THE NAME OF THE ALMĬGHTY IS BLASPHEMED AMONG THE NATIONS BECAUSE OF YOU⁰, just as it has been getting written.

²⁵Because circumcision truly is profiting when you are practicing the Law, but when you may be a transgressor of the Law, your circumcision has been becoming uncircumcision˟. ²⁶So if the uncircumcised man may be keeping the just things of the Law, will not his uncircumcision be ˡtaken into account as circumcision? ²⁷And the one who is naturally uncircumcised, when keeping the Law, will judge you, who through a ᵖletter promising to repay and circumcision, are a transgressor of the Law.

²⁸Because what is on the outside is not Yehudi, nor is what is only on the outside in the flesh circumcision, ²⁹but one is in the inside Yehudi. And circumcision of the heart^α *is* in spirit, and not by a ᵝletter promising to repay, in persons whose praise is not from men, but from the Almĭghty.

3 Then what advantage has the Yehudi? Or what is the benefit of circumcision?ʸ ²Great in every way. Firstly, indeed, in that they have been held faithful with the sayings of the Almĭghty⁰. ³So what if certain ones are unfaithful? Perhaps their unfaithfulness will undo the faithfulness of the Almĭghty?

2:24 θ Isa 52:5, Eze 36:20; (thematic). **2:25** χ Many taught that circumcision gave a Jew enough merit to cancel out their demerit. But Paul says the demerit annuls the circumcision. **2:26** λ if appropriating the merit of the fathers by circumcision were true, then it is a fair question ask if the Torah observance of the uncircumcised is counted as circumcision. Paul isn't saying it is; he is just asking. **2:27** ρ✓ The Greek word for letter was used for a promissory note. When a person had a debt they agreed to pay, they handed over a letter stating how much they owed to the creditor, who kept the letter until the debt was repaid. See Luke 16:6-7. Judaism takes on the letter to repay in the doctrine of zechut. See vs. 29; 7:6; 2 Cor. 3:6-7. The word letter might also have been used for a sentence or an indictment, but this usage is uncertain.▷ Heretical interpreters suggest the letter means the literal commandments, which they take as inseparable from condemnation, since in their view the laws only function is to condemn, and holds out no mercy for sinners. This slanderous opinion is commonly applied to the faithful in polemical arguments by those who have never truthfully read the Torah. **2:29** α περιτομὴ NNFS καρδίας NGFS. Other translations redefine circumcision by falsely locating the word "is": "circumcision [is] of the heart," but Scripture teaches both literal and heart circumcision proving that the redefinition is false. Future prophecy speaks of both. See Ezek. 44:6-9; Deut. 30:6. **2:29** β (see 2:27ρ). **3:1** γ See 1 Cor 7:18 **3:2** ρ The Yehudim have had the greater access to divine revelation because they have preserved it and have taught the Hebrew language in which it is written, and no doubt preserve some traditions helpful in understanding the texts. So they have been relatively faithful in this matter, which is without a doubt an advantage to being Jewish. But some try to coerce the faithful to follow what is considered the consensus of Jewish authority in all things. This notion is immediately contradicted by vs. 3, and the well known fact that the Jewish consensus rejects the Messiah. However, the faithful must not use Jewish rejectionism as an excuse to take no advantage of Jewish sources, nor to unfairly slander Jewish traditional contributions.

⁴May it never be! So, let the Almĭghty be getting found true, and every man a liar, as it has been getting written, "WITH THE END THAT YOU SHALL HAVE BEEN FOUND RIGHT IN YOUR WORDS,ᵃ" and "YOU WILL GET VICTORY WHEN YOU ARE JUDGED.ᵃ" ⁵But if our unrighteousness demonstrates the justice of the Almĭghty,ᵠ what will we say? "Maybe the Almĭghty who brings wrath is unjust?" (I am speaking humanly.) ⁶May it never be! Otherwise, how will the Almĭghty judge the world? ⁷Or, "when the truth of the Almĭghty, by my lie abounds to his glory, why am I also still being judged as a sinner?" ⁸Also, it is not, just as we are being ᵖslandered, and just as some are claiming us to be saying, "We should do evil so that good may come," for whom the judgment is just.

⁹What then? Are weᵞ better? Not altogetherᵘ, because we previously charged Yehudim, besides also Greeks, ᵖeach to be under sin, ¹⁰just as it has been getting written, "THERE IS NONE UPRIGHT, NOT EVEN ONE.ᵃ ¹¹There is none WHO UNDERSTAND.ᵘ There are none WHO ARE SEEKING THE ALMĬGHTY.ᵘ ¹²ALL TURN ASIDE. TOGETHER THEY HAVE BEEN CORRUPTED. NONE IS DOING KINDNESS—NOT EVEN ONE.ᵃ ¹³THEIR THROAT IS A GRAVE WHICH HAS BEEN OPENING ITSELF. THEIR TONGUES WERE SMOOTH IN DECEIT.ᵝ THE POISON OF ASPS IS UNDER THEIR LIPS.ᵞ ¹⁴Their MOUTH IS FULL OF CURSING AND BITTERNESS.ᵟ ¹⁵THEIR FEET ARE SWIFT TO SHED BLOOD. ¹⁶DESTRUCTION AND MISERY ARE IN THEIR HIGHWAYS, ¹⁷and, THE

3:4 α Psa 51:4-5, "AGAINST YOU, YOU BESIDES: I HAVE SINNED, AND THE EVIL *THING* I HAVE DONE IN YOUR EYES **WITH THE END THAT YOU SHALL HAVE BEEN RIGHT IN YOUR SPEAKING**, *AND* **PURE IN YOUR JUDGING**. BEHOLD, INTO INIQUITY I HAVE BEEN MADE TO BE <u>BORN</u>, AND INTO SIN MY MOTHER HAS MADE ME TO BE <u>CONCEIVED</u>." The underlined words mean 'to be born through the writhing agony of labor,' and 'to conceive in heat.' ▷ Not *to you, you only* (contra Anselm with respect to the divine honor). Anselm assumed all sin was an infinite offense against the honor of God, and thus by comparison *only* God, which could only be restored by an infinite compensation, the death of Christ, the God-Man, but this view meets its demise in Lev. 19:15. Judgment is not to be light or severe based on the rank of the party offended. That is Amorite doctrine, and feudalism. ▷ *With the end that,* לְמַעַן expresses result only, and not that the sin was divinely ordained, which is the Gnostic view. *Into iniquity...into sin* states that he was brought forth into a sinful environment, and not that be was born with the guilt of the original sin upon him (Pelagius contra Augustine). See Rom. 5:12, 18. See below on total depravity. Some have supposed that David discovered he was an illegitimate child, e.g. a child of rape, but I think if there is any hint of this, it is camaflauge on the real thought. In any case, this idea also refutes total depravity, and makes the same point, i.e. that his environment was toxic. **3:5 ψ** The worst sorts of human rulers know that if they find some obvious evil doers upon which they can execute punitive justice that people will then think them righteous for doing so. So they maintain their image by doing so. They are even known to frame up the innocent as evil doers so that they may appear righteous by punishing them. These are called false flag attacks. This is how evil humans view the Almĭghty. He unjustly punishes them just so that he can appear in the right. The same idea is repeated another way in vs. 7. **3:8 ρ** Paul's adversaries did not tell the truth about what he taught.

3:9 γ Paul is speaking with a corporate 'we' of the nation of Yisra·el vs. other nations. His quotations demonstrate that Yisra·el itself has drunk its fair share of the cup of evil, and that it has not been nationally more righteous. By no means does he mean that no person is righteous, but the "none" the texts speak of are the evil members of Yisra·eli society that the Psalmist was excoriating. The texts cited are: Psa. 14:1-3 (= 53:1-4); Psa. 5:9-10; 10:7; Isa. 59:7; Prov. 1:16. Paul's point is to refute Judaism's doctrine that salvation is by having Jewish identity. **3:9 μ** See BDAG: πάντως ❷ *altogether* **3:9 ρ** See BDAG: πᾶς ❶ *each*. 'Under sin' refers to the unfaithful. See Num. 15:30-31. Recognizing this distinction vs. sins of ignorance, and noting that the citations to follow are aimed at the wicked in Yisra·el, to show that the nation was not exempt among nations, proves that Paul is not teaching a doctrine of total and universal individual depravity. See *Rom. 7:14 η; Gal. 3:22 π*. **3:10 α** Psa 14:3, 53:3 (טוֹב=δίκαιος); (but not Eccl. 7:20) **3:11 μ** Psa 14:2 **3:12 α** Psa 14:3, 53:3 (טוֹב=χρηστότητα) **3:13 β** Psa 5:9 **3:13 γ** Psa 140:3 **3:14 δ** Psa 10:7 **3:14-17 θ** Isa 59:7-8

WAY OF PEACE THEY KNOW NOT.θ ¹⁸THEREλ IS NO FEAR OF THE ALMĬGHTY BEFORE their EYES."

¹⁹But we have been knowing that as much as the Law is saying to those instructed λin the Law, it is also speaking so that every mouth will have been closed and all the world will have come ρto trial before the Almĭghty. ²⁰Therefore, based on φcustomary works no flesh εwill be administered justice before him, because through the Law is βfull recognition of sin.

²¹But now apart from what is ψcustomary, the justiceκ of the Almĭghty has

---

3:18 λ Psa 36:1 **3:19** λ ἐν τῷ νόμῳ Only a little mistranslation is necessary to change the whole meaning of a text. Here many translations put "under" the law. But the Greek doesn't say "under." It says "in the Law." Paul uses "under nomos," and "in the Law" to explain two different things. For the one he means under the legal norm, which is judgment, and for the other he means those instructed in the Law, who keep a good conscience toward it, just as back in 2:12. **3:19** ρ ὑπόδικος = under justice; *brought to trial* (LSJ).

3:20 φ→works: ἔργων νόμου = *works of custom*. Paul speaks only of such works as would be used to offset demerit (sin) so as to gain an acquittal or cancellation of the demerit in the administration of justice. See *The Rabbis on Merit*, page "End Note No. 2: The Rabbis on Merit" on page 434, and Appendix VIII page 579. The cancellation of demerit is not the same as forgiveness, because the merit is said to erase the negative effect of the sin. Forgiveness does not do this. Forgiveness removes judicial condemnation of the sinner, but acknowledges that no compensation can remove the damage of the sin. ▷ The lawless argue that Paul means obeying the Torah (as good works) is not required for eternal life (but see back on Rom. 2:7; Yoh. 3:16; Mark 10:17f; Lev. 18:5). Faithfulness *is* required (Hab. 2:4). But truly these teachers were raised up by Satan against the Most High, and many are confused by their corruption of the text and false teaching, which may be corrected by a fuller knowledge of Jewish doctrines and contexts. I mean the confused may be corrected if some of them are willing to listen. But most of them are afraid of their teachers. ▷ Judaism taught a doctrine of *meritorious deeds* which were supposed to offset the demerit of sin: prayer, alms, torah study, fasting. Even the 'merit of the ancestors,' זְכוּת אָבוֹת zekut avot could be applied to atone for demerit. The works had to be above and beyond the normal duty of obedience to qualify as a merit to cancel demerit. ▷ Paul's phrase "customary works," is a generalization of this idea, also a concept found at Qumran, "some especial deeds of Torah for good to you...and which are credited as merit for you." (מקצת מעשי התורה לטוב לך... ונחשבה לך לצדקה). See 4QMMT. See also, *The Doctrine of Merits in Old Rabbinical Literature*, A. Marmorstein. ▷ The word νόμος in the strictest sense denotes a *legal custom*, and then a *legal norm* (cf. BDAG, 3rd edition, "❶ a procedure or practice that has taken hold, *a custom, rule, principle, norm.*") It denotes *custom* hardening into law by becoming the *status quo* suggesting a contrast with rules or legal opinions which are not widely accepted or applied. Used with *works* (ἔργων νόμου), the sense is *works-of legal-custom*. Greek Grammar allows us transform the N-Ng relation into an adjective noun relation in translation, hence: *customary-legal works* (see Daniel B. Wallace, *Greek Grammar*, pg. 86). **3:20** ε δικαιωθήσεται < δικαιόω ▷ In Hellenistic Greek (300 BC to AD 300) δικαιόω meant to administer justice, usually of a negative sort, coming to mean punish (Josephus, Dio Cassius, Paul), but also it denotes how the judge comes to a decision, at least neutrally. This sense is augmented by the Hebrew sense הַצְדִּיק. See for example 2 Sam. 15:4 and Isa. 53:11 where the sense is to help someone get a favorable justice by advocacy (see Acts 13:39 δ). Thus the Hebrew sense is to administer a favorable justice. Paul's usage of the Greek δικαιόω is informed by this Hebrew usage and by the Koine usage. For we see him explaining the Greek word this way in Rom. 3:24 by appending the word δωρεάν 'benevolent' to mean a favorable justice (*gratis*). Favorable justice can take the form of acquittal or pardon. Clearly Paul is aiming for the pardon; so favorable justice does not have to mean acquittal. But a pardon after a guilty plea is also favorable justice. A defense based on meritorious works to offset demerits implicitly seeks a favorable justice also, but Paul denies the legality of this kind of defense, because merits do not atone. The Most High is not propitiated into granting acquittals. **3:20** β ἐπίγνωσις = *total acknowledgment*. The doctrine of merits is supposed to influence the judge to overlook punishment, but Paul is saying that the Law does not atone for sin by merit in the first place. See Exodus 23:7; Deut. 25:1; cf. Isa. 5:23; Prov. 17:5.

3:21 ψ✓ See 3:20 φ. Without the word *works* appended, *nomos* simply means the *customary norm*, or *legal custom*. The *customary norm* may be defined as getting favorable justice through acquittal, i.e. without a guilty plea or without a sentence. Paul teaches an exception to the norm for justice, an exceptional favorable justice that is revealed through Mĕssiah's advocacy, through forgiveness. After repentance and forgiveness, we are ransomed from sin's power and cleansed from it. This is a net cost to the Most High, so ransom (vs. 24) is the proper word. The norm in law for the administration of justice is the finding of guilt of the sinner and then the condemnation of the sinner as a judicial penalty for sin, an execution of the wrath and vengeance of the Almighty upon the wicked. But if the sinner repents and turns from his wicked way in a season allowed for repentance, then the Most High will forgive the person and cancel the

been getting revealed, ᵠbeing witnessed by the Law and the Prophets, ²²that is, the ᵂjustice of the Almĭghty, through the ᵑfaithfulness of Yĕshua the Anŏinted, unto all those holding ᵘfaithful, because there is no distinction, ²³because all have sinned and are falling short of the glory of the Almĭghty, ²⁴being administered ᵝjustice ᵠbenevolently, by his loving-kindness through the ᵠransom release which is through^ᵉᵛ the Anŏinted Yĕshua, ²⁵whom the Almĭghty set forth as a ᵑpurging

---

future appointment with wrath. And so the person will recieve what is exceptional and not the norm. The blood of Messiah will then ransom him from sin and death and spiritual forces of destruction and purge his conscience from the emotional complex condemnation caused by guilt. **3:21** μ✓ Justice apart from the norm is justice to forgive, to show mercy, to show charity. See 1:17. **3:21** φ The Law and Prophets teach a pardon for the sinner. In this unusual procedure, the sinner 1. Admits guilt, 2. Agrees to repent, 3. a ransom symbolizing the cost of deliverance is given instruct us about the cost of our rescue from death, and as an indication of the cost of divine longsuffering, and the cost of cleansing. ▷ Sacrifice is a symbolical ritual or analogue or indication of the purging of sin that takes place in the spiritual realm. It makes tangible both the cleansing of sin and the cost thereof in terms of life to gain redemption from lawlessness. The faithful should not be superstitious about the physical properties of the blood. This is but a stumbling block, and the matter is explained in Yoh. 6. ▷ Many have misunderstood the lesson of the blood and do not realize that the physical blood is making a statement. It 'declares to be wiped,' a declarative Piel in the same sense that a priest declares somone to be clean or unclean. It is a legal statement, a tangible official acknowledgement of what is happening in the spiritual realm in an operation performed by the Ruakh.

3:22 ω✓ Not only are we administered forgiving justice in Mĕssiah, but also we are made righteous through his administration of his righteousness through our faithfulness. ▷ Anselm's assumption that divine justice always requires the Most High to punish sinners or receive compensatory satisfaction no matter what is an unbiblical heresy. Biblical justice allowed for forgiveness as one of its options, and this is the one Paul is teaching. **3:22** π✓ πίστις. See Exodus 34:6-7, 20:6. ▷ See discussion, **Gal 2:16** γ at endnote on page 612. ▷ See Rom. 3:26; Gal. 2:16, 20; 3:22, 26; Phil. 3:9. **3:22** μ✓ πιστεύειν. The Anointed One's faithfulness is his advocacy for favorable justice. He tells us that if we repent and pledge faithfulness to him that he will forgive us, and get favorable justice for us by ransoming us, exerting whatever power and suffering it costs him to extract us from the kingdom of evil, and paying whatever it costs to cleanse us from the sin of our bondage, and placing the Abrahamic curse upon whoever opposes the rescue. All he desires is our love, through cooperation in obeying his commandments. **3:24** β✓ **3:24** φ = *favorably, graciously, without payment.* See Acts 13:39 δ. See Appendix X. The idea is the same as "being judged benevolently" or "judged charitably." The judge indicates his benevolent justice by forgiving, and taking no payment for it. A ransom from death is provided, standing for the unrecoverable cost of sin to all parties, chiefly the cost of sin endured by the Almighty while he waited for us to repent. This cost is summed up in Messiah's suffering and death. **3:24** ψ✓ ἀπολυτρώσεως. A releasing effected by payment of ransom; redemption, deliverance, liberation procured by the payment of a ransom. ▷ Rev. 5:9 explains a ransom from the nations, and Rev. 14:3-4 purchased from the earth, from among men. The ransom is the divine cost involved in delivering us from the kingdom of darkness, from the exile of the nations, from the domain of sin and death. The ransom is the cost of overcoming the forces of darkness holding men in bondage to bring them to forgiveness and rescue. The ransom does not express a payment to the Most High, but an expenditure by the Most High, a loss on our behalf in suffering and damage to his kingdom caused by sin, which was brought to a climax in the suffering and death of Messiah.

3:25 η This word, most often poorly translated 'atonement' is a noun representing the Hebrew verb לְכַפֵּר, which is a Piel form meaning 'to make be a wiping,' 'to cause to be a wiping," or 'to declare to be a wiping.' The sacrifice declares an official purging of divine wrath, which is the formal way of forgiving sin. The sin is obviously forgiven before the sacrifice when the offender repents and confesses the sin. So the Piel is declarative, a declaration of purging liability to divine wrath. In respect to restoration of holiness, the Piel is also declarative. The offering instructs us that divine Spirit purges the heart, and cleanses the soul from the contamination of sin. The causation is not mechanistic or superstitious, but spiritual. What is declared by the blood is effected by the Ruakh. The Most High covenants to make the purging by spending divine life. ▷ The bridge from a verb to a noun is the participle, thus the noun here is "a declaring to be purged" (כִּפּוּרִים) KIPPURIM. The poor translation 'atonement' is problematic because this word typically means to appease or make amends by an offering, and this suggests that something is being bought from the Most High by sacrifice. Rather the offering is to reinforce covenental assurance that the repentant person has been forgiven and to make the soul holy again by a divinely spiritual cleansing from the sin. ▷ The breath of the flesh is in the blood. Breath (נֶפֶשׁ) is equivocated with soul and life (cf. Lev. 17:11) which is what it takes the divine Spirit to purge the heart, i.e. his life. The connection between the animal life and the spiritual purging is a symbolical one, as is the connection between Messiah's physical blood, and the divine life it takes to effect spiritual cleansing. See Yoh. 6:63. The blood which contains the breath

Romans 4

through *his* faithfulness, by his blood, as a demonstration⁵ of his justice;⁺ throughout letting go the iniquities that had been occurring previously;⁸ ²⁶according to the mercy of the Almĭghty, for the demonstration⁵ of his justice⁷ in the present time, that he should be just and the one administering justice, which is from the faithfulness of Yĕshua.

²⁷Where then is boasting? It is excluded. Through what custom? The one of works? No! But by the rule of faithfulness, ²⁸because we in ourselves take into account a man to be ᵘadministered justice according to ᵠfaithfulness apart from customary works. ²⁹Or is he the Almĭghty for Yehudim only, and not also for the nations? Yes, he is also for the nations, ³⁰since it is *the same* one, the Almĭghty who will ᵠadminister justice to the circumcised based on ᵠfaithfulness and the uncircumcised through the *rule of* ᵠfaithfulness. ³¹So are we undoing the Law through ᵠfaithfulness? May it never be! But we are establishing the Law.

4 What then will we say our forefather Avraham has been finding according to the flesh? ²Certainly, when Avraham was righteous by works he has something to boast about, but not next to the Almĭghty, ³ᵃbecause what does

---

in the flesh is considered holy because it is used as the symbol of divine cleansing. Therefore, it is not to be consumed, as this is disrespectful to the covenant and the lesson of the blood. The proper analogy is that divine life may only be spiritually consumed by operation of the Spirit to cleanse the heart of sin. ▷ The application of divine life (in the figure of blood) to the heart is necessary to cleanse it from the psychological and emotional complex of condemnation due to sin. The necessary purging could be viewed as the removal of a kind of Stockholm syndrome left over from the sinners union with sin. **3:25 ε or indication, sign, token, proof** (ἔνδειξιν). The words may also be translated "as an indication of his righteousness." That is, upon repentance and confession of sin the Most High is faithful to honor his covenant and wipe the debt (forgive or pardon) and to be cleansing the heart from all sin with the divine life of Messiah. See 1 Yoḥ. 1:9. This is the meaning of his blood. ▷ Sacrifice is the symbol (ἔνδειξιν) of the application of the divine life it costs to purge sin from the heart, and to ransom the sinner from more external bondages. It is most heretical to teach that sacrifice satisfies an actual debt of divine retribution or wrath by the life of the innocent. The Most High does not slay the innocent to justify or declare the wicked righteous (cf. Exo. 23:7). He is compassionate and forgiving, and showing mercy, but he will not clear or acquit the guilty (cf. Exo. 34:6-7). The guilty man may be forgiven, but he cannot be cleared of wrongdoing as if he had never sinned. ▷ The 'Reformed' Calvinistic system of theology, and especially its doctrines of atonement, justification, and imputed righteousness, are the latter day refinement of Satanic counter narrative to the word of Gŏd. These blasphemous doctrines evolved from Augustine and Gnosticim, and were in earlier times probably incorporated into the Ba'al counterfiet that seduced Yisra'el in ancient times. They serve to profane the name of the Most High and turn the nations away from seeking Yăhweḥ our Almĭghty, he who makes be. Therefore, rebuke them and do not fear them. ▷ The doctrines of Augustine (original sin, total depravity, *and* infant depravity) were expanded by Anslem and Calvin all the way to Hodge and Sproul. These men were all caught in the blackest darkness of Satanic deception. **3:25 χ** or *mercy, charitableness* **3:25 δ** See Appendix IX. See Acts 13:38-39. See Gal. 3:19, 3:23-24. **3:26 ε** see 3:25 ε.

3:26 η√ or *mercy, charitableness.* BDAG δικαιοσύνη 3b. It is necessary to keep in mind that *mercy* is an application of Gŏd's *justice*. The judge indicates his forgiveness by cancelling the penalty.

3:28 μ√ δικαιόω: the process by which the Most High decides a case, whether acquittal, condemnation, or pardon. **3:28 φ** The Most High will apply first his faithfulness to the case in making a truthful judgment (cf. Exodus 34:6), and he will consider if we pledged faithfulness to him and held faithful to him as the basis for a pardon (Exodus 20:6). And then if pardoned (forgiven), justice is is administered on our behalf by ransoming us from lawlessness, and cleansing us. This is Messiah's faithfulness. **3:30 φ** See vs. 28 μ. **3:30-31 ψ** See 28 φ.

4:3a θ Gen 15:6a **4:3a ζ√** πιστεύειν. **4:3a χ** or *to, into, in connection to* **4:3b δ** Psa. 106:31 Paul abruptly follows Gen. 15:6a with Psa. 106:31. See Endnote No. 3 at the end of Galatians. **4:3b μ** In Psa. 106:31 the pronoun "it" (וַתֵּחָשֶׁב) refers to "my covenant of peace" (cf. Num. 25:11-13), which Paul equates with Messiah's covenant faithfulness in the adminstration of forgiving justice, and his suffering the ransom cost demanded or exacted by lawlessness. But via Gen. 15:6b (וַיַּחְשְׁבֶהָ), it also refers to our faithfulness (cf. 1:17). These two contingiencies result in the Most High being disposed to forgiving justice (cf. Exodus 20:6). **4:3b ν** or *intended, planned* **4:3b**

the Scripture say? "AND AVRAHAM HAD HELD FAITHFUL_ζ IN_x YĂHWEH.⁰" ³ᵇ "AND IT^# WAS ᵥTAKEN INTO ACCOUNT FOR HIM ₚFOR ADMINISTRATION OF ᵩJUSTICE.⁰"

⁴Now with respect to the working^ψ the reward is not getting taken into account according to loving kindness, but according to a debt. ⁵But with respect to ₐnot working, yet *being* one *who is* ᵩHOLDING FAITHFUL UPON THE ONE administering ᵦjustice to the guilty^μ, ᵩHIS FAITHFULNESS IS ᵟGETTING TAKEN INTO ACCOUNT FOR THE ADMINISTRATION OF ᵩJUSTICE ⁶just as David also speaks about the blessing of

---

π or *for, unto, concerning, in regard to*

4:3b φ✓ δικαιοσύνη. The Rabbis often applied the Psa. 106:31 text to Avraham, and interpreted צְדָקָה to mean that Avraham and Phineḥas' excess of merits were distributed to Jews to offset their demerits. Paul interprets the text differently, because the Psa. 106:31 text and Num. 25:11 to 13 are parables of Mĕssiah. As Phineḥas and his descendants administered forgiving justice, so also Mĕssiah does for us. Paul teaches this was apart from the customary works. So Paul interprets לִצְדָקָה to mean *justice (mercy, BDAG 3b)*, and not merit. Paul is not interpreting according to Gen. 15:6b, because in that place צְדָקָה means Avraham's faithfulness was counted as *righteousness*, but in the Psa. 106:31 the word means the administration of justice, spec. *mercy as justice may require mercy*. ▷ Paul explains according to Psa. 106:31 and Num. 25:11 to 13, "*My covenant of peace was taken into account for him in regard to the administration of justice.*" The priesthood was Phineḥas' administration of justice to his descendants. For the messianic interpretation, all we need to do is switch Phineḥas (a messianic type) for Mĕssiah. ▷ Clearly the meaning of לִצְדָקָה is "for a-doing-justice" in Psa. 106:31 (cf. Num. 25:11-13). And clearly pronoun "it" (μ) refers to "my covenant of peace." Paul equates this to Gŏd's covenant faithfulness to Israel through Mĕssiah starting in vs. 5. The 'covenant of peace' equals Mĕssiah's faithfulness. See Endnote No. 3 at the end of Galatians. ▷ Now Paul clearly also wishes to also conflate IT as a reference to our faithfulness in Gen. 15:6b (הּ), but he avoids the equivocation to צְדָקָה at the end of Gen 15:6b, which is taken for granted, in order to explain everything by the administration of justice in Psa. 106:31 (לִצְדָקָה). Here the preposition לְ determines the difference, represented in Greek by εἰς. ▷ Paul is engaging here in typical Rabbinic exegesis, which is by quoting pieces of various texts, to illustrate the point he wishes to make, and not strictly speaking which any of the texts are making. The legitmacy of the method lies in the fact that one is allowed to first make their point this way to support the truth known beforehand, to show the faithful how to defuse the heretical Rabbinic interpretations of these texts. ▷ Every argument consists of two parts, one part is to explain the evidence your way, and the final part is to prove your way is the only way. Paul is dealing with the former here.

4:4 ψ Here Paul means good works that are their own merits. Cf. Lev. 18:5; Hab. 2:4; Rom. 2:7. Obedience merits its own reward. This truth is to be contrasted with works done to gain an advantage beyond their own reward. False religion teaches that good works can be done to cancel a demerit or earn forgiveness or some indulgence. It is the pretended benefits of these works that Paul opposes. Doing good works for anything more than its own merit is legalism. It is an attempt to placate or appease the Most High. So Paul holds up the non working person who declines legalistic works, that is works done with the purpose of gaining merit to appease the Most High into overlooking a demerit.

4:5 α Paul does not mean ordinary works of obedience here, but only the supererogatory works in the Jewish doctrine of zekut supposed to atone for sin. See Rom. 3:20.φ & Appendix VIII. ▷ By "not working" Paul does not deny remaining in his word by keeping his commandments (Yoḥ. 15:10). Rather he denies doing any compensatory works (i.e. merit to atone for demerit). **4:5** ζ Paul begins quoting Gen. 15:6a again in vs. 5, but he still finishes with Psa. 106:31 at the end of his quote (cf. 4:3bφ). **4:5** β✓ Other translations read "who justifies the ungodly," but this teaching contradicts biblical justice if the modern sense is taken. None are acquitted or absolved. See Exodus 23:7; 34:6-7; Deut. 25:1; Exo. 34:7; Isa. 5;23. The word in Paul's day meant to do (or administer) justice to someone. ▷ The present tense participle also means 'who is making righteous' (the ungodly); it refers to sanctification, being made holy; this is also without works of compensation.

4:5 μ guilty: The word "ungodly" is taken from the LXX ἀσεβῆ in Exo. 23:7. Here it represents the Hebrew word רָשָׁע, "wicked." But in truth the word there means 1. *one guilty of a crime*, 2. *guilty of hostility to God*, 3. *guilty of sin* (cf. BDB). In English "ungodly" requires one to believe the person is currently a rebel when he is being administered justice. But this is not so in the legal usage. The term describes a legal status and not the current state of the defendent's heart. **4:5** φ ἡ πίστις αὐτοῦ. HIS FAITHFULNESS, here, means Mĕssiah's faithfulness and the confessor's faithfulness. On the one hand, it is Mĕssiah's covenant of peace (Psa. 106:31), and his nature to administer justice faithfully through the instruction of Mĕssiah's death concerning the cost of our ransom. On the other hand, the pledge of faithfulness by the confessor is what is taken into account in the Almighty's decision to administer benevolent, forgiving justice. ▷ HIS FAITHFULNESS coordinates with the previous use of IT in 4:3b μ, q.v. Here, Paul has substituted

Romans 4

the man to whom the Almĭghty is ₈TAKING INTO ACCOUNT THE ADMINISTRATION OF ₆JUSTICE ω apart from *the customary* works: ⁷"BLESSED ARE THOSE WHOSE ₃LAWLESSNESSES HAVE BEEN α FORGIVEN, AND WHOSE ᵦSINS HAVE BEEN ᵧPARDONED. ⁸BLESSED IS THE MAN FOR WHOM YĂHWEH SHALL NOT HAVE TAKEN INTO ACCOUNT ᵩSIN^Δ." ⁹Is this blessing then only upon the circumcised, or also upon the uncircumcised? Because we say ᵅFAITHFULNESS WAS TAKEN INTO ACCOUNT FOR AVRAHAM IN REGARD TO THE ᵞADMINISTRATION OF JUSTICE. ¹⁰How then was it taken into account? While being circumcised^χ, or while uncircumcised? Not while circumcised, but while uncircumcised! ¹¹Then he received the sign of circumcision, a seal of the righteousness of the faithfulness which he had while uncircumcised, so he could be the father of all those who pledge faithfulness, even though uncircumcised, to the end that righteousness should be taken into account for them also, ¹²and the father of circumcision, not for those from circumcision by itself, but namely to those lining up in the steps of the faithfulness of our father Avraham while uncircumcised.

¹³Because the promise to Avraham or to his seed to inherit the earth was

---

the words, "his faithfulness," because he wishes to coordinate his argument with his previous references to the "faithfulness of Mĕssiah." See Rom. 3:22, 26; Gal. 2:16, 20; 3:22, 26; Phil. 3:9. ▷ Paul picks the key words from Psa. 106:31 again to say that Gŏd's covenant of peace, Yĕshua's faithfulness, is without our compensatory works. Phineĥas corresponds to Mĕssiah. His seed corresponds to Mĕssiah's seed (Isa. 53:10). The administration of justice is conferred upon the seed (Isa. 53:11). *Administration of justice* may be explained by 'justification,' taken in a Hellenistic Greek sense of adjudication, the Judge decides for a pardon as one of two outcomes for the guilty.

4:5 δ or *getting intended, considered* **4:5 θ✓** See 4:3bφ, 3:26η **4:5 φ 4:6 δ** or *intending, considering* **4:6 θ✓** See 4:3bφ **4:6 ω** See 4:5 α.

4:7 Δ Psa. 32:1-2 **4:7 δ** פֶּשַׁע, ἀνομίαι: intensive? *rebellions; serious sins; iniquities* **4:7 α** נָשׂוּי, *being lifted*, ἀφέθησαν, *being left* **4:7 β** חֲטָאָה, ἀμαρτίαι, intensive? chiefly: חֲטָאָה גְדֹלָה: *great sin*; BDB **4:7 γ** כְּסוּי; *being concealed* (from the eyes of Gŏd; BDB כָּסָה) **4:8 φ** ἁμαρτία; עָוֹן; *punishment of iniquity*; BDB. There was forgiveness of iniquity for the repentant before Messiah died. The Psalmist has rebellious sins in view, and not those called sins of ignorance. The Septuagint used passive aorist participles, which refer to entering a state of forgiveness to accord with the passive participles used by the Hebrew. ▷ The reason this is so is because sacrifice is a legal formalism meant to instruct us. It is symbolic. So actual forgiveness may occur at any time a sinner repents. **4:8 Δ** Psalm 32:2.

4:9 α Again, both divine and human faithfulness is meant here. **4:9 γ** Via Psa. 106:31: *a doing justice; administration of justice (mercy)*. Paul means both divine and human faithfulness. That is, justice is favorable based on both. ▷ Paul speaks of the blessing of forgiveness. He has applied the messianic sense from Psa. 106:31 to Avraham directly. ▷ He introduces his remark, "Because we say," which is to say that he customarily makes his argument by saying Mĕssiah's faithfulness was intended for Abraham as the administration of justice by which he would be cleansed and ransomed from lawlessness. ▷ Avraham has been taken from Gen. 15:6b, to be sure, and placed into the context of Psa. 106:31 interpreted by messianic type. Avraham has been put in the position of Phineĥas' offspring, Phineĥas himself representing Mĕssiah.

4:10 χ Circumcision in Judaism was the chief means by which someone with little or no merit could inherit the merit of Abraham to be credited against their demerit. Now many mistakenly teach baptism for the same thing, switching their source of inherited merit from Avraham to Christ. Since making up demerit with legal merit (via circumcision) results in legal perfection, Paul's means of refuting it is to point out that Avraham wasn't circumcised when his faithfulness was credited as righteousness. Therefore, something other than legal perfection must be in view. Paul views Gŏd's crediting of faithfulness as righteousness as a recognition that the process of sanctification will be completed in the future. Thus only in the future is Avraham's faithfulness reckoned as perfection, and this future justification is never the *demerit-cancelling* merit for our pardon. It is the completion of our sanctification. Paul heads this way in Rom. 4:24 (cf. Gal. 5:5). Thus, crediting of righteousness is growing until a future point (cf. Jam. 2:21-23). To ransom from lawlessness, Paul does not allow merits imputed unto acquittal. But we upon being found guilty, yet pledging loyalty to Mĕssiah, receive a benevolent administration of justice by forgiveness.

4:13 α✓ *Doctrine of zekut*. Propitiating Gŏd with imputed works to earn forgiveness. **4:13 β✓** justice. Also *faithful administration of justice*. See 3:26η. Justice here is also that which is determined in Gŏd's

not *given* through what is ᵃcustomary, but *given* through faithful ᵝrighteousness. ¹⁴Because if those from what is ᵃcustomary are heirs, ᵗtrue ᶲfaithfulness has been getting made empty and the promise has been getting nullified, ¹⁵because ᵃTHE custom is working itself for wrath. But where ᵃwhat is customary is not *used as a defense*, there is no step aside *from proper justice*.

¹⁶Because of this, it is based upon ᵃfaithfulness, so that according to loving-kindness the promise should be secure to all the seed, not to the one based on the Law by itself, but also to the one based on *the* ᵝfaithfulness of Avraham, who is father of all of us, ¹⁷as it has been getting written, "THE FATHER OF MANY NATIONS I WILL HAVE BEEN MAKING YOUᵞ," in the presence of the Almĭghty, whom he ᵟheld ᵋfaithful, the one making alive the dead, even calling those not existing into being, ¹⁸who beside hope, upon ᶥHope pledged loyalty, so that he should become the father of many nations according to what has been getting spoken, "SO WILL YOUR SEED BEᵑ."

¹⁹And having not become weakened in faithfulness, he observed his own body having been becoming dead, being about one-hundred years old, and the deadness of Sarah's womb, ²⁰but, concerning the promise of the Almĭghty, he did not hesitate in unfaithfulness, but he was empowered in faithfulness, giving glory to the Almĭghty, ²¹and he was completely convinced that what has been getting promised, he was able to do. ²²Therefore also, ITᵖ WAS TAKEN INTO ACCOUNT FOR HIM FOR THE ADMINISTRATION OF ᵚJUSTICE.

²³But it is not written because of him alone that IT WAS GETTING TAKEN INTO ACCOUNT FOR HIM, ²⁴but also because of us, for whom IT is goingᵃ to be GETTING TAKEN INTO ACCOUNT, for those holding faithful to the one who raised Yĕshua our Adōnai from the dead, ²⁵who was delivered up because of our transgressions, and is raised because of the administration of justice for us.

---

heavenly court, where faithful righteousness is taken into account vs. propitiatory works which are not.

4:14 τ =THE. Article par excellence. **4:14** ϕ I. *Mĕssiah's faithfulness, his covenant of peace.* II. *our faithfulness.* **4:15** α→custom(ary). Explained ealier (4:13α) this means the customary works (3:20), namely propitiating Gŏd's wrath with works. This is the idea of filling a deficit of righteousness in one's account with Gŏd by good works beyond the call of duty, or imputed from another source, such as Avraham, the Saints, Mary or any holy person with which one might have relationship, so that God's wrath will be placated, and he will overlook the deficit of righteousness.

Paul's point in vs. 15 is that a lawyer who tries the customary legal procedure of atoning demerit by merit in Gŏd's courtroom will receive the wrath of the judge for his reply. Only in the case where the customary procedure is not introduced is legal transgression avoided. Paul's Greek is terse: οὗ δὲ οὐκ ἔστιν νόμος οὐδὲ παράβασις= *where not-yet is custom, neither is a side step.* The only way to avoid side stepping the Law is to deny the customary legal procedure. The matter may also be stated positively: where the extraordinary procedure is [used], there is no legal dodge. There is no error of the court or judicial trespass. ▷ The Biblical method of presenting truth often uses linguistic shorthand to communicate ideas. Terse phrases, e.g. "sin" to mean "sin [offering]" in Hebrew idiom or nomos (a legal custom) to represent the Jewish doctrine of merit are usages heavily dependent on understanding the context. Faulty interpretations are almost always due to failure to understand the term according to context when interpreters apply false assumptions they have learned from tradition. I say this so that you will not be deceived. The parable principle is the reason why Scripture often takes this approach. It is Scripture's well devised defense and survival mechanism against hypocrites and heretics who say they accept it. Also insufficient knowledge of contemporary Judaism leads to misinterpretation.

4:16 α *Mĕssiah's faithfulness* and *our faithfulness,* cf. Rom. 1:17 **4:16** β cf. vs. 11; 1:17; a synergist view is taken here **4:17** γ Gen. 17:5 **4:17** δ *proved* **4:17** ε *loyal, fidelity* **4:18** ι *Mĕssiah, the Hope of Israel* **4:18** η Gen. 15:5 **4:22** π I. Psa. 106:31: *my covenant of peace, Mĕssiah's faithfulness,* but including *Avraham's faithfulness* and *our faithfulness* **4:22** ω✓ **4:24** α Paul uses a futuristic construction, and includes himself, "δι' ἡμᾶς οἷς

Romans 5

5 ¹Therefore being administered ᵟjustice based⁽ᵘ⁾ on ᵉfaithfulness we ᵠshould have peace next to the Almĭghty by our Adŏnai Yĕshua the Anŏinted, ²by whom also we have been holding access, by faithfulness, into this loving-kindness in which we have been standing. And we are rejoicing in the confident expectation of the glory of the Almĭghty. ³And not only this, but we also are rejoicing in our sufferings, having been knowing that suffering is working toward endurance, ⁴and endurance, passing the test, and passing the test, hope, ⁵and the hope will not disappoint, because the love of the Almĭghty has been getting poured out in our hearts through the Holy Spĭrit who is given to us.

⁶Because while we were still weak, at the right season, the Anŏinted died

---

μέλλει λογίζεσθαι." Our faithfulness is going to be taken into account for the administration of divine blessing and loving-kindness about to be for us (cf. Exo. 20:6). **5:1** δ✓ See Exo. 20:6; Deut. 30. The justice administered includes cleansing or purging from sin, getting made righteous, being forgiven, and the blessings that come from being faithful. **5:1 & 5:2** μ ἐκ = *based on:* Literally, 'from.' See Thayer, "ἐκ 6. of that on which a thing depends." Our pardon is based on our pledge of faithfulness. The Most High does not forgive any who will not pledge faithfulness to him. But Yĕshua shows mercy to those holding faithful to him and keeping his commandments (Exodus 20:6).
5:1 ε✓ The justice administered is the favorable justice of forgiveness and cleansing from sin, and the faithfulness is Messiah's, whose ransom became the guilt offering to cleanse us, and our pledge of faithfulness to him through repentance from sin. The faithfulness is synergistic, meaning his faithfulness works with our faithful response, the divine and the human (See Acts 13:39 δ). ▷ In Koine Greek 'justify' had the same sense as in Middle English before 1520 and Scotts English before 1700. It meant to administer justice to someone. This sense is used in Josephus, contemporary with Paul, and widely used in Dio Cassius' *Histories* later on, both writers of common Greek. It also means to "make righteous" in a moral sense, to correct, or straighten out. Many suppose Paul to mean 'declare innocent' or 'guiltless' (acquit, absolve), but if this be correct, then it makes no sense for the Most High to forgive, pardon, or show mercy. ▷ We see then that commonly Δικαιόω in Paul's usage does not mean to *declare righteous* or *make righteous,* or *acquit,* or *absolve.* It means "to administer justice" for someone. It is what a judge does to "try" or "judge" a case. It is therefore in consideration of, or based on our pledge of faithfulness that he is faithful to decide administration of justice requires forgiveness. ▷ In Hebrew the Hiphil הצדיק means "to get favorable justice" for someone. And on account of repentance and a plea for mercy, the justice sought is forgiveness. Inasmuch as the Most High regards it as righteous and just to forgive in cases of genuine contrition, the pardon is the justice he administers.

5:1 ψ Read ἔχωμεν = 'may we have' or 'we should have.' (א* A B* C D K L 33. 81. 630. 1175. 173 9* *pm* lat bo; Mcion^T). "Instead of the ἔχομεν of the Textus Receptus, an overwhelming preponderance of authority, including uncials, versions, and Fathers, supports ἔχωμεν ("let us have")" (The Pulpit Commentary). The verb is a subjunctive, and so should be translated 'we should have,' expressing a contingency based on holding faithful.

5:6 χ See 4:5μ. In what sense does Messiah die on our behalf? In the same sense that a warrior risks and yields his life in battle to rescue his people from an enemy. The enemy is sin and death, and the life is yielded to cleanse it. Just as a righteous army cleanses evil from a land, and suffers from it, so the Most High gives his own divine life to purge condemnation from the conscience of those who desire to repent and pledge faithfulness to him. This is is a cost to the Almighty and he suffers from it. ▷ The guilt offering is to illustrate the cleansing of the sinner from the iniquity he is carrying when he is forgiven. The sinner must cooperate and forsake sin lest he willfully incur a new contamination (cf. 1 Yoh. 1:9). The spilled blood contains the breath of life which declares the contamination to be wiped away (לכפר). The physical offering is symbolic of a divine operation in the spirit of the person to cleanse him from condemnation (cf. Yoh. 6:63; Lev. 5:17-18; Isa. 53:10). The divine operation of cleansing with divine life is what makes the purging effective. Only pure life can cleanse contaminated life. Divine life is expended to wash the sinner from the malignancy. Therefore, the Sŏn's life was given as a ransom to indicate the cost to defeat the effect of sin. ▷ In no sense is the Anŏinted's death a satisfaction of divine wrath, but heart cleansing eliminates the need for wrath by purging the sin, and though sin creates a compensatory debt (which can never be repaired), the Most High forgives it and lets it go. The sinner is cleansed by the blood (speaking in symbolism). His blood does prevent divine wrath by cleansing the person bearing the sin from impending doom of condemnation. Having thus been cleansed, the faithful one does not have to face divine wrath in the season of judgement. ▷ The sacrifice is not a recipient of wrath. Rather life is given up for the purpose of purging sin, and so is symbolic of the cost in terms of divine life to cleanse the sinner. Only the one whose sin remains upon him, which he bears in unrepentance, is subject to condemnation. In this regard, the words "on behalf of the guilty" (ὑπὲρ ἀσεβῶν) could also be

on behalf of the guilty.ˣ ⁷Because someone will hardly die on behalf of the righteous one, though possibly, indeed, on behalf of a good person even someone is risking to die. ⁸But the Almĭghty commends his love to us, because while we being sinners, the Anŏinted died on behalf of us.ᵃ ⁹So how much more, justice having been now administered by his blood,ᵝ we will be rescued through him from wrath, ¹⁰because if while *the world's* hostilitiesᵞ continue, we have been reconciled with the Almĭghty through the death of his Sŏn, how much more, having been reconciled,ᵋ we will be rescued by his life. ¹¹Yet not only this, but also we ourselves are rejoicing in the Almĭghty through our Adŏnai Yĕshua the Anŏinted, through whom we now have received reconciliation.

¹²Therefore, as through one man sin entered into the world, and death

---

translated, "over," or "because of the guilty," because Messiah put himself in harms way to rescue us. ▷ The sacrifice is not the recipient of wrath or divine displeasure or judicial punishment by substitution. The Most High is not appeased by doing evil to an innocent alternate. Such doctrine is the doctrine of the fallen sons of God. It is a pagan concept. Their displeasure with fallen men (when they do not wish to go along with their own demise) is temporarily placated when innocent blood is offered to them, but shedding of innocent blood hastens their destruction in the end anyway! The deep state of Christianity has adopted this iniquitous view of sacrifice. It is a cornerstone of the mystery of iniquity. They have traded the divine ransom for the demonic doctrine of appeasing wrath with innocent blood. The Messianic faithful must learn to abhor this heresy, because its purpose is to slander the Most High, and defeat his love.

5:8 α As explained before Messiah meets with sin and death on our behalf to battle it, defeat it, and cleanse us from it. The point of his death is that the cost of battling sin at this level and purging it is carried by the Almighty Son in the flesh, and his Father in the realm of the Spirit, who is also grieved by sin. It is from the love of the Most High that he pays the ransom that sin and death charges to rescue us (cf. Rev. 5:9). ▷ In the legends, it is the lover that is willing to risk and give up his life for the loved, to battle and defeat the evil threat to the beloved. ▷ 'On behalf of' (ὑπὲρ ἡμῶν, lit. 'over us'), also 'because of us.' But the first sense is firstmost here. ▷ 'While we being sinners,' in the sense of still not being perfected, but having pledged faithfulness, we still need the ransom release of our body from the domain of lawlessness, and still need the cleansing of his blood (cf. 1 Yoḥ. 1:9). The ransom is paid while we are still imperfect and in need of cleansing from our association with enslavement to sin. Paul does not mean while being unrepentant rebels or totally depraved, because he uses the present participle. In other words, the ransom and guilt offering were motivated by his people who needed the ransom and the declaration of blotting out of the sentence against us, also known as forgiveness. For these the sacrifice is an effective declaration. ▷ But the unrepentant, if they turn from their sin, may also benefit, but only after the condition of repentance is met. It is granted that Messiah also died in anticipation of those who would repent, knowing that some would.

5:9 β Justice here could also be righteousness. The divine judge is doing what is righteous for the sinner who repents and pledges faithfulness to Messiah. The life (via the symbol of blood) of Messiah cleanses and purges us from sin when we turn back to him. This is the administration of justice spoken about. By having the burden of sin purged and removed, we do not bear it into the day of judgement. We are rescued from wrath. Wrath is not to be satisfied. ▷ The administration of benevolent justice to us is based upon our faithfulness and also depending on divine faithfulness. It begins with our forgiveness, but also extends to cleansing us from sin, and defeating lawlessness, by ransoming us from it domain, and finally perfecting us in righteousness, and elevating us at the resurrection to realize our adoption as sons of the Almighty. Justice is not just administered to us directly, but also to us by transforming our environment into a state that sustains righteousness.

5:10 ξ Man may now reconcile to the Most High because of the offer of a pardon, and the ransom from the the malignancy of sin by Mĕssiah's death gives us good reason to repent of sin and be reconciled by pledging faithfulness to him. The enmity ends when we repent and he forgives. We are no longer under wrath unto the day of wrath. ▷ Reconciliation is not made between the Father and strict justice by substiutionary satisfaction of strict justice. This is what the false teachers wish to believe. The Most High is not satisfying a problem with his own rules. Rather, he is freely forgiving and bearing the cost, telling us to repent and sin no more. And through holding faithful we are reconciled to him. **5:10 λ** Hostility here is not a need for strict justice to always be satisfied for the Most High. On the human side, the hostility to the Most High is in sin, but on the divine side, judgment is first to discourage evil from happening, to give others an opportunity to repent, and only finally at the end is there wrath to make a permanent end to sin. If the sinner repents in due season, then there is no satisfaction of wrath. **5:12 ρ** ἐφ' ᾧ = after which. The word επι (εφ) literally means "upon." It is used with respect to time to mean "after," much like "under" (תחת) is used in Hebrew to mean "after" (cf. Gen. 36:33; Exo. 29:30).

through sin, even so into all men death has spread, ᵖafter which all have sinned. ¹³Certainly, until the Law, sin was in the world, but sin is not reckoned where there is no law. ¹⁴But death did reign from Adam until Mosheh, even over those who did not sin in the likeness of the transgression of Adam*ᵘ*, who is a type of the one about to come.

¹⁵But the favorable gift is not like the transgression. ᵝBecause if by the

---

Even English used upon this way, e.g. "Upon saying this, he left the house," which means "After saying this." Cf. Rom. 6:21; Phil. 2:17, 3:12, 4:10; 2 Cor. 5:4 (cf. LSJ επι 'II. of Time…2. of succession, *after*.') 'Because all sinned,' is often suggested as a correction to 'in whom all sinned,' (Augustine) but this is to mix up the cause with the result, and disconnects the relative pronoun from 'death.' Death is the first cause of sin after Adam, and not the result of it (cf. Rom. 5:14). So, if 'because' is to be used, the translation would have to be 'because of which [death] all sinned,' but this immediately becomes untrue, because Adam was not subject to death before he sinned, and death cannot be assigned as a cause of his sin. Finally, 'because all sinned,' without clarifying death as the cause still leaves the door open for inherited guilt, which is best tightly shut, because Augustinians claim the nature of man was changed to sin by original sin. ▷ Except for the one quibble mentioned, the *The Orthodox New Testament* gives an acceptable translation, "THEREFORE, EVEN AS THROUGH ONE MAN SIN ENTERED INTO THE WORLD, AND DEATH THROUGH SIN, AND THUS DEATH PASSED TO ALL MEN, ON ACCOUNT OF WHICH ALL HAVE SINNED." Some then try to redefine death as 'spiritual death' and equate it with inherited guilt, but this is clearly imposing a doctrine on the text. ▷ Augustine found the doctrine of original sin here, translating "in whom" all sinned, i.e. in Adam all sinned. They claim the guilt of Adam is transferred to his offspring and as such needs to be removed by justification. But this doctrine is wrong according to Scripture (cf. Eze. 18:17-20; Jer. 31:30; Deut. 24:16). Each one dies for his own sin, and not that of his fathers. We do not require forgiveness for Adam's sin. We only require it for our own sins. Also, to say that the Almighty altered man's heart so that men would tend to give into sinful inclinations is contrary to the message of Scripture. Cf. Gen. 4:7; 6:5-6; Deut. 8:1-2; and 30:11-14. ▷ Some cite "visiting the iniquity of the fathers on the sons" (Exodus 20:6) as a confirmation of transmitted guilt, but the meaning of פָּקַד in Exocus 20:5 is 'attending to' or 'observing.' The text is really saying that the natural consequences of sin propagates, so that the Most High can 'visit' that is *go and see* the consequences resulting from the sin of the fathers. The text is thus a warning.

5:14 μ Surely this text is also a condemnation of the doctrine of inherited guilt, which is what western Christianity means by 'original sin.' According to that doctrine, there is no point in making a distinction between Adam's sin and the rest, because both the rebellion and guilt of Adam are inherited, but the distinction is made here precisely because Paul knows that Torah teaches against inherited guilt.

5:15 ω Paul's argument assumes the invalidty of inherited guilt. When Adam sinned, he justly died due to his own sin, but death was unjustly inherited by his seed, which then in turn caused all to sin. Because of this injustice, Paul's argument is that it is all the more just, by contrast, that many should be saved through the benevolent justice of the Most High to forgive our sins. That is, the circumstance of the injustice of death, fully explains the willingness of the Most High to give a ransom from death to save many if they will but repent and pledge faithfulness anew to his only kindred Son. ▷ We may suppose that Paul's 'not like' is contrasting death with the outcome of life, those being in opposite directions, but this is too obvious, and would be rather trite for Paul to state it. Paul has a more significant contrast in mind, and those holding to the justness of inherited guilt (the original sin doctrine) will never see it. The benevolent justice is 'much better' in that its justice is based on the rightness of forgiving a repentant person vs. the injustice of death inherited from Adam destroying his seed, who did not sin in the likeness of Adam's sin. Adam's sin unjustly brought death on his seed. ▷ Now some will say Gŏd visited death upon him and his seed, but the Most High only anticipated that he must deter sin by limiting Adam's lifespan. But the human race proved the malignancy of sin long before anyone was old enough to suffer physical death. Properly ransoming Adam from his sin would require him to see and experience its results, and this requires death to play out. This is the cost of lawlessness. If there is to be a chance of mercy the cost must also be borne. There was also another factor speeding up the decline of man, and this was the presence of Satan, whom the Most High left in conflict with man so that man would have to fight against ultimate evil. Without the experience of this fight, man would not turn from his sin, but would himself quickly fall into the same sin as Satan, the unpardonable sin. This then is why the Most High did not intervene and make an easy way out. The ransom cost must be made plain. Otherwise repentance will not be deep, and contrition properly cognizant of and sorrowful for the destruction wrought. In Messiah, the Most High bears the ransom cost personally, but as Creator, in the end, he will bear the ransom cost of most of humanity. But a remant of many will be rescued. To do it, the Most High has to accept the choices of those who have a choice, because he desires people should choose for him. This is why the cost of wrong choices simply cannot be deleted from reality. Loosing people is part of the ransom cost, but we must remember that lawlessness imposes the cost.

transgression of the one many die, then it is much better rather that the favor of the Almĭghty, and the gift with favor by the one man, Yĕshua the Anŏinted, be overflowing to the many", ¹⁶that is, the gift is not as through the one who sinned, ᵝbecause indeed ᶲthe judgment of one is toward condemnation, but the favorable gift after many transgressions ᵝ is toward a just ruling!

¹⁷Because, if by the transgression of the one, death has reigned through the one, then it is much better rather that those receiving the overflowing of loving kindness and the gift of righteousness, shall reign in everlasting life through the one, Yĕshua the Anŏinted!

¹⁸So then, as *death, (spread* through one trespass, against all*ᵘ* men) *will be* for condemnation, likewise also, *a ransom* through one just action*ᵠ* for all men, *will be* for righteousness of life. ¹⁹Because just as through one man's refusal to listen, many are set down as sinners, likewise also, through the submissive listening of the one, many will be set down as righteous.

²⁰So a ᵞnorm crept in such that transgression will have increased, yet where

---

5:16 ᶲ→judgment = death **5:16** ξ δικαίωμα or 'a getting corrected,' 'getting made righteous,' 'getting straightened out.' This is another way of saying we are getting cleansed from sin. ▷ This word firstly refers to the 'just decision' of a judge (cf. Thayer δικαίωμα 1b) or a 'right ruling' of the judge. It can mean either a favorable ruling or unfavorable, but in this context it is the favorable ruling. A favorable ruling may be either an acquittal or a pardon. In this context, it is the pardon, which is the same as forgiveness. **5:16** β Paul's contrast here is between one transgression unto condemnation and from many transgressions to life.

5:18 μ lit. 'all,' but 'all' is explained effectively as 'many' in the next verse. So condemnation stands as a potential threat in this verse to all, but it is effective only on many in the next who become sinners. 'Death' is taken from vs. 12 'death has spread.' **5:18** ψ The one **just action** is his making his suffering a guilt offering yeilding up his life blood as a ransom (כֹּפֶר) for many, so that we can be cleansed from sin (נְכַפֵּר) to be released from the kingdom of death, before the kingdom of darkness is destroyed. Isa. 53:10 אִם־תָּשִׂים אָשָׁם נַפְשׁוֹ. The cleansing will result in our righteousness (cf. 1 Yoh. 1:9). The guilt offering is symbolic of a spiritual operation and the larger spiritual reality, under the figure of consuming Messiah's flesh and blood (cf. Yoh. 6:47-63). The sacrificial ransom represents the real and larger ransom cost, and in personal cost there is an overlap with the larger ransom cost, in blood, sweat, and tears that is borne by the creation, and in the Spirit of the Most High, for the ransoming of those being rescued (cf. Gen. 6:6-7). It is the separate us from the malignancy of our sins so that we are not destroyed with them. ▷ The guilt offering (Lev. 5:17-18; Isa. 53:5) is **an instruction of our peace** with the most high (מוּסַר שְׁלוֹמֵנוּ עָלָיו), which is a necessary lesson for us to understand the cost of bearing away our sins to purge them. This is the answer to the question, "Why did Messiah have to die?" He had to die to bring the enormous spiritual cost that the Most High was paying in the Spirit before us in the form of his flesh to bring the equivalent point to our attention in the physical realm. He brings this point before all men, to draw all men unto his love for his creation. This is the same lesson that the Most High put immediately before Adam after he sinned. His shame represented his guilt, and the animals slain to cover his guilt are a lesson in what the cost will be to remove his guilt, which is life. ▷ If we were to undersand the mystery of iniquity we might understand why so many are lost to rescue so few when one of God's imagers turns to evil, but this may be something that may only be understood when one is fully and completely purged of sin, or even then, perhaps never, because there is risk in creating beings like the Most High. What deceives the human heart only becomes reality when the heart chooses deceit. Until then it is not knowable (cf. Deut. 8:1-4).

5:20 λ✓ norm: *social habit, status quo.* Paul employs *nomos* here in the sense of a habit or societal norm, a force like the laws of nature. This sense crops up again at the end of Romans 7 and in Romans 8:2 as the *norm of sin and death*. In this case the social norm is viewed as having a power to increase sin. In vs. 12 Paul spoke of Adam's sin spreading death to all men. The sinfulness of man left unchecked increases. Vs. 20 is parallel to vs. 12b, 14, 15β, 16β, 17a, 18a, and 19a. Vs. 20 is the summation of all these texts. The word *nomos* here cannot possibly mean the Law of Gŏd, because wickedness increased without it (cf. Gen. 6:5-6) so that he had to destroy mankind in the deluge. Then he introduced the penalty for murder to Noah (Gen. 9:6), and evil was restrained. He taught Avraham his laws (Gen. 18:19) and evil was restrained. He gave Yisra'el his Law so that a man may do it and live through it (Lev. 18:5). Without the revelation of the Law, the faithful are unable to choose life (cf. Deut. 30:19). Death was always a choice before the Law. The Law introduced the choice of life. Without the influence of Gŏd's Law the human race would have destroyed itself long ago. What many should fear is

sin increased, loving-kindness greatly overflows. ²¹Therefore, just as sin reigns in death, so also loving-kindness will have reigned through righteousness unto everlasting life, through Yĕshua the Anŏinted our Adŏnai.

6 What then will we say? "Let us be continuing in sin so that grace will have increased?" ²May it never be! How can we who die to sin, still live in it? ³Or do you not know that as many of us as have been immersed into the Anŏinted Yĕshua, into his death we are immersed?ʸ ⁴Therefore we are jointly buried with him through immersion into death, so that just as the Anŏinted was raised from the dead through the glory of the Făther, likewise we too may walk in newness of life.

⁵Because if we have been getting jointly planted in the likeness of his death, we will surely also be in his rising, ⁶knowing this, that our old man is fastened up on the execution timber with him, so that the sinful body may be destroyed, so that we no longer are enslaved to sin, ⁷because the one who dies has been getting himself rendered justice ᵝfrom sin. ⁸But if we die with the Anŏinted, we are holding faithful, because we will also live with him, ⁹having been knowing that the Anŏinted, who is raised from the dead, need not again die. Death will not again master him. ¹⁰For the death he died, ᵞbecause of sin he died, at one time, but the life he lives, he lives ᵞbecause of the Almĭghty. ¹¹Likewise you also—be considering yourselves to be dead, on the one hand ᵞbecause of sin, but on the other hand as living ᵞbecause of the Almĭghty through⁽ᵉᵛ⁾ the Anŏinted Yĕshua.

¹²Do not let sin be reigning in your mortal body to be listening to its lusts, ¹³that is, do not let the members of your body be standing by to be tools of unrighteousness to sin, but let yourselves stand by the Almĭghty as living from the dead, and your members as tools of righteousness to the Almĭghty. ¹⁴Because sin must not master you, because you⁽ᵠ⁾are not under what is ᶲcustomary but

not the Law, but the withdrawal of knowledge of the Law as men forget it so that Gŏd can test and judge the world! (cf. Mat. 5:17-20; Hab. 2:4). The Law was given so that Yisra'el would choose life over death. See Deut. 30:19. The Law is not too hard (cf. Deut. 30:11). The Law was not given to increase transgression as the translations imply or as Justin Martyr suggests to cause Yisra'el to suffer. Rather Paul means there is a sociological rule here, a law of nature, a law of sinful mankind, that transgression will increase. See Proverbs 29:16. And this rule is what is customary for mankind. See Gen. 6:5-6.

6:3 γ Immersion cleanses the body, and so is a symbol of cleansing the heart from sin, and dying with Messiah and rising is a symbol of new life after putting sinful desires to death and leaving them in the grave. See Gal. 2:20-21 notes. ▷ Paul was fond of speaking in a Hebrew fashion, frequently using perfect from a future point of view, which to Greek grammarians would be called the proleptic aorist. In English it is necessary to render this idiom in the future perfect. Sometimes this is called prophetic perfect.

6:7 β ἀπό. Paul speaks of our administration of justice to the old man through repentance. In this sense it is punitive, because the old man is getting put to death. **6:10-11** λ *because of* or *by*. The dative is instrumental, a dative of cause. See Isa. 53:5, 8, e.g. מְחֹלָל מִפְּשָׁעֵנוּ מְדֻכָּא מֵעֲוֹנֹתֵינוּ. ▷ In vs. 11 τῇ ἁμαρτίᾳ (because of sin) is the same as in vs. 10. We should not suppose that we are "dead for sin," but "because of sin." Likewise, Messiah died 'because of sin' and not 'for sin.' See 1 Yoḥ. 2:2; 1 Cor. 15:3.

6:14 φ✓ Paul uses ὑπὸ νόμ. here to mean under the sentence of the law, condemnation. When Paul wants to say law abiding he uses: ἐννόμ. See Slater, *Lexicon to Pindar*, "1. a. custom, tradition, b. political tradition, regime." Nomos means *a norm in the sphere of law*, or that which is customary in regard to law. Strict justice, or penalty, becomes the norm because men do not repent. Human judges are to exact strict justice on the limiting principle of an eye for an eye. The purpose of this justice is to deter sin, punishing the guilty with a loss no greater than the loss they took from another. (But the code of the Amorite king Hammurabi allowed for unequal exaction of punishment based upon class and rank, and even allowed punishing a son for a father's crime.) Retributive justice on the other hand is reserved for the most heinous or incurable of situations in this life. Justice in this life is to deter sin. The wrath of the Most High in the final judgment is upon sin and all united with sin contamination to put a final end to sin. This is the

under loving-kindness.

¹⁵What then? We should sin because we are not under what is customary⁵, but under loving-kindness? May it never be! ¹⁶Have you not been knowing that whatever you yourselves stand by as slaves to listen to, its slaves you are—to whatever you are listening to, either of sin unto death, or obedience to righteousness? ¹⁷But thanks be to the Almĭghty, that though you were slaves of sin, you listened, namely from the heart to the teaching imprint which was handed over to you, ¹⁸that is, having been freed from sin, you really have become servants to righteousness. ¹⁹I speak humanly because of the weakness of your flesh. For just as you made your members stand by to be slaves to uncleanness, and by lawlessness for lawlessness, likewise now you must cause your members to stand by to be slaves to righteousness, to be made holy, ²⁰because when you were slaves of sin, you were liberated from righteousness. ²¹Therefore, what fruit did you have at that time, after which you are now ashamed? Because the end of those things is death. ²²But now having been freed from sinful rebellion and having been made servants to the Almĭghty, you having your fruit for holiness, and the end: everlasting life. ²³Because the wages of sin is death⁵, but the favorable gift of the Almĭghty is everlasting life in the Anŏinted Yĕshua our Adŏnai.

7

¹Or are you ignorant brothers? Because I am talking to those knowing custom°, that THE customary norm is ruling over man for as much time as he

---

second death. ▷ But there is an exception to the legal norm, which is that the Most High may choose to show compassion and mercy according to his great name (cf. Exodus 34), which he does for his faithful ones (cf. Exodus 20:6). Even though strict justice may be exacted on some in this life, if they repent in this life, then they receive a pardon that results in everlasting life at the resurrection of the dead. The pardon (or forgiveness) is the extraordinary justice. It is the justice that is outside the norm. But I hasten to add that this justice is just as legal and lawful as the strict justice of the legal norm. And in fact, human legal codes have recognized this also, giving king, president or governors the right to pardon or forgive a crime under the right circumstances. Since repentance and holding faithful to Messiah are a condition of the pardon, it is of course imperative that the faithful do not let sin master them. **6:15** ξ Vs. *We are not under the Law*. One can see at once from the context even without correcting the translation that he means we are not subject to condemnation, yet remain subject to obedience to righteousness (vs. 16). In Greek *nomos* connotes a legal norm against that which is exceptional. So the norm is condemnation. But forgiveness is the exception, the end of the norm for those holding faithful through repentance.

6:23 ξ The word *wages* here (ὀψώνια) specifically represents the pay a Roman soldier would receive. The service of sin is compared to serving in the military (cf. Rom. 6:13). Ultimately the pay is death. It is evident that Paul is speaking of the natural consequences of sin, and the ill will of the powers fighting against the Most High. Sin pays death and corruption by cause and effect, and the greatest

sinners, who command the rest, sacrifice the lives of those under them for their own advantage, such as it may be. There is, therefore, no divine judicial consequence in view here. Sin does not pay a judicial consequence because the wrath of the Most High is not a natural consequence of sin. The wrath of the Most High is an intervention in the natural course of sin, to put and end to it. In vs. 21, Paul refers to the consequences of sin as 'fruit,' that is poisoned, whose end is death. Not following the rules of creation results in death. Murder and the threat of blood revenge already entered the world with Qayin, long before the Gŏd's judicial sentence against Adam took effect. The point is that sin does not require a judicial sentence to deal death to those involved in it. Eventually sinners begin to murder each other. Sin transmits death to the sinner, and then via death corrupts innocent blood.
▷ At first, the Most High set a limit of 1000 years on man's lifespan, but the more powerful began to exploit and murder the innocent as they came increasingly enslaved to the corupted sons of God, so he sent the flood to remove terminally corrupted humanity, and then he reduced man's lifespan drastically so that it would not happen so quickly again. Then he began to work with Abraham. The divine dealing with history should be an object lesson to sinners, to encourage them to repent.

7:1 ω✓ Paul says he is speaking to those knowing the meaning of the Greek term *nomos* (a *legal norm:* See note on vs. 7), *what is customary*. He cannot possibly mean those having expert knowledge of Torah, because clearly from his illustrations in Romans 7, little scholarly knowledge is required. What is required is to know the Greek meaning of *nomos,* in its various

is living? ²Because the married woman has been getting held bound by what is customary to the living husband, but whenever the husband may have died, she has been getting released from THE customary norm for the husband. ³So then, while the husband is living, she will be called an adulteress if she may have come to another man. But if the husband may have died, she is free from THE customary norm. So she is not an adulteress if she comes to be with another man.

⁴Therefore my brothers, you also are made to die ᵠto THE customary norm through the body of the Anŏinted, so that you may come to another Măster, to the one raised from the dead, so that we may bear fruit for the Almĭghty. ⁵Because when we were in the flesh, the passions of sins, these through THE customary norm were working with our members to bear fruit to death. ⁶But now we are released from what is customary, dead to what was holding us, and so serve in newness of spirit and not oldness of a ˟letter promising to repay.

⁷What will we say then? Is the Law sin? May it never be! But, I would not know ⁿguiltiness except through *the* Law, because besides, I would not have had

---

senses. Paul's leading illustration is just as true in Roman Law as Jewish, and indeed among all nations. He is only showing how application of the legal norm changes when a legal exception occurs. It was not the legal norm that changed. It was only that a legal exception happened. When a legal exception happens, the legal norm does not apply. This is because the legal norm only applies to the norm.

7:4 ψ The Torah contains the principle of the legal norm, and the exception. For example, in Exodus 21:28-32, if an ox gored a person, and the ox was known to be in the habit of goring, then its owner was to be put to death with the ox. If, however, a ransom was laid on the owner by the judges or relatives of the dead person, and the ransom was paid, then the owner could go free. So we have the case of a ransom creating a legal exception, and as soon as the ransom is paid, the legal norm became illegal. No one could take vengeance on the owner of the ox. It should be noted that whether a ransoming was allowed depended on the contriteness of the offender and the inclination of the court to decide if justice called for mercy in the case. ▷ Now when Yisra'el sinned, the Most High sold her to the nations, into the power of lawlessness, hoping that lawlessness might teach his people to repent and be separated from their lawlessness, but if they would not, then they would destroy them, and he would destroy the nations after. And this outcome is the legal norm. ▷ However, Yisra'el repents. And the Most High forgives. But, there is still the problem that he had sold Israel to foreign nations, particularly their foreign gods. They became the masters. He would have to buy them back according to the terms in Isa. 52:3, "Ye were sold for nothing, and without money ye shall be ransomed." So he sent his only kindred Son, saying he would be a ransom for many. The powers killed the Son, taking the ransom. And so lawlessness by taking the ransom lost ownership, and the right to execute the norm of justice on its captives, and is to be compelled to release them to their former Master. ▷ By the body of Messiah, the Most High, compels lawlessness to return his people, and because they are ransomed, the norm of the law to condemn them does not apply. ▷ The wrath satisfaction theory, constructed by Augustine, Anselm, Calvin, Hodge and Sproul, claims that the body of Christ received the wrath of God, the norm of the law, so that the judgment would be satisfied. But this theology is derived from paganism. It is the theology of the volcano god that requires innocent blood to be appeased. Paganism appeases its gods with innocent blood to gain benefits from them or to placate them. The Almighty of Yisra'el, in stark contrast, gives his life to ransom his people from the pagan gods. The contrast could not be more plain.

7:6 ˟ or *sentence*. See 2:27. **7:7** η *guiltiness, sin*. To know sin is the same thing as feeling guilty because of it. Modern language has parsed the ancient conception of sin into factual wrong and guiltiness by using different terms, but ancient authors used the word as a synonym for guilt, indictment, and even punishment. In Hebrew the term sin could mean, sin, guilt, the penalty for sin, or a sin offering. A visit to the etymology dictionary for *sin* will show it to be tied to the concept of guilt. The term takes on the meaning of guilt feelings or a person motivated by guilty feelings due to factual sin.

7:7 θ Exo. 20:17; Deu. 5:21. In 7-14 he speaks about the state of man and his relation to the law before coming to Mĕssiah for the solution. Paul's use of nomos in these few verses merges into Law, i.e. from its fundamental sense: a norm→ a personal norm (habit) → a social norm (tradition, custom) → a legal custom → a legal norm → a legal standard . Nomos denotes the usual as compared to the unusual in the personal sphere, in the social sphere, in the legal sphere, in the theoretical sphere of a perfect society, thus Gŏd's instruction norm, i.e. the norm in the sphere of his instruction. What seems an odd shift in meaning is explained by Martin Ostwald:

> The difficulty of analysing a concept such as νόμος into its constituent elements becomes most manifest as we now turn to its uses in religious contexts. For while it is true to say that

been realizing coveting except the Law was saying, "YOU SHALL NOT COVET." ⁸Now guiltiness, taking a starting point, using the commandment, worked itself out in me as every sort of coveting. Because without the legal standard, guiltiness is ᵖinactive. ⁹So I was once ᵛalive without the legal standard, but when the command came to notice, guiltiness sprung into life, and I ᶿdied. ¹⁰And this commandment, which is meant for life, was discovered by me to be unto death, ¹¹because guiltiness had taken a starting point through the commandment, and had deceived me, and through it had caused me to die. ¹²So indeed, the Law is holy, and the commandment is holy and righteous and good.

¹³Then did what is good for me become death? It should not have been! But ᶲguiltiness, ᵀthat it would have been revealed as guiltiness through what is good for me, ᵖitself was working death, such that ᶿthe guiltiness may become exeedingly guilty using the command.

¹⁴Indeed, we have been knowing that the Law is spiritual, but I am ᵠcom-

---

the term may denote a ritual ordinance, that is an injunction that something ought to be done, or a ritual practice, that is, a statement that something is actually done as a custom, or a belief, that is a conviction that something exists or that it is right that something be done, it is always difficult and often impossible to determine in any given context which of these three notions its author had in mind. The reason for this is not far to seek. As we have seen time and again, the crucial point in νόμος is that it is something which a given society regards as a valid norm for itself...In short, however interesting for us, the question of differentiation between rule and practice was unimportant for the Greek view [understanding] of νόμος.

So we see that the practiced norm merges into a norm as a moral standard, a rule. The word νόμος cannot itself sort out its uses. Only the context it is used in can. So we see why Paul is making the distinction by the use of questions and context. As the translator however, knowing that the average reader cannot be expected to know Greek, I have to choose what kind of norm is meant for the reader using the context. This involves interpretation, but if the reader wants to try to experience the Greek, he can simply plug in the term norm in all the places they see law in other translations, and then he will see how necessary the context is to sort the meaning. See, page 40, M. Ostwald, *Nomos and the Athenian Democracy;* BDAG 3rd edition; LSJ; Thayer. See also Appendix VIII.

7:8 μ. *dead = in operative.* Paul speaks of the person without Messiah through vs. 13. The trans. *inactive* is literally *dead.* Paul means that guilt is not operating in the conscience. **7:9** ν He means he was once feeling alive about himself, approved (ν); enjoying the zest of life, not knowing he was coveting. Peoples even without the written Law know that coveting is evil (cf. Rom. 2:14-15), so Paul is speaking of a child that is developing a conscience. Paul says he died (θ) when the command came. He means his feeling of approval was killed as he came under the accusation of his conscience. **7:10-12** Paul is showing how the guilty conscience deceives itself through self condemnation. The commandment is used by guilt unto death, i.e. self destruction. Guilt uses the commandment to produce a repeating cycle of habitual self destruction and disobedience.

7:13 ξ or *sin.* Paul assumes the law is for life, and asks if it is now death. He answers the question with strong denial, and then he blames the death effect on the guilty conscience. Paul uses the word sin (ξ) both for factual wrong and a feeling of guilty condemnation that motivates one to further sin or self destruction. In respect to the sub clause (τ), it is guiltiness that is identified by the Law. But it is the guilty conscience that uses the perceived condemnation by the commandment to take on further guilt of sin. Therefore, as proved by Rom. 5:20, the Law is not to be blamed for increasing sin, but it is the self-deception of the guilty conscience concerning the Law that is to blame.

7:14 η→sin. The Greek perfect (=English pres or past perf. continuous) refers to Paul's past here. See *Gal. 3:22* π; *Rom. 3:9* ρ. **7:14** ψ→flesh = σάρκινος, Thayer no. 1. Fleshly (σάρκινός) is also a word too frequently associated with a sinful attitude, and all words like it, e.g. carnal. The DLNT has one of the few good translations, "I am made of flesh." What Paul means is that one still has a physical being that has been imprinted with the habits he acquired during one's enslavement to sin guiltiness. The flesh is like a freight train and the engineer like the conscience. The engineer tells the train to change direction, but it does not easily do so because of past inertia. ▷ The guilty conscience is involved in the commission of sin. The repentant conscience is not, and submits to the rule of God's Law (cf. Rom. 8:7). This is because the repentant person truly pledges loyalty to Him from the heart. Therefore, when the repentant person finds himself in a sin, he realizes the law is not present to condemn, but simply to objectively identify sin that needs to be cleaned out. For the sin was not the result of heart disloyalty, but a result of sin still hiding out in the flesh. **7:14** φ = *which.* The relative pronoun

posed of flesh, ᶲwhich ⁿhad been getting sold under sin. ¹⁵Certainly, what I am getting myself worked into, I do not realize, because I am not practicing what I am wanting, but what I am hating, this I do do. ¹⁶But when what I am not wanting, this I do, I agree with the Law, that it is good. ¹⁷So now, no longer am I getting myself worked into it, but sin dwelling in me. ¹⁸Because I have been knowing that good is not dwelling in me, that is, within my flesh, because the willing is present in me, but getting myself worked toward the good is not. ¹⁹So the good I am wanting, I am not doing, but the evil I am not wanting, this I am accomplishing. ²⁰But when I am doing this which I am not wanting, I am no longer working it out, but the sin dwelling in me. ²¹So, I am finding the norm with my wishing to get myself working toward good, that in me evil is present. ²²Because I myself am rejoicing in the Law of the Almĭghty in the inner man, ²³but I am seeing another norm in my members, waging war against the Law in my understanding and keeping me a prisoner to the norm which is existing in my members. ²⁴Miserable man I am! Who will rescue me from this dying body? ²⁵But thanks to the Almĭghty through Yĕshua the Anŏinted our Adŏnai! So then, indeed I myself in the mind am serving the Law of the Almĭghty, but in the flesh a norm of sin.

8 So now there is no condemnation for those belonging^ᵉᵛ to the Anŏinted Yĕshua, ²because the Law of the Spĭrit of life through^ᵉᵛ the Anŏinted Yĕshua has freed you from THE norm of ᵟsin and death.

³Because the powerlessness^ᵖ of the Law *is* in that it was being weakened through the flesh. *But* the Almĭghty, having sent his own Sŏn, in the form of

---

here serves to mark the participle (πεπραμένος) in agreement with the adjective (σάρκινός). Both have masculine endings, while 'I' (ἐγώ) is unmarked except by context. The point of grammar turns on whether 'I' is perceived as separated from the flesh, which Paul is surely doing here, presenting the habit of flesh as now responsible and not the heart. **7:25** Paul is referring to sins of ignorance, and not sins of rebellion, with which the mind is complicit. If we are loyal to Mĕssiah, he will also remove our habits when he comes, but until then we wait for the hope righteousness by faithfulness (cf. Gal. 5:5). ▷ There is no 'sin nature' inherited from Adam, but all sin proceeds from habit or the choice of the person who is rebelling. The habit is induced by the influence of death and previous sins in the environment. The sinful corruption of the environment deceives people into a sin, condemnation, sin cycle. Only truth, repentance and forgiveness can break it.

8:1 δ or *guilt; rebellion.* Now we have been freed from the legal norm of death, from the norm of guiltiness also, from the norm of rebellion. **8:3** ρ for acquittal **8:3** ζ→sin: Hebrew uses the plain word "sin" (חַטָּאת) to mean a "sin offering." The LXX translates וְלַחַטָּאת as καὶ περὶ ἁμαρτίας in Lev. 7:37, where it means "and in reference to the sin [offering]." ▷ How does a sin offering judge against sin in the flesh? The repentant person lays their hand on the offering, symbolically transferring the sin to the offering. The offering bears the sin to the altar where its blood purges the sin. The hand laying on is symbolic of the act of confessing the sin and repenting. The sin is separated from the confessor and transferred to the offering which bears it. When the animal is slain, the sin is declared to be wiped by the blood. This is symbolic of the divine life from the Spirit of the Most High to cleanse the sin. The innocence or perfection of the animal represents the Most High himself. The slaying of the animal represents that the malignancy of sin attacks the offering and kills it. Thus the loss of life (represented by blood) is caused by the lawlessness of sin, the ransom necessary to purge the sin. This represents the divine loss in dealing with our sins. The whole sin offering ceremony is symbolic of spiritual reality. At the end the sin is separated from the confessor and destroyed because the ransom (the offering) yielded up life to purge the sin. Everything in the ceremony is symbolic. In the spiritual reality, so represented, the sin is judged by purging it, which is a joint effort between the confessor and the Spirit. ▷ Now when the confessor lays his hand on the offering, he is symbolically transferring sin to it to bear for the purpose of purging it. At no time is this sin the wrath of the Almighty. The offering is not bearing wrath. It is bearing sin itself in the symbolism. The sin is being removed from the confessor so that there will be no need for divine wrath later on the confessor. The blood cleanses or purges the sin. It wipes it out. This is

sinful flesh, even *in reference to a sin offering*, has judged against sin in the flesh, ⁴so that the righteousness of the Law may be fulfilled in us, who do not walk according to the flesh but according to the Spirit.

⁵Because those who are according to the flesh set their minds on the things of the flesh, but those who are according to the Spirit, the things of the Spirit. ⁶Because the fleshly thinking leads to death, but the thinking set on the Spirit leads to life and peace, ⁷because the fleshly thinking is hostile toward the Almĭghty, because it is not subjecting itself to the Law of the Almĭghty, nor indeed is able to be. ⁸So those who are controlled by the flesh cannot please the Almĭghty.

⁹However, you are not controlled by the flesh but by the Spĭrit, if indeed the Spĭrit of the Almĭghty dwells in you. But if anyone does not have the Spĭrit of the Anŏinted, he does not belong to him. ¹⁰When the Anŏinted is in you, though the body *may become* dead because of sin, yet the spirit *may become* alive through righteousness. ¹¹And since the Spĭrit of him who raised Yĕshua from the dead dwells in you, he who raised the Anŏinted Yĕshua from the dead will also give life to your mortal bodies through his Spĭrit who dwells in you.

¹²So then, brothers, we are under obligation, not to the flesh, to live according to the flesh, ¹³because if you are living according to the flesh, you must die, but if by the Spĭrit, you are putting to death the deeds of the body, you will live.

¹⁴Because all who are being led by the Spĭrit of the Almĭghty, these become sons of the Almĭghty. ¹⁵Because you have not received *a spirit of slavery* leading to fear again, but you have received the Spĭrit for adoption as sons in whom we cry out, "Abbă! Făther!" ¹⁶The Spĭrit himself testifies with our spirit that we are children of the Almĭghty, ¹⁷and when children, heirs also, heirs of the Almĭghty and fellow heirs with the Anŏinted, if indeed we jointly suffer so that we will also have been jointly glorified.

¹⁸Because I take into account that the sufferings of this present time are not worthy to be compared with the glory that is to be revealed to us. ¹⁹Because the anxious longing of the creation waits eagerly for the revealing of the sons of the Almĭghty. ²⁰Because the creation was subjected to futility, not willingly, but because of him who subjected it, in hope ²¹that the creation itself also will be set free from its slavery to corruption, into the freedom of the glory of the children of the Almĭghty.

²²Because we have been knowing that the whole creation groans and suffers the pains of childbirth together until now. ²³And not only this, but also we our-

---

symbolic of the Spirit of the Most High forgiving sin. The sin is removed from the confessor and then wiped out. Thus sin in the flesh is judged by elimination of the sin. There is no extra judicial wrath to be satisfied by the soul of the offering itself. The cost is exacted by the lawlessness of the sin itself. ▷ And to prove this, in the case of Messiah, he was raised from the dead, because he was innocent, and performs the service of ransoming us from our union with lawlessness. ▷ In more ancient times, the confessor slew the offering. This is the confessor saying that his sin causes the death of the ransom. So again, the confessor was not pouring out divine wrath on the offering. The priest is acting for the confessor when he slays the offering.

The offering itself is acting for the Most High. ▷ As I said, the offering symbolically bears the sin to the altar where the blood wipes it out. In Eph. 2:15 when Satan focuses the enmity of sin against Messiah to destroy him, the Most high takes the opportunity to make the point that the sin caused enmities are put to death and left in the grave by him for anyone who holds faithful to him. In Col. 2:14 it is the bill of divorcement that is executed and left in the grave.

8:23 *a* See also Luke 20:36; Mat. 5:9; 2 Peter 1:4. Our adoption as 'sons of the Almighty' (בְּנֵי אֱלֹהִים) comes at the resurrection of the dead, when

selves, having the beginning fruit of the Spĭrit, even we ourselves groan within ourselves, waiting eagerly for our adoption as sons,ª the ransom release of our body. ²⁴Because to hope we are rescued, but a hope that is seen is not hope, because who hopes for what he sees? ²⁵But if we trustingly expect what we do not see, with perseverance we wait eagerly for it.

²⁶In the same way, the Spĭrit yet also helps us in our weakness, because the things we should pray for, as is necessary, we have not been knowing, but the Spĭrit himself intercedes for us with unspeakable sighing, ²⁷and he who searches the hearts has been knowing what the mind of the Spĭrit is, because he intercedes on behalf of the holy ones according to the will of the Almĭghty.

²⁸And we have been knowing that for those loving the Almĭghty, he ᵝworks along with all things for good, for those who are called according to his purpose, ²⁹because those whom ʸhe ᵖacknowledges ᵖbefore, also ᵟhe ⁱdesignates before to be conformed to the image of his Sŏn, so that he may be the firstborn⁺ in rank among many brothers. ³⁰And whom designates beforehand, also he ᵚinvites, and those whom he ᵚinvites, also he ᵘadministers justice, and whom he ᵘadministers justice, these also he will have glorified.

³¹What then shall we say to these things? If the Almĭghty *is acting* on our

---

our bodies receive the ransomed release. Please note the distinction between the term 'children' and 'sons' (cf. vs. 15-16). We are still children. The sons are the grown ups after the rite of passage, which is the resurrection of the dead, and the transformation of those who still live on that day.

8:28 β συνεργεῖ = *he works along with;* ▷ 'All things work together for good' (ESV), but 'all things' is not the subject of the verb in Greek; Gŏd is. Further, 'together' is not the only nuance of συν. But see BDAG, Slater, '1.a. along with;' Middle Liddell, 'I. along with, in company with, together with.' 'The verb is present tense, meaning Gŏd takes all things as they are, including the actions of people, good or evil, limiting their freedoms or expanding them, according to his purpose for the good of those loving him. Paul only obligates him to do this for those loving him, and not for the wicked. See Exodus 20:6.

8:29 γ→before: προγινώσκω. In time, the passage shifts the perspective to the last day, the gateway to the age to come. One must acknowledge the Son now and be acknowledged by Him now, before (8.29 π) the last day, so that on the last day he can acknowledge one (cf. Mat. 7:21-23; John 3:18). Γινώσκω is used here in the sense of personal friendship and not simply factual knowledge. The wicked are factually known. They are not known as belonging to Him. ▷ The future and gnomic aorist (8.29 ρ 2x), is accepted by the principle Greek grammarians and scientific linguists: Porter, Fanning, and Wallace, Robertson. Its increased frequency in Jewish usage (LXX and NT) is encouraged by the pervasive future use of the Hebrew perfect. Many however, continue to fight mightily against such because there is a long tradition of doctrine dependent on limiting the aorist to past tense only. ▷ The above remarks apply to 'designates' (8.29 ι) also. I have chosen a synonym instead of the traditional word which in ecclesiastical English has acquired the connotation of irrevocable fate. **8:29** φ cf. Col. 1:15 ψ.

8:30 μ✓=will have. More literally the English present tenses are future perfect, 'will have.' The passage takes a Hebrew eschatological point of view. The reader is transported to the future last day assuming the future and then it is stated what has already happened, hence the future perfect 'will have.' See notes on Eph. 2:4-8. See for example James 5:1-3. The chain of redemption begins with the definition of the faithful in vs. 28, as *those loving the Almĭghty*. This is picked up in vs. 29 with the word *whom*, referring to *those loving* Him. *Loving* is defined with a present participle (ἀγαπῶσιν), thus giving a present continuous sense (cf. Exo. 20:6). See John 3:18 for the same tense definition (ὁ πιστεύων εἰς αὐτὸν). Compare Mat. 24:13. Then follows a list of promises that will have been kept for all the faithful enduring to the end. ▷ The verb καλέω (8.30 ω) should be taken in the same sense as that in Rev. 19:9, of those who will have been called (invited) to the wedding feast of the lamb. ▷ The chain of promises may be taken in order: He acknowledges us when we repent. He designates us for transformation upon our pledge of loyalty. Then he invites us to his wedding. Then he makes us righteous, because the wedding is in his kingdom (8.30 μ). Then he glorifies us, because we will rule with him. ▷ There is ambiguity in the term "justified" (8.30 μ. *administered righteousness*), because this term may refer to being ransomed by Mĕssiah or being made righteous. The word *justified* can be made to have good sense in Middle English, and Koine Greek, which both give it the sense to administer justice (to adjudicate a case in any way), but in ecclesiastical English it has been corrupted. Therefore, the term is avoided, and the other sense explained. For those readers who want to

behalf, who is against us? ³²He who did not spare his own Sŏn, but delivered him on behalf of us all⁶, how will he not also with him freely give us all things? ³³Who will bring a charge against the Almĭghty's chosen ones? The Almĭghty is the one administering justice. ³⁴Who is the one who condemns? The Anŏinted Yĕshua is he who died, yes, more so who was raised, who is at the right hand of the Almĭghty, who also intercedes on our behalf. ³⁵Who will separate us from the love of the Anŏinted? Will tribulation, or distress, or persecution, or famine, or nakedness, or peril, or sword? ³⁶Just as it has been getting written, "FOR YOUR SAKE WE ARE BEING PUT TO DEATH ALL DAY LONG. WE ARE CONSIDERED AS SHEEP TO BE SLAUGHTERED^ψ."

³⁷But in all these things we overwhelmingly conquer through him who loves us. ³⁸Because I have been getting persuaded that neither death, nor life, nor messengers, nor principalities, nor things which have been impending, nor things to come, nor powers, ³⁹nor height, nor depth, nor any other created thing, will be able to separate us from the love of the Almĭghty, which is in the Anŏinted Yĕshua our Adŏnai.

9 I am telling the truth in the Anŏinted. I am not lying, my conscience testifies with me in the Holy Spĭrit, ²that I have great sorrow and unceasing grief in my heart. ³Because I was wishing that I myself were accursed from the Anŏinted^ψ on behalf of my brothers, my kinsmen according to the flesh, ⁴who are sons of Yisra'el, concerning whom *is* the adoption as sons, and the glory and the covenants and the giving of the Law and the service and the promises, ⁵of whom *are* the fathers, and from whom *is* the Anŏinted according to the flesh, the one being over all, Almĭghty, blessed for *all* the ages. Am‑en^μ.

⁶But it is not as though the word of the Almĭghty has been failing, because they are not all Yisra'el who are from Yisra'el. ⁷Nor are they all children because

---

try to combine the two senses, I suggest: administer righteousness (as merciful justice, and impartation of moral uprightness).

8:32 δ The Almĭghty's only kindred Son consented to become our ransom from Satan when Adam sinned (cf. Gen. 3:15), so when he became a man, he was not spared from suffering the ransom cost. Sin and death, represented by Satan and his hosts, took the ransom, and now the Most High, who had sold his people into the nations because of their transgressions, will demand the release of all who turn from their sins. ▷ See Mat. 20:28; Mark 10:45. "On behalf of us" (ὑπὲρ ἡμῶν) is explained by Messiah as λύτρον ἀντὶ πολλῶν, "a ransom in return for many." The ransom is taken by lawlessness, as the price to buy us out of the powers enslaving us to sin and death. ▷ See Rev. 5:9. ▷ The wrath payment theory claims that ἀντὶ means 'in place of' and that the wrath of God was suffered by Messiah 'in the place of' many. But in fact, ἀντὶ may only mean a legal substitution in some contexts, and certainly not in any relating to Messiah's death. Strictly speaking ἀντὶ means 'over against,' 'opposite to,' so that in Mat. 20:28 it comes to mean: *in exchange for*, or *in return for*. The word does not imply anything regarding the legal justness of the position of the payer or the collector of the ransom. But the substitution theory assumes it is a just exchange, and that God is the one paid. But the opposite is the case. The Most High is giving the ransom, not collecting it. So the circumstance is the opposite of pagan doctrine, whereby the god is appeased by the ransom. Since forgiveness happens prior to any offering, the offering itself is not making any legal payment to secure it (cf. Appendix X). **8:36 ψ** Psa. 44:22.

9:3 ψ See Exodus 32:32-33. **9:5 μ** Some want the text to say, "... flesh. The one being over all, [the] Almĭghty [be] blessed for the ages." But this is urged to deny the deity of Messiah, as if Paul suddenly expostulated a praise to God over the ideas expressed up to 'flesh,' and did not mean for the pronoun, which agrees perfectly with Messiah to refer to him. If one reads the text with the presupposition that Messiah is Almĭghty, then the grammar agreement between three words, Χριστὸς, ὁ and θεὸς plainly convey this idea. And this must be the case, because the role of Messiah as the divine ransomer requires that he be the only kindred Almĭghty (cf. Yoḣ. 1:18; Titus 2:13; Hos. 13:4, 14).

Romans 9

they are Avraham's seed, but "IN YITSHAQ YOUR SEED WILL BE NAMED." ⁸That is, it is not the children of the flesh who are children of the Almĭghty, but the children of the promise are taken into account as seed.

⁹Because this is the word of the promise, "AT THIS APPOINTED SEASON I WILL COME, AND SARAH WILL HAVE A SON." ¹⁰And not only this, but there was Rivqah also, when she had conceived by one man, our father Yitsḥaq. ¹¹Because though they were not yet born and had not done anything good or bad, so that the Almĭghty's purpose according to his choice may be continuing, not from *the customary* works but from him who calls, ¹²it was said to her, "THE OLDER WILL SERVE THE YOUNGER," ¹³just as it has been getting written, "YA'AQOV I LOVED, BUT ESAU I LOVED LESS."

¹⁴What shall we say then? There is no injustice on the side of the Almĭghty, is there? May it never be! ¹⁵Because he says to Mosheh, "I WILL HAVE MERCY ON WHOM I MAY BE HAVING MERCY, AND I WILL HAVE COMPASSION ON WHOM I MAY BE HAVING COMPASSION." ¹⁶So then it is not for the one wishing or the one running, but from the Almĭghty who has mercy, ¹⁷because the Scripture says to Pharaoh, "FOR THIS VERY PURPOSE I RAISED YOU UP, SO THAT I MAY SHOW MY POWER IN YOU, AND THAT MY NAME MAY BE PROCLAIMED THROUGHOUT ALL THE EARTH." ¹⁸So then he is having mercy on whom he intends, and he is hardening whom he intends.

¹⁹You will say to me then, "Why does he still find fault, because who has been resisting his will?" ²⁰On the contrary, who are you, man, who answers back to the Almĭghty? THE THING MOLDED WILL NOT SAY TO THE MOLDER, "WHY DID YOU MAKE ME LIKE THIS," will it? ²¹Or DOES NOT THE POTTER HAVE A RIGHT OVER THE CLAY, to make from the same lump one vessel for honorable use and another for common use? ²²What if the Almĭghty, ᵃintending to demonstrate his wrath and to make his power known, endured with much patience the vessels of wrath, which have been getting fixed up for destruction, ²³even so that he might make known the riches of his glory upon vessels of mercy, which he readies be-

---

9:7 χ Gen. 21:12 **9:9** α Gen. 18:10, 14 **9:12** β Gen. 25:23 **9:13** θ Mal. 1:2 **9:15** α Exo 33:19.

9:17 β Exo 9:16. The usual translations of Exo. 33:19 imply that the Almĭghty is fickle, because the subjunctive is not given its proper force. Rather the text implies that the Almĭghty's restoration plans are only constrained by possibility: וְחַנֹּתִי אֶת־אֲשֶׁר אָחֹן

וְרִחַמְתִּי אֶת־אֲשֶׁר אֲרַחֵם. *I will have had mercy to whom I may have mercy, and I will have had compassion to whom I may have compassion.* The future perfect interacts with the subjunctive imperfect. The Greek text clearly shows this by an aorist subjunctive on the second use of each verb. **9:20** μ Isa. 45:9 **9:20** λ Jer. 18:6.

9:19-24 χ Answer a fool according to his folly. What if Gŏd cannot be resisted? Then people are only like clay that can be molded and cannot choose to be a good product or a marred product. But the clay is resiting his will! So the assumption that the Gŏd who is cannot be resisted is folly, and people are not simply clay with no responsibility for their flaws. ▷ Paul's antagonist had suggested the idea that people were only like clay in Gŏd's hands, so in his next argument Paul uses the clay metaphor to show why Gŏd is patient with the 'clay.' He is waiting for it to repent. If clay can repent, then so can Gŏd repent of designating the clay for destruction. He can remold it into something good. Paul's analogy is from Jer. 18:1-10: ▷ The nation of Yisra'el is like clay in the hand of a potter. When any people does evil, Gŏd intends destruction for it, but if any people repents he restores it, and he repents of the destruction he intended. The vessels of destruction now become the vessels of mercy. ▷ Some of the pots of wrath in vs. 22 become the pots of mercy in vs. 23 when repentance occurs. The pots of wrath are not being predestined for wrath to enhance Gŏd's sovereignty over separate pots predestined for mercy. Not so, but Gŏd is patient, as much as can be for some pots of wrath to repent, and then his slowness to execute his wrath with them and having mercy on them if they repent is his glory. ▷ If Gŏd's sovereign mercy is fatalism then that is very unglorious. People are not just

forehand for glory, ²⁴even us, whom he also called, not from the Yehudim only, but also from the nations.ˣ

²⁵As he says also in Hosh‑ea, "I WILL CALL THOSE WHO WERE NOT MY PEOPLE, 'MY PEOPLE,' AND HER WHO HAS NOT BEEN GETTING LOVED, 'SHE WHO HAS BEEN GETTING LOVED.ᵅ' ²⁶AND IT WILL BE THAT IN THE PLACE WHERE IT WAS SAID TO THEM, 'YOU ARE NOT MY PEOPLE,' THERE THEY WILL BE CALLED SONS OF THE LIVING ALMĬGHTY.ᵝ" ²⁷And Yeshayahu cries out over Yisra'el, "THOUGH THE NUMBER OF THE SONS OF YISRA'EL MAY BE LIKE THE SAND OF THE SEA, IT IS THE REMNANT THAT WILL BE RESCUED, ²⁸BECAUSE YĂHWEḤ WILL EXECUTE HIS WORD UPON THE EARTH THOROUGHLY AND QUICKLY.ᵅ" ²⁹And just as Yeshayahu has been predicting, "EXCEPT YĂHWEḤ OF ARMIES HAD LEFT TO US A POSTERITY, WE WOULD HAVE BECOME LIKE SEDOM AND WOULD HAVE RESEMBLED AMORAH.ᵝ"

³⁰What shall we say then? We say that the nations who did not pursue ᵘjustice, have understood justice, that is ᵘadministration of justice which is based on faithfulness, ³¹but Yisra'el, pursuing what is customary for ᵘjustice administration, to the Torah has not arrived. ³²Why? Because they did not pursue ᵘadministration of justice based on faithfulness, but as if based on ʸthe customary works. They stumbled over the stumbling stone, ³³just as it has been getting written, "BEHOLD, I LAY IN TSIYON A STONE OF STUMBLING AND A ROCK OF OFFENSE, AND THE ONE HOLDING FAITHFUL UPON HIM WILL NOT BE ASHAMED.ᶲ"

10

¹Brothers, indeed, my heart's desire and prayer near to the Almĭghty on their behalf is for deliverance. ²Because I testify to them, that they have zeal for the Almĭghty, but not according to accurate knowledge, ³because they are not acknowledging the Almĭghty's justice,ᵖ and while seeking to establish their own justiceᵘ they have not submitted to the justiceᵖ of the Almĭghty. ⁴Be-

---

pots. **9:25** α Hos. 2:23 **9:26** β Hos. 1:10; **9:27-28** α Isa 10:22-23, 28:22; **9:29** β Isa. 1:9; **9:30 & 32** μ✓ **9:32** γ merit: merit for demerit **9:33** ϕ Isa 28:16, 8:14. The Jewish people have long been experts in the sphere of law and justice and in the administration of justice צדקה. This was the prophecy for Yehudah. See Gen. 49:10. But they do not perceive the Almĭghty's justice צדקה (mercy, charitableness) made plain through the faithfulness of Mĕssiah as our sin offering (cf. Rom. 7:4 and 8:3 notes), but rather they set their sights on the norm of justice (what is customary for justice, the doctrine of merit to atone for demerit). They think the Almĭghty's judicial wrath against sin is appeased by good works: צדקה (merit). In common with many, they hold the notion that if they are extra good persons then on that basis their sin is canceled out by their extra good. They did not arrive at the Torah (instruction) in Scripture for forgiveness. For they have not gone through the door of Mĕssiah's faithfulness and his justice (צדקה: mercy, charitableness), which is received by pledging one's faithfulness to him. The doctrine of demerit erasing merit falsely portrays the Almĭghty as a god of commerce or business, and sin as something that always has a compensation. ▷ The MT reads יָחִישׁ

make haste [to flee] but the LXX reads καταισχυνθῇ, will be disgraced. This corresponds to the Hebrew יָבִישׁ, which means will act disgracefully. A synonym is found in Daniel 12:2 translated in the LXX αισχύνην, in Hebrew לַחֲרָפוֹת, meaning to great reproach, or great shame. There being but one letter difference in the Hebrew represented by the LXX and that of the MT. But the great Isaiah scroll contains the MT reading. In the context of Isaiah 28 it is plain that they are fleeing divine vengeance for making a covenant with death. In Isaiah 28:18 it says those who made it will be לְמִרְמָס, trampled down, which Luke 20:18 renders λικμήσει, ground into powder. This may be compared to Mark 6:11. See Mat 21:42; Mark 12:10; Luke 20:17-18; cf. Luke 2:34-35; Daniel 2:35; Psa. 118:22; 1 Pet 2:6; Rom. 9:33; 10:11; 1 Pet 2:7; Acts 2:7; Eph. 2:20. The text refers to the necessity of holding faithful to Mĕssiah to avoid being branded as a traitor who makes haste to flee from the Almĭghty in the last day and suffering everlasting shame. So we are supposed to think of *yabish* when we read *yahish*. **10:3** ρ mercy צדקה See 3:26 η. **10:3** μ merit צדקה (see Reuben Alcalay).

10:4 Vs. *Christ is the end of the law for righteousness to everyone believing.* The Matthew 7:21

cause the Anŏinted One is the end of what is ᵅcustomary for ᵝjustice, concerning everyone ᵟpledging faithfulness.ᵞ

⁵Certainly, Moshehᵅ is describing the ᵝjustice which *results*ᵞ from *doing* the ᵟLaw, that "THE ONE WHO DOES THEM WILL LIVE ᵘTHROUGH THEM,ᶿ" ⁶yetᵋ *at the same time*,ᵖ ᵑthe ᵟadministration of justice based on ᶻFAITHFULNESS is speaking in this way:

---

prophecy is fulfilled by this abomination and others like it. The Fäther has good reasons for allowing the mistranslation of Scripture, namely that most of Scripture is being distributed, even if corrupted by unworthy translators. For the word still spreads even if partly corrupted, and brings a harvest. The faithful do ignore the mistranslations in holding faithful, even if some of what they believe is not correct. This is the imposition of exile, a corporate judgment. But see Eze. 11:16-21. When the mistranslations are corrected, then the kingdom of heaven is not far off, and the faithful will no longer have to suffer stunted growth from mistranslations of the lawless, the imposition of exile. **10:4** α→norm: *norm, tradition, custom, customary procedure:* There are two sorts of norms for justice here that Paul means among all the norms. One is legal and the other just a legal tradition. The condemnation of the sinner is the legal norm being ended on a case by case basis, because the confessor is forgiven. The traditional norm also ended, at least for those who formerly held to it, is slavery to the system of merit and demerit, wherein the merits are said to cancel out demerit, giving a defaco acquittal. **10:4** β I. *administration of justice* II. *being made righteous.* What is received, therefore, through Messiah, is extraordinary justice. The Most High finds it just to forgive the sinner who confesses and repents from sin. That is, he finds it just to show mercy. ▷ The blood of Messiah's sacrifice declares the wiping out of judicial wrath for the sin (a KIPPURIM), because the confessor is repentant. The symbolism of the blood purges the punitive sentence for sin against the sinner because of covenant violations. This blood is a covenant that the sin is forgiven. The blood also renews the covenant by which the confessor pledges to be faithful to the commandments, and the Most High promises to give everlasting life to the one holding faithful. In this respect, the blood has the same fuction as the original blood of the covenant. ▷ At no point is the blood making satisfaction or paying for the covenant violations. The blood declares the erasing of punitive sentences. Also, the blood of the renewed covenant has the same force as the blood of all covenants. It is a statement of what will happen to either party in the case of betrayal of the covenant terms. ▷ Why then did Messiah himself take the place of a covenant renewal offering, and suffer death? Because in addition to forgiving us and renewing the covenant he wants to instruct of on the cost of our healing. It costs him life to cleanse our sins. It costs him life to bring us to repentance, and it costs him life to ransom us from the powers we were sold to when we first disobeyed him. So in sacrificial death, these costs are symbolically transferred to him, and he suffers them. The symbolic is a lesson on the spiritual reality so represented. Death is caused by the malignancy of the sin that he is bearing the costs of on our behalf. ▷ Please note that the costs resulting in the death of the offering is not a judicial penalty. The sacrificial death is not involved in paying such a cost, because wrath comes from the Most High, and a sentence of judgment is withdrawn by him and forgiven without cost. The cost illustrated in the death of the offering is symbolic of only the direct cost exacted by sin itself and the forces of lawlessness holding us in bondage. ▷ In truth, forgiveness, when possible, is a relief to the forgiver, because it relieves him of having to suffer further cost by destroying his creation through vengeance. God loves his creatures and does not want to have to destroy them.

10:4 δ→faithfulness = *holding faithful* **10:4** γ *loyalty.* The *norm of justice* is that a person is acquitted because they did no wrong or because their good deeds (or another's) compensate and the wrong is overlooked for that reason. ▷ Within Judaism the doctrine of merit to atone demerit was very strong in the first four centuries AD. ▷ Mĕssiah is the end of transferring merit from the account of a righteous person to a sinner, because he forgives the penalty when people repent. Legal merit is not needed for forgiveness, but is only sought after by those wanting to plead innocence in the eyes of the law, or to convince the judge that sin is compensated for by merit or some sort of debt satisfaction, and by this reason the penalty should be changed or accounted as satisfied. ▷ In sense 10:4 β II, Mĕssiah ends the norm for being declared righteous by teaching the necessity for our faithfulness. This is to say a person cannot be reckoned righteous without being so both outwardly and inwardly. The idea of performing a merit above and beyond the call of duty, so as to offset a demerit, contaminates the deed at the heart level. Only a person truly forgiven and accepting it can receive the sanctifying righteousness of Mĕssiah and thus rise above the norm which passes for righteousness. **10:5** α *Mosheh's writing* **10:5** β I. *administration of justice, fairness, equitableness;* II. *being made righteous, justification* (in a positive sense) **10:5** γ or *is* **10:5** δ *commandments* **10:5** μ *by, because of* **10:5** θ Lev. 18:5 **10:6** ε *or and, that is* (BDAG δέ No. 2) The conjunction does not connect opposing statements. It connects a qualifying statement. **10:6** ρ BDAG δέ def. 1-3 **10:6** π *this* **10:6** σ (i.q. 10:5 β) **10:6** ζ Hab. 2:4, I. *Mĕssiah's faithfulness;* II. *our faithfulness* ▷ Paul anticipates a Jewish objection based on Lev. 18:5. The text idea is that obedience preserves spiritual life. But the Leviticus text does not say that obedience restores life after a sentence of death has been passed. That is, a guilty verdict (unto death) cannot be reversed by

⁶ᵇ "YOU SHALL NOT HAVE SAID IN YOUR HEART⁶, 'WHO WILL ASCEND INTO HEAVEN?'" This is to bring the Anŏinted *One* down, ⁷or "'WHO WILL DESCEND INTO THE ABYSS?'" This is to bring the Anŏinted *One* up from the dead. ⁸But what is it saying? "THE WORD IS NEAR YOU, IN YOUR MOUTH AND IN YOUR HEART."

⁸ᵇThis is the word of the faithfulness^α which we are proclaiming, ⁹because if you may have confessed with your mouth, Adŏnai Yĕshua, and may have ᵝpledged ᵞfaithfulness in your heart, because^δ the Almĭghty raised him from the dead, you will be rescued. ¹⁰Because by the heart one ᶿis confirmed faithful to ^αrighteousness, and by the mouth ᵠone confesses oneself unto deliverance.

¹¹Because the scripture is saying, "ANYONE ᵟCONFIRMING FAITHFULNESS TO

---

good works, either those imputed from one's own merit against demerit, or those imputed from Jewish ancestors with merit left over for others. This is because the law does not allow declaring the guilty innocent, so righteousness from elsewhere cannot be credited against the demerit. Lev. 18:5 merely summarizes the means of remaining in divine favor. See Exodus 20:6; John 14:21; 15:10. ▷ In vs. 6 Paul alludes to Hab. 2:4 (cf. Gal. 3:11b-12 where he pairs up the same two texts) which explain in parallelism the same idea as Lev. 18:5. He has already explained the messianic application of Hab. 2:4 back in Rom. 3:22. Here he is merely equivocating DOING THE LAW in Lev. 18:5 with FAITHFULNESS in Hab. 2:4, and the same results in both texts: the subject WILL LIVE.

10:6b β Deu 9:4 **10:6b** δ Deu 30:12 **10:6b** θ Deu 30:13 'cross the sea;' The point of the quoted text is that faithfulness is not too hard, (כִּי הַמִּצְוָה הַזֹּאת אֲשֶׁר אָנֹכִי מְצַוְּךָ הַיּוֹם לֹא־נִפְלֵאת הִוא מִמְּךָ וְלֹא רְחֹקָה הִוא), Deu. 30:11. Paul concludes the same, but he connects the sea with the deep or the abyss, and then death, or lawlessness, which took the ransom, so now sin's prisoner will be released upon repentance to live faithfully. Considering a person's former demerits as weighty enough to keep them enslaved to the grave denies that Messiah ransoms man from the grave, from the powers that lord it over man with death. ▷ "Who will ascend" according to the Rabbinic doctrine is based on extra merit (זְכוּת) beyond ordinary duty credited (imputed) against one's demerits. Thus, who will ascend is based on having enough merit to ascend, whether one's own or that freely bestowed from the Patriarchs. This legally imputed merit is used to discharge one's case before Gŏd with a verdict of innocent. This doctrine brings Mĕssiah down, because (1) it is not based on genuine forgiveness. It makes him and his father unforgiving. (2) It brings Mĕssiah down from his own standard of justice since he is acquitting the guilty. (3) It lowers Gŏd's righteousness to something that will compensate for sin, i.e. reverse all damages. ▷ "Who will descend," i.e. who has too much demerit to be offset by merits for an acquittal. This brings Mĕssiah up from the grave because the ability of the sinner to plead guilty, repent, and take up Mĕssiah's offer to ransom him is still being denied. ▷ Mĕssiah's ransom is a sign of Gŏd's favorable justice in forgiveness, and not a reparation (satisfaction) of the damage of sin. It shows the cost of sin. It is lawlessness that took the ransom. And so death has to let its prisoner go free.

10:8 ρ Deut 30:14. THE WORD is defined in Deut. 30:8-16 to be the commandments given through Mosheh in the plains of Moab. Paul does not quote the whole context. You have to read it to see that by WORD he means keeping the commandments in the Law. See also 1 Yoḥ. 2:3-4 and 15:10. **10:8b** α τοῦτ' ἔστιν τὸ ῥῆμα τῆς πίστεως **10:9** β *confirmed, affirmed, promised* **10:9** γ *loyalty, fealty, fidelity* **10:9** δ ὅτι Paul defines "faithfulness" as "the word" which he just connected by his quotation to Gŏd's commandments. Immediately following the word "HEART," where Paul ends his quotation, the Hebrew text continues, "TO DO IT" (לַעֲשֹׂתוֹ). So it is plain that πίστις (>πίστεως) does not simply mean belief, or trust, or even faith in the modern sense, but must mean fidelity, loyalty, faithfulness. Therefore, it must mean the same in Hab. 2:4. Paul's proof text and context spell checkmate for Calvinist, Lutheran and Augustinian interpretations. Faithfulness begins with the promise (pledge) to be loyal. It is because he was raised from the dead. It is plain that ὅτι means *because* here, and not "that," since we are not talking about believing a mere assertion in the context. Faithfulness is confirmed to the Almĭghty from the heart on the basis of the evidence of the resurrection of Mĕssiah, and not simply belief in the fact thereof. **10:9** β→faithfulness: or *held faithful*.

10:10 θ→faithful, or: *confirms oneself faithful*, πιστεύεται VPIM/P-3S **10:10** α I. *administration of justice* (as mercy via a ransom); II. *administration of righteousness,* (in a positive sense) **10:10** ψ ὁμολογεῖται V-PIM/P-3S (middle voice) Again Paul means both I and II. ▷ (10:10α.II): One is confirmed faithful in the heart unto the righteousness of sanctification, pledging to be set apart, to become holy. (α.I): Also one is confirmed faithful in the heart to the administration of favorable justice, because we have been shown mercy in the circumstance of our

Romans 11

HIM WILL NOT ᵞBE ASHAMED.ᵃ" ¹²Because there is no difference for Yehudi, besides also for Greek, because the same Adŏnai is Adŏnai of all, abounding in riches to all who call on him, ¹³because, "ALL WHO MAY CALL UPON THE NAME OF YĂHWEH WILL BE RESCUED.ᵝ"

¹⁴How then shall they have called to whom they have not confirmed faithfulness? And how shall they have pledged faithfulness for whom they have not heard? And how will they have listened without someone announcing? ¹⁵How will they have announced unless they will have been sent? Just as it has been getting written, "HOW BEAUTIFUL ARE THE FEET OF THOSE WHO BRING GOOD NEWS OF GOOD THINGS!ᵋ" ¹⁶However, they did not all listen to the good news, because Yeshayahu says, "YĂHWEH, WHO HAS HELD OUR MESSAGE FAITHFUL?ᵠ" ¹⁷So faithfulness comes from listening, and listening by the word of the Anŏinted One.

¹⁸But I ask, have they not heard? On the contrary, "THEIR VOICE HAS GONE OUT INTO ALL THE EARTH, AND THEIR WORDS TO THE ENDS OF THE WORLD.ᵃ" ¹⁹But I ask, did Yisra'el not know? First Mosheh says, "I WILL MAKE YOU JEALOUS BY THAT WHICH IS NOT A NATION. BY A NATION WITHOUT UNDERSTANDING I WILL ANGER YOU.ˣ" ²⁰And Yeshayahu is very bold and says, "I WAS FOUND BY THOSE WHO SOUGHT ME NOT. I BECAME MANIFEST TO THOSE WHO DID NOT ASK FOR ME.ᵝ" ²¹But as for Yisra'el he says, "ALL THE DAY LONG I HAVE STRETCHED OUT MY HANDS TO A DISOBEDIENT AND BACK TALKING PEOPLE.ᶿ"

11

¹I ask then, has the Almĭghty rejected his people? May it never be! For I too am a Yisra'eli, a descendant of Avraham, of the tribe of Binyamin. ²The Almĭghty has not rejected his people whom he chose before. Or have you not been knowing what the Scripture says about Eliyahu, how he pleads with the Almĭghty against Yisra'el? ³"YĂHWEH, THEY HAVE KILLED YOUR PROPHETS, THEY HAVE TORN DOWN YOUR ALTARS, AND I ALONE AM LEFT, AND THEY ARE SEEKING MY LIFE.ᶿ" ⁴But what is the oracle to him? "I HAVE KEPT FOR MYSELF SEVEN THOUSAND MEN WHO HAVE NOT BOWED THE KNEE TO BA'AL.ᵝ"

⁵In the same way then, there has also been coming to be at the present time a remnant according to the choice of loving-kindness. ⁶But if it is by loving kindnessᵠ, it is still not based on *the customary* ᵋworks! Otherwise loving-kind-

---

repentance (cf. Exodus 20:6; 34:6-7). ▷ The passive/middle verb (θ) is a severe difficulty for the many who wish the verb to mean *believe*, or *trust*, which would give the sense 'one is trusted/believed,' or 'one trusts/believes oneself' (middle voice). In fact most translations ignore the passive and give an active sense. The implied subject is the faithful person. See 1Tim. 3:16 ; Rom 3:2; 2Thes. 1:10; 1Tim. 1:11; Tit. 1:3. **10:10** θ→confirmed: or, *is held faithful* **10:11** α Isa. 28:16 **10:11** δ→HIM: or, *holding faithful upon him* **10:11** λ→ashamed = LXX = יְבוֹשׁ MT: יָחִישׁ
10:13 β Joel 2:32 **10:15** ξ Isa. 52:7; **10:16** ψ Isa. 53:1 **10:18** α Psa. 19:4 **10:19** χ Deut. 32:21 **10:20** β Isa. 65:1 **10:21** θ Isa. 65:2.
11:3 θ 1 Kings 19:10, 14 **11:4** β 1 Kings 19:18 **11:6** ψ The context or concept of 'loving kindness' is covenantal. See Exodus 20:6, viz: וְעֹשֶׂה

חֶסֶד לַאֲלָפִים לְאֹהֲבַי וּלְשֹׁמְרֵי מִצְוֹתַי, AND DOING LOVING KINDNESS (OR MERCY) TO THE THOUSANDTH GENERATION OF THOSE LOVING ME AND GUARDING MY COMMANDMENTS." For this reason, the Christian concept of 'grace' being unmerited favor bestowed on a totally depraved humanity is heresy. **11:6** ε Works means the doctrine of merit for demerit, i.e. that works atone for demerit. See Rom. 3:20. ▷ Paul disapproves of works, so called, as they are defined by the Rabbis. This does not mean ordinary obedience to the commandments, because that is doing only what is required. Works in the Jewish conception are considered doing deeds beyond the call of duty, so that they will be able to offset demerits (sins). This system is an extra-biblical system of atonement, of appeasement of divine disfavor. ▷ Since this is only what Paul means, the commandments of Torah are necessary for those seeking everlasting life (cf. Rom. 2:7; Mat. 20:16-26;

ness would not still be loving-kindness. ⁷What then? What Yisra'el is seeking, it has not obtained? Yet, the chosen obtain it, and the rest have and will have been hardened, ⁸just as it has been getting written, "THE ALMĬGHTY GIVES THEM A SPIRIT OF STUPOR, EYES TO SEE NOT AND EARS TO HEAR NOT^α" past this very day. ⁹And David says, "LET THEIR TABLE BECOME A SNARE AND A TRAP AND A STUMBLING BLOCK AND A RETRIBUTION TO THEM. ¹⁰LET THEIR EYES BE DARKENED TO SEE NOT, AND MAKE BENT THEIR BACKS CONTINUALLY^β."

¹¹I ask then, did they stumble so that they will have fallen? May it never be! But by their transgression deliverance is come to the nations, making them jealous. ¹²Now if their transgression is riches for the world and their failure is riches for the nations, how much more will their fullness be! ¹³But I am speaking to you about the nations. Inasmuch then as I am an emissary for the nations, I magnify my ministry, ¹⁴if somehow I might move to jealousy my fellow countrymen and may have rescued some of them, ¹⁵because if their rejection is the reconciliation of the world, what will their acceptance be but life from the dead?

¹⁶If the first fruit is holy, the lump is also. And if the root is holy, the branches are too. ¹⁷But if some of the branches were broken off, and you being a wild olive, were grafted in among them, and became partaker with them of the rich root of the olive tree, ¹⁸do not be rejoicing against the fallen branches, but if you rejoice against them, it is not you who supports the root, but the root that supports you. ¹⁹You will say then, "Branches were broken off so that I may be grafted in." ²⁰Quite right!? They were broken off because of their unfaithfulness, but you have been standing by your faithfulness. Do not be getting high minded, but be getting afraid, ²¹because if the Almĭghty did not spare the natural branches, he will not spare you, either.

²²Behold then the kindness and severity of the Almĭghty. To those who fell, severity, but to you, the Almĭghty's kindness, if you may be continuing in his kindness, otherwise you also will be cut off. ²³And they also, if they may not be continuing in their unfaithfulness, will be grafted in, because the Almĭghty is able to graft them in again. ²⁴Because if you were cut off from what is by nature a wild olive tree, and were grafted to the side of nature into a cultivated olive tree, how much more will these who are the natural ones be grafted into their own olive tree?

²⁵Because I am not wanting you, brothers, to be ignorant of this mystery, so that you may not be wise beyond your own wisdom, because a partial hardening has been happening to Yisra'el until THE FULLNESS OF THE NATIONS^α will have entered in. ²⁶And this way all Yisra'el will be rescued, just as it has been

---

Mark 10:17-31; Rev. 22:14; Hab. 2:4; Lev. 18:5). ▷ Besides 'works' in Judaism, the faithful should walk clear of merit in Christianity. The Church eliminated the possibility of extra good works by generally defining all possible good work as required work for polemical reasons (and then they made exceptions, especially when money was involved), thus there is no such thing as a deed beyond what is required. In order to provide the need for merit to fill in the empty blanks where demerit was forgiven (but really paid for after Anselm), the Church called on the infinite merit of Christ to be legally credited to the account of the believer. This is similar to the Jewish doctrine of the "merit of the fathers," which a Jew would obtain (from the amazingly infinite well of extra merit Abraham had) if they did not have enough merit of their own. So the Christian system is the same, just with different labels. ▷ Paul uses "works" here as an abbreviation of the "customary works" stated earlier. **11:8** α Isa 6:9-10, 29:10; **11:9-10** β Psa 69:22-23.

11:25 α Gen 48:19: וְזַרְעוֹ יִהְיֶה מְלֹא־הַגּוֹיִם

11:26 ρ Isa 59:20: וּבָא לְצִיּוֹן גּוֹאֵל; γ Zec 3:9: וּמַשְׁתִּי

getting written, "THE DELIVERER WILL COME FROM TSIYON, and he WILL REMOVE IRREVERENCE FROM YAʻAQOV. ²⁷AND THIS IS MY COVENANT WITH THEM, WHEN I SHALL HAVE TAKEN AWAY THEIR SINS."

²⁸With respect to the good news they are enemies because of you, but with respect to being chosen they are beloved for the sake of the fathers, ²⁹because the gifts and the calling from the Almĭghty are irrevocable. ³⁰Because just as you once were disobedient to the Almĭghty, yet now have been shown mercy, because of their disobedience, ³¹so these also now have been disobedient to the mercy applied to you, so that even they now may be given mercy, ³²because the Almĭghty has confined all for being disobedient, wherein he may show mercy to all.

³³Oh the deepness of the riches, and of the wisdom and knowledge of the Almĭghty! How unfathomable are his judgments and untraceable his ways! ³⁴Because WHO HAS KNOWN THE MIND OF YĂHWEH, OR WHO BECAME HIS COUNSELOR?" ³⁵Or WHO HAS FIRST GIVEN TO HIM THAT IT WILL BE PAID BACK TO HIM AGAIN?ʸ ³⁶Because from him and by means of him and for him are all things. To him be the glory for all the ages. Amen.

12

Therefore I urge you, brothers, by the mercies of the Almĭghty, to present your bodies *as a* living and holy sacrifice, acceptable to the Almĭghty, which is your reasonable worship. ²And do not be getting yourselves conformed to this age, but be getting yourselves transformed by the renewing of the mind, so that you may ξprove what the will of the Almĭghty is, that which is good and acceptable and perfect.

³Because through the loving-kindness given to me I say to everyone among you not to think beyond what it is necessary to think, but to think so as to have sound judgment, as the Almĭghty divided to each a measure of πofficial duty.

⁴Because just as we have many members in one body and all the members do

---

זאת Isa 59:21: λ אֶת־עֲוֹן הָאָרֶץ־הַהִיא בְּיוֹם אֶחָד; =? **11:27** δ Isa 27:9: הָסִר חַטָּאתוֹ בְּרִיתִי אוֹתָם **𝔊**: ὅταν ἀφέλωμαι αὐτοῦ τὴν ἁμαρτίαν. But certainly Jer. 31:34: כִּי אֶסְלַח לַעֲוֹנָם = ὅταν ἀφέλωμαι τὰς ἁμαρτίας αὐτῶν. Here the ref. has been concealed by the Septuagint choosing a dynamic translation: "when I (take away) forgive their iniquity (sins)." The connection is exposed by Ep. Alex. 8:12, where כִּי is translated ὅτι instead of ὅταν. The Hebrew may mean either, but Paul used ὅταν, which places the covenantal pardon in the future. See Lev. 26:40-45; Deut. 30:1-16. In the Ep. Alex. and LXX, Jer. 31:34 is poorly translated: ὅτι ἵλεως ἔσομαι ταῖς ἀδικίαις αὐτῶν = *because merciful I will be to their iniquities.* The reason for the confusion is the previous denial that the so called 'new covenant' is in reality a renewal of the promises to Yisra'el. See denials in Expositor's Greek Testament, and Barnes. See affirmation in Jamieson-Fausset-Brown Bible Commentary, and Adam Clarke. **11:34** ξ Isa. 40:13; 1 Cor. 2:16. **11:34** η Isa. 40:14 **11:35** γ Job 35:7; 41:11.

12:2 ξ = *check by testing, validate.* **12:3** π→duty: faithfulness. A duty or ministry that requires faithfulness. The usual translations have "faith" here leading to an unintelligible sense or bad theology, but the idea is similar to being committed a public trust. The word is used for an appointment to an office that requires responsibility and trust. The office requires the servant to be faithful, or to be one holding faithful. See 2Chron. 31:15, 18 for this usage. **12:3** χ→faith: "According to the analogy of the faith:" This is to say that the illustrations given must correspond to the truths of the faith. A prophet here is one who exposits on Scripture or who is able to illustrate a truth with Scripture for edification, exhortation, and consolation. See 1 Cor. 14:3. The normative use of this gift does not involve prediction, which is a prophet extraordinaire. The regular use of this gift requires study and prayer; expositions may occur to many mature faithful when stimulated by others. It is not standard teaching. It is often revelatory both to the prophet and the audience as something not seen in Scripture before is brought to mind. The limits of this sermonizing or making of homilies is the known facts of the faith, the most important of which is confirming and upholding the Torah of the Almĭghty. The lack of this is the main reason why this gift is ill used by many professing the faith. It occurs best in something like a moderated discussion of Scripture by those who uphold it. The activity of the Holy Spirit occurs at the subjective level, and he

not have the same function, ⁵so we, who are many, are one body through⁽ᵉᵛ⁾ the Anŏinted, and individually members one of another. ⁶We have gifts that differ according to the favor given to us. If it is prophecy, let it be ˣin agreement with the pledge of faithfulness. ⁷If it is service, let it be in his serving, or he who teaches, in his teaching, ⁸or he who exhorts, in his exhortation. If it is he who gives, let it be with liberality, or he who leads, with diligence. If it is he who shows mercy, let it be with cheerfulness.

⁹Let love be without hypocrisy. Abhor what is evil. Cling to what is good. ¹⁰Be devoted to one another in brotherly love. Give preference to one another in honor, ¹¹not lagging behind in diligence, enthusiastic in spirit, serving Yăhweн, ¹²rejoicing in confident expectation, persevering in tribulation, devoted to prayer, ¹³contributing to the needs of the holy ones, practicing hospitality.

¹⁴Be blessing those who persecute you. Be blessing and do not be cursing. ¹⁵Be rejoicing with the rejoicing, weeping with the weeping. ¹⁶Be of the same mind toward one another. Do not be haughty in mind, but associate with the lowly. Do not be getting wise beyond yourselves. ¹⁷Never pay back evil for evil to anyone. Respect what is right in the sight of all men. ¹⁸If possible, so far as it depends on you, be at peace with all men. ¹⁹Never take your own revenge, beloved, but leave room for the wrath of the Almĭghty, because it has been getting written, "VENGEANCE IS MINE. I WILL REPAY,ᶝ" says Yăhweн. ²⁰But IF YOUR ENEMY MAY BE HUNGERING, BE FEEDING HIM, AND IF HE MAY BE THIRSTING, BE GIVING HIM A DRINK, BECAUSE IN SO DOING YOU WILL HEAP BURNING COALS UPON HIS HEAD⁰.

²¹Do not be getting conquered by evil, but be getting victory over evil with good.

13

¹Let every soul be subjecting itself to the higher authorities, because there is no legitimate authority except under the Almĭghty, and those which are existing, having been getting set up under the Almĭghty, are *such*. ²So whoever resists the authority really has been opposing the ordinance of the Almĭghty, and those who have been opposing will receive condemnation against themselves, ³since rulers are not a cause of fear respecting a good deed, but against the evil deed. So do you want to have no fear of the authority? Be doing what is good and you will have praise from the same, ⁴because he is a servant of the Almĭghty to you for good. Yet if you may be doing an evil thing, be fearing, because he is not carrying the sword for nothing, because he is a servant of the Almĭghty, an avenger who brings wrath on the one doing an evil thing.

⁵Therefore it is necessary to be in subjection, not only because of wrath, but also for conscience' sake. ⁶Because of this you also pay levies, because they are ministers of the Almĭghty, attending to this very thing. ⁷Return to all what is owed them. Levy to whom levy is due, tax to whom tax is due, respect to whom respect is due, honor to whom honor is due.

⁸Be owing nothing to anyone, except to love one another, because the one

---

always points us to objective confirmations of what he is trying to teach us, mainly from Scripture. Therefore the prophet does not try to validate anything from his own private experiences.

12:19 ᶝ Deu 32:35, Psa 94:1, See App. XII. **12:20** ω Pro 25:21-22.

loving another has been filling up the Law. ⁹Indeed this, "YOU SHALL NOT COMMIT ADULTERY,ᵅ YOU SHALL NOT MURDER, YOU SHALL NOT STEAL, YOU SHALL NOT COVET," and whenever *there is* any other commandment, in this saying it is getting summed up, "YOU SHALL LOVE YOUR NEIGHBOR AS YOURSELF.ᵝ" ¹⁰Love does no wrong to a neighbor. Therefore love is the ᵞfulfilling of the Law.

¹¹Do this, having been knowing the time, that it is already the hour for you to be awakened from sleep, because now our deliverance is nearer to us than when we first pledged faithfulness. ¹²The night has advanced, yet the day has been drawing near. Therefore we should lay aside the deeds of the darkness and we should put on the weapons of light. ¹³We should walk properly as in daytime, not in revelry and drunkenness, not in sexual promiscuity and sensual liberties, not in strife and jealousy. ¹⁴But put on our Adŏnai Yĕshua the Anŏinted, and be making no provision for the flesh in regard to its lusts.

Are we not allowed to eat beef, fowl, or fish?

14 ¹Now be welcoming the one who is weak in ˣthe faithfulness but not for scrutinizing his reasoning. ²One indeed holds faithful, ᵋeating ᵞeach of these, but he who is weak eats vegetables only. ³Let not the one who is eating be despising the one who is not eating, and let not the one who is not eating be ᵟjudging the one who is eating, because the Almĭghty has welcomed him. ⁴Who are you to judge the servant of another? To his own master he stands or falls, and he will stand, for Yăhweμ is able to make him stand.

13:9 *α* Deu 5:17-21, Exo 20:13-17 **13:9** β Lev 19:18 **13:10** ν The easiest commands are listed first. See Mat. 19:16f; Mark 10:17f. Every commandment is founded on love, including the Şabbaτh commandment, priestly laws, purity laws, prohibitions against eating unclean things, and even circumcision. Gŏd also is "your neighbor," because he is watching, because the creation is his and every creature in it. Idolatry is to rob Gŏd of his due place and true character. Even the Şabbaτh was made to honor Gŏd as Creator. Keeping Şabbaτh loves our neighbors, our children, the alien, and our spouse by giving them rest. When we do not rest on it, we are at least indirectly enslaving our neighbor, and robbing them of the rest Gŏd made for them (Mark 2:27)! Therefore all commandments are based on love.

14:1 χ τῇ. The article *the* points to and emphasizes the behaviour that constitutes ideal or perfect faithfulness. **14:2** ε φαγεῖν. Cf. Wallace, page 601f. **14:2** γ √ See BDAG "πᾶς ❶ each," and also the plural is brought out, "of these." See concordance entries for *each of these*. Also "As a summation of what precedes *all this*," and "*all (of them) (in contrast to a part)*" (BDAG). Paul refers to both meat and wine.

If translated, *everything*, it cannot mean anything at all. No one holds faithful in eating that which he knows will poison or contaminate him. ▷ But Paul means all that was included within the scope of the known controversy, namely meat and wine. ▷ He is responding to a question frequently raised among Roman Jews, which he encountered, so that he does not have to repeat it or perhaps the question was put anew straight to him by correspodence or messenger. Paul answers such questions elsewhere without stating the question.

Paul was getting asked how to deal with who said they should eat vegetables only. His answer was that their excluding meat or wine is not a matter that should be argued with them. ▷ Some arguments for vegetarianism may be related to *zechut* (merit). **14:3** δ Paul is definitely implying by his choice of words, 'despising' vs. 'judging' that meat eating is lawfully permitted. In other words, a conviction to vegetarianism is a private conviction that should not be despised by others, and the vegetarian should not judge those who eat meat. Just the same, to be a conscientious objector is a private conviction not to be despised, but neither should the objector pass judgment on those who fight in war, because this is lawfully permitted. ▷ Nowhere does Paul say one must give up a food restriction conviction to please another. He who respects the conviction of another is loving his brother. It is general courtesy to eat whatever a host provides, but obligation to this custom ends at the point where conviction begins, whether it is a private conviction or conviction by the divine Law, or even a health concern. The more corrupt a culture is, the greater the offense of not eating will be, because in some cultures every house has a shrine in it, and the cook sacrifices the meal to their gods. It is forbidden by law to partake of this food. But the lawless have elevated the courtesy of eating everything a host puts in front of one to a divine absolute, and by doing so they are causing massive spiritual damage on those who are compelled to eat. The goal of the lawless is to intimidate everyone else

⁵One person decides for one ⁿ*fast* day over another *fast* day. Another decides for every ⁿ*fast* day. Let each person be fully convincing himself in his own mind. ⁶ᵃThe one setting his mind to ˣthe day is setting his mind for Yăhwe₁‌. ⁶ᵇHe who is eating, for Yăhwe₁‌ is eating, because he is giving thanks to the Almĭghty. ⁶ᶜAnd he who is not eating, for Yăhwe₁‌ he is not eating, and is giving thanks to the Almĭghty, ⁷because not one of us is living for himself, and not one is dying for himself.

⁸Because if as well we may be living, we are living for Yăhwe₁‌. If as well we may be dying, we are dying for Yăhwe₁‌. Therefore whether we may be living, *or* whether we may be dying, we are Yăhwe₁‌'s. ⁹Because to this end *the* Anŏinted died and lived again, so that he will have been Adŏnai over both the dead and the living. ¹⁰But you, why do you judge your brother? Or you again, why do you regard your brother with contempt? Because we will all stand before the judgment seat of the Almĭghty. ¹¹Because it has been getting written, "As I live, says Yăhweh, every knee will bow to me, and every tongue will give praise to the Almĭghty‡." ¹²So then each one of us will give an account of himself to the Almĭghty. ¹³Therefore, let us not be judging one another anymore, but rather determine this, not to be putting an obstacle or a stumbling block in a brother's way.

¹⁴I have been knowing, and have been getting persuaded in Adŏnai Yĕshua, that nothing is ˢsharing defilement ᵘon its own ⁿ(*to the heart*), except to him who

---

into being lawless like they are.

14:5 η Supply *fast* from the context (vs. 6c)
14:6a χ→day: Generic article. Paul means any day or every day here. The faithful set their minds for every day for Yăhwe₁‌. Both he who eats and does not eat is minding the day for Yăhwe₁‌. Vs. 6a is a guideline for every day. Vs. 6b and 6c show how both are setting their mind for Yăhwe₁‌. **14:6a** ᵀ C³ Ψ 33 𝔐 sy add 'And the one not setting his mind for the day, to Lord is not setting his mind.' The phrase was added to separate the 'day' theme from the 'eating' theme, so as to allow the issue to be redefined as a Sabbath and Sunday issue. Internal corruption is detectable in the last phrase: κυρίῳ οὐ φρονεῖ. One cannot 'not mind' a day to Adŏnai; whether eating or fasting one is minding the day to Adŏnai. To cover this up the translators of the extra clause translate 'observe' which indeed is the meaning of a completely different Greek word (τηρέω). External corruption is evident in that the omission is supported by no MSS before the Vth century. The words are lacking in: 𝔓⁴⁶ ℵ A B C²ᵛⁱᵈ D F G, etc. In addition 𝔓⁴⁶ also lacks a καὶ which probably was also used to divide the text. ▷ Judaism regards fasting as a *zechut*.

14:11 ϕ Isa 45:23 **14:14** ζ→defilement: κοινὸν = sharable, that is communicating defilement. This word does not mean 'unclean,' and is nowhere used in the Septuagint (LXX) or Apostolic Writings to mean such. It refers to the concept of sharing defilement, by the transfer of defilement from one thing to another. For this reason even clean food could acquire the property of transferring defilement, if it came into contact with something reckoned as unclean. {MT—pDLNT}

14:14 μ→own, δι' ἑαυτοῦ, *through itself, by itself*. This means by unknown accident or unintentionally. A clean food that has acquired the property of transferring defilement, that is not reckoned to have this property, cannot defile the soul, i.e. make the conscience guilty, or the soul abominable. **14:14** η→heart: See Mark 7:19a for necessary context. **14:14** λ→ λογιζομένῳ: Paul could have used the word *knowing* here. The reason he does not, is because he wants to focus on what the person subjectively thinks: his opinions, whether right or wrong. If one reckons that eating X shares defilement, then to eat it is to share the defilement with the conscience, because it is now guilty regardless of whether the opinion was right or wrong. The thing sharing defilement does not enter him by itself, by accident, but with him reckoning (knowing) it to defile him. ▷ An unclean 'food' such as pork "is unclean on its own," (through itself, or by itself) whether eaten accidentally or not. But it cannot share defilement to the soul if eaten accidentally. This is why Paul used the word κοινὸν (sharable). Because to use ἀκάθαρτος (unclean), as illegitimately put in the versions, would be to deny what is known by the law, and would be to suggest that only a wrong subjective opinion makes a 'food' unclean to the person who has an incorrect opinion. But by λογιζομένῳ Paul does not mean only subjective and incorrect opinion. He includes correct opinion also. Violating the real law likewise is sharing defilement to the soul. **14:14** θ→defilement: because it is not 'through itself' (δι' ἑαυτοῦ). See 14:14 μ. Because it is not an accident or unintentional. But if someone knowingly makes his soul abominable, then defilement is shared with it: ▷

Romans 14

is ^λtaking into account anything to be sharing defilement. To him ^θit is sharing defilement. ^15Because if through food your brother is hurt, you are no longer walking according to love. Do not be destroying with your food him on behalf of whom the Anŏinted died.

^16However, do not let what is for you a good thing be getting spoken of as evil, ^17because the kingdom of the Almĭghty is not eating and drinking, but justice and peace and joy in the Holy Spĭrit. ^18Because, he who in this way serves the Anŏinted is acceptable to the Almĭghty and approved by men. ^19So then, we should be pursuing the things which make for peace and the building up of one another.

^20Do not be tearing down the work of the Almĭghty for the sake of food. Both of these are clean ^θin the clean, but they are evil for the man who through

---

Here is what the Law does say: If someone touched a source of uncleanness and did not wash his hands then the contamination could be communicated to clothes or body. See Lev. 15:11. This is classified as a type II contamination. It is not a sin to have it. It is not a sin to touch a sick person. It was only a sin if it was communicated so as to cause damage, e.g. to the holy places. Handwashing prevented the damage. See Lev. 15:31. ▷ There is also a commandment not to make one's soul abominable or unclean by eating unclean things (Lev. 11:43-44). It was a sin to do so. This is classified as a type I impurity. Knowingly breaking the commandment defiles the soul. Intention to eat what is unclean is required to 'make one's soul abominable:' אַל־תְּשַׁקְּצוּ אֶת־נַפְשֹׁתֵיכֶם. You shall not make to be abominable your souls. ▷ Here is where the Rabbis erased the criteria of intentionality: According to the Perushim, the hands may touch some impurity, and this imparted type II ritual impurity. But if the hands now touched food, say bread, or a piece of fruit, then the type II impurity transferred to the bread or fruit, making it "sharable." Then if the person ate the bread or fruit, he was defiling his soul with a type I impurity, making his soul an abomination or unclean. ▷ The Perushim were teaching that ritual impurity (type II) was communicable to the soul by communicable hands. It became a type I impurity. The food became forbidden after being touched. Yĕshua and Paul rejected this doctrine. Mĕssiah specifically rejects this doctrine of the sharability of impurity with the soul by secondary means, i.e. unwashed hands. Paul more generally rejects the idea that type II impurity can be transferred to proper (clean) food "of itself," by accident, so as to defile the soul of the person eating it, with only the exception that if the person recognizes he actually is eating something which has become unclean by communication of defilement, then to that person it becomes defiling to the soul. ▷ Minute amounts of impurities do not defile the soul if consumed without notice. The impurity is removed by the elimination system. Therefore a type I defilement of the soul cannot occur from anything unclean that "enters of itself" into the body. ▷ See notes on Mark 7. There are two levels of contamination. Type I contaminates the soul and heart, because something unclean is consumed with intentionality. Type II contamination is that which is natural to man, but considered profane in the holy places or a risk to good health otherwise.

Paul spells out the middle voice verb used in Matthew and Mark, "on its own," "by itself" δι' ἑαυτοῦ. This means by accident, without intentionality, without being noticed. So if any contamination is shared this way, then it does not share defilement to the heart, a type I contamination. It may only share (possibly) a type II contamination that simply makes one ritually impure. Such impurity is only a sin if taken into the holy place or someone did not wash and someone else gets sick because of it. Type I impurity is always a sin. Paul is only dealing with type I defilement, however, because he is dealing with matters of the heart, condemnation and approval. Someone who contracts type I contamination with intentionality is proving themselves unfaithful to Mĕssiah. ▷ Paul does not consider second degree, accidental contamination, of itself, to confer type I impurity to the heart. But he states an exception. If a person reckons impurity to be shared with an otherwise clean food, then to that person it will share the type I contamination, because the person will not be consuming it by accident without intentionality. ▷ Therefore, it is critically important that the word κοινός does not mean itself defiled or unclean things. Paul is not saying unclean things are only unclean to those who think so. This word is never used in the Greek bible to indicate something directly unclean or unfit for food. It does not even occur in the Septuagint for matters of ritual purity or clean and unclean things. The word was used among Greek Jews before the second Temple was destroyed to mean the *communicability* of impurity. What motivated the Perushim and Rabbis to complicate the ritual purity law was the desire to be ritually holy all the time, or as much as possible, even where it was not required. The doctrine of *zechut* motivates such developments. They probably made this *zekut* (merit) at first and then made it a requirement. The Rabbis also wanted to keep the Jewish community separate from non-Jews, and the way they did this was to make their ritual purity rules difficult.

14:20 θ→clean. The Ancient Ethiopean Bible has these words ኩሉ ፡ ንጹሕ ፡ በንጹሕ (cf. John Gill and verified reading: TESTAMENTVM NOVVM CVM EPISTOLA PAVLI, ANNO M.D. XLVIII, 1548); as well codex Sinaiticus ℵ² The words τοις καθαροις (ΤΟΙΣΚΑΘΑΡΟΙΣ) were copied into the margin of Codex Sinaiticus by a corrector sometime after the 4th century and before the end of the 7th century

stumbling eats. ²¹It is good not to eat meat or to drink wine, or whatever makes your brother stumble. ²²The confidence which you have, be having as your own conviction before the Almĭghty. Happy is he who does not condemn himself in what he approves. ²³And the one who is doubting will have been condemning himself if he will have eaten, because it is not from faithfulness. And all which is not from faithfulness is sin.

15

Now we who are strong ought to bear the weaknesses of those without strength and not please ourselves. ²Let each of us be benefiting his neighbor for his good, to his edification. ³Because even the Anŏinted did not benefit himself, but as it has been getting written, "THE REPROACHES OF THOSE WHO REPROACHED YOU FELL UPON ME^ψ."

⁴Because as much as was written in earlier times was written for our instruction, so that through perseverance and the encouragement of the writings we may be having hope. ⁵Now may the Almĭghty who patiently endures and gives encouragement grant you to be of the same heart with one another according to the Anŏinted Yĕshua, ⁶so that with one accord, with one voice, you may be glorifying the Almĭghty and Făther of our Adŏnai Yĕshua the Anŏinted.

⁷Therefore, be receiving one another, just as the Anŏinted also received us to the glory of the Almĭghty. ⁸Because I am saying the Anŏinted One has been making himself a servant of the circumcision on behalf of the truth of the Almĭghty to confirm the promises to the fathers, ⁹and the nations, on account of *his* mercy, to glorify the Almĭghty, as it has been getting written, "THEREFORE I WILL GIVE PRAISE TO YOU AMONG THE NATIONS, AND I WILL SING TO YOUR NAME^α." ¹⁰And again he says, "REJOICE, YE NATIONS, WITH HIS PEOPLE^β." ¹¹And again, "LET ALL THE NATIONS BE PRAISING YĂHWEĦ, AND LET ALL THE PEOPLES PRAISE HIM^δ." ¹²Again Yeshayahu says, "THERE WILL COME THE ROOT OF YISHAI, EVEN HE WHO ARISES TO RULE THE NATIONS. UPON HIM WILL THE NATIONS PUT THEIR CONFIDENCE^θ."

¹³Now may the Almĭghty of hope fill you with all joy and peace in holding faithful, so that you will abound in hope by the power of the Holy Spĭrit.

¹⁴And, I have been getting persuaded, my brothers, even me myself about you, that also you yourselves are full of goodness, having been getting filled with all knowledge and being able also to be educating one another. ¹⁵But I have written very boldly to you on some points so as to remind you again, because of the favor that was given me from the Almĭghty, ¹⁶to be a minister of

---

AD. The deletion needs no explanation, having arisen from the desire to reinterpret the passage toward the abolishment of the Levitical laws, and we have two witnesses testifying to the missing text. The passage parallels Titus 1:15, a third witness to Paul's meaning. It is another way of stating Romans 14:14. ▷ If the conscience is clean in what you eat, then accidental unclean things do not defile the conscience. 'All is clean in the clean.' If one knows they are violating a commandment by eating the wrong thing, then the conscience is not clean, and eating defiles it. There is nothing that can make the clean conscience common (defiled) by accident. ▷ The ancient Ethiopean Church kept kosher laws, the Ṣabbaṯh, and also circumcision. They permitted the mixing of milk and meat. **15:3** ψ Psa. 69:9 **15:9** α Psa 18:49, 2 Sam 22:50 **15:10** β Deu 32:43 ⑤ **15:11** δ Psa 117:1 **15:12** θ Isa 11:10

the Anŏinted Yĕshua to the nations, doing a priestly service for the good news of the Almĭghty, that the offering of the nations will have become acceptable, who have been getting made holy by the Holy Spĭrit.

¹⁷Therefore in the Anŏinted Yĕshua I have found reason for glorying in things pertaining to the Almĭghty, ¹⁸because I will not presume to speak of anything except what the Anŏinted is getting accomplished through me, for the listening submission of the nations by word and deed, ¹⁹by the power of signs and wonders, by the power of the Spĭrit, so that from Yerushalayim and round about as far as Illyricum I have been fully proclaiming the good news of the Anŏinted.

²⁰And so I am aspiring to be proclaiming the good news, not where the Anŏinted has been *already* named, so that I may not be building on another's foundation, ²¹but as it has been getting written, "THEY WHO HAD NO NEWS OF HIM WILL SEE, AND THEY WHO HAVE NOT BEEN HEARING WILL UNDERSTAND." ²²For this reason I have often been prevented from coming to you. ²³But now, with no further place for me in these regions, and since I have had for many years a longing to come to you ²⁴whenever I may be going to Spain, I expect to see you in passing, and to have been helped on my way there by you, when I have first enjoyed your company for a while.

²⁵But now, I am going to Yerushalayim, serving the holy ones, ²⁶because Macedonia and Achaia have been pleased to make a contribution for the poor among the holy ones in Yerushalayim. ²⁷Yes, they were pleased, and they are indebted to them. Because if the nations have shared in their spiritual things, they are indebted to minister to them also in material things. ²⁸Therefore, when I have finished this, and have put my seal on this fruit of theirs, I will go on by way of you to Spain.

²⁹I have been knowing that when I come to you, I will come in the fullness of the blessing of the Anŏinted. ³⁰Now I urge you, brothers, by our Adŏnai Yĕshua the Anŏinted and by the love of the Spĭrit, to strive together with me in your prayers near to the Almĭghty on my behalf, ³¹so that I may be rescued from those who are disobedient in Yehudah, and that my service for Yerushalayim will have proven acceptable to the holy ones, ³²so that having come to you in joy by the will of the Almĭghty, I may enjoy mutual rest with you. ³³Now the Almĭghty of peace be with you all. Amen.

16 I commend to you our sister Phoebe, who is also a servant of the assembly which is in Cenchrea, ²that you will have received her belonging to Yăhweh as worthy of the holy ones, and that you will have stood by her in whatever matter she may be needing from you, also because she has been a helper of many, and of myself. ³Greet Prisca and Aquila, my fellow workers belonging ᴱⱽ to the Anŏinted Yĕshua, ⁴who on behalf of my life risked their own necks, for whom not only do I give thanks, but also all the assemblies in the nations, ⁵and the assembly in their house. Greet Epaenetus, my beloved, who is a first fruit to the Anŏinted in Asia. ⁶Greet Miryam, who does many labors for

---

15:21 χ Isa. 52:15.

you. ⁷Greet Andronicus and Eunias, my kinsmen and my fellow prisoners, who are outstanding among the emissaries, who also have been coming into the Anŏinted before me. ⁸Greet Ampliatus, my beloved belonging to Yăhwe H. ⁹Greet Urbanus, our fellow worker belonging⁽ᵉᵛ⁾ to the Anŏinted, and Stachys my beloved. ¹⁰Greet Apelles, the approved belonging⁽ᵉᵛ⁾ to the Anŏinted. Greet those who belong to Aristobulus. ¹¹Greet Herodion, my kinsman. Greet those from Narcissus, being for⁽ᵉᵛ⁾ Yăhwe H. ¹²Greet Tryphaena and Tryphosa, who are working hard for Yăhwe H. Greet Persis the beloved, who has worked very hard for Yăhwe H. ¹³Greet Rufus, chosen for Yăhwe H, and his mother and mine. ¹⁴Greet Asyncritus, Phlegon, Hermes, Patrobas, Hermas and the brothers with them. ¹⁵Greet Philologus and Eulia, Nereus and his sister, and Olympas, and all the holy ones who are with them. ¹⁶Greet one another with a holy kiss. All the assemblies of the Anŏinted greet you. ¹⁷Now I urge you, brothers, to watch for those causing dissensions and hindrances alongside the teaching which you learned, and be turning away from them, ¹⁸because such ones are slaves, not of our Adŏnai the Anŏinted but of their own appetite, and by graceful words and pleasant sounding speech they deceive the hearts of those who practice no deceit. ¹⁹Because your submissive listening has touched all, therefore I am rejoicing over you, but I want you to be wise regarding good and innocent regarding evil. ²⁰The Almĭghty of peace will soon crush Satan under your feet. The loving-kindness of our Adŏnai Yĕshua be with you. ²¹Timothy my fellow worker greets you, and Lucius and Iason and Sosipater, my kinsmen. ²²I, Tertius, who write the letter, greet you in view of Yăhwe H. ²³Gaius, my host and all the assembly *here*, greet you. Erastus, the city treasurer greets you, and Quartus, the brother.

[²⁵And to the one being able to strengthen you, according to my good news, and the proclamation of Yĕshua the Anŏinted, according to the unveiling of the mystery, that in ancient times had been getting kept secret, ²⁶and is now manifested, besides through the prophetic writings, according to the commandment of the everlasting Almĭghty, concerning obedience of faithfulness, to all the nations being made known, ²⁷by the only wise Almĭghty, through Yĕshua the Anŏinted, to whom *is* the glory for the ages of the ages, Am·en.]ᵃ

---

a [16:25-27] This passage is placed after 14:23 in many texts, after 15:33 in many others, and omitted altogether in quite a few. The word μόνῳ here does not deny the deity of the Son because 'only wise Almĭghty' is speaking collectively, as in Hos. 13:4, and then 'through' comes before Messiah to express agency, and the doxology (viz. to whom is the glory) applies to the collective reference to God and also to Messiah.

Terminal Corruption

If I should make just one argument to prove to you that what popular Christianity trusts in as a valid translation of the Scripture, or interpretation if you must, particularly the Pauline Letters, is in fact terminally corrupt idolatry and superstition, I would make it from Romans 5:1. Invariably the translations say:

Therefore, being justified by faith...

For those of you who may be misinformed, the Western Church, and particularly the Lutheran faction specializes in these definitions: In their eyes, *justified* means declared perfectly righteous in God's sight, and *faith* means believing only. And if we wish to follow the evolution of this, we can all the way the Lewis Sperry Chafer and the doctrine that says only a moment of belief is necessary and then whatever may follow does not matter because one is secure in salvation on that basis. But this is the gospel of the world, and the gospel of lawlessness.

The idolatry consists in this. That this translation is held up as the image of divine justice leads directly to a corrupt and idolatrous view of the Most High. The superstition consists in the treatment of *belief* as the magic talisman that induces a false god to deliver the charmer from sin and its consequences without doing anything. But the true Almighty does not deliver anyone who is so faithless.

The faithful know this. And it is to you whom I will speak. Satan has plenty of followers who dress themselves in the lambskins of Měssiah. They are the majority. They control the press, control the Churches, and control the translations, mostly. They have infiltrated most every group and fellowship that is trying to turn to the right way also. At least they are represented there. They are the many whom Měssiah will disown.

Gŏd does forgive sin. But on what basis? Repentance. I should point out that the world's gospel redefines this also. And in fact their translations are shot through and terminally corrupted with their redefinitions of basic concepts. That means ALL translations. The problem is this, you the faithful are still under the spell of these false translations and interpretations.

Let me draw an analogy. David was a worshiper of the true Gŏd, but he and his wife had Teraphim in the house. They did not worship the Teraphim, but they still had them. But worse than this is the trust that the faithful place in false and terminally corrupt translations that do not teach the real good news.

Know this. A justification based on legal acquittal and being found righteous before Gŏd's court, and in paying off Gŏd, so he is compensated for sin is a legalistic salvation. It is not forgiveness. You have to recognize that Měssiah forgives our sins and <u>ransoms us from lawlessness</u>. He did not pay the Făther off so that he would forgive us. But the Făther jointly suffers in the Spĭrit with Měssiah, who suffered in the flesh, to ransom us from lawlessness.

Now I would not be saying this so confidently if I did not know what the real Paul really said in Romans 5:1, and that is this:

Therefore being administered justice based on faithfulness we should have peace next to the Almĭghty by our Adŏnai Yěshua the Anŏinted, by whom also we have been holding access, by faithfulness, into this loving-kindness in which we have been standing.

To be justiced (or administered justice) by the Most High means to have one's case judged, and it is as simple as this. If one if faithful to Messiah and obeys his voice or even with a whole heart pledges faithfulness to him, even though one does not yet fully know how, then he will take the faithfulness into account and forgive us and cleanse us from sin, teach us his ways, and give us everlasting life.

So you see faithfulness works and to hold faithful to Měssiah means to obey his commandments. Because faithfulness without works is not faithfulness. What then did Paul mean when speaking badly of works. He meant only trying to use works to pay for forgiveness. This concept is called zechut in Judaism. So that was what Paul was against. And you should know that Western Christianity after Augustine and Anselm has turned the faith into a philosophical system of getting forgiveness by paying Gŏd off, that is by propitiating his wrath. But truly this is false, and Messiah died as a ransom, to ransom us from the hand of lawlessness.

The faithful one already has forgiveness, and remains in it by being faithful, and needs no theological tricks to be forgiven.

So all ye faithful, the Făther loves those who keep his commandments, which are also Měssiah's commandments. And this is how we know we know him. I have provided you with the Good News of Měssiah to strenghten the faithful to prepare you for the restoration of the kingdom, and to throw down all that exalts itself against the knowledge of the Most High, which is through our Adŏnai Yěshua.

I have provided you with spiritual weapons and armor. As I have listened to the Spĭrit, and walked in the wilderness with ears open, so also the faithful must open their ears and hear what the Spĭrit is saying in these last days. Now all glory be to he who alone is Everlasting Life and alone true Almĭghty, Yěshua the Anŏinted, and unto he also who is alone true Almĭghty, the Father, and his Spĭrit, alone true Almighty, who have been sending the only kindred Sŏn.

The Ruin and Reconstruction Heresy

A very popular means of fitting a form of evolution or long ages into scripture is based on trying to find a gap of time between Genesis 1:1 and Genesis 1:2. This theory presumes that Genesis 1:1 refers to a completed creation that existed before the present creation. Then it claims Genesis 1:2 teaches the destruction of that creation by rendering, "Then the earth became" *tohu wavohu*. However they translate it, they interpret *tohu wavohu* to mean the destruction of the former creation. The waters of vs. 2 are regarded as the result of this destruction. Then in verse three they say that six days of re-creation began.

Experts in various fields of study faithful to divine revelation have shown how everything we observe in the heavens and on the earth fit into the biblical framework of six days creation, and then a global deluge, and then as the result of more conservative processes since then. So it will only be necessary to say that the ruin and reconstruction theory is unscientific. For the details, I will refer you to the faithful experts. My task here is to show that it does not agree with the written revelation.

Creationists, though they may have excellent scientific defenses against ruin and reconstruction, have generally given an inadequate or incomplete answer to ruin and reconstruction arguments using Genesis 1:1-2. This is because most creationists have another unbiblical philosophical commitment, and this is the belief that "time" was created in Genesis 1:1. As a result they use the popular mistranslation of Genesis 1:1 wherein it is supposed to be an absolute statement. Few translations correct it. Creationists also address the "became" argument incompletely, choosing to concentrate on the waw conjunctive at the beginning of vs. 2 to show the context will not support "became," but neglecting to explain how the verb hayatah doesn't mean "became."

Let me quickly explain the waw conjunctive argument, though I will be repeating what many have said, before giving the more complete answer. There are three types of waw conjunction in Hebrew. There is the waw conjunctive, and the waw consecutive, and the waw remote. Generally the English versions neglect any distinction between the three, and choose to translate them all as "and." This is because early translators did not understand the difference, and most translators still do not understand the differences.

Waw conjunctive is the equivalent of "And," but it is a special 'and' that adds information to an existing setting without moving time forward in the narrative. The waw conjunctive may be identified as such because it is always attached to a noun phrase and almost always has a vocal shewa. The waw consecutive may be identified easily also, because it is attached to an imperfect verb with a qamets vowel. That waw means "Then" as in "Then" next such and such is happening. It moves time incrementally forward. The waw remote takes the same form as the waw consecutive in the received text. It can only be identified from the context, and it is extremely rare. This waw refers to remote time, "And then" as in back then or it is a pluperfect, "And had...." It is not necessary in addressing the ruin and reconstruction theory to explain this waw further here. We are only concerned with the waw conjunctive and consecutive.

The ruin and reconstruction theory assumes that the waw at the beginning of vs. 2 is the consecutive form. They say "the earth became" ruined after the creation of vs. 1. But the waw in vs. 2 is not the consecutive form. It is the conjunctive form indicating conditions that are at the same time as vs. 1. And so far creationists do well to point this out. But their argument is badly weakened by the mistranslation of vs. 1, which correctly goes: "In the beginning of the Almighty's creating the heavens and the earth, when the earth had been nought and nothing, ..."

Now see here that I have translated the waw conjunctive at the start of verse 2, "when." This is to prevent the reader from moving time forward by interpreting the word "and (next)." That sense is the domain of the waw consecutive. So we see that if time cannot move forward with vs. 2, then the earth cannot become something that does not fit with the setting of vs. 1.

Most creationists state this as, "In the beginning God created the heavens and the earth." Period, full stop. Then, "And the earth was without form and void." They correctly say that vs. 2 indicates a time at the same time as vs. 1, more specifically, at the very start of the creation process. So vs. 2 is not after vs. 1. It is contained within the start of vs. 1. But vs. 1 they say summarizes the whole of creation from the beginning of it to the end of it.

There is just a little problem with this. The first word is construct and should be rendered "In the beginning of." It is construct everywhere else when used with the preposition. It indicates relative time, and not absolute time. Secondly, there were no vowel points in the original texts. These points had to be correctly guessed centuries after the AD era began. The first word must be construct due to its consonant text, which is original. This means the vowel points of the second word in the text must conform to the construct state of the first word. This gives the sense of "creating of" or "creating by." Yes, that's right. The word traditionally vocalized BARA should be vocalized BERO. The first word indicates that it is not a perfect, but an infinitive construct.

These facts make the realization of the waw conjunctive at the start of verse 2 a much better argument, "In the beginning of creating by the Almighty: the heavens and the earth, when the earth had been nought and nothing, ..." So Rashi explains it and also Robert Young. But those interested in reading their philosophy of time into the text pay no attention, and as a result make the waw conjunctive explanation needlessly difficult.

Creationists do not adequately explain, "was" vs. "became." The ruin and reconstruction theory argues that the verb always indicates a change of state, and should mean "became." But this argument

is contradicted by the waw conjunctive. If a change of state was the meaning, then we would expect a waw consecutive attached to an imperfect verb. We would also expect vs. 1 to take a proper absolute form rather than the form it does. But these contradictions still leave the "became" claim to be addressed.

Hebrew does not express the verb "to be" in most cases when the text is equivocating two items. This fact has led many to assume the verb means "to become" when it is actually used, and even some translators to assume this. But the truth is that the verb can be expressed when the meaning is "to be" and not "to become." For example, in Genesis 2:18, the Most High says, "It is not good for the man to be alone" (לֹא־טוֹב הֱיוֹת הָאָדָם לְבַדּוֹ). Here the text cannot mean "to become alone" because Adam always was without a partner to that point in time. Being alone was his state since he was made. So he did not suffer a change of state to become alone. He was alone. Also to say, "become alone" would imply that the man was not at first alone and that it was never proper for him to become alone even temporarily. "Become" turns the text into a lie.

There are many texts where the sense is "to be" and not "to become," but only a very few of these have enough logical context to absolutely exclude "become." In the vast majority of the "to be" cases the probable sense is "to be." So why would Hebrew express "to be" in various tenses if typically Hebrew omits "to be" when equivocating items? The answer is that Hebrew includes the verb "to be" when the narrator or speaker wants to impart special emphasis on a state that exists. Hence in the mentioned case, the observation is not simply "Adam [is] alone. This is not good." Rather it is "It is not good for Adam to be existing alone." Emphasis is being placed on his state. But it is not implied his state changes.

"When the earth had been nought and nothing." This describes the state of the earth in the beginning of creation. It had been nought and nothing, that is it did not exist yet. Only water existed as the construction material. And analogous statement would be to say, "when his house had been a pile of lumber." The use of the word house does not imply it existed yet.

The ruin and reconstruction theory also benefits from the injudicious translation of *tohu wavhou* as formless and empty. This is construed to mean the earth exists, but its surface is unformed, and that it exists, but it is empty of inhabitants. But it is "without form" at all, and "nothing" at all is the proper sense. I have chosen same sounding words to imitate the Hebrew, "nought and nothing." I have read journal articles on these words and also performed word studies on them. Both confirm the high accuracy of my "nought and nothing" translation.

Earth as a substance does not exist until dry land is made. Though it is not stated in vs. 2, the heavens were also nought and nothing at that point also. They are created later in the passage.

Some Things Hard to Understand

"To justify" (δικαιοῦν) someone in Ancient Greek normally meant "to administer justice" to him (cf. Appendix XI, page **588**). A judge would administer justice to a *guilty* defendant by either pardon, or punishment. Either outcome would "justify" the defendant, i.e. apply justice to him. Indeed, the repentant sinner could be administered justice by a pardon (also called forgiveness). See Acts 13:38-39; Rom. 3:24, 26, 28, 30; 4:5; 5:1; 6:7; 8:30, 33; 1 Cor. 6:11; Gal. 2:16, 17; 3:24; Titus 3:7. Also "to justify" could often mean "to declare in the right," (acquit). Someone who was found **not guilty** could be justified in this sense. And finally, the term could mean "to make righteous." A repentant sinner following Gŏd's commandments is administered justice by cleansing from sin. This is reformatory justice. If the definitions are mixed up, then Paul could be easily misinterpreted as Peter observed (2 Pet. 3:16; cf. pages 420-421, 588).

The words "faith" and "believe" in the usual English versions are mistranslations. The noun (πίστις) means "faithfulness" and the verb (πιστεύειν) means "to hold faithful" to someone or to hold something faithful. The noun and verb are derived from the adjective "faithful" (πιστός), which is synonymous with the verb (πείθειν) "to obey." Often when Paul speaks of "faithfulness" (πίστις) he means Messiah's faithfulness. See Rom. 3:22, 26; Gal. 2:16, 20; 3:22, 26; Phil. 3:9. Also Rom. 1:17 ε, ω; 3:25, 28, 30, 31; 4:5, etc. Therefore, "to be administered justice by faithfulness" (Rom. 5:1) means to administer justice on the basis of Messiah's faithfulness.

Paul sometimes rejected works (cf. Rom. 3:20; Eph. 2:9; Titus 3:5) and other times he taught good works (cf. Rom. 2:7, 13; Eph. 2:10; Titus 3:8). If a reader was uninformed about the Jewish context, then he could distort Paul's meaning to be a rejection of Gŏd's commandments. Appendix VIII and notes on the relevant passages (Rom. **3:20** φ; Eph. **2:9** γ; Tit. **3:5** δ) explain that Paul is rejecting the Rabbinical doctrine of zekut, which teaches the doing of specific works of piety (merits) in order to cancel out one's demerits (sins). This doctrine is opposed to forgiveness of sins because it teaches compensation for sin. Paul opposed it because it was contrary to Messiah's ransom on our behalf. If sins could be paid for by the transfer of merits to offset demerits, or by appeasement or propitiation, then what need would there be for Gŏd's forgiveness and rescue by Mĕssiah's ransoming death? (See page 433-434).

Paul sometimes appears to be rejecting the law, e.g. (Rom. 6:14-15; Rom. 3:21; Rom. 10:4), but this appearance is due to mistranslation and misinterpretation of the Greek word *nomos* (νόμος). The word means 'a legal norm' (cf. note Rom. 7:7 θ; BDAG, 3rd ed. νόμος No. 1). The exact sense of ὑπὸ νόμον (Rom. 6:14) is *not* you are not "under law," without distinction, but you are not "under the legal norm." And the exact sense of τέλος ... νόμου (Rom. 10:4) is not "the end of the law," without distinction, but "the end of the legal norm." The legal norm calls for the condemnation of the sinner. But forgiveness introduces the legal exception to strict justice: forgiving-justice.

The word *nomos* (νόμος) also means a custom or a habit or a social norm. Paul sometimes simply uses *nomos* to to mean "the customary legal practice (Gal. 3:21). He refers to zekut by the mere use of the word *nomos* this way. In other places he expands this same idea to "customary works." Other times he refers to the same idea as just "works." If the reader is unaware of the Jewish context of these statements, he will be liable to misinterpret them, or have them misinterpreted for him by anti-law teachers.

There are a great many other things misinterpreted and or mistranslated that are corrected in this volume. The reader is best served by coming to them on his own and reading the associated notes. I have at times tried to make a list of all the mistaken translations or interpretations, but the reader would weary of reading it because it would be many thousands of lines. It is best to come across the solutions in the context.

This brief introduction of *some things hard to understand* (cf. 2 Peter 3:16) covers the most critical distortions of Paul by mainstream Christianity. It may be fairly said that the thousands of other errors not detailed here are descended from these chief errors. Most of the errors were introduced into the tradition by men who did not love Gŏd's Law, who rejected important parts of it, or who rejected it completely. As a

result they have corrupted the true message of salvation, and teach that divine wrath must be appeased in some way, neglecting confession and forgiveness.

First Corinthians

1 ¹Paul, called to be an emissary of Yĕshua the Anŏinted by the will of the Almĭghty, and Sosthenes our brother. ²To the assembly of the Almĭghty which is at Corinth, to those who have been getting made holy through the Anŏinted Yĕshua, called to be holy, along with all who call upon the name of our Adŏnai Yĕshua the Anŏinted in every place, theirs and ours. ³Loving-kindness to you and peace from the Almĭghty our Făther and Adŏnai Yĕshua the Anŏinted.

⁴I thank my Almĭghty always concerning you, for the loving-kindness of the Almĭghty which was given you through the Anŏinted Yĕshua, ⁵that in everything you are enriched in him, in all speech and all knowledge, ⁶even as the testimony concerning the Anŏinted is confirmed in you, ⁷so that you are not lacking in any gift, awaiting eagerly the revelation of our Adŏnai Yĕshua the Anŏinted, ⁸who will also confirm you to the end, blameless in the day of our Adŏnai Yĕshua the Anŏinted. ⁹The Almĭghty is faithful, through whom you are called into fellowship with his Sŏn, Yĕshua the Anŏinted our Adŏnai.

¹⁰And I am encouraging you brothers, through the name of our Adŏnai Yĕshua the Anŏinted, that you all may be speaking the same things, and *that* there may be no divisions among you, and *that* you may be, *and* have been putting yourselves in order with the same mind and with the same judgment.

¹¹Because it was made clear to me about you my brothers, by Chloes' people, that there are quarrels among you. ¹²Now I mean this, that each one of you is saying, "I am of Paul," and "I of Apollos," and "I of Keipha," and "I of the Anŏinted." ¹³Has the Anŏinted been getting divided? Paul was not fastened to an execution timber on your behalf, was he? Or were you immersed in the name of Paul? ¹⁴I thank the Almĭghty that I immersed none of you except Crispus and Gaius, ¹⁵that no man will have said you were immersed into my name. ¹⁶Now I did immerse also the household of Stephanas. Beyond that, I have not been knowing whether I immersed any other.

¹⁷For the Anŏinted did not send me to immerse, but to proclaim the good news, not in cleverness of speech, so that the execution timber of the Anŏinted may not be emptied of effect.

¹⁸Because the word of the execution timber is to those who are perishing foolishness, but to us who are being rescued it is the power of the Almĭghty, ¹⁹because it has been getting written, "I WILL DESTROY THE 'WISDOM' OF THE 'WISE,' AND THE 'CLEVERNESS' OF THE 'CLEVER' I WILL SET ASIDE". ²⁰Where is the wise man? Where is the scribe? Where is the debater of this age? Has not the Almĭghty made foolish the wisdom of the world? ²¹Because since in the wisdom of the Almĭghty, the world through its wisdom did not come to know the Al-

---

1:19 µ Isa 29:14.

mighty, the Almĭghty was well-pleased through the 'foolishness' of the message proclaimed, to rescue those holding faithful. ²²Because even Yehudim ask for signs, and Greeks search for wisdom, ²³but we are proclaiming the Anŏinted, who had been getting fastened to an execution timber, to the Yehudim a stumbling block, and to the nations foolishness, ²⁴but to those who are the called, besides Yehudim also Greeks, the Anŏinted is the power of the Almĭghty and the wisdom of the Almĭghty, ²⁵because the 'foolishness' of the Almĭghty is wiser than men, and the weakness of the Almĭghty is stronger than men.

²⁶Because observe your calling brothers, that there were not many wise according to the flesh, not many mighty, *and* not many from noble kindred, ²⁷but the Almĭghty has chosen the 'foolish things' of the world so that he may be shaming 'the wise,' and the Almĭghty has chosen the weak things of the world so that he may be shaming the things which are strong.

²⁸And the low born of the world and the things which have been getting despised, the Almĭghty has chosen himself, things being nothing, so that the things being *something*, he will have undone, ²⁹that no flesh will have boasted before the Almĭghty.

³⁰But by him, you are belonging to the Anŏinted Yĕshua, who is become wisdom to us from the Almĭghty, besides justice, also holiness and a ransom

---

1:30 ρ ἀπολύτρωσις, ransom, redemption: the price paid to free a captive, that is someone being held by a slaveholder. We were slaves in Egypt. And the nations represent the face of sin and death holding Yisra'el captive now. Yisra'el is to be ransomed and cleansed by the blood of the Passover Lamb, but the nations which do not separate from sin will be judged because the blood is not upon them to cleanse them. ▷ Mĕssiah has become all these things to us as an example, because he is the perfect one, and is the example to follow. But many take the word "become" in a different sense, reading "become...righteousness" and explain that it means perfect righteousness is legally put into the books for the faithful (who are imperfect) so that they will be legally regarded as perfect, without actually being or becoming perfect. But the Almĭghty does not care one bit about this false doctrine because the only reason for it would be to set the basis for an acquittal rather than the pardon Scripture teaches. Such legal righteousness is a fiction. It does not compensate the Almĭghty for our lack of it. Neither does Mĕssiah's death. ▷ Messiah's death was caused by the forces of evil (cf. Gen. 3:15) when he invaded the kingdom of darkness to deliver us. The price he paid was exacted by sin and death, and not by divine wrath. When the world did this to him, the Most High was pleased to use his death a a guilt offering, that is to indicate the ransom demanded by sin and to show the cost of our cleansing from sin contamination. Thus Messiah's spilled blood is indicative of the cost in divine life necessary to separate us from our sin, first literally in the cost of invading the kingdom of darkness, and secondly in the cost of cleansing the prisoners from sin. The Holy Rŭakh must suffer looking upon our sin as he excises it from us. The life of Messiah is given to us through the Spĭrit, and so his blood symbolizes the consumption of divine life (cf. Yoĥ. 6). ▷ For further explanation of the ransom see Mat. 20:28; Mark 10:45; Hos. 13:14; Isa. 43:3; Rev. 5:9; 1 Tim. 2:6. ▷ The word 'justice' could also be translated 'righteousness' or 'administration of justice.' Divine justice, aka righteousness, is not only strict justice, but it is part strict justice and part forgiving justice. The Most High also shows his righteousness (or justice) via his love by giving the ransom to rescue us from sin, and by pardoning (or forgiving) us, canceling judicial penalty against us. This is on behalf of the faithful who repent and keep his commandments. See Exodus 20:6; Rev. 22:14. But for those who are unfaithful and deceived by the serpent, his justice shows another face, because they will not be separated from their sin, and come to Messiah's cleansing. ▷ In many respects the unfaithful project what they fear onto the Almighty. They fear strict justice against themselves because they will not repent of their sins, and so since they cannot shake this fear, they who profess to know him imagine that Messiah shields them from the God of wrath by giving him innocent blood to vent his wrath on, but they misunderstand the good news and remain in their sin. The ransom is an instruction in the cost taken by sin, and the cost necessary for cleansing, not a satisfaction of the penalty. TO OBEY IS BETTER THAN SACRIFICE. The unfaithful always project upon the Most High that he demands payment or compensation for every sin. This they give to him in terms of sacrifice,

release, ³¹that just as it has been getting written, "LET HIM WHO IS REJOICING IN HIMSELF, BE REJOICING IN YĂHWEH."

2 ¹And when I came to you brothers, I did not come with eloquent speech or lofty wisdom, proclaiming to you the testimony of the Almĭghty, ²because I determined to have been knowing nothing among you except Yĕshua the Anŏinted, and him who had been getting fastened to an execution timber. ³And I was with you in weakness and in fear and in much trembling. ⁴And my message and my proclaiming were not in persuasive words of wisdom, but in demonstration of the Spĭrit and of power, ⁵that your faithfulness may not be *resting* in the wisdom of men, but in the power of the Almĭghty.

⁶Yet we do speak wisdom among those who are mature—a wisdom, however, not of this age, nor of the rulers of this age, who are passing away, ⁷but we speak the Almĭghty's wisdom according to a mystery, which has been getting hidden, which the Almĭghty planned before the ages for our glory, ⁸the wisdom which none of the rulers of this age has been understanding, because if they had understood it, they would not have fastened⁺ to an execution timber the Adŏnai of glory, ⁹but just as it has been getting written, "THERE ARE THINGS WHICH EYE HAS NOT SEEN AND EAR HAS NOT HEARD, AND WHICH HAVE NOT ENTERED THE HEART OF MAN, WHICH THE ALMĬGHTY PREPARES FOR THOSE WHO LOVE HIM."

¹⁰And to us, the Almĭghty has revealed them, through the Spĭrit, because the Spĭrit searches all things, even the deep things of the Almĭghty. ¹¹Because who among men has been knowing the things of a man, except the spirit of the man which is in him? Even so the things of the Almĭghty, no one has been knowing, except the Spĭrit of the Almĭghty. ¹²Now we have not received the spirit of the world order, but the Spĭrit which is from the Almĭghty, so that we will have been knowing the things being favored on us by the Almĭghty, ¹³which things we also

---

but it is disobedience that leads to his wrath in the first place, therefore, he forgives if we repent. And he is not appeased by the sacrifice of the disobedient. The sacrifice of the disobedient is to appease the wrath of God. **1:31** ν Jer. 9:23

2:8 ϕ Because Messiah's death is the cost to the Most High in the flesh, which sums up the total cost to the Almĭghty in bearing our sins with the hope that we might repent from them. The Scripture represents the divine longsuffering and patience, and loss added up in delaying judgment due to the effects of sins continuing to be comitted by undjudged sinners, as a ransom. The cost of giving a space for repentance and forgiveness is the continuing damage sin does to creation. The Most High bears this cost, the ransom exacted by sin, and personally so in the flesh in Messiah. And the cost even goes unto sacrificing whole nations as the cost of ransoming Yisra'el (Isa. 43:3). The loss of those nations is a loss of His creation. It is a divine loss. ▷ The divine ransom becomes most visible in Messiah's death, which the powers caused through man's sin when they reached out and struck him (cf. Gen. 3:15). Having taken the innocent blood of Messiah at the climax of divine suffering, they are more clearly compelled to yield up the captives ransomed, and then Messiah continues to bear the cost of cleansing those freed by his blood, which represents the divine life. If they had known the Most High would make so visible a point in the flesh they would not have accomodated it. And now the powers have to re-explain Messiah's death to the world as appeasement of divine wrath to deflect attention from their own demands for favors in exchange for innocent blood, and to deflect attention from the Almĭghty's manifest love in sending his Son to face the risks from sin and suffering, and continue the fight in fleshly form as a witness to his beloved people. This is a message that the evil powers did not want to get through. They would have prefered the Most High stayed at a distance. It would have made their job of deception easier.

2:9 χ Isa 64:4, 65:17; See App XII

speak, not in human teachings of wise words, but in teachings of the Spirit, comparing spiritual things with spiritual things.

¹⁴But a worldly man does not accept the things of the Spirit of the Almĭghty, because they are foolishness to him, and he cannot understand them, because they are spiritually discerned. ¹⁵Now he who is spiritual discerns in everything, and he himself is discerned by no wordly person, ¹⁶because WHO HAS KNOWN THE MIND OF YĂHWEH, THAT HE SHOULD INSTRUCT HIM?" And we have the understanding of the Anŏinted.

3 ¹And I, brothers, could not speak to you as to spiritual men, but as to worldly men, as to babes, according to the Anŏinted. ²I gave you milk to drink, not solid food, because you were not yet able to receive it. Indeed, even now you are not yet able, ³because you are still worldly, because where there is jealousy and strife among you, are you not worldly, and walking like mankind? ⁴Because when one may be saying, "I am of Paul," and another, "I am of Apollos," are you not being *like* mankind? ⁵What then is Apollos? And what is Paul? Servants through whom you pledged faithfulness, even as Yăhweh gave opportunity to each one. ⁶I planted, Apollos watered, but the Almĭghty was increasing the growth. ⁷So then neither the one who plants nor the one who waters is something, but only the Almĭghty who increases the growth.

⁸Now he who plants and he who waters are one, but each will receive his own reward according to his own labor, ⁹because we are the Almĭghty's fellow workers. You are the Almĭghty's field, and the Almĭghty's building. ¹⁰According to the loving-kindness of the Almĭghty, which was given to me, as a wise master builder I laid a foundation, and another is building upon it. But let each man be watching how he builds upon it, ¹¹because no man can lay a foundation other than the one which is laid, which is Yĕshua the Anŏinted.

¹²Then if any man builds upon the foundation with gold, silver, precious stones, wood, hay, straw, ¹³each man's work will become evident, because the day will show it, because it is to be revealed with fire, and the fire itself will test the quality of each man's work. ¹⁴If any man's work which he has built upon it remains, he will receive a reward. ¹⁵If any man's work is burned up, he will suffer loss, but he himself will be rescued, yet so as through fire.

¹⁶Have you not been knowing that you are the temple of the Almĭghty, and that the Spirit of the Almĭghty dwells in you? ¹⁷If any man destroys the temple of the Almĭghty, the Almĭghty will destroy him, for the temple of the Almĭghty is holy, and that is what you are.

¹⁸Let no man be deceiving himself. If any man among you thinks that he is wise in this age, he will have become foolish that he will have become wise, ¹⁹because the wisdom of this world is foolishness before the Almĭghty. Because

---

2:16 η Isa 40:13.

3:15 δ This is to say that a minister who is faithful himself to Mĕssiah, but who pursues a foolish course of ministry will find his work destroyed in the hour of testing. Paul said this because there needed to be ministers, but indeed they were not all really ready for it. **3:19** ψ Job 5:13

it has been getting written, "*He is* THE ONE WHO CATCHES THE WISE IN THEIR CRAFTINESS^ψ," ²⁰and again, "YĂHWEӈ KNOWS THE REASONINGS of the wise, THAT THEY ARE USELESS^ψ." ²¹So then let no one be boasting in men, because all things relate to you, ²²whether Paul or Apollos or Keipha or the world or life or death or things which have been impending or things about to be coming. All things relate to you, ²³and you relate to the Anŏinted, and the Anŏinted relates to the Almĭghty.

4 ¹Likewise, let a man be taking account of us as servants of the Anŏinted and administrators of the mysteries of the Almĭghty. ²Moreover here, it is required of administrators that each should be found faithful. ³But to me it is a very small thing that I may have been examined by you, or by any human court. In fact, I do not even examine myself, ⁴because I have been getting conscious of nothing against myself, yet I have not by this been getting justified, but the one who examines me is Yăhweӈ. ⁵Therefore do not be judging anything before the appointed time, but wait until Yăhweӈ will have come who will both bring to light the things hidden in the darkness, and disclose the motives of men's hearts, and then each man's praise will come to him from the Almĭghty.

⁶Now these things, brothers, I have applied to myself and Apollos for your sakes, that in us you will have learned not to *judge* over what has been getting written, so that no one is getting blown up over another looking down, ⁷because who is going to judge you? And what do you have that you have not received? But if you did receive it, why do you boast, as if you had not received it? ⁸You have already been getting filled! You have already become rich, you have reigned without us, and I would indeed that you have reigned so that we also will have reigned with you, ⁹because, I think, the Almĭghty has exhibited us emissaries last of all, as men condemned to death, because we have become a spectacle to the world, both to messengers and to men.

¹⁰We are fools for the Anŏinted's sake, but you are prudent for the Anŏinted. We are weak, but you are strong. You are distinguished, but we are without honor. ¹¹To this present hour we are both hungry and thirsty, and are poorly clothed, and are roughly treated, and are homeless, ¹²and we toil, working with our own hands. When we are reviled, we bless. When we are persecuted, we endure. ¹³When we are slandered, we try to conciliate. We have become as the scum of the world, the dregs of all things, even until now.

¹⁴I am not writing these things for shaming you, but for educating you as my beloved children, ¹⁵because if you may be having ten thousand tutors belonging to the Anŏinted, yet not many *would be* fathers, because through the Anŏinted Yĕshua I have begotten you by the good news. ¹⁶I exhort you therefore, be becoming imitators of me. ¹⁷For this reason I have sent to you Timothy, who is my beloved child and faithful to Yăhweӈ, who will remind you of my ways which

---

3:20 ψ Psa. 94:11; see App XII.

are in the Anŏinted, just as I teach everywhere in every assembly. ¹⁸Now some have been arrogant, as though I were not coming to you. ¹⁹But I will come to you soon, if Yăhweн shall have willed, and I will find out, not the talk^λ of those who have been getting puffed up, so much as their power, ²⁰because the kingdom of the Almĭghty does not consist in talk^λ, so much as in power. ²¹What do you desire? Shall I have come to you with a rod or with love as well as a spirit of gentleness?

5

¹It is actually reported that there is immorality among you, and immorality of such a kind as does not exist even among the nations, that someone has his father's wife. ²And you have been getting puffed up, yes you are, and have not mourned instead, in order that the one who had done this deed may be removed from your midst. ³For I, on my part, though absent in body but being near in spirit, have already been judging the one who has so committed this, as if being present. ⁴In the name of our Adŏnai Yĕshua, when you are assembled, and I with you in spirit, with the power of our Adŏnai Yĕshua, ⁵deliver such a one to Satan for the destruction of his body, so that his spirit may be rescued in the day of Adŏnai Yĕshua.

⁶Your boasting is not good. Have you not been knowing that a little leaven leavens the whole batch of dough? ⁷CLEAN OUT THE OLD LEAVEN^ε, that you may be a younger batch of dough, even as you are being deleavened.

⁷ᵇAnd because the Anŏinted our Passover has been sacrificed^η, ⁸so besides, we should be CELEBRATING THE FEAST^ε, not with old leaven, nor with the leaven of malice and wickedness, but with the unleavened bread of sincerity and truth.

4:19-20 λ=λόγος. A verse often taken out of context. Paul obviously is not diminishing the value of the written word or accurate translations.

5:7 ε Exo 12:15 **5:7b** η Exodus 12:23 states, "And Yăhweн will have passed through to strike Egypt, and he will have seen the blood upon the lintel, and upon the two doorposts, and Yăhweн will have passed over the door, and will not give the destroyer *orders* to enter into your houses to strike you." The blood on the door posts represents the pieces of a covenant sacrifice, and those going through the door are entering into the covenant. Therefore, the ceremony was a renewal of the divine covenant with the Patriarchs, with their seed, to sift out who was under the blood of the covenant and who was not, and to find out who was allied with Egypt, and who was loyal to the Most High. The circumcision represents the removal of the uncleanness of sin, and the circumcision of the heart. The blood represents cleansing by the Spirit from sin in the heart in conjunction with the faithfulness of the faithful. Thus by removing the things against which the wrath of Almĭghty may burn, the faithful have been getting themselves cleansed from the causes of wrath. Therefore, the destroyer may pass over us. The physical blood of Messiah represents the same things as the blood of the Passover lamb on the lintel and two doorposts, and that is entering the covenant of old new made. If the destroyer is to pass over, then the faithful must live the reality of the symbolism. ▷ The wrath of the destroyer is averted by applying the blood to the doorposts of the heart, and entering the covenant. No evil or unclean thing is to come through the door of our heart to dwell there. ▷ Did the destroyer pass over because the blood was a sign that the destroyer had already poured out wrath on the lamb, and the destroyer said to himself, "I will pass over, because that house has already received my wrath?" No! The destroyer passed over because the people pledged their faithfulness to the Covenant, and therefore removed the cause of wrath, symbolized by leaven and uncircumcision. ▷ The substitute for wrath doctrine is a legal superstition, and is not what the symbolism teaches. The substitution doctrine assumes that God has to settle a legal problem with himself before he can forgive any sin. The problem with this wrath satisfaction is it fails entirely to recognize that repentance itself removes the need for final wrath. It also fails to explain why the unrepentant are still going to receive wrath. After all the wrath against unrepentance and the wrath said to be poured out on the substitute are one and the same. So then, why isn't wrath for unrepentance also satisfied? If it were so easy, then we should all be universalists. **5:8** ε Deut 16:1-3

⁹I wrote you in my letter not to associate with immoral people. ¹⁰I did not at all mean with the immoral people of this world, or with the covetous and swindlers, or with idolaters, because then you would have to go out of the world. ¹¹Now, I have written to you not to be associating together, if anyone who is calling himself a brother, may be an immoral person, or covetous, or an idolater, or a reviler, or a drunkard, or a swindler—not even to be eating with such a one, ¹²because what have I to do with judging outsiders? Are you not judging those who are within the assembly? ¹³But those who are outside, the Almïghty is judging. REMOVE THE WICKED OF THEM FROM AMONG YOURSELVES.ᵉ

6 ¹Is any of you, when he is having a case against another, daring to be going to law before the unrighteous, and not before the holy ones? ²Or have you not been knowing that the holy ones will judge the world? And if the world is *henceforth* being judged by you, are you unworthy to be the smallest law courts? ³Have you not been knowing that we will judge messengers? Let alone, matters of *this* life? ⁴Surely then *for trivial* matters of *this* life—if you may have those who have been getting considered for nothing in the assembly—these *persons* you must be seating *to administer* courts! ⁵I say this to your shame. Is it so, that there is not among you one wise man who will be able to decide between his brothers, ⁶but brother goes to law with brother, and that before the unfaithful?

⁷Actually, then, it is already a defeat for you, that you have lawsuits with one another. Why not rather be wronged? Why not rather be defrauded? ⁸On the contrary, you yourselves wrong and defraud, and that your brothers. ⁹Or have you not been knowing that the unrighteous will not inherit the kingdom of the Almïghty? Do not be getting deceived! Neither fornicators, nor idolaters, nor adulterers, nor men acting like women, nor homosexuals, ¹⁰nor thieves, nor the covetous, nor drunkards, nor revilers, nor swindlers, will inherit the kingdom of the Almïghty. ¹¹And such were some of you. But you were washed. But you were set apart. But you have been administered justice in the name of Adŏnai Yĕshua the Anŏinted, and by the Spïrit of our Almïghty.

¹²"ᶠSomeone allows ᵖall things ʳfor meʳ," but not all things ʳgo together. "Someone allows all things ʳfor meʳ," but I will not let myself be ᵋcontrolled by

---

5:13 ε Deut. 13:5, 17:7,12; 21:21; 22:21, 22, 24; Jud. 20:13. **6:12 μ** *someone*: cf. 1Cor. 14:5,13. **6:12 ᶠ** These words are omitted in 1Cor 10:23 in the best and oldest mss in two places. Clearly the addition of the words was the result of early editing and not unintentional mistakes. 𝔓⁴⁶ is damaged in the corner of the page so it cannot help on this text. The saying has the quality of a maxim, and I suspect the addition of 'to me' was probably first effected in 1Cor 6:12 and later by scribal comparison into 1Cor. 10:23. This is probably why the evidence of the change shows in the 4th cent. MSS for the later passage. **6:12 ξ** Πάντα Adj-ANP vs. Adj-NNP. **6:12 ρ** The older commentators regarded the phrase a quote from an indefinite opposition, the later commentators as Paul's own saying regarding Christian liberty in adiaphora (things that do not matter), and a lot of commentators try to sit on the fence suggesting both! But the context regards unlawful sex (fornication), and so the adiaphora opinion is nonsense. The addition of the words 'to me' are surely an attempt to make Paul own the maxim himself, probably by some Gnostic scribe who supposed Paul said it, and who wanted to "clarify" the matter. **6:12 ζ** συμφέρει = *bring together, agree together*. The sense can hardly be 'profit,' a lexical selection assuming adiaphora is meant. **6:12 ς** ἐξουσιασθήσομαι = *let myself be out-authoritied or over-powered*. A future passive with a middle voice ending: ομαι! **6:12 ω** τινος = *someone*. **6:12 β** Another quote by someone who thinks it does not matter what he eats, but as gluttony

1 Corinthians 7

ᵚsomeone. ¹³"Foods are for the stomach, and the stomach is for foods^β," but the Almĭghty will also destroy this *belly* and these *foods*. And the body is not for sexual immorality, but for Adŏnai, and Adŏnai for the body. ¹⁴Now the Almĭghty has not only raised Adŏnai, but will also raise us up through his power.

¹⁵Have you not been knowing that your bodies are members of the Anŏinted? Shall I then take away the members of the Anŏinted, *that* I may make them members of a harlot? May it never be! ¹⁶Or have you not been knowing that the one who joins himself to a harlot is united in body with her? For he says, "THE TWO WILL BECOME ONE FLESH."

¹⁷But the one who joins himself to Yăhweʜ is united in spirit with him. ¹⁸Be fleeing immorality. Every other sin that a man may have committed is outside the body, but the immoral man sins against his own body. ¹⁹Or have you not been knowing that your body is a temple of the Holy Spĭrit, who is in you, whom you have from the Almĭghty, and that you are not your own? ²⁰Because you have been bought with a price. Therefore glorify the Almĭghty in your body.

7 ¹Now concerning the things about which you wrote, it is good for a man not to touch a woman. ²But because of immoralities, let each man be having his own wife, and let each woman be having her own husband. ³Let the husband be fulfilling his duty to his wife, and likewise also the wife to her husband. ⁴The wife does not have authority over her own body, but the husband does, and likewise also the husband does not have authority over his own body, but the wife does. ⁵Do not be depriving one another, except by mutual agreement for a season that you may devote yourselves to prayer. Then you may be ^λas one again, so that Satan may not be tempting you through lack of self-control ^ξon your part. ⁶But this I say by way of concession, not of command. ⁷Yet I wish that all men were even as I myself am. However, each man has his own gift from the Almĭghty, one in this manner, and another in that".

⁸But I say to the unmarried and to widows that it is good for them if they will have remained even as I. ⁹But if they do not have self-control, let them marry, because it is better to marry than to burn.

¹⁰And to those who have been getting married, I give instructions, not I, but Yăhweʜ, that the wife should not be separated from her husband ¹¹(but if she may have been separated, let her be remaining unmarried to any other, or else be reconciled to her husband), and that the husband should not send his

---

is associated with fornication, Paul argues *a fortiori* (קַל וָחֹמֶר) against 'sex is for the body and the body is for sex.' ▷ Paul's announcement of judgment is not the eschatological generality that the translations make it. It is rather a specific warning of judgment against the glutton. The demonstrative pronouns are gender marked to the supplied words belly and foods. That Adŏnai relates to and is concerned with the body is also made plain in vs. 14. **6:16** γ Gen. 2:24.

7:1-7 η Paul assumes the need for intimacy is a lack of self control. Since Paul was never married one has to disagree with him. Being in a relationship produces the need, or makes one realize it exists. Several times Paul says he is giving his opinion in this passage. It is a good thing he said that because his opinion is subjective! (vs. 6, 25, 35, 40) **7:5** λ→one = *upon the same*. **7:5** ξ→part = *of ye*. 'Your lack of self control' sounds almost like an accusation, and for this reason I have avoided this exact way of putting the genitive.

wife away.

¹²But to the rest I say, not Yăhweɦ, that if any brother has a wife who is not one of the faithful, and she consents to live with him, let him not be sending her away.ᵟ ¹³And a woman who has a husband that is not one of the faithful, and he consents to live with her, let her not be sending her husband away.

¹⁴For the husband, who is not one of the faithful, has been getting made holy through his wife, and the wife, who is not one of the faithful, has been getting made holy through her faithful husband, because otherwise your children are unclean, but now they are holy. ¹⁵Yet if the one outside the faithfulᵖ leaves, let him be leaving. The brother or the sister has not been getting held bound in such cases, but the Almĭghty has been calling us to peaceᵝ.

¹⁶For how have you been knowing, wife, whether you will rescue your husband? Or how have you been knowing, husband, whether you will rescue your wife?

¹⁷Only, as Yăhweɦ has assigned to each one, as the Almĭghty has been calling each, in this manner let him be walking. And thus I direct in all the assemblies.

¹⁸Was any man ᶿcalled who had been getting circumcised? Let him not be getting uncircumcised. Has anyone been ᵠgetting called in uncircumcision? Let him not be getting circumcised. ¹⁹Circumcision is nothing, and uncircumcision is nothing, unless *it is* keeping of the commandments of the Almĭghty.

7:12 δ Consent includes an agreement not to interfere with the faithfulness of the spouse to Mĕssiah. The unbelieving spouse must not bring idolatry into the home or otherwise make it impossible for the faithful spouse to obey Mĕssiah. **7:15 β** Existing mixed marriages with new converts in the exile are permitted to remain. The children are regarded as holy. If the faithful willingly enter into one, a severe reprimand is first given (see Nehemiah). If violations increase to threaten the community of Israel then drastic action has to be taken (as under Ezra). **7:15 π** *faithfulness*

7:18 θ *was called*(ἐκλήθη) refers to the offer of salvation made and accepted at sometime in the past. One should not undo their Jewishness if he is already a Jew and *was* called to Mĕssiah. There were many Jews in the Roman world who would have loved to do just that, by getting an uncircumcision operation, and Paul is saying that neither the message of Mĕssiah, nor what he is about to say, is to be an excuse for doing that. The aorist tense refers to the call being remote, and therefore the prohibition against undoing one's circumcision is implied to be permanent. **7:18 ψ** *has been getting called* (κέκληται): this refers to a present tense salvation call to non-Jews. The Greek perfect is equivalent to the English present perfect continuous. Paul means the non-Jew who is in the very act of getting called to Mĕssiah, who may have heard the call before, but has not decided to embrace Mĕssiah yet, or who is now just responding. Therefore, the prohibition only applies in the immediate case of a response to the good news, and not later on, after the person has already responded to the call and pledged faithfulness to Messiah and is no longer being called! The reason for the temporary prohibition is to counteract the false teaching that salvation is accomplished by the ritual of circumcision. Therefore, Paul is counseling a delay between invitations to respond to the good news and going through circumcision. Similarly, a delay is also necessary between affirming faithfulness and baptism, in the presence of the ubiquitous teaching that baptism is the means of salvation. So Paul means no more than that one should not hastily get circumcised in view of the urgency placed on it by the false teachers. The same goes for baptism. ▷ The rules for circumcision are: (1) do not ultimately refuse it and (2) eat an actual Passover sacrifice without it (Exo. 12:43-49); (3) inherit land in Israel, or expect to dwell there on a permanent basis (Gen. 17:9-14; Jos. 5:2-9; Rom. 3:1-2; 4:11); (4) fail to circumcise one's own sons (cf. no. 6) (Exo. 4:24ff; Acts 16:1-4; Gal. 2:3-6; Gal. 5:11); (5) enter the temple (Ezek. 44:6-9); or (6) fail circumcise your sons on the 8th day (Lev. 12:3). The length of a delay between conversion and circumcision should not be a matter for condemnation. But the limits of delay are set by the above texts. It is my opinion that a delay may last up to a year (till Passover) or until a new convert has resolved his conceptual issues, which may take longer. But I counsel to circumcise any new sons on the eighth day. See notes on Acts 15 and End Note No. 2 on page 362.

1 Corinthians 7

²⁰Let each man be remaining in that ᶲcalling in which he was called. ²¹Were you called while a slave? Do not be worrying about it, but if you are able also to become free, rather do that. ²²For he who was called in Yăhweh while a slave, is Yăhweh's freedman. Likewise he who was called while free is the Anŏinted's slave. ²³You were bought with a price. Do not be becoming slaves of men. ²⁴Brothers, let each man be remaining with the Almĭghty in that calling in which he was called.

²⁵Now concerning virgins I have no command of Yăhweh, but I give an opinion, as one who has been getting mercy, subject to Adŏnai, being faithful. ²⁶I think then that this is good in view of the distress, which has been impending, that it is good for a man to remain as he is. ²⁷Have you been getting held bound to an unbelieving wife? Do not be seeking to be loosed. Have you been getting loosed from a wife? Do not be seeking a wife. ²⁸But if you may marry, you have not sinned, and if a virgin may marry, she has not sinned. Yet such will have trouble in this life, and I am trying to spare you. ²⁹Yet, this I am saying, brothers, the time ᶲhas been getting shortened—yea it is, so that from now on those who have wives should be as though they had none, ³⁰and those who weep, as though they did not weep, and those who rejoice, as though they did not rejoice, and those who buy, as though they did not possess, ³¹and those who use the world, as though they did not make full use of it, because the form of this world is passing away⃰.

³²But I want you to be free from concern. One who is unmarried is concerned about the things of Yăhweh, how he will have pleased Yăhweh, ³³but one who is married is concerned about the things of the world, how he will have pleased his wife, ³⁴and he has been getting divided. And the woman who is unmarried, even the virgin, is concerned about the things of Yăhweh, that she may be holy, even in body and spirit. But one who is married is worrying for the things of the world, how she will have pleased her husband. ³⁵And this I say for your own benefit, not that I will have put a halter upon you, but to promote what is seemly, and to secure undistracted devotion to Yăhweh.

³⁶But if any man is supposing that he is being rude toward his fiancé, if she may be past age, and if it must be so, let him be doing what he wishes, he does not sin. Let them be marrying.

³⁷But he who has been standing firm in his heart, being under no constraint, but has authority over his own will, and has been deciding this in his own heart, to keep his virginity, he will do well. ³⁸So then both he who marries his fiancé does well, and he who does not marry will do better.

³⁹A wife has been getting held bound as long as her husband lives, but if her husband may have slept, she is free to be married to whom she wishes, only in

---

7:20 ᶲ Paul has strategically changed the topic. By 'calling' he means 'vocation' and not the call of salvation as in the previous verses. By this maneuver Paul has left a defense against his enemies who might hear what he wrote read aloud. So long as only a few non-Jews became proselytes the main body of dispersion Jews did not have much concern, but as soon as any suggestion arose of large numbers of non-Jews joining with Israel they became radically opposed and were likely to stir up the Gentiles in their midst to oppose such a move. The uninformed are thus led to interpret Paul's words to mean that he opposes circumcision for non Jews. Paul is equally careful in his statements in other places, e.g. Gal. 2:5 and 5:11.

7:25-31 π Paul correctly foresaw trouble ahead for the Messianic Faith. Also he is not teaching assurance that it is the last episode of trouble. For this reason he warned against being tied down, and not because he is discouraging marriage. **7:29** ᶲ→is = συνεσταλμένος ἐστίν; the presentness of the perfect participle is augmented by the present tense periphrasis.

Yăhwe<small>H</small>. ⁴⁰But in my opinion she is happier if she may have remained as she is, and I think that I also have the Spĭrit of the Almĭghty.

8 ¹Now concerning "idol offerings," we have been knowing that we all have knowledge. Knowledge makes arrogant, but love edifies. ²If anyone supposes that he has been knowing something, he has not yet known as he ought to know, ³but if anyone loves the Almĭghty, he has been getting acknowledged by him.

⁴Therefore concerning "the eating of things sacrificed to idols," we have been knowing that an idol is powerless in the world, and that there is no Almĭghty but *the* one. ⁵Because even if there are those being called gods whether in heaven or on earth, as indeed there are many gods and many lords, ⁶yet for us is one^μ Almĭghty the Făther, from whom are all things^π, and we exist for him, and one Adŏnai Yĕshua, the Anŏinted, through whom are all things^π, and we exist through him^ρ. ⁷However not all men have this knowledge, but some, with the awareness of the idol until now, eat *such food* as an idol offering, and their conscience being weak is defiled.

⁸ "But food will not commend us to the Almĭghty. We are neither the worse if we may not have eaten, nor the better if we may have eaten." ⁹But be keeping watch that in no way this 'capability'^ξ of yours may have become a stumbling block to the weak! ¹⁰Because if someone may have seen you, who have knowledge, reclining in an idol's temple, will not his conscience, if he is weak, be encouraged to eat the idol offerings? ¹¹And so through your knowledge he who is weak is going to destroy himself, the brother for whose sake the Anŏinted died. ¹²And thus, by sinning against the brothers and wounding their conscience when it is

---

8:6 μ There is one Almĭghty who is Făther in relation to one Adŏnai who is Yĕshua. There is one Yăh°we<small>H</small> who is the Făther in relation to one Yăh°we<small>H</small> who is the Sŏn. See Gen. 19:24. And one Yăh°we<small>H</small> who is the Spĭrit in relation to one Făther and one Sŏn. See Isa. 48:16 and Eph. 4:4-5. ▷ If, by a heretic, Adŏnai is reduced in meaning to master, and then it is said there is One Almĭghty without adding that it means one Almĭghty *the Făther*, so as to exclude the one Măster who is the Sŏn, then **their own interpretational rule** could equally say there is one master without adding that it means one Măster *Yĕshua* and claim that the one Almĭghty is not master for us. Such is the logical destruction of those who use the text out of context to claim there is one Almĭghty to the exclusion of the Sŏn. **8:6** π All things **he makes be** (Yăh°we<small>H</small>). **8:6** ρ Paul concedes the reasoning of the one who points out that one might be able to eat the food offered to an idol without engaging in an act of worship. This is just as one can have an idol in one's house without worshiping it, as even in Yisra'el there were idols in houses that the faithful did not worship. However, it was a sin to retain these objects because they were snares to the weak and young and innocent. For this reason it was the commandment of the Almĭghty that they be destroyed. ▷ Paul shows that the same reasoning applies to Yisra'el in exile in the midst of idolaters. If one participates in an idol feast, not worshiping the idol, but just eating the food, then a brother weak in the faith may think it OK to honor Gŏd and the idol god which he will do by eating. Even though it may be otherwise, the example will teach them this. The situation is also ambiguous. Someone may say they only eat the food, but they are really abandoning the Faith in their heart! For that possibility also, the weak may be tempted to likewise abandon the Faith. ▷ Paul gives the reasoning behind the prohibition against eating idol food even if one could eat without worshiping the idol. This shows that there are no loopholes in the prohibition. The prohibition is not just for the weak, but also for the strong lest the weak fall into transgression. See Acts 15:29; Rev. 2:14, 20; Num. 25:2; Psa. 106:28.

8:9 ξ The usual translations read ἐξουσία as "liberty" or "right," but this is misleading. Here it means a mental "power," "capability," or effective control by which the strong is able to not associate the food with the idol. The ἐξουσία does not imply legal permission, but is only used to acknowledge the mental capability of eating without honoring the deity. Acting on it is only hypothetically posed for the sake of the discussion. It appears that Paul chose this word instead of a different word like 'habit' or 'practice' because he only wanted to acknowledge the possibility of eating without honoring the false god, and without agreeing with the practice of it. The only way to see

weak, you sin against the Anŏinted.

¹³Therefore, if such food causes my brother to stumble, no, I shall not have eaten such meat ever, so that I will not have caused my brother to stumble.

9

¹Am I not free? Am I not an emissary? Have I not been *beholding Yĕshua our Adŏnai? Are you not my work in Yăhweh? ²If to others I am not an emissary, at least I am to you, because you are the seal of my emissaryship in Yăhweh. ³My defense to those who examine me is this:

⁴Do we not have a right to eat and drink? ⁵Do we not have a right to take along a sister in ᵖfaithfulness as a wife, even as the rest of the emissaries, even the brothers of Adŏnai, and Keipha? ⁶Or do only Bar-Nabba and I not have a right to refrain from working? ⁷Who at any time serves as a soldier at his own expense? Who plants a vineyard, and does not eat the fruit of it? Or who tends a flock and does not use the milk of the flock? ⁸I am not speaking these things according to human judgment, am I? Or does not the Law also say these things? ⁹Because it has been getting written in the Law of Moshˆeh, "YOU SHALL NOT MUZZLE THE OX WHILE HE IS THRESHING^λ." The Almĭghty is not only concerned about oxen, is he? ¹⁰Or is he speaking also in every way for our sake? Yes, also for our benefit it was written, because the plowman ought to plow in hope, and the thresher to thresh in hope of sharing the crops. ¹¹If we have sown spiritual things among you, is it too great to expect if we should reap things for the body from you? ¹²ªIf others share the right over you, do we not more?

¹²ᵇNevertheless, we did not use this right, but we endure all things, that we will have caused no hindrance to the good news of the Anŏinted. ¹³Have you not been knowing that those working themselves at the Temple duties eat the food of the Temple, and those attending to the altar are partakers from the altar? ¹⁴Likewise also Yăhweh has ordered for those proclaiming the good news to live off of the good news.

¹⁵But I have been using none of these things. And I have not written these things that it will have become so for me, because it would be better for me to die than that any one should void my boast. ¹⁶Because when I should myself be proclaiming the good news, there is no boast for me, because a critical need is being laid upon me. For woe is me if I may not have proclaimed the good news. ¹⁷Indeed, if I do this voluntarily, I am going to have a reward, but if against my will, then for an administration I have and will have been getting held faithful. ¹⁸What then is my reward? That, when proclaiming the good news, I will have offered the good news without charge, so as not to make use of my right in the good news.

¹⁹Because by being free from all, to all, I myself became a servant, so that I will have won more. ²⁰So to the Yehudim I have made myself as a Yehudi, that

---

to it that the capability to do so does not stumble the weak is not to do so. **9:1-3** ⱪ *or perceiving, see with the mind, know* (Thayer No. 2). The pres. perf. prog. implies more than just an initial physical seeing, but a continued sight into the mind of Mĕssiah via the Spirit which is linked to the initial seeing and call of Paul. The Greek perf. reinforces Paul's continued authority. **9:5** π +*the.* **9:9** λ Deut 25:4

I will have won Yehudim. To those subject to what is customary, as subject to what is customary, though not being myself subject to what is customary, that I will have won those subject to what is customary. ²¹To those who are without what is customary, as without what is customary, though not being without what is customary for the Almĭghty, but according to what is customary for the Anŏinted, that I will have won those without what is customary.

²²To the weak I made myself weak, that I will have won the weak. I have been becoming all these things to all men, that I may by all ways have rescued some.

²³And I am doing all things for the sake of the good news, so that I will have made myself a fellow partaker of it. ²⁴Have you not been knowing that those running on a stadium race course all run, but one receives the prize? Likewise, be running so that you shall have won. ²⁵And everyone competing *in the games* exercises self-control in all things. They therefore do it so that they will have received a perishable crown, but we an imperishable. ²⁶Likewise now indeed I run, as not one uncertain. Likewise I box, as not one beating the air, ²⁷but I beat my body and make it my slave, that in no way, having proclaimed to others, I myself will have become disqualified.

10

¹Because I do not want you to be ignorant, brothers, that our fathers were all under the cloud, and all had passed through the sea. ²And all had immersed themselves into Mosheh in the cloud and in the sea. ³And all had eaten the same spiritual food. ⁴And all had drunk the same spiritual drink, because they were drinking from the spiritual ᵖRock which followed behind them, and the rock was the Anŏinted. ⁵But, with most of them the Almĭghty was not pleased, because they were strewn in the wilderness.

⁶Now these things have become examples for us, that we should not be those who lust for evil things, as they also lusted, ⁷nor let yourselves be becoming idolaters, as some of them. As it has been getting written, "THE PEOPLE SAT DOWN TO EAT AND DRINK, AND STOOD UP TO PLAYᶜ." ⁸Nor may we be practicing sexual immorality, even as some of them practiced sexual immorality, and "TWENTY-FOUR THOUSAND_β," fell in one day. ⁹Nor yet may we test the Anŏinted One, even as some of them had dared test, and were being destroyed by the serpents. ¹⁰Nor be grumbling, as some of them grumbled, and were destroyed by the destroyer.

9:20-21 Nomos (νόμος) means "What is customary" or "what is accepted to be proper." But what some consider proper is by others not considered proper. What some consider the norm is by others foreign. Paul says he is subject to what is customary for the Almĭghty, that is, what He accepts to be proper. And that we know is His Law, the Torah. What kind of norm nomos refers to is as varied as the contexts. Here it means Jewish tradition in so far as it is not against Torah, or other traditions, or lack of them, so long as they are not against the Torah. See Rom. 3:21 note.

10:4 ρ Evidently Paul is playing on a Jewish tradition here that the rock Mosheh smote water from was taken by Yisra'el on their journey, but he does not certify the tradition. Rather he uses it to say that the Messenger of Yăhweh is the spiritual Rock that followed behind them, and also He went before them. And from his word they drank. **10:7** ς Exo 32:4-6, 19. **10:8** β Num 25:9: Greek text 23,000. **10:11** γ All ages are conceived as ending at the present time, even though the end point of many ages was still moving with time, and more ages were still to come. Every movement or kingdom may have an age named after it. Even a ruler or authority may be called an Aeon. The phrase cannot mean the hasty fulfillment of all eschatology. But the point is that the examples serve the present ages.

1 Corinthians 10

¹¹Now these things as examples were befalling those ones, and they were written for our warning, to whom the ends of the ⁷ages have been arriving. ¹²Therefore let him who thinks he has been standing be looking out lest he may have fallen. ¹³No temptation has been overtaking you except what is human. And the Almĭghty is faithful, who will not allow you to be tested over what you are able, but with the testing will make also the way of escape, that you may be able to endure it.

¹⁴Therefore, my beloved, be fleeing from idolatry. ¹⁵I speak as one to the thoughtful. Judge yourselves what I say. ¹⁶Is not the cup of blessing which we bless a fellowshipping in the blood of the Anŏinted? Is not the bread which we break a fellowshipping in the body of the Anŏinted? ¹⁷Since there is one bread, we who are many are one body, because we all partake of the one bread. ¹⁸Be looking at the nation of Yisra'el according to the flesh. Are not those eating the sacrifices fellowshippers of the altar? ¹⁹What am I saying then? That an idol offering is anything, or that an idol is anything? ²⁰But only that what the nations sacrifice is to demons, and not to the Almĭghty. And I do not want you to become sharers with the demons.

²¹You cannot drink the cup of Yăhweн and the cup of demons. You cannot partake of the table of Yăhweн and the table of demons. ²²Or do we provoke Yăhweн to jealousy? We are not stronger than he, are we?

²³"Someone allows all things^χ," but not all things go together. "Someone allows all things," but not all things edify. ²⁴Let no one be seeking his own good, but that of his neighbor.

²⁵You ⁿmay be eating all being sold in the meat market, without asking questions for the sake of such an awareness, ²⁶BECAUSE THE EARTH IS YĂHWEн'S, AND ALL IT CONTAINS.ᵟ ²⁷If one of the non-faithful invites you, and you wish to go, you ⁿmay be eating anything that is set before you, without asking questions for the sake of such an awareness.

²⁸But if anyone will have said to you, "This is dedicated to idols," do not

---

10:23 χ This translation recognizes what some others have before. Paul's statement is in fact an argument from an opposition that the faithful in Corinth were facing. Gnostic theology was just starting to form against the faithful at this time, so Paul's responses seem quick and tentative. A more severe condemnation of the makers of these arguments after they infiltrated the assemblies comes later on from Yoĥanan.

10:25 η read εσθιητε vs. εσθιετε. 𝔓⁴⁶ appears to read ΦΑΓΕΤΕ in vs. 27 which is unnoticed in NA-27. 𝔓⁴⁶ also appears with a mark over ΕϹΘΙΕΤΕ in vs. 25. Maybe it should be read ΕϹΘΙΗΤΕ. It makes no sense that Paul would order them to eat everything. Rather to give permission requires the subjunctive. ▷ It is often presumed by interpreters that the meat markets were heavily contaminated with idol meat. On the contrary, only some small amount of such meat may have been somewhere in those markets. In such case, Paul judges any link with idolatry sufficiently broken unless one is informed it is idol meat. Then it becomes forbidden. ▷ Is meat marked 'Halal' such a disclosure? The situation differs. That religion does not use a shrine or images, but merely a "prayer." If one is stuck in a situation, then there is no known Scripture ruling prohibiting eating the Halal meat. If one's conscience bothers one, by no means eat it. Mine would for several reasons not mentioned pertaining to our situation. ▷ A line between idol food and not idol food has to be drawn somewhere. Surely a Hindu who "blesses" all the food on earth in a 'prayer' cannot turn all food into idol food. ▷ Asian eating establishments: make sure the cook is not sacrificing part of the meal to an idol in the kitchen. The food is idol food if they do. ▷ Any food can be turned into idol food, whether meat or vegetable, simply by laying it in front of an

be eating it, for the sake of the one who has reported it, and for the sake of a conflict of conscience; ²⁹I mean not your own conscience, but the other. For wherein why should my allowance judge itself by another's conscience conflict?^θ

³⁰If I partake with thankfulness, why am I slandered over that for which I give thanks? ³¹Whether, then, you eat or drink or whatever you do, be doing all to the glory of the Almĭghty. ³²Be giving no offense either to Yehudim or to Greeks or to the Assembly of the Almĭghty,^χ ³³just as I also please all men in the course of all things, not seeking my own profit, but the profit of the many, so that they will have been rescued.

11

¹Be becoming imitators of me, just as I also am of the Anŏinted. ²Now I praise you because you have been remembering me in everything, and hold firmly to the traditions,^α just as I delivered them to you. ³But I want you to have been understanding that the Anŏinted is the ^βhead of every man, and the man is the head of a woman, and the Almĭghty is the head of the Anŏinted.

⁴Every man who has something down from his head while praying or prophesying, disgraces his head.^γ ⁵But every woman who has her head uncovered while praying or prophesying, disgraces her head, because she is one and the same with her whose head has been getting shaved.^ψ ⁶Because if a woman does not cover her head, let her also have her hair cut off, but if it is disgraceful for a

---

image or picture of a deity or even a 'saint' being honored. **10:25** δ Psa 24:1. **10:27** η cf. 10:25 η.

10:29 θ The allowance here (or liberty) is the freedom to eat what is in the meat market without investigating whether it passed through an idol shrine. If your pagan neighbors who invite you get their meat from the market then no investigation is required. But if someone declares that it is in fact idol meat, it is forbidden, by law, which is founded on the principle of looking out for others, and not on the principle it would always be consumed with the intent to honor an idol. Now many pagans have idols in their houses also, and to these they make offerings. These residences are classified as idol temples. So attending here is forbidden. The rule is that if others begin to say that it is offered to a foreign god then avoid it. **10:32** χ Obviously if one did not worship the Greek or Roman gods one was going to offend them when they chose to be offended. Paul only means insofar as possible. Presently another religion of force specializes in taking offense. Its offense is part of its force method. It does not worship the same Gŏd as the faithful, not withstanding the arguments that its word for their god means 'god.' Many pagans were known to worship one god, but a foreign one. The classical pagans also called their gods "god." What the Jews sacrifice in the place of the Name is permitted (cf. vs. 18-20) and therefore what Rabbis dedicate is permitted, being a lesser matter than the Temple. They themselves may prove hypocrites, but their dedications are sanctified, and they themselves because they are relatives of Mĕssiah and of the house of Ya'aqov. But the foreign religion with the political ideology of force, sacrifices and dedicates toward a foreign place and a foreign shrine and to the god of a foreign religious text, and with a foreign will. And Yitsḥaq, the foreign god hates. And if anyone will be saved, he must forsake the foreign god and be adopted to Yitsḥaq.

11:2 α Traditions: practical rules or ways for implementing observance of the Torah. Binding and loosing of the emissaries on various legal questions including overturning rabbinical errors. **11:3** β The head of someone is the authority over them. The head of a woman is her husband. **11:4** γ A head covering was regarded as an effeminate article of clothing if it was draped over the head and its purpose was not to protect the head from the elements. The use of the tallit and kippah to cover the head of a man was a later Rabbinical innovation. **11:5** ψ This was the cultural perception and so it was generally considered profane if a woman did this during an act of public piety. The emissaries liberated woman to pray and prophesy in an assembly of the faithful. The Rabbis would not permit it. But the emissaries ruled (in keeping with the cultural norm) that women should cover their head when using their new freedom to pray or prophesy in public. This ruling was motivated by the general perception. Whether it applies today or not depends on the circumstances. And strictly the ruling is only required under the law of love. See 1 Cor. 9:20-22. The Torah may not be added to nor subtracted from. No one should intend to wound the sensibilities of others.

woman to have her hair cut off or her head shaved, let her be covering her head.

⁷For a man ought not to have his head covered,⁸ since he is the image and glory of the Almĭghty, but the woman is the glory of man, ⁸because man does not originate from woman, but woman from man, ⁹because indeed man was not created for the woman's sake, but woman for the man's sake. ¹⁰Therefore the woman ought to keep control over her head, because of the *fallen* messengers.⁵ ¹¹However, in Yăhweĥ, neither is woman independent of man, nor is man independent of woman. ¹²For as the woman originates from the man, so also the man has his birth through the woman, and all things originate from the Almĭghty. ¹³Judge for yourselves: is it proper for a woman to pray to the Almĭghty uncovered?

¹⁴Is not even nature itself teaching you that if a man may style effeminate hair, it is a dishonor to him? ¹⁵But if a woman may style effeminate hair, it is a glory to her. Because her long hair has been getting given to her for a veil. ¹⁶But if one is inclined to be contentious, we have no other practice, nor have the assemblies of the Almĭghty.⁴

¹⁷Now about this directive, I do not praise you, because it is not for the better, but for the worse that you gather together. ¹⁸Because on the one hand, firstly, in your coming together in the Assembly, I hear that there are schisms among you, and in part some of it I hold faithful, ¹⁹because it is inevitable even for heresies to occur among you, with the result that also those approved will have become manifest among you. ²⁰At your coming together, therefore, at the same place, it is not Adŏnai's supper⁰ to eat, ²¹because each party its own supper takes beforehand during the eating. On the one hand one is hungry, and on the other, another is drunk.

²²Because do you not have houses to eat and to drink in? Or do you despise the Assembly of the Almĭghty, and humiliate those having nothing? What shall I have said to you? Shall I have praised you? In this I do not praise! ²³Because I

11:7 δ Paul obviously means an effeminate covering and not a hat for the elements. The law does require a distinction between men's clothing and women's clothing. In that time the greatest distinction was in how the head and hair were kept. Paul gives the reason the distinction is to be made as the principle of the matter. The distinction may be made in another way only if the principle is upheld and a distinction is made. Cultural norms are usually givens, and therefore regardless of personal opinion, the law of love should operate. **11:10** ζ Paul is reminding us of the episode in Genesis 6 where the sons of the Almĭghty transgressed the created order of things and came down to take women as wives. Keeping the distinction between men and women is important enough to remind us what happens to those who try to erase the boundaries. Bucking the cultural norms of propriety makes one a target. If rebellion is intended, they become slaves of evil spirits. Every culture that is not trying to erase the bounds has acceptable ways of making the distinctions. But some cultures are so perverse as to have no distinctions. Women should make it their aim to comply with the higher standards for a public assembly on Şabbaţhs and the highest standards if they intend to take a public role. **11:16** μ Paul appears to have also been asked about hair length and the practice of veiling women, and he abruptly transitions to consideration of the question. The additional answers are given but the questions are not stated. In Greek culture long hair (comely, beautified) was regarded as feminine. So also in most cultures. Jews were stricter about veiling women in public but Paul does not require this extremity. In fact, he appears to outright reject it as a puritanical extreme. Long hair for a women suffices to make the distinction between sexes, and he only required a head covering in the Assembly when a woman prays or speaks. She does not have to be veiled at any time, and after the prayer or prophesy she did not have to keep the covering on. **11:20** φ He speaks of their attempt at observing a Passover Seder. They were too immature in the faith to do it properly without letting their cultural feasting habits corrupt the occasion.

have received from Adŏnai what even I delivered to you, because Adŏnai Yĕshua in the night which he was getting betrayed took bread, ²⁴and having blessed, he broke it and said, "This represents my body which is getting broken^p on your behalf. Be doing this for the memorial of me^θ." ²⁵Likewise also the cup after having had supper, saying, "This is the cup of the ^μcovenant ^χrenewal, which is with my blood. Be doing this ^ζas often soever you may be drinking it, for the memorial of me." ²⁶Because as often soever you may be eating this bread and this cup you may be drinking, the death of Adŏnai you are proclaiming until he may have come. ²⁷So then who ever may be eating the bread or may be drinking the cup of Adŏnai unworthily, will be guilty of the body and of the blood of

11:24 p κλώμενον. The manuscripts are divided over this word, translated, 'getting broken.' In light of Yoh. 19:36, it is obvious that the words were meant to be a metaphorical play on breaking the bread in reference to Messiah's suffering on our behalf, and not a literal bone breaking. ▷ In favor of retaining 'getting broken' might be that an early sacerdotal glorification of the bread over what it represented favored the deletion. **11:24** θ 'Be doing...': These words are not reported in the Evangelists, but Paul must have received them from Peter. Probably Mĕssiah mentioned this to Peter after his resurrection when he was remarking on the subject of Passover. **11:25** ζ→ *as often soever you may be;* The statement is contingent on whether they have a single seder or a double seder in a year, whether they are on a journey or in a situation so as not to be able to observe Passover. The directive does not prohibit making the best of a poor situation at Passover time. However, the interpretation of 'as often as' to mean quarterly, weekly, monthly, or on some other schedule disconnected with Passover was by no means the intention of the statement. One should be careful not to treat a kiddush as communion. Those who do should be corrected. **11:25** μ→renewal = בְּרִית חֲדָשָׁה (חידושה); Jer. 31:31 **11:25** χ. = *new-made;* 'renewal' clarifies the sense, but *new-made/made-new* is the precise force of καινή and only the previous knowledge of the Scriptural contexts resolves the sense. ▷ cf. Th. 3.92 ἐκ καινῆς: anew; 'they fortified anew the city' (Thucydides. The Peloponnesian War. London, J. M. Dent; New York, E. P. Dutton. 1910); 'built afresh' (Jowett); sometimes the word *new* (καινός) is used for something old; see 1 John 2:7; Καινός clearly originates from the verb καινίζω, for which the meaning 'renew' has been carefully censored, it being suggested that only ἀνα-καινίζω has that sense. BDAG (3rd edition) has '**make new**' for its brief καινίζω entry. Accordingly an adjective would be '**made new**.' Now something 'made new,' if it be an old thing would have the same meaning as 'renew,' thus a city **made new**, could be a city renewed. The Piel Hebrew חָדַשׁ is stative causative, 'to make to be new,' thus to renew or make brand new as the context may require (witness the evident confusion in the trans. of Job 10:17). In Ezek. 18:31: עֲשׂוּ לָכֶם לֵב חָדָשׁ וְרוּחַ חֲדָשָׁה = *make for yourselves a heart made-new and a spirit made-new* = ποιησατε εαυτος καρδιαν καινην και πνευμα καινον. Who will say that the heart and spirit is so wholly new as to be brand new and never existing before? One can think of a sadistic sci-fi plot here to 'replace' the mind and spirit of people with a race of alien beings taking over their bodies in the resurrection. But it is nothing so sinister. The text means a renewing of heart and spirit to faithfulness after forgiveness (cf. Ezek. 11:19; 36:26; Job 29:20; Lam. 3:23). ▷ The apparent rarity of 'made re new' vs. 'made brand new' only shows the word is used more in the one sense than the other. The question that should be asked is 'does the thing being **made new** exist already?' And what is the former status of the thing **made new**? It is the בְּרִית עוֹלָם that is made new, which is both the covenant of old, and the everlasting covenant. ▷ *A Modern Greek and English Lexicon,* 'καινίζω to renew.' By Rev. Lowndes, Inspector General of Schools in the Ionian Islands, 1837. ▷ *Analytical Lexicon to the Septuagint,* Taylor & Eynikel, 'καινίζω to make new [τι]; to renew, to repair [τι].' See 1 Macc. 10:10; Zeph. 3:17, 'καινιεῖ σε ἐν τῇ ἀγαπήσει αὐτοῦ' = *he will renew you in his love.* Isa. 61:4, 'καινιοῦσιν πόλεις ἐρήμους' = *they will restore the desolate cities* = חִדְּשׁוּ עָרֵי חֹרֶב. ▷ The cities exist already. They need restoration. ▷ νεάζω = *be young;* νέος = *youthful, young; be new (in time).*

Adŏnai. ²⁸Now let a man be testing himself, and this way from the bread let him be eating, and from the cup let him be drinking, ²⁹because the one eating and drinking, judgment to himself will eat and will drink, if he is not discerning the body. ³⁰Because of this, among you many are sick and ill and a substantial number have fallen asleep.

³¹But if we were discerning ourselves, we would not have been judged. ³²And in being judged by Adŏnai, we are being disciplined so that we will not have been condemned with the world. ³³So then, my brothers, in coming together to eat, be waiting for one another. ³⁴If anyone is hungering, let him be eating at home so that you may not be coming together for judgment. And I myself will give commandment when I may have come about the rest of the things.

12

¹Now concerning spiritual gifts, brothers, I do not want you to be unaware. ²You have been knowing that when you were pagans, you were led astray to the dumb idols, however you were led. ³Therefore I make known to you, that no one speaking by the Spĭrit of the Almĭghty says, "Yĕshua is accursed," and no one can say, "Adŏnai Yĕshua" except by the Holy Spĭrit.

⁴Now there are varieties of gifts, but the same Spĭrit. ⁵And there are varieties of ministries, and the same Adŏnai. ⁶And there are different kinds of jobs, but the same Almĭghty who works each of these among everyone. ⁷But to each one is given the revelation of the Spĭrit for the common good. ⁸On the one hand, therefore, to one is given the word of wisdom through the Spĭrit, but to another the word of knowledge according to the same Spĭrit. ⁹To another is given courageous faithfulness by the same Spĭrit, and to another gifts of healing by the one Spĭrit, ¹⁰and to another the working of miracles, and to another prophecy, and to another the distinguishing of spirits, to another various kinds of languages, and to another the interpretation of languages.

¹¹But one and the same Spĭrit works all these things, distributing to each one individually just as he wills. ¹²Because even as the body is one and yet has many members, and all the members of the body, though they are many, are one body, so also is the Anŏinted. ¹³Because by one Spĭrit we were all immersed into one body, whether Yehudim or Greeks, whether slaves or free, and we were all made to drink of one Spĭrit.

¹⁴Because the body is not one member, but many. ¹⁵If the foot may have said, "Because I am not a hand, I am not a part of the body," it is not for this reason any the less a part of the body. ¹⁶And if the ear may have said, "Because I am not an eye, I am not a part of the body," it is not for this reason any the less a part of the body. ¹⁷If the whole body were an eye, where would the hearing be? If the whole were hearing, where would the sense of smell be? ¹⁸But now the Almĭghty has placed the members, each one of them, in the body, just as he desired. ¹⁹And if they were all one member, where would the body be? ²⁰But now there are many members, but one body. ²¹And the eye cannot say to the hand, "I have no need of you," or again the head to the feet, "I have no need of you." ²²On the contrary, it is much truer that the members of the body which seem to

be weaker are necessary. ²³And those members of the body, which we deem less honorable, on these we bestow more abundant honor, and our unseemly members come to have more abundant seemliness, ²⁴whereas our seemly members have no need of it. But the Almĭghty has so composed the body, giving more abundant honor to that member which lacked, ²⁵that there may be no division in the body, but that the members should have the same care for one another. ²⁶And if one member suffers, all the members suffer with it. If one member is honored, all the members rejoice with it.

²⁷Now you are the Anŏinted's body, and individually members of it. ²⁸And the Almĭghty has appointed in the Assembly, first emissaries, second prophets, third teachers, then miracles, then gifts of healings, helps, administrations, various kinds of languages. ²⁹All are not emissaries, are they? All are not prophets^π, are they? All are not teachers, are they? All are not workers of miracles, are they? ³⁰All do not have gifts of healings, do they? All do not speak with languages, do they? All do not interpret, do they? ³¹But earnestly be desiring the greater gifts. And I show you a still more excellent way.

13

¹If I may be speaking with the languages of men and of messengers, yet do not have love, I have been becoming a ringing brass or a clanging cymbal. ²And if I may be having prophecy, and I may have been understanding all mysteries and all knowledge, and if I may hold to every faithful pledge, so as to remove mountains, yet may not have love, I am nothing. ³And if I may have given all my possessions to feed the poor, and if I may have delivered my body so that I may boast, but am not having love, it profits me nothing.

⁴Love is patient, love is kind, and is not jealous. Love does not brag and is not arrogant, ⁵and does not act unbecomingly. It does not seek its own, is not provoked, does not take account of a wrong suffered, ⁶does not rejoice in unrighteousness, but rejoices with the truth. ⁷It always protects, always holds faithful, always hopes, always endures. ⁸Love never fails, but if there are prophecies, they will be resolved. If there are languages, they will be deciphered. If there is education, it will be demoted, ⁹because we know in part, and we prophesy in part, ¹⁰but when the perfect may have come, the partial will be unemployed.

¹¹When I was being a child, I was speaking as a child. I was thinking as a child. I was reasoning as a child. When I have been becoming a man, I have been doing away with childish things, ¹²because now we see in a mirror dimly, but then face to face. Now I know in part, but then I will know fully just as I also have been fully known. ¹³But now abide faithfulness, hope, love, these three, but the greatest of these is love.

14

¹Be pursuing love, and be desiring earnestly spiritual things, but more so that you may be prophesying. ²For one who speaks in another language

---

12:29 π *a preacher;* cf. Exo. 7:1; 1 Sam. 9:9.
14:2 θ *or so much as.* There is quite a bit more of direct revelatory prophecy at the foundational level for the faith in a backwards culture of idolatry which is necessary for its nurture. This activity occurs still, but more subjectively where the faith is established, as the goal of the Holy Spirit is to point us to Scripture as the objective source of truth rather than experienc-

does not speak to men, ⁹but to the Almĭghty, because no one *else* understands, but in his spirit he speaks mysteries.

³But one who prophesies speaks edification and exhortation and consolation to men. ⁴One who speaks in another language edifies himself, but one who prophesies edifies the assembly. ⁵Now I am wishing for you all to be speaking in other languages, but more so, that you may be prophesying, and, greater is one who is prophesying than one who is speaking in other languages, unless someone may be interpreting, so that the assembly may have received edifying.

⁶But now, brothers, if I may have come to you speaking in other languages, what will I profit you, unless I may have spoken to you either by way of revelation or of knowledge or of prophecy or of teaching? ⁷Yet even lifeless things, either flute or harp, in producing a sound, if they may not have produced a distinction in the tones, how will it be known what is played on the flute or on the harp? ⁸For if the bugle may have produced an indistinct sound, who will prepare himself for battle? ⁹So also you, unless you may have produced by the tongue speech that is clear, how will it be known what is spoken? For you will be speaking into the air. ¹⁰There are, perhaps, a great many kinds of voices in the world, and

---

es. The faithful have to learn to be faithful to those commandments which they have heard already rather than hear new commandments. ▷ While prediction does fall within the meaning of prophesy, that does not appear to be the meaning Paul is focused on. See vs. 3 for other types of speaking also considered prophecy. See remarks on Rom. 12:6 for the definition. Note the lack of a category called preacher here. A preacher was a proclaimer or an evangelist or one who called to repentance in these times. What is understood by a preacher nowadays is what was meant by a prophet then in the assembly. A prophet exhorts, comforts, and builds up with Scripture. A prophet give homilies, or illustrations using scripture. A prophet reveals new things to his audience, or has new things revealed to him which he reveals to the audience. An assembly may have more than one prophet. A prophet is not a formalized teacher. A teacher instructs new people in established doctrine and the younger in formalized instruction. Some people have both gifts, i.e. prophet-teacher. The predictive prophet has a gift extraordinaire, which is seldom seen now, both due to the backsliding assemblies into lawlessness, abuse by false prophets, and also due to the fact that there is much prophecy in Scripture currently being ignored. The true prophet is required to speak in the name of the Almĭghty and to uphold his rules and laws. ▷ The Corinthians had their priorities mixed up. They had supposed that use of other languages (literally "tongues," which is an archaic term for other languages) in their assemblies was more spiritual. Therefore, they did not regulate it or require interpretations. Paul says the spiritual goal is prophesy and not the languages, which are only the means to the end. Perhaps they supposed this because of what happened at Shavuot in Acts 2 and because the standard of pagan priestesses around them was to utter unintelligible ravings and then others interpreted them. Paul knew well that the devil would be able to exploit this naiveness if preventative measures were not taken. ▷ Paul may appear to suspect the sort of thing openly promoted by Charismatics as "tongues," (when defined as *glossolalia*). If so, he writes with foresight into the future after considering babbling priestesses of Greece and their potential for infiltrating the assembly, but he deals with it indirectly by governing the use of real foreign languages. The miracles of "tongues" in Acts 2 and everywhere else including rare stories from missionaries all involved real languages being spoken or being understood where no one learned the language. Paul says nothing that would require us to believe that the Holy Spĭrit takes control of a person's tongue to utter things with it that the person himself cannot understand. When such utterances are tested they prove to be something other than what is claimed for them. Charismatics are in abject fear of questioning their experiences because they have linked both their salvation and approval by Gŏd to them. This is a false gospel to which they are slaves, and it is why so much unrighteousness comes from them.

14:9 χ On the surface Paul appears to be correcting the problem of a real human foreign language that is untranslated, but either by foresight, prophetic inspiration, or astute cultural analysis of the threat posed to the assembly by pagan Greece, he rebukes the babble called tongues by Charasmatics simply by presuming every tongue must have a meaning and that no one is edified without knowing it. The ravings of Charasmatics have proved time and again to be false when subjected to objective tests, and thus are no

none is without meaning. ¹¹If then I have not been knowing the meaning of the voice, I will be to the one who speaks a barbarian, and the one who speaks will be a barbarian to me. ¹²So also you, since you are zealous of spiritual gifts, be seeking for the edification of the assembly, so that all of you may be prospering.

¹³Therefore let one who is speaking in another language be praying so that someone may be interpreting.ᵝ ¹⁴For if I may be praying in another language, my spirit is praying, but my understanding is unfruitful *for anyone else*. ¹⁵What is the outcome then? I will pray in the spirit and I will pray for the understanding *of others also*. I will sing in the spirit and I will sing for the understanding *of others also*. ¹⁶Otherwise if you may be blessing in the spirit *only*, how will the one who is occupying the place of the unlearned say "Amen" at your giving of thanks, since he has not been knowing what you are saying? ¹⁷For you are giving thanks well enough, but the other man is not edified. ¹⁸I thank the Almighty, I speak in languages more than you all, ¹⁹however, in the assembly I desire to speak five words because of my understanding, so that I may have instructed others also, rather than ten thousand words in another language.ᶠ

²⁰Brothers, do not be becoming children in your thinking, but in evil be being babes, and in your thinking be becoming mature. ²¹In the Law it has been getting written, "BY MEN OF OTHER LANGUAGES AND BY THE LIPS OF STRANGERS I WILL SPEAK TO THIS PEOPLE, AND EVEN SO THEY WILL NOT LISTEN TO ME, SAYS YĂH-WEH.ᵠ" ²²So then other languages are for a sign, not to those who hold faithful, but to the unfaithful, but prophecy is for a sign, not to the unfaithful, but to those who hold faithful.

²³If therefore the whole assembly may have assembled together and all may be speaking in other languages, and unlearned men or unfaithful ones may have entered, will they not say that you are being mad? ²⁴But if all may be prophesying, and an unfaithful one or an unlearned man may have entered, he is being

---

better than the legendary Pythia of Delphi and her priests who interpreted the oracle into long ambiguous prognostications. **14:13** β The text does not mean that one should pray so that he himself can interpret what he means as if he did not understand it himself, but so that someone else who knows the language and the common tongue can interpret it. As vs. 17 shows the speaker of another language is directing the speech and is giving thanks. Vs. 28 confirms that a separate translator (interpreter) is meant.

14:19 ζ Paul assumes the most optimistic interpretation of events at Corinth that he can. He is responding only to a potential threat (to which they were exposed by unregulated use of real languages) with preventative measures. They are zealous to speak in their own languages because they are so full of praise for the Almighty, and new understandings from Scripture, that they can only express it this way. He therefore encourages them for the practical benefit of all, while only laying down the rules to prevent a more sinister infiltration. **14:21** ψ Isa 28:11f. This prophecy refers to the fact that Yisrael would have to learn Aramaic and other tongues in exile where they forgot Hebrew, and that they would have to hear the word of Yăhweh later in those languages. Upon return from the exile, they had to have the Hebrew text interpreted because their fathers had been unfaithful. Having to put up with other tongues, therefore, for them was a sign of their unbelief. Likewise the other languages at the tower of Babel were a sign of judgment. Having the blessing of hearing the Scriptures prophetically opened, on the other hand, is a sign of Yăhweh's blessing to the faithful.

1 Corinthians 14

convicted by all, he is being examined by all. ²⁵The secrets of his heart are being disclosed, and so fallen on his face, he will worship the Almĭghty, declaring that the Almĭghty is certainly among you.

²⁶So what happens, brothers, when you may be coming together? Each of you is having a psalm, or is having a teaching, or is having a revelation, or is having another language, or is having interpretation. Be doing all things for edification. ²⁷If as well, anyone is speaking in another language, it should be by two or at the most three, and each in turn, and let someone be interpreting, ²⁸but if there may be no interpreter, let him be keeping silent in the assembly, and let him be speaking to himself and to the Almĭghty.ᵛ ²⁹And let two or three prophets be speaking, and let the others be passing judgment. ³⁰But if a revelation may have come to another who is sitting, let the first be keeping silent. ³¹For you can all be prophesying one by one, so that all may be learning and all may be receiving exhortation, ³²and the spirits of prophets are staying subject to prophets⸰, ³³because the Almĭghty is not an Almĭghty of confusion but of peace, as in all the assemblies of the holy ones.

³⁴Let the women be keeping quiet in the assemblies, because THEY ARE NOT PERMITTED TO CARRY ON, BUT LET THEM BE SUBJECTING THEMSELVES⸗, just as the Law says. ³⁵And if they desire to learn anything, let them be asking their own husbands at home, because it is improper for a woman to ᵞcarry on in the assembly.

³⁶Was it from you that the word of the Almĭghty first went forth? Or has it come to you only? ³⁷If anyone thinks he is a prophet or spiritual, let him be

---

14:28 ᵛ Let him speak to himself and to the Almĭghty. Again this only makes sense if a person is directing his own speech thoughts to himself and to the Almĭghty. Paul does not mean this is speech "from" the Almĭghty. Such an interpretation of "speak to himself" is completely out of the ordinary. **14:32** ϕ In paganism an evil spirit takes over the prophet. The same is true of shamanism. A true predictive prophet receives a revelation in a vision or a dream. Then they come and report it or they write it down being in control of themselves. The prophets that bring forth exposition from scripture here are generally what are today called preachers, but then there were also real prophets extraordinaire. Paul is laying down a rule for all prophets in the Assembly of whichever type. They are to be in control of their own selves. The Assembly is to give no place to the Oracle of Delphi or anything like it. ▷ By this rule Paul implicitly bans all *glossolalia* in the Assembly, and not only should it be banned in the Assembly, but also in any private practice. These psychologically induced trances deprive a person of self control and open the mind to demonic influence. There are at rare times true tongues inspired by the Spĭrit, either in speaking or in hearing, but these are confirmed to be true because the recipients of the message understand what is said, and often those giving the message do not realize that communication across a language barrier has happened until after the fact. But where a person causes himself to babble out of control and then to attribute such to Gŏd is self deceit or worse. The real evidence of the Spĭrit is the fruit of the Spĭrit.

14:34 ⸗ Isa 58:13; **14:35** ᵞ→on: "In older Gk. usu. of informal communication ranging from engagement in small talk to chattering and babbling" (cf. BDAG, pg. 582, λαλεω). The word refers to idle talk or words to no purpose other than to carry on. This may be allowed at other times, but not in the Assembly on Ṣabbath. The relevant law, (as the word law was used for any part of the law or prophets) is found in Isa. 58:13, "NOR SPEAKING WORDS," which may be justly interpreted as any improper words that would serve to profane the Ṣabbath. The LXX interprets the phrase to mean "muttering words of anger," (οὐδὲ λαλήσεις λόγον ἐν ὀργῇ) but the Hebrew text (מִמְּצוֹא חֶפְצְךָ וְדַבֵּר דָּבָר) clearly means any improper words, or one's own words exalting self rather than others. Paul singles out the women in the Corinthian assembly, not because the law did not generally apply to men also, but because those women were chiefly responsible for carrying on in other languages an appearance of spirituality that edified no one but themselves in Corinth. They "were finding their own pleasure and speaking words." Their presumption is that the Word was only to them since they were not

recognizing that the things which I write to you are Yăhweӊ's commandment. ³⁸But if anyone does not recognize this, he is not recognized.

³⁹Therefore, my brothers, be desiring earnestly to be prophesying, and do not be forbidding to be speaking in languages. ⁴⁰But let all things be getting done properly and in an orderly manner.

15

¹Now I am making known to you, brothers, the good news which I proclaimed to you, which also you received, in which also you have been standing, ²by which also you are being rescued, by which word I announced good news to you, if you are holding fast, except if not, *then* you have ᵠpledged faithfulness in vain, ³because I delivered to you as of first importance what I

---

interpreting it. The application then is not that some women cannot speak at all, but that they cannot speak contrary to the words of Isa. 58:13, and that those offending needed to be silenced and learn from their husbands in accord with Gen. 3:16.

15:2 ᵠ→faithfulness: or *held faithful.*

15:3 ρ as a ransom; see Mat. 20:28; Mark 10:45; Rev. 5:9. Sin took his life in the course of his effort to rescue us. Satan strikes the Messiah in the heel (cf. Gen. 3:15). **15:3** ξ→of, ὑπὲρ lit. *over (THAYER)*, i.e. *from, because of* (BAG 1957, BDAG 2000) cf. מן *from* Isa. 53:5. ▷ This agrees well with Isa. 53, which says, 'from our transgressions,' and 'from our iniquities.' Literally, the word means 'over our sins,' that is over the matter of or over dealing with our sins. ▷ 'And Yăhweӊ will have made meet in him the iniquity of us all' (Isa. 53:6), to battle it, to defeat it, to show the cost of cleansing it. ▷ This meeting with sin breaks down into two aspects, (1) consequence, and (2) cleansing. Firstly, in respect to consequence, a limited stroke from the sins of the people and humanity caused Messiah to suffer. Thus he carries or bears sin. It may be said, however, that all of our sins were represented in those sins directly borne by Messiah, because we all have participated in the sins of the fathers, or in smaller sins which lead to the corruptions of greater sin. Secondly, in respect to cleansing, Messiah yields up his blood, in which the life is reckoned, and the blood wipes or purges the contamination of sin that the sinner is bearing and frees him from it so that he is forgiven. That is, the sin will not be carried in him to judgment. It is cleansed by the blood. This is a spiritual operation requiring the application of divine life. See Yoӊ 6. See Lev. 5:17-18 concerning the guilt offering. ▷ The difference between the animal guilt offering and Messiah's offering is one of extent. The former only pertained to unwitting sin (וְלֹא־יָדַע). Messiah's guilt offering pertains to all sin that is confessed and repented before the Most High. Messiah is a guilt offering (cf. Isa. 53:10) that cleanses the iniquity in the sinner who repents so that he is not bearing it in the day of judgment. There is nothing superstitious in this view, because the blood that carries the breath of life is symbolic of divine life, the infusion of the Spirit that restores a person. ▷ Therefore, Messiah bears sin consequentially in the course of being a ransom and in order to cleanse the sinner who repents from bearing his iniquity to judgment. The operation is one of the cost that sin exacts or takes away from the Most High while he seeks to forgive and cleanse all who would repent. See note on Rev. 5:9. ▷ In no way is the blood of Messiah appeasing the wrath of Gŏd, and in no way is it paying off a judicial penalty. A payment is not being collected. A cost is being expended on behalf of the sinner, and that cost is collected by lawlessness. Thus ransom to effect rescue is the correct paradigm. The blood of Messiah cleanses the sinner (who repents and who has renewed faithfulness) from bearing his iniquity to the final judgment. The cleansing removes from the sinner the contamination that would cause his condemnation in the final day. ▷ The false doctrine of judicial substitution as a widely taught model of atonement is based upon the assumption that judicial punishment is equitable compensation for the wrong done by the sinner, as a rich man might pay off the debt of another to restore the loss of the person to whom the debt was owed. This is by no means the case. The law of judicial punishment, viz. an eye for an eye, was stated to limit the extent of the judicial punishment because other cultures did not. For example, the Amorites punished lower classes more harshly than those with nobility or rank, and in ways exceeding the offenses. The intent was not equitable compensation for the wronged party. The purpose of judicial punishment is to deter the increase of sin, and not to undo the effects of the wrong committed. The Most High does not exact wrath because it restores a divine balance. He exacts wrath to end sin or curtail it. Penalizing someone else on the behalf of another does not restore a divine balance because wrath never does right a wrong. Capital punishment does not raise the murdered to life. And finally, it is biblically illegal to punish the innocent for the guilty (cf. Ezek. 18:20; Exo. 23:7). ▷ Messiah is our ransom, and it is sin and death which exact the cost from Messiah to bring us to forgiveness and to purge the malignancy of sin. The wrath of God is not getting paid off in Messiah's death. But what is happening is cleansing.

also received, that the Anŏinted died^ρ on account of^ξ our sins according to the writings, ⁴and that he was buried, and that he had been getting raised ON^λ THE THIRD DAY according to the writings, ⁵and that he appeared to Keipha, then to the twelve.^{ξ} ⁶After that he appeared to more than five hundred brothers at one time, most of whom remain until now, but some have fallen asleep. ⁷Then he appeared to Yaʻaqov, then to all the emissaries. ⁸And last of all, as it were to one untimely born, he appeared to me also.

⁹For I am the least of the emissaries, who am not fit to be called an emissary, because I persecuted the Assembly of the Almĭghty. ¹⁰But by the loving-kindness of the Almĭghty I am what I am, and his loving-kindness toward me did not prove vain. But I labored even more than all of them, yet not I, but the loving-kindness of the Almĭghty with me. ¹¹Whether then it was I or they, so we proclaim, and in this way you have pledged faithfulness.

¹²Now if the Anŏinted is being proclaimed, because he had been getting raised from the dead, how do some among you say that there is no resurrection of the dead? ¹³But if there is no resurrection of the dead, not even the Anŏinted had been getting raised, ¹⁴and if the Anŏinted had not been getting raised, then our proclaiming is in vain, your faithfulness also is in vain. ¹⁵Moreover we are even found to be false witnesses of the Almĭghty, because we witnessed against the Almĭghty that he raised the Anŏinted, whom he did not raise, if in fact the dead are not raised. ¹⁶For if the dead are not getting raised, not even the Anŏinted had been getting raised. ¹⁷And if the Anŏinted had not been getting raised, your faithfulness is worthless. You are still in your sins. ¹⁸Then those also who have fallen asleep belonging to the Anŏinted have perished. ¹⁹If only in this life, we have been putting hope in the Anŏinted, we are of all men most to be pitied.

²⁰But as it is, the Anŏinted had been getting raised from the dead, the first fruits^χ of those who have been falling asleep. ²¹For since by a man came death, by a man also came the resurrection of the dead. ²²For as in Adam all die, so also in the Anŏinted all will be made alive.

²³Yet, each in his own order: the Anŏinted, the first fruits, after that those who are the Anŏinted's at his presence, ²⁴then *is* the ending, when he may be

---

15:4 λ Hos. 6:1-3; Gen. 22:4; Gen. 40:20; Exo. 19:11, etc. See Luke 24:46. **15:4** ξ This must include Mattiyah. Keipha: see Luke 24:34.

15:20 χ See also vs. 23. The time of the resurrection of Mĕssiah corresponds to the ending of the wave sheaf offering. This offering was on the day after the annual Şabbath (cf. Lev. 23:11; 15) starting the seven days of unleavened bread. Like all offerings, the day for it was from dawn to dawn. The offering was put on the altar with its burnt offering in the morning, and it burned all day, and all night (cf. Lev. 6:9-10). The offering was finished at dawn, and the priest removed the ashes from the altar. The day was on the 16th of the first month. In AD 34, this day was from Friday at dawn to the weekly Şabbath at dawn. The offering was just finishing up when Mĕssiah rose from the dead. This offering burned all night during the night part of the Şabbath. ▷ According to the Friday-Sunday doctrine, the resurrection would have been before the offering even began. See Yoḥ. 20:17 for why that verse has nothing to do with the wave offering. ▷ The theory that the resurrection was between Şabbath after noon and dusk at the end of the Şabbath also does not match any time during the wave offering. For it would be well after the offering ended by one view, and well before it by the other view. ▷ The only view which actually matches the wave offering timing is Mĕssiah's resurrection just before dawn on the Şabbath. **15:24** ψ παρα+δίδωμι = put alongside, where δίδωμι is used in a Hebrew sense (cf. נתן, *set, put*). Literally: *When he may be putting the kingdom alongside the Almĭghty*, cf. BDAG,

restoring^ψ the kingdom for the Almĭghty, that is, *the* Făther, when he shall have destroyed all contrary rule and all authority and power. ²⁵For it is necessary for him to be judging as king^ζ until he may have set all his enemies under his feet. ²⁶The last enemy that will be abolished is death, ²⁷because he WILL HAVE SET IN ORDER ALL THINGS IN UNDER HIS FEET^ψ. But when one may have said, "EVERYTHING HAS ^ΦBEEN GETTING SUBORNIDATED^ψ," *it is* clear that outside *this is* he who has subordinated all things to him. ²⁸And when all things shall have been subordinated to him, then the Sŏn himself will have been^χ submitted to him who submitted all things to him, wherein the Almĭghty may be both^π of these—in all things.

²⁹Otherwise, what will those do who are immersed on behalf of the dead—if the dead are not raised at all!^μ Why then are they immersed on their behalf? ³⁰Why are we also in danger every hour? ³¹Every day I am dying, as surely as your excellence, which I am owning, *is* through the Anŏinted Yĕshua our Adŏnai. ³²If from human motives I fought with wild beasts at Ephesus, what does it profit me? If the dead are not raised, "WE SHOULD EAT AND DRINK, FOR TOMORROW WE ARE GOING TO DIE^γ." ³³Do not be getting deceived: "Bad company corrupts good morals." ³⁴Become sober-minded as you ought, and do not be sinning, because some have no knowledge of the Almĭghty. I speak this to your shame.

³⁵But someone will say, "How are the dead raised? And with what kind of body do they come?" ³⁶You fool! That which you sow does not come to life unless it may have died, ³⁷and that which you sow, you do not sow the body which is to be, but a bare grain, perhaps of wheat or of something else. ³⁸But the Almĭghty gives it a body just as he wished, and to each of the seeds a body of its own. ³⁹All flesh is not the same flesh, but there is one flesh of men, and another flesh of beasts, and another flesh of birds, and another of fish. ⁴⁰There are also heavenly bodies and earthly bodies, but the glory of the heavenly is one, and the glory of the earthly is another. ⁴¹There is one glory of the sun, and another glory of the

---

entrust. Cf. Yoh. 16:15. **15:25** ζ βασιλεύειν means 'to be generaling,' i.e. 'to be waging war as a king,' 'to be kinging,' 'to be commanding,' 'to be judging,' i.e. to be acting as king in the manner described in vs. 24 and Psa. 110:2-7. In Psalm 110:6: יָדִין בַּגּוֹיִם *He will judge among the nations,* is clearly a sense to be taken as executing justice. Of his reign there is no end, and is being King is forever. See Luke 1:33. cf. Isa. 9:7; Dan. 2:44. Rev. 11:15. **15:27** ψ Psa 8:6: *What is man that you will remember him, and the son of Adam that you will attend to him that then you will cause him to be a little lacking compared to the gods? But glory and honor you will make him to be crowned [with]. You will give him dominion among the works of your hands. Everything you will have been putting under his feet.* **15:27** φ→set: It is evident here that the Hebrew perfect verb שָׁתָה has been given a future perfect continuous interpretation according the messianic sense of the text. Vs. 25 sets the context with allusion to Psa. 110:1. **15:28** χ will have remained.

Future as gnomic subjunctive equivalent (cf. Wallace, GGBB, pg. 571). The Sŏn has always been submitted to the Făther, and the Făther to the Sŏn, because the determinate divine will is united. **15:28** π = πᾶς = *each* (BDAG). This is to say that the Almĭghty both submits to the Almĭghty and is submitted to the Almĭghty. **15:32** γ Isa 22:13.

15:29 μ The practice of performing rites for the dead and to supply them what they need in the afterlife is well known in paganism. This is why pagan graves are filled with grave goods. This has also come into Christianity as indulgences for the benefit of the dead, and even baptism to assist the dead in Mormonism. We need no more than postulate that some Gnostic sect known to Paul and his hearers baptized on behalf of the dead in the hope of a better resurrection for them. In making the reference then, Paul is rhetorically and sarcastically *ad hominem* equivocating the anti resurrection position of his opponent, who still favors immersing converts, with the known cult.

moon, and another glory of the stars, because star differs from star in glory.

⁴²So also is the resurrection of the dead. It is sown a perishable body. It is raised an imperishable body. ⁴³It is sown in dishonor. It is raised in glory. It is sown in weakness. It is raised in power. ⁴⁴It is sown a natural body. It is raised a spiritual body. If there is a natural body, there is also a spiritual body. ⁴⁵So also it has been getting written, "The first MAN, Adam, BECAME A LIVING SOUL^λ." The last Adam is a life-giving spirit. ⁴⁶However, the spiritual is not first, but the natural, then the spiritual. ⁴⁷The first man is from the earth, earthly. The second man is from heaven. ⁴⁸As is the earthly, so also are those who are earthly. And as is the heavenly, so also are those who are heavenly. ⁴⁹And just as we have borne the image of the earthly, we will also bear the image of the heavenly.

⁵⁰Now I say this, brothers, that flesh and blood cannot inherit the kingdom of the Almĭghty, nor does the perishable inherit the imperishable. ⁵¹Behold, I tell you a mystery. We will not all sleep, but we will all be changed, ⁵²in a moment, in the twinkling of an eye, at the farthest shofar^λ, because the shofar will sound, and the dead will be raised imperishable, and we will be changed. ⁵³For this perishable must put on the imperishable, and this mortal must put on immortality. ⁵⁴But when this perishable shall have put on the imperishable, and this mortal shall have put on immortality, then will come about the saying that has been getting written, "DEATH IS SWALLOWED UP IN VICTORY^α. ⁵⁵DEATH, WHERE IS YOUR VICTORY? DEATH, WHERE IS YOUR STING?^β" ⁵⁶The ^ωprod of death is sin, and the power of sin is the norm^ρ, ⁵⁷but thanks be to the Almĭghty, who gives us the victory through our Adŏnai Yĕshua the Anŏinted.

⁵⁸Therefore, my beloved brothers, be becoming steadfast, immovable, always abounding in the work of Yăhwe H, having been knowing that your toil is not in vain in Yăhwe H.

15:52 λ Or "utmost trumpet,"(cf. 1 Yoḥ. 2:18); see that ἔσχατος means "❶ **pertaining to being at the farthest boundary of an area, farthest, ❷ last ❸ utmost, finest**" (BDAG, pg. 397), e.g. ἕως ἐσχάτου τῆς γῆς "unto the farmost part of the earth" (Isa. 48:20; Acts 1:8; 13:47). ▷ The farthest trumpet is the one that goes throughout all the land (תַּעֲבִירוּ שׁוֹפָר בְּכָל־אַרְצְכֶם, Lev. 25:9), and not only the land, but throughout all the earth. The Jubilee trumpet was the one that traveled the farthest, to every corner of the land. ▷ It cannot be the last in time, because trumpets are sounded in perpetuity. If it would be the last in a series, then no series is numbered that Paul could have known. One could say it is the lastmost trumpet pertaining to the Jubilee cycle, and this would be true enough. But this is also the farthest trumpet in the extent of its reach in the land, and this observation should not be overlooked. In fact, it seems paramount. ▷ In Matthew 24:31 this trumpet is identified as the "trumpet of great sound,"(q.v.) which most nearly fits the "trumpet blast" (שׁוֹפַר תְּרוּעָה) in Lev. 25:9. ▷ It fits that the resurrection and transformation should be on YOM KIPPURIM since it is on this day that final cleansing from sin comes (cf. Lev. 16:30). It also fits the pattern of redemption, since Messiah was born on the day of Trumpets, died when the Passover was offered, and ascended from the grave with the end of the wave offering. And the Holy Spirit was poured out on the following Shavu'ot. Thus it is fitting that the Most High will make good use of his appointed times in regard to the resurrection. **15:45** λ Gen 2:7; **15:54** α Isa 25:8

15:55 β Hos 13:14; See App XII. **15:56** ω or prick, sting, goad. Transgression is like a cattle prod unto death. Without escape, sin leads to destruction. **15:56** ρ Or "what is customary." The power of sin is the rule for humanity, but in Mĕssiah we are freed from the norm of sin so that we may become ourselves the righteousness of the Almĭghty. Rom. 7:6; 8:2; 2 Cor. 5:21.

16 ¹Now concerning the collection for the holy ones, as I directed the assemblies of Galatia, so do you also. ²Down through the FIRST OF THE ŞABBAŧHS᷆ let each one of you be putting aside a savings, whatever he can give from his prosperity, that no collections be made when I may have come. ³And when I may have arrived, whomever you may have approved, I will send them with letters to carry your gift to Yerushalayim. ⁴And if it is fitting for me to go also, they will go with me. ⁵But I will come to you after I will have gone through Macedonia, because I am going to go through Macedonia. ⁶And when arrived I will stay with you, or even spend the winter, so that you may send me on my way wherever I may be going, ⁷because I do not wish to see you now just in passing, because I hope to remain with you for some time, if Yăhweн may have permitted. ⁸But I will remain in Ephesus until Shavu'ot, ⁹because a wide door for effective service has been opening to me, and there are many adversaries.

¹⁰Now if Timothy may have come, be seeing that without fear he shall have been with you, because he is doing Yăhweн's work, as I also am. ¹¹Let no one therefore despise him. But send him on his way in peace, so that he will have come to me, because I expect him with the brothers. ¹²But concerning Apollos our brother, I encouraged him greatly, that he may come to you with the brothers, and it was not at all his desire that he may come now, but he will come when he may have found a good time. ¹³Be keeping alert. Be standing firm in the pledge of faithfulness. Be becoming men. Be getting strong. ¹⁴Let all that you do be getting done in love.

¹⁵Now I urge you, brothers (you have been knowing the household of Stephanas, that they were the first fruits of Achaia, and that they have devoted themselves for ministry to the holy ones), ¹⁶that you also may be subjecting yourselves to such men and to everyone who is joining in working and laboring. ¹⁷And I rejoice over the presence of Stephanas and Fortunatus and Achaicus, because they have supplied what was lacking on your part. ¹⁸Because they have refreshed my spirit and yours. Therefore be acknowledging such as these.

¹⁹The assemblies of Asia are greeting you. Aquila and Prisca are greeting you heartily in Yăhweн, with the assembly that is in their house. ²⁰All the brothers

---

16:2 ζ κατὰ μίαν σαββάτων. κατὰ = 'downwards.' See LSJ. Thayer II. with accusative; 1a: ***down through***. The first Şabbaŧh after Passover. Lev. 23:11-15. See also Mat. 28:1; Mark 16:2; Luke 24:1; Yoĥ. 20:1, 19; Rev. 1:10; Col. 2:16; Gal. 4:10; Rom. 14:5-6. Luke 6:1; Mat. 12; Mark 3:23; Yoĥ. 5:1, 9. Paul wanted them to save up until he arrived sometime after Shavu'ot (1 Cor. 16:8) during the seven weeks. His letter was written shortly before Passover (cf. 1 Cor. 5:8), and he expected it to arrive about the first of the Şabbaŧhs. ▷ The accusative is the object of 'putting aside saving.' Compare Mat. 28:1: εἰς μίαν σαββάτων. ▷ ***Down through;*** cf. Mat. 24:7; Mark 13:8; Luke 8:39; 9:6; 10:4, 31, 32; 13:22; 15:14; 21:11; Acts 8:1; 11:1; 15:23; 21:21; 24:12; 25:3; 26:13. Κατὰ is dynamically equiv. to 'every' with an object regarded as generic, i.e. 'down through city and village' = 'throughout cities and villages,' or 'throughout the day' may by extension mean 'every day.' But when an adjective specfies one of a class, the object is unlikely to be generic, e.g. 'down through <u>this</u> day.' 'Down through the <u>first</u> day of the Şabbaŧhs.' When 'every Şabbaŧh' is meant, the Greek word πᾶν is included. See Acts 15:21. Cf. Acts 13:27; 15:36; 17:17; 18:4; 26:11. This virtually proves that κατὰ does not mean 'every' by itself. Once again, the literal sense makes plain sense before the contrived.

are greeting you. Greet one another with a holy kiss. ²¹The greeting is in my hand, Paul. ²²If anyone is not loving Yăhweh, let him be accursed. Maran eͭthaʾ. ²³The loving-kindness of Ădŏnai Yĕshuą be with you. ²⁴My love be with you all in view of the Anŏinted Yĕshua. Amen.

16:22 μ μαρὰν ἀθά = Unvoweled Aramaic for 'Ha Ădŏn has come': מָרַן אֲתָא, Or: Maran aᵗhe̓: 'Ha Ădŏn is coming': (מָרַן אָתָא). The first word means 'The Lŏrd' (emphatic state) and the second is either a perfect or participle, depending on vowels. Hebrew, even with niqqud would be similarly ambiguous: הָאָדוֹן בָּא. The Greek transliteration is also ambiguous. Strictly it should be either ἠθά, ἐθά or ἀθή, ἀθέ. This seems intentional. Both comings have to be acknowledged.

Second Corinthians

1 ¹Paul, an emissary of the Anŏinted Yĕshua by the will of the Almĭghty, and Timothy our brother, to the assembly of the Almĭghty which is at Corinth, with all the holy ones who are throughout Achaia: ²Loving-kindness to you and peace from the Almĭghty our Făther and Adŏnai Yĕshua the Anŏinted.

³Blessed be the Almĭghty and Făther of our Adŏnai Yĕshua the Anŏinted, the Făther of mercies and the Almĭghty of all comfort, ⁴who comforts us in all our affliction so that we may be able to comfort those who are in any affliction with the comfort with which we ourselves are comforted by the Almĭghty.

⁵Because just as the sufferings of the Anŏinted are ours in abundance, so also our comfort is abundant through the Anŏinted. ⁶But when we are afflicted, it is on behalf of your encouragement and deliverance. Or if we are encouraged, it is because of your encouragement, which is working in the patient enduring of the same sufferings which we also suffer. ⁷And our hope because of you is firmly grounded, having been knowing that as you are sharers of our sufferings, so also you are sharers of our encouragement.

⁸Because we do not want you to be unaware, brothers, concerning our affliction, which came to us in Asia, that we were burdened excessively, beyond our strength, so as well to despair in ourselves even of living. ⁹But we have been ᵅholding to the sentence of death within ourselvesᵝ in order that we will not have been trusting on ourselves, but on the Almĭghty who raises the dead, ¹⁰who delivered us from so great a peril of death, and will deliver *us*—in whom we have been hoping that even further he will deliver *us*, ¹¹by you also joining on our behalf through prayer, that thanks may be given by many persons concerning us for the loving-kindness to us.

¹²Because our proud confidence is this, even the testimony of our conscience: that in holiness and the sincerity of the Almĭghty, not in fleshly wisdom but in the loving-kindness of the Almĭghty, we have conducted ourselves in the world, and especially toward you. ¹³Because we write nothing else to you than what you read and understand, and I hope you will understand until the end, ¹⁴just as you also partially did understand us, that we are your reason to be proud, as you also are ours, in the day of our Adŏnai Yĕshua.

¹⁵And in this trust I intended at first to come to you, that you may twice have received a blessing, ¹⁶that is, to pass your way into Macedonia, and again from Macedonia to come to you, and by you to be helped on my journey to Yehudah.

¹⁷So, in deciding this, therefore, was I fickle? Or that which I am deliberating, do I deliberate according to the flesh, that with me there may be yes, yes and no, no *at the same time*? ¹⁸But the Almĭghty is faithful, because our word to you is not yes and no. ¹⁹Because the Almĭghty Sŏn, the Anŏinted Yĕshua, who was proclaimed among you by us—by me and Silvanus and Timothy—was not yes and no, but yes in him has been happening. ²⁰Because as many as may be

the promises of the Almĭghty, in him they are yes. Therefore also by him is our am‹en, to the glory of the Almĭghty through us. ²¹And he who is establishing us with you in the Anŏinted, and who has anointed us, is the Almĭghty, ²²who also sealed us and gave us the Spĭrit in our hearts as a pledge.

²³But I call the Almĭghty as witness to my soul, that to spare you I came no more to Corinth. ²⁴Not that we lord it over your faithfulness, but are workers with you for your joy, because in faithfulness you have been standing firm.

2 ¹But I determined this for my own sake, that I would not come to you in sorrow again. ²Because if I cause you sorrow, who can make me glad except the one whom I made sorrowful? ³And this is the very thing I wrote you, lest, having come, I will have had sorrow from those who ought to make me rejoice, after having been trusting in you all, that my joy would be the joy of you all. ⁴Because out of much affliction and anguish of heart I wrote to you with many tears, not that you should be made sorrowful, but that you will have known the love which I have especially for you.

⁵Yet, if any has been causing sorrow, he has been causing sorrow not to me, save only in some degree, in order that I may not be weighing on all of you. ⁶Sufficient for such a one is this punishment which was inflicted by the majority, ⁷so that on the contrary you should rather forgive and comfort him, lest somehow such a one will have been overwhelmed by excessive sorrow. ⁸Therefore I urge you to reaffirm your love for him. ⁹Because for this also I wrote that I might find out your genuineness, whether you are obedient in all things. ¹⁰But whomever you are forgiving anything, I *forgive* also, because indeed whom I have been forgiving, when I have been forgiving anything, I did it for your sakes in the presence of the Anŏinted, ¹¹so that we may not be exploited by Satan, because we are not ignorant of his schemes.

¹²And having come to Troas for the good news of the Anŏinted⁸—but taking my leave of them, I went on to Macedonia. (Indeed a door had been opening *there* for me. However, in Adŏnai, ¹³I had been having no rest in my spirit in *that* I was not finding Titus my brother)⁸

¹⁴But thanks be to the Almĭghty, who always leads us in his triumph in the Anŏinted, and manifests through us the sweet aroma of the knowledge of him in every place. ¹⁵Because we are a fragrance of the Anŏinted to the Almĭghty among those who are being rescued, and among those who are perishing. ¹⁶To the one an aroma from death to death, to the other an aroma from life to life. And who is adequate for these things? ¹⁷Because we are not like the many, peddling the word of the Almĭghty, but as *men* of sincerity—but as *men* of the Almĭghty in the presence of the Almĭghty, through the Anŏinted, we speak.

2:13 θ These two verses are exceedingly difficult to decipher as Paul put his reasons stated in ( ) into the place where the hyphen occurs (2:12 δ). Doing so interrupted his narrative. Further 'in Adŏnai,' it seems, has been incorrectly joined to the preceding clause. It is clear Paul is writing off the top of his head without thinking of an audience centuries later removed from his context. **3:6** δ→renewal = בְּרִית חֲדָשָׁה; חִידוּשָׁה; See 1 Cor 11:25 note χ. cf. Jer. 31:31. See 1 Yoh. 2:7-8; 2 Yoh. 1:5; cf. Yoh. 13:34 ἐντολὴν καινήν. Jer. 31:32, 'not according to the covenant (which I had cut with their fathers in the day of my gripping by their hand to bring them out of the land of Egypt) when they had

3 Furthermore, are we the first to recommend ourselves? Or do we need, as some, written reports of recommendation to you or from you? ²You are our report, (having been getting inscribed in our hearts), being known and read by all men, ³it being apparent that you are a report from the Anŏinted, being ministered by us, *you* who have been getting inscribed not with ink, but with the Spĭrit of the living Almĭghty, not on tablets of stones, but on tablets of fleshly hearts.

⁴And such trust we have through the Anŏinted before the Almĭghty. ⁵Not that we are sufficient in ourselves to consider anything as coming from ourselves, but our sufficiency is from the Almĭghty, ⁶who also qualified us as ministers of the ᵟcovenant ᵞrenewal, not a ᵠletter promising to repay but a breath of life, because the letter promising to repay kills, but the Spĭrit gives life. ⁷And since the ministry of death in ˣletters (*which* had been getting inscribed on stones) was produced in glory, so that the sons of Yisra'el could not look steadfastly at the face of Mosheh because of the glory of his face, fading as it was, ⁸why shouldn't the ministry of the Spĭrit be even more glorious? ⁹Because when there is glory in the ministry of condemnation, how much more exceeds the ministry of righteousness in glory. ¹⁰And because it has not been getting glorified—that which has been getting glorified, in this respect, on account of the exceeding glory. ¹¹Because when what is fading away is glorious, how much more is what remains glorious. ¹²Therefore, having such expectation, we use much boldness, ¹³and not as Mosheh who put a veil over his face, so that the sons of Yisra'el would not gaze at the end of what is disappearing. ¹⁴But their minds were hardened.

---

broken my covenant and I had mastered against them.' The terms of the covenant are based on *if then's*. *If* the covenant is broken *then if* no repentance occurs *then* judgment, but *if* repentance occurs and forgiveness is given, *then* life. Whatever is according to the covenant follows an *if then*, and seeing that there are two basic *thens* both related to the same commandments, it is not the commandments that the renewed covenant is not according to, but the *if then* for judgment. ▷ In Jer. 31:32, by using the words '*not like*,' failing to mark the appositive phrase, which I put in (), and by mistranslating the second אֲשֶׁר which (instead of *when* or *because*), and by subordinating the last waw וְ (*though, although*), and by failing to give בְּעַלְתִּי *ba'al-ti* negative connotation as in the LXX (*I mastered against them, I neglected them*), the translators have managed to create extreme bias against understanding the new-made as a renewal of the old, and this despite the fact that the promise of covenant renewal is simply a repeat of the same promise going back to Deut. 30:6-8; 11-14. **3:6** λ = *new-made, made-new*. 'Renewal' is used here for the reasons stated at 1 Cor. 11:25. **3:6** ψ→*repay*. Literally *a letter*. A play on words in Greek with letters in vs. 7, that cannot be exactly reproduced in English. The word means ❷ b *a promisory note* (BDAG). **3:7** χ. See Romans 7. The letters refer to the words *You shall not bear the name of Yăhweh your Almĭghty as a worthless*

thing, *because Yăhweh will not purify the one who bears his name as a worthless thing* (Exo. 20:7). *And visiting the iniquity of the fathers upon the sons* (Exo. 20:6). This occurs again in Exodus 34:7 where it says his name is *preserving loving-kindness to the thousandmost [generation], carrying away iniquity and transgression and sin, but declaring pure not he will declare pure*. To attempt getting the debt repaid seeks to be declared pure or acquitted. Forgiveness cannot be bought. Bearing away iniquity means to take away punishment, and it cannot be bought. So the ministry of death is to leave whoever rejects forgiveness contaminated with sin so that they will die by it, because sin cannot be paid for. The sinner cannot compensate Gŏd for sin to propitiate him. **3:14** π Paul is not using the words "ancient covenant" here as opposed to "new covenant." Yoḣanan speaks of the old and new in the same context (1 John 2:7-8; 2 John 1:5-6). The new commandment is an old commandment. The author of Hebrews, misunderstanding Paul's illustration, interpreted it to mean rejection of the covenant. The ancient covenant was the בְּרִית עוֹלָם, "THE COVENANT OF OLD" or "OF ANTIQUITY" (cf. Gen. 17:7, 13, 19; 2 Sam. 23:5; 1 Chron. 16:17; Psa. 105:10; Isa. 24:5, 55:3, 61:8; Jer. 32:40, 50:5; Eze. 16:60, 37:26.) The words also mean "an everlasting covenant," but with this sense the OT translators have been able to hide its connection with the "covenant of old," allowing interpreters to argue for a replacement

Because until this day, the same veil remains over *their* comprehending of the ᵐancient covenant, it not being revealed that through the Anŏinted One the veil is removed. ¹⁵But past this day whenever Mosheh isᵉ being read, a veil lies over their heart. ¹⁶But whenever one may have turned to Yăhweɥ, the veil is undone.

¹⁷Now Yăhweɥ is the Spĭrit, and where the Spĭrit of Yăhweɥ is, there is liberty. ¹⁸But we all, who have been getting the veil removed off the face, the glory of Yăhweɥ reflecting, are getting transformed into the same image from glory to glory, exactly as from the Spĭrit of Yăhweɥ.

4 ¹Therefore, since we have this ministry, as we received mercy, we do not lose heart, ²but we have renounced things hidden because of shame, not walking in craftiness or adulterating the word of the Almĭghty, but we are by demonstration of truth commending ourselves to every person's conscience in the sight of the Almĭghty. ³And even if our good news has been getting veiled, it has been getting veiled to those who are perishing, ⁴in whose case the god of this age has blinded the minds of the unfaithful, that they *may* not see the light of the good news of the glory of the Anŏinted, who is the image of the Almĭghty. ⁵Because we do not proclaim ourselves, but the Anŏinted Yĕshua as Adŏnai, and ourselves as your servants for Yĕshua's sake. ⁶Because the Almĭghty, who said light shall shine out of darkness, is the one who has lighted *the way* in our hearts toward the light of the knowledge of the ᵞglory of the Almĭghty in the countenance of the Anŏinted.

⁷But we are holding this treasure in earthen vessels, that the surpassing greatness of power may be from the Almĭghty and not from ourselves. ⁸We are afflicted in every way, but not crushed, perplexed, but not despairing, ⁹persecuted, but not forsaken, struck down, but not destroyed, ¹⁰always carrying about in the body the dying of Yĕshua, so that the life of Yĕshua also will have been manifested in our body. ¹¹Because we who live are constantly being delivered over to death for Yĕshua's sake, so that the life of Yĕshua also will have been demonstrated in our mortal flesh. ¹²So death works in us, but life in you.

¹³But having the same spirit of faithfulness, according to what has been getting written, "I HAVE PLEDGED FAITHFULNESS, THEREFORE I HAVE SPOKEN UP^ψ," we also pledge faithfulness. Therefore we also are speaking up, ¹⁴who have been knowing that he who raised Adŏnai Yĕshua will raise us also with Yĕshua and will present us with you, ¹⁵because all things are for you, so that loving-kindness, having abounded unto many, may increase the blessing for the glory of the Almĭghty.

---

covenant with different terms rather than a renewal of the old. **3:15** ε is = may be.

4:6 γ The Făther shares his glory with the Mĕssiah because they are one. This knowledge is that if we have seen the Mĕssiah then we have seen the Făther because the Mĕssiah has the glory of the Făther. The Făther lights the way in our hearts toward his own glory in the countenance of the Sŏn. **4:13** ψ Psalm 116:10: הֶאֱמַנְתִּי כִּי אֲדַבֵּר *he-'emanti ki adabber*. He means an oral testimony, a public confession that resulted from the fact of a faithful commitment to Mĕssiah.

¹⁶Therefore, we do not lose heart, but though our outer man is decaying, yet our inner man is getting new-made again day by day. ¹⁷Because our affliction is for a brief moment, compared to the exceeding excess of the everlasting weight of glory being produced in us, ¹⁸while we look not at the things which are seen, but at the things which are not seen, because the things which are seen are temporary, but the things which are not seen are everlasting.

5 ¹Because we have been knowing that if the earthly tent which is our house may have been torn down, we are going to have a building from the Almĭghty, a house not made with hands, everlasting in the heavens. ²Because indeed in this one we are groaning, longing to be clothed with our dwelling from heaven, ³inasmuch as we, having put it on, will not be found ᵛnaked. ⁴Because indeed while we exist in this tent, we groan, being burdened, after which we do not want to be unclothed, but to be clothed, in order that what is mortal will have been swallowed up by life. ⁵Now he who prepared us for this very purpose is the Almĭghty, who gave to us the Spĭrit as a pledge.

⁶Therefore, having confidence, and having been knowing that while being in *a* home, in ˢthis body, we are away from *a* ᵞhome from Yăhwęн, ⁷because we do walk through ᵐfaithfulness, not through *our* sight. ⁸We have confidence, I say, and prefer rather to be away from *a* home, away from ˢthis body and to be in *a* home next to Yăhwęн.

⁹Therefore, also we have as our ambition, whether being in *a* home or being away from *a* home, to be pleasing to him. ¹⁰Because we must all appear before the judgment seat of the Anŏinted, so that each one will have received for his deeds in ˢthis body, according to what he has done, whether good or bad.

¹¹Therefore, having been knowing the fear of Yăhwęн, we persuade men. And by the Almĭghty we have been getting ourselves illuminated, and I hope also that we have been getting ourselves illuminated in your consciences. ¹²We are not again commending ourselves to you, but are giving you an occasion to be proud because of us, that you may be having an answer for those who are taking

---

5:3 ν The metaphor of nakedness is applied to the present body since while in it we long to be clothed with the heavenly body. We long to be clothed while in this tent (vs. 4). No account is given of the time between death and resurrection because the soul is asleep and the longing is not thought then. **5:7** π Faithfulness is based on hearing or listening to the word of the Almĭghty. See Romans 10:14-17. Sight here means our understanding of situations. We may indeed come to understand the situation after we obey, or having obeyed the first time without fully understanding, we will understand the next time. Paul does not say we never walk by sight. He means we *do* walk by faithfulness and not by sight at those times when our own sight seems to inform us contrary to faithfulness. But whenever our sight is aligned with the Scripture then faithfulness is through sight. Therefore the blind will see and be able to walk the more easily. ▷ Facing death is one of those situations when our human reasoning goes into combat mode with faithfulness. It is the nature of being flesh and blood. Facing death is a time we should especially listen to what the Almĭghty said about the resurrection. **5:6, 8, 10** ς When Paul says "the body" he evidently means our current fleshly house. So the sense is "this body" (cf. Wallace, pg. 221, Deictic Article). Other versions recognize this (ERV, EXB, GW, ICB, ISV, NOG, NCV, VOICE, WE. **5:6** γ→from; The KJV translators have taken to translating "away from *a* home from" as "absent" abstracting the reference to the word *home*. In vs. 8, the KJV avoids the word *home* in the last clause, and they changed the Greek πρὸς, meaning "toward," in the sense of "facing," or "next to" to "with," turning "in *a* home next to" into an abstraction rather than the concrete idea of "in *a* home (that is) with/ toward Yăhwęн." Furthermore in vs. 6, the word 'from' gets a corrupted sense by deleting the reference to a home, viz. "absent from" vs. "away from *a* home from

pride in outward appearance, and not in the heart. ¹³Because if we appear to be ᵏnuts, it is for the Almĭghty. If we are of sound mind, it is for you. ¹⁴Because the love of the Anŏinted binds us together, having judged this, because one has died on behalf of all, therefore we all die. ¹⁵And he died on behalf of all, that they who are living may no longer be living for themselves, but for him who died and rose on their behalf.

¹⁶Thus besides, henceforth we have been considering no one according to the flesh.ᵠ If even we had been considering the Anŏinted according to the flesh, yet we are now considering *him* no longer *this way*. ¹⁷Therefore if anyone belonging to the Anŏinted One *is* a new-made creature, old things pass away. Behold, new-made things have been becoming. ¹⁸Now all these things *are* from the Almĭghty, who has reconciled us to himself through the Anŏinted, and has given to us the ministry of reconciliation. ¹⁹As such, the Almĭghty has been through the Anŏinted One, one who reconciles to himself the world, not being one who is taking into account for them their going astray.ᶿ And he has committed to us the word of reconciliation.

²⁰Therefore, we are ambassadors on behalf of the Anŏinted, as though the Almĭghty were imploring through us. We beg you on behalf of the Anŏinted. Be reconciled to the Almĭghty. ²¹The one not having known sin, he made a ᵞsin *offering* on our behalf, ᶻso that we may ourselves become the righteousness of the Almĭghty by him.

Yăhweн." The home from Yăhweн is the resurrection body. **5:13** λ Insane or crazy. **5:16** ψ According to the flesh, in this place, means by worldly standards, social status, money, influence, position, or rank. But he who would be great must be the servant of all. As Messiah ransoms us from evil, so also we must serve to ransom others from evil. And this is how we should consider the faithful, according to their conformity to the image of Messiah. But the world measures Messiah and the faithful according to their own standards, as opportunists, and religious exploiters for worldly gain. PAR The faithful are to be conformed to the image of Messiah (vs. 17, 21) bearing sin and suffering as Moses did, imaging Messiah to the world. PAR But this estimation according to the Spirit has nothing to do with the false doctrine of imputed righteousness. Paul is not teaching us to view all the faithful as perfectly righteous. He is only telling us we should not judge value by worldly standards.

5:19 θ Literally: 'As that Almĭghty was being in Anointed [a] world reconciler to himself, not an accounter-being to them [of] the side-steps of them.' The point is about the nature of the Almĭghty expressed by his name, being compassionate and forgiving (cf. Exo. 34:6-7). He is not one to be an accounter of sins, but will forgive all he may who repent. His nature is to be a world reconciler, to get the world to repent and reconcile to him. ▷ Problem: the usual translations appear to say that the whole world is reconciled, and they just need to learn about it. This is in fact the viewpoint of many Christians. But the statement is not universalism because it is limited to the nature of the Almĭghty and does not say what actually takes place. As much of the world as will not be reconciled to him will still be judged. ▷ The difficulty here lies in the fact that all translations have construed the participle καταλλάσσων (one-reconciling) as an active verb rather than a participle adverbial adjective describing what the Almĭghty was being in Messiah. The like problem occurs with λογιζόμενος (one-accounting). Many of the versions detect the universalism of the mistaken translation and try to chop off 'God was in Christ' into an independent thought unconnected and only saying 'divinity was in Christ.' Paul uses the past tense ἦν (was being) because the death of Messiah was the height of divine ransom to the world. The opportunity will be withdrawn at the end of the age when Messiah becomes the instrument of divine judgment. Note also that παραπτώματα (going astray, erring step) is a softer word than παραβάσεων (rebellion, transgression). ▷ Now notice that the world is being reconciled to the Most High, and not the other way around. This is done by paying the ransom cost exacted by sin and suffering resulting from the divine decision to wait and not judge sin immediately in the hope that men will repent and turn from their sin and be reconciled to the Most High through forgiveness. **5:21** γ The word "sin" is used in Hebrew to mean a sin offering, and also in the Greek Septuagint. The Presbyterian Albert Barnes also explained it this way and rejected the false doctrine of imputation. For speaking the truth, they almost defrocked him as a heretic in 1836. The Church

6 ¹And working together with him, we also urge you not to receive the loving-kindness of the Almĭghty in vain—²because he says, "AT THE ACCEPTABLE TIME, I LISTENED TO YOU, AND IN THE DAY OF DELIVERANCE, I HELPED YOU.ᵋ" Behold, now is "THE ACCEPTABLE TIME,ᵋ" behold, now is "THE DAY OF DELIVERANCE.ᵋ" ³Give no cause for offense in anything, in order that the ministry will not have been faulted, ⁴but in everything we commend ourselves as servants of the Almĭghty, in much endurance, in afflictions, in hardships, in distresses, ⁵in beatings, in imprisonments, in tumults, in labors, in sleeplessness, in hunger, ⁶in purity, in knowledge, in patience, in kindness, in the Holy Spĭrit, in genuine love, ⁷in the word of truth, in the power of the Almĭghty, by the weapons of justice for the right hand and the left, ⁸throughout glory and dishonor, throughout evil report and good report, regarded as deceivers and yet true, ⁹as unknown yet well-known, as dying yet behold, we live, as punished yet not put to death, ¹⁰as sorrowful yet always rejoicing, as poor yet making many rich, as having nothing yet possessing all things.

---

teaches that a transaction happens in the atonement, whereby Mĕssiah is made sin (declared sin) and the believer is made righteousness (declared righteous). Again, this is a tricky way to turn the atonement into an acquittal and make it as if sin has been compensated for. But it will be clearly seen that Paul says "so that we might ourselves become the righteousness of the Almĭghty by him," meaning that we should become righteous through obeying the commandments with Mĕssiah's divine assistance. ▷ Not "sin" itself, but "sin offering." See CJB, OJB, TLV. In Hebrew the plain word "sin" (חַטָּאת *ḥattat*) is frequently used to mean "sin offering." The NT Greek Lexicons generally refuse to specify this usage, but the use in the LXX can be clearly seen so by comparing the Hebrew text and the Greek text. That is, ἁμαρτίας without a dispute means "sin offering" when it identifies a sacrificial victim. ▷ Reformed theology insists on removing this word from its sacrificial context and translating it just "sin," and not only that, but has tried to suppress the meaning "sin offering." This is because they want to turn the atonement into an equitable legal exchange, basically a commercial transaction in which sin gets counted as righteousness and righteousness as sin.

But Mĕssiah's death does not represent a payment or appeasement of the Father. It was evil that exacted the cost (cf. Gen. 3:15) from the Most High. The cost was paid by the Father via his Son, not as a formal agreement with evil, but as the price exacted by lawlessness, the price in suffering necessary to invade the kingdom of darkness to free its captives. The correct picture is the giving of a ransom, as a man suffers in battle to ransom those he is defending. There are no formal agreement of an exchange with the enemy. The warrior's life is the ransom cost to deliver his country. Mĕssiah's death is an indicator, a demonstration, a token, an instructive warning, of the unrecoverable costs of sin. The ransom is an instructive lesson on divine cost versus a compensation requirement, not a satisfaction of compensation. So Mĕssiah cannot be literally counted as sin, nor we as having compensated God. He does not compensate the Almĭghty for his losses due to sin or any victims. A ransom is made as an instruction of forgiveness and the cost of sin. And when a *kippur* takes place, the penalty is wiped out; forgiveness happens; in its place is an instructive demonstration. ▷ He who regards the loss from sin as fully repairable does not acknowledge sin. Since sin is not perfectly repairable, an actual forgiveness is required, i.e. a real pardon. **5:21** ζ→him: The phrase expresses the hope that the pardoned sinner will learn righteousness from the Almĭghty. This is expressed in the futuristic phrase, "so that we might ourselves become...." The wording can only mean actual real righteousness belonging to the faithful as a result of cleansing from sin, and cannot mean some kind of legal accounting or reckoning of perfect righteousness at the moment of "faith." The reason for this false doctrine has to do with the converse of the mistranslation, "to be sin." If Christ is counted to be 100% sin then the believer is to be counted 100% righteous. This theology is based on the principle that sin is a negative commodity (a debt) that can be 100% paid off so that the payment is considered equitable compensation for the debt. But "bought with a price" refers to giving a ransom that has no value in satisfying strict justice, but does have every value in indicating the unrecoverable cost of sin to all parties. The ransom price is exacted by lawlessness. And punitive justice itself is hardly compensation for the tangible loss caused by sin. Sacrificial substitution is always viewed as compensation of some sort, but Rom. 3:24 says we are administered justice without payment, meaning payment to the Most High. Indeed, the Most High is the one paying the cost to Lawlessness. That's why it is called a ransom, and why he compels the powers to give up his repentant people. **6:2** ξ Isa. 49:8;

¹¹Our mouth has been opening for you, Corinthians, our heart has been getting widened. ¹²You are not getting restrained by us, but you are getting restrained in your own affections. ¹³Yet in a like exchange—I speak as to children—be widened—yea yourselves.

¹⁴Do not be getting unequally hitched together with the unfaithful, because what partnership has righteousness and lawlessness, or what fellowship has light with darkness? ¹⁵Or what harmony has the Anŏinted with Beliyaʻal, or what has a faithful one in common with an unfaithful one? ¹⁶Or what agreement has the Temple of the Almĭghty with idols? Because we are a temple of the living Almĭghty, just as the Almĭghty said, "I WILL DWELL AMONG THEM^α AND WALK AMONG THEM, AND I WILL BE THEIR ALMĬGHTY, AND THEY WILL BE MY PEOPLE^β." ¹⁷Therefore, "'COME OUT FROM THEIR MIDST AND BE SEPARATE,' SAYS YĂHWEH^γ." And, "DO NOT BE TOUCHING WHAT IS UNCLEAN, AND I WILL WELCOME YOU." ¹⁸And, "'I WILL BE A FĂTHER TO YOU, AND YOU WILL BE SONS (AND DAUGHTERS) TO ME,' SAYS YĂHWEH OF HOSTS^θ." 7.1Therefore, having these promises, beloved, let us cleanse ourselves from all defilement of flesh and spirit, perfecting holiness in the fear of the Almĭghty.

7 ¹Make room for us in your hearts! ²We wronged no one. We corrupted no one. We took advantage of no one. ³I am not speaking for condemnation, because I have been saying before that you are in our hearts to die together and to be living together. ⁴Great is my confidence for you, great is my boasting over you. I have been getting filled with encouragement. I am overflowing with joy on top of all our affliction.

⁵Because also, when we came into Macedonia, our flesh had not been having the least relief, but we were afflicted on every side: conflicts without, fears within. ⁶But the Almĭghty, who comforts the depressed, comforted us by the presence of Titus, ⁷and not only by his presence, but also by the comfort with which he was comforted by you, as he reported to us your longing, your mourning, your zeal for me, so that I rejoiced even more.

⁸Because though I caused you sorrow by my letter, I do not regret it. Though I did regret it, because I see that that letter caused you sorrow, though only for a while. ⁹I now rejoice, not that you were made sorrowful, but that you were made sorrowful to the point of being sorry and turning your heart *from sin*, because you were made sorrowful according to the will of the Almĭghty, in order that you may not suffer loss in anything through us. ¹⁰Because the sorrow that is according to the will of the Almĭghty produces being sorry and turning of heart *from sin* without regret, leading to deliverance, but the sorrow of the world produces death. ¹¹Because look what earnestness this very thing, this reverent sorrow, has produced in you: what vindication of yourselves, what indignation, what fear, what longing, what zeal, what avenging of wrong! In everything you

---

6:16 α Exo 25:8, 29:45, Jer 31:1 Eze 37:26 **6:16** β Lev 26:12 **6:17** γ Isa 52:11 **6:18** θ 2 Sam 7:14, Isa 43:6, Hos 1:10 App XII.

demonstrated yourselves to be innocent in the matter. ¹²So although I wrote to you, it was not for the sake of the offender, nor for the sake of the one offended, but that your earnestness on our behalf may be made known to you in the sight of the Almĭghty. ¹³For this reason we have been getting encouraged. And on top of our encouragement, we rejoiced even much more at the joy of Titus, because his spirit has been getting refreshed by you all. ¹⁴Because if in anything I have been getting elated to him over you, I was not put to shame. But as we spoke all things to you in truth, so also our elation before Titus proved to be the truth. ¹⁵And his affection abounds all the more toward you, as he remembers the obedience of you all, how you received him with fear and trembling. ¹⁶I rejoice that in everything I have confidence in you.

8 ¹Now, brothers, we are making known to you the charity for the Almĭghty which has been getting given by the assemblies of Macedonia, ²that in a great ordeal of affliction, their abundance of joy and their deep poverty overflowed in the wealth of their liberality. ³Because I testify that according to their ability, and beyond their ability they gave of their own accord, ⁴begging us with much entreaty for the charity of participation in the support of the holy ones, ⁵and this, not as we had expected, but they first gave themselves to Yăhweң and then to us by the will of the Almĭghty.

⁶Consequently, we exhorted Titus, that (even as he had previously made a beginning) likewise he may also complete for you this charitable work as well. ⁷But surely as you are abounding in everything, in faithfulness and speech and knowledge, and in all diligence, and in the love back and forth between us, so also you should be abounding in this charity. ⁸I am not speaking this as a command, but through *seeing* the eagerness of others, also the genuineness of your love *you may be* confirming.

⁹Because you are knowing the loving-kindness of our Adŏnai Yĕshua, the Anŏinted One, who being rich, became poor, so that you, by that one's poverty will have become rich. ¹⁰And I am giving my judgment in this matter, because this is profiting you, who not only have acted, but even had begun to be willing from last year. ¹¹Yet, now *you should* finish to do *it* also, that just as there was the readiness to be desiring *to give*, so also the having completed *it* from what is being had *by you*. ¹²Because if the readiness is exhibiting itself, according to whatever one may be having *is* acceptable, not according to what one is not having. ¹³Because this is not for the ease of others and for your affliction, but by way of equality—¹⁴at this present time your abundance being a supply for their want, that their abundance also will have become a supply for your want, so that there will have been equality, ¹⁵as it has been getting written, "HE WHO GATHERED MUCH DID NOT HAVE TOO MUCH, AND HE WHO GATHERED LITTLE HAD NO LACK.ᵟ"

¹⁶But thanks be to the Almĭghty, who puts the same earnestness on your

---

8:15 ᵟ Exo 16:18.

behalf in the heart of Titus. [17]Because he not only accepted our appeal, but being himself very earnest, he has gone to you of his own accord. [18]And we have sent along with him the brother whose fame in the things of the good news has spread through all the assemblies, [19]and not only this, but he has also been appointed by the assemblies to travel with us in this gracious work, which is being administered by us for the glory of Yăhwe͟ʜ himself, and to show our readiness, [20]taking precaution so that no one will have faulted us in our administration of this generous gift, [21]because we have regard for what is honorable, not only in the sight of Yăhwe͟ʜ, but also in the sight of men. [22]And we have sent with them our brother, whom we have often tested and found diligent in many things, but now even more diligent, because of his great trust in you. [23]As for Titus, he is my partner and fellow worker among you. As for our brothers, they are messengers of the assemblies, a glory to the Anŏinted. [24]Therefore, openly before the assemblies, show them the demonstration of your love and of our reason for boasting about you.

9

[1]For it is superfluous for me to write to you about this ministry to the holy ones, [2]because I have been knowing your readiness, of which I am getting elated over you to the Macedonians, in that Achaia has been getting prepared since last year, and your zeal has stirred up most of them. [3]Yet, I have sent the brothers, that our elation over you will not have been made empty in this case, that, even as I was saying, you may be—have been getting prepared, [4]lest if any Macedonians may have come with me and may have found you unprepared, we (that we may not be speaking of you) will have been put to shame by this confidence. [5]So I thought it necessary to urge the brothers that they should go on ahead to you and should have arranged beforehand what has been getting promised—this blessing from you, that the same may be ready as a blessing, and not as if greed.

[6]Yet, this I say, he who is sowing sparingly will also reap sparingly, and he who is sowing on *a field of* blessings will also reap on *a field of* blessings. [7]Let each one do just as he has been himself purposing in the heart, not regretfully or from pressure, because the Almĭghty loves a cheerful giver. [8]And, the Almĭghty is able to make all loving-kindness abound to you, that always having all sufficiency in everything, you may be abounding for every good work, [9]even as it has been getting written, "HE SCATTERED ABROAD, HE GAVE TO THE POOR, HIS JUSTICE[χ] ABIDES FOREVER[μ]." [10]Now he who supplies seed to the sower and bread for food, will supply and multiply your seed for sowing and increase the harvest of your righteousness. [11]You will be enriched in everything for all liberality, which through us is producing thanksgiving to the Almĭghty. [12]Because the ministry of this service is not only fully supplying the needs of the holy ones, but is also

---

9:9 χ or *mercy, charity* as a specific form of justice **9:9** μ Psa 112:9.

overflowing through many thanksgivings to the Almĭghty.

¹³Because of the proof given by this ministry, they will glorify the Almĭghty because of your obedience to your confession of the good news of the Anŏinted, and for the liberality of your contribution to them, and to all, ¹⁴while they also, by prayer on your behalf, yearn for you because of the surpassing loving-kindness of the Almĭghty in you. ¹⁵Thanks be to the Almĭghty for his indescribable gift!

10

¹Now I, Paul, myself urge you by the meekness and gentleness of the Anŏinted, I who am meek when face to face with you, but bold toward you when absent! ²But I implore you that *I need* not be coming by to show the bold confidence, that I consider to be daring against some considering us to be walking according to the flesh. ³Because though we walk in the flesh, we do not war according to the flesh, ⁴because the weapons of our warfare are not of the flesh, but divinely powerful for the destruction of fortresses. ⁵We are destroying speculations and every lofty thing raised up against the knowledge of the Almĭghty, and we are taking every thought captive to the obedience of the Anŏinted, ⁶and we are ready to ᵃpunish all disobedience, whenever your obedience may have been fulfilled.

⁷You are seeing things according to the surface appearance. If anyone has been trusting within himself that he is the Anŏinted's, let him be considering this again within himself, that just as he is the Anŏinted's, so also are we. ⁸Because if, besides, I may have boasted somewhat further about our authority, which Yăhwe<small>H</small> has given *us* for building *you* up and not for destroying you, I will not be shamed, ⁹that I may not have appeared ever to be frightening you by means of letters, ¹⁰because they say, "His letters are surely weighty and strong, but his physical presence is weak, and his speech has been turning out as nothing." ¹¹Let such a person be considering this, that what we are in word by letters when being absent, such we are also in deed *when* being by.

¹²Because we are not bold to class or compare ourselves with some of those who commend themselves, but when they measure themselves by themselves, and compare themselves with themselves, they are without understanding. ¹³But we will not boast beyond our measure, but within the measure of the sphere which the Almĭghty apportioned to us as a measure, to reach even as far as you. ¹⁴Because we are not overextending ourselves, as if we did not reach to you, because we were the first to come even as far as you in the good news of the Anŏinted, ¹⁵not boasting beyond our measure, that is, in other men's labors, but with the hope that as your faithfulness grows, we will be, within our sphere, enlarged even more by you, ¹⁶so as to proclaim the good news even to the regions beyond you, and not to boast in what has been accomplished in the sphere of another.

¹⁷But HE WHO BOASTS, LET HIM BE BOASTING IN YĂHWE<small>H</small>.ᵑ ¹⁸Because *it is* not he who commends himself *that* is approved, but whom Yăhwe<small>H</small> commends.

10:6 *α* See Yoĥ. 20:23; 2 Chron. 30:18-21. **10:17** *η* Jer 9:22-24.

2 Corinthians 11

11 ¹I wish that you would bear with me in a little foolishness, but indeed you are bearing with me, ²because I am jealous for you with a reverent jealousy, because I betrothed you to one husband, that to the Anŏinted I may present you as a pure virgin. ³But I am afraid, lest as the serpent deceived Eve by his craftiness, your minds will have been corrupted from the simplicity and purity of devotion to the Anŏinted. ⁴Because if one comes and proclaims another Yĕshua whom we have not proclaimed, or you receive a different spirit which you have not received, or a different good news which you have not accepted, you bear this beautifully. ⁵Because I am considering myself in no way to have been falling behind in relation to the most eminent emissaries. ⁶But even if I am unskilled in speech, yet I am not so in knowledge, in fact in every way we have made this evident to you in all things.

⁷Or did I commit a sin in humbling myself, so that you may be raised up, because I proclaimed the good news of the Almĭghty to you without charge? ⁸I robbed other assemblies, taking wages from them to serve you. ⁹And when I *was* coming by to you and was in need, I was not a burden to anyone, because when the brothers came from Macedonia, they fully supplied my need, and in everything I kept myself from being a burden to you, and will continue to do so. ¹⁰As the truth of the Anŏinted is in me, this boasting of mine will not be stopped in the regions of Achaia. ¹¹Why? Because I do not love you? The Almĭghty has been knowing I do! ¹²Yet what I am doing, even I will do, so that I will have cut off an opportunity from those desiring an opportunity, that in what they are boasting, they may *only* be found *doing* just as we are *already*. ¹³Because such men are false emissaries, deceitful workers, disguising themselves as emissaries of the Anŏinted. ¹⁴And no wonder, because even Satan disguises himself as a messenger of light. ¹⁵Therefore, it is not surprising if his servants also are disguising themselves as servants of justice, whose end will be according to their deeds.

¹⁶Again I say, let no one have thought me to be foolish. Yet, if not, receive me surely even as foolish, that I also may boast a little. ¹⁷That which I am speaking, I am not speaking as Yăhweĥ would, but as in foolishness, in this confidence of boasting. ¹⁸Since many boast according to the flesh, I will boast also. ¹⁹Because you, being so wise, bear with the foolish gladly. ²⁰Because you bear with anyone if he enslaves you, if he devours you, if he takes advantage of you, if he exalts himself, if he hits you in the face. ²¹Shamefully, I am speaking as if we have been weakening. Yet, in whatever respect anyone else may be daring, in foolishness I am speaking, I daring, even I. ²²Are they Hebrews? So am I. Are they Yisra'eli? So am I. Are they descendants of Avraham? So am I. ²³Are they servants of the Anŏinted?—I speak as if insane. I more so, in far more labors, in far more imprisonments, beaten times without number, often in danger of death. ²⁴Five times I received from the Yehudim thirty-nine lashes. ²⁵Three times I was beaten with rods, once I was stoned, three times I was shipwrecked, a night and a day I had been spending in the deep. ²⁶I have been on frequent journeys, in dangers from rivers, dangers from robbers, dangers from my countrymen, dangers from the nations, dangers in the city, dangers in the wilderness, dangers on the sea,

dangers among false brothers. ²⁷I have been in labor and hardship, through many sleepless nights, in hunger and thirst, often without food, in cold and exposure. ²⁸Apart from such external things, there is the daily pressure upon me of concern for all the assemblies. ²⁹Who is weak without my being weak? Who is led into sin without my intense concern?

³⁰If one needs to be boasting, I will boast of things relating to my weakness. ³¹The Almĭghty and Făther of Adŏnai Yĕshua, he who is being blessed for *all* the ages, has been knowing that I am not lying. ³²In Dammeseq the ethnarch under Aretas the king was guarding the city *gates* of the ˣDammeseq in order to seize me, ³³and I was let down in a basket through a window in the wall, and so escaped his hands.ᵖ

12 ¹Boasting is necessary, though it is not profitable. But I will go on to visions and revelations of Yăhweh. ²I have been knowing a man belonging to the Anŏinted who, ʸfourteen years ago—whether in the body I have not been knowing, or out of the body I have not been knowing, the Almĭghty has been knowing—such a man was caught up to the third heaven. ³And I have been knowing such a man—whether in the body or apart from the body I have not been knowing, the Almĭghty has been knowing—⁴that was caught up into Paradise, and heard inexpressible words, which a man is not permitted to speak. ⁵On behalf of such a man will I boast, but on my own behalf I will not boast, except in regard to my weaknesses. ⁶Because if I may have wished to boast I will not be foolish, because I will be speaking the truth, but I refrain from this, so that no one may have considered me with more than he sees in me or hears from me.

⁷And because of the surpassing greatness of the revelations, for this reason, so that I may not be becoming conceited, there was given me a thorn in the flesh, a messenger of Satan, so that he may be harassing me—so that I may not be becoming conceited! ⁸Concerning this, I entreated Yăhweh three times that it will have departed from me. ⁹And he had been saying to me, "My loving-kindness is sufficient for you, because *my* power is perfected in weakness." Most gladly, therefore, I will rather boast about my weaknesses, that the power of the Anŏinted will have dwelt in me. ¹⁰Therefore, I am well content through weaknesses, through insults, through distresses, through persecutions, through difficulties, for the Anŏinted One's sake, because when I may be weak, then I am strong.

¹¹I have been becoming foolish. You yourselves compelled me. Actually, I should have been commended by you, because in no respect was I inferior to the most eminent emissaries, even though I am a nobody. ¹²The signs of a true emissary were performed among you with all perseverance, besides by signs, also wonders and miracles. ¹³For in what respect were you treated as inferior to the rest of the assemblies, except that I myself did not become a burden to

---

11:32 χ Prop. Dammeseqiyyim, Damascenes.
11:32 π AD 38. **12:2** γ At the beginning of the reign of Claudius (AD 41), not long before Agubus' prophecy in Acts 11:27. Galatians was written in AD 49, the first of Paul's letters. There are also things which a man is not permitted to write. See Rev. 10:4. There are also things spoken in parable which the seeing will not see and the hearing will not hear. See 2 Peter 3:15-16.

2 Corinthians 13

you? Forgive me this wrong!

¹⁴Here, for this third time I am ready to come to you, and I will not be a burden to you, because I do not seek what is yours, but you. Because children are not responsible to save up for their parents, but parents for their children. ¹⁵And I will most gladly spend and be expended for your souls. If I love you the more, am I to be loved the less?

¹⁶But be that as it may, I did not burden you myself, nevertheless, crafty fellow that I am, I took you in by deceit. ¹⁷Certainly I have not taken advantage of you through any of those whom I have been sending to you? ¹⁸I urged Titus to go, and sent the brother with him. Titus did not take any advantage of you, did he? Did we not conduct ourselves in the same spirit and walk in the same steps?

¹⁹All along, are you thinking that we are defending ourselves to you? Actually, it is in the sight of the Almĭghty that we are speaking in view of the Anŏinted, and all for your building up, beloved. ²⁰Because I am afraid, that perhaps when I come, I may have found you to be not what I am wishing and I may have been found by you to be not what you wish, that perhaps there may be strife, jealousy, angry tempers, disputes, slanders, gossip, arrogance, and disturbances. ²¹I am afraid that when I come again my Almĭghty may have humiliated me in respect to you, and I will have mourned over many of those who have been sinning beforehand, who still have not turned their heart and been sorry over the uncleanness, and illicit sex which they practice.

13

¹This is the third time I am coming to you. EVERY ₐMATTER ᵦMUST BE CONFIRMED BY THE ᵩMOUTH OF TWO WITNESSES, ᵧOR THREE^ψ. ²I have been previously saying and I am saying ahead of time, like *my* being by the second time, and being absent now, to those who have been sinning in the past, and to all the rest, that if I should come again to such, I will not spare anyone, ³since you are seeking for a test of the Anŏinted who speaks in me, and who is not weak toward you, but mighty among you. ⁴Because indeed, he was fastened to an execution timber because of weakness, yet he lives because of the power of the Almĭghty. Because we also are weak in him, yet we will live with him because of the power of the Almĭghty directed toward you.

⁵Be testing yourselves *to see* if you are in the pledge of faithfulness. Be examining yourselves! Or are you not fully knowing yourselves, that Yĕshua the Anŏinted *is* in you—unless you are unacceptable? ⁶And, I am hoping that you will realize that we ourselves are not unacceptable. ⁷And, we are praying before the Almĭghty not ᵉto have done you wrong, not even one ᵞbit. Not that we ourselves

---

13:1 ψ Deu 17:6, 19:15. **13:1** α דָּבָר. **13:1** β→confirmed: יָקוּם. **13:1** φ פִּי **13:1** γ אוֹ. **13:7** ξ→γ = ποιῆσαι ὑμᾶς κακὸν μηδέν = (we are praying...not) *to have done you wrong, no yet one*. The infinitive ποιῆσαι is followed by the accusative pronoun ὑμᾶς. How then the translations turn it into the subject I cannot tell. Taking 'you' as the object of the verb makes perfect sense. Paul is trying to justly deal with all the problems in Corinth as an impartial judge praying he will commit no error in carrying out his duty, yet it would appear that because he must pass judgment on some people that he is made to appear as harsh or unloving, and therefore is faulted in any case just for deciding justice. Paul is saying he does not care if he appears 'unacceptable' to some, so long as they end up doing what is right.

may be seen *to be* acceptable, but that you may be doing what is right, though we as unacceptable may be appearing. ⁸Because we can do nothing against the truth, but only for the truth. ⁹Because we rejoice when we ourselves may be weak, and you may be strong. This we also are praying for, that you may be fully outfitted. ¹⁰For this reason I am writing these things while absent, in order that when being by I will not have used severity, in accordance with the authority which Yăhweh gave me, for building up and not for tearing down.

¹¹Finally brothers, be rejoicing. Be getting yourselves outfitted. Be getting comforted. Be minding the same thing. Be living in peace. And the Almĭghty of love and peace will be with you.

¹²Greet one another with a holy kiss.

¹³All the holy ones greet you. ¹⁴The loving-kindness of Adŏnai Yĕshua the Anŏinted, and the love of the Almĭghty, and the fellowship of the Holy Spĭrit, be with you all.

Galatians

1 ¹Paul, an ᵃemissary—not from men nor through man, but through Yĕshua the Anŏinted^β and the Almĭghty Făther, who raised him from the dead, ²and all the brothers with me, to the assemblies of Galatia. ³Loving-kindness^γ to you and peace from our Almĭghty Făther, and ᵟAdŏnai Yĕshua the Anŏinted, ⁴who gave himself because of our sins, so that he will have rescued us from the age which has been joining itself to evil, according to the will of our Almĭghty and Făther, ⁵to whom be the glory forever and ever. Amen.

⁶I am amazed that you are so quickly deserting him who called you in the loving-kindness of the Anŏinted to a different good news, ⁷which is not another, but there are some who are disturbing you and who want to change the good news of the Anŏinted. ⁸But even though we or a messenger from heaven may be announcing to you good news contrary to that which we have proclaimed to you, let him be accursed. ⁹As we have been saying before, even now I am saying again, if anyone is announcing to you good news contrary to that which you received, let him be accursed^ψ.

¹⁰For now do I have to convince men, or the Almĭghty? Or am I striving to please men? If I were still trying to please men, I would not be a servant of the Anŏinted. ¹¹Because I would have you know, brothers, that the good news which was proclaimed by me is not according to man. ¹²For I neither received it from the hand of man, nor was I taught it, but I received it through a revelation of Yĕshua the Anŏinted.

¹³For you have heard of my former manner of life in Judaism, how I used to persecute the Assembly of the Almĭghty exceedingly and tried to destroy it.

1:1 α Apostle, phoneticized in English according to the Greek, actually means an **emissary**, one sent as an ambassador or representative of a body. Yĕshua's emissaries represent the kingdom of the Most High and the Assembly of Yisra'el. By not translating the word, and phonetically adopting it only, Christianity was able to isolate and separate the concept of apostleship from Yisra'el and the covenant of old now made new again. **1:1 β** Christ is another phonetically transferred word in English, and as such Christ does not represent the meaning of the orginal, which is **Anointed**. Prophets and kings were anointed, and so also the only kindred Son, the kindred Most High to the Father was anointed in the flesh, and so he is called **The Anointed One** in Hebrew, which is הַמָּשִׁיחַ, **Ha-Mashiaḥ**. **1:3 γ** The Greek word Χάρις goes back to the Hebrew word חֶסֶד. Ḥesed is best translated loving-kindness. This includes mercy, but it is broader in sense, including general love and blessing from the Most High. ▷ Paul is wishing that more of it will flow from the Most High to the recipients of his letter. Exodus 20:6 shows the condition of receiving divine loving-kindness is keeping the Almighy's commandments, which includes mercy and forgiveness for those who return to the commandments. So good works are required (cf. Rom. 2:7; Lev. 18:5). And for this reason the word 'grace' must be avoided, as corrupt shepherds are likely to define it as unmerited favor. Forgiveness is certainly unmerited in great degree, but in the broader definition of loving-kindness, divine favor is not unmerited. Those getting rescued by the Most High pledge faithfulness to Him, and are holding faithful to Messiah. When Paul speaks negatively of works, he is referring to a Jewish concept of merit and demerit, explained later in these notes. Christianity adopted the same philosophy that Paul opposes. **1:3 δ** The word 'Lord' is avoided, not because it has a proper meaning, but because it is so often used in the hypocrisy of the false religion that many of the faithful have come out of. Like the term Ba'al (which means **lord**) the word has become like the bronze serpent, nehushtan, being invoked so many times by deceived and deceiving hearts in the way of false religion. **1:9 ψ**. Most often what is called the gospel is either a false good news or a mixture of false doctrine with elements of truth. This is because Satan's number one operation is to confuse and redefine the good news so that men do not perceive divine forgiveness. This is accomplished by turning forgive-

¹⁴And I was advancing in Judaism beyond most of my peers among my ʸkindred, being more extremely zealous for my fathers' traditions.

¹⁵Yet, when he who had set me apart from my mother's womb, and called me through his loving-kindness, was pleased ¹⁶to ᵖreveal his Sŏn to me, that I may be proclaiming him among the nations, I did not immediately consult with flesh and blood, ¹⁷nor did I go up to Yerushalayim to those who were emissaries before me, but I went away to ᵅAravia, and returned once more to ᵝDamaseq. ¹⁸Then after three yearsᵗ I went up to Yerushalayim to become acquainted with Kᵉipha, and stayed with him fifteen days. ¹⁹But I did not see any other of the emissaries except Ya'aqov the brother of ᶻAdŏnai.

²⁰Now in what I am writing to you, I assure you before the Almĭghty that I am not lying. ²¹Then I went into the regions of Şyriaʼ and Çiliçia. ²²And I had been myself unknown by face to the assemblies of Yehudah, the ones belonging to the Anŏinted, ²³but they were only hearing, "He who once persecuted us is now proclaiming the pledge of faithfulness which he once tried to destroy." ²⁴And they were glorifying the Almĭghty because of me.

2 ¹Then by way of ᵗfourteen years I went up again to Yerushalayim with Bar-Nabba, taking Titus along also. ²And, I went up in accord with a revelation, and I set before them the good news which I am proclaiming among the nations, yet in private to those who were recognized as important, due to fear that I may be running or had run in vain.

³But not even Titus who was with me, though he was a Greek, was compelled to be circumcised, ⁴ᵗₕₐₜ ᵢₛ, ᶲthrough the false brothers who had sneaked in to spy out our liberty which we have through the Anŏinted Yĕshua, in order to bring us into bondage, ⁵to whom we did °not yield in subjection for an hour, so that the

---

ness into a payment or purchase of divine favor. This is ably accomplished by the doctrines of penal substitution and justification by faith alone through grace alone. Both repentance and true forgiveness are negated by these doctrines as effectively as Judaism in Paul's day negated the good news by doctrines of merit for demerit and imputation of the righteousness of the fathers (זְכוּת הָאָבוֹת). The divine curse rests on the Calvinist System just as asseredly as the superstitious Catholic and Rabbinic systems of merit. **1:14** γ γένος. Some members of the Messianic Faith call the Faith <u>Messianic Judaism</u>. The simple term Judaism was already considered less useful by the emissaries, because none of them ever use it to refer to the faithful. After almost 2000 years of usage referring to those who oppose Yĕshua, it is even less useful now, even misleading. To an extent Messianic Jews embracing the term Judaism have redeemed the term from the suggestion that they do not believe in Mĕssiah Yĕshua by prefixing it with 'Messianic,' because that is what will be assumed if one self identifies by the plain term Judaism. If they succeed in restoring the original definition of the term Judaism or in altering the perception of opposition to Mĕssiah by using the term with 'Messianic' that is great. But the main users of the term 'Messianic Judaism' have also succeeded in making the term suggest Jewish descent and also to a great extent unbiblical Rabbinic tradition. This makes the term somewhat misleading for the faithful who are not of Jewish descent and who do not embrace Rabbinic tradition. For this reason, I advise sticking with the designation 'Messianic Faith,' which is not slanted in those ways. See End Note No. 1. **1:16** ρ AD 36. **1:17** α AD 36. **1:17** β AD 38. **1:18** τ AD 39. **1:19** ζ or 'the Măster' **2:1** τ AD 49 (cf. 1:18) 3rd visit; 14 yrs. counting from his conversion; omitting mention of 2nd visit to Jer (Acts 11:27ff). Continued in Endnotes on page 611. **2:4** δ→is: explanatory δε. **2:4** φ→brothers: Note Paul's qualifying statement. Continued in Endnotes on page 611. **2:5** ° Codex Claromontanus omits the words "to whom not." So also the Latin Irenaeus (AD 130-202), and itala b and d. Tertullian (AD 155-240), MVict Ambst and Hier(ms) also omit the negative. Tertullian accused Marcion of adding the negative (adv Marc. 5.3). ▷This note represents a change of opinion from a former edition. I now think the words should be included. The Claromontanus reading is more advantageous to those who want to do away with the Law, because it implies

truth of the good news will have remained with you. ⁶But from those who appeared to be important (what they were makes no difference to me. The Almĭghty shows no partiality)—well, those who appeared to be important added nothing to me.

⁷But on the contrary, they saw that I have been getting held faithful with the good news to the uncircumcised, just as Peter was to the circumcised. ⁸Because he who worked in Peter as an emissary of the circumcision, also worked in me for the nations. ⁹And recognizing the loving-kindness that was given to me, Yaʻaqov and Keipha and Yoḥanan, who were recognized as pillars, gave to me and Bar-Nabba the right hand of fellowship. So we go to the nations, and they to the circumcised. ¹⁰They only asked us that we may be remembering the poor—the very thing I also was eager to do.

¹¹But when Keipha came to Antioch, I opposed him to his face, because he had been prejudicing himself. ¹²Because prior to the coming of certain men from Yaʻaqov, he was eating with the nations, but when they came, he was withdrawing and holding himself aloof, fearing those of the circumcision. ¹³And the rest of the ᵟYehudim joined him in hypocrisy, with the result that even Bar-Nabba was carried away by their hypocrisy. ¹⁴But when I saw that they were not walking straight toward the truth of the good news, I said to Keipha before all, "If you, being ᵋYehudi, live ᵞgoyishly and not like a ᵡYehudi, how is it that you are forcing the nations to become ᵡYehudi?"

¹⁵"Are we Yehudim by nature, and not sinners from the nations?ₐ" ¹⁶But we have been knowing a man ᵝis not getting administered justice based on the ᶿcustomary works; if no, *then it is* through the ᵞfaithfulness of the Anŏinted Yĕshua. Even we to the Anŏinted Yĕshua have ᵟpledged faithfulness, so that justice may be administered based on the faithfulness of the Anŏinted, and not

---

that Paul complied with his opposition out of expediency for a time without really believing it should be kept. Tertullian, therefore would be incorrect, and he himself argued vehemently against circumcision. Someone did delete the negative, perhaps Marcion, and to acknowledge such would show that there was a simple explanation of the text containing the negative that upheld the circumcision commandment, which the deleter wanted to avoid. Therefore, it might be that Tertullian is accusing Marcion of adding the negative to hide the very opposite. ▷ The negative is easier to explain. The issue is plainly and simply about forcing converts to be circumcised rather than allowing them to come to a voluntary and informed decision which they can make at a time of their own choosing without fear or compulsion. That compulsion was widely applied is evident in Josephus' narratives (e.g. *Life* 1:113). Different writers disagreed on the urgency of circumcision, much like a Catholic/Lutheran vs. Baptist debate over the urgency and meaning of baptism. Some would compel it with a threat of the fire of hell while others would allow for a delay so that the convert could understand the true meaning of the sign and not be rushed into the sign for the wrong reason or under threat. ▷ The threats aimed at compulsion demand a straightforward denial. ▷ As knowledge of compelled circumcision faded with the decline of Judean power, retaining the negative became more acceptable as 'compel' could be treated as 'encouraged' or 'urged.' Opponents simply equivocated upholding the law of circumcision with compulsion. **2:13** δ = Judeans. **2:14** ξ = Jewish; **2:14** γ goyishly < ἐθνικῶς; an exaggerated prejudicial term used to refer to Jews who ignored Judean traditions. **2:14** χ = Judean, particularly Jewish in the sense of the tribe of Judah and the territory of Judah. Continued in the Endnotes on page 612. **2:15** α Sarcasm, or objection to be answered. See Romans 3:1-18 for Paul's expanded answer to this question. It is Paul's lead in that Jews cannot be acquitted by their works, because they too are sinners. **2:16** β→justice: The administration of justice is the process of judging a case, with a view to acquitting the accused and letting him go, or finding the accused guilty, and either sentencing him, or pardoning him and releasing them. **2:16** θ→works: *works of custom, works of tradition*, ἔργων νόμου (BDAG νόμος, def. no. 1); ▷ See Appendix VIII, page 579. This refers to Judaism's legal doctrine of merit (זכות) to earn forgiveness. The doctrine teaches that a good deed cancels out (or reduces) a penalty for a bad deed. Lit. works of custom or works of tradition,

based on the customary works, because based on the customary works no flesh will be administered justice.

¹⁷But when seeking to get justice administered by the Anŏinted, we ourselves have also been found guilty, then is the Anŏinted then a minister of sin?^α May it never be! ¹⁸For if I rebuild whatever legal case I have destroyed, I prove myself to be a transgressor,^θ ¹⁹because I through what is customary, to what is customary^β died, so that I will have lived for the Almĭghty: ²⁰I have been fastening ^γmyself up on the execution timber with the Anŏinted One^μ, so I no longer live *to self*, but the Anŏinted One is living in me. What I am now living in the flesh, by faithfulness I am living, ^φthrough the *faithfulness* of the Sŏn of the Almĭghty, who loved me and delivered himself up on behalf of me. ²¹I am not setting aside the loving-kindness of the Almĭghty, because if administration of justice is through what is ^θcustomary then the Anŏinted One died needlessly.

3 ¹You foolish Galatians! Who has bewitched you, before whose eyes Yĕshua the Anŏinted was publicly portrayed as having been getting fastened to an execution timber? ²This is the only thing I want to find out from you. Did you receive the Spĭrit by *doing* the customary works, or because of a ^φfaithful listening?

---

because especial acts of piety were considered efficacious: prayer, alms, torah study, constant ritual purity. Paul generalizes rejecting any good deed supposed to lessen the administration of punitive justice. So he leaves out the qualifying words, like צדקה found in 4QMMT. This is relevant to vs. 15 in that Jews cannot end up with a righteous status through offsetting merit. **2:16 γ** Also, *pledge* or *promise*. Cf. πίστις *Jos. Ant.* Continued in Endnotes on page 612. **2:16 δ**→faithfulness: *Promised loyalty* or *pledged loyalty* (with sincere repentance and contrition) and agreement to uphold the divine covenant, obeying his commandments. Continued in Endnotes on page 613. **2:17 α** Consider a Judge that issues many pardons or a President that does so. Then such an administration is supposed by every political opponent to encourage lawlessness. That is what the charge that Mĕssiah is a minister (administrator) of sin is supposed to mean. **2:18 θ** What does Paul mean by building a case that he destroyed? He destroyed the case for acquittal by admitting guilt. For in seeking a pardon through Mĕssiah, confession of sin is necessary. If a defendant admits guilt, and then retracts the plea because he thinks he can bribe the judge he is a wicked person. **2:19 β** To "die to" something means to turn and reject it, to shun it. The legal norm is for the condemnation of the sinner. Upon repentance, the norm is canceled by forgiveness, and we are rescued from death by Messiah's ransom. **2:20 γ** middle voice perfect **2:20 μ** Paul means that his sinful self is getting put to death through repentance and faithfulness to Messiah. If we leave our sinful self behind with death, then Messiah's ransom rescues us from death. **2:20 φ**→Sŏn: *in that of the Sŏn*, τῇ τοῦ υἱοῦ Literally, "I am living, through that of the Son" (ζῶ τῇ τοῦ υἱοῦ). τῇ τοῦ = *in the of the*. The first article is a dative feminine and can only refer to the fem. word faithfulness Paul just used in ref. to himself. See Pulpit Commentary. This subtlety is profoundly difficult for traditional doctrine, and is therefore ignored in the translations; τῇ is equiv. to: ἐν τῇ πίστει. **2:21 θ**→norm: or *what is customary;* The legal norm is for acquittal or the not so legal norm is to acquire merit to cancel the demerit. The legal exception for the faithful is forgiveness and ransom from death via divine long-suffering of the ravages of our sin while bringing us to repentance. Messiah need not have died under the first system, since merit would deliver from death. But instead of strict justice we receive forgiving justice. Messiah's death, therefore demonstrates the epitome of divine suffering at the human level, and indicates the judgment being canceled by his forgiveness. ▷ By no means is Messiah suffering divine wrath as a judicial payment for sin to the Father. Being hanged with Messiah, to speak figuratively of the suffering sin causes, isn't a substitionary participation in divine wrath. It is an active participation in divine suffering caused by sin. Paul speaks using the Greek perfect, which is progressive, "I have been..." This is not some kind of mental exercise. It is an active participation in the sufferings of Messiah for the sake of the kingdom, to complete what lacks in Messiah's sufferings. **3:2 φ** or: *hearing of faithfulness, hearing about f.,* ἀκοῆς πίστεως; cf. vs. 5 (γ). See Romans 1:17 for the two faithfulnesses. One must listen faithfully. One must also hear about Mĕssiah's faithfulness instead of Judaism's doctrine of זכו (merit for demerit). For the Spĭrit does respond to genuine obedience (cf. Exodus 20:6; Yoḥ. 14:21), and not to bribes. **3:3 α**→flesh; by making up demerits with merit; **3:5 β**→works: *works of custom;* he means

³Are you so foolish? Having begun by the Spĭrit, do you now ᵃperfect yourselves in the flesh? ⁴Did you suffer so many things in vain, if indeed it was in vain? ⁵Does he then, who provides you with the Spĭrit and works miracles among you, do it because of the ᵝcustomary works, or because of a ᵞfaithful listening, just as ⁶ᵃAᴠʀᴀʜᴀᴍ ʜᴀᴅ ʜᴇʟᴅ ꜰᴀɪᴛʜꜰᴜʟ ɪɴ Yᴀ̆ʜᴡᴇʜ, ᴀɴᴅ ⁶ᵇɪᴛπ ʜᴀᴅ ʙᴇᴇɴ ᴛᴀᴋᴇɴ ɪɴᴛᴏ ᴀᴄᴄᴏᴜɴᴛ ꜰᴏʀ ʜɪᴍ ᴄᴏɴᴄᴇʀɴɪɴɢ ᵂᴛʜᴇ ᴀᴅᴍɪɴɪsᴛʀᴀᴛɪᴏɴ ᴏꜰ ᴊᴜsᴛɪᴄᴇ?

⁷Therefore, be knowing that those based on ᶲfaithfulness ᵖare sons of Aᴠraham. ⁸And when the ᴺScripture foresaw, that the Almĭghty would be administering justice for the nations based on faithfulness, it announced the good news beforehand to Aᴠraham: "ᴀʟʟ ᴛʜᴇ ɴᴀᴛɪᴏɴs ᴡɪʟʟ ʙᴇ ʙʟᴇssᴇᴅ ɪɴ ʏᴏᴜᵠ." ⁹Therefore, ᵞall those based on faithfulness are getting blessed with the faithful Aᴠraham.

¹⁰Because as many as based on the customary works are ᶓjustified, under a curse are. Because it has been getting written, "ᴄᴜʀsᴇᴅ ɪs ᴇᴠᴇʀʏᴏɴᴇ ᴡʜᴏ ᴅᴏᴇs ɴᴏᴛ sᴛᴀɴᴅ ʙʏ ᴀʟʟ ᴛʜᴇ ᴛʜɪɴɢs ᴡʜɪᴄʜ ʜᴀᴠᴇ ʙᴇᴇɴ ɢᴇᴛᴛɪɴɢ ᴡʀɪᴛᴛᴇɴ ɪɴ ᴛʜᴇ ʙᴏᴏᴋ ᴏꜰ ᴛʜᴇ ʟᴀᴡ, ᴛᴏ ᴅᴏ ᴛʜᴇᴍµ." ¹¹Now it is clear that no one may be getting himself justifiedπ by ᵃwhat is customary before the Almĭghty, because "ᴛʜᴇ ʀɪɢʜᴛᴇᴏᴜs ᴏɴᴇ ᴡɪʟʟ ʟɪᴠᴇ ʙᴀsᴇᴅ ᴏɴ ꜰᴀɪᴛʜꜰᴜʟɴᴇssᵞ." ¹²So, ᴛʜᴇ customary norm is not based on faithfulness. But "ᴡʜᴇɴ ᴏɴᴇ ᵡᴅᴏᴇs ᵖᴛʜᴇ ᴄᴏᴍᴍᴀɴᴅᴍᴇɴᴛs, ᴛʜᴇɴ ʜᴇ ᴡɪʟʟ ʟɪᴠᴇ ʙʏ ᴛʜᴇᴍᶓ."

¹³The Anŏinted ᵃransomed us from the curse, ᴛʜᴇ customary norm, having ᵖbecome a curse on behalf of usµ. Because it has been getting written, "ᴄᴜʀsᴇᴅ ɪs ᴇᴠᴇʀʏᴏɴᴇ ᴡʜᴏ ʜᴀɴɢs ᴏɴ ᴀ ᴛʀᴇᴇᵟ." ¹⁴in order that through the Anŏinted Yĕshua

---

merit to cancel demerit; **3:5** I. γ→listening: or II. hearing of faithfulness, hearing about (the) faithfulness (of Mĕssiah); **3:6a** Gen. 15:6a: **3:6b** = I. Gen. 15:6b, or = II. Psa. 106:31, where 'ɪᴛ' (π) = Our faithfulness and Mĕssiah's faithfulness. See Endnote No. 3, page 384. See on Rom. 4:3; 5:1. **3:7** ϕ See Romans 1:17. Mĕssiah's faithfulness in restoring the covenant followed by our faithful response. **3:7** ρ lit. 'these are'; **3:8** η personification; Gal. 3:22; Rom. 4:3; 9:17; Yoḥ. 7:38; **3:8** ψ Gen 12:3. **3:9** λ besides just Jews. **3:10** ξ Supply from the context. There is no ransom (or pardon) from the customary curse by the doctrine of substitutionary merit (zekuth, זְכוּת = good works to compensate for sin.) See Exodus 23:7; Deut. 25:1; Prov. 17:15. µ Deu 27:26: אָרוּר אֲשֶׁר לֹא־יָקִים אֶת־דִּבְרֵי הַתּוֹרָה־הַזֹּאת לַעֲשׂוֹת אוֹתָם ▷. Paul's opponents' theology of salvation required them to interpret Deut. 27:26 to mean that absolute legal perfection in Gŏd's sight was necessary for salvation. This is why they needed the merit of the ancestors or their own merit to cover every demerit. This doctrine was in place of admitting guilt, getting forgiven, and accepting Mĕssiah's death as our ransom, the cost of our rescue and cleansing. But Deut. 27:26 doesn't say that perfect legal merit is required for salvation. In truth Deut. 27:26 only places the curse over those who spurn the law or who commit one of the serious transgressions in the other curse passages. See Endnote No. 2, page 383. **3:11** π = administered justice.

3:11 α→means: custom, the norm **3:11** λ Hab. 2:4: The false doctrine of merit and demerit decides justice (unto a verdict of life) by offsetting faithlessness (sin, demerit) by faithfulness. But Hab. 2:4 and Lev. 18:5 show that only faithfulness merits life. Therefore it is clear that Scripture does not teach the merit for demerit doctrine. Paul quotes Hab. 2:4 and Lev. 18:5 here in the reverse order of Rom. 10:5-6 (He alludes to Hab. 2:4 in Rom. 10:6): the two texts explain each other, as they are both saying exactly the same thing. Hab. 2:4 also has a messianic sense which Paul expands into the "faithfulness of Mĕssiah," by taking אֱמוּנָתוֹ (His faithfulness) to refer back to בֹּא יָבֹא לֹא יְאַחֵר from Hab. 2:3, "He will surely come. He will not be too late." The ransomer will come. **3:12** χ cf. Heb: יַעֲשֶׂה. **3:12** ρ→commandments = them. **3:12** ζ Lev 18:5; Rom. 10:5. **3:13** α The Almĭghty sold Yisra'el to its enemies (cf. Deut. 28:68; 32:30; Judges 2:14; 4:2) because they sinned. Continued in Endnotes on page 613. **3:13** ρ→curse. Continued in the Endnotes on page 614. **3:13** µ or 'because of us,' i.e. our transgressions being the cause of his injustice. **3:13** δ Deu 21:23. **3:14** γ Since his faithfulness and our faithful response are both involved Paul apologetically omits the word "his" modifying faithfulness in Hab. 2:4. Our faithfulness is applied in the non-messianic interpretation of Hab. 2:4. It is the same as Lev. 18:5 (cf. Mark 10:17-21). His faithfulness is applied in the messianic sense for our ransoming. In Paul's view these two

Galatians 3

the blessing of Aνraham will have come to the nations, so that we will have received the promise of the Spĭrit through ʸfaithfulness.

¹⁵Brothers, I speak according to man: it is the same as a covenant which has been getting confirmed by man: no one is setting *it* aside or adding modifications to *it*. ¹⁶Now the promises were spoken to Aνraham and to his seed. He does ^λ1^not speak, "And to seeds," as if only referring to many, ^λ2^if not also to one, "AND TO YOUR SEED,^δ^" that is, the Anŏinted.

¹⁷So I am saying this: what had been becoming customary^φ^ after 430 years does not annul the covenant, which had been getting confirmed beforehand by the Almĭghty, so as to undo the promise. ¹⁸Because if the inheritance is *given* based on what is ^ψ^customary, it is no more based on the promise, but the Almĭghty has been himself favoring *it* to Aνraham by means of a promise.

¹⁹Then why the customary norm^α^ for the ʳtransgressions? ʸLoving kindness has been set forthˢ until when the Seed may have come, in connection to whom it^η^ has been getting announced, which will have been administered through messengers, by the ^χ^power of *the* Mediator. ²⁰But it is not the mediator of *the* ^μ^One, but the Almĭghty only.

²¹Then is the Law against the promises of the Almĭghty? May it never be! Because if a custom was given being able to restore life, then administration of justice could really have been based on what is customary. ²²But the Scripture has imprisoned all *who are* under sin,^π^ so that the promise will have been given because of the faithfulness of Yĕshua the Anŏinted to those who are ^α^pledging faithfulness.

²³But before the ^β^faithfulness came we were getting ourselves guarded under what is customary,^μ^ getting *our*selves locked up until ^β^the faithfulness *came*, that was about to be revealed. ²⁴Therefore THE customary ^φ^norm had been becoming our chaperon unto the Anŏinted One, so that we will have been ^ρ^administered justice based on ʸfaithfulness. ²⁵But now that the faithfulness has come, we are

---

faithfulnesses operate together in the one mention of the term here. **3:16** λ1-λ2→also: The rhetorical use of "not...but" to mean "not [only]...but [also]" is known to Hebrew and Greek. See the Lexicons. **3:16** δ Gen 13:15, 17:8, 24:7. **3:17** φ✓ *customary*. Idolatry was not necessarily the norm for Yisra'el immediately upon leaving Egypt, but this faction was evidently strong enough to coerce Aharon into cooperation. Idolatry had then certainly been on the way to becoming customary, if not continuously, then by increasing episodes of repetition that interrupted Yisra'el's fidelity to the Most High, and eventually did become THE NORM. Idolatry also resulted in the curse becoming the norm (Deut. 27:15-26; 28:16-20, 45), so that they came under the sentence of death. **3:18** ψ✓ Paul knows his enemies should agree that idolatry became the norm and that idolators will not inherit everlasting life, and so he now equivocates the severity of idolatry with the doctrine of paying for sin with imputed merit. Because it is not forgiveness, this norm is also basis for being disinherited. **3:19** α✓ *customary*. **3:19** ʳ See Endnotes, page 614. **3:19** γ χάρις חֵן or *mercy*. **3:19** η the curse. **3:19** χ Lit. 'hand,' idiom for power. **3:20** μ See Endnotes, page 615. **3:21** See Endnotes on page 615. **3:22** π See Rom. 3:9 ρ; 7:14 η. Cf. Rom. 6:14-15. 'Under sin' denotes the nations in rebellion and also the disloyal in Yisra'el. Read 'under sin,' as an adjective phrase defining who 'all' is. The italics 'who are' is only to make sure the reader does not miss this. **3:22** α See Endnotes on page 616. **3:23** β✓ The faithfulness revealed is Messiah's forgiveness and ransom, and that of whoever takes his pledge of faithfulness. See Rom. 10:4. *Came* is not meant in a dispensational sense, but in a local sense, that is when those *under sin* (vs. 22) pledge faithfulness to Messiah. **3:23** μ✓ *customary*. The curse. The progressive tense, *we were getting* points to only the unfaithful getting locked up. **3:24** φ✓ *customary*. See 3:17 φ, 3:18 ψ, 3:23 μ The curse. Propitiating Gŏd with works to gain forgiveness is what idolators do expecting their gods be placated. The evil that comes from this curse should teach those under it to turn to Mĕssiah for deliverance. **3:24** ρ✓ *Administer justice*. This is what Gŏd does as a judge. His forgiveness is based on Messiah's faithfulness and our pledge of faithfulness. **3:24** γ πίστεως;

no more under a chaperonᵝ.

²⁶For you all are becoming SONS OF THE ALMĬGHTY through the faithfulness ᶾof the Anŏinted Yĕshua. ²⁷Because as many of you as have been immersed into the Anŏinted One—you clothe yourselves with the Anŏinted One. ²⁸It does not consist in being Yehudi or Greek. It is not in being a slave or a free man, nor is it in being male or female, because you are all ᶾone through the Anŏinted Yĕshua. ²⁹And if you belong to the Anŏinted, then you are Avraham's seed, heirs according to promise.

4

¹Now I say, as long as the heir is childish, he does not differ at all from a slave although he is owner of everything, ²but he comes under guardians and managersᵘ until the appointed time set by the father. ³Likewise also we, while we were being childish, we had been getting ourselves enslaved under the elemental spiritsˣ of the world.

⁴But when the fullness of the time came, the Almĭghty sent forth his Sŏn, being born from a woman, coming under what is customaryᵠ ⁵in order that he will have ransomedᵑ those under what is customary, so that we shall have received the adoption as sons. ⁶And because you are sons, the Almĭghty has sent forth the Spĭrit of his Sŏn into our hearts, crying, "Abbă! Făther!" ⁷Therefore you are no longer a slave, but a son, and if a son, then an heir through the Almĭghty.

⁸However at that time, when you had not been knowing the Almĭghty, you were slaves to those which by nature are no gods. ⁹But now that you have come to know the Almĭghty, or rather to be known by the Almĭghty, how is it that you turn back again to the weak and worthless elemental spirits, to which you desire to be enslaved all over again? ¹⁰Days you are carefully watching, even months and seasons and years. ¹¹I am getting fearful for you, that perhaps I have been laboring over you in vain.

¹²I beg of you, brothers, be becoming as I, because I also *have become as you*. You have done me no wrong, ¹³but you have been knowing that it was because of a bodily affliction that I proclaimed the good news to you the first time. ¹⁴And that which was a trial to you, due to my bodily affliction, you did

---

the def. art. is missing here. Paul meant both Mĕssiah's faithfulness and our faithfulness. See Rom. 1:17. **3:25 β** The curse is lifted off the sinner and there is no need to propitiate Gŏd with imputed works, because there is forgiveness.

3:26 ξ 𝔓⁴⁶ 3:27 Through faithfulness we will have clothed ourselves with Mĕssiah (cf. Gal. 5:5) and therefore we are the Yaĥad of Yisra'el. The idea of clothing is stated as a fact, as a snapshot, without saying how it is done (therefore justly a proleptic aorist translated future perfect). This is because Paul is focusing on the identity of the faithful. We are the Yaĥad of Yisra'el, the seed of Avraham. **3:28 ζ** יַחַד, Deu. 33:5, yaĥad. **4:2 μ** The guardians and managers were the sons of God, but under Satan, they rebelled against the Most High and enticed man into sin during his spiritual childhood. They usurped ownership of man and man's inheritance. Now to the degree of man's sin an unrepentance, they are permitted to enslave him. The time appointed is the day of ransom release when those who repented will be liberated and those who did not will be judged. **4:3 χ** or also 'elements,' as in forces of nature and fundamental principles. Paul means all three ideas, superstitions of the elements, elementary principles, and the elemental spirits, the fallen sons of God.

4:4 φ See Endnotes page 616. **4:5 η** ἐξαγοράσῃ **to buy off, to ransom.** The Father gave him as a ransom to figuratively ransom those he was forgiving from their captivity in sin. We were formerly under the legal norm, sent into slavery by the Most High, and then we repented and he forgave us. His efforts to separate us from our sin and captivity are the ransom cost that he pays, and this cost is expressed in the flesh in Mĕssiah's death, whom the slave masters wanted to kill. But the Most High regards this as a ransom and

not despise or spit at, but you received me as the Messenger Almĭghty, as the Anŏinted Yĕshua himself. ¹⁵Where then is that sense of blessing you had? Because I bear you witness, that if possible, you would have plucked out your eyes and given them to me.

¹⁶Have I therefore been becoming your enemy by telling you the truth? ¹⁷They eagerly are seeking you, not rightly, but they are wishing to have shut you out, in order that you may be seeking them. ¹⁸But it is good always to be having zeal for good, and not only during my being by with you.

¹⁹My children, with whom I am again in labor until the Anŏinted will have been formed in you, ²⁰even I am wishing to be coming by to you now and to change my tone, because I am perplexed about you.

²¹Be telling me, you who want to be under ᵖwhat is customary, do you not listen to ᶿthe Law? ²²Because it has been getting written that Avraham had two sons, one by the slave woman and one by the free woman. ²³But the son by the slave woman has been getting begotten according to the flesh, and the son by the free woman through the promise.

²⁴These are being allegorically interpreted, because these women are two ᵅwills *for inheritance*, one ᵝfar off of the ᵑboundary of Sinai, and into slavery begetting children, which is Hagar. ²⁵Indeed, mount Sinai is in Arabia. But Arabia is ᵞin the same line with the present Yerushalayim, because she is in slavery with her children. ²⁶But the ᵟupward Yerushalayim is free. She is our mother, ²⁷be-

---

compels evil to release its captives. **4:8-11** Christians teachers regularly use this text to condemn the observance of Sabbath and feast days. But this is not what Paul is talking about at all. Continued in Endnotes on page 616.

4:21 π→customary, θ→Law: Once again Paul uses "nomos" in two different senses. The second is obvious. In the first instance Paul has equivocated two senses of nomos. He uses the phrase "under nomos" to mean under the sentence of the law. This is not something they want to be under, but Paul equivocates this with what they want to be subject to, which is the customary procedure for getting justice with Gŏd (not usually used with ὑπό in Greek): crediting merit against demerit. Paul's phrase therefore is a dammed if you answer one way and dammed if you answer the other way question for his opponents. He does mean they want to be under what is customary, which is a system whereby good deeds are credited against sin. Such a system is slavery, and many exist like it in cults and also sects of Christianity. Even the Catholic Church considered penance a partial payment for sin, and also deals in the treasury of merit, whereby the good deeds of a saint are credited against the bad deeds of a sinner so that the sinner may be saved. All of this is a false good news. And even Judaism has a similar system. It is called *zehut avot*, or the "merit of the fathers." **4:24** α: But not two covenants. In regular Greek the word means a will. In Greco-Roman culture a will often specified that some would become slaves under certain conditions (such as debts owed). Other wills stated that slaves would be set free and receive inheritances. There is one covenant of old made new, but with two wills concerning inheritance, judgment leading to condemnation for many, and forgiveness for those loyal to the Almĭghty leading to life. **4:24** β ἀπό. *far from*, LSJ, def. no. 2; BDAG 3rd, def. no. ❶ *away from*. This corresponds to Exodus 20:18, 21, "Then they stood afar off" (מֵרָחֹק). "The Targum of Jonathan says, they removed twelve miles; and so Jarchi, who observes, that this was according to the length of their camp" (John Gill); Hagar is even further. Compare Rom. 9:31, "to the Torah has not arrived." **4:24** η ὄρος. Boundary limit. Continued in the Endnotes on page 616. **4:25** γ→line: Or "in the same column," "in the same rank." The present Jerusalem stands in Rabbinic Judaism far off from Sinai. They are still fled from the glory of the Sŏn upon Mt. Sinai. The Essene sect and Qumran cult regarded Jerusalem as apostate from the true Mt. Sinai. Paul is using their own rhetoric in saying they are in line with apostate Jerusalem also, and that the faithful in Messiah stand at the top of the mountain freed from sin.

4:26 δ Or "at the top." See Isa. 2:2-3; 66:20: "the mountain will be in the top of the mountains" (בְּרֹאשׁ הֶהָרִים). "The nations shall flow unto it." "For out of Zion shall go forth the Torah, and the word of Yăhweh from Jerusalem." See Ezek. 20:40; Dan. 9:16; Joel 2:1; 3:17; Mic. 4:1-2; Zech 8:3. **4:24-28** See also Isa. 54:11-13; Zech. 1:14. As in 2Cor. 3 Paul is contrasting the sentence with the ministry of righteousness. At the foot of the mountain was a sentence of death from which the nations have fled far, and

cause it has been getting written, "REJOICE, BARREN ONE WHO DOES NOT BEAR. BREAK FORTH AND SHOUT, YOU WHO ARE NOT IN LABOR, BECAUSE MORE WILL BE THE CHILDREN OF THE DESOLATE ONE THAN OF THE ONE WHO HAS A HUSBAND^μ." ²⁸And you brothers, like Yitsḥaq, are children of promise.

²⁹But as at that time he who was born according to the flesh persecuted him who was born according to the Spirit, so it is now also. ³⁰But what does the text say? "CAST OUT THE SLAVE WOMAN AND HER SON, BECAUSE THE SON OF THE SLAVE WOMAN WILL NOT BE AN HEIR WITH THE SON OF THE FREE WOMAN.^{λ}" ³¹So then, brothers, we are not children of a slave woman, but of the free woman.

5

It was for freedom that the Anŏinted set us free! Therefore be standing firm and do not be getting yourselves held down again in a yoke of slavery. ²Behold I, Paul, say to you that if ^{ω}you may be becoming 'circumcised,' the Anŏinted will be of no benefit to you. ³And I am testifying again to every man receiving 'circumcision,' that he is a debtor to have^π done the whole Law. ⁴You have been severed from the Anŏinted, you who are administered justice ^{ξ}according to what is customary. You have fallen from loving-kindness, ⁵because we through the Spirit, by faithfulness, eagerly await the hope of righteousness.

⁶Because in the Anŏinted Yĕshua neither circumcision has a particular legal force^ψ nor uncircumcision, ^{ρ}but faithfulness working through love^μ.

⁷You were running well. Who hindered you from being persuaded by the truth? ⁸This persuasion did not come from him who calls you. ⁹A little leaven leavens the whole lump of dough. ¹⁰I have been trusting for you in Yăhweĥ, that you will adopt no other view, but the one who is disturbing you will bear his judgment, whoever he may be.

¹¹But I, brothers, ^{ρ}if when I ^{θ}am still proclaiming circumcision, ^{π}why still am

---

Israel has joined them, but on top of the mountain they ate and drank with Mĕssiah. What is customary is the sentence, but Mĕssiah is the end of what is customary for justice for everyone who affirms their faithfulness. See Romans 10:4.

4:27 μ Isa 54:1. **4:29-31** λ Gen 21:10, 12.

5:1-5 The false 'baptism' of Luther and the Pope can be rebuked in precisely these same terms. The foundation of their doctrine of salvation consists in being pure in the eyes of the Almĭghty or reckoned so before the Law. Paul is objecting to a redefinition called 'circumcision' by the false teachers which incorporated such a doctrine of merit for acquittal. His advice to delay circumcision on account of false doctrine is given in 1 Cor. 7:18-19. **5:2** ω 'You' and 'every man' (vs. 3) are thus limited to the recipients who believed the false doctrine of acquittal using merit to cancel demerit before the Law. **5:3** π Vs. present infinitive *to be doing*. Since what is customary knows no forgiveness, one is a debtor to <u>have</u> done the Torah. Thus Paul is stating an impossibility for sinful man. **5:4** ξ customary. = ἐννόμῳ. **5:5** Vs. 5 says we are waiting for perfect righteousness by holding faithful. Therefore in the eyes of the Law there is no doctrine or ritual that makes us perfect in the eyes of the Law. Instead we have forgiveness and hope for perfection later. **5:6** ψ τι ἰσχύει = has a certain power. Typical English translators construe this 'has any power,' failing to recognize that τι means 'a certain,' so that Paul is speaking of a <u>certain power</u> circumcision is said to have by the circumcision party, and not any power, as if it had none at all. That certain power was the teaching that the 'merit' of circumcision was sufficient to offset the demerit of all sin. Again the Church has at times made the same claim for baptism or other indulgences said to transfer sufficient merit to the convert to be saved. Circumcision is just a sign of the covenant, and thus a commandment to obey. It does not initiate a transfer of merit. So Paul is only rejecting a certain claim about circumcision. He is not saying it has no meaning at all. **5:6** ρ See Yoĥ. 6:27 but = unless also or if not **5:6** μ Paul's wording here is more careful than in 1Cor. 7:19. But he means the same idea. Paul is not objecting to circumcision as a commandment. He is only trying to guard against a false circumcision. We have to guard against the false baptism nowadays. See notes on 1 Cor. 7:19, and Acts 15. **5:11** ρ cf. BDAG, εἰ. The case is existing in fact.

I being persecuted? It is because the offense of ᵉthe execution timber has been getting nullified *by them*. ¹²Would that those who are troubling you would even ˣamputate themselves.

¹³Because you were called to freedom, brothers, only not freedom as an opportunity for the flesh, but through love be serving one another, ¹⁴because the whole Law has been getting fulfilled in one saying, in the statement, "YOU SHALL LOVE YOUR NEIGHBOR AS YOURSELFᵝ." ¹⁵But if you bite and devour one another, be taking care lest you may be consumed by one another.

¹⁶But I say, be walking by the Spĭrit, and you shall not have carried out the desire of the flesh. ¹⁷Because the flesh sets its desire against the Spĭrit, and the Spĭrit against the flesh, because these are in opposition to one another, so that you may not be doing the things that you may be wishing. ¹⁸But if you are led by the Spĭrit, you are not under what is customary.

¹⁹Now the deeds of the flesh are evident, which are: immorality, impurity, sensuality, ²⁰idolatry, drug use, enmities, quarreling, jealousy, outbursts of anger, selfish ambition, dissensions, factions, ²¹envying, drunkenness, carousing, and things like these, of which I forewarn you just as I have warned you before, that those who practice such things will not inherit the kingdom of the Almĭghtyˣ.

²²But the fruit of the Spĭrit is love, joy, peace, patience, kindness, goodness, faithfulness, ²³gentleness, self-control. Against such things there is no law. ²⁴Now those who belong to the Anŏinted Yĕshua fasten to an execution timber the flesh with its passions and desires. ²⁵If we are living by the Spĭrit, we should also be walking by the Spĭrit. ²⁶We should not be becoming boastful, challenging one another, or envying one another.

6

¹Brothers, if indeed someone may have been overtaken in any trespass, you who are spiritual, be restoring such a one in a spirit of gentleness, looking to yourself, lest you too may be tempted. ²Be bearing one another's burdens, and thus fulfill the Law of the Anŏinted, ³because if anyone thinks he is something when he is nothing, he deceives himself. ⁴But let each one be examining his own work, and then he will have reason for joyful satisfaction in regard to himself alone, and not in regard to another. ⁵Because each one should bear his own load. ⁶And let the one who is being taught the word be sharing all good things with him who teaches. ⁷Do not be getting yourselves deceived, the Almĭghty is not

---

See on 2:3-5; cf. Acts 16:1-4; 21:20-26. Thayer, "2. Not infrequently, when a conclusion is drawn from something that is quite certain, εἰ with the indicative is used argumentatively so as to be equivalent in sense to ἐπεί [when, since] (cf. the use of German *wenn*)." See Acts 26:23; Mark 8:12. **5:11** π→persecuted? Why is he persecuted by the same false teachers *when* he does teach circumcision to converts he knows understand it (cf. Acts 16:1-4). It is because Paul did not teach circumcision according to their doctrine just as occurred with the Anabaptists who did teach baptism, but not according to the doctrine of Luther or the Pope, and therefore were persecuted to death. **5:11** ξ→timber:

or *cross*. The false teachers undermined the message of Mĕssiah's death in their teaching of 'circumcision.' **5:11** θ we would expect imperfect here 'if I were....' if the contrary hypothesis were true. **5:13** χ Paul uses an extreme word. It should be noted that the Rabbis changed the method of circumcision from *milah* to *periah*, which is more severe to prevent undoing a circumcision. But circumcision may be undone simply by rejecting what it stands for. So Paul is correct. They may as well amputate themselves. **5:14** β Lev 19:18. **5:21** χ See 1 Cor. 6:9; Eph. 5:5-7; 1 Thess. 4:6-8.

mocked, because whatever a man may be sowing, this he will also reap. ⁸Because the one who sows to his own flesh will from the flesh reap a rotting corpse, but the one who sows to the Spĭrit will from the Spĭrit reap everlasting life.

⁹And we should not be growing weary in doing good, because in due time we will reap if we are not giving up. ¹⁰So then, while we have opportunity, we should be working good for everyone, and especially to those who are of the household of faithfulness.

¹¹See with what large letters I am writing to you with my hand. ¹²As many as desire to make a good showing in the flesh try to compel you to be 'circumcised,' only so that they may not be persecuted for the execution timber of the Anŏinted, ¹³because those who are 'circumcised' do not even keep the Law themselves, so much as they desire to have you 'circumcised,' so that they may boast in your flesh. ¹⁴But may it never be that I should boast, except in the execution timber of our Adŏnai Yĕshua the Anŏinted, through which the world has been getting fastened to an execution timber to me, and I to the world, ¹⁵because neither circumcision has a particular effect, nor uncircumcision, ᵖbut a new-made creature. ¹⁶And those who will walk by this rule, peace and mercy be upon them, even upon the Yisra'el of the Almĭghty.ᵞ

¹⁷From now on let no one be causing troubles for me, because I bear on my body the brand-marks of Yĕshua. ¹⁸The loving-kindness of our Adŏnai Yĕshua the Anŏinted be with your spirit, brothers. Amen.

6:15 ρ See Yoĥ. 6:27 but = unless also or if not **6:11-16** γ See Gal. 5:2. Since the Church itself has adopted the very same error with baptism in conferring salvation on infants and adults by virtue of the ritual of baptism, they are completely blind to understanding Paul's use of circumcision here. For Paul means a false circumcision alleged to accomplish the same things the Church asserts for baptism. ▷ Paul is speaking to an audience that believes a false definition of circumcision. So he means circumcision as defined by his audience when condemning it. This sort of usage might be placed in quotes today, to show that it represents someone else's terms. Paul would rather call what they believe to be circumcision "concision," but he must write to them and tell them their circumcision is false. ▷ Paul's opponents went through the literal act of circumcision just as the Church literally baptizes. But these circumcisions and baptisms deny what the literal act stands for because the Adversary's main attack vector against true religion is to seize upon its institutions and then to work with hypocrites within to redefine the meanings so that they may justify themselves. ▷ So long as this remains the case, Paul must be understood as against the perversions called baptism or circumcision by the false teachers and not against the commandments, because the false teachers of the Church have themselves criticized the baptism of competing Churches as not being baptism in their own estimation because their doctrine or mode do not agree. They have no excuse then for failing to see that Paul is doing the same thing.

Endnote No. 1: Faith Designations

¹Paul designated the faithful as, "The seed of Abraham," (Gal. 2:29) "The way," (Acts 24:14) "citizenship in Yisra'el," (Eph. 2:12) and "joint citizens with the holy ones," (Eph. 2:19) "sons of the Almĭghty," (Gal. 3:26) and "one (yaḥad) in the Anointed one" (Gal. 3:28). ²All true faithful are members of Yisra'el (even if in exile or self imposed exile), and Yisra'el is still a nation, but anyone regardless of origin, or birth-nationality, who pledges faithfulness to the God of Abraham, through Mĕssiah, has applied for citizenship. ³Application is only rejected for those whose allegiance proves false, who refuse to abide by the laws of Mĕssiah, who refuse to take the advice of the immigrant advocate, which is Gŏd's Spirit. ⁴Therefore Yisra'el is universally inclusive. Yisra'el is a nation of nations with a real land. And even if visible Yisra'el is not all that way right now, Gŏd has promised to make it so that the home of all the faithful is Yisra'el in his way, and on his terms. ⁵Therefore citizenship in Yisra'el embraces all humanity loyal to the Almĭghty, whereas humanist globalism will enslave all humanity disloyal to Him (cf. Hab. 2:4b; 2:5b). ⁶The Almĭghty caused the faithful to be called Messianics (Acts 11:26; cf. Acts 26:28; 1 Pet. 4:16), a term that denotes allegiance to the Anointed One:

⁷O SEED OF YISRAEL HIS SERVANT, SONS OF YA'AQOV, HIS CHOSEN ONES, HE IS YAHWEH OUR ALMĬGHTY, AND HIS ADMINISTRATIONS OF JUSTICE ARE IN ALL THE EARTH. ⁸HE *WILL* HAVE REMEMBERED FOREVER HIS COVENANT, THE WORD HE HAS MADE TO BE COMMANDED TO THE THOUSANDTH GENERATION, WHICH HE CUT WITH AVRAHAM, EVEN HIS OATH TO YITS'HAQ. ⁹THEN HE MADE IT STAND FOR YA'AQOV AS A STATUTE FOR YISRAEL, A COVENANT OF OLD, SAYING, UNTO YOU I WILL GIVE THE LAND OF CANAAN, THE PORTION OF YOUR INHERITANCE, WHILE THEY WERE MEN FEW OF NUMBER IN IT.

¹⁰THEN THEY WENT FROM NATION UNTO NATION, AND FROM ONE KINGDOM TO ANOTHER PEOPLE (אֶל־עַם אַחֵר).^χ ¹¹HE DID NOT LET ANY MAN REST FOR WRONGING THEM. THEN HE REBUKED KINGS FOR THEIR SAKE:

¹²TOUCH NOT MY ANOINTED ONES (מְשִׁיחָי, χριστῶν μου), AND DO MY SPOKESMEN NO HARM! ¹³SING TO YAHWEH ALL THE EARTH. SHOW FORTH FROM DAY TO DAY HIS DELIVERANCE. ¹⁴RECOUNT HIS GLORY AMONG THE NATIONS, HIS WONDERFUL WORKS AMONG ALL PEOPLES (PSALM 105:6-15; 1 CHR. 16:13-24).

¹⁵This then is what the term 'Christian' should mean, and 'Messianic' should mean, and since the latter connotes what it should mean better, that term I have used in Acts 11:26; 26:28; and 1 Peter 4:16. ¹⁶'Messianic' is a better term mainly because of what it doesn't connote: the anti-Law tradition of Christianity. It is up to the user of the term to properly reflect what it should mean. ¹⁷Every so often a once useful term gets its definition associated with something false. Therefore, we do better to avoid using once good terms where they might mislead. ¹⁸Avoidance of a term because it connotes what is false, however, does not mean one should explicitly deny the term applies to oneself either, since the term also connotes what is true. ¹⁹The term has simply been corrupted and can be neither positively affirmed nor positively denied. I suggest the term simply be retired, not as a ruling, but as a good suggestion.

EN1.10 χ cf. Mat. 8:11-12; 21:43.

Endnote No. 2: Deut. 27:26

CURSED IS EVERYONE WHO DOES NOT STAND BY ALL THE THINGS WHICH HAVE BEEN GETTING WRITTEN IN THE BOOK OF THE LAW, TO DO THEM.

Paul's opponents probably interpreted this passage as Christianized Gnosticism generally does, to mean that the slightest demerit, error, or sin of ignorance, brought the curse. This interpretation depends on construing the word "stand by," which is "upholds" in Hebrew to mean *keep perfectly*.

Judaism's solution consists in canceling out their demerits with their own supereragatory merit or that of the ancestors if their own is not enough. Circumcision and a repentant attitude was considered sufficient to impute the merit of the ancestors unto oneself if one's own extra merit had a shortfall with respect to the demerits. In this way they would buy themselves out of the curse.

Paul's simple answer is that such justification is not the forgiveness that comes from Mĕssiah Yĕshua, who because he is the Almighty Son, forgives sin without legal compensation, propitiation, or payment. If anyone is sorry for their sin and turns their heart from it, then he freely forgives. And then his life cleanses us from all unrighteousness as we walk in the Spirit to fulfill the righteousness of the law.

Messiah's blood sums up the ransom cost paid by the Most High to deliver us from the enemies we had fallen prey to. He suffered being cursed of men and evil to ransom us from the grip of lawlessness. See notes on Gal. 3:13. His bearing of our sin to purge it through his blood, his life, his Spirit, cleanses us. His suffering was to free us from the captivity of lawlessness.

Now once we are delivered, the passage is not saying that any sin brings on the curse, keeps it, or renews it. The reader should notice that the translation is nuanced, "stand-by all things" (ἐμμένει πᾶσιν τοῖς). BDAG, def. no. 2, ἐμμένω, "stand by." See also LSJ, "*abide by, stand by, cleave to, be true to*"; also Thayer.

This means that the loyal one considers Gŏd's law to be the standard of righteousness he should obey. It is not saying it is necessary to achieve perfection to stay clear of the curse. This point is even clearer in the Hebrew text: "Accursed is he that does not uphold the words of this Torah to do them." The text is speaking of heart commitment and not perfect outcome: "uphold..to do" (יָקִים לַעֲשׂוֹת), i.e. the pledge of loyalty. We see that the word "all" is not emphasized in the Hebrew, because it is not there. The infinitive לַעֲשׂוֹת expresses intent of the heart. The curses, therefore, were laid upon the serious transgressor, as may be seen from the list of sins connected to the other curses. And one cannot stand by these sins and escape the curse. The curse concerning the Torah at the end of the other curses is because rejection of the Torah was a serious transgression itself. But to mistakenly believe that a particular law applies to one when it does not, or to mistakenly believe that it does not apply, when it does, when yet holding faithful to the Most High and upholding the Torah everywhere one knows it does apply are not mistakes that bring one under the curse. But the Most High in due time will make clear through his Spĭrit matters, and reveal to the one holding faithful to him what is correct.

But while accepting the Torah, one may error in regard to it or sin in circumstance a sin not leading to death. Such a one is not cursed because his heart still upholds the Law. We still have forgiveness in our imperfections. Romans 7:14-25 (q.v.) explains this well. But if someone says in their heart that he has propitiation with the Most High, or special favor, or some kind of credits imputed to his account, and then commits sin willfully on that basis, then this person is under the curse and has no forgiveness.

Now it should be noted that no where does Scripture say it is necessary to perfectly keep Torah to hold faithful to Mĕssiah, and walk in the forgiveness granted by him. It is only necessary to walk with a sincere heart and not in rebellion.

Endnote No. 3: Gen. 15:6 & Psa. 106:31

Avraham held faithful in Yăhweh...
and it was taken into account for him
for $^\beta$the administration of justice [as an
example] for generation to generation,
onward the age.

וְהֶאֱמִן בַּיהוָה וַיַּחְשְׁבֶהָ לּוֹ
לִצְדָקָה לְדֹר וָדֹר עַד־עוֹלָם׃

The combination of Gen. 15:6 and Psa. 106:31 is a common theme in Jewish exegesis. Paul is no different in this regard. If one examines quotations in the emissaries writings one will see that it is not uncommon to mash up parts of various texts to make a point, e.g. Rom. 3:10-18; 9:33; 11:26-27. Paul's point can be simply stated. He is teaching his thesis from Romans 1:17, that of divine faithfulness in combination with our faithfulness. The later he obviously finds in Genesis 15:6a. And the former in the word "it" from Psa. 106:31, which stands for "my covenant of peace," and is equivalent to the divine faithfulness (cf. Exodus 34:6-7) in rendering justice in judgement. But Paul is also using the word "it" to refer to Avraham's faithfulness. By so joining the texts, he is using a Rabbinic method to illustrate his dual faithfulness point, that getting rescued from this evil age is the result of the dual contingencies of divine and human faithfulness. It is a synergism. While making his point Paul is zelous to eliminate the Rabbinic doctrine of imputed merit. For Paul, Avraham and Pinehas serve as examples for all generations, and not as sources of imputed merit. For Paul, divine forgiveness is contingent on faithfulness, and for us as well.

The Rabbis find their doctrine of zekut (זְכוּת), *merit for demerit,* in these two texts (see Appendix VIII and 434). For example, "Shemaiah taught; 'Sufficient is the faith<u>fulness</u>, with which Abraham their father <u>held faithful</u> in Me that I should divide the sea before them, as it is said: And He <u>held faithful</u> in God, and He counted it unto him (i.e. at the sea) for (doing) charity (with his children)'" (Marmorstein, page 37; see below). Psalm 106:31 is translated from Rashi by chabad.org, "It was accounted for him as a merit, for generation to generation to eternity." In Late Hebrew צְדָקָה (β→justice: *tsidaqah*) means charity (alms) or other supererogatory deeds. *Tzidaqah* earned a merit (*zekut*) for the giver (cf. Rom. 4:4), which is conceded by Paul.

But in truth, the merit is not transferable to anyone except the giver, and does not yield any extra merit to offset a demerit. Charity is transferred to the recipient, merit is left with the giver. Nevertheless, the Rabbis equivocated the two ideas. The transfer of charity was founded on Psa. 106:31, 'It was counted as charity for him from generation to generation forever.' The idea that charity was given to others was conflated with the transfer of merit, which was considered transferred with the charity, and the crediting of merit against demerit was assumed. Other kinds of deeds than charity qualified as a merit also. To get a merit, it had to be a deed beyond the ordinary duty of obedience. The idea is that extra credit was needed against demerit. For ordinary merit only is credited to the deed, and there is none left over. So one could expiate (atone for) a demerit either by one's own extra merit or by calling on the extra merit inherited from Abraham, Phinehas or other pious Jews.

The patriarchs were regarded as giving charity, but instead of money, they are giving up their extra merit to the needy to offset demerits of offspring. This was done by interpreting Psa. 106:31, 'It was counted as righteous-merit for him [to be given out] from generation to generation forever.' His deed accrued extra merit which was given to tsidaqah, as it were from a trust fund, to his needy offspring needing to atone for demerit. The idea was well developed in Judaism of the first four centuries AD (*The Doctrine of Merits in Old Rabbinical Literature*, A. Marmorstein). It is really a pagan idea of appeasement infiltrating into Judaism, a redefinition of KIPPURIM, which also mutated in Christianity into the doctrine of the imputation of Christ's righteousness.

The Rabbinic doctrine of merit depended on assumptions contrary to Gŏd's justice. The Almĭghty divided the sea for Yisra'el, not because of Avraham had merit to make them worthy, but because of his own promises.

It depended on linking Gen. 15:6b to Psa. 106:31 and interpreting the word צְדָקָה to mean charity (equivocated to merit) bestowed upon one's descendants, so Gŏd would favor them and not judge them according to their demerits. Tsidaqah was supererogatory righteousness.

When the Old Greek translation was produced in Alexandria by Jewish scholars, they translated Psa. 106:31 accurately: καὶ ἐλογίσθη αὐτῷ εἰς δικαιοσύνην. They employed the passive verb ἐλογίσθη for the Hebrew Niphal (passive: תֵּחָשֵׁב), but when they translated Gen. 15:6b they used the same wording, ignoring the fact that Gen. 15:6b has the active verb (יַחְשְׁבֶהָ), and should have been translated: καὶ ἐλογίσατο αὐτὴν αὐτῷ εἰς δικαιοσύνην, as in the LXX for 1 Sam. 1:13.[a] By making Gen. 15:6b

---

a This would not be the first example of sectarian bias in the LXX. For we see it already in the alternative chronology in the LXX adapted to Egyptian antiquity.

read the same as Psalm 106:31 in the LXX they more closely tied the texts together, but the meaning of the texts is significantly different. The Jewish Doctrine of Merits traces back at least as far as Shemaiah, leader of the Perushim in the 1st century BC. It is not unlikely that the doctrine was around when the LXX was translated, nor unlikely that the translators were influenced by the doctrine. It appears that Paul goes along with it.

But he doesn't. Paul abruptly puts the Psa. 106:31 quote at the end of Gen. 15:6a in Rom. 4:3b and Galatians 3:6b, and doesn't say the Septuagint translation is right in Gen. 15:6b. This is because he does not give a reference for his quote. But he does play along with making it look like it, because he has a messianic interpretation of Psa. 106:31 that he would like to link to Gen. 15:6a to counter the rabbinic doctrine of merits tied onto Gen. 15:6b. The Septuagint mistake makes it easier for hellenistic Jewish teachers of the Rabbinic doctrine to connect their dots, but so also it makes it easier for Paul to connect the dots to Mĕssiah. Paul's messianic explanation, therefore is according to Psa. 106:31 and Numbers 25:11-13 and not Gen. 15:6b as the Rabbis ordinarily interpreted it to be a treasury of merit for Jews with demerits, for which we can be sure he gave the usual sense: Abraham's faithfulness was counted as moral righteousness by Gŏd (cf. James 2:21-24) on its own merit (cf. Rom. 4:2). His explanation is to skip over quoting Gen. 15:6b and to cite Psa. 106:31.

Paul's abrupt transition is in the tradition of the other extraordinary rabbinic interpretations of Gen. 15:6b, the one mentioned above, and Ramban, "Then he (Abraham) regarded it (Gŏd's promise), [to be] justice for him (Gŏd)" (Nahmanides). The idea intended is that Abraham regarded the promise as God himself being just (righteous). This idea does not fit the context of Gen. 15:6b, but it surely shows a tendency to abrupt turns of interpretation on the meaning of the pronouns in the text. Paul's abrupt turn is simply to ignore Gen. 15:6b and exposit on Psa. 106:31 instead. It is sad that this Pauline, and very rabbinic, maneuver has thrown most Christian interpreters off of Paul's true goal, but it would not be so if they had not misinterpreted Gen. 15:6 in the first place or corrupted the doctrine of justification, more or less in the same spirit as Judaism. Paul was on the exact same page as Ya'aqov (aka James) for Gen. 15:6a-b, and his circle knew the messianic application of Psa. 106:31 and Numbers 25:11-3. Without that proper background, Paul is almost impossible to understand.

Paul puts the two texts together, Gen. 15:6a and Psa. 106:31. He remarks as if he is interpreting Gen. 15:6b the ordinary way in Rom. 4:2, and then he launches straightaway into his messianic interpretation based on Psa. 106:31 and Numbers 25:11-13. Psa. 106:31 plainly should be translated, "Then it was taken into account for him concerning an administration of justice from generation to generation, age-lasting." Tsidaqah, therefore, is 'an administration of justice,' or 'a doing of justice,' in this case via the priestly office. It was the job of the priests to decide legal cases on appeal (cf. Deut. 17:8-13; see End Note No. 3 at the end of Matthew). Justice in a case could be served with mercy or without it. A pardon was justice as much as punishment was. The Făther's forgiveness comes through this justice, because it is merciful justice. The word justice (צְדָקָה, δικαιοσύνη) may in fact be translated "mercy" as a specific instance of justice, based on the covenant promise to forgive our sins.

This is proved in Num. 25:12-13, "Behold I am giving to him my covenant of peace, and it will have been to him, and to his seed after him a covenant of enduring priesthood" (וְהָיְתָה לּוֹ וּלְזַרְעוֹ אַחֲרָיו בְּרִית כְּהֻנַּת עוֹלָם). Thus Psa. 106:31 is just a repeat of Num. 25:12-13. "From generation to generation" (לְדֹר וָדֹר) answers to "to his seed after him" (וּלְזַרְעוֹ אַחֲרָיו). The other parts correspond also. Most importantly is the passive construction: וְהָיְתָה לּוֹ: "And it will have been to him...." This matches exactly the Niphal in Psa. 106:31: וַתֵּחָשֶׁב לוֹ: "Then it will taken into account for him...." This identifies what 'it' refers to. "It" refers to "My covenant of peace" (אֶת־בְּרִיתִי שָׁלוֹם). The Hebrew word "it" is marked in the feminine gender to agree with "covenant." This is further filled out as "a covenant of enduring priesthood" (בְּרִית כְּהֻנַּת עוֹלָם), repeating the word covenant and then defining it. Also, if we trace down the meaning of 'priesthood' we will find that it means 'minister,' thus the verb: כָּהֵן, to minister as a priest, or the noun: כֹּהֵן, minister (cf. BDB). The word is associated with this function in Hebrew, as deputies of the king could also be called 'ministers' (כֹּהֵן). The word is used in parallel with "ministers" (cf. Isa. 61:6).

Psa. 106:31, therefore, has the following sense: "Then it (My covenant of peace) was taken into account for him for administration of justice from generation to generation, age enduring." Tzidaqah (צְדָקָה) has been substituted into the text to define 'covenant of peace,' in the meaning of juridical righteousness, defined thus by Merriam-Webster: "of or relating to the administration of justice or the office of a judge." One who brings shalom is one who makes things right, who administers a favorable justice: mercy. So the justice decided is mercy. The justice (forgivingly, mercifully) ransoms us from (now) illegal condemnation. Phinehas was a type of Mĕssiah who wiped out evil in Israel making further wrath upon Israel unnecessary. As he did well with retributive justice, Gŏd entrusted him and his offspring with this responsibility, to make peace in the administration of justice, by getting sinners to repent instead, and teaching a ransom for them. This also makes satisfaction of divine wrath unnecessary.

The covenant of peace is the covenant of reconciliation. In Paul's thinking this is equated with the faithfulness of Mĕssiah to intervene in Yisra'el and

make a way for repentant sinners to be ransomed. In Paul's messianic application, "It was taken into account for him for an administration of justice." That is, Mĕssiah's faithfulness was planned to administer benevolent justice to us, and to Abraham retroactively, and every other one who truly pledged loyalty to the Almĭghty of Israel before Mĕssiah came and demonstrated Gŏd's covenant faithfulness. But connecting this back to Gen. 15:6a, Paul is also saying that our faithfulness is taken into account for an administration of justice! So the administration of benevolent justice is synergistic, depending on both his faithfulness and our faithfulness (cf. Exodus 20:6; Rom. 2:7; Matthew 19:16; Mark 10:17).

Therefore, Paul, in the main, is not explaining Gen. 15:6b with the ordinary explanation. He is explaining his point with Psa. 106:31 and Numbers 25:11-13 in its messianic application, just as he did for Hab. 2:4. By doing such he has completely turned the tables on Judaism's theology of merit for demerit.

AVRAHAM HAD HELD FAITHFUL IN YĂHWEḤ...AND (YĂHWEḤ'S COVENANT OF PEACE/ AVRAHAM'S FAITHFULENSS) WAS TAKEN INTO ACCOUNT FOR HIM FOR βAN ADMINISTRATION OF JUSTICE.

But trailing Psalm 106:31 off of Gen. 15:6a, Paul manages to teach his dual faithfulness idea again (cf. Rom. 1:17). It is imperative the the reader understand that in Rabbinic exegesis the resulting ideas obtained from texts do not have to exactly match what they are in their first context. The texts may be adapted to illustrate other points, or extend existing points. This was a common and acceptable method, so long as the audience knew midrashic (homiletic) usage was intended.

Mĕssiah's ransoming death because of our sins was the demonstration of his favorable justice toward us, the administration of benevolent justice to cause lawlessness to release us after forgiving us. Mĕssiah is the covenant of peace. Now צדקה *tzidaqah* may be understood to mean **charity**, **mercy**, **charitableness**, OR **merit**, all as specific applications of justice (righteousness). Paul's object is to explain that Messiah's covenant faithfulness, his kippurim, his ransom shows a requirement for the penalty to now be illegal. With this token of sin's cost he forgives any penalty after considering our repentance and pledge of faithfulness.

Paul's argument is a refutation of the Jewish doctrine of the imputation (transfer) of positive merit צדקה. Paul shows that the Messianic application of Psalm 106:31 teaches an administration of merciful justice to make peace. It is mercy/justice צדקה that is getting administered from generation to generation for all those holding faithful. The last phrase in the quote above can be translated, "it was intended to him for mercy." This sense comes more naturally to the Jewish mind because *tzidaqah* (charity) is mercy for the recipient. Reuben Alcalay defintes *tzidaqah* as: "**justice**, justness, fairness, right; **merit**, good deed; true judgement; piety; **mercy**, charity, alms; **victory**" (col. 2155, The Complete Hebrew English Dictionary; cf. BDAG δικαιοσύνη no. 3b).

N.T. Wright properly and famously rebukes the doctrine of imputed merit:

> If we use the language of the law court, it makes no sense whatever to say that the judge imputes, imparts, bequeaths, conveys or otherwise transfers his righteousness to either the plaintiff or the defendant. Righteousness is not an object, a substance or a gas which can be passed across the courtroom. ...To imagine the defendant somehow receiving the judge's righteousness is simply a category mistake. That is not how language works.*

---

*N. T. Wright, *What Saint Paul Really Said*, 98.

Which Texts Does the Most High Defend?

The translation of the Good News of Messiah is based on the Greek Texts. I start with the results of text critical scholarship in the Nestle-Aland tradition, because they are clearly the most professional in comparing texts and judging which readings are likely to be original. Though they have less regard for the Torah, I can testify that in very few cases has that bias made any difference in the correct results, and where I may disagree I have expressed it in the footnotes. In fact, in the main, their results have tended to favor the defence of the Torah.

They are honest textual scientists for the most part. It is important to put some perspective on the matter. It is rare indeed that a doctrine depends on a single text or even just a few texts. So if something is flagged as uncertain, we can always go to the other texts for a repeat of the teaching that has been textually confused or lost. Also, most of the textual differences have to do with spelling of words having no effect on their sense or translation.

I am confident enough of what the Greek text is to say that there are no significant disputes that arise from the level of textual criticism. Those who would say otherwise are agents of the enemy who do not know God and who are not taught of his Spirit. The vast majority of difference with other Christians is not going to be at the level of differences in Greek texts. They are too few and not important enough.

The significant difference is going to be on how the words are translated into English, and for this I am obligated to provide sufficent proofs through the citation of dictionaries and grammars and the making of grammatical points, which the honest student will be able to verify with enough study, certainly far less study that it took me to solve problems in the first place, that have crept into the Christian tradition and corrupted the translations (not the Greek texts). Intelligent readers, led of the Spirit of the Most High, will

see that things go together for themselves.

For the Torah, Prophets, and Writings I default to the Hebrew Text. On rare occasions I find something in the BHS or BHQ apparatus that makes more sense, and only sometimes, very rarely does a problem have to be solved via the Old Greek (LXX or Septuagint). If plainly a difficulty or contradiction *that arises from the primary text itself* can be solved by simply choosing different vowel points, I consider this a legitimate way to solve a problem since the vowel points cannot lay claim to originality. Even the famous Jewish scholar Rashi tells us that the vowel points on the second word of Genesis 1:1 should be different! And this is plainly obvious based on the first word of the text and parallels in Genesis 2 and 5.

But there are those who tell us that the truth is different from what the texts say. Some favor the Old Greek over the Hebrew text because it supports the false doctrines they teach. But true doctrine can be established based on the Hebrew text alone, and so all they have suceeded in doing is showing that their doctrine based on a mistranslation or deliberate alteration of the Old Greek is in contradiction to what is clearly the primary source. That is, the Septuagint was translated from the Hebrew, and not the other way round. So in the case of a conflict we are bound to respect the tradition that came first. And I think the Most High will respect us for that and see to it that we are not put to shame in it.

This of course does not address those outside the truth altogether that say no source is sufficiently sound, but these people have no trust in the Almighty, and they have no business teaching any doctrine as certain or opposing us when we teach the faithful what the word does say. Perhaps they can come to the truth if they realize the message is supernaturally consistent with reality. My particular expertiese is to show that this is so with biblical chronology.

Now there are those, who claim to be within the ranks of the faithful, who teach deadly heresies, and they are usually soundly refuted based on the Greek texts, known widely as the New Testament, that we have received, and they can appeal to no other texts. But there are those who will not accept the Greek texts, and who argue for other texts so they can teach false doctrine. Thus they claim that Syriac Texts were the original texts and that the Greek texts were translations from Syriac. They thus make claims based on their Syriac Texts in support of their false doctrines, which are hard to verify, and often prove false, or are proven false by experts in Syriac who are not teaching their false doctrine. But let us suppose that the Syriac says what they claim, or is interpreted the way they say. This still leaves their doctrine in contradiction to what the Greek Texts say!

And so it is now critical to prove that their Syriac Texts were translated from the Greek we are using, and not the other way round. That is, the Greek Evangelists are the primary source, and not their Aramaic. Since the Greek came first, the Most High expects us to use the Greek, because he expects us to use our intelligence and know that whatever language the truth was revealed in is more accurate and less corruptible than a later translation into another language. So once again, we have to respect the historical tradition that is original and not a later tradition. And the Most High will not disaapoint us or let us be put to shame, because he has forgiven us our sins, and he shows loving kindness and mercy to his people wanting them to have the fulness of the truth. As it is written, he will bless us when we obey him and follow his commandments.

Large translations works contain tell tale signs, like taggants that disclose their sources. The constant use of 'and' at the beginning of sentences discloses a Hebrew source. The use of borrowed words or translaterations of words in the source text discloses the source. When it comes to the Syriac New Testament, called the Peshitta, however, the translators were so slavishly literal in the translation of the Greek source that they imported many features of Greek into the Aramaic translation. One of these is the use of a Syriac calque of the Greek word νόμος. Another is a calque of the word 'Evangelist,' and another is a slavish immitation of the Greek conjunction δέ. This is so much so that almost always the Syriac puts this conjunction as the second position in a sentence or clause exactly as the Greeks did. There are many more features such as these if any scholar wishes to go deep into the comparison of Syriac and Greek. Anyway, the evidence is crystal clear to a real scholar with real ears to hear and real eyes to see. The Syriac came from the Greek.

One more thing we must know about Syriac is that it is not the Aramaic used in the book of Daniel and other sections of Scripture, which is called Old Imperial Aramaic, nor is it the Aramaic used by the returnees from Babylon, nor is it the Aramaic used in Galilee at the time of Messiah. But it is a dialect of Aramaic from the region of Osroene, centered in Edessa, that became the language of the Syriac Church from the third century to seventh century AD. This Aramaic is properly called Syriac to distinguish it from the earlier Aramaic. For most of its existence Syriac was maintained and developed by the literary Syriac used to translate the Greek Evangelists, and through this process it was adapted to Greek so much so that we should call it ecclesiastical Syriac influenced by Greek. And neither this Syriac nor its literary tradition existed at the time of Messiah nor to the end of the lifetime of his first disciples. The Syriac literary tradition began with the Diatessaron, a product of the late second century AD.

That the Greek originals were written by the emissaries of Messiah themselves can be proved by any scholar who is willing to take the time to study a Greek synopsis of the four Evangelists. There is in fact one such synopsis of the resurrection accounts in the appendix on page 575. By comparing the differences in the common text one can see that the level of agreement precludes the possibility that the sources are anything except firsthand accounts of witnesses who saw and heard the same things. Anyone who did not witnesses the events or obtain firsthand information, but who translated from a hypothetical Syriac original would naturally introduce discrepancies and contradictions in the process of translation.

So I lay out these principles of sound scholarship.

Firstly, the received Hebrew text of the Tanakh in its consonant text is the hightest authority, and then its vowel pointing the next, and then the Old Greek Septuagint the next or the Samaritan Pentatuech for the first five books, and then the Greek. Then the Old Latin, and then after that Syriac might be considered. For the emissaries writings, the Greek is primary, and then old Latin, and Syriac translations may bear witness to a divergent Greek text in some cases, but these versions are only to be used to help establish the Greek text and not to be appealed as a primary text.

These sources are only to be used to help recover the Hebrew and Greek texts, and never to be appealed to as authorities outside of making a restorative contribution. And as I said before, it is not often that we even have to go beyond the received Hebrew or Greek at all for any significant matter, and even then the need to do so is motivated only by the desire to find a solution to a discrepancy that arises from the Hebrew or Greek source itself.

I do believe there is a high degree of divine preservation in the Hebrew and Greek sources, and where the Most High has let a mistake or copy error or intentional scribal alteration creep into the text, he has not moved to correct it when the evidence for how to correct it is still avaialable to scholars, and the false doctrines which motivated the corruptions can be soundly refuted by other Scriptures. He has let a little error creep in in order to test us and in order that we should excercise intelligence in our Scholarship.

We must keep in mind that adversaries of the truth often pick on obvious errors and then exaggerate their significance in order to cause the faithful to lose faith in the Scripture, and what the faithful need to do when so challenged is to return to the text and learn the true insignificance of the attack on Scripture. For some that means learning scholarship.

Other advesaries of the truth pretend to be faithful and they want to substitute their non-primary traditions for the primary tradition that the Most High is defending. What we must understand is that because these traditions are non-primary they are even more open to valid criticism than the primary tradition may be. It is a certainty that those pushing these sources on the faithful are hiding truths about their sources in the closet that they do not wish to be discovered, or that they are ignorant of and have not been taught by real scholars. Non primary sources always have a multitide of additional discrepancies and problems that primary sources do not have.

The Most High wishes for us to use our intelligence guided by his Spirit. But teachers of false doctrine always in the end wish to win their arguments by appeal to their own authority or the authorities they serve. They try to present evidence and arguments, but at the end of the day, their argument always ends with appeal to authority combined with slander against anyone who uses common sense or uses authority they do not agree with. These people are not hearing the voice of Messiah, nor are they listening to his Spirit.

The greatest problem with what one receives as Scripture isn't really the texts. It is the interpretation of the texts first, and then the translation, and then lastly the texts. There are two layers of problems. First there is the chronological problem, and secondly the problem of theological interpretations. The truth is recovered in two basic steps. First it is explained and proved to you what the correct chronology of Scripture is. Then you realize that those giving the theological explanations hold to the wrong chronology, and then you begin to suspect their theological interpretations are also wrong. Their chronological wrongness is the Most High's vote of no confidence against their theolocial errors, because they departed from the Torah and rejected Messiah.

But the aim of heretics is to be theologically wrong first and to care less about chronology because it is too difficult for them to figure out. And the Most High made it this way for them on purpose! The Ruakh is only bound to correct less obvious errors in the hearts of those who listen to him. But the false teachers are paying no attention to the basic facts that expose their appointed times as false. So why should they be corrected on the greater error?

Now it so happens that many texts are designed to conceal the chronological truth and to mislead the causual reader. This device is to snare the false teachers, most of whom give up, because they conclude that the chronology cannot be recovered, and therefore must be unimportant. The few that are left try to solve the problems with unsound methods and speculations that only serve to reduce confidence in their results. This is because they are already teaching what is false, and the Most High is not going to teach them about his chronology, because the theological is united with the chronology. He wont let you have correctness on one without correctness on the other.

But the chronology preserves the Scripture against corruption. Those indecipherable texts or texts that mislead upon a surface reading have profound and ingenious solutions that all contribute to an overall harmonious solution. For it must first be realized that the Most High has a good reason to mislead the simple who pervert good theology. Someone who is not wise and astute enough to solve his simple riddles and ciphers is not wise and astute enough to properly wage war with heretics and to arm the faithful against them.

And beleive me when I say, that many times I thought my education was done, and then the Spirit said, NOPE, just one more thing. And how do we know that the Spirit is speaking. There are two answers here. Experience listening to Him, and only the Spirit's numbers add up and give us the confidence to listen to what He said in Scripture.

The short, but profound answer as to why the chronology of Scripture is at key points not obvious and spelled out in detail that keeps a simpleton from erring is one thing: to preserve Scripture from human corruption, and to raise the confidence of the truly faithful in the texts given to us.

Ephesians

1 ¹Paul, an emissary of the Anŏinted Yĕshua through the will of the Almīghty. To the holy ones being *found* in Ephesus, even *the* faithful ones to^εν the Anŏinted Yĕshua. ²Loving-kindness to you and peace from the Almīghty our Făther and Adŏnai Yĕshua the Anŏinted.

³Blessed be the Almīghty and Făther of our Adŏnai Yĕshua the Anŏinted, the *one* having blessed us for^εν every spiritual blessing in heavenly places by the Anŏinted, ⁴just as he himself ^ξ chose us for^εν himself, through him, before the founding of the world, that we should be holy and without fault before his face, in love, ⁵having appointed us long ago for adoption as ^φ sons through Yĕshua the Anŏinted, for himself, according to the good intention of his will, ⁶for the praise of the glory of his loving-kindness by which he favored us, by the One who has been getting loved, ⁷in whom we are getting a ransomed release^ψ through his blood, the release from transgressions, according to the wealth of his loving-kindness ⁸which he has made abundant unto us, with all wisdom and intelligence, ⁹having made known to us the mystery of his will, according to his good intention, which he has determined with him ¹⁰for a dominion in the fullness of the appointed time, to gather together everything unto the Anŏinted, that which is in the heavens and that which is on the earth, ¹¹by him, by whom also we have been made heirs, in being appointed beforehand according to the determination of the one working in everything, according to the counsel of his will, ¹²so that we should be for the praise of his glory, we who have been hoping beforehand in the Anŏinted.

1:4 εν h **1:4** ξ →himself: He "chose us for himself," (Greek middle voice V-AIM-3S, BDAG ἐξελέξατο < ἐκλέγομαι, def. 1), as opposed to making us for some lesser purpose as with many other creatures. Mankind was chosen to be the pinnacle of creation, made in the image of the Almīghty, to be specially holy before Him, and to have a special relationship of love with Him. The alternatives chosen between were the purposes for each kind that He made. ▷ The divine intention for us was from time immemorial, even before the plan was made that Mĕssiah would have to die in order to preserve the divine plan for man. The realization of the plan is always contingent on the cooperation of individuals, and is aborted for many who will not cooperate, but it becomes effective for the few who do. We must also realize that the religion of determinism, of a fated type of predestination for some to be saved and others lost before even Adam sinned is a false doctrine. Who would be saved and who would be lost were not the alternatives chosen between. This is one of those issues upon which there can be no negotiation, compromise, or cooperation with those who falsely teach it. For it results in a false doctrine of salvation. ▷ The word "choice" (ἐξελέξατο) is used to express the divine plan or intent for a body of people in a non-fatalistic way. It is so used in Deut. 4:37-40 with the intent that Yisra'el should keep the commandments. See also Deut. 7:6-7, 10:15-16, 14:2. Not all Yisra'el agreed with the divine plan and so many of them lost the blessings of being chosen. Here, Paul has gone further back in time, and has widened the scope of the choice to the entire human race before creation. Clearly not all mankind agreed with the divine plain either. Paul has done this to make the point that we in Mĕssiah are being blessed according to the original plan. **1:5** φ This intent is also original. Man was created in a humble form as the image of the Almīghty with the plan that he should be raised to the same position as the *Benei ha-Elohim* (בְּנֵי הָאֱלֹהִים). See 2 Peter 1:4. **1:7** ψ See Col. 1:14; Eph. 4:30. The ransom is from lawlessness. The nations, representing slavery to sin and Satan and his hosts, hold sinners in bondage to death and corruption, because the Most High sold transgressors into their hands. See Mat. 20:28; Mark 10:45; Isa. 35:10; Hos. 13:14. The innocent blood of Messiah unto death is the cost exacted by Lawlessness, and now the Most High will demand the release of all who enter his covenant.

¹³By whom also you, having heard the word of truth, the good news of our deliverance, in whom also, having held faithful, you have been sealed with the promised Spĭrit, to the Holy One, ¹⁴who is a pledge of our inheritance until the ransom release^ψ of the possession, for the sake of the praise of his glory.

¹⁵Because of this, as that also I have heard of your faithfulness to Adŏnai Yĕshua, and love for all the holy ones, ¹⁶I am not ceasing giving thanks for you, making a remembrance in my prayers, ¹⁷so that the Almĭghty of our Adŏnai Yĕshua the Anŏinted One, the Făther of glory, will have given to you the Spĭrit of wisdom and revelation in perfect knowledge of himself, ¹⁸by having been getting enlightened the eyes of your heart, ªso that you have and will have been knowing what is the hope of his call, what is the wealth of the glory of his inheritance with the holy ones, ¹⁹and what is the overflowing greatness of his power unto us who are ᵝholding faithful, according to the working of the dominion of his strength, ²⁰which he ᵞhas and will have been making effective through the Anŏinted, *moreso* having raised him from the dead, and *moreso* having made him ^ψSIT AT HIS RIGHT *hand* in the heavens, ²¹up above every ruler and authority and power and lordship and every name being named, not only in this age but also in the one coming. ²²ᵃAnd ALL HE WILL HAVE PUT UNDER HIS FEET⁺.

2

²²ᵇAnd ᵉhe has made him head over all the Assembly, ²³which is his body, the complement of himself, who is completing in all each of these, ¹even ᵛyou, now ᵖbeing dead ªto your transgressions and iniquities, ²in which at one time you walked, according to the ᵝAeon of this world, according to the Ruler of the dominion of the air, the spirit working now in the sons of rebelliousness, ³among

---

1:14 ψ See 1:7; 4:30. **1:18** α→will = *to.* **1:19** β→faithfulness = *pledging faithfulness.* **1:20** γ→-making = *makes;* gnomic, distributive (Wallace, pg. 580); This perfect is really a future perfect, the future being supplied by the subjunctive 'will have given' (δώῃ) in vs. 17. Also Paul's prayer looks to the future for continued answer, and accordingly the perfect participle (πεφωτισμένους) is episodically completed at various points in the future. It is a means of viewing the action as a distribution of completed repetitions of enlightenment (cf. Porter), and not a singular episode of completed enlightenment in past time. This point is made clear by a large number of translations which render the text for the future (AMP, CSB, CEB, CJB, CEV, ERV, EXB, GNV, GW, GNT, HCSB, NASB, NIV, NLV, etc). In anticipation of reformed objections to the translation of 2:5 and 2:8, the perfect participle is located entirely in the future in vs. 18, and substantially so in 2:5 and 2:8 with σεσωσμένοι. Paul surely did not mean to rule out a future need for salvation, 'he who endures to the end will be saved.' The saving is by loving-kindness, but the enduring is not, because the enduring is not saving. The enduring is preserving what one has been given, which will be tested. And whether Gŏd will effect future salvation by grace does in part depend on passing the test of holding faithful now. If someone returns to sin, there is a chance Gŏd will not re-rescue him or her. Sufficient is the grace given before the testing. **1:22a** φ Psa. 8:6; ψ Psa. 110:1; 1 Cor. 15:27 **1:22a** φ כֹּל שַׁתָּה תַחַת־רַגְלָיו.

2:22b vs. 1:22a was Paul's last complete sentence unit. He begins anew with 2:22b with finite verb ἔδωκεν (ε→made), used like Hebrew נָתַן. The chapter must begin with 1:22b because 'you' (2:1 υ) is not a subject, but an object of the verb 'completing.' Therefore 1:22b continues until 2:3b where a new sentence begins with finite verb ἤμεθα. **2:1** ρ The verb ὄντας is a present participle, trans. *were* being incorrect. **2:1** α The dative lacks a preposition 'in' and therefore should be translated, 'to' and the whole phrase (ρ→iniquities) means 'being repentant.' The same is the case in 2:5 and Col. 2:13. The present participle ὄντας being repeated in three places is no accident. The word *now* is interpolated to help deprogram the jaded reformed reader of the past tense heresy used to bolster the doctrine of 'regeneration.' While it is easy to interpret 'were dead in...' away from reformed doctrine, it is only a stopgap defense because the translation is also wrong. **2:2** β Aeon: immortal. Satan.

whom we also, all at one time let ourselves be controlled by the passions of our flesh, doing the desires of the flesh, and the thoughts. ³ᵇAnd we were by nature sons of wrath, as also the rest of mankind.

⁴But the Almĭghty, being rich in mercy through his great love, with which he ᵟloveş us, ⁵and we *now* being ᵞdead to transgressions, in partnership with the Anŏinted, ᶲmakeş us ᶓlive. ᶯBecause of loving-kindness ᵝyou are *and* have been getting rescuedᵝ. ⁶Also he in partnership with the Anŏinted ᶿwill have raised us, and in partnership with the Anŏinted Yĕshua ᵞwill have seated us in the heavens, ⁷so that he will have made seen in the coming ages the overflowing wealth of his loving-kindness in goodness upon us through the Anŏinted Yĕshua.

⁸For ᶯbecause of loving-kindness ᵝyou are *and* have been getting rescued, ᵠthrough faithfulness, and ᶲthis *getting rescued* is not from you. From the Almĭghty it is a gift, ⁹not from *customary*ᵡ works⁷, so that a man will not have made himself to be boasting. ¹⁰Yea, his work we are, being created by the Anŏinted Yĕshua

---

2:4 σ See Endnote I.1; cf. CJB **2:5** λ→transgressions = *repentant*. See 2:1; Col. 2:13; **2:5** φ→live: See Endnote I.2. **2:5** ζ cf. Yoḥ. 5:24; the translations exclude the resurrection by failure to recognize the future use of the Greek aorist and perfect. **2:5** η→of = Dative of Cause, or *in, by*. **2:5** β→β: ἐστε σεσωσμένοι. The present tense helping verb 'to be' (ἐστε) emphasizes the iterative (or distributive) aspect in the perfect placed before the perfect participle σεσωσμένοι (see Walace, pg. 520 and Eph. 2:8-10 note). See Endnote I.3. **2:6** θ-γ We have here clear cases of the aorist future perfect; See Endnote I.2; Other cases are found in Mat. 1:23, 16:19, 18:18; Mark 13:20; Luke 1:68; 21:19; John 13:31-32, 17:2; Rom. 4:17, 8:30; 1 Cor 15:54; 2 Cor 5:17; Gal. 3:27; Eph. 1:3, 18, 22; 2:5, 6, 8; 4:8-9, 11; 1 John 5:11; Rev. 5:10; 10:7; 11:2, 7; 12:7; 18:2-3; 21:23. This idiom is also ubiquitous in the Law and Prophets. **2:6** γ The proleptic aorist. Wallace, pg. 564. Wallace lists συνεκάθισεν as a debatable example, Eph 2:6. But there is nothing to debate here. Being seated in heaven is future.

2:8 η→of = Dative of Cause, or *in, by*. **2:8** ρ-ρ see 2:5β. (cf. Wallace, pg. 580, gnomic/distributive perfect); Gŏd's saving activity is constant. Paul sums up all instances of divine deliverance in one statement, past, present, future. 'Getting saved' is not conceived of as a status, but of instances of deliverance from sin, from enemies, from death, or from anything evil. In every instance one is rescued from some evil by gracious divine intervention. Forgiveness of sins when we first pledged faithfulness is one such instance. The resurrection at the end is another such instance. The deliverance of the holy city from enemies in the age to come is another instance. Being rescued from something as simple as a car wreck on an icy road is also an instance. Israel has been getting rescued many times from enemies as the book of Judges teaches. ' **2:8** φ 'this *getting rescued* is not from

you.' We are getting rescued from death (cf. 2:6), which is not something we are able to accomplish. The pronoun "this" (τοῦτο) is gender inflected to refer back to the idea of getting rescued because of Gŏd's loving-kindness. For this reason the italic words *getting rescued* are necessary to keep the meaning clear, such that the pronoun does not refer to 'faithfulness.' No instance of deliverance is our own doing, but that of Gŏd alone through his agents. The gender of 'this' is neuter to encompass both the feminine gender of 'loving-kindness' and the masculine gender of 'have been getting rescued.' Thus every instance of 'getting delivered by loving-kindness' is not from us. Naturally, this excludes those cases where we are capable of delivering ourselves, and if we are we may be tested in this; cf. Phil 2:12; Acts 2:40. ▷ Paul includes future salvation in his statement also: see Mat. 24:13; see also Mark 13:13 and Luke 21:19.

2:8 ψ→faithfulness. See Rom. 1:17. "Through faithfulness" may here be understood "[when coming] through faithfulness," not as a cause, but as a necessary circumstance, the "attendant or prevailing circumstance" (διὰ BDAG, 3c); our faithfulness is meant; Rom. 2:7, 10 explains; and also Messiah's faithfulness is meant, because that also is an *attendant circumstance* of the Father's deliverance for us. It is unlikely that διὰ is "causal" (διὰ LSJ A.III), but if so then only divine faithfulness would be meant. See Exo. 20:6. Mat. 19:17-19; Mark 10:17-19; Rev. 22:14; Phil. 2:12; Mat. 24:13; Mat. 7:21-23

2:9 χ Supply *customary*. See Gal. 3:2, 5. The italic word wasn't necessary in the mental context of Paul's readers. It is to help Christians who have lost the Jewish context to realize that Paul means a particular kind of works and not all works. **2:9** γ See Appendix VIII. The Appendix explains the Jewish doctrine of zekhut that Paul is rejecting. A good work done above and beyond what Torah requires, such as charity, pious prayers, fasting, or pious study of Torah or Jewish religious literature, is said to earn a merit which may then be used to cancel out a demerit (a sin).

for good works, which the Almĭghty made ready beforehand, so that in them we will have walked.

¹¹Therefore be remembering that then you were the nations in the flesh, those being called uncircumcision by those being called circumcision in the flesh, being done by hand, ¹²because you were at that time without the Anŏinted, having been alienating yourselves from citizenship in Yisra'el, and foreigners to the covenants of the promise, hope not having and ᵘgodless ones in the world.

¹³But now, by way of the Anŏinted Yĕshua, you being formerly from far away will have been brought near by the blood^ɸ of the Anŏinted. ¹⁴Because he is the peace ᵘbetween us, who makes the two *houses* one, and who the partition fence has opened; ¹⁵ *who* the emnity^π *that was* against^γ his flesh, *that was* the customary ^νnorm for the ᵉcharges *against us,* in *the* ^ɸ*decrees contrary to us,* has reduced to ^ψno effect; so that he shall have created the two *houses*, by way of himself,

---

This is what Paul meant when denying works a role in salvation. He wasn't denying all works. He wasn't denying that keeping the commandments was necessary for eternal life (cf. Rom. 2:6-7). He was only denying that meritorious works, as Judaism taught, had any saving power against sin. **2:11-12** μ→ones (ἄθεοι): Adj., plural. LSJ. 2. godless (ones), or *without Gŏd ones;* adj. substantive. **2:13** ɸ The blood is symbolic for the living divine life cleansing us from the sins which caused excision from Yisra'el (cf. Yoḥ. 6:63). ▷ The future perfect, 'will have,' is in a spiritual sense gnomic, but in a literal sense prophetic future perfect. The house of Yisra'el will again have access to the Temple, and the presence of Yăhweḥ. **2:14** μ = ἡ εἰρήνη ἡμῶν. Literally, 'the peace of us.' By Mĕssiah's peace *offering* peace is made between the Almĭghty and each house, such that peace results between the two houses. ▷ The idea of 'offering' is taken from the sacrificial context as in Lev. 7. ▷ Paul has Isa. 53:5 in mind (מוּסַר שְׁלוֹמֵנוּ עָלָיו), 'The instruction of our wellness is upon him.' This is an instruction (an *indici, indication, sign, token* cf. Rom. 3:25 ἔνδειξιν) of our cleansing, of the forgiving justice administered to us, and the ransoming cost of it. As both houses receive forgiveness in Messiah through a renewed pledge of faithfulness to him, peace and healing results between them, and Yisra'el is thereby reunited with Yehudah. The barrier excluding the house of Yisra'el is opened (λύσας), symbolized by the division between the court of the nations and that of Jewish Yisra'el, the stick of Yehudah. Yisra'el is brought near from the nations and re-enters the everlasting covenant, the covenant of old, new made. **2:15** π This is the Gen. 3:15 emnity of Satan and all other emnities stirred up by him, including the hatreds between the two houses. When we were unfaithful we justly deserved the warrants against us, and Satan's rage and divine justice were united. But when we were sorry and turned our heart from sin, God forgave us, and sent Yeshua to teach us this. Satan did not go along with God's forgiveness. Satan predictably executed his emnity focused from our transgressions against Messiah, causing Messiah to suffer from our sins. But the Most High regards this suffering as his ransoming cost summed up from the begining of his forebearance in the flesh of Messiah. He regards his just emnity against our sin as being executed with Messiah, because he has forgiven us. And this emnity is not raised again, but Messiah was raised from the dead defeating Satan's continued emnity. The judgment put on Messiah by Satan also symbolically executes the judgment itself. The unjust judgment in light of Messiah's innocence and our being forgiven is symbolically executed with Messiah, and made ineffective. In Messiah, a just penalty is not being paid. An illegal penalty was executed. It was made illegal from the moment of our forgiveness and held over to be executed when Satan attacked Yeshua. **2:15** γ ἐν, *into, onto;* a Hebraism. The Father forgave the hostility between him and us, expressed by the demand for strict justice. This was executed on the tree. See Col. 2:14. The Son was given to ransom us from the now illegal demand of death's hands to condemn us. By taking the ransom, death's right to keep us unto condemnation was acknowledged to be illegal. So figuratively speaking, the powers who directed their hostility against Messiah to condemn him only succeeded in confirming the condemnation of condemnation. **2:15** ν = *what is customary*. BDAG, "νόμος ❶ *custom, rule, principle, norm.*" **2:15** ε BDAG, "ἐντολή ❶ an order authorizing a specific action, *writs, warrants;*" Thayer: "*charges, injunctions.*" LSJ: "*injunctions, orders.*" Friberg: "*edicts, decrees, orders.*" See Yoḥ. 11:57. Specifically a warrant is a death warrant, an order for an execution. In common English legal terms: sentences. **2:15** ɸ BDAG, "δόγμα. ❶ a *decisions* b *decrees.*" This refers to the legal opinions or decisions made by the judge. **2:15** ψ καταργέω The word καταργέω means 'to undo' or "make of no effect." The Jewish leadership issued warrants (or charges) against Messiah to arrest him so they could put him to death (cf. Yoḥ.

into one new-made man, making peace. ¹⁶And so he shall have reconciled back again the two *houses* into one body to the Almĭghty, by way of the execution timber, putting to death the hostility on it.ᵖ

¹⁷AND HAVING COME, HE HAS ANNOUNCED PEACE TO YOU, TO THOSE FAR, AND PEACE TO THOSE NEAR,ᵃ ¹⁸because through him we are both holding fast the approach by one Spĭrit to the Făther.

¹⁹So then, you are no longer aliens and strangers, but you are citizens jointly with the holy ones and sons of the house of the Almĭghty, ²⁰being built upon the foundation of the emissaries and the prophets, where Yĕshua the Anŏinted himself is the cornerstone, ²¹by whom the whole building is being joined together,

---

11:57). In doing this they were carrying out Satan's emnity against the chosen seed as prophesied in Genesis 3:15. The Most High allowed this evil and unjust plan to go foward because it would allow him to prove his love and deliverance, if we allow him to interpret matters rather than Satan. When we transgress with rebellion against the Almighty, justly deserved warrants are decided upon for our execution, and we are allowed to fall under Satan's dominion to enslave us until the execution of the charges. But when we are sorry for our sin and turn our hearts from it, Satan looses his right to execute the charges, because the Almighty forgives us. The main reason that the Son agreed to suffer and die was to show in human and fleshly form the suffering cost that was grieving the Spirit of the Most High from the moment that man sinned and he decided that he would bear the cost it would take to create the opportunity to deliver a remnant of mankind. While waiting for men to turn from sin, God suffers the damage to his creation and suffers the increase of evil. And there is also a spiritual cost in cleansing sin from our souls incumbent on the Most High. All of this cost becomes climactically visible in Messiah's suffering and death in the flesh, and serves to draw men's attention to the truth that they might be getting rescued. It is the cost of our deliverance. Now, therefore, Satan sits at the highest point of evil exacting the cost. The Most High forgives us when we repent and cancels the warrants, and the usage of warrants against us is thereafter regarded as injustice. Therefore, he takes these cancelled warrants and spiritually lays them at Satan's feet, because it was Satan that deceived mankind. Satan therefore takes these canceled warrants, and spiritually tells God it is his fault, and therefore he caused Messiah to be killed. Therefore in killing Messiah, God also regards the sentences against us as united with those against his Son, as if killed and buried in the grave, never to rise again. And because Satan exacted the cost from him at the highest level and was unjust in doing so, the Most High regards the cost as a Ransom cost, and he will demand and force Satan to give up all claims on his people and release them from dominion of evil and deliver them into the kingdom of God. When Messiah was exectued, he had in God's accounting joined with him the sentences that had been, and will be canceled by forgiveness, spiritually speaking, because the Father handed over all judgment to the Son. Therefore when Messiah was executed, the warrants were symbollically put to death also. Condemnation is condemned. Wrath is destroyed and put away. Our penalty is executed with Messiah, and he rose again escaping from condemnation, leaving condemnation dead. ▷ Cf. Rom. 3:21; 10:4. Mĕssiah is the end of the norm for justice. νόμος means what is customary, the norm (cf. BDAG, 3rd edition). Both the norm for justice and the exceptional form of justice, i.e. pardon are according to the Law. By the faithfulness of Mĕssiah the exception (a pardon) becomes the norm for the faithful, and what was the norm is made of no effect, and wiped out (cf. Col. 2:14). ▷ Anti-law doctrine tries to find the abolition of the entire law in this text, ceremonial, moral, civil. This view contradicts Paul's teaching that only the penalty has been made of no effect on us who are faithful. ▷ Reformed anti-law doctrine tries to find the abolition of the *ceremonial law* in this text. It is clear from the text that what is made of no effect results in peace with the Almĭghty. But it is mainly violation of the *moral law* by iniquity and transgression that creates hostility between man and the Almĭghty. The Reformed doctrine, therefore, has a mile wide gap in the front line of its anti-law apologetic. They would rather have some anti-law interpretation at the expense of the good news rather than simply say only the penalty is forgiven.

2:16 π The hands' of death received the ransom and illegally vented the hostility on it, but the Father regarded this as only figuratively killing condemnation, confirming his forgiveness. Then Messiah was rescued from their attempt to condemn him via his resurrection. Cf. Yoh. 3:14-15

2:17 α Isa 57:19.

growing up into a holy Temple for Yăhweh, ²²for whom also you yourselves are being built together to be a dwelling of the Almĭghty in the Spĭrit.

3 ¹**In favor of this**, I Paul, a prisoner of the Anŏinted for your sake, the nations, ²if indeed you have listened to the administration of the loving-kindness of the Almĭghty which has been given to me for you, ³because according to a revelation has been made known to me the mystery, according to what I had written before in a few words, ⁴concerning which you will be able in reading it to understand my insight in the ⸦mystery of the Anŏinted, ⁵which in other generations was not made known to the sons of men like it has been revealed now, by his holy emissaries and by his prophets in the Spĭrit: ⁶that the nations should be joint heirs and a joint body, and receivers as one from the promise through the Anŏinted Yĕshua by way of the good news, ⁷of which I have become a minister according to the gift of the loving-kindness of the Almĭghty, which has been given to me, according to the action of his might — ⁸to me, the least among the least ones of all the holy ones, has been given this loving-kindness, unto the nations to announce the unsearchable wealth of the Anŏinted, ⁹and to make enlightened everyone about what is the administration of the mystery, which has been getting hidden from the ⸰Aeons by the Almĭghty, who has created everything, ¹⁰so that the many-sided wisdom of the Almĭghty will have been made known now to the rulers and to the authorities in the heavens, by way of the Assembly, ¹¹according to the plan of the ages which he had made with the Anŏinted Yĕshua our Adŏnai, ¹²in whom we have boldness and trusting access through his faithfulness, ¹³**therefore** I ask you not to lose heart at my tribulations on your behalf, which is for your glory.

¹⁴In favor of this, I bow my knees before the Făther, ¹⁵by whom every family in heaven and on earth is summoned, ¹⁶so that he may have granted you, according to the riches of his glory, to be strengthened with power through his Spĭrit in the inner man, ¹⁷to have the Anŏinted dwell in your hearts through faithfulness, having been getting rooted and having been getting a foundation in love, ¹⁸so that you shall have been able to comprehend with all the holy ones

---

3:4 ⸦ Paul is not saying the mystery was unknown, but only that it was not in the past known "like it has been revealed now." Paul refers to the inclusion of the nations in the house of Yisrα‑el. This very point is made by Gen. 48:19. See also Rom. 11:25. Paul's argument in Rom. 9:22-26 clearly applies "NOT MY PEOPLE," which refers to exiled Yisrα‑el to the nations. Likewise, Mĕssiah said that the kingdom would be taken away from Yehudah and given to another people. That people is the exiled house of Yisrα‑el. The removal of the kingdom from Yehudah, however, is temporary. The two houses will be reunited by Mĕssiah, and will have one King, and one Kingdom. How many in the nations are descended from the exiled house of Yisrα‑el? It is not impossible that it is most of them, because Gen. 48:19 says so. But if a person is non-Jewish, and does not become Jewish, but is faithful, then he belongs to the house of Yisrα‑el. But beyond this general identification, I do not think choosing a tribal affiliation is wise unless in accord with Ezek. 47:23 or a certain knowledge of descent. Tribal identifications there will be. See Rev. 7. The alien, who becomes faithful, regardless of descent, is to be treated as the native born. Jews also are not all of one tribe, but many from the house of Yisrα‑el mixed with them. So some of them also do not know their tribe. It is claimed by the house of Yehudah that Yisrα‑el already reunited and Ezek. 37 is already fulfilled. This enmity is nothing more than the hostility between the two houses from time immemorial, trying to deny the other its inheritance. I do not return the favor. Even unbelieving Jews are allowed their inheritance. Mĕssiah will decide anything more when he comes. **3:9** ⸰ The sons of the Almĭghty. See Gen. 6; Psa. 82; Eph. 2:2.

what is the breadth and length and height and depth, [19]besides to know the love
of the Anŏinted which surpasses knowledge, that you will have been filled up to
all completion from the Almĭghty.
[20]Now to him who is able to do exceedingly abundantly beyond all that we
ask or think, according to the power that works within us, [21]to him be the glory
through the Assembly and in the Anŏinted Yĕshua to all the generations of the
age of *all* the ages. Amen.

4 [1]I therefore, the prisoner of Yăhweн, entreat you to walk in a manner worthy
of the calling with which you have been called, [2]with all humility and gentleness, with patience, tolerantly enduring one another in love, [3]being diligent
to preserve the unity of the Spĭrit in the bond of peace.
[4]There is the same[μ] body and the same Spĭrit, just as also you were called
in the same hope of your calling, [5]the same Adŏnai, the same pledge of faithfulness, the same immersion, [6]the same Almĭghty and Făther of all who is over
all and through all and in all.
[7]But to each one of us loving-kindness was given according to the measure
of the Anŏinted's gift. [8]Therefore it says, "WHEN HE WILL HAVE ASCENDED ON
HIGH, HE WILL HAVE LED CAPTIVE CAPTIVITY, AND HE WILL HAVE [δ]GIVEN GIFTS
TO MEN[ψ]." [9]Now this expression, "He will have ascended," what does it mean
except that he also will have descended into the lower parts—the earth? [10]He
who descended is himself also he who ascended far above all the heavens, so
that he will have completed all things. [11]And he gives some as emissaries, and
some as prophets, and some as announcers of good news, and some as shepherds and teachers, [12]for the equipping of the holy ones for the work of service,
to the building up of the body of the Anŏinted, [13]until we all may have attained
to the unity of [ξ]faithfulness, and of the full knowledge of the Almĭghty Sŏn, as a

4:4-6 μ or *one* and fol. There is one Spĭrit, so there can be none other, and one Măster, so there can be none other, and one Almĭghty, so there can be none other, and one Father, so there can be none other. The terms are not being used here in terms of the Făther, Sŏn (a term not used here), and Holy Spĭrit, but in the sense that all of Elŏhim is spirit, is master, is almighty, is our father. We cannot split Făther off the end of the text and say it only means Făther and not Sŏn or Spĭrit, because there is one Spĭrit and because the Făther is Spĭrit and also Măster! Měssiah is included in the Fatherhood of the Almĭghty because with him all things were made. Notice that *one body* refers to the Assembly, which is a collection of persons. No one should therefore claim that *one* means one person. Also many are immersed, and many pledge faithfulness. So no one can claim these things are done but once. These statements are placed with the statements about the Most High in order to refute the popular claims about the word *one*. And it is more effective than any formal argument could be. **4:8** ψ Psa. 68:18. לָקַחְתָּ מַתָּנוֹת בָּאָדָם: "YOU WILL HAVE TAKEN GIFTS AMONG MEN." Hebrew customarily uses the perfect for timeless statements. The idea is to put the point of view of the speaker into the future (called *deictic center*) and then look back in time at the completed act (at points in all time if necessary). In a more polished English we would put such gnomic use into the present tense, 'As one who ascends on high, he leads captive captivity, and he gives gifts to men.' However, this gnomic use overlaps the prophetic future perfect, which Paul clearly has in mind, having applied the passage with messianic reference. I think his interpretation is legitimate, so we cannot simply reduce the matter to a simple English present. **4:8** δ = לָקַחְתָּ. The Hebrew verb לקח means either 'take' or 'receive,' and clearly in this context means 'take' gifts. See also Psa. 68:19 (18), CJB. Psa. 68:18 is therefore mistranslated in every other version. **4:13** ξ +the.

perfect man, to the measure of the maturity of the completeness of the Anŏinted, ¹⁴so that we may no longer be infants, tossed here and there by waves and carried about by every wind of teaching by the trickery of men, by craftiness in deceitful scheming, ¹⁵but *by* speaking the truth in love, we shall have grown up in all aspects into him who is the head, even the Anŏinted, ¹⁶from whom the whole body, being fitted and held together by that which every joint supplies, according to the proper working of each individual part, causes the growth of the body for the building up of itself in love.

¹⁷This I am saying therefore, and I myself am testifying with Yăhweh. No longer *are* you to be walking like the nations also are walking, in the futility of their mind, ¹⁸who have been getting darkened in their understanding, *who are being*—*and* have been alienating themselves from the life of the Almĭghty, because of the ignorance that is in them, because of the hardness of their heart, ¹⁹who having been becoming unfeeling, have given themselves over to sensuality, into the practice of uncleanness, all with greed. ²⁰But you did not learn the Anŏinted in this way, ²¹if indeed you have heard him and have been taught in him, just as *the* truth is in Yĕshua, ²²that in reference to your former manner of life you lay aside the old self, which is getting corrupted in accordance with the lusts of deceit, ²³and that you be getting renewed in the spirit of your mind, ²⁴namely to put on the new-made man, which according to the Almĭghty is created in righteousness and genuine holiness.

²⁵Therefore, having laid aside falsehood, BE SPEAKING TRUTH, EACH ONE OF YOU, WITH HIS NEIGHBOR,ᵃ because we are members of one another. ²⁶BE GETTING ANGRY, AND YET DO NOT BE SINNING.ᶿ Do not let the sun be going down on your anger, ²⁷and do not be giving the Slanderer an opportunity.

²⁸Let him who steals be stealing no longer, but rather let him be laboring, performing with his own hands what is good, in order that he may be having something to share with him who has need.

²⁹Let no unwholesome word be going out from your mouth, but only such a word as is good for edification according to the need of the moment, so that it may have given loving-kindness to those who hear. ³⁰And do not be grieving the Holy Spĭrit of the Almĭghty, by whom you were sealed for the day of ᵠransom release. ³¹Let all bitterness and wrath and anger and clamor and slander be put away from you, along with all ill willed hatred. ³²And be becoming kind to one another, tender-hearted, lovingly-favoring each other, just as the Almĭghty through the Anŏinted also lovingly-favors you.

4:25 α Zech 8:16 **4:26** θ Psa 4:4 **4:30** φ The ransom price has been paid. But the ransom release is still future. The idea here is that death has taken the ransom, but has not actually released the captive yet. See Col. 1:14; Eph. 1:7, 14 **5:2** ψ See Rom. 12:1-2. The sacrifice pleasing to the Most High is to sacrifice self for the ransom of others (cf. Rev. 5:9; Mat. 20:28; Mark 10:45). This is certainly a living sacrifice of self as slowly we give of ourselves, but often the faithful risk physical death by violent means, and some suffer it before the allotted lifespan in this age. But this body is mortal and is dying. We are called to sacrifice the little time we have, the allotted time for the deliverance of others. This is the same love that motivated Messiah, and we should imitate him in it. And this is the pleasing aroma to the Most High. The ransom is the sacrifice of self, which in better days, we might by rights and lawfully satisfy, but which love calls for in these evil days to deny. It is evil that is the cause of the suffering and that creates the need for it.

5 ¹Therefore be becoming imitators of the Almĭghty, as beloved children, ²and be walking in love, just as the Anŏinted also loved you and gave himself up on our behalf, an offering and a sacrifice to the Almĭghty as a fragrant aroma^ψ. ³But do not let immorality or any impurity or greed even be getting named among you, as is proper among holy ones. ⁴And there must be no filthiness and moronic slander, or coarse jesting, which are not fitting, but rather giving of thanks. ⁵Because this you have been knowing with certainty, that no immoral or impure person or covetous man, who is an idolater, has an inheritance in the kingdom of the Anŏinted, that is of the Almĭghty. ⁶Let no one be deceiving you with empty words, for because of these things the wrath of the Almĭghty comes upon the disobedient sons. ⁷Therefore do not be becoming partakers with them, ⁸because you were formerly in darkness, but now you are light in Yăhweh. Be walking as children of light, ⁹because the fruit of the light consists in all goodness and justice and truth, ¹⁰approving what is pleasing to Yăhweh.

¹¹And do not be participating in the unfruitful deeds of darkness, but instead even be ˤcorrecting them, ¹²because the things secretly being done by them are shameful even to tell about. ¹³But all things become visible when they are exposed by the light, because everything that becomes visible is light. ¹⁴For this reason it says, "Be awaking, one who is sleeping, ¹⁴ᵇand ᵖBE RISEN from the dead, ¹⁴ᶜAND THE ANŎINTED ONE WILL SHINE ON YOUˣ."

¹⁵Therefore be watching how you walk, not as unwise men, but as ˢwise, ¹⁶ransoming the time, because the days are evil. ¹⁷So then do not be becoming foolish, but be understanding what the will of Yăhweh is.

¹⁸And do not be getting yourself drunk with wine, because that is immorally indulgent, but be getting yourself filled with the Spĭrit, ¹⁹speaking to one another in psalms and praise-songs, that is, spiritual songs, singing and making melody with your heart to Yăhweh, ²⁰always giving thanks for all things in the name of our Adŏnai Yĕshua the Anŏinted, to the Almĭghty, and to the Făther, ²¹submitting yourselves to one another in fear of the Anŏinted One, ²²wives, to your own

---

5:14b ρ Isa. 61:1a: קוּמִי. The rest of the words are added by way of explanation to explain 'be risen' from Dan. 12:1-3. **5:14c** χ = Isa. 60:1b: וּכְבוֹד יְהוָה עָלַיִךְ זָרָח = *And the glory of Yăhweh will have shone upon you.* Paul substituted 'Anŏinted One' for the divine name in his quotation. ▷ Isa 60:1a: *Be rising, be shining, because your light will have come.* Dan. 12:1-3: ¹AND IN THAT TIME ONE-WHO-IS-LIKE-GŎD (מִיכָאֵל) WILL STAND UP, THE GREAT PRINCE, WHO IS STANDING OVER THE SONS OF YOUR PEOPLE. AND THERE WILL HAVE BEEN A TIME OF TROUBLE, WHICH NEVER HAS BEEN, FROM BEING A NATION UNTIL THAT TIME.

AND IN THAT TIME WILL BE DELIVERED YOUR PEOPLE, EVERY ONE WHO IS BEING FOUND BEING WRITTEN IN THE BOOK. ²AND MANY OF THE <u>SLEEPERS</u> OF THE DUST OF THE EARTH WILL BE MADE TO <u>AWAKEN</u>, SOME TO LIFE EVERLASTING, AND SOME TO <u>SHAME</u>, TO EVERLASTING <u>CONTEMPT</u>. ³AND THE <u>UNDERSTANDING</u> ONES WILL BE MADE TO <u>SHINE LIKE THE BRIGHTNESS OF THE EXPANSE</u>, ^ψEVEN THOSE CONFIRMING HIS WORDS <u>LIKE THE STARS</u> FOR EVER AND ONWARD. | vs. 3 ψ→words = וּמְקִימֵי הַדְּבָרָיו = καὶ οἱ κατισχύοντες τοὺς λόγους μου [αυτου], LXX^{OG}; cf. Mark 8:38; Luke 9:26; Gen. 15:5. **5:15** ς cf. Dan. 12:3.

Ephesians 6

husbands, as to Yăhweҥ. ²³Because the husband is the head of the wife, as the Anŏinted also *is* the head of the Assembly, he himself *being* the Rescuer of the body. ²⁴But as the Assembly is getting itself subordinated to the Anŏinted One, so also the wives ought to be to their husbands in everything.

²⁵Husbands, be loving your wives, just as the Anŏinted also loved the Assembly and gave himself up on her behalf, ²⁶so that he might make her holy. And he cleanses by the washing of water in the word, ²⁷so that he will have presented to himself the Assembly in all her glory, having no spot or wrinkle or any such thing, but that she may be holy and blameless. ²⁸So husbands ought also to love their own wives as their own bodies. He who loves his own wife loves himself, ²⁹because no one ever hated his own flesh, but nourishes and cherishes it, just as the Anŏinted also does the Assembly, ³⁰because we are members of his body. ³¹FOR THIS CAUSE A MAN WILL LEAVE HIS FATHER AND MOTHER, AND WILL CLEAVE TO HIS WIFE, AND THE TWO WILL BECOME ONE FLESH.ᵅ ³²This mystery is great, but I am speaking with reference to the Anŏinted and the Assembly. ³³However, let each individual among you also be loving his own wife even as himself, and the wife, so that she may respect her husband.

6 ¹Children, be obeying your parents in Yăhweҥ, because this is right. ²"BE HONORING YOUR FATHER AND MOTHERᵅ," which is the first commandment with a promise, ³ "THAT IT MAY HAVE BEEN WELL WITH YOU, EVEN THAT YOU MAY LIVE LONG ON THE EARTH.ᵝ" ⁴And fathers, do not be ᶜcreating anger in your children, but be nourishing them with the discipline and advice of Yăhweҥ.

⁵Slaves, be obeying those who are your masters according to the flesh, with fear and trembling, in the sincerity of your heart, as to the Anŏinted, ⁶not by way of eye service as men pleasers, but as slaves of the Anŏinted, doing the will of the Almĭghty from the heart. ⁷With good will render service as to Yăhweҥ and not to men, ⁸having been knowing that whatever good thing each one may have done, this he will receive back from beside Yăhweҥ, whether slave or free.

⁹And masters, be doing the same things to them, relaxing threatening, having been knowing that both their Adŏnai and yours is in heaven, and there is no partiality with him.

¹⁰Finally, be getting strong in Yăhweҥ and in the strength of his might. ¹¹Put on the full armor of the Almĭghty, that you may be able to stand firm against the schemes of the Slanderer. ¹²Because our struggle is not against flesh and blood, but against the rulers, against the powers, against the world forces of this darkness, against the spiritual forces of wickedness in the heavenly places.

5:31 α Gen 2:24. **6:2** α Exo 20:12 **6:3** β Deu 5:16.

6:4 ζ →anger: παροργίζετε = *beside-anger;* cf. Rom. 10:19. The word means to generate anger of perceived injustice. Hebrew: כָּעַס = *to vex, irritate, grieve.* See Deut. 32:21. With Gŏd it is the last resort judgment for a disobedient nation to give what they perceive as theirs to their inferiors. But children are not under judgment, so they should not be compelled to obedience this way, especially since their perceptions are immature and need training. **6:11** ξ ἐλέγχω also LSJ: *disgracing, putting to shame, convincing,*

¹³Therefore, take up the full armor of the Almĭghty, that you will have been able to resist in the evil day, and having done everything, to stand firm. ¹⁴Stand firm therefore, HAVING GIRDED YOUR LOINS WITH TRUTH᷾, and HAVING PUT ON THE BREASTPLATE OF RIGHTEOUSNESS^β, ¹⁵and having shod YOUR FEET WITH THE PREPARATION OF THE GOOD NEWS OF PEACE᷾, ¹⁶in addition to all, taking up the shield of faithfulness with which you will be able to quench all the arrows of the evil one, which have been getting set on fire. ¹⁷And take THE HELMET OF DELIVERANCE^β, and the sword of the Spĭrit, which is the word of the Almĭghty. ¹⁸With all prayer and petition pray at all times in the Spĭrit, and with this in view, be on the alert with all perseverance and petition for all the holy ones.

¹⁹And pray on my behalf, that utterance will have been given to me in the opening of my mouth, to make known with boldness the mystery of the good news, ²⁰for which I am an ambassador in chains, that in proclaiming it I will have spoken boldly, as I ought to have spoken.

²¹But so that you will have been knowing also about my circumstances, what I am doing, Tychicus, the beloved brother and faithful minister to^ᴱⱽ Yăhweʜ, will make everything known to you. ²²And I have sent him to you for this very purpose, so that you will have known about us, and that he will have comforted your hearts.

²³Peace be to the brothers, and love with faithfulness, from the Almĭghty, the Făther and Adŏnai Yĕshua the Anŏinted. ²⁴Loving-kindness be with all those who love our Adŏnai Yĕshua the Anŏinted with a love incorruptible.

---

convicting, refuting. **6:14**α Isa 11:5: וְהָאֱמוּנָה אֵזוֹר | שָׁלוֹם מְבַשֵּׂר טוֹב מַשְׁמִיעַ יְשׁוּעָה אֹמֵר לְצִיּוֹן מָלַךְ
חֲלָצָיו .**6:15** | וַיִּלְבַּשׁ צְדָקָה כַּשִּׁרְיָן **6:14** β Isa 59:17: | אֱלֹהָיִךְ. **6:17** β Isa 59:17: וְכוֹבַע יְשׁוּעָה בְּרֹאשׁוֹ.
γ Isa 52:7: מַה־נָּאווּ עַל־הֶהָרִים רַגְלֵי מְבַשֵּׂר מַשְׁמִיעַ

End Note No. 1: Grammar

I.1. The Greek aorist may be used gnomically. This means it is a timelessly stated truth. For this the English employs the simple present tense. But really the Greek aorist has a perfective aspect. So the timeless truth is viewed by moving the point of speaker reference to the infinite future, and then by looking back on the truth assertion as completed (perfected). The Hebrew perfect is likewise used in this fashion. The moving to the infinite future part of Greek or Hebrew is not grammatically stated, nor is how far backward to project the perfective once the mind is in the future. These notions have to be supplied by the mind of the speaker or reader. In like manner the English gnomic present is not strictly present. That it applies to all time is a notion supplied by the mind of the speaker or listener.

I.2. cf. I.1; The Greek aorist may be used for the future, but it really overlaps in nature with I.1 (gnomic use). We can preserve the perfective notion by using the English future perfect so long as we do not try to drive the perfective aspect of the English future perfect back into the present or past of the speaker or listener, in which case it would quickly become gnomic and require an English present (cf. I.1). There is nothing grammatically to stop the Greek aorist (or Hebrew perfect) from doing this, save only the context.

I.3. The Greek perfect is a controversial tense in Greek grammar (cf. I.4). Sometimes it is translated into the simple present, present progressive, or non-progressive present perfect. The confusion may be blamed squarely on equivocation with the Latin perfect and centuries of false doctrine that exploited this equivocation. The Greek perfect is really a combination of present and perfective elements, almost exactly the same as the English present perfect progressive, also called present progressive continuous. It is only almost equivalent because in some contexts it is used as a pluperfect progressive and in other contexts a future perfect progressive. The only thing that does not change is the perfective viewpoint and the progressive nature of the internal action. Normally however it is present perfect progressive unless the context requires a pluperfect or future perfect.

I.4. The simple aorist tense may be translated into the English non-progressive present perfect. Many translations do so often indicating continuing results. This is what the grammarians claim the Greek perfect to be. But it is not so.

I.5. The Greek imperfect is almost exclusively a past progressive, best translated by the simple past of the verb 'to be,' viz. 'was,' 'were' combined with the participle form of verbs, "-ing," but in some cases, having to do with the verb "to be" itelf, the imperfect, ἤν, mimics the Hebrew verb הָיָה, and may be translated present perfect into English, and sometimes even the English simple present is valid if the concept being expressed is an equivocation and timeless truth.

End Note No. 2: On Circumcision

I. Examples for how the excision penalty in Gen. 17:14 (cf. Acts 15 translation notes) was divinely applied occur in Exodus 4:24f and Joshua 5:4f. There is no doubt from the Hebrew in Exodus 4 that Mosheh was the one threatened with the penalty, and Joshua 5 observes that it was not the uncircumcised sons who died in the wilderness. The penalty was applied to negligent or rebellious fathers who did not circumcise their sons. **II.** Gen. 17:10 "every male" needs further specification. Taken alone this statement would permit no exempt time period of seven days. The same can be said for vs. 11. Verse 12 adds the further specifications: (1) a male child eight days old; (2) throughout your generations; (3) born of the house (יְלִיד בָּיִת); (4) or bought with money from any foreigner who is not your seed. Vs. 12 is necessary to limit the scope of vs. 10-11. **III.** Vs. 13 states a collective purpose, "so that my covenant *will* have been in your flesh." The word *your* is plural referring to the collective body of Yisra'el. This purpose is achieved within the limitations of vs. 12. Within these limits, similar to the exemption of a male from days 1 to 7 there is also an exemption for an adult male convert from pagan ways outside of Avraham's house for a time period. The non compulsory exemption is implied in Exodus 12:48, "And when a sojourner sojourns with you, and he has made *ready a passover lamb* to Yăhweh, *must* be circumcised all his males. And then he may approach to do it. And he *will* have been as a native of the land, but any uncircumcised will not eat in it." This statement implies the existence of a class of uncircumcised sojourner and circumcised sojourners. The purpose of the law is to state upon which condition there could be no discrimination against the sojourner. The law encourages the sojourner to become circumcised without demanding it in threatening terms. **IV.** Why then did Paul counsel against it in the case of a new convert (cf. 1 Cor. 7:18-19 and notes)? Paul was following the precedent that circumcision is not at first required of the infant, nor at first was required of Avraham, nor was immediately required to be rectified after neglect in the wilderness. Also, Paul was speaking into a context where his opponents were pushing a salvation theology of circumcision based on a transfer of merit.

Philippians

1 ¹Paul and Timothy, servants of the Anŏinted Yĕshua, to all the holy ones belonging to the Anŏinted Yĕshua who are in Philippi, including the overseers and ministers. ²Loving-kindness to you and peace from the Almĭghty our Făther and Adŏnai Yĕshua the Anŏinted.

³I thank my Almĭghty in all my remembrance of you, ⁴always offering prayer with joy in my every prayer for you all, ⁵in view of your participation in the good news from the first day until now, ⁶having been trusting this very thing, that he who began a good work in you will perfect it as far as the day of the Anŏinted Yĕshua, ⁷because it is only right for me to feel this way about you all, because I have you in my heart; besides in my imprisonment also in the defense and confirmation of the good news, you all are partakers of loving-kindness with me, ⁸because the Almĭghty is my witness, how I long for you all with the affection of the Anŏinted Yĕshua.

⁹And this I am praying, that your love may be abounding still more and more in complete knowledge and all discernment, ¹⁰for you to be approving the things that are excellent, so that you may be sincere and blameless as far as the day of the Anŏinted, ¹¹having been getting filled with the fruit of righteousness which comes through Yĕshua the Anŏinted, to the glory and praise of the Almĭghty.

¹²And I want you to be knowing brothers, that my circumstances have been turning out for the greater progress of the good news, ¹³so that my imprisonment for the sake of the Anŏinted has become well known throughout the whole praetorian guard and to everyone else, ¹⁴and most of the brothers through Yăhweн having been getting persuaded, because of my imprisonment, to dare more so to speak the word fearlessly. ¹⁵Some, to be sure, are proclaiming the Anŏinted even from envy and strife, but some also from good will. ¹⁶The latter proclaim him out of love, having been knowing that I am appointed for the defense of the good news. ¹⁷The former proclaim the Anŏinted out of selfish ambition rather than from pure motives, thinking to cause me distress in my imprisonment. ¹⁸What then? Only that in every way, whether in pretense or in truth, the Anŏinted is proclaimed. And in this I rejoice, yes, and I will rejoice.

¹⁹Because I have been knowing that this will turn out for my deliverance through your prayers and the provision of the Spĭrit of Yĕshua the Anŏinted, ²⁰according to my earnest expectation and hope, that I will not be put to shame in anything, but that with all boldness the Anŏinted will even now as always be exalted in my body whether by life or by death.

²¹Because to me, to live is for the Anŏinted, and to die is gain. ²²But if I am to live on in *this* flesh, this will mean fruitful labor for me, and I do not know which to choose. ²³But I am hard-pressed from both directions, having the de-

---

1:23 θ Paul is speaking subjectively here. From the human point of view death is immediately followed by resurrection and the presence of Mĕssiah, which is the gain immediately realized in the subjective point of view. Objectively, from the point of view of every- one still living, the soul sleeps in the grave until the resurrection. See Daniel 12:1-2; Mat. 9:24; 10:28; John 11:11. The souls of the departed faithful are not looking down on us nor are consciously existing in heaven as taught by many. They used to teach the resurrection of the dead, but now they ignore it greatly.

sire to depart and be with the Anŏinted, because that is very much better. ᶿ ²⁴Yet to remain on in the flesh is more necessary for your sake. ²⁵And having been trusting this, I have been knowing that I will remain and continue with you all for your progress and joy in the pledge of faithfulness, ²⁶so that your proud confidence in me may be abounding through the Anŏinted Yĕshua through my coming presence with you again.

²⁷Only be conducting yourselves in a manner worthy of the good news of the Anŏinted, so that whether I come and see you or remain absent, I may be hearing of you that you are standing firm in one spirit, with one mind striving together in the faithfulness of the good news, ²⁸in no way alarmed by your opponents, which^ϕ is a demonstration of destruction for them, but of deliverance for you, and that too, from the Almĭghty. ²⁹Because to you was the favorable invitation on behalf of the Anŏinted, not only to pledge faithfulness to him but also to suffer on his behalf, ³⁰experiencing the same conflict which you saw in me, and now hear to be in me.

2 ¹If therefore there is any encouragement in connection to the Anŏinted, if there is any consolation of love, if there is any fellowship of the Spĭrit, if any affection and compassion, ²make my joy complete, so that you may be agreeing, maintaining the same love, united in spirit, intent on one purpose. ³Do nothing from selfishness or empty conceit, but with humility of mind let each of you regard one another as more important than himself. ⁴Do not look out for your own interests only, but also for the interests of others.

⁵Be having this attitude in yourselves which was also in the Anŏinted Yĕshua, ⁶who in the form^ρ of the Almĭghty being^μ, ^ξcommanded his being equal to the Almĭghty not as booty, ⁷but emptied^χ himself, taking the form of a servant, and having become in the likeness of men. ⁸And being found in composition^π as a man, he humbled himself by becoming obedient to the point of death, even death on an execution timber. ⁹Therefore the Almĭghty also highly exalts him, and favors in him the name which is above every name, ¹⁰that at the name of Yĕshua EVERY KNEE SHALL HAVE BOWED^ϕ, of those who are in heaven, and on

---

1:28 ϕ cf. faithfulness, vs. 27; Mĕssiah's faithfulness in death and our faithful response.

2:6 μ ὑπάρχων. The present participle here is a historical present because going from the form of Gŏd to the form of a servant involves a change of state. **2:6** ρ μορφῇ. Form here is the outward glory (δόξα) of the Almĭghty and not his essential nature (φύσις). Cf. Mark 16:12, pg. 571. The form of the Most High is the splendor and majesty that he ordinarily appears with. **2:6** ξ→booty: A commander has the right to his booty by virtue of his position, but Mĕssiah put his rights aside to become a man and suffer and die on our

behalf. See Yoh. 1:18. **2:6** ξ He emptied himself of his former glorious form for that of human likeness. **2:6** π. σχήματι A synonym of "form." **2:10-11** χ→toward = κατεργάζεσθε; κατ < κατά + ἐργάζομαι. The prefix specifies "down through" as to a goal. See 1 Cor. 16:2. Delieverance is represented as occurring at the end here. Cf. Mat. 24:13. Faithfulness, our work, is an attendant circumstance necessary to final delieverance. Paul's criticism of works is elsewhere related to the belief that a good deed can pay for remission of a bad deed.

earth, and under the earth, ¹¹AND EVERY TONGUE SHALL HAVE CONFESSED⁺ that, "Yĕshua the Anŏinted is Adŏnai," to the glory of the Almĭghty Făther.

¹²So then, my beloved, just as you have always obeyed, not as in my presence only, but now much more in my absence, be ˣworking toward your deliverance with fear and trembling, ¹³because it is the Almĭghty who is working in you all, even his will and his work for his good pleasure. ¹⁴Be doing all things without grumbling or disputing, ¹⁵that you may prove yourselves to be blameless and innocent, children of the Almĭghty above reproach in the midst of a crooked kindred, which also has been perverting itself, among whom you are getting enlightened as lights in the world, ¹⁶holding fast the word of life, so that in the day of the Anŏinted, I may have cause to glory because I did not run in vain nor toil in vain. ¹⁷But even if I am being poured out as a drink offering after the sacrifice and service of your faithfulness, I rejoice and share my joy with you all. ¹⁸And you also, the same thing be rejoicing and be rejoicing with me.

¹⁹But I hope in Adŏnai Yĕshua to send Timothy to you shortly, so that I also may be encouraged when I learn of your condition, ²⁰because I have no one else of kindred spirit who will genuinely be concerned for your welfare. ²¹Because they all seek after their own interests, not those of the Anŏinted Yĕshua. ²²But you know of his proven worth that he served with me in the furtherance of the good news like a child serving his father. ²³Therefore I hope to send him immediately, as soon as I may have seen how things go with me. ²⁴And I have been trusting in Yăhweн that I myself also will be coming shortly.

²⁵But I thought it necessary to send to you Epaphroditus, my brother and fellow worker and fellow soldier, who is also your messenger and minister to my need, ²⁶because he was longing for you all and was distressed because you had heard that he was sick, ²⁷because indeed he was sick to the point of death, but the Almĭghty had mercy on him, and not on him only but also on me, lest I may have had sorrow upon sorrow. ²⁸Therefore I have sent him all the more eagerly in order that when you see him again you will have rejoiced and I may be less concerned about you. ²⁹Therefore be receiving him in Yăhweн with all joy, and be holding men like him in high regard, ³⁰because he came close to death for the work of the Anŏinted, risking his life so that he will have completed what was deficient in your service to me.

2:12 ϕ Isa **2:12-18** These are hard verses for those who claim works have no place in preserving our deliverance. The key is that we are saved from the penalty of the second death through forgiveness, but also we have to continue in faithfulness to Mĕssiah. So we are working out that which was already freely granted to us by his loving-kindness. Anyone who is loyal to Mĕssiah keeps his commandments, but whoever does not affirm faithfulness to Him does not know Him, and whoever will not confirm their faithfulness by keeping his commandments does not know him either. See John 15:1-10; 1 John 2:3-4; Rom. 1:17; 2:7. Consider what the rich young ruler was told to do to have everlasting life. ▷ See Eph. 2:8: 'For by loving kindness you have been getting rescued,' or 'will have been getting rescued' since the statement is also a timeless truth. Rescuing is a divine act of deliverance, whenever we need it, and whenever the Almĭghty is willing to do it, and we should not presume to willfully rebel so as to need rescuing, to try his patience, and put him to the test. But, having been delivered, he requires us to stay away from trouble (sin). Why then was Paul negative on the place of good works in keeping our place? He wasn't. Paul did not mean good works when he spoke of 'the customary works,' (cf. Gal. 2:16), but works performed as merits in order the cancel out demerits. But as for good works, the man who does them shall live by them. For the righteous one shall live by his faithfulness (Hab. 2:4).

Philippians 3

3 ¹Finally, my brothers, be rejoicing in Yăhweh. To write the same things again is no trouble to me, and it is a safe-guard for you. ²Be watching out for the ᵃdogs, be watching out for the evil workers, be watching out for the ᵝconcision, ³because we are the circumcision, those who are worshiping in the Spirit of the Almighty and getting gloriously elevated by the Anŏinted Yĕshua and who have not been trusting in the flesh, ⁴although I myself *may be* having trust even in the flesh. If anyone else is thinking to have been trusting in the flesh, ᵟI far more: ⁵circumcised the eighth day, of the nation of Yisra'el, of the tribe of Binyamin, a Hebrew of Hebrews. According to the Law, a Perushi, ⁶according to zeal, a persecutor of the Assembly, according to the righteousness which is in the Law, being ᵗfound blameless.

⁷But whatever things were being profit to me, those things I have been

---

3:2 α A euphemism for pagans. **3:2** β A word that sounds partly like circumcision in Greek, but means "to cut up" or to "mutilate." Paul was not against legitimate circumcision. See Rom. 3:1-2; Acts 16:3; Ezek. 44:7-9; Gal. 2:5; 5:6, 11. But he was against the doctrinal redefinition of his opponents. Similar terms have been used for baptism. The baptism heresy did not surface in Paul's day, but if it did he might call the teachers, "bapcons." ▷ Philippians was written well after Galatians, where Paul used the term 'circumcision' to refer to false doctrine. It appears here that he is now taking measures to prevent confusion, because some were confused by his speaking in terms defined by the false teachers in Galatia, and so he has substituted 'concision' to refer to the false doctrine so as to preserve *circumcision* to be used for the true doctrine. Likewise those who understand baptism have done, referring to the false doctrine in qualified terms and not simply as 'baptism' when speaking of paedobaptism: Thus, "beware of the bapcons (Rome, Luther), because we are the baptists who put no confidence in outward washing." ▷ κατατομήν (cut down, cut off) vs. περιτέμνω (cut around). Paul may be describing a more severe form of 'circumcison' which amounted to mutilation. The Hebrew נָמַל, מוּל, מָלַל means to cut in the fashion of grass (cf. Psa. 90:5-6), which implies that to be well trimmed back is sufficient. The grass is not uprooted or cut below ground level, but above it a bit. Scholars distinguish between **milah** and **periah**, periah being the modern form widely practiced, whereas milah will be the ancient and biblical form. How this difference came about is easy to imagine. Some groups insisted that unless one was circumcised 'their way' then it was not valid, and of course these groups made it more severe than it had to be. Zipporah's hasty circumcision of her son with a sharp rock was considered sufficient (cf. Exo. 4:24-27). A circumcision reversal (cf. 1 Cor. 7:18) required some of the original covering of the glans to still be present, which was done by 'drawing.' See BDAG 3rd, "ἐπισπάω 3) **to pull the foreskin over the end of the penis**, *pull over the foreskin*." See also Thayer. Periah was invented to prevent the ἐπισπάω:

The Biblical command for circumcision had its scope extended by the rabbis to address the unacceptable practice of epispasm, or de-circumcision, motivated by the wish to assimilate into Greco-Roman society or possibly convert to Christianity. While the Biblical requirement is to remove the foreskin (orlah) only (Genesis 17:11), the rabbis introduced complete uncovering (peri'ah) of the corona. (Rickman, Dan. "Circumcision and its Critics," Jewish World, http://www.ynetnews.com/articles/0,7340,L-3780549,00.html)… 'Rabbah b. Isaac stated in the name of Rab: The commandment of uncovering the corona at circumcision was not given to Abraham;' (Bab. Talmud, Yevamot 71b).

The Samaritans appear to have preserved the more ancient form of *milah*. (M. Avi-Yonah, "The Samaritan Revolts against the Byzantine Empire," Eretz-Israel 4 (1956): 127-32 (Hebrew); Jacob, Son of Aaron, "Circumcision among the Samaritans," ed. W. E. Barton; in Bibliotheca Sacra 65 (1908): 695-96; Pummer, "Samaritan Rituals and Customs," in A. D. Crown, ed., The Samaritans (Tübingen: J. C. Mohr, 1988); J. Mills, Three Months' Residence at Nablus, and an Account of the Modern Samaritans (London: J. Murray, 1864); and R. Kashani, "The Samaritans: History, Tradition, and Customs," Bi-Tefutzot ha-Golah 13 (1971): 202-19.).

Paul may be describing **periah**, but it is not certain. *Periah* only replaced **milah** for certain around AD 140 after the Bar Kochba revolt, but it is possible that this tradition was innovated earlier.

3:3 γ Confidence in the flesh is the root of the problem. The false teachers taught the circumcision saved a person. But like baptism it is only a symbol of salvation. Also the false teachers taught that circumcision made a person Jewish, and their confidence was in being Jewish. **3:4** δ→blameless: All these things are listed by Paul because they are what he had put confidence in. Even being a heretic hunter was something he took pride in as well as belonging to the orthodox Perush party and being blameless in his observance.

accounting to myself as loss because of the Anŏinted. ⁸More than that, I count all things to be loss in view of the surpassing value of the knowledge of the Anŏinted Yĕshua my Adŏnai, for whom I have suffered the loss of all things, and count them but rubbish in order that I will have gained the Anŏinted, ⁹that I will have been found in him, not holding to my own ᵘjustice which is based on what is customary, but that which is through the faithfulness of the Anŏinted, the ᵏjustice which is from the Almĭghty, based on the pledge of faithfulness,ᵝ ¹⁰to know him, and the power of his resurrection and the fellowship of his sufferings, being conformed to his death, ¹¹since it is how I shall have attained to the ᵞresurrection from the dead.

¹²Not that I already had received *it* or had been getting ᵝperfected, but I pursue it yet, if even I may lay hold upon that which also I have been laid hold for by the Anŏinted Yĕshua. ¹³Brothers, I do not consider myself to have been catching up, but one thing I do: forgetting what lies behind and reaching forward to what lies ahead, ¹⁴I press on toward the goal for the prize of the upward call of the Almĭghty with the help of the Anŏinted Yĕshua. ¹⁵Therefore, as many as are mature should be thinking this, and if in anything you are thinking differently, the Almĭghty will reveal that also to you. ¹⁶However, unto what we have attained sooner,ˣ with it to be aligning.

¹⁷Brothers, be becoming imitators of me, and be keeping a look out for those who walk according to the pattern you have in us. ¹⁸Because many walk, of whom I often told you, and now tell you even weeping, as enemies of the execution timber of the Anŏinted, ¹⁹whose end is destruction, whose god is their appetite, and whose glory is in their shame, who set their minds on earthly things. ²⁰Because our citizenship is in the heavens, from which also we eagerly wait for the Rescuer, Adŏnai Yĕshua the Anŏinted, ²¹who will transform the body of our humble state into conformity with the body of his glory, by the exertion of the power that he has even to subject all things to himself.

¹ᵃTherefore, my beloved brothers whom I long for, my joy and crown, be standing firm this way in Yăhweh.

Even a good thing, such as blameless observance, is a bad thing if one takes confidence in it at the expense of knowing Mĕssiah. **3:6** τ→blameless. But clearly, Paul means only so found before men of his former sect with respect to outward observance.

3:9 μ **merit** (See צדקה Reuben Alcalay, *The Complete Hebrew English Dictionary*) or **charity**. Charity was one of the supererogatory works one could do to compensate for demerits in the Jewish system of zechut. **3:9** λ *mercy* (BDAG δικαιοσύνη 3b), a specific application of justice. **3:9** β See Romans 10:1-10 for expansion of this idea. "Mĕssiah is the end of what is customary for justice for everyone pledging faithfulness." For the repentant who pledge loyalty to Messiah, the adminstration of justice is a divine pardon, divine forgiveness. The norm for justice, on the other hand, is divine wrath. So in forgiveness the penalty is canceled. The "faithfulness of Mĕssiah" is the proper sense of πίστεως Χριστοῦ, and not "faith in M." The text refers to his faithfulness to his Făther's commandment that he should lay down his life for us, to ransom us from lawlessness, and to cleanse us from the contamination of our slavery by giving us his life. The ransom idea expresses the cost the Most High takes upon himself to bear our sin, to suffer it, while he waits for us to repent. ▷ See discussion, **Gal 2:16** γ at endnote on page 612. **3:11** γ Paul means the resurrection of the righteous. See Dan. 12:1-2. Also Phil. 2:12; Col. 1:23. Paul does not doubt his present standing, but he endures all things to remain in Mĕssiah. See also Romans 2:7; 1 John 2:3-4. **3:12** β See Gal. 3:3 and 5:5. Paul does not place confidence in legal righteousness for salvation, but perfect righteousness is hoped for in the age to come. **3:16** χ = before others.

Philippians 4

4 ¹ᵇBeloved ones, ²I urge Euodia and I urge Suntuke to live in harmony in Yăhweh. ³Indeed, true partner, I ask you also to be helping these women who have shared my struggle for the good news, together with Clement also, and the rest of my fellow workers, whose names are in the scroll of life.

⁴Be rejoicing in Yăhweh always. Again I will say, be rejoicing! ⁵Let your forbearing spirit be known to all men. Yăhweh is near. ⁶Be worrying about nothing, but in everything by prayer and supplication with thanksgiving let your requests be getting made known near to the Almĭghty. ⁷And the peace of the Almĭghty, which surpasses all comprehension, will guard your hearts and your minds in connection to the Anŏinted Yĕshua. ⁸Finally, brothers, whatever is true, whatever is honorable, whatever is right, whatever is pure, whatever is lovely, whatever is of good repute, if there is any excellence and if anything worthy of praise, let your mind be thinking these things. ⁹The things you have learned and have received and have heard and have seen in me, be practicing these things, and the Almĭghty of peace will be with you.

¹⁰But I have been rejoicing in Yăhweh greatly, in that already in advance you have revived your concern for me, after which also you were being concerned *before*, but you were yourselves lacking opportunity. ¹¹Not that I speak from a deficiency, because I have learned to be content in whatever circumstances I am. ¹²I have been knowing how to get along with humble means, and I also have been knowing how to live in prosperity. In all, and in all things I have been teaching myself the secret *of how* even to be fattening myself, even to be hungering, even to be abounding, even to be lacking. ¹³I am having strength for everything by the one who is strengthening me.

¹⁴Nevertheless, you have done well to share in my affliction. ¹⁵And you yourselves also have been knowing, Philippians, that at the first proclaiming of the good news, after I had departed from Macedonia, no assembly shared with me in the matter of giving and receiving but you alone, ¹⁶because even in Thessalonica you sent a gift more than once for my needs. ¹⁷Not that I seek the gift itself, but I seek for the profit which increases to your account. ¹⁸But I am fully having everything, and I am overflowing. I have been getting filled, having received from the hand of Epaphroditus the things from your hand, a fragrant aroma, an acceptable sacrifice, well-pleasing to the Almĭghty. ¹⁹And my Almĭghty will supply all your needs according to his riches in glory, *being* in the Anŏinted Yĕshua. ²⁰Now to our Almĭghty and Făther be the glory forever and ever. Amen.

²¹Greet every holy one in the Anŏinted Yĕshua. The brothers who are with me greet you. ²²All the holy ones greet you, especially those of Caesar's household.

²³The loving-kindness of Adŏnai Yĕshua the Anŏinted be with your spirit.

Colossians

1 ¹Paul, an emissary of Yĕshua the Anŏinted by the will of the Almĭghty, and Timothy our brother, ²to the holy ones in Colossae and faithful brothers to⁽ᵉᵛ⁾ the Anŏinted. Loving-kindness to you and peace from the Almĭghty our Făther.

³We give thanks to the Almĭghty, the Făther of our Adŏnai Yĕshua the Anŏinted, praying always for you, ⁴since we heard of your faithfulness to the Anŏinted Yĕshua and the love which you have for all the holy ones, ⁵because of the hope laid up for you in the heavens, of which you previously heard in the word of truth, the good news, ⁶which is being near to you, just as in all the world also it is constantly bearing fruit and increasing, even as in you also since the day you heard and understood the loving-kindness of the Almĭghty in truth, ⁷just as you learned it from Epaphras, our beloved fellow servant, who is a faithful servant of the Anŏinted on your behalf, ⁸and he also informed us of your love in the Spĭrit.

⁹For this reason also, since the day we heard, we have not ceased to pray for you and to ask that you may be filled with the knowledge of his will in all spiritual wisdom and understanding, ¹⁰so that you may walk in a manner worthy of Yăhweн, to please him in all respects, bearing fruit in every good work and increasing in the knowledge of the Almĭghty, ¹¹strengthened with all power according to his glorious might for the attaining of all steadfastness and patience, joyously ¹²giving thanks to the Făther, who has authorized us to share in the inheritance of the holy ones in light.

¹³Because he delivers and will have ᵘdelivered us from the domain of darkness, and will have ᵘtransferred us to the kingdom of his beloved Sŏn, ¹⁴by whom we are getting⁽ʸ⁾ a ransomed release,⁽ᵋ⁾ even the release from sins.

¹⁵And he is the image of the invisible Almĭghty, the ᵠFirstborn ᶿover all creation, ¹⁶because by him all things were created, in the heavens and

---

1:13 μ Prophetic perfect and gnomic. Compare Isa. 9:6 for proof example of this idiom. See also Eph. 2:6. **1:13** γ See 1 Yoh. 5:12, 15. **1:13** ξ ἀπολύτρωσιν a release effected by payment of a ransom. But see that this release is still future in Eph. 4:30. See Luke 21:28. The ransom is exemplified by Messiah's death, but the cost being laid down includes all the divine suffering and sacrifice (cf. Isa. 43:3).

1:15 ψ πρωτότοκος. A compound word πρῶτος + τοκος (< τίκτω) first+begotten. The word denotes a status as proved by Psa. 89:27: *Yea, my Firstborn I make him, Most High of the kings of the earth* (אַף־אָ֭נִי בְּכ֣וֹר אֶתְּנֵ֑הוּ עֶ֝לְי֗וֹן לְמַלְכֵי־אָֽרֶץ). If the Psalm refers to David, David was not the firstborn of Jesse. The context of the Psalm shows that it was authored well after David when the kingdom was overrun by enemies, and "David" is used as a surname shorthand for "House of David" (Psa. 89:3, 20, 35, 49). Such usage is seen in Ezek. 34:23; Hos. 3:5; Zech. 12:8, 10. No king is higher than Mĕssiah. He is even David's king (Psa. 110:1). Thus the Psalm refers to Mĕssiah, and it is almost certain that the Psa. inspired the thought, 'firstborn over all creation,' as a status, extending earth to 'all creation.' ▷ Now 'firstborn' is synonymous with 'first begotten,' which may be taken literally and figuratively. For the literal, as respects Mĕssiah's human nature, see Mat. 1:25; Luke 2:7. For figurative as respects the divine person of the Sŏn, see Psa. 2:7. The Firstborn status is established at a point in time when the divine person of Mĕssiah takes the position of Sŏn to the divine person of the Făther (Psa. 89:26-27; Psa. 2:7). Other figurative uses: see Job 18:13: *firstborn of death*; Isa. 14:30: *firstborn of the poor*; Polycarp 7:1: *firstborn of Satan*. ▷ This also shows the doctrine of 'eternal begetting' to be unbiblical (cf. 1 Yoh. 4:9 note). The divine person that became the Sŏn has no beginning of days, but his 'Sonship' had a beginning. See John 1:1-3; Col. 1:18; Rev. 1:5; 1 Cor. 15:23; Rom. 8:29. ▷ The "firstborn" is a status or rank designating the heir. **1:15** θ The firstborn is "over" (genitive case) the whole estate. This text illustrates one of the dangers of always trying to translate the genitive case with English "of", and has been abused to mislead many into thinking that Mĕssiah was the

Colossians 1

on earth, the visible and the invisible, whether thrones or dominions or rulers or authorities. Absolutely everything has been getting created by him, and for him. ¹⁷And he is before all things, and by him all things have been holding together.

¹⁸He is also head of the body, the Assembly *of Yisra'el*, and he is the beginning, the ᵘFirstborn ᵞof the dead, so that he himself will have come to have first place in everything, ¹⁹because in himself he pleased to have all the ᵖfullness to dwell, ²⁰and through himself to reconcile all things to himself, having been a peace maker through the blood^λ of his execution timber, through himself, whether things on earth or things in the heavens.

²¹And you, *who once were* living as they who have been alienating themselves, even *as* enemies in thought, in connection to evil deeds, ²²even now, he has reconciled in^γ his fleshly body through death^χ, *in order* to present you holy and blameless and without fault before him, ²³if indeed you are fully remaining

---

"first" created being "of" creation. The context (vs. 16-17) also refutes that misunderstanding.

1:18 γ omit ἐκ (𝔓⁴⁶ ℵ*; Ir^(lat pt)). See Rev. 1:5 where 𝔐^A reads ἐκ but Aland 27 does not (𝔓¹⁷ ℵ A C etc.) does not. **1:18** μ→dead: הַבְּכוֹר לַמֵּת = *the firstborn for the dead*. The expression is to be understood in the statue for the kinsman redeemer, Deut. 25:5: וְהָיָה הַבְּכוֹר אֲשֶׁר תֵּלֵד יָקוּם עַל־שֵׁם אָחִיו הַמֵּת וְלֹא־יִמָּחֶה שְׁמוֹ מִיִּשְׂרָאֵל = *And will have been that, the firstborn, which she will bear, he will raise up for the name of his brother, the dead one, and his name will not be blotted out from Yisrael*. Literally, the Son is the *firstborn of the dead*. He is the one who ransoms the name of all the righteous who have died who are written in the book of life. This is because as the Son lives, so we also will live.

1:19 π The translation of this verse is revised in this edition. The verb εὐδόκησεν is not passive, but active, ἐν αὐτῷ εὐδόκησεν means *in himself He pleased*, not *was pleased*, πᾶν τὸ πλήρωμα κατοικῆσαι, *all the fulness to dwell*. And *Father* is incorrectly supplied by other versions as the subject. Meyer thinks vs. 18 *will have come to have* precludes this, but the fault is his classical view or Nicene Creedal view of God and not any supposed contradiction. In verse 20 the pronouns, *himself*, are emphatic and do not refer to the Father. That the will to do this is attributed to the Father elsewhere should be no objection (against Meyer) because it was jointly decided (*F* 2 Cor. 5:19; Eph. 1:9). The objection stems out of the eternal subordinationalist doctrine and the eternal geneneration doctrine.

Further objection is based on the concept of the Sŏn reconciling the world to the Fäther by propitiating the Fäther. But this is heresy and divides the Most High against himself. Rather the Fäther and Sŏn are jointly reconciling the world to the Most High. ▷ Paul was here combating Gnostics who made the person and spirit of Mĕssiah a mere man and said that the "Mĕssiah" Spirit only dwelled with him. Not so. But the Almĭghty Sŏn condescended to limit himself to the form and perspective of a man, and while a man his identity remained the Almĭghty One, his power showing from time to time.

1:20 λ Isa. 53:5, "and the instruction of our wellness (peace) is upon him." Peace is effected by cleansing from sin through confession and forgiveness. Then his blood cleanses us. The blood represents the divine life of the Spirit which we consume (cf. Yoĥ. 6). The execution timber represents the divine life being given up to cleanse us. The blood represents the ransom price in death that purchased us for the Almĭghty out of the nations.

1:22 γ The 'in' here appears not to be instrumental 'by' but locative, that is he the divine Son took on flesh and was incarnated into a body. **1:22** χ Yeshua went through death and was raised on the other side of it (διὰ τοῦ θανάτου). His fleshly body was resurrected with flesh and blood as well as a spiritual body. Reconciliation is effected by his being a willing ransom to suffer sin's attack to come into the kingdom of darkness and show us that he was the way the truth and the life. The forces of evil did not want man to see the Almĭghty Sŏn as one of us, the Son of Man, and so they plotted to kill him. But the Most High was pleased to turn this attack around and declare it a ransom, a guilt offering, symbolic of applying his life to our hearts to cleanse us from sin. He gave his flesh for the life of the world (Yoĥ. 6:51), that is, he met sin's attack on his flesh to show us the truth that whoever holds faithful to him should not perish (cf. Yoĥ. 3:16), because as the Almĭghty Son, he defeated death's attack on his flesh and rose again. Therefore, he is able to defeat it for us.

in faithfulness, having been getting yourselves a foundation and *getting* firmly seated and not moved away from the hope of the good news that you have heard, which is proclaimed to every creature under heaven, and of which I, Paul, was made a servant.

²⁴Now I rejoice in my sufferings on your behalf, and fill up what lacks in the sufferings of the Anŏinted in my flesh, on behalf of his body, which is the Assembly of Yisra'el, ²⁵for which I became a servant according to the stewardship from the Almĭghty that was given to me for you, to fulfill the word of the Almĭghty, ²⁶the mystery which has been getting hidden from the Aeons and generations, but has now been manifested to his **holy ones**, ²⁷**to which ones** the Almĭghty willed to make known what are the riches of the glory of this mystery among the nations, which is the Anŏinted in you, the hope of glory. ²⁸And we proclaim him, educating each man and teaching each man with all wisdom, that we will have presented each man perfect in *conformity with* the Anŏinted. ²⁹And for this purpose also I labor, striving according to his power which mightily works within me.

2 ¹For I am desiring that you will have been knowing how great a struggle I have on your behalf, and for those who are at Laodicea, and for all those who have not been seeing my face in the flesh, ²that their hearts will have been encouraged, so as to be made to join together in love, and in all the wealth of full assurance of understanding, into the full knowledge of the mystery of the Almĭghty, which is the Anŏinted, ³in whom are hidden all the treasures of wisdom and knowledge.

⁴I say this in order that no one may be deceiving you with persuasive sounding arguments. ⁵For even though I am absent in body, nevertheless I am with you in heart, rejoicing to see your good discipline and the firmness of your faithfulness in the Anŏinted. ⁶As you therefore have received the Anŏinted Yĕshua, Adŏnai, in him you must be walking, ⁷having been rooting yourselves and building yourselves up in him and confirming yourselves in faithfulness, just as you were instructed, abounding in thanksgiving.

⁸Be watching out that no one captivates you through philosophy and empty deception, according to the tradition of men, according to the elementary principles of the world system, and which are not according to the Anŏinted, ⁹seeing that in him all the ᵝcomplement of the divine nature dwells bodily, ¹⁰and by him you are being—yea have been getting completed, who is the head over every ruler and authority, ¹¹by whom you also are circumcised by a circumcision

---

2:9 β→nature: Or fullness. See note on 1:19. Or "complement of Almĭghtiness," divinity: הָאֱלֹהוּת. The complement or fullness of divinity is not the 'one substance' or 'essence' of the Nicene Creed, because the Son is not generated from the Father. The fullness represents all those characteristics, traits and attributes necessary to be Almĭghty. The Son is Almĭghty alone as the Father is Almĭghty alone, as is the Spirit, and any other division by which the Most High wills to exist. See Yoḥ. 17:3; Gen. 19:24. All divisions of the Amĭghty are united into the one Almĭghty by an everlasting bond of love and faithfulness. It is the aim of the Most High to reproduce this bond of fellowship between himself and those he created in his own image, so that his faithful ones may share in the bond, while he remains the first and the last Almĭghty. ▷ For those who believe that I have created some difficulty by referring to the Most High with singular pronouns, it is not the case, because I am speaking in a Hebrew fashion where a person can speak with "I" without disclosing exactly who is represented by

made without hands, along with putting off the body of flesh$^\pi$, in *connection to the circumcision of the Anŏinted*$^\beta$, ^{12}having been buried with him in immersion, by whom also you will have been raised with him, through the faithfulness of the working of the Almĭghty, who raised him from the dead.

^{13}And you, being dead to transgressions and to the $^\theta$uncircumcision of your flesh, he will have made live together with him, granting loving-kindness to us concerning all the transgressions, ^{14}wiping out the $^\chi$writing *put into our* hand according to the decrees against us, which was hostile to us, and he has been taking it out of the way$^\rho$, having nailed it to the execution timber, ^{15}disarming the rulers and authorities. He boldly disgraced them, celebrating his triumph over them with it.

^{16}Therefore$^\alpha$, do not let any$^\chi$ be judging you in $^\beta$eating $^\gamma$and in drinking, $^\delta$either $^\varepsilon$when $^\mu$partaking of a feast, $^\eta$or new moon$^\psi$, $^\eta$or Şabbaṭhs, ^{17}which are a $^\phi$reflection of the $^\rho$things to come. And the Anŏinted One is the *reflecting*$^\psi$body.

---

the speaker. **2:11** π This is to say, they were also physically circumcised. See vs. 13. The 'body of flesh' is put for 'foreskin' as a metonymy. Paul is connecting the sign with its spiritual significance. That which is unclean is being removed from the soul. The Colossians would have readily understood 'body of flesh' to connote the sinful nature through Gnostic influence. **2:11** β This is both in flesh and in heart. See Ezek. 44:7-9; Deut. 10:16.

2:13 θ→flesh: See Eph. 2:5. Circumcision stands for the righteousness of faithfulness. It stands for circumcision of the heart. And so the commentators interpret it this way here dismissing any suggestion that they were literally circumcised. But the physical is important to the Almĭghty as is the spiritual (cf. Ezek. 44:7-9). Paul has mentioned the literal in flesh circumcision here to make his spiritual point, which is a strong suggestion that Paul still taught both literal circumcision and its true meaning. See Gal. 5:11. ▷ *Dead to* is an idiom for leaving behind their transgressions, and also the uncircumcision of their flesh. Therefore, they also were circumcised in the flesh.

2:14 χ: χειρόγραφον This was Yisra'el's bill of divorce put in her hand. See Endnotes on page 617.
2:14 ρ = midst, between. The divorce sentence stood between us and the Almĭghty.

2:16 α and **2:16** χ See Endnotes on page 617.

2:16 β→drinking: See Endnote on page 618.
2:16 ψ Νεο μηνίας means "new moon." Paul tells the Colossians that they should not let the Qumran calendar cultists judge them for celebrating "new moons," since a considerable number of the new moon denying Essene cult had professed Messiah. Even today some professors of Messiah have reinvented the same cult, rejecting the new moon feast, and all the appointed feasts connected to it, also appropriating the heritage of the priestly line of to Zadok exclusively to themselves. ▷ References to a "month" in the Scripture everywhere (excluding the LXX) mean (or refer to) the "new moon," except in Gal. 4:10 (q.v.). See Appendix XVI on page 599 for proof of this fact, which is assumed in this note. ▷ Paul explicitly specifies "new moon" here because the oridinary Greek word for "month" in non-Jewish Greek meant "month", but under the influence of the Hebrew חֹדֶשׁ Jewish authors used the Greek word in reference to the new moon. Paul did not want any doubt that he meant "new moon" here, so he appends the Greek word Νεο meaning "new." ▷ The reason for this is easy to see after we comprehend the sectarian Qumran texts, and the Yaḥad cult that produced them. The Yaḥad cult denied the new moon any role in fixing the calendar. In fact, in the heretical book of "Jubilees" they defined the new moon out of any calendar role whatsoever, assigning all calendar functions to the sun (q.v. Jubilees 2:9: *And God appointed the sun to be a great sign on the earth for days and for sabbaths and for months and for feasts and for years and for sabbaths of years and for jubilees and for all seasons of the years.*) They literally eliminated the new moon from its role in Genesis 1:14. Accordingly, the pseudo-Zadok cult condemned mainstream Jews for new moon feasts, and not only that but for all the feast days set by the appointed time of the new moon. In fact, it has been been suggested by Dead Sea Scroll scholar Rachel Elior that the Yaḥad read Gen. 1:14 without a waw וּ, viz. instead of וְהָיוּ, they changed the verb to חָיָה or יְהִי, and interpreted "lights" (מְאֹרֹת) as an intensive plural "great light." ▷ It is a certainty that Paul was countering the pseudo-Zadok cult, because besides their false calendar, they had a superstitious and speculative narrative of angels (cf. vs. 18), and they were infused with Gnostic beliefs, and they also advocated fasting on the Sabbath. All of these traits were common to the cult, including a belief in predestination, a key Gnostic doctrine. And it was a well known cult with pretentions of infiltrating the Messianic Faith then, and it has been revived with the same end today.

2:17 φ ρ ψ See Endnote on page 618. **2:18** θ θρησκεία See "Thrēskeia in 4 Maccabees" Daniel Boyarin, *Sibyls, Scriptures, and Scrolls: John Collins*

¹⁸Let no one be defrauding you, delighting in *false* humility and the ⁹superstition of the angels, which he has been perceiving, vainly detailing, getting puffed up by his fleshly mind, ¹⁹and not holding fast to the head, from whom the entire body, being supplied and held together by the joints and ligaments, grows with a growth which is from the Almĭghty. ²⁰If you have died with the Anŏinted to the elementary principles of the world, why, as if you were living in the world, do you submit yourself to decrees, such as, ²¹"You shall not have handled, you shall not have tasted, you shall not have touched!", ²²which all refer to things destined to perish with the using, in accordance with the commandments and teachings of men? ²³These are matters which have, to be sure, the appearance of wisdom in ᵋself-made superstition and self-abasement and severe treatment of the body, but are of no value against fleshly indulgence.

3 ¹If then you will have been raised up with the Anŏinted, be seeking the things above, where the Anŏinted is, sitting himself at the right hand of the Almĭghty. ²Be setting your mind on the things above, not on the things that are on earth, ³because you will have died, and your life will have been getting hidden with the Anŏinted in the Almĭghty. ⁴When the Anŏinted, who is our life, may have been revealed, then you also will be revealed with him in glory.

⁵Therefore consider the members of your earthly body as dead to immorality, impurity, passion, evil desire, and greed, which amounts to idolatry, ⁶because it is on account of these things that the wrath of the Almĭghty will come, ⁷and in them you also once walked, when you were living in them. ⁸But now you also, put them all aside: anger, wrath, malice, slander, and abusive speech from your mouth. ⁹Do not be lying to one another, having laid aside the old self with its practices, ¹⁰and having put on the new self, which is getting itself renewed into a complete knowledge according to the image of the One who created it, ¹¹which is not in being Greek or Yehudi, circumcised or uncircumcised, barbarian, Scythian, slave or freeman, but each of these. And in all of these is the Anŏinted.

¹²Therefore, as the chosen of the Almĭghty, holy and having been getting loved, dress yourselves with affections of compassion, kindness, humility, gentleness, and patience, ¹³bearing with one another, and favoring forgiveness to each other, if any may be having a complaint against anyone. Just as Yăhweн favored forgiveness to you, so also *should* you.

---

at Seventy.

2:23 ξ→superstition: ἐθελοθρησκία. Certain sects of Judaism exerted themselves in creating a mythology of angels producing much literature going into voluminous detail about their names, vocations, and activities. Paul does not speak of the 'worship of angels' as most trans. have it, but the superstition of angels. The actual worship thereof would have elicited a much stronger condemnation from Paul. ▷ The Gnostic sects would have had great difficulty with Messsiah creating the material world. For this reason Paul emphasizes this very point in Colossians.

Eventually the Gnostics blamed all of creation on what they called evil angels and attributed the giving of the Torah to angels. ▷ The Jewish Gnostic sects tended to add mystical doctrines and ascetical practices alongside Torah. It is fairly certain that they were trying to acheive some salvation benefit from those practices based on worldly principles (cf. vs. 20) which reflected a non-understanding of the good news or a mis-understanding of it. They may also have projected wordly principles onto their Torah practices also.

¹⁴And beyond all these things put on love, which is the perfect bond of unity. ¹⁵And let the peace of the Anŏinted be ruling in your hearts, to which indeed you were called in one body, and be becoming thankful.

¹⁶Let the word of the Anŏinted be richly dwelling within you, with all wisdom, teaching and reminding one another with psalms, hymns, and spiritual songs, singing with thankfulness in your hearts to the Almĭghty. ¹⁷And whatever you may be doing in word or deed, do all in the name of Adŏnai Yĕshua, giving thanks through him to the Almĭghty, the Făther.

¹⁸Wives, be submitting to your husbands, as it were being proper in Yăhweh.

¹⁹Husbands, be loving your wives, and do not be getting embittered against them. ²⁰Children, be obeying your parents in all things, because this is well-pleasing to Yăhweh. ²¹Fathers, do not be inciting anger in your children, that they may not be losing heart.

²²Slaves, in all things be obeying those who are your masters according to the flesh, not with external service, as those who please men, but with sincerity of heart, fearing Yăhweh. ²³Whatever you may be doing, be working from the heart, as for Yăhweh and not for men, ²⁴having been knowing that from Yăhweh you will receive the reward of the inheritance, °because ⸂our Adŏnai Yĕshua, the Anŏinted One is he whom⸃ you must be serving, ²⁵because he who does wrong will receive the consequences of the wrong which he has done, and that without partiality. ¹Masters, be affording to your slaves justice and fairness, having been knowing that you too have a Măster in heaven.

4 ²Be devoting yourselves to prayer, keeping alert in it with thanksgiving, ³praying at the same time for us as well, that the Almĭghty will have opened up to us a door for the word, so that we may speak forth the mystery of the Anŏinted, for which I have also been getting held bound, ⁴in order that I may make it plain, as is necessary for me to speak.

⁵Be conducting yourselves with wisdom toward outsiders, ransoming the time. ⁶Let your speech always be with loving-kindness, having been getting seasoned with salt, so that you will have been knowing how you ought to be responding to each one.

⁷As to all my affairs, Tychicus, a beloved brother and faithful deputy and fellow servant in Yăhweh, will bring you information, ⁸because I have sent him to you for this very purpose, that you will have known our circumstances and that he will have encouraged your hearts, ⁹and with him Onesimus, a faithful and beloved brother, who is one of you. They will inform you about the whole situation here.

¹⁰Aristarchus, my fellow prisoner, sends you his greetings, and Mark, the cousin of Bar-Navi, about whom you received instructions. If he may have come to you, welcome him, ¹¹and Yeshua who is called Iustos. These are the only fellow workers for the kingdom of the Almĭghty who are from the circumcision, and they have proved to be an encouragement to me.

¹²Epaphras, who is one of you, a servant of Yĕshua the Anŏinted, sends you

his greetings, always laboring earnestly on your behalf in his prayers, that you will have stood perfect and having been getting fully assured in all the will of the Almĭghty, ¹³because I bear him witness that he has much distress over you and those who are in Laodicea and Hierapolis.

¹⁴Luke, the beloved doctor, sends you his greetings, and also Demas.

¹⁵Greet the brothers who are in Laodicea, and also Nympha and the assembly that is in her house. ¹⁶And when this letter may have been read among you, also make *it* so that it shall have been read in the assembly of the Laodiceans, and the one from Laodicea, that also you shall have read. ¹⁷And say to Archippus, "Be taking heed to the ministry which you have received in Yăhwe̱н, that you may be fulfilling it."

¹⁸I, Paul, write this greeting with my own hand. Be remembering my imprisonment. Loving-kindness be with you.

The Relation of Col. 2:14 to Eph. 2:15

Who the emnity *that was against* his flesh, *that was* the customary norm for the charges *against us*, in *the* decrees *contrary to us*, has reduced to no effect (GNM: *Eph.* 2:15).

He was wiping out the writing *put into our* hand according to the decrees against us, which was hostile to us, and he has been taking it out of the way, having nailed it to the execution timber (GNM: *Col.* 2:14).

The standard English translation for these two texts was:

"Having abolished in his flesh the enmity, even the law of commandments contained in ordinances (KJV: Eph. 2:15)."

"Blotting out the handwriting of ordinances that was against us, which was contrary to us, and took it out of the way, nailing it to his cross (KJV: Col. 2:14)."

Both texts are obviously talking nearly about the same concept. And they use similar language. Both texts are central to the Good News because Paul prefaced Col. 2:14 with, "having forgiven you all trespasses," (2:13) and what follows this has every appearance of being an explanation of forgiveness. And what follows Eph. 2:15 is "And that he might reconcile both unto God in one body by the cross, having slain the enmity thereby." So whatever the enmity *is*, had to be slain for reconciliation with God to happen.

Interpreters find in these passages. I. The abolishment of the entire Torah. II. The abolishment of only the ceremonial Torah, and III. The abolishment of manmade traditions added to the Torah.

Whatever the explanation is, it has to explain forgiveness and also removal of emnity between God and man, and between the Jewish faithful and non-Jewish faithful.

Upon supposition I, the abolishment of the entire Torah, it cannot be that laws whose observance prevents emnity were abolished to prevent emnity. It cannot be that if immoralities are made to be legal by abolishing them then forgiveness of immorality still has any meaning. And it cannot be that abolishing the whole Torah will make peace between Jews and non Jews.

Upon suppositions II and III, the removal of either Jewish tradition or the ceremonial law is insufficient to explain those things which really cause hatred and emnity, which are murder and every other sort of immorality that truly brings the wrath of God. Removing either ceremonial law or traditions does not remove the cause of emnity, which is breaking the moral law. And wiping out either or both cannot result in the one new-made man or forgiveness of all transgressions, or reconciliation between God and man.

Therefore, all these interpretations defy the logic of the context, and bring great suspicion of mistranslation and misinterpretation while ignoring the rest of the context to acheive the goal of locating a text to justify rejecting whatever parts of the law one may wish to call ceremonial. Because, this is the interpretation that most of Christian history has fixed upon.

Since on the grounds of logic we have ruled out all the usual interpretations, we are left with 1. find a better original text, 2. correct the translation of the existing text, or 3. a better interpretation of the existing translation.

As we shall see, option 3 is complete failure,

because no revised interpretation can make the text say what Paul really meant to say, which is that divine judgment against our sin has been nullified while at the same time upholding the entire Torah. There is simply no way to make 'law of commandments' meaning anything except that which Christians have been taught it means, either the whole law or a good deal of it. So we will stratch that option.

There are no better texts known. There is not sufficient textual variation on these verses to produce a different translation based on textual differences. One may wish to suppose the problem is textual, which is a choice, but there is currently no evidence for it. So we move on.

This leaves us with correcting the translation so as to remove the contradictions. Let us start with Col 2:14, which only requires us to understand one word and then make the right connection. The word χειρόγραφον has generally been understood to be some kind of note of indebtedness, but according to *Tyndale Bulletin 68.2 (2017) 223-239* (q.v.) this is a dead end, and after reviewing it I agree. The word is literally 'hand-writing,' but it obviously does not mean handwriting as we know it today, because everything in ancient times was hand written. In ancient times most people did not write. They hired scribes that hand wrote, so this was taken for granted. But when one said handwriting it denoted that which one had specifically written with their own hand, usually as an oath, or a declaration, and then had put into the hand of the person to recieve it. It was reserved for the declaration or oath precisely because if anything less was to be communicated, then writing simply was not used. Oral communication was.

So the χειρόγραφον was commonly a declaration of any sort that one wrote themselves, sometimes with the assistence of a scribe, and then they put it into the hand of the person who needed the document. It was most definitely not used for the product of scribal copying of manuscripts. Anyone who used χειρόγραφον in respect to common legal codes or literary works would be given the puzzled "huh?" This fact, which is not often mentioned, is the real reason why scholars ditched the common explanation that Col. 2:14 refers to the ceremonial law and instead speculated that it refers to a debt note, and almost every modern version has adopted this, e.g. ESV, NIV, RSV, etc.

But as the *Tyndale Bulletin 68.2* points out, there is no reason to think the word specifically refers to a debt, and if that was Paul's object, he certainly has better words to communicate the idea in his vocabulary. So we can ask what was written by one's own hand and put into the hand that prevented the house of Israel from taking part in his covenant? Was it the bill of divorcement mentioned in Jeremiah 3:8? It must be, because the Torah in Deut. 24:1 requires the husband himself to write the document and put in in the hand of the wife he is dismissing to make the divorce a legal fact. And that is exactly what Paul means in Col. 2:14.

According to Tyndale Bulletin 68.2 (2017) 223-239 the χειρόγραφον was a short piece of writing with an oath in it τοῖς δόγμασιν relating to a religous regulation. And this is correct. It related to the marriage covenant. But the reason they will not connect the dots is because to do so means the covenant is reinstated for the house of Israel.

Now we can turn to Ephesians 2:15, which is like Col. 2:14:

Who the emnity *that was* against his flesh, *that was* the norm for the charges *against us,* in *the* decrees *contrary to us*, has reduced to no effect (GNM: *Eph*. 2:15).

Paul is saying that the emnity (or hatred) Messiah received in his murder by Satan's minions was the just legal norm for the sentences against us. That is, what happened to Messiah was really what we deserved for being transgressors. But since he forgave us, has spiritually speaking taken the bill of divorcement from us when we became sorry for sin and turned our heart back to him, and he has figuratively nailed it next to him so that when he was put to death, it also was put to death, not to be raised again. And as a result our past transgressions now are reduced to no effect so as to cut us off from Israel and his covenant.

What is the "law of commandments in decrees"? Here is one example, "Cursed is the one striking down his neighbor in secret. And all the people will have said. Amen" (Deut. 27:24). The decrees are these curses, i.e. (δόγμασιν). A commandment is referred to here, which is the one against murder, but instead of being positively referred to, it is negatively referred to as an accusation. And in this respect the English word "charge" can be used both positively and negatively, viz., "he was charged to keep the books in order, but he was charged when he stole from the register." So you see then that the norm for the transgressor is really a legitimate law. It is this law that places the curse. It is the law for the commandments when one rebels against them. The original language was sufficiently broad for Paul to be able to explain about Israel's divorce decree and the curses that led to her excision (cf. Isa. 50:1), but in the wake of 2000 years of heretical programming, I find it necesary to include some phrases from Col. 2:14 here in italic in Eph. 2:15 to make the point over clear to those with programmed with an anti law paradigmn.

One last reminder: Messiah suffered by the hand of Satan what we normally should suffer by the hand of God, but Messiah forgave us, so no wrath against us was called for. When wrath against him was illegally judged, he took the opportunity to kill his bill of divorcement with Israel. There is no penal substitution happening here. There is just forgiveness.

First Thessalonians

1 ¹Paul and Silvanus and Timothy, to the ⁿassembly of the Thessalonians in the Almĭghty the Făther, and Adŏnai Yĕshua the Anŏinted: loving-kindness to you and peace. ²We give thanks to the Almĭghty always for all of you, making mention of you in our prayers, ³constantly bearing in mind your work of faithfulness and labor of love and steadfastness of the hope of our Adŏnai Yĕshua the Anŏinted, in the presence of our Almĭghty and Făther, ⁴having been knowing, brothers, ʗwho have been getting loved by the Almĭghty, your ʗchoosing.

⁵Because our good news did not come to you in word only, but also in power and in the Holy Spĭrit and with full conviction, just as you have been knowing what kind of men we turned out to be among you for your sake. ⁶You also became imitators of us and Adŏnai, having received the word in much tribulation with the joy of the Holy Spĭrit, ⁷so that you became an example to all those holding faithful in Macedonia and in Achaia.

⁸Because the word of Yăhweн has been getting sounded forth from you, not only in Macedonia and Achaia, but also in every place your faithfulness before the Almĭghty has been going forth, so that we have no need to say anything, ⁹because they themselves report about us what kind of a reception we had with you, and how you turned to near the Almĭghty from idols to serve the living and true Almĭghty, ¹⁰and to wait for his Sŏn from the heavens, whom he raised from the dead, who is Yĕshua, who delivers us from the coming wrath.

2 ¹Because you yourselves have been knowing, brothers, that our coming to you had not been happening in vain, ²but after we had already suffered and been insulted in Philippi, just as you have been knowing, we were emboldened in our Almĭghty to speak to you the good news of the Almĭghty in *spite of* great opposition, ³because our exhortation does not come from error or impurity or by way of deceit, ⁴but just as we have been getting approved by the Almĭghty to be held faithful with the good news, so we are speaking, not as pleasing men but the Almĭghty, who examines our hearts. ⁵Because we never came with

---

1:1 η *assembly.* = קְהִלַּת (*qehillat*) ἐκκλησία. Assembly means the whole faithful Assembly of Yisraᵉl. An assembly 'of' a location means a local assembly of the faithful, as stated here. The word "church" is a mistranslation. In fact, "church" is derived from a different Greek word altogether, which one will find in the etymology dictionaries. The word church obscures the meaning of the original *ekklesia*, meaning 'assembly' or 'congregation,' which connects us with the concept of the Assembly of Yisraᵉl. This error has also allowed the Church to be an institution divorced from the kingdom and also claiming its own human authority. **1:4** →loved: ἠγαπημένοι. Or: *who have been being (be)loved.* Greek does not say either the verb or the tense must be stative contrary to the grammars. It seems rather likely that ongoing acts of love is the meaning rather than a *state* of love after the action is over. **1:4** ζ ἐκλογὴν = *selection, election, choice.* By grammar it is not clear whose choice it is, but by usage it is clear that it is the choice of an external agent, in this case Gŏd (cf. ASV vs. KJV). ▷ The word 'election' has been overloaded with connotation of predestination by Augustinian theology, therefore a synonym is used. The word was used in Greek to denote the *levying of troops* (cf. LSJ). The picking of select men of course depends on their continuance in honorable conduct, otherwise they find themselves rejected like king Saul.

flattering speech, as you have been knowing, nor with a pretext for greed, the Almĭghty is witness. ⁶Nor did we seek glory from men, either from you or from others, even though as emissaries of the Anŏinted we could throw our weight around. ⁷But we proved to be gentle among you, as a nursing mother may be taking care of her own children.

⁸Having likewise a fond affection for you, we were well pleased to impart to you not only the good news of the Almĭghty but also our own lives, because you had become very dear to us. ⁹Because you remember, brothers, our labor and toil, working night and day, so as not to put a burden on any of you, that we proclaimed to you the good news of the Almĭghty. ¹⁰You are witnesses, and the Almĭghty *also*, how in a holy manner, and a righteous and blameless way we were toward you who hold faithful, ¹¹even as you have been knowing, as each one of you, as a father his children, we were exhorting and encouraging and testifying, ¹²that you should walk in a way worthy of the Almĭghty who calls you into his kingdom and glory.

¹³And because of this we also give thanks to the Almĭghty without ceasing, that as you received word of the report from us of the Almĭghty, you received not the word of men, but as it is in truth, the word of the Almĭghty, which also works in you who hold faithful.

¹⁴Because you, brothers, became imitators of the assemblies of the Almĭghty that are in Yehudah, belonging to the Anŏinted Yĕshua, because you also suffered the same things under your own countrymen, even as they under the Yehudim, ¹⁵who even killed Adŏnai Yĕshua and the prophets, and drove us out. They are not pleasing to the Almĭghty, but hostile to all men, ¹⁶hindering us from having spoken to the nations, that they might be rescued, with the result that they always fill up the measure of their sins. But wrath overtakes them to the end.

¹⁷But we, brothers, having been orphaned from you for an hour's time, in person, not in spirit, were all the more eager with great desire to see your face, ¹⁸because we wanted to come to you, I, Paul, more than once, and yet Satan thwarted us. ¹⁹Because who is our hope or joy or crown of exultation? Is it not even you, at the face of our Adŏnai Yĕshua at his coming presence? ²⁰Because you are our glory and joy.

3 ¹Therefore when we could endure it no longer, we thought it best to be left behind at Athens alone. ²And we sent Timothy, our brother and the Almĭghty's fellow worker in the good news of the Anŏinted, to strengthen and encourage you as to your faithfulness, ³so that no man may be getting disturbed by these afflictions, because you yourselves have been knowing that we have been destined for this. ⁴Because indeed when we were with you, we were telling you in advance that we were going to be suffering affliction, just as also it came to pass, as you have been knowing. ⁵For this reason even I, enduring it no longer, sent in order to have found out about your faithfulness, lest somehow the Tempter had tempted you, and our labor may have been in vain.

⁶But now Timothy has come to us from you, and has brought us good news of your faithfulness and love, and that you always think kindly of us, longing to see us, just as we also long to see you. ⁷For this reason, brothers, in all our distress and affliction we were comforted about you through your faithfulness, ⁸because now we really live, if you stand firm in Yăhweн.

⁹Because what thanks can we render to the Almĭghty for you in return for all the joy with which we rejoice before our Almĭghty on your account, ¹⁰as we night and day keep praying most earnestly that we may see your face, and may complete what is lacking in your faithfulness? ¹¹Now may our Almĭghty and Făther himself and Yĕshua our Adŏnai direct our way to you.

¹²And may Yăhweн cause you to increase and abound in love for one another, and for all men, just as we also do for you, ¹³so that he may establish your hearts blameless in holiness at the face of our Almĭghty and Făther at the coming presence of our Adŏnai Yĕshua with all his holy ones.

4 ¹Finally then, brothers, we request and exhort you in Adŏnai Yĕshua, that as you received from beside us instruction as to how you ought to walk and please the Almĭghty, just as you actually do walk, that you may be excelling still more, ²because you have been knowing what commandments we gave you by Adŏnai Yĕshua. ³Because this is the will of the Almĭghty, your being made holy, that is, that you abstain from sexual immorality, ⁴for each of you to have been knowing how to possess his own vessel in holiness and honor, ⁵not in lustful passion, like the nations who have not been knowing the Almĭghty, ⁶and that no man transgress and defraud his brother in the matter, because Yăhweн is the avenger in all these things, just as we also told you before and solemnly warned you, ⁷because the Almĭghty has not called us for the purpose of impurity, but in holiness. ⁸Consequently, he who rejects this is not rejecting man but the Almĭghty who gives his Holy Spĭrit to you.

⁹Now as to the love of the brothers, you have no need for anyone to write to you, because you yourselves are taught by the Almĭghty to love one another, ¹⁰because indeed you do practice it toward all the brothers who are in all Macedonia. But we urge you, brothers, to excel still more, ¹¹and to make it your ambition to lead a quiet life and attend to your own business and work with your hands, just as we commanded you, ¹²so that you may be behaving properly toward outsiders and no one may be having *any* need.

¹³But we do not want you to be uninformed, brothers, about those who are falling asleep, that you may not be grieving, as do the rest who have no hope. ¹⁴For if we hold faithful, because Yĕshua died and rose again, even so the Almĭghty will bring with him those who are fallen asleep in Yĕshua. ¹⁵Because this

---

4:14 See Dan. 12:1-2. The state of the first death is constantly described as sleep for the soul by the Scriptures, but the second death will destroy both the body and the soul in the Lake of Fire (cf. Mat. 10:28). The wicked are not destroyed in the Lake of Fire until after they are resurrected to judgment. At present they sleep also like the faithful.

we are saying to you by the word of Yăhweh, that we, the living, still remaining until the coming presence of Yăhweh, no, shall not have preceded those fallen asleep. ¹⁶Because Yăhweh himself will descend from heaven with a shout, with the voice of the Chief Messenger^μ, and with the shofar of the Almĭghty, and the dead belonging to the Anŏinted will rise first. ¹⁷Then we who are alive and remain will be carried away in the clouds together with them to meet Yăhweh by air, and thus we will always be with Yăhweh. ¹⁸Therefore be comforting one another with these words.

5 ¹Now as to the times and the epochs, brothers, you have no need of anything to be written to you, ²because you yourselves have been knowing full well that the day of Yăhweh will come just like a thief in the night. ³When they may be saying, "Peace and security," then suddenly destruction is coming upon them just as labor pains upon a woman having a child in the womb, and no, they shall not have escaped.

⁴Yet, you, brothers, are not in darkness, that the day will have overtaken you like a thief, ⁵because you are all sons of light and sons of day. We are not of night nor of darkness, ⁶so then we should not be sleeping as others do, but we should be watching and we should be getting sober. ⁷Because those who are sleeping are sleeping in the night, and those who are getting drunk are getting

---

4:15 The living will be caught away at the very end to find those who slept in death already awakened by the resurrection of the righteous, but this will happen on the same day. See Lev. 16:30 and 1 Cor. 15:52. **4:16** μ The "Chief Messenger" is the same person as the Messenger of Yăhweh, who is Messiah himself. The Greek word "archangel" means someone over or at the head of all the angels. The title of the archangel is Mika'el, which means "Who is like Gŏd." The Messenger speaks with the voice of Yăhweh because that is who he is. Famous commentaries and commentators of the past have come to the same conclusion (Matthew Henry, John Gill, Ernst Wilhelm Hengstenberg, Vitringa, C.B. Michaelis, Rambach, Starke, Hävernick). Some seem to think that Dan. 10:13 gives the Messenger a lesser position than the Almĭghty Sŏn, "AND BEHOLD MIKA'EL, THE FIRST OF THE PRINCES, THE GREATEST FIRSTMOST HAD COME TO HELP ME" (אַחַד הַשָּׂרִים הָרִאשֹׁנִים) *achad hasarim harishonim*. By consenting to the translation, "one of the chief princes," they teach this person is just one of many in order to deny He is the מַלְאַךְ יְהוָה *mal'ak Yăhweh*. But the cardinal Hebrew word "one" also stands for "first." The phrase is not indefinite, but grammatically definite: "THE ONE (FIRST) OF THE PRINCES." The adjective following is an intensive plural based on the root *rosh* רֹאשׁ, with both an Aramaic plural and Hebrew plural on the end. See also Jude 1:9. "Many Protestant interpreters have [correctly] supposed that Christ is meant." (Albert Barnes). But Barnes supposes, "There is no evidence in the name itself, or in the circumstances referred to, that Christ is intended; and if he had been, it is inconceivable why he was not referred to by his own name." But the Messenger of Yăhweh was one to conceal his own identity (See Gen. 32:24-32; Josh. 5:13; Jud. 13:6-23). Daniel 10:5-9 is a description of Messiah (cf. Rev. 1:12-17). Then Daniel falls into a deep sleep. Another messenger wakes him (10:10-15), and after his message, Daniel becomes speechless. Messiah (aka Mika'el) touches his lips (10:16-20), and leaves the rest of the message to the other messenger (10:21-12:6). Messiah speaks again in 12:7-13. A similar pattern is found in Revelation. In 17:1 the task of a lengthly explanation is given to "one of the seven messengers." Also in 21:9. But Messiah interjects at 21:7 with a voice, and Yohanan mistakes this as coming from the messenger, and is rebuked (21:8-9). In 19:9 Yohanan makes a similar mistake after Messiah interjects with a voice. In 22:12-16 Messiah again speaks. Also confusion of persons can easily occur in Zechariah. The confusion was begun by the Rabbis who do not acknowledge the

drunk in the night. ⁸But since we are in the day, we should be getting sober, having put on the breastplate of faithfulness and love, and as a helmet, the hope of deliverance. ⁹Because the Almĭghty has not destined us for wrath, but for attainment of deliverance through our Adŏnai Yĕshua the Anŏinted, ¹⁰who died on our behalf*, that whether we may be watching or may be sleeping, we will have lived together with him. ¹¹Therefore be encouraging one another, and be building up one another, just as you also are doing.

¹²But we are requesting of you, brothers, to have been appreciating those who are diligently laboring among you, and who are standing before you in Yăhweh and educating you, ¹³and that you esteem them very highly in love because of their work. Be making peace among yourselves. ¹⁴And we urge you, brothers, be admonishing the unruly. Be encouraging the fainthearted. Be helping the weak. Be patient toward all.

¹⁵Be seeing *that* no one may have repaid anyone evil for evil, but always be pursuing good, even for one another and for all.

¹⁶Be rejoicing always! ¹⁷Be praying without ceasing. ¹⁸In everything be giving thanks, because this is the Almĭghty's will in the Anŏinted Yĕshua to you.

¹⁹Do not be quenching the Spĭrit. ²⁰Do not be despising prophecies. ²¹But be proving all things. Be holding fast to that which is good. ²²Be abstaining from every appearance of evil.

²³Now may the Almĭghty of peace himself make you to be completely holy, and may your spirit and soul and body be preserved wholly intact, blameless in the coming presence of our Adŏnai Yĕshua the Anŏinted. ²⁴Faithful is he who calls you. And he also will bring it to pass.

²⁵Brothers, be praying for us.

²⁶Greet all the brothers with a holy kiss.

²⁷I solemnly charge you by Yăhweh to have this letter read to all the brothers.

²⁸The loving-kindness of our Adŏnai Yĕshua the Anŏinted be with you.

מַלְאַךְ יְהוָה *mal'ak Yăhweh* as the Sŏn of Gŏd, and made worse by the Gnostic influence in the Church. And many have unwittingly followed them.

5:10 μ or 'concerning us,' 'for us' (ὑπὲρ ἡμῶν). Although 'for us' is readily understood, I avoid this phrase because Western theology has hijacked it for penal substitution. ▷ See Rev. 5:9. Messiah died 'for us' in the sense that a patriot sacrifices himself to deliver his country from an enemy in war. The ransom cost is exacted by the enemy, who refuses to give up his claim to ownership. ▷ But Christianity, which has morphed into a Satanically inspired cult, has changed the definitions of words and phrases by constantly associating false ideas with key phrases, so that Christians can do nothing but think of the false idea when the redefined phrases are uttered from the pulpit. The words "died for us" have been redefined to mean 'died in our place to satisfy divine wrath,' or 'died in our stead,' and this is not what ὑπὲρ ἡμῶν means in relation to Messiah's death, and much less does ἀντὶ mean such in this connection, for which see Mat. 20:28. They are popularly understood to mean 'died to pay the penalty of sin,' conceived as justly and judicially laid upon Messiah to satisfy the Father's wrath. However, Scripture in no way represents the matter like this. It is a pagan narrative imposed on the text, which is that of appeasing the god with innocent blood to gain favor and avoid wrath. ▷ Since then Christianity has become a global cult in the image of the ancient Ba'al heresy, the true faithful are forced to make a conscious effort to undersand the words of the text rightly, so as to avoid the cognitive dissonance created by Satan's counter narrative. See Mat. 20:28; Mark 10:45. See endnote on Isaiah 53.

'Justify' in Koine Greek

Dio, XVI. "You all deserve to die, yet I, for my part, will not put you all to death, but *I will administer justice to* only a few whom I have already arrested; the others I release." (Cassius Dio, 16.57.47, ca. 218 BC). [δικαιώσω].

As for the cities, some of them voluntarily came over to Caesar and received pardon, and others resisted him and *were administered justice* (Cassius Dio, 49.12.5, ca. 36 BC). [ἐδικαιώθησαν].

For in taking vengeance on the wrongdoer you will be guilty of no sin, any more than the physician is who resorts to cautery and surgery; but all men will assuredly say that the offender *has been administered justice*, because, after partaking of the same rearing and education as the rest, he plotted against you. (BC 29; Dio Cassius 52.26.8). [δικαιώσουσιν],

No. 1: In fact, even in the case of such as conspired against him, *he administered justice to* (ἐδικαίωσε) only those whose lives would have been of no profit even to themselves, while he treated the rest in such a way that for years afterward they could find no pretext true or false for attacking him (Dio Cassius, 56.40.7, ca AD 14). No. 2: And while they were descending the steps down which *those administering justice* hurled [criminals], they slipped and fell. (Dio Cassius, 58.5.6, ca. AD 30). [οἱ δικαιούμενοι].
No. 3: It was voted against him, and thusly *he was administered justice*, as well also down the Stairway he was hurled, where the rabble abused his body for three whole days and afterwards threw it into the river (Dio Cassius 58.11.5, AD 31, The Execution of Sejanus.) [δικαιωθείς].

No. 4: Of the others, *he administered justice to* a very few, who had been guilty of some overt crime not only in co-operation with Cassius but also on their own account. A proof of this is that he did not slay or deprive of his property Flavius Calvisius, [16]the governor of Egypt, but merely confined him on an island. (Dio Cassius 72.28.3, ca. AD 175). [ἐδικαίωσεν]. No. 5: But he [Amaziah] acted according to the Law of Moses, which did not *administer justice* so as to punish children for their fathers' sins. (Josephus Antiquities 9:187). [ἐδικαίωσε]. No. 6: But if she die from the blow, let him also be put to death; to lay down life for life *is the Law's administering of justice* (Josephus Antiquities 4:278). [ψυχὴν ἀντὶ ψυχῆς καταθέσθαι δικαιοῦντος τοῦ νόμου].

No. 7: But [Saturninus was] not thinking himself *to administer justice* to put [Herod's sons] to death (Josephus Antiquities, 16:368). [κτείνειν δ' οὐκ οἴεσθαι δικαιοῦν]. No. 8: And they were they from those at the destruction of the golden eagle *who had been getting administered justice* (Josephus Antiquities 17:206). [κτεί ἦσαν δὲ οἱ τῶν ἐπὶ καθαιρέσει τοῦ χρυσοῦ ἀετοῦ δεδικαιωμένων].

While the prevailing sense in extant Koine Greek was for punitive justice mainly due to the frequency with which adjudication results in a punitive outcome, it cannot be denied that acquittal is also a possible sense, or for that matter any other form of justice the judge may decide is warranted, such as forgiveness with the giving of a ransom to secure the release of the defendant from yet hostile forces. The necessary sense is illustrated in Hebrew in the case of Avşalom, and a few other usages quoted below. Avşalom was getting justice for the plantiff, the one with the complaint. Naturally he was not getting the plaintiff an acquittal or a punishment. Plaintiffs do not volunteer to come to court for those reasons. He was getting them either a hearing, or a pardon, or the overruling of an unjust judgement by showing laws were violated, as an appeals court. So we will see in biblical Hebrew that the getting of justice from the judge who administers it has a wider range of meaning than is the norm in Greek. Biblical Hebrew covers the outcome of a favorable justice. If anyone has a dispute with this conclusion then I should point out that acquitting the guilty was never considered legal justice, nor was the transfer of a sentence legal, but for illegal forces demanding a ransom for releasing a forgiven party they still wanted to punish. The giving of the ransom defines the administration of justice as forgiveness for the captive party and status of illegality for the slave holders, or whatever other judgment the sinner had been sold to.

However, if all this is objected to, the normal sense of punitive justice can be given good sense. If the king wishes to administer justice for a forgiven captive, then he can allow the enemy to administer justice to a ransom to secure the release of the captive. The enemy's attempt at strict justice would thereby be illegal, and this is why the condemnation of the Son was overturned by his resurrection. By allowing a third party to illegally administer justice, the judge effectively administers forgiving justice to the faithful by disarming the parties who still wish to destroy the faithful. This is less of a stretch than the satisfaction theory.

'Justify' in Biblical Hebrew

Then Avşalom would say, "Who will appoint me judge in the land? And unto me any man may come who has a complaint or matter for judgment, and *I will have gotten him justice*!" (2 Sam. 15:4).

Through knowing him, my righteous servant *will get justice* for many (Isa. 53:11).

And Adŏnai Yăhweң will help me. Therefore, I will not have been humiliated. Therefore, I have set my face like flint, and I known that I will not be ashamed. Near is the *one getting me justice*! Who will dispute with me? Let us stand together! Who is the master of my legal case? Let him draw near to me! Behold, Adŏnai Yăhweң will help me. Who is the one acting wickedly? Behold, all of them like *a garment will wear out. The moth will eat them* (Isa. 50:7-9).

Defend the poor and orphan; for the afflicted and needy, *get justice* (Psa. 82:3).

And those explaining wisdom will shine like the brightness of the firmament. And *those obtaining justice* for the many like the stars forever and onward (Dan. 12:3).

HALOT defines the term הַצְדִיק as: "1. **to obtain rights** [justice] **for**" and cites 2 Sam. 15:4; Isa. 50:8; Psa. 82:3; Dan. 12:3; "2. **to assist someone toward his rights**" and cites Isaiah 53:11! BDB has "1. **do justice**, in administering law." This means that the just one administers favorable justice. In his role as advocate for the guilty, he offers to lay down his life as a guilt offering.

Clearly in these contexts הַצְדִיק does not mean 'justify' in the modern sense, to prove innocent, declare guiltless, innocent, or righteous in a case. But it implies getting a favorable justice for the faithful.

Isaiah 53: The Divine Ransom

¹Who *will* have held faithful to our ˣmessage? And the Arm of Yăhweң upon who will have been revealed? ²And he will have grown up as a tender plant at his face, and as a root from the dry earth. He has no form and no majesty that we may see *in* him, and no appearance that we should desire him, ³being despised and rejected of men, a man of sorrows, and being a knower of malignancy,ⁿ and like one from whom faces are hidden, he is despised, and we will not have con-

---

Isa. 53:1 χ The message is Messiah's ransom, his self sacrifice for us, to battle and defeat our sin, and cleanse and purge the sin away from us by his blood, his life sacrifice. The message is one of divine advocacy for the repentant sinner and those who may repent. It is a message of the messianic servant's battle with sin and injustice on our behalf, wherein he gets victory over it to cleanse us of it. ▷ This view may be called the Ransom explanation or the Christus Victor explanation, but I must say that Christians often come into first contact with the ransom theory, as its enemies wish to present it, in a caricature that serves as a straw man to make it easy for them to reject it. This caricature claims that the ransom view is a payment to Satan, a formal transaction between God and the devil over captives held by Satan. But this is not correct. The cost is not a legal one, and there is no agreement to a formal transaction and exchange, because Satan has no legal claim over the forgiven. Everything Satan and sin do to exact their destructive costs is illegal and lawless by definition. And hostages cannot be held against the power of the Most High. Satan is only given season to destroy the sinner as a form of deterrence if men should fail to use the means of deterrence in the divine law or be too late for repentance. The real enemy is the intrinsic destruction wrought by our sin and Satan's exploitation of the flesh. The ransom represents the divine cost to separate us from our sin and to wipe it away. That cost is exacted by our iniquities, our transgressions and Satan's plots (which is the iniquity of the devil and bene Elohim), which the Most High must bear until he purges them, and particularly the cost of the only kindred Son, the Most High in the flesh, being the Messiah, and suffering as a man even unto death is the climax of the humanly seeable sphere of the divine battle with our sin and the powers who deceive men. To forgive and create the opportunity for it, the Almighty must suffer sin's corruption during the season of repentance. All the ransom costs are exacted by evil, that should it be eliminated too soon would deny men the opportunity to repent. So the longsuffering of the Most High is an expression of his love. **Isa. 53:3** η or 'illness,' 'sickness,' 'disease.' See Gen. 3:15 *you will bruise his heel* (תְּשׁוּפֶנּוּ עָקֵב). In the battle against sin, Messiah suffers to ransom us from it, but in the end gets the victory and crushes Satan. The ransomed of Yăhweң are bought by divine suffering from the

sidered him. ⁴But our malignancies he *will* have carried. And our sorrows—he *will* have been laden with them⸲ And we, we *will* have ᵟconsidered him being smitten, being struck by the Almĭghty, and being made to be afflicted. ⁵But he is being made to be wounded from⸲ our transgressions, being made to be bruised from⸲ our iniquities. The instruction of our wellness is upon him⸲ And in his stripes *will* have been healing for us. ⁶All of us like sheep, we have strayed, each man to his way we have turned. And Yăhweḥ has made meet with ᵋhim the iniquity of ᵖall of us. ⁷He has been oppressed, and he is being afflicted, but he does not open his mouth. As a lamb to sacrifice he is led away, and as a ewe at the face of her shearers will have been dumb, he opens not his mouth. ⁸By force of restraint, and from justice he will have been taken away, and among his

---

world system, and are being cleansed by divine life, represented by the blood of Messiah. **Isa. 53:4** ζ He is laden with our grief. The negative results of sin land on him also. This is not a judicial punishment for sin that he is burdened with. The cost is not exacted by divine justice. But, the cost is taken by sin in the face of the Most High seeking to forgive his faithful ones. It is thus a ransom cost, as when men give their lives to deliver their country in the face of evil invaders.

Isa. 53:4 δ or 'thought.' Of course he wasn't smitten by the Almighty or cursed 'of God.' It is just that the Most High allowed him to meet up in the flesh with our sin to show us his suffering in the spiritual realm. Nations and even creation is part of the ransom cost being given to rescue and purge the faithful. But he is thought by those who misunderstand to be stricken by the Almighty.

Isa. 53:5 ξ Or 'because of' (מִפְּשָׁעֵנוּ and מֵעֲוֹנֹתֵינוּ). The preposition מִן is attached witn nun assimilation. The text is assigning the cause of the servant's suffering to the effects of human sin. Messiah is longsuffering with our sin in the wider picture, and he personally suffers from it to bring it to the place of cleansing. By no means is it necessary to say this means a loading of divine wrath on Messiah to make satisfaction by proxy for divine wrath against sin. The text does not say "for our transgressions" as if a penal exchange is happening. It says "because of" or "from" our transgressions. The suffering is a ransom cost taken by sin, a cup of suffering, the same cup which was drained by Messiah's disciples, because Messiah was a servant to bear the suffering of ransoming us from our sin, and he asked his disciples to also be servants and to serve and not be served.

Isa. 53:5 μ מוּסַר שְׁלוֹמֵנוּ. Paul translates the same words as ἔνδειξιν τῆς δικαιοσύνης αὐτοῦ, "an indication of his justice" once in Rom. 3:25 and once in Rom. 3:26. ἔνδειξιν means **a pointing out or indication, a proof.** The English word *indication* is in fact based on this Greek word. Since the repentant have been forgiven, he bears our sins to cleanse them as the expression of his justice and righteousness for our particular case, that is the case for those who confess their sins. This is explained in 1 Yoḥ. 1:9. The connection between justice and wellness is this: we are made well by forgiveness and cleansing. Messiah's bearing sin and death is our instruction on the cost of this divine decision to indicate his justice (or righteousness), that is his forgiving justice and merciful righteousness. ▷ Adversaries of this truth seek only to present divine justice as strict, and never BENEVOLENT or MERCIFUL, because they perceive the Most High as someone who must be appeased at all times by the satisfaction of strict judicial justice. So they have defined the means of forgiveness as the satisfaction of strict justice! But per Exodus 23:7 and Ezek. 18:20 such a form of justice is illegal. The innocent cannot bear the guilt of the wicked.

Isa. 53:6 ε not 'laid on' but 'meet with' or 'cause to encounter' (הִפְגִּיעַ < פָּגַע). This is an active encounter with evil allowed to light upon Messiah. It is not a judicial penalty. It is recognized as unfair because Messiah was innocent. The divine appointment to meet evil is the same as men charging into battle to eliminate a dangerous and hostile force from ravaging the country. It is thus the intent to meet it and cross swords with it to ransom the people being defended from being destroyed. We hope that the righteous soldier does not die in vain, but that his purchase gains life for others. **Isa. 53:6** ρ 'the iniquity of all of us' (אֵת עֲוֹן כֻּלָּנוּ). As sin was confessed over the escape goat offering (cf. Lev. 16) to make to be wiping (לְכַפֵּר), so also Messiah bears (וְנָשָׂא) ALL OF OUR (כֻּלָּנוּ) iniquity to remove it from us. The sin of Yisra'el that encountered him is symbolic of all of our sin, which Messiah spiritually encounters to cleanse it by his blood (cf. 1 Yoḥ. 1:9). The blood represents the divine life which makes the cleansing (cf. Yoḥ. 6). It is significant that the goat of escape (לַעֲזָאזֵל > עֵז אֹזֵל > אָזַל) remains alive while the goat for cleansing the holy place dies. The first goat represents the divine life given up in suffering to remove contamination from the dwelling of the Most High (heaven and earth), and the second goat represents the sin bearer taking a journey bearing the iniquity to death, yet it remains alive. I believe this points to the resurrection of Messiah. The symbolism

generation who protests when he has been cut off from the land of the living? From the transgressions of my people is a plague for him! ⁹And he is put with the wicked, his grave however with the rich in *consequence of* his violent death, because he had not done violence and no deceit is in his mouth. ¹⁰And Yăhwєң will have been pleased to make his crushing^ω to be the malignancy when his soul makes an ᵠoffense offering. He will see seed. He will make long *his* days. And the pleasure of Yăhwєң in his hand will prosper. ¹¹The labor of his soul he will see.

---

is that of cleansing and removal. The ceremony of the leper is similar with two birds (cf. Lev. 14). The function of the second bird is not to substitute for the first bird as a receiver of divine wrath. Rather, it is for removal of sin and contamination. There is removal of the sin from the dwelling of the Most High, and removal of the sin from the people. ▷ In ancient Assyria, the ritual of the substitute king was used to prevent evil from happening to the king. The evil omen to be avoided was not considered a dispensation of just divine wrath, but rather the fickle badness of the gods and fate, whom it seems could be deceived by the procedure. Therefore the substitute king was set up to deal with it while the real king went incognito and lived as an ordinary man. In the Greek myth, there is an evil omen upon the king, and it is learned that if someone dares to die for the king, then the evil omen will be diverted, and so it comes to pass that no one is willing to die for the king except the king's wife. The evil omen is not regarded in the myth as justly deserved divine wrath. But the one who dies loves the one whom he is ransoming..

Isa. 53:10 ω *dakk'o* (דַּכְּאוֹ) The infinitive construct here is not correctly translated in the versions. Infinitive constructs are often ambiguous in Hebrew, thus either "crushing of him" or "to crush him." The suffix may operate as either an object of the infinitive or the subject. But it isn't "to crush him." It is a reference to his crushing. One way or another evil is crushing Yăhwєң. The only kindred Son reveals to us the crushing upon the Most High in the flesh. He knew it would happen, because he had properly judged what evil would do. He declares or makes this crushing of Messiah the malignancy, as representative of the whole of sin's corruption that needs to be cleansed away. ▷ Most often this verse is explained that Yah "was pleased to crush him," as if the Father was the active agent, but the Piєl helps make clear this is not the case. The Father is a passive agent getting the most good possible out of an existential reality. He is taking his crushing and making it to be the malady. This is opposite of blaming the Most High for crushing Messiah. The malady is crushing him, and not the wrath of God! It is evil that bruises the only kindred Almighty in the heel as he is destroying the works of Satan. ▷ The Piєl injects a causitive emphatic sense to the verb: TO MAKE TO BE or DECLARE TO BE, hence "TO DECLARE TO BE the crushing of him." The middle root doubling is akin to the Hiphil modification of the middle root letter and the Niphal passive combined. ▷ Think of the image of Gandalf making a way of escape over the bridge of Kasadoom, and then the whip of the balrog snags him in the heel and pulls him through death, but Gandalf is raised anew. Tolkein has correctly expressed the ransom of Messiah in the symbolism of his story. The whip represents the serpent striking out at the deliverer. It is the devil, representing sin and lawlessness that crushes Messiah.

Isa. 53:10 ψ אָשָׁם *'asham*. Transgressions are confessed onto the offense offering so that the offense offering carries or bears the sins away from the repentant soul to the altar where the transgressions are wiped away, purged, cleansed, declared null and void, both in effect as to hold any sentence over the forgiven party, and in removal of the sins contaminating effects from the faithful (cf. Lev. 16:30). This is the picture of the offense offering. The offering 'bears' the offenses until they are purged by the blood. The blood represents that the purging costs innocent life, which is the ransom for the soul. In Messiah's case, his divine life is consumed (used up) by the repentant sinner in the restorative and purging operations of the divine Spirit against our sin to remove it from us. The physical sacrifice symbolizes what is necessary in the spiritual realm to purge sin, one becoming the metaphor for the other. Messiah's suffering is a loss to himself. It is the divine expense. ▷ Please note a few points. In Isaiah 53:10 the crushing of Messiah is the malignancy, the sin, which must be purged. The sins of the leaders are representative of all of our sins, and these sins murdered Messiah in his efforts to explain the truth to Israel. He knew this would happen, and it became the ransom cost to put himself before all men, to draw us to him, and to show us the great cost in love he is bearing to bring us his rescue. The cost to the Son is but illustrative in the flesh of the total divine cost to the Most High. In otherwords, it is not the total cost, but a representative cost to the Almighty Son in the flesh. ▷ The words I have translated "the malignancy" are הֶחֱלִי in Hebrew, which are taken as a noun with definite article in Hebrew, and so vowel pointed this way. Remarkably the Septuagent translation from the Hebrew agrees, rendering the words τῆς πληγῆς, "the plague." These are the sins of the people being carried to the place of purging. The offense offering carrying the malignancy of sin represents the divine cost involved in purging away those sins, i.e. the consumption of divine live, represented by Messiah's blood. Also remarkably, the LXX states, "καὶ Κύριος βούλεται καθαρίσαι αὐτὸν τῆς πληγῆς· ἐὰν δῶτε περὶ ἁμαρτίας" (Isa. 53:10).

He shall be satisfied. In knowing him⁴, my righteous servant shall get favorable justice⁷ for many, and their iniquities, he shall carry. ¹²For such, I will make to be a portion for him among the great, and with the strong he shall make to be portioned the plunder, because he has poured out to death his soul, and with transgressors he has been numbered. And he *will* have borne the of sin of many. And for transgressors he makes an meeting.

"And YHWH willed to cleanse him of the plague ... concerning a sin offering." Though not perfectly accurate here, the LXX expresses what is being said. The offense offering bears the transgressions as the advocate unto the place of purging. At the altar it is cleansed. The offering doing the service of ransom serves to provide the life (blood) necessary for the cleansing. The offering indicates the divine cost. It serves as an instruction in the matter of making us well.

▷ Tradition has translated הֶחֱלִי as a Hiphil perfect, but this mistake turns the sentence into grammatical nonsense in combination with an incorrect interpretation of the infinitive construct before it to arrive at "YHWH has been pleased to make to be crushed him--he has made ill--if his soul makes...." This places the cause in the wrong place. All along it is made clear that Messiah is crushed from bearing our iniquities. The Most High only arragned the appointement so that Messiah would meet up with them to battle them and purge them. For this reason the suggestion that the Most High has laid a judicial penalty upon Messiah in addition to the effects of our iniquities upon him is wholly incorrect. In fact, it is a diabolical heresy. The Rock of our Salvation is not to be struck twice, once with our sins and then with divine wrath for our sins. Whoever thus persits in teaching that the son received divine wrath will not be entering into the promised land. Sin is not judicially paid for in forgiveness. It is cleansed away by the blood of Messiah, which is the ransom for many. A ransom is as a soldier enters suffers in battle for the lives of others.

Isa. 53:11 μ בְּדַעְתּוֹ. This is another infinitive construct. It is ambiguous, "in knowing of him" which may be through his knowledge or in knowing him. It is certain that the text means the latter, according to the explanation in 1 Yoh. 2:3-4. It is by beholding the divine Son of a willing heart that we are transformed into his likeness through the renewing of our minds. Or to put it another way, the seed of the word, which is manifest in the Son is sown in the willing heart and unites with it so that we will have been getting begotten of the Almighty. Some versions put this rightly. It is through knowing the divine servant that the faithful become repentant, because he draws them to the Father's forgiveness through his sacrifice.

Isa. 53:11 π צַדִּיק. The sense here is strictly 'get justice' or 'make justice' according to the story of Aḇşalom, 'father of peace.' The king's son serves as a messianic type. Even though it was with evil intent that he acted to overthrow the kingdom, he illustrates the good news. David himself is a messianic type, yet he committed a great sin. So also is Aḇşalom. So to get the parable correctly, we simply have to re-explain the elements that do not strictly speaking fit the divine analogy. Now in David's realm citizens of the kingdom were not getting their cases heard due to corruption in the kingdom (no doubt partly contributed to by the king's sin). There were injustices to be righted. Now as you can imagine one of the greatest injustices is the failure to forgive a debt that should be forgiven. Those seeking justice from Aḇşalom were those who were not getting it. So he declared that he would get justice for them by getting them a hearing. Thus debts that should be forgiven were brought to court to be enforced. Property that was being illegally retained by a stronger party was made to be returned. Injury compensation that was not being made was compelled by judgment at law, and fines that were not paid were enforced for the sake of those seeking justice and were supposed to benefit from their payment. This illustrates the meaning of the Hebrew word צַדִּיק, which means in this sense 'make justice,' or to get justice, with the connotation of it being favorable for those seeking it. ▷ So as the story proceeds, the scene changes. In the course of getting favorable justice where it was ordinarily not granted, (Please consider the norm of strict justice vs. the exception of forgiveness,) rebellion increased in the kingdom and threatened to destroy the whole kingdom. So it happened that Aḇşalom, whom the king loved dearly, died to ransom his kingdom. This was because Yo'av had him put to death knowing that failure to do so would only encourage more rebellion. But we see that it was the king's sin in this case that led to the rebellion among his sons, and thus it was at the cost of four sons that the kingdom was ransomed from the evil brought on it by the adultery, the child of adultery, Amnon, Aḇşalom, and Adoniyah. Thus the Most High gives nations and princes for the ransom of his own people, and he did not spare his own Son from intercepting the destructive train of sin on our behalf. ▷ Was the life of the son of adultery taken as a substitute for divine wrath upon the king? By no means! This view is high heresy and Satanic doctrine. The Word says, "The soul, the one sinning, it shall die. A son shall not bear on iniquity of the father, and a father will not bear on the iniquity of the son. The righteousness of the righteous is upon himself, and the wickedness of the wicked shall be upon himself" (Ezek. 18:20). In 2 Sam. 12:14 the reason is given, "because spurning you have spurned the enemies of Yăhweн in this matter, also the son the one born to you dying shall die." Thus the Most High is compelled

to take the life of the son to save his kingdom from destruction by his enemies. So the picture here is a ransom. And because this son does this service for the kingdom, David says, "I am going unto him, and he does not return unto me" (2 Sam. 12:23). And so he speaks of the resurrection of the righteous. The ransom is on account the enemies, and not on account of divine wrath, because David was forgiven.

Historical Summary

In the notes I have explained the suffering servant in terms of the ransom truth. This truth may be illustrated in many ways in the Scripture. For example the people ransomed Yonatan from Sha'ul when he wanted to exact strict justice upon him (וַיִּפְדּוּ) (cf. 1 Sam. 14:45). So the people bore the threat and risk of the king's unjustified wrath and unwise decision to deliver the kings son. Now the penal substitition metanarrative is a recent innovation of Evangelical Christianity, first starting with Anselm, and then becoming more fully developed under Calvin and Luther in the late 1500's and 1600's. The people saw the problem and so the reformation began, but seeing the problem does not mean knowing the solution. For this reason the people were deceived and their good intentions are brought to nothing by Satan's counter narrative, which re-explains the meaning of Messiah's death as a satisfaction of strict penal justice. These views do not produce the repentance and faithfulness that the Almighty is seeking, but rather they keep an accurate understanding of the truth from them, and therefore delay the urgency of repentance, which costs many their salvation, because they are still in their sins, and become hardened.

Whenever you hear a teacher say Jesus paid the penalty of sin, or that he suffered the wrath of God they are teaching heresy, and against the justice of God. This teaching results in satanically induced miasma (cognitive confusion) concerning the forgiveness of the Father, and the condition of holding faithful to him by keeping his commandments for receiving it. Also usually when Evangelicals say or hear that *Jesus died for their sin*, they only think of penal substitution, and not of Messiah meeting up with our sin to battle it, defeat it, and cleanse it, bearing its cost as he is the ransom for those he defending, just like a soldier decontaminates the war zone, assuming risk and suffering to deliver others.

Witness To The Truth

This is my testimony to all the faithful, who know the truth in part, who know Messiah Yĕshua, who says ANI HU. It is also to those who need to learn more, and also a rebuke to those who think they know something and who are leading those who never knew our Almighty into cults that attack us, and also who even lead some of the chosen astray, presenting themselves as messengers of light, but who are working for Satan.

I give it not lightly, or because I need to boast, but because I see the destruction and stunted growth happening among the faithful, and have witnessed it in myself, and I see also the destruction of those seeking, but who cannot find, because no one can give them the truth, and because none can give the truth without mixing it with error.

I grew up in an Evangelical Christian home where we were taught basic morality, the forgiveness of sin, and the Scripture, and for this reason the Spirit had a voice, and would direct us little faithful ones, and answer prayers. But I was raised in a Church and Missionary culture with loads of false doctrine added on to the basic truth. The word of man made it difficult to hear the Spirit. Coming out of my teens, I soon discovered that not all Christians agreed on what correct teaching was. I also began to discover contradictions between what I'd absorbed or was told and the Scripture.

At first I was fearful to question anything, because the first thing the Pastors do when you get out of line is to threaten your salvation, perhaps not directly, but implicitly. The only rescue I had from this was the forgiveness of sins and basic morality, but I was given a rotten intellectual foundation against it. And little did I know how rotten it was.

Firstly, what was constantly preached from the pulpit was that salvation consisted of believe only, and woe to you if there was any suggestion of adding anything to to belief except trust in God's promises. Indeed, some preached that it was only necessary to have one genuine moment of belief, and then you could not loose your salvation. But I thank the Most High that I was introduced at a young age to the book of John, and key verses, e.g. if you love me you will keep my commandments. This meant basic morality. So I

know that one had to continue in belief. It could not just be a one time experience. Nevertheless, the idea of just believing continued to dominiate my thinking for a long time. It was emotionally embedded in my mind.

Let me make it clear that I never regarded myself as outside the faithfulness necessary to salvation except for some brief occassions, and still do not. I am here speaking in theological hindsight when I use the term faithfulness, but when you trust that you have been forgiven, and then the Spĭrit tells you that you cannot commit sins that you clearly know are sins, then you listen. This does not mean the intellecual problems and the false doctrines went away, but it does mean knowing that you can walk in the loving-kindess of the Most High, and that you can so walk even when misinformed. But lies are inducements and temptations to sin, and indeed, though one may be getting rescued and still have sins of ignorance, even these can lead to corruption of the faithful walk.

Christians are constantly induced to become anti-intellecutal, but nothing destroys this false doctrine as fast as learning the facts about some particular false doctrine that leads you to the truth. It was first the pretribulation rapture delusion that went down. This was because no one claimed it was a matter of salvation. But the solution was clearly intellecual thoughtfulness in reading Scripture vs. believing dogmatism.

Matters became more serious when I encountered John Stott and John Wenham, and learned that some Christians did not believe in the eternal torment doctrine, and that they could not just be summarily shoved out of the Church as heretics. I continued in the assurance of the Spĭrit when I dismissed eternal torment. But I was also eager to embrace this newly discovered truth.

Then I discovered that the popular chronology of the Passion did not fit with the facts. He died on a Wednesday, and that thanks to Ralph Woodrow and the Companion Bible. Then Gŏd decided to introduce me to his Sabbath. First contact was via a lady in the Seventh Day Baptist Church who did bread demonstrations with the Bosch Mixer and Magic Mill. I have the Magic Mill now. But I did not know she was a Seventh Day Baptist. But somehow a tract appeared in our house when I was 15 or 16. I looked at it breifly, but it did not register with me.

When I was 20, I was taking a calculus class and I was a bus riding companion with this gorgeous Chilean girl. I did not notice this at first though. But I soon learned that she did not believe in Hell. A little bit of conversation cleared up that she did believe in Hell, just not the eternal torment doctrine. So I told her I agreed with her. Her next question was, what about the Sabbath? So when I got to my parents house, I took out the concordance and looked up all the passages. Nope, nothing specifically saying not to observe the Sabbath, except a few puzzling passages. And then after a while the Spĭrit is saying to me that I should observe the Sabbath. But then all I had been taught about keeping this law would mean I wasn't just believing anymore and I was trying to earn my salvation. But the Spĭrit answered me: your sins are forgiven are they not? Yes, and so there is nothing to fear from keeping this law. After a while this knowledge was combined with the fact that I knew it was evil for those people who threatened others with loss of salvation just for obeying a biblical command when the basis of salvation was forgiveness. A few days later I was convicted to honor the Sabbath command. But my dad was clearly of the opinion that dabbling in the law meant loss of salvation, but he really did not have the courage to say what he thought except to my mother.

First, he brought an older man to remonstrate with me about Romans 14 and Colossians 2. But I had been doing some thinking, and Romans 14 went down as fasting and Colossians 2 I do not remember what answer I gave, but the encounter was tense and confrontational. But the Spĭrit was happy with my answers, and gave me no cause for alarm. After a while, my dad took me to visit Dr. George Giakumakis: Who is this scholar?

In 1978, Young handed over responsibility for the Institute of Holy Land studies to another Evangelical Zionist, George Giakumakis, and launched the BFP, an Evangelical organization that was to engage in practical work within Israeli society and in building bridges between Israel and Evangelicals (Hanson 2012, 267).

In 1979 van der Hoeven was involved with several other Evangelicals—Robert Lindsey, the pastor of the Baptist congregation in Jerusalem; David Bivin, another North American Baptist who ran a Hebrew school in Jerusalem; Canadian couple Marvin and Merla Watson; Douglas Young; George Giakumakis; and others—in founding a small prayer community that they called the Almond Tree Branch (Ariel 1997). It was this community that, in '79, launched the first Feast of Tabernacles celebration that has since become the most visible expression of the ICEJ. The rationale for this celebration came from van der Hoeven: according to his reading of Zech. 14:15 gentiles were also commanded to gather in Jerusalem during Sukkoth and it was unscriptural, he argued, that Christians celebrated only two pilgrimage feasts (Easter and Pentecost) while three (including Sukkoth) were actually mentioned in the Bible.

I did not know any of this then. I don't think my dad knew this much either, but we both respected Dr. Giakumakis. It was in 1982 that I asked this question of George in the presence of my Dad, "Is there anything an the New Testament against the Sabbath?" The answer was an unqualified "No." I don't think my dad expected this answer. Because he was raised on the theology of rabid anti-law theologian Lewis Sperry Chafer and C.I. Scofield. Bam, west meets east. George was not confrontational like the other man, but I'm sure my dad was confronted.

The Seventh Day Adventist Church did not last long with me. The Spĭrit of Měssiah did not let me fall under the influence of what they call the spirit of prophecy. I went to the Seventh Baptist Church where there was freedom from spiritual repression. Besides E.G.W., I left the SDA's because one of their elders

proclaimed it heresy to think that Mĕssiah died on a Wednesday. I began to take up the study of Hebrew and Greek, and crossed swords more than once with Samuele Bacchiocchi, and there was a particularly disagreeable confrontation with Desmond Ford. But my study of Greek led me to propose a different reading of Colossians 2:16 to Desmond Ford at a forum with Walter Martin. I think it made it onto a radio show. A little success was all it took to keep me studying the original languages.

I did not discover things by the route many others did, but the result is often the same. I read in the Greek that Mĕssiah rose "on the first of the Sabbaths," and this was the subject of Dr. Ford's nasty rebuke in the foyer of the Old SDB Church. This did not phase me a bit, but I was always looking for the flaw in my own arguments, because when faced with a contradiction of points of view or interpretation or translation, I knew I had to gain knowledge of all the legitimate choices before giving up. Invariably the pattern was to first learn enough to get stuck, then ask the Spĭrit for an answer, and then a solution presents itself and the way forward is opened again.

In those years I crossed paths with Rivi Litvin, and Israeli follower of Yeshua who lectured in Churches. I showed her the verses in Lev. 23:15 about counting Sabbaths. She was puzzled. I don't think it crossed her mind until then either.

I married an SDB Pastor's daugher, a PK as they call them, and also an MK, because my wife was born on the mission field in British Guyana. And my father in law, who just turned 97 a few days before my 58th birthday had pretty much given up Pastoring SDB Churches by then. He had left the SDA's for pretty much the same reasons I never joined them. He had a heart for the good news, but was never a deep intellectual like myself.

My wife Valerie has a middle name, the name of an SDB lady who provided what I needed most in the SDB Church, and that is love and friendship. Though I was probably too cerebral to really realize how much I needed that. A lot of chronological research got done in her rental.

We were married and keeping the feast days, but I knew the Rabbinic calendar did not work with the Passion Chronology. So I was using the conjunction in AD 33 instead of postponement rules. But then it came to my notice that the more ancient Jewish tradition used a sighted moon to set the calendar. I went to the UC Riverside library, where I had received a degree in 1989, and looked over the Mishnah and Talmud on this. It was so. So typed in computer code to calculate this. Of course many are afraid of tradition, but tradition does preserve historical practices, and I knew very well that going against a majority testimony from the past like this would be a big monkey-wrench in the works.

I had concluded, so if the moon was sighted, then AD 33 is not going to work at all, not with Wednesday and first of the Sabbaths. I knew enough about Daniel 9 and the chronology to know that it was not going to be AD 30 to 32 either. I knew the historicist and preterist views of Daniel 9 were also bunk, because you see I was not anti-Temple nor anti-Levitical, which is of course the real reason why Daniel 9:27 is misinterpreted by the Church. Before I ran the calculation for the results, I knew that only AD 34 could work with the sighted moon if anything could work. Otherwise the whole project would end with a contradiction that could not be resolved, viz. Scripture vs. its own cultural context as made plain in traditional sources. So it was with not a little fear and hope that I ran the calculation. At once it showed it was possible. I ran it again. Yes it did check. I checked the code and ran it again. I was elated. Eventually I found Finegan's Handbook also confirmed the result. I was most thankful to the Most High that day sometime in the early 1990's.

About this time I was able to satisfactorily explain Galatians 4:10 for myself. Paul was not rejecting biblical holy days there. He was rejecting the Qumran cult's calendar. Also, before this, I was encouraged to find that the main Jewish interpretation of Shavu'ot (aka Pentecost) agreed with my research on "first of the Sabbaths." About this time a pro life doctor split off from the Riverside Church and formed a new fellowship in Lake Elsinore, because pro-abortion doctors were tolerated in that Church, a thing I was never happy about. Around then I discovered that Matthew 28:1a naturally reads in Greek, "And the later of the Sabbaths...." This was huge breakthrough.

At the same time historical research was dropping into place. The main Jewish traditional histories were in agreement, and I was learning good methodology in research. A literal interpretation is best unless proven otherwise, and one should always be careful to establish what the norms for words are in ancient languages. All too often a translation is based on someone who wants an exception to the rule so that they can rubber stamp their late tradition.

During these times I would travel to libraries in California, UCR, U of Redlands, Fuller Seminary, Loma Linda University, and La Sierra. I discovered George Smith at the Loma Linda. Later I would visit Lawrence U and U of Madison Wisconsin Libraries, and also Trinity Evangelical Divinity School. I borrowed and bought books form many places. Most of this was pre-internet or early internet. I browsed the bookshelf of every scholar I visited. Dr. David Nobel's bookshelf yielded one of Martin's books. A bookstore in Loma Linda, the Concordant Greek Text. I read reading the JBL off the stacks at UCR.

Now, I also discovered that a number of passages could be translated, "the faithfulness of Messiah" instead of "faith in Messiah." And not only that, but an important faction of top ranking scholars was in favor of this translation! It was all within the rules, and not without precedent either. The Spĭrit really did seem to be up to something here, but the theology track would lag behind the chronological one by a good ten years. You see I learned Calvinism by osmosis without actually believing in it, and also the imputed righteousness business did not make any sense to me, but I hadn't a clue how to address that problem.

I was already open to basic Arminian assumptions when a little book by Richard Rice came along, and then one by John Sanders as well as the ground

breaker Clark Pinnock. Gregory Boyd was somewhat confusing, but I get ahead of the story. This was all in the background, and it was the Spirit leading me to the chronological solution that would give me the confidence and hutzpah to tackle an even greater theological disaster in the Church. It is a good thing I was steered away from seminary, and a good thing I was led to figure the chronology first, before the theology.

With the year AD 34 in hand I was able to fit Daniel 9 together, that is, there was now enough time between the start date of the prophecy and the end date of the prophecy to fit the prescribed number of Sabbatical years. You see unlike the calendar cults that ignore historical tradition and archaeological research I paid attention to it all. And for the Churches that claimed they could explain it in accord with past history and new archaeological discoveries, well I found out where all the bodies were buried. Just for example, that Sir Robert Anderson's calculation was invalid because really the claimed month of Nisan for the start point was the last month of the old year. Or for example that the Church had corrupted the order of Ezra-Nehemiah so as to support their historicist and preterist interpretations of Daniel 9. Thank's to the Companion Bible, I was again equiped with the solution before I needed it. Nehemiah governed first. Ezra was there, of course, but not the running the government, and then 49 nine years later he went and returned with a fresh Aliyah under Artaxerxes II to take care of the disaster the previous Persian governor had caused for the Temple. So now I had the explanation of the "seven sevens" in Daniel 9, which fit perfectly into the known ancient near eastern chronology handed down to us by history and confirmed by the archaeologists digging up Mesopotamian libraries.

Having multiple instances of overlooked or unexplained or mistranslated texts all fall into line to support a single answer was good objective confirmation that the answer was correct, and not based on subjective experience, wishful thinking, made up stories like the cults, or traditions handed down from Church and Synagogue which simply did not agree with older traditions. One thing that eluded me was the answer to the misleading Hebrew exegesis of Judges 11 given by Martin Antsey.

But this was not to be the end. Zeal and the Spirit pushed me farther and harder. I could now figure when the Sabbatical year was. I so figured, and then was happy to learn that Bennedict Zuckermann had allowed for my solution as one of his two possibilities. Now I had this little book by David Cooper and also Martin Antsey's Chronology. They are good chronologies, but I had been taught by the Spirit to look for the flaws by checking every reference and every fact to see if anything was contradicted.

In other words, I war gamed as many alternate interpretations as I could think of at key points. I would look at the anomalies, because anomalies are usually evidence that someone made a mistake of some sort. I was doing this because I needed myself to be completely confident of the result. And it is necessary if one is trying to find a lost answer.

I realized that the 390 and 40 years mentioned by Ezekiel should actually exist in Israel's history, as separate periods each. I was to find out later that Rabbinical chronologists had before tried to implement the same idea. So this confirmation from the tradition was just another star lining up. They had, in fact, nearly solved the problem. But it was clear their late traditions prevented the conclusion of it. Eventually I realized that to find all these years only required a twenty year addition to the aforementioned chronologies in one place.

I was able to figure when the Jubilee was, using just two data points, and I had printed up charts by this time, an early edition of the chronology. One day I was attending to Saul a son of a year, yea two years he hath reigned, and then I read the next verses in 1 Samuel 13 and realized that Saul was blowing the Jubilee Trumpet! And just as Isaiah's prophecy had alluded to the Jubilee and Sabbatical year, so also was this text. And it was with fear and trepidation that I realized this would be a critical test of what I had already discovered! What were the chances that very year in the charts I had drawn up would be the Jubilee year? I lost no time in looking it up, and wonder of wonders, it was a Jubilee year. I was rejoicing and elated. The square for that year was colored in gold, the color I used for the Jubilee. Nothing is more joyful than working out a discovery only to find out later that the Scripture will again confirm it. This was just as dramatic as finding out that the sighted moon worked out for AD 34.

Can you imagine that just reading the Greek of the resurrection passages and taking Leviticus 23:15 seriously led to all of this? Well you would have to be in my shoes to see it, because this odyssey was like the Yam Suf opening up. And I have seen, witnessed, and do testify that honest scientific research and history does line up with what is literally in the writings of the Evangelists. And I attribute this correspondence to the work of the Almighty in text and in history, and that I have been priviledged to discover the work of his hands. I teach this so that you also can hold faithful to Mĕssiah Yĕshua, and keep his appointed times and his law fully and accurately in the knowledge that all these things bear witness to the uiltimate truth.

I teach this so that you will not be disturbed by wolves and calendar cults that seek to divide the faithful against one another with disputes about the Law. I teach this so that you will know the truth with complete certainty, and will be able to judge those who hide behind a veil of light, divinely claimed authority, and lying testimony, not so that you can figure out what is really deceiving them behind the fascade, because only the Spirit knows this, but so that you can objectively judge the teaching to be false. But the more outlandish their teaching the more likely that someone is blaspheming the witness of the Holy Spirit, and I know and bear witness that it is not I.

Now with the confidence of the leading of the Spirit throughout this pilgrimage, I have applied the same zeal and research habits to our corrupted translations and the lies in false theology that we have inherited. I knew the amount of time and effort it took

to just gain a foundation that the Spĭrit could work with. If you don't know what the alternatives are and the vocabulary is, the Spĭrit cannot point you to one or the other. That is why you need to study and apply yourself to the word.

I have been translating portions of the NT since about 1990, but to say the least, I only knew enough Greek then to get into trouble and to understand the different disputes going on in scholarship. My method of seeking the truth was not to memorize vocabulary lists or to become fluent at reading. That's a good way to just end up agreeing with what tradition gives you. No what I did instead was to use logic and reason guided by the Spĭrit to locate the focal points or key texts causing problems and then study everything in and surrounding that text, and then to copy out, and look up every Greek or Hebrew word in that text to discover if there was a solution just based on the definitions of the words given in the dictionaries. This was often combined with a word study of every occurence of key terms in the Scripture using Greek or Hebrew concordances.

This, suprisingly, led to stunningly neat solutions that reduced the apparent dissonance and entropy of the unified message of Scripture. And this was just based on the normal meanings of the words. I need not review all the solutions. They are printed up in the Good News of Messiah and my other books. This is a testimony and witness after all. So I will confine myself to the climactic points. I soon realized that the study of Greek and Hebrew grammar was critically important to my task. As a result my shelves are full of grammar books on Greek and Hebrew as well as Lexicons in both languages, including Aramaic and Syriac, and even a smattering of Latin. But these are just tools.

One has to at first loose their fear of being corrected to discover the truth one has been lied to about. As I mentioned before, one has to rest in the forgiveness of one's own sins and then as the Spĭrit directs avoid becoming corrupt by jumping back into sin. If you listen, then the Spĭrit can work with you. That is my testimony. You may be far down, but if you are sorry for your sin and turn your heart from it to the rescuer, the Almĭghty Sŏn, then he is faithful and just to forgive your sin and cleanse you from all unrighteousness. Beware, there are many spiritual abusers lurking among the faithful who will find ways to come between your conscience and the Spĭrit of the Most High. The mystery of iniquity is alive and well, and dresses itself in lambskin. Listen to the Spĭrit and your conscience, because it is He who writes the Law on your heart to know what is good and evil. It is he who brings the word of faithfulness near you.

As I mentioned before, I discovered that faith is really faithfulness, that is loyalty. I already knew that Church is Assembly, and Apostle was Emissary, and that baptism was immersion.

Now early on, in the period were I believed in believing only, I had come to the conclusion that when Paul spoke negatively of works or of the law that he meant trying to earn forgiveness by works. So then, good works and obedience was not bad in itself. But works to pay for or earn forgiveness was.

I can remember a Jewish lady. Joy was her name. In the late 1980's she invited me to her home one Sabbath and we discussed Daniel 9. I was still under the spell of Sir Robert Anderson's revised theory (BC 444 to AD 33) at the time. So we drove down toward San Diego to attend a congregation of mostly non-Jewish Sabbath observers, who also observed the Jewish feasts, like we did. And there, I entered into a conversation with the elders who were of the opinion that one had to obey and do good works to seek after everlasting life.

This definitely was not believe only, and I argued with it using with just about everything I had learned from the Scofieldites (mostly Romans 4:5), not formally, but just by causual absorption. Someone quoted 1 Timothy 6:12, "Lay hold on eternal life." And this text bothered me, because it suggested that everlasting life wasn't quite laid hold on yet. And verses 18-19 was even more bothersome,

"[18]That they do good, that they be rich in good works, ready to distribute, willing to communicate, [19] Laying up in store for themselves a good foundation against the time to come, <u>that</u> they may lay hold on eternal life" (KJV).

What was most disturbing was the word "that" (ἵνα) in vs. 19. Needless to say, I couldn't argue against the text. But I was also stymied because of a host of other interpretations I had learned from Romans 4.

I was next challenged on this at a Seventh Day Baptist Conference, where one scholar whom I respected, because he observed the Shabbat, had been to Israel and held to Mĕssiah, and had a Ph.d. in Hebrew from U.W. Madison, when I had said something down the lines of if you believed, but sinned wilfully, then you could still be saved. And he replied that he would not say that. To say the least I could still not see the error. And that week was a really low point in my life, because you see I was chasing the girls without much discretion. It was nothing very serious, since I had been well protected to that point and didn't really know how to misbehave, but serious enough to be fighting serious guilt at the intellectual level. Furthermore, there was really bad stuff happening in the culture of that Church, and hardly any restraint or rebukes were coming from the elders. I remember one friend from back home who announced she wished at one time to walk on the dark side, and did so by being promiscuous. She also told me about having gotten drunk and then being raped once while in a stupor. Somehow I excused her behavior, but my heart did not feel right about it. And though the elders turned a blind eye to the general culture, the Spĭrit did not and was still speaking to me. So a spirit of licentiousness was present in that Church. I soon realized by experiencing the guilt of kissing outside of marriage that I could not actually believe in my doctrinal position that I had confidently announced to Paul. My brief experience with real sin showed me otherwise. So I stopped. It was almost as if the Spĭrit had said, "See I told you so!"

I ended up writing letters to one of those young women for two years. Then I married her under a

huppah, and Paul officiated. But at the intellecutual level even early in our marriage I was still uttering believe only nonsense.

First I found out that faith is faithfulness. Then I noticed the word faithful, and it was obvious that that pesky word "believe" which in Greek was just the verb form of the other two words simply did not communicate the same thing. I tried out "trusting faithfulness" and "faithful trusting," and some of my friends will remember this about 20 years ago. But when I turned to Biblical Hebrew it became plain that giving support to someone was not just limited to trust or trust and believe, but could actually involve showing the loyalty by obeying the person one trusted. I noticed that scholars tried to drag this sense out of believe and faith by claiming that those two things produce good works. But this is not the same as saying whether the words contain an imperative to love and obey.

I kid you not. I looked up every form of the verb, noun, and adjective, and related words in Hebrew and looked at all their contexts. I massively did the same for the Greek equivalents, which is over 500x for just that language alone. How could I find concordance in these terms?

Now at the same time I was working on this, I was also working on the word "justify." It was plain that God does not justify the wrong doer, yet Paul is saying he justifies the ungodly. I began to locate more texts like 1 Timothy 6:12-19, such as Romans. 2:7. I had stopped repeating the believe only nonsense not long after our marriage. There is this thing however that is so deeply emotionally seated that you cannot let it go, especially when you have heard your share of Chaferites pounding the idea into your head with hell fire and brimstone for as long as you can remember. I think it takes some divine delieverance to realize that it is false doctrine at an emotional level.

After the first edition or so of GNM I realized that compounding trust with faithfulness was not the limited force of the verb in Greek. That track was in fact an uneasy compromise that scholars took in the face of evidence that the word simply was not limited to believe only. The verb was in fact derived from the adjective, faithful, as many verbs are based on adjectives, and it meant to *be faithful*. But I had to discover an English helping verb that would allow it to show its various usages in contexts switching between factual objects and the personal object of Messiah. So at first I compounded a Hebrew sense to the Greek, to affirm or confirm faithfulness. This worked perfectly from the scholars point of view of translation English, but it was a bit awkward for normal reading.

Now as I said, what kept me going in all of this was the success the Spĭrit had granted me with the chronology. And knowing that was so wrong, I was willing to suspect that the theology of these basic words could also be just as wrong! And while I had some confidence that a solution would emerge, the road was long and hard, and if I had been shown the mountain I'd have to climb at the beginning, I am not sure I would have attempted it!

So it was after pouring over some classical Greek usages that I hit on the combination, "to hold faithful" and this was just perfect because now one could hold faithful to the prophets, and this meant you believed them, or you could hold faithful to Messiah, and this meant that you obeyed him.

The emotional hinderences finally crumbled away after I read Jacob Neusner and Arthur Marmorstein's book on the Jewish doctrine of the merit of the fathers. Then it was that I knew for sure what Paul was talking about in opposing works. The man who does not work is the one who does not perform zechut to gain forgiveness. But it is still necessary to obey the commandments to remain (abide) in the favor of the Most High. Now up to this discovery in Judaism I'd known it was the answer since as far back as 1990 or so, but hadn't had the historical ammunition to make the argument convincingly. I had just what I would call a logical lacuna that would fit the explanation. And indeed, this explanation was in the domain of the old Paul perspective somewhat, but it was being confused with the old ceremonial perspective, which was now being touted as the new perspective, and it turned out that Jerome's Ceremonial Law equation is the so called new perspective. But I was now able to pull this apart and make the right distinctions.

It was in fact necessary for Gŏd to find someone who never went to seminary, never earned a Ph.d, never had to write a disseration, and then have it approved. He needed someone with the blankest slate possible and the least corruption. And I can tell you that Christian theology, translation, and tradition, is terminally corrupt. And this, of course, kept me checking every which way to be sure I wasn't contradicting some actual fact. This is why I studied them so thoroughly. I asked myself, what is it that makes these theologians so sure they have the truth in the face of contradictions. Then I keep looking and having reviewed all the facts find that there is nothing holding up their opinion at all. It must therefore, then be in error.

What prepared me for this work was the a foundation in logic thanks to Francis Schaeffer, which I took seriously, then sucessful experience in applying this to the chronological puzzle. There were a sufficient number of translational problems that had to be solved this way to prepare me. I saw the corruption in the chronology, and after finding the solution, I knew that I should not let men pressure me into one direction or the other, as they could be the problem. Well I can say, they are the problem, and now I can prove it very quickly to anyone who can still listen. For that which took years to discover from having nothing can now be your treasure.

Daniel Gregg, AD 2022.

Second Thessalonians

1 ¹Paul and Silvanus and Timothy, to the assembly of the Thessalonians in the Almĭghty our Făther and Adŏnai Yĕshua the Anŏinted: ²Loving-kindness to you and peace from the Almĭghty: the Făther and Adŏnai Yĕshua the Anŏinted.

³We ought always to give thanks to the Almĭghty for you, brothers, as is fitting, because your faithfulness is greatly enlarged, and the love of each one of you toward one another grows ever greater. ⁴Therefore, we ourselves speak proudly of you among the assemblies of the Almĭghty because of your patient endurance and faithfulness in the midst of all your persecutions and afflictions which you endure, ⁵which are a plain indication of the Almĭghty's righteous judgment, to the end that you should be found worthy^γ of the kingdom of the Almĭghty, on behalf of which indeed you are suffering. ⁶Because after all it is just for the Almĭghty to repay with affliction those who afflict you, ⁷and to give relief to you who are afflicted, and to us as well when Adŏnai Yĕshua will be revealed from heaven with his mighty messengers in flaming fire, ⁸dealing out retribution to those who have not been knowing the Almĭghty and to those who do not obey the good news of our Adŏnai Yĕshua, ⁹who will suffer the penalty of everlasting destruction from the face of Yăhweн and from the glory of his power, ¹⁰whenever he may have come to be glorified in his holy ones and to be amazed at among all those who held faithful, because our testimony to you will have been proved faithful in that day, ¹¹for which also we are always praying concerning you, that our Almĭghty will have counted you worthy of our calling, and will have fulfilled every good desire for goodness and work of faithfulness with power, ¹²in order that the name of our Adŏnai Yĕshua will have been glorified in you, and you in him, according to the loving-kindness of our Almĭghty and Adŏnai, Yĕshua the Anŏinted.

2 ¹Now we are imploring you, brothers, with regard to the ^α coming presence of our Adŏnai Yĕshua the Anŏinted and our great congregation with him, ²that you should not be quickly shaken from sensible thinking or be disturbed either by a spirit or a word or a letter as if from us, as that *says* the day of Yăhweн has been standing by. ³May no one have deceived you in any way, because *it will not be yet except the rebellion^γ may have firstly come and the man^χ of lawlessness may have been revealed*, the son of destruction, ⁴who opposes and exalts himself above all being called god or object of worship, so besides having sat himself down in the temple of the Almĭghty, *he is* displaying himself, that 'he is god^χ.'

1:5 γ cf. 1:11; Luke 20:35; Titus 3:5 note. **2:1** α or "presence," "advent." **2:3** γ or "apostacy." See Dan. 9:24, 27; Mat. 24:12, 15. Rev. 11:2; 13:1-10. **2:3** χ HE SHALL INTEND TO CHANGE THE APPOINTED TIMES AND THE LAW. AND THEY, THE HOLY ONES, WILL BE GIVEN INTO HIS HAND FOR A TIME, TIMES, AND A DIVISION OF A TIME (Dan. 7:25). **2:4** χ AND UNTO THE PRINCE OF THE *heavenly* HOST HE WILL HAVE BEEN EXALTED, AND FROM HIM, WILL HAVE BEEN EXPROPRIATED THE CONTINUAL DAILY OFFERING, AND WILL HAVE BEEN THROWN DOWN THE SITE OF HIS HOLY PLACE. AND THE HORN WILL GIVE HIMSELF A HOST OVER THE CONTINUAL OFFERING THROUGH TRANSGRESSION,

⁵Do you not remember that while I was still with you, I was telling you these things? ⁶And you have been knowing what is holding *him* now, so that in his time he may be revealed, ⁷because the ᵏ*mystery of lawlessness is already working. Only the thing now holding *him will do so* until OUT OF THE MIDST HE MAY HAVE ARISEN^ψ. ⁸And then that lawless one will be revealed whom Yăhweн will slay with the breath of his mouth and bring to an end by the appearance of his coming presence, ⁹that is, the one whose presence is in accord with the activity of Satan, with all power and signs and false wonders, ¹⁰and with all the deception of wickedness for those perishing, because they did not receive the love of the truth that they may be rescued.

¹¹And for this reason the Almĭghty will send upon them a deluding influence so that they may trust what is false, ¹²in order that they all will have been judged who did not hold faithful *to* the Truth, but took pleasure in wickedness.

¹³But we should always give thanks to the Almĭghty for you, brothers, who have been getting loved by Yăhweн, because the Almĭghty has chosen you as the first-fruit for deliverance through being made holy, by the Spĭrit and faithfulness in the truth. ¹⁴And it was for this he called you through our good news, that you may gain the glory of our Adŏnai Yĕshua the Anŏinted.

AND IT WILL CAST TRUTH DOWN TO THE GROUND. AND IT WILL HAVE ACCOMPLISHED AND WILL HAVE PROSPERED…AS FAR AS 2300 EVENING DAYBREAK [OFFERINGS], THEN THE HOLY PLACE WILL BE RIGHTED (Dan. 8:11-14). UNTIL THE END … IS POURED OUT ON THE DESOLATOR (Dan. 9:27). BETWEEN THE SEAS OF THE BEAUTIFUL HOLY MOUNTAIN…HE WILL HAVE COME TO HIS END (Dan. 11:45). UNTIL WHEN IS THE END OF THESE AMAZING WONDERS? FROM THE TIME OF BEING REMOVED THE CONTINUAL OFFERING, AND IS SET UP THE ABOMINATION OF DESOLATION, DAYS 1290 (Dan. 12:7, 11) ▷ None of this happened under Antiochus IV, because he did not perish in the place prophesied, because the Temple was restored after 1104 days, and because Messiah put fulfillment of the abomination of desolation in the future in Mat. 24:15 and Mark 13:14. Messiah means the abomination spoken of by Daniel (cf. Mat. 24:15) which refers to Dan. 8:14, 9:27, 11:31, 12:11. The Hebrew in these four places is translated into the Greek LXX with the same words used by Messiah in Mat. 24:15, e.g. βδέλυγμα τῆς ἐρημώσεως = שִׁקּוּצִים מְשֹׁמֵם. A Temple is mentioned again in Revelation 11, which according to Irenaeus was written toward the end of the reign of Domitian, AD 96. But we also have the amazing testimony of Josephus, who was eye witness to the destruction of the Temple in AD 70 that the Daniel passages were NOT fulfilled then. In AD 70, "On the 17th day of Panemus [Tammuz], the sacrifice called 'the Daily Sacrifice' had failed, and had not been offered to God for want of men to offer it (*Jos. War* 6.2.1 [94])." This was July 14, AD 70. Further, Titus gave orders that there should be no danger of destroying the city or the temple so as not to defile the Temple or offend God. He even offered to pay for the sacrifices necessary to keep the Daily going (93-95, cf. 97). Josephus reply to the rebel leader included this, "To be sure, thou hast kept this city wonderfully pure for God's sake! The temple also continues entirely unpolluted! Nor hast thou been guilty of any impiety against him, for whose assistance thou hopest. He still receives his accustomed sacrifices! Vile wretch that thou art! If any one should deprive these of thy daily food, thou wouldst esteem him to be an enemy to thee; but thou hopest to have God for thy supporter in this war whom thou hast deprived of his everlasting worship! And thou imputest those sins to the Romans, who to this very time take care to have our laws observed, and almost compel these sacrifices to be still offered to God, which have by thy means been intermitted…" Josephus's speech is as epic as any speech in history, and one is encouraged to read the following chapters in Josephus. When less than 30 days after, the Temple was burned down, there had been no abomination of desolation then nor since for the time periods prescribed in Daniel. Also at the end of the time periods the Temple will have been restored (Daniel 8:14). So not only did the daily not end for the correct time period, it was not restored after the prescribed time.

2:7 μ See End Note No. 1.

2:7 ψ "Out of the midst he can arise." The little horn arises between the other horns, or out of the midst of them. See Dan. 7:8. He comes up out of the abyss in the middle of the seventieth seven. See Dan. 9:27. "What holds *him*." See Rev. 9:1, 11:7, 13:1, 17:8; 20:1, 3. The pit is the place of confinement for evil beings. The beast that will control the man of sin is not released until the Almĭghty permits. See Luke 8:31; 2 Pet. 2:4; Yehudah 1:6.

¹⁵So then, brothers, be standing firm and be holding fast to the traditions which you were taught, whether by spoken word or by letter from us. ¹⁶Now may our Adŏnai Yĕshua the Anŏinted himself, and the Almĭghty our Făther, who has loved us and given us everlasting comfort and good hope by loving-kindness, ¹⁷comfort and strengthen your hearts in every good work and word.

3 ¹Henceforth, brothers, be praying for us that the word of Yăhweh may be spreading rapidly and may it be glorified, just as also with you, ²and that we will have been delivered from perverse and evil men, because the pledge of faithfulness is not in all. ³But Yăhweh is faithful, and he will strengthen and protect you from the evil one. ⁴And we have been trusting in Yăhweh concerning you, that you are doing and will continue to do what we command. ⁵And may Yăhweh direct your hearts into the love of the Almĭghty and into the steadfast endurance of the Anŏinted.

⁶Now we command you, brothers, in the name of our Adŏnai Yĕshua the Anŏinted, that you keep aloof from every brother who leads an unruly life and not according to the tradition which you received from beside us, ⁷because you yourselves have been knowing how you ought to follow our example, because we did not act in an undisciplined manner among you, ⁸nor did we eat anyone's bread without paying for it, but with labor and hardship we kept working night and day so that we may not be a burden to any of you, ⁹not because we do not have the right, but in order that we will have given ourselves an example for you, so you can be imitating us.

¹⁰Because even when we were with you, we used to give you this order: if anyone will not work, neither let him be eating.

¹¹Because we hear that some among you are leading an undisciplined life, doing no work at all, but acting like busybodies. ¹²Now such persons we are warning and exhorting in Adŏnai Yĕshua the Anŏinted, so that working in quietness, they may be eating their own bread.

¹³And, you, brothers, shall not have grown weary in doing good things. ¹⁴And if anyone is not obeying our instruction in this letter, be noting this, not to be mixed up with him, so that he will have been shamed. ¹⁵And yet do not be treating him as an enemy, but be reminding him as a brother.

¹⁶Now may the Adŏnai of peace himself continually grant you peace in every circumstance. Yăhweh be with you all!

¹⁷I, Paul, write this greeting with my own hand, and this is a distinguishing mark in any letter. This is the way I write.

¹⁸The loving-kindness of our Adŏnai Yĕshua the Anŏinted be with you all.

End Note No. 1: The Mystery of Lawlessness

I have explained ἔργων νόμου (customary works; aka 'the works of the law') in the notes as referring to special deeds done to gain a merit to offset a demerit (sin), either one's own extra-meritorious deeds, or merit imputed from Jewish ancestors (See Appendix VIII & below Note No. 2). This explanation was lost when the Church was seduced into rejecting parts of God's Law. Origen's view was:

"One should know that the works

which Paul repudiates and frequently criticizes are not the works of righteousness [opera iustitiae] which are commanded in the law, but those in which they boast who keep the law according to the flesh; that is, the **circumcision of the flesh, the sacrificial rituals, the observance of Sabbaths and new moon festivals** [cf. Col 2.18]. These **and works of a similar nature** are the works by which he says no one can be saved, and concerning which he says in the present passage, 'not on the basis of works; otherwise, grace would no longer be grace.' For if anyone is justified through these, he is not justified gratis. But these works are by no means sought from the one who is justified through grace; but this one should take care that the grace he has received should not be in him 'in vain' [cf. 1 Cor 15.10] . . . So then, one does not make grace become in vain who joins works to it that are worthy and who does not show himself ungrateful for the grace of God. For anyone who sins after having attained grace becomes ungrateful to him who offered the grace."—Origen, Commentary on Romans 8, 7, 6. Cited from Thomas Scheck, *Origen and the History of Justification: The Legacy of Origen's Commentary on Romans* (Notre Dame: University of Notre Dame Press, 2008), 48–49.

Jerome's view, commenting on Gal. 3:2, was:

"There are indeed many things, he says, which could under interrogation compel you to prefer the gospel to the law; but since you are senseless and are by no means able to hear these things, I should speak with simple words to you. I should ask about what is at hand: whether it was works of the law, observance of the Sabbath, the superstition of circumcision and new moons that gave you the Holy Spirit that you received? . . . . Let us consider carefully that he does not say, 'I want to learn from you' whether you 'received the Spirit by works, but instead 'by the works of the law.' For he knew that even Cornelius the centurion had received the Spirit by works but not by 'works of the law,' with which he was unacquainted. But if, on the other hand, it is said: well then, the Spirit can be received even without the 'hearing of faith,' we will respond that he [Cornelius] did indeed receive the Spirit, but by the 'hearing of faith' and by natural law, which speaks within our hearts the good things that must be done and the evils that must be avoided."—Jerome, Commentary on Galatians on 3:2. Cited from Thomas P. Scheck, trans., St. Jerome's Commentaries on Galatians, Titus and Philemon (Notre Dame: University of Notre Dame Press, 2010), 114.

So this position claims that 'works of law' are those commands which aroused foreign prejudice against Israel, and further that while salvation must include good works to receive unmerited grace, that if any of the 'Jewish ceremonial' commands are joined with good works, then unmerited grace is foreited. This is the logical consequence of believing that Paul meant the ceremonial law by his phrase ἔργων νόμου. The conclusion in Gal. 5:4, "you have fallen away from grace" wasn't wrong. What was wrong was assuming the conclusion was drawn on the ceremonial law. It wasn't. It was applied to the rabbinical doctrine of supererogatory merit to cancel out demerit (See Appendix VIII & below Note No. 2).

The 'works of law' equals 'ceremonial law' interpretation was the first logical step toward rejection of the whole Law by Christianity's gnostic extremists. Reformed soteriology is a modification of the gnostic extreme. It development began with Augustine, who was himself an ex-gnostic.

Reformed soteriology also includes moral law under the concept of 'works of the law,' (a common point with gnostics) so as to soften the objection that Scripture draws no line between moral and ceremonial law. It justifies its own keeping of moral laws by the gnostic doctrine that man has no free will, and therefore their obedience is only God working in them. Only with this explanation do they allow keeping of the moral law, condemning all others like Pelagius and Arminius.

So under the Reformed explanation, one is condemned for keeping the ceremonial laws originally rejected, and for keeping the moral law under any theory of personal righteousness that accepts free will or even a whiff of human merit. Reformed theology deals with the apparent keeping of some ceremonial laws in the apostolic age by making a transitory exception for Jews. They are only allowed to participate in those laws because it is their culture.

End Note No. 2: The Rabbis on Merit

Rabbi Arthur Marmorstein's book, *The Doctrine of Merits in Old Rabbinical Literature*, illustrates the rabbinical teachings of merit (KTAV Publishing House, New York, 1920, 1968). Marmorstein's summary states, "The latter [merit] assures [every person] of reward and saves him from punishment.... Judaism further teaches, as a supplement to the doctrine of imputed merits, the law of imputed sin (page 3-4)." R. Abbahu (AD 279-320), who was educated in Tiberius, and became president of the Caesarean School said, "For the sake of Abraham's circumcision God pardons Israel's sins. We are like a man whose case is before

the king, and his advocates defend him, likewise if a man performs the commandments, studies the Law, or does charity, even when Satan accuses him, his Torah and charity defend him" (pg. 85-86). R. Ḥama bar Ḥanina (contemporary with R. יוחנן בר נפחא, AD 180-279), head of the school of Sepphoris says, "God says to Israel: 'My children, do you desire that I shall justify you in My judgement? Recall before Me the merits of your fathers and I shall pardon you'" (pg. 80). R. Matya ben Charash (רבי מתיא בן חרש), ca. AD 150 said, "The time came when God's promise to Abraham was to be fulfilled,' [i.e. the Exodus]. Yet they had no commandments to keep; they had no observances to observe, for the merits of which they deserved to be redeemed. Therefore God gave to them two commandments (i.e. the blood of circumcision and the blood of the Pascal offering), in order that they shall be engaged with them, and shall have merits to be redeemed'" (pg. 47-48). Rabbi Tarfon (רבי טרפון), (ca. AD 70 to 135), a Cohen, on a Ṣabbaṭh afternoon in Yavneh, was attempting to answer a question with his students, "For what merit was Judah worthy to be the king among his brethren? R. Tarphon said to his students, 'Answer yourselves!' They said, 'He was worthy to become king for the advice he gave his brethren not to kill Joseph.' R. Tarphon objected to this suggestion on the ground that his advice, which saved Joseph's life, was good enough to atone for the selling of Joseph and the anxiety of his father, but never so praiseworthy as to get him the rulership. Then they suggested, 'For the merit of acknowledging his sin, and saving Tamar's life.' R. Tarphon rejected this view. The confession was sufficient to atone for his sin. A third suggestion was put forward. For he pledged himself for Benjamin. This hypothesis shared the fate of the previous one. Then they said, "Now tell us!' R. Tarphon said, 'When the tribes stood before the sea, they debated who should enter first. The leader of Judah, Nahṣon ben Aminadab, put and end to this discussion, and jumped into the waves of the sea. Therefore was he chosen to the Kingdom'" (pg. 44-45).

"Shemaiah (ca. 47-40 BC stood at Herod's trial; Jos. Ant. 14:172) and Abtalyon (who in 38 BC persuaded Jerusalem to surrender to Herod; Jos. Ant. 15:1) were the first to discuss a question bearing on the subject of merits in Rabbinical literature. The problem which agitated the mind of these two 'great men of their generation' was: 'What merit did the Israelites possess that God divided the sea before them?' Shemaiah taught, 'Sufficent is the faith[fulness], with which Abraham their father [held faithful] on Me that I should divide the sea before them, as it is said: And he [held faithful] on God, and He counted it unto him (i.e. at the sea) for (doing) charity (with his children)' (Gen. 15.6). Abtaljon says: 'Worthy is the faith[fulness], they (the Israelites themselves) [held faithful on] Me so that I shall divide the sea before them, as it is said: 'And the people held faithful (Exod. 4.31)'" (pg. 37). Hillel the Elder (d. 10 BC) in an enigmatic saying adopts both views (pg 38-39). Marmorstein cites, *We have Abraham for our Father* as representing Shemaiah's view. If Shemaiah were a Christian, he'd be a Protestant. If Abtalyon and Hillel were Christians, they would be Catholics.

.

When Did Yĕshua Rise?

The Torah tells us to count Sabbaths:

> AND YE WILL HAVE COUNTED FOR YOURSELVES IN THE TOMORROW OF THE ṢABBAṭH, FROM THE DAY OF YOUR BRINGING THE SHEAF OF THE WAVE OFFERING: SEVEN REGULAR ṢABBAṭHS SHALL BE UNTIL IN THE TOMORROW OF THE SEVENTH ṢABBAṭH YOU WILL HAVE COUNTED A FIFTIETH DAY (LEV. 23:15-16A).

Q. How many Sabbaths were counted?
A. Seven.

Q. After which Sabbath did the counting start?
A. The first day of Passover.

¹But *the* later of *the* Ṣabbaṭhs, at the dawning for *the* FIRST OF THE ṢABBAṭHS, Miryam Ha-Magdalit and the other Miryam came to look at the grave. ²And behold, a severe earthquake occurred, because the Messenger of Yăhweн descended from heaven and came, rolled away the stone and was sitting up above it. (Mat 28:1-2).

Q. What was the later Sabbath?
A. The one after the Passover Sabbath

Q. What is the first of the Sabbaths?
A. The number one Sabbath of the seventh Sabbaths that the Torah commands us to count.

Q. When did Mĕssiah rise from the dead?
A. On the later Sabbath which is the first Sabbath.

Q. Why did Messenger of Yăhweн come down from heaven and roll away the stone?
A. To show that he was already resurrected and that the tomb was empty.

Q. What happened that morning?
A. The Olah offering for the firstfruits finished burning, and the priests removed the ashes from the altar, thus Mĕssiah's resurrection is timed with the end of the burning of the offering.

Q. What is a regular Sabbath? תְמִימֹת.
A. One of the weekly Sabbaths, and not the annual Sabbath after which the seven Sabbaths are counted. Temimoṭ means that which completes, thus Sabbaths that complete a creation week.

Q. When was the sheaf brought that year and its associated Olah offering put on the altar?
A. It was brought about 9 a.m. after the Passover Sabbath, on a Friday morning that year.

Q. What is another name for this offering?
A. The firstfruits offering.

Q. Which day was the firstfruits offering?
A. Nisan 16, the morrow of the annual Sabbath.

Q. What does it mean to count a 50th day in the tomorrow of the seventh Sabbath?
A. Tomorrow is a Hebrew idiom for time after, so it means to count the 50th day however many days it takes to reach it after the seventh Sabbath.

Q. How may we prove this Hebrew idiom?
A. Because also seven regular Sabbaths are counted in the tomorrow of the annual Passover Sabbath, and this also requires tomorrow to mean time after, and not the very day after.

Q. Why was all this knowledge lost?
A. Because Christianity rejected Torah, and Jews rejected Mĕssiah, and because it was the time of Yisra'el's final exile, and in that time the word is spread to the nations because of Yisra'el's sin. And the nations have treated the Torah as an unclean thing even while professing Mĕssiah, but some have been saved.

Q. Why did the true faithful lack this knowledge for the better part of 2000 years?
A. Because the Most High is not immediately ready to restore the truth after men throw it away, a lesson that should be learned from his exiling of Yisra'el.

Q. When the truth is restored does everyone receive it?
A. No, because even when Mosheн received the Torah, not all received it, and they did not listen to the Messenger of Yăhweн. Also when he came as Mĕssiah they did not listen to him then either. And if no one can do better than the Almĭghty Sŏn, the only kindred Almĭghty who reveals the Făther, then we too expect opposition.

Q. Is this then the end of what needs restoring?
A. No, it is just the start of it.

First Timothy

1 ¹Paul, an emissary of the Anŏinted Yĕshua according to the commandment of the Almĭghty our Rescuer, and of the Anŏinted Yĕshua, who is our hope. ²To Timothy, my true child in faithfulness. Loving-kindness, mercy, and peace from the Almĭghty our Făther and the Anŏinted Yĕshua our Adŏnai.

³Just as I urged you to remain in Ephesus, *in* going to Macedonia, *I remind you again* in order that you will have instructed certain ones not to be teaching other doctrines, ⁴nor to be paying attention to myths and endless genealogies, which keep giving rise to speculations more than the administration of the Almĭghty which is in faithfulness. ⁵And, the end of our instruction is love from a pure heart and a good conscience and a sincere faithfulness.

⁶For some men, straying from these things, have turned aside to fruitless discussion, ⁷wanting to be teachers of the Law, even though they do not understand either what they are saying or the matters about which they make confident assertions. ⁸But we have been knowing that the Law is good, if one may be using it lawfully, ⁹having been realizing the fact that the Law is not ⁿlaid down on a righteous man, but for those who are lawless and rebellious, for the irreverent and sinners, for the unholy and profane, for those who kill their fathers or mothers, for murderers ¹⁰and immoral men and homosexuals and kidnappers and liars and perjurers, and whatever else is contrary to sound teaching, ¹¹according to the glorious good news of the blessed Almĭghty, with which I have been held faithful.

¹²I thank the Anŏinted Yĕshua our Adŏnai, who has strengthened me, because he considered me faithful, putting me into service, ¹³even though I was formerly a blasphemer and a persecutor and a violent aggressor. And yet I was shown mercy, because I acted ignorantly in unfaithfulness. ¹⁴And the loving-kindness of our Adŏnai was more than abundant, with the faithfulness and love which are found in the Anŏinted Yĕshua. ¹⁵It is a trustworthy statement, deserving full acceptance, that the Anŏinted Yĕshua came into the world to rescue sinners, among whom I am foremost of all. ¹⁶But for this reason I found mercy, in order that in me, firstly, Yĕshua the Anŏinted may demonstrate his perfect patience, as an example for those about to be holding faithful on him to everlasting life.

¹⁷Now to the King of the ages, immortal, invisible, the ᵅonly ᵝAlmĭghty, be honor and glory forever and ever. Am·en.

1:9 η→down: Or 'enforced on' or 'dictated to.' When a new governor is appointed to eliminate corruption in government or market places he pledges to lay down the law, i.e. to enforce the existing law against the lawless. The new chief sets out to clean up the street. But there are many pious false teachers who abuse the Law to judge the righteous as if they were common thugs, not knowing when to bind or loose, nor how to tell the difference between a sin of ignorance and one of rebellion. They use their legal opinions not to promote holiness, but because they have a spirit of control. **1:17** β Some texts add 'wise' (σοφῷ). The addition does not flow right, because it would appear that wisdom is not the only attribute to be an only attribute. **1:17** α μόνῳ The phrase here applies to the Son and Spirit as much as the Father here as in Deut. 6:4: שְׁמַע יִשְׂרָאֵל יְהֹוָה אֱלֹהֵינוּ יְהֹוָה אֶחָד = *Hear Yisrael, Yahweh is our Almĭghty, Yahweh only*. See 6:16.

¹⁸This command I entrust to you, Timothy, my son, in accordance with the prophecies previously made concerning you, that by them you may be fighting the good fight, ¹⁹holding fast to faithfulness and a good conscience, which some have rejected, and have suffered shipwreck in regard to their loyalty, ²⁰among whom are Hymenaeus and Alexander, whom I have delivered over to Satan, so that they will have been instructed not to be blaspheming.

2 ¹First of all, then, I urge that entreaties and prayers, petitions and thanksgivings, be made on behalf of all men, ²on behalf of kings, and all who are in authority, in order that we may be leading a tranquil and quiet life in all reverent devotion and dignity. ³This is good and acceptable in the sight of the Almĭghty our Rescuer, ⁴who desires all men to be rescued and to come to the knowledge of the truth.

⁵For one Almĭghty^μ *is* one mediator^ξ also for *the* Almĭghty and for men, the man, the Anŏinted Yĕshua, ⁶who gave himself as a ransom on behalf of all^μ, the testimony *borne* in their appointed times. ⁷And for this I was appointed a pro-

---

2:5 μ Cf. 1 Cor. 8:6, one Adŏnai. *One Almĭghty* refers only to the Sŏn here. *For the Almĭghty* refers to the totality of the Almĭghty. Paul uses the word *one* in respect to the Sŏn alone and the Spĭrit alone. See 1 Cor. 8:6; Eph. 4:5. As saying *one Adŏnai* in those places in respect to Mĕssiah, he says *one Almĭghty* here in respect to Mĕssiah also. In Yoĥ. 17:3, Yoĥanan applies the word *alone* separately to the Făther, *the alone true Almĭghty, and* Mĕssiah: *who you have sent*. The relative pronoun *who* must refer to *the alone true Almĭghty* also. The reason Paul can do like Yoĥanan is because he does not start with the assumption that the Almĭghty is one being, and he takes efforts to undercut this false doctrine by using the word *one* in context in such a way that it cannot refer to Făther, Sŏn, and Spĭrit all under the same usage of the word *Almĭghty* or *Adŏnai*. ▷ By the word order: εἰς καὶ, placing καὶ in the second position of the second clause Paul is forcing this καὶ into an explanatory role, meaning *even* or *also*. This equivocates the first use of Almĭghty with the word mediator. The second use of Almĭghty will therefore refer to all of the Almĭghty that is not the Sŏn of man. ▷ The Nicene Creed itself preserves the separate usage of the word *one* separately, viz. Πιστεύω εἰς ἕνα Θεόν, Πατέρα; Καὶ εἰς ἕνα Κύριον Ἰησοῦν, I hold faithful to one Almĭghty, Făther, and to one Adŏnai Yĕshua. **2:5** ξ μεσίτης Being the divine Sŏn, and the Sŏn of Man, the Mĕssiah fully understands what it is to be human and what it is to be divine. Therefore, he communicates with the Spĭrit of the Most High the human condition. And being divine he communicates with man the covenant expectations of the Most High. For this reason the Son has been descending from heaven as the Messenger of Yăhweĥ to make plain his Law, and the means of our deliverance from sin via his ransom and cleansing blood. When we repent with respect to his Law he forgives us and ransoms us from our enslavement. ▷ As the human/divine mediator he bears the attack of our sin, but he does not bear the wrath of the Most High, because we only thought he was stricken by the Most High, but we were mistaken. He was wholly innocent. Messiah entered into harms way to deliver us from the kingdom of darkness. And the Most High was pleased to make use of this attack as a guilt offering, expressing the cost to himself for our rescue. ▷ The reason so many misunderstand sacrifice is that they perceive it as an appeasement of judgment, but this is not what biblical sacrifice is. Biblical sacrifice is a symbol or indication of the cost of sin, thus a ransom, the price being taken by sin, and also the blood symbolizes our cleansing from sin and the cost in life of it. As for judgment, the worshiper is forgiven upon his repentance. The sacrifice is but a formality to instruct us on the ransom cost and the cleansing cost. **2:6** μ See Mat. 20:28; Mark 10:45; Hos. 13:14; Isa. 43:3; Rev. 5:9. ▷ The cost of the ransom was charged by sin and death and paid by the Most High to rescue his people. See Jer. 31:11, "For he will have ransomed Ya'aqov from hands stronger than he." ▷ But by no means is the ransom a price paid to the Father to satisfy wrath, because the innocent are not put to death for the guilty, nor the son for the father, nor the father for the son. Punishing the innocent for the guilty was a large part of ancient legal codes, in the same spirit that the gods seek to be placated by innocent blood. It is with great horror that the good news has been corrupted within Christianity by a pagan understanding of sacrifice wherein innocent blood is spilled to placate the gods. It is hardly an acceptable apologetic to say that Messiah *volunteered* for this job, because it still presents the Father as demanding appeasement by innocent blood. It also represents the Father as unforgiving. ▷ The only kindred Son is the ransom given by the Father to rescue his people, and not a ransom to the Father. See Yoĥ. 3:16. The Most High is love, and in

claimer and an emissary (I am telling the truth, I am not lying) as a teacher of the nations in faithfulness and truth. ⁸Therefore I want the men in every place to pray, lifting up holy hands, without wrath and dissension.

⁹Likewise, I want women to adorn themselves with proper clothing, modestly and discreetly, not with braided hair and gold or pearls or costly garments, ¹⁰but rather by means of good works, as befits women making a claim to reverent devotion. ¹¹Let a woman be learning undisturbed with entire obedience.ᶜ

¹²But I do not ᶿturn to a woman to teach, nor to be ˣtaking up arms ʸ*in preference* over a man, but to be *left* undisturbed,ᶲ ¹³because it was Adam who was first created, and then Ḥauuah. ¹⁴And it was not Adam who was deceived. But the woman being quite deceived, into ᵘtrespass had been coming. ¹⁵Womankind will be preserved through the bearing of children if they shall have continued in faithfulness and love and holiness with self-restraint.ᵠ ¹ᵃHumanly° *speaking*, faithful is the word.ᵏ

---

here there is no darkness. According to the Law, the Torah only the guilty can be put to death for their own sin. It is a lawless act to punish the innocent for the guilty. **2:11** ξ This directive was a revolutionary move back to the pre-exilic treatment of women, because the Judaism of the times was greatly against educating women. **2:12** θ→to: *require, rely on, incline to* **2:12** χ αὐθεντέω = *self-take up arms*. The term is a military idiom for taking command or leading a revolt: αυτος *(self)* + εντεα *(arms, armour, fighting gear)*. To take it upon oneself to wage war or lead a revolt. The word connotes a self appointment to wage war. It is granted that the women who wanted to do this were going into spiritual battle on behalf of the faithful, and not against men, but Paul avoids letting women lead the fight for the reasons stated, which are his guidelines, and not absolutes. **2:12** γ→over = αὐθεντεῖν ἀνδρός = *to be taking arms of/from/over man*. This is a literal translation of the genitive case, which is quite ambiguous, but from the context and other Scripture, it clearly means that a woman is not to take precedence in promotion over a man in this kind of work. It could mean 'to be taking up the arms of a man,' i.e. as if donning equipment for battle. Paul's comparison by using the word αὐθεντεῖν shows that he viewed leadership in the Assembly as spiritual combat, which it surely is. **2:12** φ A woman should be left undisturbed to pursue scholarship and also not be disturbed by promoting her over men since most women are not inclined to want this or handle the stress. The principle is the same as that women should be prepared for battle, but not be required to fight the battle. But it is no sin if out of necessity or unusual inclination that a women does fight the battle, but that should be her choice. The woman is created to nurture life in the dominion of Gŏd's creation. ▷ Too many Christians, not understanding the Torah, regard everything Paul utters as canon law. First observe that the Torah makes no prohibition of a woman teaching or leading men. It is, of course, very unusual, and against the general nature of women. But necessity demands exceptions, and Scripture provides examples. Paul states why he advises his rule to Timothy, and this reason is because of the nature and frailty of women who lead: they are more so targets of Satan's attacks. Paul says what his policy is in making appointments to positions, "I do not...." It is probably a good policy for making appointments to positions of authority. But it is not Torah. The contribution of the Torah is merely to consider the weakness of women, and apply the law of love for the sake of all. Paul did let a woman learn as long as she was submissive to the Almĭghty. All should be submissive when learning. Paul's allowing a woman to learn was a revolutionary liberation for women of that age. **2:14** μ A less severe word for sin, indicating being led astray by deception. Paul refers to the garden to make his point that women are more vulnerable to the kind of attacks that fall on spiritual leaders. **2:15** ψ Paul is countering another threat aimed at women who become scholars, namely some must have said they who intrude into scholarship will be doubly cursed when it came time to have children, or worse that they would die in childbirth. Paul gives assurance that this is not the case so long as they have good virtues. Paul's progressiveness is a departure from the well known Rabbinic repression of women and a return to the liberty according to the Law in more ancient times. **2:15** λ This clause should end chapter 2 and not begin the next. Paul's assurance that women will suffer no childbirth curse for becoming scholars is simply a human calculation based on the fact that the Law allows it. But he does not have a guarantee that women will never be troubled. But it will not be because they broke the Rabbinic taboo.

1 Timothy 3

3 ¹It is a trustworthy statement: if any man aspires to the office of overseer, it is a fine work he desires to do. ²An overseer, then, must be above reproach, the husband of one wife, temperate, prudent, respectable, hospitable, able to teach, ³not addicted to wine or a bully, but gentle, uncontentious, free from the love of money. ⁴He must be one who manages his own household well, keeping his children under control with all dignity ⁵(but if a man has not been knowing how to manage his own household, how will he take care of the assembly of the Almĭghty?), ⁶and not a new convert, lest having become conceited, he may have fallen into the condemnation of the Slanderer. ⁷And he must have a good reputation with those outside the assembly, so that he may not fall into reproach and the snare of the Slanderer.

⁸The deputies likewise must be men of dignity, not double-tongued, or addicted to much wine or greedy for dishonest gain, ⁹but holding to the mystery of ᵖfaithfulness with a clear conscience. ¹⁰And let these also first be getting tested. Then let them be serving as deputies if they are beyond reproach. ¹¹Women must likewise be dignified, not malicious gossips, but temperate, faithful in all things. ¹²Let deputies be husbands of only one wife, and good managers of their children and their own households, ¹³because those who have served well as deputies obtain for themselves a high standing and great confidence in the faithfulness which is to the Anŏinted Yĕshua.

¹⁴I am writing these things to you, hoping to come to you with speed, ¹⁵yet if I may be delaying, *I write* so that you will have been knowing how one ought to be conducting himself in the household of the Almĭghty, which is the Assembly of the living Almĭghty, *who is* the pillar and main support of the truth, ¹⁶(and by common confession, *of great importance* is the ᶲmystery for reverent devotion), who has been revealed in the flesh, has been vindicated by the Spĭrit, has been seen by messengers, has been proclaimed among the nations, was held faithful in the world, has been taken up in glory.

4 ¹But the Spĭrit explicitly says that in later times some will fall away from the pledge of faithfulness, paying attention to deceitful spirits and teachings of demons, ²by means of the hypocrisy of liars, ˣwho have been getting themselves seared in their own conscience, ³men who ᵘforbid marriage and advocate ᶲab-

---

3:9 π *the faithfulness,* cf. vs. 13. **3:16** ϕ The mystery of Mĕssiah and the Assembly. See Eph. 5:32. Mĕssiah is the pillar. See 1 Cor. 10:4. He is also the foundation stone, the tried stone. Recognizing his position and role in the Assembly of Yisra'el from the beginning is the great mystery essential for reverent devotion, which is synonymous with deep loyalty. See also Eph. 3. What Mĕssiah has done for lost and exiled Yisra'el is essential to securing our loyalty. **4:2** χ→seared: to cauterize with a red hot iron: κεκαυστηριασμένων = who have been getting themselves seared (V-RPM/P-GMP). Middle: *searing themselves;* Passive: *getting seared.* Middle/Passive: *getting themselves seared.* Probably more Middle than Passive. **4:3** ϕ→foods: The Catholic Church made it a law that no meat but fish only could be eaten on Friday. The abstinence from other meat was considered a penance, a small sacrifice in memory of the Friday crucifixion. **4:3** μ→marriage: Similarly, the Catholic Church forbids marriage for its priests. Now those rules *are* teachings of demons. ▷ Now if someone tries to place the biblical kosher laws within Paul's rebuke, then what is to prevent the equally alien interpretation of supposing that Paul is rebuking anyone who would forbid a man to marry a man? ▷ If forbidding pork is what Paul means by "teachings of demons," even though pork is forbidden by law, then is forbidding homosexual marriage also a "teaching of

staining from foods, which the Almĭghty has created to be gratefully shared in by the faithful who have been fully knowing the truth, ⁴because everything created by the Almĭghty is good, and nothing is to be rejected, after blessing being received, ⁵because it is being set apart by means of the word of the Almĭghty and intercession.

⁶In setting out these things for the brothers, you will be a good servant of the Anŏinted Yĕshua, getting yourself fed with the words of the *pledge of faithfulness* and of the good teaching which you have been closely following. ⁷But be shunning profane and old wives' tales. On the other hand, be disciplining yourself for the purpose of reverent devotion, ⁸because bodily discipline is only of little profit, but reverent devotion is profitable for all things, since it holds promise for the present life and also for the life to come. ⁹It is a trustworthy statement deserving full acceptance, ¹⁰because it is for this we are laboring and contending, in that we have been hoping on the living Almĭghty, who is the Rescuer for all men, especially of the faithful.

¹¹Be prescribing these things and be teaching. ¹²Let no one be looking down on your youthfulness, but rather in speech, conduct, love, faithfulness and purity, be becoming yourself an example for the faithful. ¹³Until I come, be paying attention to the public reading, to exhortation and teaching. ¹⁴Do not be neglecting the spiritual gift within you, which was bestowed upon you through prophetic utterance with the laying on of hands by the elders. ¹⁵Be studying these things. Be getting absorbed in them, so that your progress may be evident to all. ¹⁶Be paying close attention to yourself and to the teaching. Be remaining in these things, because by doing this, even yourself you will rescue, and those who hear you.

5 ¹You shall not have sharply rebuked an older man, but rather be appealing to him as *one's own* father, to the younger men as brothers, ²the older women as mothers, and the younger women as sisters, in all purity. ³Be honoring widows who are really widows, ⁴but if any widow has children or grandchildren, let them first be learning to practice piety in regard to their own family, and to make some return to their parents, because this is acceptable in the sight of the Almĭghty. ⁵Now she who is a widow indeed, and who has been getting left alone, has been hoping on the Almĭghty, and is continuing in entreaties and prayers night and day. ⁶But she who gives herself to wanton pleasure has been dying even while she lives. ⁷Be prescribing these things as well, so that they may be above reproach. ⁸But if anyone does not provide for his own, and especially for those of his household, he has been denying the pledge of faithfulness, and is worse than the unfaithful.

⁹Let a widow be getting herself enrolled only if she is not less than sixty years old, having been becoming the wife of one man, ¹⁰having a reputation for good works, and if she has brought up children, if she has shown hospitality to strangers, if she has washed the holy ones' feet, if she has assisted those in distress, and if she has devoted herself to every good work.

¹¹Yet be refusing younger widows, because when they may have sensual

desires in disregard of the Anŏinted, they are wanting to be ʸmarried, ¹²incurring judgment, because they have set aside their previous pledge of faithfulness. ¹³And at the same time they also learn to be idle, as they go around from house to house, and not merely idle, but also gossips and busybodies, talking about things not proper to mention. ¹⁴Therefore, I want younger widows to get married, bear children, keep house, and to favor giving the enemy no occasion for reproach, ¹⁵because some have already turned aside to follow Satan. ¹⁶If any faithful woman has dependent widows, let her be assisting them, and let not the assembly be getting itself burdened, so that it will have assisted those who are widows indeed.

¹⁷Let the elders who have been standing up well be getting considered worthy of double honor, especially those who are working hard in the word and teaching, ¹⁸because the text says, "YOU SHALL NOT MUZZLE THE OX WHILE HE IS THRESHING,ᵟ" that is, "The laborer is worthy of his wages." ¹⁹Do not be receiving an accusation against an elder except on the basis of two or three witnesses. ²⁰Those who continue in sin, be rebuking in the presence of all, so that the rest also may be fearful of sinning. ²¹I am solemnly charging you in the presence of the Almĭghty and of the Anŏinted One, Yĕshua, and of the chosen messengers, that you will have guarded these things without bias, doing nothing with partiality. ²²Do not be laying hands upon anyone too hastily, nor be sharing responsibility for the sins of others. Be keeping yourself free from sin.

²³No longer be drinking water, unless you be using a little wine for the sake of your stomach and your frequent ailments.

²⁴The sins of some men are quite evident, going before them to judgment. For others, their sins follow after. ²⁵Likewise also, deeds that are good are quite evident, and those which are otherwise cannot be concealed.

6 ¹Let all who are under the yoke as slaves be regarding their own masters as worthy of all honor, so that the name of the Almĭghty and our teaching may not be spoken against. ²And let those who have faithful masters not be getting disrespectful to them because they are brothers, but let them be serving them all the more, because those who partake of the benefit are faithful and beloved. Be teaching and be proclaiming these principles.

³If anyone is teaching a strange doctrine, and not applying himself to sound words, those of our Adŏnai Yĕshua the Anŏinted, and to teaching conforming to reverent devotion, ⁴he has been getting himself puffed up and is understanding nothing, but he has a morbid interest in controversial questions and disputes

---

demons" even though the law forbids it? **5:11** γ Either the word means 'married' or to 'take a paramour,' i.e. a secret lover. See LSJ. A.2. One may be married to a secret husband, but then the woman should not be supported by the assembly if she is married. When the assembly would find out about it, the secret relationship may have gone on for some time, and indeed it would be the first step to a life of sexual promiscuity if she should leave the first lover for another. For she would have to be cut off from support. A husband is expected to provide, and some may not. Therefore to be a widow supported by the assembly, she would have to pledge to stay unmarried as long as support was being received, and would have to give notice that she intended to support herself or be supported by a husband before entering any marriage, which would then be public. **5:18** δ Deu 25:4.

about words, out of which arise envy, strife, abusive language, evil suspicions, ⁵and wasted conflicts, having been getting themselves corrupted by men in the mind, and having been getting themselves robbed dry of the truth, who are supposing piety to be a means of gain. ⸂Be withdrawing from such as these.⸃ ⁶But reverent devotion actually is a means of great gain, when accompanied by contentment, ⁷because we have brought nothing into the world, so we cannot take anything out of it either. ⁸And if we have food and covering, with these we shall be content. ⁹But those who want to get rich fall into temptation and a snare, and many foolish and harmful desires which plunge men into ruin and destruction, ¹⁰because the love of money is a root of all sorts of evil, and some by longing for it have wandered away from the pledge of faithfulness, and have pierced themselves with many a pang.

¹¹But be fleeing from these things, O man of the Almĭghty, and be pursuing justice, reverent devotion, faithfulness, love, perseverance and gentleness. ¹²Be fighting yourself the good fight of faithfulness! Lay hold upon everlasting life to which you were called, and you made the good confession in the presence of many witnesses. ¹³I am charging you in the presence of the Almĭghty, who is giving life to all things, and of the Anŏinted Yĕshua, who testified the good confession to Pontius Pilate, ¹⁴to keep yourself the commandment without stain, without reproach until the ᵞappearance of our Adŏnai Yĕshua the Anŏinted, ¹⁵which ᵞ*appearance* in ᶿtheir own appointed times ᵋhe will display, ᵋhe who is the Blessed One, and alone Sovereign, the King of those reigning and Adŏnei of those being lords, ¹⁶who alone is having immortality, dwelling in unapproachable light—who no man has seen or is being able to see.ᵠ To him be honor and everlasting dominion! Amen.

¹⁷Be instructing those who are rich in this present age not to be conceited or to have been hoping on the uncertainty of riches, but on the Almĭghty, who richly supplies us with all things to enjoy. ¹⁸Instruct them to do good, to be rich in good works, to be generous and ready to share, ¹⁹treasuring up for themselves a good foundation for the coming time, so that they will have kept hold on everlasting life. ²⁰Timothy, guard what has been entrusted to you, avoiding worldly and empty chatter and the opposing arguments of what is falsely called

---

6:15 θ see 2:6. 'Their': plural of 'its own appointed time.' The 'appearance' will take place within the appointed times, but it is implied that which recurrence of the appointed time it will be is still undetermined. Mat. 24:36 and Mark 13:32 speaks *concerning* (Περὶ) events within the end time and not of the exact time. **6:14, 15** γ singular word; vs. 15 γ: the relative pronoun is fem. gender matched to 'appearance' in vs. 14. **6:15** ξ 'He' refers to the Almĭghty generally or collectively. Hebrew uses singular pronouns to refer to plural entities. But it may also be argued that 'he' also refers to the Son alone here, and that an additional point is being made that the Son alone is Sovereign, that is by himself. Therefore μόνος is translated 'alone' here to as to allow this point also, which the translation 'only' would exclude. See Yoħ. 17:3. ▷ Against the interpretation of Yoħ. 5:26 (q.v.) which makes the Son's life dependent on the Father, it must be said that the Son is by nature the source of life along with the Father and Spirit, and that in his humanity he only for a time yields control of this to the Father, which control was returned to him upon his resurrection. Thus dependency was a temporary arrangement. **6:16** ψ No man is able to see even the Son in his glorified state. Paul, of course means mortal man, and not those raised to life. For the being of the raised is as the 'sons of Gŏd' and not as mere men.

"knowledge," [21]which some have professed and thus gone astray from the pledge of faithfulness. Loving-kindness be with you.

Genesis Note

Genesis 1 and 2 have the most significant mistranslations, with far reaching consequences, more than probably any other place in the Torah. The most important item is the definition of the day. Here is a strictly literal translation:

[1]In the beginning of the Almïghty's creating of the heavens and the earth, [2]when the earth had been nought and nothing, and darkness was over the face of the deep, and the Spïrit of the Almïghty was making a vibrating over the face of the waters, [3]then the Almïghty says, "Let there be light!" Then there is light. Then the Almïghty sees the light, that it is good. [4]Then the Almïghty is making a division between the light and between the darkness. [5a]Then the Almïghty calls the light 'day.' [5b](And the darkness he has called 'night.') [5c]Then there is setting. Then there is daybreak. One day.

In Hebrew the sequence of the narrative is carried by what is called *waw consecutive*, here translated 'then' and with wavy underline. Normally this conjunction carries time forward, meaning 'then next' such and such happened. Another form of the conjunction is called *waw conjunctive*. These are underlined with the straight line. *Waw conjunctive* does not itself indicate a time change. It very often means at the same time as the previous statements. Vs. 5b is a special case of waw conjunctive with the perfect. It is a gnomic statement, which means it is a statement of truth that is always or customarily true, and no particular occasion is being pointed to. In English the gnomic sense is created by the present tense used in a past tense narrative, i.e. "John woke up. John ate cereal. John hates eggs. John went to work." "Hates eggs" is always true for John. It is not meant to say when he hated eggs, or even if he thought about it then. So also the Hebrew perfect is used in this manner in vs. 5b. Hebrew just uses a different convention. The narrative is in the imperfect tense. The gnomic statement is in the perfect.

Now we are ready to look at the definition of 'day.' The first definition is clearly 'light' (dawn to dusk). The second definition, 'One day' follows at the end of a sequence of setting (evening) and daybreak (dawn). Between is the period of darkness, called night. Since night alone is never called 'day,' we have to go back to the first dawn when light was created to find its beginning. Therefore, 'one day' denotes a calendar day, the time from the dawn of the first light, to the dawn of daybreak at the start of day two. In narrative English, the translation would from vs 3 to 5c: (continued on page 458).

Grammatical Codes

See Appendix II, **Special Letters**, page 536. These have two uses. The primary use is in proper nouns derived from Hebrew, which is to show how the Hebrew original was pronounced. Any reader can quickly learn this. The sec-

ondary use is in marking words that are not proper nouns with a grammatical explanation. This system is <u>not</u> completely implemented. This work is ongoing. Pay attention to the letter differences. It is not expected that anyone with less than a year of Greek will be able to safely use this apparatus. It's purpose is chiefly to document the reasoning behind renditions for apologetic ends.

(1) will, shall, should, would, WILL vs. will, shall, should: marks a subjunctive.
(2) hađ vs. had: marks a rare Koine pluperfect.
(3) *will* have: marks a proleptic interpretation. If will is dropped, it will be necessary to switch 'have' to 'has' if the subject is singular.
(4) having vs. having: 'having' marks an aorist participle.
(5) when͜ vs. when: 'when͜' marks an aorist participle, which may be converted to no. 4.
(6) had vs. had: had marks a case where either 'had' or 'has' is possible.
(7) haṣ or haṿe: 'will have' is also possible.
(8) has vs. has: see no. 6.
(9) ą, ę, į, ǫ, ų. A vowel so marked in a verb represents an aorist that is gnomic, which to approximate the Greek idea one thinks of as "have and will have" or "has and will have." In Greek and Hebrew this idea is represented by a perfective verb, but in English by the simple present tense. The present is supposed in English to be a timeless present, that is applying to all time. In Greek the perfective verb is a timeless perfective, applying to all time.

Yăhweн Appearing to Avraham

^{Gen 18.1}And Yăhweн is seen by him by the oaks of Mamre. And he is sitting *in* the door of the tent *in* the heat of the day. ²Then he lifts up his eyes. Then he looks, and behold **three men** are stationed over him. Then he sees. Then he runs to call on **them** from the door of the tent. Then he made to be bowing himself earthward. ³Then he says **Adŏnai** if please I have found favor in thine eyes, you shall not please pass by from over your servant. ⁴Will be taken please a little water. Then wash ye you-all's feet. Then repose yourselves under the tree. ⁵Then let me take a bit of bread, and ye will sustain you-all's heart, afterward ye may pass by, because therefore ye have passed by over **you-all's servant. Then they say**, yes, you may do as that you have spoken.

⁹**Then they say** to him, where is Sarah your wife? Then he says, here, in the tent. ¹⁰Then he says, returning I will return to thee according to the time of life, and behold a son will belong to Sarah, thy wife.

²⁰Then **Yăhweн says**...²¹**let me go down** please that I may see...²²**Then the men turn away from there. Then they go toward** Sedom, **but Avraham is still himself standing at the face of Yăhweн**....³²Then he says I will not destroy it for the sake of ten. ³³**Then Yăhweн goes as that he had finished speaking to Avraham**, and Avraham had returned to his place.

¹⁹·¹**Then come the two Messengers** to Sedom in the setting, and Lot is sitting in the gate of Sedom. Then Lot sees. Then he rises up to call upon **them**. Then he makes himself bow nose earthward. ²Then he says, here please **my Adŏnai** turn ye please to the house of **you-all's servant**...Then they say no.

¹³Because **we** are going to destroy this place, because has become great their outcry before the face of Yăhweн, and Yăhweн has sent us to destroy it. ¹⁶And delaying himself the two men seized hold onto his hand, and the hand of his wife, and on the hand of his two daughters **in being merciful Yăhweн upon him**....¹⁸Then says Lot unto them, no please my **Adŏnai**, behold please, **has found favor thy servant in thy eyes. And you may increase your lovingkindness**, which you **have done** with me **to make live my soul**....²¹Then he says to him, behold **I will have borne your face also for this word**, that I should not overthrow the city of which you have spoken. ²²Hurry escape to there, because I am unable to do the word until thy entering

into there....²³The sun had gone forth upon the earth, and Lot is entering Tsoar, **and Yăhwęḥ has rained on Sedom and upon Amorah brimestone and fire from Yăhwęḥ, from the heavens.** Then he overthrew these cities. ²⁹And then it had been, while the Almighty is destroying the cities of the plain that the Almighty remembers Avraham. Then he sends Lot from the midst of the overthrow **while overthrowing the cities** where Lot had dwelled in them.

****

How many of the three men were Yăhwęḥ? The simplest interpretation that makes the best sense is all three. Many say that the divine name was removed from about 134 places in Scripture, the so called changes of the Sopherim. However that may be, the scribes have vowel pointed the title Adŏnai so that we may know where those places were, or are where Adŏnai refers to the Most High. In this passage I have marked Adŏnai with the /ŏ/ where this occurs. If Adonai is not so marked it may still refer to Yăhwęḥ, or may not. Only one place is unmarked in this passage in the Hebrew (19.2).

A plural pronoun certainly refers to more than one, but a singular pronoun may refer to more than one. Remember this. The first big clue is that no distinction is made to which of the three Abraham bows down. None of the three have spoken before Abraham bows. Only Abraham speaks first, and when he does he makes himself the servant of all three! Then they answer as one.

After the meal one of them speaks to take leave and two leave. In vs. 20 Then Yăhwęḥ says... Then two of them leave, but amazingly, Abraham is still standing before Yăhwęḥ! When he finishes haggling then Yăhwęḥ leaves, going back to heaven. I know it does not say this, but in 19:24 we find out where he went.

But the two that left come to Sodom take credit for the plan to destroy the place (vs. 13), receive credit for showing mercy, and are credited for granting favor and showing mercy, and then given an offer by Lot to show more mercy, and then they take credit for tolerating him.

In 19:23 a waw conjunctive is placed before the divine name, and Yăhwęḥ destroys the place, which the two before took credit for planning. In vs. 24 Yăhwęḥ literally calls forth the judgment from Yăhwęḥ who is in heaven.

All these clues are the same type of clues that are used to identify who the Messenger is in other passages where the Messenger Yăhwęḥ appears.

How do we reconcile all of this with doctrinal traditions? Firstly, we are told that none can see Yăhwęḥ and live, and this evidently means in a certain glorified state, because Hagar and Ya'aqov, and others saw and still lived, including Mosheḥ. Secondly, we are told that no one has ever seen the Almighty in Yoḥ. 1:18, and then immediately afterward that the only kindred Almighty has revealed him. We also have the Holy Spĭrit showing himself as a dove and by other manifestations. And we have mention of the seven Spĭrits of the Almĭghty.

For lack of a better terms we can say that the Most High has many voices and can show himself in more than one place at a time. Further, singular pronouns or verb references to Him do not disclose how many persons he is. We can only say for sure that the Sŏn when completely limiting himself to his human state is truly one person in the sense that we experience ourselves as single persons. In a fully glorified state or partially glorified state we have no idea and should not speculate on it.

These revelations only lead me to propose a definition clarification of only kindred ($\mu o\nu o\gamma\varepsilon\nu\tilde{\eta}$), and that is that this term refers to human kinship by being born of woman as well as kinship to the Almĭghty being in nature Almĭghty. Because the Spĭrit is kindred to Almĭghty but not kindred to man. The Most High is only kindred to man in the Sŏn.

Second Timothy

1 ¹Paul, an emissary of the Anŏinted Yĕshua by the will of the Almĭghty, according to the promise of life, from that ζ which is in the Anŏinted Yĕshua, ²to Timothy, my beloved son. Loving-kindness, mercy and peace from the Almĭghty the Făther and the Anŏinted Yĕshua our Adŏnai.

³I thank the Almĭghty, whom I serve with a clear conscience the way my forefathers did, as I constantly remember you in my prayers night and day, ⁴longing to have seen you, (having been remembering your tears,) that I may be filled with joy, ⁵because I am mindful of the sincere faithfulness within you, which first dwelt in your grandmother Lois, and your mother Eunice, and I have been getting persuaded that it is in you as well.

⁶And for this reason I remind you to kindle afresh the gift of the Almĭghty which is in you through the laying on of my hands, ⁷because the Almĭghty has not given us a spirit of timidity, but of power and love and discipline. ⁸Therefore you shall not have been ashamed of the testimony of our Adŏnai, or of me his prisoner, but join with me in suffering for the good news according to the power of the Almĭghty, ⁹who rescues us, and calls with a holy calling, not according to our works ξ, but according to his own purpose, even loving-kindness which was given to us by the Anŏinted Yĕshua in times before times most immemorial, ¹⁰but now has been revealed by the appearing of our Rescuer the Anŏinted Yĕshua, who undoes death, and brings life and immortality to light through the good news, ¹¹for which I am appointed a proclaimer and an emissary and a teacher.

¹²For this reason I also am suffering these things, but I am not getting ashamed, because I have been knowing in whom I have been holding faithful, and I have been getting persuaded, in that he is able to guard my μconsignment unto that day. ¹³Be holding fast the pattern of sound words which you have heard from beside me, in the faithfulness and love, according to love in the Anŏinted Yĕshua. ¹⁴This good consignment you must now guard through the Holy Spĭrit who dwells in us.

¹⁵You have been knowing this, that all who are in Asia turned away from me, among whom are Phygelus and Hermogenes. ¹⁶Yăhweн grant mercy to the house of Onesiphorus, because he often refreshed me, and was not ashamed of my chains, ¹⁷but when he was in Rome, he eagerly searched for me, and found me. ¹⁸Yăhweн grant to him to find mercy from beside Yăhweн on that day. And you know very well what services he rendered at Ephesus.

1:9 ζ τῆς genitive of origin, meaning 'of that imcomparable Everlasting Life that belongs to Mĕssiah's divinity. **1:9** ξ = our former evil works. Cf. Ezek. 18:22. **1:12** μ "A deposit, a trust, or thing consigned to [some]one's faithful keeping" (Thayer). The idea is that Paul has consigned his soul for safekeeping to the Almĭghty. **1:13-14** Paul entrusts his legacy to Timothy, "the pattern of sound words which you have heard from me."

2 Timothy 2

2 ¹You therefore, my son, be getting yourself strong in the loving-kindness, according to that which is in the Anŏinted Yĕshua. ²And the things which you have heard from beside me in the presence of many witnesses, these entrust to faithful men, who will be able to teach others also. ³Suffer hardship with me, as a good soldier of the Anŏinted Yĕshua. ⁴No one serving as a soldier is entangling himself in the matters of this life, so that he might please the one who enlisted him as a soldier. ⁵And also if anyone may be competing as an athlete, he is not being crowned unless he may have competed lawfully. ⁶The hard-working farmer ought to be the first to receive his share of the crops. ⁷Be minding what I say, because Yăhweh will give you understanding in everything.

⁸Be remembering Yĕshua the Anŏinted, who had been getting raised from the dead, a descendant of David, according to my good news, ⁹for which I am suffering hardship even to imprisonment as a criminal, but the word of the Almĭghty has not been getting imprisoned. ¹⁰For this reason I am enduring all things for the sake of the chosen, that they also will have made a target of the deliverance which is through the Anŏinted One, Yĕshua, with everlasting glory. ¹¹It is a trustworthy statement, because if we died with him, we will also live with him. ¹²If we endure, we will also reign with him. If we deny him, he also will deny us. ¹³If we are faithless, he remains faithful, because he cannot deny himself.

¹⁴Be reminding them of these things, and solemnly charge them in the presence of the Almĭghty not to wrangle about words, which is useless, and leads to the ruin of the hearers. ¹⁵Be diligent to present yourself approved to the Almĭghty as a workman who does not need to be ashamed, interpreting the word of truth straightly. ¹⁶But be avoiding worldly and empty chatter, because it will lead to further irreverence, ¹⁷and their talk will spread like gangrene. Among them are Hymenaeus and Philetus, ¹⁸men who have gone astray from the truth, saying the resurrection to have already been happening, and thus they upset the faithfulness of some. ¹⁹Nevertheless, the firm foundation of the Almĭghty has been standing, having this seal. Yăhweh knows those who are his, and let everyone who is naming the name of Yăhweh shun iniquity.

²⁰Now in a large house there are not only gold and silver vessels, but also vessels of wood and of earthenware, and some to honor and some to dishonor. ²¹Therefore, if a man will have cleansed himself from these things, he will be a vessel for honor, having been getting himself made holy, useful to the Măster, having been getting himself prepared for every good work. ²²Now be fleeing from youthful lusts, and be pursuing justice, faithfulness, love and peace, with those who call on Yăhweh from a pure heart. ²³But be refusing foolish and ignorant investigations, having been knowing that they are producing fights. ²⁴And, Yăhweh's servant ought not to be fighting, but to be gentle to all, able to teach, patient when wronged, ²⁵with gentleness instructing those setting themselves in opposition, ʸlest ever the Almĭghty will have offered to them *the chance of*

2:25 γ→ever: See LSJ μήποτε (& Albert Barnes). The idea is that their opposition is preventing Gŏd from offering them repentance, a turning from sin, Gŏd's circumcision of their hearts. Gŏd is

being sorry and turning their heart *from sin* into a ᵋfull knowledge of the truth, ²⁶and they will have returned to their senses out of the snare of the Slanderer, *after* having been captured alive by him for that one's will.

3 ¹But be realizing this, that in the last days difficult times will come, ²because men will be lovers of self, lovers of money, boastful, arrogant, revilers, disobedient to parents, ungrateful, unholy, ³unloving, irreconcilable, malicious gossips, without self-control, brutal, haters of good, ⁴treacherous, reckless, having been getting themselves puffed up, lovers of pleasure rather than lovers of the Almĭghty, ⁵holding to a form of piety, although they have been themselves contradicting its power. So be turning away from these.

⁶Because among them are those who enter into households and captivate weak women who have been getting themselves heaped up with sins, led on by various impulses, ⁷always learning and never able to come to the knowledge of the truth. ⁸And just as Iannas and Iambre⁺ opposed Moshᵉh, so these ones also are opposing the truth, men who have been getting themselves depraved in the mind, rejected as regards the pledge of faithfulness. ⁹But they will not make further progress, because their folly will be obvious to all, as also that of those men came to be.

¹⁰But you followed my teaching, conduct, purpose, faithfulness, patience, love, perseverance, ¹¹persecutions, and sufferings, such as happened to me at Antioch, at Iconium and at Lystra, what persecutions I endured, and out of them all Yăhwe⎕ delivered me! ¹²And indeed, all who desire to live holy *lives* according to the Anŏinted Yĕshua will be persecuted. ¹³But evil men and impostors will continue to worsen, deceiving and being deceived.

¹⁴You, however, be remaining in the things you have learned and that ᵗʷere proved faithful to you, having been knowing alongside whom you have learned, ¹⁵and that from childhood you have been knowing the holy writings which are able to give you the wisdom that leads to deliverance through faithfulness, from that which is in the Anŏinted Yĕshua. ¹⁶Every writingᵂ ᶿinspired by the Almĭghty is ᵖprofitable for teaching, for reproof, for correction, *and* for training in righteousness, ¹⁷so that the man of the Almĭghty may be adequate, having been getting himself outfitted for every good work.

---

quite willing to circumcise the hearts of sinners if they would but first circumcise their own hearts to the truth. See Acts 5:31, 11:18; Deut. 30:6; 10:16; Jer. 4:4. **2:25** ε→truth; So long as men refuse to circumcise their hearts with the little truth they have seen, Gŏd cannot complete the job of circumcising their hearts with the full truth (ἐπίγνωσιν ἀληθείας).

3:8 φ Incorrectly thought to be Pharaoh's magicians in Jewish tradition, Paul, however, does not say they were magicians. These two were in fact the two Hyksos Pharaohs that opposed Moses: Yanassi and Maybre Sheshi. Moses fled from the one after he killed the taskmaster, and the other was the Pharaoh of the Exodus. **3:14** π→you = ἐπιστώθης (V-AIP-2S) < πιστόω = be proved faithful, from πιστός. **3:16** ω or *text*. The English term *Scripture* (< Latin = text, a writing) is unsuitable here because the sense *divinely inspired* is already built into the meaning of the term. **3:16** θ→Almĭghty: θεόπνευστος Adj. = *Almĭghty-(breathed, winded, spirited)*. In the Greek writers the term is applied to their seers and poets. **3:16** ρ Other manuscripts read 'also profitable.' But καί is omitted by the old Latin (it vgᵈ), Syriac (syᵖ), Ambrosiaster, Origin, Clement, and Tertullian. Against καί are these points: 1) Original presence of καί is necessary to the translation, 'all Scripture *is* God breathed <u>and *is*</u> profitable....' But "All Scripture is inspired" is a tautologous repetition, therefore an unlikely expression based on anachronistic usage of

2 Timothy 4

4 ¹I solemnly charge you in the presence of the Almĭghty and of the Anŏinted Yĕshua, who is to judge the living and the dead, and by his appearing and his kingdom, ²proclaim the word, be ready in season and out of season, reprove, rebuke, exhort, with great patience and instruction.

³Because the time will come when they will not endure sound doctrine, but wanting to have their ears tickled, they will accumulate for themselves teachers in accordance to their own desires, ⁴and will turn away their ears from the truth, and will turn aside to myths.

⁵But you, be getting sober in all things. Endure hardship. Do the work of one announcing good news. Fulfill your ministry.

⁶Because I am already getting poured out as a drink offering, and the time of my departure has been standing by. ⁷I have been fighting the good fight. I have been finishing the course. I have been watching over the pledge of faithfulness. ⁸Henceforth there is getting laid up for me the crown of righteousness, which Yăhwᴇн, the righteous Judge, will award to me on that day, and not only to me, but also to all who have been loving his appearing.

⁹Make every effort to come to me soon, ¹⁰because Demas, having loved this present age, has deserted me and gone to Thessalonica. Crescens has gone to Galatia, Titus to Dalmatia. ¹¹Only Luke is with me. Pick up Mark and be bringing him with you, because he is useful to me for service. ¹²But Tychicus I have sent to Ephesus. ¹³When you come be bringing the cloak which I left at Troas with Carpus, and the scrolls, especially the parchments. ¹⁴Alexander the copper-smith did me much harm. Yăhwᴇн will repay him according to his deeds. ¹⁵Be guarding against him yourself, because he vigorously opposed our teaching.

¹⁶At my first defense no one supported me, but all deserted me. May it not be considered against them. ¹⁷Yet, Yăhwᴇн stood with me, and strengthened me, in order that through me the proclamation will have been fully accomplished, and all the nations will have heard. And I was delivered out of the lion's mouth. ¹⁸Yăhwᴇн will deliver me from every evil deed, and will bring me safely to his heavenly kingdom. To him be the glory forever and ever. Amen.

¹⁹Greet Prisca and Aquila, and the household of Onesiphorus. ²⁰Erastus remained at Corinth, but Trophimus I left sick at Miletus. ²¹Make every effort to come before winter. Eubulus greets you, also Pudens and Linus and Claudia and all the brothers.

²²Yăhwᴇн be with your spirit. Loving-kindness be with you.

γραφή. 2) The proper sense with καί is either, 'every writing is inspired by God, and profitable....' (predicate adjective) or 'every writing inspired by God is also profitable ....' (attributive adjective). The first sense is simply not true. ▷ See Heinrich Meyer. ▷ Paul's statement was motivated by informal gnostic teachings later formalized as a full rejection of the Torah and Prophets. They would piously agree that the writings transmitted by the Jews were inspired by God, but then they would deny its application by their doctrinal system. ▷ In vs. 14-15 only writings up to Mĕssiah are in view. ▷ Paul's wording strongly implies a rebuke to many who would concede that all the Torah, Prophets, Writings, and Evangelists were inspired, but that only certain lately inspired writings were useful for "teaching, for reproof, for correction, for training in righteousness." This position was what the Gnostics preached when they elevated their own writings and teachings. It is also the position of Christianity, which teaches the inspiration of the Torah and Prophets, but denies that all of it is profitable for training in righteousness.

Modern Christians claim that only the New Testament (or even a smaller part of it in the case of dispensationalists) is useful for defining valid commandments. ▷ The common translation shifts Paul's emphasis from explaining what inspiration means to making the claim for inspiration in the first place. The latter was not in dispute, but translating and interpreting Paul to be focused on it is a diversionary tactic.

Counting to Ṣabbath

In Hebrew, "first day unto the Ṣabbath" takes the form: יוֹם אֶחָד בְּשַׁבָּת. The point of this essay is to show that translation of the phrase to Greek normally requires (1) a separate preposition for בְּ, and (2) the word Ṣabbath is in its literal sense, שַׁבָּת, and (3) Ṣabbath is singular, and not plural. With these usages demonstrated, it will be plain that Ṣabbath does not mean 'week' in the Hebrew idiom. It should also be plain that by the normal rules μια [ημερα] των σαββατων does not represent this idiom, but rather "the first day of the Ṣabbaths" based upon "day of/for the Ṣabbaths" only meaning the Ṣabbath day. This is explained elsewhere (cf. Acts 20:6-7 notes).

The idiom בְּשַׁבָּת does not occur with the 6th or 7th day, either in Syriac or Hebrew. This is a huge clue that Ṣabbath is being retained in its literal sense. What we see for the 6th and 7th days are עֶרֶב שַׁבָּת and שַׁבָּת respectively, which is not 'eve of the week' or 'week.' Thus if Ṣabbath means week in usages for days 1-5, then strangely it changes to its literal sense as soon as we come to day 6 and 7! It is rather the case that it means 'week' in none of the cases.

First note what Gesenius' Hebrew Lexicon says on the usage of the preposition בְּ.

בְּ No. "(4) of motion to a place: *ad, an* (etwas) hin, *to, unto, upon*. This Beth differs from אֶל in this signification properly and generally, in that אֶל implies motion to a place, whether the end be arrived at or not, nach (etwas) hin. בְּ in this sense signifies the reaching the end and remaining at it. It nearly approaches in meaning to עַד *usque ad*, unto, which is however properly used, when the termination and end of the motion or action has to be more accurately stated: bis an (etwas) hin [to go up to (something)]; although the later writers appear to like to use עַד for אֶל; Gen. 11:4, רֹאשׁוֹ בַשָּׁמַיִם "a tower, whose head may reach unto heaven" (not less correctly Jer. 51:9; "her judgment reacheth unto heaven," אֶל הַשָּׁמַיִם comp. Winer, Exeget. Stud. pg. 53)."

So now we are ready to state the meaning of the idiom: בְּאֶחָד בְּשַׁבָּת. This plainly translates, "On one unto the Sabbath," and Sabbath does not mean "week." Compare "Sabbath unto Sabbath" (Isa. 66:23, MT). The preposition has the force of unto. The conclusion is made all the more plainer by the fact that we typically see "eve of the Sabbath" עֶרֶב שַׁבָּת for the sixth day of the week and not *שֵׁשׁ בְּשַׁבָּת. Neither do we see "seventh unto the Sabbath." We only see Sabbath (שַׁבָּת) in that case. But it is perfectly easy to say "sixth day of the week," and "seventh day of the week." These two cases are not observed at Qumran or in Seder Olam, the Mishnah, or in Syriac (cf. ܫܒܐ). These exceptions show that the idiom בְּשַׁבָּת means to count days 'unto Ṣabbath' and not 'in a week.'

Qumran 4Q252 shows the following usages:

C1 L4	באחד בשבת	on one unto Ṣ.
C1 L7	יום חמשה בשבת	day five unto Ṣ.
C1 L8	שולשה בשבת	three unto Ṣ.
C1 L9	יום הרביעי	day fourth
C1 L9	יום החמישי	day fifth
C1 L10	יום הששי	day sixth
C1 L11	יום רביעי לשבת	day fourth to Ṣ.
C1 L11	יום רביעי	day fourth
C1 L12	לשבת	to Ṣ.
C1 L13	יום אחד בשבת	day one unto Ṣ.
C1 L17	באחד בשב׳	on one unto Ṣ.
C2 L2	באחד בשבת	on one unto Ṣ.
C2 L3	באחד בשבת	on one unto Ṣ.

The Greek translators of the LXX, it appears, had no consistent way of translating the preposition. But they normally tried to supply one, even if it was not correct for the Hebrew:

Exo 16:5	יוֹם יוֹם	ἡμέραν εἰς ἡμέραν
1Chr 12:22	יוֹם בְּיוֹם	ἡμέραν ἐξ ἡμέρας
2Chr 8:13	יוֹם בְּיוֹם	ἡμέρας ἐν ἡμέρα
2Chr 30:21	יוֹם בְּיוֹם	ἡμέραν καθ' ἡμέραν
Isa 66:23	שַׁבָּת בְּשַׁבַּתּוֹ	σάββατον ἐκ σαββάτου, correct to: Sabbath in its ceasing.
1Chr 27:1	חֹדֶשׁ בְּחֹדֶשׁ	μῆνα ἐκ μηνός, but possibly: חֹדֶשׁ בְחֹדֶשׁ.
Lev 25:53	שָׁנָה בְּשָׁנָה	ἐνιαυτὸν ἐξ ἐνιαυτοῦ
Deu 14:22	שָׁנָה בְּשָׁנָה	ἐνιαυτὸν κατ' ἐνιαυτόν
Jud 16:20	כְּפַעַם בְּפַעַם	ὡς ἅπαξ καὶ ἅπαξ

The LXX translators rendered "into" (εἰς) "from" (ἐκ) "with" (ἐν) and "down to" (κατ').

We would expect the בשבת idiom to strongly reject the ablative option (ἐκ) if it were used for counting days of the week in Greek. This is because the idiom אחד בשבת counts days 'unto the Şabbath' and not 'from' a previous Şabbath. Neither could an ablative specify distance from a Şabbath going before it in time, because then "one from the Şabbath" would mean Friday.

To propose a means of translating אחד בשבת into Greek which agrees with both counting to the Şabbath and the LXX choices for the preposition, we would have to choose either εἰς or ἐν or κατα. It would appear that εἰς fits best. Thus, "first day to the Şabbath" in Greek would appear as "μίαν ἡμέραν εἰς το σάββατον," using κατα "down to" or more as a pure Hebraism, "μιᾷ ἡμέρα ἐν τῷ σαββάτῳ." This last version would make it difficult to understand in Greek as is evidenced with the difficulty the LXX translators had with translating the preposition.

Though μιᾷ τῶν σαββάτων in Ecclesiastical Greek is taken to mean Sunday, it should be now clear that it is no reproduction of אחד בשבת. And the meaning 'week' for שבת is clearly ruled out by the Hebrew usages. So also is an ad hoc ablative interpretation, "one day from the Şabbath" which is challenged by the plural, the fact that it is classical Greek, by the fact that "day of the Şabbaths" already has a meaning that is grammatically confirmed by parallel texts (Mat. 26:17; Mark 14:12; Luke 22:7), and by the fact that 'from the Şabbath' is not the way the Hebrew idiom for counting days works.

Moreso, the external chronology (Mat. 12:40; Mark 8:31; Luke 24:21, 23:54; and Mat. 28:1) shows that the Ecclesiastical Church has lied about the chronology Friday-Sunday. The solutions, therefore, must be based on contemporary evidence untouched by their corruptions. By setting aside the corrupt tradition, we are able to abide by all historical and grammatical norms, as well as all astronomical and chronological norms.

It is not just matters of chronology that the majority of Christianity has corrupted and suppressed for many centuries. It is not just the meaning of the word Şabbath. It is also the meaning of the noun faithfulness, and the verb to hold faithful. It is also the administration of divine justice, and the place of good works and obeying the divine Law in the way of salvation. It is the need to maintain good works and obedience to remain in the faith vs. false doctrines of merits to compensate for sin. The corruption of the faith concerns everything important.

Gŏd has allowed this corruption to happen because the human race is corrupt. Many people will accept a corrupt version of Gŏd's word because it appeals to their flesh. Also, Satan has used this to weaken the majority of Christians (cf. Dan. 7:25). Gŏd has allowed it to encourage the half committed to spread the remaining truth they have not corrupted further among the nations. He has used the corrupt Christianity to reach others who are earnest about living the truth. Yisra'el was exiled because it corrupted Gŏd's word. What little of the word they took with them benefited the nations. This is same reason why all the translations have become progressively more and more corrupt. And the nations are benefiting from the crumbs.

But the time arrives when the rescue operation must be mounted. The Almĭghty requires the errors to be substantially corrected before he will return the listeners to Tsiyon. He will only rescue Yisra'el on the basis of the truth, truth which will cause most Christians to betray one another. This side effect he wanted to avoid as long as possible. But to save the remnant he must now allow it. Because Satan escalates his war to destroy humanity. And the only weapon that can defeat him is truth, the Word of the Almĭghty.

Titus

1 ¹Paul, a servant of the Almĭghty, and an emissary of Yĕshua the Anŏinted, concerning the faithfulness of the chosen of the Almĭghty and a full knowledge of the truth, which is according to reverent devotion ²based on the hope of everlasting life, which the Almĭghty, who cannot lie, promised long ago. ³And in the proper season, he has revealed his word by means of public proclamation, with which I am held faithful according to the commandment of the Almĭghty, our Rescuer.

⁴To Titus, my true child in a common faithfulness: loving-kindness and peace from the Almĭghty, the Făther and the Anŏinted Yĕshua our Rescuer.

⁵In favor of this I left you in Crete, that you may set in order the remaining things, and will have appointed elders throughout the cities as I directed you: ⁶if any man be above reproach, the husband of one wife, having faithful children, not accused of debauchery or rebellion, ⁷because the overseer must be above reproach as the Almĭghty's steward, not arrogant, not quick-tempered, not addicted to wine, not a bully, not greedy for money, ⁸but hospitable, loving what is good, sensible, just, devout, self-controlled, ⁹holding fast the faithful word which is in accordance with the teaching, that he may be able both to exhort in sound doctrine and to refute those who contradict.

¹⁰Because there are many rebellious men, empty talkers and deceivers, especially those of the circumcision, ¹¹who must be silenced because they are upsetting whole families, teaching things they should not teach, to favor shameful profit.

¹²One of themselves, a prophet of their own, said, "Cretans are always liars, evil beasts, lazy gluttons." ¹³This testimony is true. For this cause be reproving them severely that they may be healthy in the pledge of faithfulness, ¹⁴not paying attention to Yehudi myths and commandments of men who turn away from the truth.

¹⁵ ˣAll things are clean in the clean, but to those who have been making themselves defiled and unfaithful, nothing is clean, but even the mind and the

---

1:12 χ The quotation is from Epimenidies. "While tending his father's sheep, Epimenides is said to have fallen asleep for fifty-seven years in a Cretan cave sacred to Zeus, after which he reportedly awoke with the gift of prophecy (Diogenes Laërtius i. 109-115). Plutarch writes that Epimenides purified Athens after the pollution brought by the Alcmeonidae, and that the seer's expertise in sacrifices and reform of funeral practices were of great help to Solon in his reform of the Athenian state. The only reward he would accept was a branch of the sacred olive, and a promise of perpetual friendship between Athens and Cnossus (Plutarch, Life of Solon, 12; Aristotle, Ath. Pol. 1)" (The Encyclopedia). The quotation comes from this context. In the poem, Minos addresses Zeus thus: "They fashioned a tomb for you, holy and high one, Cretans, always liars, evil beasts, idle bellies. But you are not dead: you live and abide forever, For in you we live and move and have our being." Thus it is established that the poet was a pagan idolater. It is quite clear then that Paul deliberately took the poet out of context to make a sarcastic but true point about Cretans. It is with a similar design that Yehudah 1:14 (Jude) quotes from "Enoch." ▷ See also Jude 1:14.

1:15 χ→in the clean: In an effort to appear spiritual various strains of Christianity added to the Law by forbidding foods that were permitted according to the Law. These were the commandments of men: see vs. 14. These things are clean in the clean because they do not recognize them as commandments, and therefore the conscience is not defiled to eat them. It remains clean. The phrase also has the further sense

Titus 2

conscience has been getting defiled in them. ¹⁶They profess to have been knowing the Almĭghty, but by their works they are contradicting themselves, being detestable and disobedient, and unapproved for any good work.

2 ¹But as for you, be speaking the things which are fitting for sound doctrine. ²Older men are to be temperate, dignified, sensible, sound in faithfulness, in love, in perseverance.

³Older women likewise are to be reverent in their behavior, not malicious gossips, nor having been enslaving themselves to much wine, teaching what is good, ⁴that they may be encouraging the young women to love their husbands, to love their children, ⁵to be sensible, pure, workers at home, kind, being subject to their own husbands, that the word of the Almĭghty may not be dishonored.

⁶Likewise be urging the young men to be wise minded. ⁷In all things show yourself to be an example of good deeds, with purity in teaching, dignified, ⁸healthy in speech which is beyond contradiction, in order that the contrary will have been put to shame, having nothing to be saying about us.

⁹Urge servants to be subject to their own masters in everything, to be well-pleasing, not argumentative, ¹⁰not pilfering, but showing all good faithfulness that they may be making attractive the teaching of the Almĭghty our Rescuer in every respect.

¹¹Because the ᵖloving-kindness of the Almĭghty has appeared, a rescuing ᵖone for all men, ¹²instructing us, so that having denied irreverence and worldly desires, sensibly and righteously and reverently, we shall have lived in the present age, ¹³looking forward to the blessed hope and the appearing of the glory

---

of Rom. 14:14, 20. All things (including the accidentally contaminated) are clean in the conscience of the clean, because being eaten with a clean conscience they cannot defile it. A sin of ignorance cannot make the conscience guilty unless the matter is revealed. As soon as someone knowingly violates the commandment (cf. Rom. 14:14), then the conscience is unclean.

2:11 ᵖ The adjective *saving* is taken as a noun substantive: *a saving one*. It's gender refers to 'loving-kindness,' hence 'a saving [loving kindness].

2:13 η→Gŏd: See Isa. 9:6: אֵל גִּבּוֹר *El Gibbor*. And Mĕssiah is also called the reverse: גַּבְרִיאֵל (Mighty man of Gŏd). See Luke 1. And also מִיכָאֵל *Micha'el* (Who is like Gŏd). See Dan. 12:1. Jude. 1:9. 1 Thess. 4:16. Gen. 48:16; Jud. 13:18. "THEN IT WAS IN MY SEEING (I DANIᴇL) THE VISION, THEN I SOUGHT UNDERSTANDING. AND BEHOLD, ONE STANDING OPPOSITE ME AS THE APPEARANCE OF A STRONG MAN (גֶּבֶר, *gaver*). THEN I HEARD THE VOICE OF A MAN (אָדָם, *'adam*) AMID THE ULAI RIVER. THEN HE CALLED OUT. THEN THE MIGHTY MAN OF GŎD SAID (וַיֹּאמַר גַּבְרִיאֵל, *Wayyomar Gavri'el*), 'MAKE THIS ONE UNDERSTAND THE VISION.' THEN ONE [ANOTHER MESSENGER] CAME NEAR MY STATION, AND WHEN HE CAME I HAD BEEN TERRIFIED. THEN I FELL ON MY FACE. THEN HE SAID TO ME, 'UNDERSTAND SON OF MAN, BECAUSE FOR THE TIME OF THE END IS THE VISION.' AND WHILE HE WAS SPEAKING WITH ME, I HAD BEEN ASLEEP ON MY FACE EARTHWARD. THEN HE TOUCHED ON ME. THEN HE MADE ME STAND AT MY STATION.... THEN I WAS STILL SPEAKING IN PRAYER, AND THE MAN, THE MIGHTY MAN OF GŎD (גַּבְרִיאֵל, *Gavri'el*) WHOM I HAD SEEN IN THE VISION IN THE BEGINNING, [*I MYSELF*] BEING WEARIED WITH WEARINESS, WAS TOUCHING ME AT THE TIME OF THE AFTERNOON OFFERING...THEN I LIFTED MY EYES. THEN I SAW, AND BEHOLD ONE MAN DRESSED IN LINEN, AND HIS HIPS BEING GIRDED WITH GOLD OF UPHAZ....AND I HAD FALLEN ASLEEP ON MY FACE, AND MY FACE EARTHWARD. AND BEHOLD A HAND [OF ANOTHER MESSENGER] HAD TOUCHED ME....FOR NOW I HAVE BEEN SENT TO YOU." (Dan. 8:15-18; 9:21; 10:5, 9-10; 11). There is a vision, a visitation, and a vision. In the first vision, the man is introduced, and then the message turned over to another. In the visitation it is the man only. In the last vision, the man is seen, and heard, but again the message is given over to another. The man in linen then interrupts the messenger in 10:16-19. Then the messenger continues after the man in linen departs. "AND BEHOLD, [ONE] AS THE LIKENESS OF A SON OF MAN

of our ⁿgreat Gŏd and Rescuer, the Anŏinted Yĕshua, ¹⁴who gave himself on our behalf, that he may ransom^α us from all lawlessness and may purify for himself a people as his own special possession, zealous for good deeds.

¹⁵These things be speaking and be exhorting and be reproving with all authority. Let no one be disregarding you.

3

¹Be reminding them to be subject to rulers, to authorities, to be obedient, to be ready for every good deed, ²to malign no one, to be uncontentious, gentle, showing every consideration for all men.

³Because we also once were foolish ourselves, disobedient, deceived, enslaved to various lusts and pleasures, spending our life in malice and envy, hateful, hating one another. ⁴But when kindness and generosity was shown by our Almĭghty Rescuer, ⁵he rescued us, not by *the customary* works^β, those which we had practiced for merit^μ, but according to his mercy, through the washing of rebirth and renewing by the Holy Spĭrit, ⁶whom he pours out upon us richly

---

WAS TOUCHING ON MY LIP....THEN I SAID TO THE ONE STANDING IN FRONT OF ME, ADŎNI [MY LŎRD]...AND HOW IS ABLE THE SERVANT OF MY ADŎNI, THIS *WAY* TO SPEAK WITH MY ADONI *LIKE* THIS?" (10:17). The one in the likeness of a son of man is the one who would become Mĕssiah. He is called Adŏni and the prophet is his servant. But the messenger who finishes the message is simply a fellow servant. "TRULY, THOU ART A GŎD MAKING HIMSELF HIDDEN, ALMĬGHTY OF YISRA∙EL, SAVIOR" (Isa. 45:15). ▷ But this is not easy to understand. The man seen at first in the vision implies that at some point another gave the rest of the message. The narrative switches speakers with barely a clue as to who is speaking. Such is also the case in Zechariah and Revelation. The only way to tell which is the son of man is by the description, the role, and the manner of address. The identifications are made by the context, parallelism, and repeat phrases, and subtle clues. But the pieces cannot be connected together while relying on translators to decide what ambiguous phrases mean based on their traditions. So I am telling you what I wish had been told me years ago. The puzzle may be solved when they are out of the way. Why does the Almĭghty hide himself so? It is the parable principle again, and the weed principle.

2:14 α Lawlessness exacts or charges the ransom price (cf. Hos. 13:14; Rev. 5:9). This is the price that Messiah pays in the flesh to invade the kingdom of darkness to set men free. In Gen. 3:15 it is the serpent that strikes the chosen seed on the heel who then crushes his head. He is the Almĭghty Son, the only kindred of the Father, who has been descending from heaven to ransom Yisra'el. His wound in the heel is the price extorted by lawlessness. The spilled blood of Messiah is also symbolic of the cost in divine life necessary to cleanse our hearts of the malignancies of sin. The word used here translated 'ransom' (λυτρώσηται < λύτρον) is the price to free a slave from bondage. It is those keeping the slave in bondage that collect the price. In the Septuagint, this word often represents the Hebrew גָּאַל and פָּדָה. A Redeemer is a person who pays a price to deliver someone from bondage. A kinsman redeemer is a person who delivers the family name of his brother from extinction or death. ▷ It should not go without notice that modern Christianity has turned the message of redemption backwards, claiming that the price paid was to satisfy the wrath of an angry god. Satan's major flipping of the narrative began with the former Gnostic Augustine (died AD 430), and then was further developed by Anselm of Canterbury (died AD 1109) in *Cur Deus Homo*, and then has infected the whole of the Christian religion through Calvinism (AD 1500's to present). But in more ancient times it was not so. The ransom paradigm of the good news was understood much more widely then. And it is still understood by a minority of Christians.

3:5 δ In the Law, the Almighty says, "I am doing loving-kindness to the thousandth generation to those loving me and to those keeping my commandments" (Exodus 20:6; Deu. 7:9). The loving-kindness חֶסֶד is his mercy, his forgiveness, his grace, or his reward for a job well done. It is quite clear that these benefits are for those holding faithful to the Almighty. Faithfulness yields works. What then does Paul mean by "not from works?" He does not mean obedience cooperating with divine loving-kindness. Rather he means the Rabbinical doctrine of *zekut* (See Appendix VIII and 434) by which personal merits or imputed merit transferred to one's account from exceptionally pious Jews is applied to personal demerits (sins) to cancel them out. This doctrine is diametrically opposed to the forgiveness of sins because it turns it into a transaction by which the Almĭghty is compensated for sin. In fact, it is not even forgiveness at all. So this is what Paul meant by saying "not from works." But there are many false teachers who suppose Paul meant walking in grace required no obedience to God's commandments. They misinterpret these words to mean that remaining (or abiding) in His favor requires

through Yĕshua the Anŏinted our Rescuer, ⁷so that having been administered justice done by that one's loving-kindness we shall have become heirs according to the hope of everlasting life. ⁸This is a faithful statement. And about these things I am wanting you to be affirming completely, so that those who have been holding faithful to the Almĭghty may be taking care to engage in good deeds. These things are good and profitable for men.

⁹But be shunning foolish controversies and genealogies and strife and disputes about the ˣLaw, because they are unprofitable and worthless. ¹⁰Be rejecting a ᵖdivisive man after a first and second warning, ¹¹having been knowing that such a man has been getting himself perverted and is sinning, being self-condemned.

¹²When I may have sent Artemas or Tychicus to you, hurry to come to me at Nicopolis, because I have been deciding to winter there. ¹³Diligently help Zenas the lawyer and Apollos on their way so that nothing may be lacking for them. ¹⁴And let our people also be learning to engage in good deeds to meet pressing needs, that they may not be unfruitful.

¹⁵All who are with me greet you. Greet those who love us in faithfulness. Loving-kindness be with you all.

---

no obedience. These teachers are fools who believe in neither repentance nor forgiveness, who expect Gŏd to acquit them from the good deeds of a pious Jew. Salvation is not all by unmerited favor. It is by a combination of merited favor and unmerited favor. And one is required to participate in the merited favor to receive the gift of the unmerited favor. The false teachers have made Christians to fear listening to any Scripture which contradicts them. Therefore they are disobedient and persecute those who want to be obedient. **3:5** μ (צדקה, δικαιοσύνη) *merit, charity.* **3:9** χ There were many disputes about the Law among the faithful, who upheld the law. The disputing was not that of the faithful opposing those who were anti-Law or who thought part or all of it was abolished. But the disputes referred to were on matters of interpretation of how to observe it. For there will always be factions. And Paul does not condemn legitimate discussion or proof of points, but rather divisive and abusive dispute with parties condemning parties or slandering each other in a spirit of enmity. Such disputing is now as widespread in the Messianic Faith as it is among Jewish factions in Judaism or among Christians debating positions of the eschatology of the Second Coming. ▷ If a difference cannot be reasonably discussed or explained, then one should take a pass on it. Many are so far adrift from the truth on many subjects, and immature at the same time, that only a little attempt at reasonable discussion with them quickly exposes a divisive attitude. The only time any teacher should ever allow it is if these immaturities are exposed alongside the truth for the sake of others. **3:10** ρ αἱρετικὸν = hairetikon = heretic. Originally this word meant (1) someone who caused divisions among the faithful over issues that do not matter (adiaphora), chiefly by elevating personal convictions to be a point of division among brothers, or by making people enemies over trivial disputes; (2) someone who introduced false doctrine into an Assembly or among the faithful. But the Church added a third definition (3) anyone who caused a division away from whatever they taught. Then they claimed such a person was a heretic and upsetting the unity of the Church, and that their difference with the majority should be swept away no matter what for the sake of 'unity.' This is because in wordly eyes all differences do not matter so long as everyone is building the tower together. It is the same paradigm that claims all nations are equal, all cultures are equal. It is a paradigm that refuses to recognize irreconcilable differences in order to centralize and amass power. It is the spirit of lawlessness, the operating principle of the Antichrist, and the engine of false traditions. ▷ But someone who causes a division by introducing truth among the faithful where heresy has been accepted as the norm is not a *hairetikon*. Only wordly Christians who are devoid of the truth listen to calls for unity when they should be examining the facts to see if they, their teachers, or their ancestors have been led astray on a matter. The spiritual, on the other hand, listen to the Spirit, and are willing to correct the matters in which they are erring.

Philemon

1 ¹Paul, a prisoner of the Anŏinted Yĕshua, and Timothy our brother, to Philemon our beloved brother and fellow worker, ²and to Apphia our sister, and to Archippus our fellow soldier, and to the assembly in your house. ³Loving-kindness to you and peace from the Almĭghty, our Făther and Adŏnai Yĕshua the Anŏinted.

⁴I am thanking my Almĭghty always, making mention of you in my prayers, ⁵hearing of your love, and the faithfulness which you have toward Adŏnai Yĕshua, and toward all the holy ones, ⁶so that the fellowship of your faithfulness will have become effective in the complete knowledge of every good thing which is in you for the Anŏinted's sake, ⁷because I have much joy and comfort in your love, because the hearts of the holy ones have been getting refreshed through you, brother.

⁸Therefore, though I have much boldness in view of the Anŏinted to command you to do what is proper, ⁹yet for love's sake I rather appeal—being such a one as Paul, the elderly, and now also a prisoner of the Anŏinted Yĕshua:

¹⁰I appeal to you for my child, whom I have begotten in my imprisonment, Onesimus, ¹¹who formerly was useless to you, but now is useful both to you and to me. ¹²I have sent him back to you in person, that is, as if sending my own heart, ¹³whom I wanted to keep with me, that on your behalf he may be ministering to me in my imprisonment for the good news, ¹⁴but without your consent I did not want to do anything, that your goodness may not be as by compulsion, but of your own free will.

¹⁵Because perhaps he was for this reason parted from you for a while, that you should have him back forever, ¹⁶no longer as a slave, but more than a slave, a beloved brother, especially to me, but how much more to you, both in the flesh and in Yăhweh.

¹⁷If then you regard me *as* a partner, receive him as you would me. ¹⁸But if he has wronged you in any way, or owes you anything, be charging that to my account.

¹⁹I, Paul, write with my own hand. I will repay (where I should be saying to you that you owe to me even your own self). ²⁰Yes, brother, let me benefit from you in view of Yăhweh. Refresh my heart in view of the Anŏinted.

²¹Having been getting persuaded in your listening, I write to you, having been knowing that you will do even more than what I say.

²²And at the same time also be preparing me lodging, because I hope that through your prayers I will be given to you.

²³Epaphras, my fellow prisoner belonging to the Anŏinted Yĕshua, greets you, ²⁴and Mark, Aristarchus, Demas, and Luke, my fellow workers.

²⁵The loving-kindness of Adŏnai Yĕshua the Anŏinted be with your spirit.

Philemon

(continued from Genesis Note page 444)

³Then the Almȋghty said, "Let there be light!" Then there was light. Then the Almȋghty saw the light, that it was good. ⁴Then the Almȋghty was making a division between the light and between the darkness. ⁵ᵃThen the Almȋghty called the light 'day.' ⁵ᵇ(And the darkness he calls 'night.') ⁵ᶜThen there was setting. Then there was daybreak. One day.

The remaining five days proceed to relate what was created during the daytime, and then each ends with the refrain, "Then there is setting. Then there is daybreak. The {2nd, 3rd, 4th, 5th, 6th} day." The seventh day is then presented as dawn to dusk without an ending night. The refrain is omitted.

Now in terms of creation days, the Ṣabbaṯh is introduced with the night of the sixth day:

³¹Then the Almȋghty sees all which he had made. And behold, it was very good. Then there is setting. Then there is daybreak. The sixth day. ²:¹Then are finished the heavens and the earth, and all their hosts. ²Then the Almȋghty declares to be finished on the seventh day his work which he had done. Then the Almȋghty rests on the seventh day from all his work which he had done. ³Then the Almȋghty declares to be blessed the seventh day. Then he declares it to be holy, because on it he had rested from all his work, which the Almȋghty had created to do. ⁴ᵃThese are the histories of the heavens and the earth in their being created.

The implication of "the Almȋghty sees all" is that he stopped working before the night of the sixth day, so the Ṣabbaṯh rest began with the night of the sixth day. But he waits until the seventh day to *declare* it finished. The verb tense is a rare usage called a "declarative Piˑel," e.g. Lev. 13:3 טִמֵּא. Also צִדֵּק and נִקָּה. The LXX and SP both missed this and altered their versions to "finished on the sixth day." Therefore, in terms of the creation calendar days the Ṣabbaṯh was the night of the sixth day with the seventh day. The seventh day was simply dawn to dusk. This produces an interesting symmetry in the account. The first definition of day was the 'light,' which is dawn to dusk, and at the end of the account, the seventh day is dawn to dusk again. The first literal day begins the first calendar day. The last literal day ends the Ṣabbaṯh, which incorporated the night of the sixth day.

It is critical to understand that the KJV, "And the evening and the morning were the {1st, 2nd, 3rd, 4th, 5th, 6th} day" is pure fantasy. The verb, translated 'were' (underlined) has been relocated, pluralized, and made past tense. This allows the reader to improperly invert the time line implicitly redefining evening and morning as well. But, "Then it *is* setting. Then it *is* daybreak" corresponds to the Hebrew.

It is also evident that many recent translators are also wording the text with the KJV idea in their head. A footnote in the ESV Study Bible on Gen. 1:5c tries to correct the mistaken idea, "The order—evening, *then* morning—helps the reader to follow the flow of the passage: after the workday (vv. 3-5a) there is an evening, and then a morning, implying that there is a nighttime (the worker's daily rest) in between. Thus the reader is prepared for the next workday to dawn."

Ya'aqov

1 ¹Ya'aqov, a servant of the Almĭghty, and of Adŏnai Yĕshua *the* Anŏinted, to the twelve tribes who are dispersed abroad, greetings. ²Consider it all joy, my brothers, when you may have encountered various trials, ³knowing that the testing of your faithfulness produces endurance. ⁴And let endurance be having its perfect result, that you may be perfect and complete, lacking in nothing. ⁵But if any of you lacks wisdom, let him be asking from beside the Almĭghty, who gives to all men generously and without reproach, and it will be given to him. ⁶But let him be asking in trusting faithfulness without any doubting, for the one who doubts has been getting likened to the surf of the sea getting wind blown and being wind tossed. ⁷For let not that man be expecting that he will receive anything from beside Yăhweн, ⁸being a double-minded man, unstable in all his ways.

⁹But let the brother of humble circumstances be glorying in his high position. ¹⁰And let the rich man glory in his humiliation, because like flowering grass he will pass away. ¹¹For the sun rises with a scorching wind, and withers the grass. And its flower falls off, and the beauty of its appearance is destroyed. So also the rich man in the midst of his pursuits will fade away.

¹²Blessed *is the* man who perseveres under trial, because once he has been approved, he will receive the crown of life, which he has promised to those who love him. ¹³Let no one be saying when he is tempted, "I am being tempted by the Almĭghty." For the Almĭghty cannot be tempted by evil, and he himself does not tempt anyone. ¹⁴But each one is tempted when he is carried away and enticed by his own lust. ¹⁵Then when lust has conceived, it gives birth to sin. And when sin is completely finished, it brings forth death. ¹⁶Do not be getting deceived, my beloved brothers.

¹⁷Every good thing bestowed and every perfect gift is from above, coming down from the Făther of lights, with whom there is no variation, or shifting shadow. ¹⁸In the exercise of his will he brought us forth by the word of truth, so that we may be, as it were, the first fruits among his creatures. ¹⁹You must have been knowing *this*, my beloved brothers. So let everyone be quick to hear, slow to speak and slow to anger. ²⁰For the anger of man does not achieve the justice of the Almĭghty.

²¹Therefore putting aside all filthiness and all that remains of wickedness, in humility receive the word implanted, which is able to rescue your souls. ²²But be becoming yourselves doers of the word, and not merely hearers who delude themselves. ²³For if anyone is a hearer of the word and not a doer, he has been getting likened to a man who looks at his natural face in a mirror, ²⁴because once he has looked at himself and has been going away, he has immediately forgotten what kind of person he was. ²⁵But one who looks intently at the perfect Law, the Law of liberty, and abides by it, not having become a forgetful hearer but an effectual doer, this man will be blessed in what he does.

²⁶If anyone thinks himself to be religious, and yet does not bridle his tongue but deceives his heart, this man's religion is worthless. ²⁷This is pure and undefiled religion in the sight of our Almĭghty and Făther: to visit orphans and widows in their distress, and to keep oneself unstained by the world.

2 ¹My brothers, do not be holding the faithfulness of our glorious Adŏnai Yĕshua the Anŏinted with discrimination. ²For if a man may have come into your congregation with a gold ring in fine clothes, and there also may have come in a poor man in dirty clothes, ³and you may have paid special attention to the one who is wearing the fine clothes, and you may have said, "You be sitting here in a good place," and you say to the poor man, "You stand over there, or be sitting down by my footstool," ⁴have you not made distinctions among yourselves, and become judges with evil motives?

⁵Listen, my beloved brothers: did not the Almĭghty choose the poor of this world to be rich in faithfulness and heirs of the kingdom which he promised to those who love him? ⁶But you have dishonored the poor man. Is it not the rich who oppress you and personally drag you into court? ⁷Do they not blaspheme the fair name by which you have been called? ⁸If, however, you are fulfilling the royal Law, according to the text, "YOU SHALL LOVE YOUR NEIGHBOR AS YOURSELF,ᵖ" you are doing well. ⁹But if you discriminate, you are committing sin and are convicted by the Law as transgressors.

¹⁰ For whoever may have kept the whole Law and yet may have become fallen in *connection to* one point, he will ᵝhave been becoming guilty of all^ψ. ¹¹For he who said, "You shall not commit adultery," also said, "You shall not commit murder." Now if you do not commit adultery, but do commit murder, you ᵝhave been becoming a transgressor of the Law.

¹²So be speaking and so be acting, as those who are to be judged by the Law of liberty. ¹³For judgment will be merciless to one who has shown no mercy. Mercy triumphs over judgment.

¹⁴What use is it, my brothers, if a man may be saying he is having faithfulness, but he may be having no works? Can that 'faithfulness' rescue him? ¹⁵If a brother or sister may be without clothing and in need of daily food, ¹⁶and one of you may have said to them, "Be going in peace, be getting warmed and be getting filled," and yet you may not have given them what is necessary for their body, what use is that? ¹⁷Even so that 'faithfulness,' if it may be having no works, is dead by itself.

2:8 ρ Lev. 19:18 **2:10** ψ Or "completely guilty." The text speaks here of a willful offense and not of a sin of ignorance. 'To fall' is the result of transgression here, a passive/reflexive being built into the lexical sense. The use here is more suited to Hebrew thought pattern. Paul uses in Gal. 5:4 as less ambiguous term in Greek: ἐξεπέσατε = *fallen away*. The saying is gnomic or proverbial. The Rabbis had a similar saying. The text is often used to attack the faithful who keep watch to do the commandments, saying they are guilty of all if one mistake is made, but this gnostic interpretation fails to recognize the difference between sin and sin, the sin of ignorance and the transgression. Compare 1 John 1:6-10 with 1 John 3:4-9 and Numbers 15:22-31. **2:10,11:** β→-becoming: the use of the perfect continuous here is less harsh than an aorist would be. It suggests the possibility of turning back and the non-finality of the transgression.

¹⁸But someone will say, "Do you really have faithfulness? I also include works. Show me your faithfulness without the works, if you can, but I will show you my faithfulness by my works!" ¹⁹You hold *it* faithful that one[x] Almĭghty exists? You do amazingly well! The demons also are holding *it* faithful, and shudder.

²⁰But are you willing to recognize, you foolish fellow, that the pledge of faithfulness without works is useless? ²¹Was not Avraham our father [y]administered justice based on works, when he offered up Yitsḣaq his son on the altar? ²²You see that the faithfulness was working with his works, and as a result of the works, [π]faithfulness is completed. ²³And the text was fulfilled which says, "AND AVRAHAM HAD HELD FAITHFUL IN YĂHWEH. AND IT WAS TAKEN INTO ACCOUNT

2:19 χ Read εἷς θεός ἐστιν (B 614. 630. 1505. 1852 al). This is the correct reading because nowhere does the Scripture say, "God is one," but it says "one Gŏd is" or the Most High is "Gŏd alone." This text was obviously corrupted by those who held to the homoousion doctrine set out in the Nicene Creed.

2:18-24 Some attempt is made here in the translation to unify the senses of the Greek verb *pisteuo* in English, which has three senses, 1. believe [with a datum of belief as the object], 2. affirm (or confirm) faithfulness [with the person to whom loyalty is committed as the object], and 3. trust or reliance [with a promise of the person trusted as the object]. The translation has to be varied according to the context, i.e. meanings 1-3. Linguistic unity is achieved in Greek and more so in Biblical Hebrew which influenced the usage, where the verb אמן means "to support." 1. To support a datum = believe. 2. To support a person = loyalty, fidelity. 3. To put support on a person's promise = trust. Ya'aqov address the hypocrite who says he has fidelity in vs. 14-17. In vs. 19 he gives an example of applying the wrong definition (#1). *Pisteuo* that the Almĭghty is One takes a datum of belief as the object, i.e. the truth of his unity. This clearly is not loyalty. No example is given distinguishing trust from loyalty, but Ya'aqov is arguing for loyalty, which can only be expressed in works confirming genuine faithfulness. An example of trust without loyalty may be provided. One can trust the opposite team to follow the rules most of the time, but that does not mean loyalty to the opposite team. This is really support of something they promised to do, and not support to them, and so is a variation of the datum of belief for an object. ▷ There are many who give the definition of "believe only" and "belief" to the verb and noun. This is helped greatly by mistranslation. Others, more studious, realizing a problem define the terms as "trusting only" and "trust," which is to say a person who acts on a belief has trust vs. one who does not. Someone says, "There are no cars coming down the road," and the person who trusts goes into the road whereas the one who only believes it does not. But this trust is not fidelity or loyalty because the action taken to confirm that trust exists does not involve obedience. For example one who trusts they have eternal life therefore sacrifices his life for Mĕssiah. But often the sacrifice made is not real fidelity because it involves no obedience. Only the things that the Almĭghty has commanded confirm real fidelity.

2:21 γ→justice: As a result of his keeping his pledge of faithfulness, the Most High reaffirmed the promise. See Gen. 22:15-18. This was the result that Gŏd judged just based upon his faithfulness, and so he administered justice by declaring his promise to Avraham. **2:22** π→completed: Genuine faithfulness, (fidelity, loyalty) is confirmed by its works. We may ask an antinomian Christian how they can identify legalism or salvation by works, and they will say if anyone is observed keeping certain old laws then they must be a legalist. All legalists are going to hell they say. But in fact they are expressing hatred for the renewed covenant. ▷ Real love of Mĕssiah is confirmed by obedience to his commandments (cf. Yoḣ. 14:21; 15:10). If they are keeping some commandments, then how is this not the same as the one who keeps certain old laws. So then their litmus test for legalism is arbitrary. It excludes their own keeping of certain commandments, and includes others keeping laws they don't agree with. ▷ The real legalist is the one who claims that the divine law must be perfectly satisfied to be saved (which denies real forgiveness), and then who think it may be satisfied by a substitute for real perfection, since they realize they themselves are imperfect. Judaism and Catholicism claims that merits of others may be credited to the imperfect. So for example, in Judaism, the merit of Avraham is credited to the account of less than perfect Jews. Or the Church of Rome once credited the merit of saints to those who went astray during times of persecution so that they would have enough merit for heaven. If works of self or others are used as credits to achieve perfection in Gŏd's sight, then this is legalism. Even the crediting of the good works of Christ, as taught by Protestants, to the account of Christians, is legalism. ▷ But when we keep the old laws not for acquittal before Gŏd, but to be righteous as he requires, then they condemn us while they are relying on the law keeping of others to gain an acquittal for themselves. And if this is their attitude, we must understand that neither the love of the Almĭghty nor a knowledge of the Good News of real pardon is in them, because if they knew the good news, then they would have repented, and they would not have condemned repentance in

FOR HIM FOR THE ADMINISTRATION OF JUSTICE;" and he was called the beloved of the Almĭghty. ²⁴You see that a man is getting administered justice based on works, and not by ᵖa pledge of faithfulness alone.

²⁵And in the same way was not Raḥav the harlot also made righteous by works, when she received the messengers and sent them out by another way? ²⁶For just as the body without a spirit is dead, so also ᵖfaithfulness without works is dead.

3 ¹Let not many be becoming teachers, my brothers, having been knowing that as such we will incur a stricter judgment. ²For we all stumble in many ways. If anyone does not stumble in what he says, he is a perfect man, able to bridle the whole body as well.

³Now if we put the bits into the horses' mouths so that they may obey us, we direct their entire body as well. ⁴Behold, the ships also, though they are so great and are driven by strong winds, are still directed by a very small rudder, wherever the inclination of the pilot desires.

⁵So also the tongue is a small part of the body, and yet it boasts of great things. Behold, how great a forest is set aflame by such a small fire! ⁶And the tongue is a fire, the very world of iniquity. The tongue is set among our members as that which defiles the entire body, and sets on fire the course of life, and is set on fire by Geihinnom. ⁷For every class of wild animals besides also of birds, from reptiles besides also of creatures of the sea, is getting tamed, or has been getting overpowered by mankind. ⁸But no one can tame the tongue. It is a restless evil and full of deadly poison. ⁹With it we bless Yăhweḥ who is our Făther; and with it we curse men, who have been getting made according to the likeness of the Almĭghty. ¹⁰From the same mouth come both blessing and cursing. My brothers, these things ought not to be this way.

¹¹Does a fountain send out from the same opening both fresh and bitter water? ¹²Can a fig tree, my brothers, produce olives, or a vine produce figs?

---

others. **2:23** γ Gen. 15:6a + Psa. 106:30.

2:24 ρ→alone: Or "belief alone," or "trust alone." It is clear that he does not mean faithfulness when making the negation as faithfulness cannot be alone without works. This is the statement that caused Luther to reject this book because his false theological system is flatly contradicted here. Now in Romans 4 there is no contradiction to what is stated here, since Paul speaks of Mĕssiah's faithfulness without our works in administering justice to us through his sacrifice. Paul isn't saying our faithfulness is without good works. ▷ If it should be suggested that in some sense our faithfulness is without works, then Paul only means the sort of work that is done as a merit for the purpose of canceling a demerit. But no one truly faithful can be guilty of this because everyone knows that the Almĭghty forgave our demerits through Mĕssiah and not through the customary works. Therefore faithfulness is allowed to show itself by good works, and is not valid with works removed. ▷ The contradiction occurs only if the Protestant system is assumed where 'believe only' is lawlessly promoted in place of a true affirmation of faithfulness to Mĕssiah. ▷ Paul is only speaking of the need to depend on Mĕssiah's faithfulness in obtaining forgiveness without our works. He is denying the system of penances, and not faithfulness toward the Almĭghty.

2:26 π The synonyms fidelity or loyalty could be substituted throughout for faithfulness. The Hebrew and Greek concept of πίστις (אֱמוּנָה) included works. That real faithfulness exists is confirmed by its works. Loyalty begins in the heart, but it is only confirmed to be real by outward obedience. Speaking of a true loyalty without works is a contradiction of the definition. What Ya'aqov means is the mere profession of it with no works to confirm it. See vs. 14-19.

Neither can salt water produce fresh.

¹³Who among you is wise and understanding? Let him show by his good behavior his deeds in the gentleness of wisdom. ¹⁴But if you have bitter jealousy and selfish ambition in your heart, do not be getting arrogant and so be lying against the truth. ¹⁵This wisdom is not that which comes down from above, but is earthly, natural, demonic. ¹⁶For where jealousy and selfish ambition exist, there is disorder and every evil thing. ¹⁷But the wisdom from above is first pure, then peaceable, gentle, reasonable, full of mercy and good fruits, unwavering, without hypocrisy. ¹⁸And the seed whose fruit is justice is sown in peace by those who make peace.

4 ¹What is the source of quarrels and conflicts among you? Is not the source your pleasures that wage war in your members? ²You lust and do not have, so you commit murder. And you are envious and cannot obtain, so you fight and quarrel. You do not have because you do not ask. ³You ask and do not receive, because you ask with wrong motives, so that you may spend it on your pleasures.

⁴You adulteresses, have you not been knowing that friendship with the world is hostility toward the Almĭghty? Therefore whoever may have wished to be a friend of the world makes himself an enemy of the Almĭghty. ⁵ᵃOr do you think that the Scripture speaks to no purpose? ⁵ᵇ"The Spĭrit He causes to dwell in us abhors envy.ᵡ" ⁶ᵃBut he gives a greater loving-kindness. ⁶ᵇTherefore it says, "THE ALMĬGHTY IS OPPOSED TO THE PROUD, BUT GIVES LOVING-KINDNESS TO THE HUMBLE.ᵠ" ⁷Submit therefore to the Almĭghty. Resist the Slanderer and he will flee from you. ⁸Draw near to the Almĭghty and he will draw near to you. Cleanse your hands, you sinners, and purify your hearts, you double-minded. ⁹Be miserable and mourn and weep. Let your laughter be turned into mourning, and your joy to gloom. ¹⁰Humble yourselves in the presence of Yăhweh, and he will exalt you.

¹¹Do not be speaking against one another, brothers. He who speaks against a brother, or judges his brother, speaks against the Law, and judges the Law. But if you judge the Law, you are not a doer of the Law, but a judge of it. ¹²There is only one Lawgiver and Judge, the One who is able to rescue and to destroy, but who are you who judges your neighbor?

¹³Be coming now, you who say, "Today or tomorrow, we will go to such and such a city, and spend a year there and engage in business and make a profit." ¹⁴Yet you do not know what your life will be like tomorrow. You are just a vapor that appears for a little while and then vanishes away. ¹⁵Instead, you ought to say, "If Yăhweh may have willed, then we will live and do this or that." ¹⁶But as it is, you boast in your arrogance. All such boasting is evil. ¹⁷Therefore, to one

---

4:5b χ Ya'aqov may not be introducing his formal quote so soon as 5b (cf. 5a), but in 6b. That is, 5a refers to 6b. Nevertheless, see Bauckham, R. *The Jewish World around the New Testament*, who says the sense of the quotation is given in Num. 11:25-29, and 5b is perhaps from a lost book of Eldad and Medad, which possibly stated the point as 5b does.

4:6 ψ Prov 3:34, Psa 138:6 see App XII.

who has been knowing the right thing to do, and does not do it, to him it is sin.

5 ¹Be coming now, you rich, weep and howl for your miseries which are coming upon you. ²Your riches have and will have been decaying and your clothes have and will have been becoming moth-eaten. ³Your gold and your silver have and will have been getting tarnished. And their rust will be a witness against you and will consume your flesh like fire. It is in the last days that you have stored up your treasure! ⁴Look, the pay of the laborers who reap your fields, which has been getting withheld by you, cries out. And the outcry of those who do the harvesting has been coming into the ears of Yăhweh ʐTseva'oṭh. ⁵You have lived luxuriously on the earth and led a life of wanton pleasure. You have fattened your hearts in a day of slaughter. ⁶You have condemned and put to death the righteous man. He does not resist you.

⁷Be patient, therefore, brothers, until the coming presence of Yăhweh. Behold, the farmer waits for the precious produce of the soil, being patient about it, until it may have received the early and later rains. ⁸You too be patient. Strengthen your hearts, because the coming presence of Yăhweh has been drawing near. ⁹Do not be complaining, brothers, against one another, that you yourselves may not be judged. Behold, the Judge has been standing right at the door. ¹⁰As an example, brothers, of suffering and patience, take the prophets who spoke in the name of Yăhweh. ¹¹Behold, we count those blessed who endured. You have heard of the endurance of Iyov and have seen the outcome of Yăhweh's dealings, that Yăhweh is full of compassion and is merciful.

¹²But above all, my brothers, do not be swearing, either by heaven or by earth or with any other oath. And, let your yes be yes, and your no, no—so that you will not have fallen under judgment.

¹³Is anyone among you suffering? Let him be praying. Is anyone cheerful? Let him be singing praises.

¹⁴Is anyone among you sick? Let him call for the elders of the assembly, and let them pray over him, anointing him with oil in the name of Yăhweh. ¹⁵And the prayer offered in faithfulness will restore the one who is sick, and Yăhweh will raise him up. Even if *it is* sins which he had been committing, they will be forgiven him. ¹⁶Therefore, be confessing your sins to one another, and be praying for one another, so that you will have been healed. The effective prayer of a righteous man can accomplish much. ¹⁷Eliyahu was a man with a nature like ours, and he prayed earnestly that it may not rain. And it did not rain on the earth for three years and six moons. ¹⁸And he prayed again, and the sky poured rain, and the earth produced its fruit.

¹⁹My brothers, if any among you may have been deceived from the truth, and someone may have turned him back, ²⁰let him be knowing that he who has turned back a sinner from the error of his way will rescue his soul from death, and will cover a multitude of sins.

5:4 ʐ "Hosts" or "Armies." But the Hebrew צְבָאוֹת *Tseva'oṭh* was transliterated in the Greek: Σαβαὼθ *sebaoth*.

First Peter

1 ¹Peter, an emissary of Yĕshua the Anŏinted One, to the chosen ʸaliens among the dispersion of Pontus, Galatia, Cappadocia, Asia, and Bithynia, ²according to the ᵋforeknowledge of the Almĭghty Făther, in connection to being made holy by the Spĭrit, with respect to obedience and a sprinkling of the blood of Yĕshua *the* Anŏinted. Loving-kindness to you and peace be multiplied.

³Blessed be the Almĭghty and Făther of our Adŏnai Yĕshua *the* Anŏinted, who according to his great mercy has caused us to be ᶚbegotten anew to a living hope through the resurrection of Yĕshua *the* Anŏinted from the dead, ⁴to obtain an inheritance which is imperishable and undefiled and will not fade away, having been getting taken care of in heaven for you, ⁵who are protected by the power of the Almĭghty, through faithfulness, for a deliverance ready to be revealed in the last time. ⁶In this you greatly rejoice, even though now for a little while, if necessary, you have been distressed by various trials, ⁷that the proof of your faithfulness, being more precious than gold, which is perishable, even though tested by fire, will have been found to result in praise and glory and honor at the revelation of Yĕshua the Anŏinted.

1:1 γ παρεπιδήμοις = *alongside-alien*: גֵּרִים. LXX: Gen. 23:4 = גֵּר־וְתוֹשָׁב. Peter means non-Jews dwelling with the Jewish dispersion in these regions. **1:2** ξ πρόγνωσιν = *before knowledge*. This is knowledge of future things before the future occurs. The source of the knowledge is normally found in the present. For example, a traitor comes to a general and tells him the battle plan of his enemy. The knowledge is gained in the present, but it is fore-knowledge of the enemy actions. He sets his own plan to counter what the enemy will do. Likewise, what his own troops will do according to his plan is fore-knowledge of what will happen. ▷ Viewed this way "foreknowledge" is exactly the same thing as *predetermination* (cf. BDAG, 3rd. ed πρόγνωσις def. no. 2). The only difference between man's predetermination and Gŏd's is that He has planned for every contingency, including free will decisions made by others in the course of executing his plan. Any possible agents that might upset his plan are restrained or pushed in a direction that agrees with the planned outcome. Any that do not thwart the plan are allowed whatever choice they make. For the decisions of others he does allow, all contingencies arising from them lead to his predetermined goal. Only that which the Almĭghty has predetermined by way of a promise to others or himself can be termed an absolute knowledge of events before they happen. ▷ Many want "foreknowledge" to be something that has its source in a timeless eternity by divine predetermination of every event (Augustine/Calvin) or by passive divine observation from a viewpoint in eternity of every event that isn't already determined by divine decree (Arminius). But there is absolutely no requirement in the Greek meaning of this word for these philosophic additions to the meaning of the word. Simple knowledge of the future by knowing what the current plans are fits the meaning of the term. ▷ Foreknowledge may be gained not only by discovering the plans of others or by making one's one plan, but also by giving enough forethought to current events to logically predict their outcome. Foreknowledge may be gained also by a combination of predetermination and calculations based on observation plus intervention. ▷ This foreknowledge (ξ) refers to knowing in advance that if the good news were presented to the nations, and their bondage to evil broken by Mĕssiah's ransom, multitudes would affirm faithfulness to the Mĕssiah, be forgiven, and become part of Israel. Therefore, according to this knowledge, the Almĭghty set up a plan to save a remnant of nations, and to include them with his people. He knew this would be the case, because all men are created in the image of the Almĭghty, and therefore all are equally likely to respond if allowed the opportunity. ▷ Therefore, by knowing some would repent if presented with the message, the Almĭghty caused the message to be presented, and therefore he foreknew that many would repent. Therefore the ger-toshavim added to Israel are added according to divine foreknowledge. The Almĭghty also dynamically calculates so that a maximum number of people will decide to freely follow him while minimizing the losses, and while keeping all his past promises. The losses are part of the ransom cost. See Isa. 43:3. **1:3** ζ →anew: see 1 Pet. 1:22-23.

⁸And though you have not seen him, you love him, and though you do not see him now, but pledge faithfulness, you greatly rejoice with joy inexpressible and will have been getting glorified, ⁹obtaining yourself the goal$^\psi$ of your faithfulness: the deliverance of your souls.

¹⁰As to this deliverance, the prophets who prophesied of the loving-kindness that would come to you, made careful search and inquiry, ¹¹seeking to know what person or time the Spĭrit of the Anŏinted with them was indicating as He predicted the sufferings of the Anŏinted and the glories to follow. ¹²It was revealed to them that they were not serving themselves, but you, in these things which now have been announced to you through those who proclaimed the good news to you by the Holy Spĭrit sent from heaven—things into which *angelic* messengers long to look.

¹³Therefore, gird your minds for action, keep sober in spirit, fix your hope completely on the loving-kindness to be brought to you at the revelation of Yĕshua the Anŏinted. ¹⁴As obedient children, do not be conformed to the former lusts, which were yours in your ignorance, ¹⁵but like the Holy One who called you, be holy yourselves also in all your behavior, ¹⁶because it has been getting written, "YOU SHALL BE HOLY, BECAUSE I AM HOLY$^\lambda$." ¹⁷And if you address as Făther, the One who impartially judges according to each man's work, conduct yourselves in fear during the time of your stay upon earth, ¹⁸having been knowing that you were not ransomed with perishable things like silver or gold from your futile way of life, inherited from your forefathers, ¹⁹but with precious blood, as of a lamb unblemished and spotless, the blood of the Anŏinted One, ²⁰who surely had been getting recognized before—before the founding of the world, but is manifested in these last times for the sake of you ²¹who through him are faithful ones to the Almĭghty, who raised him from the dead and gave him glory, so that your faithfulness and hope are in the Almĭghty.

²² Having been purifying your souls, by submission to the truth, into a sincere brotherly affection, love one another from purity of heart, $^\zeta$to the maximum, ²³having been $^\theta$getting yourselves begotten again not of $^\delta$corrupted seed but uncorrupted, by the word of the Almĭghty, living $^\phi$and remaining *in you.*

1:9 ψ τέλος or *end.* **1:16** λ Lev. 11:44 **1:22-23** The word order cannot be helped because readers will either doubt it or not understand it fully if meaning is sacrificed for the sake of prose. A less strict version: *While you have been purifying your souls into a state of brotherly affection, you must love one another from a pure heart to the maximum extent possible, by means of submission to the truth, while you have been getting yourselves begotten anew, again, not from seed which is corrupted, but which is not corrupted, which seed is the same as the word of the Almĭghty, and by the seed remaining in you.* **1:22** ζ ἐκτενῶς = *as stretched out, fervently.* **1:23** θ→begotten.

The verb is middle voice (reflexive) passive. There is both an external agent and an internal agent in this case. The external agent is the word. The internal is our consenting to its being united with our hearts. ▷ The passage is a precise definition of what he means to be begotten again (cf. John 3, 15, parable of the sower). **1:23** δ The adjective is re-derived from the verb here because the 'able' ending does not capture the sense. The seed that is corrupt is already corrupt, and not just able to be corrupted. Corrupt seed is the lying word of the devil by which the sons of darkness are being begotten. **1:24** λ Isa 40:6-8.

²⁴Because, "ALL FLESH IS LIKE GRASS, AND ALL ITS GLORY LIKE THE FLOWER OF GRASS. THE GRASS WILL HAVE WITHERED, AND THE FLOWER WILL HAVE FALLEN OFF, ²⁵BUT THE WORD OF YĂHWEH ABIDES FOREVER.ᵞ" And this is the word which was proclaimed to you.

2 ¹Therefore, putting aside all malice and all guile and hypocrisy and envy and all slander, ²like newborn babes, long for the pure milk of the word, that by it you will have grown into deliverance, ³if you have tasted the kindness of Yăhweh.

⁴And coming to him, the living stone, which has been getting rejected by men, but choice and precious in the sight of the Almĭghty, ⁵you also, as living stones, are being built up as a spiritual house for a holy priesthood, to offer up spiritual sacrifices acceptable to the Almĭghty through Yĕshua the Anŏinted. ⁶Because this is contained in Scripture, "BEHOLD I LAY IN TSIYON A CHOICE STONE, A PRECIOUS CORNER STONE, AND HE WHO HOLDS FAITHFUL UPON HIM, NO HE SHALL NOT HAVE BEEN ASHAMED.ᵅ" ⁷This precious valued one, then, is for you who hold faithful. But for those who are disloyal, "THE STONE WHICH THE BUILDERS REJECTED, THIS BECAME THE VERY CORNER STONE,ᵝ" ⁸and, "A STONE OF STUMBLING AND A ROCK OF OFFENSE.ᵞ" Being disobedient, they stumble at the Word, to which also they were disposed. ⁹But you are A CHOSEN KINDRED,ᶿ A ROYAL PRIESTHOOD,ᵘ A HOLY NATION, A PEOPLE FOR THE ALMĬGHTY'S OWN POSSESSION,ᵘ that you may proclaim the excellencies of him who has called you out of darkness into his marvelous light, ¹⁰because you once were NOT A PEOPLE,ᵟ but now you are THE PEOPLE OF THE ALMĬGHTY. You had NOT BEEN RECEIVING MERCY,ᵖ but now you HAVE RECEIVED MERCY.ᵖ

¹¹Beloved, I urge you as aliens and strangers to abstain from fleshly lusts, which wage war against the soul. ¹²Keep your behavior excellent among the nations, so that in the thing in which they slander you as evildoers, they may on account of your good deeds, as they observe them, have glorified the Almĭghty in the day of visitation.

¹³Submit yourselves to every human institution through Yăhweh, whether to a king as the one in authority, ¹⁴or to governors as sent by him for the punishment of evildoers and the praise of those who do right. ¹⁵Because such is the will of the Almĭghty that by doing right you may silence the ignorance of foolish men. ¹⁶Act as free men, and do not use your freedom as a covering for evil, but use it as servants of the Almĭghty. ¹⁷Honor all men. Be loving the brotherhood, be fearing the Almĭghty, be honoring the king.

¹⁸Servants, be submissive to your masters with all respect, not only to those who are good and gentle, but also to those who are unreasonable, ¹⁹because this finds favor, when for the sake of conscience toward the Almĭghty a man

---

2:6 α Isa 28:16 **2:7** β Psa 118:22 **2:8** γ Isa 8:14 **2:9** θ Deu 7:6, 14:2, Exo 19:5, Isa 43:20, Deu 4:20, 10:15 **2:9** μ Exo 19:6, Deu 7:6 **2:10** δ Hos 1:6, 9-10, **2:10** ρ Hos 2:23

1 Peter 2

bears up under sorrows when suffering unjustly. ²⁰Because what credit is there if, when you sin and are harshly treated, you endure it with patience? But if when you do what is right and suffer for it, and you patiently endure it, then this finds favor with the Almĭghty.

²¹Because you have been called for this purpose, since the Anŏinted also suffered over^α you, leaving you an example so that you may follow in his steps, ²²WHO COMMITTED NO SIN, NOR WAS ANY DECEIT FOUND IN HIS MOUTH.^α ²³And while being insulted, HE DID NOT INSULT IN RETURN.^λ While suffering, he uttered no threats, but kept entrusting himself to him who judges righteously. ²⁴And he himself bore^μ our sins^ξ in his body on the tree, so that having died to sin we may live for righteousness. BY HIS WOUNDS YOU ARE HEALED,^β ²⁵because you were

---

2:21 α ὑπὲρ or 'on behalf of you.' The faithful also have a role in suffering to ransom what is good from evil; see 1 Pet. 4:13; Rom. 8:17; 2 Cor. 1:5-7; Philippians 3:10; 2 Tim. 1:8; Col. 1:24; Rev. 11:7-12. The servant serves by ransoming many. See Mat. 20:28; Mark 10:45. See Eph. 5:16; Col. 4:5. **2:22** α Isa 53:9; **2:23** λ Isa 53:7.

2:24 μ Isa 53:6, 8, 10; To bear sins means to suffer from it, from its attack in the course of serving the Most High. The Almighty Son came to deliver his people from sin, and to do so he took upon himself the risks of taking human flesh, as the Son of man. See Mat. 20:28; Mark 10:45. See note on Rev. 5:9. See Mat. 5:10-12; 1 Pet. 2:21. To bear one's own sin means to suffer its consequences. Even the faithful end up bearing their own sin, even after forgiveness. But Yĕshua bore sin's attack to serve us being wholly innocent. ▷ Now a distinction must be sharply defined between bearing a judicial penalty for sin and bearing the built in destructiveness of sin. When forgiveness occurs judicial penalty is cancelled just as a debt is forgiven. No repayment is required. But getting free of sin's malignancy is another matter. The point of the sacrificial *kippurim* (wiping) is to cleanse the malignancy. So in this respect the offering bears the sin to cleanse it. Obviously a great deal of spiritual symbolism is involved here. The point is made in Yoḥ. 6. Divine life is required to cleanse sin's malignancy. So divine life in Messiah crossed swords with sin in the flesh to give us a window on the divine sacrifice in the spiritual realm as the Spirit of the Almighty suffered from our rebellions. ▷ Divine life is sufficiently powerful to cleanse any sin from a sinner, however the Most High isn't willing, generally, to separate this purging from repentance and a pledge of faithfulness, so that to die to sin signifies both initial repentance and continuing repentance. The return to the Shepherd is through holding faithful to him. ▷ The offering that bears sin is never bearing a divinely appointed judicial sentence or penalty for the guilty. This idea is heresy. The offering is not bearing wrath. The offering is bearing the logical malignancy of sin to cleanse it and remove it from the sinner who repents. Judicial sentence or strict justice is forgiven, so there is no judicial penalty to be paid in terms of divine wrath. There is only sin cleansing to be dealt with in the spiritual realm as indicated by the sacrifice. ▷ This is the messianic victory that ransoms us from the destruction of sin, (aka Christus Victor). ▷ The penal substitution theory is a satanically inspired attack and corruption of the meaning of sacrifice. It presents a character assassination of the Almighty, presenting him as demanding strict justice via innocent blood in every case where it cannot be executed on the unrepentant sinner himself. It damages his love and casts his law into a purely negative role, which is exactly what Satan desires. **2:24** ξ It says 'our sins,' and firstly this means bearing the collective sin of Israel, and humanity in general, as the direct cause of Messiah's suffering, exacted by evil men for giving us the truth. The sinfulness common to mankind caused the corruptions of the religious authorities that took his life. The Most High was already suffering this cost in the Spirit, but as the Son of Man he showed it to us in the person of Messiah. Secondly, part of the cost of dealing with sin is the cost to cleanse it, to separate sin from the sinner who repents. This cost is expressed in terms of the spilled blood of Messiah (blood represents the breath of life), divine life in this case. Both aspects of the cost are summed up in the term ransom, which is the divine price paid to give us freedom. The cost is exacted or charged by lawlessness, by sin and evil. It is not a judicial cost imposed by the Father as a penalty for sin. **2:24** β Isa 53:5. By his stripes you are healed. This is the ransom again. In serving us and loving us sin attacks Messiah. By entering the domain of Satan's kingdom to destroy its works he took upon himself the risk of counter attack. He showed us also the cost of cleansing our sin in divine terms in the flesh. His stripes in the flesh are not all of his stripes, but also all of his forbearing sin in the Spirit before he became human are part of the stripes. He meets up with our sin to battle it, and personally so for whoever repents and cooperates with him in the Spirit through keeping his commandments. Messiah is a warrior battling an evil bear. He is wounded by the bear, but he manages to give his beloved bride just enough time to step out of the path of the bear claw. And like the best tales, the hero survives because he is worthy. So the Most High restores him and rescues him through death. **2:25** δ Isa 53:6 **2:25** ρ Eze 34:23.

continually STRAYING LIKE SHEEP, but now you have returned to the ᴾSHEPHERD and Overseer of your souls.

3 ¹In the same way, you wives, be submissive to your own husbands so that even if any of them are disobedient to the word, they may be won without a word by the behavior of their wives, ²as they observe your chaste and respectful behavior. ³Let it not be outside behavior, braiding the hair, and wearing gold jewelry, or putting on worldly garments, ⁴so much as the hidden person of the heart, with the imperishable quality of a gentle and quiet spirit, which is precious in the sight of the Almĭghty. ⁵Because in this way in former times the holy women also, who hoped in the Almĭghty, used to adorn themselves, being submissive to their own husbands. ⁶Thus Sarah obeyed Avraham, calling him lord, and you have become her children if you do what is right without being frightened by any fear.

⁷You husbands likewise, live with your wives in an understanding way, as with a weaker vessel, since she is a woman, and grant her honor as a fellow heir of the loving-kindness of life, so that your prayers may not be hindered.

⁸To sum up, let all be harmonious, sympathetic, brotherly, kindhearted, and humble in spirit, ⁹not returning evil for evil, or insult for insult, but giving a blessing instead, because you were called for the very purpose that you might inherit a blessing. ¹⁰Because, LET HIM WHO MEANS TO LOVE LIFE AND SEE GOOD DAYS REFRAIN HIS TONGUE FROM EVIL AND HIS LIPS FROM SPEAKING GUILE. ¹¹AND LET HIM TURN AWAY FROM EVIL AND DO GOOD. LET HIM SEEK PEACE AND PURSUE IT, ¹²BECAUSE THE EYES OF YĂHWEH ARE UPON THE RIGHTEOUS, AND HIS EARS ATTEND TO THEIR PRAYER, BUT THE FACE OF YĂHWEH IS AGAINST THOSE WHO DO EVIL.

¹³And who is there to harm you if you may have become zealous for what is good? ¹⁴But even if you should suffer for the sake of righteousness, you are blessed. AND THEIR FEAR YOU SHALL NOT HAVE FEARED, NOR YET SHALL YOU HAVE BEEN TROUBLED, ¹⁵but sanctify the Anŏinted as Adŏnai in your hearts, always being ready to make a defense to everyone who asks you to give an account for the hope that is in you, yet with gentleness and reverence, ¹⁶and keep a good conscience so that in the thing in which you are slandered, those who insult your good behavior in accord with the Anŏinted may be put to shame.

¹⁷Because it is better, if the Almĭghty should will it so, that you suffer for doing what is right rather than for doing what is wrong. ¹⁸Because the Anŏinted also suffered because of⁺ sins at one time, the just on behalf of the unjust, in order that he might bring us to the Almĭghty, having been put to death in the flesh, but made alive by the Spĭrit, ¹⁹by which *Spĭrit*, also, to the spirits in prison, as One who had been departed *in death*, he proclaimed *victory*, ²⁰who formerly

---

3:6 θ Gen 18:12 **3:10-12** ψ Psa 34:12-16 **3:14** ξ Isa 8:12. **3:18** φ = περὶ, or 'concerning' sins. Messiah allowed himself to be attacked by sin to ransom us from evil back to the Most High. His blood represents the divine expenditure necessary to cleanse us from sin. **3:19** Literal text, "by which [Spĭrit] also to the spirits in prison, having been departed [in death], He proclaims [the victory]." See Luke 8:31; Genesis 6. The prison, an abyss, is the place of confinement for evil spirits that would threaten the divine plan if allowed to roam. The departure in death and the resurrection of Messiah proclaims the frustration of their plans to corrupt the seed of men and prevent the Messiah. The abyss is not the grave where Messiah was (cf. Mat. 12:40) or the Lake of Fire. We only need suppose that

ns disobeyed, while the Almĭghty was patiently waiting in the days of Noaĥ, during the construction of the ark, into which a few, that is, eight souls, were delivered through water, ²¹which figuratively now delivers you, a ⁵purifying immersion, not by the removal of filth from the flesh, but the pledge to the Almĭghty of a good conscience, because of the resurrection of Yĕshua the Anŏinted, ²²who is at the right hand of the Almĭghty, having departed to heaven, where messengers and authorities and powers have been subjected to him.

4

¹Therefore, since the Anŏinted has suffered in the flesh, arm yourselves also with the same purpose, because he who has suffered in the flesh has been ceasing from sin, ²so as to live the rest of the time in the flesh no longer for the lusts of men, but for the will of the Almĭghty. ³Because the time that has been passing by is sufficient for you to have been carrying out the desire of the nations, who have been conducting themselves in sensuality, lusts, drunkenness, carousals, drinking parties and abominable idolatries. ⁴And in all this, they are surprised that you do not run with them into the same excess of dissipation, and they malign you, ⁵but they will give account to him who is ready to judge the living and the dead. ⁶Because the good news has for this purpose been proclaimed even to those who are ˢ'dead,' so that ᵠsurely *though* they may have been condemned in the flesh according to man's *opinion*, ᵟyet they may be living in the spirit according to the Almĭghty.

---

the evil spirits in the abyss heard news of the good news the Holy Spĭrit was announcing around the world by the word of the emissaries. ▷ The prejudicial translation "preached" is an interpretation. It was not the good news that was preached, but victory that was *proclaimed*. The Greek word simply means *proclaimed* or *announced*. We have to gather from the context what was proclaimed or announced. Peter is teaching on the subject of the suffering of the righteous, and the victory achieved through it. The faithful suffer like Noaĥ suffered the destruction of the world, and especially from the vexation of the sons of Elohim who tried to overcome all mankind. He suffered in obedience to Yăhweĥ, symbolically being buried by the water, and then coming through it victorious. What is proclaimed concerning the fallen evil spirits (and to them) is a warning to any other spirits that might rebel in similar fashion that judgment awaits them, because the Sŏn of Man overcame them by rising from the dead. Peter teaches on this grand drama so that we may have an assured hope in our sufferings of victory, even though it seems as if death and dying are surrounding us. ▷ Through the Spĭrit, Yĕshua proclaims victory to all the evil principalities as a warning to them that if they overstep the limits of evil permitted to them, then they will be the more severely judged, because they have been defeated by the resurrection of the Sŏn. ▷ It is taught by Catholic interpreters and many Protestants that Christ descended into Hell and preached to the departed spirits of the dead the good news . The doctrine is called, "the harrowing of hell." This doctrine is a false doctrine. **3:21** ζ→immersion: The ESV mistranslates, "Baptism, which now corresponds to this, now saves you..." If we simply drop out the appositive then the text says, "Baptism...now saves you." But this version is impossible and all the others like it, which is nearly every version in existence. They all imply that water baptism saves. The word ἀντίτυπον means "anti-typically," or in plain English "figuratively." Friberg classes the word as an adverb. Often adjectives act as adverbs, i.e. the late man, or the man came late. The words "a purifying immersion," are not water baptism at all, but like Yĕshua's words, "And an immersion I have to be immersed with" (Luke 12:50). Here he refers to his death using the term βάπτισμα. The same non-literal sense is in 1 Peter 3:21, "a washing," which can only be seen in English by using an indefinite article. The confusion can be seen by rendering Luke 12:50 without the article, "Now I have baptism to be baptized with." Without the article it appears much more to be water baptism. But with the indefinite article and the context, it clearly is not, just like in 1 Peter 3:21. ▷ Why this indefinite use of baptism, i.e. a baptism is not seen by translators is that they have not been translating. They have been copying from the mistranslations of the past. And the sources of these were influenced by Rome and Luther. Their doctrine was that water baptism does save. So, of course, they wanted the text to say just that.

4:6 ξ The meaning of 'dead' is not literal, but rather legal judgment, in the sentence of death. The nations are 'dead' in sin (cf. Eph. 2:1), but if anyone turns to Mĕssiah, he becomes 'dead' in Mĕssiah (cf.

⁷The end of all things has been coming near. Therefore, be of sound judgment and sober spirit for the purpose of prayer. ⁸Above all, keep fervent in your love for one another, BECAUSE LOVE COVERS A MULTITUDE OF SINS.ᵚ ⁹Be hospitable to one another without complaint. ¹⁰As each one has received a special gift, employ it in serving one another, as good stewards of the many sided loving-kindness of the Almĭghty. ¹¹Whoever speaks, let him speak, as it were, the utterances of the Almĭghty. Whoever serves, let him do so as by the strength which the Almĭghty supplies, so that in all things the Almĭghty may be glorified through Yĕshua the Anŏinted, to whom belongs the glory and dominion forever and ever. Am̆en.

¹²Beloved, do not be getting surprised at the fire among you, happening to you for testing, *as if* a strange thing is befalling you. ¹³But to the degree that you share the sufferings of the Anŏinted, be rejoicing, so that also at the revelation of his glory, you will have rejoiced with *great* exultation. ¹⁴If you are insulted for the name of the Anŏinted, you are blessed, because the Spĭrit of glory and of the Almĭghty rests upon you. ¹⁵By no means let any of you be suffering as a murderer, or thief, or evildoer, or a troublesome meddler, ¹⁶but if anyone suffers as a ᵋMessianic, let him not be getting ashamed, but in that name let him be glorifying the Almĭghty.

¹⁷Because it is time for judgment to begin with the household of the Almĭghty, and if it begins with us first, what will be the outcome for those disobeying the good news of the Almĭghty?

¹⁸AND IF IT IS WITH DIFFICULTY THAT THE RIGHTEOUS IS RESCUED, WHAT WILL BECOME OF THE IRREVERENT MAN AND THE SINNER?^λ ¹⁹Therefore, let those also who suffer because they obey the will of the Almĭghty, be entrusting their souls to a faithful Creator, in doing what is right.

Gal. 2:20), and 'dead' to the world, and the world counts them as 'dead' by passing condemnation on them. So the 'dead' who have the good news preached to them, and who affirm faithfulness to Mĕssiah become alive to the Almĭghty, and 'dead' to the world.

4:6 ψ-δ The μὲν...δὲ construction = 'surely (on the one hand)...yet (on the other).

4:8 ω Prov. 10:12 שִׂנְאָה תְּעוֹרֵר מְדָנִים וְעַל כָּל־פְּשָׁעִים תְּכַסֶּה אַהֲבָה; 'Hatred makes strifes to be stirred up, but over all transgressions love will make be covered.' cf. James 5:20; Peter is speaking of past transgressions for which they have been forgiven by Mĕssiah. A spirit of hatred will revive offenses that have been repented of, but love will conceal them. ▷ It is key to note that the transgressions in Prov. 10:12 are old strifes or contentions that could be revived by mentioning them, so the later half of the verse quoted by Peter must refer also to old transgressions. See Jer. 31:34 where the Most High follows the same advice. The text certainly does not mean ignoring a new sin or one that is unrepented. Lev. 19:17 tells us we should reprove our neighbor for these lest we bear his sin also.

4:16 ξ Lit. 'Anointedian': מְשִׁיחִי. Cf. Psalm 105:15: מְשִׁיחָי *meshiḥai* = *my anointed ones;* LXX: χριστῶν. A follower of Yĕshua the Mĕssiah. The word 'Christian' has suffered from redefinition. Thankfully, there is a word in English with an original sense that has not yet been so corrupted. While it is permitted to avoid the term 'Christian,' because it has been mixed with error, one should not say they are 'not a Christian' because the term still carries a primary truth, namely that one is a follower of Yĕshua the Mĕssiah, and to say 'not a Christian' will say to the one who hears it that one is not a follower of Mĕssiah. Some Messianics are so offended by the word 'Christian' that they will not use it. This is permitted. But to say one is 'not a Christian' is to give offense against the truth that one follows Mĕssiah. This is not permitted. See Mat. 10:33. The nature of a corrupt term is that it still contains the truth and we must not offend on that truth, but neither do we have to use it at all where we might communicate the corrupt part of it. See Acts 11:26.

4:18 λ Prov 11:31 ⓕ, Luke 23:31.

1 Peter 5

5 ¹Therefore, I exhort the elders among you, as your fellow elder and witness of the sufferings of the Anŏinted, and a partaker also of the glory that is to be revealed, ²shepherd the flock of the Almĭghty among you, exercising oversight not under compulsion, but voluntarily, according to the will of the Almĭghty, and not for sordid gain, but with eagerness, ³nor yet as lording it over those allotted to your charge, but proving to be examples to the flock. ⁴And when the Chief Shepherd appears, you will receive the unfading crown of glory.

⁵You younger men, likewise, be subject to your elders. And all of you, clothe yourselves with humility toward one another, because THE ALMĬGHTY IS OPPOSED TO THE PROUD, BUT GIVES LOVING-KINDNESS TO THE HUMBLE.ᵖ ⁶Humble yourselves, therefore, under the mighty hand of the Almĭghty, that he may exalt you at the proper time, ⁷casting all your anxiety upon him, because he cares for you.

⁸Be of sober spirit. Be on the alert. Your adversary, the Slanderer, prowls about like a roaring lion, seeking someone to devour. ⁹But resist him, firm in your faithfulness, having been knowing that the same experiences of suffering are being accomplished by your brothers who are in the world. ¹⁰And after you have suffered for a little while, the Almĭghty of all loving-kindness, who called you to his everlasting glory through the Anŏinted, will himself perfect, confirm, strengthen and establish you. ¹¹To him be dominion forever and ever. Amen.

¹²Through Silvanus,ᶜ our faithful brother (because so I consider him), I have written to you briefly, exhorting and testifying that this is the true loving-kindness of the Almĭghty. Stand firm in it!

¹³The assembly which is in Bavel,ᵝ chosen together with you, sends you greetings, and so does my son, Mark. ¹⁴Greet one another with a kiss of love. Shalom be to you all who are in the Anŏinted.

5:5 π Prov 3:34; **5:12** ς It seems quite probable that Peter is disclosing that Silvanus was his amanuensis for this letter, or at least possible as Daniel Wallace allows after a review of the usages. See Acts 15:23. The practice was common enough. Paul used a professional scribe (cf. Rom. 16:22). Also, second Peter makes no mention of a scribe, and the differences in Greek and style between the two books well justify the conclusion that Peter employed a writer for his first book, but not for the second. ▷ Two questions are also answered by the close association Silvanus had with Paul. The first is the use of the LXX, which Peter approved as adequate for the purposes of the letter, and second it has been noted that there is evidence of Pauline influence in the expression of the ideas. The mention of Silvanus' involvement may indeed be Peter's way of approving of Paul in his first letter, whereas in the second a more explicit defense is given. **5:13** β Babylon upon the Euphrates still had a very large Jewish community. So it would appear that Peter went to the dispersion there, or had recently been there when the letter was written.

End Note No. 1: Cosmological Note

¹Modern physics is highly philosophical, religious, and fulls of sects. ²To know this you only have to read up on the history of physics ideas. ³Cosmological and quantum explanations range from rational to mystical. ⁴Don't call it science, because modern theories are not based on science anymore. They are religions. ▷ ⁵Mathematics guarantees truth no more than ordinary language. ⁶Words are misused or deceivingly defined. A humble number line may have 'negative numbers.' The negative and positive numbers may be used to represents directions in space, for instance to the left and to the right. ⁷Or they may be used to represent directions in time, the past, the present, and the future. But being able to travel leftward in space does not make time travel possible. ⁸Imaginary numbers have nothing 'imaginary' about them. The $\sqrt{-1} = i$ does not have valid physical interpretation in terms of claiming the side length of a square is the square

root of a negative number; i really specifies which way a vector points in space, and the properties of adding and multiplying complex numbers allows one to rotate and scale figures in space. [9]The equation for the side of a square of area 16 is $x^2 = 16$, with two solutions {-4, +4}, but the -4 solution does not make physical sense. [10]So math makes sense only if its physical application makes sense. [11]Mystical math may be used to justify imaginary physics. And a good deal of modern physics is just that, mystical and imaginary. [12]So, do not be deceived by astrophysicists doing mathematics. Their interpretations of the math are just as fallible as someone who uses ordinary language to deceive with logical fallacies. [13]But their skill in math is like an orator with language. [14]Beware of accepting their conclusions based on their skill level. ▷ [15]When i and $-i$ stand for rotations they are not 'imaginary,' but as a side length of a square $\sqrt{-1}$ is certainly 'imaginary.' One can call $\sqrt{-1}$ imaginary and then use it to do valid rotations in space. [16]Or one can use the negative numbers and the possibility of traveling left to imply that time travel is also possible, which is nonsense. ▷ [17]Relativity math, when it works truthfully, is mislabeled, just as imaginary math when it works is mislabeled. [18]Space and time when understood conceptually as 3 orthogonal directions, and regular intervals between events is the correct label for what is called 'space-time.' The 'space-time' math General Relativity, when it truthfully works, works in terms in absolute space and absolute time. GR 'space-time' semantics is simply mislabeling in such a case to get people to accept the mystical philosophy that space and time are relative, and more particularly that a fixed constant speed of light is the fixed speed of information in Creation. [19]What they really do is change the meter length and the duration of the second depending on either velocity or the nearness of mass. [20]By varying the meter and the second the GR idea is able to keep the speed of light a constant wherever one measures it with these mis-defined meters and seconds. By doing so, they conceal the fact that c varies in terms of space and time measured by universal standards. ▷ [21]To the atheistic world view c is a universal constant because they need it to be so to prevent a Cosmology from arising that agrees with Scripture. That is the reason the math of GR is mislabeled in terms of locally varying length and time. Length divided by time equals velocity. GR cleverly redefines length and time to be different at every point in space so that the ratio of length λ traveled in time τ by light is always a constant. ▷ Quantum entanglement proves that c is not the information speed limit, which is called 'spooky' action at a distance. Time travel or predestination are invoked to reject the obvious explanation that information traveled from one of the entangled quanta to the other faster than c. [22]Gravity also goes faster than c. So do the thoughts of the Almȳghty. ▷ Now let us say that when one of an entangled pair of quanta is measured on one side of the universe, then Almȳghty instructs the other quanta to assume a state correlated with the first quanta. He can do this because he is not subject to light speed as a limit. After a while the Almȳghty grows bored of personally instructing the other quanta to respond, and so creates a law that automatically does this. He can create this law because he is the Almȳghty.

How fast does starlight come to us? Firstly our farthest spacecraft are almost 24 light hours away from earth. This observation means that light must have been locally faster during creation week since I'd expect starlight to reach earth in 12 hours or less starting at dawn on the 4th day. I suggest that the local speed of light was locally faster by $\rho_o * c$ (ρ_o free parameter), and that at the fall of man it slowed to c in time τ (free parameter) before modern measurements. The zone of slow light extends to radius r (free parameter) from star sized masses beyond which light-speed increases by some function of gravity field effect F_g. At less than r only a slight gravity field effect occurs mathematically equivalent to F_g = GR, but in absolute space and time. Unlike Setterfield's CDK theory, I believe light is still faster beyond r. Light carries information about what we see, and I assume that the Almȳghty did not intend for that information to be radically outdated. He created man in his own image, and the Cosmos is not radically outdated from the divine perspective, so we may not expect it to be radically outdated for man either. There is a slight out-dating of what we see, but this is due to the fall of man and net increase in entropy. The Cosmos was made for man and the glory of the Almȳghty, and not to wait billions of years to see it. ▷ A related question is how the galaxies and stars were put into their current configurations? This was a creative process on day four. There is room here for acceleration of physical processes in the cosmos during day four to model colliding galaxies or quasar ejections from galaxy cores to form new galaxies. ▷ The nearest proposal to my light speed ideas is the theory put forth as a scientific hypothesis by Dr. Bryan M. Johnson, Ph.d in theoretical astrophysics (2018 ICC, *Towards a Young Universe Cosmology*). ▷ I would include Setterfield's CDK theory with the limitations specified above, and I would translate GR time dilation solutions into absolute space and time, and apply them only to the creative process, explaining the matter as faster physics and not changes in time. I would place the dynamics of Halton Arp's observations into day four, specifying that the rates at which physics occurred where sped up in absolute time. The results were then integrated into the finished cosmos on day four, which we are now seeing in nearly real time. ▷ There are a lot of free parameters, because these represent what we don't know. What we really know about the origin of the Cosmos is revealed in Scripture. There is room in creation for extra unknown field effects beyond the known ones (magnetism, electric, nuclear, etc.). There is still room for different explanations of gravity at great distances. There is still room for complex sets of laws governing light under various conditions. Creation is not necessarily simple or complex, but it depends on a union of simplicities and complexities. Parsimony is not an absolute law, but a way to choose between two or more explanations of the same thing when forming a working hypothesis. The laws of logic and keeping Scripture in the evidence category rank higher.

The use of *one* with Almighty

What does the Shema mean? What does it mean to say, Yăhweн is our Almĭghty, Yăhweн eḥad?

"One" in Greek and Hebrew has a particularizing force, that is pointing out a particular or certain one amongst many. To see this, put the definite article "the" in front of one to see if it makes sense. This will remove internal numerical sense incorrectly imputed by English and point out external pointing sense. For example, Jer. 24:2a: הַדּוּד אֶחָד תְּאֵנִים טֹבוֹת מְאֹד. "The basket, *the* one *with* very good figs." But not "the basket *is* one *with* very good figs." The text goes on the mention, "The basket, *the* one *with* very bad figs," but not "The basket *is* one *with* very bad figs." This usually gets translated, "the one...the other." So with this idea in mind, that of pointing out "the one" with respect to another. Also Exodus 17:12 מִזֶּה אֶחָד וּמִזֶּה אֶחָד.

LXX, Deut. 6:4b, "Yăhweн *the* one is" vs. another
LXX, Zech 14:9a, "Will be Yăhweн *the* one"
LXX, Zech 149b, "and his name *the* one"
Mark 2:7 "except one, the Almĭghty"
Mark 10:18, "except one, the Almĭghty"
Mark 12:29, "Yăhweн *the* one is" v. another
Mark 12:32, "*the* one is, and not is **another** besides"

This text explains 'one' in contrast to another: οὐκ ἔστιν **ἄλλος** πλὴν αὐτοῦ.

Luke 18:19, "except one, the Almĭghty"
Rom 3:30, "*the* one, the Almĭghty *is* who" v. other
1 Cor 8:4, "except *the* one"
1 Cor 8:6, "one Almĭghty, the Făther"
1 Cor 8:6, "one Adŏnai Yĕshua"
Gal 3:20, "the Almĭghty *the* one is"
Eph 4:4-6, "*the* one" = "the same" v. different
1 Tim, 2:5, "*the* one Almĭghty is also the one m."
Jas 2:19, "*the* one Almĭghty exists"

"The one" may become "only" or "alone" in:

Mark 2:7, "except only the Almĭghty" (cf. Lk 5:21)
Mark 10:18, "except only the Almĭghty"
Mark 12:29, "Yăhweн only is"
Mark 12:32, "only he is"
Luke 18:18, "except only the Almĭghty"
Gal. 3:20, "the Almĭghty only is"

The reason "only" or "alone" are used in translation is that it is easier to explain the Greek and Hebrew usage of "the one," and even Luke 5:21 takes a shot at using the Greek word for *only* parallel to Mark 2:7.

Contrary to what one might expect from a Rabbinic Jew, Paul uses one numerically when separately making mention of Father, Son, and Spirit, in. 1 Cor. 8:6, Eph. 2:4-6, and 1 Tim. 2:5. In each case "one" directly modifies its noun, but still it gives no internal sense of unitary being, except where the modified noun is known to be unitary, as is clear from 'one body,' 'one immersion,' 'one hope,' but many are called.

The word 'same' may be used to translate these cases: Rom 3:30 and Eph 2:4-6.

And "the one" is a pure particularizing sense, i.e. "a certain," because it follows ὅτι. Jas 2:19: ὅτι ὁ θεὸς εἷς ἐστίν = *that the one Almĭghty exists*. In Hebrew adjectives follow the nouns they modify. This is why Jas. 2:19 has εἷς after θεὸς. Even in this form Mĕssiah's brother means one exists as opposed to another Almĭghty.

In the Shema, "Yahweн [is] *the* one," the previous part of the text defines what 'one' refers to: our Almĭghty. So in no case does 'one' function to define a unitary nature for the divine being. Rather it functions to point out that He is the one vs. others.

From everlasting "Yăhweн *was* our Almĭghty, Yăhweн *was* the One. Presently, Yăhweн *is* our Almĭghty, Yăhweн *is* the One. And Yăhweн will have become the king over all the earth, and in that day shall become Yăhweн *the* one, and his name *the* one, and *the* one pillar in the earth. And he will be THE COMING ONE to everlasting and beyond.

There is one other matter to touch on, and that is the collective use of pronouns in Hebrew. "Then says to **him** Edom, **thou** shall not pass through **me**, lest with the sword **I** come out to meet **thee**." Israel's answer was, "On the highway we will go, and if **thy** water we drink, **I** or **my** livestock, then **I** will have paid their price, only nothing more. On **my** feet, **I** wish to pass through. (Num. 20:18). In another place it says, "I am, and there is no one else" (Zeph. 2:15), and in another, "I am and there is no one besides me" (Isa. 47:8). The Most High at the first said, "See therefore that I, **I AM**, and there is no Almĭghty with **me**" (Deut. 32:39). In every case here, the highlighted pronouns are collective singular, a singular pronoun used to represent a collective union, one voice speaking for every voice in the union.

And now the Almĭghty Word speaks, the Almĭghty Sŏn, with mercy and forgiveness in his right hand for all who are sorry for their sins and turn their hearts from evil, becoming faithful to Him, who is at the side of His Făther in heaven, sending forth his Spĭrit to convict the world of sin, righteousness, and judgment, and to persuade you that his words are true, because he told those of old, unless you hold faithful because I AM, you will die in your sins. In his left hand judgment is waiting, judgment in favor of the sons of Yisra'el who obey his laws and keep his covenant. Amen.

So now little faithfuls with the knowledge given to me I encourage you to learn by listening to the Spirit so that you will not be caught up in fruitless arguments with the enemy, but may learn to refute him soundly once, and turn away from him and serve the the Shepherd for the good of the flock.

Second Peter

1 ¹Sim'on Peter, a servant and emissary of Yĕshua the Anŏinted, to those who equally as us have been allotted *to keep* a pledge of faithfulness in the justice of our Almĭghty and Rescuer, Yĕshua the Anŏinted. ²Loving-kindness and peace be multiplied to you in the full knowledge of the Almĭghty, and of Yĕshua our Adŏnai, ³as his divine power has been getting given to us for everything pertaining to life and reverent devotion, through the true knowledge of him who called us by his own glory and excellence, ⁴through which he himself has been gifting to us, his precious and very great promises, in order that through these you will have become partakers of the ᶿdivine nature, having escaped the corruption that is in the world because of lust.

⁵But due to this same reason, having brought to bear all diligence, supply with your faithfulness virtue, and with virtue knowledge, ⁶and with your knowledge, self-control, and with your self-control, steadfast endurance, and with your steadfast endurance, devoted reverence; ⁷and with your devoted reverence, brotherly friendship, and with your brotherly friendship, love. ⁸Because if these things are being under your control and are increasing, they render you neither useless nor unfruitful in the true knowledge of our Adŏnai Yĕshua the Anŏinted. ⁹Because he who does not come by these things is blind, being short-sighted, having forgotten his purification from his former sins. ¹⁰Therefore, brothers, be the more diligent to make certain about his calling and choosing you, because as long as you practice these things, no, you will not have stumbled, ¹¹because in this way the entrance into the everlasting kingdom of our Adŏnai and Rescuer Yĕshua the Anŏinted will be abundantly supplied to you.

¹²Therefore, I will always be ready to remind you of these things, even though you have been knowing them, and have been getting firmly set in the truth, which is near by. ¹³And I consider it right, as long as I am in this earthly

---

1:4 θ→nature: Mankind is created in the image of the Almĭghty. This means man is like Him, male and female. But the image is not equally expressed in all, nor equally grown up in all. It is the divine intent for the image of himself to be expressed to a great extent, greater than any have attained in their present state, except the one who came down from heaven, even the Sŏn of the Almĭghty, who has been, and is in the complete image of the Făther. Murder is wrong because mankind is identified with the image, the likeness of the Almĭghty. For every person the plan is to become sons of the Almĭghty. ▷ We must distinguish between the divine natures. The word Elohim may mean "Almĭghty" or "Mĭghty Ones." The Almĭghty is unique. He is omnipotent as the word almighty says. He is the Creator, the originator of life, the ruler of all, and the one to whom all worship is due (See note on Yoh. 1:1). The divine nature to be imparted to us does not include the attributes exclusive to the Creator. But as far as we know, it is supposed to include everything else at the resurrection far beyond Adam and Hauvah. ▷ But there are some teachers who are careless in talking about "becoming elohim" without pointing out that they mean only a higher existence, that is "mighty ones," and not the Almĭghty, so that people confuse their doctrine with Gnostics that really do claim to become equal to the Almĭghty. There are some teachers actually secretly promoting this self-idolatry. No teacher who cannot explain the difference between elohim (mighty ones) and Elohim (Almĭghty) should be confusing the weak, who will suppose they are a cultist if they hear such talk. The mystery of iniquity has sunk into the so called Church. There are careless statements on this matter in the Catholic Catechism and in Orthodox Churches also. Likewise there are careless statements about this in Torah confessing Assemblies and Churches. More than once I have pointed out that there is no Elohim (Almĭghty) before Yăhweh, and that there shall be none after, to someone who has said "we become Elohim," and they are at a loss to explain that Scripture. When this occurs, you know that they are swimming in the murky waters between Orthodoxy and idolatry.

dwelling, to stir you up by way of reminder, ¹⁴having been knowing that the laying aside of my earthly dwelling is imminent, as also our Adŏnai Yĕshua the Anŏinted has made clear to me. ¹⁵And I will also be diligent that at any time after my departure you may be able to call these things to mind.

¹⁶Because we did not follow myths which have been getting made to appear as wisdom, when we made known to you the power and coming presence of our Adŏnai Yĕshua the Anŏinted, but we were eyewitnesses of that one's majesty. ¹⁷Because when he received honor and glory from beside the Almĭghty Făther, such an utterance as this was made to him by the Majestic Glory, "This is my beloved Sŏn with whom I am well-pleased"—¹⁸and we ourselves heard this utterance made from heaven when we were with him on the holy mountain.

¹⁹And so we hold firmly the prophetic word, to which you do well to pay attention, as to a lamp shining in a dark place, until the day may have dawned and the light bearer may have arisen in your hearts. ²⁰But know this first of all, that no prophecy of Scripture is let loose by mere coincidence, ²¹because no prophecy was ever made by an act of human will, but men moved by the Holy Spĭrit spoke from the Almĭghty.

2

¹But false prophets also arose among the people, just as there will also be false teachers among you, who will secretly introduce destructive heresies, even denying the Măster who bought them, bringing swift destruction upon themselves. ²And many will follow their sensuality, and because of them, the way of the truth will be maligned. ³And in their greed they will exploit you with false words. Their judgment from long ago is not idle, and their destruction is not asleep.

⁴Because if the Almĭghty did not spare messengers when they sinned, but with chains of blackness, ⁿconfining them, he handed them over to be ᶿguarded for judgment, ⁵and did not spare the ancient world, but only eight *including* Noaĥ, a proclaimer of justice he watched over, when he brought a deluge upon the world of the irreverent, ⁶and if he condemned the cities of Sedom and Amorah to destruction by reducing them to ashes, having been making them an example to those who would live in irreverence thereafter, ⁷and if he rescued righteous Lot, oppressed by the sensual conduct of unprincipled men ⁸(because by what he saw and heard that righteous man, while living among them, felt his righteous soul tormented day after day with their lawless deeds), ⁹then Yăhweĥ has been knowing how to rescue the reverent from temptation, and to keep the unrighteous

---

2:4 η→confining: "Tartarizing." In Greek mythology, Tartarus Τάρταρος Tartaros is the deep abyss that is used as a dungeon of torment and suffering for the wicked and as the prison for the Titans. The Titans were the Greek equivalent of the sons of the Almĭghty who disobeyed in the days of Noaĥ. Peter turned the noun into a participle (ταρταρώσας). So a literal translation would be "tartarizing," "throwing down to tartarus." Tartarus is used for the abyss in Enoch 20:2, where Uriel is said to be the angel over the abyss, but Avaddon is the messenger of the abyss (cf. Rev. 9:11). LSJ defines it as "the *nether world* generally;" Slater, "*the underworld.*" Middle Liddel: "a dark abyss, as deep below Hades as earth below heaven, the prison of the Titans." Peter is careful to define it as a holding place pending judgment. But no doubt the evil spirits regarded such confinement as "torment" (cf. Mat. 8:29). Perhaps there was a pecking order in the prison. But all is speculation.

2:4 θ→judgment: See Gen. 6:1-4; Jude 1:6; Luke 8:31; Rev. 9:1-2, 11; 20:1-3.

under punishment for the day of judgment, ¹⁰and especially those who indulge the flesh in its corrupt desires and despise authority.

¹⁰ᵇDaring, self-willed, they do not tremble when they blaspheme majesties, ¹¹whereas messengers who are greater in might and power do not bring a blaspheming judgment against them before Yăhweң. ¹²But these *are* like unreasoning animals, which have been getting begotten as creatures of instinct, for capture and destruction, by whatever *powers* they are ignorant *of* slandering. According to the destruction of those creatures, indeed, they will be destroyed, ¹³getting done injustice *as* the wage of injustice.

¹³ᵇThey count it a pleasure to revel in the daytime. They are stains and blemishes, reveling in their deceptions, as they carouse with you, ¹⁴having eyes full of adultery and that never cease from sin, enticing unstable souls, having a heart having been getting itself trained in greed, accursed children.

¹⁵Forsaking the right way they have gone astray, having followed the way of Bil'am, the son of Be'or, who loved the wages of injustice. ¹⁶But he received a rebuke for his own transgression, because a dumb donkey, speaking with a voice of a man, restrained the madness of the prophet. ¹⁷These are springs without water, and mists driven by a storm, for whom the black darkness has been getting reserved. ¹⁸Because speaking out arrogant words of vanity they entice by fleshly desires, by sensuality, those who barely escape from the ones who live in error, ¹⁹promising them freedom *while* they themselves *are* slaves, being under the control of corruption, because by what anyone has been getting subdued, by this he has been getting enslaved.

²⁰Because if after they have escaped the defilements of the world by the full knowledge of our Adŏnai and Rescuer Yĕshua the Anŏinted, they are again entangled in them, having been getting themselves diminished, the last state has been becoming worse for them than the first. ²¹Because it would be better for them not to have been fully knowing the way of justice, than having known it, to turn away from the holy commandment delivered to them. ²²The thing has been befalling them for which the proverb is true, "A DOG RETURNS TO ITS OWN VOMIT,ᵠ" and, "A sow, after washing, returns to wallowing in the mire."

3 ¹This is now, beloved, the second letter I am writing to you in which I am stirring up your sincere mind by way of reminder, ²that you should remember the words having been spoken beforehand by the holy prophets and the commandment of the Măster and Rescuer spoken by your emissaries.ᵡ

³Know this first of all, that in the last days mockers will come with their mocking, following after their own lusts, ⁴and saying, "Where is the promise of his coming presence? Because ever since the fathers fell asleep, all continues just as it was from the beginning of creation.ᵘ"

⁵Because this willfully escapes their notice, that the heavens ʸwere existing

---

2:22 ψ Prov 26:11. **3:2** χ Peter is writing to Paul's disciples in this letter, as in the first. It is likely that Paul has died by this point in time, and so he refers to Paul and his associates calling them "your emissaries."

of old—and the ᵝland—out of water and through water, ᵋ*the land* having been ᶲstanding together by the word of the Almĭghty, ⁶through which word the ᵘarrangement also at that time, by water, being deluged had perished.

⁷But the present heavens and earth by his word have been getting reserved—*and are so*—for fire being guarded for the day of judgment and destruction of irreverent men.

⁸But do not let this one fact be escaping your notice, beloved, that WITH YĂHWEH ONE DAY IS AS A THOUSAND YEARS, AND A THOUSAND YEARS AS ONE DAY.ᵠ ⁹Yăhweh is not slow about his promise, as some count slowness, but is patient toward you, not willing for any to perish but for all to come to being sorry and turning their hearts *from sin*.

¹⁰But the day of Yăhweh will come like a thief, in which the heavens will pass away with a roar and the elements will be destroyed with intense heat, and the earth and its works will be burned up.

¹¹*Since* all these things are getting dissolved in this way, what areas *of life* is it being needed to be taking under control for you *to be* in holy conduct and reverent devotion, ¹²awaiting and being urgent for the presence of the day of the Almĭghty, on account of which the heavens will be dissolved by burning, and the elements getting burned are melting down? ¹³But according to his promise we are looking for a new-made heavens and a new-made earth, in which justice dwells. ¹⁴Therefore, beloved, since you look for these things, be diligent to be found by him in peace, spotless and blameless, ¹⁵and be regarding the patience of our Adŏnai to be for deliverance, just as also our beloved brother Paul, according to the wisdom given him, wrote to you, ¹⁶as also in all his letters, speaking in them of these things, in which are some things hard to understand, which the untaught and unstable distort, as also other writings, to their own destruction.

¹⁷You therefore, beloved, knowing this beforehand, be guarding lest, being carried away by the error of unprincipled men, you may have fallen from your own steadfastness. ¹⁸But be growing in the loving-kindness and knowledge of our Adŏnai and Rescuer Yĕshua the Anŏinted. To him be the glory, even now and to the day everlasting. Amen.

3:4 μ See Cosmology Note at the end of 1 Peter. Several ideas of the 'religion' of modern physics must be discarded. The first is the absolute of uniformitarianism: all things continue at constant rates. And the second is that Okkam's razor means that simplicity overrules complexity. Rather simplicity is the better explanation of the same evidence (not theories). The rules of physics can be described by mathematics, but the rules are not designed to work the same everywhere or every direction. The final point is that everything can be related to an absolute frame of reference with a standard unit of time, and within an absolute Euclidean space which the Almĭghty alone fully comprehends. **3:5** γ→existing: The word ἦσαν does not speak of mere 'existence' unless it be qualified 'out of water and through water,' for mere existence itself is irrelevant to the argument, being denied by none. The state of existence is thus described as 'out of water and through water.' The plural of the verb 'were existing' comprehends both the heavens and the earth, which are both the subject. **3:5** ξ→together: the supplied words 'the land' (it, she) are necessary to connect gender inflected participle with its referent β: γῆ. **3:5** φ→together. The active participle refers to the land being all in 'one place' (אֶל־מָקוֹם אֶחָד), Gen. 1:9. The original super continent is called Pangaea. **3:6** μ = κόσμος = *order, arrangement*. The land was split up and moved away from one another. **3:8** ψ Psa 90:4.

First Yoḥanan

1 ¹What was from the beginning, what we have been hearing, what we have been seeing with our eyes, what we looked upon and our hands handled, concerning the Word of Life —²and the Life was manifested, and we have been seeing and testify and proclaim to you the ᵝEverlasting Life, which was with the Făther and was manifested to us—³what we have been seeing and have been hearing we are proclaiming to you also, so that you also may be having fellowship with us. And indeed our fellowship is with the Făther, and with his Sŏn Yĕshua the Anŏinted. ⁴And these things we write so that our joy will have been getting filled up.

⁵And this is the message we have been hearing from him and announce to you, that the Almĭghty is light, and in him there is no darkness at all. ⁶If we may have said that we have fellowship with him and still may be walking in the darkness, we lie and do not practice the truth, ⁷but if we may be walking in the light as he himself is in the light, we have fellowship with one another, and the blood of Yĕshua his Sŏn cleanses us from all sin.ᶲ

1:2 β→Life: See 5:20. Dan. 12:7. The Sŏn is *Ḥayyei Olam* חַיֵּי עוֹלָם (life everlasting) as the Făther is *Ḥayyei Olam*. 1 John 1:2, τὴν ζωὴν τὴν αἰώνιον = הַחַיֵּי הָעוֹלָם *ha-hayyei ha-olam* = the everlasting life. He is the everlasting life because he is Almĭghty.

1:5-7 ϕ The blood *cleanses* us from all sin. The tense is present tense. The translation could read "cleansing us from all sin." So it does not mean that the job is finished yet. Physical blood cleanses for ritual purification, but blood is more than just a physical substance. The breath of life is in the blood. So blood represents life. The life of Mĕssiah is the divine life, life everlasting. It is this life that he imparts to us that cleanses our soul of sin, which causes death. ▷ The animal sin offerings could 1. Declare to be wiped out the penalty of a sin of ignorance. It was forgiven, and the Almĭghty does the forgiving. The ceremony was an instruction and symbǫl of the spiritual. 2. Effect ritual cleansing by blood. Again this was symbolic. It costs life to battle sin. Sin exacts a ransom. But physical blood could not *cleanse* the soul, because the sentient life of the animal is a lower form of life, and such life does not cleanse the human created in the image of Gŏd. But the Spirit of the Most High cleansed the soul in conjunction with the symbol. Now the life of Mĕssiah, being Everlasting Life, represented by his blood (or present with it), has the power to cleanse us from every sin, because he was raised. Mĕssiah's soul cleansing divine life purifies us, not as being dead, but as a sacrificed part of himself given to us. This is a living sacrifice. Therefore, the living sacrifice of Mĕssiah cleanses us from all sin. We only need cooperate with him through repentance. This is why Mĕssiah said we must consume him, because it is a spiritual matter.

Cf. John 6:51-63. He is the Savior, but whoever does not acknowledge that he is Everlasting Life does not know he has the power to do this. There is no superstition attached to the power of the physical here. The physical flesh and blood profit nothing, but it is the spiritual reality represented by the sacrifice that counts (cf. Yoḥ. 6:63). ▷ If a soul was bearing a sin of ignorance, then he will bear his sin (Lev. 5:17). If the sin is not confessed and cleansed, then he will bear his iniquity unto the final judgment. The guilt offering was established to cleanse the fatal contamination of condemnation from the soul, through the life that is in the blood, which cleanses the soul. The operation of the offering is really indicative of and symbolic of a spiritual divine cost of cleansing. By cleansing sin any future penalty is avoided. That is, it is forgiven. The operation of the blood yielded upon in the death of the animal is to cleanse. An illustration: symbolically, the blood is spilled and exposed to the air, which is the wind and represents the Spirit. The spilled blood is not yet 'dead' when it declares the wiping (kippurim). It symbollically unites with the Spirit and it is the Spirit that cleanses the heart. ▷ Mĕssiah's blood (his life) similarly cleanses the sinner from bearing his iniquity. But there are some differences. Cleansing by Messiah may be from all sin, and not just sins one does not know about when committing them. One who commited a willful sin or rebellion was not allowed near the altar (cf. Numbers 15:30). He was cut off from the people. Therefore, the cleansing through Messiah allows covenant renewal and rejoining the holy people. Again, the physical blood of Messiah is symbolic, and there is no need for physical contact with it. It is the spiritual divine life represented by it that counts. The flesh profits nothing.

1 Yoḥanan 1

⁸If we may have said that we have no sin, we are deceiving ourselves, and the truth is not in us. ⁹When we may be confessing our sins, he is faithful and righteous, so that he shall have forgiven us our sins and he shall have cleansed us from all unrighteousness. ¹⁰If we may have said that we have not been sinning, we make him a liar, and his word is not in us.

2 ¹My little children, I am writing these things to you that you will not have sinned. And if anyone may have sinned, we have an advocate with the Father, Yĕshua the Anŏinted the righteous. ²And he *the* cleansing⁽ᵖ⁾ is concerning our sins, and not concerning ours only, but also concerning the whole world⁽ᵡ⁾.

³And by this we are knowing that we have been knowing him, if we may be keeping his commandments. ⁴The one who says, "I have been knowing him," and does not keep his commandments, is a liar, and the truth is not in him; ⁵but whoever may be keeping his word, truly in him the love of the Almĭghty has been getting accomplished. By this we know that we are in him: ⁶the one who is claiming he remains in him ought himself to be walking in the same way he walked.

2:2 ρ ἱλασμός from כִּפֻּרִים, KIPPURIM in **Pi‘el** a declaring of: a wiping out, a cleansing, a purging (cf. Lev. 16:30). The noun in Hebrew is an intensive plural (cf. Lev. 25:9; Num. 5:8). The object of כִּפֻּרִים KIPPURIM is to declare symbolically a purging of sin or ritual impurity, which is in reality effected by the Spirit of the Most High. The lexicons omit specifying the declatory grammatical function of the **Pi‘el**, which should not be omitted in translation. See Jastrow, Aramaic: "**Pi.** כִּפֵּר, כִּיפֵּר [*to wipe out,*] *to forgive...* **Pa.** 1 כַּפֵּר) *to wipe out, efface...***Ithpe.** אִתְכַּפַּר, אִיכּ׳ 1) *to be wiped out, obliterated,* 2. *to be forgiven.*" See HALOT, "I . Akk. *kapāru* **to wipe off,** *kuppuru* **to cleanse ritually.**" ▷ The Greek term ἱλασμός is used in the LXX as a synonym of סְלִיחוֹת (forgivenesses) and cleansing (καθαρισμός). In as much as forgiveness purges the liability to a debt, the two terms are closely related. It is not to placate God or appease the Most High by wrath satisfaction upon the innocent. See also C.H. Dodd, *The Bible and the Greeks*. Dodd shows that the LXX translators understood KIPPURIM as meaning cleansing (καθαρισμός) in sacrificial texts. Jacob Milgrom understood the texts this way also. But the **Pi‘el** conjugation specifies the declatory or indicative nature of sacrifice, and this was generally misunderstood with the loss of understanding the **Pi‘el** (see Appendix X). ▷ The definition 'cover' (vs. purging, cleansing, wiping) was for a time argued by many. This is taken from BDB, which nevertheless also supplies Aramaic, "كَفَرَ ,مَفَ **Pa.** *wash away, rub off,* whence כִּפֵּר, כֹּפֶר of *washing away, obliteration of sin...*" So despite 'cover' the correct definition is also cited. The supposed biblical evidence for 'cover' (Gen. 6:14) actually makes perfect sense with the proper sense, "And you will have **wiped** it inside and outside with pitch" (**Qal**). ▷ The 'cover' definition has often been cited apologetically so to say that the Levitical service only 'covered' sin to make the claim that Messiah's sin offering stands for a fundamentally different result. But BDB admits, "of foll.; orig. mng. dub., but most prob. *cover...*" In other words, the meaning is based on an Arabic derivation of doubtful application. But the Aramaic and Akkadian derivation is much more secure, and the usages in the Tanakh parallels with cleansing point in the right direction. **2:2** χ 'Concerning (περί) the whole world.' Yoḥannan included this because the Gnostics claimed (and their Calvinist offspring later) that only the elect or chosen would be able to repent and enter into the covenant, and thus receive forgiveness, and accordingly be included under the KIPPURIM. Yoḥannan is careful to use the word 'concerning' (περί), because any who are of the world may be rescued on the contingency that they confess and repent of their sins, which is the exact same contingency concerning our cleansing (cf. 1 Yoḥ. 1:9). Yoḥannan is also careful to use the noun 'cleansing' and not a verb. In other words, he is the cleansing. The Yarden river is there, but will one pledging faithfulness to Messiah dip himself in the river? ▷ Yoḥannan's words are an insurmountable problem for the view of limited 'atonement,' because only the predestined are allowed to enter the river, and not the whole world. Yoḥannan's words do not lead to universalism because the contingencies of cleansing are the same for us and the world. Not all will enter the river. But if one eliminates the contingency of loving the Most High and keeping his commandments, then one will obviously end up a universalist.

⁷Beloved, I am not writing a new-made commandment to you, but an old commandment which you have had from the beginning; the old commandment is the word which you have heard. ⁸On the other hand, I am writing a new-made commandment to you, which is true in him and in you, because the darkness is passing away, and the true light is already shining. ⁹The one who says he is in the light and yet hates his brother is in the darkness until now. ¹⁰The one who loves his brother remains in the light and there is no cause for stumbling in him. ¹¹But the one who hates his brother is in the darkness and walks in the darkness, and has not been knowing where he is going because the darkness has blinded his eyes.ᶿ ¹²I am writing to you, little children, because your sins have been getting forgiven you for his name's sake. ¹³I am writing to you, fathers, because you have been knowing him who is from the beginning. I am writing to you, young men, because you have been getting victory over the evil one. I have written to you, children, because you have been knowing the Făther. ¹⁴I have written to you, fathers, because you have been knowing him who is from the beginning. I have written to you, young men, because you are strong, and the word of the Almĭghty abides in you, and you have been getting victory over the evil one.

¹⁵Do not be loving the world, nor the things in the world. If anyone may be loving the world, the love of the Făther is not in him. ¹⁶For all that is in the world, the lust of the flesh and the lust of the eyes and the boastful pride of life, is not from the Făther, but is from the world. ¹⁷And the world is passing away, and also its lusts; but the one who does the will of the Almĭghty abides forever.

¹⁸Children, it is a ᵝcritical moment. And just as you heard that Anti-Mĕssiah is coming, even now many anti-Mĕssiahs have been rising up. From this we know that it is a critical moment. ¹⁹They went out from us, but they were not from us, because if they were from us, they ᵖwould have had been remaining with us. But therein it shall have been shown that they all are not from us.

2:7-11 θ What Yoḣanan writes here may be considered a commentary on what he recorded in John 13:34-35. See note there. First the new commandment is a guideline for the golden rule, "LOVE YOUR NEIGHBOR AS YOURSELF," wherein Mĕssiah commanded us to have especial love for the brothers and sisters affirming faithfulness to him. So it is really an old commandment with a new understanding. Yoḣanan was addressing a situation in which gnostic Christians were hating their "brothers" in Mĕssiah who were keeping the commandments of Mĕssiah. This situation occurs today, wherein many Christians and Christian sects hate the faithful who keep the Şabbath or any other commandments they refuse to consider. They are full of criticism, condemnation, discrimination, and hatred of every form for the faithful in Mĕssiah. They have centuries of theological refinements and traditions that cause them to behave like this. Often nowadays they do not even realize they are doing it. But if any of them have the Spĭrit of Mĕssiah they will be convicted of the truth and though they may still disagree on the commandments they will not persecute the faithful. **2:18** β→moment: It was the 'utmost hour,' (cf. BDAG ἔσχατος, "❸ *utmost* "). But since so many have thought that he meant the last hour before the Second Coming, I have given the idiomatic sense of the words. A commander says to his men before the battle, "Men, it is the final hour. The fate of our land will be determined in today's battle." So it was then. The Gnostics had departed from the Messianic Faith, and they were busy integrating their philosophy of salvation with pagan ideas and lawlessness. In Yoḣanan's day, it was an all out spiritual war against false doctrine. It was the last hour. The truth won, but barely. The Gnostics were forced to the fringe or had to remake themselves to continue to be perceived as Christians. Their lawlessness adopted a new form that passed for Christianity among those not paying attention to the changing definitions. **2:19** ρ→have = ἄν = would have; See LSJ.

²⁰But you have an anointing from the Holy One, and you have been knowing everything. ²¹I have not written to you because you have not been knowing the truth, but because you have been knowing it, and because no lie is of the truth. ²²Who is the liar but the one who denies that Yĕshua is the Anŏinted? This is the anti-Mĕssiah, the one who denies the Făther and the Sŏn. ²³Whoever denies the Sŏn does not have the Făther. The one who agrees with the Sŏn has the Făther also. ²⁴As for you, let that be remaining in you which you heard from the beginning. If what you heard from the beginning shall have remained in you, you also will remain in the Sŏn and in the Făther.

²⁵And this is the promise which he himself made to us: everlasting life.

²⁶These things I have written to you concerning those who are trying to deceive you. ²⁷And *as for* you, the anointing which you received from him ᵃremains in you, and you are having no need wherein ᵟsome should be teaching you, but as his anointing is teaching you about all things, and is true, and is not a lie, also just as it has taught you, you are remaining in him.

²⁸And now, little children, be remaining in him, so that when he may have been manifested, we may have had confidence and may not have been ashamed before him at his coming presence. ²⁹If you have been knowing that he is righteous, you know that everyone also practicing righteousness, from him, has been getting begotten.

3 ¹See what love the Făther has been giving us, so that we shall have been called children of the Almĭghty. And *such* we are. For this reason the world does not know us, because it did not know him. ²Beloved, now we are children of the Almĭghty, and it has not appeared as yet what we will be. We have been knowing that when he shall have been shown, we will be like him, because we will see him just as he is.

³And everyone who has this hope fixed on him purifies himself, just as he is pure. ⁴Everyone who practices sin also practices lawlessness, and sin is lawlessness. ⁵And you have been knowing that he appeared so that he will have taken away sins, and in him there is no sin. ⁶Anyone remaining in him does not sin. Anyone sinning has not been perceiving him, nor yet has he been knowing him.

2:27 α *remains in you:* The deceivers were claiming Gŏd's anointing in them took precedence in matters of teaching, urging their teaching to be accepted on the basis of their claim to being anointed of Gŏd. **2:27** δ τις *some:* Yoḣanan means those teachers promoting themselves by claiming the anointing of Gŏd. The word τις does not mean anyone at all, but just some certain ones who imply they have spiritual knowledge beyond verifiable facts, and who use this assumed position as the reason why they should be teaching, and why their teaching should be accepted. Yoḣanan urges us to remain in the anointing already in us when faced with this kind of spiritual challenge from deceivers.

3:3-6 Cf. 1 John 1:8-9. There are several Hebrew words for sin, and generally one Greek word was used to represent all of them. The Scripture distinguishes between transgression (or iniquity) which are in the category of serious sin, and sins of ignorance or unforeseen circumstances. See Numbers 15:29-31. No one who is getting begotten of the Almĭghty commits transgression or iniquity. No one who knows the Almĭghty lives in rebellion. Yet all the faithful have sins, which are bad habits, things they are ignorant of.

⁷Little children, let no one be deceiving you. The one who practices righteousness is righteous, just as he is righteous. ⁸The one practicing sin is of the Slanderer, because the Slanderer sins since the beginning. The Almĭghty Sŏn appeared for this purpose, that he shall have destroyed the works of the Slanderer.

⁹Any one ᵠwho has been getting begotten from the Almĭghty is not practicing sin, because his ᶠseed is remaining in him—and he is not able to be sinning in that he has been getting begotten from the Almĭghty. ¹⁰By this the children of the Almĭghty and the children of the Slanderer are obvious: anyone who does not practice righteousness is not of the Almĭghty, nor the one who does not love his brother.

¹¹For this is the message which you have heard from the beginning, that we should be loving one another; ¹²not as Qayin, who was of the evil one, and slew his brother. And in favor of what did he slay him? Because his deeds were evil, and his brother's were righteous. ¹³Do not be getting surprised, brothers, if the world hates you. ¹⁴We have been knowing that we have been passing out of death into life, because we love the brothers. He who does not love abides in death. ¹⁵Everyone who hates his brother is a murderer. And you have been knowing that no murderer has everlasting life remaining in him.

¹⁶By this we have been knowing love, because he laid down his life on our behalf. And we ought to lay down our lives on behalf of the brothers. ¹⁷And, whoever may be having the world's goods, and may be seeing his brother in need and may have closed his heart against him, how does the love of the Almĭghty remain in him? ¹⁸Little children, may we not be loving with word or with tongue, but in deed and truth.

3:9 ψ→begotten = γεγεννημένος (V-RPM/P-NMS). The perfect participle is gnomic and distributive (cf. Wallace, pg. 580; Gnomic Perfect). In a Hebrew sense, future perfect: will have been getting begotten. ▷ In a customary English sense: is getting begotten. According to the figure of speech, begetting a child is an episodic activity. The seed must remain in the womb to unite with the ovum. Multiple tries may be required. How much seed is needed is unknown. In the ancient view, every try is a begetting. The modern scientific view that begetting (conception) happens at an instant when sperm and egg meet is liable to mislead us as to the sense of the figure of speech Yoḥanan is using. Yoḥanan means the seed has to remain united with the heart. Only this way will the end result be the birth of sons and daughters of the Almĭghty. ▷ The distributive character of the perfect tense depends on how the verb is viewed, e.g. whether 'to be begotten' is viewed as an instant, or as an activity of the parents. The latter would be the case long ago, and even though the literal science is no longer viewed this way, the figurative use of the literal for spiritual matters must still be based on the ancient view of the literal. Each episode of adding seed in the begetting is a completed action, but it is distributive in that the same action needs to be repeated until success results or the one begetting gives up trying. Thus the word 'getting' is used where necessary to break the reader's erring intuition with certain verbs unfairly viewed as instantaneous actions. ▷ The perfect may be understood as either moving to the far future and viewing all the tries as completed, or as reading in the present and viewing all tries up to the present as completed. If one has heard the word then one should not sin. If one sins, the begetting did not work, and another try is needed. **3:9** ζ His seed remains in him. And the seed is his word, which is his commandments (Mat 13:19ff; Luke 8:11; 1 Pet. 1:23); it is just this statement that proves the activity of *begetting* is meant, and not being born [cf. Menken, *Novum Testamentum*; Vol. 51, Fasc. 4 (2009), pp. 352-368]. The word does not passively stay in the faithful, but the faithful have to remain in his words for the word to remain in them. The one who has the word in his heart, and who holds faithful to Mĕssiah does not sin, and cannot sin, because the word unites with his heart.

¹⁹We will know by this that we are of the truth, and will persuade our heart before him, ²⁰in whatever our heart may be condemning us, because the Almĭghty is greater than our heart, and is knowing all things. ²¹Beloved, if our heart may not be condemning us, we have confidence before the Almĭghty, ²²and that which^ψ we may be asking we are receiving from him, because we are keeping his commandments and doing the things that are pleasing in his sight."

²³And this is his commandment, that we shall have held faithful to the name of his Sŏn Yĕshua the Anŏinted, that is, we should be loving one another, just as he commanded us. ²⁴ᵃAnd the one keeping his commandments remains in him, and he in him. ²⁴ᵇAnd we know by this that he remains in us, by the Spĭrit whom he has given us.

4 ¹Beloved, do not be holding faithful every spirit, but be testing the spirits to see whether they are from the Almĭghty, because many false prophets have been going out into the world. ²By this you know the Spĭrit of the Almĭghty: every spirit who agrees with Yĕshua the Anŏinted—*the one* having been coming in flesh, from the Almĭghty is.^θ ³And every spirit that does not agree with Yĕshua, the Anŏinted One, who in the flesh has been coming, is not from the Almĭghty.

3:22 ψ The text is not the superlative "whatever." The emphasis is on receiving because we keep his commandments. See *Mark 11:22* x-refs.

3:19-22 η If anyone ever says that love is completely unconditional, then they are not reading the Scripture. Yohanan is repeating here what is true from Exodus 20:6: "AND DOING LOVING-KINDNESS TO THE THOUSANDTH GENERATION OF THOSE LOVING ME AND TO THE KEEPERS OF MY COMMANDMENTS." **3:23-24b** Among Christians are a lot of teachers of the Gnostic system of belief. These have gone out from the truth (cf. 1 John 2:19). They are very clever at equivocating and redefining what Scripture says. As they understand holding faithful to Mĕssiah to mean believing only what they view as promises contingent on nothing but belief, they say that this is what Yohanan must mean Mĕssiah's commandment is, and nothing more. So by changing one definition, they engage in circular equivocation to avoid the very truth that is being taught. But the vast majority of those who once embraced the Messianic Faith at the very beginning have long since (going back to the days of Yohanan) departed from the true faith.

4:3 θ The usual translation of this verse causes a difficult problem. In fact the problem is insoluble. A person may "confess" that he came in the flesh, even sincerely, but otherwise be a false teacher. So what good does it do if someone comes with the right confession, but then teaches that salvation is an acquittal of sin? Or a person may confess that Mĕssiah came in the flesh, but then teach men to pray to the 'saints'. The second statement in vs. 3 has not this problem. We can be sure that someone who denies he came in the flesh is not from Gŏd by the one test alone. ▷ The key to this text is solved in the Greek, but I will give the practical lesson first. The first is this: "having been coming in the flesh" is a descriptive phrase. So we have two characters here, one is the Mĕssiah who has been coming in the flesh. The other is the Mĕssiah that has not been coming in the flesh. False teachers teach another Mĕssiah, one who has not been coming in the flesh vs. the true Mĕssiah who has been coming in the flesh. ▷ (Mĕssiah appeared as a man in Gen. 18:1; 32:24; Jos. 5:13; Dan. 3:25; 8:16; 9:21; Zech. 1:8, 10. It may be that many or all of the cases where he is called the ANGEL OF THE LORD, he also took form in human flesh besides the angelic body, such as walking with Adam in the garden. He assumed human flesh permanently between his conception and resurrection, and on a part time basis after his return to heaven.) ▷ Next we have the word usually translated "confesses" which is weak in English. The word means literally "to say the same thing as." So what the text says is the one who says the same thing as the Mĕssiah who has been coming in the flesh vs. a false Mĕssiah who has not been coming in the flesh. Thereby our problem is solved. One who teaches only that Mĕssiah came in the flesh, but also teaches against things Mĕssiah said is not giving agreement to him. He is not "confessing" Him in the original sense. ▷ Thayer: ὁμολογέω 1. prop. *to say the same thing as another*, i.e. *to agree with, assent*. LSJ, I. *agree with, say the same thing as*. Literally, "Every spirit that same-says-as Yĕshua Mĕssiah in flesh having been coming, from the Almĭghty is." Also LSJ 3. *agree or promise to do, promise, make an agreement, come to terms*. So confession has the idea of "agrees to." It is synonymous with "covenants with." So everyone who covenants with the Mĕssiah that has been coming in the flesh is from the Almĭghty. Therefore a confession is more than just assent to a single doctrine. ▷ Yohanan's point is that the spirit from Gŏd confesses the Mĕssiah who has been coming in the flesh, and not some other Mĕssiah. The true confession involves heartfelt agreement to Mĕssiah. This

And this is the spirit of the anti-Mĕssiah, of which you have been hearing that it is coming, and now it is already in the world.

⁴You are from the Almĭghty, little children, and have been getting victory over them, because greater is he who is in you than he who is in the world. ⁵They are from the world. Therefore, they speak as from the world, and the world listens to them. ⁶We are from the Almĭghty. He who knows the Almĭghty listens to us. He who is not from the Almĭghty does not listen to us. By this we know the spirit of truth and the spirit of error.

⁷Beloved, we should be loving one another, for love is from the Almĭghty, and ⁿeveryone loving has been getting begotten of the Almĭghty and is knowing the Almĭghty. ⁸The one who does not love does not know the Almĭghty, for the Almĭghty is love. ⁹By this the love of the Almĭghty was manifested in us, that the Almĭghty has been sending his only ᵘkindred Sŏn into the world so that we shall

---

involves everything, to be sure, but Yoḥanan qualified the confession with confession to the Mĕssiah having been coming in the flesh. Why is this? This is because Ebionites, Cerenthians, Marcionites, and other Gnostics were denying that the Almĭghty truly became a man in Yĕshua. They also denied his every appearance before he was born of a virgin. Some argued that the Mĕssiah was just a divine spirit that inhabited a mere man from his baptism to just before he died. Then the divine spirit left. Clearly they denied the divine spirit become flesh. Others argued that Mĕssiah was divine, but that he only appeared to be a man, and was not in fact a man of flesh. ▷ All these heretical theories ended up denying that the person of Yĕshua himself was identified as Elohim, yet one who limited his perspectives to experience living as a man. How this is done is as great a mystery as the Almĭghty's creation of living beings with souls in the first place. But there is no logical reason to deny the Almĭghty Sŏn's ability to become man. He became man so that man could relate to him. ▷ The word ὁμολογέω appears to be somewhat like πιστεύω in usage. One may agree with a person, in which case the agreement is with everything the person says. But one may agree to a fact or datum or statement of fact. In that case the agreement is not a personal loyalty. With this in mind, the observation of H.A.W. Meyer's NT Commentary is the foundation of this comment: "The form of the object is explained by the polemic against Docetism; it is to be translated either: "Jesus Christ as come in the flesh" (Lücke, de Wette, Düsterdieck, Ebrard, etc.); or: "Jesus, as Christ [having been] come[ing] in the flesh;" the last interpretation has this advantage, that it not only brings out more clearly the reference to the Cerinthian Docetism,[254] but it makes it more easy to explain how the apostle in 1 John 4:3 can designate the object simply by τὸν Ἰησοῦν. It might, however, be still more suitable to take Ἰησοῦν ... ἐληλυθότα as one object = "the Jesus Christ who came in the flesh," so that in this expression the individual elements on which John here relied in opposition to Docetism have been gathered into one; so perhaps Braune, when he says: "the form is that of a substantive objective sentence," and "in ἐν σ. ἐλ. it is not a predicate, but an attributive clause that is added."" (Meyer, 1John 4:3). So we see that if the key phrase is taken as a predicate, i.e. "confesses Y.M. [is] having come in the flesh," then the construction is that of taking a datum as an object. It is better that Mĕssiah himself be confessed, and the other phrase be taken to modify his nature. Then the logical problem disappears. ▷The result is that Yoḥanan is not telling us that agreement to a single doctrine confirms a spirit is from the Almĭghty. He is saying that it is agreement to (ὁμολογέω) the Almĭghty Sŏn, which represents everything. Besides this, he is emphasizing to us that the divine nature having come in the flesh is part of it, because that is where the heretics were attacking the faith.

4:7 η 'everyone,' evidently, is limited to the faithful: cf. 1 Yoḥ. 2:29; 3:9; 5:1, 4, 18.

4:9 μ The Greek word μονογενής means an only relation, an only kindred within a given relationship (cf. BDAG, 3rd). Thus the Făther has only one Sŏn, who is kindred with him. The Rŭaḥ HaQodesh is also kindred with the Făther, but the Spĭrit is not in the Sŏn relationship. The Greek word stresses not just "only-ness," but also kinship. μονο means "only" but γενής from γένος means "race, stock, kin" (LSJ). The usage for Mĕssiah is exclusive to Yoḥanan. See Yoḥ. 1:14, 18; 3:16, 18, and here 1 Yoḥ. 4:9, where kinship with the Făther is also stressed. The Sŏn is of like kind with the Făther, Elohim, Almĭghty. The sense of μονογενής is not the only one of his own kind, but the only who is a Sŏn of like kind with the Făther. Thus the word is used in Luke 7:12, "an only kin son." The son was the only one of the class son-kindred to his mother. See also Luke 8:42; 9:38; ▷ The reason that translators have failed to stress the γένος part of μονογενής is that it was for many centuries thought that the word meant "only begotten," thus deriving the last part of the word from Greek root γεννάω (to beget), instead of correct one: γένος, (kind, kin, genus) from γίνομαι. Retreating from this error texts were changed from "only begotten Son" to "only Son." Out of some 52 translations, 37 mostly recent put "only Son," and 15 mostly older versions put "only begotten Son." (The Old Latin also translates with just the word only.) We see here that the mistake is only half corrected. It is admitted that the ending does not mean "begotten," but neither is the correct sense restored! If Yoḥanan

have lived through him. ¹⁰In this is love, not that we had been loving the Almĭghty, but that he loved us and sent his Sŏn *to be a* ᶿwiping away concerning our sins. ¹¹Beloved, if the Almĭghty so loved us, we also ought to love one another. ¹²No one has been beholding the ᵖAlmĭghty at any time. If we may be loving one another, the Almĭghty is abiding in us, and the love of him, having been getting perfected in us, is. ¹³By this we know that we abide in him and he in us, because he has been giving us of his Spĭrit. ¹⁴And we have been ourselves beholding and we are bearing witness that the Făther has been sending the Sŏn to be the Rescuer of the world. ¹⁵Whoever may have confessed, ᵞseeing that Yĕshua is the Sŏn, the Almĭghty One, the Almĭghty remains in him, and he in the Almĭghty. ¹⁶And we have been knowing, and we have been holding faithful the love which the Almĭghty has *invested* in us. The Almĭghty is love, and the one who is remaining in *that* love is remaining in the Almĭghty, and the Almĭghty is remaining in him.

¹⁷By this, love has and will have been getting perfected with us,ᵅ so that we

---

had meant to say "only Sŏn" the word μόνος would have sufficed. Yoḣanan certainly knew how to use that word; ▷ Proof is to be found in John 3:18. "Only Son of Gŏd" makes no sense without some further specification. There are many "SONS OF GŎD." See Gen. 6:2; Job 1:6; 2:1. Readers are apt to read something unique into the translation "only Son" without the text saying so. See also Romans 8:19; Luke 20:36. The ending -γενης is the missing specification. Mĕssiah is the only kindred Son of the Făther. Kindred means kin to the Făther as *Elohim*. Făther and Son share the relation of being Almĭghty. So in Yoḣ. 1:18, "the only kindred Almĭghty," more pointedly explains what "only kindred Sŏn" means. It may be possible to translate Yoḣ. 1:18 as "only kindred one, the Almĭghty who has been in the bosom of the Făther," but some sensibly object to making the adjective μονογενης into a substantive here, and suppose that otherwise the text only says, "the only Almĭghty," which would exclude the Făther. Restoring the ending to μονογενης solves the difficulty. The adjective need not be substantive, because "only kindred Almĭghty" explains everything; ▷ The incorrect interpretation "only begotten" led to the doctrine of eternal "begetting" in order to explain how the Sŏn was begotten without being created. This doctrine of eternal generation was promoted by Gregory of Nazianzus (A.D. 329 - 390), and followed by Ŏrigen and Jerome. In fact it was the "sonship" of the Sŏn that was begotten in time (as an adopted status), and not the Sŏn himself. And this is spoken of in a different text. See Psalm 2:7. This was an adopted and conferred status relationship between the Sŏn and the Făther. Both are Yăhweн, and at some point the Sŏn and the Făther decided what roles they would take (toward humanity) in the one Almĭghty.

4:10 ᶿ "Wiping away." See 2:2. The text is informed by the Hebrew term כִּפֶּר kipper. The word properly means "to declare to be wiped" (Piel). Asphalt was wiped onto the ark (Qal). The derivation of the word from the idea of "cover" is not correct, especially when the idea that the Levitical sin offerings only covered sin which was not actually first forgiven (cf. Appendix X). The cognate Akkadian *kaparu* means "wipe off," but the Hebrew is used in the sense of "wipe away." Three related ideas are involved in the Piel (declatory) wiping away, 1. declaring a penalty wiped, and 2. declaring heart cleansing by the life of Messiah, 3. declaring ritual cleansing by sacrificial blood. The later idea is that of ritual cleansing of ritual impurity. As applied to Mĕssiah, KIPPURIM means two straightforward ideas: 1. A sign that he wiped out our sin penalty by forgiving it, and 2. *a* sign that his life (represented by his blood) cleanses us from all sin. The indicated cleansing is in fact spiritual by his divine life. The word *sins* may be taken as wiping away *sin penalties*, or wiping away *sins* themselves. Both ideas are correct, but the completion of the wiping away of the sin so symbolized is eschatological. The wiping of the sin penalty is complete upon pledge of faithfulness to Mĕssiah in genuine repentance, and comes before the offering that declares it. Messiah's offering does not declare the wiping received by a confessor until after he confesses and repents.

4:12 π He speaks of the Făther here. No one has ever seen the Făther, but anytime Yăhweн was seen by the Adam, or the fathers, or on the mountain, or as the Messenger of Yăhweн, it was the Almĭghty Sŏn that was seen; **4:15** λ This is the same idea as in Romans 10:9. Note that ὅτι is translated "because," "seeing that," and supplies the reason for confirming our faithfulness to Him. Paul includes confessing Adŏnai Yĕshua. Without that confession, acknowledging him as Savior is likely to fall apart, because only Yăhweн is our Savior. **4:17** α By remaining in him, love will have been getting *accomplished* or *completed*. See vs. 16. Since the saying is *a* truism, it may be stated, 'By this, love has been getting accomplished.' The Greek perfect is extensive/distributive/gnomic (Wallace, pg. 580). Hebrew idiom uses a future perfect is such cases also. This is to say that Gŏd's love is completed by us every time we act in love. For this use of the perfect see Yoḣ. 5:24; Eph. 2:6, 8; **4:17** β Read εσομεθα; **4:17** γ In the age to come, we are changed to our perfected state, and will rule and reign with Mĕssiah over the earth.

may be having confidence in the day of judgment, because as he is, so also we ᵝwill be in this ᵞworld. ¹⁸There is no fear in love, but perfect love casts out fear, because fear involves punishment, and the one who fears has not been getting perfected in love.

¹⁹We love, because he first loved us. ²⁰If someone may have said, "I love the Almĭghty," and may be hating his brother, he is a liar. Because the one who does not love his brother whom he has been seeing, cannot love the Almĭghty whom he has not been seeing. ²¹And this commandment we have from him, that the one who loves the Almĭghty should be loving his brother also.

5 ¹Everyone holding faithful, because Yĕshua is the Anŏinted One, has been getting begotten of the Almĭghty. And whoever loves the One who has begotten, also loves the one who has been getting begotten from him. ²By this we know that we are loving the children of the Almĭghty, when we may be loving the Almĭghty and may be observing his commandments. ³For this is the love of the Almĭghty, that we should be keeping his commandments, and his commandments are not burdensome, ⁴because everyone who has been getting begotten from the Almĭghty is getting victory over the world, and this is the victory that ᶿwill have gotten victory over the world—our faithfulness. ⁵And who is the one who is getting victory over the world, except the one holding faithful, because Yĕshua is the Almĭghty Sŏn!

⁶This is the one who came by water and blood, Yĕshua the Anŏinted, not with the water only, but with the water and with the blood. ⁷And it is the Spĭrit who bears witness, because the Spĭrit is the truth. ⁸For there are three that bear witness, the Spĭrit and the water and the blood, and the three are in agreement. ⁹If we receive the witness of men, the witness of the Almĭghty is greater. Because the witness of the Almĭghty is this, that he has been bearing witness about his Sŏn. ¹⁰The one holding faithful to the Almĭghty Sŏn is having this witness in himself. The one who is not holding faithful to the Almĭghty has been making him a liar, because he has not been holding faithful to the witness that the Almĭghty has been witnessing about his Sŏn. ¹¹And the witness is this, that the Almĭghty has ᶿoffered us everlasting life, and this Life is in his Sŏn. ¹²The one ᵘholding to the Sŏn is ᵖholding to Life. ᶴThe one not ᵘholding to the Almĭghty Sŏn, is not ᵖholding to Life.

5:4 θ→have: a gnomic aorist participle, as in giving an example in English. 'Do it this way Sam, which has always worked,' or more commonly 'works,' or more emphatically, 'that will have worked.' **5:11** θ δίδωμι See LSJ A.3 *offer;* Middle Liddel I.1 *to offer,* 3. *to offer.* Slater: *make an offer.* BDAG, 3rd. 16. *offer.* Yohanan has defined 'eternal life' as being in the Son following his statement in 1:2 and 5:20; **5:12** ξ or 'the one not laying hold of the Almĭghty Son, is not laying hold on the Life.' See LSJ, ἔχω 'A. Trans. have, hold: I. *possess, acquire, get.* 11. keep up, maintain; II. hold, 1. hold; 2. hold fast.' Cf. Heb. נָחַל *to receive any* thing as a possession, to possess; 2. to receive as an inheritance. The present tense may be used to refer to the future, e.g. 'Mĕssiah is coming.' 'Bob is having his art displayed at the Museum.' 'We are having dinner with your Grandparents.' Thus, 'getting the Life' and 'not getting the Life' refer to the future. In Hebrew: הַנּוֹחֵל אֶת בֶּן הָאֱלֹהִים, הוּא נוֹחֵל הַחַי = the one possessing the Son, he is inheriting the life; **5:12** μ or *holding fast;* π or *inheriting.* **5:12** π *getting;* see same word ἔχομεν in vs. 15. Clearly the answers to prayers are obtained in the future of asking.

¹³These things I have written, so that you will have been knowing that you are inheriting eternal life, to those holding faithful to the name of the Almĭghty Sŏn.

¹⁴And this is the confidence which we are having before him, that if we may be asking anything according to his will, he is listening to us. ¹⁵And if we have been knowing that he is listening to us in whatever we may be asking, we have been knowing that we are ᵗgetting the requests which we have been making requested from him.

¹⁶If anyone shall have seen his brother sinning a sin not leading to death, he will ask, and the Almĭghty will give him life (that is, for those sinning not to death). There is sin leading to death. I do not say that he should make request for this. ¹⁷All unrighteousness is sin, and there is sin not leading to death.

¹⁸We have been knowing that no one who has been getting begotten of the Almĭghty is sinning, but he who is begotten of the Almĭghty is watching over ᵋhimself and the evil one is not touching him. ¹⁹We have been knowing that we are of the Almĭghty, and the whole world is laying in the power of the evil one. ²⁰And we have been knowing that the Almĭghty Sŏn comes, and has been giving us understanding, in order that we may be knowing THE TRUE ONEᵖ, and we are in THE TRUE ONE—in his Sŏn Yĕshua the Anŏinted. This one is THE TRUE ALMĬGHTY and ᶴEverlasting Life. ²¹Little children, guard yourselves from idols.

5:17 The sin that leads to death is the sin with the high hand against the truth (cf. Num. 15:30-31; Gal. 5:19-21; 1Cor. 6:9-10). The sin with the high hand is anti-faith, or faithlessness. One who is truly committed to Gŏd does not sin this kind of sin.

5:18 ε Some mss read "him" here, but I have judged the traditional reading ἑαυτὸν correct. The idea is parallel to 5:4. It is easier to explain how *himself* got changed to *him* than the reverse. Also unlikely is the use of the verb *beget* for the Sŏn when Yoĥanan constantly uses it for the faithful person. See also 1 Yoĥ. 3:3. Yoĥanan's purpose is to counter Gnostic doctrines which have evolved into the Calvinistic doctrines.

5:20 π The adjective 'TRUE' here is a substantive, that is it is treated as a noun, a person. What it refers to is explained in the last of the three uses in the verse, "THE TRUE ALMĬGHTY," so we can explain the first two uses by suppling ONE to make the personal reference clear. The parallel usage of 'in THE TRUE ONE' and 'in his Son' completely identify "the true one" with "his Son. That is, what follows, 'in' in the first clause is equated with what follows 'in' in the second clause. The first usage of 'THE TRUE ONE' includes the Father, who is unseen, but the second usage is narrowed down to the Son. Finally, in the last usage, Yoĥanan says, "This one is THE TRUE ALMĬGHTY." "This one" refers to the Son which was just mentioned in the previous clause. ▷ The background for this text is Yoĥ. 17:3, where the Son says, "And this is everlasting life, that they may be knowing you, the *one who is alone* true Almĭghty and the one whom you have sent, Yĕshua the Anŏinted One." The Father by himself (alone) is the true Almĭghty. And so also the Son by himself (alone) is the true Almĭghty. The divinity of the Son is not dependent on that of the Father. The Son, in himself, is the fulness of divinity. See Col. 1:29; 2:9. Here in 1 Yoĥ. 5:20, Yoĥanan is interpreting his own statement in his previous book (Yoĥ. 17:3). The Son alone is the true Almĭghty, and by knowing the Son, we know the Father, because the Son's nature is just like the Father's nature. ▷ In 1 Yoĥ. 1:2, the Word of Life (1:1) is identified as the Everlasting Life, which was with the Father. So the Everlasting Life, likewise, in 5:20 is the true Almĭghty. The Life that was with the Father is not the Father, but the Son. ▷ The Nicene Creed (AD 325) leads Meyer to claim: "It is only the Father of Jesus Christ that is the true God." And it also led Augustine to rearrange the words in Yoĥ. 17:3 so that they would agree with the Nicene Creed. And plainly the Greek text does not agree with the Nicene Creed in 17:3, because either it means 'only true God' and does not include the Son, or it means 'alone true God' and applies to the Son as a separate and independent instance of divinity, but by no means can it refer to one divine essence. Meyer seeks to rescue the Creed by claiming the Son is an eternal generation of the Father. Indeed, the Creed claims so based upon the corruption of Yoĥ. 1:18, viz. 'only begotten' (q.v.), but this is only a clever way of saying 'emanation,' and it is certain that the origin of the 'same being' (homoousion) doctrine is the Gnostics. Because this is where the term comes from, and we see that in the end it leads to diminishing Messiah's divinity to the level of emanation. This then is the real heresy of the Trinity doctrine as defined by Nicea. **5:20** ζ →Life: See back at 1 Yoĥ. 1:2. Yoĥanan's meant to connect his closing with his opening.

End Note No. 1: The Nicene Idolatry

Christians confess the Trinity Doctrine, which is Gŏd the Făther, Gŏd the Sŏn, and Gŏd the Holy Spĭrit, "three persons" in One Gŏd.

In this form, the errors are relatively harmless, but still harmful. The word *person*, as applied to the Făther or the Spĭrit in the sense that humans understand *person* as a singular being, is speculation, because *person* in that sense is only revealed in the humanness of the Sŏn. The words *Trinity* and *three* also are misleading, because these presume to count up the number of *persons* in the One Almĭghty. In rejecting the word *person* we are only rejecting its implications in terms of composition of being and not the spiritual qualities of persons, i.e. that they hear, speak, see, etc. In rejecting *three* we are rejecting the number restriction in terms of persons, but not the number of divine roles, which are certainly person-like differentiations (to use a simile), Făther, Sŏn and Spĭrit. But only the Sŏn is a person in the singular being sense of a human. The Spĭrit is described as seven spirits. See note on Mat. 28:20.

The real harm in the Trinity Doctrine comes from the Nicene Creed in the words *one substance* and *begotten before all worlds*. The only text in the entire Scripture to speak of "one Almĭghty" in reference to all of Gŏd is James 2:19, q.v., and in that place it means one and no others, and does not mean to define the composition of the Almĭghty. Other examples explained: In Mal. 2:10 אֵל אֶחָד means *the same Gŏd*, and אָב אֶחָד means *the same Făther*. In Deu. 6:4 and Zech. 14:9 we have, יְהוָה אֶחָד *Yăhwe**ꞪJ only*, and *his name only*, וּשְׁמוֹ אֶחָד. The word is used as an adverb, meaning *only* or *alone* (Mark 2:7; 10:18; 12:32; Luke 18:19; Gal. 3:20), or as an adjective meaning *the same* (Yoh. 10:30; Rom. 3:30; 1 Cor. 8:6; 12:6; Eph. 4:5-6). Some texts involve textual corruptions (Mat. 19:17; James 2:19). *One Almĭghty* applies to the Sŏn alone in 1 Tim. 2:5, q.v., as *one Adŏnai* in 1 Cor. 8:6. So, you see, the Scripture does not seek to explain the nature of the Almĭghty with the word אֶחָד. Rather it is explaining that he is exclusively Almĭghty, the same Almĭghty with respect to the faithful, or one member in contrast to other members, 1 Tim. 2:5, *supra*. Paul deliberately goes about using the word אֶחָד these ways, clearly to show his disagreement with the "God is one [being]" doctrine, but even this way "God is one" might mean it in the sense of a marriage. Many have indeed replaced the more correct explanation of adverbial usage of אֶחָד with the example of marriage, but can hardly be blamed in the face of corrupt translations. This explanation does have its proper place.

Because, the Scripture does disclose in what manner the Făther and the Sŏn are one in Yoh. 17:11, which is how *one* is used in Gen. 2:24, and teaches that the faithful are to join the Most High in this kind of union. So all the uses of אֶחָד in Scripture are far away from describing a singularity of being.

The grandday error is *beggoten before all worlds* (Καὶ εἰς ἕνα Κύριον Ἰησοῦν Χριστόν, τὸν Υἱὸν τοῦ Θεοῦ τὸν μονογενῆ, τὸν ἐκ τοῦ Πατρὸς γεννηθέντα πρὸ πάντων τῶν αἰώνων... ὁμοούσιον τῷ Πατρί; Nicene Creed 381)

So the Church added its philosophy to the description of Gŏd. The Church codified this in the Nicene Creed. What must be repudiated is the doctrine of the "eternal generation of the Sŏn," in that creed, which is squarly contradicted by Yoh. 17:3; Col. 1:19; Yoh. 3:14, 16; 5:44; 1 Yoh 5:20.

And the doctrine of the ὁμοούσιον (homoousion) must interpreted in a way that is unacceptable to most theologians in order to hold true. ▷ Firstly, *homoousion* means "same being." We may say that a certain rock is the same rock as another rock of the same type. One lump of coal is the same rock as another lump of coal. To prevent this understanding, the interpretation the Church puts on the words is "one substance," and that means, they say, the persons of the Trinity are all the exact same essence, substance, being, rather than separated beings with the same nature. With our rock analogy the theologians disallow three rocks of the same type, and insist "same" means the same rock, one rock. This description of Gŏd must be rejected. Scripture nowhere says that he is the same being in this sense. See Yoh. 17:3, which disproves the homoousion doctrine, and also Col. 1:19. ▷ Secondly, the doctrine of eternal generation must be rejected. *Monogenes* does not mean "only begotten." It means "only kindred," (Yoh. 1:14, 18; 3:16, 18; 5:44; 1 Yoh. 4:9) which is to say the Sŏn is the only chip of like kind to the Făther and Spĭrit. The shared nature is what is common to the individual Almĭghtiness of each one. The divine nature of the Sŏn is not derived. Also, the eternal generation doctrine comes from the Gnostic doctrine of emanations (aka generations) of Gŏd. Something begotten is derived from something not-begotten. Something begotten is physically dependent on something not-begotten. So whenever they interpret begotten as something beyond the virgin birth, they are endorsing a pagan philosophy! ▷ What makes the Făther, Sŏn, and Spĭrit One Almĭghty is not some kind of physical constraint of beingness. That is idolatry, because he has no constraints like that. That the everlasting entity who became the Sŏn and man succeeded in doing so, proves that the Almĭghty is not limited to being a simple unitary being. But like a marriage the oneness is a relationship intelligently maintained based on loyalty, love, and common purpose. This is how Měssiah defines the matter in Yoh. 17:11, 21. This is not to say that the Almĭghty cannot ever be one in some physical way, or spiritually joined in a *one essence* outside of human experience. But like a marriage, the degree of bond must vary to accommodate the revealed individuality of the Făther, Sŏn and Spĭrit. No creed has any business trying to define what is unknown and unrevealed about the Almĭghty. ▷ What does Scripture actually say about the unity of Gŏd? "Hear Yisra'el, Yăhweʜ is our Almĭghty, Yăhweʜ only" (Deu. 6:4). This statement is made not to define the one Almĭghty (cf. Jam. 2:19) any more than "one city" tells us what the population is, but to say he is the only

Almĭghty versus false gods. We say, 'One Almĭghty is' meaning he is the one Almĭghty, because there is one Almĭghty versus any false god, i.e. the only Almĭghty. He is identified by his name Yăhweн. Yet we see Him refer to himself as 'us' in Gen. 1:26, 3:22, 11:7; Isa. 6:8. Also Gen. 19:24 teaches more than one entity is Yăhweн. How is this possible? Easily, just as stated above 'One Almĭghty' is a statement about his relation to other gods, and not a statement revealing how many entities he himself chooses to exist as. We can say there is one school in a certain town having one school of engineering, one school of art, and one school of medicine, i.e. several schools are one school. Usually we call the one school a university. ▷ Yăhweн says, "I am Yăhweн, and there is yet none. Besides me there is no almighty" (Isa. 45:5). We should be careful here to understand that in Hebrew one entity may speak for all entities in a union, or a union of entities may speak as one using singular pronouns, *I*, *me*, *myself*, and further that a compound entity may be referred to with singular 3rd person pronouns. This is called the **collective singular**. Thus Yisra'el says, "Why have you made us ascend from Egypt to kill me, and my sons, and my livestock with thirst?" (Exo. 17:3). Or a city says, "I am, and no one is besides me" (Zeph. 2:15). Or a nation says to a nation, "Edom said to him, 'Thou shall not pass over through me, lest with sword I come out to meet thee.'" (Num. 20:18). Such language can reveal nothing about the entity speaking except it be revealed elsewhere. Therefore, the Almĭghty may use such words and be himself more than one entity. ▷ If the Almĭghty is more than one entity, then only one of these entities is truly one person, namely Yĕshua the Mĕssiah, since he became a man. For 'person' has no sense except that which humans know in themselves and perceive in other humans. Every **normal** human person is unitary in being. Every human person has but one self, one consciousness, and one awareness of mind. ▷ An entity may subdivide, combine, or recombine. A purely non-human entity may do this as he sees fit. Surely the Almĭghty can do this within the limits of logic. He became a man, or rather part of himself did, speaking with a *collective singular*. It stands to reason that since humans are one self that further subdivision of a human is not normally possible. We see that the Holy Spĭrit subdivides seven ways. Of the Făther we are not told. ▷ Now we come to the Nicene Creed where the Church says that Gŏd is all of the 'same being' (homoousion). We see here that if 'being' has any of the senses familiar to humans, such as 'one person,' then it contradicts Scripture. Scripture no where makes such a claim, but the claim is inferred from the Isaiah passages, viz. "I am He" and "There is none besides Me." But we may just as well infer that he is one person from such words as to infer that he is the 'same being.' Judaism actually does make this inference.

Let us make no inference at all, but rely on the other scriptures that reveal the Almĭghty as more than one entity. And this the Hebrew allows as demonstrated above with the *collective singular*. Because the use of a singular pronoun by an entity in no way reveals the entity to be singular in being. It should be noted, then, that the Nicene statement is only acceptable if it is meaningless, i.e. it means 'one being' in a sense wholly unknown to humans. But if this is the case, and it is not in Scripture, or the Scripture may be explained without appeal to the *one being* creed, then such a claim has no place in a creed. How then are the entities of the Almĭghty united? How are they one? The answer is in Yoh. 17:11, 21. Făther, Sŏn and Spĭrit are one in mutual love, loyalty, and purpose, which is a bonding humans can participate in without themselves being Almĭghty. The bonding of oneness is relational because it is spiritual. Any spiritual glue beyond this is idolatry, because it bases unity on something that does not constrain the Almĭghty. It also strikes at the heart of divine perfection, which is perfect everlasting love. ▷ What then is the fate of the Nicene Creed, that was supposed to be perfect, and express perfect orthodoxy, and carry perfect authority? The creed teaches the eternal begetting of the Sŏn, yet scholarly authorities have by near consensus agreed that *monogenes* does not mean 'only begotten.' The Creed most certainly teaches that it does mean that. Yet the only begotten error has been eliminated from most modern translations since the 1950's. So the Creed is flawed, and only true insofar as some of its assertions are actually in agreement with Scripture. As such it has no authority on its own.

The eternal generation doctrine is in fact the left overs of a previous Gnostic attack on the full divinity of Messiah. This attack is still reverberating to this day in the poor apologetics based on the creed. You will hear Unitarians basing their arguments on singular pronouns, and Trinitarians not pointing this out, because to do so will destroy their own *one being* doctrine. Trinitarians ably prove the deity of Messiah, but fail to explain how the Unitarians are wrong with their key arguments.

As I said, Scholars concluded that μονογενῆ involves no sense of *begetting*. It in fact means *only kindred*. But because the wrong sense was used in the greatest and most important creed of the Church, they try to conceal this discovery. Instead of correcting *only begotten* to *only kindred*, they just deleted the *begotten* part. Thus the ESV leaves us with *only Son* and *only God* where it formerly said *only begotten Son* or *only begotten God*.

The reason they do not want to restore the correct sense to the text is that to do so would destroy both the *one being* doctrine and the *eternal generation* doctrine in their Creed. It would be to admit that the established authority, the Church, erred, and not just the Catholic Church, but Protestants also.

Only kindred means a sole kindred in relation to someone else (cf. Luke 7:12; 8:42; 9:38)

Continued After 3 Yohanan.

Second Yoḥanan

1 ¹The elder to the ᵏchosen ladyship and her children, whom I love in truth, and not only I, but also all who have been knowing the truth, ²for the sake of the truth which dwells in us and will be with us forever. ³Loving-kindness, mercy and peace ᴧwill be with us, from beside the Almĭghty, the Fäther and from beside Yĕshua the Anŏinted, the Sŏn of the Fäther, in truth and love.

⁴I was very glad that I have been finding some of your children walking in truth, just as we have received commandment from beside the Fäther.ᶲ ⁵And now I implore you, O ladyship, not as writing to you a new-made commandment, but the one which we have had from the beginning, that we should be loving one another. ⁶And this is love, that we should be walking according to his commandments. This is the commandment, just as you all have heard from the beginning,ˣ that you all should be walking in it.

⁷Because many deceivers have gone out into the world, those who do not agree with Yĕshua the Anŏinted coming in the flesh.ᶯ This is the deceiver and the

---

1:1 μ→ladyship. The words are a metaphorical code for the Assembly. The word χυρία is not a simply word for 'lady' as it appears in English, by which an ordinary woman may be called. It is derived as a feminie form of χύριος, which means lord or master. So it is a designation of exaltation ascribing authority and power to the body addressed. To convey this, I have translated it 'ladyship.' The Assembly is the bride of Messiah, his ladyship, and her children are the faithful to Messiah. Notice that in vs. 5-6, he addresses the Assembly as 'ladyship' and then he uses a plural 'you all' in vs. 6. ▷ Yoḥanan does not desire to mention the Assembly's enemies by name here, or enter into the toxicity of rhetoric. Rather he focuses on the positive assertion against the Adversary's claims. Those who agree with sound teaching (vs. 9) are included in the bride of Messiah, his Ladyship. The enemies of the Assembly were pretentiously claiming to be the Assembly while denying the commandments of the Most High. Yoḥanan is countering them by addressing the faithful as χυρία. ▷ With a similar goal, Yoḥanan uses the word 'chosen.' The word 'chosen' (Ἐχλεχτῇ) is to counter the Gnostic doctrine of 'election,' also known as predestination. But the Gnostics were somewhat bolder than many who believe in the doctrine of predestination at present, who allow others outside their control to be 'elect.' The Gnostics frequently claimed (or implied) that they were the 'elect' and no one else was. ▷ Yoḥanan, of course, does not mean Gnostic election, which is equivalent to divine fate determined in timeless eternity before the temporal ages existed. Rather he means election based on holding faithful to Messiah and keeping his commandments (cf. Deut. 8:1-4), which is not a matter predetermined by the Most High, but only in the heart of the faithful (Deut. 8:2). ▷ This letter was most likely a congregational cover letter for 1 Yoḥ. See 3 Yoḥ.

1:3 λ→us: Yoḥanan's introduction uses the future indicative here rather than the customary, "may be with you." The reason is not far to seek. Yoḥanan is assuring the recipient that loving-kindness is with us, and not the opposition, because the opposition was lawless. **1:4** ξ Yoḥanan specifies the commandment from the Fäther because the lawless were explaining away Yĕshua's general statements regarding the Torah (Mat. 5:17-20), saying that Mĕssiah did not repeat many of the commandments, and therefore they were abolished. Therefore, he goes back to what the Fäther said from the beginning so that there will be no explaining away what Yoḥanan teaches. ▷ He refers to *some of your children*, which is to imply that some were not. The opinion that he had only met some on whom he could remark, so as to imply nothing of the others, is erroneous. There were many who were leaving the truth. Only some were left. **1:5** This is a stark exhortation, once again, aimed at the key issue over which many were falling away. **1:6** χ The lawless were in the habit of completely misunderstanding the words of Mĕssiah concerning the new commandment. Mĕssiah meant no more than the original commandment renewed with a fresh explanation. The lawless were saying that the new commandment replaced the law. But the law gives the substance of love by specific commandments. Yoḥanan corrects this misunderstanding. See Yoḥ. 13:34.

1:7 η Yoḥanan identifies the Gnostics here as the source of the lawless teaching, because they also denied that the Almĭghty Sŏn took on flesh. At that time one could identify the lawless this way, by this test. Their argument was to separate human personhood of Messiah from the divine anointing, which they would allow in him, but not to be him.

But the Gnostics have since changed out their false doctrines for more subtle false doctrines, keeping the one constant: lawlessness. ▷ It should be said that the Gnostics managed to get their doctrine into much of Christianity. One need only mention the Nestorians. And their influence is even felt in the Nicene Creed,

anti-Mĕssiah. ⁸Be watching yourselves, that you all may not have lost what we have accomplished, but that you all shall have received a full reward. ⁹Anyone who goes too far and does not remain in the teaching of the Anŏinted, does not have the Almīghty. The one who remains in the teaching, he has both the Făther and the Sŏn. ¹⁰If anyone comes to you all and does not bring this teaching, be ye not receiving him into the house, and be ye not be telling him to be rejoicing, ¹¹because the one who gives him a happy greeting participates in his evil deeds.

¹²Having many things to write to you all, I do not want to do so with paper and ink, but I hope to come to you all and speak face to face, that our joy will have been getting filled up.

¹³The children of your chosen sister greet you.

---

because the doctrine of the eternal generation of the Son, based on the mistranslation "only begotten Son," implies that the Son is a derived emanation of the Most High, rather than the only kindred Almighty (Yoh. 1:18; cf. Yoh. 17:3). Also the doctrine of Christ's two natures tends toward the denial of the Most High limiting himself to a human existence in the person of Messiah. ▷ The problem with Gnostic Christianity is their adoption of Greek philosophies of perfection in Gŏd. viz. whatever can change is imperfect, and therefore the Most High never changes in the degree of his knowledge, or any other attribute. Having restricted the Most High to exercising his omnipotence is all ways and with total determination, and at all times, they have made it logically impossible for the Most High to take on himself the limitation of a man. So long as the Most High can exist as more than one person, the only essential attribute that the Mĕssenger of Yăhweн need retain to still be divine is love and faithfulness. The other attributes can suffer temporary suspension, but Mĕssiah does allow us to see those other attributes peek through even in his flesh, so that we may know who he is, and that those other attributes still belong to him, even when his Făther is taking care of them for him. **1:9-11** δ Yoĥanan means that we should walk in the commandments. This is the original teaching which is part of Yăhweн's name, which represents Him, and how we know we know Him. See Mat. 28:18-20 and note. See Exodus 20:6. See Exodus 33-34 and 1 John 2:3-4. See John 14:21, 15:10. He refers to the teaching in vs. 6, as positively stated, and not the false doctrine in vs. 7. ▷ It is without a doubt that the Gnostic teachers were promoting legal heresies as litmus tests to say who belonged to them as elect, and who was on the outside, among the lost, and pagan. Since this period is over the historical horizon, I should only give examples of the spirit of the false teaching. And I will do so in terms of the calendar here. Many cults and semi-cults promote their exclusive liturgy as necessary for salvation, because they find salvation in perfectionism or some philosophy allowing them to legally claim it, and so a ritual is promoted to tie them to it. The more dogmatic the cult, the more they want their followings to keep their specific ritual or be condemned. One might have to say the Sacred Name a certain way, or engage in the proper meditations and ablutions. But nothing makes fertile heresies as much as creating calendar divisions does, and by division I mean passing condemnation on those who disagree, yet hold to Messiah. ▷ If one has Messiah, and one has repented of the obvious transgressions, then calendar ignorance, or any other sin of ignorance is not going to be a cause of condemnation. Only willful iniquity is a cause of condemnation after receiving Messiah, and pledging faithfulness to him. And those who promote heresies and so treat other followers of Messiah as pagans, and who cast condemnation on them for not receiving their particular calendar teaching are showing that they fail to understand the good news at all! ▷ For this reason, I do not judge others who sin ignorantly. I give some examples. Many do Shavuot on a Sunday all the time. Some observe Christmas. Some Easter, some lunar Sabbaths, and some neglect all the new moons with a solar calendar. These are serious problems. The cultist overlooks forgiveness in Messiah and fails to observe the difference between ignorance and iniquity. ▷ With this said, however, the farther away one goes from properly observing biblical instruction, the more likely it is that one does not understand the good news or listen to the Spirit, and the even more likely it is that the teachers and avid promoters of heresies do not. With the measure you use, you will be judged. I will not put up with a heretical teaching for a minute, but I will have compassion and mercy on those caught in a trap of error who may know the good news and be loyal to Messiah. They are not to be summarily excommunicated as the cultists would do. ▷ And I will have opinions about who fails to understand the good news and who does not, and I will not join in supporting them, and the worse their teaching the stronger it will be, but let no one think I reject a confessor of Messiah just for being ignorant and following the teaching of someone who does not know Messiah. But whoever does not listen to the Spirit of Messiah does not belong to him. So you can examine yourselves. Are you heeding the truth the Spirit brings to your notice or not? Not I, but the Spirit, and if I am used, them I am glad I've been a blessing. **1:13** 'Chosen sister' refers to another congregation of the Assembly whom Yoĥanan is writing from and the children are the faithful of it.

Third Yoḥanan

1 ¹The elder to the beloved Gaius⁷, whom I truly love. ²Beloved, I am praying in all respects for you to be prospering and to be in good health, just as your soul is prospering, ³because I was very glad when brothers came and bore witness about you in the truth, even as you are walking in truth ᵠ. ⁴I am having no greater joy than this, that I may be hearing about my children walking in the truth.

⁵Beloved, you are acting faithfully in whatever work you may have done for the brothers, and especially when they are strangers ᵑ. ⁶And they testify to your love before the Assembly ᶻ, and you will do well to send them on their way in a manner worthy of the Almighty, ⁷because they went out for the sake of ᵂthe name, receiving nothing from the nations ˣ. ⁸Therefore we ought to support such men, that we may be co-workers with the truth.

⁹I wrote something to the assembly, but Diotrephes ᵠ, who loves to be first over them ᵅ, is not welcoming us. ¹⁰For this reason, when I may have come, I will call attention to his deeds which he does, gossiping about us with evil words ᶿ, and not satisfied with this, neither does he himself receive the brothers ᵏ, and ᵖthose wanting *to hear* he hinders, and he casts *them* out of the ˣassembly place. ¹¹Beloved, do not be imitating what is evil, but what is good. The one who does good is from the Almighty. The one who does evil has not been seeing the Almighty.

¹²Demetrius has been receiving a confirming testimony from everyone, and from the truth itself, and we also testify, and you have been knowing that our witness is true. ¹³I had many things to write to you, but I am not willing to write to you with pen and ink, ¹⁴but I hope to see you immediately, and we will speak face to face. Shalom be to you. The friends greet you. Be greeting the friends by name.

1:1 γ According to the best theory Gaius received the letters 1-3 Yoḥ. in a packet delivered by Demetrius (vs. 12; cf. ESV Study Bible note). The third letter was to him. Gaius was under Diotrephes, but Yoḥanan is by passing him (cf. vs. 9) to elevate the asssembly in Gaius' house (cf. 2 Yoḥ. 1:10). The second letter was to the assembly in Gaius' house. And the first letter was a general letter all assemblies. **1:3** φ Yoḥanan did not know Gaius personally.

1:5 η Yoḥanan uses the word "brothers" to mean traveling ministers of the word (cf. vs 3, 5, 6-8, 10) who did missionary work. Gaius had for his part treated them well. **1:6** ζ = the larger Assembly of the faithful; not Diotrephes' assembly. **1:7** ω הַשֵּׁם = Yāhweḥ.

1:7 χ = the unconverted. **1:9** ψ Diotrephes was not an arch-heretic, but simply a controlling elder with money and an assembly place over which he had total control. He thought the congregants should hear him or support him only and not the missionaries ministering to the unconverted, so he used various underhanded means to unwelcome them. His interest was in maintaining position, power, and the flow of money to his own interests. And he was willing to malign others to keep it coming to his ends. See notes on Rev. 2:4. **1:9** α = the majority of faithful at his place of worship under the spell of his oratory **1:10** θ The gossip was whatever he could get most of his congregation to believe to the end that he remained the sole shepherd supported by them. **1:10** λ cf. vs. 5-8. The "brothers" here were traveling ministers, announcing the good news to the unconverted, and teachers skilled in the word who went from assembly to assembly.

1:10 π The congregants who attended his assembly place. **1:10** χ→place: ἐκκλησίας. He could only send them out of the assembly place to go elsewhere. He did not have the power to excommunicate.

Contintued from after 1 Yohanan.

To see this we only need to break the word into its parts, only (μόνος) and kin (γένος). The second part γένος means *kin*. Look this up in the classical Lexicon. Or separately in ANLEX (Friberg):

γένος, ους (or ως), τό, dative γένει (1) of common ancestry, *posterity, descendant, family* (RV 22.16); (2) of common identity as an ethnic group *race, people, nation*(AC 7.19); of common identity of believers *nation, people*(1P 2.9); (3) members of a family circle **kindred**, *relatives, (extended) family*(AC 7.13); (4) of a distinctive species of something *kind, class* (1C 12.10).

Kin is a word in English that can be used as a noun or adjective, e.g. *my kin brother*, or *my kin*. The word *kindred* is also an exact synonym. So if we put the two together we get *only kindred*. And this is the sense the word is normally used in Greek.

Only kin(dred) is the no nonsense ordinary meaning of the word. And in this sense it means the only kindred Son of the Almighty is of like nature to the Almighty, or in metaphorical terms a genetic copy. In fact the word genetic is derived from γένος also. This means that the Son is of like being to the Father. We could correctly term this ὁμοιούσιος (similar being). So in Yoh. 1:18, he is the *only kindred Almighty*, being of the same kind as the Father, in being Almighty. Father and Son of of similar being, not the same being as the creed claims.

For this reason, though knowing the truth, Church scholars wish to avoid the plain sense, and suggest that the term means *unique* or a *special one*. In regard to the latter, it may be observed that when a father has an only kindred child, then this child is also *special*. So by reading the contexts one might be deceived into thinking μονογενής means an *only special one*. Also scholars suggest *one-of-a-kind* so as to avoid the fact that kindred means a common identity based on similarity. But we can avoid all these attempts to nuance the term away from its plain and common sense, *only kindred*, by examining the usage of the term γένος alone.

The proper Hebrew word here is explained by Strong's Dictionary:

מִשְׁפָּחָה mishpâchâh, mish-paw-khaw'; from H8192 (compare H8198); a family, i.e. circle of relatives; figuratively, a class (of persons), a species (of animals) or sort (of things); by extension a tribe or people:—family, kind(-red).

The same Hebrew word is aligned with γένος in Jeremiah 8:3; 10:25, and 31:1. This recommends the translation into Hebrew as מִשְׁפַּחְתּוֹ הַיָּחִיד, *kindred of him the only*, e.g. Yoh. 3:18 could be translated into Hebrew: לְשֵׁם מִשְׁפַּחְתּוֹ הַיָּחִיד שֶׁהוּא בֶּן־הָאֱלֹהִים.

The one holding faithful to him is not getting judged, but the one who is not now confirming his faithfulness has been getting judged, because he has not been holding faithful <u>to the name of the only kindred Almighty Son</u>.

The Hebrew translates slightly differently than the GNM text, viz. "to the name of <u>his</u> only kindred, <u>who is</u> the Almighty Son." 'His" refers to the Father. The reason for adding *his* and *who is* is that Hebrew is weak in case endings and adjectives, and extra words are necessary to reproduce the sense.

We see then that μονογενής is an explanation of the meaning of τοῦ υἱοῦ τοῦ θεοῦ, being positioned to explain the meaning of son, viz: τοῦ μονογενοῦς υἱοῦ τοῦ θεοῦ. So no matter how anyone reads it, i.e. 'the only kindred Son of the Almighty,' or 'the only kindred Almighty Son,' i.e. is clear that the word son is a kinship term as explained in the article at the end of Luke.

I now refer the reader to the note on Yoh. 17:3, which should be seen. Since the Father, Son, and Spirit(s) exist alone and separately as Almighty, the *One Amighty* creed (or *The Almighty is One*) must speak of supra-being unity as the term אֶחָד is used in Gen. 2:24 to speak of marriage, only not on the level of flesh as spoken there, but on the level of spirit. The unity consists of mutual love and faithfulness to the others in the union, such that there is always a perfect agreement upon what the determinate will of the Almighty will be, and also perfect agreement on the use of what is regarded as the collective omnipotence. For Messiah said that all the Father has are his also. *One* cannot be interpreted to mean *one immutable being*, however it is used. But the term *one* is used in the senses already outlined earlier.

We do not know if, when, or how, the independent members of the One Almighty overlap, merge, or combine, except in the case of Messiah, who really existed as man and Almighty. Clearly omnipotence and glory can be for a time suspended leaving Messiah in his humanness, Almighty as to his identity, but dependent on His Father for his power. We are not told how this happens or is restored, and we'd not understand it in any case, or could not understand it due to our nature.

But the error of the Church and Christianity in general of adopting the Nicene Creed with eternal generation makes the Son always dependent on the Father, and thus less than him on a permanent basis.

And the one being doctrine also restricts the Almighty into existing in an unchangeable homostasis, as if somehow this restriction were binding on his nature. It is really the same as making the Creator philosophically in the image of the creation to impose this restriction when the Scripture does not. The only imposition on his nature is what his thoughts allow or do not allow.

The only essential truth that need to be gained from confessing *One Almighty* is that the Most High, speaking collectively, will always come to agreement on his determinate will, and the determinate use of his power, and he alone is Almighty, and there are no others outside this onness.

Yehudah

1 ¹Yehudah⁵, a servant of Yĕshua the Anŏinted and brother of Ya'aqov⁴, to those who are the called, having been getting loved in the Almĭghty Făther, and having been getting watched over by Yĕshua the Anŏinted: ²May mercy and peace and love be multiplied to you.

³Beloved, while I was making every effort to write you about our shared deliverance, I felt the necessity to write to you, appealing that you contend earnestly for the pledge of faithfulness which was once for all delivered to the holy-ones, ⁴because certain persons have crept in unnoticed, those who long beforehand have been getting written about for this condemnation, irreverent persons who turn the loving-kindness of our Almĭghty into licentiousness and who are denying THE ONLY ONE⁷, our Măster and Adŏnai, Yĕshua the Anŏinted.

⁵Now I desire to remind you, who have been knowing everything, that Yăhweн, at one time having rescued the people out of the land of Mitsrayim, at a second time destroyed those who did not hold faithful. ⁶As well, the messengers who did not keep their own domain, but who abandoned their own abode, he has been keeping in eternal bonds under darkness for the great day of judgment. ⁷Similarly, Sedom and Amorah and the cities around them, (who in the same way as these *messengers* indulged in gross sexual immorality and went after strange flesh), are getting themselves set forth as an example, undergoing the penalty of eternal fire.

⁸Indeed, in the same manner these dreamers defile the flesh and reject

---

1:1 ξ Yehudah is commonly known as "Jude" in English. **1:1** ψ This book is the work of Yehudah, the brother of Ya'aqov (who does not call himself an emissary). See Mat. 13:55; Mark 6:3. It would appear certain that Yehudah wrote after Peter's letters, and that he incorporated material from second Peter, sometime between AD 64 and 96. Vs. 3 would appear to indicate a date after most of the emissaries had died, perhaps all except Yoĥanan, yet it is just possible that he too was already passed from the scene. **1:4** π THE ONLY ONE refers to an only Son or kin, הַיָחִיד. The meaning is the only son or kin of the Almĭghty. He is the only Almĭghty kin. If Messiah were a mere man, he could not be called the only kin in respect to humanity, since every other human is kin to us. The kinship is expressly with the Most High. ▷ 𝔓72 cent. III-IV reads ἡμῶν (*of us*) after τὸν μόνον (*the only one [of us]*), which is an Arian alteration of the text. For without it the text can only read the way I have explained, or *the only master and lord of us*, which should be unacceptable to Arians since it excludes God himself, or unacceptable to everyone else, because it excludes the Făther. So Yehudah has left no way to read the text acceptable to Arians (aka Gnostics). ▷ τὸν μόνον represents the Hebrew יָחִיד, meaning *only one* which the LXX mistakenly translates with *beloved* in Gen. 22. Gen. 22:2 specifies, *your son, the only one who you have favored*, and Gen 22:12, 16, repeat *your son, the only one* with *who you have favored* being an implicit limitation necessary to make *only one* true, because Ishmael, who was disinherited was also a kin son, just not within the limitation of beloved. ▷ The term יָחִיד is explained by the translation *only kindred*, μονογενής, and the referent of kinship by υἱοῦ τοῦ θεοῦ, the *Almĭghty Sŏn*. In this respect the term cannot take reference to mere human kinship, because the whole human race is kin to another another, but to be exclusive it must also be limited to divine kinship.

1:5-8 Yehudah refers to the narrative in Genesis 6. There, the sons of the Almĭghty left their heavenly places and came down and took wives from among mankind. These relationships were forbidden just as the immorality in Sedom and Amorah was forbidden. Strange flesh means alien flesh. They pursued relations that the Almĭghty did not intend for them. ▷ These mighty rebels of the spiritual realm are now imprisoned in the abyss in order to keep them from causing trouble on earth. They are in eternal bonds, which means permanent bonds that do not decay or break, but some of them will be released in the last day in order to further the Almĭghty's purpose to destroy

authority and revile majesties. ⁹But Miḵa'el, Prince over messengers, when he disputed with Satan over the ⁵body of Mosheh did not pronounce against him a railing judgment, but said, "YĂHWEH REBUKE YOU.ᵠ" ¹⁰But these men revile the things which they have not been perceiving, and the things which they do know naturally—like unreasoning animals—by these things they corrupt themselves.

¹¹Woe to them! Because they have gone the way of Qayin, and for pay they have rushed headlong into the error of Bil'am, and perished in the rebellion of Qoraḥ. ¹²These men are those who are hidden reefs in your love feasts when they feast with you without fear, caring for themselves, clouds without water, carried along by winds, autumn trees without fruit, doubly dead, uprooted, ¹³wild waves of the sea, casting up their own shame like foam, wandering stars, for whom the

---

rebellious mankind. Other evil messengers are not in bonds, and these powers influence mankind toward evil, being careful to work by deception, and not use their powers too directly to corrupt men lest they also end up in bonds. ▷ As the cities of the Yarden underwent everlasting fire, so also these heavenly beings are destined. Everlasting fire means a fire that burns continually. Even so everlasting fires eventually go out, just as those that burned those cities have gone out.

1:9 ψ Zech 3:2; **1:9** ⟨→Mosheh: See Zechariah 3:2. The Messenger of Yahweh disputed with Satan over the dirty garments of the High Priest Yeshua which represented the sins of Yisra'el. Like the Assembly is the "body of Messiah," and Messiah bore our sins (suffered from our sins), so also the Assembly is Yisra'el, which is the "body of Mosheh" and the High Priest was bearing the sins of the whole body, the body of Mosheh, and was being accused by Satan to prevent the restoration of the kingdom. So by this parable, the dispute in Zechariah 3 was over the "body of Moses," which is to say the sins of Yisra'el, and the raising of the nation from the deadness of exile. See Zech. 3:9; Hos. 6:1-2. ▷ Yehudah was also quite aware that he is connecting his drash on Zechariah 3 with Deut. 34:6, where we may note that Yahweh himself buried Mosheh. Yehudah's drash is also saying that Miḵa'el (One who is like God) is the same person who buried Moses, and the same person who rebuked Satan concerning opposition to the restoration of Yisra'el in Zech. 3:2 (who is the Messenger of Yahweh). See also 1 Thess. 4:16. ▷ Gnostic Christians were fast multiplying at the time of writing. They denied the Messenger of Yahweh. Yehudah's drash teaches that the Messenger of Yahweh, Yahweh, Miḵa'el, and Messiah Yeshua are all the same person. 'Cults' are not to blame for identifying Miḵa'el as Messiah. But this identification was recognized by older commentators. The uncreated Messenger is the Most High in a physical form that communicates with mankind. See also 1 Thess. 4:16. Compare Col. 2:18. ▷ As a descendant of David, Yehudah had to be careful about any open advocacy of the kingdom. Emperor Domitian had his grandson's arrested based upon an accusation by heretics and he interrogated them intending to put them to death. But upon hearing their answers he let them go (Eusebius, Church History, Book III, ch. 19-20).

1:14 ϕ For hypothetical use of indicative see Mat. 11:21, 23; 24:43; 25:27; Luke 10:13; 19:23; John 4:10; John 5:46; 1 Cor 5:10; Gal 4:15. This usage may be regarded as under Hebrew influence of an irreal perfect, "would have." For example Numbers 22:33, אֹתְכָה הָרַגְתִּי וְאוֹתָהּ הֶחֱיֵיתִי, "you I [would] have killed, and her I [would] have kept alive." This is translated by the LXX: σὲ μὲν ἀπέκτεινα ἐκείνην δὲ περιεποιησάμην, "you indeed I [would] have killed, and her [would] have kept alive." We see in both cases the Greek verb is not maked by the conditional particle ἄν, which in proper Greek would have to say, "σὲ μὲν [ἄν] ἀπέκτεινα ἐκείνην δὲ [ἄν] περιεποιησάμην." So we see that if the LXX translators did not consider their Greek too atrocious to write, then we may accept that this Semitized usage of the Greek was acceptable to Hellenistic Jewish audiences, if for no other reason, then as a kind of dramatic effect, since Balaam speaks properly in Numbers 22:29, "ἤδη ἂν ἐξεκέντησά σε." ▷ In any case, the quotation is from the false Enoch. ▷ Yehudah's aim is to rebuke the heretics from their own prophet. ▷ But why did Yehudah make the point of judgment from psuedo-Enoch? Because he is using their own canon to establish the point of God's judgment, with which they cannot now argue. ▷ Rejecting the book of psuedo-Enoch in no way means that the book cannot be made useful in some way for understanding the context of Jewish apocalyptic thinking. But most of the essential points affirmed by the disciples are implicit in Genesis 6 already, i.e. the sons of the Almighty came down and took wives, and then begat the giants, nephilim, both before and after the Deluge. Undoubtedly, there were other commentaries on Genesis 6 from the period which were not preserved, but with no vain speculations into angels. So, Yeshua and his disciples may just have been confirming which commentaries on Genesis 6 were correct. They were not sourcing any of them as authoritative, nor specifically giving commentary on Enoch unless they were flipping the script for polemical purposes. ▷ Oth-

black darkness has been getting reserved to time immemorial.

¹⁴But ᶲwould have prophesied even *the* 'seventh from Adam,' Ḥanok̠, to these! Saying, "Behold Yăhweh will have come with ten thousands of his holy ones, ¹⁵to accomplish judgment on all and to convict every soul concerning all their irreverent deeds (BY WHICH THEY HAVE BEEN IRREVERENT, AND CONCERNING ALL THE HARSH THINGS WHICH IRREVERENT SINNERS HAVE SPOKEN) against him."

¹⁶These are grumblers, finding fault, following after their own lusts. They speak arrogantly, flattering people to favor gaining an advantage.

¹⁷But you, beloved, remember the words that have been getting spoken beforehand by the emissaries of our Adŏnai Yĕshua the Anŏinted, ¹⁸that they were saying to you, "In the last time there will be mockers, following after their own irreverent lusts." ¹⁹These are the ones who cause divisions, worldly-minded, devoid of the Spĭrit.

²⁰But you, beloved, building yourselves up with your holiest faithfulness, praying in the Holy Spĭrit, ²¹keep yourselves in the love of the Almĭghty, waiting anxiously for the mercy of our Adŏnai Yĕshua the Anŏinted for everlasting life.

²²And be having mercy on some, who are doubting. ²³Be rescuing others, snatching them out of the fire. And on some be having mercy with fear, hating even the garment having been getting polluted by the flesh. ²⁴But to the one who is able to guard you without fail, and confirm you in the presence of his glory blameless with great joy, ²⁵to the only ᵘ wise Almĭghty, to our Rescuer, be glory, majesty, dominion and authority, even now and for *all* the ages. Amen.

---

er false teachings in Enoch: (a) Enoch's eschatology lasts 4900 years or 70 generations of 70 years. Enoch divides this into 10 mega cycles of 490 years. He claims to be born during the first 490 years, which is false. The real Enoch was born in year 623. (b) Since 4900 years have gone by, this Enoch is a false prophet. (c) Nowhere does Enoch recognize the Messenger of YHWH, (d) and nowhere does he recognize who Miḵa'el is, (d) like most Christian eschatology, Enoch has no place for the restoration of the kingdom of Israel, but looks for the tribulation to occur next. (e) Enoch's calendar does not agree with Scripture. (f) There were giants, but Enoch's giants were absurdly tall (cf. Deut. 3:11). ▷ See also Col. 2:16-18 and Gal. 4:10, where Paul has Pseudo-Enoch in mind. In Enoch, Miḵa'el always appears as a created Angel, and never is the Messenger of Yăhweh mentioned. Failure to acknowledge the Messenger of YHWH alone is grounds for dismissing the book. ▷ Often the claim is made that the disciples or Yeshua quoted from the book of pseudo-Enoch based on a similarity of content, but that position assumes that pseudo Enoch is the only source of such material. It may be that Yeshua read other now lost commentaries on Genesis 6 to which he had no objections, but that these commentaries were also used as unattributed sources by pseudo-Enoch, but mixed with false teachings. ▷ It is not beyond reason to suppose that the disciples regularly met up in Jewish culture to read Genesis 6 commentary. It is not impossible that their style of stating the few ideas they agreed with was influenced by the literary culture surrounding Genesis 6. But having heard Yeshua they were able to state things correctly.

1:23 The literary connections with Zech. 3:2 and 3:4 are very definite here, "A BRAND PLUCKED FROM FIRE" and "FILTHY GARMENTS." Compare this with Jude 1:9 and Zech. 3:1. **1:25** μ A collective reference to the Most High is meant here. See Hos. 13:4. וֵאלֹהִים זוּלָתִי לֹא תֵדָע וּמוֹשִׁיעַ אַיִן בִּלְתִּי.

Yăhweh our Righteousness

Měssiah Yĕshua, who is the promised Branch, is alone true Almĭghty beside his Făther, who also is alone true Almĭghty (Yoĥ. 17:3). In him by himself is everlasting life just as everlasting life is also separately in his Făther. From everlasting the power of life was his. When he gave up his life for three days, it was restored to him by the Făther, his only kindred Almĭghty (Yoĥ. 5:44), who is like him in every way that matters. Therefore, he has the name above all names:

Behold days are coming—an utterance of of Yăhweh: And I will have raised up for Dauid a Branch of Righteousness. And he who is king will have reigned, and he will have acted wisely. And he will have executed judgement and justice in the earth. In his days Yehudah will be rescued and Yisra'el will dwell securely. **And this is his name which they will proclaim**: Yăhweh, our Righteousness. JEREMIAH 23:5-6.

Now the vowel points in the parallel passage must be corrected, so that it reads:

In those days, and in that time, I will cause to branch out for Dauid a Branch of Justice, and he will have executed judgment and justice in the earth. In those days Yehudah will be rescued and Yerushalayim will dwell securely. **And this is what he will be called by her**: Yăhweh, our Justice. JEREMIAH 33:15-16.

Why did the vowel points get corrupted? Because those putting in the vowel points did not know Měssiah. The text as pointed by Karaite Jews literally translates, "And this [is] what (he/it) will call to her: YHWH our righteousness." Only two versions have corrected this mistake (TLV and CEB). The Qal pointing in the MT should be corrected to be Niphal pointing: יִקְרָא.

Now, deniers will say that ordinary people are given theophoric names, and also places are given theophoric names, and therefore will imply there is nothing special about Měssiah being called **Yăhweh, our Righteousness**, and besides they will sow confusion by fencing off the mistranslation of Jer. 33:16 against Jer. 23:6.

Let us deal with a few place names first:

Then Avraham called the name of that place Yăhweh **will see to it**, because it will be said today in the mountain of Yăhweh he himself saw to it. GENESIS 22:14.

And the name of the city from [that] day [will be] **Yăhweh [is] there**. EZEKIEL 48:35.

And secondly, let me dispose of some alleged cases of theophoric place naming:

Then Mosheh built an altar. Then he called [upon] his name, **Yăhweh, my banner**. EXODUS 17:15.

Then he erected there an altar. Then he called to him, **Gŏd, Almĭghty of Yisra'el**. GENESIS 33:20.

One thing will be clear about the first two place names, and that is that no one will ever suppose that divinity is being ascribed to a place, because the name is in remembrance of what the Most High has done or will have done in the specified place. In the second two cases, the problem was mistranslation, which proves the rule in the first two cases.

Let me now turn to theophoric names. Ordinary people are given theophoric names. For example Yehu means "Yăhweh exists." But it should be noticed that in no case was a theophoric name ever given to a mere human with the full name Yăhweh. The name is always shortened down and combined with another word to make it a saying. Even when the name is put at the end of a theophoric name it is never spelled full.

But what is to stop anyone from spelling it full? Nothing, other than the sense that it would be inappropriate to use the name this way, because it would suggest divinity of the person so ascribed to whoever heard the person addressed.

So we see that the only exception to the shortening of the divine name in theophoric names is to the name of Měssiah himself. Měssiah may be called **Yăhweh, our Righteousness** because that is who he is, and it is probably for this reason that the Jeremiah 33:16 text was tampered with by the scribes. But the Jeremiah 23:6 text was not tampered with, and the reason it could not be is that the words **his name** occur in that text making it clear that **his name** is so called and not something else. But in place of **his name** the relative pronoun **what** occurs in Jeremiah 33:16. But it would be clear at once to anyone reading Jeremiah 33:16, having read 23:6 first, that **what** refers to **his name**.

Revelation

1 ¹The Revelation ᵃof Yĕshua the Anŏinted, which the Almĭghty gave him to show to his servants what things must quickly happen. And ᵟHe ˣput *it* in signs, having sent *it* through ᶿHis ᶯMĕssenger, to his servant Yohanan, ²who witnessed the word of the Almĭghty, and the testimony of Yĕshua the Anŏinted, as much as he saw. ³Blessed is the one reading and those who are listening to the words of the prophecy, and keeping the things having been getting written in it, as ᵠthe appointed season is near.

⁴Yohanan to the seven assemblies that are in Asia. Loving-kindness to you and peace, from the Almĭghty, THE ONE BEING^ω and THE ONE WHO HAS BEEN^η and **THE COMING ONE**^χ; and from the seven^β Spĭrits who are before his throne, ⁵and from Yĕshua the Anŏinted, the ^λfaithful witness, the ^ρfirst-born of the dead, and the ruler of the kings of the earth. To him who loves us, and who has released us from our sins by his blood, ⁶who also has made us a ^αkingdom, priests to the Almĭghty, even to his Făther, to him be the glory and the dominion for *all* the ages of the ages. Amen.

1:1 α *or about*. The book is as much a revealing about him as it is a revelation from him concerning the future. There are as many as 500 allusions to the Law and Prophets in revelation. **1:1** χ→signs: This means to explain by symbolism **1:1** θ = the Almĭghty, the Father **1:1** η The special Mĕssenger of Yăhweĥ is meant (aka Angel of the LORD, מַלְאַךְ יְהוָה), who is the same as Mĕssiah. Other messengers appear in the narrative, but these are delegates of the chief Mĕssenger, whose parts are reckoned as the testimony of the one Mĕssenger, which is why just one Messenger is indicated. All the other messengers belong to Mĕssiah (cf. Mat. 16:27; 25:31). **1:3** ψ→season: An idiomatic reference to the season of the fall feasts, יָמִים שֶׁל יְרָאָה, which are a reflection of things to come, which must have been near when the book was completed and sent out. ▷ Some things were to happen "quickly" which are the words to the seven assemblies. Other things in the distant future would happen "quickly" when they arrived on the scene of prophetic history. ▷ Or "because the critical time is near." Also the article may be generic, "because the critical time is near," i.e. the dangerous time or season. See LSJ.

For the short term predictions the appointed time was near. For other prophecies a critical time of fulfillment was near. What happens at such junctures depends on the out come of contingencies. Fulfillment is more likely at such times. The appointed prophetic times are also linked to the Scriptural Calendar and its seasons. So once a year, particularly nearing the autumnal equinox, the season of the latter day feasts approaches. The meaning of the phrase is two fold. That is whether the actual time is near or not, the season for it is frequently enough near, and the only way to prepare spiritually for it is ahead of the actual time by watching out for the season. ▷ None of the commentators gives a fully satisfactory answer to the notion that the season is near. This is probably because they neglect the fact of the fall feast days, which we were intended to keep, and it is these observances which remind us of past restorative interventions by the Almĭghty, and also keep us prepared for the future. It is the connection to the feast days that keep us connected with Mĕssiah's restorative work in history and the here and now for the remnant of Yisra'el and keep us from the extremes of a purely humanistic eschatology which neglects the hope of the age to come (and justifies it by an arbitrary allegorical hermeneutic) and the extreme of a purely pessimistic eschatology (in which salvation is purely a matter of waiting after believing the "correct" doctrines) which has no relevance to being salt in the earth. ▷ Scripture often hints at a truth that takes a key to unlock, either by parable or by coming at the matter indirectly. These are the mysteries of the kingdom of heaven. The biggest clue that the key has not been properly used is that the wrong door is used, i.e. the results of the interpretation are contradictory. **1:4** β Isa 11:2, Zech 3:9 **1:4** ω Yoĥ. 1:18; 3:13; 6:46; 8:47; Rev. 1:8; 4:8; 11:17; 16:5; Cf. Exo. 3:14 LXX **1:4** η Yoĥ. 1:1, 15, 27 **1:4** χ Psa. 118:26; Mat. 11:3; 21:9; 23:39; Mark 11:9; Luke 7:19, 20; 13:35; 19:38; Yoĥ. 6:14; 12:13; Rev. 1:8; 4:8; 11:17? Cf. Hab. 2:3 יָבֹא **1:5** λ Psa 89:37, Jer 42:5, Isa 55:4. **1:5** ρ Col. 1:18; Psa 89:27 **1:6** α Exo 19:6, Isa 61:6.

⁷Behold, HE IS COMING WITH THE CLOUDS°, and every^β eye will see him, even those who HAVE PIERCED HIM^ψ. AND ALL THE TRIBES^μ OF THE EARTH WILL MOURN OVER HIM. Yes. Amen. ⁸"I am^θ the ^γAleph and the ^δTau," says Yăhweн the Almĭghty, "THE ONE BEING and THE ONE WHO HAS BEEN and **THE COMING ONE**, the ^ρAll-powerful."

⁹I, Yoнanan, your brother and fellow partaker in the tribulation and kingdom and patient endurance in Yĕshua, came to be on the island called ^θPatmos, because of the word of the Almĭghty and the testimony of Yĕshua. ¹⁰I came to be in the Spirit on ^φYăhweн's day, AND I HEARD BEHIND ME^α A LOUD VOICE AS OF A TRUMPET^β, ¹¹saying, "Write in a scroll what you see, and send it to the seven assemblies, to Ephesus, and to Smyrna, and to Pergamum, and to Thyatira, and to Sardis and to Philadelphia, and to Laodicea."

¹²And I turned to see the voice that was speaking with me. And having turned I saw seven golden ^εmenorahs. ¹³And in the middle of the menorahs *was* one like a Sŏn of Man, who had been getting dressed down to the feet, and had been getting girded across his breast with a golden sash. ¹⁴And his head and hairs were ^αwhite like white wool, like snow, and his eyes^β were like a fiery flame, ¹⁵and his feet^δ were like whited bronze, as had been getting fired in a furnace, and his voice^θ was like the sound of many waters. ¹⁶And in his right hand he held seven stars, and out^λ of his mouth proceeded a sharp two-edged sword, and his countenance was like the sun shining in its strength.

¹⁷And when I saw him, I fell^α at his feet as if dead. And he laid his right

---

1:7 α Dan 7:13 **1:7** β Isa 40:5 **1:7** ψ Zech 12:10-14 **1:7** μ Gen 12:3, 28:14. **1:8** γ-δ Greek: Alpha and Omega **1:8** θ Isa 41:4, 46:6 **1:8** ρ Amos 3:13 ⓢ.

1:9 θ Irenaeus said, "The Revelation was seen not long ago, but almost in our own age, towards the end of the reign of Domitian." Domitian reigned AD 81-96. Irenaeus, born in Asia Minor, lived ca AD 130-AD 202. He was discipled around Ephesus where Yoнanan spent his last years. Irenaeus was only one generation removed from Yoнanan, the link being Polycarp of Smyrna (AD 69-155). An earlier date for Revelation before AD 70 is motivated by rejection of the prophetic plan to restore the kingdom to Yisra'el. Early date proponents reject a future temple and seek to confine that mentioned in Rev. 11:1 to symbolism relating to the Second Temple. Besides rejecting the divine Law, the allegorical system of interpretation required to justify this assumption is arbitrary and breaks down into self contradictions. So then, there are no good reasons to reject the testimony of Irenaeus. **1:10** φ→day; The Şabbath. Or this may be read, "Adŏnai's Day" (Lord's Day). The Şabbath is the special day for worship and resting unto Him, set apart and made holy for that purpose from creation. The usage came about due to the fact that the special restorative act of the resurrection happened on the Şabbath, but Gnostics soon corrupted this use and applied it to Sunday. See "first of the Şabbaths" (Acts 20:7; 1 Cor. 16:2; Mat. 28:1; Mark 16:2; Luke 24:1; Yoн. 20:1, 19). Also see Rom. 14:4-6; Gal. 4:10; Col. 2:16. **1:10** α Eze 3:12 **1:10** β Exo 19:16. This can be no other than the Şabbath day. The Şabbath is a day to Yăhweн because he rested on that day after creation. See Exodus 16:25. In the Hebrew there the possessive is formed with a lamed: "הַיּוֹם לַיהוָה *hay-yom le-Yăh-weн*" and that is what we see with the dative here: ἐν τῇ κυριακῇ ἡμέρᾳ, which answers to the Hebrew: "בְּיוֹם לַיהוָה *bay-yom le-Yăhweн*". The Greek text may be re-ordered like the Hebrew: "ἐν ἡμέρᾳ τῇ κυριακῇ." This is not the phrase for the future "day of the Lŏrd" which is "ἡμέρα τοῦ κυρίου" (cf. 2Thess. 2:2). Against this, the book of Revelation is not only about the day of judgment, and indeed the first part is not about it at all. The fact of the resurrection on the Şabbath leaves only one possibility for this passage: the seventh day. **1:12** ξ Zech 4:2, Exo 25:37; **1:14** α Dan 7:9; **1:14** β Dan 10:5, 6; **1:15** δ Eze 1:27, 8:2 **1:15** θ Eze 43:2 **1:16** λ Isa 49:2; Compare Daniel 10:5-6; 7:9a.

1:17 α Eze 1:28, Dan 8:17, 10:8 **1:17** β Isa 44:6:

hand upon me, saying, "Do not be fearing. I AM THE FIRST AND THE LAST,[β] ¹⁸and the living one. And I became dead, and behold, I am alive for *all* the ages of the ages, and I have the keys of death and of the grave. ¹⁹Write therefore the things which you saw, and the things which are, and which are about to happen after these things. ²⁰ As for the mystery of the ⁷seven stars which you saw in my right hand, and the seven golden menorahs: the seven stars are the ᵀmessengers of the seven assemblies, and the seven menorahs are the seven assemblies."

2 ¹"For the messenger of the assembly in Ephesus write: 'These things says the one taking hold of the seven stars in his right hand, the one who walks[α] among the seven golden menorahs: ²I have been knowing your deeds and toil and patient endurance, and that you cannot endure evil men, and you put to the test those who call themselves emissaries, and they are not, and you find them to be false, ³and you have patient endurance, and endure because of my name, and have not been tiring. ⁴But I have this against you, that you have abandoned your θfirst love. ⁵Be remembering therefore from where you have been falling, and be sorry and turn your hearts *from sin*, and do the former works, but if not, I am coming quickly to you, and I will remove your menorah out of its place—unless you shall have been sorry and turned your hearts *from sin*[ψ]. ⁶But this you do have in your favor, that you hate the deeds of the ᶲNicolaitans, which I also hate. ⁷He who is having an ear, should hear what the Spirit says to the assemblies. To

---

THUS HAS SAID YĂHWEH, KING OF YISRA'EL, EVEN ITS RANSOMER, YĂHWEH OF ARMIES, 'I AM FIRST, AND I AM LAST, AND APART FROM ME THERE IS NO ALMIGHTY.' The Most High is speaking here with the collective 'I' and a collective 'me' as is sometimes the case in Hebrew. The Father is the ransomer as much as the Son, because both are giving the ransom. **1:20** γ→stars: See Daniel 12:3. Also 8:10. Famous people are called "stars." See Jude 1:13 for false teachers being called "wandering stars." **1:20** τ The stars are the messengers Yohanan used to communicate with the assemblies (cf. Acts 6:3). Since Yohanan, the last living emissary, was exiled to Patmos, he had seven messengers delegated to the seven assemblies to carry communication between himself and the congregations. This way he was able to receive communication on the conditions in the assemblies, and to send advice, counsel, and decisions appealed to him. This arrangement is like that of the seven deacons appointed in Acts 6:3. ▷ *Lampstands.* Each lampstand has seven branches. The Temple is said to have held four in the court of the women during Tabernacles. And of course there is the menorah in the holy place. Menorah, מְנוֹרָה means "lampstand" (λυχνίαν). They number seven, which is also indicative of their construction (ἑπτὰ λυχνίας). The use of this symbol for the seven assemblies is in striking contrast to crosses used on Churches stripped of their connection to worship at Yisra'el's Temple.

2:1 α Deu 23:14; **2:7** β Gen 2:9; **2:4** θ See Yoh.

15:10; 2 Yoh. 1:5-6, 9-11. Love is loyalty expressed by keeping the commandments (cf. Exo. 20:6). One can only conclude that a compromise of a lesser sort than the Gnostics had taken over, though in the end just as deadly. The chief sin of the Perushim was their love of money. See Luke 16:14-17 and notes (cf. 1 Tim. 6:10, 17). The leaders of the Ephesian Assembly had fallen into the same error. Their error was not a doctrinal one (cf. vs. 2-3, 6), so much as a spirit of compromise for the sake of monetary gain. Their first love was supposed to be faithfulness to Messiah, but they were lowering his standards to expand the numbers of the congregation and attract revenue from members who should be rebuked for sin. They had not commited the lawless apostacy of the gnostics, but they were letting compromise decide when money was at stake. Eventually, this course would lead to lawlessness. **2:5** ψ Nothing less than salvation is at stake. They must repent. **2:6** ϕ The word means "conquering the people." This refers to the Gnostics, whose teaching crept in. But their method of spreading heresy had to have been an authoritarian regime which enslaved the weak and put the faithful out of the assemblies. So they were overcoming the people by intimidation, compromise, and making them complicit with their transgressions. They were radically anti-law, and the Scripture they reinterpreted with out of control symbolism. The assembly of Ephesus was commended for hating this worse heresy than their own.

the one getting victory, I will grant to eat from the tree of life,^β which is in the Paradise of the Almĭghty.'"

⁸"And for the messenger of the assembly in Smyrna write: 'The first and the last, who was dead, and has come to life, says this: ⁹I have been knowing your tribulation and your poverty, but you are rich, and the blasphemy by those who say they are Yehudim and are not, but are a ᵃcongregation of Satan. ¹⁰Do not be fearing what you are about to suffer. Behold, the Slanderer is about to cast some of you into prison, that you may be tested, and you will have tribulation ten days. Be becoming faithful until death, and I will give you the crown of life. ¹¹He who is having an ear, should hear what the Spĭrit says to the assemblies. He who ᵝis getting victory shall not have been hurt by the second death.'"

¹²"And for the messenger of the assembly in Pergamum write: 'The one who has the sharp two-edged sword says this: ¹³I have been knowing where you dwell, where Satan's throne is, and you hold fast my name, and did not deny my faithfulness, even in the days of Antipas, my witness, my faithful one, who was killed among you, where Satan dwells. ¹⁴But I have a few things against you, because you have there some who hold the teaching of Bil'am,^φ who taught Balaq to put a stumbling block before the sons of Yisra'el, to eat idol offerings, and to commit acts of immorality. ¹⁵Thus you also have some who in the same way hold the teaching of the Nicolaitans. ¹⁶Be sorry and turn your hearts *from sin* therefore, or else I am coming to you quickly, and I will make war against them with the SWORD OF MY MOUTH.^λ ¹⁷He who is having an ear, should hear what the Spĭrit says to the assemblies. To him who is getting victory, to him I

2:9 α Or "synagogue of Satan." See Yoh. 8:31-44 for what Měssiah said to some Jews who only professed their faithfulness to Měssiah, but they had not truly affirmed faithfulness to him in their hearts (Yoh. 8:31). It was evident they would not continue in his word, which included confessing he was the Almĭghty Sŏn (Yoh. 8:58-59). The group that most fits this description at the time of Revelation is the later Ebionites, who were prevalent in Asia Minor, who confessed the Law was still valid, and taught its observance, but who denied that Měssiah was the Almĭghty Creator come in the flesh, and especially the heretic Cerinthus, a Gnostic Jewish-Christian contemporary with Yohanan, who taught that angels created the world, and that the Nazarene was a mere man inhabited by the Christ spirit between his baptism and crucifixion. There is also a prophetic reference to the growing power of Rabbinic Judaism here, and also a reference to a synchretistic Hellenized Judaism (cf. Goodenough, Hershel Shanks), such as might have produced the Synagogue mosaics with Helios riding his chariot through the zodiac. But the immediate emphasis appears to be to a group like Cerinthus, since it was currently the main threat and attack avenue of Satan on the faithful, which was similar to the Watchtower Society or the Mormons, except that they kept to outward Torah observance;

Such Torah observant Gnostics are still infiltrating the Messianic Faith, who still have an aversion to the Almĭghty taking a physical form, denying that Měssiah appeared as the *Malak Yăhweh* (מלאך יהוה), and denying that the human soul and spirit of Měssiah is in fact Elohim, similar to the ancient Nestorian error; ▷ Stern identified the 'synagogue of Satan' as non-Jews or Gentiles only, but this position only would seem to be justified by the desire to avoid the vacuous charge of antisemitism or racism for criticism of the beliefs of some Jews, when really false teaching about Měssiah is the reason for condemnation. Many equivocate non-Jewish Torah observance with *syn. of S.*, making a cultural exception for Jews, and no exception for anyone who teaches obligatory Torah observance. But this position is based on anti-law heresy, which is the teaching of the other synagogue of Satan, the sons of antinomian gnosticism. **2:11 β** "AND YOU SHALL REMEMBER ALL THE WAY WHICH YĂHWEH YOUR ALMĬGHTY HAS MADE YOU WALK THIS FORTY YEARS IN THE WILDERNESS FOR THE SAKE OF AFFLICTING YOU, FOR TESTING YOU, TO KNOW THAT WHICH IS IN YOUR HEART, IF YOU WOULD KEEP HIS COMMANDMENTS OR NOT" (Deut. 8:2).

2:14 φ Num 25:2, 31:16 **2:16 λ** Isa 49:2, 11:4
2:17 θ Exo 16:33: The hidden manna was that manna

will give some of the manna, which has been getting hidden, and I will give him a white stone, and a new-made name having been getting written on the stone which no one has been knowing but he who receives it.'"

¹⁸"And for the messenger of the assembly in Thyatira write: 'The Almĭghty Sŏn, who has EYES LIKE A FLAME OF FIRE, AND HIS FEET ARE LIKE BURNISHED BRONZE, says this: ¹⁹I have been knowing your deeds, and your love and faithfulness and service and perseverance, and that your deeds of late are greater than at first. ²⁰But I have this against you, that you tolerate the woman Izavel, who calls herself a prophetess. Then she teaches and leads my servants astray, so that they commit acts of immorality and eat idol offerings. ²¹And I have given her time that she might have been sorry and turn her heart *from sin*, but she does not want to be sorry and turn her heart from her immorality. ²²Behold, I am casting her upon a deathbed, and those committing adultery with her into great tribulation, unless they will have been sorry and turned their hearts from her deeds. ²³And I will kill her children with pestilence. Then all the assemblies will know that I AM HE WHO SEARCHES THE MINDS AND HEARTS. THEREFORE I WILL GIVE TO EACH ONE OF YOU ACCORDING TO YOUR DEEDS.

²⁴But I say to you, the rest who are in Thyatira, who do not hold this teaching, who have not known the ᵖdeep things of Satan, as they call them—I place no other burden on you. ²⁵Nevertheless what you have, hold fast until I may have come. ²⁶And he who is getting victory, and he who keeps my deeds until the end, TO HIM I WILL GIVE AUTHORITY OVER THE NATIONS. ²⁷THEN HE WILL RULE THEM WITH A ROD OF IRON, AS THE VESSELS OF THE POTTER ARE BROKEN TO PIECES. As I also have been receiving authority beside my Făther, ²⁸therefore, I will give him the morning star. ²⁹He who is having an ear, should hear what the Spĭrit says to the assemblies.'"

3 ¹"And for the messenger of the assembly in Sardis write: 'He who has the SEVEN SPĬRITS OF THE ALMĬGHTY, and the seven stars, says this: I have been knowing your deeds, that you have a name that you are alive, but you are dead. ²Be becoming watchers, and strengthen the things that remain, which have been

---

which was kept in a pot in the holy place, at the face of the ark of testimony, as a witness. **2:17** ρ The white stone (or brilliant stone) was probably that used for the Urim and Thumin to inquire of the Almĭghty. The symbolism speaks of a right of access to the divine council.

2:18 Dan 10:6 **2:20** φ =Jezebel. Not her real name, but a substitution to indicate her true character. She leads the servants astray. She employed doctrinal deception to induce them to consume idol sacrifices. There were many such deceivers. In a similar manner the cup and unleavened bread of fellowship in the Passover Seder were changed into an atoning sacrifice by the Church of Rome. The bread is said to be the real body of Christ and the wine his real blood.

They lifted the "host" which was the bread so that it could be worshiped. **2:23** δ Jer 17:10 **2:24** ρ→Satan; They really said the "deep things of God" (cf. 1 Cor. 2:10: τὰ βάθη τοῦ Θεοῦ). This was doctrine deceiving the saved that they could not loose their salvation by participating in idol sacrifice or by being sexually immoral. Gnosis is knowing that evil is harmless to the soul (as they claim) by proving loyalty to the doctrine through participation, i.e. knowing by experiencing it. The once saved always saved teachers are they who tolerate the false doctrine, which has evolved from its crude start. It's modern forms are layered over with thick layers of theological whitewash and centuries of mistranslation and misinterpretation. See 13:8 and 17:8. **2:26-27** ψ Psa. 2:8-9. **3:1** α Isa 11:2, Zec 3:9

Revelation 3

about to die, because I have not been finding your deeds having been getting completed in the sight of my Almĭghty. ³Be remembering therefore what you have been receiving and heard, and be keeping *it*, and be sorry and turn your heart *from sin*. If therefore you may not have kept watch, I will come like a thief, and you shall not have known at what hour I will come upon you.'

⁴'But you have a few people in Sardis who have not soiled their garments, and they will walk with me in white,ᵅ because they are worthy. ⁵He who is getting victory will thus be dressed in white garments. And I WILL NOT ERASE HIS NAME FROM THE SCROLL OF LIFE,ᵞ and I will confess his name before my Făther, and before his messengers. ⁶He who is having an ear, should hear what the Spĭrit says to the assemblies."'

⁷"And for the messenger of the assembly in Philadelphia write: 'He who is holy, who is true, who has the KEY OF DAUID, WHO OPENS AND NO ONE WILL SHUT, AND WHO SHUTS AND NO ONE OPENS,ᵖ says this: ⁸I have been knowing your deeds. Behold, I have been putting before you a door, having been getting opened, which no one can shut, because you have *but* little power, and have kept my word, and have not denied my name. ⁹Behold, I shall be causing those of the ᶲcongregation of Satan, those declaring themselves to be Yehudim,ᵠ and are not, but do lie—behold, I will make them so that they will come and will bow down before your feet, and they shall have known that I have loved you.'

¹⁰'Because you have kept the word of my perseverance, I also will keep you from the hour of testing, that hour which is about to come upon the whole inhabited world, to test those who dwell in the earth. ¹¹Then I am going to ᶲcome

---

3:4 α Dan 11:35, 12:10 **3:5** γ Exo 32:32-33, Psa 69:28, Dan 12:1, Mal 3:16: It is possible to have one's name erased from the book. This threat proves false the Calvinist doctrine that a fall from grace is impossible. This doctrine they call, "Perseverance of the Saints," but it is falsely named. Scripture teaches the holy ones must persevere, or endure until the end. See Matthew 24:13. The most common logical fallacy (deception) is equivocation. Equivocation takes a term that expresses a true or correct idea and then shifts its meaning to another false idea.

3:7 ρ Isa 22:22 **3:9** ϕ See Rev. 2:9 **3:9** ψ The statement is a parable. They were in fact outward Jews, but they were not worshiping the true Almĭghty (cf. Yoh. 8:44; 1 Yoh. 5:11-12) according to the meaning of the word Jew: יְהוּדִים etymology uncertain (HALOT), but from verb root יָדָה meaning 'to confess' or 'to praise.' Leah said, אוֹדֶה אֶת־יְהוָה = *I will make confessed Yahweh*. There were a few theophoric names before the Exodus (i.e. Yah-ḵeved, יוֹכֶבֶד Yah is glory). I conjecture Yehudah was one of them, thus, the fem. participle, 'she who confesses': יוֹדָה, Qal, fem. part., *confessor, confessing*, has been put with יְהוּ, *Yahu = Yahu confessor*. In the mas. plural. יוֹדִים = *confessors*. (The reduction of יְהוּ to יְהוּ being neglected.) Thus the meaning of the plural word Yehudim, is 'Yah confessors.' I do not think the fut. Hoph. theory is correct, 'he who is being made confessed' because in that form, Yehudah would mean 'she who is being made to confessed, i.e. we would expect יוּדָה and not דָּה. The theory that the ending is a denominative is used to cover this, thus simply a noun, confessor or praiser. This will leave with a remnant passive, 'he is made to be confessor' (Hophal) which begs the question of who 'he' is. Thus the passive I reject in favor of interpreting the waw as part of the divine name, and thus the name Yehudah encodes the full sense of Leah's confession: 'Yahu, she who confesses.' The plural is evidently, 'Yahu, they who confess.' Clearly the denial of Mĕssiah or his deity makes those saying they are Yehudim, not confessors of Yah. Denying they are Yehudim, therefore, is nothing so trivial as saying they have no Jewish descent, and that is regardless of whether my etymological extension is correct. The trouble is that Leah's coined word is non-standard in the first place. **3:11** ϕ→*quickly*: This saying, like 22:7 and 22:12 must be taken in the context of the preceding verse. When the tribulation comes he will hasten his coming.

quickly! Be holding fast what you do have, in order that no one will have taken your crown.'

¹²'He who is getting victory, I will make him a pillar in the temple of my Almĭghty, and he will never have to go out from it anymore. And I will write upon him the name of my Almĭghty, and the name of the city of my Almĭghty, the new-made Yerushalayim, which comes down out of heaven from my Almĭghty, and my new-made name. ¹³He who is having an ear, should hear what the Spĭrit says to the assemblies.'

¹⁴"And for the messenger of the assembly in Laodicea write: 'The Am·en, the faithful and true witness, the head of the creation of the Almĭghty, says this: ¹⁵I have been knowing your deeds, that you are neither cold nor hot. I would that you were cold or hot. ¹⁶So because you are lukewarm, and neither hot nor cold, I will spit you out of my mouth. ¹⁷Because you say, "I am rich, and have been becoming wealthy, and have need of nothing," and you have not been knowing that you are wretched and miserable and poor and blind and naked, ¹⁸I am advising you to buy from beside me gold, having been getting fired by fire, so that you will have become rich, and white garments, so that you will have gotten dressed, and that the shame of your nakedness will not have been revealed, and eye salve to anoint your eyes, that you may be seeing.'

¹⁹'Those whom I may be loving as friends, I reprove and discipline. Be getting zealous therefore, and be sorry and turn your heart *from sin*. ²⁰Behold, I have been standing at the door and I am knocking. If anyone may have heard my voice and shall have opened the door, I will come in to him, and I will dine with him, and he with me. ²¹He who is getting victory, I will grant to him to sit down with me on my throne, as I also got victory and sat down with my Făther on his throne. ²²The one having an ear, should hear what the Spĭrit says to the assemblies."'

4 ¹After these things I looked, and behold, a door had been standing open in heaven, and the first voice which I had heard, like the sound of a ʸtrumpet speaking with me, said, "Come up here. Then I will show you what must take place after these things." ²Immediately I was in the Spĭrit, and behold, a throne was standing in heaven, and one^α sitting on the throne. ³And he who was sitting was like a jasper stone and a sardius in appearance. And there was a rainbow^β around the throne, like an emerald in appearance.

⁴And around the throne were twenty-four thrones. And upon the thrones I saw twenty-four elders sitting, who ^η had been wearing on themselves white robes, and upon their heads golden crowns. ⁵And from the throne proceed FLASHES OF LIGHTNING AND SOUNDS AND PEALS OF THUNDER.ᵃ And there were seven menorahs of fire burning before the throne, which are the seven Spĭrits of the Almĭghty.

4:1 γ See Rev. 1:10. So Mĕssiah speaks; **4:2** α | *been dressing themselves* **4:5** α Exo 19:16; Eze 1:26; **4:3** β Eze 1:28; **4:4** η→dressed: or *have*

⁶And before the throne there was, as it were, a SEA OF GLASS^α like crystal, and in the center and around the throne, FOUR LIVING CREATURES^β FULL OF EYES^θ in front and behind. ⁷AND THE FIRST CREATURE WAS LIKE A LION, AND THE SECOND CREATURE LIKE A CALF, AND THE THIRD CREATURE HAD A FACE LIKE THAT OF A MAN, AND THE FOURTH CREATURE WAS LIKE A FLYING EAGLE.^α ⁸And the four living creatures, each one of them having six wings, are full of eyes around and within, and day and night they do not cease to say, "Holy, holy, holy, is Yăhweh the Almĭghty, the all powerful, THE ONE WHO HAS BEEN and THE ONE BEING and **THE COMING ONE.**" ⁹And when the living creatures give glory and honor and thanks to him who sits on the throne, to him who lives for *all* the ages of the ages, ¹⁰the twenty-four elders will fall down before him who sits on the throne. Then they will worship him who lives for *all* the ages of the ages. Then they will cast their crowns before the throne, saying, ¹¹"Worthy are you, our Adŏnai and our Almĭghty, to receive glory and honor and power, because you have created all things, and because of your will they have been, and were created."

5

¹Then I saw in the right hand of him who sat on the throne a scroll having been getting written inside and on the back, having been getting sealed up with seven seals. ²Then I saw a mighty messenger proclaiming with a loud voice, "Who is worthy to open the scroll and to break its seals?" ³And no one in heaven, or on the earth, or under the earth, was able to open the scroll, or to look into it. ⁴Then I was weeping greatly, because no one was found worthy to open the scroll, or to look into it. ⁵And one of the elders said to me, "Do not be weeping! Behold, the Lion, THE ONE BEING from the tribe of Yehudah, the Root of David, has gotten victory so he can open the scroll and its seven seals."

⁶Then I saw at the middle, between the throne and the four living creatures, and in the middle of the elders, a Lamb who had been standing, like one which had been getting slain, having seven horns and seven eyes, which are the ^φseven Spĭrits of the Almĭghty, who have been getting sent out into all the earth. ⁷Then he came; then he had been receiving it out of the right hand of him who sat on the throne. ⁸And when he had taken the scroll, the four living creatures and the twenty-four elders fell down before the Lamb, having each one a harp, and golden bowls full of incense, which are the prayers of the holy ones. ⁹Then they

---

4:6 α Eze 1:22, Exo 24:10 **4:6** β Eze 1:5 **4:6** θ Eze 1:18, 10:12 **4:7** α Eze 1:10, 10:14.

5:6 φ see Yoh. 16:13 note. It is revealed here that the *entity called the Holy Spĭrit has a seven fold nature, and explains the reason why I have *'d the word *entity in the note on Yoh. 16:13. The humanly understood word "person" is too limiting to describe the Făther and Spĭrit. It is only strictly correct when applied to the Sŏn, who still remains mysteriously united with the Făther and Spĭrit. It appears that on a higher level personhood is divisible and multipliable. See Zech. 3:9; 4:10. See also Yoh. 1:1. Also, in Hebrew a plural entity may speak with a singular "I."

5:9 α ἠγόρασας = purchased. But elsewhere we are informed that the nature of the purchase is a ransom. Cf. Isa. 51:11; Hos. 13:14; Mat. 20:28; Mark 10:45. The avoidance of the specific word for ransom (λύτρον) suggests the heavenly choir is aware that the meaning of the word *ransomed* is easily overlooked and should be explained in other words. Doubtless this is true as Christians now are of the heretical belief that Messiah was ransoming them from the wrath of God by paying the penalty of wrath. But this is not so. ▷ The purchase is 'for the Almĭghty' and 'from every tribe and tongue and people and nation.' The currency is the blood of Messiah, that is the cost in divine life to

sang a new-made song, saying, "Worthy are you to take the scroll, and to break its seals, because you were slain, then you did purchase[a] for the Almĭghty with your blood men from every tribe and tongue and people and nation. [10]And you make them to be a kingdom and priests to our Almĭghty. Then they will reign upon the earth."

[11]Then I looked. Then I heard the voice of many messengers around the throne and the living creatures and the elders. Then the number of them was ten-thousand ten-thousands, even thousands of thousands, [12]saying with a loud voice, "Worthy is the Lamb that had been getting slain to receive power and riches and wisdom and might and honor and glory and blessing." [13]And every created thing which is in heaven and on the earth and under the earth and on the sea, and all things in them, I heard saying, "To him who sits on the throne, and to the Lamb, be blessing and honor and glory and dominion for *all* the ages of the ages." [14]And the four living creatures were saying, "Amen." And the elders had fallen down and had worshiped. [6.1]Then I saw when the Lamb broke one of the seven seals. Then I heard one of the four living creatures saying as with a voice of thunder, "Be coming."

6

[1b]Then I looked, and [2]behold, a white horse, and the one sitting on it holding a bow, and a crown was given to him. Then he went forth being victorious, and so that he will have gotten victory.

---

bring the faithful to repentance and to cleanse them from their servitude in the nations. The cost is exacted by lawlessness. So the idea explained in the song is in every way the ransom described by Messiah, 'a ransom for many.' ▷ The ransom is represented here as from the nations who are holding Yisra'el captive. See also 14 :3-4. The transaction is not a formal one since the ransom is exacted by lawlessness by taking innocent blood for the release of the captives. The devil and his hosts regard depriving innocent blood of life as more valuable to them than letting the faithful who have given their loyalty to the Most High go free, because they are motivated by getting even with the Most High for passing judgement on them. They had no intention of freeing the ransomed either, but the Most High compels them to (as Pharoah). See Isa. 49. Thus he will enforce the ransom terms on them. ▷ The ransom is the price paid in terms of suffering (cf. 1 Peter 2:21) and death to free men from sin. This includes the necessity of divine life, represented by the blood of Messiah, to cleanse us from sin, because the Most High has to look on our sin to excise it from us, because the uncleanness of our exile clings to us until cleansed. It may be noted that a multitude of evils are exacting the cost, because sin has spread to all creation. But Satan is the most responsible. The ransom is no formal (or legal) transaction with him, but the Most High allowed Satan to murder Messiah taking innocent blood, as the devil is in the habit of doing, as an indication of the divine cost of our wellness, an instruction regarding our healing (cf. Isa. 53:5; Isa. 43:3). The death of Messiah is the climax of the cost, who was declared wholly innocent by his resurrection from the dead. The Most High compels the devil to give up his pretentions of ownership over the repentant sinner because he took innocent blood. In the Almighty's view, he took the ransom, something the devil never really intended to do on God's terms. The ransom explanation is not agreed to by Satan, but it is imposed on him, because Satan is just an extention of the intrinsic cost of sin. ▷ By the climax of Messiah's suffering, and his resurrection, the narrative, or motif, of the suffering and risk taking conquering hero who delivers his beloved, and is in the end rewarded with life, along with his beloved, is made plain to all men. Messiah's sacrifice is lifted up to all to draw all to the love of the Most High. The same ransoming theme is repeated the world over in fiction, story, myth, and legend, as well as in reality. It produces the best kind of stories because they all express love and the sacrifice given to right wrong and cleanse evil. ▷ But Satan has cast darkness over Christianity by rewritting the narrative of Messiah's death in terms of divine appeasement and wrath satisfaction by innocent blood. This is exactly what Satan himself practices as god of this world. He has caused religion to remake the Most High into his own image.

6:1b-2 The seals correspond to the seven years in Dan. 9:27. The conqueror is the man of lawlessness.

³And when he broke the second seal, I heard the second living creature saying, "Be coming." ⁴Then another, a red horse, went out, and to him who sat on it, it was granted to take peace from the earth, and that men should slay one another. Then a great sword was given to him. ⁵And when he broke the third seal, I heard the third living creature saying, "Be coming." Then I looked, and behold, a black horse, and he who sat on it had a yoke^ξ in his hand. ⁶Then I heard as it were a voice in the center of the four living creatures saying, "A quart of wheat for a dinar, and three quarts of barley for a dinar. And you shall not have harmed the oil and the wine." ⁷And when he broke the fourth seal, I heard the voice of the fourth living creature saying, "Be coming." ⁸Then I looked, and behold, an ashen horse, and he who sat on it had the name Death, and the grave was following with him. And authority was given to them over a fourth of the earth, to kill with sword and with famine and with pestilence and by the wild beasts of the earth.

⁹And when he broke the fifth seal, I saw underneath the altar the souls of those who had been getting slain because of the word of the Almĭghty, and because of the testimony which they had maintained. ¹⁰Then they cried out with a loud voice, saying, "How long, O Adŏnai, holy and true, will you refrain from judging and avenging our blood on those who dwell on the earth?" ¹¹Then there was given to each of them a white robe. Then they were told that they will rest for a little while longer, until *the murder of* their fellow servants and their brothers, those being about to be killed, even as they, will have been completed also.

¹²Then I looked when he broke the sixth seal, and there was a great earthquake, and the sun became black as sackcloth made of hair, and the whole moon became like blood, ¹³and the stars of heaven fell to the earth, as a fig tree casts its unripe figs when shaken by a great wind. ¹⁴And the heaven was split apart like a scroll when it is rolled up, and every mountain and island were moved out of their places. ¹⁵And the kings of the earth and the great men and the commanders and the rich and the strong and every slave and free man, hid themselves in the caves and among the rocks of the mountains. ¹⁶Then they said to the mountains and to the rocks, "Fall on us and hide us from the presence of him who sits on the throne, and from the wrath of the Lamb, ¹⁷because the great day of their wrath has come, and who is able to stand?"

7

¹After this I saw four messengers, which had been standing at the four corners of the earth, holding back the four winds of the earth, so that no wind may be blowing on the earth or on the sea or on any tree. ²Then I saw ˣanother

---

6:5 ξ a yoke of scales. **6:9** The base of the altar was where the life was poured out. The symbolism is similar to Hevel's blood crying out from the ground. The souls may not actually awaken, but they are represented as crying out for justice and then going back to sleep.

7:2 x→sun: The same person as the "MAN IN LINEN" (Ezek. 9:4) who has the seal of the Almĭghty. See also Mal. 4:2, "SUN OF RIGHTEOUSNESS." Cf. Psa. 84:11; Ezek. 43:1: the eastern gate is for Měssiah. The Branch צֶמַח *tsemah* is rendered "riser" in Greek: Ἀνατολήν, Zech. 3:8. The morning star rises out of the sun. This alludes to the helical rising of the king planet on Sept. 1, 2 B.C. This Messenger is the messenger of

Messenger ascending from the rising of the sun, having the seal of the living Almĭghty. Then he cried out with a loud voice to the four messengers to whom it was granted to harm the earth and the sea, ³saying, "You will not have harmed the earth or the sea or the trees, until we may have sealed the servants of our Almĭghty on their foreheads."

⁴Then I heard the number of those who had been getting sealed. One hundred and forty-four thousand had been getting sealed from every tribe of the sons of Yisra'el. ⁵From the tribe of Yehudah, twelve thousand had been getting sealed, from the tribe of Re'uven twelve thousand, from the tribe of Gad twelve thousand, ⁶from the tribe of Asher twelve thousand, from the tribe of Naphtali twelve thousand, from the tribe of Menasheh twelve thousand, ⁷from the tribe of Şim'on twelve thousand, from the tribe of Levi twelve thousand, from the tribe of Yissashkar twelve thousand, ⁸from the tribe of Zevulun twelve thousand, *and* from the tribe of Yosef twelve thousand. From the tribe of Binyamin, twelve thousand had been getting sealed.

⁹After these things I looked, and behold, *there was* a great multitude, such *as* no one was able to number it, out of every nation, even tribes and peoples and tongues, who had been standing before the throne and before the Lamb, who had been getting dressed in white robes. And palm branches *were* in their hands. ¹⁰Then they were crying out with a loud voice, saying, "Deliverance belongs to our Almĭghty who sits on the throne, and to the Lamb."

¹¹And all the messengers had been standing around the throne and around the elders and the four living creatures. Then they fell on their faces before the throne and worshiped the Almĭghty, ¹²saying, "Amen! Blessing and glory and wisdom and thanksgiving and honor and power and might, be to our Almĭghty for *all* the ages of the ages. Amen."

¹³Then one of the elders began to say, saying to me, "These who have been getting dressed in the white robes, who are they, and from where have they come?" ¹⁴Then I had been saying to him, "Sir, you have been knowing." Then he said to me, "These are the ones coming out of the great tribulation. And *then*, they have washed their robes and made them white in the blood of the Lamb. ¹⁵For this reason, they are before the throne of the Almĭghty. So then, they serve him day and night in his temple, and he who sits on the throne will spread his tabernacle over them. ¹⁶They will hunger no more, neither thirst anymore, neither will the sun have beaten down on them, nor any heat, ¹⁷because the Lamb in the center of the throne will be their shepherd. Then he will guide them to springs of the water of life. Then the Almĭghty will wipe every tear from their eyes."

8 ¹And when he opened the seventh seal, there was silence in heaven for about half an hour. ²Then I saw the seven messengers who had been standing

---

the covenant. See Mal. 3:1. The Sŏn of man commands the four horses and the four chariots. See Zech. 1:8-17; | 6:5. These are the four messengers sent to the four points of the compass.

before the Almĭghty. Then seven trumpets were given to them. ³And another messenger came. Then he stood at the altar, holding a golden incense bowl. Then much incense was given to him, that he may add it to the prayers of all the holy ones upon the golden altar which was before the throne. ⁴Then the smoke of the incense, with the prayers of the holy ones, went up before the Almĭghty out of the messenger's hand. ⁵Then the messenger had been receiving the incense bowl. Then he filled it with the fire of the altar. Then he threw it to the earth. Then there followed peals of thunder and sounds and lightning and an earthquake.

⁶And the seven messengers who had the seven trumpets prepared themselves that they may have sounded them. ⁷And the first sounded. Then there came hail and fire, which had been getting mixed with blood. Then they were thrown to the earth, and a third of the earth was burned up, and a third of the trees were burned up, and all the green grass was burned up. ⁸And the second messenger sounded, and something like a great mountain burning with fire was thrown into the sea. Then a third of the sea became blood. ⁹Then a third of the creatures, which were in the sea and had life, died, and a third of the ships were destroyed.

¹⁰And the third messenger sounded. Then a great star fell from heaven, burning like a torch. Then it fell on a third of the rivers and on the springs of waters. ¹¹And the name of the star is called Wormwood. Then a third of the waters became wormwood, and many men died from the waters, because they were made bitter. ¹²And the fourth messenger sounded. Then a third of the sun and a third of the moon and a third of the stars were smitten, so that a third of them shall have been darkened; also the day shall not have shone for a third of it, and the night in the same way.

¹³Then I looked. Then I heard an eagle flying in mid-heaven, saying with a loud voice, "Woe, woe, woe, to those who dwell on the earth, because of the remaining trumpet blasts of the three messengers who are about to sound!"

9

¹And the fifth messenger sounded. Then I saw a star from heaven which had been falling to the earth. Then the key of the abyss was given to him. ²Then he opened the abyss. Then smoke went up out of the well shaft, like the smoke of a great furnace. Then the sun and the air were darkened by the smoke of the well shaft. ³And out of the smoke came forth locusts upon the earth. Then power was given them, as the scorpions of the earth have power. ⁴Then they were told that they should not hurt the grass of the earth, nor any green thing, nor any tree, but only the men who do not have the seal of the Almĭghty on their foreheads. ⁵Then it was ordered to them, that they will not have killed them, but that they will be tormented for five moons. And their torment was like the torment of a scorpion when it may have stung a man. ⁶And in those days men will seek death and will not find it. When they will long to die, then death flees from them.

⁷And the appearance of the locusts was like horses, which have been getting ready for battle. And on their heads, as it were, crowns like gold, and their faces

were like the faces of men. ⁸And they had hair like the hair of women, and their teeth were like the teeth of lions. ⁹And they had breastplates like breastplates of iron, and the sound of their wings was like the sound of chariots, of many horses rushing to battle. ¹⁰And they have tails like scorpions, and stings. And in their tails is their power to hurt men for five moons. ¹¹They have as king over them, the messenger of the abyss. His name in Hebrew is Avaddon, and in the Greek he has the name Apollyon.

¹²The first woe is past. Behold, two woes are still coming after these things.

¹³And the sixth messenger sounded. Then I heard a voice from the four horns of the golden altar which is before the Almĭghty, ¹⁴one saying to the sixth messenger who had the trumpet, "Release the four messengers who have been getting held bound at the great river Euphrates." ¹⁵Then the four messengers, who had been getting ready for the hour and day and new moon and year, were released, so that they might kill a third of mankind. ¹⁶And the number of the armies of the horsemen was two ten-thousand ten-thousands. I heard the number of them.

¹⁷And this is how I saw in the vision the horses and those who sat on them: the riders had breastplates the color of fire and of hyacinth and of brimstone, and the heads of the horses are like the heads of lions, and out of their mouths proceed fire and smoke and brimstone. ¹⁸A third of mankind was killed by these three plagues, by the fire and the smoke and the brimstone, which proceeded out of their mouths. ¹⁹For the power of the horses is in their mouths and in their tails, because their tails are like serpents and have heads, and with them they do harm.

²⁰And the rest of mankind, who were not killed by these plagues, had not been sorry and turned their hearts from the works of their hands, so as not to worship demons, and the idols of gold and of silver and of brass and of stone and of wood, which can neither see nor hear nor walk, ²¹and they had not been sorry and turned their hearts from their murders nor of their drug trafficking nor of their immorality nor of their thefts.

10

¹Then I saw another mighty Messenger coming down out of heaven, who has been getting himself dressed with a cloud, and a rainbow upon

10:1 Again this Messenger is Mĕssiah himself. For ordinary messengers are not described, but only the Mĕssenger of Yăhwe͇h is ever described. ▷ Some commentaries go to great lengths to explain that this vision is not of Mĕssiah himself. Ellicott believes the words 'another mighty angel' prevents it, although some MSS omit the word, 'another.' An inspection of the same commentary at Gen. 32:24 reveals a denial that the 'man' there was in fact the Almĭghty, though the text says it in Gen. 32:30. Rather Ellicot thinks the Almĭghty was only mediated ('mediately by His messenger') via an angel. Ellicot further implies that an angel cannot also be a man by citing Hos. 12:4. Rather the opposite is true: the man is also messenger because 'angel' need not imply a genus. It only need imply a function, as seen with Yoĥanan's seven messengers to the seven assemblies who were men. It should not be supposed that the 'incarnation' of Mĕssiah only happened when he was born of a virgin, or that Mĕssiah or the faithful are forever limited to be mere 'men.' But the faithful shall become as the stars of heaven, as the 'sons of the Almĭghty' which is a lot more than the faithful currently are. Nor should it be supposed that the Almĭghty is incapable of taking human flesh at one moment and then 'angelic' at the next. ▷ Barnes claims nothing can be argued here for Mĕssiah. ▷ Gill

his head, and his face like the sun, and his feet like pillars of fire, ²and he has in his hand a little scroll which has been getting opened. Then he placed his right foot on the sea and his left on the land. ³Then he cried out with a loud voice, as when a lion roars, and when he had cried out, the seven peals of thunder uttered their voices. ⁴And when the seven peals of thunder had spoken, I was about to be writing. Then I heard a voice from heaven saying, "Seal up the things which the seven peals of thunder have spoken, and you shall not have written them."

⁵And the Messenger whom I saw, which had been standing on the sea and on the land lifted up his right hand to heaven, ⁶then swore by him who lives for *all* the ages of the ages, who created heaven and the things in it, and the earth and the things in it, and the sea and the things in it, that there will be no more delay, ⁷but in the days of the voice of the seventh messenger, when he may be about to be sounding, then the mystery of the Almĭghty will have been finished, as he proclaimed to his servants the prophets.

⁸And the voice which I heard from heaven, I heard again speaking with me, and saying, "Be going, take the scroll which has been getting opened in the hand of the Messenger who has been standing on the sea and on the land." ⁹Then I went to the Messenger, telling him to give me the little scroll. And he said to me, "Take it, and eat it. Then it will make your stomach bitter, but in your mouth it will be sweet as honey." ¹⁰Then I took the little scroll out of the Messenger's hand. Then I ate it. Then it was in my mouth sweet as honey, and when I had eaten it, my stomach was made bitter. ¹¹Then they said to me, "You must prophesy again concerning many peoples and nations and tongues and kings."

11

¹When a measuring rod was given to me like a staff, then the Messenger stood ⁺by saying, "Be rising and measure the ᵠtemple of the Almĭghty, and the altar, and those worshiping in it. ²And the court which is outside the temple exclude, and you shall not have measured it, because it will have been given to the nations, and the holy city they will tread under foot for forty-two moons.ᵖ"

³"When I will grant authority to my two witnesses, then they will prophesy for twelve hundred and sixty days, having been getting dressed in sackcloth.

---

says it is Mĕssiah. ▷ Meyer denies it, citing the oath in 10:6 as 'not appropriate to Christ.' But a form of this oath appears in Dan. 12:7 spoken by the man clothed in linen. One may as well suppose that it was not appropriate for Mĕssiah to pray to the Father either. ▷ The Pulpit Commentary claims, "Wherever our Lord is referred to in the Revelation, it is always in a mode which cannot possibly be mistaken." But there are several cases of mistaken identity in the book already! Nor did they bother to ask Miryam Magdalene about this first. ▷ The Rabbis rejected Mĕssiah because he did not meet their expectations, and the commentaries seek to tame, fence in, and restrict Mĕssiah, so that he stays within their expectations.

11:2 π יְרָחִים Also, Rev. 13:5; See Appendix XVI. Cf. Dan. 7:25: "a time, times, and part of a time." Some put "half a time," but "half of" is more precise than the Aramaic word פְּלַג implies. The beast will achieve a political takeover of Israel before the persecution commences (Dan. 7:25), just over two months, in my reckoning. They will enter the outer courts during those two months, leaving the Temple itself alone, and the worshippers, but on the spring equinox the beast will defile the Temple, begin to murder Israel, and this will continue as indicated in the chart on page 534. The days associated with the first and last new moons do not have to be the whole month, as it is Hebrew custom to count inclusively, a part of a period, the whole parts, and a part at the end. Daniel 7:25 is worded the way it is to let us know that the 4th year after the first three is a partial one.

⁴THESE ARE THE TWO OLIVE TREES AND THE TWO MENORAHS THAT HAVE BEEN STANDING BEFORE THE 'ADŌNAI OF THE EARTH.θ ⁵And if anyone desires to harm them, fire proceeds out of their mouths. Then it devours their enemies. And if anyone may have desired to harm them, in this manner he needs to be killed. ⁶These have the power to have shut up the heaven, in order that rain may not be falling during the days of their prophesying. And they have power over the waters to be turning them into blood, and to strike the earth with every plague, as often as they may have desired."

⁷"And when they may have finished their testimony, the beast that comes up out of the abyss will make war with them. Then he will get victory over them. Then he will kill them. ⁸And their dead bodies will lie in the street of the great city which mystically is called Sedom and Mitsrayim, where also their 'Adōnai was fastened to an execution timber. ⁹Then those from the peoples and tribes and tongues and nations are going to look at their dead bodies for three and a half days, and will not permit their dead bodies to be laid in a tomb. ¹⁰And those who dwell on the earth are going to rejoice over them. Then they are going to be merry, and they will send gifts to one another, because these two prophets tormented those who dwell on the earth.

¹¹And after the three and a half days the breath of life from the Almĭghty came into them. Then they stood on their feet, and great fear fell upon those who were looking at them. ¹²Then they heard a loud voice from heaven saying to them, "Come up here." Then they went up into heaven in the cloud. Then their enemies beheld them. ¹³Also in that hour there was a great earthquake, and a tenth of the city fell. Then seven thousand *leading* names among men were killed in the earthquake, and the rest were terrified. Then they gave glory to the Almĭghty in heaven.

¹⁴The second woe has passed. Behold, the third woe is coming swiftly.

¹⁵And the seventh messenger sounded, then there arose loud voices in heaven, saying, "The kingdom of the world has become the kingdom of our Adŏnai, and of his Anŏinted, and he will reign for *all* the ages of the ages."

¹⁶And the twenty-four elders, who sit on their thrones before the Almĭghty, fell on their faces. Then they worshiped the Almĭghty, ¹⁷saying, "We give you thanks, Yăhweн, Almĭghty of Hosts, THE ONE BEING and THE ONE WHO HAS BEEN, because you have been taking up your great power and will have reigned. ¹⁸And the nations have raged. Then your wrath has come, and the appointed time for the dead to be judged, and to give the reward to your servants the prophets and to the holy ones and to those who fear your name, the small and the great, and to destroy those who destroy the earth."

11:4 θ Zech 4:14. See Mat. 17:1-13; Luke 9:28-36; Zech. 4:14; Mark 16:5; Luke 24:4.

11:11 This sign corresponds to three literal days (daylight periods). The extra half day is the night after the third day. This manner of explaining "THREE DAYS AND THREE NIGHTS" counters the Friday-Sunday chronology using a sunset epoch. Mosheн and Ęliyaнu bear witness to the resurrection of Mĕssiah. See "Jacob's Trouble" on page 534.

Revelation 12

¹⁹Then the temple of the Almĭghty which is in heaven was opened. Then the ark of his covenant was seen in his temple, and there were flashes of lightnings and voices and thunders and an earthquake and great hail.

12 ¹And a great sign was seen in heaven: a woman having been getting dressed with the sun, and the moon under her feet, and on her head a crown of twelve stars.§ ²And being with child, then she cries out, being in labor and in pain to give birth.

³Then another sign was seen in heaven: and behold, a great red serpent having seven heads and ten horns, and on his heads were seven royal crowns. ⁴And his tail sweeps along a third of the stars of heaven. And he will have thrown them to the earth.

But the serpent had been standing before the woman being about to give birth, so that when she may have given birth he might devour her child.

⁵Then she gave birth to a son, a male child, who is going to rule all the nations with a rod of iron. Then her child was caught up next to the Almĭghty and next to his throne. ⁶And the woman fled into the wilderness, where she has there a

---

12:1-2 ξ Mĕssiah was born when the sun was in the constellation of the virgin and the new moon was under its feet. This alignment happened on the new moon day of the seventh month, *Yom Teruah*, September 1, 2 BC. (See Luke 3:1, 23 for determination of the year). The metaphor speaks of the sun during its month in the constellation of the virgin, and the moon being nearby under the feet was a new moon at the beginning of the seventh month. For the sun spends one month each out of the months of the year in each constellation, and the moon passes out of the sun on the new moon for each month. The significance of this day is that it is a biblical holy day that the Most High commanded Yisra'el to observe. It is commonly known as the *Feast of Trumpets*. Therefore, Messiah's birth occurred upon that holy day, and since Messiah is the greater, the reality that makes the reflection, the holy day reflects the light of his birth date. ▷ Using a planetarium program like Stellarium, we can reproduce the alignments pictured in the text for Tishri 1, in the year 2 BC. It is a matter of tracking the position of the sun and moon backwards into the year 2 BC using the computer program until the alignment matches that in the text. ▷ One can also fashion 12 stars over the head of Virgo into a crown, but it is also evident that the 12 stars represent the 12 tribes of Yisra'el. ▷ Virgo, of course, means 'virgin.' The same constellation is called *beṭhulah* in Hebrew, which means 'maiden' in Hebrew, a more common term for 'virgin,' which is *almah* in Hebrew. ▷ Messiah also said that he is the "bright dawn star" (cf. Rev. 22:16). It happened on that same day that the dawn star *Tzedeq* in Hebrew, meaning 'righteous' or 'just one, that wandering star which is called by the Romans 'Jupiter,' first appeared in the morning after its disappearance. This was the star that was seen in the rising, the standard 12 degrees separated from the sun at dawn (cf. Mat. 2:2, 9-10). Since *Tzedeq* has a 12 year cycle, spending one year in each constellation before repeating, it is clear that the dawn star only rose as described by the Magi on Tishri 1 in the year 2 BC. To find another match would be too far from the correct range of years.

12:3 'Serpent' is translated from δράκων. See BDAG. In the LXX it is aligned with the Hebrew word תַּנִּין, *tannin* which also means a serpent. Facing off against Virgo is the constellation of Hydra. Hydra is a many headed serpent from out of the sea. It is the largest constellation, stretching over one-third of the heavens. The serpent used king Herod as his instrument to try to kill the Messiah

12:5 μ See "Jacob's Trouble" on page 534. Many suppose that 1260 days are equal to the 42 months (Rev. 11:2; 13:5), and then divide the days by the months to arrive at 30 days per month for every month. Besides contradicting the appointment of the moon, *the lesser light*, to mark appointed times (cf. Gen. 1:14-16, because months have 29 *as well as* 30 days), the assumption that the two periods measure the same time period is incorrect. The 42 months are about 1239 days because months vary between 29 and 30 days, and pertain to the dominion of the beast over the whole world, but the 1260 days pertains to the duration of the refuge. Since the text does not say the time periods are the same, it is unwise to claim so when it is easily explained in terms of the actual cycles of the moon. ▷ Some believe also that 150 days are to be divided into exactly 5 months during the deluge, but on account of both the 17th day of the 2nd month and the 17th day of the 7th month being within the 150 day count (due to inclusive counting), the five months are really 149 days. During this period there

place having been getting prepared by the Almĭghty, so that there she may be fed there for one thousand two hundred and sixty days͵ͭ.

⁷And^λ there will have been war in heaven, ͫMiƙa'el and his messengers waged war with the serpent. And the serpent and his messengers waged war. ⁸And they were not strong enough, and there was no longer a place found for them in heaven. ⁹Then the great serpent was thrown down, the serpent of old who is called the Slanderer and Satan, the one deceiving the whole world. He was thrown down to the earth, and his messengers were thrown down with him.

¹⁰Then I heard a loud voice in heaven, saying, "Now the deliverance, and the power, and the kingdom of our Almĭghty and the authority of his Anŏinted have come, because the slanderer of our brothers has been thrown down, who accuses them before our Almĭghty day and night. ¹¹And they will have gotten victory over him through the blood of the Lamb and through the word of their testimony, and they will not have loved their life even to death. ¹²For this reason, be rejoicing, heavens and you who tabernacle in them. Woe to the earth and the sea, because the Slanderer has come down to you, having great wrath, who has been knowing that he has only a short time."

¹³Then when the serpent saw that he was thrown down to the earth, he persecuted the woman who gave birth to the male child. ¹⁴Then the two wings of the great eagle were given to the woman, in order that she may be flying into the wilderness to her place, where she was fed for a time and times and half a time, from the presence of the serpent. ¹⁵Then the serpent poured water like a river out of his mouth after the woman, so that he will have caused her to be swept away with the flood. ¹⁶Then the earth helped the woman. Then the earth opened its mouth. Then it swallowed up the river which the serpent poured out of his mouth. ¹⁷Then the serpent was enraged with the woman. Then he went off to make war with the rest of her offspring, who keep the commandments of the Almĭghty and hold to the testimony of Yĕshua.

---

were four 30 day months and one 29 day month, which is within the natural variations of the moon's cycle. ▷ The deluge data are also fatal to the so called Enoch Calendar, because in that system months 2, 4, and 5 have 30 days each, but at the end of months 3 and 6 is an extra day, beyond the normal 30. There is really no way to come up with less than 152 days because of these two extra days. ▷ Also in the Enoch/Qumran calendar the actual days needed to count 42 months would be 1274 days, due to the 14 extra days at the end of months 3, 6, 9, and 12, which would exceed the time allotted for the refuge. **12:7** λ see vs. 13-14; μ See Daniˑel 12:1; Jude 1:9; 1 Thess. 4:16; 1 Cor. 15:52; Luke 1.

12:14 In the last days the house of Yehudah and the house of Yisraˑel will be reunited on the mountains of Yisraˑel. A faithful and true remnant who watches for the open door will return to the land and will inherit it (Rev. 3:8; Isa 49:22). And these will be kept out of the tribulation. For them the covenant of old is renewed when Yăhweʜ remembers his covenant. Many who are come lately to a realization of this truth, and many who are also insincere will join them at the last moment, when they come out of the nations barely escaping (and most who try at the very end will fall as the Jews tried to escape too late and perished in the Holocaust), but it will not be to settle in the land of Israel, but to come into the wilderness where the faithful remnant will go, where the rebels, and disloyal who flee for their skins only will be purged out and the untested will be tested and made to pass under the rod, and be brought into the bond of the covenant. (See Ezekiel 20 ; Dan. 11:34-41).

Revelation 13

13 ¹Then he stood on the sand of the seashore. Then I SAW A BEAST COMING UP OUT OF THE SEA,ᵃ having TEN HORNSᵝ and seven heads, and on his horns were ten royal crowns, and on his heads were blasphemous names. ²And the beast which I saw was like a LEOPARD,ᵞ and his feet were like those of a bear, and his mouth like the mouth of a LION.ᵞ Then the serpent gave him his power and his throne and great authority. ³And I saw one of his heads as if it had been getting slain, and his fatal wound was healed. Then the whole earth was amazed and followed after the beast. ⁴Then, they worshiped the serpent, because he gave his authority to the beast. Then they worshiped the beast, saying, "Who is like the beast, and who is able to wage war with him?"ᵤ

⁵Then THERE WAS GIVEN TO HIM A MOUTH SPEAKING ARROGANT WORDS AND BLASPHEMIES.ᵃ Then authority to act for FORTY-TWO MOONSᶿ was given to him. ⁶Then he opened his mouth in blasphemies against the Almighty, to blaspheme his name and his tabernacle, that is, those who dwell in heaven. ⁷Then IT WAS GIVEN TO HIM TO MAKE WAR WITH THE HOLY ONES AND TO GET VICTORY OVER THEM.ᶿ Then, authority over every tribe and people and tongue and nation was given to him. ⁸And they will worship him, all those dwelling upon the earth, whose names will not have been getting written in the Lamb's book of life, who had been getting slain, *which is* from the founding of the world. ⁹If anyone has an ear, let him hear. ¹⁰If anyone is for captivity, to captivity he goes. If anyone kills with the sword, with the sword he must be killed. Here is the perseverance and the faithfulness of the holy ones.

¹¹Then I saw another beast coming up out of the earth. And he had two horns like a lamb. Then he spoke as a serpent. ¹²And he exercises all the authority of the first beast in his presence. Then, he makes the earth and those who dwell in it to worship the first beast, whose fatal wound was healed. ¹³Then, he performs great signs, so that he may even be making fire come down out of heaven to the earth in the presence of men. ¹⁴Then, he deceives those who dwell on the earth

---

13:1 α Dan 7:3, Isa 27:1 **13:1** β Dan 7:7,24 **13:2** γ Dan 7:4-6 **13:4** μ cf. Exo 15:11, Psa 89:8 **13:5** α Dan 7:8, 11, 20 **13:5, 7** θ Dan 7:25 **13:8** See Rev. 17:8. Scholars have long disagreed what "from the founding of the world" refers back to. Clarity is missing or has been deleted from the text by an early scribe. Grammatically, the phrase could refer to either those "whose names will not have been getting written," or the one "who had been getting slain," or "the Lamb's book of life." Scholars commonly pick one of the first two choices, and by their disagreement show that it is unclear what "from the foundation of the world" refers back to. Only the third choice, "the Lamb's book of life" is free from difficulties. ▷ The book of life was "from the founding of the world" (cf. Exo. 32:33). ▷ If the worshipers were the object then it would have to read something like, "whose names will not have been getting written...from the last generations before the end of the age." They were not alive at the founding of the world so denying their names were written then makes no sense. Grammar only permits the text to refer to those who "will worship" the beast, and hence the perfect is future perfect: "will not have." ▷ The second option is also contrary to fact. The Lamb wasn't slain then, and the parallel passage in Rev. 17:8 omits the phrase allowing for only the other two choices. Perhaps that would be an option if we could take the meaning as an equivalent to a declarative Piel, "who had been *declared* to be getting slain," in reference to Gen. 3:15. We would then be forced to either interpret 17:8 differently or to suppose that this option had dropped out of this other text due to scribal omission. Having "from the founding of the world" refer to "the Lamb's book of life" agrees with all the facts as they stand. See textual conjecture at 17:8 to explain how the confusion started. ▷ The apostates, which will have been erased from the book (Rev. 3:5; Exo. 32:33; cf. Yoh. 5:24; Phil. 4:3) appear not to be included among the beast

because of the signs which it was given him to perform in the presence of the beast, telling those who dwell on the earth to make an image to the beast who had the wound of the sword, then had come to life. ¹⁵Then it was granted to him to give breath to the image of the beast, so that the image of the beast shall also have spoken, and shall have caused as many as who may not have worshiped the image of the beast *that* they will have been killed. ¹⁶Then he causes all, the small and the great, and the rich and the poor, and the free men and the slaves, that they will have put a mark on their right hand, or on their forehead, ¹⁷even so that no one will be able to have bought or sold, except the one who has the mark, either the name of the beast, or the number of his name. ¹⁸Here is wisdom. He who has understanding—he must calculate the number of the beast, because the number is that of a man. And his number is six hundred and sixty-six.

14

¹Then I looked, and behold, the Lamb had been standing on Mount Tsĭyon, and with him one hundred and forty-four thousand, having his name, even the name of his Fǎther having been getting written on their foreheads. ²Then I heard a voice from heaven, like the sound of many waters and like the sound of loud thunder, and the voice which I heard was like harpists playing on their harps. ³Then they sang a new-made song before the throne and before the four living creatures and the elders. And no one could learn the song except the one hundred and forty-four thousand who had been getting purchased⸠ from the earth. ⁴These are the ones who have not become *ritually* unclean with women, because they have kept themselves ⸡chaste as virgins. These are the ones who follow the Lamb wherever he may be going. These have been purchased⸠ from among men as first fruits to the Almĭghty and to the Lamb. ⁵And no lie was found in their mouth. They are blameless.

⁶Then I saw another messenger flying in mid-heaven, having the everlasting good news to proclaim to those who live on the earth, and to every nation and tribe and tongue and people. ⁷And he said with a loud voice, "Fear the Almĭghty, and give him glory, because the hour of his judgment has come, and worship

---

worshipers. It appears that the beast will not accept traitors (cf. Rev. 17:17; Amos 9:9-10).

14:3-4 ⸠→ransomed; see 5:9. Often this word is rendered 'redeemed,' but it means 'purchased,' and in context it is a ransom purchase. 'Earth' is put more concisely for the nations mentioned in 5:9. In 5:9 it is explained that the purchase is 'for the Almighty,' and 'from' the nations. The Son is not paying something demanded by the Father, but he is paying the cost exacted by lawlessness to cleanse and separate us from lawlessness. ▷ In all cases where the word 'redeemed' might be used, the correct term is 'ransomed,' because 'redeemed' has lost this meaning in English largely due to commercial use, as in coupons. It may be fair to say that 'redeemed' used to include the meaning of ransom. The term ransom correctly connotes the lawlessness of the captive holder, generally sin. And it is also correct to observe that the legal transactional connotation of redeemed has been theologically transferred to the heretical notion of buying back man from the penalty of sin (the wrath of God) by a coupon (Christ) who pays the penalty. This view is an abomination. See note on 5:9. **14:4** ⸡→virgins; A masculine term for virgins. The text refers to Deut. 23:9-10. Men going to war were required to abstain and keep ritually pure. It is possible that this war will require actual virgins though. See Num. 31:3. Psa. 149:6-9; Psa. 110; Rev. 17:14; 19:14, 19. 1 Sam. 21:5; 2 Sam. 11:11; cf. Lev. 15:18; 1QM 7.3-7. The 140,000 are specially chosen to execute vengeance upon the enemies of Messiah in the end of days.

Revelation 14

him who made the heaven and the earth and sea and springs of waters." ⁸And another messenger, a second one, followed, saying, "Fallen, fallen⁰ *is* Bavel the great, she who has been making all the nations to be drunk with the wine of the passion of her immorality." ⁹And another messenger, a third one, followed them, saying with a loud voice, "If anyone worships the beast and his image, and receives a mark on his forehead or upon his hand, ¹⁰he also will drink of the wine of the wrath of the Almĭghty, which has been getting mixed in full strength in the cup of his anger. And he will be tormented with fire and brimstone in the presence of the holy messengers and in the presence of the Lamb. ¹¹ᵃAnd the smoke of their torment is rising unto ages of ages.ᵖ"

¹¹ᵇ"And those who are worshiping ᵘ the beast and its image have no rest, day and night°, and whoever receives the mark of its name. ¹²In this circumstanceⁿ is the endurance of the holy ones who guard the commandments of the Almĭghty and the faithfulness ofˢ Yĕshua."

¹³Then I heard a voice from heaven, saying, "Write, 'Blessed are the dead

---

14:8 θ The message is prophetic-perfect, but with double meaning. She is spiritually fallen. She will have fallen.

14:11a π "And the smoke that tormented them kept rising unto the ages of the ages." Smoke implies fire: the fire that burned them kept going unto the ages of the ages. A parable: a prison guard wanted to torment a prisoner. "Light me a smoke," he said to a fellow guard and hold the prisoner. He burned the prisoner a few times with the smoke. The guard proceeded to slowly puff the smoke of the prisoner's torment and then placed it in an ash tray still burning. Behold, the smoke of his torment was still burning. ▷ Eternal torment is not taught here. The smoke or fire that tormented them to death continues to rise unto the ages of the ages. The space of time for the torment is relatively brief. See Isa. 34:8-10. "NIGHT-TIME AND DAYTIME IT WILL NOT BE QUENCHED. UNTO THE AGE THE SMOKE WILL RISE. FROM GENERATION TO GENERATION IT WILL BE DESOLATE. FOR THE DURATION OF DURATIONS NONE WILL PASS THROUGH IT." The LXX glosses the Hebrew, "εἰς τὸν αἰῶνα χρόνον...εἰς χρόνον πολύν" = "to the time-age...to much time." Speaking of Edom εἰς τὸν αἰῶνα χρόνον and the smoke of its burning, evidently does not mean forever. ▷ We should also note that "everlasting" is commonly used in English to refer to "everlasting fires," such as coal mine fires that burn continuously, and natural gas fires that never go out. Also torches and other memorial fires that burn continuously are called "eternal fires," which clearly are not eternal in the philosophic sense, nor if anyone was burned by them would they survive very long. ▷ This judgment is not for all men, but only the beast worshipers.

14:11b μ The present progressive takes us back to the time before they were destroyed. Otherwise the text would say 'worshiped' (past tense). Also the mention of 'its image' clues us in on this temporal shift, because the images to the beast are destroyed when their worshipers are destroyed. The Torah requires the destruction of the images (Deut. 7:5; 1 Chron. 14:12; Num. 33:52). **14:11 ρ** Those who worship the beast have no rest either day or night from the slavery they have been subjected to. They will be required to do service to the beast at all times and in all places. A modern example of this servitude may be found in North Korea. There will be no regard for their personal needs or emotions, but they will be enslaved and forced to constantly honor the idols of the beast. They will be subjected to the severest punishments if they fail to please the beast and his enforcers. **14:12 η** Ὧδε = 'Here [is the endurance]....' See BAG, 1957, "b. w. the local mng. [of 'here' weakened, *in this case, at this point, on this occasion, under these circumstances*." The language is expanded here to emphasize contemporaneity with vs. 11. 'Here is the endurance' refers to the period of time when the beast worshippers are still worshiping the beast and its image. This circumstance is one in which the holy ones have to endure (cf. vs. 12), and this fact shows that vs. 12 precedes vs. 11a on the time line. In as much as the faithful only have to endure suffering until the end (cf. Mat. 24:13) when they are rescued, the time frame of vs. 11b is placed in the period when the followers of the beast are still worshiping it and its image, before the firey judgment falls on them. It is during this time that the faithful will suffer, and will have to endure it. ▷ If these facts would be noticed, the argument against eternal torment would be easier. These false teachers would have us believe that the images being worshiped and the worshiping go on into all eternity. **14:12 δ** or 'faithfulness to Yĕshua'; the objective genitive is also possible here.

who die in Yăhweh from now on!'" "Yes," says the Spirit, "that they may be refreshed from their labors, because their deeds follow after them." ¹⁴Then I looked, and behold, a white cloud, and sitting on the cloud was one like a son of man, having a golden crown on his head, and a sharp sickle in his hand. ¹⁵And another messenger came out of the temple, crying out with a loud voice to him who sat on the cloud, "Put in your sickle and reap, because the hour to reap has come, because the harvest of the earth is ripe." ¹⁶Then he who sat on the cloud swung his sickle over the earth. Then the earth was reaped.

¹⁷And another messenger came out of the temple which is in heaven, and he also had a sharp sickle. ¹⁸And another messenger, the one who has power over fire, came out from the altar. Then he called with a loud voice to him who had the sharp sickle, saying, "Put in your sharp sickle, and gather the clusters from the vine of the earth, because her grapes are ripe." ¹⁹Then the messenger swung his sickle to the earth. Then he gathered the clusters from the vine of the earth. Then he threw them into the great wine press of the wrath of the Almighty. ²⁰Then the wine press was trodden outside the city. Then blood came out from the wine press, up to the horses' bridles, for a distance of one thousand six hundred stadia.

15

¹Then I saw another sign in heaven, great and marvelous, seven messengers who had seven plagues, which are the last, because in them the wrath of the Almighty is finished. ²Then I saw, as it were, a sea of glass having been getting mixed with fire, and those getting victory over the beast and over his image and over the number of his name, who had been standing on the sea of glass, holding harps of the Almighty. ³Then they sang the song of Mosheh the servant of the Almighty and the song of the Lamb, saying, "Great and marvelous are your works, Yăhweh the Almighty of Hosts. Righteous and true are your ways, thou King of the nations. ⁴Who will not have feared, O Yăhweh, and glorified your name? For you uniquely are holy, because all the nations will come. Then they will worship before you, because your righteous acts have been revealed."

⁵After these things I looked. Then the temple of the tabernacle of testimony in heaven was opened. ⁶Then the seven messengers who had the seven plagues came out of the temple, who had been getting dressed in linen, clean and bright, and who had been getting sashed around their breasts with golden sashes. ⁷And one of the four living creatures gave to the seven messengers seven golden bowls full of the wrath of the Almighty, who lives for *all* the ages of the ages. ⁸Then the temple was filled with smoke from the glory of the Almighty and from his power. And no one was able to enter the temple until the seven plagues of the seven messengers were finished. ¹⁶·¹ᵃThen I heard a loud voice from the temple, saying to the seven messengers, "Be going and be pouring out the seven bowls of the wrath of the Almighty into the earth."

Revelation 16

16 ¹ᵇThen the first *one* went. Then he ²poured out his bowl into the earth. Then it became a loathsome and malignant sore upon the men who had the mark of the beast and who worshiped his image. ³And the second poured out his bowl into the sea. Then it became blood like that of a dead man, and every living thing in the sea died.

⁴And the third poured out his bowl into the rivers and the springs of waters. Then they became blood. ⁵Then I heard the messenger of the waters saying, "Righteous are you, THE ONE BEING and THE ONE WHO HAS BEEN, Holy One, because you did judge these things, ⁶because they poured out the blood of holy ones and prophets, and you have been giving them blood to drink. They deserve it."

⁷Then I heard the altar saying, "Yes, Yăhweн the Almĭghty, the All-Powerful, true and righteous are your judgments." ⁸And the fourth poured out his bowl upon the sun. Then it was given to it to scorch men with fire. ⁹Then men were scorched with fierce heat. Then they blasphemed the name of the Almĭghty who has the power over these plagues, and they had not been sorry and turned their hearts *from sin*, so as to give him glory. ¹⁰And the fifth poured out his bowl upon the throne of the beast. Then his kingdom had been getting darkened. Then they gnawed their tongues because of pain. ¹¹Then they blasphemed the Almĭghty of heaven because of their pains and their sores, and they had not become sorry and turned their hearts from their deeds. ¹²And the sixth poured out his bowl upon the great river, the ᵠPerat. Then its water was dried up, so that the way will have been prepared for the kings from the east.

¹³Then I saw coming out of the mouth of the serpent and out of the mouth of the beast and out of the mouth of the false prophet, three unclean spirits like frogs, ¹⁴because they are spirits of demons, performing signs, which go out to the kings of the whole world, to gather them together for the war of the great day of the Almĭghty, the All-Powerful. ¹⁵("Behold, I am coming like a thief. Blessed is the one who stays awake and keeps his garments, lest he may be walking about naked—then men may be seeing his shame.")ᶘ ¹⁶Then they gathered them together to the place which in Hebrew is called Har-Megiddo.

¹⁷And the seventh poured out his bowl upon the air. Then a loud voice came out of the temple from the throne, saying, "It has been happening." ¹⁸Then there were flashes of lightning and sounds and peals of thunder. And there was a great earthquake, such as there had not occurred since man came to be upon the earth, so great an earthquake was it, and so mighty. ¹⁹Then the great city was split into three parts, and the cities of the nations fell. And Baᵥel the great was remembered before the Almĭghty, to give her the cup of the wine of his fierce wrath. ²⁰And every island fled away, and the mountains were not found. ²¹And huge hailstones, about one hundred pounds each, came down from heaven upon men. Then men blasphemed the Almĭghty because of the plague of

---

16:12 ψ The Euphrates. **16:15** ζ See 1 Thess. 5. The language is symbolic (see Rev. 1:1). It means staying spiritually awake, and not neglecting obedience to the commandments. The righteous acts of the holy ones are the white garments (cf. Rev. 3:4; 19:8).

the hail, because its plague was extremely severe.

17 ¹Then one of the seven messengers who had the seven bowls came. Then he spoke with me, saying, "Come here, I will show you the judgment of the great harlot who sits on many waters, ²with whom the kings of the earth have been fornicating—then those who dwell on the earth are made drunk with the wine of her fornication."

³Then he carried me away in the Spirit into a wilderness. Then I saw a woman sitting on a scarlet beast, full of blasphemous names, having seven heads and ten horns. ⁴And the woman has been getting dressed in purple and scarlet, and she has been getting adorned with gold and precious stones and pearls, having in her hand a gold cup full of abominations and of the unclean things of her fornication, ⁵and upon her forehead a name has been getting written, "Mystery, Bavel the great, the mother of harlots and of the abominations of the earth." ⁶Then I saw the woman drunk with the blood of the holy ones, and with the blood of the witnesses of Yĕshua. And when I saw her, then I wondered greatly. ⁷Then the messenger said to me, "Why do you wonder? I will tell you the mystery of the woman and of the beast that carries her, which has the seven heads and the ten horns. ⁸The beast that you saw, was, and is not, and is about to come up out of the abyss, and to go to destruction. ⁸ᵇThen those who dwell on the earth will be amazed, *those* whose names that will not have been getting written in the scroll of life, *which is* ⁸ᶜfrom the founding of the world, seeing the beast, in that he was, and is not and will be.

17:8 θ→world: see 13:8. To better explain the connection of "from the founding of the world," the words *which is* are supplied. The scroll of life is the nearest antecedent. Due to the poor transmission history of Revelation and its slow acceptance by Christians tolerating gnostic doctrines (cf. Rev. 2:20-24), I hold out for the possibility that a relative pronoun has been dropped out of the text here and in 13:8: e.g. [ὅ] ἀπὸ καταβολῆς κόσμου, *which is from the foundation of the world.* Considering the editorializing nature of the variants in 13:8 and 17:8 (cf. NA-27), I do not think a change of the text by a scribe by the omission of a single letter is too much to suggest. The text is difficult to interpret as it stands suggesting a change was made by an early scribe who believed the predestination heresy (a key doctrine of gnostics). The theory that all the names of the elect throughout history were written in the book at the foundation of the world is contradicted by Yoh. 5:24; Deut. 8:2; Mat. 24:13; Col. 1:23. Only in this respect would it make sense to reference the names of the non-elect as being omitted at that time since the decision would have been made then. But Yoh. 5:24 makes it quite clear that the decision getting us moved from the book of death to the book of life is holding faithful to Mĕssiah by keeping his commandments (cf. Yoh. 15:10; Rev. 22:14). The names of those who pledge faithfulness to Mĕssiah are written in the book (cf.Phil. 4:3). Also names of traitors will be erased (cf. Rev. 3:5). Mĕssiah warns he will erase the name of the sinner; it is false doctrine to suggest the decision which names would be in the book, and which would not be is an eternal decree or from (or before) the foundation of the world (cf. Gen. 6:6; 22:12); knowledge of perseverance is by keeping the commandments (cf. 1 Yoh. 2:3-4) ▷ The perfect progressive negative statement logically implies the opposite for the faithful. Names will have been getting written in the book of life. And the book dates from the foundation of the world. The Calvinist/ Gnostic wants the book to date from eternity past, and the list of names to be fixed without possible alteration from eternity past. This heresy is rooted in the belief that exhaustive particular foreknowledge is imposed upon the Almighty by necessity in the present (which is denied in Gen. 18:21), and in the belief that the Almighty is the particular cause of all events future (which is denied in Gen. 6:6, 22:12; Deut. 8:2 and other places). The result is a loveless man-made god imprisoned by a mechanical realty fated to be. But future *knowledge* is not ontologically real, but consists only of present plans to implement in the future. Present knowledge is ontologically real and is gained by observation. The two forms of knowledge must be distinguished. Of the set of all future contingencies, the outcome matrix is collectively determined by all sentient beings making choices. When the Almighty

Revelation 17

⁹Here is the mind which has wisdom. The seven heads are seven mountains on which the woman sits⁽ᵃ⁾, ¹⁰and they are seven kings⁽ᵝ⁾. Five have fallen⁽ᵞ⁾, one is⁽ᵟ⁾, the other has not yet come⁽ᵉ⁾; and when he shall have come, it is necessary for him to continue some little while⁽ⁿ⁾. ¹¹And the beast which was and is not⁽ˣ⁾, is himself also an eighth, and is one of the seven, and he goes to destruction⁽ᵠ⁾. ¹²And the ten horns which you saw are ten kings, who have not yet received a kingdom, but they receive authority as kings with the beast for one hour. ¹³These have one purpose and they give their power and authority to the beast.

¹⁴These will wage war against the Lamb, and the Lamb will get victory over them, because he is Adŏnai of adonim and King of kings, and those who are with him are the called ones, and chosen ones, and faithful ones."

¹⁵Then he said to me, "The waters which you saw where the harlot sits, are peoples and multitudes and nations and tongues. ¹⁶And the ten horns which you saw, and the beast, these will hate the harlot. Then they will make her as

---

wants a particular outcome to be ensured, then he uses his power to block all the contingencies which fail to achieve his plan while intervening where necessary. Since he is loving, he is minimalist. Divine causation is limited to make room for the freedom of those he loves so that the actual future outcome is a combination of divine choice and the choices of others. He allows evil moral choices to run a course for a time so that those holding faithful will learn a lesson. For these reasons, "from the foundation of the world" does not mean "before the foundation of the world," and "from the foundation" refers to the opening of the book, and not names being there already. See Rev. 2:24.

17:9 α The seven mountains correspond to seven empires that kept Yisra'el in bondage or oppressed her mightily. These are: I. The Egyptians, II. The Assyrians, III. The Babylonians, IV. The Persians, V. The Greeks, VI. The Romans, and VII. The Islamic Dominion. ▷ Remarkably Alford's commentary has this almost right, "Egypt is fallen, the first head of the beast that persecuted God's people, Ezekiel 29, 30; Nineveh is fallen, the bloody city, Nahum 3:1-34.3.19 ; Babylon is fallen, the great enemy of Israel, Isaiah 21:9 ; Jeremiah 50, 51, al.: Persia is fallen, Daniel 10:13 ; Daniel 11:2 ; Græcia is fallen, Daniel 11:3-27.11.4 . Thus, and as it seems to me thus only, can we do justice to the expression. Nor is any force done thus to βασιλεῖς , but on the contrary it is kept to its strict prophetic import, and to the analogy of that portion of prophecy which is here especially in view. For in Dan 7:17 we read these great beasts which are four are four kings, מלכין ; not βασιλεῖαι , as LXX and Theodotion), the one is (the Roman), the other (required to complete the seven) is not yet come." But Alford did not recognize the seventh dominion, which cannot be the Byzantines. **17:10 β** Representative kings are I. Pharaoh Sheshi, II. Tiglath-Pileser, III. Belshazzar, IV. Darius the Mede, V. Antiochus IV, VI. Emperor Domitian, and VII. Sultan Mehmed II.

17:10 γ Egypt, Assyria, Babylon, Persia, *and* Greece. **17:10 δ** Rome, at the time of the Revelation. **17:10 ζ** The Muhammadans. **17:10 η** ὀλίγον αὐτὸν δεῖ μεῖναι Alford's comment: "The ὀλίγον, as in ref. 1 Pet. 1:6, gives the idea of some space not assigned, but vaguely thus stated as "some little time." The idea given is rather that of duration than of non-duration. Herodotus, iv. 81, says of the river Exampæus, τοῦ καὶ ὀλίγον τι πρότερον τούτων μνήμην εἴχον, but it was twenty-nine chapters back. See for the usage of this book itself, ch. 2:14, 3:4; not 12:12, where the context decides ὀλίγον to be emphatic. Here, the stress is on δεῖ μεῖναι, and not on ὀλίγον: on the fact of some endurance, not on its being but short." ▷ Thus the prophecy means that this seventh empire will remain for some space, which is to say a long time, and that is indeed the case, because the Islamic Dominion has remained the longest. **17:11 χ** 'It was' implies it was one of the five fallen empires. The obvious choice is Babylon, because it was the Babyonian hegemony that was cut short at 66 1/2 years. 'Is not' means that city and empire is buried in the sands of Mesopotamia until the time of its restoration, which the late king of Iraq tried to restore, but he was hunted down and slain. I believe the wounding of the beast to have a double reference. It was wounded when Babylon fell to Persia, but it will arise again after the Islamic Dominion, and be dramatically wounded again, and then after the world rejects the kingdom of the Almighty, the Beast will receive a miraculous recovery and the whole world will be deceived by him. **17:11 φ** It is a clue here that the destruction of the beast is mentioned before the 10 kings, because this beast is dealt a fatal wound that prevents it from arising out of its time. In as much as the goal of this beast is to prevent the establishment of the kingdom of the Almighty, it arises now to forstall the restoration of all Yisra'el. But this beast will be dealt a fatal wound (cf. Isa. 49:5-23; 49:24-26), and

one who has been getting desolated and naked, and will eat her flesh and will burn her up with fire. ¹⁷For the Almĭghty has put it in their hearts to execute his purpose by having a common purpose, and by giving their kingdom to the beast, until the words of the Almĭghty should be fulfilled. ¹⁸And the woman whom you saw is the great city, which reigns over the kings of the earth."

18

¹After these things I saw another messenger coming down from heaven, having great authority, and the earth was illumined with his glory. ²Then he cried out with a mighty voice, saying, "Fallen! Fallen *will be* Baveḻ the great! And she will have become a dwelling place of demons and a prison of every unclean spirit, and a prison of every unclean bird, which has been getting hated. ³For all the nations have and will have been drinking of the wine of the passion of her fornication, and the kings of the earth fornicate̞ with her, and the merchants of the earth become̞ rich by the wealth of her sensuality."

⁴Then I heard another voice from heaven, saying, "Come out of her, my people, that you will not have participated in her sins and that you may not have received of her plagues, ⁵because her sins have piled up as high as heaven, and the Almĭghty will have remembered her iniquities. ⁶Pay her back even as she has paid, and give back to her double according to her deeds. In the cup which she has mixed, mix twice as much for her. ⁷To the degree that she has glorified herself and has lived sensuously, to the same degree give her torment and mourning, because she says in her heart, 'I SIT AS A QUEEN AND I AM NOT A WIDOW, AND NO, I SHALL NOT HAVE SEEN MOURNING.' ⁸For this reason in one day her plagues will come, pestilence and mourning and famine, and she will be burned up with fire, because Yăhweḥ Almĭghty who judges her is strong.

⁹"Then the kings of the earth, who fornicated and lived sensuously with her, will weep and lament over her when they may be seeing the smoke of her burning, ¹⁰having been standing at a distance because of the fear of her torment, saying, 'Woe, woe, the great city, Baveḻ, the strong city! For in one hour your judgment has come.'

¹¹"And the merchants of the earth weep. Then they mourn over her, because no one buys their cargoes any more, ¹²cargoes of gold and silver and precious stones and pearls and fine linen and purple and silk and scarlet, and every kind of citron wood and every article of ivory and every article made from very costly wood and bronze and iron and marble, ¹³and cinnamon and spice and incense and perfume and frankincense and wine and olive oil and fine flour and wheat and cattle and sheep, and cargoes of horses and chariots and slaves and human lives. ¹⁴And the fruit you long for has gone from you, and all things that were luxurious and splendid have passed away from you, and men will no longer find them.

¹⁵"The merchants of these things, who became rich from her, will stand at a distance because of the fear of her torment, weeping and mourning, ¹⁶saying,

---

will only return with its wound healed after all the tribes are restored to Yisra'el in the time of Yisra'el's | final testing. Because Yisra'el will be restored in the third day, i.e. the third milennium. **18:7** ç Isa 47:7.

'Woe, woe, the great city, she who has been getting dressed in fine linen and purple and scarlet, and has been getting adorned with gold and precious stones and pearls, ¹⁷because in one hour such great wealth has been laid waste!'

¹⁷ᵇ"And every ship-master and every passenger and sailor, and as many as make their living by the sea, stood at a distance. ¹⁸Then they were crying out as they saw the smoke of her burning, saying, 'What city is like the great city?' ¹⁹Then they threw dust on their heads. Then they were crying out, weeping and mourning, saying, 'Woe, woe, the great city, in which all who had ships at sea became rich by her wealth, because in one hour she has been laid waste!' ²⁰Be rejoicing over her, O heaven, and you holy ones, and emissaries, and prophets, because the Almighty has pronouwnced judgment for you against her."

²¹Then a strong messenger took up a stone like a great millstone. Then he threw it into the sea, saying, "Thus will Bavel, the great city, be thrown down with violence, and no, she shall not have been found any longer. ²²And the sound of harpists and musicians and flute-players and trumpeters, no, they shall not have been heard in you any longer, and no craftsman of any craft shall have been found in you any longer, and the sound of a mill, no, it shall not have been heard in you any longer, ²³and the light of a lamp, no, it shall not have shone in you any longer, and the voice of the bridegroom and bride, no they shall not have

---

18:23 φ ἐν τῇ φαρμακείᾳ σου; φαρμακεία = *pharmakeia*, e.g. **medicine**. Literally, the administering of drug poisons. Previous usage is literal: *Gal. 5:20; Rev. 9:21*, and subsequent usage *Rev. 21:8; 22:15*. The text can also be read, "with your drugging" or "into your drugging" implying also that Babylon was setting LXX an example and was herself on drugs also. See LXX, MT: Isa. 47:9, 12; 2 Chron. 33:6; 2 Kings 9:22; 2 Mac. 10:13; Deu. 18:10; Exo. 7:11, 22; 22:18. Psa. 57:58; 58:5; Mal. 3:5; Dan. 2:2; Jer. 27:9. ▷ But in this case a metaphorical usage also appears. One can say the nations are drugged by lies. The word 'venumry,' 'poisoning,' or 'medicine' will also bring out the metaphoric usage. The Greek word is equivalent to the Latin *veneficium*, which means **poisoning, magic, sorcery, drug-making**, and *venenum* means **remedy, poison, magic drug**, or **abortive**, equivalent to φαρμακον. Both the Greek and Latin terms had a negative or dangerous usage and a usage that was considered beneficial, such as in **remedy** or **cure**, but this usage is called metaphoric in the Greek Lexicons and not assigned the first definition. LSJ, "φαρμακεία A. use of drugs, esp. of *purgatives, use of any kind of drugs, potions* or *spells*. 2. *poisoning* or *witchcraft*. II. metap. *remedy*." LSJ "φαρμακον A. drug, whether healing or noxious. 2. healing remedy, medicine. 3. enchanted potion, philtre, charm, spell. 4. poison. 5. lye." LSJ "φαρμακος A. poisoner, sorcerer, magician." LSJ "φαρμακευω A. administer a drug or medicine. 2. practice enchantments, practice sorcery. II. purge... by emetic [vomiting agent]. 2. *drug a person, give him a poisonous* or *stupefying drug*." The Greek and Latin terms each cover **poisoning, medicine**, and **sor-** **cery** usages. What seems to be the case is that the English word sorcery never meant poisoning by means of drugs, but there is an attempt to expand the English word sorcery to include all that the Greek and Latin do by those studying the drug connections to Babylon. The Old Greek (LXX) will bear out the usages, and the contexts do not contradict the use of some chemical agent to produce a result, such as the Egyptian priests may have used to subdue the serpents they used as rods, or to turn water into blood, or to lure frogs, but we cannot rule out non scientific means such as using evil spirits. Inflections of the Greek φαρμακεία stand next to the Hebrew בְּכֶשֶׁף in the LXX, which is generally translated 'sorcery,' but it is likely this English definition is deficient because the LXX translators clearly understood the word to mean drugs, or potions with drugs. It is possible the inclusion of drugs in the Hebrew definition has simply been lost. Whether the LXX translators be charged with error in choosing the term or not, the Greek term is not affected, so the usage here in Revelation in the literal sense refers to the use of medicines or harmful drugs or as is increasingly clear in this age *harmful medicine*. In ancient Rome, physicians were urged to make their own remedies, increasingly so, because the drug market was corrupted over time so that chances are if one trusted it, one could get poisoned or poison their patients. The drug merchants only cared about the money they made, and in those times licit and illicit substances were found in the same markets often with no disclosure of the harm they could cause, which is also increasingly so today! As I write this, a poisonous potion is being pushed on the nations by a union of evil commercial and political

been heard in you any longer, because your merchants had been the oligarchs of the earth, because all the nations have been led astray by your drugging⁰. ²⁴And in her will have been found the blood of prophets and of holy ones and of all who have been getting slain on the earth."

19

¹After these things I heard, as it were, a loud voice of a great multitude in heaven, saying, "Hallelu Yah! Deliverance and glory and power belong to our Almĭghty, ²BECAUSE HIS JUDGMENTS ARE TRUE AND RIGHTEOUS⁰, because he has judged the great harlot who was corrupting the earth with her immorality, and HE HAS AVENGED THE BLOOD OF HIS SERVANTS ON HER.ᵝ" ³And a second time they had been saying, "Hallelu Yah! And HER SMOKE RISES UP INTO THE AGES OF THE AGES.ᵠ"

⁴Then the twenty-four elders and the four living creatures fell down and had worshiped the Almĭghty who sits on the throne, saying, "Amen. Hallelu Yah!"

⁵And a voice came from the throne, saying, "Be praising our Almĭghty, all you his servants, you who fear him, the small and the great."

⁶Then I heard, as it were, the voice of a great multitude and as the sound of many waters and as the sound of mighty peals of thunder, saying, "Hallelu Yah! Because Yăhweн our Almĭghty, the All Powerful One, reigns.

⁷"May we be rejoicing and may we be glad. And we will give the glory to him, because the marriage of the Lamb has come and his bride has made herself ready." ⁸And it was given to her, that she shall have gotten herself dressed in fine linen, pure bright, because the fine linen is the righteous acts of the holy ones.ᵘ

⁹Then he says to me, "Write, 'Blessed are those who have and will have been getting invited to the marriage supper of the Lamb.'" Then he says to me, "These are true words of the Almĭghty." ¹⁰Then I fell at his feet to worship him. Then he says to me, "Be seeing you don't! I am a fellow servant of yours and your brothers who hold the testimony of Yĕshua. Worship the Almĭghty, because the testimony of Yĕshua is the spirit of prophecy."

¹¹Then I saw heaven having been getting opened. And behold, a white horse, and he who sat upon it is called faithful and true. And with justice he judges and wages war. ¹²And his eyes are a ᵅflame of fire, and upon his head are many royal crowns. And he is having a name, which has been getting written, which no one has been knowing except himself. ¹³And he has been getting dressed with a robe which has been getting immersedᵝ in blood, and his name has been getting called the Word of the Almĭghty. ¹⁴And the armies which are in heaven, who had been getting dressed in fine linen, white and clean, were following him on white horses. ¹⁵And from his mouth comes a sharp sword, so that with it he will have struck down the nations. And he will shepherd them with a rod of iron. And he treads the wine press of the fierce wrath of the Almĭghty, the All Powerful One.

---

powers in order to gain absolute power and control. Thus everything is being done in the spirit of Babylon and the medicinal potion is quite literal.

19:2 α Psa 19:9 **19:2** β Deu 32:43 **19:3** ψ Isa 34:10. **19:8** μ Isa 61:10. **19:12** α Dan 10:6 **19:13** β Isa 34:6.

Revelation 20

¹⁶Then on his robe, even on his thigh he has a name, which has been getting written, "King of kings, and Adŏnai of adonim."

¹⁷Then I saw a messenger, who had been standing in the sun, and he cried out with a loud voice, saying to all the birds which fly in mid-heaven, "Come, assemble for the great supper of the Almĭghty, ¹⁸in order that you may eat the flesh of kings and the flesh of commanders and the flesh of mighty men and the flesh of horses and of those who sit on them and the flesh of all men, besides free men also slaves, even small and great." ¹⁹Then I saw the beast and the kings of the earth and their armies, who had been getting assembled to make war against him who sat upon the horse, and against his army.

²⁰Then the beast was seized, and with him the false prophet who performed the signs in his presence, by which he deceived those who had received the mark of the beast and those who worshiped his image. These two were thrown alive into the lake of fire which burns with brimstone. ²¹And the rest were killed with the sword which came from the mouth of him who sat upon the horse, and all the birds were filled with their flesh.

20 ¹Then I saw a messenger coming down from heaven, having the key of the abyss and a great chain in his hand. ²Then he laid hold of the serpent, the serpent of old, who is the Slanderer, (that is, Satan). Then he bound him for a thousand years. ³Then he threw him into the abyss. Then he shut it. Then he sealed it over him, so that he will not have deceived the nations any longer, until the thousand years may have been completed. After these things he must be released for a short time.

⁴Then I saw thrones. Then they sat upon them, and judgment was given to them. And I saw the souls of those who had been getting beheaded because of the testimony of Yĕshua and because of the word of the Almĭghty, and those who had not worshiped the beast or his image, and had not received the mark upon their forehead and upon their hand. And they had come to life. Then they reigned with the Anŏinted for a thousand years.

⁵The rest of the dead lived not again until the thousand years shall have been completed. This is the first resurrection. ⁶Blessed and holy is the one who has a part in the first resurrection. Over these the second death has no power, but they will be priests of the Almĭghty and of the Anŏinted and they will reign with him for a thousand years.

⁷And when the thousand years shall have been completed, Satan will be released from his prison. ⁸Then he will go out to deceive the nations which are in the four corners of the earth, Gog and Magog, to gather them together for the war. The number of them is like the sand of the seashore. ⁹Then they went up on the broad plain of the earth. Then they surrounded the camp of the holy ones and the city, which has been getting loved. Then fire came down from heaven, and it devoured them. ¹⁰And the Slanderer who deceived them was thrown into the lake of fire and brimstone, where the beast and the false prophet are also.

Then they will be tormented day and night for the ages of the ages.

¹¹Then I saw a great white throne and him who sat upon it, from whose presence earth and heaven fled away, and no place was found for them. ¹²Then I saw the dead, the great and the small, who had been standing before the throne, and scrolls were opened. And another scroll was opened, which is the scroll of life. Then the dead were judged from the things which had been getting written in the scrolls, according to their deeds.

¹³When the sea gave up the dead which were in it, and death and the grave gave up the dead which were in them, then they were judged, every one of them according to their deeds. ¹⁴Then death and the grave were thrown into the lake of fire. (This is the second death, the lake of fire. ¹⁵And if anyone's name will not have been found having been getting written in the scroll of life, he will have been thrown into the lake of fire.)

20:10 μ Note that this lengthly torment is applied only to the devil and his minions. There is no mention of men here, but only the false prophet. The beast and the false prophet were consigned 'alive' to the lake of fire at the beginning of the thousand years. See Rev. 19:20. They are still being tormented there at the end of the thousand years. All the lost of mankind are sent to the lake of fire after they are raised to be judged, but nothing is said about them being alive there or tormented. The justice of the Almighty does not require that, because his punitive justice is only an expression of the measure of his wrath, and not a positive compensation for His irreparable loss. Judicial punishment cannot restore loss. It is chiefly to deter and limit the extent evil men are allowed to harm creation by removing them. Evil is tolerated and suffered when there are some who might repent, but when the season of repentance is ended then evil is removed. The lake of fire is divine vengeance on the devil and his messengers, but for men the wrath must be somewhat lesser, and the fire is a means of disposing of the condemned.

20:15 ξ Or, "And if anyone's name is not found having been getting written in the scroll of life, he is thrown into the lake of fire," (English gnomic) or "And if anyone's name has not been found having been getting written in the scroll of life, he has been thrown into the lake of fire" (Hebrew gnomic). The warning in vs. 15 should be taken in a wider temporal sense. The scroll of life was also checked before the thousand years at the resurrection of the righteous. So I have marked it off in (). It will also be checked at the resurrection of the unrighteous as a formality. ▷ This last judgment is a formality because the season of repentance is up until the first death. It appears not all of the judged will be lawless rebels, but some will be relatively innocent victims, and many will simply have been deceived. The sins of Satan and Adam can be blamed for this, and also the sins of all who sinned as a result of their sins. That there is a last judgment for MANY is a result of divine suffering sin in the hope that MANY will repent before their end, because it is written, "For I am Yähweh your Almighty, the holy one of Yisra'el, your deliverer. I will have given your ransom. Mitsrayim, Cush, and Seva instead of you. Because you will have been precious in my eyes you have been honored, and I will have loved you, and I will have given men instead of you, and people instead of your soul" (Isa. 43:3-4). ▷ By no means am I suggesting a transfer of condemnation from Adam, but we can look back for causes. The Most High would have desired that all be saved, but such is the nature of sin that it destroys both life and opportunity. ▷ We may inquire about the most innocent of victims, but we should keep in mind that every rebel and every great sinner was once an innocent victim, and that sin is not destructive because the Most High made it judicially destructive, but because it IS destructive by nature, and judicial intervention is to put an end to it. If the Most High seeks to save the rebel, then there is a cost for this, a cost of suffering what the rebel will do while waiting for his repentance. If the Most High seeks to save the rebel then the more innocent may be his ransom. So you see the cost cannot be eliminated. So which way will one have it? Destroy the wicked now to prevent the innocent from ever existing and being destroyed by their sin, or to give the wicked a chance to repent, and then have their sin visited upon the following generations, and then they have to have their existence ended? ▷ Would it be fair for the Most High to take some of the most innocent souls and to recreate them in a better circumstance? I'm not sure of that when most every less innocent sinner is also a victim. But it isn't up to us to draw the line and place the limits and decide the final judgment. It may be that to make exceptions is itself a logical contagion.

21 ¹Then I saw a new-made⁰ heaven and a new-made earth, because the first⁰ heaven and the first earth passed away, and there was no longer any sea. ²And I saw the holy city, new-made Yerushalayim, coming down out of heaven from the Almĭghty, having been getting ready as a bride who had been getting adorned for her husband. ³Then I heard a loud voice from the throne, saying, "Behold, the tabernacle of the Almĭghty is among men.⁰ Then he will tabernacle with them. Then they will be his people. Then the Almĭghty himself will be among them, *as* their Almĭghty. ⁴Then he will wipe away every⁰ tear from their eyes. And there will no longer be any death.⁰ There will no longer be any mourning, or crying, or pain, because the first things will have passed away."

⁵Then he who sits on the throne said, "Behold, I am making all things new-made." Then he says, "Write, for these words are faithful and true." ⁶Then he said to me, "It has been happening! I am the Aleph and the Tau, the beginning and the end. I will give to the one who thirsts from the spring of the water of life freely.⁰ ⁷He who is getting victory will inherit these things. Then I will be his Almĭghty and he will be my son. ⁸But for the cowardly and unfaithful and the ones having been becoming abominable and murderers and immoral persons and drug traffickers and idolaters and all liars, their part will be in the lake that burns with fire and brimstone, which is the second death."

⁹Then one of the seven messengers who had the seven bowls full of the seven last plagues, came. Then he spoke with me, saying, "Come here, I will show you the bride, the wife of the Lamb."

¹⁰Then he carried me away in the Spĭrit to a great and high mountain, and showed me the holy city,⁰ Yerushalayim, coming down out of heaven from the Almĭghty, ¹¹having the glory of the Almĭghty. Her⁰ brilliance was like a very costly stone, as a stone of crystal-clear jasper. ¹²It had a great and high wall, with twelve gates, and at the gates twelve messengers. And names had been getting engraved on them, which are those of the twelve tribes of the sons of Yisra'el. ¹³There were three gates on the east and three gates on the north and three gates on the south and three gates on the west.⁰ ¹⁴And the wall of the city had twelve foundation stones, and on them were the twelve names of the twelve emissaries of the Lamb.

¹⁵And the one speaking with me was having a gold measuring rod, so that he may measure the city, and its gates and its wall. ¹⁶And the city is laid out as a square, and its length is as great as the width. Then he measured the city with the rod, twelve thousand stadia. Its length and width and height are equal. ¹⁷Then he measured its wall, one hundred and forty-four cubits, according to human measurements, which are also a messenger's measurements. ¹⁸And the material of the wall was jasper. And the city was pure gold, like clear glass. ¹⁹The foundation stones of the city wall had been getting adorned with ev-

---

21:1 α Isa 65:17; 66:22; 2Pet 3:13; ρ Rev 20:11 | λ Isa 55:1 **21:10** β Eze 40:2 **21:11** α Isa 54:11 **21:3** δ Eze 37:27. **21:4** β Isa 65:19 θ Isa 25:8 **21:6** | **21:13** μ Eze 48:31

ery kind of precious stone.ᵖ The first foundation stone was jasper, the second, sapphire, the third, chalcedony, the fourth, emerald, ²⁰the fifth, sardonyx, the sixth, sardius, the seventh, chrysolite, the eighth, beryl, the ninth, topaz, the tenth, chrysoprase, the eleventh, jacinth, and the twelfth, amethyst. ²¹And the twelve gates were twelve pearls. Each one of the gates was a single pearl. And the street of the city was pure gold, like transparent glass.

²²And I saw no temple in it, because Yăhwᴇн Almĭghty, the All-Powerful, and the Lamb, is its temple. ²³And the city has no need of the sun or of the moon, that they should shine upon it, because the glory of the Almĭghty will have illumined it, even its lamp is the Lamb.

²⁴When the nations will walk by its light, also the kings of the earth will bring their glory into it. ²⁵And its gates, no, they shall not have been shut at *the* end of the day, because there will be no night there. ²⁶Then they will bring the glory and the honor of the nations into it⁶. ²⁷And no, nothing⁹ sharing defilement shall have entered into it, or those practicing abomination or falsehood, except those having been getting written in the Lamb's scroll of life.

22

¹Then he showed me a river of the WATER OF LIFEᵅ, clear as crystal, coming from the throne of the Almĭghty, even of the Lamb, ²in the middle of its broad avenue. AND ON THE NEAR SIDE AND ALSO THE FAR SIDE OF THE RIVER, TREES OF LIFEᵞ, PRODUCING TWELVE FRUITS, YIELDING ITS FRUIT ACCORDING TO EACH NEW MOON. AND THE LEAVES OF THE TREES ARE FOR THE HEALING OF THE NATIONS⁶. ³AND THERE WILL NO LONGER BE ANY CURSEᵉ. And the throneᵞ of the Almĭghty, even of the Lamb will be in it, and his servants will serve him. ⁴Thenᵘ they will see his face, and his ᶿname will be on their foreheads. ⁵And there will no longer be any night. And they will not have need of the light of a lamp and the light of the sun, because Yăhwᴇн the Almĭghty will shine upon them. Then they will reign for *all* the ages of the ages.

⁶Then he said to me, "These words are faithful and true. And Yăhwᴇн, the Almĭghty of the ᵋholy prophets, sent his Messengerᶿ to show to his servants what must happen quickly."

The messenger stops speaking, and Messiah interjects:

⁷ "And behold, I am going to come quickly. Blessed is he who heeds the words

---

21:21 ρ Isa 54:11, 12; **21:23** Isa 60:19-20 **21:26** β Isa 60:11 **21:27** θ Isa 52:1, Eze 44:9.

22:1 α Zech 14:8, Eze 47:1f, Psa 46:4 **22:2** β Eze 47:12: וְעַל־הַנַּחַל יַעֲלֶה עַל־שְׂפָתוֹ מִזֶּה וּמִזֶּה כָל־עֵץ־מַאֲכָל לֹא־יִבּוֹל עָלֵהוּ וְלֹא־יִתֹּם פִּרְיוֹ לָחֳדָשָׁיו יְבַכֵּר כִּי מֵימָיו מִן־הַמִּקְדָּשׁ הֵמָּה יוֹצְאִים וְהָיוּ פִרְיוֹ לְמַאֲכָל וְעָלֵהוּ לִתְרוּפָה. **22:2** γ Gen 2:9 **22:3** δ Zech 14:11: וְחֵרֶם לֹא יִהְיֶה־עוֹד. **22:3** λ Zech 14:9, 16 **22:4** μ Psa 17:15, Job 19:26, Exo 24:10-11, **22:4** θ Eze 9:4, Num 6:27 **22:5** α Isa 24:23, 60:19, Eze 48:35; **22:6** ξ→prophets: Other manuscripts read "spirits of the prophets," which I guess is influenced by 1Cor. 14:32 with the intent to indicate NT prophets as opposed to OT prophets. See Scrivener 1894 text. **22:6** θ Gen 48:16, Isa 48:16, 63:9, Gen 16:13; **22:7** φ The Messiah himself makes an audible interjection. Messiah interrupts, but Yohanan was mistaken about where his voice came from and supposed the messenger had

Revelation 22

of the prophecy of this scroll⸰."

Yoḥanan misidentifies who is speaking:

⁸And I, Yoḥanan, am the one who heard and saw these things. And when I heard, and I had seen, I fell down to worship at the feet of the messenger who showed me these things. ⁹Then he says to me, "Be seeing that you do not! I am a fellow servant of yours and of your brothers the prophets and of those who heed the words of this scroll. Worship the Almĭghty."

Mĕssiah resumes his closing words:

¹⁰Then he says to me, "You shall not have sealed up the words of the prophecy of this scroll⸲ᵟ as the appointed season is near. ¹¹The one who does wrong, must still do wrong. And the one who is filthy, must still be filthy. And the one who is righteous, must still practice righteousness. And the one who is holy, must still be holy. ¹²Behold, I am going to come quickly, and my reward is with me, TO RENDER TO EVERY MAN ACCORDING TO WHAT HE HAS DONEᵠ. ¹³I am the Aleph and the Tav, THE FIRST AND THE LAST, the beginning and the end. ¹⁴Blessed are those ᵏkeeping his commandments, wherein it will be their rightᵖ to eat of the tree of life, and they shall have entered by the gates into the city. ¹⁵Left out are the dogs and the drug traffickers and the fornicators and the murderers and the idolaters, and everyone who loves and practices lying. ¹⁶I, Yĕshua, have sent my messenger to testify to you these things for the assemblies. I am the rootᵅ and the kindred of David, the bright dawnᶿ star. ¹⁷And the Spĭrit and the bride say, 'Be coming.' And let the one listening say, 'Be coming.' And let the one who is thirsting be coming. Let the one desiring take the water of life freelyᵖ. ¹⁸I testify to everyone hearing the words of the prophecy of this scroll: if anyone may have added to them, the Almĭghty will add to him the plagues which have been getting written in this scroll, ¹⁹and if anyone may have taken away from the words of the scroll of this prophecy, the Almĭghty will take away his part from the tree of life and from the holy city, which have been getting written in this scroll." ²⁰He who testifies to these things says, "Yes, I am going to come ᵖquickly."

Yoḥanan's closing words:

²⁰ᵇAmen. Be coming, Adŏnai Yĕshua.
²¹The loving-kindness of Adŏnai Yĕshua be with all. Amen.

---

spoken to him. This resulted in the misunderstanding in vs. 8-9. The messenger is offended and drops off speaking. Mĕssiah speaks in vs. 10-20. Yoḥanan writes 20b-21. **22:10** δ Dan 12:4; **22:12** ψ Psa 62:12, Rom 2:6; **22:11** Ezek 3:27, Dan 12:10; **22:13** Isa 41:4, 44:6, 48:12; **22:14** λ→commandments. This is the earliest attested reading, found in Tertullian (ca AD 220) and Cyprian (ca AD 258 and possibly a bit earlier). The other reading "washing their robes" is found earliest in a Sahidic translation dating no earlier than AD 250). The cursive ending of Vaticanus (B, 4th century) reads "keeping his commandments." Permission to eat from the tree of life is previously mentioned in Rev. 2:4-7 in conjunction with overcoming the heresy of the assembly of Ephesus. This heresy was the abandonment of their first love, which is faithfulness to the Almĭghty through keeping his commandments (cf. Exo. 20:6). See also Mat. 19:17; Rom. 2:6-7. On the lower probability that "washing their robes" is correct, the meaning can only be the same as "keeping his commandments" (cf. Rev. 19:8). Besides being of later date, and being disconfirmed

by Rev. 2:4-7, the suspicion is great that the text was deliberately altered to the washing figure of speech so that it could be more easily reinterpreted away from keeping the commandments. The Sahidic text is especially under this suspicion because Egypt was hotbed of early gnostic activity.

22:14 ρ Rev 2:7 **22:16** α Isa 11:1 **22:16** θ Zech 6:12, Mat 2:2, Rev 2:28; **22:17** ρ Isa 55:1; cf. 21:6. Isa. 55:1 explains, "Buy without money" to those having no money. So there is a currency for the waters of life. The currency is repentence (cf. Rev. 3:18-19; Lev. 18:5; Hab. 2:4). The money that those thirsting for righteousness do not have is merit to pay for demerit. Isa. 55:7, "Let the wicked leave his way, and a man of iniquity his intentions. And let him return to Yahweh. And he will have mercy on him, and unto our Almighty, because he will abundantly forgive." **22:19** Deu 4:2, 12:32 **22:20** ρ Hab 2:3. **22:20** ρ The futuristic use of the present. See Wallace. When these events begin to unfold then his coming is not far off. See 22:7, 12. It appears that ἐξάπινα (Isa. 48:3), "SUDDENLY" is used similarly to ταχύ here. Cf. 1Thess. 5:2-4. See Strong's: "(by surprise) suddenly." ▷ "FOR THE VISION IS STILL FOR THE APPOINTED TIME, AND HE WILL BREATHE AT THE END, AND HE WILL NOT BE FALSE. IF HE DELAYS HIMSELF, WAIT FOR HIM. FOR COMING HE WILL COME: HE WILL NOT BE TOO LATE" (Hab. 2:3). ▷ See 2 Peter 3:1-12. The calculus of the second coming is in the infinite wisdom of the Almighty balanced between his mercy, his justice, the spread of repentance and the spread of sin. When Daniel's 70th 7 begins to unfold, the promise is an assurance, despite all the evil of the rebellion, that a soon and quick coming, relative to the ages leading up to it, is assured. To claim that "soon," meant in a human sense, is not soon enough, or that the writer was mistaken, or that the text may not mean quickly when these things *begin* to happen, is externally an attack on this testimony, and internally to take the writer for an idiot unfamiliar with the divine perspective on *soon* as exposited by Peter.

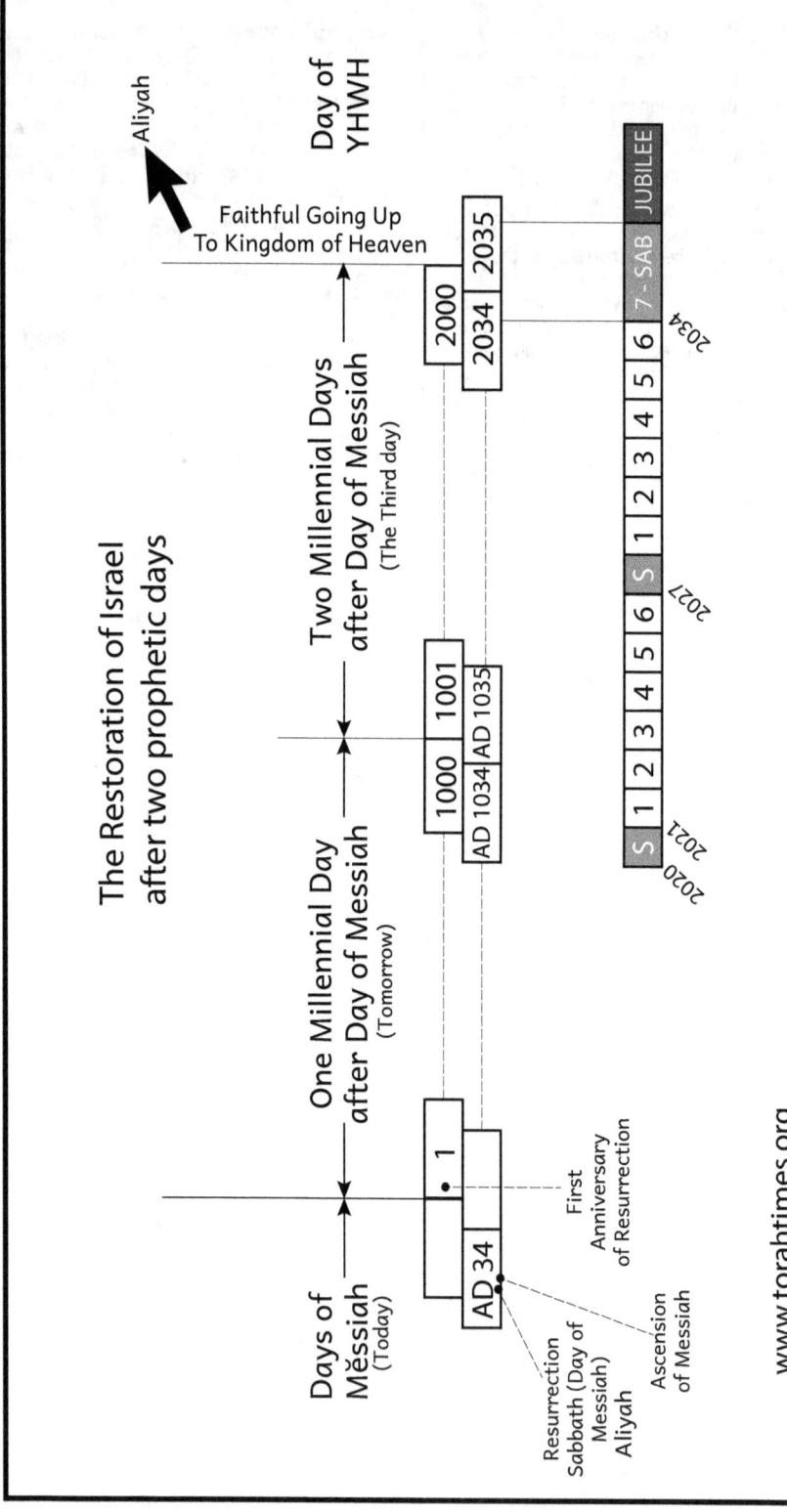

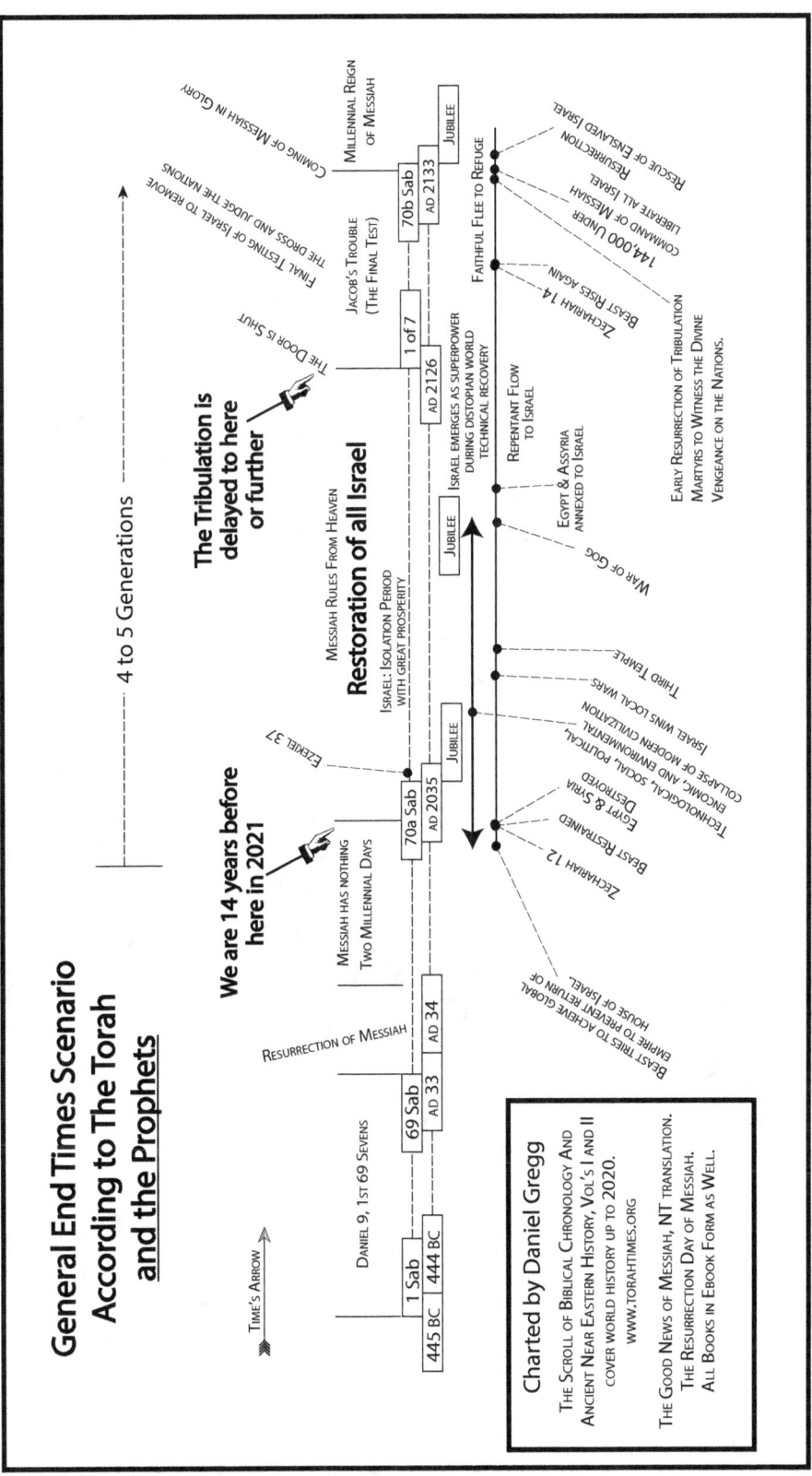

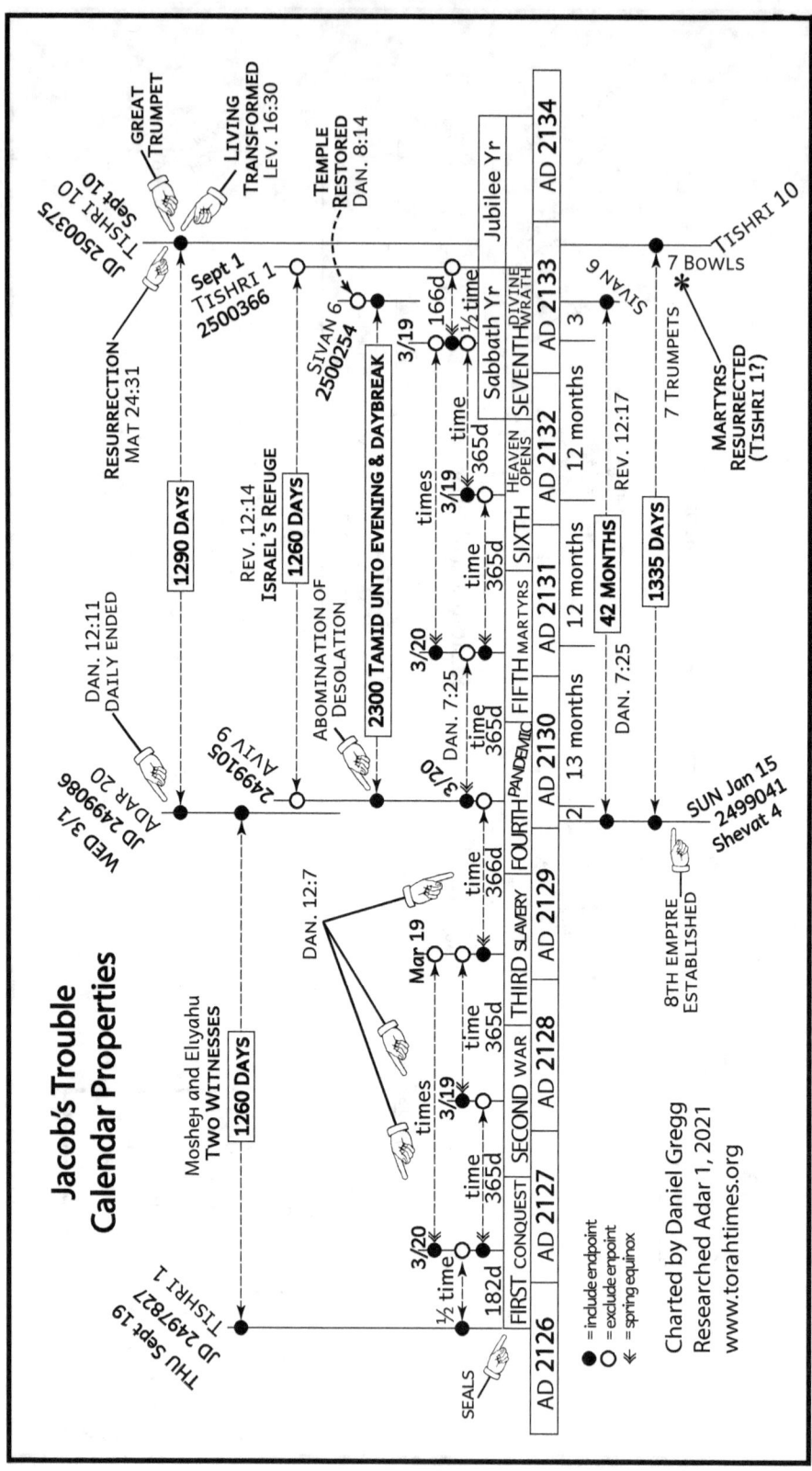

Appendices

Appendix Ia: Names of Moons

¹The first day of the year, called ʸ*tequfat ha-shanah*, is the first day on which the apparent sun first sets due west (or just north of west) at the end of winter. ²There are 12 or 13 new moons in a year. ³Each new moon occurs with a sighting of the first light of a new moon by naked eye made in Israel[χ]. ⁴If the new moon following the 12th new moon in a year has all of the 15th day thereafter before the beginning day of the year, then it becomes the 13th new moon.

⁵But if the 15th day is even partly after the beginning day of the year, then it is the first month[ξ]. The new moons are as follows, most of the names being of Babylonian origin, except where noted as pre-exilic:

⁶·¹The first new moon was called *Aviv*, (אָבִיב, green ears) before the exile, and *Nisan*, (נִיסָן) flowers, from *nitsan* (נִיצָן) after the exile. Day 15 and day 21 are annual Şabbaths.

⁶·²The second moon is called *Iyyar* (אִיָּר, rosette, blossom). In this month is the second Passover. Before the exile *Ziv* (זִו) from זָהיו, *splendour*).

⁶·³The third moon is called *Sivan* (סִיוָן, season, time). Shavu'ot, falls on the 6th, 7th, or 8th day of this month, counted 50 days starting on Aviv 16.

⁶·⁴The fourth moon is not named in Scripture; the Rabbis call it Tammuz. We call it *Shoshannim* (שׁוֹשַׁנִּים, lilies).

⁶·⁵The fifth moon is called Av (אָב, father).

⁶·⁶The sixth moon is called *Elul* (harvest, search). אֱלוּל

⁶·⁷The seventh moon is called *Tishri* (beginning). Day 1, 10, 15, and 22 are annual Şabbaths. Day one begins Şabbatical years. תִּשְׁרֵי

⁶·⁸The eighth moon is called *Heshvan* (חֶשְׁוָן, eighth month).

⁶·⁹The ninth moon is *Kislev* (כִּסְלֵו, cloudy?, Orion). Hanukkah[λ] begins on day 25. Observance is customary, but not obligatory.

⁶·¹⁰The tenth moon is *Tevet* (טֵבֵת, unknown meaning).

⁶·¹¹The eleventh moon is *Shevat* (שְׁבָט, strike).

⁶·¹²The twelfth moon is *Adar* (אֲדָר, unknown meaning). The 14th day is Purim[π] except when *Adar* II occurs.

⁶·¹³The thirteen moon is *Adar Sheni*. The 14th day is [π]Purim.

I.1 γ תְּקוּפַת הַשָּׁנָה. Also: ,תְּשׁוּבַת הַשָּׁנָה לִתְשׁוּבַת הַשָּׁנָה לִתְקֻפוֹת הַיָּמִים. Exo. 34:22; 1Sam. 1:20; Exo. 13:10. This is called the spring equinox. The words mean "circuit of the year." ▷ Due to refraction this is often one day before a spring equinox calculated by modern geometric methods. The definition assumes the simplest ancient observational method, which may be done without calculation. The point used for sunset is anywhere suitable in the holy land. A long line of observation running due west to the horizon is all that is needed. **I.5** ξ The Rabbis state the rule equivalently in terms of the 16th day after the new moon: all of the 16th day must be in the new year: The key point is sunset on the 15th day. The top of the sun should be seen setting west or north of west to be included in the new year. As a consequence, the 16th day after the new moon should be entirely in the new year. **I.3** χ For less than the ideal observational conditions that occasionally occur authorities consider astronomical calculations, and sometimes even local new moon observations if news from Israel is not available. **I.6.9** λ Celebrated from 165 BC. Mentioned in 1 Mac. 4:52; Yoḥ. 10:22. **I.6.12-13** π Purim is mentioned in Est. 9;26-32, and Yoḥ. 5:1. The day is not kept holy as a Şabbath.

Appendix Ib: The Rabbinic Calendar

This calendar started in AD 358/359. It uses calculations which often miss the new moon day. It has postponement rules to avoid Yom Kippur landing on certain days. It has fixed month lengths rather than allowing them to vary with the moon. And in the last 1660 years its equinox date has drifted 7 days later than the true equinox. These errors cause it to miss the true dates 86% of the time. The Rabbinic calendar was promoted to advance rabbinic control and authority over Jewish communities that used local observation in the diaspora. The Rabbis acknowledge that Jewish practice prior to the fourth century AD was to fix every new moon day after the first visual sighting of the new crescent. And above all, the original calendar confirms the testimony of Messiah. For these reasons we do not follow the Modern Rabbinic calendar that Messiah be acknowledged in all things.

Appendix II: Special Letters

ḣ, H = ח like /ch/ in Bach (note the curls)
ch = ḣ
ƙ, K = כ ,ך like /ch/ in Bach
v = ב like /v/ in vase
ʋ = ו u, w, v. The v is modern. The letter is made to look ambiguous so readers have a choice, e.g. Daʋid = Daweed or Daveed or David.

i = אִי or אִ like /ee/ in feet
ᴇ = אֵ like /ey/ in they
ts = צ, ץ like ts in sits (only in combination)
Ş = Sh. ṯh = t. Ḙ = ᴇ.
a = ע
ɣ = u
ҫ,Ç = k, K or q, Q.
ᴇн = ᴇh

Ordinary letters:

a = /a/ as in father
b = /b/ as in bat
c = unused
d = /d/ as in dish
e = /e/ as in egg
f = /f/ as in face
g = /g/ as in golden
h = /h/ as in hat
i = like /i/ in hit
j = unused
k = like /k/ in kite
l = like /l/ in lamb
m = like /m/ in moon
n = like /n/ in nice
o = like /o/ in note
p = like /p/ in post
q = like /ck/ in fleck
r = like /r/ in Spanish
s = like /s/ in sing
t = like /t/ in time
u = like /u/ in flute
v = not used, see v, ʋ above
w = only used in the divine name
x = not used
y = like /y/ in yes
z = like /z/ in zipper

Appendix III: The Adultery Story

The story of the woman caught in adultery may be a genuine incident in the life of Měssiah, but it clearly was not included by Yoḥanan in the place where we find it in John 7:53-8:11, and if it occurred at all, it happened at another time. The passage has been inserted into the context of the last great day (cf. John 7:37), on which the final water libation was poured out and on which the four great lamps in the court of the women were lit. This was the eighth day assembly, Shemini 'Atseret (cf. Num. 29:35). Měssiah made the connection between the water libation ceremony and himself, and the also lighted *menorot*, saying "I am the light of the world" (John 8:12). Further, in John 8:20, the setting is still in the Temple treasury, which was in the court of the women, where the four great lamps were stationed. It cannot be that the remarks in 7:37-39 and 8:12-59 are separated by a day (cf. 7:53-8:2 below.)

There is some controversy as to whether the water libation was poured on the eighth day and the menorot lit then also. But the eighth day is loosely speaking part of the seven day feast of Sukkot, and by virtue of being last is identified in John 7:37. Nor could the seventh day of the feast be called "great" because it was like the other five days after the first day. But the eighth day was the great day because it was a holy convocation like the first day, and an annual Şabbaṭh was on this day. Therefore the final water libation was poured on this day and the final lighting of the four lamps in the women's court. There would be none of these things on Tishri 23. Further, it would make no sense at all to not have the four menorah lit and the water libation done on the last day, when the people were still in attendance.

To suppose that John 8:12 took place on a day when the lamps had ceased to be lit is certainly to impute a sense of bad timing to Měssiah. To make matters worse, the supposed Tishri 23 date that year was the weekly Şabbaṭh. The last great day, Tishri 22, had come on Friday in AD 32. To suppose that the women had been put on trial on the weekly Şabbaṭh would be a scandal itself.

The Adultery Story does not appear in any of the earliest manuscripts. It is missing from $\mathfrak{P}^{66}$ (ca. 200) and $\mathfrak{P}^{75}$. Also from Sinaiticus, Vaticanus, Alexandrinus, Ephraemi, and many other texts. The oldest mss to have it is Codex Bezae (5th century, with exemplar in 2nd Cent.). The greatest scholars have long ago concluded that the section does not belong in John chapter 8, including Bruce Metzger, famed textual expert. It is supposed by some that the story was one of the many memories related in the era of the emissaries to men after them. Some of these stories were recorded by Papias (ca. 95-120 AD) and it may be that the Adultery Story was one of these that was noted in the margin of some mss of John and mistakenly copied into the text at a point supposed by a scribe who had little realization of how it would disrupt the chronology of the passage. The story is also variously positioned in the book of John by those mss that do have it. The main reason that the passage is put into the main text of Bible Translations, and only remarked upon in a note that some texts do not have it, is tradition and fear of the lack of support by the Bible buying and reading public. In other words, what goes into translations is based on fear of what the readers might think, and is not an objective standard. Here is the passage printed in the Appendix:

⁵³And everyone went to his home.

8 ¹But Yěshua went to the Mount of Olives. ²And early in the ᵀmorning he came again into the temple, and all the people were coming to him, and he sat down and was teaching them. ³And the scribes and the Perushim brought a woman caught in adultery, and having set her in the midst, ⁴they said to him, "Teacher, this woman had been getting caught committing adultery, in the very act. ⁵Now in the Law Mosheh commanded us to stone such women. What then do you say?" ⁶And they were saying this, testing him, in order that they might have grounds for accusing him. But Yěshua stooped down, and with his finger wrote on the ground.

⁷But when they persisted in asking him, he straightened up, and said to them, "He who is without Sin among you, let him be the first to throw a stone at her." ⁸And again he stooped down, and wrote on the ground.

8:2 τ On Şabbaṭh, Tishri 23, AD 32 if it is placed at John 7:53-8:11, but wherever it is placed it would certainly not go here. See chronological notes. ▷ There is nothing contrary to the Law in Měssiah's handling of the case. The Law requires the witnesses to be non-complicit in the crime and also not malicious. The Law requires two or three witnesses, but who were required to cast the stones. When Měssiah called for them they would not appear. So the case was closed and the woman freed.

⁹And when they heard it, they were going out one by one, beginning with the older ones, and he was left alone, and the woman, where she was, in the midst.

¹⁰And straightening up, Yĕshua said to her, "Woman, where are they? Did no one condemn you?" ¹¹And she said, "No one, Adŏnai." And Yĕshua said, "Neither do I condemn you. Go your way. From now on Sin no more."

Appendix IV

Introduction to 'The Alexandrian Letter'
also known as 'Hebrews'

¹This letter, believed by many to be Scripture, by tradition was attributed to Paul, but this attribution, now being proved false, leaves us with the likely alternative that the comment in the Muratorian Fragment should be applied, wherein "A Letter to the Alexandrians, forged in Paul's name, to *further* the heresy of Marcion" is mentioned, and the letter under the title 'Hebrews' is omitted in the same source. ²We need not require that Paul's name must be on the letter to explain the comment in the Fragment, but rather the promoters of the letter may easily have ascribed it to Paul by oral fiat, reinforced by remarks suggesting a connection to Paul, which were probably planted there by the real author for that purpose. ³Neither do we require it to be supposed that the letter was composed as a support for the full blown heresy of Marcionism, but rather Marcion's name may likely be anachronistically applied to the theological school of which he later became the leader, i.e. the author of our Muratorian Fragment represented a school of thought which saw the seeds of Marcionism in the letter, and therefore exposed its real purpose to be for that end. ⁴It is well known that Marcion taught a split of a New Testament from the Old Testament as he falsely termed the New Made Covenant of Old, but it is certain that this idea was thought of earlier than Marcion, and for this we have no other certain candidate than this anonymous letter. ⁵Inasmuch as the Alexandrian Christians were especially fond of the letter, and came up themselves with the theory that it was written in Hebrew and then translated to Greek, so as to defend the assumed Pauline authorship against the obvious non-Pauline style of the Greek, and also as they themselves ascribed its destination to 'Palestinian' Jewish Christians, while at the same time the rest of Western Christianity rejected the letter, we will do well to call this anonymous letter, 'The Alexandrian Letter' after the community most taken in by the author's deception. ⁶It is in fact quite probable that the letter never reached Messianic Jews in Galilee, Syria and the east until later, and if it had, it was at first summarily rejected. ⁷Now while MANY regard the letter as theologically definitive for 'faith,' the introduction and notes supplied for the text show why we should not be shaken by the opinions of THE MANY who have adopted important elements of the lawless teachings of the Marcionite heresy (cf. Mat. 7:21-23; Dan. 9:27).

⁸No one knows who the author was. Since the 16th century, it has been widely acknowledged that Paul was not the author, but the author (in my opinion) wished us to believe he was Paul. See 13:19, 23. ⁹No one knows where it was written, but the author wished us to think somewhere in Italy. See 13:24. ¹⁰And

even to whom it was written is disputed, but the author wished us to think it was the Jews. The alleged primary recipients may not have ever existed, except that it was first received as authentic for the supposed recipients by third party Christians in Alexandria. The ascribed title 'Hebrews' was not part of the original work. [11]It does not appear in the earliest canonical list, the Muratorian Canon, except perhaps as the mysterious *Letter of the Alexandrians* said to be "forged in Paul's name to *further* the heresy of Marcion." [12]The book is best named after the party that first embraced it and defended it, hence it is hereafter to be called, 'The Alexandrian Letter.' [13]In any case, suspicion is so great that it may as well be called so, and be given that title until someone proves better.

[14]Scholars admit that Hebrews has strong traces of Alexandrian origin, which was the chief place where the epistle was accepted. [15]The Alexandrians claimed that Paul wrote it in Hebrew and that it was translated into Greek by another, but scholars have rightly rejected this Hebrew to Greek translation theory also. [16]It appears to have been written between AD 110 and 130 (most likely near AD 123) since it copies phrases from Clement of Rome who lived just before this time (dying in AD 99). [17]And if the book had been written at any earlier time, then the allusions to Clement of Rome are very difficult to explain, because Clement's letter shows far more respect for the Temple and Levites than the author. [18]Clement could never have argued for the legality of the Levitical service if he had read and accepted the author's assumptions. So the reverse must be true. [19]The author read Clement of Rome and alluded to him. [20]Grammatical arguments taken from Hebrews and the book's failure to mention the destruction of the Temple are no proof of an earlier date, as the same manners of expression are found in other sources written after the Temple was destroyed, implying a continued operation of the services at a reduced level. [21]Or also possible, like pseudo-Enoch, the anachronisms could be part of the deception.

[22]Augustine (ca. 397, *On Christian Doctrine*, Book ii, chapter 8: "*quatuordecim Epistolis Pauli Apostoli*"), and his synod, the third council of Carthage (AD 397), by fiat decreed Hebrews canonical (*Sunt autem Canonicae Scripturae hae:*) and written by Paul: "*Epistolae Pauli Apostoli xiii., ejusdem ad Hebraeos una,*" along with the Wisdom of Solomon, Ecclesiasticus, Tobit, Judith, and 1 and 2 Maccabees. His canon had 72 books. [23]He also denied the Law and was a former Gnostic. [24]He had Pelagius's teaching condemned (who was the Arminius of his day). [25]He was the first Church father to deny the מַלְאַךְ יְהוָה (Mal'aƙ Yăhweн) was Yăhweн himself appearing in the form of a messenger, whereas his predecessors had all accepted Him, and referred to the Messenger of Yăhweн in their defenses of Messiah's deity. [26]Dependent upon his theological legacy are Calvin, who burned Servitus, and Luther, who persecuted the Anabaptists. [27]In every way Augustine took many, who professed the faith, to a greater level of depravity and corruption. He was a watershed man, standing at the junction of Roman persecution of Christians and Roman Ecclesiastical persecution

of Christians. So if there is one person singularly unqualified to canonize the Alexandrian Letter, it is Augustine. ²⁸For it was he that was a great corrupter of Christianity, promoting predestination, total depravity, irresistible grace, perseverance of the saints (i.e. salvation cannot be lost), and very likely that the atonement was only for the predestinated ones. ²⁹These doctrinal heresies singularly disqualify Augustine from making any authoritative pronouncements.

The Author's False Gospel

³⁰Let us begin where the author at 10:5 mis-quotes Psalm 40:6, "SACRIFICE AND OFFERING YOU HAVE NOT DESIRED, BUT *a body you have prepared for me*." ³¹What the Alexandrian Letter quotes is the author's own invention. The phrase "a body you have prepared for me" appears in no Hebrew version or Greek version of Scripture prior to its first appearance in this letter. The versions of the author's day were unified in reading "MY EARS YOU HAVE OPENED," which is a phrase meaning the Almĭghty has caused David to listen and obey. ³²This fact is confirmed by the next verse, "THEN I HAD SAID, 'BEHOLD I HAVE COME; IN THE ROLL OF THE SCROLL IT IS WRITTEN ABOUT ME: TO DO YOUR WILL O ALMĬGHTY, I *WILL* HAVE DELIGHTED, AND YOUR LAW *shall be* IN MY INNER BEING.'" ³³The text is all about obeying. But the Alexandrian Letter's author has ignored the context and the original text and has changed the text to a reading agreeable to his teaching. He also omitted the part about the Law. ³⁴The text speaks of the duties of the king (cf. Deut. 17:18-20).

³⁵The point of the Psalm is based on the Scripture teaching that "TO OBEY IS BETTER THAN SACRIFICE" (1 Sam. 15:22). ³⁶The author of the Alexandrian Letter has completely corrupted this point by substituting the sacrifice of Měssiah where obedience is expected. He has substituted a sacrifice for sacrifice where obedience is expected. ³⁷But in vain is the sacrifice offered by the person seeking to compensate for disobedience with no intention of repenting. Not even the sacrifice of Měssiah is desired in place of obedience.

³⁸It is written, "AND RIGHTEOUSNESS IT WILL BE FOR US WHEN WE KEEP WATCH TO DO ALL THIS COMMANDMENT BEFORE THE FACE OF YĂHWEĦ OUR ALMĬGHTY, AS THAT HE HAS COMMANDED US" (Deut. 6:25). ³⁹Many interpret this to mean that one has to keep all of the Law perfectly to be saved. Then they explain it is only a theory, because no one ever has, except Měssiah. ⁴⁰Then they argue that Měssiah kept the Law for us, so that Gŏd is said to put the righteousness of Měssiah in the believer's account . ⁴¹Are they then saying the sinner is acquitted of sin? Is not this sort of substitution the same as replacing obedience with sacrifice? ⁴²But this fictitious righteousness is not according to the Name of the Almĭghty. (See Mat. 28:19-20.) ⁴³For the Law and Prophets always teach us that He wants real personal righteousness, and it is actual righteousness that He recognizes. He forgives. ⁴⁴He does not acquit the guilty, but pardons in

repentance. ⁴⁵But the fictitious substitute law-keeping only serves lawlessness and the miscarriage of justice.

⁴⁶What they teach is that sacrifice equals obedience (the Satisfaction Theory of Atonement), because when the Almĭghty desired obedience they gave him a substitute. And that is the false gospel they teach. ⁴⁷The true good news requires repentance from sin. ⁴⁸When a person sins, there are consequences to the sin, both on the sinner and also on those sinned against. ⁴⁹Many will die because Adam sinned, even many who did not willfully break a commandment like Adam. ⁵⁰This is because Adam's sin causes death, and death causes many to go astray. (See Rom. 5:12-14).

⁵¹Consider the murderer. The Scripture calls for the death penalty. But is the victim of the murder compensated? Not at all. They are not brought back to life ᶲ. ⁵²In like manner the Almĭghty suffers irreparable loss from sin. There is no "undo." The Almĭghty at one time wished there was an undo. (See Genesis 6:6). But many teach as if there is a divine undo that erases all the losses due to sin. ⁵³Many teach that forgiveness is based on Gŏd being compensated for sin. That is the error. Gŏd is not compensated. ⁵⁴A substitute for righteousness cannot objectively compensate him. His loss still remains.

⁵⁵If Gŏd could be compensated, then sin would not matter. If the victim's suffering could be undone, then sin would not matter. ⁵⁶Many have believed that Gŏd is being compensated by the sacrifice of Mĕssiah. ⁵⁷And for this reason obedience does not matter to those who have trusted in this false doctrine. (It is granted that many believe the doctrine without trusting in it to excuse sin.) ⁵⁸But such is no better than claiming sacrifice is equal to obedience. Such is the mystery of iniquity.

⁵⁹But obedience is better than the sacrifice, and the Almĭghty has made receiving the benefit of the ransom from lawlessness contingent on holding faithful to Mĕssiah, which begins with an honest pledge to follow and obey him. ⁶⁰By obedience to the commandments we confirm our faithfulness to Mĕssiah. (See 1 John 2:3-4 and Deut. 8:1-2). ⁶¹If anyone professes belief in the sacrifice while continuing in transgression and in disloyalty to Mĕssiah, then their belief in the sacrifice is in vain. Messiah's suffering is not going to ransom them.

⁶²So, when many teach that it is necessary to credit the righteousness of Mĕssiah to the believer's account, via a divine exchange, whereby sin is imputed to Mĕssiah and his righteousness to us, then will it not be said that Gŏd is fully compensated? ⁶³Rather, sin's cost is borne by Mĕssiah to suffer it and cleanse it, but not wrath due to our sin. For he is a sin offering, carrying sin, and not being punished for sin.

⁶⁴Through long evolution of corruption, Paul's letters have been remade to teach these false doctrines via mistranslation and misinterpretation. ⁶⁵Now, the reader may look up the relevant verses in the *Good News of Mĕssiah* to see

---

IV.51 ϕ Also, if the victim did not know the good news, then the murderer ended their opportunity to repent and turn to life. The sin of the murderer denied the victim the possibility of being in the resurrection of the righteous.

what Paul really said. [66]However, there is no way to fix the translation of The Alexandrian Letter, or to soundly interpret what he says to be agreeable with Scripture. [67]According to the author, the sacrifice of Mĕssiah has cleansed the heart, rendering literal obedience unimportant (cf. 1:3; 9:28-10:1-4, 10, 14, 16, 18, 19).

[68]And according to false teachers, the substitute obedience is as good as the real thing. Other denominations argue the same way. [69]The heart is transformed and cleansed of all sin at baptism, and thereby the believer is perfected, which in their view means to be made inwardly and mystically righteous, to satisfy the 'demand' of the Law. [70]But this is not the Name of the Almĭghty, because he loves those who keep his commandments. [71]He does not absolve sin on any other basis, whether by tricky bookkeeping, or mystery righteousness which cannot be verified, and in fact is disconfirmed by their objective disobedience. [72]Since sin cannot be acquitted, we depend on forgiveness. (See Mat. 28:19-20 note).

[73]The author's solution to the sin problem is the sacrifice of Mĕssiah. The author rejects the Levitical services, supposing they had offered a solution for the sin problem that failed. Mĕssiah, he says, solves the sin problem by cleansing away all sin. [74]This is indeed a leap of logic when it is evident that believers are still less than perfect. [75]Nor does it undo the past consequences of sins on others. But final cleansing is still in the future.

[76]The true good news is this. The Almĭghty forgives our sins upon confession and repentance (1 Yoḥ. 1:9). He sent is son to ransom us from our enslavement by sin, and to cleanse us from all unrighteousness by his life, represented by his blood, which is through his faithfulness in response to our faithfulness (cf. Rom. 1:17). [77]His sacrifice does not compensate for the loss due to sin. The Almĭghty instituted sacrifice as an instructional sign of spiritual realities beyond the offering itself. [78]He freely forgives us compensation for the unrepayable loss he has suffered. [79]Such loss would require an "undo" to be actually compensated for. It would be better that sin had never happened, yet the followers of Augustine claim that sin was predestined to happen for the glory of Gŏd. [80]This doctrine is refuted by Deuteronomy 8:1-2. The Almĭghty tests Yisra·el to see if they will obey him or not. If he tests them, then he does not plan for them to fail for his glory.

[81]Now since sin's effects cannot be objectively erased, then engaging in sin with the expectation that Gŏd will be compensated by the sacrifice is a foolish doctrine. [82]And replacing obedience with sacrifice to compensate is equal to rebellion. That is what the author has done. That is what ancient Yisra'el tried to do when the Almĭghty said to bring no more vain offerings. That is exactly what many try to do with the sacrifice of Mĕssiah. It is how King Saul tried to appease the Almĭghty for his disobedience. And he was rejected.

[83]The true good news is that the Almĭghty does not require compensation. He freely forgives us our sins. (If he were fully compensated then it would not be forgiveness. [84]Compensation is not based on loving-kindness or mercy. Compensation is just a business transaction.) What he requires is holding faithful to him, defined as genuine repentance. [85]Sacrifice does not make up for the lack of

these things. He loves those who keep his commandments.

[86]As for Deut. 6:25, it is not what THE MANY claim it means. Rather, it means we should keep a watch to do all the commandments. It is a commandment to watch over the commandments. And this special commandment is a general one, and very important, like the command to love. [87]If we keep watch, then this commandment is singled out for special notice that it will be righteousness for us. It must then be a very important commandment! But, it is not a statement that to be saved one must be perfectly righteous.

[88]The one who does not respond to forgiveness by pursuing righteousness does not love the Almĭghty. Neither has such a one affirmed faithfulness to the Sŏn. [89]But that person, if they profess the Sŏn, depends on sacrifice to replace obedience. The Holy One of Yisraᵉl is not compensated by such. Mĕssiah's sacrifice treated this way is in vain.

[90]For this reason we reject the Alexandrian Letter, and also the apologetics of its defenders, because they still follow the same false doctrine. [91]The offering of Mĕssiah is explained as the other offerings in Appendix X. Messiah did not take on himself the wrath of the Most High. [92]Neither does the death of the wicked nor the death of Mĕssiah, or his merits, positively compensate Gŏd for the loss suffered.

[93]The death of Mĕssiah declares merciful justice. It is not strict justice of payment or compensation to God

Not Only a New Covenant, but an Old One

[95] "BEHOLD, THE DAYS ARE COMING, UTTERS YӐHWEH, WHEN I *WILL HAVE CONFIRMED* WITH THE HOUSE OF YISRAᵉL AND WITH THE HOUSE OF YEHUDAH A COVENANT RENEWAL,^χ NOT ACCORDING TO^ψ THE COVENANT (WHICH I HAD CONFIRMED WITH THEIR FATHERS IN THE DAY OF MY GRASPING THEM BY THE HAND TO BRING THEM OUT OF THE LAND OF EGYPT) WHEN^ξ THEY HAD BROKEN MY COVENANT, AND I HAD BEEN HUSBAND AGAINST THEM, UTTERS YӐHWEH. [96]BUT THIS IS THE

IV.95 χ or "RENEWAL COVENANT," adj. + n. The adj. חֲדָשָׁה *hadashah* is derived from the Piel verb חָדַשׁ *hadash*, 'make to be new.' "A right spirit renew within me" (Psa. 51:10). "Renew the kingdom there" (1 Sam. 11:14). "Renew our days as of old" (Lam. 5:21). "New moon" means the same as "renewed moon." A covenant of old made anew is a renewed covenant. See 1 Cor 11:25 χ note. **IV.95 ψ** Correctly rendered "not according to" in KJV, ASV, JUB. Wrongly using the word "like": ESV, HCSB, NASB, NIV, and many other versions. The difference is subtle but important. It means not according to the terms of the covenant for disobedience, because obedience will happen and other terms of the same covenant will apply: terms for blessing. The faithful bride is blessed. **IV.95 ξ** Or "BECAUSE," "IN THAT." The key to proper understanding of the verse is to connect "NOT ACCORDING TO THE COVENANT" with the last two clauses of the verse indicating a condition of unfaithfulness. The parentheses are inserted to help the reader do this. This refers to the provision of the covenant that applies under a condition of rebellion (the curse), under which renewal, allowing renewed blessing is unlawful. Two covenants are not being contrasted, but two agreed upon provisions: the blessing and the curse. The covenant renewal is not confirmed according to the provision for the curse, because Yisra'el will repent and be forgiven, according to the provision for blessing. If anyone does not repent, the curse remains in force, and the covenant cannot be renewed for them. Mĕssiah died on a tree to ransom us from the powers that would try to execute the curse after the Most High forgave us. He rises to put the blessing into effect for all who repent. So, the making of a renewal is not according to the covenant [provision] for rebels when he acts as judge and sells them to Lawlessness, as the husband whose wife has committed adultery,

COVENANT WHICH I ⁵CUT WITH THE HOUSE OF YISRA‑EL AFTER THOSE DAYS, SAYS YĂHWEH: I *WILL* HAVE PUT MY LAW IN THE MIDST OF THEM, AND UPON THEIR HEART I WILL WRITE IT. [97]THEN, I *WILL* HAVE BEEN THE ALMĬGHTY FOR THEM. AND THEY WILL BE A PEOPLE FOR ME. AND THEY WILL NOT TEACH ANY MORE, EACH MAN HIS NEIGHBOR, AND EACH MAN HIS BROTHER, SAYING, 'KNOW YĂHWEH,' BUT ALL OF THEM WILL KNOW ME, FROM THE LEAST OF THEM TO THE GREATEST, SAYS YĂHWEH, BECAUSE I WILL FORGIVE THEIR INIQUITY, AND THEIR SIN I WILL NOT REMEMBER ANY MORE." (Jer. 31:31-34).

[98] "THEN, I *WILL* HAVE REMEMBERED FOR THEM THE COVENANT OF THE FIRST ONES, WHEN I HAD BROUGHT THEM OUT FROM THE LAND OF EGYPT, BEFORE THE EYES OF THE NATIONS, TO BE ALMĬGHTY FOR THEM. I AM YĂHWEH. THESE ARE THE STATUTES AND THE JUDGMENTS AND THE INSTRUCTIONS WHICH YĂHWEH HAD GIVEN BETWEEN HIM AND BETWEEN THE SONS OF YISRA‑EL ON MOUNT SINAI BY THE HAND OF MOSH‑EH" (Lev. 26:45-46). [99] "THEN YĂHWEH YOUR ALMĬGHTY *WILL* HAVE CIRCUMCISED YOUR HEART AND THE HEART OF YOUR SEED, TO LOVE YĂHWEH YOUR ALMĬGHTY WITH ALL YOUR HEART AND ALL YOUR SOUL, SO THAT YOU *WILL* HAVE LIVED" (Deut. 30:6).

[100]The solution to Paul's parable in 2 Cor. 3 is that the word "old" or "antiquity" is the translation of עוֹלָם. "I *WILL* HAVE CONFIRMED FOR THEM A COVENANT OF PEACE, A COVENANT OF OLD. IT WILL BE WITH THEM" (Eze. 37:26). "THEN, I *WILL* HAVE <u>REMEMBERED</u> MY COVENANT WITH YOU <u>IN THE DAYS OF YOUR YOUTH</u>. THEN, I *WILL* HAVE CONFIRMED FOR YOU THE COVENANT <u>OF OLD</u>!" (Eze. 16:60). "TSIYON, THEY ASK FOR THE WAY! THITHER ARE THEIR FACES. COME. THEN YOU *WILL* HAVE BEEN JOINED TO YĂHWEH. THE COVENANT OF OLD WILL NOT BE FORGOTTEN." (Jer. 50:5).

[101]First He remembers. Second He does not forget. (See Lev. 26:44-45). "THEN, I WILL REMEMBER FOR THEM THE COVENANT OF THE FIRST ONES, WHEN I HAD MADE THEM GO OUT FROM THE LAND OF EGYPT." (Lev. 26:45). "INCLINE YOUR EARS, AND COME TO ME. LISTEN, AND THEN YOUR SOULS WILL LIVE! AND LET ME CONFIRM FOR YOU THE COVENANT OF OLD, THE LOVING-KINDNESSES OF DAVID WHICH ARE FAITHFUL" (Isa. 55:3).

[102]The parallelisms show that *a covenant renewal of the covenant of old is* intended. Here are some examples that show עוֹלָם being used in the sense of "old," "antiquity." See Gen. 49:26, "HILLS OF ANTIQUITY," and Amos 9:11, "AS IN DAYS OF OLD," (cf. Micah 7:14; Isa. 63:9, 11; Deut. 32:7); "A NAME OF OLD," (Isa. 63:12). Prov. 22:28, "DO NOT REMOVE THE BOUNDARY OF OLD," (cf. 23:10). "GATES OF OLD," (Psa. 24:7). "LIKE THE DEAD OF OLD," (Psa. 143:3; Lam. 3:6). "TO THE PEOPLE OF OLD," (Eze. 26:20). "IN THE WAY OF OLD," (Psa. 139:24).

---

but it is according to the provision for blessing. For the rebel, the covenant is only negative. The blessing cannot be renewed because he is unrepentant and under judgment.

IV.96 ⁵ Not "will cut" or "will make," but present tense "cut." "These are the words of the covenant which Yăhweh commanded Mosh‑eh to cut with the sons of Yisra‑el in the land of Moav, besides the covenant which he had cut with them in Horev." (Deu. 29:1). This was a covenant renewal made with additional explanations and promises. The promise in Deu. 30:6 is the same one as writing the law on the heart. The ESV has a heading for Deu. 29, "The Covenant Renewed in Moab." This was after those days when they rebelled in the wilderness. See notes on Mat. 26:28 and Mark 14:24.

"THE PATH OF OLD," (Job 22:15), "THE PATHS OF OLD," (Jer. 6:16). "THE WASTE PLACES OF OLD," (Isa. 58:12; 61:4). The grammar is the same with the phrase "COVENANT OF OLD," which may also be translated "EVERLASTING COVENANT," but terms such as "REMEMBER," and "DO NOT FORGET," point backwards in time. Also phrases like "DAYS OF YOUR YOUTH," and grammatical parallelisms, "A COVENANT OF PEACE, A COVENANT OF OLD." (See Num. 25:12; cf. Psa. 106:31).

[103] These all show that a covenant of old is being renewed, and when the covenant of old is renewed, it is truly everlasting.

Summary of Errors

[104.1] The author rejects the Levitical Law.
[104.2] The author divides Scripture into opposing Testaments.
[104.3] The author advances a theory of atonement whereby sacrifice is substituted for obedience.
[104.4] The author claims the Law was given by angels.
[104.5] The author denies that Joshua gave Israel rest.
[104.6] The author redefines the Şabbaṯh.
[104.7] The author ascribes High Priestly status to Mĕssiah.
[104.8] The author dispenses with the Levitical Law using a tortured interpretation of Melchizedek.
[104.9] The author misquotes and takes Jer. 31:31-34 out of context.
[104.10] The author misplaces a number of items in the Tabernacle, including the altar of incense and items said to be in the ark.
[104.11] The author gets his details wrong on the ratification of the covenant of old at Mt. Sinai.
[104.12] The author teaches perfectionism, and then argues via logical fallacy that the Levitical service is no good.
[104.13] The author's contextual definition of *pistis* tends toward action based on trust in promises (i.e. *courage* only), excludes fidelity to the Levitical Law (regarded as apostasy), and appears to include holding faithful to his doctrine, and opinions on Church government.
[104.14] The author equivocates the daily offering with the sin offering, and then replaces 'the continual' worship offering with Christ contrary to Dan. 8.

[105] There are quite a number of other errors of lesser importance pointed out in the notes, which would be too tedious to list here.

The Alexandrian Letter
also known as Hebrews

1 ¹In many ways, and in many manners, the Almighty has spoken of old, to the fathers, in the Prophets. ²In these last days, he has spoken to us by a Son, whom he designates heir of all things, through whom also he made the ˣages, ³who being the radiance of the glory, and an exactly duplicated impress of his nature, *who* besides upholding all things by the word of his power, ᶿwhen

---

1:1-2 χ But see Gen. 1:1-3: "IN THE BEGINNING OF THE ALMĬGHTY'S CREATING OF THE HEAVENS AND THE EARTH, WHEN THE EARTH HAD BEEN UNFORMED AND NOTHING...THEN THE ALMĬGHTY SAID, 'LET IT BECOME LIGHT.'" The setting assumes the existence of time already. Nothing is said about making it anywhere in Scripture. See 11:3 note. The beginning is the start of this creation, not time. ▷ Some are fond of saying God is outside of time, but as other concepts lack certain properties, so time doesn't have an outside to be in.

1:3 θ→sin: But see 1 Yoħ. 1:8-9 where cleansing is explained as continuing. The author explains cleansing as already finished as if caused by the offering itself. But actual cleansing of sin happens with confession and repentance unto obedience. The sacrificial offering only made a declaration of wiping (see Appendix X), certifying what already happened by the Spirit through forgiveness. Messiah's offering symbolizes the same **declaration** for all our transgressions. Like the other offerings, the actual forgiveness and spiritual cleansing represented by the symbolism occurs when confession and repentance is made through the Spĭrit. ▷ But since death still rules in the body and the physical realm and wars against and contaminates the spirit, it is necessary to continue confessing and getting purged of sin. This is why we afflict our souls on YOM KIPPURIM once a year. Final cleansing (perfection of the soul) is not completed till the age to come on YOM KIPPURIM when the Jubilee trumpet is blown announcing the ransomed release of the body. (See Zech. 3:9, 1 Cor. 13:10, Lev. 16:30; 1 Cor. 15:52; 1 Yoħ. 1:8-10, 3:3, Phil. 3:12 and Gal. 5:5). ▷ The author ignores the Scriptures that say the offerings are effective for declaring forgiveness, and claims they are not effective for declaring cleansing of the soul. But the Scripture says the confessor is forgiven (cf. Lev. 4:20, 26, 31, 35; 5:10, 13, 16, 18; 6:7; Num. 15:25, 26,) for sins of ignorance. ▷ Also the author implicitly denies the offerings declared any wiping, e.g. forgiveness by 1. Omitting any affirmation that they did, and 2. Stating they only concerned the flesh or the body (Heb. 9:10), when the symbolism represents spiritual truth, and 3. Stating the only effect is to remind of sin (Heb. 10:3), when in fact they remind of cleansing and forgiveness, and 4. Stating that the Levitical service was useless (Heb. 7:18), when ritual assurance of cleansing and forgiveness is very important. Though the author does not directly state that Levitical offerings declared no forgiveness, his various statements taken together teach this, and this is what Christians have concluded the author meant. ▷ Forgiveness and major cleansing vs. final forgiveness and perfect cleansing of the soul to make a person perfectly righteous are two different operations. The author denies a declatory function for both for the Levitical offerings (of an existing spiritual reality, and of one that will be), and argues that only the latter was **effected** by Messiah's offering (saying it now is), faulting the sin offerings for failure to effect perfect righteousness. Someone will argue then that Christians do not appear to be perfectly righteous, and that therefore Messiah's blood does not effect perfect cleansing, since a good deal of sinful ignorance remains in Christians. Therefore this sin is not cleansed, but Messiah's offering can only remind us of it (to use words of the author aimed at the Levitical offerings). It is only cleansed when confessed and reformed, and we do not see that complete yet. ▷ Truly, Messiah's blood will effect complete cleansing of the life in terms of perfect righteousness, but this is only because his blood represents his living divine life, which he will give to us as a living sacrifice (cf. Yoħ 6:63). When the Temple is restored in this age (cf. Rev. 11:1; Mat. 24:15; 2 Thess. 2:3-4; Dan. 9:27), and in the one to come (Ezek. 40-48; Zech. 14:20-21; Mal. 3:3-4; Jer. 33:17-22), the sin offerings will have the same declatory assurance originally promised in the Scripture for sins of ignorance. They will assure the confessor they are forgiven, or have been as Leviticus states. And it is these offerings that teach us the meaning of *kippurim* (a declaring of wiping away, cf. Ap. X). If these terms do not mean what they say in Torah, then there is no assurance that they mean what they say with respect to Messiah. **1:3 μ** The author uses this phrase taken from Psalm 110:1 to convey finality at the cross for his cleansing doctrine at a fixed point in time. But reading that text we must realize that the enemies are not yet subdued. Messiah's sitting at the right hand was not a resting from work already finished, but rather it is an appointment to administration as the right hand of the Almighty, to finish the work of executing justice on earth. (See 1 Cor. 15:26-28). ▷ The underlined text parallels Clement of Rome: 1 Clement 36:2 (to the Corinthians), "Who being the brightness of His majesty, is so much greater than angels, as He hath inherited a

he made cleansing of sin, "sat down at the right hand of the Majesty on high, ⁴as one who <u>is so much better than the messengers</u>, <u>as he has been inheriting a more excellent Name</u> than they. ⁵Because to which of the messengers did he at some time say, "YOU ARE MY SON, TODAY I HAVE BEEN BRINGING YOU FORTH$^\alpha$." And again, "I WILL BE A FATHER TO HIM AND HE WILL BE A SON TO ME$_\beta$"?

⁶And again, whenever he may have brought the firstborn into the inhabited earth, he says, "AND LET ALL THE $^\phi$messengers OF THE ALMIGHTY WORSHIP HIM$^\alpha$." ⁷And about the messengers he would say, $^\psi$"WHO MAKES HIS MESSENGERS SPIRITS, AND HIS MINISTERS A FLAME OF FIRE$^\beta$."

⁸But to the Son, "YOUR THRONE, ALMIGHTY, IS FOR THE AGE OF THE AGE, AND THE RIGHTEOUS SCEPTER IS THE SCEPTER OF HIS KINGDOM. ⁹YOU HAVE LOVED JUSTICE AND HATED LAWLESSNESS. THEREFORE THE ALMIGHTY, YOUR ALMIGHTY, HATH ANOINTED YOU WITH THE OIL OF GLADNESS ABOVE YOUR COMPANIONS$^\psi$."

¹⁰And, "YOU, $^\chi$ADONAI, IN THE BEGINNING DID LAY THE FOUNDATION OF THE EARTH, AND THE HEAVENS ARE THE WORKS OF YOUR HANDS. ¹¹THEY WILL PERISH,

---

more excellent name." The author has borrowed from Clement of Rome, representing Clement's words as if Paul's from an earlier time, placing a *terminus a quo* of ca. AD 96 for composition of the Alexandrian Letter. If questioned about the words, the author (See notes on Heb 2:3, 13:19, 23) would be able to say (and certainly his defenders do say) that Clement must have known of Paul's last letter and included phrases in his letter to the Corinthians just before he died (ca. AD 99). By this explanation the many have been deceived. But this hypothesis is not possible, since it would require Clement to be complicit with the author's heresy. On the contrary, Clement speaks favorably of the Levitical priests. See extended quote from Clement in the notes for Heb. 7:10. **1:5** α Psa. 2:7; **1:5** β 2 Sam. 7:14; 1 Chr. 17:13.

1:6 α Deu 32:43, Psa 97:7; β Psa 104:4; **1:6** φ For Deut. 32:43, the Old Greek (LXX) reads "SONS OF THE ALMIGHTY," i.e. בני אלהים. Michael Heiser makes a good case that the phrase בני אלהים is original to the Hebrew there, and also in Deut. 32:8. The author alters "SONS" to "messengers," which is copied by the later Odes of Solomon 2:43. Clearly the argument of 1:5 fails with "SONS," so the author discarded that reading. **1:7** ψ 1 Clem. 36:3. The literary dependency of the author on Clement is shown by the fact that Clement is much shorter than vs. 3-14: 1 Clem 36:2-5: "Through Him let us look steadfastly unto the heights of the heavens; through Him *we behold as in a mirror His faultless and most excellent visage*; through Him the eyes of our hearts were opened; through Him our foolish and darkened mind springs up unto the light; through Him the Master willed that we should taste of the immortal knowledge, 2b <u>who being the brightness of His majesty is so much greater than angels, as He hath inherited a more excellent name</u>. 3 FOR SO IT IS WRITTEN, <u>Who maketh His angels spirits and His ministers a flame of fire</u>. 4 but of His Son the Master said thus, <u>Thou art My Son, I this day have begotten thee</u>. Ask of Me, and I will give Thee the Gentiles for Thine inheritance, and the ends of the earth for Thy possession. 5 AND AGAIN HE SAITH UNTO HIM, <u>Sit Thou on My right hand, until I make Thine enemies a footstool for Thy feet</u>." ▷ Again, the underlined portions are the common text. The author borrows the words in nearly the same order, only swapping vs. 3 and 4. The author then greatly expands upon Clement, adding many other quotations and phrases between the Clement material. Clement himself is not dependent on the author, but introduces his text with an allusion to 2 Cor. 3:18. The italic texts are allusions or quotations of Scripture (2 Cor. 3:18; Psa. 104:4; Psa. 2:7-8; Psa. 110:1). Clement introduces two of his quotations in citation format, which is indicated by the small capitals. He quotes more of Psalm 2 than Hebrews. This also shows that Clement is resorting to Scripture and not to Hebrews for his texts.

1:8-9 ψ Psa 45:6-7; **1:10-12** θ Psa. 102:25-27; **1:10** χ The divine name and nomina sacra markings I omit from this book. The definition of profane is to mix what is holy with what is perverse. The holy is indeed holy, but it really hurts to see the author walk all over what is holy to make his profane points in the context. An individual quote or sentence on its own may be error free, but elsewhere in the context the author is exploiting it to make a heretical point. One cannot really use a system devised for an evil purpose to explain the truth. For example, creationists cannot really redeem the evolutionary geological column, secular plate tectonic theory, or cosmological relativity as foundations for explaining the truth. These theories pervert their very foundations in their assumptions, their mathematics, classifications, and mechanisms. To use any part of them uncritically is to risk repeating hidden error, and if one suspects error in them, then to trust parts of these theories without mastering the right answer is folly. For one cannot see the folly their authors put into them unless one knows the right answer. One's own speculation apart from them would indeed be less

BUT YOU REMAIN. AND THEY ALL WILL BECOME OLD AS A GARMENT. ¹²AND AS A MANTLE YOU WILL ROLL THEM UP. AS A GARMENT THEY WILL ALSO BE CHANGED. BUT YOU ARE THE SAME, AND YOUR YEARS WILL NOT COME TO AN END.⁰." ¹³But to which of the messengers has he ever been saying, "BE SITTING^β AT MY RIGHT HAND, WHILE I SHALL HAVE SET THINE ENEMIES A FOOTSTOOL FOR YOUR FEET"? ¹⁴Are they not all ministering spirits, sent out to render service for the sake of those who will inherit salvation?

2 ¹For this reason we must pay much closer attention to what we have heard, lest we will have drifted away, ²because if the word spoken through messengers was confirmed, and every transgression and disobedience received a just recompense, ³how will we escape neglecting such great salvation which at the beginning was received through Adonai, ᵃbeing confirmed to us by those hearing him, ⁴bearing witness for the Almighty, in signs besides also wonders, and in many miracles and in distributions of the Holy Spirit according to his own will.ˣ

⁵Because he did not subject to messengers the inhabited world to come, concerning which we are speaking. ⁶But one has testified somewhere, saying, "WHAT

---

risky. Even including this book in the appendix was a hard choice, but a necessary one, because we have to put some effort into deconstructing the false world view. **1:13 β** Psa. 110:1; 1 Clem. 36:5; ▷ But they are not all mere angels of the created order. There is one Messenger of Yăhweӊ who is the Sŏn, who is Yăhweӊ. The author's argument is a poor argument for the divinity of Mĕssiah. His angel argument has much in common with Gnostic assumptions.

2:1-4 χ The Messianic Faith, once delivered to the saints, teaches that the Messenger of Yăhweӊ (also called: Angel of the LORD) is in fact the same person as the Sŏn of the Almĭghty. He is identified as Yăhweӊ in the Scripture. Now the author claims the word was received of old through messengers, as distinct from the Sŏn (also implied in 1:1), when in fact, the Messenger that delivered the word was almost always the Sŏn: (Gen. 16:7-11; 21:17; 22:11-15; 31:11; 48:16; Exo. 3:2; 14:19; 23:20-23; 32:34; 33:2; Num. 20:16; 22:22-35; Jud. 2:4; 5:23; 6:11-22; 13:3-21; 2 Sam. 24:16-17; 1 Ki. 19:5-7; 2 Ki 1:3, 15; 19:35, etc). I can think of a few possible exceptions, like when an angel guided Lot out of Sedom, or when a long portion of Daniel 11 was assigned to another angel. All the other times it was the Sŏn who appeared as a messenger that delivered the word. (The Gnostics denied this. They said the 'Angel of the Lord' was a fallen being that had created the material world. They then said that the Mĕssiah spirit came upon the son of man at his baptism, and then left before his death.) It would appear then, that in his supposed efforts to defend the divinity of Mĕssiah, that the author was also attacking anyone who identified the Messenger of Yăhweӊ with the Sŏn. This sort of argument is still with us today. It is assumed that all angels are created beings, and therefore the Angel of Yăhweӊ cannot be Adŏnai. But the truth is that the appearing of the Messenger of Yăhweӊ in the Scripture is not just a strong argument for the divinity of Mĕssiah. It is the strongest argument. And it was put to such use by all those before Augustine against Arians and Eunomians. Our author here completely neglects this and gives us the weakest of arguments, because his object is to undermine the Messenger of the Covenant. For to which of the messengers did He say "YOU ARE MY SŎN?" He said this to the special Messenger of Yăhweӊ who is the Sŏn, who is Yăhweӊ (Cf. 1:5). **2:3 α→**us: Maybe the author's intent in writing these words was in anticipation of the objection that Paul was not a first generation disciple. Then the author (while concealing himself as the true author) would say that Paul was collectively classing himself with the Jewish people in making the remark, which is the apology offered in the commentaries defending Pauline authorship. The author would then point out the lack of Paul's standard opening for letters to gentiles, and claim it was absent because he was trying to "more humbly" persuade Jews. Thus the author could justify the apparent anonymity of his fraud. Then he could point to 13:19 and 23 as his "proof" it was written by Paul. The rescuing argument was built in. (Paul was indeed concerned about false teachers faking a letter in his name. See Gal. 6:11; 2 Thess. 2:2; 3:17.) The author's fraud was not entirely successful, but the Alexandrian Letter was rejected everywhere in the west, and especially at Rome. ▷ The chief early argument for the canonicity of the letter was that Paul wrote it, but when scholarship more carefully examined the style and found it was not Paul's, the requirement for Pauline authorship in determining canonicity was quietly dropped also. The new argument for canonicity was long tradition since the 4th century. It is quite clear that an anonymous writing with no tradition behind it could never be accepted. So now it is clear that the deception for Pauline authorship, described above,

IS MAN, THAT YOU REMEMBER HIM? OR THE SON OF MAN, THAT YOU ARE CONCERNED ABOUT HIM? ⁷YOU *WILL* HAVE MADE HIM FOR A LITTLE WHILE LOWER THAN THE MESSENGERS. YOU *WILL* HAVE CROWNED HIM WITH GLORY AND HONOR, AND *WILL* HAVE APPOINTED HIM OVER THE WORKS OF YOUR HANDS. ⁸YOU *WILL* HAVE PUT ALL THINGS IN SUBJECTION UNDER HIS FEET^ψ," because in subjecting all things to him, he *will* have left nothing that is not subject to him. But now we do not yet see all things having been getting themselves subjected to him.

⁹But we do see Yĕshua having been getting made lower than the messengers, having been getting crowned with glory and honor after his suffering and death, in order that by the loving-kindness of the Almighty he will have tasted death on behalf of everyone.

¹⁰Because it was fitting for him, for whom are all things, and through whom are all things, in bringing many sons to glory, to ⁿperfect the leader of their salvation through sufferings, ¹¹because besides the sanctifier also those being sanctified are all from one, for which reason he is not ashamed to call them brethren, ¹²saying, "I WILL PROCLAIM YOUR NAME TO MY BROTHERS. IN THE MIDST OF THE CONGREGATION I WILL SING YOUR PRAISE^α." ¹³And again, "I WILL HAVE BEEN TRUSTING IN HIM^ψ." And again, "BEHOLD, I AND THE CHILDREN WHOM ADONAI HAS GIVEN ME^β." ¹⁴Since then the children have been sharing in flesh and blood, he himself likewise also partook of the same, that through death he might render powerless him who had the power of death, that is, the Slanderer, ¹⁵and might deliver those who through fear of death were subject to slavery all their lives. ¹⁶Because assuredly he does not give help to messengers, but he takes hold of the seed of Avraham. ¹⁷Therefore, he had to be likened to his brethren

---

was needed to get it accepted in the first place.

2:5-8 ψ Psa 8:4-6. The author's argument here is flawed. He quotes Psalm 8 because it says the Sŏn of Man was "FOR A LITTLE WHILE LOWER THAN MESSENGERS." Once again the author is attempting to say that the Sŏn never took the form of a messenger. He also took the form of a man, to be sure, and finally became a man, to be sure. The author counts on the ignorance of his audience concerning the Messenger of Yăhweḥ. Denial that the מלאך יהוה was Mĕssiah became widespread in the Church after Augustine. Before then it was principally Gnostics that attacked the Messenger.

2:10 η The notion of the perfecting of Mĕssiah is a Gnostic idea. The author *does* state that Mĕssiah was without sin, but that does not acquit him of inconsistency for pandering to Gnostic ideas. The Gnostics taught that the divine "Mĕssiah" spirit came upon the Christ at his baptism and departed before the man died. Clearly then the "man" would need perfecting since he would not be Gŏd. **2:12** α Psa 22:22 **2:13** ψ Isa. 8:17 **2:13** β Isa 8:18 **2:17** α See vs. 10. Part of the perfecting of the Sŏn included "that he might become a merciful and faithful high priest." This supposition makes better sense if the author secretly believes the Spirit came upon the man Yĕshua, and that he denies the soul, the person of Yĕshua, is Yăhweḥ. This extremely heretical Nestorian view is Gnostic, and it is current in the Aramaic Primacy sect, part of which even has pretentions to Torah fidelity. They speak in every way to conceal it. ▷ The high priest theology here and elsewhere in this book is unique to this author. The Scripture knows nothing of it. Though, perhaps the author is hardly to be blamed. Clement of Rome comes up with a similar notion (1 Clem 36:1), but he clearly cannot mean as a replacement for the Levitical high priest. For he assigns that one his legitimate position (cf. 40:5; 41:2). The Mĕssiah and high priest are kept separate in Scripture. See 1 Samuel 2:35. Also, Zechariah 6:12-13 where there are two thrones, one for Mĕssiah and one for the high priest. "AND THERE WILL HAVE BEEN A PRIEST UPON HIS THRONE, AND THE COUNSEL OF PEACE WILL BE BETWEEN THE TWO OF THEM." Due to the influence of Hebrews even these verses have been misinterpreted or mistranslated. "AND I WILL HAVE RAISED UP FOR ME A FAITHFUL PRIEST. ACCORDING TO WHAT IS IN MY HEART AND IN MY SOUL HE WILL DO. AND I WILL HAVE BUILT FOR HIM A FAITHFUL HOUSE. AT THE FACE OF MY MĔSSIAH HE HIMSELF WILL HAVE WALKED ALL THE DAYS" (1 Sam. 2:35)! **2:17** λ According to 1:3 this was accomplished, and then he sat down at the right hand. The author conceives of the

in all things, that he might become a merciful and faithful high priest^α in things pertaining to the Almighty, to purge^λ the sins of the people. ¹⁸Because in that he had been suffering himself, as tested, he is able to help those being tested.

3 ¹Therefore, holy brethren, partakers of a heavenly calling, look to the Anointed One, the Emissary and High Priest of our confession, ²who is faithful to him who appointed him, as also Mosh•eh *was* in all His house, ³because he has been getting counted worthy of more glory than Mosh•eh, inasmuch as the builder of the house has more honor than the house. ⁴Because every house is built by someone, but the builder of all things is the Almighty. ⁵Now Mosh•eh was faithful in all His house as a servant, for a testimony of those things which were to be spoken later, ⁶but the Anointed is faithful as a Son over His house, whose house we are, if we may have held fast our confidence and the boast of our hope firm until the end.^{χ}

⁷Therefore, just as the Holy Spirit says, "TODAY IF YOU MAY HAVE HEARD HIS VOICE, ⁸YOU SHALL NOT HAVE HARDENED YOUR HEARTS AS WHEN THEY PROVOKED ME, AS IN THE DAY OF TRIAL IN THE WILDERNESS, ⁹WHERE YOUR FATHERS TRIED ME BY TESTING ME, AND SAW MY WORKS FOR FORTY YEARS. ¹⁰THEREFORE I WAS ANGRY WITH THIS GENERATION, AND SAID, 'THEY ALWAYS GO ASTRAY IN THEIR HEART. AND THEY DID NOT KNOW MY WAYS', ¹¹AS I SWORE IN MY WRATH, 'THEY WILL NOT ENTER MY REST^ψ.'" ¹²Be watching, brethren, lest there should be in any one of you an evil, unfaithful heart, that falls away from the living Almighty. ¹³But be encouraging one another day after day, as long as it is still called "Today," lest any one of you will have been hardened by the deceitfulness of sin, ¹⁴because we have been becoming partakers of the Anointed, ^{α}if we may have held fast the beginning of courage firm until the end. ¹⁵While it is said, "TODAY IF YOU MAY HAVE HEARD HIS VOICE, YOU SHALL NOT HAVE HARDENED YOUR HEARTS, AS WHEN THEY PROVOKED ME^β." ¹⁶Because certain ones, hearing, bitterly provoked! But not all those who came out of Egypt through Mosh•eh. ¹⁷And with whom was he angry for forty years? Was it not with those who sinned, whose bodies fell

---

offering itself, as a sacrificial offering, as purging the sin of the people. But in this respect he is incorrect. Sacrificial offering is only a declaring to be wiped out that recognizes a reality that came about through confession and repentance. At the same time the Most High forgives sins. As such, the offering that follows it is only symbolic of that reality. But 9:22 claims that the sacrifice itself is the cause of forgiveness, or that which enacts forgiveness. But this is not so, but Prov. 16:6 states: בְּחֶסֶד וֶאֱמֶת יְכֻפַּר עָוֹן. *By loving-kindness and faithfulness iniquity will be made to be wiped away.* See also 1 Yoḥ. 3:3. And 1 Yoḥ. 1:9 says that forgiveness happens with confession.

3:1-6 χ cf. Num. 12:7. The author emphasizes faithfulness as mere confidence in the promise and acting in confidence, i.e. courage of conviction. The Scriptural definition is holding faithful to Měssiah, i.e. to affirm and confirm faithfulness to him by keeping his commandments. See Hebrews 11:1. Courage of conviction is a side effect of faithfulness to Měssiah. But by itself it becomes humanism. The 'can do' spirit of America without faithfulness to Měssiah by giving him credit is idolatry and reliance on self. **3:7-11** ψ Psa 95:7-11 **3:14** α→end: Again we see the author's narrow definition of πίστις to mean just 'a holding faithful' equal to courage (ὑπόστασις). See 11:1. This is a possible meaning of the word in many contexts. (See Mat. 9:2; 17:20; 21:21; Luke 7:50; 8:25, 50; 17:5-6, 19; 18:42; John 11:40; Acts 14:9; 1 Cor 12:9). But it is too narrow and off Scriptural emphasis, which is faithfulness to Měssiah shown by loving him, by keeping his commandments. The parallel use of the terms (3:18 γ and 3:19 θ) show the author's focus. Unfaithfulness for the author is lack of persuasion with respect to his doctrine. Unfaithfulness in the biblical definition is rejecting Gŏd's covenant. **3:15** β Psa. 95:7-8.

in the wilderness? ¹⁸And to whom did he swear that they should not enter his rest, except to those who were ʸnot obedient? ¹⁹And so we see that they were not able to enter because of ᶿunfaithfulness.

4 ¹Therefore, we should fear lest, while a promise remains of entering his rest, any one of you should be appearing to have been falling short of it, ²because indeed we are those who have been getting good news announced to us, just as they also, but the word they heard did not profit them, because it had not been getting united with faithfulness in those who heard, ³because having held faithful, we do enter that rest, just as he has been saying, "As I swore in my wrath, they will not enter my rest^α," and yet his works have existed since the founding of the world. ⁴Because he had been saying somewhere concerning the seventh day, "And the Almighty rested on the seventh day from all his works^β," ⁵and again in this passage, "They will not enter my rest^γ."

⁶When therefore it is remaining for some to enter it. And those who formerly had good news preached to them failed to enter because of not trusting. ⁷He again fixes a certain day today, saying through David after so long a time just as he has been saying, "Today if you may have heard his voice, you shall not have hardened your hearts^α." ⁸For if Yehoshua had given them rest, he would not have spoken of another rest after those days^χ. ⁹There remains therefore a Şabbaṯh rest for the people of the Almighty, ¹⁰because the one who enters his rest himself also rests from his works, just as the Almighty from his own^β.

¹¹We should be diligent then to enter that rest, lest anyone should fall into the same example of not trusting, ¹²because the word of the Almighty is living and active and sharper than any two-edged sword, and piercing as far as the division of soul and spirit, besides joints and marrow, and able to judge the thoughts and intentions of the heart. ¹³And there is no creature hidden from his sight, but all things are naked and have been getting laid bare to the eyes of him with whom we have to do.

¹⁴Since then we have a great high priest who has been passing through the heavens, Yeshua the Almighty Son, we should be holding fast to our confession, ¹⁵because we do not have a high priest who cannot sympathize with our weaknesses, but one who had been getting tested in every way, in every manner, without sin. ¹⁶We may therefore be drawing near with confidence to the throne of kindness, wherein we shall have received mercy and shall have found loving kindness for timely help.

5 ¹Because every high priest, being taken from among men, is appointed on behalf of men in things pertaining to the Almighty, in order that he may be

---

3:18 γ. ἀπειθέω **3:19** θ. ἀπιστία **4:3** α Psa 95:11; **4:4** β Gen 2:2-3; **4:5** γ Psa 95:11. **4:7** α Psa 95:7-8. **4:8** χ But the Scripture says that Yăhweӊ did give them rest through Yehoshua "ACCORDING TO ALL WHICH HE SWORE TO THEIR FATHERS" (Jos. 21:44). (See Jos. 1:13, 15; 11:23; 14:15; 22:4; 23:1). They also had salvation rest under Yehoshua because all that generation walked in the way of Yăhweӊ (Jud. 2:7-12). Yehoshua gave them rest as Yăhweӊ had promised. Therefore, the premise of the author's argument is wrong. **4:10** β The Şabbaṯh rest is redefined by the author.

offering gifts, besides also sacrifices concerning sins, ²he can deal gently with the ignorant and misguided, since he himself also is beset with weakness, ³and because of it he is obligated to offer sacrifices for sins, as for the people, so also for himself. ⁴And no one receives the honor to himself, unless he is called by the Almighty, even as Aharon was. ⁵Likewise even the Anointed did not glorify himself so as to become a high priest, but *he was so glorified by* him who said to him, "YOU ARE MY SON, TODAY I HAVE BEEN BRINGING YOU FORTH^α," ⁶just as he says also in another passage, "YOU ARE A priest FOREVER in the order of Malkitsedeq^β."

⁷In the days of his flesh, he offered up prayers, besides also supplications with loud crying and tears to the One able to rescue him from death, even as one who is heard because of piety. ⁸Although he was the Son, ^αhe learned submission from the things which he suffered. ⁹And as one who is perfected, he becomes to all those who submit to him a cause of everlasting salvation, ¹⁰being addressed by the Almighty as a high "priest in the order of Malkitsedeq^β." ¹¹Concerning him we have much to say, and it is hard to explain, since you have been becoming dull of hearing, ¹²because though by this time you ought to be teachers, you have need again for someone to teach you the elementary principles of the sayings of the Almighty, and you have been happening to need milk and not solid food. ¹³Because everyone partaking of milk only, is inexperienced in the word of righteousness, because he is an infant. ¹⁴But solid food is for the perfect, who because of practice have been getting their senses trained to discern good, besides also evil.^γ

5:5 α Psa 2:7. **5:6** β Psa 110:4. But Psalm 110:4 translates, "YOU ARE A MINISTER FOREVER CONCERNING MY CAUSE O MY KING OF JUSTICE," or "IN MY MANNER O MY KING OF JUSTICE." See Gesenius' Hebrew Lexicon. Non-Levitical administrators of the kingdom were sometimes called *cohen* (minister) because they dispensed justice like a priest judging a case (see 2 Sam. 8:18). The Davidic king acted in the manner of a priest judging a case. The Hebrew may also mean "my matter (my cause)." That is, Messiah serves justice for the cause of the Father. Service at the altar was limited to the Levitical priests, but the judicial function was permitted to non-Levitical administrators, and so came to be performed by the king, and ultimately by Messiah. The equivocation of the ministry of justice as a competing (or replacement) priesthood to that of Aharon by the author is completely unfounded. Rather, the non-Levitical minister cooperated with the Levitical minister, and both operated at the same time. ▷ The author wishes us to read the text 'in the order of' (τάξιν LXX), but this rendition of the Hebrew דִּבְרָתִי *divrati* is by no means certain. The only other exact instance of this word is in Job 5:8 where it means "my cause." See Gesenius' Hebrew-Chaldee Lexicon: דִּבְרָה (*divarah*). And see also Eccl. 3:18, 7:14, 8:2 for usages of the same word in Hebrew. The definition "manner" appears to apply only in Psalm 110:4 and raises my suspicion that it was custom made to keep the author of Hebrews out of trouble. None of my reference tools have any other example of the definition "manner." Also, the word *malkitsedeq* מַלְכִּי צֶדֶק may not refer at all to the priest in Gen. 14. The word מַלְכִּי *malki* naturally means "my king of" (cf. Psa. 74:12). And צֶדֶק *tsedeq* means "justice" or "righteousness." See for instance Deu. 16:20. Thus אַתָּה-כֹהֵן לְעוֹלָם עַל-דִּבְרָתִי = "You are a minister forever concerning my cause, my King of justice." This sense fits the context of Psa. 110:4 much better. כֹהֵן *cohen* means "minister" as in 2 Sam. 8:18. Messiah is the Father's viceroy to execute justice on earth. All judgment has been committed to the Son. Yoh. 5:22. **5:8** α→submission: Another phrase unique to this author, acceptable to the Gnostic belief that the 'son of man' evolved to perfection. Messiah was born submissive to the will of the Father, as he was submissive before being born of a virgin. He was not one in need of testing to see if he would obey the commandments or not (cf. Deut. 8:1-2). **5:10** β Psa 110:4. **5:14** γ This illustration appears to be aimed at observance of the Law, while the solid food is 'knowledge' that the Temple system is obsolete.

Appendix IV: Alex. Let. 6

6 ¹Therefore, leaving the elementary teaching about the Anointed, we should be pressing on to perfection, not laying again a foundation of being sorry and turning the heart from ᵅdead works and of faithfulness upon the Almighty, ²of instruction about washings, besides laying on of hands, besides the resurrection of the dead, and everlasting judgment. ³And this we will do, if the Almighty may be permitting.

⁴Because in the case of those who have once been enlightened, having tasted besides, of the heavenly gift, and have been made partakers of the Holy Spirit, ⁵and have tasted the good word of the Almighty, besides the powers of the age to come, ⁶and then have fallen away, it is ᶲimpossible to renew them again to being sorry and turning the heart *from sin*, since they again fasten to an execution timber for themselves the Almighty Son, and put him to ᵠopen shame. ⁷Because ground that drinks the rain which often falls upon it, and brings forth vegetation useful to those for whose sake it is also tilled, receives a blessing from the Almighty, ⁸but if it yields thorns and thistles, it is worthless and close to being cursed, and it ends up being burned. ⁹But, beloved, we have been getting persuaded for better things concerning you, and things that accompany salvation, though we are speaking in this way. ¹⁰Because the Almighty is not unjust so as to forget your work and the love which you have shown toward his name, in having ministered and in still ministering to the holy ones. ¹¹And we desire that each one of you show the same diligence so as to realize the full assurance of hope until the end, ¹²that you will not have become sluggish, but imitators of those who through faithfulness and patience inherit the promises.

¹³Because when the Almighty made the promise to Avraham, since he could swear by no one greater, he swore by himself, ¹⁴saying, "I WILL SURELY BLESS YOU, AND I WILL SURELY MULTIPLY YOUᵂ." ¹⁵And thus, having patiently waited, he obtained the promise, ¹⁶because men swear by one greater than themselves, and with them an oath given as confirmation is an end of every dispute. ¹⁷In the same way the Almighty, desiring even more to show to the heirs of the promise the unchangeableness of his purpose, interposed with an oath, ¹⁸in order that by two unchangeable things, in which it is impossible for the Almighty to lie, we may be having strong encouragement, we who have fled for refuge in laying hold of the hope set before us. ¹⁹This hope we have as an anchor of the soul, a

---

6:1 α→works: 'Dead works' is a phrase unique to the author. It appears that he defines it as Jewish observances. Cf. 9:13-14 and 6:4-6 and 13:9-13. But by Jewish observances, he does not mean traditions. He means the Law itself. **6:6** ϕ But see Mĕssiah's teaching on blasphemy of the Holy Spirit, which is really the only unforgivable sin. The author judges rejection of Mĕssiah, acceptance of the Law, and particularly support for the Levitical service as all equally rejection of the Mĕssiah. Christians usually interpret the author this way. ▷ The author's criteria for concluding a person cannot be saved after backsliding is faulty. In all probability he equates falling away with literal obedience to commandments he attributes to the "old testament," such as the Sabbath and food laws, or any respect for the Temple and its services. **6:6** ψ→shame: The author and his converts probably accused the Jewish Christians of profaning Mĕssiah because they supported the Temple. This point is indeed what modern interpreters also take away from this passage. **6:14** λ Gen 22:17. **6:19** ϕ→veil: Entering within the veil is a doctrine unique to this author, as is the idea of the forerunner. Forerunner also fits in with Gnostic teaching. See earlier remarks on Psa. 110:4. The high priest enters in the veil once a year. The promise in Lev. 16:30 is "FOR IN THAT DAY HE

sure hope, besides also steadfast, and one which ⁺enters within the veil, ²⁰where Yeshua has entered as a forerunner on our behalf, having become a high "priest FOREVER in the order of Malkitsedeq^β."

7 ¹Because this Malkitsedeq, king of Şalem, priest of the Gŏd Most High, who met Avraham as he was returning from the slaughter of the kings, and blessed him; ²to whom also Avraham apportioned a tenth part of all the spoils, was first of all, by the translation of his name, "king of justice," and then also king of Şalem, which is king of peace; ³without patriarchy, without matriarchy, without pedigree, having neither beginning of days nor a life end. But ᵠhaving been getting made a copy to the Almighty Son, he abides a priest as the continual one^α.

⁴Now be observing how great this man was to whom Avraham, the patriarch, gave a tenth of the choicest spoils. ⁵And those indeed of the sons of Levi who receive the priest's office, have commandment in the Law to collect a tenth from the people, that is, from their brethren, although these have been going out from Avraham. ⁶But the one whose genealogy is not getting traced from them has been collecting a tenth from Avraham, and has been blessing the one who had the promises. ⁷But without any dispute the lesser is blessed by the greater. ⁸But in hither case mortal men receive tithes, and in thither case one receives them, of whom it is witnessed that he lives on. ⁹And, in a word, through Avraham even Levi, who received tithes, has been paying tithes, ¹⁰because he was still in the loins of his father when Malkitsedeq met him^γ.

WILL DECLARE A WIPING AWAY FOR YOU, CONCERNING CLEANSING YOU FROM ALL YOUR SINS. AT THE FACE OF YĂHWEH YOU WILL BE CLEAN." Obviously no one has been perfected yet. Therefore, this promise is also eschatological in regard to final perfection. On a future Day of Atonement, the Spĭrit will finally cleanse the hearts of all Yisra'el from all sin and will complete the promise of inscribing the Law on the heart, on the basis of the forgiveness and the ransomed release of Mĕssiah, and the cleansing power of his blood (divine life). But the author has hijacked this promise, claiming it was fulfilled in his day. It has to be perfectly clear that the author means that final cleansing was effected. And this Gnostic doctrine has been taken into the Church under the claim of being "made righteous." See Heb. 10:14. **6:20 β** Psa 110:4.

7:1-3 α See earlier note on Psalm 110:4. The speculation is an argument from silence. Without a doubt Malkitsedeq was descended from Noah. The unfounded claim of perpetual priesthood for him is supposed by the author to support his priesthood replacement doctrine. **7:3 ψ→**copy: ἀφωμοιωμένος: from-same. APO+HOMO. See LSJ, a *copy;* Thayer: *facsimile*. Since the writer has discarded all Mĕssiah's appearances as the Angel of Yahweh, he is reduced to finding an appearance in Melchizedek.

7:7-10 γ In the author's day, the Levites still collected some tithes. The altar before the destroyed Temple was likely still used in reduced fashion between about AD 90 and 130 after a hiatus between AD 70 and 90. But the Emperor Hadrian sought to remove it all just before the second Revolt. See Clement of Rome's remarks on the Levitical service. The author's argument is clearly aimed at undermining or replacing the income of the Levites. ▷ Clement writes, "These things therefore being manifest to us, and since we look into the depths of the divine knowledge, it behooves us to do all things in [their proper] order, which the Lord has commanded us to perform at stated times. He has enjoined offerings [to be presented] and service to be performed [to Him], and that not thoughtlessly or irregularly, but at the appointed times and hours. Where and by whom He desires these things to be done, He Himself has fixed by His own supreme will, in order that all things being piously done according to His good pleasure, may be acceptable unto Him. Those, therefore, who present their offerings at the appointed times, are accepted and blessed; for inasmuch as they follow the laws of the Lord, they sin not. For his own peculiar services are assigned to the high priest, and their own proper place is prescribed to the priests, and their own special ministrations devolve on the Levites. The layman is bound by the laws that pertain to laymen" (Chap. XL). ▷ "Let every one of you, brethren, give thanks to Gŏd in his own order, living in all good conscience, with becoming gravity, and not going beyond the rule of the ministry prescribed to him. Not in every place, brethren, are the daily sacrifices offered, or the peace-offerings, or the sin-offerings and the trespass-offerings, but in Jerusalem only. And

¹¹Surely then, if perfection had been through the Levitical priesthood, because by it the people have been getting the Law set forth, what further need was there for another priest to arise in the order of Malkitsedeq, and not be designated according to the order of Aharon? ¹²Because when the priesthood is changed, of necessity there takes place a change of law also.^π

¹³Because the one concerning whom these things are being spoken has been belonging to another tribe, from which no one has been approaching the altar. ¹⁴Because it is evident that our Lord had been arising from Yehudah, a tribe with reference to which Mosheh spoke nothing concerning priests. ¹⁵And it is still exceedingly evident, since another priest is arising, according to the likeness of Malkitsedeq, ¹⁶who not according to a law of ⁺fleshly commandment has been becoming so, but according to the power of an indestructible life.

¹⁷Because it is witnessed of him, "YOU ARE A ˣpriest UNTO THE AGE^θ in the order of Malkitsedeq." ¹⁸Because, on the one hand, ^λthere is a setting aside of a former commandment because of its weakness and uselessness, ¹⁹because the Law made nothing perfect, and on the other hand there is a bringing in of a better hope, through which we draw near to the Almighty, ²⁰and inasmuch as it

---

even there they are not offered in any place, but only at the altar before the temple, that which is offered being first carefully examined by the high priest and the ministers already mentioned. Those, therefore, who do anything beyond that which is agreeable to His will, are punished with death. Ye see, brethren, that the greater the knowledge that has been vouchsafed to us, the greater also is the danger to which we are exposed" (Chap. XLI).

7:11-12 π A straw man argument is assumed for the Levitical service to justify its replacement. Then the author brings in his theology of Psalm 110:4 to provide a replacement, saying the Law is changed. But see Jeremiah 33:17-22 where the Levitical priesthood is not changed. See also Ezekiel 40-48 and Malachi 3:3-4. Ecclesiastical scribes deleted the Jeremiah passage from his versions of the Septuagint. ▷ Měssiah's offering is easily harmonized with the Levitical service in that KIPPURIM means "a declaring to be wiped away." The offerings for sin were intended to confirm forgiveness for sins of ignorance. The offering of Měssiah was intended for all sin which forgiveness could not be assured by the Temple, i.e. covenant breaking sin, and serves for all sin in those times in which there is no Temple. See Acts 13:38-39. Read carefully Leviticus 4-6. In as much as sin is declared to be wiped away in the symbolism of the sacrifice, it is confession, repentance, and the divine Spirit that purges sin before the offering itself declares it. Since Messiah himself, in the Spirit, is what the sacrifice in the flesh points to, it is of course his divine life that purges sin from the faithful and his divine self that forgives (cf. Yoh. 6:63). The objections to the Levitical service, besides mere hatred of the Torah, are substantially based on the supposition that the offerings effect in themselves forgiveness and cleansing of the heart. But this is superstition, and the confusing of the sign and symbol with the spiritual reality for which it stands. We have seen the same error with the claimed efficaciousness for circumcision, baptism, and the Eucharist. Even the concept such as salvation by "belief" or "believing" is in the same category. None of these things are magic wands effecting forgiveness or purification of sins.

7:16 φ Scripture nowhere calls any commandment fleshly. (See Lev. 19:30; 26:2; Eze. 23:38; 45:17. A spiritual observation: Lev. 4:20, 26, 31, 35; 5:10, 13, 16, 18; 6:7; 19:22; Num. 15:25, 26, 28, "And it has been forgiven," (וְנִסְלַח). The offerings are declatory assurance of wiping away sin and penalty. It is the Spirit that forgives the confessor beforehand. **7:17** θ Psa 110:4). **7:17** x Heb. כֹּהֵן = *minister*, as in a political appointee. **7:18** λ→uselessness: A direct contradiction to Lev. 4-6, where it is explained how the Levitical offerings declare the wiping away for sins of ignorance, i.e. forgiveness and cleansing. The author exaggerates the intended purpose of the Levitical offerings to perfection and then he says they are good for nothing. The 'Reformation' evolution of this thinking via Anselm leads to the compensation view of Měssiah's ransom, where sacrifice replaces obedience to the commandments. See introductory remarks. (See 1 Sam. 15:22; Mat. 9:13; 12:7. See Psa. 50:8-14; 51:16-17; Isa 1:11; Jer. 6:20; 7:21-23; Mic. 6:6-8; Hos. 6:6). ▷ The author's argument here is his own opinion and it fails all the rules of logical reasoning. "The Law made nothing perfect" is but a straw man argument. One cannot deduce from this that a commandment must be set aside. The author's better hope is opposed to the Law.

was not without an oath. ²¹Because they surely are having been becoming priests ⁿwithout an oath, but he ⁿwith an oath through the One who said to him, "ADONAI HAS SWORN AND WILL NOT CHANGE HIS MIND, 'YOU ARE A ˣpriest UNTO THE AGE.'"

²²And so much the more also the Anointed One has been becoming the guarantee of a ᵋbetter covenant. ²³And those surely ᶻare many, who have been becoming priests, *but* because of death ᵞare getting prevented from continuing, ²⁴but he, on the other hand, because he abides to the time immemorial, holds his priesthood permanently.

²⁵Hence, also, he is able to rescue completely those who draw near to the Almighty through him, since he always lives to make intercession on their behalf.

²⁶For it was fitting that we should have such a high priest, holy, innocent, undefiled, having been getting separated from sinners and exalted above the heavens, ²⁷who does not need, daily, like those high priests, to offer up sacrifices, first concerning his own ᵖsins, and then the ᵖsins of the people, because this he did at one time when he offered up himself.

²⁸Because the Law appoints men as high priests who are ˣweak, but the saying of the oath, which came after the Law, appoints a Son, ᵞwho has been getting perfected, unto the age.

8

¹Now the main point in what has been said is this. We have such a high priest who has taken his seat at the right hand of the throne of the Majesty in the heavens, ²a servant in the sanctuary, and in the trueˣ Tabernacle, which the Lord pitched, not manˣ.

³Because every high priest is appointed to offer gifts besides also sacrifices. Hence it is necessary that this high priest also have something he will have offered. ⁴Now if he were on earth, he would not be a priest at all, since there are those

---

7:21 η→oath: an attempt to de-legitimize, but see Mal. 2:4-7; 4:4; θ Psa 110:4; χ see note 7:17 χ. **7:22** ξ→covenant: Scripture nowhere calls the new made covenant a better covenant than the original covenant. (See Rom. 10 & Deu. 30). It is in fact the covenant of old new made. **7:23** ζ→becoming: the periphrastic present plus pres. perf. continuous indicate that an altar had been restored at the Temple site several decades after AD 70 until ca. AD 132. λ→getting: present participle. Surely the imperfect would be used if no services were currently being conducted. **7:26-27** ρ But there was no daily sin offering. The daily offering was a worship offering. The sin offerings were regularly offered on the new moon day. The author claims the function of the Levitical offerings was abolished once for all with the offering of Mĕssiah. Obviously this is not so since the Temple is to be restored to Israel. The sin offerings give assurance by the declatory wiping of sins of ignorance. Mĕssiah's offering addresses the issue of greater sins for which there was no Temple offering in the same type of symbolism. (See Zech. 14:20-21; Mal. 3:1-4; Dan. 8:13-14; Ezek. 40-48; Jer. 33:17-22). **7:28** χ By stating a legally irrelevant fact the author attacks the Levitical service (cf. Mal. 2:4-8). **7:28** θ Psa. 110:4, but the Hebrew is speaking of Mĕssiah as a minister of justice to enforce the Law and execute its justice upon the nations (cf. Psa. 110:4-6); see earlier remarks. **7:28** γ→perfected: it seems the author is taking the Gnostic viewpoint that Christ evolved to godhood, which is complete heresy. Even trying to make it refer to a resultant state: 'who has been being perfected' still suggests a perfecting process in the past. There is no way to rescue the language from the suggestion that the starting point was less than perfect.

8:1-2 χ But the Law says TO RESPECT THE SANCTUARY AND KEEP HIS ŞABBAŧHS (Lev 19:30; 26:2). The glory of Yăhweң dwelled in the Holiest Place and Yăhweң also spoke face to face with Mosheң there. Also, Yăhweң appeared next to the altar of incense in the Holy Place. The earthly dwelling was just as true as the heavenly one. It is to be likened as the Almĭghty's summer home among his people. What was pitched by man was according to the word of the Almĭghty. The author's implied *put down* of the earthly sanctuary must be rejected. For there the Almĭghty has chosen to put his name, and there he will yet put his name.

who offer the gifts according to the Law, ⁵which serve a copy and shadow of the heavenly things, just as Mosheh had been getting divinely instructed, when he was about to erect the Tabernacle, because, "BE SEEING," he says, "THAT YOU MAKE ALL THINGS ACCORDING TO THEIR PATTERN WHICH WAS SHOWN YOU ON THE MOUNTAIN.ᵖ"

⁶But now he has been obtaining a different ministry, by as much as he is also the mediator of a ᵘbetter will, which has been getting made into law by ᵟbetter promises.

⁷Because if that first testament was faultless, there would have been no occasion sought for a second, ⁸because finding fault with them, he says, "BEHOLD, THE DAYS ARE COMING, SAYS ADONAI, WHEN I WILL EFFECT A ᵝnew-made COVENANT WITH THE HOUSE OF YISRA'EL AND WITH THE HOUSE OF YEHUDAH, ⁹NOT ᶲlike THE COVENANT WHEN I COVENANTED WITH THEIR FATHERS, ᵠon THE DAY WHEN I TOOK THEM BY THE HAND TO LEAD THEM OUT OF THE LAND OF EGYPT; ᵘFor THEY DID NOT CONTINUE IN MY COVENANT, AND I ᵖdid not care for THEM, SAYS ADONAI, ¹⁰BECAUSE THIS IS THE COVENANT WHICH I ᵚwill COVENANT WITH THE HOUSE OF YISRA'EL AFTER THOSE DAYS, SAYS ADONAI. I WILL PUT MY LAWS INTO THEIR MINDS, AND I WILL WRITE THEM UPON THEIR HEARTS. AND I WILL BE THEIR ALMIGHTY, AND THEY WILL BE MY PEOPLE. ¹¹AND THEY SHALL NOT HAVE TAUGHT EVERYONE HIS FELLOW CITIZEN, AND EVERYONE HIS BROTHER, SAYING, 'KNOW ADONAI,' BECAUSE ALL WILL KNOW ME, FROM THE LEAST TO THE GREATEST OF THEM, ¹²BECAUSE I WILL FORGIVE THEIR INIQUITIES, AND I SHALL HAVE REMEMBERED THEIR SINS NO MOREᵠ." ¹³By saying, "new-made COVENANT," he has been making the first old. And what is getting old also is aging, near disappearanceʸ.

9

¹Now even the ᵅfirst testament had regulations of divine worship, besides the earthly sanctuary, ²because there was a tabernacle prepared, the outer one, in which besides the menorah was also the table and the sacred bread, which is called the Holy Place. ³And behind the second veil, there was a tabernacle which is called the Holy of Holies, ⁴havingᵋ a golden ᵝaltar of incense, and the ark of

---

8:5 ρ Exo 25:40; **8:6** μ-δ The author equivocates the meaning of covenant with the notion of a will and testament. The translation reflects this. The author's error is great. No greater promises can be made than those in Deuteronomy 30, and Paul quotes the passage in Romans 10. The word which he preached was the word of faithfulness according to the definitions given in Deut. 30:6, 11-14. **8:7-12** β-φ-ψ-μ-π-ω The places underlined and not in small caps are where the text has been falsely interpreted. The corrected text appears in the introductory remarks. Corrections: β = renewal; See 1 Cor 11:25 note χ. φ = according to; ψ = in; μ = when, because; π = was master against; ω = do. **8:8-12** ψ Jer 31:31-34; **8:13** γ See introduction. But the new covenant is really a covenant renewal of the covenant of old. The covenant of old (ברית עולם) was already ancient before the prophet announced a renewal. In the messianic age, Měssiah comes to restore Yisra‑el from exile (Deut. 30), and to remember his covenant (Lev. 26:44-45), the covenant of old, which is made new by the blood of Měssiah.

9:1 α = first [testament]; Or will. The standard meaning of this word in Greek is a will, but through Hebrew usage came to mean covenant. In this case the author means will. (See 9:16-18). A covenant does not require the death of the covenant maker for effectiveness. Only a will does. **9:4** β→incense, θυμιατήριον: Philo and Josephus use the word to mean 'altar of incense.' The author has misplaced the golden altar of incense. It belonged to the first compartment of the Tabernacle, the Holy Place. An attempt to define this object as a hand held incense burner used on the Day of Atonement isn't likely, because the author is describing the standard furniture constantly stationed in the Tabernacle. If an incense burner were meant,

the covenant, having been getting covered on all sides with gold, ᶲin which was a golden jar havingᶝ the manna, and Aharon's rod which budded, and the ᶿtables of the covenant. ⁵And above it were the Keruvim of glory overshadowing the mercy seat, but of these things we cannot now speak in detail.

⁶Now when these things had been getting prepared thus, the priests are continually entering the outer tabernacle, performing the divine worship, ⁷but into the second only the high priest enters, once a year, not without taking blood, which he brings concerning himself and the sins of the people committed in ignorance.

⁸This *is* clarifying, by the Holy Spirit, *that* the way into the Holiest Place had not yet been getting revealed, while the first tabernacle was still standing, ⁹which is a parable for the time which has been already existing. Accordingly gifts besides also sacrifices are offered which cannot make the worshiper ᵅperfect in conscience, ¹⁰since they relate only to food and drink and various washings, ᵝregulations for the body imposed until a time of reformation. ¹¹But when the Anointed appeared as a high priest of the good things to come, he entered through the greater and more perfect Tabernacle, not made with hands, that is to say, not of this creation, ¹²and not through the blood of goats and calves, but through his own blood, he entered the Holy Place at one time, having obtained everlasting redemption.

¹³Because if the blood of goats and bulls and the ashes of a heifer sprinkling those who have been getting defiled, make one holy for the cleansing of the ᶲflesh,

---

which is a minor object, then the golden altar upon which incense was offered daily would be inexplicably omitted. Also, the supposition of a special incense pan is tradition, which in any case by the same tradition wasn't kept in the most Holy Place. **9:4** ξ ἔχουσα (cf. ζ): The author is not acquitted by 1 Kings 6:22, so as to allow reinterpretation of the word 'having' (ξ). For that verse is mistranslated "belonging to" (*owning*) in many versions, but it says "TOWARD THE ORACLE," לדביר, which is shortened from לפני העדות (*toward the face of the testimony*) or לפני הפרכת (*toward the face of the atonement place*), besides possibly meaning simply *next to the oracle*. See Exodus 30:6, 36. But Yăhweң met in two places; the oracle was not confined to the Holiest Place. He spoke from above the ark. But the Mĕssenger of Yăhweң would appear next to the altar of incense (cf. Luke 1:11) so that the words in 1 Kings 6:22 may imply either that the altar was (1) toward the face of the Holiest Place, but still within the Holy Place, or (2) next to the space at its right side where the oracle also spoke in the form of the Mĕssenger. In no case does the ל reasonably mean *owning* or *possessing* (ξ), so as to exclude the location in this context, because the word is not so ambiguous in relation to the ark. Put it like this: *the most special room of my house is possessing a fancy table and a cedar hope chest*, and it is clear that no linguistic rationalization can put either item in another room! And if the ל means "belonging to" in 1 Kings 6:22, it would surely then mean beside the golden incense altar (cf. 1 Sam. 3:10, 21), where the Mĕssenger was actually seen speaking, and not hidden by the curtain. **9:4** θ None of these items save only the tablets were placed inside the ark (See Num 17:10; Exo 16:33: 1 Ki 8:9; 2 Chr 5:10). **9:4** φ→which = ἐν ᾗ (RelPro-DFS): The relative pronoun is feminine to agree with the words ark: κιβωτὸν τῆς διαθήκης. There is no doubt that the author claims all the following items to be in the ark.

9:9 α→conscience: But this was not the purpose of the Levitical service. The author's alternative does not make a person perfect in conscience either (as he falsely implies) since the perfection of conscience is a matter of obedience to the commandments (which have to be learned) and not a matter of sacrifice. **9:10** β→body: The author claims the Levitical offerings only relate to "regulations for the body." But this simply is not true. The sin offerings had to do with guilt, which is a very spiritual matter, and forgiveness of sins of ignorance was declared through them. The continual offering was a worship offering and the Almĭghty ordained them for his spiritual worship. The author clearly means these offerings are to be ended because he thinks Mĕssiah's appearing is the "time of reformation," and so the Law is no longer imposed. **9:13-14** φ The presumption that the Levitical service only stood for cleansing of the flesh is an error. But Leviticus 4-6 says that when the offering is made the

¹⁴how much more will the blood of the Anointed, who through the everlasting Spirit offered himself without blemish to the Almighty, cleanse your conscience from dead works to serve the living Almighty?

¹⁵And for this reason he is the mediator of a new-made testament, in order that since a death has taken place for the redemption of the transgressions that were committed under the first testament, those who have been getting called will have received the promise of the everlasting inheritance. ¹⁶Because where a testament is, there must of necessity be the death of the one who made it, ¹⁷because a testament is valid only when men are dead, because it is never in force while the one who made it lives⁴.

¹⁸Therefore even the first testament had not been getting inaugurated without blood, ¹⁹because when every commandment was spoken by Mosheh to all the people according to the Law, he took the blood of the calves and the ᵚgoats, with ᵚwater and ᵚscarlet wool and ᵚhyssop, and sprinkled besides the ᵚbook itself also all the people, ²⁰saying, "THIS IS THE BLOOD OF THE COVENANT WHICH THE ALMIGHTY COMMANDS YOUᵃ."

²¹And in the same way he sprinkled both the Tabernacle and all the vessels of the ministry with the bloodˣ. ²²And according to the Law, almost all things are cleansed with blood, and without shedding of blood there is no forgivenessᵠ.

---

worshiper *has been forgiven* for sins of ignorance, or "is forgiven" in timeless English, which is to say the offering is a ceremonial assurance of forgiveness. And by this there is declatory assurance (or confirmation) of forgiveness and cleansing. The author errs greatly in denying the assurance that the offerings for sins of ignorance provided the confessor of his forgiveness. By doing so, he also removes any objective foundation for believing that Měssiah's offering confirms our forgiveness. **9:15-17** μ This whole line of argument is based on the assumption that the covenant was a will or testament. In a will one gets the inheritance only when the will maker dies. The assumption begs the question of how the 'first covenant' was valid before the covenant maker died. Yisra'el inherited the land, but the covenant maker did not have to die for this to happen.

9:19 ω Exodus 24 describes the ratification of the covenant. There is no mention that blood was sprinkled on the book, nor goats sacrificed, nor scarlet wool or hyssop involved in the ceremony. The author has confused other passages with what happened in Exodus 24. But only oxen were mentioned (פרים) in Exo. 24:5. The blood was sprinkled on the people in Exo. 24:8. The scarlet and hyssop belong to passages like Lev. 14:6, 49; or Num. 19:6, passages concerning the cleansing from leprosy of either man or house, and the preparation of the ashes of the red heifer, to be used for cleansing procedures. **9:20** α Exo 24:8; **9:21** χ Again the author is incorrect. Oil was generally used for anointing the Tabernacle items. Blood was only used on the ark, the ground, and the altar. (See Exodus 40:9).

9:22 ψ or 'release [from sin].' This is a titanic lie, and it is based on a superstitious view of the effect of sacrifices. Truly forgiveness occurs upon confession and repentance (1 Yoh. 1:9). The sacrificial lesson is only confirmatory and instructive. See note *2:17* λ on Prov. 16:6. The coal off the altar that purged the iniquity of Isaiah symbolized an immediate spiritual operation without blood (cf. Isa. 6:7), because the divine presence had immediately revealed things deep in Yesha'yahu's heart that even he had walled off. Lev. 5:11-13 is also a declaratory offering without blood. It is termed a "memorial" (אַזְכָּרָתָה). This flour offering contained no oil or spice, which affliction symbolizes the bearing of sin. The sin is declared to be purged, 'on the fires of Yăhweḥ' (עַל אִשֵּׁי יְהוָה). David was also forgiven according to 2 Sam. 12:13; Psa. 32:5. Yet, he brought no offering for it. We should not overlook Matthew 9:2; Mark 2:5, "your sins are getting forgiven"; and Luke 5:20, (ἀφέωνται), "you sins have been getting forgiven you." How is it that the Son of man proclaims forgiveness of sins without the shedding of blood? It is because he is the Almighty Son. How are the man's sins getting forgiven without a substitutionary payment in blood to satisfy the wrath of God? It is because that doctrine is wrong. Sin is not paid for. It is forgiven and cleansed, and sacrifice was given to teach us that and indicate the cost of our ransom. Sacrifice is the agent of forgiveness no more than baptism or Eucharist. The blood declares and confirms forgiveness. It does not put a hex on God to make him do it, nor does the lack of it prevent him from forgiving. See Appendix X, 584.

²³Therefore it was necessary for the copies of the things in the heavens to be cleansed with these, but the heavenly things themselves with better sacrifices than these᠆ᵘ.

²⁴Because the Anointed did not enter a Holy Place made with hands, a ᶜcopy of the true one, but into heaven itself, now to appear in the presence of the Almighty on our behalf. ²⁵Nor was it that he should be offering himself repeatedly, as the high priest enters the Holy Place year by year with blood not his own. ²⁶Otherwise, he would have needed to suffer often since the founding of the world, but now once at the ᶠconsummation of the ages he has been manifesting himself to abolish sin by the sacrifice of himselfᵖ. ²⁷And inasmuch as it is appointed for men to die once and after this comes judgment, ²⁸so the Anointed also, having been offered once to take away the sins of many, will appear a second time for salvation without reference to sin, to those who eagerly await him.

¹⁰·¹For the Law, since it has a shadow of the good things to come and not the image of matters, can never by the same sacrifices throughout a year, which they offer as ˣthe continual, make perfect those who draw nearˡ.

9:23 μ The notion that heaven itself needed to be cleansed with sacrifices (plural) is unique to this author. It would appear that the heavenly Sanctuary never was defiled in the first place and had no need of cleansing. Or if it was, then the fire from the Most High was the agent of cleansing and not physical blood.

9:24-25 ς The Law does not say the pattern shown on the mount was a *copy* of the layout in heaven. It was a blueprint for the earthly Sanctuary, and some items are similar to those in heaven. The idea that what is supposed to take place on earth must also take place in heaven based on these similarities is fallacious. Cleansing sacrifice is necessary for what is earthly, not what abides in heaven. **9:26** ξ See 10:37 for the author's belief in the very soon coming. This word is used in Mat. 13:39, 40, 49; 24:3; 28:20. It refers to the consummation of the age at the second coming. The author incorrectly teaches it was the consummation then. **9:26** ρ The author supposes final cleansing has come. Not so according to Scripture. See 1 Yoḥ. 1:9 and Zech. 3:9-10. But it was not the end of the ages then. Nowhere does Scripture claim Mĕssiah came at the end of the ages. See 10:37.

10:1 χ→continual = הַתָּמִיד **10:1** λ The argument is a variation of the lie that it is useless to keep any commandments of the Torah because one cannot keep them all perfectly. In this case, the author lies that the Levitical service is useless because it could not perfect the sinner. Truly, the Levitical service was not meant to perfect the sinner. The commandments were not meant to be kept only if all could be kept perfectly. ▷ Firstly, we are given here a dry crust, 'the law has a shadow of good things,' but it is meant only to distract the reader long enough to swallow the next lie, 'and not the image of matters.' What the author means by 'shadow' is explained in 9:10, the shadow only relates to the physical, and as a true Gnostic would say, was a concessionary to the material realm, and one must by all means set it aside to embrace the truly spiritual so as to reconnect with the pleroma. ▷ But truly 'the image' (εἰκόνα) is a word that also means 'an icon,' 'a picture,' or 'representation,' and thus it has the same meaning as 'shadow,' which was translated 'reflection' over in Col. 2:17. In fact, we may consider the author's point of view here a reinterpretation of Col. 2:17, since the wording is almost the same, viz. ἅ ἐστιν σκιὰ τῶν μελλόντων vs. Σκιὰν γὰρ ἔχων ὁ νόμος τῶν μελλόντων ἀγαθῶν. Having equated the shadow with the physical, the author proceeds to deny that the law contains the image of the spiritual. ▷ But the Torah surely does reflect the spiritual in the symbolism of the Levitical offerings, because the symbols have spiritual meanings. The forgiveness of sins is a spiritual operation of the divine Spirit. One cannot read Lev. 4-5 and say the offerings do not represent this. When the blood is applied to the altar, the symbolism is declaratory that sin is being removed from the confessor (who laid his hand on the offering) and blotted out by the blood. Truly, the confessor is forgiven in the spiritual realm before he brings the offering by the Spirit of the Most High, because he has confessed and repented. The offering is brought to represent this to the whole world. ▷ The reason the ceremony was limited to sins of ignorance was that transgression and iniquity caused a break in the covenant, whereas sins of ignorance did not. Iniquities were also forgiven upon repentance, and this is indicated by the second goat in Lev. 16, wherein these sins are carried away, giving the people assurance that these sins also may be cleansed. And this is a spiritual message. But people must realize that it is harder. If they will not afflict their souls and repent, then the spiritual assurance drawn from the symbolism of the ceremony will be for nought, and they will be cut off from the people. Because it is through confession and repentance to the Most High

10

²Otherwise, would they not have ceased to be offered, because the worshipers, having once been getting cleansed, would no longer have had consciousness of sins?ʸ ³But in those sacrifices there is aᵗ reminder of sins year by year. ⁴Because it is impossible for the blood of bulls and goats to take away sins.

⁵Therefore, when he comes into the world, he says: "SACRIFICE AND OFFERING YOU HAST NOT DESIRED, BUT ˣa body you have prepared for me. ⁶WHOLE-ASCENDING SACRIFICE, AND SACRIFICE FOR SIN YOU HAVE NOT ASKED FOR. ⁷SO I SAID, 'BEHOLD, I HAVE COME. IN THE ROLL OF THE BOOK IT HAS BEEN GETTING WRITTEN OF ME TO DO YOUR WILL, O ALMIGHTY. [*YOUR LAW IS WITHIN MY HEART*].'"

⁸After saying above, "SACRIFICES AND OFFERINGS AND WHOLE ASCENDING SACRIFICES EVEN FOR SIN YOU HAVE NOT DESIRED, NOR HAVE YOU ASKED FOR," which are offered according to the Law, ⁹then he had been saying, "BEHOLD, I HAVE COME TO DO YOUR WILL O ALMIGHTY, [*YOUR LAW IS WITHIN MY HEART*]ᵠ."

---

that transgression is forgiven.

10:2 γ The argument is a straw man since the author is rhetorically assuming that sacrifices are supposed to do something they were never meant to. He builds an erring expectation for the Levitical service and then attacks it on the basis that it did not reach this expectation. But, in fact the offerings confirmed forgiveness of the confessor and his cleansing from sin.

10:3-4 π That the author means 'only a reminder' is clear from Heb. 9:10. We must understand that stating what they *only* do excludes everything not mentioned. The author clearly means to exclude forgiveness or pardon from the messaging of the offerings for sins of ignorance. The usual rationalization offered to support the author against the plain statements of Leviticus is that "atonement" only means "to cover" sin. But KIPPURIM means to "to declare to be wiped away" (See 1 Yoḥ 4:10 note). The sinner is under condemnation. He confesses and repents. The condemnation is forgiven, and the Spirit of Messiah cleanses him. This reality is then indicated by the sacrificial cermony. See Appendix X. ▷ The meaning of KIPPURIM is the same with respect to Messiah's offering for iniquity (1 Yoḥ 2:2, 4:10; Rom. 3:25; Lev. 25:9). The alleged alteration of meaning in the term has no foundation in fact. The only limitation of the Levitical offerings was limitation to sins of ignorance, but this was not a fault. It was by design. Messiah's offering is for all other sins. See Acts 13:39 note. ▷ If "atonement" is allowed to mean only 'cover' in respect to the Levitical service, then what justification is there for it to mean anything else in respect to Messiah's offering? And we should note that postulating the meaning "cover" in contrast to some later forgiveness or remission is a denial that forgiveness occurs in the spiritual realm after confession and repentance (cf. 1 Yoḥ. 1:9).

10:5-7 ζ Psa 40:6-8; **10:5 χ→**prepared: The original Psalm reads, "BUT MY EARS YOU HAVE OPENED" (אָזְנַיִם כָּרִיתָ לִי). The reading is unique to this author and occurs nowhere in the Hebrew text nor in the Greek Septuagint (LXX: ὠτία δὲ κατηρτίσω μοι). The original text points to obedience for the king rather than sacrifice (cf. Deut. 17:18-20). The author has changed it to point to another sacrifice. The Scripture says that TO OBEY IS BETTER THAN SACRIFICE (1 Sam 15:22; Hos 6:6). But the lawless substitute sacrifice for obedience because they think that sacrifice compensates the Almĭghty for their disobedience. But in no way is this view of Messiah's death acceptable. The Almĭghty is not compensated for sin any more than the victim of a murder is brought back to life when the murderer is punished. Messiah did not suffer to pay the penalty we deserved. He suffered as a ransom to deliver us from Lawlessness which held us in bondage. The penalty is forgiven. The ransom also teaches that sin extorts a great cost. It is a warning instruction against sin, and not a compensation for sin. The false doctrines of Augustine, and Anselm of Canterbury led to false doctrines of imputed righteousness taught by Luther and Calvin as a means of making restitution to the Almĭghty. The whole theory falls to pieces as soon as we realize that the consequences of sin are not all undone. The forgiveness of the sin of one person does not undo the eternal death it caused to the other. Sacrifice does not compensate the Almĭghty for the loss caused by lawlessness. ▷ I have included the end of the quote that the author has left off since it is relevant to the author's deception replacing obedience with sacrifice: וְתוֹרָתְךָ בְּתוֹךְ מֵעָי.

10:8-9 ψ Psa. 40:6-8. But the author has left out the closing phrase of 40:8 because he has argued that the sacrifices and offerings that were not wanted have been replaced with another sacrifice, namely Christ, rather than acknowledging the point of King David, wherein it is obedience that is wanted instead of sacrifice (cf. Deut. 17:18-20). **10:9b-13 δ** The covenant of the first ones (Lev. 26:45) cannot be removed, because it will be remembered when Israel repents in exile (cf. Deut. 30:1-6). This is the 'covenant of old' (בְּרִית עוֹלָם). The Messiah died to make this covenant new, like an old commandment is made new (cf. 1 Yoḥ. 2:7-8). The author writes against Jer. 33:17-22

⁹ᵇHe takes away the first in order that he will have established the second.ᵟ ¹⁰By this will we have been getting made holy through the sacrifice of the body of the Anointed at one time. ¹¹And, on the one hand every priest has been standing, daily ministering and offering time after time the same sacrifices, which can never take away sins, ¹²but on the other hand, he, having offered one sacrifice concerning sins as the continual, sat down at the right hand of the Almighty, ¹³henceforth waiting while his enemies will have been made a footstool for his feet.

¹⁴Because by one offering he has been perfecting ᶲas the continual those who are getting made holy. ¹⁵And the Holy Spirit also bears witness to us, because after what he had been saying, *he said*, ¹⁶"THIS IS THE COVENANT THAT I ᶲwill COVENANT WITH THEM AFTER THOSE DAYS, SAYS ADONAI. I WILL PUT MY LAWS UPON THEIR HEART, AND UPON THEIR MIND I WILL WRITE THEM, ¹⁷AND THEIR LAWLESS DEEDS I WILL REMEMBER NO MORE.ᶴ"

¹⁸Now where there is release from these things, there is no longer any offering for sin. ¹⁹Since therefore, brethren, we have confidence to enter the Holy Place by the blood of Yeshua, ²⁰by a recent and living way which he dedicated for us through the veil, that is, his flesh, ²¹and since we have a great Priest over the house of the Almighty, ²²we should be drawing near with a sincere heart in full certainty of confidence, having been getting our hearts sprinkled clean from an evil conscience and having been getting our bodies washed with pure water.

---

and all the prophecies predicting a restoration of the Temple in the age to come. His denial of the value of the Levitical offerings as instructive spiritual lessons removes the foundation for the meaning of Mĕssiah's offering and its spiritual lesson.

10:14 ϕ→continual: The author has transferred the false supposition that sacrifice perfects the person to Mĕssiah's offering, and has replaced the continual offering with it (cf. Num. 28:3; Dan. 8:11, 12-13). But this is not what the continual offering (הַתָּמִיד) meant. The continual offering was a worship offering and did not pertain to perfection of the worshipers. The Almĭghty did not desire sacrifice, not even Mĕssiah, as a substitute for obedience. He was pleased with it as a means of communicating the lesson of sacrifice when the powers thought it was to their advantage to take the life of the only kindred Son (cf. Isa. 53:10-11), but as we see, the mechanism for perfection is stated in vs. 16, which writing of the Law upon the heart is not the continual offering or Mĕssiah's offering. It is in fact through "knowing him" that we get favorable justice. The correct analogy of Mĕssiah's blood with respect to perfection is life by his resurrection power through repentance and the cleansing of the divine Spĭrit (cf. Psalm 32 and 51). **10:16** ϕ The author wishes us to think that the covenant was made when Mĕssiah came, but in fact the renewal began when the forty years were at an end on the plains of Moav (cf. Deut. 29:1; Mat. 26:28; Mark 14:24; Rom. 10:8; Deut. 30:14). This is what Jeremiah means by '*after those days.*' We should read the Hebrew imperfect (אֶכְרֹת) as '*I am covenanting*' or '*I do covenant.*' Also, the renewal is not yet complete, because he is not finished writing the Law on the hearts of all the faithful. But the author teaches his converts that they are already getting perfected by sacrifice, redefining obedience in terms of sacrifice. **10:16-17** ξ Jer. 31:33-34.

10:18 ς The author considers the Law already written on the heart. He claims one may enter the Holy Place because one is purified from sin. The point is that he considers himself pure, body and soul (cf. vs.22). But the true good news teaches forgiveness, and a future purification from sin in the age to come (cf. Gal. 5:5). The author's definition of holding faithful is inadequate, since he clearly contradicts outward faithfulness by making the claim to be perfected while in the flesh (cf. Gal. 3:3). ▷ The author considers perfection a done deal. But the promises are not complete. Hearts are not perfectly cleansed or perfectly circumcised, nor are sins of ignorance at an end. The Temple service will be restored in the ages to come both for sins of ignorance and worship. And the offerings will teach the same lessons they were meant to teach when first given to Yisra'el. There are many Christians to this day that believe all sins of all mankind were forgiven at the cross. All they have to do is accept it. But this is not so. Mĕssiah died to ransom every person. But the forgiveness is not effective without holding faithful to Mĕssiah. Many will hear in that day, "I NEVER ACKNOWLEDGED YOU," (Mat. 7:23) because they never fulfilled the condition of their pardon to repent of sin, and be cleansed by the life of Messiah.

²³We should be holding fast the confession of our hope without wavering, because he who promised is trustworthy, ²⁴and we should be concentrating on how to stimulate one another to love and good deeds, ²⁵not forsaking our own congregating, as is the habit of some, but encouraging one another, and all the more, as you see the day drawing near.

²⁶Because if we go on sinning willfully after receiving the knowledge of the truth, there no longer remains a sacrifice for sins, ²⁷but a certain terrifying expectation of judgment, and the fury of a fire which will consume the adversaries.

²⁸Anyone who has set aside the Law of Mosheh dies without mercy ON THE TESTIMONY OF TWO OR THREE WITNESSES.ᵟ ²⁹How much severer punishment do you think he will deserve who has trampled under foot the Almighty Son, and has regarded as unclean the blood of the covenant by which he was sanctified, and has insulted the Spirit of grace?

³⁰Because we have been knowing him who said, "VENGEANCE IS MINE, I WILL REPAY.ᵅ" And again, "ADONAI WILL JUDGE HIS PEOPLE.ᵝ" ³¹It is a terrifying thing to fall into the hands of the living Almighty. ³²But be reminding yourselves of the former days, in which, having been enlightened, you endured much conflict in sufferings, ³³This *was* indeed by insults, besides also by tribulations, some being made public examples, or such having been made fellowshippers with those likewise being survivors. ³⁴Because you showed sympathy to the prisoners, and accepted joyfully the seizure of your property, knowing that you have for yourselves a better possession and an abiding one. ³⁵Therefore, you shall not have thrown away your confidence, which has a great reward, ³⁶because you have need of endurance, so that when you have done the will of the Almighty, you will have received what was promised.

³⁷ "FOR YET IN A VERY VERY LITTLE WHILEᵅ…THE ONE COMING WILL COME, AND WILL NOT DELAY.ᵝ" ³⁸"BUT my RIGHTEOUS ONE WILL LIVE BY FAITHFULNESS.ᶿ"

10:28 δ Deut. 17:6 **10:30** α Deu 32:35 **10:30** β Deu 32:36.

10:37 α Isa 10:25, cf. 26:20 **10:37** α The first part of the quote in 10:37 is spliced from Isa. 10:25; cf. 26:20, "FOR IN A VERY LITTLE WHILE, AND WILL HAVE ENDED INDIGNATION AND MY ANGER BY THEIR DESTRUCTION." The text refers to Assyria. See Isa. 10:24. **10:37** β Hab 2:3. The Hebrew Hab. 2:3 says, "BECAUSE COMING HE WILL COME. HE WILL NOT BE TOO LATE." The author felt this was not soon enough, so he interprets the words 'will not be too late' (לֹא יְאַחֵר, literally, 'no he makes to be late,' which means Messiah will not unnecessarily delay his rescue from the final Babylon), to mean time-wise *soon* with no consideration for things that might make Messiah later than he thinks, such as the salvation of the nations. The author therefore speeds things up by prefixing Isa. 10:25 to his text. But it has been two millennia. Messiah has been necessarily delayed on account of the nations, but he will not make himself be [too] late.

So the passage of time shows the author has greatly erred. **10:38** θ Hab 2:4b. Paul never cites Hab. 2:4 the way the author does. In Hab. 2:4b the author deviated from both Hebrew and the LXX. The Hebrew says: BUT THE RIGHTEOUS ONE BY HIS FAITHFULNESS WILL LIVE. The LXX reads "my faithfulness," which is a legitimate interpretation of "HIS FAITHFULNESS." "His" refers to the Almighty. But the author has transposed this to "My righteous one." Paul would not have written such as it undermines his exposition on the "FAITHFULNESS OF MESSIAH," which is his covenant faithfulness. See Rom. 1:17; 3:21-25; Gal. 2:16; 3:11. **10:38** μ Hab 2:4a 𝔊. The last quote occurs only in the LXX; it is a poor attempt to translate Hab. 2:4a, which in Hebrew properly goes: BEHOLD, ONE BEING PROUD: HE WILL NOT HAVE BEEN UPRIGHT IN HIS SOUL. The proud one in Hab. 2:4a is Babylon or its leader antiMessiah. It isn't God's soul that is mentioned there. In only a collective derivative sense does the text refer to an apostate Christian identified with Babylon.

"And if he may have shrunk back, my soul has no pleasure in him.ᵘ" ³⁹But we are not of those who shrink back to DESTRUCTION,ᵖ but are of FAITHFULNESS to the preserving of the soul.ᵖ

11 ¹Now ᵐholding faithful is the ᵖcourage of things hoped for, the testimony of things not seen, ²because by it the men of old gained approval. ³By holding faithful we perceive the ᶿages to have been getting made ready by the word of the Almighty, so that what is being perceived has not been becoming out of things which are visible. ⁴By holding faithful, Hevel offered to the Almighty a better sacrifice than Qayin, through which he obtained the testimony that he was righteous, the Almighty testifying about his gifts, and through it, though he is dead, he still speaks.

⁵By ˣholding faithful Ḥanok was taken up so that he should not see death. And he was not found because the Almighty took him up, because he had been getting the testimony, before his being taken up, to have been pleasing the

---

10:39 ρ Isa. 10:25. **11:1** π πίστις. ρ ὑπόστασις = *courage; resolution; steadiness;* (LSJ B.II.4; cf. Heb. 3:14). The author's stated definition is only half the truth, but also, 'holding faithful' is fidelity to Gǒd's commandments in things presently seen. Holding faithful is not just courage, or trust in an unseen promise or truth, but the actual doing of the commandments. The author's misdirection is at the context level and not with the unaffected semantics of πίστις. But it does open the door to the long road to defining the term πίστις as 'belief' or 'trust' only taken from Latin to English. The author's definition construes 'holding faithful' to mean action based on trusting. The trust-action is the objective testimony of the unseen promise. The holding faithful is the courage of the heart. ▷ The πίστις word group means, 1. faithful, 2. faithfulness, 3. holding faithful. What it means is based on the context. Scripturally, saving *faithfulness* means fidelity to Gǒd by a. keeping his commandments, b. trusting his promises. This application is imparted from the context. For example, holding faithful means something different to a soldier in the Roman army. Holding faithful can also mean the power of positive thinking if that is the context. It could just mean a firm trusting. It could mean only obeying certain commandments and not others. And this author probably has not rejected the idea that holding faithful to Gǒd means keeping his commandments, but he has rejected the levitical commandments, and he has shifted the emphasis toward trust based action with a view to future promises. So while he may yet believe holding faithful may mean fidelity to the commandments, he has not stated it in his definition. And his examples generally steer away from simple obedience toward action based on trust, though sometimes it is difficult to figure out what the one holding faithful was doing to aim at the promise, and thus the meaning appears to slide back into general obedience, as is the case of Enoch, who probably did not know what Gǒd intended before it happened. ▷ The reason the author can use his examples is that 'holding faithful' for him is a fluid dispensational concept. He has already told us that a change of law occurs respecting the priesthood. ▷ The shift in meaning or application to a future hope over present obedience is a Gnostic one, motivated by rejection of the physical world for a spritual one liberated from the physical. This is why the author does not interpret the Levitical service according to its spiritual meanings. But, to give his spiritual lesson he uses his disconnected concept of 'faith.' **11:1** π I think it better to use a participle throughout the passage to translate πίστις; it should be taken as a noun: 'a holding faithful,' and has the same sense as 'faithfulness.' Another good gloss would be 'holding firm.' **11:3** θ αἰῶνας = *eons, aeons;* Ages is often translated "worlds," but the primary sense of the Greek word is "aeons." The alleged creation of time is a favorite argument used to shore up false doctrines. Further, we have here a contradiction to Gen. 1:1-3 and 2 Peter 3:5. The heavens and earth were created out of water, which is a visible material. Gnostics would much prefer a Gǒd that made time and not one that created with something material (which they attributed to another Gǒd). The Almǐghty can certainly make stuff out of nothing because he is all powerful. But the world was not made from nothing. It was made from water. It is sufficient to affirm that he made the heavens and earth from water. ▷ The author seems to be equivocating holding to his definition of creation to holding faithful. It is usually the case when major parts of the Law are rejected that what constitutes 'holding faithful' is redefined by the traditions of men.

11:5 χ Πίστει *by holding firm.* The author is still aiming at receiving a promise, but Ḥanok's being taken up seems to be disconnected from Ḥanok's expectations.

Almighty. ⁶And without holding faithful it is impossible to please him, because it is necessary to hold faithful to make the approach to the Almighty, that he is, and that he is a rewarder of those who seek him. ⁷By holding faithful⁺ Noaĥ, being divinely instructed by the Almighty about things not yet seen, in reverence prepared an ark for the salvation of his household, by which he condemned the world, and became an heir of the righteousness which is according to faithfulness.

⁸By holding faithful Avraham, when he was called, listened by going out to a place which he was to receive for an inheritance. And he went out, not knowing where he was going. ⁹By holding faithful he lived as an alien in the land of promise, as in a foreign land, dwelling in tents with Yitsĥaq and Ya'aqov, fellow heirs of the same promise, ¹⁰because he was looking for the city which has foundations, whose architect and builder is the Almighty. ¹¹By holding faithful even Sarah herself received ability to conceive, even beyond the proper time of life, since she considered him faithful who had promised. ¹²Therefore, also, there was born of one man, and these as one having been becoming dead, even as many descendants AS THE STARS OF HEAVEN IN NUMBER, AND INNUMERABLE AS THE SAND WHICH IS BY THE SEASHORE.ʸ

¹³All these died holding faithful, without receiving the promises, but having seen them and having welcomed them from a distance, and having confessed that they were strangers and exiles on the earth, ¹⁴because those who say such things make it clear that they are seeking a country of their own. ¹⁵And indeed if they were thinking of that one from which they went out, they would have had opportunity to return. ¹⁶But as it is, they desire a better one, that is, a heavenly one. Therefore the Almighty is not ashamed to be called their Almighty, because he has prepared a city for them.

¹⁷By holding faithful Avraham, when he was tested, had been offering up Yitsĥaq, and he who had received the promises was offering up his only kindred, ¹⁸concerning whom it was said, "IN YITSĤAQ YOUR DESCENDANTS WILL BE CALLED.ʸ" ¹⁹He considered that the Almighty is able to resurrect even from the dead, from which he also received him back as a type.

²⁰By holding faithful Yitsĥaq blessed Ya'aqov and Esau, even regarding things to come. ²¹By holding faithful Ya'aqov, as he was dying, blessed each of the sons

---

11:6 In the context of Scripture, "seek Him" means via repentance, keeping the commandments, and honestly reading Scripture. But the author's parallelism emphasizes *seek* as believing God's promises.

11:7 1 Clement 9:4, "Noah, being found faithful, by his ministration preached regeneration unto the world, and through him the Master saved the living creatures that entered into the ark in concord" (Νωε πιστος ευρεθεις). The author has altered Clement's use of the adjective "faithful" with the verb 'being found' to turn it around to point to action based on trust in a future promise. But Clement is referring to Noah's faithful living, which is why he received the commission to build the ark. Clement is focused on Noah's general obedience in life. The author switches this to the trusting courage that caused Noah to build the ark. ▷ The author's examples do not really concord with what Messiah upholds as important, the commandments (cf. Lev. 18:5; Mat. 20:16; Rev. 22:14).

11:12 y Gen 22:17.

11:16 The author has redefined the promise of the land of Israel to a heavenly country. Yes, the land of Israel will be heavenly in the age to come, but I think this is not what the author meant, because the letter was written in the context of increasing non-Jewish animosity toward Jerusalem. At the time Jewish Christians were praying toward Jerusalem, and were visiting the Temple area, and there may have been some services after AD 70 before the final revolt in AD 132.

11:18 y Gen. 21:12. **11:21** Others have pointed out

of Yosef, and bowed down on the top of his staff. ²²By holding faithful Yosef, when he was dying, made mention of the exodus of the sons of Yisra'el, and gave orders concerning his bones.

²³By Holding faithful, Mosheh having been born, was hidden three months by his parents, because they saw he was a beautiful child. And they were not afraid of the king's edict. ²⁴By holding faithful Mosheh, when he had grown up, refused to be called the son of Pharaoh's daughter, ²⁵choosing rather to endure ill-treatment with the people of the Almighty, than to enjoy the passing pleasures of sin, ²⁶considering the reproach of the Anointed greater riches than the treasures of Egypt, because he was looking to the reward. ²⁷By holding faithful he left Egypt, not fearing the wrath of the king, because he endured, as seeing him who is unseen. ²⁸By holding faithful he had been keeping the Passover and the sprinkling of the blood, so that he who destroyed the first-born might not touch them.

²⁹By holding faithful they passed through the Red Sea as though they were passing through dry land. And the Egyptians, when they attempted it, were drowned. ³⁰By holding faithful the walls of Yeriho fell down, after they were encircled for seven days. ³¹By holding faithful Rahav the harlot did not perish along with those who were disobedient, after she had welcomed the spies in peace.

³²And what more may I be saying? Because time will fail me if I tell of Gid'on, Baraq, Shimshon, Yiphtah, of David besides also Shemu'el and the prophets, ³³who by holding faithful conquered kingdoms, performed acts of justice, obtained promises, shut the mouths of lions, ³⁴quenched the power of fire, escaped the edge of the sword, from weakness were made strong, became mighty in war, put foreign armies to flight. ³⁵Women received back their dead by resurrection, and others were tortured, not accepting their release, in order that they might obtain a better resurrection, ³⁶and others experienced mockings and scourgings, yes, also chains and imprisonment. ³⁷They were stoned. They were sawn in two. They were tempted. They were put to death with the sword. They went about in sheepskins, in goatskins, being destitute, afflicted, ill-treated, ³⁸men of whom the world was not worthy, wandering in deserts and mountains and caves and holes in the ground.

³⁹And all these, having gained approval through their holding faithful, did not receive what was promised, ⁴⁰because the Almighty had provided something

---

that the author has his facts wrong here. Gen. 47:31 says, "Then Yisra'el worshiped upon the head of the bed" (וַיִּשְׁתַּחוּ יִשְׂרָאֵל עַל־רֹאשׁ הַמִּטָּה). The error is that the text does not say "staff," and that this event is not connected to the blessing of the sons. The error is derived from the LXX, "καὶ προσεκύνησεν Ἰσραηλ ἐπὶ τὸ ἄκρον τῆς ῥάβδου αὐτοῦ" reading הַמַּטֶּה for הַמִּטָּה. **11:29-31** 1 Clement 12:1, "Through faithfulness and hospitality Rahab the harlot was saved." Again Clement is focused on general faithfulness, and the author refocuses on a situational holding faithful, which is courage founded upon a promise.

11:35 Some of the author's references are found only in apocryphal sources. See the margin of Nestle-Aland for a complete list of sources. Scripture does not cite apocryphal sources authoritatively like this. **11:39-40** See 12:23 where he does declare the spirits of the saints perfected. The Gnostic point of view does not care about the visible, or the outward, or the material. The perfection being claimed is an inward mystical perfection of the spirit. See 10:14.

better for us, so that apart from us they will not have been made perfect.

12 ¹Therefore, since we have so great a cloud of witnesses surrounding us, having laid aside every weight, and the sin which so easily entangles us, we should be running with endurance the race that is set before us, ²fixing our eyes on Yeshua, the founder and perfecter of the faith, who for the joy set before him endured the execution timber, despising the shame. At the right hand, besides, of the throne of the Almighty he has been sitting. ³Surely, consider for yourselves, him who had been enduring such hostility by sinners against himself, so that you will not have grown weary and lose heart.

⁴You have not yet resisted to the point of shedding blood in your striving against sin. ⁵And you have been forgetting yourselves the exhortation which is addressed to you as sons, "MY SON, DO NOT BE REGARDING LIGHTLY THE DISCIPLINE OF ADONAI, NOR BE FAINTING WHEN YOU ARE REPROVED BY HIM, ⁶BECAUSE THOSE WHOM ADONAI LOVES HE DISCIPLINES, AND HE SCOURGES EVERY SON WHOM HE RECEIVES^ψ." ⁷It is for discipline that you endure. The Almighty deals with you as with sons, because what son is there whom his father does not discipline? ⁸But if you are without discipline, of which all have been becoming partakers, then you are illegitimate children and not sons.

⁹Furthermore, we had earthly fathers to discipline us, and we respected them. Shall we not much more be subject to the Father of spirits, and live? ¹⁰Because they disciplined us for a short time as seemed best to them, but he disciplines us for our good, that we may share his holiness. ¹¹All discipline for the moment seems not to be joyful, but sorrowful, yet to those who have been getting trained by it, afterward it yields the peaceful fruit of righteousness.

¹²Therefore, strengthen the hands that have been getting weak and the knees that have been getting feeble, ¹³and be making straight paths for your feet, so that the limb which is lame will not have been put out of joint, but rather will have been healed. ¹⁴Be pursuing peace with all men, and the sanctification without which no one will see the Lord. ¹⁵See to it that no one comes short of the grace of the Almighty, that no root of bitterness springing up may be troubling *you*, and by it many will have been defiled, ¹⁶that there be no immoral or irreverent person like Esau, who sold his own birthright for a single meal, ¹⁷because you have been knowing that even afterwards, when he desired to inherit the blessing, he was rejected, because he found no place for being sorry and turning his heart *from sin*, though he sought for it with tears.

¹⁸Because you have not been approaching what is getting handled, that is to a fire which had been burning, and to darkness and gloom and whirlwind, ¹⁹and to the blast of a trumpet and the sound of words which those who heard begged that no further word should be spoken to them, ²⁰because they could not bear the command, "IF EVEN A BEAST MAY HAVE TOUCHED THE MOUNTAIN,

---

12:5-6 ψ Prov 3:11-12. **12:17** But this is not true. Esau did repent after his brother left, as a careful reading of Genesis will show. **12:20** α Exo 19:12-13;

IT WILL BE STONED.ᵃ" ²¹And so terrible was the sight, that Mosheh said, "I AM FULL OF FEARᵝ and trembling."

²²But you have been approaching Mount Tsiyon and to the city of the living Almighty, the heavenly Yerushalayim, and to myriads of messengers, ²³to the whole gathering and to the assembly of the first-born who have been getting enrolled in heaven, and to the Almighty Judge of all, and to the spirits of righteous men ᶓwho had been getting made perfect, ²⁴and to Yeshua, the mediator of a newᵛ testament, and to the sprinkled blood, which speaks better than Hevel's.

²⁵Be seeing to it that you may not have refused him who is speaking, because if those did not escape when they refused him who divinely instructed them on earth, much less will we escape who turn away from him who warns from heaven. ²⁶And his voice shook the earth then, but now it has been getting promised, saying, "YET ONCE MORE I WILL SHAKE NOT ONLY THE EARTH, BUT ALSO THE HEAVEN.ᵃ" ²⁷And this expression, "YET ONCE MORE,ᵃ" denotes the removing of those things which can be shaken, as of things which had been getting created, in order that those things which cannot be shaken will have remained. ²⁸Therefore, *since we are* receiving a kingdom which cannot be shaken, we may be having the gratitude, by which we may be serving the Almighty acceptably with reverence and awe, ²⁹because our Almighty is a consuming fire.

13

¹Let love of the brethren be continuing. ²Do not be neglecting to show hospitality to strangers, because by this some have entertained messengers without knowing it. ³Be remembering the prisoners, as though having been getting imprisoned with them, and those who are ill-treated, since you yourselves also are in the body.

⁴Let marriage be held in honor among all, and let the marriage bed be undefiled, because fornicators and adulterers the Almighty will judge. ⁵Let your character be free from the love of money, being satisfied with the things on

---

12:21 β Deu 9:19. The most scholars can do for the source of this quote is cite Deut. 9:19 and 1 Macc. 13:2 to complete it. But the Deut. passage does not apply, because Mosheh was fearful of wrath because Yisra∙el had sinned, not because of the sight of the smoke and fire on the mountain. We can only conclude the author made this up or misremembered in order to further his put down of the Sinai covenant. **12:23** ξ→perfect: τετελειωμένων, V-RPM/P-GMP; or *having perfected themselves.* Once again the author is claiming perfection of the saints. It is a perfection that he denies to anyone before the cross. See 11:40. It is a perfection that he denies the Levitical offerings could accomplish. Really, this is a straw man argument, as those offerings declared forgiveness of sins of ignorance, but not perfectionism. Scholars attempting to rescue the author from his perfectionism error have proposed that the word means "consecrate," in places like 10:14, but this argument makes nonsense out of the author's earlier denial. The Levitical offerings never "consecrated" the ones offering? And then the claim in 10:14 would be no more than what the offerings already did for the priests. The phrase in the LXX is "τελειώσεις αὐτῶν τὰς χεῖρας" (you will complete their hands) and Hebrew, "תְּמַלֵּא יָדָם" (you will fill their hands) (Exo. 29:35). Such a notion is refuted by 10:2 where the kind of cleansing is supposed to relieve the worshiper of "consciousness of sins." The author's perfection teaching also falls into line with Gnostic doctrine. **12:24** ν νέας *brand new* **12:25-27** α Hag 2:6. The author has spiritualized Tsiyon and Yerushalayim. In vs. 28 he speaks of the kingdom, and like the Gnostics he disconnects this from the created order. The creation vanishes and only his "unshakable" spiritualization remains. What then of the promised restoration of Yisra∙el and the reign of Mĕssiah on the throne of David?

13:5 α Deu 31:6 ,8; **13:6** β Psa 118:6. **13:7** α Present participle. These were their current leaders. This is not any proof the readers know the author, but rather a clue that he does not know them, and a hint that they should keep their leaders under scrutiny

hand, because he himself has been saying, "I WILL NEVER HAVE DESERTED YOU, NOR WILL I EVER HAVE FORSAKEN YOU^α," ⁶so that we confidently say, "ADONAI IS MY HELPER, I WILL NOT BE AFRAID. WHAT WILL MAN DO TO ME?_β"

⁷Be remembering those ᵃleading you, who have spoken the word of the Almighty to you, of whom observing the outcome of *their* conduct, be imitating faithfulness. ⁸Yeshua the Anointed is the same yesterday and today, and to time immemorial^μ. ⁹Do not be getting carried away by varied and strange teachings, because it is good for the heart to be strengthened by grace, not by foods, through which those who were thus occupied were not benefited. ¹⁰We have an altar, from which those who serve the tabernacle have no right to eat, ¹¹because the bodies of those animals whose blood is brought into the Holy Place by the high priest as an offering for sin, are burned outside the camp. ¹²Therefore Yeshua also, that he might sanctify the people through his own blood, suffered outside the gate. ¹³Hence, we should be going out to him outside the camp, bearing his reproach.

¹⁴Because here we do not have a lasting city, but we are seeking the city which is to come. ¹⁵Through him then, we should be offering up a sacrifice of praise to the Almighty, that is, the fruit of lips that give thanks to his name. ¹⁶And do not be getting forgetful of doing good and sharing, because with such sacrifices the Almighty is pleased. ¹⁷Be obeying your leaders, and be submitting to them, because they keep watch over your souls, as those who will give an account, so that they may be doing this with joy and not with grief, because this would be unprofitable for you. ¹⁸Be praying for us, because we trust that we have a good conscience, desiring to conduct ourselves honorably in all things. ¹⁹And I urge you all the more to do this, that I will have been restored to you the sooner.

---

lest they do not line up with the author's doctrine. Also alleged to be evidence that the readers know the author is cited at 6:9-10; 10:34; 13:7,9, 18-19, 23. This is what the author wants us to believe, but since neither original recipients, or their time, or their place can be verified, the author's suggested existence of original recipients could be part of the fraud. ▷ Who was the audience of this letter? What was their altar? It is my opinion that the letter was produced as a fraud from the very start. There was no original audience. There were no original recipients. Like the "Sunday letter from heaven," it was "discovered" by the author: "Behold brothers what I have found: it appears that Paul wrote a last letter to the Jews...." This was after all the emissaries were passed away, and Timothy and Clement of Rome. There would be no way to cross examine him except by literary forensics and a thorough and correct knowledge of Scripture. The author, like some false teachers in the Messianic Faith now, appears to be a secret Gnostic. In public they claim to assert the Deity of Messiah, but leave clues to the contrary. In secret they teach that the Spirit of the Almighty only dwelled with the man spirit of Yeshua. This is like Nestorianism. The classic Gnostics claimed the Spirit came on him at baptism and left before he died. But do not be surprised by false teachers that conceal the most false of their beliefs, who disclose them only to their inner circle, or which you can find only after digesting a lot of their material! ▷ It appears that after a hiatus between AD 70 and AD 90 that the altar at the Temple was restored between AD 90 and 130. Clement speaks favorably of this ca. AD 96, and then the Alexandrian Letter speaks negatively of it ca. AD 123. Christians began to remove pro-Temple elders from leadership and began to replace them with new leadership which was anti-Temple. This new leadership then set up new altars outside of Jerusalem, which Clement rebukes. It is the author's aim in this section to piously justify and drag Christians into an anti-Temple attitude.

13:8 μ cf. Mal. 3:6.

13:17-19 The author is alluding to Paul's imprisonment. He does not mean that Paul was not then freed, but that being freed, he had been imprisoned for some time, and for some other reason, he could not immediately make the journey. Tradition puts Paul's death in AD 64, and he was under house arrest until at least AD 61 or 62. There is a window of opportunity for his release and then a later rearrest during the Neronian persecution. The author exploits this gap to suggest that Timothy had meanwhile been arrested and then released so that both Paul and Timothy were

⁲⁰Now *may* the Almighty of peace, who lead up from the dead the great Shepherd of the sheep with the blood of the everlasting covenant, even Mĕssiah our Lord, ²¹equip you in every good thing to do his will, working in us that which is pleasing in his sight, through Yeshua the Anointed, to whom be the glory forever and ever. Amen. ²²But I urge you, brethren, be bearing with this word of exhortation, because I have written to you briefly. ²³Take notice that our brother ᶳTimothy has been getting released, with whom, if he may be coming soon, I will see you. ²⁴Greet all of your leaders and all the saints. Those from ᶳItaly greet you. ²⁵Grace be with you all.

---

free, expecting to see the recipients of the letter (cf. vs. 23). By including this he hopes the letter will be accepted as Pauline.

13:23 ξ It is very likely that this remark was also written by the author in the hopes that the audience would assume Paul was the author. The pseudo-author could point to Phil. 1:7 and 2:24, concluding that Paul had been recently released and was hoping soon to be restored to the community of the recipients (cf. vs. 19). By AD 123, around when the pseudo-author must have written, Timothy would have been dead, according to tradition martyred in AD 97, and could not contradict him. **13:24 ζ** The author gives Paul's last known place of residence, Italy, as an indication of the place the letter was written. The destination is not named by the author, as this would likely open the author to cross-examinations, but it is left to be assumed that he wrote to Jews somewhere outside of Italy. The author could claim that the letter was somehow copied and distributed in Rome, where Clement supposedly made use of it, and then died in AD 99. This is the probable backstory to establish for the author that he had located a genuine letter of Paul some 60 years after Paul was martyred at Rome, allegedly composed in the chaos of the Great Fire of Rome, soon after blamed on Christians, and then first recovered only by Clement, who was dead by AD 123 and could not say he did not know the letter. But the letter was first presented in none of these places as far as we know. It was certainly brought to Alexandria to deceive the Christians there. And we need no other argument for this except that the author contradicts Scripture. When it got back to Rome, it was rejected as spurious. Apparently the backstory was not good enough for the Roman Christians. Probably, someone knew that there was no Hebrews in Clement of Rome's personal library.

Appendix V: Additions to Mark

The longer ending of Mark, set forth below, I regard as spurious. See note on Mark 16:8. The vocabulary, style, and theology of the longer ending does not agree with that of Mark in general. The long ending has the appearance of being cobbled together from the other Evangelists along with the unknown author's own interpretations. Most scholars do not consider it genuine, and I refer you to their explanations. My own remarks are noted below.

Note the imperative of immersion to salvation, much like the false doctrine of circumcision to salvation. Note the emphasis on belief and unbelief and that signs define believers from unbelievers. Not so. True faith is loyalty to the Almĭghty demonstrated by obeying his commandments. The spurious writer's remarks on the unbelief of Yĕshua's Yehudi disciples reek of ill will toward the tribe of Yehudah. I do not read a word of harsh rebuke mentioned in vs. 14, not in any Evangelist. They were only rebuked for slowness to believe the Scripture, but never for slowness to realize it had been fulfilled from the reports that reached their ears. Rather, Yĕshua persuaded them by gently presenting the evidence that he was alive, and indeed was the Almĭghty Sŏn who had died, but now lived.

The Longer Ending

⟦⁹And rising early on the first ᵅSabbath, he was seen first by Miryam Ha-Magdalit, from whom he had been casting out seven demons.ᵝ ¹⁰This oneᵞ going,ᵟ announced it to those who had been with him,ᶿ who were mourning and weeping. ¹¹And these ones,ᵘ having heard that he lives and was ᵖseen by her, held *it* untrustworthy.ᵚ

¹²And after these things,ᵅ he was seen in another form by two from among them, who were traveling in the country.ᵝ ¹³And these ones, having gone back, announced to the rest, but neither these did they hold trustworthy.ᵞ ¹⁴Later,ᵟ when they were reclining, he was seen by the eleven.ᶿ And he rebuked their unfaithfulness, and hardness of heart, because they had not held faithful those who had seen him having been getting

---

16:9 α The author uses the singular here when it is supposed to be "the first of the Sabbaths." See 16:2. He also uses the ordinal adjective "first" instead of the cardinal "one" used elsewhere. This suggests the author thought the word meant "week." **16:9** β This is copied from Luke 8:2. The mention here is inappropriate, and if Mark had thought to mention it, he would have put it at 15:40 where he first mentions her. The author's motivation is probably due to a doctrine of signs and wonders. See vs. 17. **16:10** γ Heinrich Meyer notes: "Foreign to Mark is here—(1) ἐκείνη, which never occurs (comp. Mark 4:11, Mark 7:15, Mark 12:4 f., Mark 14:21) in his Gospel so devoid of emphasis as in this case." **16:10** δ "πορευθεῖσα, which word Mark, often as he had occasion for it, never uses, while in this short section it occurs three times (Mark 16:10, 12, 15)." See Heinrich Meyer. **16:10** θ "Moreover, (3) the circumlocution τοῖς μετ' αὐτοῦ γενομένοις, instead of τοῖς μαθηταῖς αὐτοῦ (the latter does not occur at all in the section), is foreign to the Gospels. The μαθηταί in the more extended sense are meant, the apostles and the rest of the companions of Jesus; the apostles alone are designated at Mark 16:14 by οἱ ἕνδεκα as at Luke 24:9; Luke 24:33; Acts 2:14." See Heinrich Meyer. **16:11** μ "An unemphatic stands κἀκεῖνοι in Mark 16:11, but not at ver 13, as also ἐκείνοις in Mark 16:13 and ἐκεῖνοι, at Mark 16:20 are emphatic." See Heinrich Meyer. **16:11** π "The fact that θεάομαι, apart from this section does not occur in Mark, forms, considering the frequency of the use of the word elsewhere, one of the signs of a strange hand." See Meyer, 16:14. **16:11** ω The author introduces a theme of Jewish unfaithfulness here alien to Mark, and he keeps repeating it. The author's use of ἀπιστία (unfaithfulness) never appears in the Evangelists applied to the disciples in an absolute sense. See vs. 13-14. The Evangelists never represent their disbelief as anything but temporary, and as a matter to be gently corrected by a more tangible presentation of the evidence. The pseudo-author rebukes the alleged unfaithfulness harshly as if it was a great spiritual deficiency. But when they were rebuked, they were only rebuked for slowness to believe the Scripture, but never for slowness to realize it had been fulfilled from the reports that reached their ears. Rather, Yĕshua persuaded them by gently presenting the evidence that he was alive and indeed was the Almighty Sŏn who had died but now lived. Meyer states, "ἀπιστεῖν does not occur in Mark except here and at Mark 16:16, but is altogether of rare occurrence in the N. T. (even in Luke only in chap. 24:41 [but not used absolutely there])."

16:12 α Meyer, "μετὰ ταῦτα: (after what was narrated in Mark 16:9-11) does not occur at all in Mark, often as he might have written it: it is an expression foreign to him. How long after, does not appear. According to Luke, it was still on the same day." **16:12** β This inclusion is taken from the ending of Luke. Meyer, "Mark 16:12-13. A meager statement of the contents of Luke 24:13-35, yet provided with a traditional explanation (ἐν ἑτέρᾳ μορφῇ), and presenting a variation (οὐδὲ ἐκείνοις ἐπίστευσαν) which betrays as its source[184] not Luke himself, but a divergent tradition." **16:13** γ Meyer comments on the following words, which to me seem to have the tinge of anti-Jewishness, as he deals with the ill-advised efforts of the Church Fathers to explain the text: "οὐδὲ ἐκείνοις ἐπιστ: not even them did they [hold faithful.] A difference of the tradition from that of Luke 24:34, not a confusion with Luke 24:41, which belongs to the following appearance (in opposition to Schultheiss, Fritzsche, de Wette). It is boundless arbitrariness of harmonizing to assume, as do Augustine, de consens. evang. iii. 25, Theophylact, and others, including Kuinoel, that under λέγοντας in Luke 24:34, and also under the unbelievers in the passage before us, we are to think only of some, and those different at the two places; while Calvin makes the distribution in such a manner, that they had doubted at first, but had afterwards believed! Bengel gives it conversely. According to Lange, too, they had been believing, but by the message of the disciples of Emmaus they were led into new doubt. Where does this appear? According to the text, they believed neither the Magdalene nor even the disciples of Emmaus. De Wette wrongly thinks (following Storr, Kuinoel, and others) here and repeatedly, that an interpolator would not have allowed himself to extract so freely. Our author, in fact, wrote not as an interpolator of Mark (how unskillfully otherwise must he have gone to work!), but independently of Mark, for the purpose of completing whose Gospel, however, this fragment was subsequently used." **16:14** δ

raised upᵏ.

¹⁵And he said to them, "Go into all the world, announcing the good news to all creation. ¹⁶The one having ᵝheld *it* faithful and having been immersed will be rescued, but the one having ᵝheld *it* unfaithful will be condemned. ¹⁷These ᵃsigns will accompany those having ᵝheld *it* faithful: In my name they will cast out demons. They will speak with new-made languages. ¹⁸They will pick up serpents. And if they should drink something deadly, it can by no means harm them. Upon the sick they will lay hands, and they will get well."

¹⁹So then Adŏnai Yĕshua, after speaking to them was taken up into heaven and sat down at the right hand of the Almĭghty. ²⁰And these, having gone out, proclaimed everywhere, Adŏnai working with them and the word confirming through the accompanying signs.]]

The Expositor's Bible supposes that the ending has been cobbled together with the help of the other three evangelists: "Mark 16:9-20 may be divided into three parts corresponding more or less to sections in John, Luke, and Matthew, and not improbably based on these; Mark 16:9-11, answering to John 20:14-18; John 20:12-14, answering to Luke 24:13-35; Luke 24:15-18, answering to Matthew 28:19. Mark 16:19-20 wind up with a brief reference to the ascension and the subsequent apostolic activity of the disciples."

Meyer, "Mark 16:14. Ὕστερον: not found elsewhere in Mark, *does not* mean: *at last* (Vulgate, Luther, Beza, Schulthess, and many others), although, according to our text, this appearance was the last (comp. Matthew 21:37), but: *afterwards, subsequently* (Matthew 4:2; Matthew 21:29; John 13:36), which certainly is a very indefinite specification. [Note: it simply means *later*.]"
▷ "The narrative of this appearance confuses very different elements with one another. It is manifestly (see Mark 16:15) the appearance which according to Matthew 28:16 took place on the mountain in Galilee; but ἀνακειμένοις (*as they reclined at table*) introduces an altogether different scenery and locality, and perhaps arose from a confusion with the incident contained in Luke 24:42 f., or Acts 1:4 (according to the view of συναλιζόμενος as *convescens*); while also the reproaching of the unbelief is here out of place, and appears to have been introduced from some confusion with the history of Thomas, John 20, and with the notice contained in Luke 24:25; for which the circumstance mentioned at the appearance on the mountain, Matthew 28:17 (οἱ δὲ ἐδίστασαν), furnished a certain basis." **16:14** θ "Αὐτοῖς τοῖς ΕΝΔΕΚΑ: *ipsis undecim*. Observe the ascending gradation in the three appearances—(1) to Mary; (2) to two of His earlier companions; (3) to the eleven themselves. Of other appearances in the circle of the eleven our author knows nothing; to him this was the only one. See Mark 16:19." **16:14** μ The pseudo-author keeps hammering in his theme of unbelief and hardness of heart. One can almost feel that he has an ax to grind against Jewish unbelief. It appears that his conclusion has prejudiced his perception of all Jews so that he has projected it onto the disciples also.

16:16-17 β→**faithful;** The pseudo-author's definition of 'faith' is incorrect. He regards it as believing facts rather than pledging loyalty to Mĕssiah. The evidence is the aorist used in vs. 17. One cannot be spoken of as having held faithful until the last day. Also see that the use of the verb in 16:9-14 applies only to trusting the facts reported by others. **16:17** α In fact none of these signs are necessary to confirm if one has affirmed faithfulness to Yĕshua, and the evidence is the fruit of the Spĭrit, and a changed life in obedience to the commandments. Signs are easily faked or easily reported by those teaching a false theology, and such reports are accepted by those who want their ears tickled with assurances based on something less than a genuine commitment to Mĕssiah. Such signs were more to break the ice with pagans than a confirmation to the faithful. But the author presents it as confirmation for the faithful. ▷ The author also preaches a doctrine of condemnation for a lack of baptism. The Scripture nowhere objectively states the matter this way.

16:19-20 The author has completely bypassed the sign of the faith, which is the resurrection on the third day. This is the sign for the faithful. The other signs where to open the ears of the unconverted so that they would listen long enough to understand it.

Appendix VI: Resurrection Account Harmony

M1-10 = Mat. 28:1-10; R1-8 = Mark 16:1-8; L1-12 = Luke 24:1-12; Y1-18 = John 20:1-18
Common text: underlined. See notes in separate accounts.

 R1And when the ṢABBAṭH was past, Miryam Ha-Magdalit, and Miryam the mother of Ya'aqov, and Shelomit, bought spices, that having come, they might anoint him. 0.1But M1*the later of the* Ṣabbaṭhs, at the dawning, R2very 0.2early, 0.3on 0.4the 0.5FIRST 0.6OF-THE 0.7ṢABBAṭHS, 0.8Miryam Ha-Magdalit M1and the other Miryam 0.9are coming M1to look at the grave, Y1darkness still being, L1in the θdepth of dawn 1.0upon the tomb, L1bringing the spices which they had prepared, R3when they were saying to themselves, "Who will roll away the stone for us from the door of the tomb?" M2And behold, a severe earthquake occurred, because the Messenger of Yăhweh descended from heaven, and *he* came, rolled away the stone, and was sitting up above it. M3And his appearance had been like lightning, and his garment as white as snow. M4And those guarding shook because of fear of him, and became like dead men. 1.1When R4they looked up, 1.2they are seeing R4that 1.3the stone 1.4has been getting rolled away 1.5from the tomb, R4although it had been extremely large.

 M5And the messenger, having begun to speak, said to the women, "Do not be afraid, because I have been knowing that you are looking for Yĕshua who had been getting fastened up on an execution timber. M6He is not so here, because he has risen, just as he said. Come, see the place where he was lying. M7And having gone quickly, tell his disciples that he has risen from the dead. And behold, he is going before you into Galil, there you will see him. Behold, I have told you."

 1.6And when-they-entered R5the tomb, L3they did not find the body of Adŏnai Yĕshua. L4And it happened that while they were perplexed about this, behold, two men suddenly stood near them in dazzling apparel; R5They saw a young man sitting at the right, one who has been dressing himself in a white robe, and they were really frightened. R6And he says to them, "Do not be frightened. You are looking for Yĕshua Ha-Natsri, who had been getting fastened up on an execution timber. L5And as the women were terrified and bowed their faces to the ground; the men said to them, "Why do you seek the living One among the dead? 1.7He has risen. He is not so here. R6Behold, here is the place where they laid him. L6Remember how he spoke to you while he was still in Galil, L7saying that the Sŏn of Man must be delivered into the hands of sinful men, and be fastened up on an execution timber, and the third day rise again."

 R7But go, tell his disciples and Peter, 'He is going before you into Galil. There you will see him, just as he said to you.'" 1.8And when they went out, R8they fled M8quickly 1.9from the tomb, M8with fear and great joy, R8because trembling and amazement had been gripping them, and they said nothing to anyone, because they were being in a state of awe.

 L8Then they remembered his words, and returned from the tomb, M8and they

ran to report it to his disciples. ⁽ʸ²⁾And so *Miryam Ha-Magdalit* is running and is coming to Şim'on Peter, and to the other disciple whom Yĕshua was loving. And *she* is saying to them, "They have taken away my Adŏnai out of the tomb, and we have not been knowing where they have laid him." ⁽ᴸ⁹⁾And *they* reported all these things to the eleven and to all the rest. ⁽ᴸ¹⁰⁾Now they were Miryam Magdalene and Yohanna and Miryam the mother of Ya'aqov. Also the other women with them were telling these things to the emissaries. ⁽ᴸ¹¹⁾And these words appeared to them as nonsense, and they were holding them to be unfaithful.

⁽ᴸ¹²⁾But ²·⁰Peter, ⁽ᴸ¹²⁾having risen, ⁽ʸ³⁾therefore went forth; ⁽ᴸ¹²⁾he ran to the tomb, ⁽ʸ³⁾and the other disciple, and they were going to the tomb *[The women following them back after reporting everything they knew to all]*. ⁽ʸ⁴⁾And the two were running together, and the other disciple ran ahead faster than Peter, and came to the tomb first, ⁽ʸ⁵⁾and stooping and looking in, he saw the linen wrappings lying there, but he did not go in. ⁽ʸ⁶⁾Şim'on Peter therefore also came, following him, and entered the tomb, ⁽ᴸ¹²⁾and when he stooped sideways, ⁽ʸ⁶⁾and ²·¹he sees ²·²the linen wrappings ⁽ᴸ¹²⁾alone, ⁽ʸ⁶⁾lying there, ⁽ʸ⁷⁾and the face-cloth, which had been on his head, not lying with the linen wrappings, but which had been wrapped up in one place. ⁽ʸ⁸⁾So the other disciple who had first come to the tomb entered then also, and he saw and he held faithful. (⁽ʸ⁹⁾For they had not yet been understanding the Scripture, that he needs to rise from the dead.) ⁽ᴸ¹²⁾And he *[Peter]* went away, wondering to himself what has been happening. ⁽ʸ¹⁰⁾So the disciples went away again to their own friends.

[Then the women arrived back at the tomb] ⁽ʸ¹¹⁾But Miryam had been standing outside the tomb weeping, and so, as she wept, she stooped and looked into the tomb, ⁽ʸ¹²⁾and she beheld two messengers in white sitting, one at the head, and one at the feet, where the body of Yĕshua had been lying. ⁽ʸ¹³⁾And they are saying to her, "Woman, why are you weeping?" She is saying to them, "Because they have taken away my Adŏnai, and we have not been knowing where they have laid him." ⁽ʸ¹⁴⁾When she had said this, she turned backwards, and sees Yĕshua, who had been standing there, and had not been knowing that it was Yĕshua. ⁽ʸ¹⁵⁾Yĕshua said to her, "Woman, why are you weeping? Whom are you seeking?" Supposing him to be the gardener, she said to him, "Sir, if you have carried him away, tell me where you have laid him, and I will take him away." ⁽ʸ¹⁶⁾Yĕshua is saying to her, "Miryam!" When she turned around, that one is saying to him in Hebrew, "Rabboni!" (which means, Teacher). ⁽ʸ¹⁷⁾Yĕshua is saying to her, "Stop clinging to me, because not yet, have I been ascending to the Făther, but go to my brothers, and say to them, 'I am going to ascend to my Făther and your Făther, and my Almĭghty and your Almĭghty.'" ⁽ʸ¹⁸⁾Then *Miryam Ha-Magdalit* is coming, announcing to the disciples, "I have been seeing Adŏnai," and that he had said these things to her.

⁽ᴹ⁹⁾And behold, Yĕshua met *the rest of* them saying, "Be Rejoicing!" And they came up and took hold of his feet and worshiped him. ⁽ᴹ¹⁰⁾Then Yĕshua says to them, "Do not be afraid. Go and take word to my brothers so that they will have left for Galil, and there they will see me."

__Common Text__: 0.1 M δὲ R καὶ Υ δὲ L δὲ 0.2 M - R πρωΐ L - Y πρωΐ 0.3 M εἰς R dative L dative Y dative 0.4 M the R τῇ L τῇ Y τῇ 0.5 M μίαν R μιᾷ L μιᾷ Y μιᾷ 0.6 M - R τῶν L τῶν Y τῶν 0.7 M σαββάτων R σαββάτων L σαββάτων Y σαββάτων 0.8 M Μαρία ἡ Μαγδαληνὴ M - L - Y Μαρία ἡ Μαγδαληνὴ 0.9 R ἔρχονται M ἦλθεν L ἦλθον Y ἔρχεται. 1.0 M -- R ἐπὶ τὸ μνημεῖον L ἐπὶ τὸ μνῆμα Y εἰς τὸ μνημεῖον 1.1 M -- R καὶ L δὲ Y καὶ 1.2 M -- R θεωροῦσιν L εὗρον Y βλέπει 1.3 M -- R ὁ λίθος L τὸν λίθον Y τὸν λίθον 1.4 M -- R ἀποκεκύλισται L ἀποκεκυλισμένον Y ἠρμένον 1.5 M -- R -- L ἀπὸ τοῦ μνημείου Y ἐκ τοῦ μνημείου 1.6 M -- R καὶ εἰσελθοῦσαι L καὶ εἰσελθοῦσαι Y -- 1.7 M -- R ἠγέρθη οὐκ ἔστιν ὧδε L 6 οὐκ ἔστιν ὧδε ἀλλ᾽ ἠγέρθη 1.8 M Καὶ ἀπελθοῦσαι R Καὶ ἐξελθοῦσαι 1.9 M ἀπὸ τοῦ μνημείου R ἀπὸ τοῦ μνημείου L -- Y -- 2.0 M -- R -- L Πέτρος Y ὁ Πέτρος 2.1 M -- R -- L βλέπει Y θεωρεῖ 2.2 M -- R -- L τὰ ὀθόνια Y τὰ ὀθόνια

Summary: The women go to the tomb. The Messenger of YHWH moves the stone. He speaks to them. They go into the tomb. Two men speak to them. They flee in confusion, saying nothing. They recover and return to make a report. Peter and John investigate, and are followed back by the women. The men leave. Miryam M. arrives back at the tomb mourning. Yeshua appears to Miryam M., and then the other women who followed her back.

Appendix VII: Luke 22:17-25

Luke reports the cup and bread in a different order than Matthew and Mark. (The Greek conjunctions do not have to imply strict chronological order.) The evidence is that this cup in Luke is the same cup of blessing (cf. 1 Cor. 10:16), and not an additional cup, because it is joined with vs. 18 (= Mark 14:25), which occurs in Mark joined with the same cup. This means that Luke reported the cup first and then the unleavened bread. Because vs. 18 is parallel to Mark 14:25, it cannot truly be argued that Luke is reporting an earlier cup in the meal.

Codex Bezae (D[05]) and itala a d ff[2] i l: omit: 19b *which is given for you; do this for my memorial. 20 And in the same way he took the cup after they had eaten, saying, "This cup which is poured out for you is the renewed covenant in my blood.* Itala b, c, reorder the verse order to 19,17,18. The Syriac also shows evidence of a shorter text. The Greek scribes conflated the text with the words from 1Cor. 11:24-25, and thus created the sequence cup-bread-cup, treating the first cup as an earlier cup in the meal. But this is evidently a mistake because the first cup in Luke is identified by vs. 18 as the second cup in Mark (cf. Mark 14:25). The contradiction can be seen by creating a synopsis of the conflated version of *Luke* (italic) , Mark (non-italic), **Common text (bold)**, and [ ] that should be omitted.

[[17Lk]*And having taken a cup, having given thanks, he said, "Take this, divide for yourselves.* [18Lk]*<u>Because I am saying to ye that no from now on I may not drink from the fruit of the vine until when the kingdom of Gŏd have have come.</u>"*] [22Mk]**And** while they are eating, [C]**he took some bread,** [C]**blessing, broke and gave to them**, and [C]**said**, "Take; [CO.]**this represents my body,** [LK][[19b]*which is given on behalf of you. Do this for my memorial.*] [23MK]**And** taking **a cup** [[LK20]*likewise, after they had eaten,]* [MK]having given thanks he gave to them, and they all drank from it. [24]And he **said** to them, "**This is** my blood, [[LK20]*the cup]*, **of the** [[LK20]*new*] **covenant,** [[LK20]*in my blood]* which is getting itself poured out on behalf of many, *[ye]*. [25MK]<u>Amen, I say to you, no I will not drink again of the fruit of the vine until that day when I drink it new in the kingdom of Gŏd.</u>"

Now compare vs. 18 from Luke with vs. 25 from Mark. The association shows that Luke's first cup is really the cup of blessing. It is extremely unlikely that Yĕshua would have duplicated the same statement after two different cups. It is also unlikely that Luke would have reported two cups, even though a Seder contained four.

The longer version of Luke is explained by the scribes supposing that Luke reported an earlier cup in the meal, and that their text was deficient in omitting the cup after the bread. They supposed that this deficiency could be repaired by conflating the text with 1Cor. 11:24-25, and were further motivated by the observation that the words, "Do this at my memorial" are not reported in any of the gospels. They were also motivated by the fact that the word "new" is not reported in Matthew or Mark in front of the word "covenant." What they did not observe very carefully was that Luke 22:18 does not allow the original cup mentioned by Luke to become an earlier cup in the meal, unless it be assumed that Yĕshua made the same statement twice, and this is as unlikely as thinking that Luke meant to mention two cups, and then confuse the reader by putting vs. 18 after vs. 17 instead of after vs. 20. This contradiction was not lost on all the scribes. The editors of itala[b,e] syr[c] and syr[c] all reordered the text to 19, 17, 18, an attempt to justify correcting Luke's 'incorrect' order. 19, 17, 18 is the actual order. Luke simply reported the cup before the bread without regard to its true chronological order.

Finally, the reasoning of Bruce Metzger and his committee for favoring the longer version (a minority of the committee dissented) includes this reasoning, "The rise of the shorter version can be accounted for in terms of the theory of *disciplina arcana*, i.e. in order to protect the Eucharist from profanation, one or more copies of the gospel of Luke, prepared for circulation among non-Christian readers, omitted the sacramental formula after the beginning words" (pg. 176, *A Textual Commentary on the Greek New Testament*).

Notice that the shorter version is not attributed to accident. The committee did recognize that the difference is too large, and in a too important text to be attributed to an unnoticed accident of transmission. This means they have to come up with a deliberate reason to justify how the shorter text was created. But their opinion has the appearance of a *just so story*, and leads to the contradiction in the Majority text implied by the position of vs. 18.

I would suggest that Luke himself left out "This is my blood of the covenant," precisely because such words require more explanation to non-Jews than he wanted to put in, and that Luke favored an oral explanation be given to converts. In other words, Luke himself was concerned about a misunderstanding. And of course, he would be right, because Yoḥanan finds the need to omit any mention of the cup, and later we find the *transubstantiation* and *real presence* doctrines as corrupt explanations which would justify not focusing on the Eucharistic words. The Jews themselves had problems enough with Yĕshua's saying (cf. John 6).

Finally, if "Do this for my memorial," is not contained in any of the gospels, then where did Paul obtain the words? I suggest that he learned them from Peter (cf. Gal. 1:18) at the time of Passover in AD 39. There needs be no explanation why Luke left the words out. Matthew and Mark leave them out also. That may not explain why they were left out, but it certainly justifies the shorter text.

Luke and John were meant for circulation among non-Jews. I think this explains the brief account of Luke, and John's omitting it.

Appendix VIII: Works of the Law

The New Perspective on Paul has given us many valuable insights, but it has done a disservice by claiming that Jews did not believe meritorious works could cancel their demerits. This doctrine was surely part of first century Judaism. Even if we had no direct evidence for it, we would have to fill in the logical lacuna in the Pauline argument by supposing it.

While we cannot map out what each and every sect or faction believed, it is apparent that the sect Paul was dealing with in Galatians believed in the justifying merit of at least some works to offset sins. And further, Paul expands the same arguments in Romans. So we cannot say the problems Paul addresses were trivial issues only to be faced off in some backwater of Judaism (See End Note No. 2, page 434).

The problems Paul addresses are in fact the main issues. It is the idea that certain deeds considered especially meritorious can be saved up for oneself or others against the day of judgment. In the Church this takes the form of indulgences. For example, during the Roman persecutions, many Christians lapsed into apostasy, while many other Christians confessed Christ and died as martyrs. When the lapsed repented they were given long penances. On the other hand, the martyrs had an excess of merit. This came to be called the treasury of merit. To this treasury they added the merit of Christ. The idea then was that the lapsed could draw on the treasury of merit to shorten their penances. It went so far as that the merit of a particular martyr could be applied to the penance of a particular lapsed person.

If the god who perverts justice by these legalisms sounds like the commercial god of the Satisfaction Theory of Atonement, it is the same concept on the same theme. They paint an image of Gŏd as if he has to be bought off in order to forgive. I have explained elsewhere that Mĕssiah's KIPPURIM does not buy off the Almĭghty. The KIPPURIM declares the wiping out of the sentences against us, and demonstrates the cost of our rescue through a ransoming sacrifice. (See Appendix X, page 584).

A snapshot of Judaism will illustrate the problem. Like I said, we do not know what each and every sect believed, but what we find in Judaism well illustrates the theme of merits, that must have come and gone in other forms in the past. If for no other reason we would have to presume these doctrines existed simply because they are so useful to Satan in perverting the justice of the Almĭghty and in painting a false image of Gŏd which he hopes men will accept.

Judaism has a concept of זְכוּת *zekut*. This term means, "merit, credit" (cf. Reuben Alcalay, *The Complete Hebrew Dictionary*). This also occurs as זְכוּת אָבוֹת *zekut avot*, which means "merit of the ancestors." *Zekut* is the Jewish *treasury of merits*. The basic concept is that one performs an extraordinary deed of righteousness, above and beyond simple Torah observance, and this deed is a *zekut* that can be credited to others (or oneself) against the day of judgment or disaster. Commonly, charity, prayer, fasting, and devotion to Torah study were considered to contribute to *zekut*. And if one appreciated the righteousness of the ancestors, while being a sinner oneself, then the ancestors' *zekut* could be credited to one's account. *Zekut* can also be collectively credited to Yisrǎel to be drawn on in times of great crisis to obtain great miracles on behalf of the nation. Jacob Neusner (author of 900+ books) explains:

> The family, called 'Israel,' could draw upon the family estate, consisting of the inherited *zekhut* of the matriarchs and patriarchs in such a way as to benefit today from the heritage of yesterday. This notion involved very concrete problems. If 'Israel, the family' sinned, it could call upon the *'zekhut'* accumulated by Abraham and Isaac at the binding of Isaac (Genesis 22) to win forgiveness for that sin. True, 'fathers will not die on account of the sin of the sons,' but children may benefit from the *zekhut* of the forebears" (Jacob Neusner, *Theological and Philosophical Premises of Judaism*, pg. 193).

The binding of Isaac does not point to *zekut* as the solution to the sin problem. It points directly to Mĕssiah. So we see in both Judaism and Christianity a "treasury of merit," which perverts the justice of the Almĭghty and paints him as a person that must be bought off in order to remember his covenant.

While the above is a snapshot of Judaism, the concept of works of the law reckoned for righteousness of a transferable nature shows up in the Dead Sea Scrolls. 4QMMT states that *some particular deeds of the law are reckoned for righteousness*. Why some particular ones and not all deeds? Probably because these deeds were thought to accrue a superabundance of merit, and those doing them would be made to feel secure. Ordinary deeds didn't count, since it was only doing what was required in the first place.

But we do not have to define exactly what the theology of Paul's opponents was. This is because he denies that *any* customary works are regarded by the Almĭghty in judging the case. This would include any works of the law also treated as a means of appeasement. Paul is denying a whole concept regardless of the particulars of how it is implemented. We have seen how Judaism implements the idea with *zekut*, and that the Church has the *treasury of merit*. As for particulars, it is clear that the Church places great merit in baptism and Judaism in circumcision (cf. End Note No. 2, pg. 434).

Now I turn to the Protestant *treasury of merit*. It is but a variation of the Catholic one. I have described this before. The idea is that the righteousness of Christ is credited to the account of the believer, and thus the believer's case is discharged by acquittal. This again is the same concept as *zekut*. The merit of another is transferred to the believer for the sake of acquittal. Like the Rabbis' doctrine, this commercial use of merit is disguised from that of individual works by appealing

to others' works. So it is not recognized as working for forgiveness. But it is all the same an attempt to satisfy justice by someone's works.

Messiah's righteousness (by way of following his example) is surely counted to us, but only in like manner as that of Avraham's faithfulness. It was counted when he obeyed, and pledging his loyalty was the beginning of his obedience (Gen. 15:6; James 2:21-24). Righteousness will be counted to us through our steps of obedience while we wait for perfect righteousness by continued faithfulness (Gal. 5:5; Rom. 4:24; Rev. 19:8; 3:4, 5, 18; 6:11; 7:9). And none of it is a legal credit against sin. Sin is not forgiven by crediting positive merits. It is forgiven because the Almĭghty is merciful. Nor is sin forgiven because satisfaction was made for his wrath. See **Rom. 5:18** ψ note. That also would be a form of payment.

In the Good News of Messiah (GNM) all usages compounded with the word works (ἔργων νόμου) are translated as **the customary works**. Now more literally this is *the works-of custom of* or *the works of custom."* However, it is grammatically acceptable to regard this as a genitive of quality with a qualitative noun such as custom. So *the works of custom* becomes *the customary works*. In Greek this phrase appears without the article, but it is regarded as definite on account of the genitive construction. When Paul refers to **the customary works** he is speaking directly of the doctrine of zechut, and nothing else. Also when he is speaking of works in a negative sense without the word custom attached, he is still speaking of the customary works, the doctrine of zechut. And the GNM supplies the word customary in some cases to make this clear.

The Abstract Use of ב and ל.

The abstract use of these two Hebrew prepositions and their corresponding Greek words, ἐν and εἰς is exceedingly important and exceedingly delicate in the translation of key passages. The discussion was begun in "Appendix XVI: The New Moon" on page 599. Here that discussion must be expanded. The translations 'in' is unjustly put for ἐν in many cases, and then exploited theologically on the basis of the narrower sense of meaning in Modern English. Let's start with the lesser known definitions ἐν of in in BDAG:

❽ **marker denoting the object to which something happens or in which something shows itself, or by which something is recognized, *to, by, in connection with*:**

❸ **marker of extension toward a goal that is understood to be within an area or condition, *into*.**

Not infrequently ἐν is also translated *by, with, among, because of, on, in*. But these glosses would not be controversial because they are not at the focal point of theological controversies. They make clear however that the Greek word and its Hebrew counterpart do not simply mean 'in' as understood in English. The above definition number ❽ needs to be extended a bit. The abstract usage means: *in the sphere of, in relation to, or in regard to, in view of*.

Even though this is the full definition for the sake of succinctness and brevity equivalent translations recommend themselves in Greek. Most commonly, I would suggest *to* and *for*. Examples:

1 Cor. 4:17 faithful to Yăhweh
Eph. 1:1 faithful to the Anŏinted.
Eph. 1:15 your faithfulness to Adŏnai
Eph. 6:21 and faithful servant to Yăhweh
Col. 1:2 faithful brothers to the Anŏinted
Col. 1:4 your faithfulness to the Anŏinted
1 Tim 3:13 which is to the Anŏinted

Sometimes *for:*

Eph. 1:3 having blessed us for every spiritual
Eph. 1:4 chose us for himself
Rom 16:11 being for Yăhweh
Rom 16:12 working hard for Yăhweh
Rom 16:12 worked very hard for Yăhweh
Rom 16:13 chosen for Yăhweh
1 Cor 4:10 prudent for the Anŏinted
Phil 1:13 for the sake of the Anŏinted

Often *through:*

Rom 3:24 through the Anŏinted
Rom 6:11 through the Anŏinted
Rom 6:23 through the Anŏinted
Rom 8:2 through the Anŏinted
Rom 12:5 through the Anŏinted
1 Cor 1:2 through the Anŏinted
etc.

Often *belonging to:*

Rom 8:1 those belonging to the Anŏinted
Rom 16:2 belonging to Yăhweh
Rom 16:3 belonging to the Anŏinted
Rom 16:8 belonging to Yăhweh
Rom 16:9 belonging to the Anŏinted
Rom 16:10 belonging to the Anŏinted
etc.

Sometimes *in view of:*

Rom 9:1 in view of the Anointed
Rom 15:17 in view of the Anointed

Rom 16:22 in view of Yăhweн
1 Cor 16:24 in view of the Anŏinted
2 Cor 12:19 in view of the Anŏinted

Sometimes *in connection to:*

Phil 2:1 in connection to the Anŏinted
Phil 4:7 in connection to

Sometimes *into:*

Rom 16:7 coming into the Anŏinted

Probably the greatest abuse of the translation "in" is in the combination "in Christ" taken in the meaning of a positional union with Christ so that all the attributes of Christ are imputed to the one said to be in Christ. So for instance, since Christ is sinless, then one in Christ is viewed as sinless by God.

Apparatus Notes

Abbreviations:

MT = majority translation tradition = ASV, AMP, AMPC, BRG, CEB, CEV, CJB, CSB, DARBY, DLNT, DRA, EHV, ERV, ESV, ESVUK, EXB, GNV, GW, GNT, HCSB, ICB, ISV, PHILLIPS, JUB, AKJV, LEB, MSG, MEV, MOUNCE, NOG, NABRE, NASB, NASB1995, NCB, NCV, NET, NIRV, NIV, NIVUK, NKJV, NLV, NLT, NMB, NRSV, NRSVA, NRSVACE, NRSVCE, NTE, OJB, RGT, RSV, RSVCE, TLB, TLV, VOICE, WE, WEB, WYC, YLT.

PT = popular translations = ASV, CJB, ESV, HCSB, KJV, NASB, NIV, NKJV, NRSV, RSV.

✓ = check footnoted word in text in "Translation Concordance" on page 604. If a single word follows the check mark, then it means check the Concordance under that entry.

v. = versus
p = partly correct

le = Lemming effect

db = Traditional Doctrinal Bias

— = except for

a = translation shows awareness of the problem, but unsucessfully repaired it.
{ } = versus

Tagged so far.

Mat 1:25
Mark 7:19 in detail
Luke 24:21 in detail
Luke 24:39
Rom 14:14

Nomos with the article and without

Greek words with or without the article do not behave like English. According to Daniel Wallace there are at least ten ways a Greek word can be definite without having the article. What I want to do here is zero in on the word *nomos* when it does and does not have the article, which can be mystifying if someone tries to impose expectations based on the English definite article. Nomos (νόμος) is a qualitative noun, meaning 'custom' or 'norm.' It is a substantive defined by its quality of 'being the custom' or 'being the norm.'

This means that when Paul speaks of νόμος he is almost never meaning "a custom", but whatever custom he is focused on in his context, as if the reader isn't supposed to know. English complicates the picture further by turning nouns without the article into abstract nouns or when the noun is without the article, but cannot be indefinite into a reference to the whole class specified by the noun.

Thus **custom is beneficial* means in English custom in general or as a whole class is beneficial. So we see upon omitting the article with the Greek and then translating into English we have, **For not through custom is the promise to Abraham* (Rom. 4:13a). One would thus believe that Paul is talking about tradition or custom in general as a whole class, which clearly isn't the case.

But omission of the article in Greek with a qualitative noun does not turn it into a reference to the whole class like English. Daniel Wallace states

> Qualitative: It is akin to a generic noun in that it focuses on the *kind*. Further like a generic, *it emphasizes class traits*. <u>Yet, unlike generic nouns, a qualitative noun often has in view one individual rather than the class as a whole</u> (GGBB, pg. 244).

Wallace gives the example *God is a love and *God is the love. Clearly either translation is incorrect. Since love is an abstract noun, he gives another example with life: *In him was life* vs. *a life and vs. presumably *the life. But if we say *Life was in him* then the abscence of the article almost begs the question, so what? What is special about life being in a person? This is because life in general is not meant but a specific kind of the class life.

Wallace gives another example, **God has spoken to us in Son* vs. *in a son*, and presumably *the Son would also be possible. The word *son* is qualitative, expressing kinship.

I don't think Wallace has a good solution to translating a qualitative noun without the article when the author has something definite in mind, that at times can also be indefinite, or at least of explaining it to non scholars. Yes we can choose to make plain in English what is open to choice in Greek, but then the simple might think we are not being fair with the Greek or translating concordantly or literally. Or worse the reader might not determine what is specifically being talked about based on the quality of the noun.

When Wallace is talking about ways of translating various cases into English he often supplies helping phrases that help determine if a case is being used in a particular sense. Really he is just helping the student expand his understanding of the semantic range of the cases to match that of the Greek.

Something similar needs to be done here. So I propose helping the reader choose whether something is definite or not by the helping words *what is, that which is, or the thing which is*. This will be unnecessary with abstract nouns, viz. *God is love* is the best we are going to do, although some sense as *God is especially love*, or *God is the very essence of love* might carry the Greek better. With qualitative nouns the helping phrases will break the English tendency to refer to the whole class and let the reader assume a specific reference, thus:

"In him was *that which is* life." "God has spoken to us in *he who is* Kin." See now rather than having it decided for you, viz. 'the Son,' you get to decide by figuring out who particularly the Kin is. This device is especially important in 1 Cor. 9:20-21:

> [20]So to the Yehudim I have made myself as a Yehudi, that I will have won Yehudim. To those subject to *what is* custom*ary*, as subject to *what is* custom*ary*, though not being myself subject to *what is* custom*ary*, that I will have won those subject to *what is* custom*ary*. [21]To those who are without *what is* custom*ary*, as without *what is* custom*ary*, though not being without *what is* custom*ary* for the Almighty, but according to *what is* custom*ary* for the Anŏinted, that I will have won those without *what is* custom*ary*.

Without this English gloss we come off believing with English linguistic blinders that Paul is speaking about the whole class of custom in each usage, when it is really a specific thing depending on each situation. But if we put the definite article in then he sounds like he is contradicting himself, because then it appears he is talking about the same custom in each mention.

What the Greek is asking the reader to do in the case of anarthrous nouns is to consider a special definite case of the class represented by the noun if it may be discovered. If not then it is indefinite or generic referring to the whole class, or the reader is able to hold out that it is definite even if he has not discovered why. English demands the writer determine the case for the reader. But this is damaging because Paul often refers to some particular customs, and not just "the custom" or "a custom" or generic "custom." That is, sometimes he is combining the customary curse and the doctrine of zechut under the same anarthrous usage! For this reason we have to use the English workaround: [what is] custom[ary]. This allows the reader to exercise their mind on the context in the same way a Greek speaker would.

Now that we have come up for an acceptable gloss without the article, the usage with the article needs to be explained better. THE νόμος is 'THE custom' or 'THE norm," that is the norm or custom *par excellence*, the one known before in the context. The reason for the article is to place emphasis moreso than to make definite.

Appendix IX: Forgiveness

In this edition 0.5.2.4 this note has been revised. Some years ago the Spirit impressed upon me that my penal substitution theology was incorrect, but everything did not change instantly, because I had to work through a lot of thinking and various places that thinking was expressed in writing. It is almost as if the Spirit was waiting to the last to correct this. Perhaps this is because atonement theology is where Christianity has dug its deepest hole, and one has to reach many ledges first before one can exit the pit. I Daniel grew up in the den of the teaching that forgiveness only occurs when the offering is made, and was taught that this is when the penalty of sin is paid for. But I have come to learn that the Most High forgives before and after the offering in relation to serious sins for which the person is knowingly guilty. Forgiveness happens when confession is made and the person repents. And this happens because the purpose of sacrifice and atonement is not to pay for sin.

The purpose of the sacrifice is to "declare (*something*) to be wiped away" (לכפר). This is one of the nuances of the **Piel**, a declarative **Piel**. The purpose has to do with wiping out sin, that is cleansing it from the confessor, and removing it from him. See Rom. 8:3 note.

The sacrifice is also an indication of suffering that sin causes. Messiah's suffering is an indication of divine suffering on a human level exacted from the Most High like a ransom as he suffers our sins waiting for us to repent. See Rom. 7:4 note. The Almighty is waiting to deliver us, and Messiah is the epitome of the divine and human ransom cost suffered in hope of restoration. The offering is a declaration of the wiping out of any penalty that is the Most High's benevolent justice.

So as Israel looked upon the suspended serpent, the Most High wants us to see the suffering our sins have caused as a lesson on the cost of our forgiveness and cleansing from sin, as a lesson on the strict justice we are being forgiven, the cost of it, and a declaration of benevolent justice, which is the favorable justice of forgiveness.

But by no means is the sacrifice paying for or satisfying strict justice. By no means is the offering suffering the wrath of God. The offering may be showing what the wrath of God could be, but isn't for us. The suffering visited on Messiah was caused by the transgressions of men. It wasn't the wrath of God. The Most High only uses this suffering to show his suffering on a human level, as the ransom, and as indication of the consequence of sin that he is forgiving. But the offering is not actually paying for or making compensation for sin.

Appendix X: What is Atonement?

"Atonement" is a word that should be banned, because it is most often used to convey the pagan idea of *propitiation* or *appeasement* of the deity by some sort of gift or exchange, usually innocent blood in exchange for the guilty. It should be banned, because this idea has nothing to do with the Scriptural teaching on KIPPURIM. Particularly in respect of the false doctrine of substitutionary atonement should the word be banned. See translation and exegesis of Isaiah 53 at the end of 1 Thessalonians. To say that the offering of sacrifice is to provide an alternative subject for divine wrath so that favor can be shown to the offerer is heresy. So what does the biblical term really mean?

The Hebrew verb *kāphar* (כָּפַר) Qal, properly means "to wipe away," with close synonyms being "to cleanse," "to purge," and "to purify" (See 1 Yoh. **2:2** χ note), or as a noun, "a wiping away," "cleansing," "purging," and "purification." Besides the definitions cited in 1 Yoh. we can add the one given in the margin of BDB "also Assyrian *kuppuru*, **purify**." The **Piel** stem adds an emphatic stative idea, expressed by a passive infix "to be" and also a causitive idea, usually expressed by "make," but in this case it is a legal making, and thus is a declarative **Piel**. Thus the meaning of the common **Piel** conjugation is "to declare to be wiped away," or in a noun form, a "declaration of wiping away." For example, when the priest pronounces someone to be clean or unclean, the Hebrew conjugation is the verb for 'clean' (וְטִהֲרוֹ) or 'unclean' (וְטִמֵּא) in the **Piel** conjugation. Truly, the subject of the priest's exam is already clean or unclean. The priest is merely making an official statement that this is indeed the case, viz. "And he will have declared him to be clean," or "And he will have declared him to be unclean." Leviticus 13 is the place to look for these examples.

With this idea in mind consider Leviticus 17:11, "Because the blood, which is with breath, declares to be wiping," and consider the fact that the worshipper has already purified himself or herself before the offering is made. So we see that "to declare to be wiped away" in respect to sin is an official notice by a symbolical ceremony on that which is already true through confession and repentance from sin, and the forgiveness of the Most High. Now, just as a qualification, it is not in every case that KIPPURIM must be declarative of a previous reality, but in the cases of applying the blood directly to a holy object (or subject) that has become impure, there is a simultaneous ritual cleansing of the impure object (or subject) cojoined with the application of the blood, and this is effected by the divine Spirit. So the blood is symbolic of the divine Spirit, which is acting immediately in conjunction with the application of the blood. In this connection, the Greek equivalents to KIPPURIM may lack the declarative nuance (cf. Rom. 3:25; 1 Yoh. 2:2, 4:10,) but this lack is immediately made up for by the fact that Messiah himself is the agent of the cleansing in the Spirit, and so I have chosen not to indicate the delcarative nuance in these texts.

So what wiping away does the blood declare? In the first place it is equivalent to a declaration of forgiveness. The blood symbolizes the purging of any divine retribution or judgment against the confessor. To be sure, the repentant worshipper is already forgiven by the time the offering is brought, and in fact, in conjunction with the offering is the refrain, "And he has been forgiven," (וְנִסְלַח). Leviticus 4 is the place to look for these examples. In Hebrew it is always in the perfect tense, "And he has been forgiven." One may endeavor to translate this future perfect, "And he will have been forgiven," but the perfect is the most attemporal of Hebrew tenses. In English we might put it, "And he is forgiven" which is merely stating a fact without saying when the fact became true. For example, David was forgiven (נָשָׂאתָ, **LXX:** ἀφίημι) when he confessed his sin (Psa. 32:5), and not when he brought any offerings. In fact, he could not bring any offerings, because it was only allowed for sins of ignorance. Nevertheless, he was forgiven. In this respect, with Messiah's offering, his sin is "declared to be wiped away" because Messiah's offering declares the cleansing for all sins more serious than those of ignorance. So we see that David was forgiven before the offering that declared it, and also cleansed before the offering.

So we see that the condition of forgiveness is confession and repentance, and this agrees with 1 Yoḥ. 1:9. It is partaking of the Spirit that effects the cleansing in conjunction with the faithfulness of the confessor (cf. Yoḥ. 6:63). So now, let us put the symbology of the sacrifice in the correct terms. (1) The confessor lays his hand on the sin offering. This means symbolically that his sin is taken off of him and placed onto the offering which bears it. The suffering of the offering is symbolic of the cost of the sin, which is a malignacy, a miasma. (2) When the offering is slain, this is symbolic of the effect of sin and lawlessness. It kills the innocent. The offering stands for all the innocent that are harmed, including the Most High. The priest wields the knife as a proxy for the confessor. The confessor is symbolically confessing that his sin kills. (3) The blood of the offering becomes separated from its flesh, with the breath (of life) still in it. This is symbolic of the offering reverting to its separate parts, the dust of the earth, and the breath of life (cf. Gen. 2:7) נִשְׁמַת חַיִּים, which is the divine contribution to the creation of all flesh. The blood is applied to the altar, which symbolically declares the sin to be purged, and any penalty for it. Thus the sin is symbollically removed from the sinner, forgiven, and purged. Now the reality so symbolized is that of the divine Spirit in covenant faithfulness cleansing the heart of the confessor in conjunction with the faithfulness of the confessor. So the blood represents the operation of the Spirit, the giving of divine life to cleanse.

When the sinner has confessed and been cleansed by the Spirit, the offering represents the removal and cleansing of the sin, along with its cost. The blood represents the divine life needed to effect the cleansing. It is sin/lawlessness that causes all the damages and death in the symbolism and in reality. It is divine life imparted to the confessor with renewed faithfulness that removes it.

And with this accomplished, there is no requirement for divine wrath, because wrath is only for the unrepentant.

The death of the offering does not symbolize the effect of divine wrath. And not a word is said about the offering being punished in anyone's place. But the death of the offering is to be viewed as a symbolic ransom, which in reality is the cost exacted by lawlessness in the operation of separating the confessor from his sin. This reality is climatically realized by Messiah's ransom (cf. Rev. 5:9 notes) to compel the powers to return his people out of bondage where he had sold them because of their transgressions. So in this view every sacrificial offering symbolizes the ransom cost to lawlessness in order to separate the sinner from his sin. And in Messiah's case, his death is the actual ransom so symbolized.

In this view the offering is assisting the faithful to remove sin from the faithful, and to remove the faithful from the domain of lawlessness, so when the day of judgment comes, only the domain of lawlessness is judged.

Now let us see why the substititionary payment of divine wrath is not justice, and why sin really has to be forgiven. To understand this we must comprehend two kinds of justice. There is merciful justice and compensatory justice. Compensatory justice happens when the injured party is completely compensated or paid off for a loss. This happens when a third party pays someone's monetary debt, or a thief makes restitution. The injured party is fully repaid and ends with no net loss.[a] In this regard see note on Mat. 5:38.

Compensation is not what is happening through the death of Mĕssiah. To use an extreme example, the law demands the death of the murderer. This punitive justice does not restore the life of the murder victim. All sin has consequences, some more, some less. The punishment of the sinner does not undo the consequences of those sins. No punitive justice positively compensates the injured parties. The murder victim is not compensated, and the Almĭghty to whom the victim belonged in the first place is not compensated for the loss. To claim that a substitutionary death satisfies the justice of God still leaves the injustice done to the victim of sin uncompensated. This violates God's own law, because it is favoritism in justice to the mighty in disfavor of the lowly.

The punitive penalty of sin is *ordinarily* justly deserved wrath and anger made effective against the sinner. But it does not compensate the losses caused by the sin. Punitive justice, in fact, is a further loss. It is a loss to the one who suffers and dies. We may also say punitive justice is a loss to the Almĭghty, because in having to execute strict justice he loses what he created in his image. Substitution makes the claim that God always seeks punitive justice.

The Satisfaction Theory of 'atonement' claims that the Almĭghty is compen-

---

[a] The gospel is presented this way by Evangelical and Fundamentalist Protestants. But this kind of illustration needs to be rejected completely. It corrupts the good news of Mĕssiah. In the parable of the unforgiving servant, the debt is unpaid when the king forgives the debt. The Almĭghty is not recovering his losses by forgiveness. Invariably the satisfaction heresy uses payment words, which should by all means be avoided except when the ransom we have in Messiah is clearly being explained, where the payment is collected by evil. KIPPURIM is not divine debt recovery.

sated for all his loss, i.e. sin is expiated from the timeline as if undone, and full retribution regarded as satisfied. It accomplishes this by claiming that Gŏd sees the sinner as completely righteous after the 'atonement' is made when the sinner *believes*. So righteousness is imputed to the sinner past, present, and future, going back to the day of conception. Because of this the sinner is acquitted. Gŏd sees no net loss from the person because he only sees righteousness. But this is only legal trickery and philosophy. It in no way erases the objective fact that Gŏd is in a position of net loss due to sin. The theory effectively teaches that forgiveness is not forgiveness, because Gŏd has been fully paid the debt he is owed by the righteousness of another. So we must reject the Satisfaction Theory.

KIPPURIM is an instructional ritual procedure (מוּסָר) to which the Almighty has officially and symbolically attached his mercy to declare a *wipe out* of the retributive penalty of the repentant sinner, and to teach a cleansing of sin from the heart. By divine promise, God's forgives when a repentant sinner confesses his sin, and afterward the sacrificial offering is presented to delcare it. The sacrifice is an ***instructional warning*** of sin's consequences required after our forgiveness (מוּסַר שְׁלוֹמֵנוּ), symbolizing a ransoming of the repentant one from suffering a death of retributive wrath after forgiveness still being sought by the powers of lawlessness. Lawlessness seeks retribution after the Most High has forgiven its prisoner. So, the sacrifice does not suffer divine retribution. It is innocent. It is only dies because of the sin it bears to symbolize the ransom cost exacted by sin and death. The ransom is a ***symbolic token*** (ἔνδειξιν) of the forgiving justice the Most High is giving us to cleanse us from sin, and buy us out of the domain of the powers. The ransom receives no objective wrath from the Most High. The ransom is His ***indication*** (ἔνδειξιν) of choosing benevolent justice for us.

The ransom is never satisfaction of strict justice. It is a demonstration (ἔνδειξιν) of our forgiveness (cf. Rom. 3:25-26). Divine justice consists of either his mercy *or* his wrath, not just wrath. The ransom is a sign (**indici**) of his mercy so we know what mercy we are receiving. Since we are ransomed and cleansed, there is no cause for future wrath, because we will have become circumcised in the heart.

Our pardon is conditioned on our holding faithful to Měssiah. In this manner he has administered benevolent justice to us, not strict justice, but merciful justice (Rom. 3:24). The Almighty's righteousness requires forgiving justice for us, because we have confessed and repented.

The normal legal justice for sin is retributive death. When a person repents, this kind of death is forgiven. The wrath and anger of the Almĭghty is wiped away by his own act of forgiving. This purging of the penalty is declared by the ransoming death of Měssiah at the hands of evil men, meant by them to be retributive, but meant by the Father to ransom the faithful from illegal death. Retributive death is not satisfied. Rather it is completely forgiven. Wrath is forgiven. KIPPURIM declares the retributive penalty to be erased, not satisfied.

Měssiah's ransom of the faithful is taught in Scripture (cf. *Gal.* 3:13 note; Hos. 13:14; *Mat.* 20:28; *Mark* 10:45; 1 Tim. 2:6). The <u>Ransom Theory</u> was the chief belief of pre Augustinian Christendom.

It should be understood that the evil powers are compelled to abide by heavens' rules of ransom. While they are not formally paid the ransom, they took it anyway, and so they loose their power to serve as God's proxy in executing divine wrath on a person for transgression as soon as the person repents and calls upon the Almighty for rescue. Those powers that refuse face immediate judgment and confinement to the abyss.

So Měssiah's death is a ransom from retributive wrath, which sin, death, and Satan, still seek to execute on the faithful even after they are forgiven. Because, the Most High thought it just to sell us over to their justice when we were transgressors, but now that we have confessed and repented, his mercy renders their justice unlawfull. Satan or his cohorts may be the kidnappers who enslaved man, but the devil is only a tool of God's retributive wrath. So long as man is content to dwell under death, the ransom is not effective, but when he repents, the ransom of Měssiah's death is applied, and retributive death has to release him. The ransom is an illustration of the great cost that the Almǐghty had to suffer to convince us to return to him. We sinned against him, and he takes a net loss to get us back. The ransom indicates enormity of the price the Almǐghty Sǒn had to pay to retrieve us as well as the net loss caused to himself, including the Father, by all the consequences of our sins.

The Son drank the cup of suffering caused by our sins, not divine vengeance or wrath. The Son became a curse (in the eyes of many), but he was not accursed *of God*, because he was innocent. The Son met up with death for us so that we could get rescued from it. He did not pay a retributive penalty for us, nor did he compensate the Father for his sin loss. He is a instruction of our peace, God's actual forgiveness (Isa. 53:5). Through his stripes we are purchased out of evil and by his blood we are cleansed.

Appendix XI: The Meaning of Justify

(See page 325: Some Things Hard to Understand). The meaning of the word mistranslated "justify" is essential to a proper understanding of the good news. Any *divine* court case may end with 1. Condemnation of the accused, 2. Acquittal of the accused, 3. Pardon of the accused. In human courts the power to pardon is often very limited, usually being reserved for a chief executive or a king. The infinitive verb δικαιοῦν **di-kay-oon** means 'to administer justice,' 'to justice,' 'to judge rightly.' The following texts show its usage in this general sense: Luke 18:14; Acts 13:38-39; Rom. 3:20, 24, 26, 28, 30; 5:1, 9; 8:30, 33; Gal. 2:16, 17; 3:8, 11, 24; 5:4. The case of the repentant person seeking to be judged correctly in Měssiah, or justiced, or administered justice, is never an acquittal. It is always a pardon. Pardon means forgiveness. The accused is still

guilty, but the accused is forgiven.

In BDAG, 3rd edition, "δικαιόω 1. **to take up a legal cause**, *show justice, do justice, take up a cause*." The authors of this lexicon (having a Lutheran legacy) are trying to conceal the meaning of the word while including it. By 'legal cause' they mean a judicial matter requiring a judgment, something we call a *legal case* nowadays. Notice that the definition does not specify an outcome to the case. It is simply the judging of the case. The outcome can be any one of the three listed above. A judge "takes up a legal case" when he decides he will hear it or try it.

At the bottom of the entry for δικαιόω in Thayer's Lexicon, "*to do one justice, to condemn, punish, to have justice done one's self, to suffer justice, be treated rightly.*" These meanings are certainly not acquittal or justifying the guilty. But they fit what Messiah did. He administered his favorable justice to us through Messiah's ransom (cf. Rom. 3:24). Thayer, by placing this definition last, effectively keeps it out of sight. But this was the normal sense in Paul's day (cf. McGrath below). In the online LSJ lexicon, "*pronounce judgment, do a man right or justice*, chastise, punish, pass sentence on, have right done one."

Alister E. McGrath in *Iustitia Dei* states, "It is clear that the passive meaning of the verb is '*to have justice done one*'" (pg. 13). McGrath rejects this meaning because the LXX uses it to mean "justify." But who says that Paul used it the way the LXX does? McGrath does not consider that Paul may have used the verb the way it was in normal Greek. Neither did English translators or previous interpreters going back to Augustine. A similar problem attends *nomos*. Paul uses it with the variety in normal Greek. The LXX uses it in nearly all cases to mean *Torah*.

John Owen exposes the facts also, "**Δικαιόω** is the word used to the same purpose in the New Testament, and that alone. Neither is this word used in any good author whatever to signify the making of a man righteous by any applications to produce internal righteousness in him; but either to absolve and acquit, to judge, esteem, and pronounce righteous; or, on the contrary, to condemn. So Suidas, Δικαιοῦν δυὸ δηλοῖ, τὸ τε κολάζειν, καὶ τὸ δίκαιον νομίζειν· — 'It has two significations; to punish [κολάζειν], and to account righteous.' And he confirms this sense of the word by instances out of Herodotus, Appianus, and Josephus. And again, Δικαιῶσαι αἰτιατικῇ, καταδικάσαι, κολάσαι, δίκαιον νομίσαι with an *accusative case;* that is, when it respects and affects a subject, a person, it is either *to condemn* and *punish*, or *to esteem* and *declare righteous:* and of this latter sense he gives pregnant instances in the next words. Hesychius mentions only the first signification. Δικαιούμενον, κολαζόμενον, δικαιῶσαι, κολάσαι. They never thought of any sense of this word but what is forensic. And, in our language, to be justified was commonly used formerly for to be judged and sentenced; as it is still among the Scots. One of the articles of peace between the two nations at the surrender of Leith, in the days of Edward VI., was, 'That if any one committed a crime, he should be justified by the law, upon his trial.' And, in general, δικαοῦσθαι is "jus in judicio auferre;" and δικαιῶσαι is "justum censere,

declarare pronuntiare;" and how in the Scripture it is constantly opposed unto "condemnare," we shall see immediately" (*Doctrine of Justification by Faith*).

Owen's fault here is not that he does not know the facts, but that he fails to apply the proper definition. This is because he believed with the other reformers that Měssiah acquitted us. Owen correctly points out that the word may mean "declare righteous" at law. But he fails to see that it is complete lawlessness to do so for a person unless they are actually righteous. He has overlooked the sense he gives above "to judge," which does not mean condemn, but it does mean to try a case or decide a case.

Exactly like Greek and Latin, the word "justify" in middle English means "to administer justice": "justifien (v.) Also justefien; p.ppl. i) justified. 1 (a) To administer justice; execute (laws); (b) to judge (matters), adjudicate; (c) to punish an offender; bring (sb.) to justíce, punish; correct (sb. or his heart); refl. discipline (oneself)..... 5. [**Corrupt**] (a) To acquit (the guilty); (b) of Gǒd: to absolve (the sinner) by His free gift of divine forgiveness and grace and for man's faith in Christ; also, to win Gǒd's grace for (sb.)." For example, "If Robert þe Brus of Scotland wolde nouȝt be *iustifiede*, and make amendes vnto kyng Edward.. þat þe sentence shulde be pronouncede þrouȝ all Engeland" (Middle English Dictionary). This dictionary is online at the University of Michigan. Obviously the wrong definition (no. 5) is in the dictionary also, but the right one is no. 1.

Let us now apply this in Rom. 3:24, "being administered justice benevolently, by his lovingkindness through the ransom which is in the Anǒinted Yěshua." The sense is "administered justice" or "adjudicated." The word benevolent means to bestow a gift without payment. BDAG defines, "$\delta\omega\rho\epsilon\grave{\alpha}\nu$ ❶ **pertaining to being freely given, *as a gift, without payment, gratis*.**" Isa. 52:3 says, "For nothing you have been sold, and not with silver you will be ransomed." No one is paying the judge to administer favorable justice to us, but the judge of all bears the cost of the ransom. Therefore, it would be incorrect to claim the Son of the Judge is paying a penalty to the judge. Rather the Judge sent his own Son to be the ransom, to suffer the cost exacted by lawlessness holding his people in bondage, in order to free them.

A ransom is a price paid to recover a lost soul, not a price paid to satisfy the penalty of sin. It is men that are being ransomed, and the payment is not made to God, but it is made by God to win the loyalty of men, to draw all men unto himself.

Appendix XII: Quotations

Ancient quotation standards were very different than modern standards, especially when dealing with material from several different languages, and the fact that most of the material quoted was from memory. Like modern quotes the author may insert bracketed material into the quote, an explanation, a transition. But there was no standard for bracketing additions. In this text you will see some words no longer in small capitals between the quotation marks. This represents material that would be bracketed in a modern quote. As a matter of course the biblical writers took great liberties with their quotes, and therefore the expectation of the ancient reader was more tolerant. No one would charge an author with deceptive misquoting unless the idea communicated was false or the words quoted could not be reasonably found or inferred from their source texts. Sometimes a detail was misremembered in making a quotation (e.g. 1 Cor. 10:8).

When an author says something is written, the standard is that most of the quote is written somewhere. When the author says the Scripture says something, it means at least that it communicates the idea. Often an author will create a mash up of Scripture, which would require a lot of brackets, ellipses, and other devices, making it pointless to render the quote in a modern format, or according to modern standards.

The ancient reader expected to see pronoun switches to apply the quote more specifically to the topic. Often enough, an author will insert a synonym into a quote for an original word, for didactic or homiletical reasons. For example, instead of "go across the sea," Paul quotes Deuteronomy 30:13 as "descend into the abyss." This effect would require a complicated apparatus to make it conform to modern standards, i.e. "Who will go across the sea [or descend into the abyss]?" The idea is the same: who will go to some remote place? For his homily Paul equivocates sea and abyss, taking his point off the depths of the sea. The abyss is a jail for evil persons waiting for the last judgment. These things make for a very creative literary art.

Often a whole theme of Scripture will be summarized as part of a quote. This sort of paraphrasing on a theme occurs frequently.

In order to know whether a quote is unjustly used or altered, one has to know the Scriptures, and the Scriptural themes, as well as the expected standards. This is like having to consult an original source for a modern quote to see if the author quoted exactly or if the author altered it or falsely attributed it. For example, the author of Hebrews quotes Psa. 40:6 and alters the words "ears you have opened" to "body," a crime covered up by some late versions of the LXX. The author then alters the Scriptural teaching that obedience is better than sacrifice in order to make a point contrary to the text quoted. Generally, the book of Hebrews is a mine of quotes used to make doctrinally erroneous points, e.g. See Hebrews 1:13, 2:1-2. The Law was not given by angels.

Sometimes there are several possible Scriptures that an author could have in mind when quoting. Some are appropriate and others are not. And sometimes modern editors have chosen the wrong attribution for antinomian reasons. A number of these have been fixed.

To simplify things for the modern reader when seeking the source of a quote, it might be better for the reader to consider a quote a rephrasing of a Scriptural theme rather then try to locate all the parts and understand all the rephrasing. It is better to become acquainted with the Scriptural theme being quoted by reading the Scripture in general.

I have added a number of quote citations not in the usual study Bibles, that would be regarded as quotes by ancient criteria. Also quite a number of allusions are highlighted, but not all, because the text would look hacked up if all the allusions were marked, especially in the book of Revelation, which has virtually no quotes, but more allusions to Scripture than any other book.

Appendix XIII
Appointed Times vs. Counterfeits

The appointed times of Yăhweḥ according to the Messianic Faith, which were ordained by divine commandment, and those traditional times† which meet with divine approval but are not mandated.

True Appointed Time	Corruption or Counterfeit
1. Şabbath	Sunday
2. Passover	Easter
3. Shavuot/Pentecost	Whitsunday (50 days after Easter)
4. Yom Teruah/Trumpets	Christmas/Epiphany
	New Year's Day
5. †Season of Teshuvah/ †Yam‑ei Ratson †Days of Awe	Lent
6. Yom Kippur	Ash Wednesday
7. Sukkot/Tabernacles	Michaelmas/Harvest Home
8. †Ḥanukkah	Advent
9. †Purim	Mardi Gras/Carnival
10. Sabbatical year	Central Bank and Fiat Currency
11. Jubilee year	Corporate Facism

Yom Teruah is the new year for Sabbatical and Jubilee years. It is the new year for the agricultural year, and the new year for the kings of Yehudah. The Most High favored this day with deeper historical meaning because on this day Mĕssiah was born. It is a day for blowing horns, trumpets, shofars. It announces a new beginning.

The season of Teshuvah is a traditional 40 days from the first of Elul to Yom Kippur. Teshuvah means repentance. During this time Mĕssiah fasted for 40 days and 40 nights. The Days of Awe are the 10 days from Tishri to Yom Kippur.

Ḥanukkah is a traditional feast commemorating the dedication of the temple after it was recovered from the Syrians by the Maccabees. The Church custom of Advent might be seen to be a corruption of lighting the candles during Ḥanukkah. Mĕssiah was conceived on the 6th (or possibly 7th) day of Ḥanukkah. This feast is mentioned in Yoḥ. 10:22.

Purim is meant by the feast in Yoḥ. 5:1.

What makes a man made appointed time a corruption? There are several ways to tell. If the man made time competes with the divinely ordained, then it is in opposition to the true appointed time. If the man made time teaches a false version of history, then it is a corruption.

Observing and keeping the true appointed times of Yăhweḥ our Almĭghty is an important way we show our loyalty to him, by honoring the Most High on the anniversaries of the times he acted in history.

Appendix XIV: Appointed Times

AD 2021	Seventh New Moon	SEP 9 *AF-R*	1 of 7 and 36 of 50
↓	Yom Kippurim	SEP 18	
↓	Sukkot	SEP 23 and SEP 30	
↓	Ḥannukah	DEC 1 to DEC 8	
AD 2022	Purim	MAR 17+ *BZ*	1988
↓	New Moon day Aviv	APR 3 *AG-N*	MAR 19=
↓	Passover	APR 17 and APR 23	YEAR 6161
↓	Shavuot	JUN 6	366 days
↓	Seventh New Moon	SEP 28 *AF-W*	2 of 7 and 37 of 50
↓	Yom Kippurim	OCT 7	
↓	Sukkot	OCT 12 and Oct 19	
↓	Ḥannukah	DEC 20 to DEC 27	
AD 2023	Purim	MAR 7	1989
↓	New Moon Aviv	MAR 23+ *BZ-R*	MAR 20=
↓	Passover	APR 6+ and APR 12+	YEAR 6162
↓	Shavuot	MAY 26+	365 days
↓	Seventh New Moon	SEP 17 *AG-N*	3 of 7 and 38 of 50
↓	Yom Kippurim	SEP 26	
↓	Sukkot	OCT 1 and OCT 8	
↓	Ḥannukah	DEC 10 to DEC 17	
AD 2024	Purim	FEB 25	1990
↓	New Moon Aviv	MAR 12 *AG-T*	MAR 19=
↓	Passover	MAR 26 and APR 1	YEAR 6163
↓	Shavuot	MAY 15	365 days
↓	Seventh New Moon	SEP 5+ *BG-R*	4 of 7 and 39 of 50
↓	Yom Kippurim	SEP 14+	
↓	Sukkot	SEP 19+ and SEP 26+	
↓	Ḥannukah	NOV 28 to DEC 5	
AD 2025	Purim	MAR 15	1991
↓	New Moon Aviv	MAR 31 *AG-M*	MAR 19=
↓	Passover	APR 14 and APR 20	YEAR 6164
↓	Shavuot	JUNE 3	365 days
↓	Seventh New Moon	SEP 24+ *BF-W*	5 of 7 and 40 of 50
↓	Yom Kippurim	OCT 3+	
↓	Sukkot	OCT 8+ and OCT 15+	
↓	Ḥannukah	DEC 17 to DEC 24	
AD 2026	Purim	MAR 4	1992
↓	New Moon Aviv	MAR 21 *AG-S*	MAR 19=
↓	Passover	APR 4 and APR 10	YEAR 6165
↓	Shavuot	MAY 24	366 days

↓	Seventh New Moon	Sep 13+ *BG-S* 6 of 7 and 41 of 50	
↓	Yom Kippurim	Sep 22+	
↓	Sukkot	Sep 27+ and Oct 4+	
↓	Ḥannukah	Dec 6 to Dec 13	
AD 2027	Purim	Feb 22- *AC*	1993
↓	New Moon Aviv	Mar 10 *AG-W*	**Mar 20**
↓	Passover	Mar 24 and Mar 30	**Year 6166**
↓	Shavuot	May 13	**365 days**
↓	Seventh New Moon	Sep 3 *AF-F* 7 of 7 and 42 of 50	
↓	Yom Kippurim	Sep 12	Sabbath Year
↓	Sukkot	Sep 17 and Sep 24	
↓	Ḥannukah	Nov 25 to Dec 2	
AD 2028	Purim	Mar 11	1994
↓	New Moon Aviv	Mar 28 *AG-T*	**Mar 19=**
↓	Passover	Apr 11 and Apr 17	**Year 6167**
↓	Shavuot	May 31	**365 days**
↓	Seventh New Moon	Sep 21 *AF-R* 1 of 7 and 43 of 50	
↓	Yom Kippurim	Sep 30	
↓	Sukkot	Oct 5 and Oct 12	
↓	Ḥannukah	Dec 13 and Dec 20	
AD 2029	Purim	Feb 28	1995
↓	New Moon Aviv	Mar 17 *AG-S*	**Mar 19=**
↓	Passover	Mar 31 and Apr 6	**Year 6168**
↓	Shavuot	May 20	**365 days**
↓	Seventh New Moon	Sep 11 *AF-T* 2 of 7 and 44 of 50	
↓	Yom Kippurim	Sep 20	
↓	Sukkot	Sep 25 and Oct 1	
↓	Ḥannukah	Dec 2 and Dec 9	
AD 2030	Purim	Feb 17	1996
↓	New Moon Aviv	Mar 6 *AG-W*	**Mar 19 =**
↓	Passover	Mar 20 and Mar 26	**Year 6169**
↓	Shavuot	May 20	**366 days**
↓	Seventh New Moon	Aug 31+ *BF-S* 3 of 7 and 45 of 50	
↓	Yom Kippurim	Sep 9+	
↓	Sukkot	Sep 14+ and Sep 21+	
↓	Ḥannukah	Nov 22 to Nov 29	
AD 2031	Purim	Mar 8	1997
↓	New Moon Aviv	Mar 25 *AG-T*	**Mar 20**
↓	Passover	Apr 8 and Apr 14	**Year 6170**
↓	Shavuot	May 28	**365 days**
↓	Seventh New Moon	Sep 19 *AF-F* 4 of 7 and 46 of 50	
↓	Yom Kippurim	Sep 28	

↓	Sukkot	OCT 3 AND OCT 10	
↓	Hannukah	DEC 11 TO DEC 18	
AD 2032	Purim	FEB 26	1998
↓	New Moon Aviv	MAR 13 *AZ-S*	MAR 19 =
↓	Passover	MAR 27 AND APR 2	YEAR 6171
↓	Shavuot	MAY 16	365 DAYS
↓	Seventh New Moon	SEP 7+ *BF-T* 5 of 7 and 47 of 50	
↓	Yom Kippurim	SEP 16+	
↓	Sukkot	SEP 21+ AND SEP 28+	
↓	Hannukah	NOV 29 TO DEC 6	
AD 2033	Purim	MAR 16	1999
↓	New Moon Aviv	APR 1 *AZ-F*	MAR 19=
↓	Passover	APR 15 AND APR 21	YEAR 6172
↓	Shavuot	JUNE 4	365 DAYS
↓	Seventh New Moon	SEP 26 *AF-M* 6 of 7 and 48 of 50	
↓	Yom Kippurim	OCT 5	
↓	Sukkot	OCT 10 AND OCT 17	
↓	Hannukah	DEC 18 TO DEC 25	
AD 2034	Purim	MAR 6	2000
↓	New Moon Aviv	MAR 22 *AG-W*	MAR 19 =
↓	Passover	APR 5 and APR 11	YEAR 6173
↓	Shavuot	MAY 25	366 DAYS
↓	Seventh New Moon	SEP 15 *AF-F* 7 of 7 and 49 of 50	
↓	Yom Kippurim	SEP 24	Sabbath Year
↓	Sukkot	SEP 29 and OCT 6	
↓	Hannukah	DEC 7 to DEC 14	
AD 2035	Purim FEB 23	**THIRD MILLENNIUM**	2001
↓	New Moon Aviv	MAR 12 *AF-M*	20 MAR=
↓	Passover	MAR 26 AND APR 1	YEAR 6174
↓	Shavuot	MAY 15	365 DAYS
↓	Seventh New Moon	SEP 4 *AG-T* 1 of 7 and 50 of 50	
↓	Yom Kippurim	SEP 13	Jubille Year
↓	Sukkot	SEP 18 AND SEP 25	
↓	Hannukah	NOV 26 TO DEC 3	
AD 2036	Purim	MAR 13	

Calendar Notes and Admonitions

No. 1: All Annual Sabbaths begin at sunset the day before that listed. All dates correspond to the daylight portion of a day. For example, a new moon date is given in the daylight portion of the day, but the new crescent will be seen in the beginning of night before the day listed. In the case of the seventh month, the Sabbath for the feast will begin with sunset before the day listed and extend to sunset on the day listed. But in the case of the new moon offerings and

the new moon feast day, the day is calculated from dawn on the day listed to dawn beginning the next day. In otherwords, the new moon is seen in the night at the head of the new moon feast day. All days are counted from dawn to dawn, but the Sabbath begins with the night of the calendar day previous to the day of the Sabbath.

No. 2: A + sign after a date means the calculated or predicted new moon sighting is not certain and the date could be the next day. While it is calculated as probably as possible, the results of visual observation should be consulted in these cases. It should be understood that dates considered certain do not factor in cloudy skies which may prevent the new moon from being seen in a location. It is judged acceptable at this time to rely on calculations which predict a certain sighting of the moon if skies are clear. In the time span of this calendar it is acceptable to use the dates indicated without checking witnesses if witnesses prove to be unavailable, or inclement conditions prevent witnesses from seeing the moon. Since there is no Temple operating and no altar any error is an error of ignorance and will be overlooked. An error because of uncertainty in the new moon date is not to be regarded as transgression.

There is great transgression in the calendar errors of many, but not in the matter above. Those who adopted counterfiet appointed times transgress the law. The obvious example here is the ecclesiastical calendar promoted by the Chuches. But also those who go by the moon alone and ignore Sabbaths are guilty of great transgression. And also those who go by the sun alone and ignore the news moons. At this time I grant a dispensation to observers of the Rabbinical calendar, and also a dispensation to those following Church calendar traditions who are in ignorance of the law, but still hold faithful to Messiah, because they are in the infancy of their faith and or have circumstances and communities around them that do not see the truth. And it is the perogative of the Most High to sort the sheep from the goats. But certain leaders, both Rabbis and churchmen who actively promote their calendar errors I give no dispensations, and those who convert from following Torah to afterward following a corrupt calendar, I allow no dispensations. They are personally guilty of transgression after knowing the truth, and are to be held unfaithful. They are to be called to repentance. These are of course general observations. Anyone who wilfully ignores the truth is guilty of transgression. I say this because the faithful will have to listen to the Spirit of the Most High and exercise discretion in who to judge and who not to, erring on the side of mercy, knowing that we ourselves have before fallen into error because we were misled.

A − sign after a date means it could be before for the same reason. That is the new moon could be seen on the previous day under the most perfect and pristine of conditions with observers of gifted eyesight. Such sightings are considered hard or difficult sightings. But they happen.

No. 3: the codes *AF, AG, BF*, etc. in are italics technical new moon codes. The hypehnated codes are for the weekday of the day listed. That is: -N,M,T,W,R,F,S are weekdays after new moon codes, suN, Mon, Tue, Wed, thuR, Fri, Sabbath. Checking both the weekday and the date helps prevent error in comprehending the date.

No. 4: Years **6160-6174** count from creation. All these years begin on the spring equinox, or tequfah. This is the day on which the sun completes its annual circuit and begins it anew. See No. 6 below.

No. 5: Years **1987-2000** count the final years of the second millennium after Messiah's death and resurrection. Year **2001** is the first year of the **THIRD MILLENNIUM**. What we are looking for here is NOT the second coming

of Messiah, but the restoration of the house of Israel in the third day after Messiah's resurrection. See Hosea 6:1-3. And when this happens, Israel will become a light to all nations to seek Messiah and his goodness in the latter days.

No. 6: Dates marked **MAR 19** or **MAR 20** are dates of the spring equinox, and the beginnings of years with each year length specified: **365** or **366 DAYS**. These equinox days are often one day before equinox dates marked in most calendars, because they are based on modeling visual observation used in ancient times. The mwain factor is when looking for the day that the sun reaches the western limit of heaven is that of atmospheric refraction which raises the apparent sun in the sky and allows it to align with west sooner than those using a mathematical method that omits refraction.

No. 7: Small cap feasts are annual Sabbaths. Indented dates are not. The Sabbath year cycle count 1 to 7 and the Jubilee year cycle count, 1 to 50 is also indicated. It should be understood that the Jubilee count begins again in the 50th year, so that year 1 of the new cycle is the same year as year 50 of the old cycle.

Appendix XV: Indefinite Future Perfect

[1]The *Good News of Mĕssiah* uses the future perfect in ways that some English speakers may not expect. If a reader is having difficulty, usages 'will have been' may be simplified to 'will be,' or 'will have' to 'will.' [2]These future perfects are termed the 'indefinite future perfect.' What this means is that the future point in time has to be gained from the context, because it is not explicitly defined. [3]What is usually seen in English is 'X will have been done by the time Y happens.' Sometimes it is 'By the time Y happens, X will have been done.' [4]In the indefinite future perfect the underlined phrase is omitted, and the future point with respect to which the perfect tense is past is left indefinite. It is unstated. [5]When a simple future is used, 'X will happen,' no definite point in the future need be stated in English. [6]The odd usage consists in using the indefinite future perfect will the same sense as the simple future, without stating a definite future point. [7]Why use the future perfect? The simple future looks forward; the future perfect locates the point of view in the future of the event and looks backward to it. This is a way of representing the event as more tangible, more concrete, or more certain. [8]Readers should never assume that the indefinite future perfect in terms of *time* has any other meaning than the simple future. [9]In some cases the use of the future perfect may imply to some readers that the stated event must take place before another stated event, as in 'Jill walks to school. Jill will have eaten lunch later.' If the underlined word is omitted (hence an indefinite future perfect), some readers will assume lunch was eaten before she walked to school. [10]There are therefore some cases where later (or some other time adverb) may have to be supplied to alter what some English readers will assume based on the English construction.

[11]English teachers aim to teach English norms. That's good. But it's no good for translators who need unusual English to represent a non-English text they are translating literally. [12]The translator often does not have a choice but to translate literally, because someone will say he is translating incorrectly if he does not translate literally. [13]Thus an unusual English form must be used to show that the translation is correct with some explanatory footnotes if necessary. Every good English translation of Scripture deviates radically from normal English. Nobody speaks ESV English, 'For Gŏd so loved the world....' But perhaps the GW version does, "Gŏd loved the world this way...." No one speaks with 'for' anymore, which really means 'because.'

[14]The indefinite future perfect will be hard for some to grasp in this version. That is because it is unusual English. Here is a 'normal' future perfect: 'I will have finished your project by Monday.' It is a definite future perfect because a definite later time is stated after using it. Example 2: "Joan said, 'Please finish the project by Monday.' Jill replied, 'I will have finished it.'" Jill has left off the later deadline because the context already had it. Example 3: 'He will have glorified his people [at some future point].' Here we see that an indefinite future is definitely stated as the later point. [15]So if we keep in mind that all future perfects, without a definite statement of later time, must gain either a definite later time from the context, or failing that assume an indefinite future, as if 'by some future point,' were tacked onto the use of the future perfect, then the logic of the sense will be clear.

[16]There are of course many Hebrew and Greek idioms in the Scripture that are not normal English. The first future perfect in the Scripture is Gen. 1:14, 'And they will have been for signs and for appointed

times, and for days and years [by some future point].' So leaving off this phrase is unusual English, but still makes sense. In fact, it gets us closer to the way the original writers of Scripture were thinking. And every so often it makes an important difference.

[17] Greek has also an explicit future perfect. See Mat. 18:18 in CSB, DLNT, ISV, MOUNCE, NET, NLV, NTE, OJB, TLV, Aramaic Bible in Plain English, and WEB. None of these versions saw the need to indicate the future point: 'will have been bound [by the time you finish binding it],' but all leave it indefinite.

[18] The future perfect works by transporting the mental viewpoint of the audience to the future and then by looking back from that assumed viewpoint at the completed event. With such use of the perfect in Hebrew, the verb is in the perfect tense. The future perfect idea must be gained from the context. [19] The same is the case with the future use of the aorist tense in Greek, except in the passage just mentioned, where the future perfect idea is fully conjugated and the translators are obliged to acknowledge it.

[19] I am anticipating being contradicted by the English Teaching Establishment or Translating Guild, which will insist that English can only be used in certain ways and not in certain other ways that break their rules. I think they have forgotten how language came to be. English was transformed by the Saxon, Norse, and Norman invasions of England. And if you go back further in time, one will find that many grammatical features were added and subtracted. The point is that the rules were being broken when it happened, just as war breaks the rules and changes languages.

[20] Also, literary forms of language preserve more unusual forms of language than spoken forms, and people learn such forms by the reading of literature that they would never use in everyday speech, e.g. thee, thou, hath, hadst, etc. Furthermore, the KJV, a very popular version, is frequently complained about because it is in archaic English!

[21] So, I am going to call the future perfect illustrated above, 'The Indefinite Future Perfect.' This means the future perfect is used without a future point being definitely stated: 'The marooned man will have been rescued by the end of the week.' If this is a perceived violation of rules (that are assumed to make this construction impossible), then my answer to that is that English is going to adopt an additional tense for literary use by the rules of war. [22] The reason is that this has enormous apologetical value in disposing of a myriad of deceptive arguments that rely on excluding the use of the future perfective idea.

[23] Plainly a good many Scriptures make plain sense with the future perfect idea. Without it, interpreters have been compelled to resort to sophistic reasoning usually used to support some false doctrine. The most common is that salvation has no dependence on our faithfulness and is therefore completely assured without it. The future idea is ignored, and such statements treated as if they are past tense, and therefore not subject to any future contingency.

[24] If the future perfect be overlooked, then Isa. 9:6, for example, would have to be rendered, "For a child was born to us; a son was given to us...." This text is plainly in the perfect in Hebrew and the aorist in Greek. Apologists for Judaism loose no time in claiming that the text refers to a birth that had already occurred rather than pointing to Měssiah in the future. Christian translators often try to soften the blow by using the present tense, "A child is born...." However, this is a faulty apologetic since the Hebrew perfect really is used for the future quite frequently. Thus a future perfect quite properly expresses the sense, "For a child will have been born to us; a son will have been given to us...."

[25] The applications are many. "And whom he will have administered justice, these also he will have glorified" (Rom. 8:30). The future perfect idea here allows Paul to include those who have not yet come to Messiah, and also to refer to a completely future idea of glorification. "[He] will have raised us" (Eph. 2:6) refers to the actual resurrection of the dead and not to some mystical spiritual event, "he has raised us."

[26] I note also that the aorist subjunctive also lends itself readily to the future perfect idea, "so that he will (may) have made seen in the coming ages the overflowing wealth of his loving-kindness" (Eph. 2:7). For the future subjunctives I often render 'will' have' in different type, i.e. 'will' to make clear that this future perfect is subjunctive. There is in Greek also a present subjunctive, and I have avoided including the perfect idea (have) into any of these.

[27] In Hebrew and Greek, the future perfect idea looks back from the future to its past. In terms of absolute time, it may be any time. It may look back past our present. Now in English we would use a future in past construction to show this, "He would have...." In Hebrew and Greek the idea could be gnomic looking all the way fact from the infinite future to the infinite past. Thus the sense becomes gnomic (a truism for all time). See page 400.

[28] The future perfect is a powerful idea for opening the possibilities of Scripture interpretations that have been lost for many generations. It is an idea essential to Hebrew (and Greek) obvious to those knowing those languages. It was unnecessarily lost in translation.

Appendix XVI: The New Moon

In all places where the Hebrew word חֹדֶשׁ and its Greek equivalents are used, the meaning always makes reference to the "new moon." Even if the affected meaning in the context is a "month," it is the context that must bear this out in relation to the sense of "new moon." If the context does not indicate particularly otherwise, then the meaning is literally the "new moon." And if the literal sense doesn't seem to make sense, it is a metaphorical sense related to the new moon, as we shall see.

In general, in those cases where a particular day after a new moon is not indicated, the text is referring to the new moon itself. In this regard, matters have been confused by translators trying to use the word "month" when they should use the words "new moon," and to cause further injury they have represented two prepositions used in Hebrew as conforming to expectations for the use of the word "month," when the same prepositions in Hebrew have meanings that make perfect sense of the texts when the rendering is properly "new moon."

The two prepostions are בּ and לּ. Both these prepositions are used in Hebrew with a greater abstraction than beginning students of Hebrew will recognize, who are given the definitions "in" and "to" respectively for these two prepositions. And using only these two definitions, they will find it impossible to understand many usages, and also difficult to conceive how Hebrew goes from those two senses to the many others listed in the Lexicon!

So for the sake of brevity and this discussion, I will supply two definitions that are needed. The first preposition, בּ, denotes **proximity**, thus define this as "in connection with," and a good rendering for our new moon study with be the gloss "with." You will see how this works in a bit. The second, לּ, denotes "with respect to," and has the practical sense of "after." All these definitions are found in the Lexicon. The problem is not that they are not there, but that translators failed to apply them. When we do so, things begin to make sense.

So let us see how this plays out in various texts. Genesis 7:11 goes like this, "In the sixth hundreth year of the life of Noah *in connection* with the second **new moon**, on the seventeenth day *after* the **new moon**, on this day all the springs of the great deep had split apart." Now we could have translated every occurrence of בּ in this text as "with," viz. "With the sixth hundred year...with the 17th day...with this day...." But I will not do this because it is not necessary. The preposition is denoting proximity and not the containing in a space that English might imply. You will see that English contrains us into a sense too spacial. "In the second new moon," or worse "on the second new moon" contradicts what follows, whereas, "With the second new moon" does not, because it means in connection with, allowing us to think in proximity terms.

Likewise, "after the new moon" is strictly speaking, "with respect to the new moon." More literally, the Hebrew word for new moon is a word meaning 'newing,' being a noun derived from a particiPle: חֹדֶשׁ.

So if I were to translate Gen. 7:11 thus, "with the second renewing, on the seventeenth day after the renewing" then you see everything makes sense, and it does refer to the new moon.

I will now introduce three other Hebrew idioms. We have "a new moon of days" (Gen. 29:14) חֹדֶשׁ יָמִים, which is an idiom for 30 days without respect to the actual moon phases. Also we have "a moon of days" (2 Kings 15:13) יֶרַח־יָמִים. Both these usages are not literal, but they indicate time by using new moon and moon as a metaphor. A metaphor is a non literal equivalency between two objects seeking to ascribe one of the properties of one object to the other rather than all of them. The property of moon and new moon sought after is the time for it to complete one cycle of days rounded up to 30. Another idiom is like it from Numbers 3:15, "from the son of a new moon and upward." It has the same meaning as the previous idioms, which is 30 days, but a son of 30 days is a child that is at least 31 days old. This also is a metaphor since the new moon doesn't actually give birth. The ideal property ascribed to days is the time for the moon to renew itself, 30 days.

Let me now cover some important texts. In Exodus 12:2 we have "This new moon for you is the first of the new moons. First it is for you with respect to the new moons of the year." And Exodus 12:3 states, "On the tenth after this new moon..." and 12:6, "until on the fourteenth day after this new moon...between the settings."

Exodus 23:15 is a text of interest, "After the appointed time of the new moon of Ha-Aviv, because with it you had gone out from Egypt." This requires us to recognize that the absolute state לְמוֹעֵד should be reduced to לְמוֹעֵד, because it is in the construct state. In like manner, Exodus 34:18 is rendered, "...after the appointed time of the new moon of Ha-Aviv, because with the new moon of Ha-Aviv you had gone out from Egypt."

Numbers 9:22 can be difficult to grasp in the MT Hebrew text, but this translation should clear things up "or *after* a couple days or *after* a new moon, or *after* a year *of* days in making long the cloud over the tabernacle. The progression of the text sorts out the difference. "After" is implied by vs. 20-21, "And it is that the cloud would be a number of days over the tabernacle. By the mouth of Yahweh they settled in camp, and by the mouth of Yahweh they pulled out. And it is that would be the cloud from setting until daybreak, and the cloud had ascended in the daybreak, and they had pulled out, or *after* a daytime and a nighttime, and the cloud had ascended, and they had pulled out." The daybreak in which the cloud ascended to signal pulling out was not counted in the time for encampment. Thus it is after the time specified that they set out. It should be noted that when they were in camp a couple of days, it was from setting before the first of the days until daybreak after the second of the days. Thus three nights came between. The days are not calendar days, but temporal waymarks. Likewise the new moon is a temporal

waymark, through which they stayed, and the morning after which they pulled out. I should point out that the LXX reads "a new moon of days" indicating that the Hebrew source lacked the second אֶת, and in that case it is simply a metaphor for 30 days.

Another real interesting case is Numbers 28:14, "This is the ascending offering of the new moon [feast] in its renewing with respect to new moons of the year." Certainly the Hebrew בְּחָדְשׁוֹ should be an infinitive construct בְּחַדְּשׁוֹ, "in its making to be new."

Of interest will be Deut. 16:1, "Watch for the new moon of Ha-Aviv, and you will have done Passover for Yâhweh your Almighty, because with the new moon of Ha-Aviv, Yâhweh your Almighty had made you go out from Egypt at night." Also Exodus 19:1, "On the third new moon, after the going out of the sons of Yisra'el from the land of Egypt, on this day, they had entered the wilderness of Sinai."

In Numbers 10:10 and 28:11 it speaks of "On the heads of your new moons..." or "In the beginnings of your new moons." The new moon can be said to have two beginnings, when it is seen in the evening, and when the ascending offerings are made just after dawn on the new moon day. But this is probably not what this means when we examine the case of an enumeration of new moons, for example שִׁבְעָה חֳדָשִׁים in 1 Sam. 6:1. The new moon is still in view here, but it is the meaning is "[days belonging to] seven new moons." Again this is a metaphor since "seven new moons" does not make literal sense. This is almost the same meaning as "seven months," but it refers to the new moon unlike the word "month" which is inaccurate in that it does not refer to the new moon. So our Numbers passages would be understood as, "In the beginning of [days belonging to] your new moons..." (Num. 10:10; 28:11). Thus "new moon" is a metaphor for a month, but such a metaphor that the days indicated are in relation to an actual new moon.

Finally, after the example of Numbers 28:14 given above, Isaiah 66:23 should be translated with a pair of infinitive constructs, "And it will have been after the sufficientness of the new moon in the renewing of it, and the sufficientness of the Sabbath in the ceasing of it, that shall come all flesh to bow themselves down at my face, says Yâhweh."

So now when we turn to matters Greek, BDAG (2000) states the following, "μήν ❶ month, ...❷ new moon." And Thayer states, "1. a month, 2. the time of the new moon, new moon, (barbarous Lat. novilunium; after the use of the Hebr. חֹדֶשׁ, which denotes both a 'month' and a 'new moon.'" The Latin word used here means simply "new moon" (Derived from novus ("new") + lūna ("the Moon") + -ium (abstract noun-forming suffix). The reason for this comment is that the Romans also expressed time in terms of their Calends, which was the day of the new moon, and the primitive Roman calendar was orginally based on actual lunations.

The Lexicons of Jewish Greek Literature are misdirecting us in putting the order of the definitions as they do. The first definition of the Greek word in NT and LXX usage is "new moon," and this is clearly under the influence of the Hebrew. Clearly, in the Hebrew texts the sense "new moon" is always in view, and the meaning "month" is only derived under the influence of context. The overturning of this biblical paradigm to put forth "month" in most places, except where the context is so strong (cf. LXX) that misdefinition cannot overturn "new moon," is a grand mistake. It is an error that certainly has its origins in ignorance of Hebrew and reliance on Greek outside Jewish Greek Literature. It is an error that defies the evidence, once exposed to view, and should it continue can only be ascribed to willfully perpetuating the spiritual darkness under which Christendom operates. Probably the only place a Greek word truly means "month" disconnected from the new moon is Galatians 4:10, and there it is speaking about the heretical solar calendar found at Qumran, and in the books of pseudo-Enoch and Jubilees, which indeed was not related to the new moon.

In non-biblical Greek, or non-Jewish secular Greek, the word almost exclusively and literally means "month" except in some very rare context demanding cases.

The Moon's Place in the Calendar

Let us turn to the Hebrew word for moon, which takes two forms, one poetic and one not יָרֵחַ and יֶרַח. The longer form is poetic. That this is certainly the word for the physical moon is made plain by an easy word study of the poetic form where the usage is not aimed at marking a time period. As for the regular form, it is regularly mistranslated 'month.' But it still means 'moon,' and in the clocking of time ancient people spoke of so many 'moons.' One can think of a 'month' as a 'moonth.' One can speak of so many 'new moons' which takes reference to new moons (חֳדָשִׁים) that pass by. But 'moons,' on the other hand, have no reference to a part of the cycle, and 'moon' is put for the whole cycle or part of one. Thus 1 Kings 6:38, "In the moon of Bul. It is the eighth new moon. The house had been finished." So moon of Bul specifies the whole 'moonth,' but in the eighth new moon specifies the first day. Also, 1 Kings 8:2, "In the moon of the-ever flowing, in the feast day. It is the seventh new moon." And so we now come to Psalm 104:19, "He has made the moon for appointed times. The sun has known its entering." The Psalmist uses the poetic form for moon alongside the sun. There is no doubt that it refers to the physical moon (cf. Greek: σελήνην). And this proves that the moon is correctly tied being the light sign for the מוֹעֲדִים in Gen. 1:14, that is the appointed times of the Yâhweh's feast days. He made the moon for appointed times in the beginning.

Appendix XVII: Priestly Rotations

I. Lewin's Calculation

Thomas Lewin caculated the 8th division to begin on 16 May, BC 7. And I calculated it to begin again later on 6 July, BC 3. These dates are on the same rotational solution since they differ by exactly 24 weeks. Converting these dates to the corresponding Julian day numbers yields: 1,719,002 and 1,720,514. The difference in the two dates is 1,512. Dividing by 24 yields 63:

$$(1,720,514 - 1,719,002)/24 = 63$$

The even result of the division with no remainder means both services of the 8th division occur a multiple of 24 weeks apart, precisely 63 × 24 days.

II. Qumran Documents

The Dead Sea Scrolls confirm the dates of the priestly rotations, which before their discovery, could only be figured using *Seder Olam* (ca. AD 165). Without *Seder Olam*, in theory, the correct rotations could be determined based on Luke's nativity chronology and Revelation 12:1-2 because he mentions the new moon in Luke 1:36, but this text is ignorantly mistranslated, so that it is doubtful if anyone could reconstruct matters without some additional historical help.

The relevant Dead Sea documents are 4Q320-4Q321, and these record a six year span of priestly rotations. It is perfectly obvious from the documents without having to do any astronomy calculations that the rotations are listed continuously, without annually restarting, without gaps, or without skipped weeks. But like the perpetual 7 day cycle for the week, a perpetual 24 week cycle is for each complete rotation of the divisions, and then it begins anew at no. 1 again, until it reaches no. 24, and then it begins again on the very next week with no. 1. That was the only way to ensure all the priests were treated fairly, as required (cf. Deut. 18:8).

While the documents were produced by the Qumran sect, which diagreed with the Pharisees (cf. Mat. 23:1-3) on calendar matters, the Qumran documents have shown a great deal of agreement with mainstream Judaism of the day. They kept Sabbath on the same day as other Jews, and observed laws concerning the clean and the unclean, and also observed circumcision. And in fact, on a good many points their Judaism was stricter and more ascetic than the mainstream. Their main point of disagreement, however, was when the major festivals should be observed. But on the point of perpetual rotations for the priests, they were correct, and this is proved by Deut. 18:8 and a careful examination of the beginning of the priestly rotations when Solomon's Temple was inaugurated, which proves only to agree with the truth asserted here, and with none of the annual schemes that restart the divisions in conjunction with the first week of Tishri or Nisan. And anything else proves too arbitrary to consider. And as far as we know, the Qumran sect was simply recording the rotations exaclty as they were followed in the Second Temple period by all Jews.

The perpetual rotation fact itself would be useless alone, since there would be no way of knowing where they began and ended. However, the authors of these documents have done us the service of plotting Egyptian lunar dates along with the priestly divisions, and also they have done us the service of starting the six year span just after the spring equinox.

Using this data, John P. Pratt, *Dead Sea Scrolls May Solve Mystery*, determines division no. 22 (Gamul) to the week after the spring equinox in 42 BC. But I myself have confirmed his calculations. Although, there are several solutions, historical constraints rule out the extra solutions. And the solution that remains agrees with the *Seder Olam* sychronization point, and the required synchronization point used in Luke. This gives three independent witnesses attesting to the same rotational pattern. No competing theory of continuous rotations has ever been proposed.

III. Pseudo-Enoch Calendar

So what is the Enoch calendar? It uses a year length of 364 days. The months of the year begin in the first seven day week which is entirely after the spring equinox on a Wednesday. For example, in AD 34, the year Messiah died and rose again, the first day of the Enoch Calendar would be on Wednesday, March 31, because the spring equinox was the previous week on March 22.

Months are 30 days long. At the end of every third month or quarter year there is an extra day, making that month 31 days long. This extra quarterly day is called a *Hodesh*, but clearly not meaning 'new moon' for them, but rather denoting a pseudo solstice or pseudo equinoctal day. Whenever the first day of the year might fall into the same week with the spring equinox, then an extra week is intercalated in the spring to keep the first day of the year in the week following the week with the spring equinox. The Enoch calendar does not follow the phases of the moon, which almost always disagree with it. For this reason, the new moon falls on random dates in the Pseudo-Enoch calendar.

It is only necessary, therefore, to observe that that the calendar in Scripture fixes the first day of a month on that day when the moon reappears after a conjunction. The Mishnah agrees with this along with Josephus and Philo. We also see that חֹדֶשׁ means "new moon" in Biblical Hebrew (see Appendix XVI).

A more fundamental proof is from Genesis. It states in Genesis 1:14 that the lights in heaven are for "appointed times" (לְמוֹעֲדִים). There were two lights created, a greater light (the sun), and a lesser light (the moon). And these lights were made to govern the appointed times. It says in Exodus 23:15, "The feast of unleavened bread you shall keep. Seven days you shall eat unleavened bread just as I have commanded you <u>after the appointed time of the new moon of Ha-Aviv</u>, because <u>with it</u> you had gone out from Egypt."

A disproof of the Enoch calendar comes from the deluge account. From the 17th day of the 2nd month through the 17th day of the 7th month is 150 days. But in the Enoch calendar, from one date to the other is not less than 152 days, even counting exclusively. However, using the real moon, a span of five months may contain four 30 day months and one 29 day month. This will make

149 days. We arrive at 150 days by inclusive counting, that is counting both the 17th day of the 2nd month and the 17th day of the 7th month. The reason the pseudo Enoch calendar goes over the limit is their extra day at the end of months 3 and 6.

The Enoch calendar does not keep to the Genesis 1:14 definitions, because the first day of its month is not fixed by the light in heaven for the month. The only body with a cycle close to 30 days is the moon, and the moon gives light, yet in Pseudo-Enoch this light is not used for the appointed times.

Apologists for the pseudo-Enoch calendar cite Jude 1:14 as a claim for the canoncity of pseudo-Enoch, which contains the Qumran calendar. The answer to this is to translate that the real Enoch "would have prophsied to these" (but not really) and then supply the words of Pseudo-Enoch. Hebrew is a language lacking explict forms for moods, and we see this influnece in the Evangelists. It is like English when we abbreviate, "He would have prophesied" to "He'd have prophesied." Jude puts words into the real Enoch's mouth because he knows that Enoch would agree with his apologetic of using their own sources against them.

The real problem with advocates of the Qumran calendar is their spiritual darkness. For this reason they cannot be reasoned out of their position.

IV. Falsification of Pseudo-Enoch Calendar

❶ According to 2 Chronicles 3:2, "Then he began to build with the second new moon, in the second day, in the fourth year of his reign." The second day of the second month in the Pseudo-Enoch Calendar is always a Sabbath, so how do they explain Solomon building on the Sabbath, i.e. figuratively plunging in the golden shovel at the Temple site? But in the Biblical Calendar, in the 4th year of Solomon, which was 1019 BC, the second day after the new moon was the first weekday (5/1/1019 BC), the day after the Sabbath, which is a perfect time to begin an important building project.

The 2 Chronicles 3:2 text is an explanation of 1 Kings 6:1 בְּחֹדֶשׁ זִו הוּא הַחֹדֶשׁ הַשֵּׁנִי, which should be translated, "with the new moon of Ziv. It was the second new moon." This did not mean Ziv was the second new moon of the year, as supposed, because then the text would be in contradiction to 2 Chronicles 3:2. Rather, in the expected place for the day of the month, it says "the second new moon," which is the second new moon feast day. We see this, because the exact same words are used in 1 Sam. 20:27, הַחֹדֶשׁ הַשֵּׁנִי, to mean the second new moon day feast, i.e. the second day after the new moon was sighted was also a new moon feast. So while Ziv is the second new moon of the year, the text is talking about the *second new moon feast day* of that month. Scholars, having thought the Hebrew Text was in contradiction, favored the Old Greek, which omits the words "the second" in 2 Chron. 3:2, and so the pseudo-Enoch calendar apologists predictably argued against the Hebrew, but as we see, knowing Hebrew more precisely than they do vindicates the Hebrew text!

Second Refutation of Qumran Calendar

❷ According to Yoḥanan 19:14 Messiah died on the prepration of the Passover. This preparation day is also mentioned in Mat. 27:62; Mark 15:42; Luke 23:54; Yoḥ. 19:31, and Yoḥ. 19:42. This was a day before a Sabbath that year (Mark 15:42; Yoḥ. 19:31). There are only two possibilities, (1) it was the weekly Sabbath, and accordingly the first day of unleavened bread was Friday or the weekly Sabbath, or (2) it was an annual Sabbath, and accordingly the first day of unleavened bread was earlier in the week. Upon the first possibility, the Qumran calendar is refuted for each sub view, since their unleavened bread began on Tuesday at sunset.

Now let us explore the second. Various counts of three days, and three days and three nights have been worked out proposing the first day of unleavened bread to start on Wednesday at sunset and Thursday at sunset. But the Qumran calendar has the first day of unleavened bread starting on Tuesday at sunset, and this would have to begin an annual Sabbath. Accordingly the Qumran calendar must place the crucifixion on Tuesday afternoon or claim the texts cited above are lies. So let's go with preserving the texts cited. Now there are only two possibilities for the resurrection day, and these are "first day of the week" which is Sunday, and "first day of the Sabbaths" which was the weekly Sabbath. On the first possibility, the Qumran calendar would place Messiah *five days and five nights* in the grave. On the second, it would be *four days and four nights*. And this contradicts the many passages which say Messiah would rise in three days. Therefore, the Pseudo-Enoch (aka Zadoq, aka Essene, aka Qumran, aka Jubilees) Calendar contradicts the testimony of Yĕshua (cf. Rev. 19:10).

Third Refutation of Qumran Calendar

Denying of the Testimony of Yeshua

❸ The Pseudo-Enoch calendar begins the counting of 50 days to the feast of weeks (Shavu'ot, Pentecost) on the 26th day of their first month. From this it is clear that they wait to begin their counting till the day after the weekly Sabbath which falls immediately after the last day of unleavened bread. And it logically follows that the number one day of their seven Sabbaths will be counted on the 2nd day of their 2nd month, well away from all Passion chronologies. But this in no way agrees with the resurrection accounts that place Messiah's resurrection, "On the [number] one [day] of the Sabbaths," which must be the Sabbath immediately after the first day of unleavened bread, and not the third Sabbath afterward. It would be mighty helpful if they could change their calculation of Shavu'ot so that the first of the Sabbaths could be when the Evangelists say it was. But too bad for them, their calculation is based on the Dead Sea Scrolls, and it is too late for them to change their avenue of deception.

V. Falsification of Lunar Sabbath Heresy

Rejecting of the Testimony of Yeshua

The lunar sabbath heresy teaches that the Sabbath day is determined by the moon, and not by counting continuous and unbroken seven day cycles going back to the first Sabbath commemorating the creation of the world in six days. The lunar sabbath doctrine designates days after the new moon to be sabbaths. They are days 1, 8, 15, 22, and 29 after every new moon. Their claim to be biblical rests upon conflating the 15th of the first month,

and the 15th and 22nd days of the seventh month mentioned in the Torah with their assumed lunar Sabbath doctrine, making these days equal to weekly Sabbaths. These days are the first day of unleavened bread, the first day of tabernacles, and the last great day.

The only chronology of Messiah's death and resurrection compatible with the lunar sabbath doctrine is the traditional Friday to Sunday doctrine, in which the 15th day after the first new moon is regarded as both the weekly sabbath and the feast day sabbath on the same day. So if the Friday to Sunday tradition is proved false, then also the lunar sabbath doctrine will be proved false.

All four Evangelists indicate that Messiah died on the day before a Sabbath. All four Evangelists indicate that Messiah was raised by dawn on the weekly Sabbath, and all four Evangelists count Messiah's sojourn in the grave as three days. Thus Mat. 28:1 says the resurrection was "the later of the Sabbaths," and Mark 16:2, "very early on the first of the Sabbaths," and Luke 23:54b, "Then the Sabbath was dawning," and Yoḥ. 20:1, "on the first of the Sabbaths...early, darkness still being."

Yoḥanan times matters with two Sabbaths (19:31 and 20:1). Mark does the same (Mark 16:1 and 16:2) and Luke also (Luke 23:56 and 24:1). And Matthew mentions the 'later' Sabbath which alludes to the one earlier. Obviously if the resurrection was on the Sabbath on the third day, and obviously since there was an earlier Sabbath just two days before, that was the 15th of the month, then clearly the weekly Sabbath upon which the resurrection of Messiah occurred was not the 15th day of the month. Accordingly, the lunar Sabbath doctrine is refuted by the testimony of Messiah.

Appendix XVIII: Do we need Tradition?

There are many who claim to go by Scripture only when they are teaching their doctrines. And we find various groups teaching opposing doctrines with the same claim that they are using Scripture only. Can the same Scriptures teach assertions that contradict each other? Of course not. If it does, then it cannot be Scripture at all, because a true Scripture from the Most High would be consistent with itself. And those seeking to prove things from Scripture to show that they are right and the opposers are wrong are counting on everyone to agree with them that Scripture gives one message, and one answer, because if it gives two, then what is the point of claiming to be more right than anyone else?

They need us to assume this if their proof from Scripture is to have moral validity. Now that we have got this out of the way, let us now turn to the next step. Those saying they go by Scripture are claiming divine authority for their teaching whenever they quote it to prove their doctrines. But we have the Catholic Bibles, the Greek Orthodox Bibles, and the Protestant Bibles, and the Jewish Bibles, and many other Bibles. And invariably every opinion turns on either a varying translation of a text or a varying interpretative paradigm, or what creed or tradition says the Scripture is supposed to mean even if it does not say it.

Let's take your King James Only cult as an example. Who translated the KJV? Men. Where did they get the definitions of the Hebrew and Greek words in English that they used? Dictionaries, written by men. And where did the men who wrote the dictionaries get all their definitions? Other dictionaries and or living usages of actual spoken language or word studies and linguistic research conducted by men figuring logically what words must mean so that a text will make good sense. And all of this activity is based on a language tradition outside the resulting product called Scripture. So a tradition was needed to produce the thing that is called Scripture. And by claiming that a translation is error free, the KJV only cult is also claiming that none of the elements that went into producing it were mistaken.

But we come to the replacement of the word Passover in the Greek Text with the word Easter in the KJV and we see the beginning of lies. But how do we know it is a lie? Well we have to go back and look up the Greek word in a dictionary, which were written by men, and so in saying Easter is a lie we are relying the tradition received in the dictionary that the word means Passover. So we are relying on a source outside what is called Scripture to show that it is not Scripture.

Matters get even more dicey when opponents agree upon what the text says, but they disagree on what the text means. For example Scripture speaks of *Sabbaths*. Some think this means Sunday, as in Europe they number their calendars with Sunday as the seventh day. Some think this means the 1st, 8th, 15th, 22nd, and 29th days after a new moon, and this is called the lunar Sabbath interpretation, and some think it means Saturday dawn to Sunday dawn, and the rest of us think it means sunset on Friday to dusk on Saturday. How do we know who is right? Well again, we have to resort to that dictionary produced by men called the tradition. When was the Sabbath historically kept back in days of old? We do best to consult the people that Messiah related to, the Jews of his day, the people he debated with, the Pharisees, and even the people he rebuked more, the Sadducees. Which view of the Sabbath was the prevailing view of the culture that Yeshua dealt with? Does he dispute it? Do the Evangelists seek to explain the correct timing of Sabbath when they use the term against a culture they disagree with, or do they bypass this step and take it for granted that their audiences need no special sectarian instruction?

We can be sure that anyone who uses a term and publishes a history using the term is trying to use that term so that their audience will understand what it means. We can be sure of this, because every sect that disagrees with the prevailing norm hastens to point out just exactly what they think the term means.

The difference between promoting a lying interpretation or tradition, and correcting a lying interpretation or translation that has become the status quo is this. The lying interpretation cannot show any historical norm

for its assertions in the history and language norms surrounding the writing of the original text. But in uncovering and correcting error that has become the status quo, or in refuting lying sectarian interpretations, we consult the language and interpretive norms of the times contemporary with the writing of the text, and we find our interpretation of the text is confirmed by the norms of the past.

So we do need tradition. We need the norms of the past to know what the text means, and to correct it, if it has departed from past norms. When we watch Messiah interacting with past sects, we see what he agrees with and what he corrected.

Why does Scripture appear to give incomplete information on some topics? Or information scattered here and there that just seems to be incidentally mentioned? Such information is often needed to understand just what the Most High expects of us in giving us certain commandments, or what is meant when Scripture makes certain theological points or gives informational instruction. The reason that matters may seem incomplete or more often scattered around and not seemly intended for formal instruction in *how to, or exactly what to believe* is this: The surrounding culture and tradition to the biblical statements or commandments takes the norms derived therefrom for granted, and does not need to repeat them in Scripture.

So if we can recover the norms and cultural framework in which the contemporaries of Scripture would see matters then we can sort out which interpretations are correct, and which are not. And you will see that cults and sectarians wish to cut themselves off from all norms of the past which could cross-examine them and expose their innovations as the lies they are.

Now I will point out that there are many who claim to do just this, and they are correct in identifying the methodology. And they are correct in presuming that contemporary Scripture in the past was aimed at establishing the divine norms and only correcting world norms which might be assumed, by revealing the biblical norm so that the outside norm would not make the biblical norm impossible for contemporary readers to understand. For we see that cults bring a secretive understanding to the text that is known only to them, because the text does not specifically endorse their interpretation over against what one would normally assume from other contemporary information.

As I said, there are many to claim to use the right methodology. They often speak of context, and historical interpretation, but then they fail to practice what they preach, because they often ignore finding out what the original norm was in favor of a relatively modern tradition which contradicts such analysis. That is, they claim to sit in the seat of Moses, but then they don't sit in the seat of Moses, and they do and teach otherwise. So if you want to discover the truth you have to bypass these hypocrites. Many of them come with high academic degrees. And their hypocrisy can be quite selective.

Thankfully, the Most High has provided us a means to overthrow the errors of the past cobbled together in rebellious hearts and spoon fed to the innocent who were then deceived and became corrupt like them. And it consists in this. Firstly, listening to the Holy Spirit, and then weeding out improper interpretations by a proper application of historical norms. It may take a prophet to get most started, but once started, one should not have to be a prophet to understand which interpretations and translations are correct.

Translation Concordance

†This is a partial listing only for dagger marked terms. Use Young's Analytical Concordance to locate remaining instances. One will occasionally find that an instance has a different underlying Greek word or that an existing Greek word was not translated the way stated in this Concordance. This is because in some cases the list was obtained from an existing Greek word concordance and that some terms are translated with more than one English word. Terms are in alphabetic order, but related terms are also nearby, and the underlined portion is how the term was alphabetized. The purpose of this concordance is not to provide an exahaustive scholarly study tool, but to give the student a view on the scope and extent of multi word mistranslations that have been corrected in the Good News of Messiah with theological significance. For the many singular instances of mistranslation I refer the reader to the text and footnotes.

A /*/ item means there is a footnote explaining the text.

<u>administer</u> justice
  vs. *justify*
δικαιόω
δικαιοσύνη
Acts 13:38, 39
Rom 3:20, 24, 26, 28, 30; 4:3b, 5 (2x), 6, 9, 22, 25; 5:1, 9; 8:30 (2x), 33; 9:30, 31, 32; 10:6
1 Cor 6:11
Gal 2:16 (3x); 2:21; 3:6, 8, 17, 21, 24;

5:4
Titus 3:7

†**Adŏnai**
  vs. *Lord*
KC 722x
Mat *7:21
See also Yăhweĥ.

<u>Almĭghty</u> **Sŏn**
  vs. *son of God*
YY τοῦ ΘY
Mat 4:3, 6; 8:29; 14:33; 26:33, 63;

27:40, 43, 54
Mark 1:1; 3:11; 15:39
Luke 1:35; 4:3, 9, 41; 8:28; 22:70
Yoĥ. *1:34, 49; 3:18; 5:25; 9:35; 10:36; 11:4, 27; 19:7; 20:31
Acts 8:37; 9:20
Rom 1:4
2 Cor 1:19
Gal 2:20
Eph 4:13
1 Yoĥ 3:8; 4:15; 5:5,

10, 12, 13, 20
Rev 2:18

†*alone*
  vs. *one*
¹εἰς *only*
²εἰς *alone*
³εἰς *same*
⁴εἰς *one*
⁵μόνος *alone*
⁶μόνος *only*
⁷μόνος *uniquely*
Mark 10:18²; 12:29¹, 32¹

Luke 18:19²;
Yoĥ 16:32⁵ (2x); 17:3⁵
Rom 3:30³
Rom *16:27⁶
1 Cor 8:4⁴, 6⁴
Gal 3:20¹
Eph 4:4³ (3x), 5³ (3x), 6³
1 Tim *1:17⁶; 2:5⁴ (2x); *6:15⁵, 16⁵
Jam *2:19⁴
Jude *1:4⁶, *25⁶
Rev 15:4⁷

604

†Anŏinted
vs. *Christ*
Χριστός 538x

Mat 1:1, 16, 17, 18; 2:4; 11:2, etc.

assembly
vs. *church*
ἐκκλησία, 114x

Mat 16:18; 18:17 (2x)
Acts 5:11; 7:38; 8:1, 3; 9:31; 11:22, 26; 12:1, 5; 13:1; 14:23, 27; 15:3, 4, 22, 41; 16:5; 18:22; 19:32, 39, 41; 20:17, 28
Rom 16:1, 4, 5, 16, 23
1 Cor 1:2; 4:17; 6:4; 7:17; 10:32; 11:16, 18, 22; 12:28; 14:4, 5, 12, 19, 23, 28, 33, 34, 35; 15:9; 16:1, 19 (2x)
2 Cor 1:1; 8:1, 18, 19, 23, 24; 11:8, 28; 12:13
Gal 1:2, 13, 22
Eph 1:22; 3:10, 21; 5:23, 24, 25, 27, 29, 32
Phil 3:6; 4:15
Col 1:18, 24; 4:15, 16
1Thes *1:1; 2:14
2 Thes 1:1, 4
1 Tim 3:5, 15; 5:16
Philemon 1:2
Jam 5:14
3 Yoh 1:6, 9, 10
Rev 1:4, 11, 20 (2x); 2:1, 7, 8, 11, 12, 17, 18, 23, 29; 3:1, 6, 7, 13, 14, 22; 22:16

based on
vs. *by, of*,
ἐκ, ἐξ

Rom 3:20, 30; 4:16 (3x); 5:1; 9:30, 32 (2x); 10:6
Gal 2:16 (4x); 3:7, 8, 9, 10, 11, 12, 18 (2x), 21, 24
Phi 3:9

†because
vs. *that*
ὅτι

¹*in that*
²*so that*

?ambiguous
³*seeing that*
Mat 9:28
Mar 11:23², 24²
Luke 1:45¹
Yoh 4:21¹; 5:38; 8:24³; 10:38; 11:15; 11:42³; 13:19¹; 14:10³, 11³; 16:30; 17:21; 19:35⁷
Acts 14:22; 27:25¹
Rom 6:8; 9:30⁷, 32; 10:9 (2x)
1 Cor 1:18; 13:5⁷
Gal 3:7⁷
1 Thes 4:14
1 Yoh 5:1, 5

getting begotten
vs. *born*
γεννάω

Yoh 3:6 (2x), 8; 8:41; 9:32
Acts 22:3, 28
Gal 4:23
2 Pet 2:12
1 Yoh 2:29; *3:9 (2x); 4:7; 5:1 (2x), 4, 18

on behalf of
vs. *for*
ὑπέρ

Mark 14:24
Yoh 6:51; 10:11, 15; 11:50, 51, 52; 13:37, 38; 15:13; 17:19; 18:14
Acts 8:24; 15:26; 21:26
Rom 1:5; 5:6, 7 (2x), 8; 8:27, 31, 32, 34; 9:3; 10:1; 14:15; 15:8, 30; 16:4
1 Cor 11:24; 15:29 (2x)
2 Cor 1:6, 11; 5:14, 15 (2x), 20 (2x), 21; 7:12; 8:16; 9:14; 12:5 (2x), 13
Gal 2:20; 3:13
Eph 3:13; 5:2, 25; 6:19
Phil 1:29 (2x)
Col 1:7, 24 (2x); 2:1; 4:12
1 Thes 5:10
2 Thes 1:5
1 Tim 2:1, 2, 6
Tit 2:14
Phm 1:13
1 Pet 3:18
1 Yoh 3:16 (2x)

beside
vs. *from*
παρά, 194x

¹*at the side of* ᵈᵃᵗ
²*from beside* ᵃᵇˡᵃᵗ
³*beside* ᵍᵉⁿ, ᵃᶜᶜ

⁴מִיָּד
⁵עַל־יָד
⁶לִפְנֵי
מִלִּפְנֵי

Mat 2:4⁶, 7⁶,16⁶; 4:18; 10:27¹ (3x); 21:42²; 22:25⁶;
Mark 3:21; 8:11; 12:11
Luke 1:30¹, 37¹; 6:19; 8:49; 10:7; 18:27¹ (2x)
Yoh *1:6², 14², 39¹, 40³; 4:9³, 40¹, 52³ 5:34², 41³, 44³, 44², 6:45³, 46², 7:29²; 8:26³, 38², 40², 9:16², 33²; 10:18²; 14:17¹, 23¹, 25¹, 15:15², 26² (2x), 16:27², 28²; 17:5¹ (2x), 8¹; 19:25¹
Acts 2:33³; 3:2³,⁴, 5², 4:35³; 5:2³; 7:16³, 58³; 9:2⁴, 43¹; 10:6¹,⁵, 22³, 32³,⁵; 16:13³,⁵; 17:9³,⁴; 18:3¹, 18:13³; 20:24²; 21:7¹,8¹, 16¹; 22:3³, 5³,⁴; 24:8³; 26:8¹, 10²,⁴; 28:14¹, 22³
Rom 1:25³, 26³

†besides, as well as
vs. *both, and*
τε, 215x

List under Acts 15:5

choice, choosing, chosen
vs. *election, elect*
ἐκλογή, 7x
ἐκλεκτός, 23x

Mat 20:16; 22:14; 24:22, 24, 31
Mark 13:20, 22, 27
Luke 18:7; 23:35
Acts 9:15
Rom 8:33; 9:11; 11:5, 7, 28; 16:13
Col 3:12
1 Thes 1:4

1 Tim 5:21
2 Tim 2:10
Titus 1:1
1 Pet 1:1; 2:4, 6, 9
2 Pet 1:10
2 Yoh 1:1, 13
Rev 17:14

congregation
vs. *synagogue*
συναγωγή, 56x

Mat 4:23, etc.

customary, cf. norm
νόμος vs. *law*

what is customary ³⁴ˣ
Rom *3:21; 4:13, 14, 15²ˣ; 6:14, 15; 7:2, 6; 9:31; 10:4
1 Cor 9:20⁴ˣ, 21⁵ˣ
Gal 2:19²ˣ, 21; 3:11, 17, 18, 21, 23; 4:4, 5, 21; 5:4, 18
Phil 3:9

customary ¹⁴ˣ
Rom *3:20, 28; 4:6; 9:11, 32; 11:6
Gal 2:16³ˣ; 3:2, 5, 10
Eph 2:9²
Titus 3:5²

norm ⁷ˣ
Rom 5:20; 7:21, 23 23, 25; 8:1⁴
1 Cor 15:56⁴

customary norm ⁹ˣ
Rom 7:1, 2, 3, 4, 5
Gal 3:13, 19, 24
Eph 2:15

custom ³ˣ
Rom 3:27; 7:1;
Gal 3:21

rule ¹ˣ Rom 3:27

dead to trans.
vs. *dead in*
νεκρούς τοῖς π.

Eph *2:1, *5
Col 2:13

each of these
vs. *everything*
vs. *all*
¹πάντας
²πάντα
³πᾶσιν

Rom 3:9¹; 14:1², 20²
1 Cor 12:6²; 15:28²
Eph 1:23²

Col 3:11², 11³

emissary
vs. *apostle*
ἀπόστολος

Mat 10:2
Mar 3:14; 6:30
Luke 6:13; 9:10; 11:49; 17:5; 22:14; 24:10
Yoh 13:16
Acts 1:2, 26; 2:37, 42, 43; 4:33, 35, 36, 37; 5:2, 12, 18, 29, 40; 6:6; 8:1, 14, 18; 9:27; 11:1; 14:4, 14; 15:2, 4, 6, 22, 23; 16:4
Rom 1:1; 11:13; 16:7
1 Cor 1:1; 4:9; 9:1, 2, 5; 12:28, 29; 15:7, 9
2 Cor 1:1; 8:23; 11:5, 13; 12:11, 12
Gal 1:1, 17, 19
Eph 1:1; 2:20; 3:5; 4:11
Phil *2:25
Col 1:1
1 Thes 2:6
1 Tim 1:1; 2:7
2 Tim 1:1, 11
Titus 1:1
1 Pet 1:1
2 Pet 1:1; 3:2
Jude 1:17
Rev 2:2; 18:20; 21:14

†execution timber
vs. *cross*
¹σταυρός, 27x
²σταυρόω, 46x

Mat 10:38¹; 20:19², etc.

†to hold faithful
vs. *to believe*
=*to pledge f.*
=*to promise f.*
=*to pledge loyalty*
=*to pledge allegiance*
=*to give support*
πιστεύειν 244x

Mat 8:13; 9:28; 14:31; 16:8; 18:6, 10; 21:22, 25, 32 (3x); 24:23, 26; 27:42
Mark 1:15; 5:36; 9:23 (2x), 24 (2x), 42; 11:23, 24, 31; 13:21; 15:32
Luke 1:20, 45; 8:12, 13, 50; 16:11;

20:5; 22:67; 24:25
Yoh 1:7, 12, 50;
2:11, 22, 23, 24;
3:12 (2x), 15, 16,
18 (3x), 36; 4:21,
39, 41, 42, 48,
50; 5:24, 38, 44,
46 (4x); 6:29, 30,
35, 36, 40, 47, 64
(2x), 69; 7:31, 38,
39; 8:24, 30, 31,
45, 46; 9:18, 35,
36; 10:25, 26, 37,
38 (2x), 42; 11:14,
25, 26 (2x), 27, 40,
45, 48; 12:11, 36,
37, 38, 39, 42, 44
(2x), 46; 13:19;
14:1 (2x), 10, 11
(2x), 12, 29; 16:9,
27, 30, 31; 17:8,
20, 21; 19:35;
20:8, 25, 27, 29
(2x), 31 (2x)

† **to hold unfaithful**
vs. *to disbelieve*
ἀπιστεύειν

Luke 24:11

† **faithful**
vs. *believer*
πιστός 67x
ἀληθινός

Mat 6:30; 8:26;
24:45; 25:21 (2x),
23 (2x)
Mark 5:34; 10:52;
11:22
Luke 12:28, 42; 16:10
(2x), 11, 12; 19:17
Yoh 7:28

little faithful one(s)
vs. *of little faith*
ὀλιγόπιστ(οι) 6x

Mat *6:30; 8:26;
14:31; 16:8; 17:20
Luke 12:28

† **unfaithful**
vs. *unbelieving*
ἄπιστος, 23x

Mat 17:17
Mark 9:19
Luke 9:41; 12:46
Yoh 20:27

† **faithfulness**
vs. *faith, belief*
πίστις 243x

Mat 9:2, 22; 23:23.
Luke 7:50; 8:48; 17:5,

6, 19; 18:8b, 42;
22:32
Acts 3:16 (2x); 6:5, 7;
11:24; 13:8; 14:9,
22, 27; 15:9; 16:5;
20:21; 24:24;
26:18
Rom 1:17
ἀλήθεια
Yoh 1:14, 17b

† **faithlessness**
vs. *unbelief*
ἀπιστία

Mat 13:58
Mark 6:6

good news
vs. *gospel*
εὐαγγέλιον 76x

Mat 4:23; 9:35;
24:14; 26:13
Mark 1:1, 14, 15;
8:35; 10:29;
13:10; 14:9
Acts 15:7; 20:24
Rom 1:1, 9, 16; 2:16;
10:16; 11:28;
15:16, 19; 16:25
1 Cor 4:15; 9:12, 14
(2x), 18 (2x), 23;
15:1
2 Cor 2:12; 4:3, 4;
8:18; 9:13; 10:14;
11:4, 7
Gal 1:6, 7, 11; 2:2, 5,
7, 14
Eph 1:13; 3:6; 6:15,
19
Phil 1:5, 7, 12, 16, 27
(2x); 2:22; 4:3, 15
Col 1:5, 23
1 Thes 1:5; 2:2, 4, 8,
9; 3:2
2 Thes 1:8; 2:14
1 Tim 1:11
2 Tim 1:8, 10; 2:8
Philemon 1:13
1 Pet 4:17
Rev 14:6

**being sorry, [and]
turning the heart
[from sin]**
= *repentance*
¹μετανοίας, 22x
²μετανοέω, 34x

Mat 3:2¹, 8¹, 11¹;
4:17²; 11:20², 21²;
12:41²
Mark 1:4¹,15²; 6:12²
Luke 3:3¹, 8¹; 5:32¹;
10:13²; 11:32²;

13:3², 5²; 15:7², 7¹,
10²; 16:30²; 17:3²,
4¹; 24:47¹
Acts 2:38²; 3:19²;
5:31¹; 8:22²;
11:18¹; 13:24¹;
17:30²; 19:4¹;
20:21¹; 26:20², 20¹
Rom 2:4
2 Cor 7:9¹, 10¹; 12:21²
1 Tim 2:25
2 Pet 3:9¹
Rev 2:5¹ (2x), 16¹, 21¹
(2x), 22¹; 3:3¹, 19¹;
9:20¹, 21¹; 16:9¹,
11¹

† **holy ones**
vs. *saint(s)*
ἅγιος , 235x

Mat 27:52
Acts 9:13, 32, 41;
26:10
Rom 1:7; 8:27; 12:13;
15:25, 26, 31;
16:2, 15, etc.

I AM
vs. *I am he*
ἐγώ εἰμι, 14x

Mat 14:27, 1x
Mark *6:50; 13:6;
14:62, 3x
Luke 21:8; 22:70;
*24:39, 3x
Yoh *6:20; 8:24, 28,
58; 13:19; 18:5-6,
8, 7x

† **immerse**
vs. *baptize*
βαπτίζω, 81x

Mat 3:6, 11 (2x), 13,
14, 16; 20:22 (2x),
23 (2x); 28:19
Mark 1:4, 5, 8 (2x),
9; 6:14, 24; 7:4;
10:38, 39 (2x)
Luke 3:7, 12, 16 (2x),
etc.

justice
= admin. of justice
= justification
= righteousness
= make righteous
= admin. of r.
= justicing
= juridical r.
= charity
= mercy

δικαιοσύνη, 92x

kindred
vs. *generation*
γενεά

Mat 11:16; 12:39,
41, 42, 45; 16:4;
17:17; 23:36;
*24:34
Mark 8:12 (2x), 38;
9:19; 13:30
Luke 7:31; 9:41;
11:29 (2x), 30, 31,
32, 50, 51; 16:8;
17:25; *21:32
Acts 2:40; 8:33
Phil 2:15

only kindred
vs. *only begotten*
μονογενής

Luke 7:12; 8:42; 9:38
Yoh 1:14, 18; *3:16,
18; *5:44;
1 Yoh *4:9

later
vs. *after, end
evening*
¹ὀψέ *later*
²ὀψέ *late*
³ὄψιμος *later*
⁴ὄψιος, *late*
⁵ὄψιος, *later*

Mat 8:16⁴; 14:15⁴,
23⁴; 16:2⁴; 20:8⁴;
26:20⁵; 27:57⁴;
*28:1¹
Mark 1:32⁵; 4:35⁵;
6:47⁵; 11:11⁴, 19¹;
14:17⁵; 13:35²;
15:42⁴;
Yoh 6:16⁵; 20:19⁵
Jam 5:7³

lawless
vs. *without law*
ἀνόμως 2x

Rom 2:12 (2x)

† **letter [to repay]**
vs. *letter*
¹γράμματος, 3x
²γράμμα, 3x
³γράμματι, 1x
⁴γράμμασιν, 1x

Luke 16:6²; 7²
Rom *2:27¹, 29³; 7:6¹
2 Cor 3:6¹, 6², 7⁴

† **loving-kindness,
favor**
vs. *grace*
χάρις, 157x

† **messenger**
vs. *angel*
ἄγγελος 176x

Mat 1:20, etc.

new-made
vs. *[brand] new*
καινός

Mat 9:17; 13:52;
26:29 (*28); 27:60
Mark 1:27; 2:21, 22;
14:25(*24)
Luke 5:36 (2x), 38;
22:16
Yoh 13:34; 19:41
Acts 17:19, 21
1 Cor *11:25
2 Cor *3:6; 5:17 (2x)
Gal 6:15
Eph 2:15; 4:23
2 Pet 3:13 (2x)
1 Yoh 2:7, 8
2 Yoh 1:5
Rev 2:17; 3:12 (2x);
5:9; 14:3; 21:1
(2x), 2, 5

new moon, moon
vs. *month*
¹μηνός *new moon*
²μῆνας *moons*
³μηνός *month*
⁴νουμηνία *new moon*

Luke *1:24¹, *26¹,
*36¹, 56¹; 4:25²
Yoh 4:35²
Acts *7:20²; 18:11²;
19:8²; 20:3²;
28:11²
Col *2:16⁴
Gal *4:10³
Jam 5:17²
Rev 9:5², 10², 15¹;
11:2²; 13:5²; 22:2¹

next to
or *near to,
before, to near*
πρός

Yoh 1:1, 2; 13:3
Acts 4:24; 12:5
Rom 4:2; 5:1; 10:1;
15:30
2 Cor 3:4; 13:7
Phil 4:6
1 Thes 1:8
1 Yoh 1:2; 3:21
Rev 12:5 (2x)

norm, cf. *customary*

ransom
vs. *redeem*
¹λύτρον

606

²λυτρόω
³ἀντίλυτρον
⁴ἐξαγοράζω
⁵ἀπολύτρωσις
⁶λύτρωσις

Mat *20:28¹;
Mark *10:45¹;
Luke 1:68⁶; 2:38⁶; 21:18⁵; 24:21²;
Rom 3:24⁵; 5:18 (italics); 8:23⁵;
1 Cor 1:30⁵;
Eph 1:7⁵, 14⁵; 4:30⁵; 5:16⁴
Gal 3:13⁴; 4:5⁴
Col 1:14⁵; 4:5⁴
1 Tim 2:6³
Tit 2:14²
1 Pet 1:18²;

†**rescued**
vs. *saved*
σώζω 108x
σωτήρ 24x

But left unchanged:
Luke 7:50; 8:48; 17:19; 18:42

Also, **deliver**.

sabbaths
vs. *week*
¹σαββάτων
²σαββάτου

ᴸˣˣExo 20:8¹; 35:3¹
ᴸˣˣLev 23:15¹, 38¹; 24:8¹
ᴸˣˣNum 15:32¹, 33¹; 28:9¹
ᴸˣˣDeut 5:12¹, 15¹
ᴸˣˣNeh 10:33¹ [34]
ᴸˣˣIsa 58:13¹
ᴸˣˣJer 17:21¹, 22¹, 24¹, 27¹
ᴸˣˣEze 22:26¹; 46:1¹,4¹, 12¹
Mat *28:1¹ (2x)
Mark *16:2¹
Luke 4:16¹; *18:12²; *24:1¹
Yoh *20:1¹, *19¹
Acts 13:14¹; 16:13¹; *20:7¹
1 Cor *16:2¹
Col 2:16¹

same heart
or *same passion*
ὁμοθυμαδόν

Acts 1:14; 2:46; 4:24; 5:12; 7:57; 8:6; 12:20; 15:25; 18:12; 19:29
Rom 15:6

take into account
vs. *imputed*
λογίζομαι 41x
¹take into account
²consider
³think

Luke 22:37²
Yoh 11:50¹
Acts 19:27²
Rom 2:3¹, 26¹; 3:28¹; 4:3¹, 4¹, 5¹, 6¹, 8¹, 9¹, 10¹, 11¹, 22¹, 23¹, 24¹; 6:11²; 8:18¹, 36²; 9:8¹; 14:14¹
1 Cor 4:1¹; 13:5¹, 11³
2 Cor 3:5²; 5:19¹; 10:2², 2², 7², 11²; 11:5²; 12:6²
Gal 3:6¹
Phil 3:13²; 4:8³
2 Tim 4:16²
Jas 2:23¹
1 Pet 5:12²

†**unto that place**
vs. *in that p.*
ἐκεῖ

Mat *8:12; 13:42, 50; 22:13; 24:51
Luke 13:28

†**getting victory**
vs. *overcoming*
νικάω, 28x

Rev 2:11, 17, etc

will have 143x
vs. *past tense*
¹future aorist
²gnomic aorist
³gnomic perfect
⁴future perfect

Mat 4:16¹ (2x); 5:31 16:19⁴ (2x); 18:15¹, 18 (2x)⁴
Mark 4:39⁴; 9:12¹ (3x), 13¹; 11:24²; 13:20¹ (4x); 15:36¹
Luke 1:20¹, 68¹ (2x), 69¹; 2:11¹, 12⁴; 13:12⁴; 19:40⁴; 21:19¹
Yoh 1:12² (2x), 13², *18²; 5:26², 27²; 6:37¹; 11:41²; 13:31¹ (2x), 32¹; 15:6¹, 8¹, 15¹; 16:11¹; 17:2³, 10³, 22³, 22⁴, 23² (2x), 24³ (2x), 25² (3x), 26² (2x) 20:23⁴ (2x), 29¹
Acts 7:43¹; 15:17⁴; 28:26¹
Rom 4:17⁴; 5:19²; 6:3²,

4², 6², 7², 8²; 8:29² (2x), 30² (5x), 30¹; 9:23²; 11:7², 7¹, 8²; 14:23¹
1 Cor 2:9²; 9:17³; 15:27¹ (2x), 27⁴
2 Cor 5:17²
Gal 3:19¹; 27²
Eph 1:18³, 20³, 22a¹; 2:4², 5², 6¹ (2x), 13², 14², 4:8¹ (3x), 9¹ (2x), 11², 24²
Col 1:13¹,², 2:1⁴, 12¹, 13¹; 3:1¹, 3¹, 3⁴
2 Thes 1:10¹
Jam 5:2³ (2x), 3³
1 Pet 1:8⁴, 24¹
1 Yoh 4:17³; 5:4²
Jude 1:14¹
Rev 5:4, 10²; 10:7¹; 11:2¹, 17¹; 12:4¹, 7¹, 11¹ (2x); 18:2¹ (3x), 3³, 3² (2x), 5¹; 24¹; 19:8³; 20:15¹; 21:4¹, 23¹;

would have, 15x
ᴸˣˣGen 26:10
ᴸˣˣNum 22:33
ᴸˣˣPsa 73:15; 124:3, 4
Mat 11:21, 23; 24:43 (2x); 25:27
Luke 10:13; 19:23, 42
Yoh 4:10; 5:46; 8:19; 9:41
1 Cor 5:10
Gal 4:15
*Jude 1:14

† **Yȧhweh**
vs. *Lord*
$\overline{KC}$ 722x

See also Adōnai.

† **Yĕshua**
vs. *Jesus*
$\overline{IC}$ 923x

Mat *1:1

End Notes

Luke 21:32 ξ The text is based on Jer. 33:23-26. See also Mark 13:30; Mat. 24:34. "Going past." See Mat. 5:17-19 notes. ▷ This verse is reassurance that Yisra'el will not pass away even though a calamity ten times greater than the fall of Yerushalayim in 587 B.C. was going to take place. After reading many commentaries, and seeing they were confused, clueless, or only had a half answer, I had to ask Adōnai for the answer. Afterward I found my way to Lange's Commentary, where I picked up some promising leads. ▷ Between the deportation of Yehudah in 597 BC and the final destruction of the First Temple in 587 BC, this prophecy came to Yirmeyahu: "²³THEN WAS THE WORD OF YȦHWEH TO YIRMEYAHU, SAYING, ²⁴'HAVE YOU NOT SEEN WHAT THIS PEOPLE HAVE MADE TO BE SAID, SAYING, 'THE TWO FAMILIES (*kindreds*, הַמִּשְׁפָּחוֹת) WHICH YȦHWEH HAD CHOSEN, AMONG THEM—THEN HE WILL REJECT THEM.' AND MY PEOPLE THEY WILL DESPISE FROM BEING AGAIN A NATION BEFORE THEIR FACES.' ²⁵THUS HAS SAID YȦHWEH, 'IF MY COVENANT BY DAY AND NIGHT, PRESCRIBED STATUTES OF THE HEAVENS AND EARTH, I HAVE NOT ESTABLISHED, ²⁶ALSO THE SEED OF YA'AQOV AND DAVID MY SERVANT I WILL REJECT, FROM TAKING FROM ITS SEED, THOSE RULING OVER THE SEED OF AVRAHAM, YITSḤAQ, AND YA'AQOV, BECAUSE I WILL RETURN THEIR CAPTIVITY, AND I WILL HAVE MADE TO BE MERCY UPON THEM'" (Jer. 33:23-26). ▷ Yĕshua must have been thinking in terms of these very verses in view of the coming destruction. Mark 13:30 runs parallel to Jer. 33:24, and Mark 13:31 runs parallel to Jer. 33:25. The matter is repeated in Mat. 24:34 and Luke 21:32. His oath as to the preservation of the seed of Avraham as a nation in his sight is as sure as his word governing the celestial clock-work of the heavens. So he says in Mark 13:31, "Heaven and earth may pass away, but my words will not pass away." The reason that the commentators have not completely connected the dots is that they think Yȧhweh finished

with the historic nation of Yisra'el in AD 70 and AD 135, and therefore, they have completely missed out on the reassurance of this text. ▷ I should point out that the verses quoted above (Jer. 33:23-26) where omitted from the LXX (Septuagint) along with Jer. 33:14-22 because the corrupted Church had rejected the divine law. The omission is relevant because the text is material to the interpretation the "generation" passage in Matthew, Mark, and Luke. ▷ We obtain a huge clue to the meaning of γενεά (family clan vs. generation) in Jer. 8:3, "DEATH WILL HAVE BEEN CHOSEN ABOVE LIFE BY ALL THE REMNANT THAT IS REMAINING FROM THIS EVIL KINDRED IN ALL THE PLACES THEY ARE LEFT, WHERE I HAVE MADE THEM BANISHED, UTTERS YĂHWEH OF HOSTS." Now here the words τῆς γενεᾶς ἐκείνης in the LXX stand parallel to הַמִּשְׁפָּחָה הַזֹּאת, and it is evident that the LXX translator has represented הַמִּשְׁפָּחָה, "FAMILY CLAN" with γενεᾶς in the Greek text. ▷ For the rest here I simply cite Lange's Commentary on Mt. 24:34 where he cites Alford: "...it may be well to shew that γενεά has in Hellenistic Greek the meaning of a race or family of people. See Jer. 8:3 in LXX.; compare Matthew 23:36 with Matthew 24:35, ἐφονεύσατε ... but this generation did not slay Zacharias—so that the whole people are addressed: see also Matthew 12:45, in which the meaning absolutely requires this sense (see note there): see also Luke 17:25; Matt. 17:17; Luke 16:8, where γενεά is predicated both of the υἱοὶ τουα αἰῶνος τούτου and the υἱοὶ τοῦ φετός Acts 2:40; Phil. 2:15. In all these places, γενεά=γένος or nearly so; having it is true a more pregnant meaning, implying that the character of one generation stamps itself upon the race, as here in this verse also.... The continued use of παρέρχομαι in Matthew 24:34, 35, should have saved the commentators from the blunder of imagining that the then living generation was meant, seeing that the prophecy is by the next verse carried on to the end of all things; and that, as matter of fact, the Apostles and ancient Christians did continue to expect the Lord's coming, after that generation had passed away." ▷ The cause of the misunderstanding or mistranslation of Mat. 24:34, Mark 13:30, and Luke 21:32 is the deletion of Yisra'el in the theologies of the interpreters. But the deleters also deleted the passage from the Greek Septuagint, namely Jer. 33:14-26, by which the texts may be easily understood. When does Jer. 33:14-26 disappear from view? Enough of this passage appears in the Hebrew fragments 4QJer^c (200 BC - AD 100) to conclude that the passage was present in the texts at the time of the Dead Sea Scrolls (33:16-20 is attested, but the fragment cuts off after vs 20.) The other DSS fragments could have come from scrolls containing the passage. The passage, however, is missing from the LXX. There is no convincing evidence that this was because there were two Hebrew originals, a longer one, and a shorter one. Despite what Immanuel Tov says, I believe Shemaryahu Talmon is correct. And I suppose that Jer. 33:14-26 disappeared from the text when it was redacted by Christian scribes after AD 135, or perhaps a little before by Jewish Gnostics from Alexandria who rejected the Temple and Levitical Priesthood. After the political repression of Hadrian, contrary LXX texts were not to be found. For almost no amount of reinterpretation can deprive this text of its force for the future continuance of the line of David and the Levitical priests, or the nation of Yisra'el. The text was quietly restored later in history after the anti-Levitical tradition was solidly in place. ▷ This quiet admission of the scholars is one witness for the text. The other witness is that the deleted text explains everything we need to know about Mĕssiah's comments concerning his kindred.

Luke 24:21 Many texts add "today", but this is clearly redundant. The reading follows NA-27: ἀλλά γε καὶ σὺν πᾶσιν τούτοις τρίτην ταύτην ἡμέραν ἄγει ἀφ' οὗ ταῦτα ἐγένετο. ▷ Codex Bezae reads 'a third day passes by' (τριτην ημεραν) omitting 'this.' Tischendorf's *Novum Testamentum* notes that the word 'this' (ταύτην) is omitted in, "D al⁵ a b c e f ff²·ᵛⁱᵈ l vg Aug^{cons} et^{loh}", an impressive number of old Latin mss in addition to D. This omission is an attempt to get the text to mean, "a third day is passing by," though it is still ambiguous, "a third day passes by" (historical present). I became suspicious of D's edits at Mark 16:2 when it became evident that the D scribe was not simply copying. One by one, D's edits have been abandoned as better solutions have appeared to me. ▷ The text literally goes "a third, this day, *time* passes by." But they wish to make it read, "this third day passes" making that very day the third day. This is wrong, τριτην is a substantive adjective to be understood as "a third one," i.e. "a third [day]." It is in the accusative and must be a verbal object and not a subject. Time passed a third day when that day arrived, i.e. the daylight part of the Sabbath. The kernal sentence is "A third day it passes by." The words "*this day*" are appositive: "A third day, this day, it passes by." ▷ It (*time*) passed the third day at dawn on the Şabbath reckoning from Wednesday sunrise. The present tense (ἄγει) is clearly a historical present, i.e. just passed. For the men would have no cause to be concerned if the third day were not terminated, and the objection could surely be made that they should wait to the end of the third day before expressing such despair. The present indicates that the third day has "just passed." ▷ The remark is not only against the Friday-Sunday tradition, but against Wednesday to Sunday also, or Tuesday to Sabbath (q.v. Qumran Calendar). The resurrection could not have been late on the Şabbath or just after sunset, because the women would have to go to the tomb on Sunday instead of the "first of the Şabbaths" as stated. And the walk to Emmaus would also have to take place on Sunday instead of the Şabbath. Counting from Wednesday, Sunday is the 5th day. The counting is always inclusive, 'today, tomorrow, the third day' (cf. Luke 13:32; Gen. 40:13, 18, 19; Hos. 6:1-2). So in that case, it would not be that the third day had just passed. In all the Messianic types of death and resurrection the counting is inclusive. ▷ The verb ἄγει is a 'historical present.' It transports

us back to the moment that the third day passes at daybreak for dramatic effect (cf. Wallace Exegetical Syntax, pg. 526). The third day passed at daybreak because the three days are reckoned according to days for sacrifices (see Lev. 6:9-10; 7:15). **24:28** ψ This was literally true since he was going to return to the Fåther.

Yoh. 11:50 ψ ὑπὲρ. Cf. vs. 51. See 18:14. ▷ The observation in vs. 48 was quite correct. If Messiah had continued to win disciples without meeting up with the internal transgression and corruption of Yisra'el's leadership, the Romans would come and take away their place and nation due to the mounting internal conflict. The Almighty Son knew there was a better way to secure his kingdom than to just take over right away. Giving himself over to the Romans for crucifixion would ransom the nation, and not only Yehudah, but scattered Yisra'el as well. As it turned out, judgment by the Romans was delayed from AD 34 to AD 70. This was Qayafa's estimation of the ransom. But the real enemy was Satan and the powers under him, the sins of the people and the world. And that is what exacted the ransom cost on Messiah in the flesh. ▷ It was Satan who was in control of the kingdoms of the world and he had power over the Romans also. The first deal the devil wanted to make with Messiah was to give him the kingdoms of the world in exchange for worshiping him (cf. Mat. 4:8-9; Luke 4:5-7). The deal was that he would give up the kingdoms of the world voluntarily in exchange for Messiah's submission. But Yĕshua had a counter offer. He would volunteer to fall into Satan's hands, agreeing not to call up twelve legions of messengers and take his kingdom away by force and set up the kingdom of the Most High immediately, and allow them to slay him, if Satan would just leave his people Yisra'el alone to have the opportunity to decide whom they would serve, the Most High or sin and Satan. Being the liar and cheat he was, Satan 'agreed,' (see No. 3 below) knowing in his heart that he would not keep to the terms, and that he would simply deceive Yisra'el as the rest of the nations, and then he would destroy Yisra'el first in his rage against the Most High. ▷ Therefore Messiah was ransoming Yisra'el while Yisra'el was still in the grasp of Rome and the nations abroad from the power of Satan to destroy them in their exile, while Yisra'el was still yet in its sin in exile. He was ransoming for them the opportunity to be persuaded to repent and pledge their faithfulness to him, and this is what the last 2000 years is all about, the spread of the good news to all nations to persuade all who may listen before the day of Yăhweh. Satan and the gods of the nations are opposed to this invasion of the truth upon their territory, but they had agreed to take Messiah's life and let Yisra'el alone, and the Most High has consequently compelled them to yield for his emissaries to persuade the nations to pledge faithfulness to Messiah. The Most High is forcing the powers to abide by the terms they agreed to. ▷ When the time runs out, and the captives have made their choices, he will appear to set up his kingdom, and he will demand their release from the nations. ▷ The ransom explained this way makes every bit of sense, but it is common that the ransom is explained in ways that do not make sense, because Church fathers earlier than Augustine corrupted it, and these explanations are used as straw men to reject the ransom truth by its enemies who run from the straw men straight to Anselm. These objections are now disposed of in favor of the original truth: ▷ **1.** For example, the devil was said to have the right to hold man, but this is not true. He held man by force of deception, and the power of sin and condemnation. ▷ **2.** Others say the deity of Messiah was concealed from Satan, and so that Satan was deceived into thinking he could keep Yĕshua's soul in the power of death, and so readily agreed to the deal. But Satan knew exactly who Messiah was. Even the demons knew. Satan simply thought he would be weak in the flesh. That is why he tempted him to use divine power to avoid hunger. Also, in the end the devil will know his time is short. What does motivate the devil is a sense of personal vengeance upon the Creator and his creation. Therefore he bargains for the opportunity to deprive innocent blood of life as long as he can. If Satan is proud of one thing, it is his ability to deceive and kill people created by the Most High. Satan wants to take as many into destruction with him as he can. He is ultimately corrupt, and totally depraved in that sense, a murderer from the beginning. His emotional fix is to take innocent life forever. If he was deceived, it was not by God, but by his own nature. So he bargains for more time to keep doing what he does. This involves its own blindness, and is quite predictable. It is only in his own hidden wisdom that the Most High holds back using force to end it all, opting to let persuasion have a chance longer. This is a trade off, because the devil is also given longer, but what is best is in the hidden wisdom of the Most High. What the Most High gets out of this is the right to justly compel the devil to leave sinners for a season so that they can be persuaded to repent and pledge faithfulness to Messiah. The Most High gets more time to show mercy, which is his nature. But it comes with a cost. That is the ransom. ▷ **3.** One huge objection is the notion that innocent blood was being offered to a despot, but we have to remember that Satan was already using man's sin to exact the cost of destruction in creation. He was already taking life. But the Most High used his advantage to determine that it would be his life for the others. Satan is really representing the power of sin, so the nature of the agreement is really in the divine knowledge that sin is going to take the cost no matter what, and that the Most High will represent the cost taken as a ransom. So there is no contractual agreement or covenant with death. Rather the ransom is the divine view of the matter in the light of sin's destructive cost. What Satan has taken from Gŏd, is thus identified as a ransom, and release will be imposed on him. ▷ **4.** Finally, there is the claim that there is no direct effect on man in the ransom. But this is wrong. The selfless love of the Most High counts in persuading men, and his spilled blood represents the gift of divine life that cleanses us from our sin. The removal of our sin from us rescues us, because those who bear sin unto the

day of judgment will be destroyed with their sin. The purging cost is the ransom cost.

Acts 15:1 χ→not = *may not have been;* ● **15:1** η→be = *are not able to have been;* ● **15:1** λ The key texts are Gen. 17:9-14: "⁹And the Almĭghty said to Aᵥraham, 'And thou my covenant thou shall keep, thou and thine seed after thee through their generations. ¹⁰This is my covenant which ye shall keep, between me and between ye, and between thine seed after you: being circumcised every male *boy* belonging to ye, ¹¹so that ye will have been circumcised *in* the flesh of your_p foreskins. And it will have been as a sign of the covenant between me and between ye: ¹²a son of eight days will be circumcised belonging to ye, every male *boy* throughout your_p generations, one born of the house, or bought by money from any stranger, who is not from thine seed. ¹³Being circumcised, shall be circumcised one born of thine house or bought by thine money. And it will have been my covenant in your_p flesh for an everlasting covenant. ¹⁴And an uncircumcised male *boy*, which one will not circumcise the flesh of his foreskin, then that soul will have gotten itself cut off from its people. He has broken my covenant." ▷ The pronoun *one* is 3ms in Hebrew, i.e. 'which he (one = the father) will not circumcise.' The Niphal text לֹא יִמּוֹל should be pointed Qal לֹא יָמוּל. And נִכְרְתָה is reflexive-passive: *he will have gotten himself cut off* suggesting responsibility. In vs. 14 "my covenant" ambiguously refers to the covenant *sign* or the covenant itself, but this is not explicitly stated because the offense is serious and possibly a result of rebellion against the covenant itself. The offender is the father who fails to circumcise his son, and the penalty is applied to him, not the child (cf. Josh. 5:4-9; Exodus 4:24 where Mosheh is threatened with death for his neglect, and not his son.) The offense may be neglect or rebellion and the threat or execution of the penalty is according to the circumstances. If the case is neglect, then the excision does not threaten salvation. But the father may be divinely penalized even in a case of neglect. ▷ Exodus 12:44, "⁴⁴And every servant of a man bought with money, when you may have circumcised him, then he may eat in it." Exodus 12:48, "And when sojourns with you a sojourner (יָגוּר אִתְּךָ גֵּר), and he has made ready a passover *lamb* to Yăhweн, must be circumcised every male of his, and then he may come near to do it, and he will have been as the native of the land, but any uncircumcised man may not eat in it." ▷ A sojourner is required to keep the Sabbath (cf. Exodus 20:10), and abstain from leaven during the Passover (Exo. 12:19). The implication is that the sojourner should obey all laws from which he is not temporarily exempt, including to afflict his soul on Yom Kippur. ▷ There is one category of persons in Aᵥraham's house that was exempt from a compelled circumcision: clearly someone not bought with money who is not his physical seed (cf. Rom. 2:26) nor born in his house, but who are nevertheless adopted (Isa. 52:3; Gal. 3:29; cf. Gen. 12:16) into his house by pledging faithfulness to the Almĭghty of Aᵥraham. The commandment is only compelled upon all born in his house, to every eight day son, whether bought or not. So the uncircumcised man redeemed by faithfulness without money is required to circumcise his sons born after he comes into Aᵥraham's house, even if he himself has not yet chosen to be circumcised. Exodus 12:48 makes it clear that the adult sojourner should choose to be circumcised without it being forced upon him. But he still has to circumcise his sons on the eighth day because of the imperative and the excision penalty for neglect of sons. ▷ The Holy Spirit shows this to be the case in how he speaks in Gen. 17:23, "Then Aᵥraham takes Yishma‛el, his son, and all born of his house, and all bought with his money, every male one, among the men of the house of Aᵥraham. Then he circumcised the flesh of their foreskins on that very day, just as the Almĭghty had spoken with him." Clearly, 'every male one among the men of the house' (כָּל־זָכָר בְּאַנְשֵׁי בַיִת, πᾶν ἄρσεν τῶν ἀνδρῶν τῶν ἐν τῷ οἴκῳ) makes no sense unless some of the men may be exempt from compulsion because they are neither born or bought with money into his house. Some, indeed, were acquired without money (cf. Gen. 12:16). ▷ Mĕssiah the king buys his bondservants without money from among the nations (Isa. 52:3; 1 Cor. 6:20; 7:23; 2 Pet. 2:1). Therefore, all so acquired belong to the house of Yisra‛el, and are adopted as seed. ▷ If the sojourner wants to eat the Passover offering, then like Aᵥraham his whole house is required to be circumcised with him (natural offspring still in his house). ▷ In special circumstances circumcision was radically enforced when it had been neglected (Josh. 5:2-9), by special command of the Almĭghty. ▷ The covenant of circumcision is an eternal covenant sign of the eternal covenant. This is the same as having an agreement for a sign of an agreement: זֹאת בְּרִיתִי... וְהָיָה לְאוֹת בְּרִית. Gen. 17:10-11, "This is my covenant...and it will have been for a sign of the covenant." See. Gen. 17:13. Therefore uncircumcision does not break the covenant. It breaks the covenant sign. Uncircumcision of the heart (not holding faithful to the Almĭghty) on the other hand breaks the covenant. See End Note No. 2, page 400.

Acts 15:5 β τε = *besides, as well as;* ▷ β This Greek enclitic particle (τε) is constantly used by Luke, and its meaning is obvious as may be seen in Acts **1:**1, 8, 13, 15; **2:**9, 10, 11, 33, 37, 40, 43, 46; **4:**13, 14, 27, 33; **5:**14, 19, 24, 35, 42; **6:**7, 12, 13; **7:**26; **8:**3, 12, 13, 25, 28, 31, 38; **9:**2, 3, 15, 18, 24, 29; **10:**22, 28, 33, 39; **11:**21, 26; **12:**6, 12, 17; **13:**1, 4, 11, 46, 52; **14:**1, 5, 11, 12, 21, 31; **15:**3, 4, 5, 6, 9, 32, 39; **16:**13, 23, 34; **17:**4, 10, 14, 19, 26; **18:**4, 5, 26; **19:**2, 3, 6, 10, 11, 12, 17, 18, 27, 29; **20:**3, 7, 11, 21, 35; **21:**12, 18, 20, 25, 28, 30, 31, 37; **22:**4, 7, 8, 23; **23:**5, 10, 24, 28; **24:**3, 5, 10, 15, 23, 27; **25:**2, 16, 23, 24; **26:**3, 4, 10, 11, 14, 16, 20, 22, 23, 30; **27:**1, 3, 5, 8, 17, 20, 21, 29, 43; **28:**2, 23. It is also used in Luke 2:16; 12:45; 14:26; 15:2; 21:11; 22:66; 23:12; 24:20; Paul uses it in Romans 1:12, 14, 16, 20, 26, 27; 2:9, 10, 19; 3:9; 7:7; 10:12; 14:8; 16:26; 1 Cor. 1:24, 30; 4:21; 2 Cor. 10:8; 12:12; Eph. 3:19; Phil. 1:7; Also Matthew 3x: 22:10; 27:48; 28:12. John 2:15; 4:42; 6:18; Jam.3:7;

Jud. 1:6; Rev. 19:18. Also Alex. Let. 1:3; 2:4, 11; 4:12; 5:1, 7, 14; 6:2, 4, 5, 19; 8:3; 9:1, 2, 9, 19; 10:33; 11:32; 12:2. ▷ Firstly, they were already instructed to obey the commandments. See Matthew 28:18-20; 5:17-20. Secondly, the Assembly was placing no urgency on the specific of circumcision. So "besides to keep the law of Mosheh" is a concessionary statement, as if to say, "We know you give this directive in general, but you gotta make sure they are circumcised for salvation." Possibly, those who wanted an emphasis on circumcision at the council were not the same ones who wanted it for salvation. See vs. 1.

Acts 15:9 ψ τῇ πίστει, or "with the pledge of f." ▷ The purification of the heart is a joint project between the Spirit and the repentance of the sinner. Vs. 8 speaks of the Almighty knowing the heart, and this without a doubt refers to a willing and penitent heart. See 1 Yoh. 3:3-6. The intake of the Spirit is the intake of divine life, symbolized by the application of Messiah's blood to cleanse sin (cf. 1 Yoh. 1:6-10; Yoh. 6). A ransom is taken by the malignancy of sin in blood and flesh to cleanse it. The symbols instruct us in the spiritual cost of our cleansing, an instruction of our wellness. ▷ We should look to Lev. 16:30 for the definition of KIPPURIM, "Because on that day, he will declare to be wiping (yeKaPPayR) for ye for making to be cleansed (leTaHayR) ye from all your sins, at the face of Yăhweh, ye shall be clean." The effect of the KIPPURIM (intensive plural) is to declare a cleansing of the sinner. The context defines the meaning of KIPPURIM in terms of the Hebrew word for cleansing. KIPPURIM means 'a declaring to be wiped' or making so, and TaHayR means 'to declare to be cleansed.' The wiping and the cleansing are synonymous. We also see the frequent connection of the two words in the law of the leper (cf. Lev. 14). Sin may be described as a malignancy, a leprousy that clings to the sinner. ▷ The Yom Kippurim text is an eschatological promise for the day of transformation and resurrection (1 Cor. 15:52). Until then the cleansing is continuous (1 Yoh. 1:9; Yoh. 6), because we have not received the final purification yet. But we have been cleansed from a condemned conscience before the Most High through the life of Messiah, the life of the Spirit, under the symbol of his blood, which contains the breath of life. ▷ The object of KIPPURIM is the sin to be cleansed so that divine wrath will not come upon the sinner at a later date because of the presence of sin. The object of KIPPURIM is never the Almighty or his wrath. The Most High is not being placated or bought with a gift of blood. Nor is he taking a payment for sin or penalty. But life is given to cleanse the sin, and this is what biblical sacrifice for sin teaches. The removal of sin costs life. The reason for this is the malignancy of sin. Lawlessness exacts the price, the ransom. ▷ The reader will note that the word 'atonement' has been avoided here. Likewise I try to avoid the word 'expiation.' This is because 'atonement' has been redefined by Satan's counter narrative to mean placating the deity with innocent blood by giving the deity a substitute to vent his wrath upon. This is not what the Scripture teaches, but it is what modern Christianity in the last 500 years or so has mostly taught, going back to Anselm. This narrative flipping defition of condemning the innocent in place of the guilty contradicts divine justice (cf. Exo. 23:7; Ezek. 18:20). This view is one of the highest blasphemy's against the name of the Most High (cf. Exo. 34), and it is high heresy to teach it, yet many well meaning Christians ignorantly believe it, and ignorantly teach it, and they do not realize how opposed this view is to divine forgiveness. I am mourning over this doctrine because it has affected my life so much.

Gal 2:1 τ AD 49 (cf. 1:18) 3rd visit; 14 yrs. counting from his conversion; omitting mention of 2nd visit to Jer (Acts 11:27ff). ▷ We do not in fact know for sure how many times Paul visited Jerusalem after his conversion, because every visit may not be mentioned. In fact, he is not trying to give us a comprehensive chronology because he omitted the Acts 11 charity mission. From the writings we can determine that he was in Jerusalem at the stoning of Stephen (AD 34), and when he was commissioned to go to Damascus, probably living in the city this whole time. Then he was converted at Damascus (AD 36), and then went to Arabia. After three years, counting from his conversion, and so it would be the fourth year (AD 39), he went to Jerusalem to visit Peter (first recorded visit). In Acts is mentioned the charity mission (AD 43), visit no. 2. In this letter he mentions the Titus visit (fall AD 48), no 3, and he omits the Jerusalem Council, because it had not happened yet, which resolved matters publically, mostly likely in the summer of AD 49, visit no. 4. In AD 52 there is visit no. 5, and in AD 57 visit no. 6. Though Paul did not mean to mention every visit, it seems he meant to mention every significant interaction with Peter, and the recorded visits may well be all of them. We know for certain that all the visits mentioned in Galatians preceded the Jerusalem Council because of the lateness the passion year in AD 34. Those arguing that matters came later face two insurmountable objections. The first is there is not enough time to sandwitch 17 years before Paul's sojourn at Corinth and AD 34. So the 3 and 14 years must not be added consecutively. They must count from the same point, Paul's conversion. Secondly, compelled circumcision is still an issue in this book, and if the Council had already happened, Paul would have certainly mentioned it rather then write in Galatians 2:6, an argument from silence indicating he is sticking with his position in any case.

Gal 2:4 φ→brothers: Note Paul's qualifying statement. Paul was not opposed to circumcision. He was opposed the false circumcision as a merit (זְכוּת) of justification. Many churches preach the same heresy with baptism. Paul was not opposed to a true circumcision, but only to a circumcision to make a person a Jew, which was equated with saved status in the eyes of its teachers. ▷ Since we do not have details on Paul's opposition in Galatia, we have to reconstruct things from a broader knowledge of Rabbinic Judaism selecting common elements from it that are incompatible with the good news. This excercise is useful in that it plots a reasonable trajectory for Paul's arguments without leading to the anti-Torah

conclusions of Christianity. In fact, we will find that Christianity is in its own way guilty of importing the same false philosophies as Rabbinic Judaism into the good news. So a Rabbinic teacher would say that the non Jews in Galatia needed to be circumcised because circumcision was necessary to impute the righteousness of the fathers to the convert to protect them from their own demerits. Circumcision was said to be the instrument by which a favored status was attained with God, so as to deliver the soul from the gates of hades. So it is no wonder that Paul opposed it. The transfer of merit is anti-forgiveness, anti-repentance, and anti-faithfulness. It bases the converts duty on a single act, and makes divine favor something that is paid for by someone else's merit. There is a parallel doctrine within Christianity concerning baptism, which is said to be the instrument by which justification is imputed to the convert. Justification teaches that the convert has become fully righteous in God's eyes. So if one is not baptised, then one has not received the grace of justification, and hence one is on the road to Hell. Apart from Catholics and Lutherans, many Christians discard the connection between baptism and justification and replace it with faith or believe only. But in this form the doctrine still teachers a transfer of merit from Christ so as to make the demerits of the converts judicially invisible to the Most High, the Judge of all. The effect of this doctrine is to render an acquittal before God, i.e. just as if the convert had never sinned. But if one is acquitted, then who needs forgiveness? Or for that matter who needs a life of faithful repentance after an acquittal? But the Torah says the guilty will not be acquitted (Exo. 23:7). The guilty will not be cleared of their offenses (Exo. 34:7). So this leaves only divine pardon, another word for forgiveness, as the only positive outcome for the guilty. A pardon does not relieve the finding of guilt. It only relieves the sentence for the crime, and opens the way for cleansing.

Gal 2:14 χ = Judean, particularly Jewish in the sense of the tribe of Judah and the territory of Judah. What Paul is really arguing for is that it is acceptable to be of the sons of Yisra'el without being Jewish in that sense. ▷ Judean Jews did not eat with non-Jews. Others Jews did. The closer in time Judea came to the AD 66-70 revolt the more the stricter parties took over. According to Scripture someone who was not circumcised was supposed to choose of his own free will to be circumcised, at least without civil coercion. The Judean party did not succeed in completely quashing non-conformity, because even Josephus successfully resisted calls for forced circumcision (cf. *Life*, 1:113). See Acts 15. Though circumcision was strongly encouraged, except in certain circumstances, a non Jew who lacked it could not be considered faithless if he upheld the Torah (cf. Rom. 2:26). ▷ Paul's charged rhetoric was plain in meaning to contemporary parties, but the logic must be explained to us at cultural temporal distance. If K·eipha took the important step to disagree with the Pharisees' Judaism over the issue of eating with the uncircumcised, and thus incur their judgement of living like a goy, then why is he walking back on this, which tends to also go along with their religio-political agenda on the issue of forcing circumcisions? Shouldn't he be aware of their greater error? The answer is that he most assuredly was aware of their error, and that of Rabbinical Judaism in general concerning the imputation of merit and the placing of circumcision in this scheme. But the reason he walked back table fellowship was because he feared the Rabbinical faction that had accepted Yeshua as Messiah, but who did not accept him as the only kindred Almighty. He feared the trouble and schism they would cause if he confronted them directly. Yoḥannan 8:30-59 reveals a conversation Yeshua had with this faction when he wrote his book well after these events, where he did confront them directly, and they tried to kill him. This faction was guilty of theological deicide, if not with the stoning, then with their doctrine. The point is that the Rabbinical deity denying faction existed for a time under the tent of the Nazarenes, before they departed, and became the Ebionite faction. These tended to uncritical acceptance of Rabbinic doctrines. Eventually K·eipha would realize that his going along with the circumcision faction could not be accomplished without confusing matters, even if he hoped they would come to a real knowledge of Messiah. K·eipha was afraid to officially toss them out of the Assembly, and as a result Satan had a channel to challenge the Assembly with Rabbinical doctrines. ▷ We may suppose that Peter was keeping peace among the factions by dividing the missions of Paul and himself, and also by the early weakness of the Ebionite faction, which kept its deity denying and forced circumcision doctrines quiet, but eventually they gained courage and brought forced circumcision into the open enough to place pressure on Paul's mission in late AD 48. Paul sought affirmation and received it then, and the circumcision faction held its tongue because of Peter's status. But shortly after, while Peter was visiting Antioch, men from Ya'aqov came affirming the opposite. Thus Peter would have perceived a major loss of support for his Cornelius revelation, and rather than trusting what he knew and realizing that his status as first among Messiah's disciples was a major force in keeping the circumcision faction in check, he instead feared them, and accomodated them in Antioch. But he must have shortly reflected and regretted his action after finding Ya'aqov was still on his side, and this comes out at the Council.

Gal 2:16 γ Also, *pledge* or *promise*. Cf. πίστις *Jos. Ant.* Subjective genitive. See Wallace, *Syntax*. See Hay, David M. *JBL*, vol. 108, no. 3, 1989, pp. 461-476. ▷ In the first and simplest sense justice is getting administered for us through the faithfulness of Messiah. He is completely fair in justice, forgiving those whom he should and not forgiving those whom he should not. From the divine point of view, Messiah is the only kindred Almighty (Yoḥ. 1:18), and thus possesses the whole nature of Yähweʜ. So he is faithful to doing righteousness in judgement. This faithfulness of Messiah is the same faithfulness stated in Exodus 34:6, "Then Yähweʜ passed by his face. Then

he called out, Yăhweh, Yăhweh, the Mighty one merciful and benevolent, slow with anger, and great with loving-kindness and faithfulness." Divine faithfulness is expresed by the word אֱמֶת in Hebrew, which is a derivative of the verb אָמַן, *to be faithful*. It is not faithfulness to another here that is expressed, but his own *fidelity*, *soundness*, and *trueness* in judgement. He is completely fair and just. He is true in this sense. As we say a wheel is true when it spins without a wobble, so the Almighty is true in justice. The same trueness or faithfulness belongs to Messiah, and it is with the same faithfulness we are getting administered justice. Thus, if we are to be forgiven, we must confess and repent from our sins and pledge faithfulness to him, because the Most High shows mercy and loving-kindness to those loving him and keeping his commandments (Exodus 20:6). He will not acquit the guilty (Exodus 34:7), and he will let its consequences go to the third and fourth generation while he keeps watch, but if anyone repents, he will pardon them and cleanse them from all unrighteousness. ▷ Now is these respects, administering justice by compensating for sin with the customary works is not within the true justice of the Most High. It is not the faithfulness of Messiah to judge this way. The Most High does not want compensation. He wants repentance. ▷ We can also take this faithfulness from the human side of Messiah, that is the divine faithfulness expressed in the human form and limitation. The Almighty decides that he will pardon us if Messiah pledges (cf. Isa. 53:10: אִם־תָּשִׂים אָשָׁם נַפְשׁוֹ) to ransom us from sin and death. Messiah therefore takes up this command (Yoh. 10:18) from the Father, to lay down his life, and this is called **His faithfulness** on our behalf. ▷ Messiah's sacrifice of himself is the climax of the declaration of divine cost, divine suffering endured, to bring repentance and forgiveness to us. Whenever the Most High forgives sin and iniquity, he wants the repentant one, who returns to faithfulness, to realize the cost of sin. For this reason a sacrifice is required in making the official declaration of purging the condemnation. The sacrifice symbolizes both the divine cost and the human cost of sin, and indeed also the cost of divine patience until the sinner repents and seeks him while the offer of forgiveness is still possible. The loss of an animal is allowed to make the point. Forgiving justice, a pardon, is costly to the Most High. Knowing that sinful man would attack his only kindred Son in the flesh, the Most High, with the Son's agreement, suffered the limitations of the flesh to bring us the truth as a man, and in the course of matters was predictably attacked. The Most High was therefore pleased to appoint his crushing as the offense sacrifice, to show the divine cost in the flesh, that is to show the cost exacted by our sins in the Most High's efforts to bring us to repentance and forgiveness. ▷ Sacrifice is a ransom cost, that is either an animal dying that symbolizes the actual ransom cost, or Messiah dying that both symbolizes the whole cost to the Most High, and indeed is in itself part of the actual ransom cost, the worst part of it. The ransom cost is that which sin and death does to pillage his kingdom, his creation, while hoping that men will repent and come to forgiveness during the season of forgiveness. The Most High will not allow this to go on too long, until too many are beyond forgiveness. Indeed, even before death takes them, their minds become so corrupt that he sends a delusion among them that they should believe the lie.

Gal 2:16 δ→faithfulness: *Promised loyalty* or *pledged loyalty* (with sincere repentance and contrition) and agreement to uphold the divine covenant, obeying his commandments. Paul now lays down the condition of our pardon. We must promise loyalty to Messiah, then "justice may be administered from the faithfulness of Messiah." Strong 4100: πιστεύω < πίστις, "to have faith"; *faith*< *fei*, *Middle English*, fidelity, loyalty; to make a pledge of loyalty (to). See also: https://www.etymonline.com/word/faith. See *JBL* above. ▷ The justice administered is forgiving justice, the decision of the judge to cancel retribution upon seeing that the sinner is repentant. The foundation of the gospel of merit, zechut, or imputed merit, is the assumption that the Most High always demands retribution for sin if he is not in some way paid off. This kind of gospel amounts to using works to placate the Almighty, and indeed someone else's works in both Judaism and Christianity if the convert does not have enough works to satisfy strict justice. Penal justice is the norm, the legal norm, but forgiveness cancels this norm. Forgiving justice is also legal, though, because it falls within the righteousness of the Most High to forgive without requiring satsifaction for a punitive debt. If a punitive debt is upheld by heaven then a righteous person cannot pay it for another, because the Torah says, "From a false matter you will keep far. And the innocent and righteous do not kill, because I will not declare the wicked righteous" (Exodus 23:7; cf Ex. 34:6-7). Torah does not permit the acquittal of the guilty by slaying the righteous. Animal offerings for sin, therefore, were not the innocent taking an unremitted retribution upon the sinner in their stead. Rather the animal offerings declare the wiping of the debt, the purging of the debt, in the same action as giving a demonstration of the cost of sin, the ransom taken by sin. This is the forgiving justice, first wiping the debt, and then indicating the cost of the sin. The blood of the sacrifice declares the wiping of the debt. The blood also symbolizes the divine life necessary to cleanse the heart.

Gal 3:13 α The Almighty sold Yisra'el to its enemies (cf. Deut. 28:68; 32:30; Judges 2:14; 4:2) because they sinned. Evil powers are the enemy slaveholders (Psa. 82; cf. Yoh. 8:34). The curse is the Law's pronouncement that the sinner (traitor) is delivered to the enemy to carry out God's justice. Should the sinner repent, the Most High will forgive and lift the curse. He will cancel the sentence, purge the debt, or wipe the punitive penalty, indicating this via the ransom sacrifice. But the enemy will still try to kill him declaring it their right to execute strict justice. But his justice decided to forgive us, and the ransoming sacrifice rescues us from death's attempt to destroy us. Thus Messiah ransoms us from the enemy, in that the enemy is forced to submit to God's forgiving justice

making their desire to execute strict justice of no effect. For it was Gŏd's justice that turned the sinner over to them in the first place, and therefore Gŏd has the right of ransom from them when he forgives us. The enemy tried to execute its "justice" upon Mĕssiah, but he escaped from condemnation by rising from the dead. ▷ It is very important to realize the ransom is paid by the Almĭghty and not to him; Mĕssiah's death is a net cost to all of Gŏd. ▷ Messiah's ransom is the sacrifice. When the powers reached out and struck the only kindred Son, the Father was pleased to declare it the ransom for many. To declare to sin and death the debt of the faithful one wiped away, purged, and demand a release, making his execution of strict justice via the powers unnecessary, so the powers have to release the person from enslavement to sin. Therefore, Messiah's blood releases the repentant from bondage.

Gal 3:13 *p*→curse. He was only regarded as accursed, there being many hanged who were innocent. Deut. 21:22-23 only says the that one guilty is accursed "of Gŏd" "if there is in a man the sin of a death sentence." Therefore, Paul leaves out the words "of Gŏd." Isaiah 53:4 clarifies, "We had thought him being stricken, smitten by the Almĭghty," but it was wicked men who did this, and a misunderstanding people who regarded it as deserved. ▷ Deut 21:23 says in Hebrew, "because an accursed one of the Almighty is the one being hanged" (כִּי־קִלְלַת אֱלֹהִים תָּלוּי). This is because a sin with the judgment of death was in the man, and he had not repented, but was wicked and rebellious to the end. So to confer the extra degree of divine displeasure the judges ordered the body of the rebel to be hanged, but not past sunset lest the land be made unclean by too long a display. The text does not say EVERYONE who is hanged is accursed (πᾶς κρεμάμενος). This notion comes from the Septuagint (LXX) mistranslation, and the translators were not careful to consider when modifying the text that an innocent person might be hanged and get regarded as a curse. Paul finds that it suits him to leave the word EVERYONE, but he deletes the words "of the Almighty" so that we know that Messiah was not judicially cursed in heaven's sight, but only in the sight of the wicked. Everyone hanged is regarded as accursed by someone, surley those who did the hanging. So Paul finds it useful to leave that part of the mistranslation uncorrected, because it is still true in a general sense. ▷ But the Most High made use of the injustice he knew Messiah would suffer and appointed it an offense offering to show the cost he was suffering, a cost collected by sin and death, as he made every effort to bring us to repentance and forgiveness. So this cost taken by sin and death on our behalf from Messiah is the divine ransom cost exacted by sin and death upon the only kindred Almighty in the flesh. Because it says, "Yăhwe╄ will have been pleased to make (or declare) his crushing the disease when he appoints his soul an offense offering" (Isa. 53:10, וַיהוָה חָפֵץ דַּכְּאוֹ הֶחֱלִי אִם־תָּשִׂים אָשָׁם נַפְשׁוֹ). Messiah's crushing is the culmination of evil's attack on the divine seed (Gen. 3:15). This is the climax of the ransom cost exacted upon the one who had been coming into the world to deliver us. The disease (חֳלִי) is sin and death. Cf. Hos. 13:14, "From the hand of She'ol I will ransom them; from death I shall redeem them. I will be your plagues death. I will be your destruction She'ol. Compassion will be hidden from my eyes." Messiah's suffering was the ransom cost, but rising from the dead he has vengeance in mind for sin and death. Also it says, "But he was wounded from our transgressions" (Isa. 53:5). Thus, it was sin that took the ransom. The only kindred Son became cursed by sin and death to ransom us from sin and death. ▷ The judicial penalty for sin is *declared wiped out* (כִּפֶּר) when the innocent victim demonstrates by example the unrecoverable ransom cost of sin which is getting forgiven. See Albert Barnes notes (cf. 2 Cor. 5:21γ). The ransom blood declares the wiping of the debt, because the Most High only ransoms from sin and death those who repent and pledge loyalty to him, whom he has forgiven. ▷ The penalty transfer teachers (aka penal substitution Calvinists) claim that strict justice, the curse, was legally transferred to Messiah, and suffered by him to satisfy an unalterable divine demand for strict justice, so that Messiah received divine wrath. But this is illegal according to Torah, "Keep far from a false matter, and the innocent and righteous slay not, because I will not declare the wicked one righteous." (Exodus 23:7). So it is illegal to slay an innocent person to justify a wicked person. It is an abomination to the Most High. Yet this is what the deep mystery of iniquity has brought into the Church. What is legal is to pardon and forgive a guilty person. Such is not acquittal or clearing of wrongdoing. The Most High did not say he would never leave the guilty unpunished. He said he would not clear or acquit the guilty of wrongdoing (Exodus 34:7). Penalty transfer teachers are guilty of making a mockery of divine justice, just as it is a mockery for the son to die for the sin of the father. This is not to be narrowly interpreted. It is a mockery for anyone to be put to death for another sinner, the guiltless for the guilty. ▷ Messiah's sacrifice is therefore a ransom demanded by sin and death to secure our release from sin and death, not a judicial payment demanded by his Father. Penalty payment is not forgiveness. ▷ He 'ransomed us from the curse, the customary norm.' The slaveholders, the foreign powers, wish to execute strict justice (the curse) after the prisoners repent and are forgiven because Satan is forever an Accuser, but Messiah ransoms us from this fate by allowing them to vent their illegal justice on him and we will go free into everlasting life on the last day, because he himself escaped from the grave.

Gal 3:19 ʳ The earliest texts are corrupted here to an extent that indicates more than some innocent mistake: 𝔓[46] (ca. 200) Τί οὖν ὁ νόμος τῶν πραξεων ἄχρις οὗ ἔλθῃ τὸ σπέρμα ; D* it[ar] it[d] it[f] it[o] vg (Ambrose) Pelagius Jerome Augustine[9/21] Speculum: παραδόσεων χάριν ἐτέθη; ℵ A B C D²: παραβάσεων χάριν προσετέθη. I can only make a good guess to

restore the text. The original was probably: Τί οὖν ὁ νόμος τῶν παραβάσεων. Χάρις προσετέθη....which was then changed to the traditional text, differing by but one letter. It should be noted that the word ΧΑΡΙC is completely lacking in 𝔓⁴⁶, and two other words also are modified. ▷ The level of corruption of the text indicates that its first corruptors understood the sense and did not like it, but did not hit on the most economical way to change it at first. But I will hazard to explain the trajectory here. ▷ A favorite Gnostic theme was to say the Torah was given to increase transgression (but see *Rom. 5:20*; *Rom 7:8*), and in favor of this at the final step they changed the text to "Why then the law? In favor of transgressions it was added until...", but this radical perversion was not hit upon without first going through the previous experimental changes first. And truly ΧΑΡΙC when used as a preposition, ΧΑΡΙΝ, means **to favor the advantage of something**, and so to show this I have likewise rendered all eight texts where it is used thus (Luke 7:47; Eph. 3:1, 14; 1 Tim. 5:14; Titus 1:5, 11; 1 Yoh. 3:12; Jude 1:16). Translators are in the habit of rendering the word "by reason of" so as to convey no sense of *favoring* in the usage, because they need to conceal the radical nature of the Gnostic rejection of the Torah, because then it becomes too obvious that the modern text properly rendered conveys a malignant hatred for the Torah. ▷ This again refers to the customary norm of the curse, the section in the law which formally states curses for severe transgressions. The question is why the curses should not be applied to transgressors since they are in the law. Paul is going to answer that there is a 'grace' period at present until the judgment is held, during which repentance is possible. And the faithful are no longer technically under the sentence of law, because the faithful are forgiven, and Mĕssiah has paid the ransom for us who did transgress to those unto whom he sold Yisra'el, who were allowed to execute the curse before the time on the unfaithful. Therefore the curse is lifted off the faithful by forgiveness. However, it still will apply to the unrepentant. Paul has already explained how Mĕssiah ransomed transgressors from the curses through his faithfulness for those who in repentance affirm faithfulness to him (3:13-14). He **bears with** the transgressions of the repentant (cf. Rom. 3:25; Lev. 16:10, 21-22; See Appendix IX). The same idea is expanded in 3:23-25 and 4:4-5.

Gal 3:20 μ→One = unity, yahad, יחד; This is aimed at the Dead Sea Scroll Sect called "The Yaḥad," or like teachers who exported their doctrine into Galatia after adopting the Mĕssiah. The term Yaḥad means Unity, One, or "the thing which is One," (cf. "catholic" universal). I take "not the mediator of One" to mean that the Yaḥad overseer, claiming the mantle of Mosh'eh, is not our mediator. The Yaḥad mediator determined who was anathema (cursed) under the law for transgressions (Deut. 27:15-26; 28:16-19) and who was not. And I take the words "But the Almĭghty is [the] One," to mean that Mĕssiah is the true Mediator of the covenant, who is our forgiver and who meets and mediates with death to ransom us (cf. Mat. 20:28). The Yaḥad overseer claimed the mantle of Mosh'eh. The Yaḥad ruled with harsh authority placing curses on anyone who disagreed with their legal rulings (cf. Gal. 1:8-9). The fear of being anathematized by the priestly hierarchy of the Yaḥad kept its members in line. ▷ Exegesis of the following passage probably has much to do with the Yaḥad sect: "THEN HE SAID, "YĂH-WEH FROM SINAI HAD COME. AND HE HAD APPEARED FROM SE'IR TO THEM. HE HAD SHINED FORTH FROM MOUNT PARAN. AND HE HAD BROUGHT TEN THOUSANDS OF HOLY ONES. FROM HIS RIGHT HAND WAS A FIERY LAW FOR THEM. YES, HE LOVES THE PEOPLE. ALL HIS HOLY ONES ARE IN YOUR HAND. AND THEY HAD BEEN LED TO YOUR FEET. ONE LIFTS UP AT YOUR WORDS. MOSH'EH COMMANDED TO US A LAW, A POSSESSION OF THE ASSEMBLY OF YA'AQOV. WHEN HE WAS WITH YESHURUN [THE UPRIGHT] HE HAD BECOME KING (מֶלֶךְ). IN HIS MAKING BE GATHERED THE HEADS OF THE PEOPLE (רָאשֵׁי עָם) HE HAD MADE ONE [YAHAD יָחַד] THE TRIBES OF YISRA'EL" (Deut. 33:2-5). Mĕssiah is the one who makes the tribes Yaḥad, and not the Bishops of the sect with the anathemas, for whom this text was proof of their right to authoritarian succession (cf. Papal succession taken from Mat. 16:18). See also Isa 49:6.

Gal 3:21 This passage illustrates the possible variations in the meaning of "nomos." First Paul means the whole law and all of its instruction. None of it contradicts the promises of the good news. ▷ In the second instance he says if there was a customary practice (a norm, or tradition). He means any theoretical law or rule if kept. But keeping any law does not restore life. It only preserves the life one already has. Supposing that keeping a law could restore life, then a strict justice would demand a complete reversal of sin damages. And this is the problem. No such compensation is possible. It is customary for people to assume that loss of life due to sin, damages, etc, can be repaired and compensated for by keeping the commandments. Such compensations are called *penance*, *zekut*, or some other *treasury of merit*. In the last instance "nomos" means what is the actual customary practice for justice. This is Judaism's doctrine of merit for demerit. ▷ There is no commandment for making a compensatory justice in the law that can restore life. There are no laws for a murderer to keep to restore life to the victim and to erase the victim's suffering. ▷ The translation "justice" instead of righteousness is critical (unless one is able to understand BDAG def. No. 2: **juridical correctness**, but the normal English reader cannot), and to realize that Paul is speaking of *compensatory* justice, i.e. the kind that undoes the damages, "restores life." Another way to translate the noun δικαιοσύνη would be **administration of justice**: BDAG No. 1, "the practice of judicial responsibility with focus on fairness." This would make it coordinate

with the verb δικαιόω "*to administer justice*," again BDAG No. 1, "to do justice." The noun and the verb derive from the same adjective (δίκαιος, just, right), hence verb: be just (as a judge) and noun: the quality of being just (as a judge).

3:22 α→faithfulness: or, *holding faithful*. Under sin means the same as under law, the same as under the penalty or sentence of law. But, Messiah's death ransoms us from death, the hands of lawlessness (cf. Hos. 13:14), and the powers that the unrepentant have been sold to. The ransom is an instructive in the cost of our healing, our wellness, and is not not a satisfaction of compensation or wrath. The cost of sin is forgiven outright. Lawlessness is represented as causing the death of the offering, because the offering bears the natural consequence of sin confessed onto it (not a wrathful one). The blood released by the the innocent (perfect) victim represents the divine life lost purging and cleansing sin. The offering represents the Most High who is the innocent victim of sin. The priest's knife represents the sinner's burden taking the life of the victim. Abraham's knife represented lawlessness, which is why the Most High altered his order, and supplied a ram to make the point. Later he would let lawlessness itself make the point. To the question, why does an innocent sacrifice (representing the Most High) have to die? The answer is that our sins have required it, and not the wrath of God!

4:4 ϕ He did not come judicially under the legal norm in the sight of the Făther as justly deserved, but he was put under the legal norm by the forces of evil condemning him. Měssiah's death was regarded by the authorities as a due penalty under strict justice (the norm). But he was innocent, so this reason is incorrect. In Isaiah 53:4 it states, "And we had thought him being stricken, being made smitten of the Almighty." The clear implication is that he wasn't struck by the Most High, but by injustice motivated by evil. This is in the same sense that Měssiah was cursed. He was cursed by men and regarded as accursed by men, but he was not accursed 'of Gŏd.' See Gal. **3:13** ρ. Moreover, Isa. 53:10 is supposed by many to say that the Most High put his wrath on Měssiah, but this is due to mistranslation. It says, "And Yăhweн has been pleased to make to be crushing of him the malignancy, when his soul makes a guilt offering." The malignancy is the bruise of sin prophesied in Gen. 3:15. The Most High declared the attack on Měssiah to be the fulfilment of Gen. 3:15. The mistranslation is in the infinitive construct, 'to make to be crushing of him' into pleased 'to crush him.' The correct translation is a reference to his crushing. The incorrect translation has the Most High crushing him.

Gal 4:8-11 Christians teachers regularly use this text to condemn the observance of Sabbath and feast days. But this is not what Paul is talking about at all. Back in 3:20 (μ) Paul identified the false teachers as the Qumran calendar cult, which is enjoying a modern revival under various names such as the Zadok calendar. See page 602. The same evil spirits lie in back of this now that were then. ▷ The Qumran calendar consisted of a 364 day *year*. The year was divided into four quarters, which were their **seasons**. Each quarter had 3 **months**, the first month being 30 days, the second month being 30 days, and the third being 31 days. The quarter had 91 days. And four quarters made 91 x 4 = 364 days. They say the 31st days are **days** for marking the equinoxes and solstices. So we have all the elements of Paul's rebuke here, days, months, seasons, and years. And none of them refer to the Biblical Calendar. ▷ Paul's fear was that the level of truth denial and ignorance of Torah needed to keep this calendar cult going was indicative that those getting persuaded in this error were indeed falling from away from the truth and back into influence by spirits of paganism, albeit pious spirits making a pretense of being orthodox teachers of the 'real' Torah. ▷ The calendar was evidence that they were equally committed to other Qumran teachings that perverted justice, 4QMMT, some extraordinary works of the law (מקצת מעשי התורה) which by which a person is supposed to be reckoned righteous (See 'Paul "Works of the Law" and MMT', by Martin Abegg, BIBLICAL ARCHAEOLOGY REVIEW 20:6, November/December 1994.) But now this doctrine has spread to the Church as a whole wherever they teach justification by the imputation of legal righteousness. See 1 Cor 16:2; Col. 2:16. ▷ Paul appears to observe the distinction between 'new moon' and 'month' in Greek unlike the normal Jewish usage. See Col. 2:16. See page 599. And this is plainly obvious because the Qumran Calendar months did not begin with new moons. ▷ Paul speaks of the 'poor elements' they were enslaved to. See **4:3** χ. This includes the logical fallacies of mathemtatical perfection they ascribe to their calendar.

Gal **4:24** η ὅρος. Boundary limit. By switching the breathing marks (*orous* to *horous*), we can read the text "at the boundary limit of Sinai" (ἀπὸ PG ὅρους NGNS Σινᾶ NGNS). See Exodus 19:12. וְהִגְבַּלְתָּ "AND YOU WILL HAVE SET BOUNDS." Yet on the morrow, the seventy are allowed to go up the mountain and they see the Almĭghty. *Off of the boundary* is associated with exclusion and condemnation, and going up the mountain with release from condemnation. The Greek word "boundary" is not matched with the Hebrew verb in Exo. 19:12, but it is matched with it in Deut. 19:14 and Zech. 9:2, LXX, and very extensively as a noun. The Hebrew noun from the verb is usually matched with the Greek word spelled ὅρος by the LXX, but not used in this spelling by Paul. He uses it as commonly spelled in Greek ὅρος, inflected gen. ὅρους. ▷ The text may be logically interpreted agreeable to Torah without supposing that ὅρος means 'bound,' or ἀπὸ 'far off.' We are on firm ground with διαθῆκαι = wills, dispositions as this is the default meaning of the word in Greek. It follows as a logical consequence if διαθῆκαι means covenants, i.e. 'old covenant' vs. 'new covenant,' then the interpretation must be an attack on the 'covenant of old.' Therefore, διαθῆκαι does not mean this. One covenant, 'the covenant of old' produces two outcomes, two wills leading to two inheritances, one for life (by being renewed) and one for death. Both results come from Mt. Sinai. Paul strategically mentions only one explicit outcome from Mt. Sinai,

leaving the other to be assumed. When he speaks of the Jerusalem above, he means to implicitly connect the reader to the other outcome, the top of Mt. Sinai. So imagine the two outcomes of the covenant, the one for death in line with the present Jerusalem, drawing a line north from the base of the mountain, and the other outcome in line with the Jerusalem above, drawing a vertical line from the base to the top of the mountain, a renewed Jerusalem, the covenant renewed. This sense is implicit. We may accuse Paul of leaving the interpretation agreeable to Torah only implicit, saying it is incompletely stated. This allows anti-Torah interpreters to exploit it. Explicitly stating only a negative half of the truth does not logically exclude the positive half from being similarly connected. Making the negative half the only outcome depends on argument from silence, i.e. interpreting silence to mean total exclusion of life from Sinai. The allegory is a species of parable, which is liable to be misunderstood by those without ears to hear, perhaps by its design.

Why does Paul place emphasis on Arabia? Firstly, he is merely stating a fact. Secondly, he is alluding to his opposition by the place of their origin, which is Arabia, the land of Damascus. And this is also probably why he remarks on his three year sojourn in Arabia as part of his resume. The Essenes were a secretive sect that was forced out of the land because their heresies were not accepted, so they made their exile a point of piety, tying in with Ezekiel 20.

Col 2:14 χ: χειρόγραφον = hand+writing. But not 'handwriting' in the modern English sense, because all writing in ancient times was by hand. Rather this word had a more specific sense, and this was a piece of writing that could be placed in the hand or written by one's <u>own</u> hand, וְכָתַב לָהּ, usually some kind of declatory note (cf. Tyndale Bulletin 68.2 (1917) 223-239). The writing put in the hand of Yisra'el by the Most High was the: סֵפֶר כְּרִיתֻת וְנָתַן בְּיָדָהּ, the divorce document that had been put into her hand. See Deut. 24:1. This is referred to in Jer. 3:8, and the causes of it in Isa. 50:1.

The χειρόγραφον is the divorce document for transgressions. This is figuratively nailed to the execution timber with Messiah (cf. Eph. 2:14-16 notes). The divorce decree is figuratively executed alongside Messiah, meaning it gets wiped out or extinguished. At the same time Messiah is reckoned as the ransom for Yisra'el from the power of the grave. The hands of death receive the ransom, which they try to condemn, but Messiah escapes from it rising on the third day. Cf. Hos. 13:14; Rev. 5:9; 14:4; Mat. 20:28; Mark 10:45. The picture is forgiveness and then ransom from an illegal fate. Messiah is not taking our place for the first death, because we still suffer it. Messiah is not taking anyone's place in the second death, because he did not suffer it. After forgiveness there is no penalty to be paid. To show that the excision penalty (כְּרִיתֻת) is canceled, the writing in the hand is wiped out—"executed" by nailing it to the execution timber. The condemnation death is seeking now becomes unlawful. Messiah is given as a ransom to show death's hand must release us from its condemnation. The ransoming sacrifice declares our divorcement was wiped out. Further, the hand of death was unable to condemn Messiah proving the excision, the cutting off, had been put to death. Messiah, however, rose again, and was not successfully condemned. See Rev. 5:9. ▷ The text does not say the bill of divorce was nailed to the tree to pay the penalty of spiritual adultery by a substitute, but to wipe them out (ἐξαλείψας). This is the effect of כִּפֻּרִים (kippurim) as in the guilt offering (Lev. 5:17-19). The burden of sin that the sinner is carrying to judgment is declared to be wiped out and expunged. It is not paid for. The price paid in life goes toward removing the malignancy of sin from the sinner. The blood price symbolizes the greater price of divine forbearance in suffering sins while waiting for men to repent. So the price is a ransom lawlessly exacted by sin, and not a judicial penalty prescribed by the Almighty. When the king forgives debts, no second party pays the king to cover his loss (cf. Mat. 18:23-35).

Col 2:16 α The connection between vs. 14-15 and vs. 16-22 relating to the Colossian critics was probably some kind of system or philosophy of merit in the meld of Judaism and Gnosticism. Only history knows exactly what, but two more well known examples will suffice to show some possibilities. The judging could be motivated by or related to Rabbinic Judaism's ancient doctrine of merit (זְכוּת). Judaism then taught that deeds performed above and beyond the minimal requirements of the Torah were credits which could be used to offset demerits (sin). In the light of the Father's forgiveness of sin, and Messiah's suffering the example of the fate that was forgiven us, by ransoming us from a judicially illegal destruction the Adversary still seeks, the Father made plain that he does not require a credit system to forgive our demerits (sins). The faithful did not need to earn any credits by performing man-made duties outside the Torah, by fasting on feasts, new moons, or Sabbaths, because Messiah's death explains the Father's forgiveness. His death is the climax of the divine cost expended to ransom us from lawlessness, and to cleanse us from sin by his life. ▷ The Church's system of penance is like the zekuth system. ▷ Judaism also derives a transfer of merit from the Patriarchs (זְכוּת אָבוֹת), and likewise Protestant Christianity teaches the same concept under the guise of the legal imputation of Christ's righteousness to the account of the believer. ▷ It was considered a merit to deny oneself certain privileges that were lawful in order to earn a merit that could be used to offset or cancel out a demerit.

2:16 χ τις or 'a certain one,' 'someone.' Therefore, because they, his readers should understand the good news laid out in Col. 2:13-14, that their debt and sentence had been wiped out through Messiah, they should accordingly understand that they should not let those who did not understand their getting rescued impose on them a system of merit incompatible with the truth. ▷ It was those who did not understand who were doing the judging, and in

this regard the text could be translated 'a certain one' or 'someone' that they had reported, and that Paul was referring to. But it may be that Paul more generalized his injunction to 'any,' because in truth he regarded them as mature enough in Messiah to make their own judgments, because they did understand the good news, and had sufficient grasp of Torah to know where the lines should be drawn. And he is with this in mind simply reminding them of the power they have in Messiah to reject false doctrine.

Col 2:16 β→drinking: Scribes changed the Greek text from "eating and in drinking," to "eating or in drinking," (cf. γ) and translators further changed it to "food or in drink." Further it was neglected that the Greek conjunction (δ) is pragmatically subordinating in its first use, "whether, either," and not coordinating "or," with a previous element (See also J. Payne-Smith, Syriac pg. 4: ܐܘ, ‹either—or, if or no›. See also Jastrow א. Also, they failed to take note of the literal sense "in part of" (δ-ε-μ) which suggests sharing or partaking and obscured it with words like "regarding," (Syriac: portion: ܚܦܕܝ). The first change was made in the text to deceive *the many* concerning the holy days, to make the text say no one should judge them for neglecting them. But the text only says no one should judge you for enjoying a feast on the holy days. (Fasting may be viewed as gaining the necessary merit against an indulgence). The reason they had to change the text is obvious. Translated rightly it is a powerful testimony that the Assembly was indeed keeping the holy days. ▷ The sequence, "either ... or ... or" (δ-η-η) introduces a subordinate clause, which is to say, it only explains when the judging was occurring. (The translational paradigm is found in BDAG 3rd edition. See "ἤ...ἤ...ἤ".) This means that *the many* cannot use this text to say they should not be judged for Sabbath breaking. For linguistic purists, concordance is achieved with the word "whether:" Let no one judge you in eating and in drinking, whether in part of a feast, whether new moon, whether Sabbaths. See also Gal. 4:10; Cor. 16:2. Rev. 1:10.

Col 2:17 φ A shadow is an outline made by an object and light. (A reflection is simply a more detailed image made by an object and light.) A primitive speaker will say, "Look, my shadow in the mirror!" The holy days are the reflection of him because these seasons teach Mĕssiah from his birth to his death and resurrection, and our future benefits in his life. ▷ I have retired the word "shadow" because of its constant polemical use in the anti-Law narrative where it has gained that connotation in the ears of the Church. The reflection maker is Mĕssiah. The appointed times are a reflection of things to come. ▷ BDAG quotes an ancient Greek author, "the water served as a mirror suggesting that the grove was twofold, one real and the other a reflection (σκιᾶς)." See also LSJ, "2. *reflection, image.*" ● **2:17** ρ Messiah's reflection (or shadow) is his law that proceeds before his comings and remains after his goings, and reminds us of his presence. The literal text here is ungrammatical in English: "which things is a reflection of about to be coming things." The NIV and several other minor versions illegitimately translate "are a shadow of things that <u>were</u> to come," casting the whole sense in the prophetic past, obviously to avoid any sense of current or future relevance of the appointed times. ● **2:17** ψ The original word σῶμα indicates a body that makes the reflection. The word σκιά means both shadow and reflection (cf. LSJ). The Greek words σκιά and σῶμα are used in Greek to refer to reflection and the thing making the reflection. See both words in BDAG, 3rd ed.

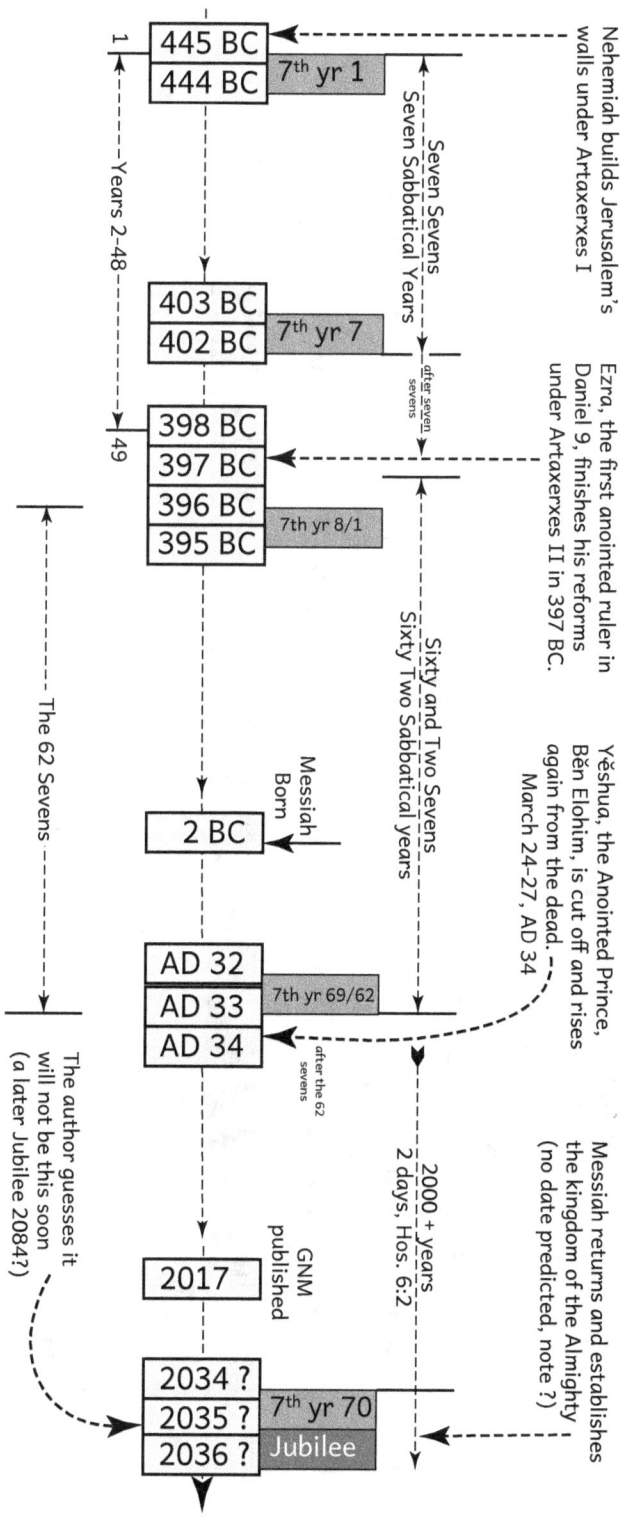

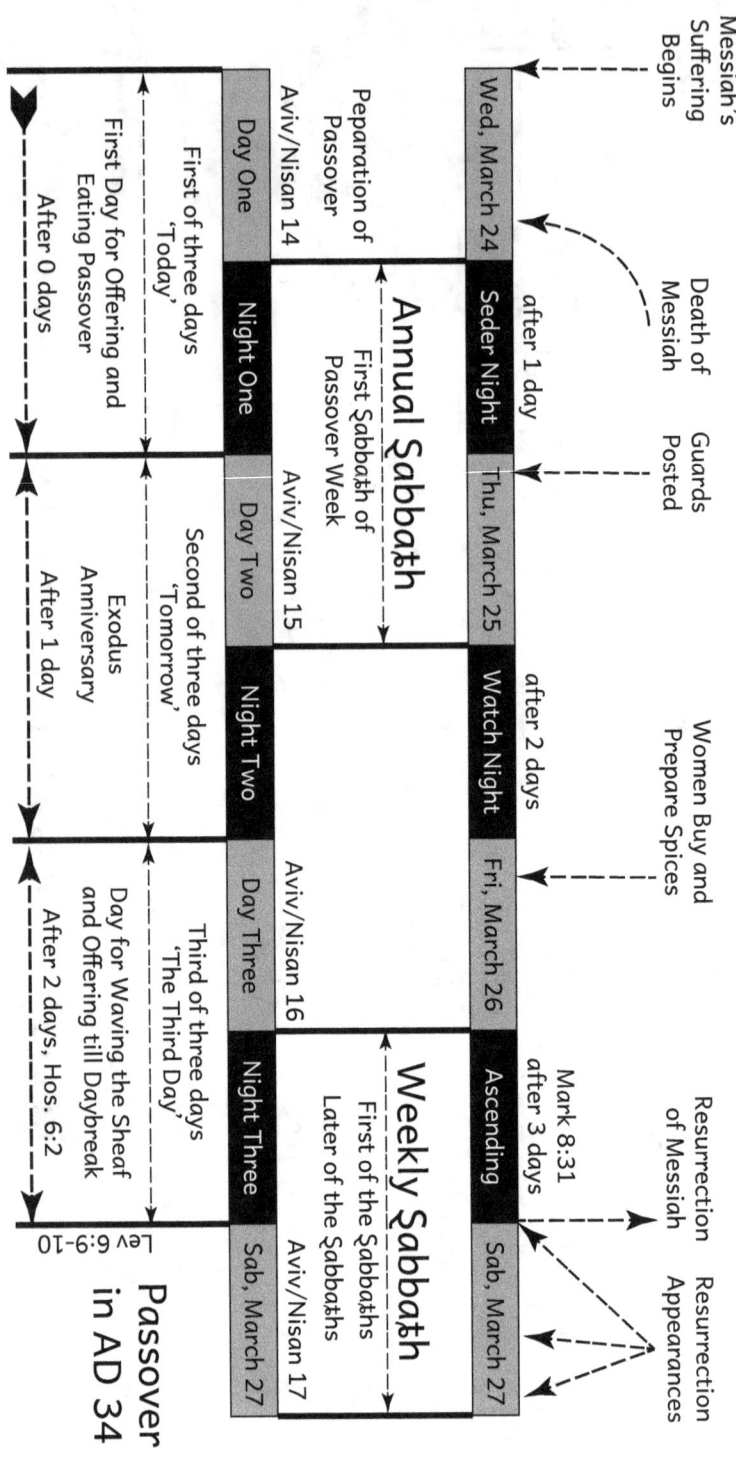

www.ingramcontent.com/pod-product-compliance
Lightning Source LLC
Chambersburg PA
CBHW071947110526
44592CB00012B/1027